American Payroll Association

2013 Edition

By Michael P. O'Toole, Esq.
Senior Director of Publications, Education, and Government Relations

In the preparation of this text, every effort has been made to offer the most current, correct, and clearly understandable information possible. Nonetheless, inadvertent errors can occur, and tax rules and regulations are constantly changing.

This text is intended to provide authoritative information in regard to the subject matter covered and can be used as a training tool. As such, it is not an evaluation device upon which to base performance reviews and/or promotions.

This material is distributed with the understanding that the publisher and author are not engaged in rendering legal, accounting, or other professional services. If legal advice or other professional assistance is required, the service of your attorney or certified public accountant should be sought. Readers are encouraged to consult with appropriate professional advisors for advice concerning specific matters before making decisions affecting their individual operations. The publisher disclaims any responsibility for positions taken by practitioners in their individual cases or for any misunderstanding on the part of readers. The information in this text is current as of February 1, 2013.

Please visit our Web site at www.americanpayroll.org

ISBN: 978-1-934951-59-0

Printed in the United States

ANSWER KEY

TABLE OF CONTENTS

SECTION 1: THE EMPLOYER-EMPLOYEE RELATIONSHIP

Review Questions

1. The factors used in determining whether an employer has the right to direct or control the financial aspects of a worker's activities (i.e., whether the worker can suffer a profit or loss) include:

   - Whether the worker has made a significant financial investment in performing the work
   - Whether the worker has business expenses that are unreimbursed
   - Whether the worker makes his or her services available to the general market
   - Whether the worker is paid on a regularly recurring basis or by the job

2. The four categories of statutory employees are:

   - Agent-drivers or commission-drivers
   - Full-time life insurance salespersons
   - Homeworkers
   - Traveling or city salespersons

3. The two categories of statutory nonemployees are:

   - Qualified real estate agents
   - Direct sellers

4. Temporary workers are hired, screened, and trained by the temporary help agency to provide services for clients. They are employees of the temporary help agency, which sets their wages and has the sole right to hire and fire. The agency is also responsible for all payroll taxes.

   Leased employees are hired, trained, and qualified by a leasing company, which provides workers for a client company. The client pays a fee to the leasing company to cover the cost of payroll, benefits, etc.

5. Employers should make sure they are dealing with a financially secure and reputable company before entering into a contract, since the temporary help agency or leasing company's financial failure could lead to the client company becoming liable for any withholding or employment taxes that remain unpaid.

6. a. The three parts of the ABC test are:

   - The worker is free from control or direction in performing the work both by agreement and in reality (Absence of control).
   - The work is performed outside the usual course of the company's business or away from any of the employer's facilities (Business—unusual and/or away).
   - The worker is customarily engaged in an independent trade, occupation, or business (Customarily independent contractor).

   b. The ABC test is used by many states to determine a worker's employment status under state unemployment insurance laws.

7. Form I-9 is used to verify that an individual has the legal right to work in the United States. The Immigration Reform and Control Act of 1986 makes it illegal for an employer to hire an unauthorized worker.

8. Although the client company may have the right to hire and fire the workers, set wage levels, and supervise their work, the workers are generally employees of the leasing company, which is responsible for withholding federal income tax and social security and Medicare taxes, as well as paying the employer's share of social security, Medicare, and FUTA taxes.

9. The factors courts and the DOL consider when making an employment status determination under the FLSA include:

    - how much control the employer has over how the work is performed;
    - whether the worker has the chance to make a profit or risks a loss based on how skillfully the work is performed;
    - whether the worker invests in tools or materials required to perform the work or hires helpers;
    - whether the work requires a special skill;
    - how permanent the working relationship is; and
    - whether the work performed is an integral part of the employer's business operation.

10. Employers would rather use workers who are not employees to perform services for them because employers must withhold income and employment taxes from employees' wages, and pay employment taxes with their own funds. Employers also must pay federal and state unemployment taxes based on their employees' wages. If a worker is an employee, most companies have their own list of benefits and other entitlements that are provided to employees but not to independent contractors.

11. A social security card that does not contain language saying that employment is not work-authorized is proof of an employee's authorization to work in the U.S., but not proof of identity.

12. Factors that the IRS does not consider important in making worker classification determinations include part-time or full-time work, the location of the work, and hours of work.

13. The employer must report each new hire's name, address, social security number, and first day of work for which compensation is paid, as well as the employer's name, address, and federal employer identification number.

14. In general, employers must report new hires within 20 calendar days of the date of hire. Employers that report magnetically or electronically must send 2 transmissions per calendar month which are 12-16 days apart.

15. The name of the program offered by U.S. Citizenship and Immigration Services that employers can use to verify the employment authorization status of new hires is the E-Verify Program.

True or False Questions

1. True

2. False   Their earnings must consist solely of commissions to be exempt from FUTA tax.

3. True

4. False   If telemarketers work under the direction and control of a company, they are employees of that company.

5. True

6. True

7. True

8. False   If an employer uses the E-Verify program, new hires must enter their SSN in Section 1 of Form I-9.

9. False   Managers and executives are classified as employees, for tax purposes, although they are exempt under most wage-hour and labor relations laws.

10. True

11. True

12. True

13. False   Part-time employees are covered under the federal payroll tax laws if they meet the common law test for employment status.

14. True

15. False   Employers cannot demand specific documents to prove an employee's eligibility to work. New hires can produce any approved documents that prove identity and work authorization.

16. False   The IRS cannot require an employer to show that more than 25% of its industry treated similarly situated workers as independent contractors.

17. True

18. True

19. False   Multistate employers can designate one state in which they have employees as the state to which they will report all new hires.

20. False   The employer must retain the employee's Form I-9 for one year after the employee's last day of employment.

Multiple Choice Questions

1.	c	7.	c
2.	b	8.	c
3.	a	9.	a
4.	b	10.	a
5.	c	11.	c
6.	b	12.	c

SECTION 2: FEDERAL AND STATE WAGE-HOUR LAWS

Review Questions

1. The five major areas regulated by the Fair Labor Standards Act are:

    - Minimum wage
    - Overtime
    - Child labor
    - Equal pay
    - Recordkeeping

2. Under enterprise coverage, all the employees of a business are covered by the FLSA so long as at least two employees of the business are engaged in interstate commerce or involved in the production of goods or services for interstate commerce, and the business has annual gross sales of at least $500,000. Individual employees can be covered even if the business is not a covered enterprise if the employee is engaged in interstate commerce or the production of goods for interstate commerce.

3. Exempt employees do not have to be paid the required minimum wage or overtime pay, and the employer does not have to keep certain records detailing their work, while nonexempt employees must be paid the required minimum wage and overtime pay and the employer must keep detailed records of their work hours and wage payments.

4. The time limit is two years after the alleged violation or three years if the violation was willful.

5. The plan is called the "Belo" plan, named after the company involved in the Supreme Court's decision, and the plan guarantees a fixed salary for irregular hours that includes a set amount of overtime pay.

6. "Compensable time" is defined as all hours during which the employee is under the employer's control, even if the time is unproductive, so long as the time spent is for the employer's benefit.

7. The following categories of employees make up the "white collar" exemption under the FLSA:

    - Administrative
    - Executive
    - Professional
    - Computer-related professional
    - Outside sales

8. The following questions must be answered to properly calculate overtime pay:

    - What is the employee's workweek?
    - What constitutes hours worked?
    - What payments made to the employee are considered wages?
    - What is the employee's regular rate of pay?

9. The regular rate of pay is an hourly rate of pay determined by dividing the total regular pay actually earned for the workweek by the total number of hours worked. For salaried nonexempt employees, the regular rate of pay is the employee's salary divided by the number of hours the salary is intended to compensate.

10. Yes. In order for the computer professional exemption to apply to an hourly paid employee, the employee would have to be paid at least $27.63 per hour.

11. To qualify as an administrative employee:

   - The employee's primary duty must be the performance of office or nonmanual work directly related to the management or general business operations of the employer or the employer's customers; and
   - The employee's primary duty must include the exercise of discretion and independent judgment regarding matters of significance.

12. The following conditions must be met for an employer to apply the tip credit to the minimum wage:

   - The employee must be a "tipped employee," which is an employee working in an occupation in which he or she regularly receives at least $30 per month in tips.
   - The employee must receive at least as much in tips as the credit taken by the employer.
   - The employee must be informed about the tip credit provisions of the law before the credit is taken.
   - All tips received by the employee must be kept by the employee, although tip pooling may be required among employees who are customarily and regularly tipped.
   - Credit card tips must be given to the employee by the next payday.

13. All the following conditions must be met for attendance at meetings, lectures, seminars, and training sessions to be considered nonwork time:

   - The meeting, lecture, etc., is not held during the employee's regular work hours.
   - Attendance is voluntary.
   - The meeting, lecture, etc., is not directly related to the employee's job.
   - The employee does not perform any productive work for the employer while attending.

14. No minors under age 18 can work in a job that has been declared hazardous by the Wage and Hour Division. Some minors age 16 and 17 are exempt from these restrictions under student learner or apprenticeship programs, under an exception for loading paper balers and compactors, or under an exception for 17-year-olds who work with wood products under the supervision of a parent and meet several other requirements.

15. Employers can be fined up to $11,000 for each violation of the child labor restrictions and up to $50,000 for each violation that causes the death or serious injury of a minor.

True or False Questions

1. False   Employers must comply with whichever law is more beneficial to the employee.

2. True

3. True

4. False   An important sounding job title does not exempt an employee from the minimum wage and overtime pay provisions of the FLSA. The employee's actual duties and salary must meet the tests of the exemption.

5. True

6. True

7. True

8. False   The FLSA does not require overtime pay for hours worked on Sunday, unless the total hours worked for the workweek exceed 40.

9. False   Under the FLSA, employers are not required to give rest periods to employees. However, rest periods may be required by state law.

10. False   Bona fide meal periods during which the employee is completely relieved from duty are not working time.

11. False   The FLSA does not require the employer to pay for hours not worked because of illness.

12. True

13. False   To determine gross earnings, the total overtime earnings are added to the total regular earnings.

14. True

15. False   The Oregon state minimum hourly wage is higher than the federal minimum wage, so Sharon must be paid the state minimum wage of $8.95.

16. True

17. True

18. True

19. True

20. False   Taxicab drivers are only exempt from the overtime pay requirements.

21. True

22. False   In addition to wages paid in the form of cash, employees may be paid in other forms as well. They may be paid partly in room, board, or other facilities provided by the employer. These facilities must primarily benefit the employee, not the employer, in order to be classified as wages.

23. True

24. False   Where service charges are automatically added to customers' bills and then turned over to the employee, these amounts are not tips and are considered wages when determining whether the minimum wage has been paid.

25. False   When employees are required to wear uniforms that cannot be worn as regular "street cloth-ing" and their cost and maintenance would put the employee below the minimum hourly wage, the employer must pay for the purchase, cleaning, and repair of the uniforms. If the uniform can be worn off the job, the employer need not reimburse the employee, even if the employee's wages go below the minimum.

Multiple Choice Questions

1.	b	6.	b
2.	b	7.	b
3.	d	8.	d
4.	d	9.	b
5.	a	10.	b

Problems

1. Step 1: Calculate total earnings due if overtime pay is required for hours worked over 8 in a day.

   Regular pay: $10 x 85 hours = $850
   Overtime hours: [5 x (9 − 8)] + [4 x (10 − 8)] = 13
   Overtime premium rate: $10 x .5 = $5
   Overtime premium pay: $5 x 13 hours = $65
   Total earnings: $850 + $65 = $915

   Step 2: Calculate total earnings due if overtime pay is required for hours worked over 80 in the 14-day work period.

   Regular pay: $10 x 85 hours = $850
   Overtime hours: 85 − 80 = 5
   Overtime premium rate: $10 x .5 = $5
   Overtime premium pay: $5 x 5 hours = $25
   Total earnings: $850 + $25 = $875

   Step 3: David must be paid the higher of the result in Step 1 or 2 — $915.

2. Regular pay: $9.00 x 47 hours = $423.00
   Overtime hours: 47 − 40 = 7
   Overtime premium rate: $9.00 x .5 = $4.50
   Overtime premium pay: $4.50 x 7 = $31.50
   Total earnings: $423.00 + $31.50 = $454.50

3. Regular pay: $12 x 42 hours = $504.00
   Overtime hours: 42 − 40 = 2
   Overtime premium rate: $12.00 x .5 = $6.00
   Overtime premium pay: $6.00 x 2 = $12.00
   Total earnings: $504.00 + $12.00 = $516.00

4. Regular pay: ($10 + $1) x 45 hours = $495
   Overtime hours: 45 − 40 = 5
   Overtime premium rate: $11.00 x .5 = $5.50
   Overtime premium pay: $5.50 x 5 = $27.50
   Total earnings: $495.00 + $27.50 = $522.50

5. Regular hourly pay: $10.00 x 44 hours = $440.00
    Total regular pay: $440 + $38.00 = $478.00
    Regular rate of pay: $478 ÷ $44.00 = $10.86
    Overtime hours: 44 − 40 = 4
    Overtime premium rate: $10.86 x .5 = $5.43
    Overtime premium pay: $5.43 x 4 = $21.72
    Total earnings: $478.00 + $21.72 = $499.72

6. Regular pay: $9.50 x 48 hours = $456.00
    Overtime hours: 48 − 40 = 8
    Overtime premium rate: $9.50 x .5 = $4.75
    Overtime premium pay: $4.75 x 8 = $38.00
    Discretionary bonus: $100.00
    Total earnings: $456.00 + $38.00 + $100.00 = $594.00

7. Regular pay: ($10.00 x 24 hours) + ($12.00 x 20 hours) = $240.00 + $240.00 = $480.00
    Regular rate of pay: $480.00 ÷ 44 hours = $10.91
    Overtime hours: 44 − 40 = 4
    Overtime premium rate: $10.91 x .5 = $5.46
    Overtime premium pay: $5.46 x 4 = $21.84
    Total earnings: $480.00 + $21.84 = $501.84

8. Regular rate of pay: $520.00 ÷ 40 hours = $13.00
    Regular pay: $13.00 x 49 hours = $637.00
    Overtime hours: 49 − 40 = 9
    Overtime premium rate: $13.00 x .5 = $6.50
    Overtime premium pay: $6.50 x 9 = $58.50
    Total earnings: $637.00 + $58.50 = $695.50

9. Hours worked in a year: 52 weeks x 40 hours = 2,080
    Regular rate of pay: $23,400 ÷ 2,080 = $11.25
    Regular pay: $11.25 x 48 hours = $540.00
    Overtime hours: 48 − 40 = 8
    Overtime premium rate: $11.25 x .5 = $5.63
    Overtime premium pay: $5.63 x 8 = $45.04
    Total earnings: $540.00 + $45.04 = $585.04

10. Yearly earnings: $1,500 x 12 months = $18,000
    Hours worked in a year: 52 weeks x 40 hours = 2,080
    Regular rate of pay: $18,000 ÷ 2,080 = $8.65
    Regular pay: $8.65 x 49 hours = $423.85
    Overtime hours: 49 − 40 = 9
    Overtime premium rate: $8.65 x .5 = $4.33
    Overtime premium pay: $4.33 x 9 = $38.97
    Total earnings: $423.85 + $38.97 = $462.82

11. Yearly earnings: $1,000 x 24 = $24,000
    Hours worked in a year: 52 weeks x 32 hours = 1,664
    Regular rate of pay: $24,000 ÷ 1,664 = $14.42
    Regular pay: $14.42 x 42 hours = $605.64
    Overtime hours: 42 − 40 = 2
    Overtime premium rate: $14.42 x .5 = $7.21
    Overtime premium pay: $7.21 x 2 = $14.42
    Total earnings: $605.64 + $14.42 = $620.06

12. Yearly earnings: $2,500 x 12 months = $30,000
Hours worked in a year: 52 weeks x 35 hours = 1,820
Regular rate of pay: $30,000 ÷ 1,820 = $16.48
Regular pay: $16.48 x 43 hours = $708.64
Overtime hours: 43 − 40 = 3
Overtime premium rate: $16.48 x .5 = $8.24
Overtime premium pay: $8.24 x 3 = $24.72
Total earnings: $708.64 + $24.72 = $733.36

13. Regular piecework earnings: $0.50 x 840 units = $420.00
Regular rate of pay: $420.00 ÷ 46 hours = $9.13
Overtime hours: 46 − 40 = 6
Overtime premium rate: $9.13 x .5 = $4.57
Overtime premium pay: $4.57 x 6 = $27.42
Total earnings: $420.00 + $27.42 = $447.42

14. Regular piecework earnings: $2.00 x 326 units = $652.00
Production bonus: $0.50 x 26 units = $13.00
Total piecework earnings plus bonus: $652.00 + $13.00 = $665.00
Regular rate of pay: $665.00 ÷ 43 hours = $15.47
Overtime hours: 43 − 40 = 3
Overtime premium rate: $15.47 x .5 = $7.74
Overtime premium pay: $7.74 x 3 = $23.22
Total earnings: $652.00 + $13.00 + $23.22 = $688.22

15. Regular piecework earnings: $0.30 x 1,560 units = $468.00
Overtime piece rate: $0.30 x 1.5 = $0.45
Overtime earnings: $0.45 x 212 = $95.40
Total earnings: $468.00 + $95.40 = $563.40

SECTION 3: TAXABLE AND NONTAXABLE COMPENSATION

Review Questions

1. The following conditions must be met for an employer to use the vehicle cents-per-mile method of valuing an employee's personal use of an employer-provided car.

   - The employer must expect the employee to regularly use the vehicle while conducting the employer's business, or the vehicle must actually be driven at least 10,000 miles and be used primarily by employees.
   - The fair market value of the vehicle cannot exceed $16,000 for cars placed in service in 2013.
   - If the employee pays for fuel, the mileage rate is reduced by $.055 per mile.

2. A benefit whose value is so small that accounting for it would be unreasonable or impracticable.

3. The three special valuation methods are:

   - Annual lease value method
   - Vehicle cents-per-mile method
   - Commuting method

4. a. $90,000 - $50,000 = $40,000

   b. $.15 per $1,000 of the taxable value of the coverage

5. $2,000. If the employer provides more than $2,000 in group-term life insurance to an employee's dependent, the value of the total amount including the first $2,000 becomes taxable to the employee. However, if the difference between the Table I value of the insurance and the amount paid by the employee in after-tax dollars is considered de minimis, then there is no income for the employee.

6. Taxable: When the employer has a nonaccountable plan because it does not require the employee to substantiate business travel expenses and to return any amount not spent by the employee on business within a reasonable period of time.

   Nontaxable: When the employer has an accountable plan and the employee is required to substantiate business travel expenses and refund the balance of the advance not used within a reasonable period of time.

7. Yes. The method allowed by the IRS is called "grossing-up."

8. Outplacement services are not included in employees' income under the following circumstances:

   - The employer derives a substantial business benefit from providing the outplacement services other than providing the compensation (e.g., a positive corporate image, an attractive benefit that encourages new hires).
   - The employees do not have the choice of accepting cash rather than the outplacement services (e.g., a higher severance payment if the services are refused).
   - The employees would be able to deduct the cost of the outplacement services as a business expense on their personal tax returns.

9. In the private sector, a control employee is an employee who:

   - is a corporate officer earning at least $100,000 in 2013 (indexed annually);
   - is a director;
   - earns at least $205,000 in 2013 (indexed annually); or
   - is a 1% owner.

   In the public sector, a control employee is an employee who:

   - is an elected official; or
   - earns more than a federal employee at Executive Level V ($145,700 through April 6, 2013; $146,400 after April 6.2013).

10. The two types of deductible job-related moving expenses are:

    - transportation and storage of household goods, and
    - expenses of moving the employee and his or her family from the old home to the new home (not meals)

11. If a reimbursement is made under an "accountable plan," the amount reimbursed is excluded from income and is not subject to federal income tax withholding or social security, Medicare, and FUTA taxes. If the reimbursement is made under a "nonaccountable plan," the reimbursement or the excess amount is included in income and is subject to federal income tax withholding and social security, Medicare, and FUTA taxes.

12. If an employer regularly fails to comply with the requirements for reimbursing or advancing amounts paid or incurred by employees for business expenses, the IRS will consider this a "pattern of abuse" and will treat all payments as being made under a nonaccountable plan.

13. Five years.

14. When a manufacturer pays a bonus to sales employees working for a retailer to get them to "push" its products, the bonus is not wages because it is being paid by a third party, not the employer (for services performed for the third party), and is not subject to federal income tax withholding or social security, Medicare, and FUTA taxes. The bonus is taxable income to the sales employees, however, and must be reported on their personal income tax return.

15. Exclusion limitation: The excluded amount of dependent care assistance cannot exceed $5,000 in a year or the employee's earned income for the year, whichever is less.

    When expenses are incurred: An employer's dependent care expenses are treated as incurred when the care is provided, not when payments are made to the employee or third party.

    Written plan: The dependent care assistance program must be a separate, written plan of the employer and it must be designed solely for the employees' benefit.

    No discrimination: The program must not discriminate in favor of highly compensated employees.

    Notification: Eligible employees must receive reasonable notification of the availability and terms of the program.

    Annual statement: The employer must give the employee a statement each year by January 31 showing the dependent care assistance provided by the employer during the previous year (Box 10 of Form W-2).

16. When companies change ownership, key executives are often provided with "golden parachutes" to soften their landing should they be terminated by the new owner. The tax law defines a "parachute payment" as compensation that is paid to an officer, shareholder, or highly compensated employee only after a change in corporate ownership or control and that is at least three times the employee's average compensation during the five most recent tax years.

True or False Questions

1. False   The Internal Revenue Code does not define the term "fringe benefits," although it includes several examples.

2. True

3. False   The goods or services must be offered for sale to customers in the employer's line of business in which the employee normally works.

4. True

5. True

6. True

7. False   Restaurant employers wishing to participate in a TRDA must agree with the IRS on a certain tip percentage based on the charge tips it reported and an IRS formula to determine cash tips. Also, 75% of the employees at each establishment must agree to report the tip percentage agreed on in the TRDA.

8. True

9. False   The annual lease value does not include the value of employer-provided fuel.

10. False   If an employee uses a company aircraft for business and personal use, the value of the personal use is included in the employee's income.

11. True

12. True

13. True

14. False   During the 12-month period immediately following the move, the employee must work for at least 39 weeks in the general location of the new workplace. The employee does not have to work for the same employer for 39 weeks, nor do the 39 weeks have to be consecutive.

15. False   Cash gifts or gift certificates with a cash value are never de minimis fringes. They are included in income and are taxable to the employee.

16. True

17. False   Scholarships and fellowships covering tuition and related fees are excluded from an individual's income if the individual is a candidate for a degree at an educational institution.

18. True

19. True

20. True

21. True

22. True

23. False   Gifts provided to employees must be included in the employees' income unless they can be excluded as a de minimis fringe benefit or as a gift between relatives that is not based on the employer-employee relationship.

24. False   This exclusion was repealed in 1996.

25. True

26. False   Special rules and limitations apply to combined business and pleasure travel outside the United States. Even though the trip is primarily for business, if the trip has any element of pleasure, the cost of traveling to and from the destination must be allocated between the business and personal portions of the trip.

27. False   To deduct travel expenses, an employee must be in travel status. The employee must usually be away from home "overnight." Overnight does not literally mean 24 hours. It is a period of time longer than an ordinary work day during which rest or relief from work is required. The deduction may also be available to employees who travel from their residence to a temporary work location and return home on the same day. In addition, the deduction may be available to employees staying overnight near where the employee lives if certain requirements are met that show the employer benefits from the overnight stay.

28. True

29. True

30. True

Multiple Choice Questions

1.	c	10.	b
2.	d	11.	a
3.	b	12.	a
4.	d	13.	b
5.	a	14.	d
6.	b	15.	b
7.	a	16.	b
8.	c	17.	a
9.	d		

Problems

1. Annual lease value = $6,850
   Taxable amount: $6,850 x 40% = $2,740

2. Personal use: 100% - 70% = 30%
   Personal mileage: 12,000 miles x .30 = 3,600 miles
   Taxable amount: (3,600 miles x $0.565) = $2,034.00

3. Step 1:   2 x $75,000 = $150,000
   Step 2: $150,000 - $50,000 = $100,000
   Step 3: $100,000 ÷ $1,000 = 100
   Step 4:   Bill is 39 years old as of 12-31-13
   Step 5: $0.09 x 100 = $9.00 monthly taxable coverage

4. Step 1:   2 x $78,000 = $156,000
   Step 2: $156,000 - $50,000 = $106,000
   Step 3: $106,000 ÷ $1,000 = 106
   Step 4:   Bill is 39 years old as of 12-31-13
   Step 5: $0.09 x 106 = $9.54 monthly taxable coverage
   Step 6: $9.54 - $5.00 = $4.54 monthly taxable coverage for May - December

5. a. Total tax % = 25% + 5% + 6.2% + 1.45% = 37.65%
       Gross-up % = 100% - 37.65% = 62.35%
       Gross earnings = $4,500 ÷ .6235 = $7,217.32

   To check:
       FITW = 25% x $7,217.32 = $1,804.33
       SITW = 5% x $7,217.32 = $360.87
       Soc. Sec. = 6.2% x $7,217.32 = $447.47
       Medicare = 1.45% x $7,217.32 = $104.65

   $7,217.32 - $1,804.33 - $360.87 - $447.47 - $104.65 = $4,500.00

   b. Soc. Sec. tax on $1,500 = .062 x $1,500 = $93
       Total to be grossed-up = $4,500 + $93 = $4,593
       Total tax % = 25% + 5% + 1.45% = 31.45%
       Gross-up % = 100% - 31.45% = 68.55%
       Gross earnings = $4,593 ÷ .6855 = $6,700.22

   To check:
       FITW = 25% x $6,700.22 = $1,675.06
       SITW = 5% x $6,700.22 = $335.01
       Soc. Sec. = 6.2% x $1,500 = $93.00
       Medicare = 1.45% x $6,700.22 = $97.15

   $6,700.22 - $1,675.06 - $335.01 - $93.00 - $97.15 = $4,500.00

6. Total tax % = 25% + 3.5% + 6.2% + 1.45% = 36.15%
   Gross-up % = 100% - 36.15% = 63.85%

a.	Gross earnings = $6,000 ÷ .6385 =	$9,397.02
b.	FITW = 25% x $9,397.02 =	- 2,349.26
c.	SITW = 3.5% x $9,397.02 =	- 328.90
d.	Soc. Sec. = 6.2% x $9,397.02 =	- 582.62
e.	Medicare = 1.45% x $9,397.02 =	- 136.26
f.	Check:	$6,000.00

7. Moving, packing, and storage = $2,800.00
   Travel expenses during move (no meals):
      $1,500 - $150 =   + 1,350.00
   Total qualified reimbursement $4,150.00

SECTION 4: HEALTH, ACCIDENT, AND RETIREMENT BENEFITS

Review Questions

1. Family and Medical Leave Act.

2. Cafeteria plan.

3. Only if the §401(k) plan existed prior to the effective date of the Tax Reform Act of 1986.

4. 12 weeks (26 weeks if the child, spouse, or parent is a covered military servicemember suffering a serious injury or illness).

5. The status changes that allow a cafeteria plan to permit an employee to change a cafeteria plan benefit election during the year are:

   - marital status changes – marriage, divorce, death of spouse, legal separation, or annulment
   - changes in the number of dependents – birth, adoption, placement for adoption, or death of a dependent
   - employment status changes (applies to employee, spouse, dependent, or adult child under 27) – termination or commencement of employment, strike or lockout, starting or ending an unpaid leave of absence, change in worksite, change from full-time to part-time, exempt to nonexempt, or salaried to hourly status
   - change in dependent or adult child status – any event that causes an employee's dependent or adult child under 27 to become covered or lose coverage (e.g., attainment of a certain age)
   - residence change – a change in the place of residence of the employee, spouse, dependent, or adult child under 27
   - adoptions – the commencement or termination of an adoption proceeding

6. Cafeteria plans must satisfy the following three nondiscrimination tests:

   - eligibility test
   - contributions and benefits test
   - concentration test

7. The three major types of health insurance plans offered by employers are:

   - traditional health insurance (fee-for-service)
   - Health Maintenance Organizations
   - Preferred Provider Organizations

8. "The diagnosis, cure, mitigation, treatment, or prevention of disease, or for the purpose of affecting any structure or function of the body."

9. To be nondiscriminatory in terms of eligibility, an employer-provided group health insurance plan must benefit:

   - at least 70% of all employees;
   - at least 80% of all employees who are eligible to participate in the plan (if at least 70% of all employees are eligible to participate); or
   - a classification of employees that the Secretary of the Treasury finds not to be discriminatory.

In terms of benefits, an employer-provided group plan is nondiscriminatory if all the benefits provided to highly compensated employees are provided to all other participating employees. Plans may have limits on benefits, but they must be uniform for all participants when based on employer contributions and must not be proportionately based on employee compensation.

10. Sick pay may take many forms, but its essential purpose is to replace the wages of an employee who cannot work because of a nonjob-related illness or injury. Workers' compensation, however, deals with payments to employees who cannot work because of job-related injuries or illness.

11. Information an employer should provide a third-party payer of sick pay includes:

    - the total wages paid by the employer to the employee during the calendar year before the third party begins making payments (helps determine whether the social security and FUTA wage bases have been met);
    - the last month in which the employee worked for the employer (helps determine how long the third party is responsible for social security and Medicare taxes); and
    - employee contributions made to the cost of the insurance after taxes have been withheld (helps determine how much of each disability payment is taxable).

12. While an employer's business generally determines its classification code, and the more dangerous the business the higher the dollar value assigned to that code, some employees may be assigned a different or less costly code because of the duties they perform. Employees who work exclusively in an office, outside sales employees, and drivers and their helpers may be assigned a "standard exception classification." Such classifications generally carry a significantly lower dollar value than other employee classifications.

13. A pre-tax contribution is one that is made from an employee's wages before the taxes on those wages are calculated, while an after-tax contribution is made after the tax is calculated. A pre-tax contribution will result in higher take-home pay for the employee.

14. The payroll department must maintain accurate records of:

    - hours worked
    - compensation earned
    - date of birth
    - date of hire

15. A defined contribution plan sets up individual accounts for each employee, with a set amount being contributed into the account by the employer and/or the employee periodically. The employee's retirement benefit depends on the amount of money in his or her account at retirement, which is determined by the contribution amounts and any investment gains or losses. Other characteristics of defined contribution plans include:

    - the plan provides for a contribution formula involving the employer and/or the employees
    - employer contributions are made no less frequently than annually (usually more often)
    - being able to see how much is in their accounts makes the plan easy to understand for employees
    - no need for actuarial calculations
    - annual reports must be filed with the IRS and the Department of Labor

True or False Questions

1. True

2. True

3. False   A pre-tax contribution will result in more take-home pay for the employee.

4. True

5. False   In this case, cafeteria plans are exempt from the nondiscrimination tests.

6. True

7. True

8. False   Only the premium portion of overtime is excluded. The straight time portion is included.

9. False   Employers can require eligible employees to use any paid vacation, personal, sick, medical, or family leave as part of the 12-week guaranteed leave.

10. True

11. True

12. False   Employer contributions to an accident or health insurance plan for the benefit of its employees and their spouses, dependents, and adult children under age 27 are not wages and are not subject to federal income tax withholding or social security, Medicare, and FUTA taxes.

13. True

14. True

15. False   Health insurance provided for employees through a third-party insurance company must not discriminate in favor of highly compensated employees.

16. True

17. True

18. False   The general rules for depositing withheld federal income, social security, and Medicare taxes do apply to sick pay, although the party liable for depositing the taxes may change.

19. True

20. True

21. True

22. True

23. False   Once selected, benefits cannot be changed during the plan year unless the cafeteria plan permits the employee to make a change if there is a change in status that causes the employee or the employee's spouse, dependent, or adult child under age 27 to lose or gain coverage under the plan, or premiums or coverage are significantly altered by the insurance carrier or the employer.

24. True

25. False   An employee may not be reimbursed for amounts spent on over-the-counter drugs that are not prescribed by a licensed physician through her health FSA.

Multiple Choice Questions

1.	c	14.	c
2.	c	15.	b
3.	b	16.	d
4.	c	17.	c
5.	b	18.	d
6.	a	19.	a
7.	c	20.	c
8.	a	21.	b
9.	b	22.	c
10.	d	23.	c
11.	d	24.	c
12.	c	25.	c
13.	b		

Problems

1. a. $1,000 x 6 months x 60% = $3,600
    b. $1,000 x 10 months x 60% = $6,000

2. a. $900 x 6 months x 2/3 = $3,600
    b. $900 x 7 months x 2/3 = $4,200
    c. $900 x 7 months x 1/3 = $2,100

3. a. If the contribution is pre-tax:

Regular wages	$600.00
Medical and dental	- 25.00
FITW	- 71.00
Soc. Sec. ($600 - 25) x 6.2%	- 35.65
Medicare ($600 - 25) x 1.45%	- 8.34
SITW $71.00 x 10%	- 7.10
Net Pay:	$452.91

   b. If the contribution is after-tax:

Regular wages	$600.00
FITW	- 76.00
Soc. Sec. ($600 x 6.2%)	- 37.20
Medicare ($600 x 1.45%)	- 8.70
SITW ($76.00 x 10%)	- 7.60
Medical and dental	- 25.00
Net Pay:	$445.50

4. a. §408(k)
    b. §501(c)(18)(D)
    c. §457(b)
    d. §403(b)
    e. §401(k)
    f. §401(a)
    g. §408(p)

5. a. $7,500 — the lesser of 15% x $50,000 ($7,500) or $17,500 (annual dollar limit effective for 2013).
    b. $17,500 — the lesser of 15% x $120,000 ($18,000) or $17,500 (annual dollar limit effective for 2013).

6. $5,500 — the lesser of $27,500 x 100% or $5,500 annual applicable dollar limit for 2013.

7. a. Federal income taxable wages

Gross wages ($38,000 ÷ 24):	$1,583.33
Cafeteria plan ($125 ÷ 2):	- 62.50
§401(k) plan ($1,583.33 x .05):	- 79.17
Taxable wages:	$1,441.66

    b. Social security taxable wages

Gross wages ($38,000 ÷ 24):	$1,583.33
Cafeteria plan ($125 ÷ 2):	-62.50
Taxable wages	$1,520.83

    c. Medicare taxable wages

Gross wages ($38,000 ÷ 24):	$1,583.33
Cafeteria plan ($125 ÷ 2):	- 62.50
Taxable wages:	$1,520.83

    d. FUTA taxable wages

Gross wages ($38,000 ÷ 24):	$1,583.33
Cafeteria plan ($125 ÷ 2):	- 62.50
Taxable wages:	$1,520.83

8. a. Federal income taxable wages

Gross wages:	$3,760.00
Cafeteria plan:	- 75.00
§401(k) plan ($3,760 x .075):	- 282.00
Taxable wages:	$3,403.00

    b. Social security taxable wages

Gross wages:	$3,760.00
Cafeteria plan:	-75.00
Taxable wages:	$3,685.00

    c. Medicare taxable wages

Gross wages:	$3,760.00
Cafeteria plan:	-75.00
Taxable wages:	$3,685.00

    d. FUTA taxable wages

Gross wages:	$3,760.00
Cafeteria plan:	-75.00
Taxable wages:	$3,685.00

9.   Gross wages: $650.00

        Cafeteria plan ($650 x 6%):   -39.00

        Taxable wages: $611.00

        FITW: - 31.00

        Soc. Sec. ($611.00 x 6.2%):   - 37.88

        Medicare ($611.00 x 1.45%):   -8.86

        Net Pay: $533.26

10. Gross wages: $900.00

        Cafeteria plan: - 10.00

        §401(k) plan ($900 x 6%):   - 54.00

        FITW: - 101.00

        Soc. Sec. [($900 - $10) x 6.2%]:   - 55.18

        Medicare [($900 - $10) x 1.45%]: - 12.91

        Net pay: $666.91

SECTION 5: PAYING THE EMPLOYEE

Review Questions

1. State laws govern how often employers must pay employees.

2. Advantages of direct deposit for an employer include:

   - prevents lost and stolen checks
   - employees do not have to take time out of their work day to cash or deposit their paycheck
   - employers do not have to file/store cashed checks and related documents
   - better control of check stock

   Disadvantages of direct deposit for an employer include:

   - direct deposit is not a paperless system, since employers still may have to provide employees with a written statement of hours worked and deductions from gross pay, as well as collect a written authorization form, depending on their policies and procedures
   - direct deposit cannot be made mandatory in many states
   - employer cannot dictate the financial institution that the employee uses in most states
   - employer's loss of interest on payroll funds before paychecks clear

3. State escheat laws govern the treatment of unclaimed paychecks. Under these laws, employers are generally required to:

   - try to locate and contact the employee
   - file an annual report with the state where the employee resides that includes the employee's name, last known address, amount of the check, and the related payday
   - hold the checks for a certain length of time before turning them over to the state as abandoned property

4. Prenotification involves sending zero dollar amounts through the ACH network as a test before the first actual direct deposit for an employee. If such a "prenote" is used (it is an optional procedure), it must be sent at least 6 business days before any actual pay is sent through the network. This is a test of the accuracy of the information in the authorization agreement.

5. Authorization agreements (where they are in paper form) still must be signed, checked for accuracy, and retained, and employees using direct deposit must be given statements on payday showing the compensation they earned and the deductions taken for the pay period. Some employers do use electronic pay statements in meeting that requirement.

6. The main problem is whether to recompute weekly or biweekly paychecks for exempt salaried employees who are earning a certain amount annually. Employers are free to reduce exempt salaried employees' pay when faced with an extra payday, so long as there is no contract guaranteeing a certain amount of pay each weekly or biweekly pay period and the employee's pay is not reduced below the minimum required by state or federal law. Employers may also face a hostile reaction from salaried employees whose pay is reduced in this manner.

7. The benefits for employers in paying employees with electronic paycards include:

    *   reduced costs for manual checks, lost and stolen checks, stop payment orders, fraudulent cashing of duplicate checks, paycheck production and handling, and bank reconciliation fees
    *   enhanced efficiency by eliminating paper paychecks
    *   all employees are eligible for electronic funds transfer
    *   increased employee productivity as less time is spent cashing paychecks
    *   reduction of escheat issues.

8. A branded paycard has either a MasterCard®, Visa®, or Discover Network®, logo imprinted on it and is accepted wherever cards issued by these companies are accepted.

9. The following are the steps involved in establishing an electronic funds transfer:

    *   The employee must give authorization for direct deposit by designating the financial institution(s) to which the employee's pay will be transferred, the type of account to which the pay will be transferred, the number of the account, and the financial institution's routing number

    *   The employer prepares an automated file of direct deposit records which is sent to a financial institution with the ability to process the file, known as the Originating Depository Financial Institution (ODFI).

    *   The ODFI processes the file through the Automated Clearing House (ACH) operator.

    *   The ACH operator processes electronic payments between the ODFI and the financial institutions designated by the employees to receive the payments and coordinates the financial settlement between the participating financial institutions.

    *   The Receiving Depository Financial Institutions (RDFI) designated by the employees accept the electronic payments and post them to their customers' (the employees') accounts.

    *   On payday, the employees receive an information statement containing the same data that would have been shown on the pay stub, had the employee been paid by check.

10. Disadvantages for an employer in paying employees by paycheck include:

    *   lost or stolen checks
    *   unclaimed or uncashed checks
    *   employee time off needed to cash checks
    *   storage of cashed checks and related documents
    *   early preparation of vacation checks
    *   reconciliation of bank account with outstanding checks

True or False Questions

1. False   These matters are left up to the individual states.

2. True

3. False   Most states have a separate set of rules governing when employees must be paid when they separate from employment, either through discharge, layoff, or resignation.

4. False   More than 15 states have no statutory provisions dealing with paying wages owed to deceased employees.

5. True

6. True

7. False   A biweekly salary is paid every two weeks.

8. True

9. True

10. False   There is no minimum number required. Each state has its own regulations and requirements regarding mandatory direct deposit.

11. False   The FLSA does not regulate the frequency of wage payments. Each state regulates when employees must be paid.

12. True

13. True

14. False   When selecting a paycard vendor, it is very important for an employer to determine whether the vendor can comply with state wage payment requirements.

15. False   Reduced escheat issues is an important employer benefit of implementing a paycard program.

Multiple Choice Questions

1.	c	9.	d
2.	b	10.	b
3.	a	11.	c
4.	b	12.	b
5	a	13.	c
6.	c	14.	b
7.	c	15.	a
8.	c		

SECTION 6: WITHHOLDING TAXES _____

Review Questions

1. Employee's Withholding Allowance Certificate

2. Employers must retain each employee's Form W-4 for at least four years after the date the last tax return was due using information from the form, which is April 15 of the following year (e.g., if an employee files an amended W-4 in 2013, the previous W-4 must be retained until at least April 15, 2018).

3. Constructive payment indicates the point in time when an employee has the ability to control the payments for services from an employer.

4. The date of actual or constructive payment is important because it determines when wages are taxed and reported and at what rates.

5. A Form W-4 filed by a newly hired employee must be put into effect by the employer for the first wage payment after the form is filed.

6. Form W-4 tells the employer how many withholding allowances the employee is claiming and the employee's marital status. The number of allowances and marital status help determine the amount of federal income tax to withhold from the employee's wages. Form W-4 also notifies the employer whether the employee is claiming exempt from withholding. In addition, it may indicate that the employee wants an additional dollar amount withheld beyond the amount that is calculated on the withholding allowances and marital status claimed.

7. In order to be exempt from withholding, the employee must certify that:

   - he or she had a right to a refund of all federal income tax withheld in the prior year because the employee had no tax liability,

   - he or she expects to have no tax liability in the current year, and

   - he or she cannot be claimed as a dependent on someone else's income tax return if the employee will have more than $1,000 in income (including at least $350 in nonwage income) in 2013.

8. The employer must submit Form W-4 to the IRS in the following situations:

   - the IRS directs the employer to do so in a written notice to the employer; or

   - the IRS directs the employer to do so in published guidance, such as a revenue procedure.

9. Types of payments that are treated as supplemental wage payments include:

   - reported tips;
   - overtime pay;
   - bonuses;
   - back pay;
   - commissions;
   - payments made under reimbursement or other expense allowance arrangements that are made under a nonaccountable plan;
   - nonqualified deferred compensation payments included in wages;

- noncash fringe benefits;
- sick pay paid by a third party as an agent of the employer;
- amounts includible in gross income under IRC §409A;
- income recognized on the exercise of a nonstatutory stock option;
- wages imputed for health coverage of someone who is not a spouse, dependent, or adult child under age 27 of an employee; and
- wages recognized on the lapse of restrictions on restricted property transferred from an employer to an employee.

10. The withholding exemption would apply to the supplemental wages as well, so no withholding for federal income tax would be done.

11. Generally all nonperiodic payments of all or any portion of the balance of a recipient's account in a qualified deferred compensation plan are eligible rollover distributions other than:

- substantially equal periodic payments made over the lifetime or life expectancy of the employee or his or her beneficiary, or made for a specified period of at least 10 years,
- any minimum distribution that is required under IRC §401(a)(9) regarding qualified plans,
- distributions not included in gross income (e.g., return of an employee's after-tax contributions), except for net unrealized appreciation of employer securities,
- returns of amounts deferred under a §401(k) or §403(b) plan that exceed the elective deferral limits,
- loans treated as deemed distributions,
- dividends paid on employer securities, or
- distributions of the cost of current life insurance coverage.

12. Payers must generally withhold 28% of reportable nonpayroll payments during 2013 if payees fail to furnish payers with their taxpayer identification number or the IRS notifies them to withhold. This withholding is referred to as backup withholding.

13. The employer social security tax rate for wages paid in 2013 is 6.2%.

14. No. Advance payments of the Earned Income Credit were eliminated for wages paid after December 31, 2010.

15. Employers must provide notification of the right to the earned income credit by giving the employees one of the following:

- Copy B of Form W-2, Wage and Tax Statement (IRS-supplied forms have the required EIC statement on the back of Copy B; substitutes used for this purpose must have the required statement on the back of the employee copy),
- Notice 797, Possible Federal Tax Refund Due to the Earned Income Credit, or
- a written statement with the exact same wording as Notice 797.

True or False Questions

1. True

2. False   Wages are considered constructively paid only if they are made available to the employee without "substantial limitation or restriction."

3. True

4. True

5. True

6. False   Under the principle of constructive payment, an employee is considered to have been paid wages when they are actually or constructively paid, not when they are earned or payable.

7. True

8. False   The required rate for backup withholding in 2013 is 28%.

9. True

10. True

11. True

12. True

13. False   Employees cannot indicate on their W-4 form that they wish to have a flat amount of tax withheld rather than an amount based on the number of withholding allowances that can be claimed.

14. True

15. True

16. False   For wage payments equaling or exceeding the maximum amount, the percentage method of withholding must be used.

17. True

18. True

19. True

20. True

Multiple Choice Questions

1.	b	11.	a
2.	a	12.	d
3.	b	13.	d
4.	b	14.	b

5. d	15. a
6. b	16. b
7. b	17. b
8. c	18. d
9. b	19. a
10. b	20. b

Problems

1. a.

Semimonthly wages ($1,800 ÷ 2):	$900.00
Allowance value:	-162.50
Wages subject to withholding:	$737.50
Percentage method formula:	-464.00
	273.50
	x .15
	$ 41.03
	+37.20
FITW:	$ 78.23

b.

Monthly wages ($42,500 ÷ 12):	$3,541.67
Allowance value ($325.00 x 3):	- 975.00
Wages subject to withholding:	2,566.67
Percentage method formula:	- 2,179.00
	387.67
	x .15
	$ 58.15
	+148.70
FITW:	$206.85

c.

Weekly wages ($27,500 ÷ 52):	$528.85
Allowance value ($75.00 x 2):	- 150.00
Wages subject to withholding:	378.85
Percentage method formula:	- 214.00
	164.85
	x .15
	$ 24.73
	+17.20
FITW:	$ 41.93

2. a.

Quarterly wages ($72,000 ÷ 4):	$18,000.00
Allowance value ($975.00 x 4):	-3,900.00
Wages subject to withholding:	14,100.00
Percentage method formula:	-6,538.00
	7,562.00
	x .15
	$ 1,134.30
	+446.30
FITW:	$1,580.60

b. Weekly wages [($2,650 x 12) ÷ 52]: $611.54
    Allowance value: - 75.00
    Wages subject to withholding: 536.54
    Percentage method formula: - 214.00
     322.54
     x .15
     $ 48.38
     +17.20
    FITW: $ 65.58

c. Biweekly wages ($53,000 ÷ 26): $2,038.46
    Allowance value ($150.00 x 3):   -450.00
    Wages subject to withholding: 1,588.46
    Percentage method formula: - 1,006.00
     582.46
     x .15
     $87.37
     +68.70
    FITW: $156.07

3. $49.00

4. Annual wages = $1,200 x 26 payroll periods = $31,200

Withholding using the percentage method:

Gross wages: $31,200.00
Allowance value ($3,900 x 3):   - 11,700.00
Wages subject to withholding: $19,500.00
Percentage method formula: - 8,300.00
     $11,200.00
     x .10
     $1,120.00

Withholding per payroll period = $1,120.00 ÷ 26 = $43.08

5. Annual wages = $6,000 x 12 payroll periods = $72,000

Withholding using the percentage method:

Gross wages: $72,000.00
Allowance value ($3,900 x 2):   - 7,800.00
Wages subject to withholding: $64,200.00
Percentage method formula: -38,450.00
     $25,750.00
     x .25
     6,437.50
     + 4,991.25
     $11,428.75

Withholding per payroll period = $11,428.75 ÷ 12 = $952.40

6. $2,000 x 25% = $500

7. a. FITW on regular wages = $30
    b. FITW on supplemental wages = $1,000 x 25% = $250
    c. FITW on total wages $30 + $250 = $280

8. Total of latest wages and bonus ($1,200 + $750) = $1,950
    FITW on total amount (wage-bracket method) =   254
    FITW from latest wage payment =   - 125
    FITW from supplemental wage payment = $ 129

9. a. Using the flat rate method:
    FITW on regular wages = $ 65
    FITW on supplemental wages ($100 x 25%) =   + 25
    Total FITW = $65 + $25 = $ 90

    b. Using the aggregate method:
    FITW on $700 ($600 in regular wages plus $100 bonus) = $80

10. Social security: $430 x 6.2% = $26.66

    Medicare: $430 x 1.45% = $6.24

11. Weekly wages: $36,000 ÷ 52 = $692.31

    Social security: $692.31 x 6.2% = $42.92

    Medicare: $692.31 x 1.45% = $10.04

12. Social security wage limit: $113,700
    Wages paid to date ($2,500 x 45):   -112,500
    Social security taxable wages this pay: 1,200
        x 6.2%
    Social security tax to withhold: $74.40

    Medicare taxable wages this pay: $2,500
        x 1.45%
    Medicare tax to withhold: $36.25

13. Social security wage limit: $113,700
    Wages paid to date ($9,500 x 21):   -199,500
    Social security taxable wages this pay: 0
    Social security tax to withhold: $0.00

    Medicare taxable wages this pay: $9,500
        x 1.45%
    Medicare tax to withhold: $ 137.75

    Total Medicare taxable wages through this pay: ($9,500 x 22): $209,000
    Additional Medicare tax threshold: -200,000
    Additional Medicare taxable wages this pay: 9,000
        x 0.9%
    Additional Medicare tax to withhold: $81.00

SECTION 7: UNEMPLOYMENT INSURANCE _____

Review Questions

1. The normal credit against FUTA tax liability equals the amount of an employer's required contributions that are timely paid into a certified state unemployment insurance fund. It is also called the 90% credit because the amount of the credit is limited to 90% of the 6.0% FUTA tax rate.

2. The following individuals can sign an employer's Form 940:

    *   the individual owning the business, if it is a sole proprietorship,
    *   the president, vice president, or other principal corporate officer authorized to act, if the employer is a corporation (including a limited liability company treated as a corporation),
    *   an authorized member, partner, or officer of an unincorporated association or partnership (including a limited liability company treated as a partnership) having knowledge of the organization's affairs
    *   the owner or principal officer authorized to act, if it is a single member limited liability company treated as a disregarded entity, or
    *   a fiduciary if the employer is a trust or estate.

3. A Form 940 that is mailed through the U.S. Postal Service is considered filed at the time it is postmarked by the U.S. Postal Service.

4. Employers that cease doing business must file a Form 940 for the portion of the last calendar year they were in business and check Box d in the upper right hand corner of page 1 indicating no future returns will be filed. The employer must also attach a statement to the form including the following information: the location where required records will be kept; who is responsible for keeping the records; and the name and address of the purchaser of the business or the fact that there was no purchaser or that the purchaser's name is unknown.

5. Unless there is reasonable cause and no willful neglect, late payment of tax owed as shown on Form 940 results in an "addition to tax," the amount of which depends on how late the payment is made. The amounts are:

    *   5% of any unpaid tax shown on the return (after accounting for credits) for each month or fraction of a month that the payment is late, up to a maximum of 25%, and
    *   an additional 0.5% per month of any unpaid tax that is not shown on the return but for which the IRS has issued a notice and demand, if the tax is not paid within 21 calendar days of the notice and demand (10 business days if the amount is at least $100,000), up to a maximum of 25%.

6. The four factors used by employers in allocating employees who work in more than one state for purposes of unemployment insurance are:

    *   Are services "localized?"
    *   Does the employee have a "base of operations?"
    *   Is there a "place of direction or control?"
    *   What is the employee's "state of residence?"

7. The following employers are not subject to FUTA tax:

   - federal, state, and local government employers, including their political subdivisions,

   - Indian tribes; and

   - nonprofit religious, charitable, or educational organizations that are tax-exempt.

8. Following is a list of several FUTA exempt payments:

   - sick or disability pay paid more than six calendar months after the last month the employee worked for an employer;

   - sickness or injury payments made under a state workers' compensation law or a law in the nature of a workers' compensation law;

   - payments made under a deferred compensation plan, except elective deferrals to the plan;

   - noncash payments to an employee for work done outside the employer's trade or business;

   - qualified moving expense reimbursements;

   - death or disability retirement benefits;

   - noncash payments to agricultural workers;

   - reimbursements for, or provision of deductible dependent care assistance;

   - value of group-term life insurance coverage;

   - value of deductible meals and lodging provided by the employer;

   - wages owed to a deceased employee and paid to a beneficiary after the year of the employee's death; and

   - tips not reported by an employee to an employer (generally if less that $20 a month).

9. Following is a list of several types of employment that are exempt from FUTA:

   - work on a foreign ship outside the U.S.;

   - work done by students for the school where they attend classes or for an organized camp;

   - work performed as student nurses or hospital interns;

   - life insurance agents who receive only commissions;

   - newspaper deliverers under age 18 who deliver directly to customers;

   - certain nonimmigrant aliens working under F, J, M or Q visas;

   - work performed for a spouse or child;

   - work performed by a child under age 21 for his or her parents;

   - work performed by an inmate of a penal institution;

- work performed by an election worker who is paid less than $1,600 in 2013;

- work performed by alien agricultural workers under an H-2A visa; and

- work performed by statutory nonemployees.

10. Employers that make an error on Form 940 need to file an amended return. They do this by filing a new Form 940 for the year being amended with the correct numbers. Box a in the upper right corner of page 1 indicating an amended return should be checked. The form should be accompanied by a statement as to why the amended return is necessary.

11. The four methods used to determine an employer's unemployment insurance experience rating are:

- Reserve ratio
- Benefit ratio
- Benefit-wage ratio
- Payroll stabilization

12. The voluntary contribution option is often made unavailable to:

- new employers,
- negative reserve balance employers, and
- employers that have not paid state taxes on time.

13. When faced with a claim for unemployment benefits, the employer should:

- be complete and truthful in listing the grounds for an employee's termination when responding to forms and notices from the unemployment benefits agency;

- document any and all evidence of misconduct that may be needed to challenge a claim for benefits;

- respond to notices and requests for information within the time frame allowed;

- detail any final payments made to terminated employees, since they may disqualify the employee, at least temporarily; and

- urge the unemployment agency to make sure the claimant is looking for work.

14. The following standards must be met for employees to be eligible for unemployment benefits:

- earning a certain amount of wages in the "base period";

- being involuntarily unemployed for reasons other than misconduct connected with their work;

- filing a claim for benefits;

- registering for work with the state employment security office;

- being physically and mentally able to work;

- be looking for and available for work (other than during time spent on job training or jury duty);

- not being unemployed because of a labor dispute other than a lockout;

- being truthful in applying for benefits.

True or False Questions

1. True

2. True

3. False   The employer receives the normal credit for timely payments it makes.

4. True

5. False   Nonprofit and public sector employers may choose the direct reimbursement method or the experience-rated method to satisfy their state unemployment insurance liability.

6. True

7. True

8. True

9. False   The employer must file Form 940 annually, no later than January 31 following the close of the calendar year.

10. True

11. False   If the employer's FUTA tax liability is more than $500, a deposit is required.

12. False   If the FUTA tax deposit due date falls on a Saturday, the deposit is due on the next business day.

13. True

14. False   FUTA tax is based on the first $7,000 in wages paid to each employee in 2013.

15. True

16. True

17. False   If an employee works for more than one employer, the wage limit must be applied to the wages paid by each employer.

18. True

19. False   Employers that have a great deal of turnover generally have a higher experience rate.

20. True

21. False   The period for which a terminated employee is eligible to claim benefits is known as the "benefit year."

22. True

23. False   Employees whose hours are reduced are also eligible, so long as they are not earning more than the weekly benefit amount.

Multiple Choice Questions

1.	a	10.	b
2.	c	11.	c
3.	b	12.	c
4.	a	13.	d
5.	d	14.	c
6.	b	15.	a
7.	a	16.	b
8.	c	17.	b
9.	b			

Problems

1. a. $14,000 x .006 = $84

   b. No, because the liability did not exceed $500.

2. a. $70,000 x .006 = $420

   b. $70,000 x .032 = $2,240

   c. $420 + $2,240 = $2,660

3. a. $7,000 x 5 x 6.0% = $2,100

   b. $7,000 x 5 x 5.4% = $1,890

   c. $2,100 - $1,890 = $210

4. Six employees earned $7,000 or more during the first quarter.

   Taxable wages:
$7,000 x 6 =	$42,000
	+ 6,000
	+ 3,150
	+ 4,600
	+ 5,400
Total taxable wages:	$61,150

   1st quarter FUTA liability = $61,150 x .006 = $366.90

5. a. $6,000 x .049 = $294

    b. $1,000 x .049 = $49

    c. $7,000 x .006 = $42

6. a. $6,600 x .006 = $39.60

    b. $7,000 x .006 = $42

7. a. Gross FUTA tax:

Total wages paid during 2013 =	$72,680.00
Wages paid in excess of $7,000:	-26,230.00
Total taxable wages:	46,450.00
Rate of tax:	x 6.0%
Amount of gross FUTA tax:	$ 2,787.00

    b. State tax credit:

Total taxable wages:	$46,450.00
Credit against tax:	x 5.4%
Total credit:	$ 2,508.30

    c. Net FUTA tax: $2,787.00 - $2,508.30 = $278.70

8. Four employees earned $7,000 or more during the first quarter.

Taxable wages:	
David Jones	$ 7,000
Sheryl Smith	7,000
Johnny Foster	7,000
Melissa Denney	5,400
Jackie Stewart	7,000
Kathy Jensen	4,300
Paul Thornton	2,600
Total	$40,300

    1st quarter FUTA tax liability: $40,300 x .006 = $241.80

9. See the completed Form 940 on pages 39 and 40.

10. a.　First quarter:

$1,800 x 10 x 3 months =	$ 54,000
$2,000 x 6 x 3 months =	36,000
$1,000 x 4 x 3 months =	12,000
FUTA taxable wages:	$102,000

Net 1st quarter FUTA tax: $102,000 x .006 = $612

Second quarter:

$1,600 x 10 x 1 month =	$16,000
$1,000 x 6 x 1 month =	6,000
$1,000 x 4 x 3 months =	12,000
FUTA taxable wages:	$34,000

Net 2nd quarter FUTA tax: $34,000 x .006 = $204

Third quarter:

$1,000 x 4 x 1 month =	$4,000

Net 3rd quarter FUTA tax: $4,000 x .006 = $24

b.　Taxable wages　　　　　　　　　　　　FUTA Tax

1st Quarter	$102,000	
2nd Quarter	34,000	
3rd Quarter	4,000	
Total	$140,000 x 2.0% =	$2,800

Less year-to-date liability	-840
($612 + $204 + $24)	
4th quarter liability	$1,960

11.　See the completed Form 940 on pages 41 and 42, and the completed Schedule A on page 43.

12.　See the completed Form 940 on pages 44 and 45, and the completed Schedule A on page 46.

Problem 9

Form **940 for 2012:** Employer's Annual Federal Unemployment (FUTA) Tax Return

850112

Department of the Treasury — Internal Revenue Service

OMB No. 1545-0028

Employer identification number (EIN) 2 2 – 3 4 1 2 3 4 5

Name *(not your trade name)* Fine Arts

Trade name *(if any)*

Address 31 West Street
Number   Street   Suite or room number

Tulsa   OK   98243
City   State   ZIP code

Type of Return
(Check all that apply.)

- [ ] **a.** Amended
- [ ] **b.** Successor employer
- [ ] **c.** No payments to employees in 2012
- [ ] **d.** Final: Business closed or stopped paying wages

Instructions and prior-year forms are available at *www.irs.gov/form940.*

Read the separate instructions before you complete this form. Please type or print within the boxes.

Part 1:   Tell us about your return. If any line does NOT apply, leave it blank.

1a If you had to pay state unemployment tax in one state only, enter the state abbreviation .   **1a** O K

1b If you had to pay state unemployment tax in more than one state, you are a multi-state employer .   **1b** [ ] Check here. Complete Schedule A (Form 940).

2 If you paid wages in a state that is subject to **CREDIT REDUCTION** .   **2** [ ] Check here. Complete Schedule A (Form 940).

Part 2:   Determine your FUTA tax before adjustments for 2012. If any line does NOT apply, leave it blank.

3 Total payments to all employees .   **3** 69000 . 00

4 Payments exempt from FUTA tax .   **4** .

Check all that apply: **4a** [ ] Fringe benefits   **4c** [ ] Retirement/Pension   **4e** [ ] Other
4b [ ] Group-term life insurance   **4d** [ ] Dependent care

5 Total of payments made to each employee in excess of $7,000 .   **5** 27000 . 00

6 Subtotal (line 4 + line 5 = line 6) .   **6** 27000 . 00

7 Total taxable FUTA wages (line 3 – line 6 = line 7) (see instructions) .   **7** 42000 . 00

8 FUTA tax before adjustments (line 7 x .006 = line 8) .   **8** 252 . 00

Part 3:   Determine your adjustments. If any line does NOT apply, leave it blank.

9 If ALL of the taxable FUTA wages you paid were excluded from state unemployment tax, multiply line 7 by .054 (line 7 × .054 = line 9). Go to line 12 .   **9** .

10 If SOME of the taxable FUTA wages you paid were excluded from state unemployment tax, OR you paid ANY state unemployment tax late (after the due date for filing Form 940), complete the worksheet in the instructions. Enter the amount from line 7 of the worksheet .   **10** .

11 If credit reduction applies, enter the total from Schedule A (Form 940) .   **11** .

Part 4:   Determine your FUTA tax and balance due or overpayment for 2012. If any line does NOT apply, leave it blank.

12 Total FUTA tax after adjustments (lines 8 + 9 + 10 + 11 = line 12) .   **12** 252 . 00

13 FUTA tax deposited for the year, including any overpayment applied from a prior year   **13** 252 . 00

14 Balance due (If line 12 is more than line 13, enter the excess on line 14.)
- If line 14 is more than $500, you must deposit your tax.
- If line 14 is $500 or less, you may pay with this return. (see instructions) .   **14** .

15 Overpayment (If line 13 is more than line 12, enter the excess on line 15 and check a box below.) .   **15** .

► You **MUST** complete both pages of this form and **SIGN** it.   Check one: [ ] Apply to next return. [ ] Send a refund.

Next ▶

For Privacy Act and Paperwork Reduction Act Notice, see the back of Form 940-V, Payment Voucher.   Cat. No. 11234O   Form **940** (2012)

Problem 9 continued

850212

Name *(not your trade name)*	Employer identification number (EIN)
Fine Arts	22-3412345

Part 5: Report your FUTA tax liability by quarter only if line 12 is more than $500. If not, go to Part 6.

16 Report the amount of your FUTA tax liability for each quarter; do NOT enter the amount you deposited. If you had no liability for a quarter, leave the line blank.

16a **1st quarter** (January 1 – March 31) . . . . 16a   82 . 80

16b **2nd quarter** (April 1 – June 30) . . . . 16b   91 . 80

16c **3rd quarter** (July 1 – September 30) . . . . 16c   46 . 20

16d **4th quarter** (October 1 – December 31) . . . . . . 16d   31 . 20

17 Total tax liability for the year (lines 16a + 16b + 16c + 16d = line 17) 17   252 . 00   Total must equal line 12.

Part 6: May we speak with your third-party designee?

Do you want to allow an employee, a paid tax preparer, or another person to discuss this return with the IRS? See the instructions for details.

☐ **Yes.**   Designee's name and phone number

Select a 5-digit Personal Identification Number (PIN) to use when talking to IRS

☒ **No.**

Part 7: Sign here. You MUST complete both pages of this form and SIGN it.

Under penalties of perjury, I declare that I have examined this return, including accompanying schedules and statements, and to the best of my knowledge and belief, it is true, correct, and complete, and that no part of any payment made to a state unemployment fund claimed as a credit was, or is to be, deducted from the payments made to employees. Declaration of preparer (other than taxpayer) is based on all information of which preparer has any knowledge.

✗ Sign your name here

Print your name here

Print your title here

Date   /   /

Best daytime phone   405-918-1111

Paid Preparer Use Only

Check if you are self-employed . . . ☐

Preparer's name		PTIN	
Preparer's signature		Date	/ /
Firm's name (or yours if self-employed)		EIN	
Address		Phone	
City	State	ZIP code	

Form **940** (2012)

Problem 11

Form **940 for 2012:** **Employer's Annual Federal Unemployment (FUTA) Tax Return**

850112

Department of the Treasury — Internal Revenue Service

OMB No. 1545-0028

Employer identification number (EIN) 8 6 – 2 3 4 5 6 7 8

Name *(not your trade name)* Conrow Lumber Company

Trade name *(if any)*

Address 1234 San Francisco Street

Number Street Suite or room number

San Francisco CA 56789-1234

City State ZIP code

Read the separate instructions before you complete this form. Please type or print within the boxes.

Type of Return
(Check all that apply.)

☐ **a.** Amended

☐ **b.** Successor employer

☐ **c.** No payments to employees in 2012

☐ **d.** Final: Business closed or stopped paying wages

Instructions and prior-year forms are available at *www.irs.gov/form940.*

Part 1: **Tell us about your return. If any line does NOT apply, leave it blank.**

1a If you had to pay state unemployment tax in one state only, enter the state abbreviation . **1a** ☐ ☐

1b If you had to pay state unemployment tax in more than one state, you are a multi-state employer . . . . **1b** ☒ Check here. Complete Schedule A (Form 940).

2 If you paid wages in a state that is subject to **CREDIT REDUCTION** . . . . **2** ☒ Check here. Complete Schedule A (Form 940).

Part 2: **Determine your FUTA tax before adjustments for 2012. If any line does NOT apply, leave it blank.**

3 Total payments to all employees . . . . **3** 600000 . 00

4 Payments exempt from FUTA tax . . . . . . **4** .

Check all that apply: **4a** ☐ Fringe benefits **4c** ☐ Retirement/Pension **4e** ☐ Other
4b ☐ Group-term life insurance **4d** ☐ Dependent care

5 Total of payments made to each employee in excess of $7,000 . . . . **5** 460000 . 00

6 Subtotal (line 4 + line 5 = line 6) . . . . **6** 460000 . 00

7 Total taxable FUTA wages (line 3 – line 6 = line 7) (see instructions) . . . . . **7** 140000 . 00

8 FUTA tax before adjustments (line 7 x .006 = line 8) . . . . **8** 840 . 00

Part 3: **Determine your adjustments. If any line does NOT apply, leave it blank.**

9 If ALL of the taxable FUTA wages you paid were excluded from state unemployment tax, multiply line 7 by .054 (line 7 × .054 = line 9). Go to line 12 . . . . . . **9** .

10 If SOME of the taxable FUTA wages you paid were excluded from state unemployment tax, OR you paid ANY state unemployment tax late (after the due date for filing Form 940), complete the worksheet in the instructions. Enter the amount from line 7 of the worksheet . . **10** .

11 If credit reduction applies, enter the total from Schedule A (Form 940) . . . . . **11** 735 . 00

Part 4: **Determine your FUTA tax and balance due or overpayment for 2012. If any line does NOT apply, leave it blank.**

12 Total FUTA tax after adjustments (lines 8 + 9 + 10 + 11 = line 12) . . . . . . **12** 1575 . 00

13 FUTA tax deposited for the year, including any overpayment applied from a prior year . **13** 1575 . 00

14 Balance due (If line 12 is more than line 13, enter the excess on line 14.)
 • If line 14 is more than $500, you must deposit your tax.
 • If line 14 is $500 or less, you may pay with this return. (see instructions) . . . **14** .

15 Overpayment (If line 13 is more than line 12, enter the excess on line 15 and check a box below.) . . . . . . **15** .

▶ You **MUST** complete both pages of this form and **SIGN** it.

Check one: ☐ Apply to next return. ☐ Send a refund.

Next ▶

For Privacy Act and Paperwork Reduction Act Notice, see the back of Form 940-V, Payment Voucher. Cat. No. 11234O Form **940** (2012)

Problem 11 continued

850212

Name *(not your trade name)*	Employer identification number (EIN)
Conrow Lumber Company	86-2345678

Part 5: Report your FUTA tax liability by quarter only if line 12 is more than $500. If not, go to Part 6.

16 Report the amount of your FUTA tax liability for each quarter; do NOT enter the amount you deposited. If you had no liability for a quarter, leave the line blank.

16a	**1st quarter** (January 1 – March 31)	**16a**	672 . 00
16b	**2nd quarter** (April 1 – June 30)	**16b**	84 . 00
16c	**3rd quarter** (July 1 – September 30)	**16c**	42 . 00
16d	**4th quarter** (October 1 – December 31)	**16d**	777 . 00

17 **Total tax liability for the year** (lines 16a + 16b + 16c + 16d = line 17) **17**   1575 . 00   Total must equal line 12.

Part 6: May we speak with your third-party designee?

Do you want to allow an employee, a paid tax preparer, or another person to discuss this return with the IRS? See the instructions for details.

☐ **Yes.**   Designee's name and phone number

Select a 5-digit Personal Identification Number (PIN) to use when talking to IRS

☒ **No.**

Part 7: Sign here. You MUST complete both pages of this form and SIGN it.

Under penalties of perjury, I declare that I have examined this return, including accompanying schedules and statements, and to the best of my knowledge and belief, it is true, correct, and complete, and that no part of any payment made to a state unemployment fund claimed as a credit was, or is to be, deducted from the payments made to employees. Declaration of preparer (other than taxpayer) is based on all information of which preparer has any knowledge.

✗ Sign your name here

Print your name here

Print your title here

Date   /   /

Best daytime phone

Paid Preparer Use Only   Check if you are self-employed . . . ☐

Preparer's name		PTIN	
Preparer's signature		Date	/ /
Firm's name (or yours if self-employed)		EIN	
Address		Phone	
City	State	ZIP code	

Form **940** (2012)

Problem 11 continued

Schedule A (Form 940) for 2012:

Multi-State Employer and Credit Reduction Information
Department of the Treasury — Internal Revenue Service

860312

OMB No. 1545-0028

Employer identification number (EIN) | 8 6 – 2 3 4 5 6 7 8

Name *(not your trade name)* | Conrow Lumber Company

See the instructions on page 2. File this schedule with Form 940.

Place an "X" in the box of EVERY state in which you were required to pay state unemployment tax this year. For states with a credit reduction rate greater than zero, enter the FUTA taxable wages, multiply by the reduction rate, and then enter the credit reduction amount for that state. If any states do not apply to you, leave them blank.

Postal Abbreviation	FUTA Taxable Wages	Reduction Rate	Credit Reduction	Postal Abbreviation	FUTA Taxable Wages	Reduction Rate	Credit Reduction
☐ AK	.	× .000	.	☐ NC	.	× .006	.
☐ AL	.	× .000	.	☐ ND	.	× .000	.
☐ AR	.	× .006	.	☐ NE	.	× .000	.
☒ AZ	35000 . 00	× .003	105 . 00	☐ NH	.	× .000	.
☒ CA	105000 . 00	× .006	630 . 00	☐ NJ	.	× .006	.
☐ CO	.	× .000	.	☐ NM	.	× .000	.
☐ CT	.	× .006	.	☐ NV	.	× .006	.
☐ DC	.	× .000	.	☐ NY	.	× .006	.
☐ DE	.	× .003	.	☐ OH	.	× .006	.
☐ FL	.	× .006	.	☐ OK	.	× .000	.
☐ GA	.	× .006	.	☐ OR	.	× .000	.
☐ HI	.	× .000	.	☐ PA	.	× .000	.
☐ IA	.	× .000	.	☐ RI	.	× .006	.
☐ ID	.	× .000	.	☐ SC	.	× .000	.
☐ IL	.	× .000	.	☐ SD	.	× .000	.
☐ IN	.	× .009	.	☐ TN	.	× .000	.
☐ KS	.	× .000	.	☐ TX	.	× .000	.
☐ KY	.	× .006	.	☐ UT	.	× .000	.
☐ LA	.	× .000	.	☐ VA	.	× .000	.
☐ MA	.	× .000	.	☐ VT	.	× .003	.
☐ MD	.	× .000	.	☐ WA	.	× .000	.
☐ ME	.	× .000	.	☐ WI	.	× .006	.
☐ MI	.	× .000	.	☐ WV	.	× .000	.
☐ MN	.	× .000	.	☐ WY	.	× .000	.
☐ MO	.	× .006	.	☐ PR	.	× .000	.
☐ MS	.	× .000	.	☐ VI	.	× .015	.
☐ MT	.	× .000	.				

Total Credit Reduction. Add all amounts shown in the *Credit Reduction* boxes. Enter the total here and on Form 940, line 11 . . . .

735 . 00

For Privacy Act and Paperwork Reduction Act Notice, see the last page of Form 940.   Cat. No. 16997C   Schedule A (Form 940) 2012

Problem 12

Form **940 for 2012:** **Employer's Annual Federal Unemployment (FUTA) Tax Return**

850112

Department of the Treasury — Internal Revenue Service

OMB No. 1545-0028

Employer identification number (EIN) 8 2 – 4 0 2 0 3 0 4

Name *(not your trade name)* MiloSuisse Textured Yarns

Trade name *(if any)*

Address 1000 East State Street
Number   Street   Suite or room number

Campton   FL   13579-2468
City   State   ZIP code

Type of Return
(Check all that apply.)

☐ **a.** Amended
☐ **b.** Successor employer
☐ **c.** No payments to employees in 2012
☐ **d.** Final: Business closed or stopped paying wages

Instructions and prior-year forms are available at *www.irs.gov/form940.*

Read the separate instructions before you complete this form. Please type or print within the boxes.

Part 1: **Tell us about your return. If any line does NOT apply, leave it blank.**

1a	If you had to pay state unemployment tax in one state only, enter the state abbreviation .	1a ☐ ☐
1b	If you had to pay state unemployment tax in more than one state, you are a multi-state employer	1b ☒ Check here. Complete Schedule A (Form 940).
2	If you paid wages in a state that is subject to **CREDIT REDUCTION**	2 ☒ Check here. Complete Schedule A (Form 940).

Part 2: **Determine your FUTA tax before adjustments for 2012. If any line does NOT apply, leave it blank.**

3	Total payments to all employees	3	995500 . 00
4	Payments exempt from FUTA tax	4	56000 . 00	
	Check all that apply: **4a** ☒ Fringe benefits **4c** ☐ Retirement/Pension **4e** ☐ Other **4b** ☒ Group-term life insurance **4d** ☐ Dependent care		
5	Total of payments made to each employee in excess of $7,000	5	589500 . 00	
6	Subtotal (line 4 + line 5 = line 6)	6	645500 . 00
7	Total taxable FUTA wages (line 3 – line 6 = line 7) (see instructions)	7	350000 . 00
8	FUTA tax before adjustments (line 7 x .006 = line 8)	8	2100 . 00

Part 3: **Determine your adjustments. If any line does NOT apply, leave it blank.**

9	If ALL of the taxable FUTA wages you paid were excluded from state unemployment tax, multiply line 7 by .054 (line 7 x .054 = line 9). Go to line 12	9	.
10	If SOME of the taxable FUTA wages you paid were excluded from state unemployment tax, OR you paid ANY state unemployment tax late (after the due date for filing Form 940), complete the worksheet in the instructions. Enter the amount from line 7 of the worksheet . .	10	.
11	If credit reduction applies, enter the total from Schedule A (Form 940)	11	1491 . 00

Part 4: **Determine your FUTA tax and balance due or overpayment for 2012. If any line does NOT apply, leave it blank.**

12	Total FUTA tax after adjustments (lines 8 + 9 + 10 + 11 = line 12)	12	3591 . 00
13	FUTA tax deposited for the year, including any overpayment applied from a prior year	13	3591 . 00
14	Balance due (If line 12 is more than line 13, enter the excess on line 14.) • If line 14 is more than $500, you must deposit your tax. • If line 14 is $500 or less, you may pay with this return. (see instructions)	14	.
15	Overpayment (If line 13 is more than line 12, enter the excess on line 15 and check a box below.)	15	.

▶ You **MUST** complete both pages of this form and **SIGN** it.   Check one: ☐ Apply to next return.   ☐ Send a refund.

Next ▶

For Privacy Act and Paperwork Reduction Act Notice, see the back of Form 940-V, Payment Voucher.   Cat. No. 11234O   Form **940** (2012)

Problem 12 continued

Name (not your trade name)	Employer identification number (EIN)
MiloSuisse Textured Yarns	82-4020304

Part 5: Report your FUTA tax liability by quarter only if line 12 is more than $500. If not, go to Part 6.

16 Report the amount of your FUTA tax liability for each quarter; do NOT enter the amount you deposited. If you had no liability for a quarter, leave the line blank.

16a	**1st quarter** (January 1 – March 31)	16a	1075 . 00
16b	**2nd quarter** (April 1 – June 30)	16b	650 . 00
16c	**3rd quarter** (July 1 – September 30)	16c	350 . 00
16d	**4th quarter** (October 1 – December 31)	16d	1516 . 00

17 Total tax liability for the year (lines 16a + 16b + 16c + 16d = line 17) 17 | 3591 . 00 | Total must equal line 12.

Part 6: May we speak with your third-party designee?

Do you want to allow an employee, a paid tax preparer, or another person to discuss this return with the IRS? See the instructions for details.

☐ **Yes.**   Designee's name and phone number

Select a 5-digit Personal Identification Number (PIN) to use when talking to IRS

☒ **No.**

Part 7: Sign here. You MUST complete both pages of this form and SIGN it.

Under penalties of perjury, I declare that I have examined this return, including accompanying schedules and statements, and to the best of my knowledge and belief, it is true, correct, and complete, and that no part of any payment made to a state unemployment fund claimed as a credit was, or is to be, deducted from the payments made to employees. Declaration of preparer (other than taxpayer) is based on all information of which preparer has any knowledge.

✗ Sign your name here

Print your name here

Print your title here

Date   /   /

Best daytime phone

Paid Preparer Use Only

Check if you are self-employed . . . ☐

Preparer's name		PTIN	
Preparer's signature		Date	/ /
Firm's name (or yours if self-employed)		EIN	
Address		Phone	
City	State	ZIP code	

Form **940** (2012)

Problem 12 continued

Schedule A (Form 940) for 2012:

860312

Multi-State Employer and Credit Reduction Information
Department of the Treasury — Internal Revenue Service

OMB No. 1545-0028

See the instructions on page 2. File this schedule with Form 940.

Employer identification number (EIN) | 8 | 2 | – | 4 | 0 | 2 | 0 | 3 | 0 | 4 |

Name *(not your trade name)*   MiloSuisse Textured Yarns

Place an "X" in the box of EVERY state in which you were required to pay state unemployment tax this year. For states with a credit reduction rate greater than zero, enter the FUTA taxable wages, multiply by the reduction rate, and then enter the credit reduction amount for that state. If any states do not apply to you, leave them blank.

Postal Abbreviation	FUTA Taxable Wages	Reduction Rate	Credit Reduction	Postal Abbreviation	FUTA Taxable Wages	Reduction Rate	Credit Reduction
☐ AK	.	× .000	.	☐ NC	.	× .006	.
☐ AL	.	× .000	.	☐ ND	.	× .000	.
☐ AR	.	× .006	.	☐ NE	.	× .000	.
☒ AZ	91000 . 00	× .003	273 . 00	☐ NH	.	× .000	.
☒ CA	84000 . 00	× .006	504 . 00	☐ NJ	.	× .006	.
☐ CO	.	× .000	.	☐ NM	.	× .000	.
☐ CT	.	× .006	.	☐ NV	.	× .006	.
☐ DC	.	× .000	.	☐ NY	.	× .006	.
☐ DE	.	× .003	.	☐ OH	.	× .006	.
☒ FL	119000 . 00	× .006	714 . 00	☐ OK	.	× .000	.
☐ GA	.	× .006	.	☐ OR	.	× .000	.
☐ HI	.	× .000	.	☐ PA	.	× .000	.
☐ IA	.	× .000	.	☐ RI	.	× .006	.
☐ ID	.	× .000	.	☐ SC	.	× .000	.
☐ IL	.	× .000	.	☐ SD	.	× .000	.
☐ IN	.	× .009	.	☐ TN	.	× .000	.
☐ KS	.	× .000	.	☐ TX	.	× .000	.
☐ KY	.	× .006	.	☐ UT	.	× .000	.
☐ LA	.	× .000	.	☐ VA	.	× .000	.
☐ MA	.	× .000	.	☐ VT	.	× .003	.
☐ MD	.	× .000	.	☐ WA	.	× .000	.
☐ ME	.	× .000	.	☐ WI	.	× .006	.
☐ MI	.	× .000	.	☐ WV	.	× .000	.
☐ MN	.	× .000	.	☐ WY	.	× .000	.
☐ MO	.	× .006	.	☐ PR	.	× .000	.
☒ MS	.	× .000	.	☐ VI	.	× .015	.
☐ MT	.	× .000	.				

Total Credit Reduction. Add all amounts shown in the *Credit Reduction* boxes. Enter the total here and on Form 940, line 11 . . . . | 1491 . 00 |

For Privacy Act and Paperwork Reduction Act Notice, see the last page of Form 940.   Cat. No. 16997C   Schedule A (Form 940) 2012

SECTION 8: DEPOSITING AND REPORTING WITHHELD TAXES

Review Questions

1. Monthly depositors must deposit their accumulated tax liability for each calendar month by the 15th of the following month.

    Semiweekly depositors must deposit their payroll tax liability for wages paid on Wednesday, Thursday and Friday by the following Wednesday. The payroll tax liability for wages paid on Saturday, Sunday, Monday, and Tuesday must be paid by the following Friday.

    If an employer's accumulated payroll tax liability reaches $100,000 on any day during a monthly or semi-weekly deposit period, the liability must be deposited by the close of the next business day.

2. Under the "shortfall" rule, employers are not penalized for depositing a small amount less than the entire amount of their deposit obligation. An employer satisfies its deposit obligation if the shortfall is no more than the greater of $100 or 2% of the entire amount due and the shortfall is made up by the appropriate "make-up" date.

3. Beginning with payroll tax deposits based on wages paid after December 31, 2010, they may not be mailed because they must be made by electronic funds transfer through the Electronic Federal Tax Payment System. Federal tax deposit coupons and paper checks are no longer acceptable as a method of deposit.

4. Schedule R (Form 941), *Allocation Schedule for Aggregate Form 941 Filers,* is filed to allocate the aggregate information reported on Form 941 to each of the reporting agent's clients.

5. Individuals who are responsible for collecting, accounting for, and paying over withheld income and employment taxes and who willfully fail to do so are subject to an additional penalty equal to the total amount of the taxes owed. This is known as the "Trust Fund Recovery Penalty" or the "100% penalty."

6. If a Form W-2c cannot be delivered to an employee after a reasonable effort to do so has been made, the employer must keep the form for four years or maintain an electronic file containing the information on the form for the same time period.

7. Employers that have a payroll tax liability of up to $1,000 in a calendar year file Form 944, *Employer's Annual Federal Tax Return,* rather than Form 941, *Employer's Quarterly Federal Tax Return.*

8. Take the following steps to obtain an EIN by phone:

    *   complete Form SS-4 before calling;

    *   call 800-829-4933;

    *   provide the requested information from Form SS-4; and

    *   if requested by the IRS representative, mail or fax Form SS-4 within 24 hours to the IRS at the address provided by the representative.

9. The lookback period is the 12-month period ending June 30 of the previous year.

10. March 5, 2013 through June 30, 2013.

11. Mark's deposit obligation as of July 12 is $110,000. It must be deposited by the close of the next business day (Monday, July 15). Mark becomes a semiweekly depositor for the rest of 2013 and all of 2014.

12. The following are the penalties for not making payroll tax deposits on time:

    • 2% of the undeposited amount if it is deposited within 5 days of the due date;
    • 5% of the undeposited amount if it is deposited within 6-15 days of the due date;
    • 10% of the undeposited amount if it is deposited more than 15 days after the due date; or
    • 15% of the undeposited amount if it is not paid within 10 days after the employer receives its first IRS delinquency notice or on the same day that a notice and demand for payment is received.

13. An employer that will no longer be in business and will not be paying wages subject to federal income withholding, social security, and Medicare taxes should do the following:

    • check the box on Line 17 when completing its last Form 941 indicating that it will not file any returns in the future;
    • enter the date that final wages were paid;
    • attach a statement showing the address where the employer's records will be kept, the name of the person keeping the records, and, if the business has been sold or transferred, the name and address of the new owner and the date of the sale or transfer;
    • file the Form 941 by the end of the first month after the end of the quarter during which the employer stopped paying wages; and
    • file Schedule D (Form 941), *Report of Discrepancies Caused by Acquisitions, Statutory Mergers, or Consolidations,* if the employer is no longer in business as the result of a statutory merger or consolidation, or if it qualifies as a predecessor or successor after an acquisition.

14. Enter on Line 7 the difference between the total security and Medicare taxes on Line 5e and the amount actually withheld from employees' wages and paid by the employer that is due to rounding to the nearest penny.

15. Schedule B records an employer's payroll tax liability, not its deposits. Semiweekly depositors at any time during a quarter must file a Schedule B with Form 941.

16. Form 945, *Annual Return of Withheld Federal Income Tax.*

17. Unless an employer has reasonable cause and is not guilty of willful neglect, late filing of Form 941 or other employment tax returns results in an "addition to tax," the amount of which depends on how late the return is filed. The amount is: 5% of the amount of tax required to be shown on the return (after accounting for deposits and credits) for each month or fraction of a month that the return is late, to a maximum of 25% (15% per month to a maximum of 75% of the unpaid tax if the late filing is fraudulent).

18. The purpose of backup withholding is to ensure that income tax is paid on income reported on Forms 1099.

19. The amounts compared by the SSA include:

    • social security wages,
    • social security tips, and
    • Medicare wages and tips.

20. The general penalties for failure to file information returns on time and with correct information are as follows:

- $30 per return if the failure to file or provide correct information is corrected within 30 days after the due date, with a maximum penalty of $250,000 a year ($75,000 for small businesses);

- $60 per return if the failure to file or provide correct information is corrected more than 30 days after the due date but before August 1 of the same year the return is due, with a maximum penalty of $500,000 a year ($200,000 for small businesses); and

- $100 per return if the failure to file or provide correct information is not corrected by August 1, with a maximum penalty of $1,500,000 ($500,000 for small businesses).

True or False Questions

1. True

2. False   New employers are classified as monthly depositors.

3. False   At least 98% of the tax liability (or the liability - $100, if that is less) must be deposited to avoid a late payment penalty.

4. True

5. True

6. False   Form SS-4 is filed with the IRS, not the SSA.

7. False   This scenario creates 2 separate deposit obligations that must be satisfied by the same day.

8. True

9. False   For calendar year 2013, the payroll tax deposit lookback period is July 1, 2011 - June 30, 2012.

10. False   The employer is a monthly depositor for 2013 because its total payroll tax liability for the 2013 lookback period is less than $50,000.

11. True

12. False   Forms 941 sent by U.S. mail are considered timely if postmarked no later than the form's due date.

13. True

14. True

15. False   The employer has the option to either deposit the amount or pay it with Form 941.

16. True

17. False   When recovering undercollections from employees, each employee must be treated separately, so an overcollection of taxes from one employee cannot be used to offset an undercollection from another.

18. True

19. False   Allocated tips should not be included in Box 1, 5, or 7 of Form W-2, but they should be included in Box 8.

20. False   In general, employers wishing to use substitute W-2 forms should not send a sample to the IRS for approval prior to use.

21. True

22. True

23. False   Nonprofit organizations engaged in a trade or business are not exempt from Form 1099 reporting requirements.

24. False   Forms 1099 must be sent to the IRS Service Center listed on the 1099 series instructions.

25. True

Multiple Choice Questions

1.	c	14.	b
2.	d	15.	b
3.	a	16.	d
4.	d	17.	b
5.	c	18.	d
6.	c	19.	c
7.	b	20.	d
8.	b	21.	a
9.	a	22.	c
10.	d	23.	a
11.	b	24.	c
12.	c	25.	b
13.	a		

Problems

1.
J	Sick pay not included as income
C	Value of group-term life insurance over $50,000
E	Section 403(b) elective deferrals
EE	Designated Roth contributions to a governmental 457(b) plan
Q	Nontaxable combat pay
D	Section 401(k) elective deferrals
G	Section 457(b) elective deferrals
W	Health savings account contributions
T	Adoption benefits
AA	Designated Roth contributions to a Section 401(k) plan

P	Excludable moving expense reimbursements paid to employees
F	Section 408(k)(6) elective deferrals
H	Section 501(c)(18)(D) elective deferrals
DD	Value of employer-provided health coverage
Y	Deferrals under a Section 409A nonqualified deferred compensation plan
B	Uncollected Medicare tax on tips
R	Medical savings account contributions
A	Uncollected social security tax on tips
V	Nonstatutory stock options
BB	Designated Roth contributions to a Section 403(b) plan
L	Nontaxable part of employee business expense reimbursements
K	Tax on excess golden parachute payments
Z	Income under Section 409A on a nonqualified deferred compensation plan
M	Uncollected social security tax on value of group-term life insurance coverage over $50,000
N	Uncollected Medicare tax on value of group-term life insurance coverage over $50,000
S	SIMPLE retirement account contributions

2. See the completed Form 941 on page 52—53.

3. See the completed Form 941 on page 54—55.

4. See the completed Form 941 and Schedule B on pages 56—58.

5. See the completed Forms W-2 and Form W-3 on pages 59—61.

6. a. No penalty is imposed for 13 of the failures to provide correct information (i.e., the greater of 10 or 0.5% x 2,600 = 13).

   Late returns subject to penalty: 40 - 13 = 27

   b. 27 x $60 = $1,620 since the corrections were made more than 30 days after the due date (March 31) but before August 1.

7. a. No penalty is imposed for 10 of the failures to provide correct information (i.e., the greater of 10 or 0.5% x 1,400 = 7).

   Late returns subject to penalty: 30 - 10 = 20

   b. 20 x $60 = $1,200 since the corrections were made more than 30 days after the due date (March 31) but before August 1.

8. (50 x $100 maximum penalty) = $5,000 since the returns were filed after August 1.

9. 380 - 249 = 131 returns subject to penalty.

Problem 2

Form 941 for 2013: **Employer's QUARTERLY Federal Tax Return**
(Rev. January 2013)
Department of the Treasury — Internal Revenue Service

950113

OMB No. 1545-0029

Employer identification number (EIN) ☐☐ – ☐☐☐☐☐☐☐

Name (not your trade name) Allied Steel Products

Trade name (if any)

Address

Number   Street   Suite or room number

City   State   ZIP code

Report for this Quarter of 2013
(Check one.)

☐ **1:** January, February, March
☐ **2:** April, May, June
☐ **3:** July, August, September
☒ **4:** October, November, December

Instructions and prior year forms are available at *www.irs.gov/form941*.

Read the separate instructions before you complete Form 941. Type or print within the boxes.

Part 1: Answer these questions for this quarter.

1	Number of employees who received wages, tips, or other compensation for the pay period including: *Mar. 12* (Quarter 1), *June 12* (Quarter 2), *Sept. 12* (Quarter 3), or *Dec. 12* (Quarter 4) **1**	18
2	Wages, tips, and other compensation **2**	83254 . 90
3	Income tax withheld from wages, tips, and other compensation **3**	8991 . 49
4	If no wages, tips, and other compensation are subject to social security or Medicare tax ☐ Check and go to line 6.	

		Column 1		Column 2	
5a	Taxable social security wages	83254 . 90	× .124 =	10323 . 61	
5b	Taxable social security tips	.	× .124 =	.	
5c	Taxable Medicare wages & tips	83254 . 90	× .029 =	2414 . 39	
5d	Taxable wages & tips subject to Additional Medicare Tax withholding	.	× .009 =	.	

5e	Add Column 2 from lines 5a, 5b, 5c, and 5d **5e**	12738 . 00
5f	Section 3121(q) Notice and Demand—Tax due on unreported tips (see instructions) **5f**	.
6	Total taxes before adjustments (add lines 3, 5e, and 5f) **6**	21729 . 49
7	Current quarter's adjustment for fractions of cents **7**	.
8	Current quarter's adjustment for sick pay **8**	.
9	Current quarter's adjustments for tips and group-term life insurance **9**	.
10	Total taxes after adjustments. Combine lines 6 through 9 **10**	21729 . 49
11	Total deposits for this quarter, including overpayment applied from a prior quarter and overpayment applied from Form 941-X or Form 944-X filed in the current quarter **11**	21729 . 49
12a	COBRA premium assistance payments (see instructions) **12a**	.
12b	Number of individuals provided COBRA premium assistance	
13	Add lines 11 and 12a **13**	21729 . 49
14	Balance due. If line 10 is more than line 13, enter the difference and see instructions **14**	.
15	Overpayment. If line 13 is more than line 10, enter the difference [.] Check one: ☐ Apply to next return. ☐ Send a refund.	

▶ You MUST complete both pages of Form 941 and SIGN it.

For Privacy Act and Paperwork Reduction Act Notice, see the back of the Payment Voucher.   Cat. No. 17001Z   Form **941** (Rev. 1-2013)

Problem 2 continued

950213

Name *(not your trade name)*	Employer identification number (EIN)
Allied Steel Products	

Part 2: Tell us about your deposit schedule and tax liability for this quarter.

If you are unsure about whether you are a monthly schedule depositor or a semiweekly schedule depositor, see Pub. 15 (Circular E), section 11.

16 Check one:

☐ Line 10 on this return is less than $2,500 or line 10 on the return for the prior quarter was less than $2,500, and you did not incur a $100,000 next-day deposit obligation during the current quarter. If line 10 for the prior quarter was less than $2,500 but line 10 on this return is $100,000 or more, you must provide a record of your federal tax liability. If you are a monthly schedule depositor, complete the deposit schedule below; if you are a semiweekly schedule depositor, attach Schedule B (Form 941). Go to Part 3.

☒ **You were a monthly schedule depositor for the entire quarter.** Enter your tax liability for each month and total liability for the quarter, then go to Part 3.

Tax liability:	Month 1	9654 . 87
	Month 2	5866 . 35
	Month 3	6208 . 27
	Total liability for quarter	21729 . 49	Total must equal line 10.

☐ **You were a semiweekly schedule depositor for any part of this quarter.** Complete Schedule B (Form 941), Report of Tax Liability for Semiweekly Schedule Depositors, and attach it to Form 941.

Part 3: Tell us about your business. If a question does NOT apply to your business, leave it blank.

17 If your business has closed or you stopped paying wages . . . . ☐ Check here, and

enter the final date you paid wages [/ /] .

18 If you are a seasonal employer and you do not have to file a return for every quarter of the year . . ☐ Check here.

Part 4: May we speak with your third-party designee?

Do you want to allow an employee, a paid tax preparer, or another person to discuss this return with the IRS? See the instructions for details.

☐ Yes. Designee's name and phone number [ ] [ ]

Select a 5-digit Personal Identification Number (PIN) to use when talking to the IRS. ☐ ☐ ☐ ☐ ☐

☒ No.

Part 5: Sign here. You MUST complete both pages of Form 941 and SIGN it.

Under penalties of perjury, I declare that I have examined this return, including accompanying schedules and statements, and to the best of my knowledge and belief, it is true, correct, and complete. Declaration of preparer (other than taxpayer) is based on all information of which preparer has any knowledge.

X

Sign your name here		Print your name here	
		Print your title here	
Date [/ /]		Best daytime phone	

Paid Preparer Use Only   Check if you are self-employed . . . ☐

Preparer's name		PTIN	
Preparer's signature		Date	[/ /]
Firm's name (or yours if self-employed)		EIN	
Address		Phone	
City		State	ZIP code

Form **941** (Rev. 1-2013)

Problem 3

Form **941 for 2013:** Employer's QUARTERLY Federal Tax Return
(Rev. January 2013)   Department of the Treasury — Internal Revenue Service

950113

OMB No. 1545-0029

Employer identification number (EIN) ☐☐ – ☐☐☐☐☐☐☐

Name *(not your trade name)* Value Carpet Center

Trade name *(if any)*

Address
Number   Street   Suite or room number
City   State   ZIP code

Report for this Quarter of 2013
(Check one.)

☐ 1: January, February, March
☐ 2: April, May, June
☒ 3: July, August, September
☐ 4: October, November, December

Instructions and prior year forms are available at *www.irs.gov/form941.*

Read the separate instructions before you complete Form 941. Type or print within the boxes.

Part 1:   Answer these questions for this quarter.

1	Number of employees who received wages, tips, or other compensation for the pay period including: *Mar. 12* (Quarter 1), *June 12* (Quarter 2), *Sept. 12* (Quarter 3), or *Dec. 12* (Quarter 4)	1	
2	Wages, tips, and other compensation	2	36000 . 00
3	Income tax withheld from wages, tips, and other compensation	3	5800 . 00
4	If no wages, tips, and other compensation are subject to social security or Medicare tax	☐ Check and go to line 6.	

		Column 1		Column 2
5a	Taxable social security wages	34000 . 00	× .124 =	4216 . 00
5b	Taxable social security tips	.	× .124 =	.
5c	Taxable Medicare wages & tips	36000 . 00	× .029 =	1044 . 00
5d	Taxable wages & tips subject to Additional Medicare Tax withholding	.	× .009 =	.

5e	Add Column 2 from lines 5a, 5b, 5c, and 5d	5e	5260 . 00
5f	Section 3121(q) Notice and Demand—Tax due on unreported tips (see instructions)	5f	.
6	Total taxes before adjustments (add lines 3, 5e, and 5f)	6	11060 . 00
7	Current quarter's adjustment for fractions of cents	7	.
8	Current quarter's adjustment for sick pay	8	.
9	Current quarter's adjustments for tips and group-term life insurance	9	.
10	Total taxes after adjustments. Combine lines 6 through 9	10	11060 . 00
11	Total deposits for this quarter, including overpayment applied from a prior quarter and overpayment applied from Form 941-X or Form 944-X filed in the current quarter	11	11060 . 00
12a	COBRA premium assistance payments (see instructions)	12a	.
12b	Number of individuals provided COBRA premium assistance		
13	Add lines 11 and 12a	13	11060 . 00
14	Balance due. If line 10 is more than line 13, enter the difference and see instructions	14	.
15	Overpayment. If line 13 is more than line 10, enter the difference [.] Check one: ☐ Apply to next return. ☐ Send a refund.		

▶ You MUST complete both pages of Form 941 and SIGN it.   Next ▶

For Privacy Act and Paperwork Reduction Act Notice, see the back of the Payment Voucher.   Cat. No. 17001Z   Form **941** (Rev. 1-2013)

Problem 3 continued

Name *(not your trade name)*
Value Carpet Center

Employer identification number (EIN)

950213

Part 2: Tell us about your deposit schedule and tax liability for this quarter.

If you are unsure about whether you are a monthly schedule depositor or a semiweekly schedule depositor, see Pub. 15 (Circular E), section 11.

16 Check one: ☐ Line 10 on this return is less than $2,500 or line 10 on the return for the prior quarter was less than $2,500, and you did not incur a $100,000 next-day deposit obligation during the current quarter. If line 10 for the prior quarter was less than $2,500 but line 10 on this return is $100,000 or more, you must provide a record of your federal tax liability. If you are a monthly schedule depositor, complete the deposit schedule below; if you are a semiweekly schedule depositor, attach Schedule B (Form 941). Go to Part 3.

☒ **You were a monthly schedule depositor for the entire quarter.** Enter your tax liability for each month and total liability for the quarter, then go to Part 3.

Tax liability:	Month 1	3900 . 00
	Month 2	3900 . 00
	Month 3	3260 . 00
	Total liability for quarter	11060 . 00	Total must equal line 10.

☐ **You were a semiweekly schedule depositor for any part of this quarter.** Complete Schedule B (Form 941), Report of Tax Liability for Semiweekly Schedule Depositors, and attach it to Form 941.

Part 3: Tell us about your business. If a question does NOT apply to your business, leave it blank.

17 If your business has closed or you stopped paying wages . . . . ☐ Check here, and

enter the final date you paid wages [/ /].

18 If you are a seasonal employer and you do not have to file a return for every quarter of the year . . ☐ Check here.

Part 4: May we speak with your third-party designee?

Do you want to allow an employee, a paid tax preparer, or another person to discuss this return with the IRS? See the instructions for details.

☐ Yes. Designee's name and phone number

Select a 5-digit Personal Identification Number (PIN) to use when talking to the IRS. ☐ ☐ ☐ ☐ ☐

☒ No.

Part 5: Sign here. You MUST complete both pages of Form 941 and SIGN it.

Under penalties of perjury, I declare that I have examined this return, including accompanying schedules and statements, and to the best of my knowledge and belief, it is true, correct, and complete. Declaration of preparer (other than taxpayer) is based on all information of which preparer has any knowledge.

X Sign your name here

Print your name here

Print your title here

Date [/ /]

Best daytime phone

Paid Preparer Use Only   Check if you are self-employed . . . ☐

Preparer's name		PTIN	
Preparer's signature		Date	/ /
Firm's name (or yours if self-employed)		EIN	
Address		Phone	
City		State		ZIP code	

Page **2**

Form **941** (Rev. 1-2013)

55

Problem 4

Form **941 for 2013:** Employer's QUARTERLY Federal Tax Return
(Rev. January 2013)

950113

Department of the Treasury — Internal Revenue Service

OMB No. 1545-0029

Employer identification number (EIN) 4 3 – 1 2 3 4 5 6 7

Name *(not your trade name)* Bimms & Ferrow, Inc.

Trade name *(if any)*

Address 3456 Mid West Street
Number   Street   Suite or room number

Kansas City   KS   25783
City   State   ZIP code

Report for this Quarter of 2013
(Check one.)

- [ ] 1: January, February, March
- [ ] 2: April, May, June
- [X] 3: July, August, September
- [ ] 4: October, November, December

Instructions and prior year forms are available at *www.irs.gov/form941*.

Read the separate instructions before you complete Form 941. Type or print within the boxes.

Part 1:   Answer these questions for this quarter.

1	Number of employees who received wages, tips, or other compensation for the pay period including: *Mar. 12* (Quarter 1), *June 12* (Quarter 2), *Sept. 12* (Quarter 3), or *Dec. 12* (Quarter 4)	1	
2	Wages, tips, and other compensation	2	2400000 . 00
3	Income tax withheld from wages, tips, and other compensation	3	360000 . 00
4	If no wages, tips, and other compensation are subject to social security or Medicare tax		[ ] Check and go to line 6.

		Column 1		Column 2	
5a	Taxable social security wages . .	2000000 . 00	× .124 =	248000 . 00	
5b	Taxable social security tips . . .	.	× .124 =	.	
5c	Taxable Medicare wages & tips . .	2400000 . 00	× .029 =	69600 . 00	
5d	Taxable wages & tips subject to Additional Medicare Tax withholding	.	× .009 =	.	

5e	Add Column 2 from lines 5a, 5b, 5c, and 5d	5e	317600 . 00
5f	Section 3121(q) Notice and Demand—Tax due on unreported tips (see instructions) . .	5f	.
6	Total taxes before adjustments (add lines 3, 5e, and 5f)	6	677600 . 00
7	Current quarter's adjustment for fractions of cents	7	.
8	Current quarter's adjustment for sick pay	8	.
9	Current quarter's adjustments for tips and group-term life insurance	9	.
10	Total taxes after adjustments. Combine lines 6 through 9	10	677600 . 00
11	Total deposits for this quarter, including overpayment applied from a prior quarter and overpayment applied from Form 941-X or Form 944-X filed in the current quarter . . .	11	677600 . 00
12a	COBRA premium assistance payments (see instructions)	12a	.
12b	Number of individuals provided COBRA premium assistance . .		
13	Add lines 11 and 12a	13	677600 . 00
14	Balance due. If line 10 is more than line 13, enter the difference and see instructions . .	14	.
15	Overpayment. If line 13 is more than line 10, enter the difference	.	Check one: [ ] Apply to next return. [ ] Send a refund.

▶ You MUST complete both pages of Form 941 and SIGN it.

Next ▶

For Privacy Act and Paperwork Reduction Act Notice, see the back of the Payment Voucher.   Cat. No. 17001Z   Form **941** (Rev. 1-2013)

Problem 4 continued

950213

Name *(not your trade name)*	Employer identification number (EIN)
Bimms & Ferrow, Inc.	43-1234567

Part 2: Tell us about your deposit schedule and tax liability for this quarter.

If you are unsure about whether you are a monthly schedule depositor or a semiweekly schedule depositor, see Pub. 15 (Circular E), section 11.

16 Check one: ☐ Line 10 on this return is less than $2,500 or line 10 on the return for the prior quarter was less than $2,500, and you did not incur a $100,000 next-day deposit obligation during the current quarter. If line 10 for the prior quarter was less than $2,500 but line 10 on this return is $100,000 or more, you must provide a record of your federal tax liability. If you are a monthly schedule depositor, complete the deposit schedule below; if you are a semiweekly schedule depositor, attach Schedule B (Form 941). Go to Part 3.

☐ **You were a monthly schedule depositor for the entire quarter.** Enter your tax liability for each month and total liability for the quarter, then go to Part 3.

Tax liability: Month 1 _____ .

Month 2 _____ .

Month 3 _____ .

Total liability for quarter _____ .   Total must equal line 10.

☒ **You were a semiweekly schedule depositor for any part of this quarter.** Complete Schedule B (Form 941), Report of Tax Liability for Semiweekly Schedule Depositors, and attach it to Form 941.

Part 3: Tell us about your business. If a question does NOT apply to your business, leave it blank.

17 If your business has closed or you stopped paying wages . . . . ☐ Check here, and

enter the final date you paid wages   ___ / ___ / ___ .

18 If you are a seasonal employer and you do not have to file a return for every quarter of the year . . ☐ Check here.

Part 4: May we speak with your third-party designee?

Do you want to allow an employee, a paid tax preparer, or another person to discuss this return with the IRS? See the instructions for details.

☐ Yes. Designee's name and phone number _____ _____

Select a 5-digit Personal Identification Number (PIN) to use when talking to the IRS. ☐ ☐ ☐ ☐ ☐

☒ No.

Part 5: Sign here. You MUST complete both pages of Form 941 and SIGN it.

Under penalties of perjury, I declare that I have examined this return, including accompanying schedules and statements, and to the best of my knowledge and belief, it is true, correct, and complete. Declaration of preparer (other than taxpayer) is based on all information of which preparer has any knowledge.

X   Sign your name here _____

Print your name here _____

Print your title here _____

Date   ___ / ___ / ___

Best daytime phone _____

Paid Preparer Use Only

Check if you are self-employed . . . ☐

Preparer's name	_____	PTIN	_____
Preparer's signature	_____	Date	___ / ___ / ___
Firm's name (or yours if self-employed)	_____	EIN	_____
Address	_____	Phone	_____
City	_____	State ____	ZIP code _____

Form **941** (Rev. 1-2013)

Problem 4 continued

Schedule B (Form 941):

Report of Tax Liability for Semiweekly Schedule Depositors

960311

OMB No. 1545-0029

(Rev. June 2011)   Department of the Treasury — Internal Revenue Service

(EIN)
Employer identification number   4 3 – 1 2 3 4 5 6 7

Name *(not your trade name)*   Bimms & Ferrow, Inc.

Calendar year   2 0 1 3   *(Also check quarter)*

Report for this Quarter...
(Check one.)

- [ ] **1:** January, February, March
- [ ] **2:** April, May, June
- [X] **3:** July, August, September
- [ ] **4:** October, November, December

Use this schedule to show your TAX LIABILITY for the quarter; DO NOT use it to show your deposits. When you file this form with Form 941 or Form 941-SS, DO NOT change your tax liability by adjustments reported on any Forms 941-X. You must fill out this form and attach it to Form 941 or Form 941-SS if you are a semiweekly schedule depositor or became one because your accumulated tax liability on any day was $100,000 or more. Write your daily tax liability on the numbered space that corresponds to the date wages were paid. See Section 11 in Pub. 15 (Circular E), Employer's Tax Guide, for details.

Month 1

									Tax liability for Month 1
1		9		17		25			
2		10		18		26			228400 . 00
3		11		19		27			
4		12		20		28			
5		13		21		29			
6		14		22		30			
7		15	114200 . 00	23		31	114200 . 00		
8		16		24					

Month 2

									Tax liability for Month 2
1		9		17		25			
2		10		18		26			226400 . 00
3		11		19		27			
4		12		20		28			
5		13		21		29			
6		14		22		30			
7		15	113600 . 00	23		31	112800 . 00		
8		16		24					

Month 3

									Tax liability for Month 3
1		9		17		25			
2		10		18		26			222800 . 00
3		11		19		27			
4		12		20		28			
5		13		21		29			
6		14		22		30	110900 . 00		
7		15	111900 . 00	23		31			
8		16		24					

Fill in your total liability for the quarter (Month 1 + Month 2 + Month 3) ▶
Total must equal line 10 on Form 941 or Form 941-SS.

Total liability for the quarter

677600 . 00

For Paperwork Reduction Act Notice, see separate instructions.   Cat. No. 11967Q   **Schedule B (Form 941)** (Rev. 6-2011)

Problem 5

a Employee's social security number 486-11-3245	OMB No. 1545-0008		
b Employer identification number (EIN) 12-3456789		**1** Wages, tips, other compensation 39500.00	**2** Federal income tax withheld 5925.00
c Employer's name, address, and ZIP code Sanchez Corporation 640 San Francisco St., Ste. 6 Sacramento, CA 35123		**3** Social security wages 42500.00	**4** Social security tax withheld 2635.00
		5 Medicare wages and tips 42500.00	**6** Medicare tax withheld 616.25
		7 Social security tips	**8** Allocated tips
d Control number		**9**	**10** Dependent care benefits 1000.00
e Employee's first name and initial Last name Suff. David V Sandoval		**11** Nonqualified plans	**12a** Code D	3000.00
4213 Central Avenue		**13** Statutory employee ☐ Retirement plan ☑ Third-party sick pay ☐	**12b** Code
Sacramento, CA 35814		**14** Other	**12c** Code
			12d Code
f Employee's address and ZIP code			

15 State	Employer's state ID number	**16** State wages, tips, etc.	**17** State income tax	**18** Local wages, tips, etc.	**19** Local income tax	**20** Locality name
CA	985-4321	39500.00	1777.50			

Form **W-2** Wage and Tax Statement   **2013**   Department of the Treasury—Internal Revenue Service
Copy 2—To Be Filed With Employee's State, City, or Local Income Tax Return

a Employee's social security number 234-56-7890	OMB No. 1545-0008		
b Employer identification number (EIN) 12-3456789		**1** Wages, tips, other compensation 28481.50	**2** Federal income tax withheld 4272.23
c Employer's name, address, and ZIP code Sanchez Corporation 640 San Francisco St., Ste. 6 Sacramento, CA 35123		**3** Social security wages 30481.50	**4** Social security tax withheld 1889.85
		5 Medicare wages and tips 30481.50	**6** Medicare tax withheld 441.98
		7 Social security tips	**8** Allocated tips
d Control number		**9**	**10** Dependent care benefits
e Employee's first name and initial Last name Suff. William T Foster		**11** Nonqualified plans	**12a** Code C	481.50
123 University Heights		**13** Statutory employee ☐ Retirement plan ☑ Third-party sick pay ☐	**12b** Code D	2000.00
Sacramento, CA 35123		**14** Other	**12c** Code
			12d Code
f Employee's address and ZIP code			

15 State	Employer's state ID number	**16** State wages, tips, etc.	**17** State income tax	**18** Local wages, tips, etc.	**19** Local income tax	**20** Locality name
CA	985-4321	28481.50	1281.67			

Form **W-2** Wage and Tax Statement   **2013**   Department of the Treasury—Internal Revenue Service
Copy 2—To Be Filed With Employee's State, City, or Local Income Tax Return

Problem 5 continued

a Employee's social security number 987-65-4321		OMB No. 1545-0008	
b Employer identification number (EIN) 12-3456789		**1** Wages, tips, other compensation 31800.00	**2** Federal income tax withheld 4770.00
c Employer's name, address, and ZIP code Sanchez Corporation 640 San Francisco St., Ste. 6 Sacramento, CA 35123		**3** Social security wages 34200.00	**4** Social security tax withheld 2120.40
		5 Medicare wages and tips 34200.00	**6** Medicare tax withheld 495.90
		7 Social security tips	**8** Allocated tips
d Control number		**9**	**10** Dependent care benefits
e Employee's first name and initial Last name Suff. Helen G Roseville 7000 Mt. Pleasant Rd. Sacramento, CA 35900		**11** Nonqualified plans	**12a** Code D 2400.00
		13 Statutory employee ☐ Retirement plan ☑ Third-party sick pay ☐	**12b** Code
		14 Other Co Veh 1800.00 Ed Asst 2500.00	**12c** Code
			12d Code
f Employee's address and ZIP code			

15 State CA	Employer's state ID number 985-4321	**16** State wages, tips, etc. 31800.00	**17** State income tax 1431.00	**18** Local wages, tips, etc.	**19** Local income tax	**20** Locality name

Form **W-2** Wage and Tax Statement   2013   Department of the Treasury—Internal Revenue Service
Copy 2—To Be Filed With Employee's State, City, or Local Income Tax Return

a Employee's social security number 246-80-1357		OMB No. 1545-0008	
b Employer identification number (EIN) 12-3456789		**1** Wages, tips, other compensation 18000.00	**2** Federal income tax withheld 2700.00
c Employer's name, address, and ZIP code Sanchez Corporation 640 San Francisco St., Ste. 6 Sacramento, CA 35123		**3** Social security wages 19000.00	**4** Social security tax withheld 1178.00
		5 Medicare wages and tips 19000.00	**6** Medicare tax withheld 275.50
		7 Social security tips	**8** Allocated tips
d Control number		**9**	**10** Dependent care benefits
e Employee's first name and initial Last name Suff. Beryl Horstmann 1212 Forest Ridge Dr. Sacramento, CA 35196		**11** Nonqualified plans	**12a** Code D 1000.00
		13 Statutory employee ☐ Retirement plan ☑ Third-party sick pay ☐	**12b** Code
		14 Other Ed Asst 800.00	**12c** Code
			12d Code
f Employee's address and ZIP code			

15 State CA	Employer's state ID number 985-4321	**16** State wages, tips, etc. 18000.00	**17** State income tax 540.00	**18** Local wages, tips, etc.	**19** Local income tax	**20** Locality name

Form **W-2** Wage and Tax Statement   2013   Department of the Treasury—Internal Revenue Service
Copy 2—To Be Filed With Employee's State, City, or Local Income Tax Return

Problem 5 continued

DO NOT STAPLE

33333	**a** Control number	For Official Use Only ▶ OMB No. 1545-0008	

| **b** Kind of Payer (Check one) | 941 ☒ CT-1 ☐ | Military ☐ Hshld. emp. ☐ | 943 ☐ Medicare govt. emp. ☐ | 944 ☐ | **Kind of Employer** (Check one) | None apply ☒ State/local non-501c ☐ | 501c non-govt. ☐ State/local 501c ☐ | Federal govt. ☐ | Third-party sick pay (Check if applicable) ☐ |

c Total number of Forms W-2 4	**d** Establishment number	**1** Wages, tips, other compensation 117781.50	**2** Federal income tax withheld 17667.23
e Employer identification number (EIN) 12-3456789		**3** Social security wages 126181.50	**4** Social security tax withheld 7823.25
f Employer's name Sanchez Corporation		**5** Medicare wages and tips 126181.50	**6** Medicare tax withheld 1829.63
640 San Francisco St., Ste. 6		**7** Social security tips	**8** Allocated tips
Sacramento, CA 35123		**9**	**10** Dependent care benefits 1000.00
g Employer's address and ZIP code		**11** Nonqualified plans	**12a** Deferred compensation 8400.00
h Other EIN used this year		**13** For third-party sick pay use only	**12b**
15 State CA	Employer's state ID number 985-4321	**14** Income tax withheld by payer of third-party sick pay	
16 State wages, tips, etc. 117781.50	**17** State income tax 5030.17	**18** Local wages, tips, etc.	**19** Local income tax
Contact person		Telephone number	For Official Use Only
Email address		Fax number	

Under penalties of perjury, I declare that I have examined this return and accompanying documents and, to the best of my knowledge and belief, they are true, correct, and complete.

Signature ▶   Title ▶   Date ▶

Form **W-3** Transmittal of Wage and Tax Statements   **2013**   Department of the Treasury Internal Revenue Service

Send this entire page with the entire Copy A page of Form(s) W-2 to the Social Security Administration (SSA). Photocopies are not acceptable. Do not send Form W-3 if you filed electronically with the SSA.
Do not send any payment (cash, checks, money orders, etc.) with Forms W-2 and W-3.

Reminder

Separate instructions. See the 2013 General Instructions for Forms W-2 and W-3 for information on completing this form.

Purpose of Form

A Form W-3 Transmittal is completed only when paper Copy A of Form(s) W-2, Wage and Tax Statement, is being filed. Do not file Form W-3 alone. Do not file Form W-3 for Form(s) W-2 that were submitted electronically to the SSA (see below). All paper forms **must** comply with IRS standards and be machine readable. Photocopies are **not** acceptable. Use a Form W-3 even if only one paper Form W-2 is being filed. Make sure both the Form W-3 and Form(s) W-2 show the correct tax year and Employer Identification Number (EIN). Make a copy of this form and keep it with Copy D (For Employer) of Form(s) W-2 for your records. The IRS recommends retaining copies of these forms for four years.

E-Filing

The SSA strongly suggests employers report Form W-3 and Forms W-2 Copy A electronically instead of on paper. The SSA provides two free e-filing options on its Business Services Online (BSO) website:

• **W-2 Online.** Use fill-in forms to create, save, print, and submit up to 50 Forms W-2 at a time to the SSA.

• **File Upload.** Upload wage files to the SSA you have created using payroll or tax software that formats the files according to the SSA's *Specifications for Filing Forms W-2 Electronically (EFW2)*.

W-2 Online fill-in forms or file uploads will be on time if submitted by March 31, 2014. For more information, go to *www.socialsecurity.gov/ employer* and select "First Time Filers" or "Returning Filers" under "BEFORE YOU FILE."

When To File

Mail Form W-3 with Copy A of Form(s) W-2 by February 28, 2014.

Where To File Paper Forms

Send this entire page with the entire Copy A page of Form(s) W-2 to:

Social Security Administration
Data Operations Center
Wilkes-Barre, PA 18769-0001

Note. If you use "Certified Mail" to file, change the ZIP code to "18769-0002." If you use an IRS-approved private delivery service, add "ATTN: W-2 Process, 1150 E. Mountain Dr." to the address and change the ZIP code to "18702-7997." See Publication 15 (Circular E), Employer's Tax Guide, for a list of IRS-approved private delivery services.

For Privacy Act and Paperwork Reduction Act Notice, see the separate instructions.

Cat. No. 10159Y

SECTION 9: OTHER DEDUCTIONS FROM PAY

Review Questions

1. According to Form 668-W, when determining take-home pay the employer should allow the payroll deductions that were in effect when the levy notice was received.

2. Employers that fail to withhold and pay over an amount not exempt from levy after receiving Form 668-W are liable for the full amount required to be withheld, plus interest from the wage payment date. In addition, the employer is liable for a penalty equal to 50% of the amount recoverable by the IRS after the failure to withhold and remit.

3. CCPA stands for Consumer Credit Protection Act. It provides the legal framework around which state child support withholding laws have been constructed and limits the amount that can be withheld for child support.

4. When the law of the state where the employee works requires that health insurance be deducted to determine the employee's disposable earnings.

5. Yes. Payments to independent contractors constitute property subject to a child support withholding order.

6. The federal garnishment maximum applies no matter how many garnishments are received for an employee.

7. The lesser of the amount stated on the garnishment order up to 15% of an employee's disposable earnings or the excess of the employee's disposable earnings over 30 times the federal minimum wage may be garnished to satisfy a delinquent federal agency loan unless the employee consents in writing to a higher amount.

8. 50%, because it is more beneficial to the employee.

9. Following are some of the voluntary deductions which are not subtracted from earnings in calculating disposable pay:

    *   health insurance premiums (unless state law says otherwise)
    *   life insurance premiums
    *   union dues
    *   retirement plan contributions
    *   United Way contributions
    *   other charitable contributions
    *   savings plan deductions, etc.

10. Under a medical child support order, a noncustodial parent is required to provide health insurance for the child by enrolling the child in the parent's employer-sponsored health insurance plan. The order may also provide for automatic enrollment of the child if the parent fails to accomplish the enrollment.

11. Under these requirements, each state's laws must:

- prohibit insurers from denying medical insurance under a parent's coverage to a child because the child was born out of wedlock, is not a dependent on the parent's income tax return, or does not live with the parent or in the insurer's service area;
- where a qualified medical child support order exists, require insurers and employers to allow the parent to enroll the child without restrictions, and to enroll the child themselves if the parent does not do it;
- where a qualified medical child support order exists, require employers to withhold the employee's share of health insurance premiums and pay it to the insurer;
- require insurers to make it easier for custodial parents to submit and collect on claims where the non-custodial parent's insurer carries the child's coverage; and
- permit state Medicaid agencies to garnish an employee's wages so the state can be reimbursed for payments made to the employee on behalf of a child who is eligible for Medicaid.

True or False Questions

1. False   You must use the table for married filing separate with one exemption if the employee does not submit a statement of filing status and exemptions.

2. False   The Consumer Credit Protection Act imposes a lower limit depending on the amount of the employee's disposable earnings in relation to the minimum wage, and various state laws also have more severe restrictions.

3. False   The exempt amount is subtracted from the employee's "take-home pay."

4. True

5. True

6. False   Employers are liable for the full amount required to be withheld.

7. True

8. False   Voluntary deductions are not subtracted from gross pay to determine disposable earnings, which only take into account deductions required by law, but they are subtracted to determine take-home pay.

9. False   An employer is only required to garnish an employee's wages by order of a court, not the creditor.

10. True

11. True

12. True

13. True

14. True

15. True

16. True

17. False   Employers must withhold child support from payments made to independent contractors when required to do so by order of a court or state child support enforcement agency.

18. False   Government employees are subject to child and spousal support withholding orders on the same basis as private sector employees.

19. False   Employers are prohibited by the CCPA from terminating an employee because the employee's earnings have been subjected to garnishment for any one indebtedness.

20. True

Multiple Choice Questions

1.	c	9.	a
2.	b	10.	b
3.	d	11.	c
4.	b	12.	a
5.	c	13.	b
6.	d	14.	d
7.	c	15.	a
8.	c		

Problems

1. Continue withholding according to the order unless and until you receive notification in writing from the court or issuing agency that a change is necessary.

2. John's take-home pay: $351.75
   ($500.00 - $148.25)
   Exempt amount: -192.31
   (Taken from 2013 table)
   Amount subject to levy: $159.44

3. Matthew's take-home pay: $1,157.85
   ($2,000.00 - $842.15)
   Exempt amount: -1,158.33
   (Taken from 2013 table)
   Amount subject to levy: $ 0.00

4. a. David's take-home pay: $2,262.57
      ($3,500.00 - $1,237.43)
      Exempt amount: - 1,666.67
      (Taken from 2013 table)
      Amount subject to levy: $595.90

   b. David's new take-home pay: $2,269.10
      ($3,500.00 - $1,300.90 + $70.00)
      Exempt amount: -1,991.67
      (Taken from 2013 table)
      Amount subject to levy: $277.43

Note: David's §401(k) deduction changed from $70 to $140 when he changed his elective deferral rate from 2% to 4%. His health insurance deduction increased from $50 to $70 when the premiums were raised. In figuring David's take-home pay, the employer cannot deduct the $70 increase in the §401(k) deduction because it was the result of a voluntary increase. The $20 increase in the health insurance deduction may be counted because it was the result of an increase in the cost of coverage, not a change in coverage chosen by the employee.

    c.   David's net pay after changes:
        Net pay = Exempt amount - §401(k) deduction increase
        Net pay = $1,991.67 - $70.00 = $1,921.67

5.
Gross pay ($8.50 x 40):	$340.00
Federal income tax:	- 33.00
State income tax:	- 3.30
Social security tax:	- 21.08
Medicare tax:	- 4.93
Disposable earnings:	$277.69

6.
Regular pay ($7.50 x 48):	$360.00
Overtime premium:	+30.00
Gross pay:	390.00
Federal income tax:	- 58.50
State income tax:	- 11.70
Social security tax ($390 x 6.2%):	- 24.18
Medicare tax ($390 x 1.45%):	- 5.66
Disposable earnings:	$289.96

7.   Week one:
Regular pay ($10.00 x 43):	$430.00
Overtime premium (0.5 x $10 x 3):	+ 15.00
Total:	445.00

Week two:
Regular pay ($10.00 x 39):	390.00
Total earnings (2 weeks):	835.00

Federal income tax:	-125.25
State income tax:	- 25.05
Social security tax ($835 x 6.2%):	- 51.77
Medicare tax ($835 x 1.45%):	- 12.11
Disposable earnings:	$620.82

8.   The lesser of:
    $320.00 x 25% = $80.00 or
    $320 - $217.50 = $102.50

Therefore, the maximum amount of Jane's disposable earnings that can be garnished is $80.00.

9. Gross pay: $2,600.00
   Federal income tax: - 390.00
   State income tax: - 195.00
   Social security tax ($2,570 x 6.2%): - 159.34
   Medicare tax ($2,570 x 1.45%): <u>- 37.27</u>
   Disposable pay: $1,818.39

   The lesser of:
   $1,818.39 x 25% = $454.60 or
   $1,818.39 - $471.25 = $1,347.14

   Therefore, the maximum amount of Don's disposable earnings that can be garnished is $454.60. However, since $150 of Don's disposable earnings are already subject to a child support withholding order and a federal tax levy, only $304.60 is subject to garnishment ($454.60 - $150).

SECTION 10: RECORDKEEPING AND RECORD RETENTION

Review Questions

1. Where employees are exempt from overtime pay requirements for time spent receiving remedial education, the employer must keep, in addition to other required records, records of the hours spent by each employee receiving such remedial education and the wages paid for those hours.

2. Willful violations of the recordkeeping requirements can bring a criminal penalty of up to $10,000 and/or imprisonment for up to 6 months, although a jail sentence can be imposed only for second and subsequent convictions.

3. These records must be kept for at least four years after the due date of the tax (or the date the tax is paid, if later) for the return period to which the records relate.

4. 3 days

5. Following is a list of the records that must be kept for three years after the last date of entry for each covered employee under the FLSA:

    *   name, as it appears on the employee's social security card;
    *   home address, including apartment number, if any, and Zip code;
    *   date of birth, if under age 19;
    *   sex and occupation (for use in determining Equal Pay Act compliance);
    *   the beginning of the employee's workweek (time and day);
    *   regular rate of pay for overtime weeks, the basis for determining the rate, and any payments excluded from the regular rate;
    *   hours worked each workday and workweek;
    *   straight-time earnings (including straight-time pay for overtime hours);
    *   overtime premium earnings;
    *   additions to and deductions from wages for each pay period;
    *   total wages paid for each pay period; and
    *   date of payment and the pay period covered.

6. Following is a list of records that must be kept for at least two years from their last date of entry under the FLSA:

    *   basic employment and earning records that support the data for each nonexempt employee's hours of work, basis for determining wages, and wages paid (e.g., time or production cards);
    *   order, shipping, and billing records showing customer orders, shipping and delivery records, and customer billings; and
    *   records substantiating additions to or deductions from employees' wages, including purchase orders, operating cost records, wage assignments, and garnishments.

7. In addition to other required records, hospitals and residential care facilities whose employees have a work period of 14 consecutive days (rather than 7 for other employees) must keep records of the time and day on which the 14-day period begins, hours worked each day and each 14-day period, and straight-time and overtime premium earnings paid in each 14-day period. They also must keep a copy of the written agreement between the hospital and the employee allowing use of the 14-day work period or a memorandum summarizing its terms if the agreement is oral.

8. Employers that use the tip credit to pay part of a tipped employee's minimum wage must keep, in addition to other required records, the following:

   - some notation of the records showing that the employee's wages are determined partly by tips;
   - the amount reported by the employee to the employer as tips (weekly or monthly), which may be taken from IRS Form 4070;
   - the amount of the tip credit taken by the employer;
   - hours worked and straight-time earnings for time worked other than as a tipped employee; and
   - hours worked and straight-time earnings for time worked as a tipped employee.

9. The procedures are generally aimed at achieving one goal—making it easy for the IRS to determine the employer's correct tax liability.

10. Employers must retain the completed Form I-9, *Employment Eligibility Verification,* for at least three years after the date of hire or one year after the date of termination, whichever is later.

11. The advantages of micromedia storage over paper storage include:

    - less space needed for storage
    - reduced storage costs
    - less chance of losing individual documents
    - increased durability

12. The main problem is one of quality control—the camera may not photograph 100% of every document, the image may be partially unreadable, and verification of the image after it develops can be a time-consuming process.

13. Whatever method an employer uses to create and preserve its employment and payroll records, it should have a policy governing record retention, retrieval, and destruction. The written policy should clearly state how long records are to be retained (and how the containers should be labeled), how they can be retrieved (especially important if records are stored off site), and when and how they should be disposed of.

14. The Privacy Rule.

15. The Department of Health and Human Services.

True or False Questions

1. False   Payroll records may be retained in any form, including microfilm, microfiche, paper, or computerized.

2. True

3. False   72 hours.

4. True

5. False   The employer remains ultimately responsible for the recordkeeping requirements.

6. True

7. False   Certain records relating to overtime pay requirements, including hours worked, need not be kept for exempt "white collar" employees. However, employers must include in their records the basis on which wages are paid so that each employee's total earnings for each pay period can be calculated.

8. True

9. True

10. False   The records required by the FLSA may be stored by the employer either at the work site or at a central location where its records are customarily maintained.

11. True

12. False   Form W-4 must be retained by the employer for at least four years after the date the last return was filed using the information on the form (i.e., the employee's personal income tax return for the last year during which the Form W-4 was in effect, which is due the following April 15).

13. True

14. True

15. False   The various federal and state laws generally do not require that records be kept in any particular form and often specifically allow record retention on micromedia, digitally, or electronically.

Multiple Choice Questions

1.	a	6.	b
2.	d	7.	b
3.	b	8.	a
4.	c	9.	b
5.	d	10.	c

SECTION 11: PAYROLL ACCOUNTING

Review Questions

1. Management, stockholders, investors, employees, and auditors would be interested in the financial records of a business.

2. Subsidiary ledgers are used for a single type of account and are subordinate to the general ledger. For example, entries documenting payroll expenses and liabilities may be contained in a subsidiary ledger known as the Payroll Register. Other subsidiary ledgers that contain entries for several accounts might include Accounts Payable, Accounts Receivable, and Fixed Assets.

3. In most companies, a "chart of accounts" lists each account by name and number, with the number being used to identify accounts in an automated system.

4. Asset, Liability, Expense, Revenue, and Equity.

5. If payroll expenses are recorded functionally, entries must be based on the processes supported by the expenses (e.g., manufacturing, sales, administration). This means that the payroll would have to be distributed into different labor distribution expense accounts and a separate Labor Distribution Subsidiary Ledger would have to be kept. Recording payroll expenses by type of pay can be done where the payroll register breaks down employees' wages into regular and overtime pay.

6. Internal controls

7. Under accrual accounting, revenue is recognized and recorded when earned and expenses are recognized and recorded when incurred. Accrual entries are made at the end of an accounting period to estimate payroll expenses and liabilities incurred between the end of the last payroll period and the accounting period end.

8. Accruals generally are estimates, so they must be corrected by reversing entries during the next accounting period when the actual expenses and liabilities are recorded.

9. In preparing to file quarterly Forms 941 and annual Form 940, employers should verify the following:

    * that FUTA, social security, and Medicare tax deposits for the quarter equal the current tax rates for each, multiplied by the taxable wages for each;
    * the total Form 941 tax deposits and COBRA premium assistance payments for the quarter equal the liability section for Form 941 (Line 13 of Form 941 equals Line 16 of Form 941 or the "Total liability for the quarter" line of Schedule B, whichever applies), although monthly depositors may pay their lawful $100 or 2% deposit shortfall with Form 941, in which case total deposits would not equal the liability;
    * total FUTA tax deposits equal Part 4, Line 13 and Part 5, Line 17 of Form 940.

10. Earnings per share show the company's net income divided by the weighted average number of outstanding shares of stock.

11. The purposes of an external audit include:

    • to determine the accuracy of financial statements,
    • to depict the company's financial condition and determine whether the notes to financial statements accurately summarize the company's accounting policies and procedures,
    • to guard against any possible conflict of interest,
    • to safeguard the company's assets, and
    • to provide an objective opinion as to the fairness of the financial statements.

12. The job of a company's internal auditor is to review the efficiency of the organization's internal control procedures and to identify weaknesses in the controls.

13. A balance sheet is a statement of the financial position of a business at a specific period in time. It is an itemized list showing the business's assets, liabilities, and owner's equity.

14. Revenue has the effect of increasing owner's equity.

15. Expenses have the effect of decreasing owner's equity.

16. The journal is used to list all the necessary information about a transaction in one place. The journal is the first accounting record of business transactions and is therefore referred to as a record of original entry.

True or False Questions

1. True

2. True

3. False   Payroll taxes are always reported on a calendar year basis.

4. False   The income statement summarizes the organization's revenues, expenses, and earnings for the current and preceding fiscal years.

5. True

6. False   Accounts payable are liabilities.

7. False   Assets must equal liabilities plus owner's equity.

8. False   The property owned by a business is known as assets.

9. True

10. True

11. True

12. True

13. True

14. True

15. False   Revenue appears on the income statement.

16. True

17. True

18. True

19. True

20. True

21. False   The general ledger is the record of final entry.

22. False   The payroll expense journal will debit an expense account for the labor costs (salary expense) and credit a liability account (accrued salaries/wages).

23. True

24. False   Payroll checks that cannot be delivered should be returned to a department other than payroll and be locked up until the employee returns and can receive the check.

25. True

26. True

Multiple Choice Questions

1.	b	12.	d
2.	c	13.	d
3.	a	14.	c
4.	d	15.	c
5.	a	16.	b
6.	a	17.	b
7.	a	18.	b
8.	b	19.	d
9.	c	20.	d
10.	b	21.	d
11.	a		

Problems

1. a. Cash   Asset
   b. Loan payable to a bank Liability
   c. Delivery equipment Asset
   d. Account payable to a creditor Liability
   e. Office furniture Asset
   f. Owner's financial interest Owner's Equity
   g. Petty cash Asset
   h. Mortgage payable to a bank Liability
   i. FUTA taxes payable Liability

2.

	Accounts	Income Statement	Balance Sheet
a.	Accounts payable		✓
b.	Accounts receivable		✓
c.	Advertising expense	✓	
d.	Cash		✓
e.	Salaries payable		✓
f.	Duplicating equipment		✓
g.	Paul Morris, capital		✓
h.	Miscellaneous expense	✓	
i.	Office furniture		✓
j.	Rent expense	✓	

3. a. Accounts receivable   Debit
   b. Social security tax payable   Credit
   c. Sales   Credit
   d. Sales tax payable   Credit
   e. Accounts payable   Credit
   f. Wage garnishments payable   Credit
   g. Payroll taxes expense   Debit
   h. Professional fees payable   Credit
   i. Freight expense   Debit
   j. Life insurance premiums payable Credit

4.

Date	Item	Debit	Credit
Jan 6, 2013	Wages/salary expense	$50,000.00	
	Social security tax payable		$ 3,100.00
	Medicare tax payable		725.00
	Federal income tax payable		7,500.00
	State income tax payable		750.00
	City income tax payable		375.00
	Life insurance premiums payable		200.00
	Health insurance premiums payable		120.00
	Credit union contributions payable		100.00
	Savings Bond deductions payable		350.00
	Wages/salaries payable		36,780.00

5.

Date	Item	Debit	Credit
Jan 13, 2013	Payroll taxes expense	$ 4,380.00	
	Social security tax payable		$ 2,480.00
	Medicare tax payable		580.00
	FUTA tax payable		240.00
	SUTA tax payable		1,080.00

6.

a.

Date	Item	Debit	Credit
Jan 13, 2013	Wages/salaries expense	$30,000.00	
	Social security tax payable		$ 1,860.00
	Medicare tax payable		435.00
	Federal income tax payable		4,500.00
	Wages/salaries payable		23,205.00

b.

Date	Item	Debit	Credit
Jan 13, 2013	Payroll taxes expense	$ 3,285.00	
	Social security tax payable		$ 1,860.00
	Medicare tax payable		435.00
	FUTA tax payable		180.00
	SUTA tax payable		810.00

c.

Date	Item	Debit	Credit
Jan 20, 2013	Wages/salaries payable	$23,205.00	
	Cash		$23,205.00

7.

Date	Item	Debit	Credit
Jan 6, 2013	Wages/salaries expense	$16,400.00	
	Social security tax payable		$ 1,016.80
	Medicare tax payable		237.80
	Federal income tax payable		2,460.00
	State income tax payable		246.00
	Life insurance premiums payable		30.00
	Health insurance premiums payable		22.00
	Wages/salaries payable		12,387.40
Jan 6, 2013	Payroll taxes expense	$ 1,795.80	
	Social security tax payable		$ 1,016.80
	Medicare tax payable		237.80
	FUTA tax payable		98.40
	SUTA tax payable		442.80
Jan 6, 2013	Wages/salaries payable	$12,387.40	
	Cash		$12,387.40

8.

a.

Date	Item	Debit	Credit
Jan 25, 2013	Accrued payroll expense	$80,000.00	
	Accrued payroll liability		$80,000.00

To record the estimated salaries due from Jan. 22 – Jan. 25

Date	Item	Debit	Credit
Jan 25, 2013	Accrued payroll tax expense	$9,000.00	
	Accrued social security tax payable		$ 4,960.00
	Accrued Medicare tax payable		1,160.00
	Accrued FUTA tax payable		480.00
	Accrued SUTA tax payable		2,400.00

To record the estimated payroll tax expenses on wages from Jan. 22 – Jan. 25.

b.

Date	Item	Debit	Credit
Jan 26, 2013	Accrued payroll liability	$80,000.00	
	Accrued payroll expense		$80,000.00

To record the reversal of the estimated salaries from Jan. 22 – Jan. 25.

Date	Item	Debit	Credit
Jan. 26, 2013	Accrued social security tax payable	$ 4,960.00	
	Accrued Medicare tax payable	$ 1,160.00	
	Accrued FUTA tax payable	480.00	
	Accrued SUTA tax payable	2,400.00	
	Accrued payroll tax expense		9,000.00

To record the reversal of the estimated payroll tax expenses from Jan. 22 – Jan. 25.

9.

a.

Item	Debit	Credit
Vacation expense	$4,000	
Vacation liability payable		$4,000

To record the employees' accrual of vacation leave for the month of January.

b.

Item	Debit	Credit
Vacation liability payable	$ 900	
Cash		$ 900

To record the employees' actual use of vacation leave.

SECTION 12: PAYROLL SYSTEMS AND TECHNOLOGY _____

Review Questions

1. Other company systems that interface with payroll include:

    -   human resources,
    -   benefits,
    -   accounting,
    -   bank reconciliation,
    -   direct deposit,
    -   time and attendance, and
    -   general ledger.

2. Commonly used payroll system edits include:

    -   warning that a check is being generated for a terminated employee,
    -   report for new hires,
    -   error message when no check is generated for an active employee,
    -   error message for negative net pay,
    -   error message for negative deductions,
    -   report when compensation exceeds certain amounts,
    -   report for excessive overtime (or any overtime in some companies), and
    -   report when rate of pay changes.

3. The payroll department's customers include:

    -   employees,
    -   other departments
    -   upper management, and
    -   federal, state and local government agencies

4. Reasons why an integrated payroll, human resources, and benefits system would benefit a company include:

    -   streamlining functions that make up the highest percentage of cost in most organizations,
    -   storing complete data in a single separate database, which means that the information needed to make intelligent business decisions is readily available, and
    -   significant improvements in existing systems are often impossible, because most of their time and energy is spent supporting necessary interfaces among the existing systems' databases.

5. Representatives of the following departments should be included on the system selection and implementation project team:

    -   payroll,
    -   human resources,
    -   benefits,
    -   accounting,
    -   tax,

- budget/finance,
- data processing/MIS, and
- facilities.

6. A successful automated payroll system must:

   - provide for compliance with federal, state, and local withholding, depositing, and reporting requirements,
   - issue timely and accurate paychecks and/or make accurate direct deposits and payroll card account deposits,
   - maintain adequate records of all data and transactions,
   - prepare internal reports, and
   - guarantee the security of the system.

7. Slow response time to needed changes and emergency requirements.

8. Advantages of using an in-house automated payroll system include:

   - control of the system
   - convenient access
   - downtime can be reduced
   - system security
   - scheduling flexibility
   - interactive applications

9. A Current Situation Analysis should include the following components:

   - documentation of all work flow into/out of the current system,

   - documentation of the procedures for maintenance, including who is called, response time, and average downtime,

   - identify who receives information from the payroll system, how often, and whether they are using it,

   - along with the end users, identify and prioritize complaints, problems, and restrictions,

   - identify any actual or potential compliance problems,

   - document any manual processes that might be eliminated by automation, and

   - identify all costs of the current system—tax updates, corporate policy changes, computer time, paper, system shutdowns, etc.

10. A Request for Proposal should include the following:

    - the employer's purpose in issuing the request,
    - specific payroll information—size, frequency, union vs. nonunion, salaried and hourly,
    - functional requirements of a new system now and in the future,
    - number of fields required for earnings and deductions,
    - whether human resources and benefits will be integrated with the payroll system and what interfaces will be required,
    - training needs and whether this should be included in the bid,
    - level of support (maintenance) expected,
    - contract terms and conditions, and
    - instructions to vendor on how to submit proposal.

11. Common mistakes made during selection of a new payroll system include:

    - not including representatives of all the potential user departments,
    - failing to provide enough time for project team members to work on their system selection duties,
    - failing to prioritize needs and desires,
    - making decisions without sufficient input,
    - failing to consider all the costs associated with a new system,
    - making on-site visits only to customers referred by a vendor or service provider,
    - failing to thoroughly check for signs of obsolescence,
    - failing to negotiate performance guarantees, and
    - not considering future company needs—shortsightedness.

12. Four environmental concerns that need to be addressed regarding new system hardware are:

    - need for climate controlled rooms,
    - power surges, or spikes,
    - dirt, and
    - humidity.

True or False Questions

1. True

2. True

3. True

4. True

5. False   Documentation is a very important part of a company's overall control mechanisms.

6. True

7. True

8. False   An automated time and attendance system can often reduce the errors inherent in a manual timekeeping system.

9. True

10. False   An automated time and attendance system should integrate with an employer's human resources, payroll, and cost accounting systems.

11. False   The initial step in selecting a new payroll system is to put together a project team or task force.

12. True

13. False   The final test before going live with a new system is called parallel testing.

14. True

15. True

Multiple Choice Questions

1.	b	9.	a
2.	b	10.	c
3.	a	11.	d
4.	b	12.	b
5.	b	13.	d
6.	b	14.	c
7.	b	15.	a
8.	d		

SECTION 13: MANAGING A PAYROLL DEPARTMENT

Review Questions

1. Tasks and relationships.

2. The fundamental skills that most managers must master to be successful include:

    *   strategic planning/organizing,
    *   staffing,
    *   giving directions,
    *   controlling progress, and
    *   reporting to upper management.

3. Activities that must be defined during the planning and organizing process include:

    *   goals and objectives,
    *   the time frame, and
    *   the subtasks.

4. In developing a job description, the payroll manager must answer the five following questions:

    *   What are the educational requirements needed to perform the job?
    *   What knowledge/skills must the applicant have before being offered the job?
    *   What training opportunities can be offered to the new employee?
    *   What is the level of supervision required on the job?
    *   How much communication and interaction with other employees will be necessary?

5. Interview questions should be open-ended and force applicants to explain past behavior rather than questions that call for one word answers.

6. If their delegation is unsuccessful, they must do the work themselves, which tends to result in unfulfilled employees and burned out managers.

7. Four communication skills managers must possess when directing employees are:

    *   listening,
    *   providing feedback,
    *   coaching, and
    *   leading.

8. Three qualities that can help make a payroll manager a strong leader include:

    *   having a vision,
    *   building team support, and
    *   seeking partners.

9. Often the best performers are driven by a personal need to succeed and be the best rather than by money or other incentives.

10. Possible rewards for employees who have demonstrated leadership potential include:

    - public recognition,
    - promotion to supervisory positions,
    - leadership roles (projects, teams or tasks), and
    - taking them into your confidence (seeking their input).

11. A payroll manager's report to upper management should have the following characteristics:

    - include only the relevant information,
    - the information should be produced in a timely manner, and
    - it should be written clearly but briefly.

12. There are several things the payroll manager can do to ensure that the lessons a crisis has taught are not forgotten:

    - conduct a meeting of the team to discuss the crisis and determine which of the problems that occurred during the crisis are preventable;
    - initiate a plan to prevent those problems that can be prevented from reoccurring;
    - list the successful results of the crisis management operation and include them in a "Crisis File" for future reference;
    - list all the issues that were not satisfactorily resolved and formulate procedures to resolve them; and
    - express your appreciation to your staff once again for their hard work during the crisis.

13. The four combinations of time categories should be:

    - urgent and important—crisis management, immediate attention needed;
    - not urgent but important—planning and prevention activities;
    - urgent but not important—pressing activities that may be easy to accomplish; and
    - not urgent and not important—easily accomplished, time-wasting activities.

14. Following are the characteristics that define effective teams and team players:

    - the team has clear and specific goals and objectives,
    - team meetings have a relaxed atmosphere where members can offer help and share experiences;
    - each member has a role in reaching the team's goals;
    - team members listen without judging and with interest in what others are saying;
    - there is civilized disagreement among team members, who criticize constructively;
    - decisions are reached by a consensus of support, not unanimity, with even disagreeing members pledging to support the final decision;
    - there is open communication and trust among members;
    - each member has a clear assignment;
    - all members are responsible for the team's success or failure;
    - the team builds networks with employees outside the team and asks for their feedback;
    - the team contains a diversity of employee styles—contributors, collaborators, communicators, and challengers; and
    - the team performs a formal or informal self-assessment.

15. When conducting performance appraisals, managers often make these common mistakes:

    - guilt over negative evaluations,
    - no accountability for the manager, and
    - improper application of standards

16. Some of the forms of guidance in interpreting tax laws, other than IRS regulations, include:

    - Revenue Procedures
    - Revenue Rulings
    - Private Letter Rulings
    - Publications
    - Announcements, Notices, and News Releases
    - Field Service Advice, Service Center Advice, Internal Legal Memoranda

17. Union contract obligations can affect the following areas of payroll processing:

    - dues checkoffs,
    - fringe benefit contributions,
    - upcoming layoffs,
    - wage increases,
    - probationary employees, and
    - overtime and other premium pay.

18. Once the type of meeting has been determined, the manager leading the meeting should take the following steps:

    - prepare an agenda,
    - keep the meeting on track,
    - promote participation, and
    - keep written records.

19. The four stages of team development are:

    - forming,
    - storming,
    - norming, and
    - performing.

True or False Questions

1. False   Most payroll managers achieve their position because of their technical proficiency.

2. True

3. True

4. True

5. False   Timely completion of subtasks will lead to attainment of the objectives.

6. True

7. False   At all times during the hiring process—from job analysis through interviewing and orientation, the payroll manager must keep in mind the legal requirements surrounding the process.

8. True

9. False   The payroll manager must decide which employee will be assigned the responsibility for each task or portion of a task in the department.

10. False   Use a different training method before resorting to discipline.

11. False   Training can improve skills and knowledge, not attitude.

12. True

13. True

14. True

15. True

16. True

17. True

18. False   Counseling should not be used by a payroll manager when an employee has a severe personal problem. The employee should be referred to an appropriate employee counseling program if the employer has an Employee Assistance Program.

19. False   While most payroll managers do not like to think about it, crisis management is one of the most important leadership tests they will have.

20. True

21. False   Managers who are constantly moving from crisis to crisis, or who fail to delegate properly, have no time to focus on the payroll department's overall mission of quality service or their own personal goals and objectives.

22. True

23. False   Performance evaluations are a formal way of giving feedback. They provide a form and written record of how employees are performing relative to present goals that are designed to help the department and company meet their overall business goals.

24. True

25. False   The final stage of team development is performing.

Multiple Choice Questions

1.	c	11.	c
2.	b	12.	d
3.	a	13.	b
4.	c	14.	c
5.	d	15.	d
6.	a	16.	b
7.	d	17.	a
8.	c	18.	d
9.	d	19.	c
10.	a		

SECTION 14: PAYROLL FOR U.S. EMPLOYEES ABROAD AND ALIENS IN THE U.S.

Review Questions

1. Reasonable housing expenses do not include the following:

    *   telephone and cable television charges,
    *   capital expenditures such as mortgage payments or furniture,
    *   cost of domestic labor such as a maid or gardener, and
    *   lavish or extravagant expenses under the circumstances.

2. An employee's tax home is the location of his or her regular place of business. If there is none, the employee's tax home is where the employee regularly lives.

3. Whether an expatriate employee is a bona fide resident of a foreign country depends on the following factors:

    *   whether the employee brings his or her family and they intend to make the foreign country their home for the duration of the assignment;
    *   purchase of a home or signing a long-term lease in the foreign country;
    *   involvement in the culture and social life of the foreign country;
    *   the terms of the employment agreement regarding the foreign assignment; and
    *   the type of visa or residence permit secured by the employee.

4. This test is met if the expatriate employee has a foreign tax home and is physically present in a foreign country (or countries) for 330 full days during any consecutive 12-month period.

5. Foreign earned income is income earned by an employee from sources within a foreign country while that employee has a foreign tax home and qualifies for the foreign earned income exclusion under the bona fide residence or physical presence test. Earned income includes all compensation, such as wages, salaries, commissions, bonuses, tax reimbursements, cost of living allowances, educational reimbursements, professional fees, etc., paid for personal services rendered, including noncash payments.

6. Totalization agreements are agreements between the U.S. and another country under which expatriate employees working "temporarily" in the foreign country would be subject to U.S. social security tax only. Wages earned by employees working "permanently" in the foreign country would be subject only to the foreign country's social security taxes. The reverse is also true for foreign employees working in the U.S.

7. Income tax treaty benefits include:

   - nondiscrimination clauses allowing resident aliens to qualify for the foreign earned income and housing cost exclusions under the bona fide residence test as well as the physical presence test;
   - a partial or total exemption from taxation by the foreign country for an employee's wages for personal services performed in the treaty country if the employee's stay is short and certain other requirements are met;
   - wages received by a U.S. teacher or professor in a treaty country are exempt from foreign taxes under most treaties for temporary periods of up to 2 or 3 years;
   - amounts received by U.S. residents for study, research, or business and technical training are generally exempt from the treaty country's income tax; and
   - to avoid double taxation, tax treaties provide for credits and deductions to reduce taxes imposed by the foreign country.

8. An education allowance is added compensation for an expatriate so the employee can send his or her children to a private or boarding school.

9. Tax protection plans attempt to guarantee that the employee will be reimbursed by the employer to the extent that the employee's combined income and social security taxes in the U.S. and the foreign country exceed the amount the employee would have paid if living and working in the U.S.

10. Tax equalization plans ensure that all expatriates continue to incur a tax burden equal to what they would incur if they were living and working in the U.S., regardless of the actual foreign tax liability.

11. The following factors generally indicate an employee's domicile:

    - where the employee votes;
    - where the employee maintains a residence;
    - where the employee's immediate family lives and where children attend school;
    - whether the employee owns a new abode or has a short-term lease;
    - where the employee returns after vacations or other leaves from work;
    - the state issuing the employee's driver's license; and
    - where bank accounts and business associations are maintained.

12. Some of the factors that generally indicate residency include:

    - physical presence;
    - where family members live and children attend school;
    - where the employee works, has business interests, and owns property; and
    - where bank accounts and business interests are maintained.

13. Under the Internal Revenue Code, an alien qualifies as a resident if he or she meets either one of two tests—the lawful permanent resident test or the substantial presence test.

14. The substantial presence test to determine an alien's tax status requires the following:

    - that the alien be present in the U.S. for at least 31 days during the current calendar year; and
    - that the total of the number of days of U.S. presence during the current calendar year, plus one-third of the U.S. days during the first preceding calendar year, plus one-sixth of the U.S. days during the second preceding calendar year, be at least 183 days (no rounding allowed—fractions must be used).

15. The specific conditions that must be satisfied for the "commercial traveler" exemption to apply are as follows:

- the nonresident alien employee is in the U.S. for no more than a total of 90 days during the taxable year;
- compensation received for work performed in the U.S. totals no more than $3,000 during the taxable year; and
- the nonresident alien is employed by: a U.S. employer in a foreign country or a U.S. possession or by a foreign employer not engaged in a trade or business in the U.S.

True or False Questions

1. True

2. False   The total exclusion is up to the first $97,600 of foreign earned income in 2013.

3. True

4. False   For purposes of the §911 exclusions, all territories of the U.S., including Guam, are not considered foreign countries.

5. True

6. True

7. False   Travel and living expense reimbursements for employees on a temporary foreign assignment may be excluded from income as reimbursed employee business travel expenses if they are provided under an accountable plan.

8. True

9. True

10. False   Reimbursements for nondeductible moving expenses incurred for a move from the U.S. to a foreign country are included in foreign earned income.

11. True

12. True

13. False   The foreign earned income exclusion is available to each spouse to the extent that each spouse actually has foreign earned income.

14. True

15. True

16. True

17. True

18. False   Employers cannot require nonresident aliens to produce their social security cards as proof of authorization to work in the U.S. The alien can produce any approved document to show work authorization.

19. False   In general, social security and Medicare taxes apply to all wages paid for work performed in the U.S., regardless of the citizenship or residency status of the employee (unless exempted by a totalization agreement).

20. True

21. True

22. True

Multiple Choice Questions

1.	c	11.	a
2.	b	12.	c
3.	d	13.	c
4.	b	14.	a
5.	c	15.	c
6.	d	16.	b
7.	b	17.	d
8.	b	18.	d
9.	d	19.	a
10.	b	20.	c

SECTION 15: PREPARING FOR THE CPP EXAM

Practice Test Number 1

1.	a	14.	b
2.	c	15.	d
3.	a	16.	c
4.	c	17.	a
5.	c	18.	c
6.	b	19.	b
7.	c	20.	c
8.	a	21.	c
9.	c	22.	c
10.	b	23.	c
11.	b	24.	c
12.	d	25.	b
13.	c		

Practice Test Number 2

1.	c	14.	a
2.	a	15.	d
3.	b	16.	b
4.	d	17.	a
5.	b	18.	c
6.	d	19.	a
7.	d	20.	a
8.	d	21.	b
9.	d	22.	d
10.	d	23.	d
11.	d	24.	c
12.	c	25.	c
13.	c		

Practice Test Number 3

1.	c	14.	b
2.	b	15.	b
3.	b	16.	d
4.	c	17.	c
5.	c	18.	c
6.	b	19.	c
7.	d	20.	b
8.	d	21.	c
9.	a	22.	c
10.	d	23.	c
11.	a	24.	b
12.	c	25.	c
13.	a		

Practice Test Number 4

1.	c	14.	d
2.	b	15.	c
3.	a	16.	c
4.	d	17.	a
5.	a	18.	b
6.	d	19.	b
7.	a	20.	c
8.	b	21.	b
9.	d	22.	c
10.	a	23.	a
11.	c	24.	d
12.	c	25.	b
13.	a		

APPENDIX—FEDERAL WITHHOLDING TABLES, FORMS, AND INSTRUCTIONS

TABLE OF CONTENTS

If the number of withholding allowances is:	ALLOWANCE TABLE FOR WAGES PAID IN 2013							
	And wages are paid –							
	WEEKLY	BIWEEKLY	SEMI-MONTHLY	MONTHLY	QUARTERLY	SEMI-ANNUALLY	ANNUALLY	DAILY OR MISC.
	The total amount of withholding allowances for the payroll period is:							
0	$ -	$ -	$ -	$ -	$ -	$ -	$ -	$ -
1	75.00	150.00	162.50	325.00	975.00	1,950.00	3,900.00	15.00
2	150.00	300.00	325.00	650.00	1,950.00	3,900.00	7,800.00	30.00
3	225.00	450.00	487.50	975.00	2,925.00	5,850.00	11,700.00	45.00
4	300.00	600.00	650.00	1,300.00	3,900.00	7,800.00	15,600.00	60.00
5	375.00	750.00	812.50	1,625.00	4,875.00	9,750.00	19,500.00	75.00
6	450.00	900.00	975.00	1,950.00	5,850.00	11,700.00	23,400.00	90.00
7	525.00	1,050.00	1,137.50	2,275.00	6,825.00	13,650.00	27,300.00	105.00
8	600.00	1,200.00	1,300.00	2,600.00	7,800.00	15,600.00	31,200.00	120.00
9	675.00	1,350.00	1,462.50	2,925.00	8,775.00	17,550.00	35,100.00	135.00
10	750.00	1,500.00	1,625.00	3,250.00	9,750.00	19,500.00	39,000.00	150.00

Percentage Method Tables for Income Tax Withholding

(For Wages Paid in 2013)

TABLE 1—WEEKLY Payroll Period

(a) SINGLE person (including head of household)—				(b) MARRIED person—			
If the amount of wages (after subtracting withholding allowances) is:		The amount of income tax to withhold is:		If the amount of wages (after subtracting withholding allowances) is:		The amount of income tax to withhold is:	
Not over $42		$0		Not over $160		$0	
Over—	But not over—		of excess over—	Over—	But not over—		of excess over—
$42	—$214 . .	$0.00 plus 10%	—$42	$160	—$503 . .	$0.00 plus 10%	—$160
$214	—$739 . .	$17.20 plus 15%	—$214	$503	—$1,554 . .	$34.30 plus 15%	—$503
$739	—$1,732 . .	$95.95 plus 25%	—$739	$1,554	—$2,975 . .	$191.95 plus 25%	—$1,554
$1,732	—$3,566 . .	$344.20 plus 28%	—$1,732	$2,975	—$4,449 . .	$547.20 plus 28%	—$2,975
$3,566	—$7,703 . .	$857.72 plus 33%	—$3,566	$4,449	—$7,820 . .	$959.92 plus 33%	—$4,449
$7,703	—$7,735 . .	$2,222.93 plus 35%	—$7,703	$7,820	—$8,813 . .	$2,072.35 plus 35%	—$7,820
$7,735		$2,234.13 plus 39.6%	—$7,735	$8,813		$2,419.90 plus 39.6%	—$8,813

TABLE 2—BIWEEKLY Payroll Period

(a) SINGLE person (including head of household)—				(b) MARRIED person—			
If the amount of wages (after subtracting withholding allowances) is:		The amount of income tax to withhold is:		If the amount of wages (after subtracting withholding allowances) is:		The amount of income tax to withhold is:	
Not over $85		$0		Not over $319		$0	
Over—	But not over—		of excess over—	Over—	But not over—		of excess over—
$85	—$428 . .	$0.00 plus 10%	—$85	$319	—$1,006 . .	$0.00 plus 10%	—$319
$428	—$1,479 . .	$34.30 plus 15%	—$428	$1,006	—$3,108 . .	$68.70 plus 15%	—$1,006
$1,479	—$3,463 . .	$191.95 plus 25%	—$1,479	$3,108	—$5,950 . .	$384.00 plus 25%	—$3,108
$3,463	—$7,133 . .	$687.95 plus 28%	—$3,463	$5,950	—$8,898 . .	$1,094.50 plus 28%	—$5,950
$7,133	—$15,406 . .	$1,715.55 plus 33%	—$7,133	$8,898	—$15,640 . .	$1,919.94 plus 33%	—$8,898
$15,406	—$15,469 . .	$4,445.64 plus 35%	—$15,406	$15,640	—$17,627 . .	$4,144.80 plus 35%	—$15,640
$15,469		$4,467.69 plus 39.6%	—$15,469	$17,627		$4,840.25 plus 39.6%	—$17,627

TABLE 3—SEMIMONTHLY Payroll Period

(a) SINGLE person (including head of household)—				(b) MARRIED person—			
If the amount of wages (after subtracting withholding allowances) is:		The amount of income tax to withhold is:		If the amount of wages (after subtracting withholding allowances) is:		The amount of income tax to withhold is:	
Not over $92		$0		Not over $346		$0	
Over—	But not over—		of excess over—	Over—	But not over—		of excess over—
$92	—$464 . .	$0.00 plus 10%	—$92	$346	—$1,090 . .	$0.00 plus 10%	—$346
$464	—$1,602 . .	$37.20 plus 15%	—$464	$1,090	—$3,367 . .	$74.40 plus 15%	—$1,090
$1,602	—$3,752 . .	$207.90 plus 25%	—$1,602	$3,367	—$6,446 . .	$415.95 plus 25%	—$3,367
$3,752	—$7,727 . .	$745.40 plus 28%	—$3,752	$6,446	—$9,640 . .	$1,185.70 plus 28%	—$6,446
$7,727	—$16,690 . .	$1,858.40 plus 33%	—$7,727	$9,640	—$16,944 . .	$2,080.02 plus 33%	—$9,640
$16,690	—$16,758 . .	$4,816.19 plus 35%	—$16,690	$16,944	—$19,096 . .	$4,490.34 plus 35%	—$16,944
$16,758		$4,839.99 plus 39.6%	—$16,758	$19,096		$5,243.54 plus 39.6%	—$19,096

TABLE 4—MONTHLY Payroll Period

(a) SINGLE person (including head of household)—				(b) MARRIED person—			
If the amount of wages (after subtracting withholding allowances) is:		The amount of income tax to withhold is:		If the amount of wages (after subtracting withholding allowances) is:		The amount of income tax to withhold is:	
Not over $183		$0		Not over $692		$0	
Over—	But not over—		of excess over—	Over—	But not over—		of excess over—
$183	—$927 . .	$0.00 plus 10%	—$183	$692	—$2,179 . .	$0.00 plus 10%	—$692
$927	—$3,204 . .	$74.40 plus 15%	—$927	$2,179	—$6,733 . .	$148.70 plus 15%	—$2,179
$3,204	—$7,504 . .	$415.95 plus 25%	—$3,204	$6,733	—$12,892 . .	$831.80 plus 25%	—$6,733
$7,504	—$15,454 . .	$1,490.95 plus 28%	—$7,504	$12,892	—$19,279 . .	$2,371.55 plus 28%	—$12,892
$15,454	—$33,379 . .	$3,716.95 plus 33%	—$15,454	$19,279	—$33,888 . .	$4,159.91 plus 33%	—$19,279
$33,379	—$33,517 . .	$9,632.20 plus 35%	—$33,379	$33,888	—$38,192 . .	$8,980.88 plus 35%	—$33,888
$33,517		$9,680.50 plus 39.6%	—$33,517	$38,192		$10,487.28 plus 39.6%	—$38,192

Percentage Method Tables for Income Tax Withholding (continued)

(For Wages Paid in 2013)

TABLE 5—QUARTERLY Payroll Period

(a) SINGLE person (including head of household)—

If the amount of wages (after subtracting withholding allowances) is:

The amount of income tax to withhold is:

Not over $550 . . . . $0

Over—	But not over—		of excess over—
$550	—$2,781 . .	$0.00 plus 10%	—$550
$2,781	—$9,613 . .	$223.10 plus 15%	—$2,781
$9,613	—$22,513 . .	$1,247.90 plus 25%	—$9,613
$22,513	—$46,363 . .	$4,472.90 plus 28%	—$22,513
$46,363	—$100,138 . .	$11,150.90 plus 33%	—$46,363
$100,138	—$100,550 . .	$28,896.65 plus 35%	—$100,138
$100,550	. . . .	$29,040.85 plus 39.6%	—$100,550

(b) MARRIED person—

If the amount of wages (after subtracting withholding allowances) is:

The amount of income tax to withhold is:

Not over $2,075 . . . . $0

Over—	But not over—		of excess over—
$2,075	—$6,538 . .	$0.00 plus 10%	—$2,075
$6,538	—$20,200 . .	$446.30 plus 15%	—$6,538
$20,200	—$38,675 . .	$2,495.60 plus 25%	—$20,200
$38,675	—$57,838 . .	$7,114.35 plus 28%	—$38,675
$57,838	—$101,663 . .	$12,479.99 plus 33%	—$57,838
$101,663	—$114,575 . .	$26,942.24 plus 35%	—$101,663
$114,575	. . . .	$31,461.44 plus 39.6%	—$114,575

TABLE 6—SEMIANNUAL Payroll Period

(a) SINGLE person (including head of household)—

If the amount of wages (after subtracting withholding allowances) is:

The amount of income tax to withhold is:

Not over $1,100 . . . . $0

Over—	But not over—		of excess over—
$1,100	—$5,563 . .	$0.00 plus 10%	—$1,100
$5,563	—$19,225 . .	$446.30 plus 15%	—$5,563
$19,225	—$45,025 . .	$2,495.60 plus 25%	—$19,225
$45,025	—$92,725 . .	$8,945.60 plus 28%	—$45,025
$92,725	—$200,275 . .	$22,301.60 plus 33%	—$92,725
$200,275	—$201,100 . .	$57,793.10 plus 35%	—$200,275
$201,100	. . . .	$58,081.85 plus 39.6%	—$201,100

(b) MARRIED person—

If the amount of wages (after subtracting withholding allowances) is:

The amount of income tax to withhold is:

Not over $4,150 . . . . $0

Over—	But not over—		of excess over—
$4,150	—$13,075 . .	$0.00 plus 10%	—$4,150
$13,075	—$40,400 . .	$892.50 plus 15%	—$13,075
$40,400	—$77,350 . .	$4,991.25 plus 25%	—$40,400
$77,350	—$115,675 . .	$14,228.75 plus 28%	—$77,350
$115,675	—$203,325 . .	$24,959.75 plus 33%	—$115,675
$203,325	—$229,150 . .	$53,884.25 plus 35%	—$203,325
$229,150	. . . .	$62,923.00 plus 39.6%	—$229,150

TABLE 7—ANNUAL Payroll Period

(a) SINGLE person (including head of household)—

If the amount of wages (after subtracting withholding allowances) is:

The amount of income tax to withhold is:

Not over $2,200 . . . . $0

Over—	But not over—		of excess over—
$2,200	—$11,125 . .	$0.00 plus 10%	—$2,200
$11,125	—$38,450 . .	$892.50 plus 15%	—$11,125
$38,450	—$90,050 . .	$4,991.25 plus 25%	—$38,450
$90,050	—$185,450 . .	$17,891.25 plus 28%	—$90,050
$185,450	—$400,550 . .	$44,603.25 plus 33%	—$185,450
$400,550	—$402,200 . .	$115,586.25 plus 35%	—$400,550
$402,200	. . . .	$116,163.75 plus 39.6%	—$402,200

(b) MARRIED person—

If the amount of wages (after subtracting withholding allowances) is:

The amount of income tax to withhold is:

Not over $8,300 . . . . $0

Over—	But not over—		of excess over—
$8,300	—$26,150 . .	$0.00 plus 10%	—$8,300
$26,150	—$80,800 . .	$1,785.00 plus 15%	—$26,150
$80,800	—$154,700 . .	$9,982.50 plus 25%	—$80,800
$154,700	—$231,350 . .	$28,457.50 plus 28%	—$154,700
$231,350	—$406,650 . .	$49,919.50 plus 33%	—$231,350
$406,650	—$458,300 . .	$107,768.50 plus 35%	—$406,650
$458,300	. . . .	$125,846.00 plus 39.6%	—$458,300

TABLE 8—DAILY or MISCELLANEOUS Payroll Period

(a) SINGLE person (including head of household)—

If the amount of wages (after subtracting withholding allowances) divided by the number of days in the payroll period is:

The amount of income tax to withhold per day is:

Not over $8.50 . . . . $0

Over—	But not over—		of excess over—
$8.50	—$42.80 . .	$0.00 plus 10%	—$8.50
$42.80	—$147.90 . .	$3.43 plus 15%	—$42.80
$147.90	—$346.30 . .	$19.20 plus 25%	—$147.90
$346.30	—$713.30 . .	$68.80 plus 28%	—$346.30
$713.30	—$1,540.60 . .	$171.56 plus 33%	—$713.30
$1,540.60	—$1,546.90 . .	$444.57 plus 35%	—$1,540.60
$1,546.90	. . . .	$446.78 plus 39.6%	—$1,546.90

(b) MARRIED person—

If the amount of wages (after subtracting withholding allowances) divided by the number of days in the payroll period is:

The amount of income tax to withhold per day is:

Not over $31.90 . . . . $0

Over—	But not over—		of excess over—
$31.90	—$100.60 . .	$0.00 plus 10%	—$31.90
$100.60	—$310.80 . .	$6.87 plus 15%	—$100.60
$310.80	—$595.00 . .	$38.40 plus 25%	—$310.80
$595.00	—$889.80 . .	$109.45 plus 28%	—$595.00
$889.80	—$1,564.00 . .	$191.99 plus 33%	—$889.80
$1,564.00	—$1,762.70 . .	$414.48 plus 35%	—$1,564.00
$1,762.70	. . . .	$484.03 plus 39.6%	—$1,762.70

SINGLE Persons—WEEKLY Payroll Period

(For Wages Paid through December 2013)

And the wages are—		And the number of withholding allowances claimed is—										
At least	But less than	0	1	2	3	4	5	6	7	8	9	10
		The amount of income tax to be withheld is—										
$ 0	$55	$0	$0	$0	$0	$0	$0	$0	$0	$0	$0	$0
55	60	2	0	0	0	0	0	0	0	0	0	0
60	65	2	0	0	0	0	0	0	0	0	0	0
65	70	3	0	0	0	0	0	0	0	0	0	0
70	75	3	0	0	0	0	0	0	0	0	0	0
75	80	4	0	0	0	0	0	0	0	0	0	0
80	85	4	0	0	0	0	0	0	0	0	0	0
85	90	5	0	0	0	0	0	0	0	0	0	0
90	95	5	0	0	0	0	0	0	0	0	0	0
95	100	6	0	0	0	0	0	0	0	0	0	0
100	105	6	0	0	0	0	0	0	0	0	0	0
105	110	7	0	0	0	0	0	0	0	0	0	0
110	115	7	0	0	0	0	0	0	0	0	0	0
115	120	8	0	0	0	0	0	0	0	0	0	0
120	125	8	1	0	0	0	0	0	0	0	0	0
125	130	9	1	0	0	0	0	0	0	0	0	0
130	135	9	2	0	0	0	0	0	0	0	0	0
135	140	10	2	0	0	0	0	0	0	0	0	0
140	145	10	3	0	0	0	0	0	0	0	0	0
145	150	11	3	0	0	0	0	0	0	0	0	0
150	155	11	4	0	0	0	0	0	0	0	0	0
155	160	12	4	0	0	0	0	0	0	0	0	0
160	165	12	5	0	0	0	0	0	0	0	0	0
165	170	13	5	0	0	0	0	0	0	0	0	0
170	175	13	6	0	0	0	0	0	0	0	0	0
175	180	14	6	0	0	0	0	0	0	0	0	0
180	185	14	7	0	0	0	0	0	0	0	0	0
185	190	15	7	0	0	0	0	0	0	0	0	0
190	195	15	8	0	0	0	0	0	0	0	0	0
195	200	16	8	1	0	0	0	0	0	0	0	0
200	210	16	9	1	0	0	0	0	0	0	0	0
210	220	17	10	2	0	0	0	0	0	0	0	0
220	230	19	11	3	0	0	0	0	0	0	0	0
230	240	20	12	4	0	0	0	0	0	0	0	0
240	250	22	13	5	0	0	0	0	0	0	0	0
250	260	23	14	6	0	0	0	0	0	0	0	0
260	270	25	15	7	0	0	0	0	0	0	0	0
270	280	26	16	8	1	0	0	0	0	0	0	0
280	290	28	17	9	2	0	0	0	0	0	0	0
290	300	29	18	10	3	0	0	0	0	0	0	0
300	310	31	20	11	4	0	0	0	0	0	0	0
310	320	32	21	12	5	0	0	0	0	0	0	0
320	330	34	23	13	6	0	0	0	0	0	0	0
330	340	35	24	14	7	0	0	0	0	0	0	0
340	350	37	26	15	8	0	0	0	0	0	0	0
350	360	38	27	16	9	1	0	0	0	0	0	0
360	370	40	29	17	10	2	0	0	0	0	0	0
370	380	41	30	19	11	3	0	0	0	0	0	0
380	390	43	32	20	12	4	0	0	0	0	0	0
390	400	44	33	22	13	5	0	0	0	0	0	0
400	410	46	35	23	14	6	0	0	0	0	0	0
410	420	47	36	25	15	7	0	0	0	0	0	0
420	430	49	38	26	16	8	1	0	0	0	0	0
430	440	50	39	28	17	9	2	0	0	0	0	0
440	450	52	41	29	18	10	3	0	0	0	0	0
450	460	53	42	31	20	11	4	0	0	0	0	0
460	470	55	44	32	21	12	5	0	0	0	0	0
470	480	56	45	34	23	13	6	0	0	0	0	0
480	490	58	47	35	24	14	7	0	0	0	0	0
490	500	59	48	37	26	15	8	0	0	0	0	0
500	510	61	50	38	27	16	9	1	0	0	0	0
510	520	62	51	40	29	17	10	2	0	0	0	0
520	530	64	53	41	30	19	11	3	0	0	0	0
530	540	65	54	43	32	20	12	4	0	0	0	0
540	550	67	56	44	33	22	13	5	0	0	0	0
550	560	68	57	46	35	23	14	6	0	0	0	0
560	570	70	59	47	36	25	15	7	0	0	0	0
570	580	71	60	49	38	26	16	8	1	0	0	0
580	590	73	62	50	39	28	17	9	2	0	0	0
590	600	74	63	52	41	29	18	10	3	0	0	0

Publication 15 (2013)

SINGLE Persons—WEEKLY Payroll Period

(For Wages Paid through December 2013)

And the wages are–		And the number of withholding allowances claimed is—										
At least	But less than	0	1	2	3	4	5	6	7	8	9	10
		The amount of income tax to be withheld is—										
$600	$610	$76	$65	$53	$42	$31	$20	$11	$4	$0	$0	$0
610	620	77	66	55	44	32	21	12	5	0	0	0
620	630	79	68	56	45	34	23	13	6	0	0	0
630	640	80	69	58	47	35	24	14	7	0	0	0
640	650	82	71	59	48	37	26	15	8	0	0	0
650	660	83	72	61	50	38	27	16	9	1	0	0
660	670	85	74	62	51	40	29	17	10	2	0	0
670	680	86	75	64	53	41	30	19	11	3	0	0
680	690	88	77	65	54	43	32	20	12	4	0	0
690	700	89	78	67	56	44	33	22	13	5	0	0
700	710	91	80	68	57	46	35	23	14	6	0	0
710	720	92	81	70	59	47	36	25	15	7	0	0
720	730	94	83	71	60	49	38	26	16	8	1	0
730	740	95	84	73	62	50	39	28	17	9	2	0
740	750	97	86	74	63	52	41	29	18	10	3	0
750	760	100	87	76	65	53	42	31	20	11	4	0
760	770	102	89	77	66	55	44	32	21	12	5	0
770	780	105	90	79	68	56	45	34	23	13	6	0
780	790	107	92	80	69	58	47	35	24	14	7	0
790	800	110	93	82	71	59	48	37	26	15	8	0
800	810	112	95	83	72	61	50	38	27	16	9	1
810	820	115	96	85	74	62	51	40	29	17	10	2
820	830	117	99	86	75	64	53	41	30	19	11	3
830	840	120	101	88	77	65	54	43	32	20	12	4
840	850	122	104	89	78	67	56	44	33	22	13	5
850	860	125	106	91	80	68	57	46	35	23	14	6
860	870	127	109	92	81	70	59	47	36	25	15	7
870	880	130	111	94	83	71	60	49	38	26	16	8
880	890	132	114	95	84	73	62	50	39	28	17	9
890	900	135	116	97	86	74	63	52	41	29	18	10
900	910	137	119	100	87	76	65	53	42	31	20	11
910	920	140	121	102	89	77	66	55	44	32	21	12
920	930	142	124	105	90	79	68	56	45	34	23	13
930	940	145	126	107	92	80	69	58	47	35	24	14
940	950	147	129	110	93	82	71	59	48	37	26	15
950	960	150	131	112	95	83	72	61	50	38	27	16
960	970	152	134	115	96	85	74	62	51	40	29	17
970	980	155	136	117	99	86	75	64	53	41	30	19
980	990	157	139	120	101	88	77	65	54	43	32	20
990	1,000	160	141	122	104	89	78	67	56	44	33	22
1,000	1,010	162	144	125	106	91	80	68	57	46	35	23
1,010	1,020	165	146	127	109	92	81	70	59	47	36	25
1,020	1,030	167	149	130	111	94	83	71	60	49	38	26
1,030	1,040	170	151	132	114	95	84	73	62	50	39	28
1,040	1,050	172	154	135	116	97	86	74	63	52	41	29
1,050	1,060	175	156	137	119	100	87	76	65	53	42	31
1,060	1,070	177	159	140	121	102	89	77	66	55	44	32
1,070	1,080	180	161	142	124	105	90	79	68	56	45	34
1,080	1,090	182	164	145	126	107	92	80	69	58	47	35
1,090	1,100	185	166	147	129	110	93	82	71	59	48	37
1,100	1,110	187	169	150	131	112	95	83	72	61	50	38
1,110	1,120	190	171	152	134	115	96	85	74	62	51	40
1,120	1,130	192	174	155	136	117	99	86	75	64	53	41
1,130	1,140	195	176	157	139	120	101	88	77	65	54	43
1,140	1,150	197	179	160	141	122	104	89	78	67	56	44
1,150	1,160	200	181	162	144	125	106	91	80	68	57	46
1,160	1,170	202	184	165	146	127	109	92	81	70	59	47
1,170	1,180	205	186	167	149	130	111	94	83	71	60	49
1,180	1,190	207	189	170	151	132	114	95	84	73	62	50
1,190	1,200	210	191	172	154	135	116	97	86	74	63	52
1,200	1,210	212	194	175	156	137	119	100	87	76	65	53
1,210	1,220	215	196	177	159	140	121	102	89	77	66	55
1,220	1,230	217	199	180	161	142	124	105	90	79	68	56
1,230	1,240	220	201	182	164	145	126	107	92	80	69	58
1,240	1,250	222	204	185	166	147	129	110	93	82	71	59

| $1,250 and over | Use Table 1(a) for a **SINGLE person** on page 44. Also see the instructions on page 42. |

MARRIED Persons—WEEKLY Payroll Period

(For Wages Paid through December 2013)

And the wages are–		And the number of withholding allowances claimed is—										
At least	But less than	0	1	2	3	4	5	6	7	8	9	10
		The amount of income tax to be withheld is—										
$ 0	$160	$0	$0	$0	$0	$0	$0	$0	$0	$0	$0	$0
160	165	0	0	0	0	0	0	0	0	0	0	0
165	170	1	0	0	0	0	0	0	0	0	0	0
170	175	1	0	0	0	0	0	0	0	0	0	0
175	180	2	0	0	0	0	0	0	0	0	0	0
180	185	2	0	0	0	0	0	0	0	0	0	0
185	190	3	0	0	0	0	0	0	0	0	0	0
190	195	3	0	0	0	0	0	0	0	0	0	0
195	200	4	0	0	0	0	0	0	0	0	0	0
200	210	5	0	0	0	0	0	0	0	0	0	0
210	220	6	0	0	0	0	0	0	0	0	0	0
220	230	7	0	0	0	0	0	0	0	0	0	0
230	240	8	0	0	0	0	0	0	0	0	0	0
240	250	9	1	0	0	0	0	0	0	0	0	0
250	260	10	2	0	0	0	0	0	0	0	0	0
260	270	11	3	0	0	0	0	0	0	0	0	0
270	280	12	4	0	0	0	0	0	0	0	0	0
280	290	13	5	0	0	0	0	0	0	0	0	0
290	300	14	6	0	0	0	0	0	0	0	0	0
300	310	15	7	0	0	0	0	0	0	0	0	0
310	320	16	8	1	0	0	0	0	0	0	0	0
320	330	17	9	2	0	0	0	0	0	0	0	0
330	340	18	10	3	0	0	0	0	0	0	0	0
340	350	19	11	4	0	0	0	0	0	0	0	0
350	360	20	12	5	0	0	0	0	0	0	0	0
360	370	21	13	6	0	0	0	0	0	0	0	0
370	380	22	14	7	0	0	0	0	0	0	0	0
380	390	23	15	8	0	0	0	0	0	0	0	0
390	400	24	16	9	1	0	0	0	0	0	0	0
400	410	25	17	10	2	0	0	0	0	0	0	0
410	420	26	18	11	3	0	0	0	0	0	0	0
420	430	27	19	12	4	0	0	0	0	0	0	0
430	440	28	20	13	5	0	0	0	0	0	0	0
440	450	29	21	14	6	0	0	0	0	0	0	0
450	460	30	22	15	7	0	0	0	0	0	0	0
460	470	31	23	16	8	1	0	0	0	0	0	0
470	480	32	24	17	9	2	0	0	0	0	0	0
480	490	33	25	18	10	3	0	0	0	0	0	0
490	500	34	26	19	11	4	0	0	0	0	0	0
500	510	35	27	20	12	5	0	0	0	0	0	0
510	520	36	28	21	13	6	0	0	0	0	0	0
520	530	38	29	22	14	7	0	0	0	0	0	0
530	540	39	30	23	15	8	0	0	0	0	0	0
540	550	41	31	24	16	9	1	0	0	0	0	0
550	560	42	32	25	17	10	2	0	0	0	0	0
560	570	44	33	26	18	11	3	0	0	0	0	0
570	580	45	34	27	19	12	4	0	0	0	0	0
580	590	47	35	28	20	13	5	0	0	0	0	0
590	600	48	37	29	21	14	6	0	0	0	0	0
600	610	50	38	30	22	15	7	0	0	0	0	0
610	620	51	40	31	23	16	8	1	0	0	0	0
620	630	53	41	32	24	17	9	2	0	0	0	0
630	640	54	43	33	25	18	10	3	0	0	0	0
640	650	56	44	34	26	19	11	4	0	0	0	0
650	660	57	46	35	27	20	12	5	0	0	0	0
660	670	59	47	36	28	21	13	6	0	0	0	0
670	680	60	49	38	29	22	14	7	0	0	0	0
680	690	62	50	39	30	23	15	8	0	0	0	0
690	700	63	52	41	31	24	16	9	1	0	0	0
700	710	65	53	42	32	25	17	10	2	0	0	0
710	720	66	55	44	33	26	18	11	3	0	0	0
720	730	68	56	45	34	27	19	12	4	0	0	0
730	740	69	58	47	35	28	20	13	5	0	0	0
740	750	71	59	48	37	29	21	14	6	0	0	0
750	760	72	61	50	38	30	22	15	7	0	0	0
760	770	74	62	51	40	31	23	16	8	1	0	0
770	780	75	64	53	41	32	24	17	9	2	0	0
780	790	77	65	54	43	33	25	18	10	3	0	0
790	800	78	67	56	44	34	26	19	11	4	0	0

A-8

MARRIED Persons—WEEKLY Payroll Period

(For Wages Paid through December 2013)

And the wages are–		And the number of withholding allowances claimed is—										
At least	But less than	0	1	2	3	4	5	6	7	8	9	10
		The amount of income tax to be withheld is—										
$800	$810	$80	$68	$57	$46	$35	$27	$20	$12	$5	$0	$0
810	820	81	70	59	47	36	28	21	13	6	0	0
820	830	83	71	60	49	38	29	22	14	7	0	0
830	840	84	73	62	50	39	30	23	15	8	0	0
840	850	86	74	63	52	41	31	24	16	9	1	0
850	860	87	76	65	53	42	32	25	17	10	2	0
860	870	89	77	66	55	44	33	26	18	11	3	0
870	880	90	79	68	56	45	34	27	19	12	4	0
880	890	92	80	69	58	47	35	28	20	13	5	0
890	900	93	82	71	59	48	37	29	21	14	6	0
900	910	95	83	72	61	50	38	30	22	15	7	0
910	920	96	85	74	62	51	40	31	23	16	8	1
920	930	98	86	75	64	53	41	32	24	17	9	2
930	940	99	88	77	65	54	43	33	25	18	10	3
940	950	101	89	78	67	56	44	34	26	19	11	4
950	960	102	91	80	68	57	46	35	27	20	12	5
960	970	104	92	81	70	59	47	36	28	21	13	6
970	980	105	94	83	71	60	49	38	29	22	14	7
980	990	107	95	84	73	62	50	39	30	23	15	8
990	1,000	108	97	86	74	63	52	41	31	24	16	9
1,000	1,010	110	98	87	76	65	53	42	32	25	17	10
1,010	1,020	111	100	89	77	66	55	44	33	26	18	11
1,020	1,030	113	101	90	79	68	56	45	34	27	19	12
1,030	1,040	114	103	92	80	69	58	47	35	28	20	13
1,040	1,050	116	104	93	82	71	59	48	37	29	21	14
1,050	1,060	117	106	95	83	72	61	50	38	30	22	15
1,060	1,070	119	107	96	85	74	62	51	40	31	23	16
1,070	1,080	120	109	98	86	75	64	53	41	32	24	17
1,080	1,090	122	110	99	88	77	65	54	43	33	25	18
1,090	1,100	123	112	101	89	78	67	56	44	34	26	19
1,100	1,110	125	113	102	91	80	68	57	46	35	27	20
1,110	1,120	126	115	104	92	81	70	59	47	36	28	21
1,120	1,130	128	116	105	94	83	71	60	49	38	29	22
1,130	1,140	129	118	107	95	84	73	62	50	39	30	23
1,140	1,150	131	119	108	97	86	74	63	52	41	31	24
1,150	1,160	132	121	110	98	87	76	65	53	42	32	25
1,160	1,170	134	122	111	100	89	77	66	55	44	33	26
1,170	1,180	135	124	113	101	90	79	68	56	45	34	27
1,180	1,190	137	125	114	103	92	80	69	58	47	35	28
1,190	1,200	138	127	116	104	93	82	71	59	48	37	29
1,200	1,210	140	128	117	106	95	83	72	61	50	38	30
1,210	1,220	141	130	119	107	96	85	74	62	51	40	31
1,220	1,230	143	131	120	109	98	86	75	64	53	41	32
1,230	1,240	144	133	122	110	99	88	77	65	54	43	33
1,240	1,250	146	134	123	112	101	89	78	67	56	44	34
1,250	1,260	147	136	125	113	102	91	80	68	57	46	35
1,260	1,270	149	137	126	115	104	92	81	70	59	47	36
1,270	1,280	150	139	128	116	105	94	83	71	60	49	38
1,280	1,290	152	140	129	118	107	95	84	73	62	50	39
1,290	1,300	153	142	131	119	108	97	86	74	63	52	41
1,300	1,310	155	143	132	121	110	98	87	76	65	53	42
1,310	1,320	156	145	134	122	111	100	89	77	66	55	44
1,320	1,330	158	146	135	124	113	101	90	79	68	56	45
1,330	1,340	159	148	137	125	114	103	92	80	69	58	47
1,340	1,350	161	149	138	127	116	104	93	82	71	59	48
1,350	1,360	162	151	140	128	117	106	95	83	72	61	50
1,360	1,370	164	152	141	130	119	107	96	85	74	62	51
1,370	1,380	165	154	143	131	120	109	98	86	75	64	53
1,380	1,390	167	155	144	133	122	110	99	88	77	65	54
1,390	1,400	168	157	146	134	123	112	101	89	78	67	56

$1,400 and over — Use Table 1(b) for a **MARRIED person** on page 44. Also see the instructions on page 42.

SINGLE Persons—BIWEEKLY Payroll Period

(For Wages Paid through December 2013)

And the wages are—		And the number of withholding allowances claimed is—										
At least	But less than	0	1	2	3	4	5	6	7	8	9	10
		The amount of income tax to be withheld is—										
$ 0	$105	$0	$0	$0	$0	$0	$0	$0	$0	$0	$0	$0
105	110	2	0	0	0	0	0	0	0	0	0	0
110	115	3	0	0	0	0	0	0	0	0	0	0
115	120	3	0	0	0	0	0	0	0	0	0	0
120	125	4	0	0	0	0	0	0	0	0	0	0
125	130	4	0	0	0	0	0	0	0	0	0	0
130	135	5	0	0	0	0	0	0	0	0	0	0
135	140	5	0	0	0	0	0	0	0	0	0	0
140	145	6	0	0	0	0	0	0	0	0	0	0
145	150	6	0	0	0	0	0	0	0	0	0	0
150	155	7	0	0	0	0	0	0	0	0	0	0
155	160	7	0	0	0	0	0	0	0	0	0	0
160	165	8	0	0	0	0	0	0	0	0	0	0
165	170	8	0	0	0	0	0	0	0	0	0	0
170	175	9	0	0	0	0	0	0	0	0	0	0
175	180	9	0	0	0	0	0	0	0	0	0	0
180	185	10	0	0	0	0	0	0	0	0	0	0
185	190	10	0	0	0	0	0	0	0	0	0	0
190	195	11	0	0	0	0	0	0	0	0	0	0
195	200	11	0	0	0	0	0	0	0	0	0	0
200	205	12	0	0	0	0	0	0	0	0	0	0
205	210	12	0	0	0	0	0	0	0	0	0	0
210	215	13	0	0	0	0	0	0	0	0	0	0
215	220	13	0	0	0	0	0	0	0	0	0	0
220	225	14	0	0	0	0	0	0	0	0	0	0
225	230	14	0	0	0	0	0	0	0	0	0	0
230	235	15	0	0	0	0	0	0	0	0	0	0
235	240	15	0	0	0	0	0	0	0	0	0	0
240	245	16	1	0	0	0	0	0	0	0	0	0
245	250	16	1	0	0	0	0	0	0	0	0	0
250	260	17	2	0	0	0	0	0	0	0	0	0
260	270	18	3	0	0	0	0	0	0	0	0	0
270	280	19	4	0	0	0	0	0	0	0	0	0
280	290	20	5	0	0	0	0	0	0	0	0	0
290	300	21	6	0	0	0	0	0	0	0	0	0
300	310	22	7	0	0	0	0	0	0	0	0	0
310	320	23	8	0	0	0	0	0	0	0	0	0
320	330	24	9	0	0	0	0	0	0	0	0	0
330	340	25	10	0	0	0	0	0	0	0	0	0
340	350	26	11	0	0	0	0	0	0	0	0	0
350	360	27	12	0	0	0	0	0	0	0	0	0
360	370	28	13	0	0	0	0	0	0	0	0	0
370	380	29	14	0	0	0	0	0	0	0	0	0
380	390	30	15	0	0	0	0	0	0	0	0	0
390	400	31	16	1	0	0	0	0	0	0	0	0
400	410	32	17	2	0	0	0	0	0	0	0	0
410	420	33	18	3	0	0	0	0	0	0	0	0
420	430	34	19	4	0	0	0	0	0	0	0	0
430	440	35	20	5	0	0	0	0	0	0	0	0
440	450	37	21	6	0	0	0	0	0	0	0	0
450	460	38	22	7	0	0	0	0	0	0	0	0
460	470	40	23	8	0	0	0	0	0	0	0	0
470	480	41	24	9	0	0	0	0	0	0	0	0
480	490	43	25	10	0	0	0	0	0	0	0	0
490	500	44	26	11	0	0	0	0	0	0	0	0
500	520	47	28	13	0	0	0	0	0	0	0	0
520	540	50	30	15	0	0	0	0	0	0	0	0
540	560	53	32	17	2	0	0	0	0	0	0	0
560	580	56	34	19	4	0	0	0	0	0	0	0
580	600	59	36	21	6	0	0	0	0	0	0	0
600	620	62	39	23	8	0	0	0	0	0	0	0
620	640	65	42	25	10	0	0	0	0	0	0	0
640	660	68	45	27	12	0	0	0	0	0	0	0
660	680	71	48	29	14	0	0	0	0	0	0	0
680	700	74	51	31	16	1	0	0	0	0	0	0
700	720	77	54	33	18	3	0	0	0	0	0	0
720	740	80	57	35	20	5	0	0	0	0	0	0
740	760	83	60	38	22	7	0	0	0	0	0	0
760	780	86	63	41	24	9	0	0	0	0	0	0
780	800	89	66	44	26	11	0	0	0	0	0	0

SINGLE Persons—BIWEEKLY Payroll Period

(For Wages Paid through December 2013)

And the wages are—		And the number of withholding allowances claimed is—										
At least	But less than	0	1	2	3	4	5	6	7	8	9	10
		The amount of income tax to be withheld is—										
$800	$820	$92	$69	$47	$28	$13	$0	$0	$0	$0	$0	$0
820	840	95	72	50	30	15	0	0	0	0	0	0
840	860	98	75	53	32	17	2	0	0	0	0	0
860	880	101	78	56	34	19	4	0	0	0	0	0
880	900	104	81	59	36	21	6	0	0	0	0	0
900	920	107	84	62	39	23	8	0	0	0	0	0
920	940	110	87	65	42	25	10	0	0	0	0	0
940	960	113	90	68	45	27	12	0	0	0	0	0
960	980	116	93	71	48	29	14	0	0	0	0	0
980	1,000	119	96	74	51	31	16	1	0	0	0	0
1,000	1,020	122	99	77	54	33	18	3	0	0	0	0
1,020	1,040	125	102	80	57	35	20	5	0	0	0	0
1,040	1,060	128	105	83	60	38	22	7	0	0	0	0
1,060	1,080	131	108	86	63	41	24	9	0	0	0	0
1,080	1,100	134	111	89	66	44	26	11	0	0	0	0
1,100	1,120	137	114	92	69	47	28	13	0	0	0	0
1,120	1,140	140	117	95	72	50	30	15	0	0	0	0
1,140	1,160	143	120	98	75	53	32	17	2	0	0	0
1,160	1,180	146	123	101	78	56	34	19	4	0	0	0
1,180	1,200	149	126	104	81	59	36	21	6	0	0	0
1,200	1,220	152	129	107	84	62	39	23	8	0	0	0
1,220	1,240	155	132	110	87	65	42	25	10	0	0	0
1,240	1,260	158	135	113	90	68	45	27	12	0	0	0
1,260	1,280	161	138	116	93	71	48	29	14	0	0	0
1,280	1,300	164	141	119	96	74	51	31	16	1	0	0
1,300	1,320	167	144	122	99	77	54	33	18	3	0	0
1,320	1,340	170	147	125	102	80	57	35	20	5	0	0
1,340	1,360	173	150	128	105	83	60	38	22	7	0	0
1,360	1,380	176	153	131	108	86	63	41	24	9	0	0
1,380	1,400	179	156	134	111	89	66	44	26	11	0	0
1,400	1,420	182	159	137	114	92	69	47	28	13	0	0
1,420	1,440	185	162	140	117	95	72	50	30	15	0	0
1,440	1,460	188	165	143	120	98	75	53	32	17	2	0
1,460	1,480	191	168	146	123	101	78	56	34	19	4	0
1,480	1,500	195	171	149	126	104	81	59	36	21	6	0
1,500	1,520	200	174	152	129	107	84	62	39	23	8	0
1,520	1,540	205	177	155	132	110	87	65	42	25	10	0
1,540	1,560	210	180	158	135	113	90	68	45	27	12	0
1,560	1,580	215	183	161	138	116	93	71	48	29	14	0
1,580	1,600	220	186	164	141	119	96	74	51	31	16	1
1,600	1,620	225	189	167	144	122	99	77	54	33	18	3
1,620	1,640	230	192	170	147	125	102	80	57	35	20	5
1,640	1,660	235	197	173	150	128	105	83	60	38	22	7
1,660	1,680	240	202	176	153	131	108	86	63	41	24	9
1,680	1,700	245	207	179	156	134	111	89	66	44	26	11
1,700	1,720	250	212	182	159	137	114	92	69	47	28	13
1,720	1,740	255	217	185	162	140	117	95	72	50	30	15
1,740	1,760	260	222	188	165	143	120	98	75	53	32	17
1,760	1,780	265	227	191	168	146	123	101	78	56	34	19
1,780	1,800	270	232	195	171	149	126	104	81	59	36	21
1,800	1,820	275	237	200	174	152	129	107	84	62	39	23
1,820	1,840	280	242	205	177	155	132	110	87	65	42	25
1,840	1,860	285	247	210	180	158	135	113	90	68	45	27
1,860	1,880	290	252	215	183	161	138	116	93	71	48	29
1,880	1,900	295	257	220	186	164	141	119	96	74	51	31
1,900	1,920	300	262	225	189	167	144	122	99	77	54	33
1,920	1,940	305	267	230	192	170	147	125	102	80	57	35
1,940	1,960	310	272	235	197	173	150	128	105	83	60	38
1,960	1,980	315	277	240	202	176	153	131	108	86	63	41
1,980	2,000	320	282	245	207	179	156	134	111	89	66	44
2,000	2,020	325	287	250	212	182	159	137	114	92	69	47
2,020	2,040	330	292	255	217	185	162	140	117	95	72	50
2,040	2,060	335	297	260	222	188	165	143	120	98	75	53
2,060	2,080	340	302	265	227	191	168	146	123	101	78	56
2,080	2,100	345	307	270	232	195	171	149	126	104	81	59

$2,100 and over — Use Table 2(a) for a **SINGLE person** on page 44. Also see the instructions on page 42.

MARRIED Persons—BIWEEKLY Payroll Period

(For Wages Paid through December 2013)

And the wages are—		And the number of withholding allowances claimed is—										
At least	But less than	0	1	2	3	4	5	6	7	8	9	10
		The amount of income tax to be withheld is—										
$ 0	$320	$0	$0	$0	$0	$0	$0	$0	$0	$0	$0	$0
320	330	1	0	0	0	0	0	0	0	0	0	0
330	340	2	0	0	0	0	0	0	0	0	0	0
340	350	3	0	0	0	0	0	0	0	0	0	0
350	360	4	0	0	0	0	0	0	0	0	0	0
360	370	5	0	0	0	0	0	0	0	0	0	0
370	380	6	0	0	0	0	0	0	0	0	0	0
380	390	7	0	0	0	0	0	0	0	0	0	0
390	400	8	0	0	0	0	0	0	0	0	0	0
400	410	9	0	0	0	0	0	0	0	0	0	0
410	420	10	0	0	0	0	0	0	0	0	0	0
420	430	11	0	0	0	0	0	0	0	0	0	0
430	440	12	0	0	0	0	0	0	0	0	0	0
440	450	13	0	0	0	0	0	0	0	0	0	0
450	460	14	0	0	0	0	0	0	0	0	0	0
460	470	15	0	0	0	0	0	0	0	0	0	0
470	480	16	1	0	0	0	0	0	0	0	0	0
480	490	17	2	0	0	0	0	0	0	0	0	0
490	500	18	3	0	0	0	0	0	0	0	0	0
500	520	19	4	0	0	0	0	0	0	0	0	0
520	540	21	6	0	0	0	0	0	0	0	0	0
540	560	23	8	0	0	0	0	0	0	0	0	0
560	580	25	10	0	0	0	0	0	0	0	0	0
580	600	27	12	0	0	0	0	0	0	0	0	0
600	620	29	14	0	0	0	0	0	0	0	0	0
620	640	31	16	1	0	0	0	0	0	0	0	0
640	660	33	18	3	0	0	0	0	0	0	0	0
660	680	35	20	5	0	0	0	0	0	0	0	0
680	700	37	22	7	0	0	0	0	0	0	0	0
700	720	39	24	9	0	0	0	0	0	0	0	0
720	740	41	26	11	0	0	0	0	0	0	0	0
740	760	43	28	13	0	0	0	0	0	0	0	0
760	780	45	30	15	0	0	0	0	0	0	0	0
780	800	47	32	17	2	0	0	0	0	0	0	0
800	820	49	34	19	4	0	0	0	0	0	0	0
820	840	51	36	21	6	0	0	0	0	0	0	0
840	860	53	38	23	8	0	0	0	0	0	0	0
860	880	55	40	25	10	0	0	0	0	0	0	0
880	900	57	42	27	12	0	0	0	0	0	0	0
900	920	59	44	29	14	0	0	0	0	0	0	0
920	940	61	46	31	16	1	0	0	0	0	0	0
940	960	63	48	33	18	3	0	0	0	0	0	0
960	980	65	50	35	20	5	0	0	0	0	0	0
980	1,000	67	52	37	22	7	0	0	0	0	0	0
1,000	1,020	69	54	39	24	9	0	0	0	0	0	0
1,020	1,040	72	56	41	26	11	0	0	0	0	0	0
1,040	1,060	75	58	43	28	13	0	0	0	0	0	0
1,060	1,080	78	60	45	30	15	0	0	0	0	0	0
1,080	1,100	81	62	47	32	17	2	0	0	0	0	0
1,100	1,120	84	64	49	34	19	4	0	0	0	0	0
1,120	1,140	87	66	51	36	21	6	0	0	0	0	0
1,140	1,160	90	68	53	38	23	8	0	0	0	0	0
1,160	1,180	93	71	55	40	25	10	0	0	0	0	0
1,180	1,200	96	74	57	42	27	12	0	0	0	0	0
1,200	1,220	99	77	59	44	29	14	0	0	0	0	0
1,220	1,240	102	80	61	46	31	16	1	0	0	0	0
1,240	1,260	105	83	63	48	33	18	3	0	0	0	0
1,260	1,280	108	86	65	50	35	20	5	0	0	0	0
1,280	1,300	111	89	67	52	37	22	7	0	0	0	0
1,300	1,320	114	92	69	54	39	24	9	0	0	0	0
1,320	1,340	117	95	72	56	41	26	11	0	0	0	0
1,340	1,360	120	98	75	58	43	28	13	0	0	0	0
1,360	1,380	123	101	78	60	45	30	15	0	0	0	0
1,380	1,400	126	104	81	62	47	32	17	2	0	0	0
1,400	1,420	129	107	84	64	49	34	19	4	0	0	0
1,420	1,440	132	110	87	66	51	36	21	6	0	0	0
1,440	1,460	135	113	90	68	53	38	23	8	0	0	0
1,460	1,480	138	116	93	71	55	40	25	10	0	0	0
1,480	1,500	141	119	96	74	57	42	27	12	0	0	0

MARRIED Persons—BIWEEKLY Payroll Period
(For Wages Paid through December 2013)

And the wages are—		And the number of withholding allowances claimed is—										
At least	But less than	0	1	2	3	4	5	6	7	8	9	10
		The amount of income tax to be withheld is—										
$1,500	$1,520	$144	$122	$99	$77	$59	$44	$29	$14	$0	$0	$0
1,520	1,540	147	125	102	80	61	46	31	16	1	0	0
1,540	1,560	150	128	105	83	63	48	33	18	3	0	0
1,560	1,580	153	131	108	86	65	50	35	20	5	0	0
1,580	1,600	156	134	111	89	67	52	37	22	7	0	0
1,600	1,620	159	137	114	92	69	54	39	24	9	0	0
1,620	1,640	162	140	117	95	72	56	41	26	11	0	0
1,640	1,660	165	143	120	98	75	58	43	28	13	0	0
1,660	1,680	168	146	123	101	78	60	45	30	15	0	0
1,680	1,700	171	149	126	104	81	62	47	32	17	2	0
1,700	1,720	174	152	129	107	84	64	49	34	19	4	0
1,720	1,740	177	155	132	110	87	66	51	36	21	6	0
1,740	1,760	180	158	135	113	90	68	53	38	23	8	0
1,760	1,780	183	161	138	116	93	71	55	40	25	10	0
1,780	1,800	186	164	141	119	96	74	57	42	27	12	0
1,800	1,820	189	167	144	122	99	77	59	44	29	14	0
1,820	1,840	192	170	147	125	102	80	61	46	31	16	1
1,840	1,860	195	173	150	128	105	83	63	48	33	18	3
1,860	1,880	198	176	153	131	108	86	65	50	35	20	5
1,880	1,900	201	179	156	134	111	89	67	52	37	22	7
1,900	1,920	204	182	159	137	114	92	69	54	39	24	9
1,920	1,940	207	185	162	140	117	95	72	56	41	26	11
1,940	1,960	210	188	165	143	120	98	75	58	43	28	13
1,960	1,980	213	191	168	146	123	101	78	60	45	30	15
1,980	2,000	216	194	171	149	126	104	81	62	47	32	17
2,000	2,020	219	197	174	152	129	107	84	64	49	34	19
2,020	2,040	222	200	177	155	132	110	87	66	51	36	21
2,040	2,060	225	203	180	158	135	113	90	68	53	38	23
2,060	2,080	228	206	183	161	138	116	93	71	55	40	25
2,080	2,100	231	209	186	164	141	119	96	74	57	42	27
2,100	2,120	234	212	189	167	144	122	99	77	59	44	29
2,120	2,140	237	215	192	170	147	125	102	80	61	46	31
2,140	2,160	240	218	195	173	150	128	105	83	63	48	33
2,160	2,180	243	221	198	176	153	131	108	86	65	50	35
2,180	2,200	246	224	201	179	156	134	111	89	67	52	37
2,200	2,220	249	227	204	182	159	137	114	92	69	54	39
2,220	2,240	252	230	207	185	162	140	117	95	72	56	41
2,240	2,260	255	233	210	188	165	143	120	98	75	58	43
2,260	2,280	258	236	213	191	168	146	123	101	78	60	45
2,280	2,300	261	239	216	194	171	149	126	104	81	62	47
2,300	2,320	264	242	219	197	174	152	129	107	84	64	49
2,320	2,340	267	245	222	200	177	155	132	110	87	66	51
2,340	2,360	270	248	225	203	180	158	135	113	90	68	53
2,360	2,380	273	251	228	206	183	161	138	116	93	71	55
2,380	2,400	276	254	231	209	186	164	141	119	96	74	57
2,400	2,420	279	257	234	212	189	167	144	122	99	77	59
2,420	2,440	282	260	237	215	192	170	147	125	102	80	61
2,440	2,460	285	263	240	218	195	173	150	128	105	83	63
2,460	2,480	288	266	243	221	198	176	153	131	108	86	65
2,480	2,500	291	269	246	224	201	179	156	134	111	89	67
2,500	2,520	294	272	249	227	204	182	159	137	114	92	69
2,520	2,540	297	275	252	230	207	185	162	140	117	95	72
2,540	2,560	300	278	255	233	210	188	165	143	120	98	75
2,560	2,580	303	281	258	236	213	191	168	146	123	101	78
2,580	2,600	306	284	261	239	216	194	171	149	126	104	81
2,600	2,620	309	287	264	242	219	197	174	152	129	107	84
2,620	2,640	312	290	267	245	222	200	177	155	132	110	87
2,640	2,660	315	293	270	248	225	203	180	158	135	113	90
2,660	2,680	318	296	273	251	228	206	183	161	138	116	93
2,680	2,700	321	299	276	254	231	209	186	164	141	119	96

$2,700 and over — Use Table 2(b) for a **MARRIED person** on page 44. Also see the instructions on page 42.

SINGLE Persons—SEMIMONTHLY Payroll Period

(For Wages Paid through December 2013)

And the wages are—		And the number of withholding allowances claimed is—										
At least	But less than	0	1	2	3	4	5	6	7	8	9	10
		The amount of income tax to be withheld is—										
$ 0	$115	$0	$0	$0	$0	$0	$0	$0	$0	$0	$0	$0
115	120	3	0	0	0	0	0	0	0	0	0	0
120	125	3	0	0	0	0	0	0	0	0	0	0
125	130	4	0	0	0	0	0	0	0	0	0	0
130	135	4	0	0	0	0	0	0	0	0	0	0
135	140	5	0	0	0	0	0	0	0	0	0	0
140	145	5	0	0	0	0	0	0	0	0	0	0
145	150	6	0	0	0	0	0	0	0	0	0	0
150	155	6	0	0	0	0	0	0	0	0	0	0
155	160	7	0	0	0	0	0	0	0	0	0	0
160	165	7	0	0	0	0	0	0	0	0	0	0
165	170	8	0	0	0	0	0	0	0	0	0	0
170	175	8	0	0	0	0	0	0	0	0	0	0
175	180	9	0	0	0	0	0	0	0	0	0	0
180	185	9	0	0	0	0	0	0	0	0	0	0
185	190	10	0	0	0	0	0	0	0	0	0	0
190	195	10	0	0	0	0	0	0	0	0	0	0
195	200	11	0	0	0	0	0	0	0	0	0	0
200	205	11	0	0	0	0	0	0	0	0	0	0
205	210	12	0	0	0	0	0	0	0	0	0	0
210	215	12	0	0	0	0	0	0	0	0	0	0
215	220	13	0	0	0	0	0	0	0	0	0	0
220	225	13	0	0	0	0	0	0	0	0	0	0
225	230	14	0	0	0	0	0	0	0	0	0	0
230	235	14	0	0	0	0	0	0	0	0	0	0
235	240	15	0	0	0	0	0	0	0	0	0	0
240	245	15	0	0	0	0	0	0	0	0	0	0
245	250	16	0	0	0	0	0	0	0	0	0	0
250	260	16	0	0	0	0	0	0	0	0	0	0
260	270	17	1	0	0	0	0	0	0	0	0	0
270	280	18	2	0	0	0	0	0	0	0	0	0
280	290	19	3	0	0	0	0	0	0	0	0	0
290	300	20	4	0	0	0	0	0	0	0	0	0
300	310	21	5	0	0	0	0	0	0	0	0	0
310	320	22	6	0	0	0	0	0	0	0	0	0
320	330	23	7	0	0	0	0	0	0	0	0	0
330	340	24	8	0	0	0	0	0	0	0	0	0
340	350	25	9	0	0	0	0	0	0	0	0	0
350	360	26	10	0	0	0	0	0	0	0	0	0
360	370	27	11	0	0	0	0	0	0	0	0	0
370	380	28	12	0	0	0	0	0	0	0	0	0
380	390	29	13	0	0	0	0	0	0	0	0	0
390	400	30	14	0	0	0	0	0	0	0	0	0
400	410	31	15	0	0	0	0	0	0	0	0	0
410	420	32	16	0	0	0	0	0	0	0	0	0
420	430	33	17	1	0	0	0	0	0	0	0	0
430	440	34	18	2	0	0	0	0	0	0	0	0
440	450	35	19	3	0	0	0	0	0	0	0	0
450	460	36	20	4	0	0	0	0	0	0	0	0
460	470	37	21	5	0	0	0	0	0	0	0	0
470	480	39	22	6	0	0	0	0	0	0	0	0
480	490	40	23	7	0	0	0	0	0	0	0	0
490	500	42	24	8	0	0	0	0	0	0	0	0
500	520	44	26	9	0	0	0	0	0	0	0	0
520	540	47	28	11	0	0	0	0	0	0	0	0
540	560	50	30	13	0	0	0	0	0	0	0	0
560	580	53	32	15	0	0	0	0	0	0	0	0
580	600	56	34	17	1	0	0	0	0	0	0	0
600	620	59	36	19	3	0	0	0	0	0	0	0
620	640	62	38	21	5	0	0	0	0	0	0	0
640	660	65	41	23	7	0	0	0	0	0	0	0
660	680	68	44	25	9	0	0	0	0	0	0	0
680	700	71	47	27	11	0	0	0	0	0	0	0
700	720	74	50	29	13	0	0	0	0	0	0	0
720	740	77	53	31	15	0	0	0	0	0	0	0
740	760	80	56	33	17	1	0	0	0	0	0	0
760	780	83	59	35	19	3	0	0	0	0	0	0
780	800	86	62	37	21	5	0	0	0	0	0	0

Publication 15 (2013)

A-14

SINGLE Persons—SEMIMONTHLY Payroll Period

(For Wages Paid through December 2013)

And the wages are—		And the number of withholding allowances claimed is—										
At least	But less than	0	1	2	3	4	5	6	7	8	9	10
		The amount of income tax to be withheld is—										
$800	$820	$89	$65	$40	$23	$7	$0	$0	$0	$0	$0	$0
820	840	92	68	43	25	9	0	0	0	0	0	0
840	860	95	71	46	27	11	0	0	0	0	0	0
860	880	98	74	49	29	13	0	0	0	0	0	0
880	900	101	77	52	31	15	0	0	0	0	0	0
900	920	104	80	55	33	17	1	0	0	0	0	0
920	940	107	83	58	35	19	3	0	0	0	0	0
940	960	110	86	61	37	21	5	0	0	0	0	0
960	980	113	89	64	40	23	7	0	0	0	0	0
980	1,000	116	92	67	43	25	9	0	0	0	0	0
1,000	1,020	119	95	70	46	27	11	0	0	0	0	0
1,020	1,040	122	98	73	49	29	13	0	0	0	0	0
1,040	1,060	125	101	76	52	31	15	0	0	0	0	0
1,060	1,080	128	104	79	55	33	17	0	0	0	0	0
1,080	1,100	131	107	82	58	35	19	2	0	0	0	0
1,100	1,120	134	110	85	61	37	21	4	0	0	0	0
1,120	1,140	137	113	88	64	40	23	6	0	0	0	0
1,140	1,160	140	116	91	67	43	25	8	0	0	0	0
1,160	1,180	143	119	94	70	46	27	10	0	0	0	0
1,180	1,200	146	122	97	73	49	29	12	0	0	0	0
1,200	1,220	149	125	100	76	52	31	14	0	0	0	0
1,220	1,240	152	128	103	79	55	33	16	0	0	0	0
1,240	1,260	155	131	106	82	58	35	18	2	0	0	0
1,260	1,280	158	134	109	85	61	37	20	4	0	0	0
1,280	1,300	161	137	112	88	64	39	22	6	0	0	0
1,300	1,320	164	140	115	91	67	42	24	8	0	0	0
1,320	1,340	167	143	118	94	70	45	26	10	0	0	0
1,340	1,360	170	146	121	97	73	48	28	12	0	0	0
1,360	1,380	173	149	124	100	76	51	30	14	0	0	0
1,380	1,400	176	152	127	103	79	54	32	16	0	0	0
1,400	1,420	179	155	130	106	82	57	34	18	2	0	0
1,420	1,440	182	158	133	109	85	60	36	20	4	0	0
1,440	1,460	185	161	136	112	88	63	39	22	6	0	0
1,460	1,480	188	164	139	115	91	66	42	24	8	0	0
1,480	1,500	191	167	142	118	94	69	45	26	10	0	0
1,500	1,520	194	170	145	121	97	72	48	28	12	0	0
1,520	1,540	197	173	148	124	100	75	51	30	14	0	0
1,540	1,560	200	176	151	127	103	78	54	32	16	0	0
1,560	1,580	203	179	154	130	106	81	57	34	18	2	0
1,580	1,600	206	182	157	133	109	84	60	36	20	4	0
1,600	1,620	210	185	160	136	112	87	63	39	22	6	0
1,620	1,640	215	188	163	139	115	90	66	42	24	8	0
1,640	1,660	220	191	166	142	118	93	69	45	26	10	0
1,660	1,680	225	194	169	145	121	96	72	48	28	12	0
1,680	1,700	230	197	172	148	124	99	75	51	30	14	0
1,700	1,720	235	200	175	151	127	102	78	54	32	16	0
1,720	1,740	240	203	178	154	130	105	81	57	34	18	1
1,740	1,760	245	206	181	157	133	108	84	60	36	20	3
1,760	1,780	250	209	184	160	136	111	87	63	38	22	5
1,780	1,800	255	214	187	163	139	114	90	66	41	24	7
1,800	1,820	260	219	190	166	142	117	93	69	44	26	9
1,820	1,840	265	224	193	169	145	120	96	72	47	28	11
1,840	1,860	270	229	196	172	148	123	99	75	50	30	13
1,860	1,880	275	234	199	175	151	126	102	78	53	32	15
1,880	1,900	280	239	202	178	154	129	105	81	56	34	17
1,900	1,920	285	244	205	181	157	132	108	84	59	36	19
1,920	1,940	290	249	209	184	160	135	111	87	62	38	21
1,940	1,960	295	254	214	187	163	138	114	90	65	41	23
1,960	1,980	300	259	219	190	166	141	117	93	68	44	25
1,980	2,000	305	264	224	193	169	144	120	96	71	47	27
2,000	2,020	310	269	229	196	172	147	123	99	74	50	29
2,020	2,040	315	274	234	199	175	150	126	102	77	53	31
2,040	2,060	320	279	239	202	178	153	129	105	80	56	33
2,060	2,080	325	284	244	205	181	156	132	108	83	59	35
2,080	2,100	330	289	249	208	184	159	135	111	86	62	37
2,100	2,120	335	294	254	213	187	162	138	114	89	65	40
2,120	2,140	340	299	259	218	190	165	141	117	92	68	43

$2,140 and over   Use Table 3(a) for a **SINGLE person** on page 44. Also see the instructions on page 42.

MARRIED Persons—SEMIMONTHLY Payroll Period
(For Wages Paid through December 2013)

| And the wages are— | | And the number of withholding allowances claimed is— | | | | | | | | | | |
At least	But less than	0	1	2	3	4	5	6	7	8	9	10
		The amount of income tax to be withheld is—										
$ 0	$350	$0	$0	$0	$0	$0	$0	$0	$0	$0	$0	$0
350	360	1	0	0	0	0	0	0	0	0	0	0
360	370	2	0	0	0	0	0	0	0	0	0	0
370	380	3	0	0	0	0	0	0	0	0	0	0
380	390	4	0	0	0	0	0	0	0	0	0	0
390	400	5	0	0	0	0	0	0	0	0	0	0
400	410	6	0	0	0	0	0	0	0	0	0	0
410	420	7	0	0	0	0	0	0	0	0	0	0
420	430	8	0	0	0	0	0	0	0	0	0	0
430	440	9	0	0	0	0	0	0	0	0	0	0
440	450	10	0	0	0	0	0	0	0	0	0	0
450	460	11	0	0	0	0	0	0	0	0	0	0
460	470	12	0	0	0	0	0	0	0	0	0	0
470	480	13	0	0	0	0	0	0	0	0	0	0
480	490	14	0	0	0	0	0	0	0	0	0	0
490	500	15	0	0	0	0	0	0	0	0	0	0
500	520	16	0	0	0	0	0	0	0	0	0	0
520	540	18	2	0	0	0	0	0	0	0	0	0
540	560	20	4	0	0	0	0	0	0	0	0	0
560	580	22	6	0	0	0	0	0	0	0	0	0
580	600	24	8	0	0	0	0	0	0	0	0	0
600	620	26	10	0	0	0	0	0	0	0	0	0
620	640	28	12	0	0	0	0	0	0	0	0	0
640	660	30	14	0	0	0	0	0	0	0	0	0
660	680	32	16	0	0	0	0	0	0	0	0	0
680	700	34	18	2	0	0	0	0	0	0	0	0
700	720	36	20	4	0	0	0	0	0	0	0	0
720	740	38	22	6	0	0	0	0	0	0	0	0
740	760	40	24	8	0	0	0	0	0	0	0	0
760	780	42	26	10	0	0	0	0	0	0	0	0
780	800	44	28	12	0	0	0	0	0	0	0	0
800	820	46	30	14	0	0	0	0	0	0	0	0
820	840	48	32	16	0	0	0	0	0	0	0	0
840	860	50	34	18	2	0	0	0	0	0	0	0
860	880	52	36	20	4	0	0	0	0	0	0	0
880	900	54	38	22	6	0	0	0	0	0	0	0
900	920	56	40	24	8	0	0	0	0	0	0	0
920	940	58	42	26	10	0	0	0	0	0	0	0
940	960	60	44	28	12	0	0	0	0	0	0	0
960	980	62	46	30	14	0	0	0	0	0	0	0
980	1,000	64	48	32	16	0	0	0	0	0	0	0
1,000	1,020	66	50	34	18	1	0	0	0	0	0	0
1,020	1,040	68	52	36	20	3	0	0	0	0	0	0
1,040	1,060	70	54	38	22	5	0	0	0	0	0	0
1,060	1,080	72	56	40	24	7	0	0	0	0	0	0
1,080	1,100	74	58	42	26	9	0	0	0	0	0	0
1,100	1,120	77	60	44	28	11	0	0	0	0	0	0
1,120	1,140	80	62	46	30	13	0	0	0	0	0	0
1,140	1,160	83	64	48	32	15	0	0	0	0	0	0
1,160	1,180	86	66	50	34	17	1	0	0	0	0	0
1,180	1,200	89	68	52	36	19	3	0	0	0	0	0
1,200	1,220	92	70	54	38	21	5	0	0	0	0	0
1,220	1,240	95	72	56	40	23	7	0	0	0	0	0
1,240	1,260	98	74	58	42	25	9	0	0	0	0	0
1,260	1,280	101	77	60	44	27	11	0	0	0	0	0
1,280	1,300	104	80	62	46	29	13	0	0	0	0	0
1,300	1,320	107	83	64	48	31	15	0	0	0	0	0
1,320	1,340	110	86	66	50	33	17	1	0	0	0	0
1,340	1,360	113	89	68	52	35	19	3	0	0	0	0
1,360	1,380	116	92	70	54	37	21	5	0	0	0	0
1,380	1,400	119	95	72	56	39	23	7	0	0	0	0
1,400	1,420	122	98	74	58	41	25	9	0	0	0	0
1,420	1,440	125	101	77	60	43	27	11	0	0	0	0
1,440	1,460	128	104	80	62	45	29	13	0	0	0	0
1,460	1,480	131	107	83	64	47	31	15	0	0	0	0
1,480	1,500	134	110	86	66	49	33	17	1	0	0	0
1,500	1,520	137	113	89	68	51	35	19	3	0	0	0
1,520	1,540	140	116	92	70	53	37	21	5	0	0	0
1,540	1,560	143	119	95	72	55	39	23	7	0	0	0
1,560	1,580	146	122	98	74	57	41	25	9	0	0	0
1,580	1,600	149	125	101	76	59	43	27	11	0	0	0

A-16

MARRIED Persons—SEMIMONTHLY Payroll Period
(For Wages Paid through December 2013)

At least	But less than	0	1	2	3	4	5	6	7	8	9	10
And the wages are—		And the number of withholding allowances claimed is—										
		The amount of income tax to be withheld is—										
$1,600	$1,620	$152	$128	$104	$79	$61	$45	$29	$13	$0	$0	$0
1,620	1,640	155	131	107	82	63	47	31	15	0	0	0
1,640	1,660	158	134	110	85	65	49	33	17	0	0	0
1,660	1,680	161	137	113	88	67	51	35	19	2	0	0
1,680	1,700	164	140	116	91	69	53	37	21	4	0	0
1,700	1,720	167	143	119	94	71	55	39	23	6	0	0
1,720	1,740	170	146	122	97	73	57	41	25	8	0	0
1,740	1,760	173	149	125	100	76	59	43	27	10	0	0
1,760	1,780	176	152	128	103	79	61	45	29	12	0	0
1,780	1,800	179	155	131	106	82	63	47	31	14	0	0
1,800	1,820	182	158	134	109	85	65	49	33	16	0	0
1,820	1,840	185	161	137	112	88	67	51	35	18	2	0
1,840	1,860	188	164	140	115	91	69	53	37	20	4	0
1,860	1,880	191	167	143	118	94	71	55	39	22	6	0
1,880	1,900	194	170	146	121	97	73	57	41	24	8	0
1,900	1,920	197	173	149	124	100	76	59	43	26	10	0
1,920	1,940	200	176	152	127	103	79	61	45	28	12	0
1,940	1,960	203	179	155	130	106	82	63	47	30	14	0
1,960	1,980	206	182	158	133	109	85	65	49	32	16	0
1,980	2,000	209	185	161	136	112	88	67	51	34	18	2
2,000	2,020	212	188	164	139	115	91	69	53	36	20	4
2,020	2,040	215	191	167	142	118	94	71	55	38	22	6
2,040	2,060	218	194	170	145	121	97	73	57	40	24	8
2,060	2,080	221	197	173	148	124	100	75	59	42	26	10
2,080	2,100	224	200	176	151	127	103	78	61	44	28	12
2,100	2,120	227	203	179	154	130	106	81	63	46	30	14
2,120	2,140	230	206	182	157	133	109	84	65	48	32	16
2,140	2,160	233	209	185	160	136	112	87	67	50	34	18
2,160	2,180	236	212	188	163	139	115	90	69	52	36	20
2,180	2,200	239	215	191	166	142	118	93	71	54	38	22
2,200	2,220	242	218	194	169	145	121	96	73	56	40	24
2,220	2,240	245	221	197	172	148	124	99	75	58	42	26
2,240	2,260	248	224	200	175	151	127	102	78	60	44	28
2,260	2,280	251	227	203	178	154	130	105	81	62	46	30
2,280	2,300	254	230	206	181	157	133	108	84	64	48	32
2,300	2,320	257	233	209	184	160	136	111	87	66	50	34
2,320	2,340	260	236	212	187	163	139	114	90	68	52	36
2,340	2,360	263	239	215	190	166	142	117	93	70	54	38
2,360	2,380	266	242	218	193	169	145	120	96	72	56	40
2,380	2,400	269	245	221	196	172	148	123	99	74	58	42
2,400	2,420	272	248	224	199	175	151	126	102	77	60	44
2,420	2,440	275	251	227	202	178	154	129	105	80	62	46
2,440	2,460	278	254	230	205	181	157	132	108	83	64	48
2,460	2,480	281	257	233	208	184	160	135	111	86	66	50
2,480	2,500	284	260	236	211	187	163	138	114	89	68	52
2,500	2,520	287	263	239	214	190	166	141	117	92	70	54
2,520	2,540	290	266	242	217	193	169	144	120	95	72	56
2,540	2,560	293	269	245	220	196	172	147	123	98	74	58
2,560	2,580	296	272	248	223	199	175	150	126	101	77	60
2,580	2,600	299	275	251	226	202	178	153	129	104	80	62
2,600	2,620	302	278	254	229	205	181	156	132	107	83	64
2,620	2,640	305	281	257	232	208	184	159	135	110	86	66
2,640	2,660	308	284	260	235	211	187	162	138	113	89	68
2,660	2,680	311	287	263	238	214	190	165	141	116	92	70
2,680	2,700	314	290	266	241	217	193	168	144	119	95	72
2,700	2,720	317	293	269	244	220	196	171	147	122	98	74
2,720	2,740	320	296	272	247	223	199	174	150	125	101	77

$2,740 and over	Use Table 3(b) for a **MARRIED person** on page 44. Also see the instructions on page 42.

SINGLE Persons—MONTHLY Payroll Period

(For Wages Paid through December 2013)

And the wages are—		And the number of withholding allowances claimed is—										
At least	But less than	0	1	2	3	4	5	6	7	8	9	10
		The amount of income tax to be withheld is—										
$ 0	$220	$0	$0	$0	$0	$0	$0	$0	$0	$0	$0	$0
220	230	4	0	0	0	0	0	0	0	0	0	0
230	240	5	0	0	0	0	0	0	0	0	0	0
240	250	6	0	0	0	0	0	0	0	0	0	0
250	260	7	0	0	0	0	0	0	0	0	0	0
260	270	8	0	0	0	0	0	0	0	0	0	0
270	280	9	0	0	0	0	0	0	0	0	0	0
280	290	10	0	0	0	0	0	0	0	0	0	0
290	300	11	0	0	0	0	0	0	0	0	0	0
300	320	13	0	0	0	0	0	0	0	0	0	0
320	340	15	0	0	0	0	0	0	0	0	0	0
340	360	17	0	0	0	0	0	0	0	0	0	0
360	380	19	0	0	0	0	0	0	0	0	0	0
380	400	21	0	0	0	0	0	0	0	0	0	0
400	420	23	0	0	0	0	0	0	0	0	0	0
420	440	25	0	0	0	0	0	0	0	0	0	0
440	460	27	0	0	0	0	0	0	0	0	0	0
460	480	29	0	0	0	0	0	0	0	0	0	0
480	500	31	0	0	0	0	0	0	0	0	0	0
500	520	33	0	0	0	0	0	0	0	0	0	0
520	540	35	2	0	0	0	0	0	0	0	0	0
540	560	37	4	0	0	0	0	0	0	0	0	0
560	580	39	6	0	0	0	0	0	0	0	0	0
580	600	41	8	0	0	0	0	0	0	0	0	0
600	640	44	11	0	0	0	0	0	0	0	0	0
640	680	48	15	0	0	0	0	0	0	0	0	0
680	720	52	19	0	0	0	0	0	0	0	0	0
720	760	56	23	0	0	0	0	0	0	0	0	0
760	800	60	27	0	0	0	0	0	0	0	0	0
800	840	64	31	0	0	0	0	0	0	0	0	0
840	880	68	35	3	0	0	0	0	0	0	0	0
880	920	72	39	7	0	0	0	0	0	0	0	0
920	960	76	43	11	0	0	0	0	0	0	0	0
960	1,000	82	47	15	0	0	0	0	0	0	0	0
1,000	1,040	88	51	19	0	0	0	0	0	0	0	0
1,040	1,080	94	55	23	0	0	0	0	0	0	0	0
1,080	1,120	100	59	27	0	0	0	0	0	0	0	0
1,120	1,160	106	63	31	0	0	0	0	0	0	0	0
1,160	1,200	112	67	35	2	0	0	0	0	0	0	0
1,200	1,240	118	71	39	6	0	0	0	0	0	0	0
1,240	1,280	124	76	43	10	0	0	0	0	0	0	0
1,280	1,320	130	82	47	14	0	0	0	0	0	0	0
1,320	1,360	136	88	51	18	0	0	0	0	0	0	0
1,360	1,400	142	94	55	22	0	0	0	0	0	0	0
1,400	1,440	148	100	59	26	0	0	0	0	0	0	0
1,440	1,480	154	106	63	30	0	0	0	0	0	0	0
1,480	1,520	160	112	67	34	2	0	0	0	0	0	0
1,520	1,560	166	118	71	38	6	0	0	0	0	0	0
1,560	1,600	172	124	75	42	10	0	0	0	0	0	0
1,600	1,640	178	130	81	46	14	0	0	0	0	0	0
1,640	1,680	184	136	87	50	18	0	0	0	0	0	0
1,680	1,720	190	142	93	54	22	0	0	0	0	0	0
1,720	1,760	196	148	99	58	26	0	0	0	0	0	0
1,760	1,800	202	154	105	62	30	0	0	0	0	0	0
1,800	1,840	208	160	111	66	34	1	0	0	0	0	0
1,840	1,880	214	166	117	70	38	5	0	0	0	0	0
1,880	1,920	220	172	123	74	42	9	0	0	0	0	0
1,920	1,960	226	178	129	80	46	13	0	0	0	0	0
1,960	2,000	232	184	135	86	50	17	0	0	0	0	0
2,000	2,040	238	190	141	92	54	21	0	0	0	0	0
2,040	2,080	244	196	147	98	58	25	0	0	0	0	0
2,080	2,120	250	202	153	104	62	29	0	0	0	0	0
2,120	2,160	256	208	159	110	66	33	1	0	0	0	0
2,160	2,200	262	214	165	116	70	37	5	0	0	0	0
2,200	2,240	268	220	171	122	74	41	9	0	0	0	0
2,240	2,280	274	226	177	128	79	45	13	0	0	0	0
2,280	2,320	280	232	183	134	85	49	17	0	0	0	0
2,320	2,360	286	238	189	140	91	53	21	0	0	0	0
2,360	2,400	292	244	195	146	97	57	25	0	0	0	0

SINGLE Persons—MONTHLY Payroll Period

(For Wages Paid through December 2013)

And the wages are—		And the number of withholding allowances claimed is—										
At least	But less than	0	1	2	3	4	5	6	7	8	9	10
		The amount of income tax to be withheld is—										
$2,400	$2,440	$298	$250	$201	$152	$103	$61	$29	$0	$0	$0	$0
2,440	2,480	304	256	207	158	109	65	33	0	0	0	0
2,480	2,520	310	262	213	164	115	69	37	4	0	0	0
2,520	2,560	316	268	219	170	121	73	41	8	0	0	0
2,560	2,600	322	274	225	176	127	79	45	12	0	0	0
2,600	2,640	328	280	231	182	133	85	49	16	0	0	0
2,640	2,680	334	286	237	188	139	91	53	20	0	0	0
2,680	2,720	340	292	243	194	145	97	57	24	0	0	0
2,720	2,760	346	298	249	200	151	103	61	28	0	0	0
2,760	2,800	352	304	255	206	157	109	65	32	0	0	0
2,800	2,840	358	310	261	212	163	115	69	36	4	0	0
2,840	2,880	364	316	267	218	169	121	73	40	8	0	0
2,880	2,920	370	322	273	224	175	127	78	44	12	0	0
2,920	2,960	376	328	279	230	181	133	84	48	16	0	0
2,960	3,000	382	334	285	236	187	139	90	52	20	0	0
3,000	3,040	388	340	291	242	193	145	96	56	24	0	0
3,040	3,080	394	346	297	248	199	151	102	60	28	0	0
3,080	3,120	400	352	303	254	205	157	108	64	32	0	0
3,120	3,160	406	358	309	260	211	163	114	68	36	3	0
3,160	3,200	412	364	315	266	217	169	120	72	40	7	0
3,200	3,240	420	370	321	272	223	175	126	77	44	11	0
3,240	3,280	430	376	327	278	229	181	132	83	48	15	0
3,280	3,320	440	382	333	284	235	187	138	89	52	19	0
3,320	3,360	450	388	339	290	241	193	144	95	56	23	0
3,360	3,400	460	394	345	296	247	199	150	101	60	27	0
3,400	3,440	470	400	351	302	253	205	156	107	64	31	0
3,440	3,480	480	406	357	308	259	211	162	113	68	35	3
3,480	3,520	490	412	363	314	265	217	168	119	72	39	7
3,520	3,560	500	419	369	320	271	223	174	125	76	43	11
3,560	3,600	510	429	375	326	277	229	180	131	82	47	15
3,600	3,640	520	439	381	332	283	235	186	137	88	51	19
3,640	3,680	530	449	387	338	289	241	192	143	94	55	23
3,680	3,720	540	459	393	344	295	247	198	149	100	59	27
3,720	3,760	550	469	399	350	301	253	204	155	106	63	31
3,760	3,800	560	479	405	356	307	259	210	161	112	67	35
3,800	3,840	570	489	411	362	313	265	216	167	118	71	39
3,840	3,880	580	499	417	368	319	271	222	173	124	76	43
3,880	3,920	590	509	427	374	325	277	228	179	130	82	47
3,920	3,960	600	519	437	380	331	283	234	185	136	88	51
3,960	4,000	610	529	447	386	337	289	240	191	142	94	55
4,000	4,040	620	539	457	392	343	295	246	197	148	100	59
4,040	4,080	630	549	467	398	349	301	252	203	154	106	63
4,080	4,120	640	559	477	404	355	307	258	209	160	112	67
4,120	4,160	650	569	487	410	361	313	264	215	166	118	71
4,160	4,200	660	579	497	416	367	319	270	221	172	124	75
4,200	4,240	670	589	507	426	373	325	276	227	178	130	81
4,240	4,280	680	599	517	436	379	331	282	233	184	136	87
4,280	4,320	690	609	527	446	385	337	288	239	190	142	93
4,320	4,360	700	619	537	456	391	343	294	245	196	148	99
4,360	4,400	710	629	547	466	397	349	300	251	202	154	105
4,400	4,440	720	639	557	476	403	355	306	257	208	160	111
4,440	4,480	730	649	567	486	409	361	312	263	214	166	117
4,480	4,520	740	659	577	496	415	367	318	269	220	172	123
4,520	4,560	750	669	587	506	425	373	324	275	226	178	129
4,560	4,600	760	679	597	516	435	379	330	281	232	184	135
4,600	4,640	770	689	607	526	445	385	336	287	238	190	141
4,640	4,680	780	699	617	536	455	391	342	293	244	196	147
4,680	4,720	790	709	627	546	465	397	348	299	250	202	153
4,720	4,760	800	719	637	556	475	403	354	305	256	208	159
4,760	4,800	810	729	647	566	485	409	360	311	262	214	165
4,800	4,840	820	739	657	576	495	415	366	317	268	220	171
4,840	4,880	830	749	667	586	505	424	372	323	274	226	177
4,880	4,920	840	759	677	596	515	434	378	329	280	232	183
4,920	4,960	850	769	687	606	525	444	384	335	286	238	189
4,960	5,000	860	779	697	616	535	454	390	341	292	244	195
5,000	5,040	870	789	707	626	545	464	396	347	298	250	201
5,040	5,080	880	799	717	636	555	474	402	353	304	256	207

| $5,080 and over | | Use Table 4(a) for a **SINGLE person** on page 44. Also see the instructions on page 42. |

MARRIED Persons—MONTHLY Payroll Period
(For Wages Paid through December 2013)

And the wages are—		And the number of withholding allowances claimed is—										
At least	But less than	0	1	2	3	4	5	6	7	8	9	10
		The amount of income tax to be withheld is—										
$ 0	$680	$0	$0	$0	$0	$0	$0	$0	$0	$0	$0	$0
680	720	1	0	0	0	0	0	0	0	0	0	0
720	760	5	0	0	0	0	0	0	0	0	0	0
760	800	9	0	0	0	0	0	0	0	0	0	0
800	840	13	0	0	0	0	0	0	0	0	0	0
840	880	17	0	0	0	0	0	0	0	0	0	0
880	920	21	0	0	0	0	0	0	0	0	0	0
920	960	25	0	0	0	0	0	0	0	0	0	0
960	1,000	29	0	0	0	0	0	0	0	0	0	0
1,000	1,040	33	0	0	0	0	0	0	0	0	0	0
1,040	1,080	37	4	0	0	0	0	0	0	0	0	0
1,080	1,120	41	8	0	0	0	0	0	0	0	0	0
1,120	1,160	45	12	0	0	0	0	0	0	0	0	0
1,160	1,200	49	16	0	0	0	0	0	0	0	0	0
1,200	1,240	53	20	0	0	0	0	0	0	0	0	0
1,240	1,280	57	24	0	0	0	0	0	0	0	0	0
1,280	1,320	61	28	0	0	0	0	0	0	0	0	0
1,320	1,360	65	32	0	0	0	0	0	0	0	0	0
1,360	1,400	69	36	4	0	0	0	0	0	0	0	0
1,400	1,440	73	40	8	0	0	0	0	0	0	0	0
1,440	1,480	77	44	12	0	0	0	0	0	0	0	0
1,480	1,520	81	48	16	0	0	0	0	0	0	0	0
1,520	1,560	85	52	20	0	0	0	0	0	0	0	0
1,560	1,600	89	56	24	0	0	0	0	0	0	0	0
1,600	1,640	93	60	28	0	0	0	0	0	0	0	0
1,640	1,680	97	64	32	0	0	0	0	0	0	0	0
1,680	1,720	101	68	36	3	0	0	0	0	0	0	0
1,720	1,760	105	72	40	7	0	0	0	0	0	0	0
1,760	1,800	109	76	44	11	0	0	0	0	0	0	0
1,800	1,840	113	80	48	15	0	0	0	0	0	0	0
1,840	1,880	117	84	52	19	0	0	0	0	0	0	0
1,880	1,920	121	88	56	23	0	0	0	0	0	0	0
1,920	1,960	125	92	60	27	0	0	0	0	0	0	0
1,960	2,000	129	96	64	31	0	0	0	0	0	0	0
2,000	2,040	133	100	68	35	3	0	0	0	0	0	0
2,040	2,080	137	104	72	39	7	0	0	0	0	0	0
2,080	2,120	141	108	76	43	11	0	0	0	0	0	0
2,120	2,160	145	112	80	47	15	0	0	0	0	0	0
2,160	2,200	149	116	84	51	19	0	0	0	0	0	0
2,200	2,240	155	120	88	55	23	0	0	0	0	0	0
2,240	2,280	161	124	92	59	27	0	0	0	0	0	0
2,280	2,320	167	128	96	63	31	0	0	0	0	0	0
2,320	2,360	173	132	100	67	35	2	0	0	0	0	0
2,360	2,400	179	136	104	71	39	6	0	0	0	0	0
2,400	2,440	185	140	108	75	43	10	0	0	0	0	0
2,440	2,480	191	144	112	79	47	14	0	0	0	0	0
2,480	2,520	197	148	116	83	51	18	0	0	0	0	0
2,520	2,560	203	154	120	87	55	22	0	0	0	0	0
2,560	2,600	209	160	124	91	59	26	0	0	0	0	0
2,600	2,640	215	166	128	95	63	30	0	0	0	0	0
2,640	2,680	221	172	132	99	67	34	2	0	0	0	0
2,680	2,720	227	178	136	103	71	38	6	0	0	0	0
2,720	2,760	233	184	140	107	75	42	10	0	0	0	0
2,760	2,800	239	190	144	111	79	46	14	0	0	0	0
2,800	2,840	245	196	148	115	83	50	18	0	0	0	0
2,840	2,880	251	202	153	119	87	54	22	0	0	0	0
2,880	2,920	257	208	159	123	91	58	26	0	0	0	0
2,920	2,960	263	214	165	127	95	62	30	0	0	0	0
2,960	3,000	269	220	171	131	99	66	34	1	0	0	0
3,000	3,040	275	226	177	135	103	70	38	5	0	0	0
3,040	3,080	281	232	183	139	107	74	42	9	0	0	0
3,080	3,120	287	238	189	143	111	78	46	13	0	0	0
3,120	3,160	293	244	195	147	115	82	50	17	0	0	0
3,160	3,200	299	250	201	153	119	86	54	21	0	0	0
3,200	3,240	305	256	207	159	123	90	58	25	0	0	0
3,240	3,280	311	262	213	165	127	94	62	29	0	0	0
3,280	3,320	317	268	219	171	131	98	66	33	1	0	0
3,320	3,360	323	274	225	177	135	102	70	37	5	0	0
3,360	3,400	329	280	231	183	139	106	74	41	9	0	0

MARRIED Persons—MONTHLY Payroll Period

(For Wages Paid through December 2013)

And the wages are–		And the number of withholding allowances claimed is—										
At least	But less than	0	1	2	3	4	5	6	7	8	9	10
		The amount of income tax to be withheld is—										
$3,400	$3,440	$335	$286	$237	$189	$143	$110	$78	$45	$13	$0	$0
3,440	3,480	341	292	243	195	147	114	82	49	17	0	0
3,480	3,520	347	298	249	201	152	118	86	53	21	0	0
3,520	3,560	353	304	255	207	158	122	90	57	25	0	0
3,560	3,600	359	310	261	213	164	126	94	61	29	0	0
3,600	3,640	365	316	267	219	170	130	98	65	33	0	0
3,640	3,680	371	322	273	225	176	134	102	69	37	4	0
3,680	3,720	377	328	279	231	182	138	106	73	41	8	0
3,720	3,760	383	334	285	237	188	142	110	77	45	12	0
3,760	3,800	389	340	291	243	194	146	114	81	49	16	0
3,800	3,840	395	346	297	249	200	151	118	85	53	20	0
3,840	3,880	401	352	303	255	206	157	122	89	57	24	0
3,880	3,920	407	358	309	261	212	163	126	93	61	28	0
3,920	3,960	413	364	315	267	218	169	130	97	65	32	0
3,960	4,000	419	370	321	273	224	175	134	101	69	36	4
4,000	4,040	425	376	327	279	230	181	138	105	73	40	8
4,040	4,080	431	382	333	285	236	187	142	109	77	44	12
4,080	4,120	437	388	339	291	242	193	146	113	81	48	16
4,120	4,160	443	394	345	297	248	199	150	117	85	52	20
4,160	4,200	449	400	351	303	254	205	156	121	89	56	24
4,200	4,240	455	406	357	309	260	211	162	125	93	60	28
4,240	4,280	461	412	363	315	266	217	168	129	97	64	32
4,280	4,320	467	418	369	321	272	223	174	133	101	68	36
4,320	4,360	473	424	375	327	278	229	180	137	105	72	40
4,360	4,400	479	430	381	333	284	235	186	141	109	76	44
4,400	4,440	485	436	387	339	290	241	192	145	113	80	48
4,440	4,480	491	442	393	345	296	247	198	150	117	84	52
4,480	4,520	497	448	399	351	302	253	204	156	121	88	56
4,520	4,560	503	454	405	357	308	259	210	162	125	92	60
4,560	4,600	509	460	411	363	314	265	216	168	129	96	64
4,600	4,640	515	466	417	369	320	271	222	174	133	100	68
4,640	4,680	521	472	423	375	326	277	228	180	137	104	72
4,680	4,720	527	478	429	381	332	283	234	186	141	108	76
4,720	4,760	533	484	435	387	338	289	240	192	145	112	80
4,760	4,800	539	490	441	393	344	295	246	198	149	116	84
4,800	4,840	545	496	447	399	350	301	252	204	155	120	88
4,840	4,880	551	502	453	405	356	307	258	210	161	124	92
4,880	4,920	557	508	459	411	362	313	264	216	167	128	96
4,920	4,960	563	514	465	417	368	319	270	222	173	132	100
4,960	5,000	569	520	471	423	374	325	276	228	179	136	104
5,000	5,040	575	526	477	429	380	331	282	234	185	140	108
5,040	5,080	581	532	483	435	386	337	288	240	191	144	112
5,080	5,120	587	538	489	441	392	343	294	246	197	148	116
5,120	5,160	593	544	495	447	398	349	300	252	203	154	120
5,160	5,200	599	550	501	453	404	355	306	258	209	160	124
5,200	5,240	605	556	507	459	410	361	312	264	215	166	128
5,240	5,280	611	562	513	465	416	367	318	270	221	172	132
5,280	5,320	617	568	519	471	422	373	324	276	227	178	136
5,320	5,360	623	574	525	477	428	379	330	282	233	184	140
5,360	5,400	629	580	531	483	434	385	336	288	239	190	144
5,400	5,440	635	586	537	489	440	391	342	294	245	196	148
5,440	5,480	641	592	543	495	446	397	348	300	251	202	153
5,480	5,520	647	598	549	501	452	403	354	306	257	208	159
5,520	5,560	653	604	555	507	458	409	360	312	263	214	165
5,560	5,600	659	610	561	513	464	415	366	318	269	220	171
5,600	5,640	665	616	567	519	470	421	372	324	275	226	177
5,640	5,680	671	622	573	525	476	427	378	330	281	232	183
5,680	5,720	677	628	579	531	482	433	384	336	287	238	189
5,720	5,760	683	634	585	537	488	439	390	342	293	244	195
5,760	5,800	689	640	591	543	494	445	396	348	299	250	201
5,800	5,840	695	646	597	549	500	451	402	354	305	256	207
5,840	5,880	701	652	603	555	506	457	408	360	311	262	213

$5,880 and over   Use Table 4(b) for a **MARRIED person** on page 44. Also see the instructions on page 42.

SINGLE Persons—DAILY Payroll Period
(For Wages Paid through December 2013)

And the wages are—		And the number of withholding allowances claimed is—										
At least	But less than	0	1	2	3	4	5	6	7	8	9	10
		The amount of income tax to be withheld is—										
$ 0	$12	$0	$0	$0	$0	$0	$0	$0	$0	$0	$0	$0
12	15	1	0	0	0	0	0	0	0	0	0	0
15	18	1	0	0	0	0	0	0	0	0	0	0
18	21	1	0	0	0	0	0	0	0	0	0	0
21	24	1	0	0	0	0	0	0	0	0	0	0
24	27	2	0	0	0	0	0	0	0	0	0	0
27	30	2	1	0	0	0	0	0	0	0	0	0
30	33	2	1	0	0	0	0	0	0	0	0	0
33	36	3	1	0	0	0	0	0	0	0	0	0
36	39	3	1	0	0	0	0	0	0	0	0	0
39	42	3	2	0	0	0	0	0	0	0	0	0
42	45	4	2	1	0	0	0	0	0	0	0	0
45	48	4	2	1	0	0	0	0	0	0	0	0
48	51	4	3	1	0	0	0	0	0	0	0	0
51	54	5	3	1	0	0	0	0	0	0	0	0
54	57	5	3	2	0	0	0	0	0	0	0	0
57	60	6	4	2	1	0	0	0	0	0	0	0
60	63	6	4	2	1	0	0	0	0	0	0	0
63	66	7	4	3	1	0	0	0	0	0	0	0
66	69	7	5	3	1	0	0	0	0	0	0	0
69	72	8	5	3	2	0	0	0	0	0	0	0
72	75	8	6	4	2	1	0	0	0	0	0	0
75	78	8	6	4	2	1	0	0	0	0	0	0
78	81	9	7	4	3	1	0	0	0	0	0	0
81	84	9	7	5	3	1	0	0	0	0	0	0
84	87	10	8	5	3	2	0	0	0	0	0	0
87	90	10	8	6	4	2	1	0	0	0	0	0
90	93	11	8	6	4	2	1	0	0	0	0	0
93	96	11	9	7	4	3	1	0	0	0	0	0
96	99	12	9	7	5	3	1	0	0	0	0	0
99	102	12	10	8	5	3	2	0	0	0	0	0
102	105	13	10	8	6	4	2	1	0	0	0	0
105	108	13	11	8	6	4	2	1	0	0	0	0
108	111	13	11	9	7	4	3	1	0	0	0	0
111	114	14	12	9	7	5	3	1	0	0	0	0
114	117	14	12	10	8	5	3	2	0	0	0	0
117	120	15	13	10	8	6	4	2	1	0	0	0
120	123	15	13	11	8	6	4	2	1	0	0	0
123	126	16	13	11	9	7	4	3	1	0	0	0
126	129	16	14	12	9	7	5	3	1	0	0	0
129	132	17	14	12	10	8	5	3	2	0	0	0
132	135	17	15	13	10	8	6	4	2	1	0	0
135	138	17	15	13	11	8	6	4	2	1	0	0
138	141	18	16	13	11	9	7	4	3	1	0	0
141	144	18	16	14	12	9	7	5	3	1	0	0
144	147	19	17	14	12	10	8	5	3	2	0	0
147	150	19	17	15	13	10	8	6	4	2	1	0
150	153	20	17	15	13	11	8	6	4	2	1	0
153	156	21	18	16	13	11	9	7	4	3	1	0
156	159	22	18	16	14	12	9	7	5	3	1	0
159	162	22	19	17	14	12	10	8	5	3	2	0
162	165	23	19	17	15	13	10	8	6	4	2	1
165	168	24	20	17	15	13	11	8	6	4	2	1
168	171	25	21	18	16	13	11	9	7	4	3	1
171	174	25	22	18	16	14	12	9	7	5	3	1
174	177	26	22	19	17	14	12	10	8	5	3	2
177	180	27	23	19	17	15	13	10	8	6	4	2
180	183	28	24	20	17	15	13	11	8	6	4	2
183	186	28	25	21	18	16	13	11	9	7	4	3
186	189	29	25	22	18	16	14	12	9	7	5	3
189	192	30	26	22	19	17	14	12	10	8	5	3
192	195	31	27	23	19	17	15	13	10	8	6	4
195	198	31	28	24	20	17	15	13	11	8	6	4
198	201	32	28	25	21	18	16	13	11	9	7	4
201	204	33	29	25	22	18	16	14	12	9	7	5
204	207	34	30	26	22	19	17	14	12	10	8	5
207	210	34	31	27	23	19	17	15	13	10	8	6
210	213	35	31	28	24	20	17	15	13	11	8	6
213	216	36	32	28	25	21	18	16	13	11	9	7
216	219	37	33	29	25	22	18	16	14	12	9	7

Publication 15 (2013)

SINGLE Persons—DAILY Payroll Period

(For Wages Paid through December 2013)

And the wages are—		And the number of withholding allowances claimed is—										
At least	But less than	0	1	2	3	4	5	6	7	8	9	10
		The amount of income tax to be withheld is—										
$219	$222	$37	$34	$30	$26	$22	$19	$17	$14	$12	$10	$8
222	225	38	34	31	27	23	19	17	15	13	10	8
225	228	39	35	31	28	24	20	17	15	13	11	8
228	231	40	36	32	28	25	21	18	16	13	11	9
231	234	40	37	33	29	25	22	18	16	14	12	9
234	237	41	37	34	30	26	22	19	17	14	12	10
237	240	42	38	34	31	27	23	19	17	15	13	10
240	243	43	39	35	31	28	24	20	17	15	13	11
243	246	43	40	36	32	28	25	21	18	16	13	11
246	249	44	40	37	33	29	25	22	18	16	14	12
249	252	45	41	37	34	30	26	22	19	17	14	12
252	255	46	42	38	34	31	27	23	19	17	15	13
255	258	46	43	39	35	31	28	24	20	17	15	13
258	261	47	43	40	36	32	28	25	21	18	16	13
261	264	48	44	40	37	33	29	25	22	18	16	14
264	267	49	45	41	37	34	30	26	22	19	17	14
267	270	49	46	42	38	34	31	27	23	19	17	15
270	273	50	46	43	39	35	31	28	24	20	17	15
273	276	51	47	43	40	36	32	28	25	21	18	16
276	279	52	48	44	40	37	33	29	25	22	18	16
279	282	52	49	45	41	37	34	30	26	22	19	17
282	285	53	49	46	42	38	34	31	27	23	19	17
285	288	54	50	46	43	39	35	31	28	24	20	17
288	291	55	51	47	43	40	36	32	28	25	21	18
291	294	55	52	48	44	40	37	33	29	25	22	18
294	297	56	52	49	45	41	37	34	30	26	22	19
297	300	57	53	49	46	42	38	34	31	27	23	19
300	303	58	54	50	46	43	39	35	31	28	24	20
303	306	58	55	51	47	43	40	36	32	28	25	21
306	309	59	55	52	48	44	40	37	33	29	25	22
309	312	60	56	52	49	45	41	37	34	30	26	22
312	315	61	57	53	49	46	42	38	34	31	27	23
315	318	61	58	54	50	46	43	39	35	31	28	24
318	321	62	58	55	51	47	43	40	36	32	28	25
321	324	63	59	55	52	48	44	40	37	33	29	25
324	327	64	60	56	52	49	45	41	37	34	30	26
327	330	64	61	57	53	49	46	42	38	34	31	27
330	333	65	61	58	54	50	46	43	39	35	31	28
333	336	66	62	58	55	51	47	43	40	36	32	28
336	339	67	63	59	55	52	48	44	40	37	33	29
339	341	67	63	60	56	52	48	45	41	37	33	30
341	343	68	64	60	56	53	49	45	41	38	34	30
343	345	68	64	61	57	53	49	46	42	38	34	31
345	347	69	65	61	57	54	50	46	42	39	35	31
347	349	69	65	62	58	54	50	47	43	39	35	32
349	351	70	66	62	58	55	51	47	43	40	36	32
351	353	70	66	63	59	55	51	48	44	40	36	33
353	355	71	67	63	59	56	52	48	44	41	37	33
355	357	72	67	64	60	56	52	49	45	41	37	34
357	359	72	68	64	60	57	53	49	45	42	38	34
359	361	73	68	65	61	57	53	50	46	42	38	35
361	363	73	69	65	61	58	54	50	46	43	39	35
363	365	74	70	66	62	58	54	51	47	43	39	36
365	367	74	70	66	62	59	55	51	47	44	40	36
367	369	75	71	67	63	59	55	52	48	44	40	37
369	371	75	71	67	63	60	56	52	48	45	41	37
371	373	76	72	68	64	60	56	53	49	45	41	38
373	375	77	72	68	64	61	57	53	49	46	42	38
375	377	77	73	69	65	61	57	54	50	46	42	39
377	379	78	73	69	65	62	58	54	50	47	43	39
379	381	78	74	70	66	62	58	55	51	47	43	40
381	383	79	75	70	66	63	59	55	51	48	44	40
383	385	79	75	71	67	63	59	56	52	48	44	41
385	387	80	76	72	67	64	60	56	52	49	45	41
387	389	80	76	72	68	64	60	57	53	49	45	42
389	391	81	77	73	68	65	61	57	53	50	46	42

$391 and over	Use Table 8(a) for a **SINGLE person** on page 45. Also see the instructions on page 42.

A-23

MARRIED Persons—DAILY Payroll Period

(For Wages Paid through December 2013)

And the wages are—		And the number of withholding allowances claimed is—										
At least	But less than	0	1	2	3	4	5	6	7	8	9	10
		The amount of income tax to be withheld is—										
$0	$36	$0	$0	$0	$0	$0	$0	$0	$0	$0	$0	$0
36	39	1	0	0	0	0	0	0	0	0	0	0
39	42	1	0	0	0	0	0	0	0	0	0	0
42	45	1	0	0	0	0	0	0	0	0	0	0
45	48	1	0	0	0	0	0	0	0	0	0	0
48	51	2	0	0	0	0	0	0	0	0	0	0
51	54	2	1	0	0	0	0	0	0	0	0	0
54	57	2	1	0	0	0	0	0	0	0	0	0
57	60	3	1	0	0	0	0	0	0	0	0	0
60	63	3	1	0	0	0	0	0	0	0	0	0
63	66	3	2	0	0	0	0	0	0	0	0	0
66	69	4	2	1	0	0	0	0	0	0	0	0
69	72	4	2	1	0	0	0	0	0	0	0	0
72	75	4	3	1	0	0	0	0	0	0	0	0
75	78	4	3	1	0	0	0	0	0	0	0	0
78	81	5	3	2	0	0	0	0	0	0	0	0
81	84	5	4	2	1	0	0	0	0	0	0	0
84	87	5	4	2	1	0	0	0	0	0	0	0
87	90	6	4	3	1	0	0	0	0	0	0	0
90	93	6	4	3	1	0	0	0	0	0	0	0
93	96	6	5	3	2	0	0	0	0	0	0	0
96	99	7	5	4	2	1	0	0	0	0	0	0
99	102	7	5	4	2	1	0	0	0	0	0	0
102	105	7	6	4	3	1	0	0	0	0	0	0
105	108	8	6	4	3	1	0	0	0	0	0	0
108	111	8	6	5	3	2	0	0	0	0	0	0
111	114	9	7	5	4	2	1	0	0	0	0	0
114	117	9	7	5	4	2	1	0	0	0	0	0
117	120	10	7	6	4	3	1	0	0	0	0	0
120	123	10	8	6	4	3	1	0	0	0	0	0
123	126	10	8	6	5	3	2	0	0	0	0	0
126	129	11	9	7	5	4	2	1	0	0	0	0
129	132	11	9	7	5	4	2	1	0	0	0	0
132	135	12	10	7	6	4	3	1	0	0	0	0
135	138	12	10	8	6	4	3	1	0	0	0	0
138	141	13	10	8	6	5	3	2	0	0	0	0
141	144	13	11	9	7	5	4	2	1	0	0	0
144	147	14	11	9	7	5	4	2	1	0	0	0
147	150	14	12	10	7	6	4	3	1	0	0	0
150	153	15	12	10	8	6	4	3	1	0	0	0
153	156	15	13	10	8	6	5	3	2	0	0	0
156	159	15	13	11	9	7	5	4	2	1	0	0
159	162	16	14	11	9	7	5	4	2	1	0	0
162	165	16	14	12	10	7	6	4	3	1	0	0
165	168	17	15	12	10	8	6	4	3	1	0	0
168	171	17	15	13	10	8	6	5	3	2	0	0
171	174	18	15	13	11	9	7	5	4	2	1	0
174	177	18	16	14	11	9	7	5	4	2	1	0
177	180	19	16	14	12	10	7	6	4	3	1	0
180	183	19	17	15	12	10	8	6	4	3	1	0
183	186	19	17	15	13	10	8	6	5	3	2	0
186	189	20	18	15	13	11	9	7	5	4	2	1
189	192	20	18	16	14	11	9	7	5	4	2	1
192	195	21	19	16	14	12	10	7	6	4	3	1
195	198	21	19	17	15	12	10	8	6	4	3	1
198	201	22	19	17	15	13	10	8	6	5	3	2
201	204	22	20	18	15	13	11	9	7	5	4	2
204	207	23	20	18	16	14	11	9	7	5	4	2
207	210	23	21	19	16	14	12	10	7	6	4	3
210	213	24	21	19	17	15	12	10	8	6	4	3
213	216	24	22	19	17	15	13	10	8	6	5	3
216	219	24	22	20	18	15	13	11	9	7	5	4
219	222	25	23	20	18	16	14	11	9	7	5	4
222	225	25	23	21	19	16	14	12	10	7	6	4
225	228	26	24	21	19	17	15	12	10	8	6	4
228	231	26	24	22	19	17	15	13	10	8	6	5
231	234	27	24	22	20	18	15	13	11	9	7	5
234	237	27	25	23	20	18	16	14	11	9	7	5
237	240	28	25	23	21	19	16	14	12	10	7	6
240	243	28	26	24	21	19	17	15	12	10	8	6

MARRIED Persons—DAILY Payroll Period

(For Wages Paid through December 2013)

And the wages are—		And the number of withholding allowances claimed is—										
At least	But less than	0	1	2	3	4	5	6	7	8	9	10
		The amount of income tax to be withheld is—										
$243	$246	$28	$26	$24	$22	$19	$17	$15	$13	$10	$8	$6
246	249	29	27	24	22	20	18	15	13	11	9	7
249	252	29	27	25	23	20	18	16	14	11	9	7
252	255	30	28	25	23	21	19	16	14	12	10	7
255	258	30	28	26	24	21	19	17	15	12	10	8
258	261	31	28	26	24	22	19	17	15	13	10	8
261	264	31	29	27	24	22	20	18	15	13	11	9
264	267	32	29	27	25	23	20	18	16	14	11	9
267	270	32	30	28	25	23	21	19	16	14	12	10
270	273	33	30	28	26	24	21	19	17	15	12	10
273	276	33	31	28	26	24	22	19	17	15	13	10
276	279	33	31	29	27	24	22	20	18	15	13	11
279	282	34	32	29	27	25	23	20	18	16	14	11
282	285	34	32	30	28	25	23	21	19	16	14	12
285	288	35	33	30	28	26	24	21	19	17	15	12
288	291	35	33	31	28	26	24	22	19	17	15	13
291	294	36	33	31	29	27	24	22	20	18	15	13
294	297	36	34	32	29	27	25	23	20	18	16	14
297	300	37	34	32	30	28	25	23	21	19	16	14
300	303	37	35	33	30	28	26	24	21	19	17	15
303	306	37	35	33	31	28	26	24	22	19	17	15
306	309	38	36	33	31	29	27	24	22	20	18	15
309	312	38	36	34	32	29	27	25	23	20	18	16
312	315	39	37	34	32	30	28	25	23	21	19	16
315	318	40	37	35	33	30	28	26	24	21	19	17
318	321	41	37	35	33	31	28	26	24	22	19	17
321	324	41	38	36	33	31	29	27	24	22	20	18
324	327	42	38	36	34	32	29	27	25	23	20	18
327	330	43	39	37	34	32	30	28	25	23	21	19
330	333	44	40	37	35	33	30	28	26	24	21	19
333	336	44	41	37	35	33	31	28	26	24	22	19
336	339	45	41	38	36	33	31	29	27	24	22	20
339	341	46	42	38	36	34	32	29	27	25	23	20
341	343	46	42	39	36	34	32	30	27	25	23	21
343	345	47	43	39	37	34	32	30	28	25	23	21
345	347	47	43	40	37	35	32	30	28	26	23	21
347	349	48	44	40	37	35	33	30	28	26	24	21
349	351	48	44	41	38	35	33	31	29	26	24	22
351	353	49	45	41	38	36	33	31	29	27	24	22
353	355	49	45	42	38	36	34	31	29	27	25	22
355	357	50	46	42	38	36	34	32	29	27	25	23
357	359	50	46	43	39	36	34	32	30	27	25	23
359	361	51	47	43	39	37	35	32	30	28	26	23
361	363	51	47	44	40	37	35	33	30	28	26	24
363	365	52	48	44	40	37	35	33	31	28	26	24
365	367	52	48	45	41	38	35	33	31	29	26	24
367	369	53	49	45	41	38	36	33	31	29	27	24
369	371	53	49	46	42	38	36	34	32	29	27	25
371	373	54	50	46	42	39	36	34	32	30	27	25
373	375	54	50	47	43	39	37	34	32	30	28	25
375	377	55	51	47	43	40	37	35	32	30	28	26
377	379	55	51	48	44	40	37	35	33	30	28	26
379	381	56	52	48	44	41	38	35	33	31	29	26
381	383	56	52	49	45	41	38	36	33	31	29	27
383	385	57	53	49	45	42	38	36	34	31	29	27
385	387	57	53	50	46	42	38	36	34	32	29	27
387	389	58	54	50	46	43	39	36	34	32	30	27
389	391	58	54	51	47	43	39	37	35	32	30	28
391	393	59	55	51	47	44	40	37	35	33	30	28
393	395	59	55	52	48	44	40	37	35	33	31	28
395	397	60	56	52	48	45	41	38	35	33	31	29
397	399	60	56	53	49	45	41	38	36	33	31	29
399	401	61	57	53	49	46	42	38	36	34	32	29

$401 and over   Use Table 8(b) for a **MARRIED person** on page 45. Also see the instructions on page 42.

OMB No. 1615-0047; Expires 08/31/12

Form I-9, Employment Eligibility Verification

Department of Homeland Security
U.S. Citizenship and Immigration Services

Instructions
Read all instructions carefully before completing this form.

Anti-Discrimination Notice. It is illegal to discriminate against any individual (other than an alien not authorized to work in the United States) in hiring, discharging, or recruiting or referring for a fee because of that individual's national origin or citizenship status. It is illegal to discriminate against work-authorized individuals. Employers **CANNOT** specify which document(s) they will accept from an employee. The refusal to hire an individual because the documents presented have a future expiration date may also constitute illegal discrimination. For more information, call the Office of Special Counsel for Immigration Related Unfair Employment Practices at 1-800-255-8155.

What Is the Purpose of This Form?

The purpose of this form is to document that each new employee (both citizen and noncitizen) hired after November 6, 1986, is authorized to work in the United States.

When Should Form I-9 Be Used?

All employees (citizens and noncitizens) hired after November 6, 1986, and working in the United States must complete Form I-9.

Filling Out Form I-9

Section 1, Employee

This part of the form must be completed no later than the time of hire, which is the actual beginning of employment. Providing the Social Security Number is voluntary, except for employees hired by employers participating in the USCIS Electronic Employment Eligibility Verification Program (E-Verify). **The employer is responsible for ensuring that Section 1 is timely and properly completed.**

Noncitizen nationals of the United States are persons born in American Samoa, certain former citizens of the former Trust Territory of the Pacific Islands, and certain children of noncitizen nationals born abroad.

Employers should note the work authorization expiration date (if any) shown in **Section 1.** For employees who indicate an employment authorization expiration date in **Section 1,** employers are required to reverify employment authorization for employment on or before the date shown. Note that some employees may leave the expiration date blank if they are aliens whose work authorization does not expire (e.g., asylees, refugees, certain citizens of the Federated States of Micronesia or the Republic of the Marshall Islands). For such employees, reverification does not apply unless they choose to present

in Section 2 evidence of employment authorization that contains an expiration date (e.g., Employment Authorization Document (Form I-766)).

Preparer/Translator Certification

The Preparer/Translator Certification must be completed if **Section 1** is prepared by a person other than the employee. A preparer/translator may be used only when the employee is unable to complete **Section 1** on his or her own. However, the employee must still sign **Section 1** personally.

Section 2, Employer

For the purpose of completing this form, the term "employer" means all employers including those recruiters and referrers for a fee who are agricultural associations, agricultural employers, or farm labor contractors. Employers must complete **Section 2** by examining evidence of identity and employment authorization within three business days of the date employment begins. However, if an employer hires an individual for less than three business days, **Section 2** must be completed at the time employment begins. Employers cannot specify which document(s) listed on the last page of Form I-9 employees present to establish identity and employment authorization. Employees may present any List A document **OR** a combination of a List B and a List C document.

If an employee is unable to present a required document (or documents), the employee must present an acceptable receipt in lieu of a document listed on the last page of this form. Receipts showing that a person has applied for an initial grant of employment authorization, or for renewal of employment authorization, are not acceptable. Employees must present receipts within three business days of the date employment begins and must present valid replacement documents within 90 days or other specified time.

Employers must record in Section 2:

1. Document title;
2. Issuing authority;
3. Document number;
4. Expiration date, if any; and
5. The date employment begins.

Employers must sign and date the certification in **Section 2.** Employees must present original documents. Employers may, but are not required to, photocopy the document(s) presented. If photocopies are made, they must be made for all new hires. Photocopies may only be used for the verification process and must be retained with Form I-9. **Employers are still responsible for completing and retaining Form I-9.**

Form I-9 (Rev. 08/07/09) Y

For more detailed information, you may refer to the *USCIS Handbook for Employers* (Form M-274). You may obtain the handbook using the contact information found under the header "USCIS Forms and Information."

Section 3, Updating and Reverification

Employers must complete **Section 3** when updating and/or reverifying Form I-9. Employers must reverify employment authorization of their employees on or before the work authorization expiration date recorded in **Section 1** (if any). Employers **CANNOT** specify which document(s) they will accept from an employee.

A. If an employee's name has changed at the time this form is being updated/reverified, complete Block A.

B. If an employee is rehired within three years of the date this form was originally completed and the employee is still authorized to be employed on the same basis as previously indicated on this form (updating), complete Block B and the signature block.

C. If an employee is rehired within three years of the date this form was originally completed and the employee's work authorization has expired **or** if a current employee's work authorization is about to expire (reverification), complete Block B; and:

  1. Examine any document that reflects the employee is authorized to work in the United States (see List A **or** C);

  2. Record the document title, document number, and expiration date (if any) in Block C; and

  3. Complete the signature block.

Note that for reverification purposes, employers have the option of completing a new Form I-9 instead of completing **Section 3.**

What Is the Filing Fee?

There is no associated filing fee for completing Form I-9. This form is not filed with USCIS or any government agency. Form I-9 must be retained by the employer and made available for inspection by U.S. Government officials as specified in the Privacy Act Notice below.

USCIS Forms and Information

To order USCIS forms, you can download them from our website at www.uscis.gov/forms or call our toll-free number at 1-800-870-3676. You can obtain information about Form I-9 from our website at www.uscis.gov or by calling 1-888-464-4218.

Information about E-Verify, a free and voluntary program that allows participating employers to electronically verify the employment eligibility of their newly hired employees, can be obtained from our website at www.uscis.gov/e-verify or by calling 1-888-464-4218.

General information on immigration laws, regulations, and procedures can be obtained by telephoning our National Customer Service Center at 1-800-375-5283 or visiting our Internet website at www.uscis.gov.

Photocopying and Retaining Form I-9

A blank Form I-9 may be reproduced, provided both sides are copied. The Instructions must be available to all employees completing this form. Employers must retain completed Form I-9s for three years after the date of hire or one year after the date employment ends, whichever is later.

Form I-9 may be signed and retained electronically, as authorized in Department of Homeland Security regulations at 8 CFR 274a.2.

Privacy Act Notice

The authority for collecting this information is the Immigration Reform and Control Act of 1986, Pub. L. 99-603 (8 USC 1324a).

This information is for employers to verify the eligibility of individuals for employment to preclude the unlawful hiring, or recruiting or referring for a fee, of aliens who are not authorized to work in the United States.

This information will be used by employers as a record of their basis for determining eligibility of an employee to work in the United States. The form will be kept by the employer and made available for inspection by authorized officials of the Department of Homeland Security, Department of Labor, and Office of Special Counsel for Immigration-Related Unfair Employment Practices.

Submission of the information required in this form is voluntary. However, an individual may not begin employment unless this form is completed, since employers are subject to civil or criminal penalties if they do not comply with the Immigration Reform and Control Act of 1986.

EMPLOYERS MUST RETAIN COMPLETED FORM I-9
DO NOT MAIL COMPLETED FORM I-9 TO ICE OR USCIS
Form I-9 (Rev. 08/07/09) Y Page 2

A-27

Paperwork Reduction Act

An agency may not conduct or sponsor an information collection and a person is not required to respond to a collection of information unless it displays a currently valid OMB control number. The public reporting burden for this collection of information is estimated at 12 minutes per response, including the time for reviewing instructions and completing and submitting the form. Send comments regarding this burden estimate or any other aspect of this collection of information, including suggestions for reducing this burden, to: U.S. Citizenship and Immigration Services, Regulatory Management Division, 111 Massachusetts Avenue, N.W., 3rd Floor, Suite 3008, Washington, DC 20529-2210. OMB No. 1615-0047. **Do not mail your completed Form I-9 to this address.**

OMB No. 1615-0047; Expires 08/31/12

Department of Homeland Security
U.S. Citizenship and Immigration Services

Form I-9, Employment
Eligibility Verification

Read instructions carefully before completing this form. The instructions must be available during completion of this form.

ANTI-DISCRIMINATION NOTICE: It is illegal to discriminate against work-authorized individuals. Employers CANNOT specify which document(s) they will accept from an employee. The refusal to hire an individual because the documents have a future expiration date may also constitute illegal discrimination.

Section 1. Employee Information and Verification *(To be completed and signed by employee at the time employment begins.)*

Print Name: Last	First	Middle Initial	Maiden Name

Address *(Street Name and Number)*	Apt. #	Date of Birth *(month/day/year)*

City	State	Zip Code	Social Security #

I am aware that federal law provides for imprisonment and/or fines for false statements or use of false documents in connection with the completion of this form.

I attest, under penalty of perjury, that I am (check one of the following):

☐ A citizen of the United States

☐ A noncitizen national of the United States (see instructions)

☐ A lawful permanent resident (Alien #) _____

☐ An alien authorized to work (Alien # or Admission #) _____
until (expiration date, if applicable - *month/day/year*) _____

Employee's Signature	Date *(month/day/year)*

Preparer and/or Translator Certification *(To be completed and signed if Section 1 is prepared by a person other than the employee.) I attest, under penalty of perjury, that I have assisted in the completion of this form and that to the best of my knowledge the information is true and correct.*

Preparer's/Translator's Signature	Print Name

Address *(Street Name and Number, City, State, Zip Code)*	Date *(month/day/year)*

Section 2. Employer Review and Verification *(To be completed and signed by employer. Examine one document from List A OR examine one document from List B and one from List C, as listed on the reverse of this form, and record the title, number, and expiration date, if any, of the document(s).)*

	List A	OR	List B	AND	List C
Document title:					
Issuing authority:					
Document #:					
Expiration Date *(if any)*:					
Document #:					
Expiration Date *(if any)*:					

CERTIFICATION: I attest, under penalty of perjury, that I have examined the document(s) presented by the above-named employee, that the above-listed document(s) appear to be genuine and to relate to the employee named, that the employee began employment on *(month/day/year)* _____ **and that to the best of my knowledge the employee is authorized to work in the United States. (State employment agencies may omit the date the employee began employment.)**

Signature of Employer or Authorized Representative	Print Name	Title

Business or Organization Name and Address *(Street Name and Number, City, State, Zip Code)*	Date *(month/day/year)*

Section 3. Updating and Reverification *(To be completed and signed by employer.)*

A. New Name *(if applicable)*	B. Date of Rehire *(month/day/year) (if applicable)*

C. If employee's previous grant of work authorization has expired, provide the information below for the document that establishes current employment authorization.

Document Title:	Document #:	Expiration Date *(if any)*:

I attest, under penalty of perjury, that to the best of my knowledge, this employee is authorized to work in the United States, and if the employee presented document(s), the document(s) I have examined appear to be genuine and to relate to the individual.

Signature of Employer or Authorized Representative	Date *(month/day/year)*

Form I-9 (Rev. 08/07/09) Y Page 4

LISTS OF ACCEPTABLE DOCUMENTS
All documents must be unexpired

LIST A		LIST B		LIST C
Documents that Establish Both Identity and Employment Authorization	**OR**	**Documents that Establish Identity**	**AND**	**Documents that Establish Employment Authorization**
1. U.S. Passport or U.S. Passport Card		1. Driver's license or ID card issued by a State or outlying possession of the United States provided it contains a photograph or information such as name, date of birth, gender, height, eye color, and address		1. Social Security Account Number card other than one that specifies on the face that the issuance of the card does not authorize employment in the United States
2. Permanent Resident Card or Alien Registration Receipt Card (Form I-551)				2. Certification of Birth Abroad issued by the Department of State (Form FS-545)
3. Foreign passport that contains a temporary I-551 stamp or temporary I-551 printed notation on a machine-readable immigrant visa		2. ID card issued by federal, state or local government agencies or entities, provided it contains a photograph or information such as name, date of birth, gender, height, eye color, and address		3. Certification of Report of Birth issued by the Department of State (Form DS-1350)
4. Employment Authorization Document that contains a photograph (Form I-766)		3. School ID card with a photograph		
		4. Voter's registration card		4. Original or certified copy of birth certificate issued by a State, county, municipal authority, or territory of the United States bearing an official seal
5. In the case of a nonimmigrant alien authorized to work for a specific employer incident to status, a foreign passport with Form I-94 or Form I-94A bearing the same name as the passport and containing an endorsement of the alien's nonimmigrant status, as long as the period of endorsement has not yet expired and the proposed employment is not in conflict with any restrictions or limitations identified on the form		5. U.S. Military card or draft record		
		6. Military dependent's ID card		5. Native American tribal document
		7. U.S. Coast Guard Merchant Mariner Card		
		8. Native American tribal document		6. U.S. Citizen ID Card (Form I-197)
		9. Driver's license issued by a Canadian government authority		
6. Passport from the Federated States of Micronesia (FSM) or the Republic of the Marshall Islands (RMI) with Form I-94 or Form I-94A indicating nonimmigrant admission under the Compact of Free Association Between the United States and the FSM or RMI		**For persons under age 18 who are unable to present a document listed above:**		7. Identification Card for Use of Resident Citizen in the United States (Form I-179)
		10. School record or report card		8. Employment authorization document issued by the Department of Homeland Security
		11. Clinic, doctor, or hospital record		
		12. Day-care or nursery school record		

Illustrations of many of these documents appear in Part 8 of the Handbook for Employers (M-274)

Form I-9 (Rev. 08/07/09) Y Page 5

Form **SS-4**
(Rev. January 2010)
Department of the Treasury
Internal Revenue Service

Application for Employer Identification Number

(For use by employers, corporations, partnerships, trusts, estates, churches, government agencies, Indian tribal entities, certain individuals, and others.)

▶ **See separate instructions for each line.** ▶ **Keep a copy for your records.**

OMB No. 1545-0003

EIN

Type or print clearly.

1	Legal name of entity (or individual) for whom the EIN is being requested

2 Trade name of business (if different from name on line 1)	3 Executor, administrator, trustee, "care of" name
4a Mailing address (room, apt., suite no. and street, or P.O. box)	5a Street address (if different) (Do not enter a P.O. box.)
4b City, state, and ZIP code (if foreign, see instructions)	5b City, state, and ZIP code (if foreign, see instructions)

6	County and state where principal business is located

7a Name of responsible party	7b SSN, ITIN, or EIN

8a Is this application for a limited liability company (LLC) (or a foreign equivalent)? . . . . ☐ **Yes** ☐ **No**

8b If 8a is "Yes," enter the number of LLC members . . . . ▶

8c If 8a is "Yes," was the LLC organized in the United States? . . . . ☐ **Yes** ☐ **No**

9a **Type of entity** (check only one box). **Caution.** If 8a is "Yes," see the instructions for the correct box to check.

☐ Sole proprietor (SSN) _____
☐ Partnership
☐ Corporation (enter form number to be filed) ▶_____
☐ Personal service corporation
☐ Church or church-controlled organization
☐ Other nonprofit organization (specify) ▶_____
☐ Other (specify) ▶

☐ Estate (SSN of decedent) _____
☐ Plan administrator (TIN) _____
☐ Trust (TIN of grantor) _____
☐ National Guard ☐ State/local government
☐ Farmers' cooperative ☐ Federal government/military
☐ REMIC ☐ Indian tribal governments/enterprises
Group Exemption Number (GEN) if any ▶

9b If a corporation, name the state or foreign country (if applicable) where incorporated

State	Foreign country

10 **Reason for applying** (check only one box)
☐ Started new business (specify type) ▶ _____
☐ Hired employees (Check the box and see line 13.)
☐ Compliance with IRS withholding regulations
☐ Other (specify) ▶

☐ Banking purpose (specify purpose) ▶_____
☐ Changed type of organization (specify new type) ▶_____
☐ Purchased going business
☐ Created a trust (specify type) ▶_____
☐ Created a pension plan (specify type) ▶_____

11 Date business started or acquired (month, day, year). See instructions.

12 Closing month of accounting year

13 Highest number of employees expected in the next 12 months (enter -0- if none).

If no employees expected, skip line 14.

Agricultural	Household	Other

14 If you expect your employment tax liability to be $1,000 or less in a full calendar year **and** want to file Form 944 annually instead of Forms 941 quarterly, check here. (Your employment tax liability generally will be $1,000 or less if you expect to pay $4,000 or less in total wages.) If you do not check this box, you must file Form 941 for every quarter. ☐

15 First date wages or annuities were paid (month, day, year). **Note.** If applicant is a withholding agent, enter date income will first be paid to nonresident alien (month, day, year) . . . . ▶

16 Check **one** box that best describes the principal activity of your business.
☐ Construction ☐ Rental & leasing ☐ Transportation & warehousing ☐ Health care & social assistance ☐ Wholesale-agent/broker
☐ Real estate ☐ Manufacturing ☐ Finance & insurance ☐ Accommodation & food service ☐ Wholesale-other ☐ Retail
☐ Other (specify)

17 Indicate principal line of merchandise sold, specific construction work done, products produced, or services provided.

18 Has the applicant entity shown on line 1 ever applied for and received an EIN? ☐ **Yes** ☐ **No**
If "Yes," write previous EIN here ▶

Third Party Designee	Complete this section **only** if you want to authorize the named individual to receive the entity's EIN and answer questions about the completion of this form.	
	Designee's name	Designee's telephone number (include area code) ( )
	Address and ZIP code	Designee's fax number (include area code) ( )

Under penalties of perjury, I declare that I have examined this application, and to the best of my knowledge and belief, it is true, correct, and complete.

Name and title (type or print clearly) ▶

Applicant's telephone number (include area code) ( )

Applicant's fax number (include area code) ( )

Signature ▶ Date ▶

For Privacy Act and Paperwork Reduction Act Notice, see separate instructions. Cat. No. 16055N Form **SS-4** (Rev. 1-2010)

Do I Need an EIN?

File Form SS-4 if the applicant entity does not already have an EIN but is required to show an EIN on any return, statement, or other document.[1] See also the separate instructions for each line on Form SS-4.

IF the applicant...	AND...	THEN...
Started a new business	Does not currently have (nor expect to have) employees	Complete lines 1, 2, 4a–8a, 8b–c (if applicable), 9a, 9b (if applicable), and 10–14 and 16–18.
Hired (or will hire) employees, including household employees	Does not already have an EIN	Complete lines 1, 2, 4a–6, 7a–b (if applicable), 8a, 8b–c (if applicable), 9a, 9b (if applicable), 10–18.
Opened a bank account	Needs an EIN for banking purposes only	Complete lines 1–5b, 7a–b (if applicable), 8a, 8b–c (if applicable), 9a, 9b (if applicable), 10, and 18.
Changed type of organization	Either the legal character of the organization or its ownership changed (for example, you incorporate a sole proprietorship or form a partnership)[2]	Complete lines 1–18 (as applicable).
Purchased a going business[3]	Does not already have an EIN	Complete lines 1–18 (as applicable).
Created a trust	The trust is other than a grantor trust or an IRA trust[4]	Complete lines 1–18 (as applicable).
Created a pension plan as a plan administrator[5]	Needs an EIN for reporting purposes	Complete lines 1, 3, 4a–5b, 9a, 10, and 18.
Is a foreign person needing an EIN to comply with IRS withholding regulations	Needs an EIN to complete a Form W-8 (other than Form W-8ECI), avoid withholding on portfolio assets, or claim tax treaty benefits[6]	Complete lines 1–5b, 7a–b (SSN or ITIN optional), 8a, 8b–c (if applicable), 9a, 9b (if applicable), 10, and 18.
Is administering an estate	Needs an EIN to report estate income on Form 1041	Complete lines 1–6, 9a, 10–12, 13–17 (if applicable), and 18.
Is a withholding agent for taxes on non-wage income paid to an alien (i.e., individual, corporation, or partnership, etc.)	Is an agent, broker, fiduciary, manager, tenant, or spouse who is required to file Form 1042, Annual Withholding Tax Return for U.S. Source Income of Foreign Persons	Complete lines 1, 2, 3 (if applicable), 4a–5b, 7a–b (if applicable), 8a, 8b–c (if applicable), 9a, 9b (if applicable), 10, and 18.
Is a state or local agency	Serves as a tax reporting agent for public assistance recipients under Rev. Proc. 80-4, 1980-1 C.B. 581[7]	Complete lines 1, 2, 4a–5b, 9a, 10, and 18.
Is a single-member LLC	Needs an EIN to file Form 8832, Classification Election, for filing employment tax returns and excise tax returns, or for state reporting purposes[8]	Complete lines 1–18 (as applicable).
Is an S corporation	Needs an EIN to file Form 2553, Election by a Small Business Corporation[9]	Complete lines 1–18 (as applicable).

[1] For example, a sole proprietorship or self-employed farmer who establishes a qualified retirement plan, or is required to file excise, employment, alcohol, tobacco, or firearms returns, must have an EIN. A partnership, corporation, REMIC (real estate mortgage investment conduit), nonprofit organization (church, club, etc.), or farmers' cooperative must use an EIN for any tax-related purpose even if the entity does not have employees.

[2] However, do not apply for a new EIN if the existing entity only (a) changed its business name, (b) elected on Form 8832 to change the way it is taxed (or is covered by the default rules), or (c) terminated its partnership status because at least 50% of the total interests in partnership capital and profits were sold or exchanged within a 12-month period. The EIN of the terminated partnership should continue to be used. See Regulations section 301.6109-1(d)(2)(iii).

[3] Do not use the EIN of the prior business unless you became the "owner" of a corporation by acquiring its stock.

[4] However, grantor trusts that do not file using Optional Method 1 and IRA trusts that are required to file Form 990-T, Exempt Organization Business Income Tax Return, must have an EIN. For more information on grantor trusts, see the Instructions for Form 1041.

[5] A plan administrator is the person or group of persons specified as the administrator by the instrument under which the plan is operated.

[6] Entities applying to be a Qualified Intermediary (QI) need a QI-EIN even if they already have an EIN. See Rev. Proc. 2000-12.

[7] See also *Household employer* on page 4 of the instructions. **Note.** State or local agencies may need an EIN for other reasons, for example, hired employees.

[8] See *Disregarded entities* on page 4 of the instructions for details on completing Form SS-4 for an LLC.

[9] An existing corporation that is electing or revoking S corporation status should use its previously-assigned EIN.

Instructions for Form SS-4

(Rev. January 2011)

Department of the Treasury
Internal Revenue Service

Application for Employer Identification Number (EIN)
Use with the January 2010 revision of Form SS-4

Section references are to the Internal Revenue Code unless otherwise noted.

What's New

EIN operations contact information. Contact information for EIN operations at the Philadelphia Internal Revenue Service Center has changed.
• The phone number to use for Form SS-4 applicants outside of the United States has changed to 1-267-941-1099. See the *Note* in the *Telephone* section under *How to Apply*, later.
• The ZIP code for EIN Operations at the Philadelphia Internal Revenue Service Center now includes a ZIP+4 extension. The revised ZIP code is 19255-0525.
• The Fax-TIN number for EIN Operations at the Philadelphia Internal Revenue Service Center has changed to 1-267-941-1040. See the *Where to File or Fax* table on page 2.

Federal tax deposits must be made by electronic funds transfer. Beginning January 1, 2011, you must use electronic funds transfer to make all federal tax deposits (such as deposits of employment tax, excise tax, and corporate income tax). Forms 8109 and 8109-B, Federal Tax Deposit Coupon, cannot be used after December 31, 2010. Generally, electronic fund transfers are made using the Electronic Federal Tax Payment System (EFTPS). If you do not want to use EFTPS, you can arrange for your tax professional, financial institution, payroll service, or other trusted third party to make deposits on your behalf. You also may arrange for your financial institution to initiate a same-day wire on your behalf. EFTPS is a free service provided by the Department of Treasury. Services provided by your tax professional, financial institution, payroll service, or other third party may have a fee.

To get more information about EFTPS or to enroll in EFTPS, visit *www.eftps.gov* or call 1-800-555-4477. Additional information about EFTPS is also available in Publication 966, The Secure Way to Pay Your Federal Taxes.

General Instructions

Use these instructions to complete Form SS-4, Application for Employer Identification Number (EIN). Also see *Do I Need an EIN?* on page 2 of Form SS-4.

Purpose of Form

Use Form SS-4 to apply for an EIN. An EIN is a nine-digit number (for example, 12-3456789) assigned to sole proprietors, corporations, partnerships, estates, trusts, and other entities for tax filing and reporting purposes. The information you provide on this form will establish your business tax account.

 An EIN is for use in connection with your business activities only. Do not use your EIN in place of your social security number (SSN).

Reminders

Apply online. Generally, you can apply for and receive an EIN on IRS.gov. See *How To Apply*, later.

 This is a free service offered by the Internal Revenue Service at IRS.gov.

File only one Form SS-4. Generally, a sole proprietor should file only one Form SS-4 and needs only one EIN, regardless of

the number of businesses operated as a sole proprietorship or trade names under which a business operates. However, if a sole proprietorship incorporates or enters into a partnership, a new EIN is required. Also, each corporation in an affiliated group must have its own EIN.

EIN applied for, but not received. If you do not have an EIN by the time a return is due, write "Applied For" and the date you applied in the space shown for the number. Do not show your SSN as an EIN on returns.

If you do not have an EIN by the time a tax deposit is due, send your payment to the Internal Revenue Service Center for your filing area as shown in the instructions for the form that you are filing. Make your check or money order payable to the "United States Treasury" and show your name (as shown on Form SS-4), address, type of tax, period covered, and date you applied for an EIN.

Election to file Form 944. Eligible employers may now elect to file Form 944 annually instead of Forms 941 quarterly. See *Line 14. Do you want to file Form 944?* on page 5 for details.

Electronic filing and payment. Businesses can file and pay federal taxes electronically. Use e-file and the Electronic Federal Tax Payment System (EFTPS).
• For additional information about e-file, visit IRS.gov.
• For additional information about EFTPS, visit *www.eftps.gov* or call EFTPS Customer Service at 1-800-555-4477, 1-800-733-4829 (TDD), or 1-800-244-4829 (Spanish).

Federal tax deposits. New employers that have a federal tax obligation will be pre-enrolled in EFTPS. EFTPS allows you to make all of your federal tax payments online at *www.eftps.gov* or by telephone. Shortly after we have assigned you your EIN, you will receive instructions by mail for activating your EFTPS enrollment. You will also receive an EFTPS Personal Identification Number (PIN) that you will use when making your payments, as well as instructions for obtaining an online password.

For more information on federal tax deposits, see Pub. 15 (Circular E), Employer's Tax Guide.

How To Apply

You can apply for an EIN online, by telephone, by fax, or by mail, depending on how soon you need to use the EIN. Use only one method for each entity so you do not receive more than one EIN for an entity.

Online. Taxpayers and authorized third party designees located within the United States and U.S. possessions can receive an EIN online and use it immediately to file a return or make a payment. Go to the IRS website at *www.irs.gov/businesses* and click on *Employer ID Numbers*.

 Taxpayers who apply online have an option to view, print, and save their EIN assignment notice at the end of the session. (Authorized third party designees will receive the EIN, however, the EIN assignment notice will be mailed to the applicant.)

 Applicants who are not located within the United States or U.S. possessions cannot use the online application to obtain an EIN. Please use one of the other methods to apply.

Telephone. You can receive your EIN by telephone and use it immediately to file a return or make a payment. Call the IRS at 1-800-829-4933 (toll free). The hours of operation are 7:00 a.m. to 10:00 p.m. local time (Pacific time for Alaska and Hawaii).

Cat. No. 62736F

The person making the call must be authorized to sign the form or be an authorized designee. See *Third Party Designee* and *Signature* on page 6. Also see the first *TIP* on page 2.

Note. International applicants must call 1-267-941-1099 (not toll free).

If you are applying by telephone, it will be helpful to complete Form SS-4 before contacting the IRS. An IRS representative will use the information from the Form SS-4 to establish your account and assign you an EIN. Write the number you are given on the upper right corner of the form and sign and date it. Keep this copy for your records.

If requested by an IRS representative, mail or fax the signed Form SS-4 (including any third party designee authorization) within 24 hours to the IRS address provided by the IRS representative.

 *Taxpayer representatives can apply for an EIN on behalf of their client and request that the EIN be faxed to their client on the same day. **Note.** By using this procedure, you are authorizing the IRS to fax the EIN without a cover sheet.*

Fax. Under the Fax-TIN program, you can receive your EIN by fax within 4 business days. Complete and fax Form SS-4 to the IRS using the appropriate Fax-TIN number listed below. A long-distance charge to callers outside of the local calling area will apply. Fax-TIN numbers can only be used to apply for an EIN. The numbers may change without notice. Fax-TIN is available 24 hours a day, 7 days a week.

Be sure to provide your fax number so the IRS can fax the EIN back to you.

Mail. Complete Form SS-4 at least 4 to 5 weeks before you will need an EIN. Sign and date the application and mail it to the service center address for your state. You will receive your EIN in the mail in approximately 4 weeks. Also see *Third Party Designee* on page 6.

Call 1-800-829-4933 to verify a number or to ask about the status of an application by mail.

 Form SS-4 downloaded from IRS.gov is a fill-in form, and when completed, is suitable for faxing or mailing to the IRS.

Where to File or Fax

If your principal business, office or agency, or legal residence in the case of an individual, is located in:	File or fax with the "Internal Revenue Service Center" at:
One of the 50 states or the District of Columbia	Attn: EIN Operation Cincinnati, OH 45999 Fax-TIN: 859-669-5760
If you have no legal residence, principal place of business, or principal office or agency in any state or the District of Columbia:	Attn: EIN Operation Philadelphia, PA 19255-0525 Fax-TIN: 267-941-1040

How To Get Forms and Publications

Internet. You can download, view, and order tax forms, instructions, and publications at IRS.gov.

Phone. Call 1-800-TAX-FORM (1-800-829-3676) to order forms, instructions, and publications. You should receive your order or notification of its status within 10 workdays.

DVD for Tax Products. For small businesses, return preparers, or others who may frequently need tax forms or publications, a DVD containing over 2,000 tax products (including many prior year forms) can be purchased from the National Technical Information Service (NTIS).

To order Pub. 1796, IRS Tax Products DVD, call 1-877-233-6767 or go to www.irs.gov/cdorders.

 Tax help for your business is available at www.irs.gov/businesses/.

Related Forms and Publications

The following forms and instructions may be useful to filers of Form SS-4.

- Form 11-C, Occupational Tax and Registration Return for Wagering.
- Form 637, Application for Registration (For Certain Excise Tax Activities).
- Form 720, Quarterly Federal Excise Tax Return.
- Form 730, Monthly Tax Return for Wagers.
- Form 941, Employer's QUARTERLY Federal Tax Return.
- Form 944, Employer's ANNUAL Federal Tax Return.
- Form 990-T, Exempt Organization Business Income Tax Return.
- Instructions for Form 990-T.
- Form 1023, Application for Recognition of Exemption Under Section 501(c)(3) of the Internal Revenue Code.
- Form 1024, Application for Recognition of Exemption Under Section 501(a).
- Schedule C (Form 1040), Profit or Loss From Business (Sole Proprietorship).
- Schedule F (Form 1040), Profit or Loss From Farming.
- Instructions for Form 1041 and Schedules A, B, G, J, and K-1, U.S. Income Tax Return for Estates and Trusts.
- Form 1042, Annual Withholding Tax Return for U.S. Source Income of Foreign Persons.
- Instructions for Form 1065, U.S. Return of Partnership Income.
- Instructions for Form 1066, U.S. Real Estate Mortgage Investment Conduit (REMIC) Income Tax Return.
- Instructions for Forms 1120.
- Form 2290, Heavy Highway Vehicle Use Tax Return.
- Form 2553, Election by a Small Business Corporation.
- Form 2848, Power of Attorney and Declaration of Representative.
- Form 8821, Tax Information Authorization.
- Form 8832, Entity Classification Election.
- Form 8849, Claim for Refund of Excise Taxes.

For more information about filing Form SS-4 and related issues, see:

- Pub. 15 (Circular E), Employer's Tax Guide;
- Pub. 51 (Circular A), Agricultural Employer's Tax Guide;
- Pub. 538, Accounting Periods and Methods;
- Pub. 542, Corporations;
- Pub. 557, Tax-Exempt Status for Your Organization;
- Pub. 583, Starting a Business and Keeping Records;
- Pub. 966, The Secure Way to Pay Your Federal Taxes for Business and Individual Taxpayers;
- Pub. 1635, Understanding Your EIN.

Specific Instructions

Follow the instructions for each line to expedite processing and to avoid unnecessary IRS requests for additional information. Enter "N/A" on the lines that do not apply.

Line 1. Legal name of entity (or individual) for whom the EIN is being requested. Enter the legal name of the entity (or individual) applying for the EIN exactly as it appears on the social security card, charter, or other applicable legal document. An entry is required.

Individuals. Enter your first name, middle initial, and last name. If you are a sole proprietor, enter your individual name, not your business name. Enter your business name on line 2. Do not use abbreviations or nicknames on line 1.

Trusts. Enter the name of the trust as it appears on the trust instrument.

Estate of a decedent. Enter the name of the estate. For an estate that has no legal name, enter the name of the decedent followed by "Estate."

Partnerships. Enter the legal name of the partnership as it appears in the partnership agreement.

Corporations. Enter the corporate name as it appears in the corporate charter or other legal document creating it.

Plan administrators. Enter the name of the plan administrator. A plan administrator who already has an EIN should use that number.

Line 2. Trade name of business. Enter the trade name of the business if different from the legal name. The trade name is the "doing business as" (DBA) name.

 Use the full legal name shown on line 1 on all tax returns filed for the entity. (However, if you enter a trade name on line 2 and choose to use the trade name instead of the legal name, enter the trade name on all returns you file.) To prevent processing delays and errors, use only the legal name (or the trade name) on all tax returns.

Line 3. Executor, administrator, trustee, "care of" name. For trusts, enter the name of the trustee. For estates, enter the name of the executor, administrator, or other fiduciary. If the entity applying has a designated person to receive tax information, enter that person's name as the "care of" person. Enter the individual's first name, middle initial, and last name.

Lines 4a–b. Mailing address. Enter the mailing address for the entity's correspondence. If the entity's address is outside the United States or its possessions, you must enter the city, province or state, postal code, and the name of the country. Do not abbreviate the country name. If line 3 is completed, enter the address for the executor, trustee or "care of" person. Generally, this address will be used on all tax returns.

If the entity is filing the Form SS-4 only to obtain an EIN for the Form 8832, use the same address where you would like to have the acceptance or nonacceptance letter sent.

 File Form 8822, Change of Address, to report any subsequent changes to the entity's mailing address.

Lines 5a–b. Street address. Provide the entity's physical address only if different from its mailing address shown in lines 4a–b. Do not enter a P.O. box number here. If the entity's address is outside the United States or its possessions, you must enter the city, province or state, postal code, and the name of the country. Do not abbreviate the country name.

Line 6. County and state where principal business is located. Enter the entity's primary physical location.

Lines 7a–b. Name of responsible party. Enter the full name (first name, middle initial, last name, if applicable) and SSN, ITIN (individual taxpayer identification number), or EIN of the entity's responsible party as defined below.

Responsible party defined. For entities with shares or interests traded on a public exchange, or which are registered with the Securities and Exchange Commission, "responsible party" is (a) the principal officer, if the business is a corporation, (b) a general partner, if a partnership, (c) the owner of an entity that is disregarded as separate from its owner (disregarded entities owned by a corporation enter the corporation's name and EIN), or (d) a grantor, owner, or trustor, if a trust.

For all other entities, "responsible party" is the person who has a level of control over, or entitlement to, the funds or assets in the entity that, as a practical matter, enables the individual, directly or indirectly, to control, manage, or direct the entity and the disposition of its funds and assets. The ability to fund the entity or the entitlement to the property of the entity alone, however, without any corresponding authority to control, manage, or direct the entity (such as in the case of a minor child beneficiary), does not cause the individual to be a responsible party.

If the person in question is an alien individual with a previously assigned ITIN, enter the ITIN in the space provided and submit a copy of an official identifying document. If

necessary, complete Form W-7, Application for IRS Individual Taxpayer Identification Number, to obtain an ITIN.

You must enter an SSN, ITIN, or EIN on line 7b unless the only reason you are applying for an EIN is to make an entity classification election (see Regulations sections 301.7701-1 through 301.7701-3) and you are a nonresident alien or other foreign entity with no effectively connected income from sources within the United States.

Lines 8a–c. Limited liability company (LLC) information. An LLC is an entity organized under the laws of a state or foreign country as a limited liability company. For federal tax purposes, an LLC may be treated as a partnership or corporation or be disregarded as an entity separate from its owner.

By default, a domestic LLC with only one member is disregarded as an entity separate from its owner and must include all of its income and expenses on the owner's tax return (for example, Schedule C (Form 1040)). Also by default, a domestic LLC with two or more members is treated as a partnership. A domestic LLC may file Form 8832 to avoid either default classification and elect to be classified as an association taxable as a corporation. For more information on entity classifications (including the rules for foreign entities), see the instructions for Form 8832.

If the answer to line 8a is "Yes," enter the number of LLC members. If the LLC is owned solely by a husband and wife in a community property state and the husband and wife choose to treat the entity as a disregarded entity, enter "1" on line 8b.

 Do not file Form 8832 if the LLC accepts the default classifications above. If the LLC is eligible to be treated as a corporation that meets certain tests and it will be electing S corporation status, it must timely file Form 2553. The LLC will be treated as a corporation as of the effective date of the S corporation election and does not need to file Form 8832. See the Instructions for Form 2553.

Line 9a. Type of entity. Check the box that best describes the type of entity applying for the EIN. If you are an alien individual with an ITIN previously assigned to you, enter the ITIN in place of a requested SSN.

 This is not an election for a tax classification of an entity. See Disregarded entities *on page 4.*

Sole proprietor. Check this box if you file Schedule C, or Schedule F (Form 1040) and have a qualified plan, or are required to file excise, employment, alcohol, tobacco, or firearms returns, or are a payer of gambling winnings. Enter your SSN (or ITIN) in the space provided. If you are a nonresident alien with no effectively connected income from sources within the United States, you do not need to enter an SSN or ITIN.

Corporation. This box is for any corporation other than a personal service corporation. If you check this box, enter the income tax form number to be filed by the entity in the space provided.

 If you entered "1120S" after the "Corporation" checkbox, the corporation must file Form 2553 no later than the 15th day of the 3rd month of the tax year the election is to take effect. Until Form 2553 has been received and approved, you will be considered a Form 1120 filer. See the Instructions for Form 2553.

Personal service corporation. Check this box if the entity is a personal service corporation. An entity is a personal service corporation for a tax year only if:
• The principal activity of the entity during the testing period (prior tax year) for the tax year is the performance of personal services substantially by employee-owners, and
• The employee-owners own at least 10% of the fair market value of the outstanding stock in the entity on the last day of the testing period.

Personal services include performance of services in such fields as health, law, accounting, or consulting. For more information about personal service corporations, see the Instructions for Form 1120 and Pub. 542.

 If the corporation is recently formed, the testing period begins on the first day of its tax year and ends on the earlier of the last day of its tax year, or the last day of the calendar year in which its tax year begins.

Other nonprofit organization. Check this box if the nonprofit organization is other than a church or church-controlled organization and specify the type of nonprofit organization (for example, an educational organization).

 If the organization also seeks tax-exempt status, you must file either Form 1023 or Form 1024. See Pub. 557 for more information.

If the organization is covered by a group exemption letter, enter the four-digit group exemption number (GEN) in the last entry. (Do not confuse the GEN with the nine-digit EIN.) If you do not know the GEN, contact the parent organization. See Pub. 557 for more information about group exemption letters.

If the organization is a section 527 political organization, check the box for *Other nonprofit organization* and specify "section 527 organization" in the space to the right. To be recognized as exempt from tax, a section 527 political organization must electronically file Form 8871, Political Organization Notice of Section 527 Status, within 24 hours of the date on which the organization was established. The organization may also have to file Form 8872, Political Organization Report of Contributions and Expenditures. See *www.irs.gov/polorgs* for more information.

Plan administrator. If the plan administrator is an individual, enter the plan administrator's taxpayer identification number (TIN) in the space provided.

REMIC. Check this box if the entity has elected to be treated as a real estate mortgage investment conduit (REMIC). See the Instructions for Form 1066 for more information.

State/local government. If you are a government employer and you are not sure of your social security and Medicare coverage options, go to *www.ncsssa.org/statessadminmenu.html* to obtain the contact information for your state's Social Security Administrator.

Other. If not specifically listed, check the "Other" box, enter the type of entity and the type of return, if any, that will be filed (for example, "Common Trust Fund, Form 1065" or "Created a Pension Plan"). Do not enter "N/A." If you are an alien individual applying for an EIN, see the *Lines 7a–b* instructions on page 3.
• **Household employer.** If you are an individual that will employ someone to provide services in your household, check the "Other" box and enter "Household Employer" and your SSN. If you are a trust that qualifies as a household employer, you do not need a separate EIN for reporting tax information relating to household employees; use the EIN of the trust.
• **Household employer agent.** If you are an agent of a household employer that is a disabled individual or other welfare recipient receiving home care services through a state or local program, check the "Other" box and enter "Household Employer Agent." (See Rev. Proc. 80-4, 1980-1 C.B. 581; Rev. Proc. 84-33, 1984-1 C.B. 502; and Notice 2003-70, 2003-43 I.R.B. 916.) If you are a state or local government also check the box for state/local government.
• **QSub.** For a qualified subchapter S subsidiary (QSub) check the "Other" box and specify "QSub."
• **Withholding agent.** If you are a withholding agent required to file Form 1042, check the "Other" box and enter "Withholding Agent."

Disregarded entities. A disregarded entity is an eligible entity that is disregarded as separate from its owner for federal income tax purposes. Disregarded entities include single-member limited liability companies (LLCs) that are disregarded as separate from their owners, qualified subchapter S subsidiaries (qualified subsidiaries of an S corporation), and certain qualified foreign entities. See the Instructions for Form 8832 and Regulations section 301.7701-3 for more information on domestic and foreign disregarded entities.

For wages paid on or after January 1, 2009, the disregarded entity is required to use its name and EIN for reporting and payment of employment taxes. A disregarded entity is also required to use its name and EIN to register for excise tax activities on Form 637, pay and report excise taxes reported on Forms 720, 730, 2290, and 11-C, and claim any refunds, credits, and payments on Form 8849. See the instructions for the employment and excise tax returns for more information.

Complete Form SS-4 for disregarded entities as follows.
• If a disregarded entity is filing Form SS-4 to obtain an EIN because it is required to report and pay employment and excise taxes (see above) or for non-federal purposes such as a state requirement, check the "Other" box for line 9a and write "disregarded entity" (or "disregarded entity-sole proprietorship" if the owner of the disregarded entity is an individual).
• If the disregarded entity is requesting an EIN for purposes of filing Form 8832 to elect classification as an association taxable as a corporation, or Form 2553 to elect S corporation status, check the "Corporation" box for line 9a and write "single-member" and the form number of the return that will be filed (Form 1120 or 1120S).
• If the disregarded entity is requesting an EIN because it has acquired one or more additional owners and its classification has changed to partnership under the default rules of Regulations section 301.7701-3(f), check the "Partnership" box for line 9a.

Line 10. Reason for applying. Check only one box. Do not enter "N/A." A selection is required.

Started new business. Check this box if you are starting a new business that requires an EIN. If you check this box, enter the type of business being started. Do not apply if you already have an EIN and are only adding another place of business.

Hired employees. Check this box if the existing business is requesting an EIN because it has hired or is hiring employees and is therefore required to file employment tax returns. Do not apply if you already have an EIN and are only hiring employees. For information on employment taxes (for example, for family members), see Pub. 15 (Circular E).

 You must make electronic deposits of all depository taxes (such as employment tax, excise tax, and corporate income tax) using EFTPS. See Federal tax deposits must be made by electronic funds transfer *on page 1; section 11,* Depositing Taxes, *in Pub. 15 (Circular E); and Pub. 966.*

Banking purpose. Check this box if you are requesting an EIN for banking purposes only, and enter the banking purpose (for example, a bowling league for depositing dues or an investment club for dividend and interest reporting).

Changed type of organization. Check this box if the business is changing its type of organization. For example, the business was a sole proprietorship and has been incorporated or has become a partnership. If you check this box, specify in the space provided (including available space immediately below) the type of change made. For example, "From Sole Proprietorship to Partnership."

Purchased going business. Check this box if you purchased an existing business. Do not use the former owner's EIN unless you became the "owner" of a corporation by acquiring its stock.

Created a trust. Check this box if you created a trust, and enter the type of trust created. For example, indicate if the trust is a nonexempt charitable trust or a split-interest trust.

Exception. Do not file this form for certain grantor-type trusts. The trustee does not need an EIN for the trust if the trustee furnishes the name and TIN of the grantor/owner and the address of the trust to all payers. However, grantor trusts that do not file using Optional Method 1 and IRA trusts that are required to file Form 990-T, Exempt Organization Business Income Tax Return, must have an EIN. For more information on grantor trusts, see the Instructions for Form 1041.

 Do not check this box if you are applying for a trust EIN when a new pension plan is established. Check "Created a pension plan."

Created a pension plan. Check this box if you have created a pension plan and need an EIN for reporting purposes. Also, enter the type of plan in the space provided.

 Check this box if you are applying for a trust EIN when a new pension plan is established. In addition, check the "Other" box on line 9a and write "Created a Pension Plan" in the space provided.

Other. Check this box if you are requesting an EIN for any other reason; and enter the reason. For example, a newly-formed state government entity should enter "Newly-Formed State Government Entity" in the space provided.

Line 11. Date business started or acquired. If you are starting a new business, enter the starting date of the business. If the business you acquired is already operating, enter the date you acquired the business. For foreign applicants, this is the date you began or acquired a business in the United States. If you are changing the form of ownership of your business, enter the date the new ownership entity began. Trusts should enter the date the trust was funded. Estates should enter the date of death of the decedent whose name appears on line 1 or the date when the estate was legally funded.

Line 12. Closing month of accounting year. Enter the last month of your accounting year or tax year. An accounting or tax year is usually 12 consecutive months, either a calendar year or a fiscal year (including a period of 52 or 53 weeks). A calendar year is 12 consecutive months ending on December 31. A fiscal year is either 12 consecutive months ending on the last day of any month other than December or a 52-53 week year. For more information on accounting periods, see Pub. 538.

Individuals. Your tax year generally will be a calendar year.

Partnerships. Partnerships must adopt one of the following tax years.
● The tax year of the majority of its partners.
● The tax year common to all of its principal partners.
● The tax year that results in the least aggregate deferral of income.
● In certain cases, some other tax year.

See the Instructions for Form 1065 for more information.

REMICs. REMICs must have a calendar year as their tax year.

Personal service corporations. A personal service corporation generally must adopt a calendar year unless it meets one of the following requirements.
● It can establish a business purpose for having a different tax year.
● It elects under section 444 to have a tax year other than a calendar year.

Trusts. Generally, a trust must adopt a calendar year except for the following trusts.
● Tax-exempt trusts.
● Charitable trusts.
● Grantor-owned trusts.

Line 13. Highest number of employees expected in the next 12 months. Complete each box by entering the number (including zero ("-0-")) of "Agricultural," "Household," or "Other" employees expected by the applicant in the next 12 months.

If no employees are expected, skip line 14.

Line 14. Do you want to file Form 944? If you expect your employment tax liability to be $1,000 or less in a full calendar year, you are eligible to file Form 944 annually (once each year) instead of filing Form 941 quarterly (every three months). Your employment tax liability generally will be $1,000 or less if you expect to pay $4,000 or less in total wages subject to social security and Medicare taxes and federal income tax withholding. If you qualify and want to file Form 944 instead of Forms 941, check the box on line 14. If you do not check the box, then you must file Form 941 for every quarter.

 For employers in the U.S. possessions, generally, if you pay $6,536 or less in wages subject to social security and Medicare taxes, you are likely to pay $1,000 or less in employment taxes.

For more information on employment taxes, see Pub. 15 (Circular E); or Pub. 51 (Circular A) if you have agricultural employees (farmworkers).

Line 15. First date wages or annuities were paid. If the business has employees, enter the date on which the business began to pay wages or annuities. For foreign applicants, this is the date you began to pay wages in the United States. If the business does not plan to have employees, enter "N/A."

Withholding agent. Enter the date you began or will begin to pay income (including annuities) to a nonresident alien. This also applies to individuals who are required to file Form 1042 to report alimony paid to a nonresident alien. For foreign applicants, this is the date you began or will begin to pay income (including annuities) to a nonresident alien in the United States.

Line 16. Check the one box on line 16 that best describes the principal activity of the applicant's business. Check the "Other" box (and specify the applicant's principal activity) if none of the listed boxes applies. You must check a box.

Construction. Check this box if the applicant is engaged in erecting buildings or engineering projects (for example, streets, highways, bridges, tunnels). The term "Construction" also includes special trade contractors (for example, plumbing, HVAC, electrical, carpentry, concrete, excavation, etc. contractors).

Real estate. Check this box if the applicant is engaged in renting or leasing real estate to others; managing, selling, buying, or renting real estate for others; or providing related real estate services (for example, appraisal services). Also check this box for mortgage real estate investment trusts (REITs). Mortgage REITs are engaged in issuing shares of funds consisting primarily of portfolios of real estate mortgage assets with gross income of the trust solely derived from interest earned.

Rental and leasing. Check this box if the applicant is engaged in providing tangible goods such as autos, computers, consumer goods, or industrial machinery and equipment to customers in return for a periodic rental or lease payment. Also check this box for equity real estate investment trusts (REITs). Equity REITs are engaged in issuing shares of funds consisting primarily of portfolios of real estate assets with gross income of the trust derived from renting real property.

Manufacturing. Check this box if the applicant is engaged in the mechanical, physical, or chemical transformation of materials, substances, or components into new products. The assembling of component parts of manufactured products is also considered to be manufacturing.

Transportation & warehousing. Check this box if the applicant provides transportation of passengers or cargo; warehousing or storage of goods; scenic or sight-seeing transportation; or support activities related to transportation.

Finance & insurance. Check this box if the applicant is engaged in transactions involving the creation, liquidation, or change of ownership of financial assets and/or facilitating such financial transactions; underwriting annuities/insurance policies; facilitating such underwriting by selling insurance policies; or by providing other insurance or employee-benefit related services.

Health care & social assistance. Check this box if the applicant is engaged in providing physical, medical, or psychiatric care or providing social assistance activities such as youth centers, adoption agencies, individual/family services, temporary shelters, daycare, etc.

Accommodation & food services. Check this box if the applicant is engaged in providing customers with lodging, meal preparation, snacks, or beverages for immediate consumption.

Wholesale–agent/broker. Check this box if the applicant is engaged in arranging for the purchase or sale of goods owned by others or purchasing goods on a commission basis for goods traded in the wholesale market, usually between businesses.

Wholesale–other. Check this box if the applicant is engaged in selling goods in the wholesale market generally to other businesses for resale on their own account, goods used in production, or capital or durable nonconsumer goods.

Retail. Check this box if the applicant is engaged in selling merchandise to the general public from a fixed store; by direct, mail-order, or electronic sales; or by using vending machines.

Other. Check this box if the applicant is engaged in an activity not described above. Describe the applicant's principal business activity in the space provided.

Line 17. Use line 17 to describe the applicant's principal line of business in more detail. For example, if you checked the "Construction" box on line 16, enter additional detail such as "General contractor for residential buildings" on line 17. An entry is required. For mortgage REITs indicate mortgage REIT and for equity REITs indicate what type of real property is the principal type (residential REIT, nonresidential REIT, miniwarehouse REIT).

Line 18. Check the applicable box to indicate whether or not the applicant entity applying for an EIN was issued one previously.

Third Party Designee. Complete this section only if you want to authorize the named individual to receive the entity's EIN and answer questions about the completion of Form SS-4. The designee's authority terminates at the time the EIN is assigned and released to the designee. You must complete the signature area for the authorization to be valid.

Signature. When required, the application must be signed by (a) the individual, if the applicant is an individual, (b) the president, vice president, or other principal officer, if the applicant is a corporation, (c) a responsible and duly authorized member or officer having knowledge of its affairs, if the applicant is a partnership, government entity, or other unincorporated organization, or (d) the fiduciary, if the applicant is a trust or an estate. Foreign applicants may have any duly-authorized person (for example, division manager) sign Form SS-4.

Privacy Act and Paperwork Reduction Act Notice. We ask for the information on this form to carry out the Internal Revenue laws of the United States. We need it to comply with section 6109 and the regulations thereunder, which generally require the inclusion of an employer identification number (EIN) on certain returns, statements, or other documents filed with the Internal Revenue Service. If your entity is required to obtain an EIN, you are required to provide all of the information requested on this form. Information on this form may be used to determine which federal tax returns you are required to file and to provide you with related forms and publications.

We disclose this form to the Social Security Administration (SSA) for their use in determining compliance with applicable laws. We may give this information to the Department of Justice for use in civil and/or criminal litigation, and to cities, states, the District of Columbia, and U.S. commonwealths and possessions for use in administering their tax laws. We may also disclose this information to other countries under a tax treaty, to federal and state agencies to enforce federal nontax criminal laws, and to federal law enforcement and intelligence agencies to combat terrorism.

We will be unable to issue an EIN to you unless you provide all of the requested information that applies to your entity. Providing false information could subject you to penalties.

You are not required to provide the information requested on a form that is subject to the Paperwork Reduction Act unless the form displays a valid OMB control number. Books or records relating to a form or its instructions must be retained as long as their contents may become material in the administration of any Internal Revenue law. Generally, tax returns and return information are confidential, as required by section 6103.

The time needed to complete and file this form will vary depending on individual circumstances. The estimated average time is:

Recordkeeping	8 hrs., 36 min.
Learning about the law or the form	42 min.
Preparing, copying, assembling, and sending the form to the IRS	52 min.

If you have comments concerning the accuracy of these time estimates or suggestions for making this form simpler, we would be happy to hear from you. You can write to Internal Revenue Service, Tax Products Coordinating Committee, SE:W:CAR:MP:T:T:SP, IR-6526, 1111 Constitution Avenue, NW, Washington, DC 20224. Do not send the form to this address. Instead, see *Where to File or Fax* on page 2.

SOCIAL SECURITY ADMINISTRATION
Application for a Social Security Card

Applying for a Social Security Card is easy **AND** it is free!

USE THIS APPLICATION TO APPLY FOR:
- An **original** Social Security card
- A **replacement** Social Security card
- A **change of information** on your record

IMPORTANT: You MUST provide the required evidence before we can process the application. Follow the instructions below to provide the information and evidence we need.

STEP 1 Read the instructions on this application. They contain important information about documents that can be submitted as evidence, and how to complete and submit the application.
STEP 2 Complete and sign the application using BLUE or BLACK INK. **Do not** use pencil or other colors of ink. Please write legibly. If you print this application from our website, you must print it on 8 1/2" x 11" white paper (if you live abroad and cannot obtain 8 1/2" x 11" paper, A4 size paper (8.25" x 11.7") is the only acceptable alternative).
STEP 3 Submit the completed and signed application with all required evidence to any Social Security office.

PROTECT YOUR SOCIAL SECURITY NUMBER AND CARD
Protect your SSN card and number from loss and identity theft. **DO NOT** carry the card with you. Keep it in a secure location and only take it with you when you must show the card, e.g. to obtain a new job, open a new bank account, or to obtain benefits from certain U.S. agencies. **DO NOT** allow others to use your Social Security number as their own.

HOW TO SUBMIT THIS APPLICATION
In most cases, you can mail or take this application with your evidence documents to any Social Security office. However, if you live in an area serviced by a Social Security Card Center, you may need to visit the Social Security Card Center in person for all SSN related business. We will return your documents to you. **IMPORTANT: If you are age 12 or older and have never been assigned a Social Security number before, you MUST apply in person.**

If you have any questions about this form, or about the evidence documents we need, please contact any Social Security office. A telephone call will help you make sure you have everything you need to apply for a card or change information on your record. You can find your nearest office or Social Security Card Center in your local phone directory or on our website at www.socialsecurity.gov.

ABOUT YOUR EVIDENCE DOCUMENTS
You must provide the required documents based on your type of request. If your documents do not meet these requirements, we cannot process your application.
- We need **ORIGINAL** documents or **copies certified by the custodian of the record**. We will return your documents after we have seen them.
- **We cannot accept photocopies or notarized copies of documents.**

ORIGINAL CARD: To apply for an **original card**, you will need to provide **at least** two documents to prove **age**, **identity**, and **U.S. citizenship or current lawful, work-authorized immigration status. If you are not a U.S. citizen or do not have current lawful, work-authorized immigration status, you MUST prove that you have a valid nonwork reason for requesting a card. (See HOW TO COMPLETE THIS APPLICATION, Item 3.)**

REPLACEMENT CARD: To apply for a **replacement card**, you must prove your **identity**. If you were born outside of the U.S., you will also need to prove your **U.S. citizenship or current lawful, work-authorized immigration status.**

If you need to correct information on your SSN card, or information shown in our records (e.g., a name change, or corrected date of birth), you will need to prove your **identity <u>and</u>** provide **documents that support the change and establish the reason for the change (e.g., a birth certificate to show your corrected date or place of birth)**. If you were born outside of the U.S., you also need to prove your **U.S. citizenship or current lawful, work-authorized immigration status**.

LIMITS ON REPLACEMENT SOCIAL SECURITY NUMBER (SSN) CARDS

Public Law 108-458 imposes **limits on the number of replacement SSN cards** you may receive at 3 per year and 10 in a lifetime. In determining these limits, SSA will not count changes in name (i.e., first name or surname), or changes to a restrictive legend (i.e., Valid for Work with DHS Authorization, Not Valid for Employment) shown on the SSN card. In addition, we may grant exceptions on a case-by-case basis if you provide evidence to establish a need for an SSN card **beyond these limits** (e.g., a letter from a social services agency stating you must show the SSN card in order to get benefits).

HOW TO COMPLETE THIS APPLICATION

Most items on the form are self-explanatory. Those that need explanation are discussed below. The numbers match the numbered items on the form. If you are completing this form for someone else, please complete the items as they apply to that person.

2.   Show the address where you can receive your card 10 to 14 days from now.

3.   If you check "Legal Alien **Not** Allowed to Work," you must provide a document from the U.S. Federal, State, or local government agency that explains why you need a Social Security number and that you meet <u>all</u> of the requirements for the U.S. government benefit. NOTE: Not all U.S. State or local benefits are acceptable for non-work SSN purposes. Contact SSA to see if your reason qualifies.

If you check "Other," you must provide a document from the U.S. government agency that explains why you need a Social Security number and that you meet all of the requirements for a Federal benefit except for the number.

5.   Providing race/ethnic information is voluntary. However, providing this information helps us prepare statistical reports on how Social Security programs affect people. We do not reveal the identities of individuals in these reports.

6.   Show the month, day and full (4 digit) year of birth, for example, "1998" for year of birth.

8.B.   You **must** show the mother's Social Security number only when the application is for an **original** Social Security card for a person <u>under age 18</u>. However, this item may be left blank if the mother was never assigned a Social Security number, or if you do not know the mother's Social Security number and are unable to obtain it. We will still be able to assign a number to the person under age 18.

9.B.   You **must** show the father's Social Security number only when the application is for an **original** Social Security card for a person <u>under age 18</u>. However, this item may be left blank if the father was never assigned a Social Security number, or if you do not know the father's Social Security number and are unable to obtain it. We will still be able to assign a number to the person under age 18.

13.   If the date of birth you show in item 6 is different from the date of birth you used on a prior application for a Social Security card, show the date of birth you used on the prior application and submit evidence of age to support the date of birth in item 6.

16.   If you are age 18 or older, you **must sign** the application. If you are under age 18, you or a parent or legal guardian may sign. If you are physically or mentally incapable of signing the application, generally a parent, close relative, or legal guardian may sign the application. If you cannot sign your name, you should sign with an "X" mark and have two people sign as witnesses in the space beside the mark. Please do not alter your signature by including any additional information on the signature line as this may invalidate your application. Call us if you need clarification about who can sign. (See the "IMPORTANT" note under evidence of **IDENTITY** on page 3.)

EVIDENCE DOCUMENTS WE NEED TO SEE

The following lists are not all inclusive. However, they provide examples of the types of documents we need to see. **All documents must meet the criteria shown under "ABOUT YOUR EVIDENCE DOCUMENTS" on Page 1 in order to be considered.** If you have questions or need to discuss additional documents, see "If you have any questions" also on Page 1. Some documents we **may** accept are as follows:

AGE: We prefer to see your birth certificate. However, we can accept another document that shows your age. Some of the other documents we can accept are:

- Hospital record of your birth (created at the time of your birth)
- Religious record established before age five showing your age or date of birth
- Passport
- Final Adoption Decree (the adoption decree must indicate that the birth data was taken from the original birth certificate)

Call us for advice if you cannot obtain one of these documents.

IDENTITY: We must see evidence of identity in the name you want shown on the SSN card. Generally, we prefer to see documents issued in the U.S. Documents submitted to establish identity must contain your name **AND** provide biographical information (your date of birth, age, or parents' names) **and/or** physical information (photograph, or a photograph and physical description--height, eye and hair color, etc.). Additionally, if you send a picture identity document but do not appear in person, the document **must** also show your biographical information (e.g., your date of birth, age, or parents' names). To protect your Social Security card and number, identity documents **must** be of recent issuance.

- Driver's license
- U.S. Immigration Document
- Life insurance policy
- Court-ordered Name Change
- Final Adoption Decree (**only** if not used to establish age of the applicant)
- Marriage/Divorce records
- Military ID card
- Passport
- Employee ID card
- U.S. State ID card
- Foreign ID card

For young children, we may accept medical records (clinic, doctor, or hospital) provided they are records maintained by the medical provider. We may also accept school records and ID cards.

WE CANNOT ACCEPT A BIRTH CERTIFICATE, HOSPITAL SOUVENIR BIRTH CERTIFICATE, SOCIAL SECURITY CARD OR CARD STUB, OR A SOCIAL SECURITY RECORD as evidence of identity.

IMPORTANT: If you are **applying for a card on behalf of someone else, you must provide evidence that establishes your authority to sign the application on behalf of the person to whom the card will be issued** (e.g., a minor child's birth certificate establishes the authority of a parent to sign on behalf of the child). **In addition**, we must see proof of identity for both you and the person to whom the card will be issued.

U.S. CITIZENSHIP: Generally, we can accept most documents that show you were born in the U.S. If you are a U.S. citizen born outside the U.S., show us a U.S. Consular Report of Birth, a U.S. passport, a Certificate of Citizenship, or a Certificate of Naturalization.

IMMIGRATION STATUS: We need to see a current document issued to you by the Department of Homeland Security (DHS) showing your immigration status, such as Form I-551, I-94, I-688B, or I-766. We CANNOT accept a receipt showing you applied for the document. If you are not authorized to work in the U.S., we can issue you a Social Security card only if you need the number for a valid nonwork reason. (See HOW TO COMPLETE THIS APPLICATION, Item 3.) Your card will be marked to show you cannot work. If you do work, we will notify DHS.

THE PAPERWORK/PRIVACY ACT AND YOUR APPLICATION

The Privacy Act of 1974 requires us to give each person the following notice when applying for a Social Security number.

Sections 205(c) and 702 of the Social Security Act allow us to collect the facts we ask for on this form.

We use the facts you provide on this form to assign you a Social Security number and to issue you a Social Security card. You do not have to give us these facts, however, without them we cannot issue you a Social Security number or a card. Without a number, you may not be able to get a job and could lose Social Security benefits in the future.

The Social Security number is also used by the Internal Revenue Service for tax administration purposes as an identifier in processing tax returns of persons who have income which is reported to the Internal Revenue Service and by persons who are claimed as dependents on someone's Federal income tax return.

We may disclose information as necessary to administer Social Security programs, including to appropriate law enforcement agencies to investigate alleged violations of Social Security law; to other government agencies for administering entitlement, health, and welfare programs such as Medicaid, Medicare, veterans benefits, military pension, and civil service annuities, black lung, housing, student loans, railroad retirement benefits, and food stamps; to the Internal Revenue Service for Federal tax administration; and to employers and former employers to properly prepare wage reports. We may also disclose information as required by Federal law, for example, to the Department of Homeland Security, to identify and locate aliens in the U.S.; to the Selective Service System for draft registration; and to the Department of Health and Human Services for child support enforcement purposes. We may verify Social Security numbers for State motor vehicle agencies that use the number in issuing drivers licenses, as authorized by the Social Security Act. Finally, we may disclose information to your Congressional representative if they request information to answer questions you ask him or her.

We may use the information you give us when we match records by computer. Matching programs compare our records with those of other Federal, State, or local government agencies to determine whether a person qualifies for benefits paid by the Federal government. The law allows us to do this even if you do not agree to it.

Explanations about these and other reasons why information you provide us may be used or given out are available in Social Security offices. If you want to learn more about this, contact any Social Security office.

This information collection meets the requirements of 44 U.S.C. §3507, as amended by Section 2 of the Paperwork Reduction Act of 1995. You do not need to answer these questions unless we display a valid Office of Management and Budget control number. We estimate that it will take about 8.5 to 9.5 minutes to read the instructions, gather the facts, and answer the questions. **MAIL OR TAKE THE COMPLETED FORM TO YOUR LOCAL SOCIAL SECURITY OFFICE. The office is listed under U. S. Government agencies in your telephone directory or you may call Social Security at 1-800-772-1213.** *You may send comments on our time estimate above to: SSA, 6401 Security Blvd., Baltimore, MD 21235-6401.* **Send _only_ comments relating to our time estimate to this address, not the completed form.**

SOCIAL SECURITY ADMINISTRATION
Application for a Social Security Card

Form Approved
OMB No. 0960-0066

1

NAME TO BE SHOWN ON CARD	First	Full Middle Name	Last
FULL NAME AT BIRTH IF OTHER THAN ABOVE	First	Full Middle Name	Last
OTHER NAMES USED			

2 MAILING ADDRESS — Do Not Abbreviate

Street Address, Apt. No., PO Box, Rural Route No.

City	State	ZIP Code

3 CITIZENSHIP (Check One)

☐ U.S. Citizen   ☐ Legal Alien Allowed To Work   ☐ Legal Alien **Not** Allowed To Work (See Instructions On Page 2)   ☐ Other (See Instructions On Page 2)

4 SEX — ☐ Male   ☐ Female

5 RACE/ETHNIC DESCRIPTION (Check One Only - Voluntary)

☐ Asian, Asian-American or Pacific Islander   ☐ Hispanic   ☐ Black (Not Hispanic)   ☐ North American Indian or Alaskan Native   ☐ White (Not Hispanic)

6 DATE OF BIRTH _____ Month, Day, Year

7 PLACE OF BIRTH _____ (Do Not Abbreviate) City _____ State or Foreign Country   FCI

Office Use Only

8

A. MOTHER'S NAME AT HER BIRTH — First | Full Middle Name | Last Name At Her Birth

B. MOTHER'S SOCIAL SECURITY NUMBER (See instructions for 8B on Page 2) → ☐☐☐ - ☐☐ - ☐☐☐☐

9

A. FATHER'S NAME → First | Full Middle Name | Last

B. FATHER'S SOCIAL SECURITY NUMBER (See instructions for 9B on Page 2) → ☐☐☐ - ☐☐ - ☐☐☐☐

10 Has the applicant or anyone acting on his/her behalf ever filed for or received a Social Security number card before?

☐ Yes (If "yes", answer questions 11-13.)   ☐ No (If "no," go on to question 14.)   ☐ Don't Know (If "don't know," go on to question 14.)

11 Enter the Social Security number previously assigned to the person listed in item 1. → ☐☐☐ - ☐☐ - ☐☐☐☐

12 Enter the name shown on the most recent Social Security card issued for the person listed in item 1. → First | Middle Name | Last

13 Enter any different date of birth if used on an earlier application for a card. → _____ Month, Day, Year

14 TODAY'S DATE _____ Month, Day, Year

15 DAYTIME PHONE NUMBER ( ) — Area Code   Number

16 I declare under penalty of perjury that I have examined all the information on this form, and on any accompanying statements or forms, and it is true and correct to the best of my knowledge.

YOUR SIGNATURE ►

17 YOUR RELATIONSHIP TO THE PERSON IN ITEM 1 IS:

☐ Self   ☐ Natural Or Adoptive Parent   ☐ Legal Guardian   ☐ Other (Specify) _____

DO NOT WRITE BELOW THIS LINE (FOR SSA USE ONLY)

NPN			DOC	NTI	CAN			ITV
PBC	EVI	EVA	EVC	PRA	NWR	DNR	UNIT	
EVIDENCE SUBMITTED					SIGNATURE AND TITLE OF EMPLOYEE(S) REVIEWING EVIDENCE AND/OR CONDUCTING INTERVIEW			
					_____ DATE			
					DCL _____ DATE			

Form SS-5 (12-2005)   ef (12-2005)   Destroy Prior Editions   Page 5

Form **SS-8**	**Determination of Worker Status for Purposes**	OMB. No. 1545-0004

Form **SS-8**
(Rev. August 2011)

Department of the Treasury
Internal Revenue Service

Determination of Worker Status for Purposes of Federal Employment Taxes and Income Tax Withholding

OMB. No. 1545-0004

For IRS Use Only:
Case Number:

_____

Earliest Receipt Date:

Name of firm (or person) for whom the worker performed services	Worker's name
Firm's mailing address (include street address, apt. or suite no., city, state, and ZIP code)	Worker's mailing address (include street address, apt. or suite no., city, state, and ZIP code)

Trade name	Firm's email address	Worker's daytime telephone number	Worker's email address
Firm's fax number	Firm's website	Worker's alternate telephone number	Worker's fax number
Firm's telephone number (include area code)	Firm's employer identification number	Worker's social security number	Worker's employer identification number (if any)

Note. If the worker is paid for these services by a firm other than the one listed on this form, enter the name, address, and employer identification number of the payer. ▶ _____

Disclosure of Information

The information provided on Form SS-8 may be disclosed to the firm, worker, or payer named above to assist the IRS in the determination process. For example, if you are a worker, we may disclose the information you provide on Form SS-8 to the firm or payer named above. The information can only be disclosed to assist with the determination process. If you provide incomplete information, we may not be able to process your request. See *Privacy Act and Paperwork Reduction Act Notice* on page 6 for more information. **If you do not want this information disclosed to other parties, do not file Form SS-8.**

Parts I–V. All filers of Form SS-8 must complete all questions in Parts I–IV. Part V must be completed if the worker provides a service directly to customers or is a salesperson. If you cannot answer a question, enter "Unknown" or "Does not apply." If you need more space for a question, attach another sheet with the part and question number clearly identified. Write your firm's name (or workers' name) and employer identification number (or social security number) at the top of each additional sheet attached to this form.

Part I	**General Information**

1 This form is being completed by: ☐ Firm ☐ Worker; for services performed _____ to _____ .
   (beginning date)   (ending date)

2 Explain your reason(s) for filing this form (for example, you received a bill from the IRS, you believe you erroneously received a Form 1099 or Form W-2, you are unable to get worker's compensation benefits, or you were audited or are being audited by the IRS). _____
_____
_____

3 Total number of workers who performed or are performing the same or similar services: _____ .

4 How did the worker obtain the job? ☐ Application ☐ Bid ☐ Employment Agency ☐ Other (specify) _____

5 **Attach copies of all supporting documentation (for example, contracts, invoices, memos, Forms W-2 or Forms 1099-MISC issued or received, IRS closing agreements or IRS rulings).** In addition, please inform us of any current or past litigation concerning the worker's status. If no income reporting forms (Form 1099-MISC or W-2) were furnished to the worker, enter the amount of income earned for the year(s) at issue $ _____ .

   If both Form W-2 and Form 1099-MISC were issued or received, explain why. _____
_____

6 Describe the firm's business. _____
_____

For Privacy Act and Paperwork Reduction Act Notice, see page 6.   Cat. No. 16106T   Form **SS-8** (Rev. 8-2011)

Part I **General Information** (continued)

7   If the worker received pay from more than one entity because of an event such as the sale, merger, acquisition, or reorganization of the firm for whom the services are performed, provide the following: Name of the firm's previous owner: _____

Previous owner's taxpayer identification number: _____ Change was a: ☐ Sale ☐ Merger ☐ Acquisition ☐ Reorganization

☐ Other (specify) _____

Description of above change: _____

_____

Date of change (MM/DD/YY): _____

8   Describe the work done by the worker and provide the worker's job title. _____

_____

9   Explain why you believe the worker is an employee or an independent contractor. _____

_____

10   Did the worker perform services for the firm in any capacity before providing the services that are the subject of this determination request?

☐ Yes   ☐ No   ☐ N/A

If "Yes," what were the dates of the prior service? _____

If "Yes," explain the differences, if any, between the current and prior service. _____

_____

11   If the work is done under a written agreement between the firm and the worker, attach a copy (preferably signed by both parties). Describe the terms and conditions of the work arrangement. _____

_____

Part II **Behavioral Control** (Provide names and titles of specific individuals, if applicable.)

1   What specific training and/or instruction is the worker given by the firm? _____

2   How does the worker receive work assignments? _____

3   Who determines the methods by which the assignments are performed? _____

4   Who is the worker required to contact if problems or complaints arise and who is responsible for their resolution? _____

5   What types of reports are required from the worker? Attach examples. _____

6   Describe the worker's daily routine such as his or her schedule or hours. _____

_____

7   At what location(s) does the worker perform services (for example, firm's premises, own shop or office, home, customer's location)? Indicate the appropriate percentage of time the worker spends in each location, if more than one. _____

8   Describe any meetings the worker is required to attend and any penalties for not attending (for example, sales meetings, monthly meetings, staff meetings). _____

9   Is the worker required to provide the services personally? . . . . ☐ Yes   ☐ No

10   If substitutes or helpers are needed, who hires them? _____

11   If the worker hires the substitutes or helpers, is approval required? . . . . ☐ Yes   ☐ No

If "Yes," by whom? _____

12   Who pays the substitutes or helpers? _____

13   Is the worker reimbursed if the worker pays the substitutes or helpers? . . . . ☐ Yes   ☐ No

If "Yes," by whom? _____

| **Part III** | **Financial Control** (Provide names and titles of specific individuals, if applicable.) |

1 List the supplies, equipment, materials, and property provided by each party:

The firm: _____

The worker: _____

Other party: _____

2 Does the worker lease equipment, space, or a facility? . . . . ☐ **Yes** ☐ **No**

If "Yes," what are the terms of the lease? (Attach a copy or explanatory statement.) _____

_____

3 What expenses are incurred by the worker in the performance of services for the firm? _____

_____

4 Specify which, if any, expenses are reimbursed by:

The firm: _____

Other party: _____

5 Type of pay the worker receives: ☐ Salary   ☐ Commission   ☐ Hourly Wage   ☐ Piece Work

☐ Lump Sum   ☐ Other (specify) _____

If type of pay is commission, and the firm guarantees a minimum amount of pay, specify amount. $ _____

6 Is the worker allowed a drawing account for advances? . . . . ☐ **Yes** ☐ **No**

If "Yes," how often? _____

Specify any restrictions. _____

_____

7 Whom does the customer pay? . . . . ☐ Firm   ☐ Worker

If worker, does the worker pay the total amount to the firm? ☐ **Yes**   ☐ **No**   If "No," explain. _____

_____

8 Does the firm carry workers' compensation insurance on the worker? . . . . ☐ **Yes** ☐ **No**

9 What economic loss or financial risk, if any, can the worker incur beyond the normal loss of salary (for example, loss or damage of equipment, material)? _____

_____

_____

10 Does the worker establish the level of payment for the services provided or the products sold? . . . . ☐ **Yes** ☐ **No**

If "No," who does? _____

| **Part IV** | **Relationship of the Worker and Firm** |

1 Please check the benefits available to the worker: ☐ Paid vacations   ☐ Sick pay   ☐ Paid holidays

☐ Personal days   ☐ Pensions   ☐ Insurance benefits   ☐ Bonuses

☐ Other (specify) _____

2 Can the relationship be terminated by either party without incurring liability or penalty? . . . . ☐ **Yes** ☐ **No**

If "No," explain your answer. _____

3 Did the worker perform similar services for others during the time period entered in Part I, line 1? . . . . ☐ **Yes** ☐ **No**

If "Yes," is the worker required to get approval from the firm? . . . . ☐ **Yes** ☐ **No**

4 Describe any agreements prohibiting competition between the worker and the firm while the worker is performing services or during any later period. Attach any available documentation. _____

_____

5 Is the worker a member of a union? . . . . ☐ **Yes** ☐ **No**

6 What type of advertising, if any, does the worker do (for example, a business listing in a directory or business cards)? Provide copies, if applicable. _____

7 If the worker assembles or processes a product at home, who provides the materials and instructions or pattern? _____

_____

8 What does the worker do with the finished product (for example, return it to the firm, provide it to another party, or sell it)? _____

_____

9 How does the firm represent the worker to its customers (for example, employee, partner, representative, or contractor), and under whose business name does the worker perform these services? _____

_____

10 If the worker no longer performs services for the firm, how did the relationship end (for example, worker quit or was fired, job completed, contract ended, firm or worker went out of business)? _____

_____

Form **SS-8** (Rev. 8-2011)

Part V   **For Service Providers or Salespersons.** Complete this part if the worker provided a service directly to customers or is a salesperson.

1   What are the worker's responsibilities in soliciting new customers? _____

2   Who provides the worker with leads to prospective customers? _____

3   Describe any reporting requirements pertaining to the leads. _____

4   What terms and conditions of sale, if any, are required by the firm? _____

5   Are orders submitted to and subject to approval by the firm? . . . . ☐ **Yes**   ☐ **No**

6   Who determines the worker's territory? _____

7   Did the worker pay for the privilege of serving customers on the route or in the territory? . . . . ☐ **Yes**   ☐ **No**

    If "Yes," whom did the worker pay? _____

    If "Yes," how much did the worker pay? . . . . $ _____

8   Where does the worker sell the product (for example, in a home, retail establishment)? _____

9   List the product and/or services distributed by the worker (for example, meat, vegetables, fruit, bakery products, beverages, or laundry or dry cleaning services). If more than one type of product and/or service is distributed, specify the principal one. _____

10   Does the worker sell life insurance full time? . . . . ☐ **Yes**   ☐ **No**

11   Does the worker sell other types of insurance for the firm? . . . . ☐ **Yes**   ☐ **No**

    If "Yes," enter the percentage of the worker's total working time spent in selling other types of insurance . . . . . _____ %

12   If the worker solicits orders from wholesalers, retailers, contractors, or operators of hotels, restaurants, or other similar establishments, enter the percentage of the worker's time spent in the solicitation . . . . _____ %

13   Is the merchandise purchased by the customers for resale or use in their business operations? . . . . ☐ **Yes**   ☐ **No**

    Describe the merchandise and state whether it is equipment installed on the customers' premises. _____

Sign Here ▶	Under penalties of perjury, I declare that I have examined this request, including accompanying documents, and to the best of my knowledge and belief, the facts presented are true, correct, and complete.
	_____ Title ▶ _____ Date ▶ _____
	Type or print name below signature.

Form **SS-8** (Rev. 8-2011)

General Instructions

Section references are to the Internal Revenue Code unless otherwise noted.

Purpose

Firms and workers file Form SS-8 to request a determination of the status of a worker for purposes of federal employment taxes and income tax withholding.

A Form SS-8 determination may be requested only in order to resolve federal tax matters. If Form SS-8 is submitted for a tax year for which the statute of limitations on the tax return has expired, a determination letter will not be issued. The statute of limitations expires 3 years from the due date of the tax return or the date filed, whichever is later.

The IRS does not issue a determination letter for proposed transactions or on hypothetical situations. We may, however, issue an information letter when it is considered appropriate.

Definition

Firm. For the purposes of this form, the term "firm" means any individual, business enterprise, organization, state, or other entity for which a worker has performed services. The firm may or may not have paid the worker directly for these services.

If the firm was not responsible for payment for services, be sure to enter the name, address, and employer identification number of the payer on the first page of Form SS-8, below the identifying information for the firm and the worker.

The Form SS-8 Determination Process

The IRS will acknowledge the receipt of your Form SS-8. Because there are usually two (or more) parties who could be affected by a determination of employment status, the IRS attempts to get information from all parties involved by sending those parties blank Forms SS-8 for completion. Some or all of the information provided on this Form SS-8 may be shared with the other parties listed on page 1. The case will be assigned to a technician who will review the facts, apply the law, and render a decision. The technician may ask for additional information from the requestor, from other involved parties, or from third parties that could help clarify the work relationship before rendering a decision. The IRS will generally issue a formal determination to the firm or payer (if that is a different entity), and will send a copy to the worker. A determination letter applies only to a worker (or a class of workers) requesting it, and the decision is binding on the IRS. In certain cases, a formal determination will not be issued. Instead, an information letter may be issued. Although an information letter is advisory only and is not binding on the IRS, it may be used to assist the worker to fulfill his or her federal tax obligations.

Neither the Form SS-8 determination process nor the review of any records in connection with the determination constitutes an examination (audit) of any federal tax return. If the periods under consideration have previously been examined, the Form SS-8 determination process will not constitute a reexamination under IRS reopening procedures. Because this is not an examination of any federal tax return, the appeal rights available in connection with an examination do not apply to a Form SS-8 determination. However, if you disagree with a determination or you have additional information concerning the work relationship that you believe was not previously considered, you may request that the determining office reconsider the determination.

Completing Form SS-8

Answer all questions as completely as possible. Attach additional sheets if you need more space. Provide information for **all** years the worker provided services for the firm. Determinations are based on the entire relationship between the firm and the worker. Also indicate if there were any significant changes in the work relationship over the service term.

Additional copies of this form may be obtained on IRS.gov or by calling 1-800-TAX-FORM (1-800-829-3676).

Fee

There is no fee for requesting a Form SS-8 determination letter.

Signature

Form SS-8 must be signed and dated by the taxpayer. A stamped signature will not be accepted.

The person who signs for a corporation must be an officer of the corporation who has personal knowledge of the facts. If the corporation is a member of an affiliated group filing a consolidated return, it must be signed by an officer of the common parent of the group.

The person signing for a trust, partnership, or limited liability company must be, respectively, a trustee, general partner, or member-manager who has personal knowledge of the facts.

Where To File

Send the completed and signed Form SS-8 to the address below for the firm's location. Faxed, photocopied, or electronic versions of Form SS-8 are not acceptable for the initial request for the Form SS-8 determination. However, only for cases involving federal agencies, send Form SS-8 to the Internal Revenue Service, Attn: CC:CORP:T:C, Ben Franklin Station, P.O. Box 7604, Washington, DC 20044. **Do not submit Form SS-8 with your tax return as that will delay processing time.**

Firm's location:	Send to:
Alaska, Arizona, Arkansas, California, Colorado, Hawaii, Idaho, Illinois, Iowa, Kansas, Minnesota, Missouri, Montana, Nebraska, Nevada, New Mexico, North Dakota, Oklahoma, Oregon, South Dakota, Texas, Utah, Washington, Wisconsin, Wyoming, American Samoa, Guam, Puerto Rico, U.S. Virgin Islands	Internal Revenue Service Form SS-8 Determinations P.O. Box 630 Stop 631 Holtsville, NY 11742-0630
Alabama, Connecticut, Delaware, District of Columbia, Florida, Georgia, Indiana, Kentucky, Louisiana, Maine, Maryland, Massachusetts, Michigan, Mississippi, New Hampshire, New Jersey, New York, North Carolina, Ohio, Pennsylvania, Rhode Island, South Carolina, Tennessee, Vermont, Virginia, West Virginia, all other locations not listed	Internal Revenue Service Form SS-8 Determinations 40 Lakemont Road Newport, VT 05855-1555

Instructions for Workers

If you are requesting a determination for more than one firm, complete a separate Form SS-8 for each firm.

 Form SS-8 is not a claim for refund of social security and Medicare taxes or federal income tax withholding.

If the IRS determines that you are an employee, you are responsible for filing an amended return for any corrections related to this decision. A determination that a worker is an employee does not necessarily reduce any current or prior tax liability. For more information, call 1-800-829-1040.

Time for filing a claim for refund. Generally, you must file your claim for a credit or refund within 3 years from the date your original return was filed or within 2 years from the date the tax was paid, whichever is later.

Filing Form SS-8 does not prevent the expiration of the time in which a claim for a refund must be filed. If you are concerned about a refund, and the statute of limitations for filing a claim for refund for the year(s) at issue has not yet expired, you should file Form 1040X, Amended U.S. Individual Income Tax Return, to protect your statute of limitations. File a separate Form 1040X for each year.

On the Form 1040X you file, do not complete lines 1 through 22 on the form. Write "Protective Claim" at the top of the form, sign and date it. In addition, enter the following statement in Part III: "Filed Form SS-8 with the Internal Revenue Service Office in (Holtsville, NY; Newport, VT; or Washington, DC; as appropriate). By filing this protective claim, I reserve the right to file a claim for any refund that may be due after a determination of my employment tax status has been completed."

Filing Form SS-8 does not alter the requirement to timely file an income tax return. Do not delay filing your tax return in anticipation of an answer to your SS-8 request. In addition, if applicable, do not delay in responding to a request for payment while waiting for a determination of your worker status.

Instructions for Firms

If a **worker** has requested a determination of his or her status while working for you, you will receive a request from the IRS to complete a Form SS-8. In cases of this type, the IRS usually gives each party an opportunity to present a statement of the facts because any decision will affect the employment tax status of the parties. Failure to respond to this request will not prevent the IRS from issuing a determination letter based on the information he or she has made available so that the worker may fulfill his or her federal tax obligations. However, the information that you provide is extremely valuable in determining the status of the worker.

If you are requesting a determination for a particular class of worker, complete the form for one individual who is representative of the class of workers whose status is in question. If you want a written determination for more than one class of workers, complete a separate Form SS-8 for one worker from each class whose status is typical of that class. A written determination for any worker will apply to other workers of the same class if the facts are not materially different for these workers. Please provide a list of names and addresses of all workers potentially affected by this determination.

If you have a reasonable basis for not treating a worker as an employee, you may be relieved from having to pay employment taxes for that worker under section 530 of the 1978 Revenue Act. However, this relief provision cannot be considered in conjunction with a Form SS-8 determination because the determination does not constitute an examination of any tax return. For more information regarding section 530 of the 1978 Revenue Act and to determine if you qualify for relief under this section, visit IRS.gov.

Privacy Act and Paperwork Reduction Act Notice. We ask for the information on Form SS-8 to carry out the Internal Revenue laws of the United States. This information will be used to determine the employment status of the worker(s) described on the form. Subtitle C, Employment Taxes, of the Internal Revenue Code imposes employment taxes on wages, including income tax withholding. Sections 3121(d), 3306(a), and 3401(c) and (d) and the related regulations define employee and employer for purposes of employment taxes imposed under Subtitle C. Section 6001 authorizes the IRS to request information needed to determine if a worker(s) or firm is subject to these taxes. Section 6109 requires you to provide your taxpayer identification number. Neither workers nor firms are required to request a status determination, but if you choose to do so, you must provide the information requested on this form. Failure to provide the requested information may prevent us from making a status determination. If any worker or the firm has requested a status determination and you are being asked to provide information for use in that determination, you are not required to provide the requested information. However, failure to provide such information will prevent the IRS from considering it in making the status determination. Providing false or fraudulent information may subject you to penalties. Generally, tax returns and return information are confidential, as required by section 6103. However, section 6103 allows or requires the IRS to disclose or give the information shown on your tax return to others as described in the Code. Routine uses of this information include providing it to the Department of Justice for use in civil and criminal litigation, to the Social Security Administration for the administration of social security programs, and to cities, states, the District of Columbia, and U.S. commonwealths and possessions for the administration of their tax laws. We also may disclose this information to other countries under a tax treaty, to federal and state agencies to enforce federal nontax criminal laws, or to federal law enforcement and intelligence agencies to combat terrorism. We may provide this information to the affected worker(s), the firm, or payer as part of the status determination process.

You are not required to provide the information requested on a form that is subject to the Paperwork Reduction Act unless the form displays a valid OMB control number. Books or records relating to a form or its instructions must be retained as long as their contents may become material in the administration of any Internal Revenue law.

The time needed to complete and file this Form SS-8 will vary depending on individual circumstances. The estimated average time is: Recordkeeping, 23 hrs., 55 min.; Learning about the law or the form, 1 hr., 48 min.; Preparing the form, 5 hrs., 03 min.; and Sending the form to the IRS, 48 min. If you have comments concerning the accuracy of these time estimates or suggestions for making this form simpler, we would be happy to hear from you. You can write to the Internal Revenue Service, Tax Products Coordinating Committee, SE:W:CAR:MP:T:M:S, 1111 Constitution Ave. NW, IR-6526, Washington, DC 20224. Do not send the tax form to this address. Instead, see *Where To File* on page 5.

Social Security Administration

Form Approved
OMB No. 0960-0565

EMPLOYER REPORT OF SPECIAL WAGE PAYMENTS

PART I - TO BE COMPLETED BY SSA/EMPLOYER:

Tax Year	Employee Name	Employee's SSN	SSA Claim Number *(To be completed by SSA)*

Employer	Address

PART 2 - TO BE COMPLETED BY EMPLOYER:

Employees are sometime paid wages *in a year* subsequent to the year that the wages were earned. The most common types of payments are accumulated (for prior years) vacation pay or sick pay paid after retirement; deferred compensation; severance pay (when paid on account of retirement) and bonuses--paid pursuant to a prior agreement or contract.

Wages which are earned in a year prior to the year they are paid usually do not affect benefits payable under the Social Security annual earnings test. However, for the Social Security Administration to pay benefits accurately, these prior year amounts must be reported to us. The above named individual has filed for Social Security benefits. To ensure that correct Social Security benefits are paid, please complete the information below and return this form to the Social Security Administration. (Please see reverse side for instructions for the completion of this form.)

1. Employer Identification Number (EIN)	2. Retirement date (MM/DD/YYYY)	3. Date employee last performed services (MM/DD/YYYY)

If the dates in items 2 and 3 are not the same, please explain the difference.

4. For wages paid to the employee in the "tax year" (see Part I above), enter the amount that was for services performed prior to the tax year; or was not attributable to services rendered during the tax year; or was paid on account of retirement: ➡ $_____

Check the type(s) of wages paid in the tax year but for services performed in a prior year or were paid on account of retirement.

☐ Vacation Pay   ☐ Sick Pay   ☐ Severance Pay

☐ Bonus   ☐ Deferred Compensation

☐ Other *(Explain)* _____

5. Will payments listed in item "4" be made for years after the tax year?   ☐ Yes   ☐ No

If answered Yes, please show the amounts and years in which these amounts will be paid, if known.

Amount	Year	Amount	Year

6. Nonqualified deferred compensation and section 457 plans only. If payments and deferrals occurred during the tax year, enter the amount of wages earned by the employee during the tax year. $_____

Signature ▶

Title	Date	Phone Number
		(___) ___ - ____

Form **SSA-131** (8-2001) Destroy Prior Editions EF (06-2002)   (Over)

EMPLOYER INSTRUCTIONS FOR COMPLETING SPECIAL WAGE PAYMENT FORM

1. Provide the EIN that was used or will be used to report the employee's wages on the Form W-2.

2. Enter the date the employee retired. Enter "Not Retired" if the employee has not retired.

3. Enter the date that the employee last performed services; was not expected to return to work; and was not subject to recall to render additional services. This date should be the same as or earlier than the date in item "2." Enter "Not Retired" if the employee has not retired.

4. Enter the wages that were paid to the employee in the tax year that were for services that were performed in years prior to the tax year or that were paid on account of retirement.

   Examples (not all inclusive) of payments to be included:

   - Payments in lieu of vacation that were earned in a year prior to the tax year.

   - Accumulated sick payments which were paid in a lump sum based on "retirement" as the sole condition of payment.

   - Accumulated sick payments paid at or after the date in item 3, which were earned in a year prior to the tax year.

   - Payments "on account of retirement"--dismissal, severance or termination pay paid because of retirement.

   - Bonuses which are paid pursuant to a prior contract, agreement or promise causing the employee to expect such payments regularly; or announced to induce the employee to work more steadily, rapidly or efficiently or to remain with the employer.

   - Stock Options.

   Do not include in item "4" payments:

   - For annual, sick, holiday or vacation pay if used (absence from work) prior to the date of retirement (earlier of items "2" or "3").

   - That were reported or will be reported under "Nonqualified Plans" on the Form W-2.

   - That were deducted from the employee's wages and paid to a deferred compensation plan (e.g., 401k).

   - Employees health and dental plan benefits (non-covered/non-taxable for Social Security Wages).

   - Bonuses *earned* and *paid* in the tax year.

5. Check whether payments listed in item 4 will be made for years after the tax year. If yes, please show the amounts and years in which these will be paid, if known.

6. **Nonqualified deferred compensation and section 457 plans only.** If you were unable to report nonqualified deferred compensation or section 457 plan payments and deferrals (contributions) on Form W-2 because both payments and deferrals occurred during the year, show the amount of wages **earned** by the employee during the tax year. Generally, the wages earned will be the compensation reported in block 1 of Form W-2 less payments from a nonqualified deferred compensation (or 457) plan, but including any amounts deferred under the plan during the tax year (See IRS Publication 957).

Paperwork/Privacy Act Notice: This report is authorized by regulation 20 CFR 404.702. The information that you provide will be used in making a determination regarding the amount of Social Security benefits payable to the above named individual. While your response is voluntary, if you do not respond we may not be able to make a correct determination regarding the amount of Social Security benefits payable to the above named individual for the year in question.

We may also use the information you give us when we match records by computer. Matching programs compare our records with those of other Federal, State, or local government agencies. Many agencies may use matching programs to find or prove that a person qualifies for benefits paid by the Federal Government. The law allows us to do this even if you do not agree to it.

Explanations about these and other reasons why information you provide us may be used or given out are available in Social Security Offices. If you want to learn more about this, contact any Social Security Office.

PAPERWORK REDUCTION ACT: This information collection meets the clearance requirements of 44 U.S.C. §3507, as amended by Section 2 of the Paperwork Reduction Act of 1995. You are not required to answer these questions unless we display a valid Office of Management and Budget control number. We estimate that it will take you about 20 minutes to read the instructions, gather the necessary facts, and answer the questions.

Form **SSA-131** (8-2001) EF (06-2002)

Statement Concerning Your Employment in a Job
Not Covered by Social Security

Employee Name _____ **Employee ID#** _____

Employer Name _____ **Employer ID#** _____

Your earnings from this job are not covered under Social Security. When you retire, or if you become disabled, you may receive a pension based on earnings from this job. If you do, and you are also entitled to a benefit from Social Security based on either your own work or the work of your husband or wife, or former husband or wife, your pension may affect the amount of the Social Security benefit you receive. Your Medicare benefits, however, will not be affected. Under the Social Security law, there are two ways your Social Security benefit amount may be affected.

Windfall Elimination Provision

Under the Windfall Elimination Provision, your Social Security retirement or disability benefit is figured using a modified formula when you are also entitled to a pension from a job where you did not pay Social Security tax. As a result, you will receive a lower Social Security benefit than if you were not entitled to a pension from this job. For example, if you are age 62 in 2012, the maximum monthly reduction in your Social Security benefit as a result of this provision is $383.50. This amount is updated annually. This provision reduces, but does not totally eliminate, your Social Security benefit. For additional information, please refer to Social Security Publication, "Windfall Elimination Provision."

Government Pension Offset Provision

Under the Government Pension Offset Provision, any Social Security spouse or widow(er) benefit to which you become entitled will be offset if you also receive a Federal, State or local government pension based on work where you did not pay Social Security tax. The offset reduces the amount of your Social Security spouse or widow(er) benefit by two-thirds of the amount of your pension.

For example, if you get a monthly pension of $600 based on earnings that are not covered under Social Security, two-thirds of that amount, $400, is used to offset your Social Security spouse or widow(er) benefit. If you are eligible for a $500 widow(er) benefit, you will receive $100 per month from Social Security ($500 - $400=$100). Even if your pension is high enough to totally offset your spouse or widow(er) Social Security benefit, you are still eligible for Medicare at age 65. For additional information, please refer to Social Security Publication, "Government Pension Offset."

For More Information

Social Security publications and additional information, including information about exceptions to each provision, are available at www.socialsecurity.gov. You may also call toll free 1-800-772-1213, or for the deaf or hard of hearing call the TTY number 1-800-325-0778, or contact your local Social Security office.

I certify that I have received Form SSA-1945 that contains information about the possible effects of the Windfall Elimination Provision and the Government Pension Offset Provision on my potential future Social Security Benefits.

Signature of Employee _____ **Date** _____

Form **SSA-1945** (05-2012)

Information about Social Security Form SSA-1945 Statement Concerning Your Employment in a Job Not Covered by Social Security

New legislation [Section 419(c) of Public Law 108-203, the Social Security Protection Act of 2004] requires State and local government employers to provide a statement to employees hired January 1, 2005 or later in a job not covered under Social Security. The statement explains how a pension from that job could affect future Social Security benefits to which they may become entitled.

Form SSA-1945, **Statement Concerning Your Employment in a Job Not Covered by Social Security,** is the document that employers should use to meet the requirements of the law. The SSA-1945 explains the potential effects of two provisions in the Social Security law for workers who also receive a pension based on their work in a job not covered by Social Security. The Windfall Elimination Provision can affect the amount of a worker's Social Security retirement or disability benefit. The Government Pension Offset Provision can affect a Social Security benefit received as a spouse, surviving spouse, or an ex-spouse.

Employers must:

-   Give the statement to the employee prior to the start of employment;
-   Get the employee's signature on the form; and
-   Submit a copy of the signed form to the pension paying agency.

Social Security will not be setting any additional guidelines for the use of this form.

Copies of the SSA-1945 are available online at the Social Security website, www.socialsecurity.gov/form1945. Paper copies can be requested by email at oplm.oswm.rqct.orders@ssa.gov or by fax at 410-965-2037. The request must include the name, complete address and telephone number of the employer. Forms will not be sent to a post office box. Also, if appropriate, include the name of the person to whom the forms are to be delivered. The forms are available in packages of 25. Please refer to Inventory Control Number (ICN) 276950 when ordering.

Form **SSA-1945** (05-2012)

22222	Void ☐	**a** Employee's social security number	For Official Use Only ▶ OMB No. 1545-0008

b Employer identification number (EIN)	**1** Wages, tips, other compensation	**2** Federal income tax withheld
c Employer's name, address, and ZIP code	**3** Social security wages	**4** Social security tax withheld
	5 Medicare wages and tips	**6** Medicare tax withheld
	7 Social security tips	**8** Allocated tips
d Control number	**9**	**10** Dependent care benefits

e Employee's first name and initial	Last name	Suff.	**11** Nonqualified plans	**12a** See instructions for box 12
			13 Statutory employee ☐ Retirement plan ☐ Third-party sick pay ☐	**12b**
			14 Other	**12c**
				12d
f Employee's address and ZIP code				

15 State	Employer's state ID number	**16** State wages, tips, etc.	**17** State income tax	**18** Local wages, tips, etc.	**19** Local income tax	**20** Locality name

Form **W-2** Wage and Tax Statement   **2013**

Copy A For Social Security Administration — Send this entire page with
Form W-3 to the Social Security Administration; photocopies are **not** acceptable.

Department of the Treasury—Internal Revenue Service
**For Privacy Act and Paperwork Reduction
Act Notice, see the separate instructions.**

Cat. No. 10134D

Do Not Cut, Fold, or Staple Forms on This Page

	a Employee's social security number	OMB No. 1545-0008		
22222				

b Employer identification number (EIN)		**1** Wages, tips, other compensation	**2** Federal income tax withheld
c Employer's name, address, and ZIP code		**3** Social security wages	**4** Social security tax withheld
		5 Medicare wages and tips	**6** Medicare tax withheld
		7 Social security tips	**8** Allocated tips
d Control number		**9**	**10** Dependent care benefits
e Employee's first name and initial Last name Suff.		**11** Nonqualified plans	**12a** Code
		13 Statutory employee ☐ Retirement plan ☐ Third-party sick pay ☐	**12b** Code
		14 Other	**12c** Code
			12d Code
f Employee's address and ZIP code			

15 State Employer's state ID number	**16** State wages, tips, etc.	**17** State income tax	**18** Local wages, tips, etc.	**19** Local income tax	**20** Locality name

Form **W-2** Wage and Tax Statement   **2013**   Department of the Treasury—Internal Revenue Service

Copy 1—For State, City, or Local Tax Department

a Employee's social security number			Safe, accurate, FAST! Use	IRS e~file	Visit the IRS website at www.irs.gov/efile

OMB No. 1545-0008

b Employer identification number (EIN)		**1** Wages, tips, other compensation	**2** Federal income tax withheld
c Employer's name, address, and ZIP code		**3** Social security wages	**4** Social security tax withheld
		5 Medicare wages and tips	**6** Medicare tax withheld
		7 Social security tips	**8** Allocated tips
d Control number		**9**	**10** Dependent care benefits
e Employee's first name and initial Last name Suff.		**11** Nonqualified plans	**12a** See instructions for box 12
		13 Statutory employee ☐ Retirement plan ☐ Third-party sick pay ☐	**12b**
		14 Other	**12c**
			12d
f Employee's address and ZIP code			

15 State Employer's state ID number	**16** State wages, tips, etc.	**17** State income tax	**18** Local wages, tips, etc.	**19** Local income tax	**20** Locality name

Form **W-2** **Wage and Tax Statement**   **2013**   Department of the Treasury—Internal Revenue Service

Copy B—To Be Filed With Employee's FEDERAL Tax Return.
This information is being furnished to the Internal Revenue Service.

Notice to Employee

Do you have to file? Refer to the Form 1040 Instructions to determine if you are required to file a tax return. Even if you do not have to file a tax return, you may be eligible for a refund if box 2 shows an amount or if you are eligible for any credit.

Earned income credit (EIC). You may be able to take the EIC for 2013 if your adjusted gross income (AGI) is less than a certain amount. The amount of the credit is based on income and family size. Workers without children could qualify for a smaller credit. You and any qualifying children must have valid social security numbers (SSNs). You cannot take the EIC if your investment income is more than the specified amount for 2013 or if income is earned for services provided while you were an inmate at a penal institution. For 2013 income limits and more information, visit *www.irs.gov/eitc*. Also see Pub. 596, Earned Income Credit. **Any EIC that is more than your tax liability is refunded to you, but only if you file a tax return.**

Clergy and religious workers. If you are not subject to social security and Medicare taxes, see Pub. 517, Social Security and Other Information for Members of the Clergy and Religious Workers.

Corrections. If your name, SSN, or address is incorrect, correct Copies B, C, and 2 and ask your employer to correct your employment record. Be sure to ask the employer to file Form W-2c, Corrected Wage and Tax Statement, with the Social Security Administration (SSA)

to correct any name, SSN, or money amount error reported to the SSA on Form W-2. Be sure to get your copies of Form W-2c from your employer for all corrections made so you may file them with your tax return. If your name and SSN are correct but are not the same as shown on your social security card, you should ask for a new card that displays your correct name at any SSA office or by calling 1-800-772-1213. You also may visit the SSA at *www.socialsecurity.gov*.

Cost of employer-sponsored health coverage (if such cost is provided by the employer). The reporting in box 12, using code DD, of the cost of employer-sponsored health coverage is for your information only. **The amount reported with code DD is not taxable.**

Credit for excess taxes. If you had more than one employer in 2013 and more than $7,049.40 in social security and/or Tier I railroad retirement (RRTA) taxes were withheld, you may be able to claim a credit for the excess against your federal income tax. If you had more than one railroad employer and more than $3,709.20 in Tier II RRTA tax was withheld, you also may be able to claim a credit. See your Form 1040 or Form 1040A instructions and Pub. 505, Tax Withholding and Estimated Tax.

(Also see *Instructions for Employee* on the back of Copy C.)

a Employee's social security number		OMB No. 1545-0008	This information is being furnished to the Internal Revenue Service. If you are required to file a tax return, a negligence penalty or other sanction may be imposed on you if this income is taxable and you fail to report it.	
b Employer identification number (EIN)			1 Wages, tips, other compensation	2 Federal income tax withheld
c Employer's name, address, and ZIP code			3 Social security wages	4 Social security tax withheld
			5 Medicare wages and tips	6 Medicare tax withheld
			7 Social security tips	8 Allocated tips
d Control number			9	10 Dependent care benefits
e Employee's first name and initial Last name Suff.			11 Nonqualified plans	12a See instructions for box 12
			13 Statutory employee Retirement plan Third-party sick pay	12b
			14 Other	12c
				12d
f Employee's address and ZIP code				

15 State Employer's state ID number	16 State wages, tips, etc.	17 State income tax	18 Local wages, tips, etc.	19 Local income tax	20 Locality name

Form **W-2** **Wage and Tax Statement**

2013

Department of the Treasury—Internal Revenue Service

Safe, accurate, FAST! Use   *IRS e-file*

Copy C—For EMPLOYEE'S RECORDS (See *Notice to Employee* on the back of Copy B.)

Instructions for Employee (Also see *Notice to Employee,* on the back of Copy B.)

Box 1. Enter this amount on the wages line of your tax return.

Box 2. Enter this amount on the federal income tax withheld line of your tax return.

Box 5. This amount may be required to be entered on Form 8959. See Form 1040 instructions to determine if you are required to complete Form 8959.

Box 6. This amount includes the 1.45% Medicare Tax withheld on all Medicare wages and tips shown in Box 5, as well as the 0.9% Additional Medicare Tax on any of those Medicare wages and tips above $200,000.

Box 8. This amount is **not** included in boxes 1, 3, 5, or 7. For information on how to report tips on your tax return, see your Form 1040 instructions.

You must file Form 4137, Social Security and Medicare Tax on Unreported Tip Income, with your income tax return to report at least the allocated tip amount unless you can prove a smaller amount with adequate records. If you have records that show the actual amount of tips you received, report that amount even if it is more or less than the allocated tips. On Form 4137 you will figure the social security and Medicare tax owed on the allocated tips shown on your Form(s) W-2 that you must report as income and on other tips you did not report to your employer. By filing Form 4137, your social security tips will be credited to your social security record (used to figure your benefits).

Box 10. This amount is the total dependent care benefits that your employer paid to you or incurred on your behalf (including amounts from a section 125 (cafeteria) plan). Any amount over $5,000 is also included in box 1. Complete Form 2441, Child and Dependent Care Expenses, to compute any taxable and nontaxable amounts.

Box 11. This amount is (a) reported in box 1 if it is a distribution made to you from a nonqualified deferred compensation or nongovernmental section 457(b) plan or (b) included in box 3 and/or 5 if it is a prior year deferral under a nonqualified or section 457(b) plan that became taxable for social security and Medicare taxes this year because there is no longer a substantial risk of forfeiture of your right to the deferred amount. This box should not be used if you had a deferral and a distribution in the same calendar year. If this happens and you are or will be age 62 by the end of the calendar year, your employer should file Form SSA-131 with the Social Security Administration and give you a copy.

Box 12. The following list explains the codes shown in box 12. You may need this information to complete your tax return. Elective deferrals (codes D, E, F, and S) and designated Roth contributions (codes AA, BB, and EE) under all plans are generally limited to a total of $17,500 ($12,000 if you only have SIMPLE plans; $20,500 for section 403(b) plans if you qualify for the 15-year rule explained in Pub. 571). Deferrals under code G are limited to $17,500. Deferrals under code H are limited to $7,000.

However, if you were at least age 50 in 2013, your employer may have allowed an additional deferral of up to $5,500 ($2,500 for section 401(k)(11) and 408(p) SIMPLE plans). This additional deferral amount is not subject to the overall limit on elective deferrals. For code G, the limit on elective deferrals may be higher for the last 3 years before you reach retirement age. Contact your plan administrator for more information. Amounts in excess of the overall elective deferral limit must be included in income. See the "Wages, Salaries, Tips, etc." line instructions for Form 1040.

Note. If a year follows code D through H, S, Y, AA, BB, or EE, you made a make-up pension contribution for a prior year(s) when you were in military service. To figure whether you made excess deferrals, consider these amounts for the year shown, not the current year. If no year is shown, the contributions are for the current year.

A—Uncollected social security or RRTA tax on tips. Include this tax on Form 1040. See "Other Taxes" in the Form 1040 instructions.

B—Uncollected Medicare tax on tips. Include this tax on Form 1040. See "Other Taxes" in the Form 1040 instructions.

C—Taxable cost of group-term life insurance over $50,000 (included in boxes 1, 3 (up to social security wage base), and 5)

D—Elective deferrals to a section 401(k) cash or deferred arrangement. Also includes deferrals under a SIMPLE retirement account that is part of a section 401(k) arrangement.

E—Elective deferrals under a section 403(b) salary reduction agreement

(continued on back of Copy 2)

a Employee's social security number		
	OMB No. 1545-0008	

	1 Wages, tips, other compensation	**2** Federal income tax withheld
b Employer identification number (EIN)		
c Employer's name, address, and ZIP code	**3** Social security wages	**4** Social security tax withheld
	5 Medicare wages and tips	**6** Medicare tax withheld
	7 Social security tips	**8** Allocated tips
d Control number	**9**	**10** Dependent care benefits
e Employee's first name and initial Last name Suff.	**11** Nonqualified plans	**12a** C o d e
	13 Statutory employee ☐ Retirement plan ☐ Third-party sick pay ☐	**12b** C o d e
	14 Other	**12c** C o d e
		12d C o d e
f Employee's address and ZIP code		

15 State Employer's state ID number	**16** State wages, tips, etc.	**17** State income tax	**18** Local wages, tips, etc.	**19** Local income tax	**20** Locality name

Form **W-2** Wage and Tax Statement

2013

Department of the Treasury—Internal Revenue Service

Copy 2—To Be Filed With Employee's State, City, or Local Income Tax Return

Instructions for Employee *(continued from back of Copy C)*

F—Elective deferrals under a section 408(k)(6) salary reduction SEP

G—Elective deferrals and employer contributions (including nonelective deferrals) to a section 457(b) deferred compensation plan

H—Elective deferrals to a section 501(c)(18)(D) tax-exempt organization plan. See "Adjusted Gross Income" in the Form 1040 instructions for how to deduct.

J—Nontaxable sick pay (information only, not included in boxes 1, 3, or 5)

K—20% excise tax on excess golden parachute payments. See "Other Taxes" in the Form 1040 instructions.

L—Substantiated employee business expense reimbursements (nontaxable)

M—Uncollected social security or RRTA tax on taxable cost of group-term life insurance over $50,000 (former employees only). See "Other Taxes" in the Form 1040 instructions.

N—Uncollected Medicare tax on taxable cost of group-term life insurance over $50,000 (former employees only). See "Other Taxes" in the Form 1040 instructions.

P—Excludable moving expense reimbursements paid directly to employee (not included in boxes 1, 3, or 5)

Q—Nontaxable combat pay. See the instructions for Form 1040 or Form 1040A for details on reporting this amount.

R—Employer contributions to your Archer MSA. Report on Form 8853, Archer MSAs and Long-Term Care Insurance Contracts.

S—Employee salary reduction contributions under a section 408(p) SIMPLE plan (not included in box 1)

T—Adoption benefits (not included in box 1). Complete Form 8839, Qualified Adoption Expenses, to compute any taxable and nontaxable amounts.

V—Income from exercise of nonstatutory stock option(s) (included in boxes 1, 3 (up to social security wage base), and 5). See Pub. 525 and instructions for Schedule D (Form 1040) for reporting requirements.

W—Employer contributions (including amounts the employee elected to contribute using a section 125 (cafeteria) plan) to your health savings account. Report on Form 8889, Health Savings Accounts (HSAs).

Y—Deferrals under a section 409A nonqualified deferred compensation plan

Z—Income under section 409A on a nonqualified deferred compensation plan. This amount is also included in box 1. It is subject to an additional 20% tax plus interest. See "Other Taxes" in the Form 1040 instructions.

AA—Designated Roth contributions under a section 401(k) plan

BB—Designated Roth contributions under a section 403(b) plan

DD—Cost of employer-sponsored health coverage. **The amount reported with Code DD is not taxable.**

EE—Designated Roth contributions under a governmental section 457(b) plan. This amount does not apply to contributions under a tax-exempt organization section 457(b) plan.

Box 13. If the "Retirement plan" box is checked, special limits may apply to the amount of traditional IRA contributions you may deduct.

Box 14. Employers may use this box to report information such as state disability insurance taxes withheld, union dues, uniform payments, health insurance premiums deducted, nontaxable income, educational assistance payments, or a member of the clergy's parsonage allowance and utilities. Railroad employers use this box to report RRTA compensation, Tier I tax, Tier II tax, Medicare tax and Additional Medicare Tax.

Note. Keep **Copy C** of Form W-2 for at least 3 years after the due date for filing your income tax return. However, to help **protect your social security benefits,** keep Copy C until you begin receiving social security benefits, just in case there is a question about your work record and/or earnings in a particular year.

		a Employee's social security number		
Void ☐		OMB No. 1545-0008		

b Employer identification number (EIN)	**1** Wages, tips, other compensation	**2** Federal income tax withheld
c Employer's name, address, and ZIP code	**3** Social security wages	**4** Social security tax withheld
	5 Medicare wages and tips	**6** Medicare tax withheld
	7 Social security tips	**8** Allocated tips
d Control number	**9**	**10** Dependent care benefits
e Employee's first name and initial Last name Suff.	**11** Nonqualified plans	**12a** See instructions for box 12
	13 Statutory employee ☐ Retirement plan ☐ Third-party sick pay ☐	**12b**
	14 Other	**12c**
		12d
f Employee's address and ZIP code		

15 State Employer's state ID number	**16** State wages, tips, etc.	**17** State income tax	**18** Local wages, tips, etc.	**19** Local income tax	**20** Locality name

Form **W-2** Wage and Tax Statement

2013

Department of the Treasury—Internal Revenue Service

For Privacy Act and Paperwork Reduction Act Notice, see separate instructions.

Copy D — For Employer

Employers, Please Note—

Specific information needed to complete Form W-2 is available in a separate booklet titled the 2013 General Instructions for Forms W-2 and W-3. You can order those instructions and additional forms by calling 1-800-TAX-FORM (1-800-829-3676). You also can get forms and instructions at IRS.gov.

Caution. *Do not send the SSA Forms W-2 and W-3 that you have printed from IRS.gov. The SSA is unable to process these forms. Instead, you can create and submit them online. See E-filing, later.*

Due dates. By January 31, 2014, furnish Copies B, C, and 2 to each person who was your employee during 2013. By February 28, 2014, send Copy A of Form(s) W-2 and W-3 to the SSA. However, if you file electronically, the due date is March 31, 2014. See the separate instructions.

Need help? If you have questions about reporting on Form W-2, call the information reporting customer service site toll free at 1-866-455-7438 or 304-263-8700 (not toll free). For TTY/TDD equipment for persons who are deaf, hard of hearing, or have a speech disability, call 304-579-4827 (not toll free). The hours of operation are 8:30 a.m. to 4:30 p.m. Eastern time.

E-filing. If you file 250 or more Form(s) W-2, you must file electronically. E-filing can save you time and effort, even if you are not required to do so. Employers may now use the SSA's W-2 Online service to create, save, print, and submit up to 50 Form(s) W-2 at a time over the Internet. For information, visit SSA's Employer W-2 Filing Instructions & Information website at *www.socialsecurity.gov/employer.*

Future developments. Information about any future developments affecting Form W-2 and its instructions (such as legislation enacted after we release them) will be posted at *www.irs.gov/w2.*

DO NOT STAPLE

33333	**a** Control number	**For Official Use Only ▶** OMB No. 1545-0008

| **b**
Kind
of
Payer
(Check one) | 941 ☐   Military ☐   943 ☐   944 ☐
CT-1 ☐   Hshld. ☐   Medicare
emp.   govt. emp. ☐ | **Kind**
of
Employer
(Check one) | None apply ☐   501c non-govt. ☐
State/local ☐   State/local 501c ☐   Federal govt. ☐
non-501c | Third-party
sick pay
(Check if
applicable) ☐ |

c Total number of Forms W-2	**d** Establishment number	**1** Wages, tips, other compensation	**2** Federal income tax withheld
e Employer identification number (EIN)		**3** Social security wages	**4** Social security tax withheld
f Employer's name		**5** Medicare wages and tips	**6** Medicare tax withheld
		7 Social security tips	**8** Allocated tips
		9	**10** Dependent care benefits
		11 Nonqualified plans	**12a** Deferred compensation
g Employer's address and ZIP code			
h Other EIN used this year		**13** For third-party sick pay use only	**12b**
15 State Employer's state ID number		**14** Income tax withheld by payer of third-party sick pay	
16 State wages, tips, etc.	**17** State income tax	**18** Local wages, tips, etc.	**19** Local income tax
Contact person		Telephone number	For Official Use Only
Email address		Fax number	

Under penalties of perjury, I declare that I have examined this return and accompanying documents and, to the best of my knowledge and belief, they are true, correct, and complete.

Signature ▶ _____   Title ▶ _____   Date ▶ _____

Form **W-3** **Transmittal of Wage and Tax Statements**   **2013**   Department of the Treasury
Internal Revenue Service

Send this entire page with the entire Copy A page of Form(s) W-2 to the Social Security Administration (SSA). Photocopies are not acceptable. Do not send Form W-3 if you filed electronically with the SSA.
Do not send any payment (cash, checks, money orders, etc.) with Forms W-2 and W-3.

Reminder

Separate instructions. See the 2013 General Instructions for Forms W-2 and W-3 for information on completing this form.

Purpose of Form

A Form W-3 Transmittal is completed only when paper Copy A of Form(s) W-2, Wage and Tax Statement, is being filed. Do not file Form W-3 alone. Do not file Form W-3 for Form(s) W-2 that were submitted electronically to the SSA (see below). All paper forms **must** comply with IRS standards and be machine readable. Photocopies are **not** acceptable. Use a Form W-3 even if only one paper Form W-2 is being filed. Make sure both the Form W-3 and Form(s) W-2 show the correct tax year and Employer Identification Number (EIN). Make a copy of this form and keep it with Copy D (For Employer) of Form(s) W-2 for your records. The IRS recommends retaining copies of these forms for four years.

E-Filing

The SSA strongly suggests employers report Form W-3 and Forms W-2 Copy A electronically instead of on paper. The SSA provides two free e-filing options on its Business Services Online (BSO) website:

• **W-2 Online.** Use fill-in forms to create, save, print, and submit up to 50 Forms W-2 at a time to the SSA.

• **File Upload.** Upload wage files to the SSA you have created using payroll or tax software that formats the files according to the SSA's *Specifications for Filing Forms W-2 Electronically (EFW2).*

W-2 Online fill-in forms or file uploads will be on time if submitted by March 31, 2014. For more information, go to *www.socialsecurity.gov/ employer* and select "First Time Filers" or "Returning Filers" under "BEFORE YOU FILE."

When To File

Mail Form W-3 with Copy A of Form(s) W-2 by February 28, 2014.

Where To File Paper Forms

Send this entire page with the entire Copy A page of Form(s) W-2 to:

Social Security Administration
Data Operations Center
Wilkes-Barre, PA 18769-0001

Note. If you use "Certified Mail" to file, change the ZIP code to "18769-0002." If you use an IRS-approved private delivery service, add "ATTN: W-2 Process, 1150 E. Mountain Dr." to the address and change the ZIP code to "18702-7997." See Publication 15 (Circular E), Employer's Tax Guide, for a list of IRS-approved private delivery services.

For Privacy Act and Paperwork Reduction Act Notice, see the separate instructions.

Cat. No. 10159Y

DO NOT CUT, FOLD, OR STAPLE THIS FORM

44444	For Official Use Only ▶ OMB No. 1545-0008		

a Employer's name, address, and ZIP code	c Tax year/Form corrected / **W-2**	d Employee's correct SSN

e Corrected SSN and/or name (Check this box and complete boxes f and/or g if incorrect on form previously filed.) ☐

Complete boxes f and/or g only if incorrect on form **previously filed** ▶

f Employee's **previously reported** SSN

b Employer's Federal EIN

g Employee's **previously reported** name

h Employee's first name and initial | Last name | Suff.

Note: Only complete money fields that are being corrected (exception: for corrections involving MQGE, see the Instructions for Forms W-2c and W-3c, boxes 5 and 6).

i Employee's address and ZIP code

Previously reported	Correct information	Previously reported	Correct information
1 Wages, tips, other compensation	1 Wages, tips, other compensation	2 Federal income tax withheld	2 Federal income tax withheld
3 Social security wages	3 Social security wages	4 Social security tax withheld	4 Social security tax withheld
5 Medicare wages and tips	5 Medicare wages and tips	6 Medicare tax withheld	6 Medicare tax withheld
7 Social security tips	7 Social security tips	8 Allocated tips	8 Allocated tips
9 Advance EIC payment	9 Advance EIC payment	10 Dependent care benefits	10 Dependent care benefits
11 Nonqualified plans	11 Nonqualified plans	12a See instructions for box 12	12a See instructions for box 12
13 Statutory employee ☐ Retirement plan ☐ Third-party sick pay ☐	13 Statutory employee ☐ Retirement plan ☐ Third-party sick pay ☐	12b	12b
14 Other (see instructions)	14 Other (see instructions)	12c	12c
		12d	12d

State Correction Information

Previously reported	Correct information	Previously reported	Correct information
15 State	15 State	15 State	15 State
Employer's state ID number	Employer's state ID number	Employer's state ID number	Employer's state ID number
16 State wages, tips, etc.	16 State wages, tips, etc.	16 State wages, tips, etc.	16 State wages, tips, etc.
17 State income tax	17 State income tax	17 State income tax	17 State income tax

Locality Correction Information

Previously reported	Correct information	Previously reported	Correct information
18 Local wages, tips, etc.	18 Local wages, tips, etc.	18 Local wages, tips, etc.	18 Local wages, tips, etc.
19 Local income tax	19 Local income tax	19 Local income tax	19 Local income tax
20 Locality name	20 Locality name	20 Locality name	20 Locality name

For Privacy Act and Paperwork Reduction Act Notice, see separate instructions.

Copy A—For Social Security Administration

Form **W-2c** (Rev. 2-2009)

Corrected Wage and Tax Statement

Cat. No. 61437D

Department of the Treasury
 Internal Revenue Service

Notice to Employee

This is a corrected Form W-2, Wage and Tax Statement, (or Form W-2AS, W-2CM, W-2GU, W-2VI or W-2c) for the tax year shown in box c. If you have filed an income tax return for the year shown, you may have to file an amended return. Compare amounts on this form with those reported on your income tax return. If the corrected amounts change your U.S. income tax, file Form 1040X, Amended U.S. Individual Income Tax Return, with Copy B of this Form W-2c to amend the return you already filed.

If you have not filed your return for the year shown in box c, attach Copy B of the original Form W-2 you received from your employer and Copy B of this Form W-2c to your return when you file it.

For more information, contact your nearest Internal Revenue Service office. Employees in American Samoa, Commonwealth of the Northern Mariana Islands, Guam, or the U.S. Virgin Islands should contact their local taxing authority for more information.

Employers, Please Note:

Specific information needed to complete Form W-2c is given in the separate *Instructions for Forms W-2c and W-3c.* You can order those instructions and additional forms by calling 1-800-TAX-FORM (1-800-829-3676).

You can also get forms and instructions from the IRS website at *www.irs.gov.* Electronic filing of Form W-2c is preferred. For information on how to file electronically, go to the Social Security Administration website at *www.socialsecurity.gov/employer.*

DO NOT CUT, FOLD, OR STAPLE

55555	a Tax year/Form corrected ---------------- / W- ----------------	For Official Use Only ▶ OMB No. 1545-0008

b Employer's name, address, and ZIP code

c Kind of Payer (Check one)

941/941-SS	Military	943	944/944-SS
☐	☐	☐	☐

	CT-1	Hshld. emp.	Medicare govt. emp.
	☐	☐	☐

Kind of Employer (Check one)

None apply	501c non-govt.
☐	☐

State/local non-501c	State/local 501c	Federal govt.
☐	☐	☐

Third-party sick pay

(Check if applicable) ☐

d Number of Forms W-2c	**e** Employer's Federal EIN	**f** Establishment number	**g** Employer's state ID number
Complete boxes h, i, or j **only** if incorrect on last form filed.	**h** Employer's **incorrect** Federal EIN	**i Incorrect** establishment number	**j** Employer's **incorrect** state ID number

Total of amounts previously reported as shown on enclosed Forms W-2c.	Total of corrected amounts as shown on enclosed Forms W-2c.	Total of amounts previously reported as shown on enclosed Forms W-2c.	Total of corrected amounts as shown on enclosed Forms W-2c.
1 Wages, tips, other compensation	1 Wages, tips, other compensation	2 Federal income tax withheld	2 Federal income tax withheld
3 Social security wages	3 Social security wages	4 Social security tax withheld	4 Social security tax withheld
5 Medicare wages and tips	5 Medicare wages and tips	6 Medicare tax withheld	6 Medicare tax withheld
7 Social security tips	7 Social security tips	8 Allocated tips	8 Allocated tips
9 Advance EIC payments	9 Advance EIC payments	10 Dependent care benefits	10 Dependent care benefits
11 Nonqualified plans	11 Nonqualified plans	12a Deferred compensation	12a Deferred compensation
14 Inc. tax w/h by third-party sick pay payer	14 Inc. tax w/h by third-party sick pay payer	12b HIRE exempt wages and tips	12b HIRE exempt wages and tips
16 State wages, tips, etc.	16 State wages, tips, etc.	17 State income tax	17 State income tax
18 Local wages, tips, etc.	18 Local wages, tips, etc.	19 Local income tax	19 Local income tax

Explain decreases here:

Has an adjustment been made on an employment tax return filed with the Internal Revenue Service?   ☐ Yes   ☐ No

If "Yes," give date the return was filed ▶

Under penalties of perjury, I declare that I have examined this return, including accompanying documents, and, to the best of my knowledge and belief, it is true, correct, and complete.

Signature ▶   Title ▶   Date ▶

Contact person	Telephone number	For Official Use Only
Email address	Fax number	

Form **W-3c** (Rev. 12-2011)   **Transmittal of Corrected Wage and Tax Statements**   Department of the Treasury Internal Revenue Service

Purpose of Form

Use this form to transmit Copy A of **Form(s) W-2c,** Corrected Wage and Tax Statement (Rev. 2-2009). Make a copy of Form W-3c and keep it with Copy D (For Employer) of Forms W-2c for your records. File Form W-3c even if only one Form W-2c is being filed or if those Forms W-2c are being filed only to correct an employee's name and social security number (SSN) or the employer identification number (EIN). See the 2012 General Instructions for Forms W-2 and W-3 for information on completing this form.

When To File

File this form and Copy A of Form(s) W-2c with the Social Security Administration as soon as possible after you discover an error on Forms W-2, W-2AS, W-2GU, W-2CM, W-2VI, or W-2c. Provide Copies B, C, and 2 of Form W-2c to your employees as soon as possible.

For Paperwork Reduction Act Notice, see separate instructions.

Where To File

If you use the U.S. Postal Service, send Forms W-2c and W-3c to the following address:

**Social Security Administration
Data Operations Center
P.O. Box 3333
Wilkes-Barre, PA 18767-3333**

If you use a carrier other than the U.S. Postal Service, send Forms W-2c and W-3c to the following address:

**Social Security Administration
Data Operations Center
Attn: W-2c Process
1150 E. Mountain Drive
Wilkes-Barre, PA 18702-7997**

Cat. No. 10164R

20**12**

General Instructions for Forms W-2 and W-3

(Including Forms W-2AS, W-2GU, W-2VI, W-3SS, W-2c, and W-3c)

Department of the Treasury
Internal Revenue Service

Section references are to the Internal Revenue Code unless otherwise noted.

What's New

Future developments. The IRS has created a page on IRS.gov for information about Forms W-2 and W-3 and their instructions, at *www.irs.gov/w2*. Information about any future developments affecting Forms W-2 and W-3 and their instructions (such as legislation enacted after we release them) will be posted on that page.

Employee social security tax withholding. The 4.2% rate of social security tax withholding (for employees only) is extended for wage payments made in 2012. See *Box 4—Social security tax withheld* on page 14.

New title for instructions. The title of the Instructions for Forms W-2 and W-3 has been changed to the General Instructions for Forms W-2 and W-3. These instructions now include instructions for U.S. possessions and corrected wage and tax statements. The separate Instructions for Forms W-2AS, W-2GU, W-2VI, and W-3SS, and the Instructions for Forms W-2c and W-3c will not be updated. In these instructions, references to Forms W-2 and W-3 include Forms W-2AS, W-2GU, W-2VI, and W-3SS, respectively, unless otherwise noted.

Form W-3, Kind of Employer. The specific instructions for the checkboxes in box b, Kind of Employer, of Form W-3 (box c for Form W-3c) include examples for various types of section 501(c) organizations. For more information, see *Box b—Kind of Employer* on page 18.

Form W-3c, box b. Box b of Form W-3c has been expanded to include an additional line for name, address, and ZIP code.

Form W-3c, Kind of Employer. Box c of Form W-3c has been expanded to include a new section, Kind of Employer, which contains five new checkboxes. All filers are required to check one of these new checkboxes. For more information, see *Box c—Kind of Employer* on page 23.

Form 944-SS discontinued. Form 944-SS will no longer be issued by the IRS after 2011. Reference to Form 944-SS has been removed from these instructions, except in the *General Instructions for Forms W-2c and W-3c* section. On Form W-3SS, in box b, Kind of Payer, the 944-SS checkbox has been replaced with a 944 checkbox. For more information, see the 2012 Instructions for Form 944.

Foreign agricultural workers. You must report on Form W-2 compensation of $600 or more that you pay to H-2A visa agricultural workers. See *Foreign agricultural workers* on page 8 for details.

Reporting the cost of group health insurance coverage. You must report the cost of employer-sponsored health coverage in box 12 using code DD. However, transitional relief applies to certain employers and certain types of plans. For more information, see *Code DD—Cost of employer-sponsored health coverage* on page 17.

Reminders

Get it done faster...
E-file your Forms W-2 with the SSA.
See page 2.

Automatic extension for e-filers. Receive an automatic filing extension by e-filing your Forms W-2 with the Social Security Administration (SSA). The due date for e-filing 2012 Form W-2 Copy A with the SSA is extended to April 1, 2013. See *E-filing* on page 2.

Business Services Online (BSO). The SSA has enhanced its secure BSO website to make it easier to register and navigate. Use BSO's online fill-in forms to create, save, and submit Forms W-2 and W-2c to the SSA electronically. BSO lets you print copies of these forms to file with state or local governments, distribute to your employees, and keep for your records. BSO generates Form W-3 automatically based on your Forms W-2. You also can use BSO to upload wage files to the SSA, check on the status of previously submitted wage reports, and take advantage of other convenient services for employers and businesses. Visit the SSA's Employer W-2 Filing Instructions & Information website at *www.socialsecurity.gov/employer* for more information about using BSO to save time for your organization. Here you also will find forms and publications used for wage

Aug 21, 2012   Cat. No. 25979S

reporting, information about verifying employee social security numbers online, how to reach an SSA employer services representative for your region, and more.

 Preview BSO by viewing a brief online tutorial. Go to www.socialsecurity.gov/bso/bsowelcome.html and click on "Tutorial."

Correcting wage reports. You can use BSO to create, save, print, and submit Forms W-2c, Corrected Wage and Tax Statement, online for the current year as well as for prior years. After logging in to BSO, navigate to the Electronic Wage Reporting home page and click on the "Forms W-2c/W-3c Online" tab. See *E-filing* below and *E-filing Forms W-2c and W-3c* on page 20.

Distributions from governmental section 457(b) plans of state and local agencies. Generally, report distributions from section 457(b) plans of state and local agencies on Form 1099-R, Distributions From Pensions, Annuities, Retirement or Profit-Sharing Plans, IRAs, Insurance Contracts, etc. See Notice 2003-20 for details. You can find Notice 2003-20 on page 894 of Internal Revenue Bulletin 2003-19 at *www.irs.gov/pub/irs-irbs/ irb03-19.pdf.*

Earned income credit (EIC) notice (not applicable to Forms W-2AS, W-2GU, and W-2VI). You must notify employees who have no income tax withheld that they may be able to claim an income tax refund because of the EIC. You can do this by using the official IRS Form W-2 with the EIC notice on the back of Copy B or a substitute Form W-2 with the same statement. You must give your employee Notice 797, Possible Federal Tax Refund Due to the Earned Income Credit (EIC), or your own statement that contains the same wording if (a) you use a substitute Form W-2 that does not contain the EIC notice, (b) you are not required to furnish Form W-2, or (c) you do not furnish a timely Form W-2 to your employee. For more information, see section 10 in Pub. 15 (Circular E), Employer's Tax Guide.

Electronic statements for employees. Furnishing Copies B, C, and 2 of Forms W-2 to your employees electronically may save you time and effort. See Pub. 15-A, Employer's Supplemental Tax Guide, for additional information.

E-filing. The SSA encourages all employers to *e-file.* E-filing can save you time and effort and helps ensure accuracy. You must *e-file* if you are required to file 250 or more Forms W-2 or W-2c. If you are required to *e-file* but fail to do so, you may incur a penalty.

Waiver from e-filing. You can request a waiver from this requirement by filing Form 8508, Request for Waiver From Filing Information Returns Electronically. Submit Form 8508 to the IRS at least 45 days before the due date of Form W-2, or 45 days before you file your first Form W-2c. See Form 8508 for information about filing this form.

The SSA's BSO website makes e-filing easy by providing two ways to submit your Forms W-2 or W-2c Copy A and Forms W-3 or W-3c information.
• If you need to file 50 or fewer Forms W-2 or 5 or fewer Forms W-2c at a time, you can use BSO to create them online. BSO guides you through the process of creating

Forms W-2 or W-2c, saving and printing them, and submitting them to the SSA when you are ready. You do not have to wait until you have submitted Forms W-2 or W-2c to the SSA before printing copies for your employees. BSO generates Form W-3 or W-3c automatically based on your Forms W-2 or W-2c.
• If you need to file more than 50 Forms W-2 or more than 5 Forms W-2c, BSO's "file upload" feature might be the best e-filing method for your business or organization. To obtain file format specifications, visit the SSA's Employer W-2 Filing Instructions & Information website at *www.socialsecurity.gov/employer* and click on "E-Filing Format." This information is also available by calling the SSA's Employer Reporting Branch at 1-800-772-6270 (toll free).

 If you e-file, do not file the same returns using paper forms.

For more information about e-filing Forms W-2 or W-2c and a link to the BSO website, visit the SSA's Employer W-2 Filing Instructions & Information website at *www.socialsecurity.gov/employer.*

In a few situations, reporting instructions vary depending on the filing method you choose. For example, you can include every type of box 12 amount in one employee wage record if you upload an electronic file. If you file on paper or create Forms W-2 online, you can include only four box 12 amounts per Form W-2. See the *TIP* for Copy A on page 15.

Form 944. Use the "944" checkbox in box b of Form W-3 or Form W-3SS if you filed Form 944, Employer's ANNUAL Federal Tax Return. Also use the "944" checkbox if you filed Formulario 944(SP), the Spanish-language version of Form 944.

Forms W-2 for U.S. possessions. In these instructions, reference to Forms W-2 and W-3 includes Forms W-2AS, W-2GU, W-2VI, and W-3SS, unless otherwise noted. These instructions are not applicable to wage and tax statements for Puerto Rico or the Commonwealth of the Northern Mariana Islands. Form W-2AS is used to report American Samoa wages paid by American Samoa employers, Form W-2CM is used to report the Commonwealth of the Northern Mariana Islands (CNMI) wages paid by CNMI employers, Form W-2GU is used to report Guam wages paid by Guam employers, and Form W-2VI is used to report U.S. Virgin Islands (USVI) wages paid by USVI employers. Do not use these forms to report wages subject to U.S. income tax withholding. Instead, use Form W-2 to show U.S. income tax withheld.

Military differential pay. Employers paying their employees while they are on active duty in the United States uniformed services should treat these payments as wages subject to income tax withholding. See *Military differential pay* on page 9.

Military Spouses Residency Relief Act (MSRRA). You may be required to report wages and taxes on a form different from the form you generally use if an employee claims residence or domicile under MSRRA in a different jurisdiction in one of the 50 states, the District of Columbia, American Samoa, the Commonwealth of the

Northern Mariana Islands, Puerto Rico, or the U.S. Virgin Islands.

Under MSRRA, the spouse of an active duty servicemember (civilian spouse) may keep his or her prior residence or domicile for tax purposes (tax residence) when accompanying the servicemember spouse, who is relocating under military orders, to a new military duty station in one of the 50 states, the District of Columbia, or a U.S. possession. Before relocating, both spouses must have had the same tax residence.

For example, if a civilian spouse is working in Guam but properly claims tax residence in one of the 50 states under MSRRA, his or her income from services would not be taxable income for Guam tax purposes. Federal income taxes should be withheld and remitted to the IRS. State and local income taxes may need to be withheld and remitted to state and local tax authorities. You should consult with state, local, or U.S. possession tax authorities regarding your withholding obligations under MSRRA.

Nonqualified deferred compensation plans. You are not required to complete box 12 with code Y (deferrals under a section 409A nonqualified deferred compensation plan). Section 409A provides that all amounts deferred under a nonqualified deferred compensation (NQDC) plan for all tax years are includible in gross income unless certain requirements are satisfied. See *Nonqualified deferred compensation plans* on page 9.

Substitute forms. You may use an acceptable substitute form instead of an official IRS form.

Form W-2. If you are not using the official IRS form to furnish Form W-2 to employees or to file with the SSA, you may use an acceptable substitute form that complies with the rules in Pub. 1141, General Rules and Specifications for Substitute Forms W-2 and W-3. Pub. 1141 is a revenue procedure that explains the requirements for format and content of substitute Forms W-2 and W-3. Your substitute forms must comply with the requirements in Pub. 1141.

Form W-2c. If you are not using the official IRS form to furnish Form W-2c to employees or to file with the SSA, you may use an acceptable substitute form that complies with the rules in Pub. 1223, General Rules and Specifications for Substitute Forms W-2c and W-3c. Pub. 1223 is a revenue procedure that explains the requirements for format and content of substitute Forms W-2c and W-3c. Your substitute forms must comply with the requirements in Pub. 1223.

Need Help?

Help with e-filing. If you have questions about how to register or use BSO, call 1-800-772-6270 (toll free) to speak with an employer reporting specialist at the SSA. The hours of operation are Monday through Friday from 7:00 a.m. to 7:00 p.m. Eastern time. If you experience problems using any of the services within BSO, call 1-888-772-2970 (toll free). To speak with the SSA's Employer Services Liaison Officer (ESLO) for the U.S. Virgin Islands, call 1-212-264-1117 (not a toll-free number). For Guam or American Samoa, call 1-510-970-8247 (not a toll-free number). For all other employers, contact the ESLO that services your region.

For a complete telephone listing, visit the SSA's Employer W-2 Filing Instructions & Information website at *www.socialsecurity.gov/employer*.

Information reporting customer service site. The IRS operates a centralized customer service site to answer questions about reporting on Forms W-2, W-3, 1099, and other information returns. If you have questions about reporting on these forms, call 1-866-455-7438 (toll free). The hours of operation are Monday through Friday from 8:30 a.m. to 4:30 p.m. Eastern time.

Hearing impaired TTY/TDD equipment. Telephone help is available using TTY/TDD equipment. If you have questions about reporting on information returns (Forms 1096, 1097, 1098, 1099, 3921, 3922, 5498, W-2, W-2G, and W-3), call 1-304-579-4827. For any other tax information, call 1-800-829-4059.

Employment tax information. Detailed employment tax information is given in:
* Pub. 15 (Circular E), Employer's Tax Guide,
* Pub. 15-A, Employer's Supplemental Tax Guide,
* Pub. 15-B, Employer's Tax Guide to Fringe Benefits, and
* Pub. 51 (Circular A), Agricultural Employer's Tax Guide.
* Pub. 80 (Circular SS), Federal Tax Guide for Employers in the U.S. Virgin Islands, Guam, American Samoa, and the Commonwealth of the Northern Marianas.

You also can call the IRS with your employment tax questions at 1-800-829-4933 or visit IRS.gov and type "Employment Taxes" in the search box.

How To Get Forms and Publications

Internet. You can access IRS.gov 24 hours a day, 7 days a week to:
* Download, view, and order tax forms, instructions, and publications.
* Access commercial tax preparation and *e-file* services.
* Research your tax questions online.
* See answers to frequently asked tax questions.
* Search publications online by topic or keyword.
* View Internal Revenue Bulletins published in the last few years.
* Sign up to receive local and national tax news by email.

 Do not download Copy A of Forms W-2, W-3, W-2c, or W-3c from IRS.gov and then file them with the SSA. The SSA accepts only e-filed reports and the official red-ink versions (or approved substitute versions) of these forms. For information about e-filing, see E-filing *on page 2.*

Free tax services. To find out what services are available, get Pub. 910, IRS Guide to Free Tax Services. It contains lists of free tax information sources, including publications, services, and free tax education and assistance programs. It also has an index of over 100 TeleTax topics (recorded tax information) you can listen to on your telephone. Accessible versions of IRS published products are available on request in a variety of alternative formats.

General Instructions for Forms W-2 and W-3 (2012)   -3-

DVD of tax products. You can order Publication 1796, IRS Tax Products DVD, and obtain:

- Current-year forms, instructions, and publications.
- Prior-year forms, instructions, and publications.
- Tax Map: an electronic research tool and finding aid.
- Tax law frequently asked questions.
- Tax Topics from the IRS telephone response system.
- Internal Revenue Code—Title 26 of the U.S. Code.
- Fill-in, print, and save features for most tax forms.
- Internal Revenue Bulletins.
- Toll free and email technical support.
- Two releases during the year.

-The first release will ship the beginning of January 2012.

-The final release will ship the beginning of March 2012.

Purchase the DVD from National Technical Information Service (NTIS) at *www.irs.gov/cdorders* for $30 (no handling fee) or call 1-877-233-6767 toll free to purchase the DVD for $30 (plus a $6 handling fee).

Mail. You can send your order for forms, instructions, and publications to the following address. You should receive a response within 10 days after your request is received.

Internal Revenue Service
1201 N. Mitsubishi Parkway
Bloomington, IL 61705-6613

Phone. Many services are available by phone.
- *Ordering forms, instructions, and publications.* Call 1-800-829-3676 to order current-year forms, instructions, and publications, and prior-year forms and instructions. You should receive your order within 10 days.
- *TTY/TDD equipment.* If you have access to TTY/TDD equipment, call 1-800-829-4059 to order forms and publications.

Common Errors on Forms W-2

Forms W-2 provide information to your employees, the SSA, the IRS, and state and local governments. Avoid making the following errors, which cause processing delays.

Do not:
- Omit the decimal point and cents from entries.
- Make entries using ink that is too light. Use only black ink.
- Make entries that are too small or too large. Use 12-point Courier font, if possible.
- Add dollar signs to the money-amount boxes. They have been removed from Copy A and are not required.
- Inappropriately check the "Retirement plan" checkbox in box 13. See *Retirement plan* on page 17.
- Misformat the employee's name in box e. Enter the employee's first name and middle initial in the first box, his or her surname in the second box, and his or her suffix (such as "Jr.") in the third box (optional).

General Instructions for Forms W-2 and W-3

Who must file Form W-2. Every employer engaged in a trade or business who pays remuneration, including noncash payments of $600 or more for the year (all amounts if any income, social security, or Medicare tax was withheld) for services performed by an employee must file a Form W-2 for each employee (even if the employee is related to the employer) from whom:
- Income, social security, or Medicare tax was withheld.
- Income tax would have been withheld if the employee had claimed no more than one withholding allowance or had not claimed exemption from withholding on Form W-4, Employee's Withholding Allowance Certificate.

If you are required to file 250 or more Forms W-2 or want to take advantage of the benefits of e-filing, see *E-filing* on page 2.

Who must file Form W-3. Anyone required to file Form W-2 must file Form W-3 to transmit Copy A of Forms W-2. Make a copy of Form W-3; keep it and Copy D (For Employer) of Forms W-2 with your records for 4 years. Be sure to use Form W-3 for the correct year. If you are filing Forms W-2 electronically, see *E-filing* on page 2.

Household employers. Even employers with only one household employee must file Form W-3 to transmit Copy A of Form W-2. On Form W-3 check the "Hshld. emp." checkbox in box b. For more information, see Schedule H (Form 1040), Household Employment Taxes, and its separate instructions. You must have an employer identification number (EIN). See *Box b—Employer identification number (EIN)* on page 12.

Who may sign Form W-3. A transmitter or sender (including a service bureau, reporting agent, paying agent, or disbursing agent) may sign Form W-3 (or use its PIN to e-file) for the employer or payer only if the sender satisfies both of the following.
- It is authorized to sign by an agency agreement (whether oral, written, or implied) that is valid under state law; and
- It writes "For (name of payer)" next to the signature (paper Form W-3 only).

 Use of a reporting agent or other third-party payroll service provider does not relieve an employer of the responsibility to ensure that Forms W-2 are furnished to employees and that Forms W-2 and W-3 are filed with the SSA, correctly and on time.

Be sure that the payer's name and EIN on Forms W-2 and W-3 are the same as those used on the Form 941, Employer's QUARTERLY Federal Tax Return; Form 943, Employer's Annual Federal Tax Return for Agricultural Employees; Form 944; Form CT-1, Employer's Annual Railroad Retirement Tax Return; or Schedule H (Form 1040) filed by or for the payer.

When to file. If you file using paper forms, you must file Copy A of Form W-2 with Form W-3 by February 28, 2013. However, if you e-file, the due date is automatically extended to April 1, 2013. You may owe a penalty for each Form W-2 that you file late. See *Penalties* on page 10. If you terminate your business, see *Terminating a business* on page 10.

Extension to file. You may request an automatic extension of time to file Form W-2 with the SSA by sending Form 8809, Application for Extension of Time To File Information Returns, to the address shown on Form 8809. You must request the extension before the due date of Forms W-2. You will have an additional 30 days to file. See Form 8809 for details.

 Even if you request an extension of time to file Form W-2, you still must furnish Form W-2 to your employees by January 31, 2013. But see Extension of time to furnish Forms W-2 to employees *on page 5.*

Where to file paper Forms W-2 and W-3. File Copy A of Form W-2 with Form W-3 at the following address.

**Social Security Administration
Data Operations Center
Wilkes-Barre, PA 18769-0001**

 If you use "Certified Mail" to file, change the ZIP code to "18769-0002." If you use an IRS-approved private delivery service, add "Attn: W-2 Process, 1150 E. Mountain Dr." to the address and change the ZIP code to "18702-7997." See Pub. 15 (Circular E) for a list of IRS-approved private delivery services.

 Do not send cash, checks, money orders, or other forms of payment with the Forms W-2 and W-3 that you submit to the SSA. Employment tax forms (for example, Form 941 or Form 943), remittances, and Forms 1099 must be sent to the IRS.

Copy 1. Send Copy 1 of Form W-2, if required, to your state, city, or local tax department. For more information concerning Copy 1 (including how to complete boxes 15 through 20), contact your state, city, or local tax department.

American Samoa. File Copy 1 of Form W-3SS and Forms W-2AS at the following address.

**American Samoa Tax Office
Executive Office Building
First Floor
Pago Pago, AS 96799**

For additional information about Form W-2AS, see *www.americansamoa.gov*.

Guam. File Copy 1 of Form W-3SS and Forms W-2GU at the following address.

**Guam Department of Revenue and Taxation
P.O. Box 23607
GMF, GU 96921**

For additional information about Form W-2GU, see *www.guamtax.com*.

United States Virgin Islands. File Copy 1 of Form W-3SS and Forms W-2VI at the following address.

**Virgin Islands Bureau of Internal Revenue
6115 Estate Smith Bay
Suite 225
St. Thomas, VI 00802**

For additional information about Form W-2VI, see *www.viirb.com*.

Commonwealth of the Northern Mariana Islands. File Form OS-3710 and Copy 1 of Forms W-2CM at the following address.

**Division of Revenue and Taxation
Commonwealth of the Northern Mariana Islands
P.O. Box 5234 CHRB
Saipan, MP 96950**

Forms OS-3710 and W-2CM are not IRS forms. For additional information about Form W-2CM, see *www.cnmidof.net*.

Shipping and mailing. If you file more than one type of employment tax form, group Forms W-2 of the same type with a separate Form W-3 for each type, and send them in separate groups. See the specific instructions for box b of Form W-3 on page 18.

Prepare and file Forms W-2 either alphabetically by employees' last names or numerically by employees' social security numbers. Do not staple or tape Form W-3 to the related Forms W-2 or Forms W-2 to each other. These forms are machine read. Staple holes or tears interfere with machine reading. Also, do not fold Forms W-2 and W-3. Send the forms to the SSA in a flat mailing.

Furnishing Copies B, C, and 2 to employees. Generally, you must furnish Copies B, C, and 2 of Form W-2 to your employees by January 31, 2013. You will meet the "furnish" requirement if the form is properly addressed and mailed on or before the due date.

If employment ends before December 31, 2012, you may furnish copies to the employee at any time after employment ends, but no later than January 31, 2013. If an employee asks for Form W-2, give him or her the completed copies within 30 days of the request or within 30 days of the final wage payment, whichever is later. However, if you terminate your business, see *Terminating a business* on page 10.

You may furnish Forms W-2 to employees on IRS official forms or on acceptable substitute forms. See *Substitute forms* on page 3. Be sure the Forms W-2 you provide to employees are clear and legible and comply with the requirements in Pub. 1141.

Extension of time to furnish Forms W-2 to employees. You may request an extension of time to furnish Forms W-2 to employees by sending a letter to:

**Internal Revenue Service
Information Returns Branch, Mail Stop 4360
Attn: Extension of Time Coordinator
240 Murall Drive
Kearneysville, WV 25430**

Mail your letter on or before the due date for furnishing Forms W-2 to employees. It must include:
• Your name and address,

- Your EIN,
- A statement that you are requesting an extension to furnish "Forms W-2" to employees,
- The reason for delay, and
- Your signature or that of your authorized agent.

 Requests for an extension of time to furnish recipient statements for more than 10 payers must be submitted electronically. See Publication 1220, Part D, Sec. 4.

Undeliverable Forms W-2. Keep for 4 years any employee copies of Forms W-2 that you tried to but could not deliver. However, if the undelivered Form W-2 can be produced electronically through April 15th of the fourth year after the year at issue, you do not need to keep undeliverable employee copies. Do not send undeliverable Forms W-2 to the SSA.

Taxpayer identification numbers (TINs). Employers use an employer identification number (EIN) (00-0000000). Employees use a social security number (SSN) (000-00-0000). When you list a number, separate the nine digits properly to show the kind of number. Do not accept an IRS individual taxpayer identification number (ITIN) in place of an SSN for employee identification or for Form W-2 reporting. An ITIN is only available to resident and nonresident aliens who are not eligible for U.S. employment and need identification for other tax purposes. You can identify an ITIN because it is a 9-digit number beginning with the number "9" with either a "7" or "8" as the fourth digit and is formatted like an SSN (for example, 9NN-7N-NNNN). Do not auto populate an ITIN into *box a— Employee's social security number* on Form W-2. See section 4 of Pub. 15 (Circular E).

 An individual with an ITIN who later becomes eligible to work in the United States must obtain an SSN from the Social Security Administration.

The IRS uses SSNs to check the payments that you report against the amounts shown on employees' tax returns. The SSA uses SSNs to record employees' earnings for future social security and Medicare benefits. When you prepare Form W-2, be sure to show the correct SSN for each employee. For information about verifying SSNs, see section 4 of Pub. 15 (Circular E) or visit the SSA's Employer W-2 Filing Instructions & Information website at *www.socialsecurity.gov/employer*.

 Form W-2 e-filed with the SSA must contain the same TINs as shown on all copies of Form W-2 furnished to employees.

Special Reporting Situations for Form W-2

Adoption benefits. Amounts paid or expenses incurred by an employer for qualified adoption expenses under an adoption assistance program are not subject to federal income tax withholding and are not reportable in box 1. However, these amounts (including adoption benefits paid from a section 125 (cafeteria) plan, but not including adoption benefits forfeited from a cafeteria plan) are subject to social security, Medicare, and railroad

retirement taxes and must be reported in boxes 3 and 5. (Use box 14 if railroad retirement taxes apply.) Also, the total amount must be reported in box 12 with code T.

For more information on adoption benefits, see Notice 97-9, 1997-1 C.B. 365, which is on page 35 of Internal Revenue Bulletin 1997-2 at *www.irs.gov/pub/irs-irbs/ irb97-02.pdf*. Advise your employees to see the Instructions for Form 8839, Qualified Adoption Expenses.

Agent reporting. Generally, an agent who has an approved Form 2678, Employer/Payer Appointment of Agent, should enter the agent's name as the employer in box c of Form W-2 and file only one Form W-2 for each employee. However, if the agent (a) is acting as an agent for two or more employers or is an employer and is acting as an agent for another employer, and (b) pays social security wages to an individual on behalf of more than one employer, and (c) the total of the individual's social security wages from these employers is greater than the social security wage base, the agent must file separate Forms W-2 for the affected employee reflecting the wages paid by each employer.

On the Form W-2 the agent should enter the following in box c of Form W-2.

(Name of agent)
Agent for (name of employer)
Address of agent

Each Form W-2 should reflect the EIN of the agent in box b. An agent files one Form W-3 for all of the Forms W-2 and enters its own information in boxes e, f, and g of Form W-3 as it appears on the agent's related employment tax returns (for example, Form 941). Enter the client-employer's EIN in box h of Form W-3 if the Forms W-2 relate to only one employer (other than the agent); if not, leave box h blank. See Rev. Proc. 70-6, 1970-1 C.B. 420; Notice 2003-70, 2003-43 I.R.B. 916, available at *www.irs.gov/irb/2003-43_IRB/ar09.html*; and the Instructions for Form 2678 for procedures to be followed in applying to be an agent. For state and local health and welfare agencies wishing to act as agents under section 3504, see Rev. Proc. 80-4, 1980-1 C.B. 581.

 Generally, an agent is not responsible for refunding excess social security or railroad retirement (RRTA) tax withheld from employees. If an employee worked for more than one employer during 2012 and had more than $4,624.20 in social security and Tier I RRTA tax withheld, he or she should claim the excess on the appropriate line of Form 1040, Form 1040A, or Form 1040NR. If an employee had more than $3,194.10 in Tier II RRTA tax withheld from more than one employer, the employee should claim a refund on Form 843, Claim for Refund and Request for Abatement.

Archer MSA. An employer's contribution to an employee's Archer MSA is not subject to federal income tax withholding or social security, Medicare, or railroad retirement taxes if it is reasonable to believe at the time of the payment that the contribution will be excludable from the employee's income. However, if it is not reasonable to believe at the time of payment that the contribution will be excludable from the employee's income, employer contributions are subject to income tax withholding and social security and Medicare taxes (or railroad retirement taxes, if applicable) and must be reported in boxes 1, 3, and 5. (Use box 14 if railroad retirement taxes apply.)

You must report all employer contributions to an Archer MSA in box 12 of Form W-2 with code R. Employer contributions to an Archer MSA that are not excludable from the income of the employee also must be reported in box 1.

An employee's contributions to an Archer MSA are includible in income as wages and are subject to federal income tax withholding and social security and Medicare taxes (or railroad retirement taxes, if applicable). Employee contributions are deductible, within limits, on the employee's Form 1040.

For more information, see Pub. 969, Health Savings Accounts and Other Tax-Favored Health Plans, and Notice 96-53, which is found on page 5 of Internal Revenue Bulletin 1996-51 at *www.irs.gov/pub/irs-irbs/ irb96-51.pdf*.

Clergy and religious workers. For certain members of the clergy and religious workers who are not subject to social security and Medicare taxes as employees, boxes 3 and 5 of Form W-2 should be left blank. You may include a minister's parsonage and/or utilities allowance in box 14. For information on the rules that apply to ministers and certain other religious workers, see Pub. 517, Social Security and Other Information for Members of the Clergy and Religious Workers, and *Section 4–Religious Exemptions and Special Rules for Ministers* in Pub. 15-A.

Deceased employee's wages. If an employee dies during the year, you must report the accrued wages, vacation pay, and other compensation paid after the date of death. Also report wages that were available to the employee while he or she was alive, regardless of whether they actually were in the possession of the employee, as well as any other regular wage payment, even if you may have to reissue the payment in the name of the estate or beneficiary.

If you made the payment after the employee's death but in the same year the employee died, you must withhold social security and Medicare taxes on the payment and report the payment on the employee's Form W-2 only as social security and Medicare wages to ensure proper social security and Medicare credit is received. On the employee's Form W-2, show the payment as social security wages (box 3) and Medicare wages and tips (box 5) and the social security and Medicare taxes withheld in boxes 4 and 6. Do not show the payment in box 1.

If you made the payment after the year of death, do not report it on Form W-2, and do not withhold social security and Medicare taxes.

Whether the payment is made in the year of death or after the year of death, you also must report it in box 3 of Form 1099-MISC, Miscellaneous Income, for the payment to the estate or beneficiary. Use the name and taxpayer identification number (TIN) of the payment recipient on Form 1099-MISC. However, if the payment is a reissuance of wages that were constructively received by the deceased individual while he or she was still alive, do not report it on Form 1099-MISC.

Example. Before Employee A's death on June 15, 2012, A was employed by Employer X and received $10,000 in wages on which federal income tax of $1,500 was withheld. When A died, X owed A $2,000 in wages and $1,000 in accrued vacation pay. The total of $3,000 (less the social security and Medicare taxes withheld) was paid to A's estate on July 20, 2012. Because X made the payment during the year of death, X must withhold social security and Medicare taxes on the $3,000 payment and must complete Form W-2 as follows.

- Box a – Employee A's SSN
- Box e – Employee A's name
- Box f – Employee A's address
- Box 1 – 10000.00 (does not include the $3,000 accrued wages and vacation pay)
- Box 2 – 1500.00
- Box 3 – 13000.00 (includes the $3,000 accrued wages and vacation pay)
- Box 4 – 546.00 (4.2% of the amount in box 3)
- Box 5 – 13000.00 (includes the $3,000 accrued wages and vacation pay)
- Box 6 – 188.50 (1.45% of the amount in box 5)

 Employer X also must complete Form 1099-MISC as follows.

- *Boxes for recipient's name, address, and TIN—the estate's name, address, and TIN.*
- *Box 3: 3000.00 (Even though amounts were withheld for social security and Medicare taxes, the gross amount is reported here.)*

If Employer X made the payment after the year of death, the $3,000 would not be subject to social security and Medicare taxes and would not be shown on Form W-2. However, the employer would still file Form 1099-MISC.

Designated Roth contributions. Under section 402A, a participant in a section 401(k) plan, under a 403(b) salary reduction agreement, or in a governmental 457(b) plan that includes a qualified Roth contribution program, may elect to make designated Roth contributions to the plan or program in lieu of elective deferrals. Designated Roth contributions are subject to federal income tax withholding and social security and Medicare taxes (and railroad retirement taxes, if applicable) and must be reported in boxes 1, 3, and 5. (Use box 14 if railroad retirement taxes apply.)

Section 402A requires separate reporting of the yearly designated Roth contributions. Designated Roth contributions to 401(k) plans will be reported using code AA in box 12; designated Roth contributions under 403(b) salary reduction agreements will be reported using code BB in box 12; and designated Roth contributions under a governmental section 457(b) plan will be reported using Code EE in box 12. For reporting instructions, see *Code AA, Code BB,* and *Code EE* on page 17.

Educational assistance programs. Employer-provided educational assistance that qualifies as a working condition benefit is excludable from an employee's wages. For employer-provided educational assistance that does not qualify as a working condition benefit, a $5,250 exclusion may apply if the assistance is provided under an educational assistance program under section 127. See Pub. 970, *Tax Benefits for Education*, and section 2 of Pub. 15-B for more information. Also see *Box 1—Wages, tips, other compensation* on page 12.

Election workers. Report on Form W-2 payments of $600 or more to election workers for services performed in state, county, and municipal elections. File Form W-2 for payments of less than $600 paid to election workers if social security and Medicare taxes were withheld under a section 218 (Social Security Act) agreement. Do not report election worker payments on Form 1099-MISC.

If the election worker is employed in another capacity with the same government entity, see Rev. Rul. 2000-6, which is on page 512 of Internal Revenue Bulletin 2000-6 at *www.irs.gov/pub/irs-irbs/irb00-06.pdf.*

Employee business expense reimbursements. Reimbursements to employees for business expenses must be reported as follows.
* Generally, payments made under an accountable plan are excluded from the employee's gross income and are not reported on Form W-2. However, if you pay a per diem or mileage allowance and the amount paid for substantiated miles or days traveled exceeds the amount treated as substantiated under IRS rules, you must report as wages on Form W-2 the amount in excess of the amount treated as substantiated. The excess amount is subject to income tax withholding and social security and Medicare taxes. Report the amount treated as substantiated (that is, the nontaxable portion) in box 12 using code L. See *Code L— Substantiated employee business expense reimbursements* on page 16.
* Payments made under a nonaccountable plan are reported as wages on Form W-2 and are subject to federal income tax withholding and social security and Medicare taxes.

For more information on accountable plans, nonaccountable plans, amounts treated as substantiated under a per diem or mileage allowance, the standard mileage rate, the per diem substantiation method, and the high-low substantiation method, see Pub. 463, *Travel, Entertainment, Gift, and Car Expenses*; Pub. 1542, *Per Diem Rates*; and section 5 of Pub. 15 (Circular E).

Employee's social security and Medicare taxes paid by employer. If you paid your employee's share of social security and Medicare taxes rather than deducting them from the employee's wages, you must include these payments as wages subject to federal (or American Samoa, Guam, or U.S. Virgin Islands) income tax withholding and social security, Medicare, and federal unemployment (FUTA) taxes. The amount to include as wages is determined by using the formula contained in the discussion of *Employee's Portion of Taxes Paid by Employer* in section 7 of Pub. 15-A.

 This does not apply to household and agricultural employers. If you pay a household or agricultural employee's social security and Medicare taxes, you must include these payments in the employee's

wages for income tax withholding purposes. However, the wage increase due to the tax payments is not subject to social security, Medicare, or FUTA taxes. For information on completing Forms W-2 and W-3 in this situation, see the Instructions for Schedule H (Form 1040) and section 4 of Pub. 51 (Circular A).

Foreign agricultural workers. You must report compensation of $600 or more paid in a calendar year to an H-2A visa agricultural worker for agricultural labor. If the H-2A visa agricultural worker furnishes a valid taxpayer identification number, report these payments in box 1 of Form W-2. If the worker does not furnish a valid taxpayer identification number, report the payments on Form 1099-MISC. See *Form 1099-MISC*, below.

On Form W-2, no amount should be reported in boxes 3 or 5. In most cases, you do not need to withhold federal income tax from compensation paid to H-2A visa agricultural workers. Employers should withhold federal income tax only if the H-2A visa agricultural worker and the employer agree to withhold. The H-2A visa agricultural worker must provide a completed Form W-4. If the employer withholds income tax, the employer must report the tax withheld in box 2 of Form W-2 and on line 6 of Form 943. See Publication 51 (Circular A).

Form 1099-MISC. If the H-2A visa agricultural worker fails to furnish a taxpayer identification number to the employer, and the total annual payments made to the H-2A visa agricultural worker are $600 or more, the employer must begin backup withholding on the payments made until the H-2A visa agricultural worker furnishes a valid taxpayer identification number. Employers must report the compensation paid and any backup withholding on Forms 1099-MISC and Form 945. See the 2012 Instructions for Form 1099-MISC and the 2012 Instructions for Form 945.

For more information, visit the Foreign Agricultural Workers page on IRS.gov.

Fringe benefits. Include all taxable fringe benefits in box 1 of Form W-2 as wages, tips, and other compensation and, if applicable, in boxes 3 and 5 as social security and Medicare wages. Although not required, you may include the total value of fringe benefits in box 14 (or on a separate statement). However, if you provided your employee a vehicle and included 100% of its annual lease value in the employee's income, you must separately report this value to the employee in box 14 (or on a separate statement). The employee can then figure the value of any business use of the vehicle and report it on Form 2106, Employee Business Expenses. Also see Pub. 15-B for more information.

 If you used the commuting rule or the vehicle cents-per-mile rule to value the personal use of the vehicle, you cannot include 100% of the value of the use of the vehicle in the employee's income. See Pub. 15-B.

Golden parachute payments (not applicable to Forms W-2AS, W-2GU, or W-2VI). Include any golden parachute payments in boxes 1, 3, and 5 of Form W-2. Withhold federal income, social security, and Medicare taxes as usual and report them in boxes 2, 4, and 6, respectively. Excess parachute payments are also subject to a 20% excise tax. If the excess payments are considered wages, withhold the 20% excise tax and include it in box 2 as income tax withheld. Also report the excise tax in box 12 with code K. For definitions and additional information, see Regulations section 1.280G-1 and Rev. Proc. 2003-68, 2003-34 I.R.B. 398, available at *www.irs.gov/irb/2003-34_IRB/ar16.html*.

Government employers. Federal, state, and local governmental agencies have two options for reporting their employees' wages that are subject to only Medicare tax for part of the year and both social security and Medicare taxes for part of the year.

The first option (which the SSA prefers) is to file a single set of Forms W-2 per employee for the entire year, even if only part of the year's wages are subject to both social security and Medicare taxes. Check "941" (or "944") or "941-SS" in box b of Form W-3. The wages in box 5 of Form W-2 must be equal to or greater than the wages in box 3 of Form W-2.

The second option is to file one set of Forms W-2 for wages subject only to Medicare tax and another set for wages subject to both social security and Medicare taxes. Use a separate Form W-3 to transmit each set of Forms W-2. For the Medicare-only Forms W-2, check "Medicare govt. emp." in box b of Form W-3. For the Forms W-2 showing wages subject to both social security and Medicare taxes, check "941" (or "944") or "941-SS" in box b of Form W-3. The wages in box 5 of Form W-2 must be equal to or greater than the wages in box 3 of Form W-2.

Group-term life insurance. You must include in boxes 1, 3, and 5 the cost of group-term life insurance that is more than the cost of $50,000 of coverage, reduced by the amount the employee paid toward the insurance. Use the table in section 2 of Pub. 15-B to determine the cost of the insurance. Also, show the amount in box 12 with code C. For employees, you must withhold social security and Medicare taxes, but not federal income tax. For coverage provided to former employees, the former employees must pay the employee part of social security and Medicare taxes on the taxable cost of group-term life insurance over $50,000 on Form 1040. You are not required to collect those taxes. However, you must report the uncollected social security tax with code M and the uncollected Medicare tax with code N in box 12 of Form W-2.

Health savings account (HSA). An employer's contribution (including an employee's contributions through a cafeteria plan) to an employee's HSA is not subject to federal income tax withholding or social security, Medicare, or railroad retirement taxes (or FUTA tax) if it is reasonable to believe at the time of the payment that the contribution will be excludable from the employee's income. However, if it is not reasonable to believe at the time of payment that the contribution will be excludable from the employee's income, employer contributions are subject to federal income tax withholding, social security and Medicare taxes (or railroad retirement taxes, if applicable), and FUTA tax and must be reported in boxes 1, 3, and 5 (use box 14 if railroad retirement taxes apply), and on Form 940,

Employer's Annual Federal Unemployment (FUTA) Tax Return.

You must report all employer contributions (including an employee's contributions through a cafeteria plan) to an HSA in box 12 of Form W-2 with code W. Employer contributions to an HSA that are not excludable from the income of the employee also must be reported in boxes 1, 3, and 5. (Use box 14 if railroad retirement taxes apply.)

An employee's contributions to an HSA (unless made through a cafeteria plan) are includible in income as wages and are subject to federal income tax withholding and social security and Medicare taxes (or railroad retirement taxes, if applicable). Employee contributions are deductible, within limits, on the employee's Form 1040. For more information about HSAs, see Notice 2004-2, Notice 2004-50, and Notice 2008-52. Notice 2004-2, 2004-2 I.R.B. 269, is available at *www.irs.gov/irb/ 2004-02_IRB/ar09.html*. Notice 2004-50, 2004-33 I.R.B. 196, is available at *www.irs.gov/irb/2004-33_IRB/ ar08.html*. Notice 2008-52, 2008-25 I.R.B. 1166, is available at *www.irs.gov/irb/2008-25_IRB/ar10.html*. Also see Form 8889, Health Savings Accounts (HSAs), and Pub. 969.

Lost Form W-2—reissued statement. If an employee loses a Form W-2, write "REISSUED STATEMENT" on the new copy and furnish it to the employee. You do not have to add "REISSUED STATEMENT" on Forms W-2 provided to employees electronically. Do not send Copy A of the reissued Form W-2 to the SSA. Employers are not prohibited (by the Internal Revenue Code) from charging a fee for the issuance of a duplicate Form W-2.

Military differential pay. Employers paying their employees while they are on active duty in the United States uniformed services should treat these payments as wages. Differential wage payments made to an individual while on active duty for periods scheduled to exceed 30 days are subject to income tax withholding, but are not subject to social security, Medicare, and unemployment taxes. Report differential wage payments in box 1 and any federal income tax withholding in box 2. Differential wage payments made to an individual while on active duty for 30 days or less are subject to income tax withholding, social security, Medicare, and unemployment taxes, and are reported in boxes 1, 3, and 5. See Rev. Rul. 2009-11, 2009-18 I.R.B. 896, available at *www.irs.gov/irb/ 2009-18_IRB/ar07.html*.

Moving expenses. Report moving expenses as follows.
• Qualified moving expenses that an employer paid to a third party on behalf of the employee (for example, to a moving company) and services that an employer furnished in kind to an employee are not reported on Form W-2.
• Qualified moving expense reimbursements paid directly to an employee by an employer are reported only in box 12 of Form W-2 with code P.
• Nonqualified moving expense reimbursements are reported in boxes 1, 3, and 5 (use box 14 if railroad retirement taxes apply) of Form W-2. These amounts are subject to federal income tax withholding and social security and Medicare taxes (or railroad retirement taxes, if applicable).

General Instructions for Forms W-2 and W-3 (2012)   -9-

For more information on qualified and nonqualified moving expenses, see Pub. 521, Moving Expenses.

Nonqualified deferred compensation plans. Section 409A provides that all amounts deferred under a nonqualified deferred compensation (NQDC) plan for all tax years are currently includible in gross income unless certain requirements are met. Generally, section 409A is effective with respect to amounts deferred in tax years beginning after December 31, 2004, but deferrals made prior to that year may be subject to section 409A under some circumstances.

It is not necessary to show amounts deferred during the year under an NQDC plan subject to section 409A. If you report section 409A deferrals, show the amount in box 12 using code Y. For more information, see Notice 2008-115, 2008-52 I.R.B. 1367, available at *www.irs.gov/irb/ 2008-52_IRB/ar10.html.*

Income included under section 409A from an NQDC plan will be reported in box 1 and in box 12 using code Z. This income is also subject to an additional tax of 20% that is reported on Form 1040. For more information on amounts includible in gross income and reporting requirements, see proposed Regulations section 1.409A-4, 2008-51 I.R.B 1325, and Notice 2008-115. For information on correcting failures to comply with section 409A and related reporting, see Notice 2008-113, 2008-51 I.R.B. 1305, available at *www.irs.gov/irb/ 2008-51_IRB/ar12.html*; Notice 2010-6, 2010-3 I.R.B 275, available at *www.irs.gov/irb/2010-3_IRB/ar08.html*; and Notice 2010-80, 2010-51 I.R.B. 853, available at *www.irs.gov/irb/2010-51_IRB/ar08.html.*

Railroad employers (not applicable to Forms W-2AS, W-2GU, or W-2VI). Railroad employers must file Form W-2 to report their employees' wages and income tax withholding in boxes 1 and 2. Electronic reporting may be required; see *E-filing* on page 2. If you have employees covered under the Federal Insurance Contributions Act (FICA) (social security and Medicare) and the Railroad Retirement Tax Act (RRTA), you must file a separate Form W-3 to transmit the Forms W-2 for each group of employees.

For employees covered by social security and Medicare, complete boxes 3, 4, 5, 6, and 7 of Form W-2 to show the social security and Medicare wages and the amounts withheld for social security and Medicare taxes. On the Form W-3 used to transmit these Forms W-2, check the "941" checkbox in box b.

For employees covered by RRTA tax, report the Tier I and Tier II taxes withheld in box 14 of Form W-2. Label them "Tier I tax" and "Tier II tax." Boxes 3, 4, 5, 6, and 7 apply only to covered social security and Medicare wages and taxes and are not to be used to report railroad retirement wages and taxes. On the Form W-3 used to transmit these Forms W-2, check the "CT-1" checkbox in box b.

Repayments. If an employee repays you for wages received in error, do not offset the repayments against current year wages unless the repayments are for amounts received in error in the current year. Repayments made in the current year, but related to a prior year or years, must be repaid in gross, not net, and require

special tax treatment by employees in some cases. You may advise the employee of the total repayments made during the current year and the amount (if any) related to prior years. This information will help the employee account for such repayments on his or her federal income tax return.

If the repayment was for a prior year, you must file Form W-2c with the SSA to correct only social security and Medicare wages and taxes. Do not correct "Wages, tips, other compensation" in box 1, or "Federal income tax withheld" in box 2, on Form W-2c. File the "X" return that is appropriate for the return on which the wages were originally reported (Form 941-X, 943-X, 944-X, or CT-1X). Correct the social security and Medicare wages and taxes for the period during which the wages were originally paid. For information on reporting adjustments to Form 941, Form 941-SS, Form 943, Form 944, or Form CT-1, see section 13 of Pub. 15 (Circular E) or section 9 of Pub. 51 (Circular A).

 Tell your employee that the wages paid in error in a prior year remain taxable to him or her for that year. This is because the employee received and had use of those funds during that year. The employee is not entitled to file an amended return (Form 1040X) to recover the income tax on these wages. Instead, the employee is entitled to a deduction (or a credit, in some cases) for the repaid wages on his or her Form 1040 for the year of repayment. Refer your employee to Repayments in Pub. 525.

Scholarship and fellowship grants. Give a Form W-2 to each recipient of a scholarship or fellowship grant only if you are reporting amounts includible in income under section 117(c) (relating to payments for teaching, research, or other services required as a condition for receiving the qualified scholarship). Also see Pub. 15-A and Pub. 970. These payments are subject to federal income tax withholding. However, their taxability for social security and Medicare taxes depends on the nature of the employment and the status of the organization. See *Students, scholars, trainees, teachers, etc.,* in section 15 of Pub. 15 (Circular E).

Sick pay. If you had employees who received sick pay in 2012 from an insurance company or other third-party payer and the third party notified you of the amount of sick pay involved, you may be required to report the information on the employees' Forms W-2. If the insurance company or other third-party payer did not notify you in a timely manner about the sick pay payments, it must prepare Forms W-2 and W-3 for your employees showing the sick pay. For specific reporting instructions, see *Sick Pay Reporting* in section 6 of Pub. 15-A.

SIMPLE retirement account. An employee's salary reduction contributions to a SIMPLE (savings incentive match plan for employees) retirement account are not subject to federal income tax withholding but are subject to social security, Medicare, and railroad retirement taxes. Do not include an employee's contribution in box 1, but do include it in boxes 3 and 5. (Use box 14 if railroad retirement taxes apply.) An employee's total contribution also must be included in box 12 with code D or S.

An employer's matching or nonelective contribution to an employee's SIMPLE retirement account is not subject to federal income tax withholding or social security, Medicare, or railroad retirement taxes, and is not to be shown on Form W-2.

For more information on SIMPLE retirement accounts, see Notice 98-4, 1998-1 C.B. 269. You can find Notice 98-4 on page 25 of Internal Revenue Bulletin 1998-2 at *www.irs.gov/pub/irs-irbs/irb98-02.pdf.*

Successor/predecessor employers. If you buy or sell a business during the year, see Rev. Proc. 2004-53 for information on who must file Forms W-2 and employment tax returns. Rev. Proc. 2004-53, 2004-34 I.R.B 320, is available at *www.irs.gov/irb/2004-34_IRB/ar13.html.*

Terminating a business. If you terminate your business, you must provide Forms W-2 to your employees for the calendar year of termination by the due date of your final Form 941, 944, or 941-SS. You also must file Forms W-2 with the SSA by the last day of the month that follows the due date of your final Form 941, 944, or 941-SS. If filing on paper, make sure you obtain Forms W-2 and W-3 preprinted with the correct year. If e-filing, make sure your software has been updated for the current tax year.

However, if any of your employees are immediately employed by a successor employer, see *Successor/predecessor employers,* earlier. Also, for information on automatic extensions for furnishing Forms W-2 to employees and filing Forms W-2, see Rev. Proc. 96-57, which is on page 14 of Internal Revenue Bulletin 1996-53 at *www.irs.gov/pub/irs-irbs/irb96-53.pdf.*

 Get Schedule D (Form 941), Report of Discrepancies Caused by Acquisitions, Statutory Mergers, or Consolidations, for information on reconciling wages and taxes reported on Forms W-2 with amounts reported on Form 941, Form 941-SS, Form 943, or Form 944.

Uniformed Services Employment and Reemployment Rights Act of 1994 (USERRA) makeup amounts to a pension plan. If an employee returned to your employment after military service and certain makeup amounts were contributed to a pension plan for a prior year(s) under the USERRA, report the prior year contributions separately in box 12. See the *TIP* above Code D on page 15. You also may report certain makeup amounts in box 14. See *Box 14—Other* on page 17.

Instead of reporting in box 12 (or box 14), you may choose to provide a separate statement to your employee showing USERRA makeup contributions. The statement must identify the type of plan, the year(s) to which the contributions relate, and the amount contributed for each year.

Penalties

The following penalties apply to the person or employer required to file Form W-2. The penalties apply to both paper filers and e-filers.

 Use of a reporting agent or other third-party payroll service provider does not relieve an employer of the responsibility to ensure that Forms W-2 are furnished to employees and that Forms W-2 and W-3 are filed with the SSA, correctly and on time.

Failure to file correct information returns by the due date. If you fail to file a correct Form W-2 by the due date and cannot show reasonable cause, you may be subject to a penalty as provided under section 6721. The penalty applies if you:

- Fail to file timely,
- Fail to include all information required to be shown on Form W-2,
- Include incorrect information on Form W-2,
- File on paper forms when you are required to *e-file,*
- Report an incorrect TIN,
- Fail to report a TIN, or
- Fail to file paper Forms W-2 that are machine readable.

The amount of the penalty is based on when you file the correct Form W-2. The penalty is:

- $30 per Form W-2 if you correctly file within 30 days (by March 30 if the due date is February 28); the maximum penalty is $250,000 per year ($75,000 for small businesses, defined on page 11).
- $60 per Form W-2 if you correctly file more than 30 days after the due date but by August 1, 2013; the maximum penalty is $500,000 per year ($200,000 for small businesses).
- $100 per Form W-2 if you file after August 1, 2013, or you do not file required Forms W-2; the maximum penalty is $1,500,000 per year ($500,000 for small businesses).

 If you do not file corrections and you do not meet any of the exceptions to the penalty, the penalty is $100 per information return. The maximum penalty is $1,500,000 per year.

Exceptions to the penalty. The following are exceptions to the failure to file correct information returns penalty.

1. The penalty will not apply to any failure that you can show was due to reasonable cause and not to willful neglect. In general, you must be able to show that your failure was due to an event beyond your control or due to significant mitigating factors. You also must be able to show that you acted in a responsible manner and took steps to avoid the failure.

2. An inconsequential error or omission is not considered a failure to include correct information. An inconsequential error or omission does not prevent or hinder the SSA/IRS from processing the Form W-2, from correlating the information required to be shown on the form with the information shown on the payee's tax return, or from otherwise putting the form to its intended use. Errors and omissions that are never inconsequential are those relating to:

- A TIN,
- A payee's surname, and
- Any money amounts.

3. De minimis rule for corrections. Even though you cannot show reasonable cause, the penalty for failure to

file correct Forms W-2 will not apply to a certain number of returns if you:
• Filed those Forms W-2 on or before the required filing date,
• Either failed to include all of the information required on the form or included incorrect information, and
• Filed corrections of these forms by August 1, 2013.

If you meet all of the de minimis rule conditions, the penalty for filing incorrect information returns (including Form W-2) will not apply to the greater of 10 information returns (including Form W-2) or one-half of 1% of the total number of information returns (including Form W-2) that you are required to file for the calendar year.

Small businesses. For purposes of the lower maximum penalties shown in parentheses on page 10, you are a small business if your average annual gross receipts for the 3 most recent tax years (or for the period that you were in existence, if shorter) ending before the calendar year in which the Forms W-2 were due are $5 million or less.

Intentional disregard of filing requirements. If any failure to file a correct Form W-2 is due to intentional disregard of the filing or correct information requirements, the penalty is at least $250 per Form W-2 with no maximum penalty.

Failure to furnish correct payee statements. If you fail to provide correct payee statements (Forms W-2) to your employees and cannot show reasonable cause, you may be subject to a penalty as provided under section 6722. The penalty applies if you fail to provide the statement by January 31, 2013, if you fail to include all information required to be shown on the statement, or if you include incorrect information on the statement.

The amount of the penalty is based on when you furnish the correct payee statement. This penalty is an additional penalty and is applied in the same manner, and with the same amounts, as the penalty for failure to file correct information returns by the due date (section 6721), described on page 10.

Exceptions to the penalty. An inconsequential error or omission is not considered a failure to include correct information. An inconsequential error or omission cannot reasonably be expected to prevent or hinder the payee from timely receiving correct information and reporting it on his or her income tax return or from otherwise putting the statement to its intended use. Errors and omissions that are never inconsequential are those relating to:
• A dollar amount,
• A significant item in a payee's address, and
• The appropriate form for the information provided, such as whether the form is an acceptable substitute for the official IRS form.

See *Exceptions to the penalty* in *Failure to file correct information returns by the due date*, on page 10, for additional exceptions to the penalty for failure to file correct payee statements.

Intentional disregard of payee statement requirements. If any failure to provide a correct payee statement (Form W-2) to an employee is due to intentional disregard of the requirements to furnish a correct payee

statement, the penalty is $250 per Form W-2 with no maximum penalty.

Civil damages for fraudulent filing of Forms W-2. If you willfully file a fraudulent Form W-2 for payments that you claim you made to another person, that person may be able to sue you for damages. You may have to pay $5,000 or more.

Specific Instructions for Form W-2

How to complete Form W-2. Form W-2 is a multi-part form. Ensure all copies are legible. Send Copy A to the SSA; Copy 1, if required, to your state, city, or local tax department; and Copies B, C, and 2 to your employee. Keep Copy D, and a copy of Form W-3, with your records for 4 years.

Enter the information on Form W-2 using black ink in 12-point Courier font. Copy A is read by machine and must be typed clearly with no corrections made to the entries and with no entries exceeding the size of the boxes. Entries completed by hand, in script or italic fonts, or in colors other than black cannot be read by the machines. Make all dollar entries on Copy A without the dollar sign and comma but with the decimal point (00000.00). Show the cents portion of the money amounts. If a box does not apply, leave it blank.

Send the whole Copy A page of Form W-2 with Form W-3 to the SSA even if one of the Forms W-2 on the page is blank or void. Do not staple Forms W-2 together or to Form W-3. File Forms W-2 either alphabetically by employees' last names or numerically by employees' SSNs.

Calendar year basis. The entries on Form W-2 must be based on wages paid during the calendar year. Use Form W-2 for the correct tax year. For example, if the employee worked from December 21, 2012, through January 4, 2013, and the wages for that period were paid on January 5, 2013, include those wages on the 2013 Form W-2.

Multiple forms. If necessary, you can issue more than one Form W-2 to an employee. For example, you may need to report more than four coded items in box 12 or you may want to report other compensation on a second form. If you issue a second Form W-2, complete boxes a, b, c, d, e, and f with the same information as on the first Form W-2. Show any items that were not included on the first Form W-2 in the appropriate boxes. Also, see the *TIP* for Copy A (Form W-2) on page 15.

Do not report the same federal, American Samoa, Guam, or U.S. Virgin Islands tax data to the SSA on more than one Copy A.

 For each Form W-2 showing an amount in box 3 or box 7, make certain that box 5 equals or exceeds the sum of boxes 3 and 7.

Void. Check this box when an error is made on Form W-2 and you are voiding it because you are going to complete a new Form W-2. Do not include any amounts shown on "Void" forms in the totals you enter on Form W-3. See *Corrections* on page 20.

Box a—Employee's social security number. Enter the number shown on the employee's social security card.

If the employee does not have a card, he or she should apply for one by completing Form SS-5, Application for a Social Security Card. The SSA lets you verify employee names and SSNs online or by telephone. For information about these free services, visit the Employer W-2 Filing Instructions & Information website at *www.socialsecurity.gov/employer*. If you have questions about using these services, call 1-888-772-6270 (toll free) to speak with an employer reporting specialist at the SSA.

If the employee has applied for a card but the number is not received in time for filing, enter "Applied For" in box a on paper Forms W-2 filed with the SSA. If e-filing, enter zeros (000-00-0000 if creating forms online or 000000000 if uploading a file).

Ask the employee to inform you of the number and name as they are shown on the social security card when it is received. Then correct your previous report by filing Form W-2c showing the employee's SSN. If the employee needs to change his or her name from that shown on the card, the employee should call the SSA at 1-800-772-1213.

If you do not provide the correct employee name and SSN on Form W-2, you may owe a penalty unless you have reasonable cause. For more information, see Publication 1586, Reasonable Cause Regulations & Requirements for Missing and Incorrect Name/TINs.

ITINs for aliens. Do not accept an ITIN in place of an SSN for employee identification or for work. An ITIN is only available to resident and nonresident aliens who are not eligible for U.S. employment and need identification for other tax purposes. You can identify an ITIN because it is a 9-digit number, beginning with the number "9" with either a "7"or "8" as the fourth digit, and is formatted like an SSN (for example, 9NN-7N-NNNN). An individual with an ITIN who later becomes eligible to work in the United States must obtain an SSN.

 Do not auto-populate an ITIN into box a.

Box b—Employer identification number (EIN). Show the EIN assigned to you by the IRS (00-0000000). This should be the same number that you used on your federal employment tax returns (Form 941, Form 941-SS, Form 943, Form 944, Form CT-1, or Schedule H (Form 1040)). Do not use a prior owner's EIN. If you do not have an EIN when filing Forms W-2, enter "Applied For" in box b; do not use your SSN. You can get an EIN by applying online at IRS.gov, by calling the toll-free number, 1-800-829-4933, or by filing Form SS-4, Application for Employer Identification Number. Also see *Agent reporting* on page 6.

Box c—Employer's name, address, and ZIP code. This entry should be the same as shown on your Form 941, Form 941-SS, Form 943, Form 944, Form CT-1, or Schedule H (Form 1040). The U.S. Postal Service recommends that no commas or periods be used in return addresses. Also see *Agent reporting* on page 6.

Box d—Control number. You may use this box to identify individual Forms W-2. You do not have to use this box.

Boxes e and f—Employee's name and address. Enter the name as shown on your employee's social security card (first name, middle initial, last name). If the name does not fit in the space allowed on the form, you may show the first and middle name initials and the full last name. It is especially important to report the exact last name of the employee. If you are unable to determine the correct last name, use of the SSA's Social Security Number Verification System may be helpful. Separate parts of a compound name with either a hyphen or a blank. Do not join them into a single word. Include all parts of a compound name in the appropriate name field. For example, for the name "John R Smith-Jones", enter "Smith-Jones" or "Smith Jones" in the last name field. If the name has changed, the employee must get a corrected social security card from any SSA office. Use the name on the original card until you see the corrected card. Do not show titles or academic degrees, such as "Dr.,""RN," or "Esq.," at the beginning or end of the employee's name. Generally, do not enter "Jr.,""Sr.," or other suffix in the "Suff." box on Copy A unless the suffix appears on the card. However, the SSA still prefers that you do not enter the suffix on Copy A.

Include in the address the number, street, and apartment or suite number (or P.O. box number if mail is not delivered to a street address). The U.S. Postal Service recommends that no commas or periods be used in delivery addresses. For a foreign address, give the information in the following order: city, province or state, and country. Follow the country's practice for entering the postal code. Do not abbreviate the country name.

Third-party payers of sick pay filing third-party sick pay recap Forms W-2 and W-3 must enter "Third-Party Sick Pay Recap" in place of the employee's name in box e. Do not file the recap Forms W-2 and W-3 electronically. Also, do not enter the employee's SSN in box a. See *Sick Pay Reporting* in section 6 of Pub. 15-A.

Box 1—Wages, tips, other compensation. Show the total taxable wages, tips, and other compensation (before any payroll deductions) that you paid to your employee during the year. However, do not include elective deferrals (such as employee contributions to a section 401(k) or 403(b) plan) except section 501(c)(18) contributions. Include the following.

1. Total wages, bonuses (including signing bonuses), prizes, and awards paid to employees during the year. See *Calendar year basis* on page 11.

2. Total noncash payments, including certain fringe benefits. See *Fringe benefits* on page 8.

3. Total tips reported by the employee to the employer (not allocated tips).

4. Certain employee business expense reimbursements (see *Employee business expense reimbursements* on page 7).

5. The cost of accident and health insurance premiums for 2%-or-more shareholder-employees paid by an S corporation.

6. Taxable benefits from a section 125 (cafeteria) plan if the employee chooses cash.

7. Employee contributions to an Archer MSA.

8. Employer contributions to an Archer MSA if includible in the income of the employee. See *Archer MSA* on page 6.

9. Employer contributions for qualified long-term care services to the extent that such coverage is provided through a flexible spending or similar arrangement.

10. Taxable cost of group-term life insurance in excess of $50,000. See *Group-term life insurance* on page 8.

11. Unless excludable under *Educational assistance programs* (see page 7), payments for non-job-related education expenses or for payments under a nonaccountable plan. See Pub. 970.

12. The amount includible as wages because you paid your employee's share of social security and Medicare taxes. See *Employee's social security and Medicare taxes paid by employer* on page 7. If you also paid your employee's income tax withholding, treat the grossed-up amount of that withholding as supplemental wages and report those wages in boxes 1, 3, 5, and 7. No exceptions to this treatment apply to household or agricultural wages.

13. Designated Roth contributions made under a section 401(k) plan, a section 403(b) salary reduction agreement, or a governmental section 457(b) plan. See *Designated Roth contributions* on page 7.

14. Distributions to an employee or former employee from an NQDC plan (including a rabbi trust) or a nongovernmental section 457(b) plan.

15. Amounts includible in income under section 457(f) because the amounts are no longer subject to a substantial risk of forfeiture.

16. Payments to statutory employees who are subject to social security and Medicare taxes but not subject to federal income tax withholding must be shown in box 1 as other compensation. See *Statutory employee* on page 17.

17. Cost of current insurance protection under a compensatory split-dollar life insurance arrangement.

18. Employee contributions to a health savings account (HSA).

19. Employer contributions to an HSA if includible in the income of the employee. See *Health savings account (HSA)* on page 8.

20. Amounts includible in income under an NQDC plan because of section 409A. See *Nonqualified deferred compensation plans* on page 9.

21. Payments made to former employees while they are on active duty in the Armed Forces or other uniformed services.

22. All other compensation, including certain scholarship and fellowship grants (see page 10). Other compensation includes taxable amounts that you paid to your employee from which federal income tax was not withheld. You may show other compensation on a separate Form W-2. See *Multiple forms* on page 12.

Box 2—Federal income tax withheld. Show the total federal income tax withheld from the employee's wages for the year. Include the 20% excise tax withheld on excess parachute payments. See *Golden parachute payments* on page 8.

For Forms W-2AS, W-2GU, or W-2VI, show the total American Samoa, Guam, or U.S. Virgin Islands income tax withheld.

Box 3—Social security wages. Show the total wages paid (before payroll deductions) subject to employee social security tax but not including social security tips and allocated tips. If reporting these amounts in a subsequent year (due to lapse of risk of forfeiture), the amount must be adjusted by any gain or loss. See *Box 7—Social security tips* and *Box 8—Allocated tips* on page 14. Generally, noncash payments are considered to be wages. Include employee business expense reimbursements reported in box 1. If you paid the employee's share of social security and Medicare taxes rather than deducting them from wages, see *Employee's social security and Medicare taxes paid by employer* on page 7. The total of boxes 3 and 7 cannot exceed $110,100 (2012 maximum social security wage base).

Report in box 3 elective deferrals to certain qualified cash or deferred compensation arrangements and to retirement plans described in box 12 (codes D, E, F, G, and S) even though the deferrals are not includible in box 1. Also report in box 3 designated Roth contributions made under a section 401(k) plan, under a section 403(b) salary reduction agreement, or under a governmental section 457(b) plan described in box 12 (codes AA, BB, and EE).

Amounts deferred (plus earnings or less losses) under a section 457(f) or nonqualified plan or nongovernmental section 457(b) plan must be included in boxes 3 and/or 5 as social security and/or Medicare wages as of the later of when the services giving rise to the deferral are performed or when there is no substantial forfeiture risk of the rights to the deferred amount. Include both elective and nonelective deferrals for purposes of nongovernmental section 457(b) plans.

 Wages reported in box 3 include:

• *Signing bonuses an employer pays for signing or ratifying an employment contract. See Rev. Rul. 2004-109, 2004-50 I.R.B 958, available at www.irs.gov/irb/2004-50_IRB/ar07.html.*

• *Taxable cost of group-term life insurance over $50,000 included in box 1. See* Group-term life insurance *on page 8.*

• *Cost of accident and health insurance premiums for 2%-or-more shareholder-employees paid by an S corporation, but only if not excludable under section 3121(a)(2)(B).*

• *Employee and nonexcludable employer contributions to an MSA or HSA. However, do not include employee contributions to an HSA that were made through a cafeteria plan. See* Archer MSA *on page 6 and* Health savings account (HSA) *on page 8.*

• *Employee contributions to a SIMPLE retirement account. See* SIMPLE retirement account *on page 10.*

• *Adoption benefits. See* Adoption benefits *on page 6.*

Box 4—Social security tax withheld. Show the total employee social security tax (not your share) withheld, including social security tax on tips. For 2012, the amount should not exceed $4,624.20 ($110,100 × 4.2%). Include only taxes withheld (or paid by you for the employee) for 2012 wages and tips. If you paid your employee's share, see *Employee's social security and Medicare taxes paid by employer* on page 7.

Box 5—Medicare wages and tips. The wages and tips subject to Medicare tax are the same as those subject to social security tax (boxes 3 and 7) except that there is no wage base limit for Medicare tax. Enter the total Medicare wages and tips in box 5. Be sure to enter tips that the employee reported even if you did not have enough employee funds to collect the Medicare tax for those tips. See *Box 3—Social security wages*, on page 13, for payments to report in this box. If you paid your employee's share of taxes, see *Employee's social security and Medicare taxes paid by employer* on page 7.

If you are a federal, state, or local governmental agency with employees paying only the 1.45% Medicare tax, enter the Medicare wages in this box. See *Government employers* on page 8.

Example of how to report social security and Medicare wages. You paid your employee $140,000 in wages. Enter in box 3 (social security wages) 110100.00 but enter in box 5 (Medicare wages and tips) 140000.00. There is no limit on the amount reported in box 5. If the amount of wages paid was $110,100 or less, the amounts entered in boxes 3 and 5 would be the same.

Box 6—Medicare tax withheld. Enter the total employee Medicare tax (not your share) withheld. Include only tax withheld for 2012 wages and tips. If you paid your employee's share of the taxes, see *Employee's social security and Medicare taxes paid by employer* on page 7.

Box 7—Social security tips. Show the tips that the employee reported to you even if you did not have enough employee funds to collect the social security tax for the tips. The total of boxes 3 and 7 should not be more than $110,100 (the maximum social security wage base for 2012). Report all tips in box 1 along with wages and other compensation. Include any tips reported in box 7 in box 5 also.

Box 8—Allocated tips (not applicable to Forms W-2AS, W-2GU, or W-2VI). If you are a food or beverage establishment, show the tips allocated to the employee. See the Instructions for Form 8027, Employer's Annual Information Return of Tip Income and Allocated Tips. Do not include this amount in boxes 1, 3, 5, or 7.

Box 9. Do not enter an amount in box 9.

Box 10—Dependent care benefits (not applicable to Forms W-2AS, W-2GU, or W-2VI). Show the total dependent care benefits under a dependent care assistance program (section 129) paid or incurred by you for your employee. Include the fair market value (FMV) of care in a daycare facility provided or sponsored by you for your employee and amounts paid or incurred for dependent care assistance in a section 125 (cafeteria) plan. Report all amounts paid or incurred (regardless of any employee forfeitures), including those in excess of the $5,000 exclusion. This may include (a) the FMV of benefits provided in kind by the employer, (b) an amount paid directly to a daycare facility by the employer or reimbursed to the employee to subsidize the benefit, or (c) benefits from the pre-tax contributions made by the employee under a section 125 dependent care flexible spending account. Include any amounts over $5,000 in boxes 1, 3, and 5. For more information, see Pub. 15-B.

 An employer that amends its cafeteria plan to provide a grace period for dependent care assistance may continue to rely on Notice 89-111 by reporting in box 10 of Form W-2 the salary reduction amount elected by the employee for the year for dependent care assistance (plus any employer matching contributions attributable to dependent care). Also see Notice 2005-42, 2005-23 I.R.B. 1204, available at www.irs.gov/irb/2005-23_IRB/ar11.html.

Box 11—Nonqualified plans. The purpose of box 11 is for the SSA to determine if any part of the amount reported in box 1 or boxes 3 and/or 5 was earned in a prior year. The SSA uses this information to verify that they have properly applied the social security earnings test and paid the correct amount of benefits.

Show distributions to an employee from a nonqualified plan or a nongovernmental section 457(b) plan. Also report these distributions in box 1. Make only one entry in this box. Distributions from governmental section 457(b) plans must be reported on Form 1099-R, not in box 1 of Form W-2.

If you did not make distributions this year, show deferrals (plus earnings or less losses) under a nonqualified or any section 457(b) plan that became taxable for social security and Medicare taxes during the year (but were for prior year services) because the deferred amounts were no longer subject to a substantial risk of forfeiture. Also report these amounts in boxes 3 (up to the social security wage base) and 5. Do not report in box 11 deferrals included in boxes 3 and/or 5 and deferrals for current year services (such as those with no risk of forfeiture).

 *If you made distributions and also are reporting any deferrals in box 3 and/or 5, do not complete box 11. See Pub. 957, Reporting Back Pay and Special Wage Payments to the Social Security Administration, and Form SSA-131, Employer Report of Special Wage Payments, for instructions on reporting these and other kinds of compensation earned in prior years. However, **do not file Form SSA-131 if this situation applies but the employee will not be age 62 or older by the end of that year.***

Unlike qualified plans, NQDC plans do not meet the qualification requirements for tax-favored status for this purpose. NQDC plans include those arrangements traditionally viewed as deferring the receipt of current compensation. Accordingly, welfare benefit plans, stock option plans, and plans providing dismissal pay, termination pay, or early retirement pay are not NQDC plans.

General Instructions for Forms W-2 and W-3 (2012)   **-15-**

Report distributions from NQDC or section 457 plans to beneficiaries of deceased employees on Form 1099-MISC, not on Form W-2.

Military employers must report military retirement payments on Form 1099-R.

 Do not report special wage payments, such as accumulated sick pay or vacation pay, in box 11. For more information on reporting special wage payments, see Pub. 957.

Box 12—Codes. Complete and code this box for all items described below. Note that the codes do not relate to where they should be entered in boxes 12a through 12d on Form W-2. For example, if you are only required to report code D in box 12, you can enter code D and the amount in box 12a of Form W-2. Report in box 12 any items that are listed as codes A through EE. Do not report in box 12 section 414(h)(2) contributions (relating to certain state or local government plans). Instead, use box 14 for these items and any other information that you wish to give to your employee. For example, union dues and uniform payments may be reported in box 14.

 On Copy A (Form W-2), do not enter more than four items in box 12. If more than four items need to be reported in box 12, use a separate Form W-2 to report the additional items (but enter no more than four items on each Copy A (Form W-2)). On all other copies of Form W-2 (Copies B, C, etc.), you may enter more than four items in box 12 when using an approved substitute Form W-2. See Multiple forms *on page 12.*

Use the IRS code designated below for the item you are entering, followed by the dollar amount for that item. Even if only one item is entered, you must use the IRS code designated for that item. Enter the code using a capital letter(s). Use decimal points but not dollar signs or commas. For example, if you are reporting $5,300.00 in elective deferrals under a section 401(k) plan, the entry would be D 5300.00 (not A 5300.00 even though it is the first or only entry in this box). Report the IRS code to the left of the vertical line in boxes 12a through 12d and the money amount to the right of the vertical line.

See the *Form W-2 Reference Guide for Box 12 Codes* on page 24. See also the detailed instructions next for each code.

Code A—Uncollected social security or RRTA tax on tips. Show the employee social security or Railroad Retirement Tax Act (RRTA) tax on all of the employee's tips that you could not collect because the employee did not have enough funds from which to deduct it. Do not include this amount in box 4.

Code B—Uncollected Medicare tax on tips. Show the employee Medicare tax or RRTA Medicare tax on tips that you could not collect because the employee did not have enough funds from which to deduct it. Do not include this amount in box 6.

Code C—Taxable cost of group-term life insurance over $50,000. Show the taxable cost of group-term life insurance coverage over $50,000 provided to your employee (including a former employee). See *Group-term*

life insurance on page 8. Also include this amount in boxes 1, 3 (up to the social security wage base), and 5.

Codes D through H, S, Y, AA, BB, and EE. Use these codes to show elective deferrals and designated Roth contributions made to the plans listed. Do not report amounts for other types of plans. See the example for reporting elective deferrals under a section 401(k) plan, later.

The amount reported as elective deferrals and designated Roth contributions is only the part of the employee's salary (or other compensation) that he or she did not receive because of the deferrals or designated Roth contributions. Only elective deferrals and designated Roth contributions should be reported in box 12 for all coded plans; except, when using code G for section 457(b) plans, include both elective and nonelective deferrals.

For employees who were 50 years of age or older at any time during the year and made elective deferral and/or designated Roth "catch-up" contributions, report the elective deferrals and the elective deferral "catch-up" contributions as a single sum in box 12 using the appropriate code, and the designated Roth contributions and designated Roth "catch-up" contributions as a single sum in box 12 using the appropriate code.

 If any elective deferrals, salary reduction amounts, or nonelective contributions under a section 457(b) plan during the year are makeup amounts under the Uniformed Services Employment and Reemployment Rights Act of 1994 (USERRA) for a prior year, you must enter the prior year contributions separately. Beginning with the earliest year, enter the code, the year, and the amount. For example, elective deferrals of $2,250 for 2010 and $1,250 for 2011 under USERRA under a section 401(k) plan are reported in box 12 as follows:

D 10 2250.00, D 11 1250.00. A 2012 contribution of $7,000 does not require a year designation; enter it as D 7000.00. Report the code (and year for prior year USERRA contributions) to the left of the vertical line in boxes 12a through 12d.

The following are not elective deferrals and may be reported in box 14, but not in box 12.
• Nonelective employer contributions made on behalf of an employee.
• After-tax contributions that are not designated Roth contributions, such as voluntary contributions to a pension plan that are deducted from an employee's pay. See the instructions on page 17 for Code AA, Code BB, and Code EE for reporting designated Roth contributions.
• Required employee contributions.
• Employer matching contributions.

Code D—Elective deferrals under section 401(k) cash or deferred arrangement (plan). Also show deferrals under a SIMPLE retirement account that is part of a section 401(k) arrangement.

Example of reporting excess elective deferrals and designated Roth contributions under a section 401(k) plan. For 2012, Employee A (age 45) elected to defer $18,300 under a section 401(k) plan. The employee also made a designated Roth contribution to the plan of

$1,000, and made a voluntary (non-Roth) after-tax contribution of $600. In addition, the employer, on A's behalf, made a qualified nonelective contribution of $2,000 to the plan and a nonelective profit-sharing employer contribution of $3,000.

Even though the 2012 limit for elective deferrals and designated Roth contributions is $17,000, the employee's total elective deferral amount of $18,300 is reported in box 12 with code D (D 18300.00). The designated Roth contribution is reported in box 12 with code AA (AA 1000.00). The employer must separately report the actual amounts of $18,300 and $1,000 in box 12 with the appropriate codes. The amount deferred in excess of the limit is not reported in box 1. The return of excess salary deferrals and excess designated contributions, including earnings on both, is reported on Form 1099-R.

The $600 voluntary after-tax contribution may be reported in box 14 (this is optional) but not in box 12. The $2,000 nonelective contribution and the $3,000 nonelective profit-sharing employer contribution are not required to be reported on Form W-2, but may be reported in box 14.

Check the "Retirement plan" box in box 13.

Code E—Elective deferrals under a section 403(b) salary reduction agreement.

Code F—Elective deferrals under a section 408(k) (6) salary reduction SEP.

Code G—Elective deferrals and employer contributions (including nonelective deferrals) to any governmental or nongovernmental section 457(b) deferred compensation plan. Do not report either section 457(b) or section 457(f) amounts that are subject to a substantial risk of forfeiture.

Code H—Elective deferrals under section 501(c) (18)(D) tax-exempt organization plan. Be sure to include this amount in box 1 as wages. The employee will deduct the amount on his or her Form 1040.

Code J—Nontaxable sick pay. Show any sick pay that was paid by a third-party and was not includible in income (and not shown in boxes 1, 3, and 5) because the employee contributed to the sick pay plan. Do not include nontaxable disability payments made directly by a state.

Code K—20% excise tax on excess golden parachute payments (not applicable to Forms W-2AS, W-2GU, or W-2VI). If you made excess "golden parachute" payments to certain key corporate employees, report the 20% excise tax on these payments. If the excess payments are considered to be wages, report the 20% excise tax withheld as income tax withheld in box 2.

Code L—Substantiated employee business expense reimbursements. Use this code only if you reimbursed your employee for employee business expenses using a per diem or mileage allowance and the amount that you reimbursed exceeds the amount treated as substantiated under IRS rules. See *Employee business expense reimbursements* on page 7.

Report in box 12 only the amount treated as substantiated (such as the nontaxable part). Include in boxes 1, 3 (up to the social security wage base), and 5 the part of the reimbursement that is more than the amount treated as substantiated.

Code M—Uncollected social security or RRTA tax on taxable cost of group-term life insurance over $50,000 (for former employees). If you provided your former employees (including retirees) more than $50,000 of group-term life insurance coverage for periods during which an employment relationship no longer exists, enter the amount of uncollected social security or RRTA tax on the coverage in box 12. Also see *Group-term life insurance* on page 8.

Code N—Uncollected Medicare tax on taxable cost of group-term life insurance over $50,000 (for former employees). If you provided your former employees (including retirees) more than $50,000 of group-term life insurance coverage for periods during which an employment relationship no longer exists, enter the amount of uncollected Medicare tax or RRTA Medicare tax on the coverage in box 12. Also see *Group-term life insurance* on page 8.

Code P—Excludable moving expense reimbursements paid directly to employee. Show the total moving expense reimbursements that you paid directly to your employee for qualified (deductible) moving expenses. See *Moving expenses* on page 9.

Code Q—Nontaxable combat pay. If you are a military employer, report any nontaxable combat pay in box 12.

Code R—Employer contributions to an Archer MSA. Show any employer contributions to an Archer MSA. See *Archer MSA* on page 6.

Code S—Employee salary reduction contributions under a section 408(p) SIMPLE plan. Show deferrals under a section 408(p) salary reduction SIMPLE retirement account. However, if the SIMPLE plan is part of a section 401(k) arrangement, use code D. If you are reporting prior year contributions under USERRA, see the *TIP* above Code D on page 15.

Code T—Adoption benefits. Show the total that you paid or reimbursed for qualified adoption expenses furnished to your employee under an adoption assistance program. Also include adoption benefits paid or reimbursed from the pre-tax contributions made by the employee under a section 125 (cafeteria) plan. However, do not include adoption benefits forfeited from a section 125 (cafeteria) plan. Report all amounts including those in excess of the $12,650 exclusion. For more information, see *Adoption benefits* on page 6.

Code V—Income from the exercise of nonstatutory stock option(s). Show the spread (that is, the fair market value of stock over the exercise price of option(s) granted to your employee with respect to that stock) from your employee's (or former employee's) exercise of nonstatutory stock option(s). Include this amount in boxes 1, 3 (up to the social security wage base), and 5.

This reporting requirement does not apply to the exercise of a statutory stock option, or the sale or disposition of stock acquired pursuant to the exercise of a statutory stock option. For more information about the taxability of employee stock options, see Pub. 15-B.

Code W—Employer contributions to a health savings account (HSA). Show any employer contributions (including amounts the employee elected to contribute using a section 125 (cafeteria) plan) to an HSA. See *Health savings account (HSA)* on page 8.

Code Y—Deferrals under a section 409A nonqualified deferred compensation plan. It is not necessary to show deferrals in box 12 with code Y. For more information, see Notice 2008-115. However, if you report these deferrals, show current year deferrals, including earnings during the year on current year and prior year deferrals. See *Nonqualified deferred compensation plans* on page 9.

Code Z—Income under section 409A on a nonqualified deferred compensation plan. Enter all amounts deferred (including earnings on amounts deferred) that are includible in income under section 409A because the NQDC plan fails to satisfy the requirements of section 409A. Do not include amounts properly reported on a Form 1099-MISC, corrected Form 1099-MISC, Form W-2, or Form W-2c for a prior year. Also, do not include amounts that are considered to be subject to a substantial risk of forfeiture for purposes of section 409A. For more information, see Regulations sections 1.409A-1 through 1.409A-6 and Notice 2008-115.

The amount reported in box 12 using code Z is also reported in box 1 and is subject to an additional tax reported on the employee's Form 1040. See *Nonqualified deferred compensation plans* on page 9.

For information regarding correcting section 409A errors and related reporting, see Notice 2008-113, Notice 2010-6, and Notice 2010-80.

Code AA—Designated Roth contributions under a section 401(k) plan. Use this code to report designated Roth contributions under a section 401(k) plan. Do not use this code to report elective deferrals under code D. See *Designated Roth contributions* on page 7.

Code BB—Designated Roth contributions under a section 403(b) plan. Use this code to report designated Roth contributions under a section 403(b) plan. Do not use this code to report elective deferrals under code E. See *Designated Roth contributions* on page 7.

Code DD—Cost of employer-sponsored health coverage. Use this code to report the cost of employer-sponsored health coverage. **The amount reported with code DD is not taxable.** Additional reporting guidance, including information about the transitional reporting rules that apply, is available on the Affordable Care Act Tax Provisions page of IRS.gov.

Code EE—Designated Roth contributions under a governmental section 457(b) plan. Use this code to report designated Roth contributions under a governmental section 457(b) plan. Do not use this code to report elective deferrals under code G. See *Designated Roth contributions* on page 7.

Box 13—Checkboxes. Check all boxes that apply.
● ***Statutory employee.*** Check this box for statutory employees whose earnings are subject to social security and Medicare taxes but not subject to federal income tax withholding. Do not check this box for common-law employees. There are workers who are independent contractors under the common-law rules but are treated by statute as employees. They are called statutory employees.

1. A driver who distributes beverages (other than milk), or meat, vegetable, fruit, or bakery products; or who picks up and delivers laundry or dry cleaning if the driver is your agent or is paid on commission.

2. A full-time life insurance sales agent whose principal business activity is selling life insurance or annuity contracts, or both, primarily for one life insurance company.

3. An individual who works at home on materials or goods that you supply and that must be returned to you or to a person you name if you also furnish specifications for the work to be done.

4. A full-time traveling or city salesperson who works on your behalf and turns in orders to you from wholesalers, retailers, contractors, or operators of hotels, restaurants, or other similar establishments. The goods sold must be merchandise for resale or supplies for use in the buyer's business operation. The work performed for you must be the salesperson's principal business activity.

For details on statutory employees and common-law employees, see section 1 in Pub. 15-A.
● ***Retirement plan.*** Check this box if the employee was an "active participant" (for any part of the year) in any of the following.

1. A qualified pension, profit-sharing, or stock-bonus plan described in section 401(a) (including a 401(k) plan).

2. An annuity plan described in section 403(a).

3. An annuity contract or custodial account described in section 403(b).

4. A simplified employee pension (SEP) plan described in section 408(k).

5. A SIMPLE retirement account described in section 408(p).

6. A trust described in section 501(c)(18).

7. A plan for federal, state, or local government employees or by an agency or instrumentality thereof (other than a section 457(b) plan).

Generally, an employee is an active participant if covered by (a) a defined benefit plan for any tax year that he or she is eligible to participate in or (b) a defined contribution plan (for example, a section 401(k) plan) for any tax year that employer or employee contributions (or forfeitures) are added to his or her account. For additional information on employees who are eligible to participate in a plan, contact your plan administrator. For details on the active participant rules, see Notice 87-16, 1987-1 C.B. 446; Notice 98-49, 1998-2 C.B. 365; section 219(g)(5); and Pub. 590, Individual Retirement Arrangements (IRAs). You can find Notice 98-49 on page 5 of Internal Revenue Bulletin 1998-38 at *www.irs.gov/pub/irs-irbs/ irb98-38.pdf*. Also see Notice 2000-30, which is on page 1266 of Internal Revenue Bulletin 2000-25 at *www.irs.gov/pub/irs-irbs/irb00-25.pdf*.

 Do not check this box for contributions made to a nonqualified or section 457(b) plan.

● ***Third-party sick pay.*** Check this box only if you are a third-party sick pay payer filing a Form W-2 for an insured's employee or are an employer reporting sick pay payments made by a third party. See *Sick Pay Reporting* in section 6 of Pub. 15-A.

Box 14—Other. If you included 100% of a vehicle's annual lease value in the employee's income, it also must be reported here or on a separate statement to your employee. You also may use this box for any other information that you want to give to your employee. Label each item. Examples include state disability insurance taxes withheld, union dues, uniform payments, health insurance premiums deducted, nontaxable income, educational assistance payments, or a member of the clergy's parsonage allowance and utilities. In addition, you may enter the following contributions to a pension plan: (a) nonelective employer contributions made on behalf of an employee, (b) voluntary after-tax contributions (but not designated Roth contributions) that are deducted from an employee's pay, (c) required employee contributions, and (d) employer matching contributions.

If you are reporting prior year contributions under USERRA (see the *TIP* above Code D on page 15 and *Uniformed Services Employment and Reemployment Rights Act of 1994 (USERRA) makeup amounts to a pension plan* on page 10), you may report in box 14 makeup amounts for nonelective employer contributions, voluntary after-tax contributions, required employee contributions, and employer matching contributions. Report such amounts separately for each year. Railroad employers, see page 9.

Boxes 15 through 20—State and local income tax information (not applicable to Forms W-2AS, W-2GU, or W-2VI). Use these boxes to report state and local income tax information. Enter the two-letter abbreviation for the name of the state. The employer's state ID numbers are assigned by the individual states. The state and local information boxes can be used to report wages and taxes for two states and two localities. Keep each state's and locality's information separated by the broken line. If you need to report information for more than two states or localities, prepare a second Form W-2. See *Multiple forms* on page 12. Contact your state or locality for specific reporting information.

Specific Instructions for Form W-3

How to complete Form W-3. The instructions under *How to complete Form W-2* on page 11 generally apply to Form W-3. Use black ink for all entries. Scanners cannot read entries if the type is too light. Be sure to send the entire page of the Form W-3.

 Amounts reported on related employment tax forms (for example, Form W-2, Form 941, Form 941-SS, Form 943, or Form 944) should agree with the amounts reported on Form W-3. If there are differences, you may be contacted by the IRS and SSA. Retain your reconciliation information for future reference. See Reconciling Forms W-2, W-3, 941, 941-SS, 943, 944, CT-1, and Schedule H (Form 1040) *on page 19.*

Box a—Control number. This is an optional box that you may use for numbering the whole transmittal.

Box b—Kind of Payer. Check the box that applies to you. Check only one box. If you have more than one type of Form W-2, send each type with a separate Form W-3. **Note.** The "Third-party sick pay" indicator box does not designate a separate kind of payer.

941 or 941-SS. Check this box if you file Form 941 or Form 941-SS and no other category applies. A church or church organization should check this box even if it is not required to file Form 941, Form 941-SS, or Form 944.

Military. Check this box if you are a military employer sending Forms W-2 for members of the uniformed services.

943. Check this box if you are an agricultural employer and file Form 943 and you are sending Forms W-2 for agricultural employees. For nonagricultural employees, send their Forms W-2 with a separate Form W-3, checking the appropriate box.

944. Check this box if you file Form 944 (or Formulario 944(SP), its Spanish-language version), and no other category applies.

CT-1. Check this box if you are a railroad employer sending Forms W-2 for employees covered under the Railroad Retirement Tax Act (RRTA). Do not show employee RRTA tax in boxes 3 through 7. These boxes are only for social security and Medicare information. If you also have employees who are subject to social security and Medicare taxes, send that group's Forms W-2 with a separate Form W-3 and check the "941" checkbox on that Form W-3.

Hshld. emp. Check this box if you are a household employer sending Forms W-2 for household employees and you did not include the household employee's taxes on Form 941, Form 941-SS, Form 943, or Form 944.

Medicare govt. emp. Check this box if you are a U.S., state, or local agency filing Forms W-2 for employees subject only to the 1.45% Medicare tax. See *Government employers* on page 8.

Box b—Kind of Employer. Check the box that applies to you. Check only one box unless the second checked box is "Third-party sick pay." See Pub. 557, Tax-Exempt Status for Your Organization, for information about 501(c) (3) tax-exempt organizations.

None apply. Check this box if none of the checkboxes discussed next apply to you.

501c non-govt. Check this box if you are a non-governmental tax-exempt section 501(c) organization. Types of 501(c) non-governmental organizations include private foundations, public charities, social and recreation clubs, and veterans organizations. For additional examples of 501(c) non-governmental organizations, see chapters 3 and 4 of Pub. 557, Tax-Exempt Status for Your Organization.

State/local non-501c. Check this box if you are a state or local government or instrumentality. This includes cities, townships, counties, special-purpose districts, public schools districts, or other publicly-owned entities with governmental authority.

State/local 501c. Check this box if you are a state or local government or instrumentality, and you have received a determination letter from the IRS indicating that you are also a tax-exempt organization under section 501(c)(3).

Federal govt. Check this box if you are a Federal government entity or instrumentality.

Box b—Third-party sick pay. Check this box if you are a third-party sick pay payer (or are reporting sick pay payments made by a third party) filing Forms W-2 with the "Third-party sick pay" checkbox in box 13 checked. File a single Form W-3 for the regular and "Third-party sick pay" Forms W-2. See *941 or 941-SS* on this page.

Box c—Total number of Forms W-2. Show the number of completed individual Forms W-2 that you are transmitting with this Form W-3. Do not count "Void" Forms W-2.

Box d—Establishment number. You may use this box to identify separate establishments in your business. You may file a separate Form W-3, with Forms W-2, for each establishment even if they all have the same EIN; or you may use a single Form W-3 for all Forms W-2 of the same type.

Box e—Employer identification number (EIN). Enter the nine-digit EIN assigned to you by the IRS. The number should be the same as shown on your Form 941, Form 941-SS, Form 943, Form 944, Form CT-1, or Schedule H (Form 1040) and in the following format: 00-0000000. Do not use a prior owner's EIN. See *Box h—Other EIN used this year* on page 19.

If you do not have an EIN when filing your Form W-3, enter "Applied For" in box e, not your social security number (SSN), and see *Box b—Employer identification number (EIN)* on page 12.

Box f—Employer's name. Enter the same name as shown on your Form 941, Form 941-SS, Form 943, Form 944, or Form CT-1.

Box g—Employer's address and ZIP code. Enter your address.

Box h—Other EIN used this year. If you have used an EIN (including a prior owner's EIN) on Form 941, 941-SS, Form 943, Form 944, or Form CT-1 submitted for 2012 that is different from the EIN reported on Form W-3 in box e, enter the other EIN used. Agents generally report the employer's EIN in box h. See *Agent reporting* on page 6.

Contact person, telephone number, fax number, and email address. Include this information for use by the SSA if any questions arise during processing.

 The amounts to enter in boxes 1 through 19, described next, are totals from only the Forms W-2 (excluding any Forms W-2 marked "VOID") that you are sending with this Form W-3.

Boxes 1 through 8. Enter the totals reported in boxes 1 through 8 on the Forms W-2.

Box 9. Do not enter an amount in box 9.

Box 10—Dependent care benefits (not applicable to Forms W-2AS, W-2GU, and W-2VI). Enter the total reported in box 10 on Forms W-2.

Box 11—Nonqualified plans. Enter the total reported in box 11 on Forms W-2.

Box 12a—Deferred compensation. Enter the total of all amounts reported with codes D through H, S, Y, AA, BB, and EE in box 12 on Forms W-2. Do not enter a code.

 The total of Form W-2 box 12 amounts reported with Codes A through C, J through R, T through W, Z, and DD is not reported on Form W-3.

Box 13—For third-party sick pay use only. Third-party payers of sick pay (or employers using the optional rule for Form W-2 described in section 6 of Pub. 15-A) filing third-party sick pay recap Forms W-2 and W-3 must enter "Third-Party Sick Pay Recap" in this box.

Box 14—Income tax withheld by payer of third-party sick pay. Complete this box only if you are the employer and have employees who had federal income tax withheld on third-party payments of sick pay. Show the total income tax withheld by third-party payers on payments to all of your employees. Although this tax is included in the box 2 total, it must be separately shown here.

Box 15—State/Employer's state ID number (territorial ID number for Forms W-2AS, W-2GU, and W-2VI). Enter the two-letter abbreviation for the name of the state or territory being reported on Form(s) W-2. Also enter your state- or territory-assigned ID number. If the Forms W-2 being submitted with this Form W-3 contain wage and income tax information from more than one state or territory, enter an "X" under "State" and do not enter any state or territory ID number.

Boxes 16 through 19 (not applicable to Forms W-2AS, W-2GU, and W-2VI). Enter the total of state/ local wages and income tax shown in their corresponding boxes on the Forms W-2 included with this Form W-3. If the Forms W-2 show amounts from more than one state or locality, report them as one sum in the appropriate box on Form W-3. Verify that the amount reported in each box is an accurate total of the Forms W-2.

Reconciling Forms W-2, W-3, 941, 941-SS, 943, 944, CT-1, and Schedule H (Form 1040)

Reconcile the amounts shown in boxes 2, 3, 5, and 7 from all 2012 Forms W-3 with their respective amounts from the 2012 yearly totals from the quarterly Form 941 or 941-SS or annual Form 943, Form 944, Form CT-1 (box 2 only), and Schedule H (Form 1040). When there are discrepancies between amounts reported on Forms W-2 and W-3 filed with the SSA and on Form 941, 941-SS, Form 943, Form 944, Form CT-1, or Schedule H (Form 1040) filed with the IRS, you will be contacted to resolve the discrepancies.

To help reduce discrepancies on Forms W-2:
- Report bonuses as wages and as social security and Medicare wages on Form W-2, and on Forms 941, 941-SS, 943, 944, and Schedule H (Form 1040).
- Report both social security and Medicare wages and taxes separately on Forms W-2 and W-3, and on Forms 941, 941-SS, 943, 944, and Schedule H (Form 1040).
- Report social security taxes withheld on Form W-2 in box 4, not in box 3.
- Report Medicare taxes withheld on Form W-2 in box 6, not in box 5.

- Do not report a nonzero amount in box 4 if boxes 3 and 7 are both zero.
- Do not report a nonzero amount in box 6 if box 5 is zero.
- Do not report an amount in box 5 that is less than the sum of boxes 3 and 7.
- Make sure that the social security wage amount for each employee does not exceed the annual social security wage base limit ($110,100 for 2012).
- Do not report noncash wages that are not subject to social security or Medicare taxes as social security or Medicare wages.
- If you use an EIN on any quarterly Form 941 or Form 941-SS for the year (or annual Forms 943, 944, CT-1, or Schedule H (Form 1040)) that is different from the EIN reported in box e on Form W-3, enter the other EIN in box h on Form W-3.

To reduce the discrepancies between amounts reported on Forms W-2 and W-3, and Forms 941, 941-SS, 943, 944, CT-1, and Schedule H (Form 1040):
- Be sure that the amounts on Form W-3 are the total amounts from Forms W-2.
- Reconcile Form W-3 with your four quarterly Forms 941 or 941-SS (or annual Forms 943, 944, CT-1, or Schedule H (Form 1040)) by comparing amounts reported for:

    1. Income tax withholding (box 2).

    2. Social security wages, Medicare wages and tips, and social security tips (boxes 3, 5, and 7). Form W-3 should include Form 941 or 941-SS or Forms 943, 944, or Schedule H (Form 1040) adjustments only for the current year. If the Form 941, Form 941-SS, Form 943, or Form 944 adjustments include amounts for a prior year, do not report those prior year adjustments on the current year Forms W-2 and W-3.

    3. Social security and Medicare taxes (boxes 4 and 6). The amounts shown on the four quarterly Forms 941 or 941-SS (or annual Form 943, Form 944, or Schedule H (Form 1040)), including current year adjustments, should be approximately twice the amounts shown on Form W-3.

Amounts reported on Forms W-2 and W-3, and Forms 941, 941-SS, 943, 944, CT-1, or Schedule H (Form 1040) may not match for valid reasons. If they do not match, you should determine that the reasons are valid. Retain your reconciliation information in case you receive inquiries from the IRS or the SSA.

General Instructions for Forms W-2c and W-3c

Applicable forms. Use with the February 2009 revision of Form W-2c and the December 2011 revision of Form W-3c.

Purpose of forms. Use Form W-2c to correct errors on Form W-2, W-2AS, W-2CM, W-2GU, W-2VI, or W-2c filed with the SSA. Also use Form W-2c to provide a corrected Form W-2, W-2AS, W-2CM, W-2GU, W-2VI, or W-2c to employees.

Corrections reported on Form W-2c may require you to make corrections to your previously filed employment tax

returns using the corresponding "X" form, such as Form 941-X, Adjusted Employer's QUARTERLY Federal Tax Return or Claim for Refund; Form 943-X, Adjusted Employer's Annual Federal Tax Return for Agricultural Employees or Claim for Refund; Form 944-X, Adjusted Employer's ANNUAL Federal Tax Return or Claim for Refund; or Form CT-1X, Adjusted Employer's Annual Railroad Retirement Tax Return or Claim for Refund. See section 13 of Pub. 15 (Circular E) for more information. If you are making corrections to a previously filed Schedule H (Form 1040), see Pub. 926, Household Employer's Tax Guide. If an employee repaid you for wages received in a prior year, also see *Repayments* on page 9.

Do not use Form W-2c to report corrections to back pay. Instead, see Pub. 957, Reporting Back Pay and Special Wage Payments to the Social Security Administration, and Form SSA-131, Employer Report of Special Wage Payments.

Do not use Form W-2c to correct Form W-2G, Certain Gambling Winnings. Instead, see the General Instructions for Certain Information Returns for the current reporting year.

Use Form W-3c to send Copy A of Form W-2c to the SSA. Always file Form W-3c when submitting one or more Forms W-2c.

E-filing Forms W-2c and W-3c. The SSA encourages all employers to *e-file* using its secure BSO website. E-filing can save you effort and helps ensure accuracy. See *E-filing* on page 2 for more information.

Where to file paper Forms W-2c and W-3c. If you use the U.S. Postal Service, send Forms W-2c and W-3c to:

    Social Security Administration
    Data Operations Center
    P.O. Box 3333
    Wilkes-Barre, PA 18767-3333

If you use a carrier other than the U.S. Postal Service, send Forms W-2c and W-3c to:

    Social Security Administration
    Data Operations Center
    Attn: W-2c Process
    1150 E. Mountain Drive
    Wilkes-Barre, PA 18702-7997

See Pub. 15 (Circular E) for a list of IRS-designated private delivery services.

 Do not send Forms W-2, W-2AS, W-2GU, or W-2VI to either of these addresses. Instead, see Where to file paper Forms W-2 and W-3 *on page 4.*

When to file. File Forms W-2c and W-3c as soon as possible after you discover an error. Also provide Form W-2c to employees as soon as possible.

How to complete. If you file Forms W-2c and W-3c on paper, make all entries using dark or black ink in 12-point Courier font, if possible, and make sure all copies are legible. See *How to complete Form W-2* on page 11.

If any item shows a change in the dollar amount and one of the amounts is zero, enter "-0-." Do not leave the box blank.

Who may sign Form W-3c. Generally, employers must sign Form W-3c. See *Who may sign Form W-3* on page 4 for more information.

Special Situations for Forms W-2c and W-3c

HIRE wages and tips paid to qualified employees. Employers who hired a qualified employee under the HIRE Act must report the amount of social security wages and tips paid after March 18, 2010, and before January 1, 2011, for which the employer claimed the payroll tax exemption. A qualified employee is one who:
• Was hired after February 3, 2010, and before January 1, 2011;
• Was not hired to replace another employee unless the other employee separated from employment voluntarily or for cause (including downsizing);
• Was not a family member or other related individual of the employer; and
• Signed Form W-11, Hiring Incentives to Restore Employment (HIRE) Act Employee Affidavit, or other similar statement under penalties of perjury, certifying under penalties of perjury that he or she had not worked more than 40 hours during the 60 days prior to beginning employment.

Report any corrections to the amount of wages and tips paid to the qualified employee for which you claimed the payroll tax exemption in box 12 using code CC. This will include wages and tips paid to the qualified employee from April 1, 2010, through December 31, 2010, for which you claimed the payroll tax exemption, plus wages and tips paid to the qualified employee from March 19, 2010, through March 31, 2010, for which you claimed a payroll tax credit. The amount may not exceed $106,800 (2010 maximum social security wage base). For more information, visit IRS.gov and enter "Payroll Tax Exemption for Hiring Unemployed Workers" in the search box.

Undeliverable Forms W-2c. See *Undeliverable Forms W-2* on page 5 for more information.

Correcting Forms W-2 and W-3

Corrections. Use the current version of Form W-2c to correct errors (such as incorrect name, SSN, or amount) on a previously filed Form W-2 or Form W-2c. File Copy A of Form W-2c with the SSA. To *e-file* your corrections, see *Correcting wage reports* on page 2.

If the SSA issues your employee a replacement card after a name change, or a new card with a different social security number after a change in alien work status, file a Form W-2c to correct the name/SSN reported on the most recently filed Form W-2. It is not necessary to correct the prior years if the previous name and number were used for the years prior to the most recently filed Form W-2.

File Form W-3c whenever you file a Form W-2c with the SSA, even if you are only filing a Form W-2c to correct an employee's name or SSN. However, see *Employee's*

incorrect address on Form W-2, later, for information on correcting an employee's address. See *Correcting an incorrect tax year and/or EIN incorrectly reported on Form W-2 or Form W-3*, below, if an error was made on a previously filed Form W-3.

If you discover an error on Form W-2 after you issue it to your employee but before you send it to the SSA, check the "Void" box at the top of the incorrect Form W-2 on Copy A. Prepare a new Form W-2 with the correct information, and send Copy A to the SSA. Write "CORRECTED" on the employee's new copies (B, C, and 2), and furnish them to the employee. If the "Void" Form W-2 is on a page with a correct Form W-2, send the entire page to the SSA. The "Void" form will not be processed. Do not write "CORRECTED" on Copy A of Form W-2.

If you are making a correction for a previously filed Form 941, Form 941-SS, Form 943, Form 944, Form 944-SS, or Form CT-1, use the corresponding "X" form, such as Form 941-X, Form 943-X, Form 944-X, or Form CT-1X for the return period in which you found the error. See section 13 of Pub. 15 (Circular E) for more details. If you are making corrections to a previously filed Schedule H (Form 1040), see Pub. 926. Issue the employee a Form W-2c if the error discovered was for the prior year.

Correcting an employee's name and/or SSN only. If you are correcting only an employee's name and/or SSN, complete Form W-2c boxes d through i. Do not complete boxes 1 through 20. Advise your employee to correct the SSN and/or name on his or her original Form W-2.

If your employee is given a new social security card following an adjustment to his or her resident status that shows a different name or SSN, file a Form W-2c for the most current year only.

Correcting an employee's name and SSN if the SSN was reported as blanks or zeros and the employee name was reported as blanks. If you need to correct an employee's name and SSN, and the SSN was reported as blanks or zeros and the employee's name was reported as blanks, do not use Form W-2c to report the corrections. You must contact the SSA at 1-800-772-6270 for instructions.

Correcting an incorrect tax year and/or EIN incorrectly reported on Form W-2 or Form W-3. To correct an incorrect tax year and/or EIN on a previously submitted Form W-2 or Form W-3, file one Form W-3c along with a Form W-2c for each affected employee. Enter the tax year and EIN originally reported, and enter in the "Previously reported" boxes the money amounts that were on the original Form W-2. In the "Correct information" boxes, enter zeros. Prepare a second Form W-3c along with a second Form W-2c for each affected employee. Enter zeros in the "Previously reported" boxes, and enter the correct money amounts in the "Correct information" boxes. Enter the correct tax year and/or correct EIN.

Correcting more than one Form W-2 for an employee. There are two ways to prepare a correction for an employee for whom more than one Form W-2 was filed under the same EIN for the tax year. You can (1) consider all the Forms W-2 when determining the amounts to enter on Form W-2c or (2) file a single Form W-2c to correct only the incorrect Form W-2.

However, state, local, and federal government employers who are preparing corrections for Medicare Qualified Government Employment (MQGE) employees also must follow the instructions in the *CAUTION* for state, local, and federal government employers on page 22.

Correcting more than one kind of form. You must use a separate Form W-3c for each type of Form W-2 (Form W-2, W-2AS, W-2CM, W-2GU, W-2VI, or W-2c) being corrected. You also must use a separate Form W-3c for each kind of payer/employer combination in box c. If you are correcting more than one kind of form, please group forms of the same kind of payer/employer combination, and send them in separate groups.

Employee's incorrect address on Form W-2. If you filed a Form W-2 with the SSA that reported an incorrect address for the employee, but all other information on the Form W-2 was correct, do not file Form W-2c with the SSA merely to correct the address.

However, if the address was incorrect on the Form W-2 furnished to the employee, you must do one of the following.
• Issue a new, corrected Form W-2 to the employee that includes the new address. Indicate "REISSUED STATEMENT" on the new copies. Do not send Copy A of Form W-2 to the SSA.
• Issue a Form W-2c to the employee that shows the correct address in box i and all other correct information. Do not send Copy A of Form W-2c to the SSA.
• Reissue the Form W-2 with the incorrect address to the employee in an envelope showing the correct address or otherwise deliver it to the employee.

Two Forms W-2 were filed under the same EIN, but only one should have been filed.

Example. Two Forms W-2 were submitted for Mary Smith under the same EIN for the same tax year. One Form W-2 correctly reported social security wages of $20,000. The other Form W-2 incorrectly reported social security wages of $30,000. There are two ways to correct this situation.
• File a Form W-3c along with one Form W-2c, entering $50,000 in box 3 under "Previously reported" and $20,000 in box 3 under "Correct information," or
• File a Form W-3c along with one Form W-2c, entering $30,000 in box 3 under "Previously reported" and $0.00 in box 3 under "Correct information."

Two Forms W-2 were filed under the same EIN, but wages on one were incorrect.

Example. Two Forms W-2 were submitted for Mary Smith under the same EIN for the same tax year. One Form W-2 correctly reported social security wages of $20,000. The other Form W-2 incorrectly reported social security wages of $30,000, whereas $25,000 should have been reported. There are two ways to correct this situation.
• File a Form W-3c along with one Form W-2c, entering $50,000 in box 3 under "Previously reported" and $45,000 in box 3 under "Correct information," or

• File a Form W-3c along with one Form W-2c, entering $30,000 in box 3 under "Previously reported" and $25,000 in box 3 under "Correct information."

Specific Instructions for Form W-2c

Box a—Employer's name, address, and ZIP code. This entry should be the same as shown on your Form 941, 941-SS, 943, 944, 944-SS, CT-1, or Schedule H (Form 1040).

Box b—Employer's Federal EIN. Show the correct nine digit EIN assigned to you by the IRS in the format 00-0000000.

Box c—Tax year/Form corrected. If you are correcting Form W-2, enter all four digits of the year of the form you are correcting. If you are correcting Form W-2AS, W-2CM, W-2GU, W-2VI, or W-2c, enter all four digits of the year you are correcting, and also enter "AS,""CM,""GU,""VI," or "c" to designate the form you are correcting. For example, "2010" and "GU" shows that you are correcting a 2010 Form W-2GU.

Box d—Employee's correct SSN. You must enter the employee's correct SSN even if it was correct on the original Form W-2. If you are correcting an employee's SSN, you also must complete boxes e through i.

Box e—Corrected SSN and/or name. Check this box only if you are correcting the employee's SSN, name, or both SSN and name. You also must complete boxes d and f through i.

Box f—Employee's previously reported SSN. Complete this box if you are correcting an employee's previously reported incorrect SSN and/or name. If the previous SSN was reported as blanks or not available, then box f should be all zeroes.

Box g—Employee's previously reported name. Complete this box if you are correcting an employee's previously reported incorrect SSN and/or name. You must enter the employee's previously reported full name in box g exactly as it was previously reported. If the previous reported name was reported as blanks or not available, then box g should be all blanks.

 *For boxes f and g, If both the previous SSN and the previous name were reported as blanks, **do not** use Form W-2c. Contact the SSA at 1-800-772-6270.*

Box h—Employee's first name and initial, Last name, Suff. Always enter the employee's correct name. See *Boxes e and f—Employee's name and address* on page 12 for name formatting information.

Box i—Employee's address and ZIP code. Always enter the employee's correct address. See *Boxes e and f—Employee's name and address* on page 12 for address formatting information.

 You must enter the employee's full name in boxes g and h.

Boxes 1 through 20. For the items you are changing, enter under "Previously reported" the amount reported on the original Form W-2 or on a prior Form W-2c. Enter under "Correct information" the correct amount.

Do not make an entry in any of these boxes on Copy A unless you are making a change. However, see the *CAUTION* for state, local, or federal government employers below.

Box 2—Federal income tax withheld. Use this box only to make corrections because of an administrative error. (An administrative error occurs only if the amount you entered in box 2 of the incorrect Form W-2 was not the amount you actually withheld.) If you are correcting Forms W-2AS, W-2CM, W-2GU, or W-2VI, box 2 is for income tax withheld for the applicable U.S. possession.

Boxes 5 and 6. Complete these boxes to correct Medicare wages and tips and Medicare tax withheld. State, local, or federal government employers also should use these boxes to correct MQGE wages. Box 5 must equal or exceed the sum of boxes 3 and 7.

 A state, local, or federal government employer correcting only social security wages and/or social security tips (boxes 3 and/or 7) for an MQGE employee also must complete Medicare wages and tips in box 5. Enter the total Medicare wages and tips, including MQGE-only wages, even if there is no change to the total Medicare wages and tips previously reported.

Boxes 8 through 11. Use these boxes to correct allocated tips, an advance EIC payment (before 2011), dependent care benefits, or deferrals and distributions relating to nonqualified plans.

Box 12—Codes. Complete these boxes to correct any of the coded items shown on Forms W-2. Examples include uncollected social security and/or Medicare taxes on tips, taxable cost of group-term life insurance coverage over $50,000, elective deferrals (codes D through H, S, Y, AA, BB, and EE), sick pay not includible as income, and employee business expenses. See *Box 12—Codes* on page 15 for the proper format to use in reporting coded items from box 12 of Forms W-2.

Employers should enter both the code and dollar amount for both fields on Form W-2c.

If a single Form W-2c does not provide enough blank spaces for corrections, use additional Forms W-2c.

Box 13. Check the boxes in box 13, under "Previously reported," as they were checked on the original Form W-2. Under "Correct information," check them as they should have been checked. For example, if you checked the "Retirement plan" box on the original Form W-2 by mistake, check the "Retirement plan" checkbox in box 13 under "Previously reported," but do not check the "Retirement plan" checkbox in box 13 under "Correct information."

Box 14. Use this box to correct items reported in box 14 of the original Form W-2 or on a prior Form W-2c. If possible, complete box 14 on Copies B, C, 1, and 2 of Form W-2c only, not on Copy A.

Boxes 15 through 20—State/local taxes. If your only changes to the original Form W-2 are to state or local data, do not send Copy A of Form W-2c to the SSA.

Instead, send Form W-2c to the appropriate state or local agency and furnish copies to your employees.

Correcting state information. Contact your state or locality for specific reporting information.

Specific Instructions for Form W-3c

Do not staple or tape the Forms W-2c to Form W-3c or to each other. File a separate Form W-3c for each tax year, for each type of form, and for each kind of payer/employer combination. (The "Third-party sick pay" indicator box does not designate a separate kind of payer or employer.) Make a copy of Form W-3c for your records.

In the money boxes of Form W-3c, total the amounts from each box and column on the Forms W-2c you are sending.

Box a—Tax year/Form corrected. Enter all four digits of the year of the form you are correcting and the type of form you are correcting. For the type of form, enter "2," "2AS,""2CM,""2GU,""2VI,""2c,""3,""3SS," or "3c." For example, entering "2010" and "2" indicates that all the forms being corrected are 2010 Forms W-2.

Box b—Employer's name, address, and ZIP code. This should be the same as shown on your Form 941, Form 941-SS, Form 943, Form 944, Form 944-SS, Form CT-1, or Schedule H (Form 1040). Include the suite, room, or other unit number after the street address. If the Post Office does not deliver mail to the street address and you use a P.O. box, show the P.O. box number instead of the street address.

 The IRS will not use Form W-3c to update your address of record. If you wish to change your address, file Form 8822 or Form 8822-B. To get this or any other IRS form, call 1-800 TAX-FORM (1-800-829-3676) or visit IRS.gov.

Box c—Kind of Payer. Check the box that applies to you. Check only one box. If your previous Form W-3 or Form W-3SS was checked incorrectly, report your prior incorrect payer type in the "Explain decreases here" area below boxes 18 and 19.

941/941-SS. Check this box if you file Form 941 or Form 941-SS.

Military. Check this box if you are a military employer correcting Forms W-2 for members of the uniformed services.

943. Check this box if you file Form 943 and you are correcting Forms W-2 for agricultural employees. For nonagricultural employees, send Forms W-2c with a separate Form W-3c, generally with the 941/941-SS box checked.

944/944-SS. Check this box if you file Form 944 (or Form 944-SS for years before 2012).

CT-1. Check this box if you are a railroad employer correcting Forms W-2 for employees covered under the Railroad Retirement Tax Act (RRTA). If you also have to correct forms of employees who are subject to social security and Medicare taxes, complete a separate Form W-3c with the "941/941-SS" box or "944/944-SS" box checked instead.

Hshld. emp. Check this box if you are a household employer correcting Forms W-2 for household employees and you file Schedule H (Form 1040). If you also have to correct forms of employees who are not household employees, complete a separate Form W-3c.

Medicare govt. emp. Check this box if you are a U.S., state, or local agency filing corrections for employees subject only to Medicare taxes.

Box c—Kind of Employer. Check the box that applies to you. Check only one box. If your previous Form W-3 or W-3SS was checked incorrectly, report your prior incorrect employer type in the "Explain decreases here" area below boxes 18 and 19.

None apply. Check this box if none of the checkboxes described next apply to you.

501c non-govt. Check this box if you are a non-governmental tax-exempt 501(c) organization. Types of 501(c) non-governmental organizations include private foundations, public charities, social and recreation clubs, and veterans organizations. For additional examples of 501(c) non-governmental organizations, see chapters 3 and 4 of Pub. 557, Tax-Exempt Status for Your Organization.

State/local non 501c. Check this box if you are a state or local government or instrumentality. This includes cities, townships, counties, special-purpose districts, public schools districts, or other publicly-owned entities with governmental authority.

State/local 501c. Check this box if you are a state or local government or instrumentality, and you have received a determination letter from the IRS indicating that you are also a tax-exempt organization under section 501(c)(3).

Federal govt. Check this box if you are a Federal government entity or instrumentality.

Box c—Third-party sick pay. Check this box if you are a third-party sick pay payer (or are reporting sick pay payments made by a third party) correcting Forms W-2 with the "Third-party sick pay" checkbox in box 13 of Form W-2c under "Correct information" checked. File a separate Form W-3c for each payer/employer combination reporting "Third-party sick pay" on Form W-2c.

Box d—Number of Forms W-2c. Show the number of individual Forms W-2c filed with this Form W-3c or enter "-0-" if you are correcting only a previously filed Form W-3 or Form W-3SS.

Box e—Employer's Federal EIN. Enter the correct number assigned to you by the IRS in the following format: 00-0000000. If you are correcting your EIN, enter the incorrect EIN you used in box h.

Box f—Establishment number. You may use this box to identify separate establishments in your business. You may file a separate Form W-3c, with Forms W-2c, for each establishment or you may use a single Form W-3c for all Forms W-2c. You do not have to complete this item; it is optional.

Box g—Employer's state ID number. You are not required to complete this box. This number is assigned by the individual state where your business is located.

However, you may want to complete this item if you use copies of this form for your state returns.

Box h—Employer's incorrect Federal EIN. Your correct number must appear in box e. Make an entry here only if the number on the original form was incorrect.

Box i—Incorrect establishment number. You may use this box to correct an establishment number.

Box j—Employer's incorrect state ID number. Use this box to make any corrections to your previously reported state ID number.

Boxes 1 through 11. Enter the total of amounts reported in boxes 1 through 11 as "Previously reported" and "Correct information" from Forms W-2c.

Box 9—Advance EIC payment. Enter an amount in box 9 only if you are making a correction for years before 2011.

Box 12a—Deferred compensation. Enter the total of amounts reported with codes D through H, S, Y, AA, BB, and EE as "Previously reported" and "Correct information" from Forms W-2c.

 The total of Form W-2c box 12 amounts reported with Codes A through C, J through R, T through W, Z, and DD is not reported on Form W-3c.

Box 12b—HIRE exempt wages and tips. Enter the total of amounts reported with code CC as "Previously reported" and "Correct information" from Forms W-2c. See *HIRE wages and tips paid to qualified employees* on page 20.

Box 14—Inc. tax w/h by third-party sick pay payer. Enter the amount previously reported and the corrected amount of income tax withheld on third-party payments of sick pay. Although this tax is included in the box 2 amounts, it must be shown separately here.

Boxes 16 through 19. If your only changes to the Forms W-2c and W-3c are to the state and local data, do not send either Copy A of Form W-2c or Form W-3c to the SSA. Instead, send the forms to the appropriate state or local agency and furnish copies of Form W-2c to your employees.

Explain decreases here. Explain any decrease to amounts "Previously reported." Also report here any previous incorrect entry in box c, "Kind of Payer" or "Kind of Employer." Enclose (but do not attach) additional sheets explaining your decreases, if necessary.

Signature. Sign and date the form. Also enter your title, phone number, and the name of a person to contact. If you have a fax number and/or email address, enter them. If you are not the employer, see *Who may sign Form W-3c* on page 20.

Privacy Act and Paperwork Reduction Act Notice. We ask for the information on Forms W-2 and W-3 to carry out the Internal Revenue laws of the United States. We need it to figure and collect the right amount of tax. Section 6051 and its regulations require you to furnish wage and tax statements to employees, the Social Security Administration, and the Internal Revenue Service. Section 6109 requires you to provide your

General Instructions for Forms W-2 and W-3 (2012)   -25-

Form W-4 (2013)

Purpose. Complete Form W-4 so that your employer can withhold the correct federal income tax from your pay. Consider completing a new Form W-4 each year and when your personal or financial situation changes.

Exemption from withholding. If you are exempt, complete **only** lines 1, 2, 3, 4, and 7 and sign the form to validate it. Your exemption for 2013 expires February 17, 2014. See Pub. 505, Tax Withholding and Estimated Tax.

Note. If another person can claim you as a dependent on his or her tax return, you cannot claim exemption from withholding if your income exceeds $1,000 and includes more than $350 of unearned income (for example, interest and dividends).

Basic instructions. If you are not exempt, complete the **Personal Allowances Worksheet** below. The worksheets on page 2 further adjust your withholding allowances based on itemized deductions, certain credits, adjustments to income, or two-earners/multiple jobs situations.

Complete all worksheets that apply. However, you may claim fewer (or zero) allowances. For regular wages, withholding must be based on allowances you claimed and may not be a flat amount or percentage of wages.

Head of household. Generally, you can claim head of household filing status on your tax return only if you are unmarried and pay more than 50% of the costs of keeping up a home for yourself and your dependent(s) or other qualifying individuals. See Pub. 501, Exemptions, Standard Deduction, and Filing Information, for information.

Tax credits. You can take projected tax credits into account in figuring your allowable number of withholding allowances. Credits for child or dependent care expenses and the child tax credit may be claimed using the **Personal Allowances Worksheet** below. See Pub. 505 for information on converting your other credits into withholding allowances.

Nonwage income. If you have a large amount of nonwage income, such as interest or dividends, consider making estimated tax payments using Form 1040-ES, Estimated Tax for Individuals. Otherwise, you may owe additional tax. If you have pension or annuity income, see Pub. 505 to find out if you should adjust your withholding on Form W-4 or W-4P.

Two earners or multiple jobs. If you have a working spouse or more than one job, figure the total number of allowances you are entitled to claim on all jobs using worksheets from only one Form W-4. Your withholding usually will be most accurate when all allowances are claimed on the Form W-4 for the highest paying job and zero allowances are claimed on the others. See Pub. 505 for details.

Nonresident alien. If you are a nonresident alien, see Notice 1392, Supplemental Form W-4 Instructions for Nonresident Aliens, before completing this form.

Check your withholding. After your Form W-4 takes effect, use Pub. 505 to see how the amount you are having withheld compares to your projected total tax for 2013. See Pub. 505, especially if your earnings exceed $130,000 (Single) or $180,000 (Married).

Future developments. Information about any future developments affecting Form W-4 (such as legislation enacted after we release it) will be posted at *www.irs.gov/w4*.

Personal Allowances Worksheet (Keep for your records.)

A	Enter "1" for **yourself** if no one else can claim you as a dependent	**A** _____
B	Enter "1" if: { • You are single and have only one job; or • You are married, have only one job, and your spouse does not work; or • Your wages from a second job or your spouse's wages (or the total of both) are $1,500 or less. } . . .	**B** _____
C	Enter "1" for your **spouse**. But, you may choose to enter "-0-" if you are married and have either a working spouse or more than one job. (Entering "-0-" may help you avoid having too little tax withheld.)	**C** _____
D	Enter number of **dependents** (other than your spouse or yourself) you will claim on your tax return . . .	**D** _____
E	Enter "1" if you will file as **head of household** on your tax return (see conditions under **Head of household** above) . .	**E** _____
F	Enter "1" if you have at least $1,900 of **child or dependent care expenses** for which you plan to claim a credit . . . (**Note.** Do **not** include child support payments. See Pub. 503, Child and Dependent Care Expenses, for details.)	**F** _____
G	**Child Tax Credit** (including additional child tax credit). See Pub. 972, Child Tax Credit, for more information. • If your total income will be less than $65,000 ($95,000 if married), enter "2" for each eligible child; then **less** "1" if you have three to six eligible children or **less** "2" if you have seven or more eligible children. • If your total income will be between $65,000 and $84,000 ($95,000 and $119,000 if married), enter "1" for each eligible child . . .	**G** _____
H	Add lines A through G and enter total here. (**Note.** This may be different from the number of exemptions you claim on your tax return.) ▶ **H**	_____

For accuracy, complete all worksheets that apply.	{	• If you plan to **itemize** or **claim adjustments to income** and want to reduce your withholding, see the **Deductions and Adjustments Worksheet** on page 2. • If you are **single and have more than one job** or are **married and you and your spouse both work** and the combined earnings from all jobs exceed $40,000 ($10,000 if married), see the **Two-Earners/Multiple Jobs Worksheet** on page 2 to avoid having too little tax withheld. • If **neither** of the above situations applies, **stop here** and enter the number from line H on line 5 of Form W-4 below.

-------------------- **Separate here and give Form W-4 to your employer. Keep the top part for your records.** --------------------

Form **W-4** Department of the Treasury Internal Revenue Service	**Employee's Withholding Allowance Certificate** ▶ Whether you are entitled to claim a certain number of allowances or exemption from withholding is subject to review by the IRS. Your employer may be required to send a copy of this form to the IRS.	OMB No. 1545-0074 2013

1 Your first name and middle initial	Last name	2 **Your social security number**

Home address (number and street or rural route)	3 ☐ Single ☐ Married ☐ Married, but withhold at higher Single rate. **Note.** If married, but legally separated, or spouse is a nonresident alien, check the "Single" box.
City or town, state, and ZIP code	4 **If your last name differs from that shown on your social security card,** check here. You must call 1-800-772-1213 for a replacement card. ▶ ☐

5	Total number of allowances you are claiming (from line **H** above **or** from the applicable worksheet on page 2)	**5**	
6	Additional amount, if any, you want withheld from each paycheck	**6**	$
7	I claim exemption from withholding for 2013, and I certify that I meet **both** of the following conditions for exemption. • Last year I had a right to a refund of **all** federal income tax withheld because I had **no** tax liability, **and** • This year I expect a refund of **all** federal income tax withheld because I expect to have **no** tax liability. If you meet both conditions, write "Exempt" here . . . . ▶	**7**	

Under penalties of perjury, I declare that I have examined this certificate and, to the best of my knowledge and belief, it is true, correct, and complete.

Employee's signature
(This form is not valid unless you sign it.) ▶ _____   Date ▶ _____

8 Employer's name and address (Employer: Complete lines 8 and 10 only if sending to the IRS.)	9 Office code (optional)	10 Employer identification number (EIN)

For Privacy Act and Paperwork Reduction Act Notice, see page 2.   Cat. No. 10220Q   Form **W-4** (2013)

Deductions and Adjustments Worksheet

Note. Use this worksheet *only* if you plan to itemize deductions or claim certain credits or adjustments to income.

1	Enter an estimate of your 2013 itemized deductions. These include qualifying home mortgage interest, charitable contributions, state and local taxes, medical expenses in excess of 10% (7.5% if either you or your spouse was born before January 2, 1949) of your income, and miscellaneous deductions. For 2013, you may have to reduce your itemized deductions if your income is over $300,000 and you are married filing jointly or are a qualifying widow(er); $275,000 if you are head of household; $250,000 if you are single and not head of household or a qualifying widow(er); or $150,000 if you are married filing separately. See Pub. 505 for details . . .	**1** $ _____
2	Enter: { $12,200 if married filing jointly or qualifying widow(er) / $8,950 if head of household / $6,100 if single or married filing separately }	**2** $ _____
3	**Subtract** line 2 from line 1. If zero or less, enter "-0-"	**3** $ _____
4	Enter an estimate of your 2013 adjustments to income and any additional standard deduction (see Pub. 505)	**4** $ _____
5	**Add** lines 3 and 4 and enter the total. (Include any amount for credits from the *Converting Credits to Withholding Allowances for 2013 Form W-4* worksheet in Pub. 505.)	**5** $ _____
6	Enter an estimate of your 2013 nonwage income (such as dividends or interest)	**6** $ _____
7	**Subtract** line 6 from line 5. If zero or less, enter "-0-"	**7** $ _____
8	**Divide** the amount on line 7 by $3,900 and enter the result here. Drop any fraction	**8** _____
9	Enter the number from the **Personal Allowances Worksheet, line H, page 1**	**9** _____
10	**Add** lines 8 and 9 and enter the total here. If you plan to use the **Two-Earners/Multiple Jobs Worksheet,** also enter this total on line 1 below. Otherwise, **stop here** and enter this total on Form W-4, line 5, page 1	**10** _____

Two-Earners/Multiple Jobs Worksheet (See *Two earners or multiple jobs* on page 1.)

Note. Use this worksheet *only* if the instructions under line H on page 1 direct you here.

1	Enter the number from line H, page 1 (or from line 10 above if you used the **Deductions and Adjustments Worksheet**)	**1** _____
2	Find the number in **Table 1** below that applies to the **LOWEST** paying job and enter it here. **However,** if you are married filing jointly and wages from the highest paying job are $65,000 or less, do not enter more than "3"	**2** _____
3	If line 1 is **more than or equal to** line 2, subtract line 2 from line 1. Enter the result here (if zero, enter "-0-") and on Form W-4, line 5, page 1. **Do not** use the rest of this worksheet	**3** _____
Note.	If line 1 is **less than** line 2, enter "-0-" on Form W-4, line 5, page 1. Complete lines 4 through 9 below to figure the additional withholding amount necessary to avoid a year-end tax bill.	
4	Enter the number from line 2 of this worksheet . . . . **4** _____	
5	Enter the number from line 1 of this worksheet . . . . **5** _____	
6	**Subtract** line 5 from line 4	**6** _____
7	Find the amount in **Table 2** below that applies to the **HIGHEST** paying job and enter it here	**7** $ _____
8	**Multiply** line 7 by line 6 and enter the result here. This is the additional annual withholding needed . .	**8** $ _____
9	Divide line 8 by the number of pay periods remaining in 2013. For example, divide by 25 if you are paid every two weeks and you complete this form on a date in January when there are 25 pay periods remaining in 2013. Enter the result here and on Form W-4, line 6, page 1. This is the additional amount to be withheld from each paycheck	**9** $ _____

Table 1

Married Filing Jointly		All Others	
If wages from **LOWEST** paying job are—	Enter on line 2 above	If wages from **LOWEST** paying job are—	Enter on line 2 above
$0 - $5,000	0	$0 - $8,000	0
5,001 - 13,000	1	8,001 - 16,000	1
13,001 - 24,000	2	16,001 - 25,000	2
24,001 - 26,000	3	25,001 - 30,000	3
26,001 - 30,000	4	30,001 - 40,000	4
30,001 - 42,000	5	40,001 - 50,000	5
42,001 - 48,000	6	50,001 - 70,000	6
48,001 - 55,000	7	70,001 - 80,000	7
55,001 - 65,000	8	80,001 - 95,000	8
65,001 - 75,000	9	95,001 - 120,000	9
75,001 - 85,000	10	120,001 and over	10
85,001 - 97,000	11		
97,001 - 110,000	12		
110,001 - 120,000	13		
120,001 - 135,000	14		
135,001 and over	15		

Table 2

Married Filing Jointly		All Others	
If wages from **HIGHEST** paying job are—	Enter on line 7 above	If wages from **HIGHEST** paying job are—	Enter on line 7 above
$0 - $72,000	$590	$0 - $37,000	$590
72,001 - 130,000	980	37,001 - 80,000	980
130,001 - 200,000	1,090	80,001 - 175,000	1,090
200,001 - 345,000	1,290	175,001 - 385,000	1,290
345,001 - 385,000	1,370	385,001 and over	1,540
385,001 and over	1,540		

Form **W-4P**

Department of the Treasury
Internal Revenue Service

Withholding Certificate for Pension or Annuity Payments

OMB No. 1545-0074

20**13**

Purpose. Form W-4P is for U.S. citizens, resident aliens, or their estates who are recipients of pensions, annuities (including commercial annuities), and certain other deferred compensation. Use Form W-4P to tell payers the correct amount of federal income tax to withhold from your payment(s). You also may use Form W-4P to choose (a) not to have any federal income tax withheld from the payment (except for eligible rollover distributions or payments to U.S. citizens delivered outside the United States or its possessions) or (b) to have an additional amount of tax withheld.

Your options depend on whether the payment is periodic, nonperiodic, or an eligible rollover distribution, as explained on pages 3 and 4. Your previously filed Form W-4P will remain in effect if you do not file a Form W-4P for 2013.

What do I need to do? Complete lines **A** through **G** of the **Personal Allowances Worksheet**. Use the additional worksheets on page 2 to further adjust your withholding allowances for itemized deductions, adjustments to income, any additional standard deduction, certain credits, or multiple pensions/more-than-one-income situations. If you do not want any federal income tax withheld (see *Purpose*, earlier), you can skip the worksheets and go directly to the Form W-4P below.

Sign this form. Form W-4P is not valid unless you sign it.

Future developments. The IRS has created a page on IRS.gov for information about Form W-4P and its instructions, at *www.irs.gov/w4p*. Information about any future developments affecting Form W-4P (such as legislation enacted after we release it) will be posted on that page.

Personal Allowances Worksheet (Keep for your records.)

A Enter "1" for **yourself** if no one else can claim you as a dependent . . . . **A** _____

B Enter "1" if:
- You are single and have only one pension; or
- You are married, have only one pension, and your spouse has no income subject to withholding; or
- Your income from a second pension or a job or your spouse's pension or wages (or the total of all) is $1,500 or less.

. . . . **B** _____

C Enter "1" for your **spouse**. But, you may choose to enter "-0-" if you are married and have either a spouse who has income subject to withholding or more than one source of income subject to withholding. (Entering "-0-" may help you avoid having too little tax withheld.) . . . . **C** _____

D Enter number of **dependents** (other than your spouse or yourself) you will claim on your tax return . . . . . **D** _____

E Enter "1" if you will file as **head of household** on your tax return . . . . **E** _____

F **Child Tax Credit** (including additional child tax credit). See Pub. 972, Child Tax Credit, for more information.
- If your total income will be less than $65,000 ($95,000 if married), enter "2" for each eligible child; then **less** "1" if you have three to six eligible children or **less** "2" if you have seven or more eligible children.
- If your total income will be between $65,000 and $84,000 ($95,000 and $119,000 if married), enter "1" for each eligible child . . . . **F** _____

G Add lines A through F and enter total here. (**Note.** This may be different from the number of exemptions you claim on your tax return.) ▶ **G** _____

For accuracy, complete all worksheets that apply.
- If you plan to **itemize** or **claim adjustments to income** and want to reduce your withholding, see the **Deductions and Adjustments Worksheet** on page 2.
- If you are **single and have more than one source of income subject to withholding** or are **married and you and your spouse both have income subject to withholding** and your combined income from all sources exceeds $40,000 ($10,000 if married), see the **Multiple Pensions/More-Than-One-Income Worksheet** on page 2 to avoid having too little tax withheld.
- If **neither** of the above situations applies, **stop here** and enter the number from line G on line 2 of Form W-4P below.

-------------- Separate here and give Form W-4P to the payer of your pension or annuity. Keep the top part for your records. --------------

Form **W-4P**

Department of the Treasury
Internal Revenue Service

Withholding Certificate for Pension or Annuity Payments

▶ **For Privacy Act and Paperwork Reduction Act Notice, see page 4.**

OMB No. 1545-0074

20**13**

Your first name and middle initial	Last name	Your social security number
Home address (number and street or rural route)		Claim or identification number (if any) of your pension or annuity contract
City or town, state, and ZIP code		

Complete the following applicable lines.

1 Check here if you **do not want any** federal income tax withheld from your pension or annuity. (Do not complete line 2 or 3.) ▶ ☐

2 Total number of allowances and marital status you are claiming for withholding from each **periodic** pension or annuity payment. (You also may designate an additional dollar amount on line 3.) . . . . ▶ _____ (Enter number of allowances.)

Marital status: ☐ Single ☐ Married ☐ Married, but withhold at higher Single rate.

3 Additional amount, if any, you want withheld from each pension or annuity payment. (**Note.** For periodic payments, you cannot enter an amount here without entering the number (including zero) of allowances on line 2.) . . . . . ▶ $ _____

Your signature ▶   Date ▶

Cat. No. 10225T   Form **W-4P** (2013)

Deductions and Adjustments Worksheet

Note. Use this worksheet *only* if you plan to itemize deductions or claim certain credits or adjustments to income.

1 Enter an estimate of your 2013 itemized deductions. These include qualifying home mortgage interest, charitable contributions, state and local taxes, medical expenses in excess of 10% (7.5% if either you or your spouse was born before January 2, 1949) of your income, and miscellaneous deductions. For 2013, you may have to reduce your itemized deductions if your income is over $300,000 and you are married filing jointly or are a qualifying widow(er); $275,000 if you are head of household; $250,000 if you are single and not head of household or a qualifying widow(er); or $150,000 if you are married filing separately. See Pub. 505 for details . . . .   **1** $ _____

2 Enter: { $12,200 if married filing jointly or qualifying widow(er)
            $8,950 if head of household } . . . . . .   **2** $ _____
            $6,100 if single or married filing separately

3 **Subtract** line 2 from line 1. If zero or less, enter "-0-" . . . .   **3** $ _____

4 Enter an estimate of your 2013 adjustments to income and any additional standard deduction (see Pub. 505) . . . .   **4** $ _____

5 **Add** lines 3 and 4 and enter the total. (Include any credit amounts from the *Converting Credits to Withholding Allowances for 2013 Form W-4* worksheet in Pub. 505.) . . . .   **5** $ _____

6 Enter an estimate of your 2013 income not subject to withholding (such as dividends or interest) . .   **6** $ _____

7 **Subtract** line 6 from line 5. If zero or less, enter "-0-" . . . .   **7** $ _____

8 **Divide** the amount on line 7 by $3,900 and enter the result here. Drop any fraction . . . .   **8** _____

9 Enter the number from the **Personal Allowances Worksheet,** line G, page 1 . . . .   **9** _____

10 **Add** lines 8 and 9 and enter the total here. If you use the **Multiple Pensions/More-Than-One-Income Worksheet,** also enter this total on line 1 below. Otherwise, **stop here** and enter this total on Form W-4P, line 2, page 1 . . . .   **10** _____

Multiple Pensions/More-Than-One-Income Worksheet

Note. Complete *only* if the instructions under line G, page 1, direct you here. This applies if you (and your spouse if married filing jointly) have more than one source of income subject to withholding (such as more than one pension, or a pension and a job, or you have a pension and your spouse works).

1 Enter the number from line G, page 1 (or from line 10 above if you used the **Deductions and Adjustments Worksheet**) . . . .   **1** _____

2 Find the number in **Table 1** below that applies to the **LOWEST** paying pension or job and enter it here. **However,** if you are married filing jointly and the amount from the highest paying pension or job is $65,000 or less, do not enter more than "3" . . . .   **2** _____

3 If line 1 is **more than or equal to** line 2, subtract line 2 from line 1. Enter the result here (if zero, enter "-0-") and on Form W-4P, line 2, page 1. **Do not** use the rest of this worksheet . . . .   **3** _____

Note. If line 1 is **less than** line 2, enter "-0-" on Form W-4P, line 2, page 1. Complete lines 4 through 9 below to figure the additional withholding amount necessary to avoid a year-end tax bill.

4 Enter the number from line 2 of this worksheet . . . . **4** _____

5 Enter the number from line 1 of this worksheet . . . . **5** _____

6 **Subtract** line 5 from line 4 . . . .   **6** _____

7 Find the amount in **Table 2** below that applies to the **HIGHEST** paying pension or job and enter it here   **7** $ _____

8 **Multiply** line 7 by line 6 and enter the result here. This is the additional annual withholding needed . .   **8** $ _____

9 **Divide** line 8 by the number of pay periods remaining in 2013. For example, divide by 12 if you are paid every month and you complete this form in December 2012. Enter the result here and on Form W-4P, line 3, page 1. This is the additional amount to be withheld from each payment . . . .   **9** $ _____

Table 1				Table 2			
Married Filing Jointly		**All Others**		**Married Filing Jointly**		**All Others**	
If wages from **LOWEST** paying job or pension are—	Enter on line 2 above	If wages from **LOWEST** paying job or pension are—	Enter on line 2 above	If wages from **HIGHEST** paying job or pension are—	Enter on line 7 above	If wages from **HIGHEST** paying job or pension are—	Enter on line 7 above
$0 - $5,000	0	$0 - $8,000	0	$0 - $72,000	$590	$0 - $37,000	$590
5,001 - 13,000	1	8,001 - 16,000	1	72,001 - 130,000	980	37,001 - 80,000	980
13,001 - 24,000	2	16,001 - 25,000	2	130,001 - 200,000	1,090	80,001 - 175,000	1,090
24,001 - 26,000	3	25,001 - 30,000	3	200,001 - 345,000	1,290	175,001 - 385,000	1,290
26,001 - 30,000	4	30,001 - 40,000	4	345,001 - 385,000	1,370	385,001 and over	1,540
30,001 - 42,000	5	40,001 - 50,000	5	385,001 and over	1,540		
42,001 - 48,000	6	50,001 - 70,000	6				
48,001 - 55,000	7	70,001 - 80,000	7				
55,001 - 65,000	8	80,001 - 95,000	8				
65,001 - 75,000	9	95,001 - 120,000	9				
75,001 - 85,000	10	120,001 and over	10				
85,001 - 97,000	11						
97,001 - 110,000	12						
110,001 - 120,000	13						
120,001 - 135,000	14						
135,001 and over	15						

Additional Instructions

Section references are to the Internal Revenue Code.

When should I complete the form? Complete Form W-4P and give it to the payer as soon as possible. Get Pub. 505, Tax Withholding and Estimated Tax, to see how the dollar amount you are having withheld compares to your projected total federal income tax for 2013. You also may use the IRS Withholding Calculator at *www.irs.gov/individuals* for help in determining how many withholding allowances to claim on your Form W-4P.

Multiple pensions/more-than-one income. To figure the number of allowances that you may claim, combine allowances and income subject to withholding from all sources on one worksheet. You may file a Form W-4P with each pension payer, but do not claim the same allowances more than once. Your withholding usually will be most accurate when all allowances are claimed on the Form W-4P for the highest source of income subject to withholding and zero allowances are claimed on the others.

Other income. If you have a large amount of income from other sources not subject to withholding (such as interest, dividends, or capital gains), consider making estimated tax payments using Form 1040-ES, Estimated Tax for Individuals. Call 1-800-TAX-FORM (1-800-829-3676) to get Form 1040-ES and Pub. 505. You also can get forms and publications at *www.irs.gov/formspubs.*

If you have income from wages, see Pub. 505 to find out if you should adjust your withholding on Form W-4 or Form W-4P.

Note. Social security and railroad retirement payments may be includible in income. See Form W-4V, Voluntary Withholding Request, for information on voluntary withholding from these payments.

Withholding From Pensions and Annuities

Generally, federal income tax withholding applies to the taxable part of payments made from pension, profit-sharing, stock bonus, annuity, and certain deferred compensation plans; from individual retirement arrangements (IRAs); and from commercial annuities. The method and rate of withholding depend on (a) the kind of payment you receive; (b) whether the payments are delivered outside the United States or its commonwealths and possessions; and (c) whether the recipient is a nonresident alien individual, a nonresident alien beneficiary, or a foreign estate. Qualified distributions from a Roth IRA are nontaxable and, therefore, not subject to withholding. See page 4 for special withholding rules that apply to payments outside the United States and payments to foreign persons.

Because your tax situation may change from year to year, you may want to refigure your withholding each year. You can change the amount to be withheld by using lines 2 and 3 of Form W-4P.

Choosing not to have income tax withheld. You (or in the event of death, your beneficiary or estate) can choose not to have federal income tax withheld from your payments by using line 1 of Form W-4P. For an estate, the election to have no income tax withheld may be made by the executor or personal representative of the decedent. Enter the estate's employer identification number (EIN) in the area reserved for "Your social security number" on Form W-4P.

You may not make this choice for eligible rollover distributions. See *Eligible rollover distribution—20% withholding* on page 4.

Caution. There are penalties for not paying enough federal income tax during the year, either through withholding or estimated tax payments. New retirees, especially, should see Pub. 505. It explains your estimated tax requirements and describes penalties in detail. You may be able to avoid quarterly estimated tax payments by having enough tax withheld from your pension or annuity using Form W-4P.

Periodic payments. Withholding from periodic payments of a pension or annuity is figured in the same manner as withholding from wages. Periodic payments are made in installments at regular intervals over a period of more than 1 year. They may be paid annually, quarterly, monthly, etc.

If you want federal income tax to be withheld, you must designate the number of withholding allowances on line 2 of Form W-4P and indicate your marital status by checking the appropriate box. Under current law, you cannot designate a specific dollar amount to be withheld. However, you can designate an additional amount to be withheld on line 3.

If you do not want any federal income tax withheld from your periodic payments, check the box on line 1 of Form W-4P and submit the form to your payer. However, see *Payments to Foreign Persons and Payments Outside the United States* on page 4.

Caution. If you do not submit Form W-4P to your payer, the payer must withhold on periodic payments as if you are married claiming three withholding allowances. Generally, this means that tax will be withheld if your pension or annuity is at least $1,680 a month.

If you submit a Form W-4P that does not contain your correct social security number (SSN), the payer must withhold as if you are single claiming zero withholding allowances even if you checked the box on line 1 to have no federal income tax withheld.

There are some kinds of periodic payments for which you cannot use Form W-4P because they are already defined as wages subject to federal income tax withholding. These payments include retirement pay for service in the U.S. Armed Forces and payments from certain nonqualified deferred compensation plans and deferred compensation plans described in section 457 of tax-exempt organizations. Your payer should be able to tell you whether Form W-4P applies.

For periodic payments, your Form W-4P stays in effect until you change or revoke it. Your payer must notify you each year of your right to choose not to have federal income tax withheld (if permitted) or to change your choice.

Nonperiodic payments—10% withholding. Your payer must withhold at a flat 10% rate from nonperiodic payments (but see *Eligible rollover distribution—20% withholding* on page 4) **unless** you choose not to have federal income tax withheld. Distributions from an IRA that are payable on demand are treated as nonperiodic payments. You can choose not to have federal income tax withheld from a nonperiodic payment (if permitted) by submitting Form W-4P (containing your correct SSN) to your payer and checking the box on line 1. Generally, your choice not to have federal income tax withheld will apply to any later payment from the same plan. You cannot use line 2 for nonperiodic payments. But you may use line 3 to specify an additional amount that you want withheld.

Caution. If you submit a Form W-4P that does not contain your correct SSN, the payer cannot honor your request not to have income tax withheld and must withhold 10% of the payment for federal income tax.

Eligible rollover distribution—20% withholding. Distributions you receive from qualified pension or annuity plans (for example, 401(k) pension plans and section 457(b) plans maintained by a governmental employer) or tax-sheltered annuities that are eligible to be rolled over tax free to an IRA or qualified plan are subject to a flat 20% federal withholding rate. The 20% withholding rate is required, and you cannot choose not to have income tax withheld from eligible rollover distributions. Do not give Form W-4P to your payer unless you want an additional amount withheld. Then, complete line 3 of Form W-4P and submit the form to your payer.

Note. The payer will not withhold federal income tax if the entire distribution is transferred by the plan administrator in a direct rollover to a traditional IRA or another eligible retirement plan (if allowed by the plan), such as a qualified pension plan, governmental section 457(b) plan, section 403(b) contract, or tax-sheltered annuity.

Distributions that are (a) required by law, (b) one of a specified series of equal payments, or (c) qualifying "hardship" distributions are **not** "eligible rollover distributions" and are not subject to the mandatory 20% federal income tax withholding. See Pub. 505 for details. See also *Nonperiodic payments—10% withholding* on page 3.

Changing Your "No Withholding" Choice

Periodic payments. If you previously chose not to have federal income tax withheld and you now want withholding, complete another Form W-4P and submit it to your payer. If you want federal income tax withheld at the rate set by law (married with three allowances), write "Revoked" next to the checkbox on line 1 of the form. If you want tax withheld at any different rate, complete line 2 on the form.

Nonperiodic payments. If you previously chose not to have federal income tax withheld and you now want withholding, write "Revoked" next to the checkbox on line 1 and submit Form W-4P to your payer.

Payments to Foreign Persons and Payments Outside the United States

Unless you are a nonresident alien, withholding (in the manner described above) is required on any periodic or nonperiodic payments that are delivered to you outside the United States or its possessions. You cannot choose not to have federal income tax withheld on line 1 of Form W-4P. See Pub. 505 for details.

In the absence of a tax treaty exemption, nonresident aliens, nonresident alien beneficiaries, and foreign estates generally are subject to a 30% federal withholding tax under section 1441 on the taxable portion of a periodic or nonperiodic pension or annuity payment that is from U.S. sources. However, most tax treaties provide that private pensions and annuities are exempt from withholding and tax. Also, payments from certain pension plans are exempt from withholding even if no tax treaty applies. See Pub. 515, Withholding of Tax on Nonresident Aliens and Foreign Entities, and Pub. 519, U.S. Tax Guide for Aliens, for details. A foreign person should submit Form W-8BEN, Certificate of Foreign Status of Beneficial Owner for United States Tax Withholding, to the payer before receiving any payments. The Form W-8BEN must contain the foreign person's taxpayer identification number (TIN).

Statement of Federal Income Tax Withheld From Your Pension or Annuity

By January 31 of next year, your payer will furnish a statement to you on Form 1099-R, Distributions From Pensions, Annuities, Retirement or Profit-Sharing Plans, IRAs, Insurance Contracts, etc., showing the total amount of your pension or annuity payments and the total federal income tax withheld during the year. If you are a foreign person who has provided your payer with Form W-8BEN, your payer instead will furnish a statement to you on Form 1042-S, Foreign Person's U.S. Source Income Subject to Withholding, by March 15 of next year.

Privacy Act and Paperwork Reduction Act Notice

We ask for the information on this form to carry out the Internal Revenue laws of the United States. You are required to provide this information only if you want to (a) request federal income tax withholding from periodic pension or annuity payments based on your withholding allowances and marital status, (b) request additional federal income tax withholding from your pension or annuity, (c) choose not to have federal income tax withheld, when permitted, or (d) change or revoke a previous Form W-4P. To do any of the aforementioned, you are required by sections 3405(e) and 6109 and their regulations to provide the information requested on this form. Failure to provide this information may result in inaccurate withholding on your payment(s). Providing false or fraudulent information may subject you to penalties.

Routine uses of this information include giving it to the Department of Justice for civil and criminal litigation, and to cities, states, the District of Columbia, and U.S. commonwealths and possessions for use in administering their tax laws. We may also disclose this information to other countries under a tax treaty, to federal and state agencies to enforce federal nontax criminal laws, or to federal law enforcement and intelligence agencies to combat terrorism.

You are not required to provide the information requested on a form that is subject to the Paperwork Reduction Act unless the form displays a valid OMB control number. Books or records relating to a form or its instructions must be retained as long as their contents may become material in the administration of any Internal Revenue law. Generally, tax returns and return information are confidential, as required by section 6103.

The average time and expenses required to complete and file this form will vary depending on individual circumstances. For estimated averages, see the instructions for your income tax return.

If you have suggestions for making this form simpler, we would be happy to hear from you. See the instructions for your income tax return.

Form **W-4S**

Department of the Treasury
Internal Revenue Service

Request for Federal Income Tax Withholding From Sick Pay

▶ **Give this form to the third-party payer of your sick pay.**
▶ **Information about Form W-4S is available at *www.irs.gov/w4s*.**

OMB No. 1545-0074

2013

Type or print your first name and middle initial.	Last name	Your social security number

Home address (number and street or rural route)

City or town, state, and ZIP code

Claim or identification number (if any) . . . .

I request federal income tax withholding from my sick pay payments. I want the following amount to be withheld from each payment. (See **Worksheet** below.) . . . . $

Employee's signature ▶   Date ▶

------------------------ **Separate here and give the top part of this form to the payer. Keep the lower part for your records.** ------------------------

Worksheet (Keep for your records. Do not send to the Internal Revenue Service.)

1	Enter amount of adjusted gross income that you expect in 2013	**1**	
2	If you plan to itemize deductions on Schedule A (Form 1040), enter the estimated total of your deductions. For 2013, you may have to reduce your itemized deductions if your income is over $300,000 and you are married filing jointly or are a qualifying widow(er); $275,000 if you are head of household; $250,000 if you are single and not head of household or a qualifying widow(er); or $150,000 if you are married filing separately. See Pub. 505 for details. If you do not plan to itemize deductions, enter the standard deduction. (See the instructions on page 2 for the standard deduction amount, including additional amounts for age and blindness.)	**2**	
3	Subtract line 2 from line 1	**3**	
4	Exemptions. Multiply $3,900 by the number of personal exemptions	**4**	
5	Subtract line 4 from line 3	**5**	
6	Tax. Figure your tax on line 5 by using the 2013 Tax Rate Schedule X, Y, or Z on page 2. Do not use the Tax Table or Tax Rate Schedule X, Y, or Z in the 2012 Form 1040, 1040A, or 1040EZ instructions	**6**	
7	Credits (child tax and higher education credits, credit for child and dependent care expenses, etc.)	**7**	
8	Subtract line 7 from line 6	**8**	
9	Estimated federal income tax withheld or to be withheld from other sources (including amounts withheld due to a prior Form W-4S) during 2013 or paid or to be paid with 2013 estimated tax payments	**9**	
10	Subtract line 9 from line 8	**10**	
11	Enter the number of sick pay payments you expect to receive this year to which this Form W-4S will apply . .	**11**	
12	Divide line 10 by line 11. Round to the nearest dollar. This is the amount that should be withheld from each sick pay payment. Be sure it meets the requirements for the amount that should be withheld, as explained under *Amount to be withheld* below. If it does, enter this amount on Form W-4S above	**12**	

General Instructions

Purpose of form. Give this form to the third-party payer of your sick pay, such as an insurance company, if you want federal income tax withheld from the payments. You are not required to have federal income tax withheld from sick pay paid by a third party. However, if you choose to request such withholding, Internal Revenue Code sections 3402(o) and 6109 and their regulations require you to provide the information requested on this form. Do not use this form if your employer (or its agent) makes the payments because employers are already required to withhold federal income tax from sick pay.

Note. If you receive sick pay under a collective bargaining agreement, see your union representative or employer.

Definition. Sick pay is a payment that you receive:

• Under a plan to which your employer is a party and

• In place of wages for any period when you are temporarily absent from work because of your sickness or injury.

Amount to be withheld. Enter on this form the amount that you want withheld from each payment. The amount that you enter:

• Must be in whole dollars (for example, $35, not $34.50).

• Must be at least $4 per day, $20 per week, or $88 per month based on your payroll period.

• Must not reduce the net amount of each sick pay payment that you receive to less than $10.

For payments larger or smaller than a regular full payment of sick pay, the amount withheld will be in the same proportion as your regular withholding from sick pay. For example, if your regular full payment of $100 a week normally has $25 (25%) withheld, then $20 (25%) will be withheld from a partial payment of $80.

Caution. You may be subject to a penalty if your tax payments during the year are not at least 90% of the tax shown on your tax return. For exceptions and details, see Pub. 505, Tax Withholding and Estimated Tax. You may pay tax during the year through withholding or estimated tax payments or both. To avoid a penalty, make sure that you have enough tax withheld or make estimated tax payments using Form 1040-ES, Estimated Tax for Individuals. You may estimate your federal income tax liability by using the worksheet above.

Sign this form. Form W-4S is not valid unless you sign it.

Statement of income tax withheld. After the end of the year, you will receive a Form W-2, Wage and Tax Statement, reporting the taxable sick pay paid and federal income tax withheld during the year. These amounts are reported to the Internal Revenue Service.

(continued on back)

For Paperwork Reduction Act Notice, see page 2.   Cat. No. 10226E   Form **W-4S** (2013)

Changing your withholding. Form W-4S remains in effect until you change or revoke it. You may do this by giving a new Form W-4S or a written notice to the payer of your sick pay. To revoke your previous Form W-4S, complete a new Form W-4S and write "Revoked" in the money amount box, sign it, and give it to the payer.

Specific Instructions for Worksheet

You may use the worksheet on page 1 to estimate the amount of federal income tax that you want withheld from each sick pay payment. Use your tax return for last year and the worksheet as a basis for estimating your tax, tax credits, and withholding for this year.

You may not want to use Form W-4S if you already have your total tax covered by estimated tax payments or other withholding.

If you expect to file a joint return, be sure to include the income, deductions, credits, and payments of both yourself and your spouse in figuring the amount you want withheld.

Caution. If any of the amounts on the worksheet change after you give Form W-4S to the payer, you should use a new Form W-4S to request a change in the amount withheld.

Line 2—Deductions

Itemized deductions. For 2013, you may have to reduce your itemized deductions if your income is over $300,000 and you are married filing jointly or are a qualifying widow(er); $275,000 if you are head of household; $250,000 if you are single and not head of household or a qualifying widow(er); or $150,000 if you are married filing separately. See Pub. 505 for details.

Standard deduction. For 2013, the standard deduction amounts are:

Filing Status	Standard Deduction
Married filing jointly or qualifying widow(er)	$12,200*
Head of household	$8,950*
Single or Married filing separately	$6,100*

*If you are age 65 or older or blind, add to the standard deduction amount the additional amount that applies to you as shown in the next paragraph. If you can be claimed as a dependent on another person's return, see *Limited standard deduction for dependents,* later.

Additional amount for the elderly or blind. An additional standard deduction of $1,200 is allowed for a married individual (filing jointly or separately) or qualifying widow(er) who is 65 or older or blind, $2,400 if 65 or older **and** blind. If both spouses are 65 or older or blind, an additional $2,400 is allowed on a joint return ($2,400 on a separate return if you can claim an exemption for your spouse). If both spouses are 65 or older **and** blind, an additional $4,800 is allowed on a joint return ($4,800 on a separate return if you can claim an exemption for your spouse). An additional $1,500 is allowed for an unmarried individual (single or head of household) who is 65 or older or blind, $3,000 if 65 or older **and** blind.

Limited standard deduction for dependents. If you can be claimed as a dependent on another person's return, your standard deduction is the greater of (a) $1,000 or (b) your earned income plus $350 (up to the regular standard deduction for your filing status). If you are 65 or older or blind, see Pub. 505 for additional amounts that you may claim.

Certain individuals not eligible for standard deduction. For the following individuals, the standard deduction is zero.

• A married individual filing a separate return if either spouse itemizes deductions.

• A nonresident alien individual.

• An individual filing a return for a period of less than 12 months because of a change in his or her annual accounting period.

Line 7—Credits

Include on this line any tax credits that you are entitled to claim, such as the child tax and higher education credits, credit for child and dependent care expenses, earned income credit, or credit for the elderly or the disabled.

Line 9—Tax Withholding and Estimated Tax

Enter the federal income tax that you expect will be withheld this year on income other than sick pay and any payments made or to be made with 2013 estimated tax payments. Include any federal income tax already withheld or to be withheld from wages and pensions.

2013 Tax Rate Schedules

Schedule X—Single

If line 5 is: Over—	But not over—	The tax is:	of the amount over—
$0	$8,925	$0 + 10%	$0
8,925	36,250	892.50 + 15%	8,925
36,250	87,850	4,991.25 + 25%	36,250
87,850	183,250	17,891.25 + 28%	87,850
183,250	398,350	44,603.25 + 33%	183,250
398,350	400,000	115,586.25 + 35%	398,350
400,000	and greater	116,163.75 + 39.6%	400,000

Schedule Z—Head of household

If line 5 is: Over—	But not over—	The tax is:	of the amount over—
$0	$12,750	$0 + 10%	$0
12,750	48,600	1,275 + 15%	12,750
48,600	125,450	6,652.50 + 25%	48,600
125,450	203,150	25,865 + 28%	125,450
203,150	398,350	47,621 + 33%	203,150
398,350	425,000	112,037 + 35%	398,350
425,000	and greater	121,394.50 + 39.6%	425,000

Schedule Y-1—Married filing jointly or Qualifying widow(er)

If line 5 is: Over—	But not over—	The tax is:	of the amount over—
$0	$17,850	$0 + 10%	$0
17,850	72,500	1,785 + 15%	17,850
72,500	146,400	9,982.50 + 25%	72,500
146,400	223,050	28,457.50 + 28%	146,400
223,050	398,350	49,919.50 + 33%	223,050
398,350	450,000	107,768 + 35%	398,350
450,000	and greater	125,846 + 39.6%	450,000

Schedule Y-2—Married filing separately

If line 5 is: Over—	But not over—	The tax is:	of the amount over—
$0	$8,925	$0 + 10%	$0
8,925	36,250	892.50 + 15%	8,925
36,250	73,200	4,991.25 + 25%	36,250
73,200	111,525	14,228.75 + 28%	73,200
111,525	199,175	24,959.75 + 33%	111,525
199,175	225,000	53,884.25 + 35%	199,175
225,000	and greater	62,923 + 39.6%	225,000

Paperwork Reduction Act Notice. We ask for the information on this form to carry out the Internal Revenue laws of the United States.

You are not required to provide the information requested on a form that is subject to the Paperwork Reduction Act unless the form displays a valid OMB control number. Books or records relating to a form or its instructions must be retained as long as their contents may become material in the administration of any Internal Revenue law. Generally, tax returns and return information are confidential, as required by Code section 6103.

The average time and expenses required to complete and file this form will vary depending on individual circumstances. For estimated averages, see the instructions for your income tax return.

If you have suggestions for making this form simpler, we would be happy to hear from you. See the instructions for your income tax return.

Form **W-7**	**Application for IRS Individual Taxpayer Identification Number**	
(Rev. January 2012) Department of the Treasury Internal Revenue Service	▶ For use by individuals who are not U.S. citizens or permanent residents. ▶ See instructions.	OMB No. 1545-0074

An IRS individual taxpayer identification number (ITIN) is for federal tax purposes only.

FOR IRS USE ONLY

Before you begin:

• **Do not submit** this form if you have, or are eligible to get, a U.S. social security number (SSN).

• *Getting an ITIN does not change your immigration status or your right to work in the United States and does not make you eligible for the earned income credit.*

Reason you are submitting Form W-7. Read the instructions for the box you check. **Caution:** If you check box **b, c, d, e, f,** or **g, you must file a tax return with Form W-7 unless you meet one of the exceptions** (see instructions).

- **a** ☐ Nonresident alien required to get ITIN to claim tax treaty benefit
- **b** ☐ Nonresident alien filing a U.S. tax return
- **c** ☐ U.S. resident alien **(based on days present in the United States)** filing a U.S. tax return
- **d** ☐ Dependent of U.S. citizen/resident alien ⎫ Enter name and SSN/ITIN of U.S. citizen/resident alien (see instructions) ▶ _____
- **e** ☐ Spouse of U.S. citizen/resident alien ⎭ _____
- **f** ☐ Nonresident alien student, professor, or researcher filing a U.S. tax return or claiming an exception
- **g** ☐ Dependent/spouse of a nonresident alien holding a U.S. visa
- **h** ☐ Other (see instructions) ▶ _____

Additional information for **a** and **f**: Enter treaty country ▶ _____ and treaty article number ▶ _____

Name (see instructions)	**1a** First name	Middle name	Last name
Name at birth if different . . ▶	**1b** First name	Middle name	Last name

Applicant's mailing address	**2** Street address, apartment number, or rural route number. **If you have a P.O. box, see separate instructions.**
	City or town, state or province, and country. Include ZIP code or postal code where appropriate.

Foreign (non-U.S.) address (if different from above) (see instructions)	**3** Street address, apartment number, or rural route number. **Do not use a P.O. box number.**
	City or town, state or province, and country. Include ZIP code or postal code where appropriate.

Birth information	**4** Date of birth (month / day / year)	Country of birth	City and state or province (optional)	**5** ☐ Male ☐ Female

Other information	**6a** Country(ies) of citizenship	**6b** Foreign tax I.D. number (if any)	**6c** Type of U.S. visa (if any), number, and expiration date

6d Identification document(s) submitted (see instructions) ☐ Passport ☐ Driver's license/State I.D.
☐ USCIS documentation ☐ Other _____

Date of entry into the United States (MM/DD/YYYY)

Issued by: _____ No.: _____ Exp. date: __ / __ / __   / /

6e Have you previously received a U.S. temporary taxpayer identification number (TIN) or employer identification number (EIN)?
☐ **No/Do not know.** Skip line 6f.
☐ **Yes.** Complete line 6f. If more than one, list on a sheet and attach to this form (see instructions).

6f Enter: TIN or EIN ▶ _____ and
Name under which it was issued ▶ _____

6g Name of college/university or company (see instructions) _____
City and state _____ Length of stay _____

Sign Here Keep a copy for your records.	Under penalties of perjury, I (applicant/delegate/acceptance agent) declare that I have examined this application, including accompanying documentation and statements, and to the best of my knowledge and belief, it is true, correct, and complete. I authorize the IRS to disclose to my acceptance agent returns or return information necessary to resolve matters regarding the assignment of my IRS individual taxpayer identification number (ITIN), including any previously assigned taxpayer identifying number.		
	▶ Signature of applicant (if delegate, see instructions)	Date (month / day / year) / /	Phone number
	▶ Name of delegate, if applicable (type or print)	Delegate's relationship to applicant ▶	☐ Parent ☐ Court-appointed guardian ☐ Power of Attorney

Acceptance Agent's Use ONLY	▶ Signature	Date (month / day / year) / /	Phone
			Fax
	▶ Name and title (type or print)	Name of company	EIN
			Office Code

For Paperwork Reduction Act Notice, see separate instructions.   Cat. No. 10229L   Form **W-7** (Rev. 1-2012)

Instructions for Form W-7

(Rev. January 2013)

Department of the Treasury
Internal Revenue Service

(Use with the January 2012 revision of Form W-7.)

Application for IRS Individual Taxpayer Identification Number

Section references are to the Internal Revenue Code unless otherwise noted.

Future Developments

For the latest information about developments related to Form W-7 and its instructions, such as legislation enacted after they were published, go to *www.irs.gov/w7*.

What's New

IRS will continue to accept only original identification documents or certified copies of these documents from the issuing agency with the Form W-7 and federal tax return to the ITIN office in Austin, Texas. Applicants can go to the ITIN page at *http://www.irs.gov/Individuals/Individual-Taxpayer-Identification-Number-(ITIN)* to get additional information.

General Instructions

Purpose of Form

Use Form W-7 to apply for an IRS individual taxpayer identification number (ITIN). An ITIN is a nine-digit number issued by the U.S. Internal Revenue Service (IRS) to individuals who are required for U.S. tax purposes to have a U.S. taxpayer identification number but who do not have and are not eligible to get a social security number (SSN).

The ITIN is for federal tax purposes only. An ITIN does not entitle you to social security benefits and does not change your immigration status or your right to work in the United States. Also, individuals filing tax returns using an ITIN are not eligible for the earned income credit (EIC).

SSNs. Do not complete Form W-7 if you have an SSN or you are eligible to get an SSN. You are eligible for an SSN if you are a U.S. citizen or if you have been admitted by the United States for permanent residence or U.S. employment.

To get an SSN, see Form SS-5, Application for a Social Security Card. To get Form SS-5 or to find out if you are eligible to get an SSN, go to *www.socialsecurity.gov* or contact a Social Security Administration (SSA) office.

If you have an application for an SSN pending, do not file Form W-7. Complete Form W-7 only if the SSA notifies you that an SSN cannot be issued.

If the SSA will not issue you an SSN, you must get a letter of denial and attach it to your Form W-7. This applies whether you are attaching Form W-7 to your federal tax return or requesting an ITIN under one of the exceptions. However, students, professors, and researchers, see information for box "f," later.

Who Must Apply

Any individual who is not eligible to get an SSN but who must furnish a taxpayer identification number must apply for an ITIN on Form W-7. Examples include the following.
* A nonresident alien individual eligible to get the benefit of reduced withholding under an income tax treaty. See Pub. 515, Withholding of Tax on Nonresident Aliens and Foreign Entities.
* A nonresident alien individual not eligible for an SSN who is required to file a U.S. tax return or who is filing a U.S. tax return only to claim a refund.

* A nonresident alien individual not eligible for an SSN who elects to file a joint U.S. tax return with a spouse who is a U.S. citizen or resident alien.
* A U.S. resident alien (based on the substantial presence test) who files a U.S. tax return but who is not eligible for an SSN. For information about the substantial presence test, see Pub. 519, U.S. Tax Guide for Aliens.
* An alien spouse claimed as an exemption on a U.S. tax return who is not eligible to get an SSN.
* An alien individual eligible to be claimed as a dependent on a U.S. tax return but who is not eligible to get an SSN. To determine if an alien individual is eligible to be claimed as a dependent on a U.S. tax return, see Pub. 501, Exemptions, Standard Deduction, and Filing Information, and Pub. 519.
* A nonresident alien student, professor, or researcher who is required to file a U.S. tax return but who is not eligible for an SSN, or who is claiming an exception to the tax return filing requirement.
* A dependent/spouse of a nonresident alien U.S. visa holder, who is not eligible for an SSN.

Deceased Taxpayers

When requesting an ITIN for a deceased taxpayer, the deceased must meet all of the requirements established to get an ITIN. Also, you must write "Deceased" across the top of the Form W-7 and attach the additional documentation shown in the following chart.

IF you are:	THEN you must attach:
The surviving spouse filing an original or amended joint return with your deceased spouse	• Form W-7, • A U.S. individual income tax return, • Documentation substantiating the identity and foreign status of the deceased, and • A copy of the certificate of death.
The court-appointed executor or administrator of the deceased's estate filing an original tax return on behalf of the deceased	• Form W-7, • A U.S. individual income tax return, • Documentation substantiating the identity and foreign status of the deceased*, and • A court certificate showing your appointment.
Neither the surviving spouse nor the court-appointed executor or administrator of the deceased's estate	• Form W-7, • A U.S. individual income tax return, • Documentation substantiating the identity and foreign status of the deceased*, • Form 1310 (if a refund is due), and • A copy of the certificate of death.

* If the Form W-7 is for a deceased individual under 18 years of age, one of the documents proving identity and/or foreign status must be a birth certificate, unless a passport is submitted.

ITIN not needed for Forms 4868, 1040-ES, or 1040-ES (NR). If you are filing an application for an extension of time to file using Form 4868, or making an estimated tax payment using Form 1040-ES or Form 1040-ES (NR), do not file Form W-7 with those forms. Enter "ITIN TO BE REQUESTED" wherever your

Dec 20, 2012   Cat. No. 54092G

SSN or ITIN is requested. An ITIN will be issued only after you file a tax return and meet all other requirements.

Additional Information

Publications. In addition to Pubs. 501, 515, and 519 mentioned earlier, see Pub. 1915, Understanding Your IRS Individual Taxpayer Identification Number (ITIN), for more information.

These publications are available free from the IRS. To order the publications, call 1-800-TAX-FORM (1-800-829-3676) if you are in the United States. If you have a foreign address, write to:

Internal Revenue Service
1201 N. Mitsubishi Motorway
Bloomington, IL 61705-6613

You also can get these publications at *www.irs.gov/ formspubs*.

Telephone help. If, after reading these instructions and our free publications, you are not sure how to complete your application or have additional questions, call 1-800-829-1040 if you are in the United States. If you are outside the United States, call 267-941-1000 (not a toll-free number) or contact our overseas offices in Beijing, Frankfurt, London, or Paris.

 You cannot electronically file (e-file) a return using an ITIN in the calendar year the ITIN is issued; however, you can e-file returns in the following years. For example, if you apply for and receive an ITIN in 2012, you may not e-file any tax return using that ITIN (including prior year returns) until 2013.

If you need to file multiple year returns, you can either attach them all to your Form W-7 and submit them to the IRS, or file just the tax return which is due and wait until you receive your ITIN to file your prior year returns on paper. However, no returns may be e-filed in the calendar year in which you receive the ITIN.

How To Apply

Your application must include all of the following.

1. Your completed Form W-7.

Note. If you submit a Form W-7, all later ITIN notices and correspondence that you receive will be in English. If you prefer to receive them in Spanish, please submit Form W-7(SP).

2. Your original, valid tax return(s) for which the ITIN is needed. Attach Form W-7 to the front of your tax return. If you are applying for more than one ITIN for the same tax return (such as for a spouse or dependent(s)), attach all Forms W-7 to the same tax return. After your Form W-7 has been processed, the IRS will assign an ITIN to the return and process the return.

 There are exceptions to the requirement to include a U.S. tax return. If you claim one of these exceptions, you must submit the documentation required instead of a tax return. See the Exceptions Tables, *later.*

3. The original documents, or certified copies of these documents from the issuing agency, that support the information provided on the Form W-7. The supporting documentation must be consistent with the applicant's information provided on Form W-7. For example, the name, date of birth, and country(ies) of citizenship must be the same as on Form W-7, lines 1a, 4, and 6a.

You can submit copies of original documents if you do any of the following.
- Have the copies certified by the issuing agency.
- Have the officers at U.S. Embassies and Consulates overseas provide certification and authentication services. Contact the Consular Section, American Citizens Services of the U.S.

embassy or consulate in advance to determine the hours of operation for these services.

 Original documents you submit will be returned to you at the mailing address shown on your Form W-7. You do not need to provide a return envelope. Applicants are permitted to include a prepaid Express Mail or courier envelope for faster return delivery of their documents. The IRS will then return the documents in the envelope provided by the applicant. If your original documents are not returned within 60 days, you can call the IRS (see Telephone help *above). If you will need your documents for any purpose within 60 days of submitting your ITIN application, you may wish to apply in person at an IRS Taxpayer Assistance Center. Designated Taxpayer Assistance Centers (TACs) will be able to validate passports and National ID documents and return those documents immediately. See IRS.gov for a list of these designated TACs. All other TACs are available for assistance in completing applications and will forward documents to Austin, Texas for processing. See* Where To Apply, *later.*

Proving your "foreign status" or "identity." If you submit an original valid passport (or a certified copy from the issuing agency), you do not need to submit any other documents to prove your "foreign status" or "identity." Otherwise, you must submit at least two of the documents listed in the chart below. The documents must be current*, verify your identity (that is, contain your name), and support your claim of foreign status. At least one document must contain your photograph, but a photograph is not required if documents are submitted for a dependent under age 14 (under age 18 if a student). Do not attach expired documents.

Note. Certified copies from the issuing agency of a passport must include the U.S. visa pages if a visa is required for your Form W-7 application.

*Current original documents are:
- Civil birth certificates—since civil birth certificates do not contain an expiration date, they are considered current at all times.
- Passports and national identification cards—these documents will be considered current only if their expiration date has not passed prior to the date the Form W-7 is submitted.
- Medical records—these documents will be accepted for dependents under 6 years of age. A medical record will consist only of a shot/immunization record which documents the patient's name and chronological dates of the patient's medical history and care. The medical record must contain the child's name, date of birth, and verifiable address. In addition, the medical record must document the name, address, and phone number of the doctor, hospital, or clinic where treatment was last administered. If this information is not printed on the medical record, the medical record must be accompanied by a dated letter providing the required information on official letterhead from the Federal authority, physician, hospital, or clinic that administered the latest care of the child. If a date of entry is required for the applicant, the medical record must be from a U.S. facility.
- School records—these documents are valid for dependents under the age of 14 (under age 18 if a student) and are considered current if they are for a school term no older than 12 months from the date of the W-7 application (e.g., January 2012–December 2012 for a January 2013 application). The school record consists of an official report card or transcript issued by the school or equivalent of a Ministry of Education and signed by the school or ministry official. The record must be dated and contain the student's name, course work with grades, date of grading period(s), and school name and address. If a date of entry is required for the applicant, the school record must be from a U.S. facility.

Supporting Documentation	Can be used to establish:	
	Foreign status	Identity
Passport (the only stand-alone document)	x	x
U.S. Citizenship and Immigration Services (USCIS) photo identification	x	x
Visa issued by U.S. Department of State	x	x
U.S. driver's license		x
U.S. military identification card		x
Foreign driver's license		x
Foreign military identification card	x	x
National identification card (must be current and contain name, photograph, address, date of birth, and expiration date)	x	x
U.S. state identification card		x
Foreign voter's registration card	x	x
Civil birth certificate	x*	x
Medical records (valid only for dependents under age 6)	x*	x
School records (valid only for dependents under age 14 (under age 18 if a student))	x*	x
* Can be used to establish foreign status only if they are foreign documents.		

Note. Original documentation submitted for a dependent must include a civil birth certificate (unless a passport is submitted).

Keep a copy of your application for your records.

When To Apply

Complete and attach Form W-7 when you file the tax return for which the ITIN is needed. However, if you meet one of the exceptions described later under *h. Other*, complete and submit Form W-7 as soon as possible after you determine you are covered by that exception.

Allow 6 weeks for the IRS to notify you of your ITIN (8 to 10 weeks if you submit documents during peak processing periods (January 15 through April 30) or if you are filing from overseas). If you have not received your ITIN or correspondence at the end of that time, you can call the IRS to find out the status of your application (see *Telephone help,* earlier).

 You cannot electronically file (e-file) a return using an ITIN in the calendar year the ITIN is issued; however, you can e-file returns in the following years. For example, if you apply for and receive an ITIN in 2012, you may not e-file any tax return using that ITIN (including prior year returns) until 2013.

If you need to file multiple year returns, you can either attach them all to your Form W-7 and submit them to the IRS, or file just the tax return which is due and wait until you receive your ITIN to file your prior year returns on paper. However, no returns may be e-filed in the calendar year in which you receive the ITIN.

Where To Apply

By mail. Mail Form W-7, your tax return (or other documents required by an exception), and the documentation described in item (3) and listed in the chart under *How To Apply,* earlier to:

    Internal Revenue Service
    ITIN Operation
    P.O. Box 149342
    Austin, TX 78714-9342

 Do not use the mailing address in the instructions for your tax return.

Private delivery services. If you use a private delivery service to submit your Form W-7, use the following address:

    Internal Revenue Service
    ITIN Operation
    Mail Stop 6090-AUSC
    3651 S. Interregional, Hwy 35
    Austin, TX 78741-0000

In person. You can apply for an ITIN by bringing your completed forms and documentation to any IRS Taxpayer Assistance Center in the United States or IRS office abroad. Designated IRS Taxpayer Assistance Centers will be able to verify passports and National ID documents and return them immediately. Information on our overseas offices can be found in Pub. 1915 or at IRS.gov.

Through acceptance agent. You also can apply through an acceptance agent authorized by the IRS. An acceptance agent can help you complete and file Form W-7. To get a list of agents, visit IRS.gov and enter "*acceptance agent program*" in the search box at the top of the page.

Specific Instructions

If you are completing this form for someone else, answer the questions as they apply to that person.

Reason For Applying

You must check the box to indicate the reason you are completing Form W-7. If more than one box applies to you, check the box that best explains your reason for submitting Form W-7.

Note. If you check box "a" or "f," then box "h" may also be checked. If applicable, you also must enter the treaty country and treaty article. For more information on treaties, see Pub. 901, U.S. Tax Treaties.

a. Nonresident alien required to get an ITIN to claim tax treaty benefit. Certain nonresident aliens must get an ITIN to claim a tax treaty benefit even if they do not have to file a U.S. tax return. If you check this box to claim the benefits of a U.S. income tax treaty with a foreign country, also check box h. On the dotted line next to box h, enter the appropriate designation for Exception 1 or 2, whichever applies (see *Exception 1* and *Exception 2,* later). Identify the exception by its number, alpha subsection, and category under which you are applying (for example, enter "Exception 1d-Pension Income" or "Exception 2d-Gambling Winnings"). Also, enter the name of the treaty country and treaty article number in the appropriate entry spaces below box h and attach the documents required under whichever exception applies. For more details on tax treaties, see Pub. 901.

b. Nonresident alien filing a U.S. tax return. This category includes:
• A nonresident alien who must file a U.S. tax return to report income effectively or not effectively connected with the conduct of a trade or business in the United States, and
• A nonresident alien who is filing a U.S. tax return only to get a refund.

c. U.S. resident alien (based on days present in the United States) filing a U.S. tax return. A foreign individual living in the United States who does not have permission to work from the USCIS, and is thus ineligible for an SSN, may still be required to file a U.S. tax return. These individuals must check this box.

d. Dependent of a U.S. citizen/resident alien. This is an individual who can be claimed as a dependent on a U.S. tax return and is not eligible to get an SSN.

Note. If you live abroad and requested an Adoption Taxpayer Identification Number (ATIN) for a foreign child you adopted or who has been legally placed in your home pending adoption and that request was denied, your dependent may be eligible for an ITIN. When submitting your Form W-7, ensure you include a copy of the legal documents verifying your relationship to the child.

e. Spouse of a U.S. citizen/resident alien. This category includes:
• A resident or nonresident alien husband or wife who is not filing a U.S. tax return (including a joint return) and who is not eligible to get an SSN but who, as a spouse, is claimed as an exemption, and
• A resident or nonresident alien electing to file a U.S. tax return jointly with a spouse who is a U.S. citizen or resident alien.

f. Nonresident alien student, professor, or researcher filing a U.S. tax return or claiming an exception. This is an individual who has not abandoned his or her residence in a foreign country and who is a bona fide student, professor, or researcher coming temporarily to the United States solely to attend classes at a recognized institution of education, to teach, or to perform research.

If you check this box, you must complete lines 6c and 6g and provide your passport with a valid U.S. visa. If you are present in the United States on a work-related visa (F-1, J-1, or M-1), but will not be employed (that is, your presence in the United States is study-related), you can choose to attach a letter from the Designated School Official or Responsible Officer instead of applying with the SSA for an SSN. The letter must clearly state that you will not be securing employment while in the United States and your presence here is solely study-related. This letter can be submitted instead of a Social Security denial letter if you are filing a tax return with this Form W-7 or claiming Exception 2 (explained later).

Nonresident alien students and exchange visitors and their dependents under the Student Exchange Visitors Program (SEVP) can have their original ID certified by a SEVP-approved institution rather than mailing originals to the IRS. These are individuals admitted to the U.S. under an F, J, or M visa who receive taxable scholarships, fellowships or other grants. See IRS.gov for the procedures.

If you check this box to claim an exception under the benefits of a U.S. income tax treaty with a foreign country, also check box h. On the dotted line next to box h, enter the appropriate designation for Exception 2, explained later. Identify the exception by its number, alpha subsection, and category under which you are applying (for example, enter "Exception 2b-Scholarship Income and claiming tax treaty benefits" or "Exception 2c-Scholarship Income"). Also, enter the name of the treaty country and the treaty article number in the appropriate entry spaces below box h (if applicable) and attach the documents required under Exception 2.

g. Dependent/spouse of a nonresident alien holding a U.S. visa. This is an individual who can be claimed as a dependent or a spouse on a U.S. tax return, who is unable, or not eligible, to get an SSN, and who has entered the United States with a nonresident alien who holds a U.S. visa. If you apply for an ITIN under this category, remember to attach a copy of your visa to your Form W-7.

h. Other. If the reason for your ITIN request is not described in boxes a through g, check this box. Describe in detail your reason for requesting an ITIN and attach supporting documents.

Frequently, third parties (such as banks and other financial institutions) that are subject to information reporting and withholding requirements will request an ITIN from you to enable them to file information returns required by law. If you are requesting an ITIN for this reason, you may be able to claim one of the exceptions described later. Enter on the dotted line next to box h the exception that applies to you. Identify the exception by its number, alpha subsection (if applicable), and category under which you are applying (for example, enter "Exception 1a-Partnership Interest" or "Exception 3-Mortgage Interest"). Examples of completed Forms W-7 can be found in Pub. 1915. You will not need to attach a tax return to your Form W-7.

Exception 1. Passive income—third party withholding or tax treaty benefits. This exception may apply if you are the recipient of partnership income, interest income, annuity income, rental income, or other passive income that is subject to third party withholding or covered by tax treaty benefits. See the *Exceptions Tables*, later, for more details on Exception 1.

Information returns applicable to Exception 1 may include the following.
• Form 1042-S, Foreign Person's U.S. Source Income Subject to Withholding.
• Form 1099-INT, Interest Income.
• Form 8805, Foreign Partner's Information Statement of Section 1446 Withholding Tax.
• Schedule K-1 (Form 1065), Partner's Share of Income, Deductions, Credits, etc.

 Applicants receiving compensation for personal services performed in the United States, or issued a U.S. visa that is valid for employment, should first apply for an SSN with the SSA. You are not eligible for an ITIN if you are eligible to get an SSN.

 If you are required to file a tax return, then you are not eligible for this exception.

Exception 2. Other income. This exception may apply if:
1. You are claiming the benefits of a U.S. income tax treaty with a foreign country and you receive any of the following:
    a. Wages, salary, compensation, and honoraria payments,
    b. Scholarships, fellowships, and grants, or
    c. Gambling income, or
2. You are receiving taxable scholarship, fellowship, or grant income, but not claiming the benefits of an income tax treaty.

See the *Exceptions Tables*, later, for more details on Exception 2. Information returns applicable to Exception 2 may include Form 1042-S.

Exception 3. Mortgage interest—third party reporting. This exception may apply if you have a home mortgage loan on real property you own in the United States that is subject to third party reporting of mortgage interest. See the *Exceptions Tables*, later, for more details on Exception 3. Information returns applicable to Exception 3 may include Form 1098, Mortgage Interest Statement.

Exception 4. Dispositions by a foreign person of U.S. real property interest—third party withholding. This exception may apply if you are a party to a disposition of a U.S. real property interest by a foreign person, which is generally subject to withholding by the transferee or buyer (withholding agent). See the *Exceptions Tables*, later, for more details on Exception 4.

Information returns applicable to Exception 4 may include the following.
- Form 8288, U.S. Withholding Tax Return for Dispositions by Foreign Persons of U.S. Real Property Interests.
- Form 8288-A, Statement of Withholding on Dispositions by Foreign Persons of U.S. Real Property Interests.
- Form 8288-B, Application for Withholding Certificate for Dispositions by Foreign Persons of U.S. Real Property Interests.

Exception 5. Treasury Decision (TD) 9363. This exception may apply if you have an IRS reporting requirement under TD 9363 and are submitting Form W-7 with Form 13350. See the *Exceptions Tables*, later, for more details on Exception 5.

Line Instructions

Enter "N/A" (not applicable) on all lines that do not apply to you. **Do not** leave any lines blank.

Line 1a. Enter your legal name on line 1a as it appears on your documents. This entry should reflect your name as it will appear on a U.S. tax return.

 Your ITIN will be established using this name. If you do not use this name on the U.S. tax return, the processing of the U.S. tax return may be delayed.

Line 1b. Enter your name as it appears on your birth certificate if it is different from your entry on line 1a.

Line 2. Enter your complete mailing address on line 2. This is the address the IRS will use to return your original documents and send written notification of your ITIN.

Note. If the U.S. Postal Service will not deliver mail to your physical location, enter the U.S. Postal Service's post office box number for your mailing address. Contact your local U.S. Post Office for more information. Do not use a post office box owned and operated by a private firm or company.

Line 3. Enter your complete foreign (non-U.S.) address in the country where you permanently or normally reside if it is different from the address on line 2. If you no longer have a permanent residence, due to your relocation to the United States, enter only the foreign country where you last resided on line 3. If you are claiming a benefit under an income tax treaty with the United States, line 3 must show the treaty country.

 Do not use a post office box or an "in care of" (c/o) address instead of a street address on line 2 if you are entering just a "country" name on line 3. If you do, your application may be rejected.

Line 4. To be eligible for an ITIN, your birth country must be recognized as a foreign country by the U.S. Department of State.

Line 6a. Enter the country or countries (in the case of dual citizenship) in which you are a citizen. Enter the complete country name; do not abbreviate.

Line 6b. If your country of residence for tax purposes has issued you a tax identification number, enter that number on line 6b. For example, if you are a resident of Canada, enter your Canadian Social Security number.

Line 6c. Enter only U.S. nonimmigrant visa information. Include the USCIS classification, number of the U.S. visa, and the expiration date in month/day/year format. For example, if you have an F-1/F-2 visa with the number 123456 that has an expiration date of December 31, 2012, enter "F-1/F-2,""123456," and "12/31/2012" in the entry space. Individuals in possession of an I-20/I-94 document(s) should attach a copy to their Form W-7.

Line 6d. Check the box indicating the type of document(s) you are submitting to prove your foreign status and identity. You

must submit documents as explained in item (3) under *How To Apply*, earlier. Enter the name of the state or country or other issuer, the identification number (if any) appearing on the document(s), the expiration date, and the date on which you entered the United States. Dates must be entered in the month/day/year format. Also, you may later be required to provide a certified translation of foreign language documents.

Note. If you are submitting a passport, or a certified copy from the issuing agency, no other documentation is required to prove your "foreign status" or "identity," but ensure any visa information shown on the passport is entered on line 6c and the pages of the passport showing the U.S. visa (if a visa is required for your Form W-7) are included with your Form W-7. However, if you are submitting more than one document, enter only the information for the first document on this line. Attach a separate sheet showing the required information for the additional document(s). On the separate sheet, be sure to write your name and "Form W-7" at the top.

 The "Entry date in United States" must contain the complete date on which you entered the country for the purpose for which you are requesting an ITIN (if applicable). If you have never entered the United States, enter "Never entered the United States" on this line.

Example. You entered the United States on June 1, 2011, to visit. You returned home on July 1, 2011. You then entered the United States on August 1, 2012, to work for Company X. You want to file a return for the income you earned in the United States in 2012. You are not eligible to get a social security number. You file Form W-7 with your 2012 return. Enter "08/01/2012" on line 6d of Form W-7.

Line 6e. If you ever received a temporary taxpayer identification number (TIN) or an employer identification number (EIN), check the "Yes" box and complete line 6f. If you never had a temporary TIN or an EIN, or you do not know your temporary TIN, check the "No/Do not know" box.

A temporary TIN is a nine-digit number issued by the IRS to persons who file a return or make a payment without providing a TIN. You would have been issued this number if you filed a U.S. tax return and did not have a social security number. This temporary TIN will appear on any correspondence the IRS sent you concerning that return.

An EIN is a nine-digit number (for example, 12-3456789) assigned by the IRS to businesses, such as sole proprietorships.

Line 6f. If you have both a temporary TIN and an EIN, attach a separate sheet listing both. If you were issued more than one temporary TIN, attach a separate sheet listing all the temporary TINs you received. On the separate sheet, be sure to write your name and "Form W-7" at the top.

Line 6g. If you checked reason f, you must enter the name of the educational institution and the city and state in which it is located. You also must enter your length of stay in the United States.

If you are temporarily in the United States for business purposes, you must enter the name of the company with whom you are conducting your business and the city and state in which it is located. You also must enter your length of stay in the United States.

Signature

Who Can Sign the Form W-7

Generally, the applicant is required to sign Form W-7. The following are exceptions to this requirement.

Applicant is a dependent under 18 years of age. If the applicant is a dependent under 18 years of age, his or her parent or court-appointed guardian can sign if the child cannot. The parent or court-appointed guardian must type or print his or her name in the space provided and check the appropriate box that indicates his or her relationship to the applicant. If the individual is signing as a court-appointed guardian, a copy of the court-appointment papers showing the legal guardianship must be attached.

Adults, other than a parent or court-appointed guardian, can sign the Form W-7 only if a Form 2848, Power of Attorney and Declaration of Representative, has been signed by a parent or court-appointed guardian authorizing the individual to sign for the applicant.

Applicant is a dependent 18 years of age or older. If the applicant is 18 years of age or older, the applicant can sign or can appoint his or her parent, a court-appointed guardian, or another individual to sign. The person signing, if other than the applicant, must type or print his or her name in the space provided, check the appropriate box that indicates his or her relationship to the applicant, and attach a Form 2848.

Note. All Powers of Attorney (POA) submitted to the IRS must be in English. Any POAs received in a foreign language will be considered invalid unless accompanied by a certified English translation. The POA must clearly state the purpose for which it is intended under the "tax matters" section. For more information, go to IRS.gov.

Acceptance Agent's Use ONLY

Enter the 8-digit office code that was issued to you by the ITIN Program Office.

Paperwork Reduction Act Notice. We ask for the information on this form to carry out the Internal Revenue laws of the United States. You are required to give us the information. We need it to ensure that you are complying with these laws and to allow us to figure and collect the right amount of tax.

You are not required to provide the information requested on a form that is subject to the Paperwork Reduction Act unless the form displays a valid OMB control number. Books or records relating to a form or its instructions must be retained as long as their contents may become material in the administration of any Internal Revenue law. Generally, tax returns and return information are confidential, as required by Internal Revenue Code section 6103.

The average time and expenses required to complete and file this form will vary depending on individual circumstances. For the estimated averages, see the instructions for your income tax return.

If you have suggestions for making this form simpler, we would be happy to hear from you. See the instructions for your income tax return.

Exceptions Tables

Exception #1
Note. Federal tax withholding and/or information reporting must take place within the current tax year.

Third Party Withholding on Passive Income	**Persons who are eligible to claim Exception 1 include:**	**Documentation you must submit if you are eligible to claim Exception 1:**
	1(a) Individuals who are partners of a U.S. or foreign partnership that invests in the United States and that owns assets that generate income subject to IRS information reporting and federal tax withholding requirements; or	**1(a)** A copy of the portion of the partnership or LLC agreement displaying the partnership's employer identification number and showing that you are a partner in the partnership that is conducting business in the United States.
	1(b) Individuals who have opened an interest-bearing bank deposit account that generates income that is effectively connected with their U.S. trade or business and is subject to IRS information reporting and/or federal tax withholding; or	**1(b)** A signed letter from the bank on its official letterhead, displaying your name and stating that you have opened a business account that is subject to IRS information reporting and/or federal tax withholding on the interest generated during the current tax year.
	1(c) Individuals who are "resident aliens" for tax purposes and have opened an interest-bearing bank deposit account that generates income subject to IRS information reporting and/or federal tax withholding; or	**1(c)** A signed letter from the bank on its official letterhead, displaying your name and stating that you have opened an individual deposit account that is subject to IRS information reporting and/or federal tax withholding on the interest generated during the current tax year.
	1(d) Individuals who are receiving distributions during the current tax year of income such as pensions, annuities, rental income, royalties, dividends, etc., and are required to provide an ITIN to the withholding agent (for example, an investment company, insurance company, or financial institution, etc.) for the purposes of tax withholding and/or reporting requirements.	**1(d)** A signed letter or document from the withholding agent, on official letterhead, showing your name and verifying that an ITIN is required to make distributions to you during the current tax year that are subject to IRS information reporting or federal tax withholding.

Form W-7 (Rev. January 2013)

A-103

Exception #2		
Note. Federal tax withholding and/or information reporting must take place within the current tax year.		
2(a). Wages, Salary, Compensation, and Honoraria Payments *Claiming the benefits of a tax treaty*	**Persons who are eligible to claim Exception 2(a) include:**	**Documentation you must submit if you are eligible to claim Exception 2(a):**
	Individuals claiming the benefits of a tax treaty who: • are either exempt or subject to a reduced rate of withholding of tax on their wages, salary, compensation, and honoraria payments, **and** • will be submitting Form 8233 to the payer of the income.	• A letter of employment from the payer of the income, or • A copy of the employment contract, or • A letter requesting your presence for a speaking engagement, etc. **along with:** • Evidence (information) on the Form W-7 that you are entitled to claim the benefits of a tax treaty, and • A copy of the completed withholding agent's portion of Form 8233 attached to the Form W-7, and a letter from the Social Security Administration (SSA)*, stating that you are ineligible to receive a social security number. *If you are present in the United States and are receiving honoraria payments, you **do not** have to get a letter of denial from the SSA. A letter from the authorized school official stating the purpose of the visit and that the individual will be receiving payment in the form of an honoraria will be enough.

Exceptions Tables (continued)

Exception #2 (continued)		
Note. Federal tax withholding and/or information reporting must take place within the current tax year.		
2(b). **Scholarships,** **Fellowships, and** **Grants** *Claiming the* *benefits of a tax* *treaty*	**Persons who are eligible to claim Exception 2(b) include:** Individuals claiming the benefits of a tax treaty who: • are either exempt from or subject to a reduced rate of tax on their income from scholarships, fellowships, or grants (that is, foreign students, scholars, professors, researchers, foreign visitors, or any other individual), **and** • will be submitting Form W-8BEN to the withholding agent. **Note.** Student and Exchange Visitor Program (SEVP)-approved institutions for non-resident alien students and exchange visitors and their dependents classified under section 101(a)(15)(F), (M), or (J) of the Immigration and Nationality Act {8 U.S.C. 1101(a)(15)(F), (M), or (J)}: A certification letter is required for each Form W-7 application: primary, associated secondary (spouse), and dependent(s).¹	**Documentation you must submit if you are eligible to claim Exception 2(b):** • A letter or official notification from the college or university awarding the noncompensatory scholarship, fellowship, or grant; or • A copy of a contract with a college, university, or educational institution; **along with:** • A copy of your passport showing the valid visa issued by the U.S. Department of State, • Evidence (information) on the Form W-7 that you are entitled to claim the benefits of a tax treaty, • A copy of the W-8BEN that was submitted to the withholding agent, and • A letter from the Social Security Administration* stating that you are ineligible to receive a social security number (SSN). ¹The certification letter from a SEVP-approved institution serves as a substitute for submission of original supporting identification documents with the Form W-7. The certification letter must: • Be on original, official college, university, or institution letterhead with a verifiable address • Provide the applicant's full name and Student Exchange Visitor's Information System (SEVIS) number • Certify the applicant's registration in SEVIS • Certify that the student presented an unexpired passport, visa, or other identification documents for review • List the identification documents provided to verify identity and foreign status • Be signed and dated by a SEVIS official: Principal Designated School Official (PDSO), Designated School Official (DSO), Responsible Officer (RO), or Alternate Responsible Officer (ARO) of a certified school exchange program with a verifiable contact telephone number • Attach copies of documents used to verify the applicant's identity and foreign status from the approved list of documents presented in the Form W-7 instructions (passport must include copy of valid visa issued by the U.S. Department of State) • Attach a copy of DS-2019, Certificate of Eligibility for Exchange Visitor Status (J-1 status) and/or a copy of the I-20, Certificate of Eligibility for Non-Immigrant Student Status • Attach a copy of the Form W-8 BEN submitted to the withholding agent • Form W-7 must include the treaty country and article number that supports claiming a tax treaty benefit • Include a letter from the DSO or RO stating that the applicant will not be securing employment in the U.S. or receiving any type of income from personal services. *If you are a student on an F-1, J-1, or M-1 visa who will not be working while studying in the United States, you will not have to apply for an SSN. You will be permitted to provide a letter from the Designated School Official or Responsible Officer stating that you will not be securing employment in the United States or receiving any type of income from personal services.
2(c). **Scholarships,** **Fellowships, and** **Grants** *Not claiming* *benefits of a tax* *treaty*	**Persons who are eligible to claim Exception 2(c) include:** Individuals receiving noncompensatory income from scholarships, fellowships, or grants (that is, foreign students, scholars, professors, researchers, or any other individual) that is subject to IRS information reporting and/or withholding requirements during the current year.	**Documentation you must submit if you are eligible to claim Exception 2(c):** • A letter or official notification from the educational institution (that is, college or university) awarding the noncompensatory scholarship, fellowship, or grant; or • A copy of a contract with a college, university, or educational institution; **along with:** • A copy of your passport showing the valid visa issued by the U.S. Department of State, • A letter from the Designated School Official (DSO) or Responsible Officer (RO) stating that you are receiving noncompensatory income from scholarships, fellowships, or grants that is subject to IRS information reporting and/or federal tax withholding requirements during the current year (this letter must be attached to your Form W-7 or your application for an ITIN will be denied), and • A letter from the Social Security Administration* stating that you are ineligible to receive a social security number (SSN). *If you are a student on an F-1, J-1, or M-1 visa who will not be working while studying in the United States, you will not have to apply for an SSN. You will be permitted to provide a letter from the DSO or RO stating that you will not be securing employment in the United States or receiving any type of income from personal services.

Form W-7 (Rev. January 2013)

Exceptions Tables (continued)

Exception #2 (continued)		
Note. Federal tax withholding and/or information reporting must take place within the current tax year.		
2(d). Gambling Income *Claiming the benefits of a tax treaty*	**Persons who are eligible to claim Exception 2(d) include:** Nonresident aliens visiting the United States who: • have gambling winnings, • are claiming the benefits of a tax treaty for an exempt or reduced rate of federal tax withholding on that income, and • will be utilizing the services of a gaming official as an IRS ITIN Acceptance Agent.	**Documentation you must submit if you are eligible to claim Exception 2(d):** Your W-7, which must be submitted through the services of an appropriate gaming official serving as an IRS ITIN Acceptance Agent to apply for an ITIN under Exception 2(d). **Note.** If you do not secure the services of a gaming official, you may still file Form 1040NR at the end of the tax year with a Form W-7, attaching a copy of Form 1042-S displaying the amount of tax withheld. Your 1040NR return also should display the tax treaty article number and country under which you are claiming the treaty benefits.

Exception #3	
Note. Federal tax withholding and/or information reporting must take place within the current tax year.	
Third Party Reporting of Mortgage Interest	If you are eligible to claim Exception 3, you must submit documentation showing evidence of a home mortgage loan. This would include a copy of the contract of sale or similar documentation showing evidence of a home mortgage loan on real property located in the United States.

Exception #4	
Note. Federal tax withholding and/or information reporting must take place within the current tax year.	
Third Party Withholding—Disposition by a Foreign Person of U.S. Real Property Interest	A withholding obligation generally is imposed on a buyer or other transferee (withholding agent) when the buyer acquires a U.S. real property interest from a foreign person. In some instances, the foreign person may apply for a withholding certificate to reduce or eliminate withholding on the disposition of real property. If you are eligible to claim Exception 4, you must submit: • A completed Form 8288-B, and • A copy of the sale contract. **Note.** For the seller of the property, copies of Forms 8288 and 8288-A submitted by the buyer should be attached to Form W-7.

Exception #5	
Note. Federal tax withholding and/or information reporting must take place within the current tax year.	
Reporting obligations under TD 9363	If you are eligible to claim Exception 5, you must submit Form W-7 and Form 13350 along with a letter from your employer on corporate letterhead stating you have been designated as the person responsible for ensuring compliance with IRS information reporting requirements.

Form **W-8BEN**
(Rev. February 2006)
Department of the Treasury
Internal Revenue Service

Certificate of Foreign Status of Beneficial Owner for United States Tax Withholding
▶ Section references are to the Internal Revenue Code. ▶ See separate instructions.
▶ Give this form to the withholding agent or payer. Do not send to the IRS.

OMB No. 1545-1621

Do not use this form for:	Instead, use Form:
• A U.S. citizen or other U.S. person, including a resident alien individual	W-9
• A person claiming that income is effectively connected with the conduct of a trade or business in the United States	W-8ECI
• A foreign partnership, a foreign simple trust, or a foreign grantor trust (see instructions for exceptions)	W-8ECI or W-8IMY
• A foreign government, international organization, foreign central bank of issue, foreign tax-exempt organization, foreign private foundation, or government of a U.S. possession that received effectively connected income or that is claiming the applicability of section(s) 115(2), 501(c), 892, 895, or 1443(b) (see instructions)	W-8ECI or W-8EXP

Note: *These entities should use Form W-8BEN if they are claiming treaty benefits or are providing the form only to claim they are a foreign person exempt from backup withholding.*

• A person acting as an intermediary	W-8IMY

Note: *See instructions for additional exceptions.*

Part I Identification of Beneficial Owner (See instructions.)

1 Name of individual or organization that is the beneficial owner

2 Country of incorporation or organization

3 Type of beneficial owner: ☐ Individual ☐ Corporation ☐ Disregarded entity ☐ Partnership ☐ Simple trust
☐ Grantor trust ☐ Complex trust ☐ Estate ☐ Government ☐ International organization
☐ Central bank of issue ☐ Tax-exempt organization ☐ Private foundation

4 Permanent residence address (street, apt. or suite no., or rural route). **Do not use a P.O. box or in-care-of address.**

City or town, state or province. Include postal code where appropriate.

Country (do not abbreviate)

5 Mailing address (if different from above)

City or town, state or province. Include postal code where appropriate.

Country (do not abbreviate)

6 U.S. taxpayer identification number, if required (see instructions)
☐ SSN or ITIN ☐ EIN

7 Foreign tax identifying number, if any (optional)

8 Reference number(s) (see instructions)

Part II Claim of Tax Treaty Benefits (if applicable)

9 I certify that (check all that apply):

a ☐ The beneficial owner is a resident of _____ within the meaning of the income tax treaty between the United States and that country.

b ☐ If required, the U.S. taxpayer identification number is stated on line 6 (see instructions).

c ☐ The beneficial owner is not an individual, derives the item (or items) of income for which the treaty benefits are claimed, and, if applicable, meets the requirements of the treaty provision dealing with limitation on benefits (see instructions).

d ☐ The beneficial owner is not an individual, is claiming treaty benefits for dividends received from a foreign corporation or interest from a U.S. trade or business of a foreign corporation, and meets qualified resident status (see instructions).

e ☐ The beneficial owner is related to the person obligated to pay the income within the meaning of section 267(b) or 707(b), and will file Form 8833 if the amount subject to withholding received during a calendar year exceeds, in the aggregate, $500,000.

10 **Special rates and conditions** (if applicable—see instructions): The beneficial owner is claiming the provisions of Article _____ of the treaty identified on line 9a above to claim a _____ % rate of withholding on (specify type of income): _____ .
Explain the reasons the beneficial owner meets the terms of the treaty article: _____
_____

Part III Notional Principal Contracts

11 ☐ I have provided or will provide a statement that identifies those notional principal contracts from which the income is **not** effectively connected with the conduct of a trade or business in the United States. I agree to update this statement as required.

Part IV Certification

Under penalties of perjury, I declare that I have examined the information on this form and to the best of my knowledge and belief it is true, correct, and complete. I further certify under penalties of perjury that:
1 I am the beneficial owner (or am authorized to sign for the beneficial owner) of all the income to which this form relates,
2 The beneficial owner is not a U.S. person,
3 The income to which this form relates is (a) not effectively connected with the conduct of a trade or business in the United States, (b) effectively connected but is not subject to tax under an income tax treaty, or (c) the partner's share of a partnership's effectively connected income, **and**
4 For broker transactions or barter exchanges, the beneficial owner is an exempt foreign person as defined in the instructions.
Furthermore, I authorize this form to be provided to any withholding agent that has control, receipt, or custody of the income of which I am the beneficial owner or any withholding agent that can disburse or make payments of the income of which I am the beneficial owner.

Sign Here ▶

_____   _____   _____
Signature of beneficial owner (or individual authorized to sign for beneficial owner)   Date (MM-DD-YYYY)   Capacity in which acting

For Paperwork Reduction Act Notice, see separate instructions.   Cat. No. 25047Z   Form **W-8BEN** (Rev. 2-2006)

✿ *Printed on Recycled Paper*

Instructions for Form W-8BEN

Department of the Treasury
Internal Revenue Service

(Rev. February 2006)

Certificate of Foreign Status of Beneficial Owner for United States Tax Withholding

General Instructions

Section references are to the Internal Revenue Code unless otherwise noted.

For definitions of terms used throughout these instructions, see *Definitions* on pages 3 and 4.

Purpose of form. Foreign persons are subject to U.S. tax at a 30% rate on income they receive from U.S. sources that consists of:

- Interest (including certain original issue discount (OID));
- Dividends;
- Rents;
- Royalties;
- Premiums;
- Annuities;
- Compensation for, or in expectation of, services performed;
- Substitute payments in a securities lending transaction; or
- Other fixed or determinable annual or periodical gains, profits, or income.

This tax is imposed on the gross amount paid and is generally collected by withholding under section 1441 or 1442 on that amount. A payment is considered to have been made whether it is made directly to the beneficial owner or to another person, such as an intermediary, agent, or partnership, for the benefit of the beneficial owner.

In addition, section 1446 requires a partnership conducting a trade or business in the United States to withhold tax on a foreign partner's distributive share of the partnership's effectively connected taxable income. Generally, a foreign person that is a partner in a partnership that submits a Form W-8 for purposes of section 1441 or 1442 will satisfy the documentation requirements under section 1446 as well. However, in some cases the documentation requirements of sections 1441 and 1442 do not match the documentation requirements of section 1446. See Regulations sections 1.1446-1 through 1.1446-6. Further, the owner of a disregarded entity, rather than the disregarded entity itself, shall submit the appropriate Form W-8 for purposes of section 1446.

If you receive certain types of income, you must provide Form W-8BEN to:
- Establish that you are not a U.S. person;
- Claim that you are the beneficial owner of the income for which Form W-8BEN is being provided or a partner in a partnership subject to section 1446; and

- If applicable, claim a reduced rate of, or exemption from, withholding as a resident of a foreign country with which the United States has an income tax treaty.

You may also be required to submit Form W-8BEN to claim an exception from domestic information reporting and backup withholding for certain types of income that are not subject to foreign-person withholding. Such income includes:
- Broker proceeds.
- Short-term (183 days or less) original issue discount (OID).
- Bank deposit interest.
- Foreign source interest, dividends, rents, or royalties.
- Proceeds from a wager placed by a nonresident alien individual in the games of blackjack, baccarat, craps, roulette, or big-6 wheel.

You may also use Form W-8BEN to certify that income from a notional principal contract is not effectively connected with the conduct of a trade or business in the United States.

A withholding agent or payer of the income may rely on a properly completed Form W-8BEN to treat a payment associated with the Form W-8BEN as a payment to a foreign person who beneficially owns the amounts paid. If applicable, the withholding agent may rely on the Form W-8BEN to apply a reduced rate of withholding at source.

Provide Form W-8BEN to the withholding agent or payer before income is paid or credited to you. Failure to provide a Form W-8BEN when requested may lead to withholding at a 30% rate (foreign-person withholding) or the backup withholding rate.

Additional information. For additional information and instructions for the withholding agent, see the Instructions for the Requester of Forms W-8BEN, W-8ECI, W-8EXP, and W-8IMY.

Who must file. You must give Form W-8BEN to the withholding agent or payer if you are a foreign person and you are the beneficial owner of an amount subject to withholding. Submit Form W-8BEN when requested by the withholding agent or payer whether or not you are claiming a reduced rate of, or exemption from, withholding.

Do not use Form W-8BEN if:
- You are a U.S. citizen (even if you reside outside the United States) or other U.S. person (including a resident alien individual). Instead, use Form W-9, Request for Taxpayer Identification Number and Certification.
- You are a disregarded entity with a single owner that is a U.S. person and you are not a hybrid entity claiming treaty benefits. Instead, provide Form W-9.

Cat. No. 25576H

• You are a nonresident alien individual who claims exemption from withholding on compensation for independent or dependent personal services performed in the United States. Instead, provide Form 8233, Exemption from Withholding on Compensation for Independent (and Certain Dependent) Personal Services of a Nonresident Alien Individual, or Form W-4, Employee's Withholding Allowance Certificate.

• You are receiving income that is effectively connected with the conduct of a trade or business in the United States, unless it is allocable to you through a partnership. Instead, provide Form W-8ECI, Certificate of Foreign Person's Claim That Income Is Effectively Connected With the Conduct of a Trade or Business in the United States. If any of the income for which you have provided a Form W-8BEN becomes effectively connected, this is a change in circumstances and Form W-8BEN is no longer valid. You must file Form W-8ECI. See *Change in circumstances* on this page.

• You are filing for a foreign government, international organization, foreign central bank of issue, foreign tax-exempt organization, foreign private foundation, or government of a U.S. possession claiming the applicability of section 115(2), 501(c), 892, 895, or 1443(b). Instead, provide Form W-8EXP, Certificate of Foreign Government or Other Foreign Organization for United States Tax Withholding. However, you should use Form W-8BEN if you are claiming treaty benefits or are providing the form only to claim you are a foreign person exempt from backup withholding. You should use Form W-8ECI if you received effectively connected income (for example, income from commercial activities).

• You are a foreign flow-through entity, other than a hybrid entity, claiming treaty benefits. Instead, provide Form W-8IMY, Certificate of Foreign Intermediary, Foreign Flow-Through Entity, or Certain U.S. Branches for United States Tax Withholding. However, if you are a partner, beneficiary, or owner of a flow-through entity and you are not yourself a flow-through entity, you may be required to furnish a Form W-8BEN to the flow-through entity.

• You are a disregarded entity for purposes of section 1446. Instead, the owner of the entity must submit the form.

• You are a reverse hybrid entity transmitting beneficial owner documentation provided by your interest holders to claim treaty benefits on their behalf. Instead, provide Form W-8IMY.

• You are a withholding foreign partnership or a withholding foreign trust within the meaning of sections 1441 and 1442 and the accompanying regulations. A withholding foreign partnership or a withholding foreign trust is a foreign partnership or trust that has entered into a withholding agreement with the IRS under which it agrees to assume primary withholding responsibility for each partner's, beneficiary's, or owner's distributive share of income subject to withholding that is paid to the partnership or trust. Instead, provide Form W-8IMY.

• You are acting as an intermediary (that is, acting not for your own account, but for the account of others as an agent, nominee, or custodian). Instead, provide Form W-8IMY.

• You are a foreign partnership or foreign grantor trust for purposes of section 1446. Instead, provide Form

W-8IMY and accompanying documentation. See Regulations sections 1.1446-1 through 1.1446-6.

Giving Form W-8BEN to the withholding agent. Do not send Form W-8BEN to the IRS. Instead, give it to the person who is requesting it from you. Generally, this will be the person from whom you receive the payment, who credits your account, or a partnership that allocates income to you. Give Form W-8BEN to the person requesting it before the payment is made to you, credited to your account or allocated. If you do not provide this form, the withholding agent may have to withhold at the 30% rate, backup withholding rate, or the rate applicable under section 1446. If you receive more than one type of income from a single withholding agent for which you claim different benefits, the withholding agent may, at its option, require you to submit a Form W-8BEN for each different type of income. Generally, a separate Form W-8BEN must be given to each withholding agent.

Note. If you own the income or account jointly with one or more other persons, the income or account will be treated by the withholding agent as owned by a foreign person if Forms W-8BEN are provided by all of the owners. If the withholding agent receives a Form W-9 from any of the joint owners, the payment must be treated as made to a U.S. person.

Change in circumstances. If a change in circumstances makes any information on the Form W-8BEN you have submitted incorrect, you must notify the withholding agent or payer within 30 days of the change in circumstances and you must file a new Form W-8BEN or other appropriate form.

If you use Form W-8BEN to certify that you are a foreign person, a change of address to an address in the United States is a change in circumstances. Generally, a change of address within the same foreign country or to another foreign country is not a change in circumstances. However, if you use Form W-8BEN to claim treaty benefits, a move to the United States or outside the country where you have been claiming treaty benefits is a change in circumstances. In that case, you must notify the withholding agent or payer within 30 days of the move.

If you become a U.S. citizen or resident alien after you submit Form W-8BEN, you are no longer subject to the 30% withholding rate or the withholding tax on a foreign partner's share of effectively connected income. You must notify the withholding agent or payer within 30 days of becoming a U.S. citizen or resident alien. You may be required to provide a Form W-9. For more information, see Form W-9 and instructions.

Expiration of Form W-8BEN. Generally, a Form W-8BEN provided without a U.S. taxpayer identification number (TIN) will remain in effect for a period starting on the date the form is signed and ending on the last day of the third succeeding calendar year, unless a change in circumstances makes any information on the form incorrect. For example, a Form W-8BEN signed on September 30, 2005, remains valid through December 31, 2008. A Form W-8BEN furnished with a U.S. TIN will remain in effect until a change in circumstances makes any information on the form incorrect, provided that the withholding agent reports on Form 1042-S at least one payment annually to the beneficial owner who provided the Form W-8BEN. See the instructions for line 6

-2-

beginning on page 4 for circumstances under which you must provide a U.S. TIN.

Definitions

Beneficial owner. For payments other than those for which a reduced rate of withholding is claimed under an income tax treaty, the beneficial owner of income is generally the person who is required under U.S. tax principles to include the income in gross income on a tax return. A person is not a beneficial owner of income, however, to the extent that person is receiving the income as a nominee, agent, or custodian, or to the extent the person is a conduit whose participation in a transaction is disregarded. In the case of amounts paid that do not constitute income, beneficial ownership is determined as if the payment were income.

Foreign partnerships, foreign simple trusts, and foreign grantor trusts are not the beneficial owners of income paid to the partnership or trust. The beneficial owners of income paid to a foreign partnership are generally the partners in the partnership, provided that the partner is not itself a partnership, foreign simple or grantor trust, nominee or other agent. The beneficial owners of income paid to a foreign simple trust (that is, a foreign trust that is described in section 651(a)) are generally the beneficiaries of the trust, if the beneficiary is not a foreign partnership, foreign simple or grantor trust, nominee or other agent. The beneficial owners of a foreign grantor trust (that is, a foreign trust to the extent that all or a portion of the income of the trust is treated as owned by the grantor or another person under sections 671 through 679) are the persons treated as the owners of the trust. The beneficial owners of income paid to a foreign complex trust (that is, a foreign trust that is not a foreign simple trust or foreign grantor trust) is the trust itself.

For purposes of section 1446, the same beneficial owner rules apply, except that under section 1446 a foreign simple trust rather than the beneficiary provides the form to the partnership.

The beneficial owner of income paid to a foreign estate is the estate itself.

Note. A payment to a U.S. partnership, U.S. trust, or U.S. estate is treated as a payment to a U.S. payee that is not subject to 30% withholding. A U.S. partnership, trust, or estate should provide the withholding agent with a Form W-9. For purposes of section 1446, a U.S. grantor trust or disregarded entity shall not provide the withholding agent a Form W-9 in its own right. Rather, the grantor or other owner shall provide the withholding agent the appropriate form.

Foreign person. A foreign person includes a nonresident alien individual, a foreign corporation, a foreign partnership, a foreign trust, a foreign estate, and any other person that is not a U.S. person. It also includes a foreign branch or office of a U.S. financial institution or U.S. clearing organization if the foreign branch is a qualified intermediary. Generally, a payment to a U.S. branch of a foreign person is a payment to a foreign person.

Nonresident alien individual. Any individual who is not a citizen or resident alien of the United States is a nonresident alien individual. An alien individual meeting either the "green card test" or the "substantial presence

test" for the calendar year is a resident alien. Any person not meeting either test is a nonresident alien individual. Additionally, an alien individual who is a resident of a foreign country under the residence article of an income tax treaty, or an alien individual who is a bona fide resident of Puerto Rico, Guam, the Commonwealth of the Northern Mariana Islands, the U.S. Virgin Islands, or American Samoa is a nonresident alien individual. See Pub. 519, U.S. Tax Guide for Aliens, for more information on resident and nonresident alien status.

 Even though a nonresident alien individual married to a U.S. citizen or resident alien may choose to be treated as a resident alien for certain purposes (for example, filing a joint income tax return), such individual is still treated as a nonresident alien for withholding tax purposes on all income except wages.

Flow-through entity. A flow-through entity is a foreign partnership (other than a withholding foreign partnership), a foreign simple or foreign grantor trust (other than a withholding foreign trust), or, for payments for which a reduced rate of withholding is claimed under an income tax treaty, any entity to the extent the entity is considered to be fiscally transparent (see below) with respect to the payment by an interest holder's jurisdiction.

For purposes of section 1446, a foreign partnership or foreign grantor trust must submit Form W-8IMY to establish the partnership or grantor trust as a look through entity. The Form W-8IMY may be accompanied by this form or another version of Form W-8 or Form W-9 to establish the foreign or domestic status of a partner or grantor or other owner. See Regulations section 1.1446-1.

Hybrid entity. A hybrid entity is any person (other than an individual) that is treated as fiscally transparent (see below) in the United States but is not treated as fiscally transparent by a country with which the United States has an income tax treaty. Hybrid entity status is relevant for claiming treaty benefits. See the instructions for line 9c on page 5.

Reverse hybrid entity. A reverse hybrid entity is any person (other than an individual) that is not fiscally transparent under U.S. tax law principles but that is fiscally transparent under the laws of a jurisdiction with which the United States has an income tax treaty. See the instructions for line 9c on page 5.

Fiscally transparent entity. An entity is treated as fiscally transparent with respect to an item of income for which treaty benefits are claimed to the extent that the interest holders in the entity must, on a current basis, take into account separately their shares of an item of income paid to the entity, whether or not distributed, and must determine the character of the items of income as if they were realized directly from the sources from which realized by the entity. For example, partnerships, common trust funds, and simple trusts or grantor trusts are generally considered to be fiscally transparent with respect to items of income received by them.

Disregarded entity. A business entity that has a single owner and is not a corporation under Regulations section 301.7701-2(b) is disregarded as an entity separate from its owner.

-3-

A disregarded entity shall not submit this form to a partnership for purposes of section 1446. Instead, the owner of such entity shall provide appropriate documentation. See Regulations section 1.1446-1.

Amounts subject to withholding. Generally, an amount subject to withholding is an amount from sources within the United States that is fixed or determinable annual or periodical (FDAP) income. FDAP income is all income included in gross income, including interest (as well as OID), dividends, rents, royalties, and compensation. FDAP income does not include most gains from the sale of property (including market discount and option premiums).

For purposes of section 1446, the amount subject to withholding is the foreign partner's share of the partnership's effectively connected taxable income.

Withholding agent. Any person, U.S. or foreign, that has control, receipt, or custody of an amount subject to withholding or who can disburse or make payments of an amount subject to withholding is a withholding agent. The withholding agent may be an individual, corporation, partnership, trust, association, or any other entity, including (but not limited to) any foreign intermediary, foreign partnership, and U.S. branches of certain foreign banks and insurance companies. Generally, the person who pays (or causes to be paid) the amount subject to withholding to the foreign person (or to its agent) must withhold.

For purposes of section 1446, the withholding agent is the partnership conducting the trade or business in the United States. For a publicly traded partnership, the withholding agent may be the partnership, a nominee holding an interest on behalf of a foreign person, or both. See Regulations sections 1.1446-1 through 1.1446-6.

Specific Instructions

 A hybrid entity should give Form W-8BEN to a withholding agent only for income for which it is claiming a reduced rate of withholding under an income tax treaty. A reverse hybrid entity should give Form W-8BEN to a withholding agent only for income for which no treaty benefit is being claimed.

Part I

Line 1. Enter your name. If you are a disregarded entity with a single owner who is a foreign person and you are not claiming treaty benefits as a hybrid entity, this form should be completed and signed by your foreign single owner. If the account to which a payment is made or credited is in the name of the disregarded entity, the foreign single owner should inform the withholding agent of this fact. This may be done by including the name and account number of the disregarded entity on line 8 (reference number) of the form. However, if you are a disregarded entity that is claiming treaty benefits as a hybrid entity, this form should be completed and signed by you.

Line 2. If you are a corporation, enter the country of incorporation. If you are another type of entity, enter the country under whose laws you are created, organized, or governed. If you are an individual, enter N/A (for "not applicable").

Line 3. Check the one box that applies. By checking a box, you are representing that you qualify for this classification. You must check the box that represents your classification (for example, corporation, partnership, trust, estate, etc.) under U.S. tax principles. Do not check the box that describes your status under the law of the treaty country. If you are a partnership or disregarded entity receiving a payment for which treaty benefits are being claimed, you must check the "Partnership" or "Disregarded entity" box. If you are a sole proprietor, check the "Individual" box, not the "Disregarded entity" box.

 Only entities that are tax-exempt under section 501 should check the "Tax-exempt organization" box. Such organizations should use Form W-8BEN only if they are claiming a reduced rate of withholding under an income tax treaty or some code exception other than section 501. Use Form W-8EXP if you are claiming an exemption from withholding under section 501.

Line 4. Your permanent residence address is the address in the country where you claim to be a resident for purposes of that country's income tax. If you are giving Form W-8BEN to claim a reduced rate of withholding under an income tax treaty, you must determine your residency in the manner required by the treaty. Do not show the address of a financial institution, a post office box, or an address used solely for mailing purposes. If you are an individual who does not have a tax residence in any country, your permanent residence is where you normally reside. If you are not an individual and you do not have a tax residence in any country, the permanent residence address is where you maintain your principal office.

Line 5. Enter your mailing address only if it is different from the address you show on line 4.

Line 6. If you are an individual, you are generally required to enter your social security number (SSN). To apply for an SSN, get Form SS-5 from a Social Security Administration (SSA) office or, if in the United States, you may call the SSA at 1-800-772-1213. Fill in Form SS-5 and return it to the SSA.

If you do not have an SSN and are not eligible to get one, you must get an individual taxpayer identification number (ITIN). To apply for an ITIN, file Form W-7 with the IRS. It usually takes 4-6 weeks to get an ITIN.

 An ITIN is for tax use only. It does not entitle you to social security benefits or change your employment or immigration status under U.S. law.

If you are not an individual or you are an individual who is an employer or you are engaged in a U.S. trade or business as a sole proprietor, you must enter an employer identification number (EIN). If you do not have an EIN, you should apply for one on Form SS-4, Application for Employer Identification Number. If you are a disregarded entity claiming treaty benefits as a hybrid entity, enter your EIN.

A partner in a partnership conducting a trade or business in the United States will likely be allocated effectively connected taxable income. The partner is

-4-

required to file a U.S. federal income tax return and must have a U.S. taxpayer identification number (TIN).

You must provide a U.S. TIN if you are:
• Claiming an exemption from withholding under section 871(f) for certain annuities received under qualified plans,
• A foreign grantor trust with 5 or fewer grantors,
• Claiming benefits under an income tax treaty, or
• Submitting the form to a partnership that conducts a trade or business in the United States.

However, a U.S. TIN is not required to be shown in order to claim treaty benefits on the following items of income:
• Dividends and interest from stocks and debt obligations that are actively traded;
• Dividends from any redeemable security issued by an investment company registered under the Investment Company Act of 1940 (mutual fund);
• Dividends, interest, or royalties from units of beneficial interest in a unit investment trust that are (or were upon issuance) publicly offered and are registered with the SEC under the Securities Act of 1933; and
• Income related to loans of any of the above securities.

 You may want to obtain and provide a U.S. TIN on Form W-8BEN even though it is not required. A Form W-8BEN containing a U.S. TIN remains valid for as long as your status and the information relevant to the certifications you make on the form remain unchanged provided at least one payment is reported to you annually on Form 1042-S.

Line 7. If your country of residence for tax purposes has issued you a tax identifying number, enter it here. For example, if you are a resident of Canada, enter your Social Insurance Number.

Line 8. This line may be used by the filer of Form W-8BEN or by the withholding agent to whom it is provided to include any referencing information that is useful to the withholding agent in carrying out its obligations. For example, withholding agents who are required to associate the Form W-8BEN with a particular Form W-8IMY may want to use line 8 for a referencing number or code that will make the association clear. A beneficial owner may use line 8 to include the number of the account for which he or she is providing the form. A foreign single owner of a disregarded entity may use line 8 to inform the withholding agent that the account to which a payment is made or credited is in the name of the disregarded entity (see instructions for line 1 on page 4).

Part II

Line 9a. Enter the country where you claim to be a resident for income tax treaty purposes. For treaty purposes, a person is a resident of a treaty country if the person is a resident of that country under the terms of the treaty.

Line 9b. If you are claiming benefits under an income tax treaty, you must have a U.S. TIN unless one of the exceptions listed in the line 6 instructions above applies.

Line 9c. An entity (but not an individual) that is claiming a reduced rate of withholding under an income tax treaty must represent that it:
• Derives the item of income for which the treaty benefit is claimed, and

• Meets the limitation on benefits provisions contained in the treaty, if any.

An item of income may be derived by either the entity receiving the item of income or by the interest holders in the entity or, in certain circumstances, both. An item of income paid to an entity is considered to be derived by the entity only if the entity is not fiscally transparent under the laws of the entity's jurisdiction with respect to the item of income. An item of income paid to an entity shall be considered to be derived by the interest holder in the entity only if:
• The interest holder is not fiscally transparent in its jurisdiction with respect to the item of income, and
• The entity is considered to be fiscally transparent under the laws of the interest holder's jurisdiction with respect to the item of income. An item of income paid directly to a type of entity specifically identified in a treaty as a resident of a treaty jurisdiction is treated as derived by a resident of that treaty jurisdiction.

If an entity is claiming treaty benefits on its own behalf, it should complete Form W-8BEN. If an interest holder in an entity that is considered fiscally transparent in the interest holder's jurisdiction is claiming a treaty benefit, the interest holder should complete Form W-8BEN on its own behalf and the fiscally transparent entity should associate the interest holder's Form W-8BEN with a Form W-8IMY completed by the entity.

 An income tax treaty may not apply to reduce the amount of any tax on an item of income received by an entity that is treated as a domestic corporation for U.S. tax purposes. Therefore, neither the domestic corporation nor its shareholders are entitled to the benefits of a reduction of U.S. income tax on an item of income received from U.S. sources by the corporation.

To determine whether an entity meets the limitation on benefits provisions of a treaty, you must consult the specific provisions or articles under the treaties. Income tax treaties are available on the IRS website at *www.irs.gov.*

 If you are an entity that derives the income as a resident of a treaty country, you may check this box if the applicable income tax treaty does not contain a "limitation on benefits" provision.

Line 9d. If you are a foreign corporation claiming treaty benefits under an income tax treaty that entered into force before January 1, 1987 (and has not been renegotiated) on (a) U.S. source dividends paid to you by another foreign corporation or (b) U.S. source interest paid to you by a U.S. trade or business of another foreign corporation, you must generally be a "qualified resident" of a treaty country. See section 884 for the definition of interest paid by a U.S. trade or business of a foreign corporation ("branch interest") and other applicable rules.

In general, a foreign corporation is a qualified resident of a country if any of the following apply.
• It meets a 50% ownership and base erosion test.
• It is primarily and regularly traded on an established securities market in its country of residence or the United States.
• It carries on an active trade or business in its country of residence.
• It gets a ruling from the IRS that it is a qualified resident.

-5-

See Regulations section 1.884-5 for the requirements that must be met to satisfy each of these tests.

 If you are claiming treaty benefits under an income tax treaty entered into force after December 31, 1986, do not check box 9d. Instead, check box 9c.

Line 9e. Check this box if you are related to the withholding agent within the meaning of section 267(b) or 707(b) and the aggregate amount subject to withholding received during the calendar year will exceed $500,000. Additionally, you must file Form 8833, Treaty-Based Return Position Disclosure Under Section 6114 or 7701(b).

Line 10

Line 10 must be used only if you are claiming treaty benefits that require that you meet conditions not covered by the representations you make in lines 9a through 9e. However, this line should always be completed by foreign students and researchers claiming treaty benefits. See *Scholarship and fellowship grants* below for more information.

The following are additional examples of persons who should complete this line.
● Exempt organizations claiming treaty benefits under the exempt organization articles of the treaties with Canada, Mexico, Germany, and the Netherlands.
● Foreign corporations that are claiming a preferential rate applicable to dividends based on ownership of a specific percentage of stock.
● Persons claiming treaty benefits on royalties if the treaty contains different withholding rates for different types of royalties.

This line is generally not applicable to claiming treaty benefits under an interest or dividends (other than dividends subject to a preferential rate based on ownership) article of a treaty.

Nonresident alien who becomes a resident alien. Generally, only a nonresident alien individual may use the terms of a tax treaty to reduce or eliminate U.S. tax on certain types of income. However, most tax treaties contain a provision known as a "saving clause." Exceptions specified in the saving clause may permit an exemption from tax to continue for certain types of income even after the recipient has otherwise become a U.S. resident alien for tax purposes. The individual must use Form W-9 to claim the tax treaty benefit. See the instructions for Form W-9 for more information. Also see *Nonresident alien student or researcher who becomes a resident alien* later for an example.

Scholarship and fellowship grants. A nonresident alien student (including a trainee or business apprentice) or researcher who receives noncompensatory scholarship or fellowship income may use Form W-8BEN to claim benefits under a tax treaty that apply to reduce or eliminate U.S. tax on such income. No Form W-8BEN is required unless a treaty benefit is being claimed. A nonresident alien student or researcher who receives compensatory scholarship or fellowship income must use Form 8233 to claim any benefits of a tax treaty that apply to that income. The student or researcher must use Form W-4 for any part of such income for which he or she is not claiming a tax treaty withholding exemption. Do not use Form W-8BEN for compensatory scholarship or

fellowship income. See *Compensation for Dependent Personal Services* in the Instructions for Form 8233.

 If you are a nonresident alien individual who received noncompensatory scholarship or fellowship income and personal services income (including compensatory scholarship or fellowship income) from the same withholding agent, you may use Form 8233 to claim a tax treaty withholding exemption for part or all of both types of income.

Completing lines 4 and 9a. Most tax treaties that contain an article exempting scholarship or fellowship grant income from taxation require that the recipient be a resident of the other treaty country at the time of, or immediately prior to, entry into the United States. Thus, a student or researcher may claim the exemption even if he or she no longer has a permanent address in the other treaty country after entry into the United States. If this is the case, you may provide a U.S. address on line 4 and still be eligible for the exemption if all other conditions required by the tax treaty are met. You must also identify on line 9a the tax treaty country of which you were a resident at the time of, or immediately prior to, your entry into the United States.

Completing line 10. You must complete line 10 if you are a student or researcher claiming an exemption from taxation on your scholarship or fellowship grant income under a tax treaty.

Nonresident alien student or researcher who becomes a resident alien. You must use Form W-9 to claim an exception to a saving clause. See *Nonresident alien who becomes a resident alien* on this page for a general explanation of saving clauses and exceptions to them.

Example. Article 20 of the U.S.-China income tax treaty allows an exemption from tax for scholarship income received by a Chinese student temporarily present in the United States. Under U.S. law, this student will become a resident alien for tax purposes if his or her stay in the United States exceeds 5 calendar years. However, paragraph 2 of the first protocol to the U.S.-China treaty (dated April 30, 1984) allows the provisions of Article 20 to continue to apply even after the Chinese student becomes a resident alien of the United States. A Chinese student who qualifies for this exception (under paragraph 2 of the first protocol) and is relying on this exception to claim an exemption from tax on his or her scholarship or fellowship income would complete Form W-9.

Part III

If you check this box, you must provide the withholding agent with the required statement for income from a notional principal contract that is to be treated as income not effectively connected with the conduct of a trade or business in the United States. You should update this statement as often as necessary. A new Form W-8BEN is not required for each update provided the form otherwise remains valid.

Part IV

Form W-8BEN must be signed and dated by the beneficial owner of the income, or, if the beneficial owner is not an individual, by an authorized representative or officer of the beneficial owner. If Form W-8BEN is completed by an agent acting under a duly authorized power of attorney, the form must be accompanied by the power of attorney in proper form or a copy thereof specifically authorizing the agent to represent the principal in making, executing, and presenting the form. Form 2848, Power of Attorney and Declaration of Representative, may be used for this purpose. The agent, as well as the beneficial owner, may incur liability for the penalties provided for an erroneous, false, or fraudulent form.

Broker transactions or barter exchanges. Income from transactions with a broker or a barter exchange is subject to reporting rules and backup withholding unless Form W-8BEN or a substitute form is filed to notify the broker or barter exchange that you are an exempt foreign person.

You are an exempt foreign person for a calendar year in which:
• You are a nonresident alien individual or a foreign corporation, partnership, estate, or trust;
• You are an individual who has not been, and does not plan to be, present in the United States for a total of 183 days or more during the calendar year; and
• You are neither engaged, nor plan to be engaged during the year, in a U.S. trade or business that has effectively connected gains from transactions with a broker or barter exchange.

_____

Paperwork Reduction Act Notice. We ask for the information on this form to carry out the Internal Revenue laws of the United States. You are required to provide the information. We need it to ensure that you are complying with these laws and to allow us to figure and collect the right amount of tax.

You are not required to provide the information requested on a form that is subject to the Paperwork Reduction Act unless the form displays a valid OMB control number. Books or records relating to a form or its instructions must be retained as long as their contents may become material in the administration of any Internal Revenue law. Generally, tax returns and return information are confidential, as required by section 6103.

The time needed to complete and file this form will vary depending on individual circumstances. The estimated average time is: **Recordkeeping,** 5 hr., 58 min.; **Learning about the law or the form,** 3 hr., 46 min.; **Preparing and sending the form to IRS,** 4 hr., 2 min.

If you have comments concerning the accuracy of these time estimates or suggestions for making this form simpler, we would be happy to hear from you. You can email us at *taxforms@irs.gov*. Please put "Forms Comment" on the subject line. Or you can write to Internal Revenue Service, Tax Products Coordinating Committee, SE:W:CAR:MP:T:T:SP, 1111 Constitution Ave. NW, IR-6406, Washington, DC 20224. Do not send Form W-8BEN to this office. Instead, give it to your withholding agent.

Form **W-9**
(Rev. December 2011)
Department of the Treasury
Internal Revenue Service

Request for Taxpayer
Identification Number and Certification

Give Form to the requester. Do not send to the IRS.

Print or type
See Specific Instructions on page 2.

Name (as shown on your income tax return)

Business name/disregarded entity name, if different from above

Check appropriate box for federal tax classification:

☐ Individual/sole proprietor ☐ C Corporation ☐ S Corporation ☐ Partnership ☐ Trust/estate

☐ Limited liability company. Enter the tax classification (C=C corporation, S=S corporation, P=partnership) ▶ - - - - - - - - - - - - - - - -

☐ Exempt payee

☐ Other (see instructions) ▶

Address (number, street, and apt. or suite no.)

Requester's name and address (optional)

City, state, and ZIP code

List account number(s) here (optional)

Part I   Taxpayer Identification Number (TIN)

Enter your TIN in the appropriate box. The TIN provided must match the name given on the "Name" line to avoid backup withholding. For individuals, this is your social security number (SSN). However, for a resident alien, sole proprietor, or disregarded entity, see the Part I instructions on page 3. For other entities, it is your employer identification number (EIN). If you do not have a number, see *How to get a TIN* on page 3.

Note. If the account is in more than one name, see the chart on page 4 for guidelines on whose number to enter.

Social security number

| | | | – | | | – | | | | |

Employer identification number

| | – | | | | | | | |

Part II   Certification

Under penalties of perjury, I certify that:

1. The number shown on this form is my correct taxpayer identification number (or I am waiting for a number to be issued to me), and

2. I am not subject to backup withholding because: (a) I am exempt from backup withholding, or (b) I have not been notified by the Internal Revenue Service (IRS) that I am subject to backup withholding as a result of a failure to report all interest or dividends, or (c) the IRS has notified me that I am no longer subject to backup withholding, and

3. I am a U.S. citizen or other U.S. person (defined below).

Certification instructions. You must cross out item 2 above if you have been notified by the IRS that you are currently subject to backup withholding because you have failed to report all interest and dividends on your tax return. For real estate transactions, item 2 does not apply. For mortgage interest paid, acquisition or abandonment of secured property, cancellation of debt, contributions to an individual retirement arrangement (IRA), and generally, payments other than interest and dividends, you are not required to sign the certification, but you must provide your correct TIN. See the instructions on page 4.

Sign Here   Signature of U.S. person ▶   Date ▶

General Instructions

Section references are to the Internal Revenue Code unless otherwise noted.

Purpose of Form

A person who is required to file an information return with the IRS must obtain your correct taxpayer identification number (TIN) to report, for example, income paid to you, real estate transactions, mortgage interest you paid, acquisition or abandonment of secured property, cancellation of debt, or contributions you made to an IRA.

Use Form W-9 only if you are a U.S. person (including a resident alien), to provide your correct TIN to the person requesting it (the requester) and, when applicable, to:

1. Certify that the TIN you are giving is correct (or you are waiting for a number to be issued),

2. Certify that you are not subject to backup withholding, or

3. Claim exemption from backup withholding if you are a U.S. exempt payee. If applicable, you are also certifying that as a U.S. person, your allocable share of any partnership income from a U.S. trade or business is not subject to the withholding tax on foreign partners' share of effectively connected income.

Note. If a requester gives you a form other than Form W-9 to request your TIN, you must use the requester's form if it is substantially similar to this Form W-9.

Definition of a U.S. person. For federal tax purposes, you are considered a U.S. person if you are:

• An individual who is a U.S. citizen or U.S. resident alien,

• A partnership, corporation, company, or association created or organized in the United States or under the laws of the United States,

• An estate (other than a foreign estate), or

• A domestic trust (as defined in Regulations section 301.7701-7).

Special rules for partnerships. Partnerships that conduct a trade or business in the United States are generally required to pay a withholding tax on any foreign partners' share of income from such business. Further, in certain cases where a Form W-9 has not been received, a partnership is required to presume that a partner is a foreign person, and pay the withholding tax. Therefore, if you are a U.S. person that is a partner in a partnership conducting a trade or business in the United States, provide Form W-9 to the partnership to establish your U.S. status and avoid withholding on your share of partnership income.

Cat. No. 10231X   Form **W-9** (Rev. 12-2011)

The person who gives Form W-9 to the partnership for purposes of establishing its U.S. status and avoiding withholding on its allocable share of net income from the partnership conducting a trade or business in the United States is in the following cases:

• The U.S. owner of a disregarded entity and not the entity,

• The U.S. grantor or other owner of a grantor trust and not the trust, and

• The U.S. trust (other than a grantor trust) and not the beneficiaries of the trust.

Foreign person. If you are a foreign person, do not use Form W-9. Instead, use the appropriate Form W-8 (see Publication 515, Withholding of Tax on Nonresident Aliens and Foreign Entities).

Nonresident alien who becomes a resident alien. Generally, only a nonresident alien individual may use the terms of a tax treaty to reduce or eliminate U.S. tax on certain types of income. However, most tax treaties contain a provision known as a "saving clause." Exceptions specified in the saving clause may permit an exemption from tax to continue for certain types of income even after the payee has otherwise become a U.S. resident alien for tax purposes.

If you are a U.S. resident alien who is relying on an exception contained in the saving clause of a tax treaty to claim an exemption from U.S. tax on certain types of income, you must attach a statement to Form W-9 that specifies the following five items:

1. The treaty country. Generally, this must be the same treaty under which you claimed exemption from tax as a nonresident alien.

2. The treaty article addressing the income.

3. The article number (or location) in the tax treaty that contains the saving clause and its exceptions.

4. The type and amount of income that qualifies for the exemption from tax.

5. Sufficient facts to justify the exemption from tax under the terms of the treaty article.

Example. Article 20 of the U.S.-China income tax treaty allows an exemption from tax for scholarship income received by a Chinese student temporarily present in the United States. Under U.S. law, this student will become a resident alien for tax purposes if his or her stay in the United States exceeds 5 calendar years. However, paragraph 2 of the first Protocol to the U.S.-China treaty (dated April 30, 1984) allows the provisions of Article 20 to continue to apply even after the Chinese student becomes a resident alien of the United States. A Chinese student who qualifies for this exception (under paragraph 2 of the first protocol) and is relying on this exception to claim an exemption from tax on his or her scholarship or fellowship income would attach to Form W-9 a statement that includes the information described above to support that exemption.

If you are a nonresident alien or a foreign entity not subject to backup withholding, give the requester the appropriate completed Form W-8.

What is backup withholding? Persons making certain payments to you must under certain conditions withhold and pay to the IRS a percentage of such payments. This is called "backup withholding." Payments that may be subject to backup withholding include interest, tax-exempt interest, dividends, broker and barter exchange transactions, rents, royalties, nonemployee pay, and certain payments from fishing boat operators. Real estate transactions are not subject to backup withholding.

You will not be subject to backup withholding on payments you receive if you give the requester your correct TIN, make the proper certifications, and report all your taxable interest and dividends on your tax return.

Payments you receive will be subject to backup withholding if:

1. You do not furnish your TIN to the requester,

2. You do not certify your TIN when required (see the Part II instructions on page 3 for details),

3. The IRS tells the requester that you furnished an incorrect TIN,

4. The IRS tells you that you are subject to backup withholding because you did not report all your interest and dividends on your tax return (for reportable interest and dividends only), or

5. You do not certify to the requester that you are not subject to backup withholding under 4 above (for reportable interest and dividend accounts opened after 1983 only).

Certain payees and payments are exempt from backup withholding. See the instructions below and the separate Instructions for the Requester of Form W-9.

Also see *Special rules for partnerships* on page 1.

Updating Your Information

You must provide updated information to any person to whom you claimed to be an exempt payee if you are no longer an exempt payee and anticipate receiving reportable payments in the future from this person. For example, you may need to provide updated information if you are a C corporation that elects to be an S corporation, or if you no longer are tax exempt. In addition, you must furnish a new Form W-9 if the name or TIN changes for the account, for example, if the grantor of a grantor trust dies.

Penalties

Failure to furnish TIN. If you fail to furnish your correct TIN to a requester, you are subject to a penalty of $50 for each such failure unless your failure is due to reasonable cause and not to willful neglect.

Civil penalty for false information with respect to withholding. If you make a false statement with no reasonable basis that results in no backup withholding, you are subject to a $500 penalty.

Criminal penalty for falsifying information. Willfully falsifying certifications or affirmations may subject you to criminal penalties including fines and/or imprisonment.

Misuse of TINs. If the requester discloses or uses TINs in violation of federal law, the requester may be subject to civil and criminal penalties.

Specific Instructions

Name

If you are an individual, you must generally enter the name shown on your income tax return. However, if you have changed your last name, for instance, due to marriage without informing the Social Security Administration of the name change, enter your first name, the last name shown on your social security card, and your new last name.

If the account is in joint names, list first, and then circle, the name of the person or entity whose number you entered in Part I of the form.

Sole proprietor. Enter your individual name as shown on your income tax return on the "Name" line. You may enter your business, trade, or "doing business as (DBA)" name on the "Business name/disregarded entity name" line.

Partnership, C Corporation, or S Corporation. Enter the entity's name on the "Name" line and any business, trade, or "doing business as (DBA) name" on the "Business name/disregarded entity name" line.

Disregarded entity. Enter the owner's name on the "Name" line. The name of the entity entered on the "Name" line should never be a disregarded entity. The name on the "Name" line must be the name shown on the income tax return on which the income will be reported. For example, if a foreign LLC that is treated as a disregarded entity for U.S. federal tax purposes has a domestic owner, the domestic owner's name is required to be provided on the "Name" line. If the direct owner of the entity is also a disregarded entity, enter the first owner that is not disregarded for federal tax purposes. Enter the disregarded entity's name on the "Business name/disregarded entity name" line. If the owner of the disregarded entity is a foreign person, you must complete an appropriate Form W-8.

Note. Check the appropriate box for the federal tax classification of the person whose name is entered on the "Name" line (Individual/sole proprietor, Partnership, C Corporation, S Corporation, Trust/estate).

Limited Liability Company (LLC). If the person identified on the "Name" line is an LLC, check the "Limited liability company" box only and enter the appropriate code for the tax classification in the space provided. If you are an LLC that is treated as a partnership for federal tax purposes, enter "P" for partnership. If you are an LLC that has filed a Form 8832 or a Form 2553 to be taxed as a corporation, enter "C" for C corporation or "S" for S corporation. If you are an LLC that is disregarded as an entity separate from its owner under Regulation section 301.7701-3 (except for employment and excise tax), do not check the LLC box unless the owner of the LLC (required to be identified on the "Name" line) is another LLC that is not disregarded for federal tax purposes. If the LLC is disregarded as an entity separate from its owner, enter the appropriate tax classification of the owner identified on the "Name" line.

Other entities. Enter your business name as shown on required federal tax documents on the "Name" line. This name should match the name shown on the charter or other legal document creating the entity. You may enter any business, trade, or DBA name on the "Business name/ disregarded entity name" line.

Exempt Payee

If you are exempt from backup withholding, enter your name as described above and check the appropriate box for your status, then check the "Exempt payee" box in the line following the "Business name/ disregarded entity name," sign and date the form.

Generally, individuals (including sole proprietors) are not exempt from backup withholding. Corporations are exempt from backup withholding for certain payments, such as interest and dividends.

Note. If you are exempt from backup withholding, you should still complete this form to avoid possible erroneous backup withholding.

The following payees are exempt from backup withholding:

1. An organization exempt from tax under section 501(a), any IRA, or a custodial account under section 403(b)(7) if the account satisfies the requirements of section 401(f)(2),

2. The United States or any of its agencies or instrumentalities,

3. A state, the District of Columbia, a possession of the United States, or any of their political subdivisions or instrumentalities,

4. A foreign government or any of its political subdivisions, agencies, or instrumentalities, or

5. An international organization or any of its agencies or instrumentalities.

Other payees that may be exempt from backup withholding include:

6. A corporation,

7. A foreign central bank of issue,

8. A dealer in securities or commodities required to register in the United States, the District of Columbia, or a possession of the United States,

9. A futures commission merchant registered with the Commodity Futures Trading Commission,

10. A real estate investment trust,

11. An entity registered at all times during the tax year under the Investment Company Act of 1940,

12. A common trust fund operated by a bank under section 584(a),

13. A financial institution,

14. A middleman known in the investment community as a nominee or custodian, or

15. A trust exempt from tax under section 664 or described in section 4947.

The following chart shows types of payments that may be exempt from backup withholding. The chart applies to the exempt payees listed above, 1 through 15.

IF the payment is for . . .	THEN the payment is exempt for . . .
Interest and dividend payments	All exempt payees except for 9
Broker transactions	Exempt payees 1 through 5 and 7 through 13. Also, C corporations.
Barter exchange transactions and patronage dividends	Exempt payees 1 through 5
Payments over $600 required to be reported and direct sales over $5,000 [1]	Generally, exempt payees 1 through 7 [2]

[1] See Form 1099-MISC, Miscellaneous Income, and its instructions.

[2] However, the following payments made to a corporation and reportable on Form 1099-MISC are not exempt from backup withholding: medical and health care payments, attorneys' fees, gross proceeds paid to an attorney, and payments for services paid by a federal executive agency.

Part I. Taxpayer Identification Number (TIN)

Enter your TIN in the appropriate box. If you are a resident alien and you do not have and are not eligible to get an SSN, your TIN is your IRS individual taxpayer identification number (ITIN). Enter it in the social security number box. If you do not have an ITIN, see *How to get a TIN* below.

If you are a sole proprietor and you have an EIN, you may enter either your SSN or EIN. However, the IRS prefers that you use your SSN.

If you are a single-member LLC that is disregarded as an entity separate from its owner (see *Limited Liability Company (LLC)* on page 2), enter the owner's SSN (or EIN, if the owner has one). Do not enter the disregarded entity's EIN. If the LLC is classified as a corporation or partnership, enter the entity's EIN.

Note. See the chart on page 4 for further clarification of name and TIN combinations.

How to get a TIN. If you do not have a TIN, apply for one immediately. To apply for an SSN, get Form SS-5, Application for a Social Security Card, from your local Social Security Administration office or get this form online at *www.ssa.gov*. You may also get this form by calling 1-800-772-1213. Use Form W-7, Application for IRS Individual Taxpayer Identification Number, to apply for an ITIN, or Form SS-4, Application for Employer Identification Number, to apply for an EIN. You can apply for an EIN online by accessing the IRS website at *www.irs.gov/businesses* and clicking on Employer Identification Number (EIN) under Starting a Business. You can get Forms W-7 and SS-4 from the IRS by visiting IRS.gov or by calling 1-800-TAX-FORM (1-800-829-3676).

If you are asked to complete Form W-9 but do not have a TIN, write "Applied For" in the space for the TIN, sign and date the form, and give it to the requester. For interest and dividend payments, and certain payments made with respect to readily tradable instruments, generally you will have 60 days to get a TIN and give it to the requester before you are subject to backup withholding on payments. The 60-day rule does not apply to other types of payments. You will be subject to backup withholding on all such payments until you provide your TIN to the requester.

Note. Entering "Applied For" means that you have already applied for a TIN or that you intend to apply for one soon.

Caution: *A disregarded domestic entity that has a foreign owner must use the appropriate Form W-8.*

Part II. Certification

To establish to the withholding agent that you are a U.S. person, or resident alien, sign Form W-9. You may be requested to sign by the withholding agent even if item 1, below, and items 4 and 5 on page 4 indicate otherwise.

For a joint account, only the person whose TIN is shown in Part I should sign (when required). In the case of a disregarded entity, the person identified on the "Name" line must sign. Exempt payees, see *Exempt Payee* on page 3.

Signature requirements. Complete the certification as indicated in items 1 through 3, below, and items 4 and 5 on page 4.

1. Interest, dividend, and barter exchange accounts opened before 1984 and broker accounts considered active during 1983. You must give your correct TIN, but you do not have to sign the certification.

2. Interest, dividend, broker, and barter exchange accounts opened after 1983 and broker accounts considered inactive during 1983. You must sign the certification or backup withholding will apply. If you are subject to backup withholding and you are merely providing your correct TIN to the requester, you must cross out item 2 in the certification before signing the form.

3. Real estate transactions. You must sign the certification. You may cross out item 2 of the certification.

4. Other payments. You must give your correct TIN, but you do not have to sign the certification unless you have been notified that you have previously given an incorrect TIN. "Other payments" include payments made in the course of the requester's trade or business for rents, royalties, goods (other than bills for merchandise), medical and health care services (including payments to corporations), payments to a nonemployee for services, payments to certain fishing boat crew members and fishermen, and gross proceeds paid to attorneys (including payments to corporations).

5. Mortgage interest paid by you, acquisition or abandonment of secured property, cancellation of debt, qualified tuition program payments (under section 529), IRA, Coverdell ESA, Archer MSA or HSA contributions or distributions, and pension distributions. You must give your correct TIN, but you do not have to sign the certification.

What Name and Number To Give the Requester

For this type of account:	Give name and SSN of:
1. Individual	The individual
2. Two or more individuals (joint account)	The actual owner of the account or, if combined funds, the first individual on the account [1]
3. Custodian account of a minor (Uniform Gift to Minors Act)	The minor [2]
4. a. The usual revocable savings trust (grantor is also trustee)	The grantor-trustee [1]
b. So-called trust account that is not a legal or valid trust under state law	The actual owner [1]
5. Sole proprietorship or disregarded entity owned by an individual	The owner [3]
6. Grantor trust filing under Optional Form 1099 Filing Method 1 (see Regulation section 1.671-4(b)(2)(i)(A))	The grantor*

For this type of account:	Give name and EIN of:
7. Disregarded entity not owned by an individual	The owner
8. A valid trust, estate, or pension trust	Legal entity [4]
9. Corporation or LLC electing corporate status on Form 8832 or Form 2553	The corporation
10. Association, club, religious, charitable, educational, or other tax-exempt organization	The organization
11. Partnership or multi-member LLC	The partnership
12. A broker or registered nominee	The broker or nominee
13. Account with the Department of Agriculture in the name of a public entity (such as a state or local government, school district, or prison) that receives agricultural program payments	The public entity
14. Grantor trust filing under the Form 1041 Filing Method or the Optional Form 1099 Filing Method 2 (see Regulation section 1.671-4(b)(2)(i)(B))	The trust

[1] List first and circle the name of the person whose number you furnish. If only one person on a joint account has an SSN, that person's number must be furnished.

[2] Circle the minor's name and furnish the minor's SSN.

[3] You must show your individual name and you may also enter your business or "DBA" name on the "Business name/disregarded entity" name line. You may use either your SSN or EIN (if you have one), but the IRS encourages you to use your SSN.

[4] List first and circle the name of the trust, estate, or pension trust. (Do not furnish the TIN of the personal representative or trustee unless the legal entity itself is not designated in the account title.) Also see *Special rules for partnerships* on page 1.

*Note. Grantor also must provide a Form W-9 to trustee of trust.

Note. If no name is circled when more than one name is listed, the number will be considered to be that of the first name listed.

Secure Your Tax Records from Identity Theft

Identity theft occurs when someone uses your personal information such as your name, social security number (SSN), or other identifying information, without your permission, to commit fraud or other crimes. An identity thief may use your SSN to get a job or may file a tax return using your SSN to receive a refund.

To reduce your risk:

- Protect your SSN,
- Ensure your employer is protecting your SSN, and
- Be careful when choosing a tax preparer.

If your tax records are affected by identity theft and you receive a notice from the IRS, respond right away to the name and phone number printed on the IRS notice or letter.

If your tax records are not currently affected by identity theft but you think you are at risk due to a lost or stolen purse or wallet, questionable credit card activity or credit report, contact the IRS Identity Theft Hotline at 1-800-908-4490 or submit Form 14039.

For more information, see Publication 4535, Identity Theft Prevention and Victim Assistance.

Victims of identity theft who are experiencing economic harm or a system problem, or are seeking help in resolving tax problems that have not been resolved through normal channels, may be eligible for Taxpayer Advocate Service (TAS) assistance. You can reach TAS by calling the TAS toll-free case intake line at 1-877-777-4778 or TTY/TDD 1-800-829-4059.

Protect yourself from suspicious emails or phishing schemes. Phishing is the creation and use of email and websites designed to mimic legitimate business emails and websites. The most common act is sending an email to a user falsely claiming to be an established legitimate enterprise in an attempt to scam the user into surrendering private information that will be used for identity theft.

The IRS does not initiate contacts with taxpayers via emails. Also, the IRS does not request personal detailed information through email or ask taxpayers for the PIN numbers, passwords, or similar secret access information for their credit card, bank, or other financial accounts.

If you receive an unsolicited email claiming to be from the IRS, forward this message to *phishing@irs.gov*. You may also report misuse of the IRS name, logo, or other IRS property to the Treasury Inspector General for Tax Administration at 1-800-366-4484. You can forward suspicious emails to the Federal Trade Commission at: *spam@uce.gov* or contact them at *www.ftc.gov/idtheft* or 1-877-IDTHEFT (1-877-438-4338).

Visit IRS.gov to learn more about identity theft and how to reduce your risk.

Privacy Act Notice

Section 6109 of the Internal Revenue Code requires you to provide your correct TIN to persons (including federal agencies) who are required to file information returns with the IRS to report interest, dividends, or certain other income paid to you; mortgage interest you paid; the acquisition or abandonment of secured property; the cancellation of debt; or contributions you made to an IRA, Archer MSA, or HSA. The person collecting this form uses the information on the form to file information returns with the IRS, reporting the above information. Routine uses of this information include giving it to the Department of Justice for civil and criminal litigation and to cities, states, the District of Columbia, and U.S. possessions for use in administering their laws. The information also may be disclosed to other countries under a treaty, to federal and state agencies to enforce civil and criminal laws, or to federal law enforcement and intelligence agencies to combat terrorism. You must provide your TIN whether or not you are required to file a tax return. Under section 3406, payers must generally withhold a percentage of taxable interest, dividend, and certain other payments to a payee who does not give a TIN to the payer. Certain penalties may also apply for providing false or fraudulent information.

Instructions for the Requester of Form W-9

Department of the Treasury
Internal Revenue Service

(Rev. January 2011)
Request for Taxpayer Identification Number and Certification

Section references are to the Internal Revenue Code unless otherwise noted.

What's New

New checkboxes. Generally, for any sale of a covered security acquired by an S corporation (other than a financial institution) after December 31, 2011, brokers will be required to report gross proceeds and basis information to S corporations and may not treat them as exempt recipients. New tax classification checkboxes have been added for S corporation and Trust/estate. The Form W-9 is revised to allow S corporations sufficient time to provide new certifications to brokers indicating their non-exempt status. Also, disregarded entity was removed as a tax classification for limited liability companies.

Reminders

● The backup withholding rate is 28% for reportable payments.
● The IRS website offers TIN Matching e-services for certain payers to validate name and TIN combinations. See *Taxpayer Identification Number (TIN) Matching* on page 4.

How Do I Know When To Use Form W-9?

Use Form W-9 to request the taxpayer identification number (TIN) of a U.S. person (including a resident alien) and to request certain certifications and claims for exemption. (See *Purpose of Form* on Form W-9.) Withholding agents may require signed Forms W-9 from U.S. exempt recipients to overcome any presumptions of foreign status. For federal purposes, a U.S. person includes but is not limited to:
● An individual who is a U.S. citizen or U.S. resident alien,
● A partnership, corporation, company, or association created or organized in the United States or under the laws of the United States,
● Any estate (other than a foreign estate), or
● A domestic trust (as defined in Regulations section 301.7701-7).

A partnership may require a signed Form W-9 from its U.S. partners to overcome any presumptions of foreign status and to avoid withholding on the partner's allocable share of the partnership's effectively connected income. For more information, see Regulations section 1.1446-1.

Advise foreign persons to use the appropriate Form W-8. See Pub. 515, Withholding of Tax on Nonresident Aliens and Foreign Entities, for more information and a list of the W-8 forms.

Also, a nonresident alien individual may, under certain circumstances, claim treaty benefits on scholarships and fellowship grant income. See Pub. 515 or Pub. 519, U.S. Tax Guide for Aliens, for more information.

Electronic Submission of Forms W-9

Requesters may establish a system for payees and payees' agents to submit Forms W-9 electronically, including by fax. A requester is anyone required to file an information return. A payee is anyone required to provide a taxpayer identification number (TIN) to the requester.

Payee's agent. A payee's agent can be an investment advisor (corporation, partnership, or individual) or an introducing broker. An investment advisor must be registered with the Securities and Exchange Commission (SEC) under the Investment Advisers Act of 1940. The introducing broker is a broker-dealer that is regulated by the SEC and the National Association of Securities Dealers, Inc., and that is not a payer. Except for a broker who acts as a payee's agent for "readily tradable instruments," the advisor or broker must show in writing to the payer that the payee authorized the advisor or broker to transmit the Form W-9 to the payer.

Electronic system. Generally, the electronic system must:
● Ensure the information received is the information sent, and document all occasions of user access that result in the submission;
● Make reasonably certain that the person accessing the system and submitting the form is the person identified on Form W-9, the investment advisor, or the introducing broker;
● Provide the same information as the paper Form W-9;
● Be able to supply a hard copy of the electronic Form W-9 if the Internal Revenue Service requests it; and
● Require as the final entry in the submission an electronic signature by the payee whose name is on Form W-9 that authenticates and verifies the submission. The electronic signature must be under penalties of perjury and the perjury statement must contain the language of the paper Form W-9.

 For Forms W-9 that are not required to be signed, the electronic system need not provide for an electronic signature or a perjury statement.

For more details, see the following.
● Announcement 98-27, which is on page 30 of Internal Revenue Bulletin 1998-15 at *www.irs.gov/pub/irs-irbs/ irb98-15.pdf*.
● Announcement 2001-91, which is on page 221 of Internal Revenue Bulletin 2001-36 at *www.irs.gov/pub/ irs-irbs/irb01-36.pdf*.

Cat. No. 20479P

Individual Taxpayer Identification Number (ITIN)

Form W-9 (or an acceptable substitute) is used by persons required to file information returns with the IRS to get the payee's (or other person's) correct name and TIN. For individuals, the TIN is generally a social security number (SSN).

However, in some cases, individuals who become U.S. resident aliens for tax purposes are not eligible to obtain an SSN. This includes certain resident aliens who must receive information returns but who cannot obtain an SSN.

These individuals must apply for an ITIN on Form W-7, Application for IRS Individual Taxpayer Identification Number, unless they have an application pending for an SSN. Individuals who have an ITIN must provide it on Form W-9.

Substitute Form W-9

You may develop and use your own Form W-9 (a substitute Form W-9) if its content is substantially similar to the official IRS Form W-9 and it satisfies certain certification requirements.

You may incorporate a substitute Form W-9 into other business forms you customarily use, such as account signature cards. However, the certifications on the substitute Form W-9 must clearly state (as shown on the official Form W-9) that under penalties of perjury:

1. The payee's TIN is correct,
2. The payee is not subject to backup withholding due to failure to report interest and dividend income, and
3. The payee is a U.S. person.

You may not:

1. Use a substitute Form W-9 that requires the payee, by signing, to agree to provisions unrelated to the required certifications, or
2. Imply that a payee may be subject to backup withholding unless the payee agrees to provisions on the substitute form that are unrelated to the required certifications.

A substitute Form W-9 that contains a separate signature line just for the certifications satisfies the requirement that the certifications be clearly stated.

If a single signature line is used for the required certifications and other provisions, the certifications must be highlighted, boxed, printed in bold-face type, or presented in some other manner that causes the language to stand out from all other information contained on the substitute form. Additionally, the following statement must be presented to stand out in the same manner as described above and must appear immediately above the single signature line:

"The Internal Revenue Service does not require your consent to any provision of this document other than the certifications required to avoid backup withholding."

If you use a substitute form, you are required to provide the Form W-9 instructions to the payee only if he or she requests them. However, if the IRS has notified the payee that backup withholding applies, then you must instruct the payee to strike out the language in the certification that relates to underreporting. This instruction can be given orally or in writing. See item 2 of the *Certification* on Form W-9. You can replace "defined

below" with "defined in the instructions" in item 3 of the *Certification* on Form W-9 when the instructions will not be provided to the payee except upon request. For more information, see Rev. Proc. 83-89,1983-2 C.B. 613; amplified by Rev. Proc. 96-26, which is on page 22 of Internal Revenue Bulletin 1996-8 at *www.irs.gov/pub/ irs-irbs/irb96-08.pdf.*

TIN Applied for

For interest and dividend payments and certain payments with respect to readily tradable instruments, the payee may return a properly completed, signed Form W-9 to you with "Applied For" written in Part I. This is an "awaiting-TIN" certificate. The payee has 60 calendar days, from the date you receive this certificate, to provide a TIN. If you do not receive the payee's TIN at that time, you must begin backup withholding on payments.

Reserve rule. You must backup withhold on any reportable payments made during the 60-day period if a payee withdraws more than $500 at one time, unless the payee reserves an amount equal to the current year's backup withholding rate on all reportable payments made to the account.

Alternative rule. You may also elect to backup withhold during this 60-day period, after a 7-day grace period, under one of the two alternative rules discussed below.

Option 1. Backup withhold on any reportable payments if the payee makes a withdrawal from the account after the close of 7 business days after you receive the awaiting-TIN certificate. Treat as reportable payments all cash withdrawals in an amount up to the reportable payments made from the day after you receive the awaiting-TIN certificate to the day of withdrawal.

Option 2. Backup withhold on any reportable payments made to the payee's account, regardless of whether the payee makes any withdrawals, beginning no later than 7 business days after you receive the awaiting-TIN certificate.

 The 60-day exemption from backup withholding does not apply to any payment other than interest, dividends, and certain payments relating to readily tradable instruments. Any other reportable payment, such as nonemployee compensation, is subject to backup withholding immediately, even if the payee has applied for and is awaiting a TIN.

Even if the payee gives you an awaiting-TIN certificate, you must backup withhold on reportable interest and dividend payments if the payee does not certify, under penalties of perjury, that the payee is not subject to backup withholding.

If you do not collect backup withholding from affected payees as required, you may become liable for any uncollected amount.

Payees Exempt From Backup Withholding

Even if the payee does not provide a TIN in the manner required, you are not required to backup withhold on any payments you make if the payee is:

1. An organization exempt from tax under section 501(a), any IRA, or a custodial account under section 403(b)(7) if the account satisfies the requirements of section 401(f)(2);

2. The United States or any of its agencies or instrumentalities;

3. A state, the District of Columbia, a possession of the United States, or any of their political subdivisions, agencies, or instrumentalities;

4. A foreign government or any of its political subdivisions, agencies, or instrumentalities; or

5. An international organization or any of its agencies or instrumentalities.

Other payees that may be exempt from backup withholding include:

6. A corporation;

7. A foreign central bank of issue;

8. A dealer in securities or commodities required to register in the United States, the District of Columbia, or a possession of the United States;

9. A futures commission merchant registered with the Commodity Futures Trading Commission;

10. A real estate investment trust;

11. An entity registered at all times during the tax year under the Investment Company Act of 1940;

12. A common trust fund operated by a bank under section 584(a);

13. A financial institution;

14. A middleman known in the investment community as a nominee or custodian; or

15. A trust exempt from tax under section 664 or described in section 4947.

The following types of payments are exempt from backup withholding as indicated for items 1 through 15 above.

Interest and dividend payments. All listed payees are exempt except the payee in item 9.

Broker transactions. All payees listed in items 1 through 5 and 7 through 13 are exempt. Also, C corporations are exempt. A person registered under the Investment Advisers Act of 1940 who regularly acts as a broker is also exempt.

Barter exchange transactions and patronage dividends. Only payees listed in items 1 through 5 are exempt.

Payments reportable under sections 6041 and 6041A. Only payees listed in items 1 through 7 are generally exempt.

However, the following payments made to a corporation (including gross proceeds paid to an attorney under section 6045(f), even if the attorney is a corporation) and reportable on Form 1099-MISC, Miscellaneous Income, are not exempt from backup withholding.

● Medical and health care payments.
● Attorneys' fees.
● Payments for services paid by a federal executive agency. (See Rev. Rul. 2003-66, which is on page 1115 of Intenal Revenue Bulletin 2003-26 at *www.irs.gov/pub/ irs-irbs/irb03-26.pdf*.)

Payments Exempt From Backup Withholding

Payments that are not subject to information reporting also are not subject to backup withholding. For details, see sections 6041, 6041A, 6042, 6044, 6045, 6049, 6050A, and 6050N, and their regulations. The following payments are generally exempt from backup withholding.

Dividends and patronage dividends
● Payments to nonresident aliens subject to withholding under section 1441.
● Payments to partnerships not engaged in a trade or business in the United States and that have at least one nonresident alien partner.
● Payments of patronage dividends not paid in money.
● Payments made by certain foreign organizations.
● Section 404(k) distributions made by an ESOP.

Interest payments
● Payments of interest on obligations issued by individuals. However, if you pay $600 or more of interest in the course of your trade or business to a payee, you must report the payment. Backup withholding applies to the reportable payment if the payee has not provided a TIN or has provided an incorrect TIN.
● Payments described in section 6049(b)(5) to nonresident aliens.
● Payments on tax-free covenant bonds under section 1451.
● Payments made by certain foreign organizations.
● Mortgage or student loan interest paid to you.

Other types of payment
● Wages.
● Distributions from a pension, annuity, profit-sharing or stock bonus plan, any IRA, an owner-employee plan, or other deferred compensation plan.
● Distributions from a medical or health savings account and long-term care benefits.
● Certain surrenders of life insurance contracts.
● Distribution from qualified tuition programs or Coverdell ESAs.
● Gambling winnings if regular gambling winnings withholding is required under section 3402(q). However, if regular gambling winnings withholding is not required under section 3402(q), backup withholding applies if the payee fails to furnish a TIN.
● Real estate transactions reportable under section 6045(e).
● Cancelled debts reportable under section 6050P.
● Fish purchases for cash reportable under section 6050R.

 After 2011, backup withholding will apply to certain payment card transactions by a qualified payment card agent under section 6050W.

Joint Foreign Payees

If the first payee listed on an account gives you a Form W-8 or a similar statement signed under penalties of perjury, backup withholding applies unless:

1. Every joint payee provides the statement regarding foreign status, or

2. Any one of the joint payees who has not established foreign status gives you a TIN.

If any one of the joint payees who has not established foreign status gives you a TIN, use that number for purposes of backup withholding and information reporting.

For more information on foreign payees, see the Instructions for the Requester of Forms W-8BEN, W-8ECI, W-8EXP, and W-8IMY.

Names and TINs To Use for Information Reporting

Show the full name and address as provided on Form W-9 on the information return filed with the IRS and on the copy furnished to the payee. If you made payments to more than one payee or the account is in more than one name, enter on the first name line of the information return only the name of the payee whose TIN is shown on Form W-9. You may show the names of any other individual payees in the area below the first name line on the information return.

 For more information on the names and TINs to use for information reporting, see section J of the General Instructions for Certain Information Returns.

Notices From the IRS

The IRS will send you a notice if the payee's name and TIN on the information return you filed do not match the IRS's records. (See *Taxpayer Identification Number (TIN) Matching*, later.) You may have to send a "B" notice to the payee to solicit another TIN. Pub. 1281, Backup Withholding for Missing and Incorrect Name/TIN(s), contains copies of the two types of "B" notices.

Taxpayer Identification Number (TIN) Matching

TIN Matching allows a payer or authorized agent who is required to file Forms 1099-B, DIV, INT, K, MISC, OID, and/or PATR to match TIN and name combinations with IRS records before submitting the forms to the IRS. TIN Matching is one of the e-services products that is offered and is accessible through the IRS website. Go to IRS.gov and enter e-services in the search box. It is anticipated that payers who validate the TIN and name combinations before filing information returns will receive fewer backup withholding (CP2100) notices and penalty notices.

Additional Information

For more information on backup withholding, see Pub. 1281.

Form **668-D** (Rev. December 2001)	Department of the Treasury — Internal Revenue Service **Release of Levy/Release of Property from Levy**

To	Taxpayer(s)
	Identifying Number(s)

A notice of levy was served on you and demand was made for the surrender of:

☐ all property, rights to property, money, credits and bank deposits of the taxpayer(s) named above, except as provided in 6332(c) of the Internal Revenue Code—"Special Rule For Banks." See the back of this form regarding this exception.

☐ wages, salary and other income, now owed to or becoming payable to the taxpayer(s) named above.

The box checked below applies to the levy we served on you.

Release of Levy

☐ Under the provisions of Internal Revenue Code section 6343, all property, rights to property, money, credits, and bank deposits of the taxpayer(s) named above are released from the levy.

☐ Under the provisions of Internal Revenue Code section 6343, all wages, salary and other income now owed to or becoming payable to the taxpayer(s) named above are released from the levy.

Release of Property from Levy

☐ Under the provisions of Internal Revenue Code section 6343, all property, rights to property, money, credits, and bank deposits greater than $ _____ are released from the levy. The levy now attaches only to this amount.

☐ The last payment we received from you was $ _____ dated _____ . The amount the taxpayer still owes is $ _____ . When this amount is paid to the Internal Revenue Service, the levy is released. If you sent us a payment after the last payment date shown, subtract that from the amount you send now.

☐ Under the provisions of Internal Revenue Code section 6343, all wages, salary and other income ☐ **greater than** ☐ **less than** $ _____ each _____ now owed to or becoming payable to the taxpayer(s) named above are released from the levy.

Dated at _____   _____

                          (Place)   *(Date)*

Signature	Telephone Number	Title

Excerpts from the Internal Revenue Code

Sec. 6332 Surrender of Property Subject to Levy

(c) **Special Rule for Banks.**—Any bank *(as defined in section 408(n))* shall surrender *(subject to an attachment or execution under judicial process)* any deposits *(including interest thereon)* in such bank only after 21 days after service of levy.

* * * * * * *

Sec. 6343. Authority to Release Levy and Return Property

(a) **Release of Levy and Notice of Release.**—

(1) **In general.**—Under regulations prescribed by the Secretary, the Secretary shall release the levy upon all, or part of, the property or rights to property levied upon and shall promptly notify the person upon whom such levy was made *(if any)* that such levy has been released if—

(A) the liability for which such levy was made is satisfied or becomes unenforceable by reason of lapse of time,

(B) release of such levy will facilitate the collection of such liability,

(C) the taxpayer has entered into an agreement under section 6159 to satisfy such liability by means of installment payments, unless such agreement provides otherwise,

(D) the Secretary has determined that such levy is creating an economic hardship due to the financial condition of the taxpayer, or

(E) the fair market value of the property exceeds such liability and release of the levy on a part of such property could be made without hindering the collection of such liability.

For purposes of subparagraph (C), the Secretary is not required to release such levy if such release would jeopardize the secured creditor status of the Secretary.

(2) **Expedited determination of certain business property.**—In the case of any tangible personal property essential in carrying on the trade or business of the taxpayer, the Secretary shall provide for an expedited determination under paragraph (1) if levy on such tangible personal property would prevent the taxpayer from carrying on such trade or business.

(3) **Subsequent levy.**—The release of levy on any property under paragraph (1) shall not prevent any subsequent levy on such property.

(b) **Return of property.**—

If the Secretary determines that property has been wrongfully levied upon, it shall be lawful for the Secretary to return . . . an amount equal to the amount of money levied upon . . . any time before the expiration of 9 months from the date of such levy . . . .

(d) **Return of Property in Certain Cases.**—If—

(1) any property has been levied upon, and

(2) the Secretary determines that—

(A) the levy on such property was premature or otherwise not in accordance with administrative procedures of the Secretary,

(B) the taxpayer has entered into an agreement under section 6159 to satisfy the tax liability for which the levy was imposed by means of installment payments, unless such agreement provides otherwise,

(C) the return of such property will facilitate the collection of the tax liability, or

(D) with the consent of the taxpayer or the Taxpayer Advocate, the return of such property would be in the best interests of the taxpayer (as determined by the Taxpayer Advocate) and the United States,

the provisions of subsection (b) shall apply in the same manner as if such property had been wrongly levied upon, except that no interest shall be allowed . . . .

Form **668-D** (Rev. 12-2001)

Form 668-D
(Rev. December 2001)

Department of the Treasury — Internal Revenue Service
Release of Levy/Release of Property from Levy

To

Taxpayer(s)

Identifying Number(s)

A notice of levy was served on you and demand was made for the surrender of:

☐ all property, rights to property, money, credits and bank deposits of the taxpayer(s) named above, except as provided in 6332(c) of the Internal Revenue Code—"Special Rule For Banks." See the back of this form regarding this exception.

☐ wages, salary and other income, now owed to or becoming payable to the taxpayer(s) named above.

The box checked below applies to the levy we served on you.

Release of Levy

☐ Under the provisions of Internal Revenue Code section 6343, all property, rights to property, money, credits, and bank deposits of the taxpayer(s) named above are released from the levy.

☐ Under the provisions of Internal Revenue Code section 6343, all wages, salary and other income now owed to or becoming payable to the taxpayer(s) named above are released from the levy.

Release of Property from Levy

☐ Under the provisions of Internal Revenue Code section 6343, all property, rights to property, money, credits, and bank deposits greater than $ _____ are released from the levy. The levy now attaches only to this amount.

☐ The last payment we received from you was $ _____ dated _____ . The amount the taxpayer still owes is $ _____ . When this amount is paid to the Internal Revenue Service, the levy is released. If you sent us a payment after the last payment date shown, subtract that from the amount you send now.

☐ Under the provisions of Internal Revenue Code section 6343, all wages, salary and other income ☐ **greater than** ☐ **less than** $ _____ each _____ now owed to or becoming payable to the taxpayer(s) named above are released from the levy.

Dated at _____   _____
              (Place)   *(Date)*

Signature	Telephone Number	Title

Part 2— For Taxpayer   Cat. No. 20450C   www.irs.gov   **Form 668-D** (Rev. 12-2001)

Excerpts from the Internal Revenue Code

Sec. 6332 Surrender of Property Subject to Levy

(c) **Special Rule for Banks.**—Any bank *(as defined in section 408(n))* shall surrender *(subject to an attachment or execution under judicial process)* any deposits *(including interest thereon)* in such bank only after 21 days after service of levy.

* * * * * * *

Sec. 6343. Authority to Release Levy and Return Property

(a) **Release of Levy and Notice of Release.**—

(1) **In general.**—Under regulations prescribed by the Secretary, the Secretary shall release the levy upon all, or part of, the property or rights to property levied upon and shall promptly notify the person upon whom such levy was made *(if any)* that such levy has been released if—

(A) the liability for which such levy was made is satisfied or becomes unenforceable by reason of lapse of time,

(B) release of such levy will facilitate the collection of such liability,

(C) the taxpayer has entered into an agreement under section 6159 to satisfy such liability by means of installment payments, unless such agreement provides otherwise,

(D) the Secretary has determined that such levy is creating an economic hardship due to the financial condition of the taxpayer, or

(E) the fair market value of the property exceeds such liability and release of the levy on a part of such property could be made without hindering the collection of such liability. For purposes of subparagraph (C), the Secretary is not required to release such levy if such release would jeopardize the secured creditor status of the Secretary.

(2) **Expedited determination of certain business property.**—In the case of any tangible personal property essential in carrying on the trade or business of the taxpayer, the Secretary shall provide for an expedited determination under paragraph (1) if levy on such tangible personal property would prevent the taxpayer from carrying on such trade or business.

(3) **Subsequent levy.**—The release of levy on any property under paragraph (1) shall not prevent any subsequent levy on such property.

(b) **Return of property.**—

If the Secretary determines that property has been wrongfully levied upon, it shall be lawful for the Secretary to return . . . an amount equal to the amount of money levied upon . . . any time before the expiration of 9 months from the date of such levy . . . .

(d) **Return of Property in Certain Cases.**—If—

(1) any property has been levied upon, and

(2) the Secretary determines that—

(A) the levy on such property was premature or otherwise not in accordance with administrative procedures of the Secretary,

(B) the taxpayer has entered into an agreement under section 6159 to satisfy the tax liability for which the levy was imposed by means of installment payments, unless such agreement provides otherwise,

(C) the return of such property will facilitate the collection of the tax liability, or

(D) with the consent of the taxpayer or the Taxpayer Advocate, the return of such property would be in the best interests of the taxpayer (as determined by the Taxpayer Advocate) and the United States,

the provisions of subsection (b) shall apply in the same manner as if such property had been wrongly levied upon, except that no interest shall be allowed . . . .

Form **668-D** (Rev. 12-2001)

Form **668-D** (Rev. December 2001)	Department of the Treasury — Internal Revenue Service ## Release of Levy/Release of Property from Levy

To	Taxpayer(s)
	Identifying Number(s)

A notice of levy was served on you and demand was made for the surrender of:

☐ all property, rights to property, money, credits and bank deposits of the taxpayer(s) named above, except as provided in 6332(c) of the Internal Revenue Code—"Special Rule For Banks." See the back of this form regarding this exception.

☐ wages, salary and other income, now owed to or becoming payable to the taxpayer(s) named above.

The box checked below applies to the levy we served on you.

Release of Levy

☐ Under the provisions of Internal Revenue Code section 6343, all property, rights to property, money, credits, and bank deposits of the taxpayer(s) named above are released from the levy.

☐ Under the provisions of Internal Revenue Code section 6343, all wages, salary and other income now owed to or becoming payable to the taxpayer(s) named above are released from the levy.

Release of Property from Levy

☐ Under the provisions of Internal Revenue Code section 6343, all property, rights to property, money, credits, and bank deposits greater than $ _____ are released from the levy. The levy now attaches only to this amount.

☐ The last payment we received from you was $ _____ dated _____ . The amount the taxpayer still owes is $ _____ . When this amount is paid to the Internal Revenue Service, the levy is released. If you sent us a payment after the last payment date shown, subtract that from the amount you send now.

☐ Under the provisions of Internal Revenue Code section 6343, all wages, salary and other income ☐ **greater than** ☐ **less than** $ _____ each _____ now owed to or becoming payable to the taxpayer(s) named above are released from the levy.

Dated at _____   _____
(Place)   (Date)

Signature	Telephone Number	Title

Part 3— IRS Copy   Cat. No. 20450C   www.irs.gov   Form **668-D** (Rev. 12-2001)

Excerpts from the Internal Revenue Code

Sec. 6332 Surrender of Property Subject to Levy

(c) **Special Rule for Banks.**—Any bank *(as defined in section 408(n))* shall surrender *(subject to an attachment or execution under judicial process)* any deposits *(including interest thereon)* in such bank only after 21 days after service of levy.

*   *   *   *   *   *   *

Sec. 6343. Authority to Release Levy and Return Property

(a) **Release of Levy and Notice of Release.**—

(1) **In general.**—Under regulations prescribed by the Secretary, the Secretary shall release the levy upon all, or part of, the property or rights to property levied upon and shall promptly notify the person upon whom such levy was made *(if any)* that such levy has been released if—

(A) the liability for which such levy was made is satisfied or becomes unenforceable by reason of lapse of time,

(B) release of such levy will facilitate the collection of such liability,

(C) the taxpayer has entered into an agreement under section 6159 to satisfy such liability by means of installment payments, unless such agreement provides otherwise,

(D) the Secretary has determined that such levy is creating an economic hardship due to the financial condition of the taxpayer, or

(E) the fair market value of the property exceeds such liability and release of the levy on a part of such property could be made without hindering the collection of such liability.

For purposes of subparagraph (C), the Secretary is not required to release such levy if such release would jeopardize the secured creditor status of the Secretary.

(2) **Expedited determination of certain business property.**—In the case of any tangible personal property essential in carrying on the trade or business of the taxpayer, the Secretary shall provide for an expedited determination under paragraph (1) if levy on such tangible personal property would prevent the taxpayer from carrying on such trade or business.

(3) **Subsequent levy.**—The release of levy on any property under paragraph (1) shall not prevent any subsequent levy on such property.

(b) **Return of property.**—

If the Secretary determines that property has been wrongfully levied upon, it shall be lawful for the Secretary to return . . . an amount equal to the amount of money levied upon . . . any time before the expiration of 9 months from the date of such levy . . . .

(d) **Return of Property in Certain Cases.**—If—

(1) any property has been levied upon, and

(2) the Secretary determines that—

(A) the levy on such property was premature or otherwise not in accordance with administrative procedures of the Secretary,

(B) the taxpayer has entered into an agreement under section 6159 to satisfy the tax liability for which the levy was imposed by means of installment payments, unless such agreement provides otherwise,

(C) the return of such property will facilitate the collection of the tax liability, or

(D) with the consent of the taxpayer or the Taxpayer Advocate, the return of such property would be in the best interests of the taxpayer (as determined by the Taxpayer Advocate) and the United States,

the provisions of subsection (b) shall apply in the same manner as if such property had been wrongly levied upon, except that no interest shall be allowed . . . .

Form **668-D** (Rev. 12-2001)

Form **668-W(c)(DO)** (Rev. July 2002)	Department of the Treasury – Internal Revenue Service **Notice of Levy on Wages, Salary, and Other Income**

DATE:
REPLY TO:

TELEPHONE NUMBER
OF IRS OFFICE:

NAME AND ADDRESS OF TAXPAYER:

TO:

IDENTIFYING NUMBER*(S)*:

Kind of Tax	Tax Period Ended	Unpaid Balance of Assessment	Statutory Additions	Total
			Total Amount Due ▶	

We figured the interest and late payment penalty to _____

THIS ISN'T A BILL FOR TAXES YOU OWE. THIS IS A NOTICE OF LEVY TO COLLECT MONEY OWED BY THE TAXPAYER NAMED ABOVE.

The Internal Revenue Code provides that there is a lien for the amount shown above. Although we have given the notice and demand required by the Code, the amount owed hasn't been paid. This levy requires you to turn over to us: (1) this taxpayer's wages and salary that have been earned but not paid, as well as wages and salary earned in the future until this levy is released, and (2) this taxpayer's other income that you have now or for which you are obligated.

We levy this money to the extent it isn't exempt, as shown in the instructions. Don't offset money this person owes you without contacting us at the telephone number shown above for instructions.

If you don't owe money to this taxpayer, please call us at the telephone number at the top of this form. Instead of calling us you may complete the back of Part 3, attach it as a cover to the rest of this form, and return all parts to IRS in the enclosed envelope.

If you do owe money to this taxpayer, please see the back of this page for instructions on how to act on this notice.

Signature of Service Representative	Title

Part 1 — For Employer or other Addressee	Catalog No. 15703I	www.irs.gov	Form **668-W(c)(DO)** (Rev. 7-2002)

A-129

IF MONEY IS DUE THIS TAXPAYER

Give the taxpayer Parts 2, 3, 4 and 5, as soon as you receive this levy. Part of the taxpayer's wages, salary, or other income is exempt from levy. To claim exemptions, the taxpayer must complete and sign the Statement of Exemptions and Filing Status on Parts 3, 4, and 5 and return Parts 3 and 4 to you within 3 work days after you receive this levy. The taxpayer's instructions for completing the Statement of Exemptions and Filing Status are on the back of Part 5.

Send us the taxpayer's take home pay minus the exempt amount which is described below, on the same dates that payments are made, or are due, to the taxpayer. Unless we tell you that a deduction should not be allowed, allow the taxpayer's payroll deductions which were in effect when you received this levy in determining the take home pay. Do not allow the taxpayer to take new voluntary payroll deductions while this levy is in effect. The method of payment to the taxpayer, for example, direct deposit, has no bearing on take home pay. Direct deposit is not considered a payroll deduction.

When you send us your check, **complete the back of Part 3 of this form,** attach it to the check, and mail them to us in the enclosed envelope. **Make your check payable to United States Treasury. Please write on the check (not on a detachable stub) the taxpayer's name, identifying number**(s)**, kind of tax, and tax periods shown on Part 1, and the words "LEVY PROCEEDS."**

This levy remains in effect for all wages and salary for personal services until we send you a release of levy. Wages and salary include fees, commissions, and bonuses. If more than one payment is necessary to satisfy the levy, send additional payments to the Internal Revenue Service address shown on your copy of this levy, and make out your check as described above.

This levy remains in effect for benefit and retirement income if the taxpayer has a current fixed right to future payments, until we send you a release of levy.

For income other **than wages and salary, and benefit and retirement income as described above, this levy is effective only for funds you owe the taxpayer now.** We may issue another levy if necessary. However, this levy attaches to all obligations you owe the taxpayer at the time you receive it, even though you plan to make the payment at a later date.

INSTRUCTIONS FOR FIGURING THE AMOUNT EXEMPT FROM THIS LEVY

There are three steps in figuring the amount exempt from this levy.

1. When you receive the completed Parts 3 and 4 from the taxpayer, use item 1 of the enclosed table (Publication 1494) to figure how much wages, salary, or other income is exempt from this levy. Find the correct block on the table using the taxpayer's filing status, number of personal exemptions claimed, and pay period. Be sure you allow one exemption for the taxpayer, in addition to one for each person listed on Parts 3 and 4, unless, "I cannot claim myself as an exemption," is written next to the taxpayer's signature. If no Social Security Number is provided for a personal exemption, do not allow that exemption, unless "Less than six months old" is written in the space for that person's Social Security Number. If you don't receive the completed Parts 3 and 4, then the exempt amount is what would be exempt if the taxpayer had returned them indicating married filing separate and only the taxpayer is claimed as a personal exemption. Don't use the information on the taxpayer's Form W-4, Employee's Withholding Allowance Certificate, to determine the amount that is exempt from this levy. That information can be different from what is filed on the employee's individual income tax return.

2. If the taxpayer, or the taxpayer's spouse, is at least 65 years old and/or blind, an additional amount is exempt from this levy. To claim this, the taxpayer counts one for each of the following: (a) the taxpayer is 65 or older, (b) the taxpayer is blind, (c) the taxpayer's spouse is 65 or older, and (d) the taxpayer's spouse is blind. Then, this total (up to 4) is entered next to "ADDITIONAL STANDARD DEDUCTION" on the Statement of Exemptions and Filing Status. If the taxpayer has entered a number in this space, use item 2 of the enclosed table to figure the additional amount exempt from this levy.

3. The amount the taxpayer needs to pay support, established by a court or an administrative order, for minor children is also exempt from the levy, but the court or administrative order must have been made before the date of this levy. These children can't be claimed as personal exemptions on Parts 3, 4, and 5.

If the taxpayer's exemptions, filing status, or eligibility for additional standard deduction change while this levy is in effect, the taxpayer may give you a new statement to change the amount that is exempt. You can get more forms from an IRS office. If you are sending payments for this levy next year, the amount that is exempt doesn't change merely because the amount that all taxpayers can deduct for exemptions, filing status, and additional standard deductions on individual income tax returns changes for the new year. However, if the taxpayer asks you to recompute the exempt amount in the new year by submitting a new Statement of Exemptions and Filing Status, even though there may be no change from the prior statement, you may use the new year's exemption table. This change applies to levies you already have as well as this one. If you are asked to recompute the exempt amount and you don't have the new year's exemption table, you may order one by calling 1-800-829-3676. Ask for Publication 1494. This publication is also available at our internet site www.irs.gov The taxpayer submits the information under penalties of perjury, and it is subject to verification by the Internal Revenue Service.

Form **668-W(c)(DO)** (Rev. 7-2002)

Form **668-W(c)(DO)** (Rev. July 2002)	Department of the Treasury – Internal Revenue Service **Notice of Levy on Wages, Salary, and Other Income**

DATE:

REPLY TO:

TELEPHONE NUMBER
OF IRS OFFICE:

NAME AND ADDRESS OF TAXPAYER:

TO:

IDENTIFYING NUMBER*(S)*:

Kind of Tax	Tax Period Ended	Unpaid Balance of Assessment	Statutory Additions	Total
			Total Amount Due ▶	

We figured the interest and late payment penalty to _____

Although we asked you to pay the amount you owe, it is still not paid.

This is your copy of a Notice of Levy we have sent to collect the unpaid amount. We will send other levies if we don't get sufficient funds to pay the total amount you owe.

This levy requires the person who received it to turn over to us: your wages and salary that have been earned but not paid, as well as wages and salary earned in the future until the levy is released; and (2) your other income that the person has now or is obligated to pay you. This money is levied to the extent it isn't exempt, as explained on the back of Part 5 of this form.

If you decide to pay the amount you owe now, please **bring** a guaranteed payment *(cash, cashier's check, or money order)* to the nearest IRS office with this form, so we can tell the person who received this levy not to send us your money. Make checks and money orders payable to United States Treasury. If you mail your payment instead of bringing it to us, we may not have time to stop the person who received this levy from sending us your money.

If you have any questions or want to arrange payment before other levies are issued, please call or write us. If you write to us, please include your telephone number and the best time for us to call you.

Please see the back of Part 5 for instructions.

Signature of Service Representative	Title

Part 2 — For Taxpayer	Catalog No. 15703I	www.irs.gov	Form **668-W(c)(DO)** (Rev. 7-2002)

Excerpts from the Internal Revenue Code

Sec. 6331. LEVY AND DISTRAINT.

(b) **Seizure and Sale of Property.–**The term "levy" as used in this title includes the power of distraint and seizure by any means. Except as otherwise provided in subsection (e), a levy shall extend only to property possessed and obligations existing at the time thereof. In any case in which the Secretary may levy upon property or rights to property, he may seize and sell such property or rights to property (whether real or personal, tangible or intangible).

(c) **Successive Seizures.–**Whenever any property or right to property upon which levy has been made by virtue of subsection (a) is not sufficient to satisfy the claim of the United States for which levy is made, the Secretary may, thereafter, and as often as may be necessary, proceed to levy in like manner upon any other property liable to levy of the person against whom such claim exists, until the amount due from him, together with all expenses, is fully paid.

(e) **Continuing Levy on Salary and Wages.–**The effect of a levy on salary or wages payable to or received by a taxpayer shall be continuous from the date such levy is first made until such levy is released under Section 6343.

Sec. 6332. SURRENDER OF PROPERTY SUBJECT TO LEVY.

(a) **Requirement.–** Except as otherwise provided in this section, any person in possession of (or obligated with respect to) property or rights to property subject to levy upon which a levy has been made shall, upon demand of the Secretary, surrender such property or rights (or discharge such obligation) to the Secretary, except such part of the property or rights as is, at the time of such demand, subject to an attachment or execution under any judicial process.

(d) **Enforcement of Levy.**

(1) **Extent of personal liability**.–Any person who fails or refuses to surrender any property or rights to property, subject to levy, upon demand by the Secretary, shall be liable in his own person and estate to the United States in a sum equal to the value of the property or rights not so surrendered, but not exceeding the amount of taxes for the collection of which such levy has been made, together with costs and interest on such sum at the underpayment rate established under section 6621 from the date of such levy (or, in the case of a levy described in section 6331 (d)(3), from the date such person would otherwise have been obligated to pay over such amounts to the taxpayer). Any amount (other than costs) recovered under this paragraph shall be credited against the tax liability for the collection of which such levy was made.

(2) **Penalty for violation.**–In addition to the personal liability imposed by paragraph (1), if any person required to surrender property or rights to property fails or refuses to surrender such property or rights to property without reasonable cause, such person shall be liable for a penalty equal to 50 percent of the amount recoverable under paragraph (1). No part of such penalty shall be credited against the tax liability for the collection of which such levy was made.

(e) **Effect of honoring levy.**–Any person in possession of (or obligated with respect to) property or rights to property subject to levy upon which a levy has been made who, upon demand by the Secretary, surrenders such property or rights to property (or discharges such obligation) to the Secretary (or who pays a liability under subsection (d)(1)) shall be discharged from any obligation or liability to the delinquent taxpayer and any other person with respect to such property or rights to property arising from such surrender or payment.

Sec. 6333. PRODUCTION OF BOOKS.

If a levy has been made or is about to be made on any property, or right to property, any person having custody or control of any books or records, containing evidence or statements relating to the property or right to property subject to levy, shall, upon demand of the Secretary exhibit such books or records to the Secretary.

Sec. 6334. PROPERTY EXEMPT FROM LEVY.

(a) **Enumeration.–**There shall be exempt from levy

(4) **Unemployment benefits.–**Any amount payable to an individual with respect to his unemployment (including any portion thereof payable with respect to dependents) under an unemployment compensation law of the United States, of any State, or of the District of Columbia or of the Commonwealth of Puerto Rico.

(6) **Certain annuity and pension payments.–**Annuity or pension payments under the Railroad Retirement Act, benefits under the Railroad Unemployment Insurance Act, special pension payments received by a person whose name has been entered on the Army, Navy, Air Force, and Coast Guard Medal of Honor roll (38 U.S.C. 562), and annuities based on retired or retainer pay under chapter 73 of title 10 of the United States Code.

(7) **Workmen's compensation.–** Any amount payable to an individual as workmen's compensation (including any portion thereof payable with respect to dependents) under a workmen's compensation law of the United States, any State, the District of Columbia, or the Commonwealth of Puerto Rico.

(8) **Judgments for support of minor children.–**If the taxpayer is required by judgment of a court of competent jurisdiction, entered prior to the date of levy, to contribute to the support of his minor children, so much of his salary, wages, or other income as is necessary to comply with such judgment.

(9) **Minimum exemption for wages, salary and other income.–**Any amount payable to or received by an individual as wages or salary for personal services, or as income derived from other sources, during any period, to the extent that the total of such amounts payable to or received by him during such period does not exceed the applicable exempt amount determined under subsection (d).

(10) **Certain service-connected disability payments.–**Any amount payable to an individual as a service-connected (within the meaning of section 101(16) of title 38, United States Code) disability benefit under-

(A) subchapter II, III, IV, V, or VI of chapter 11 of such title 38, or

(B) Chapter 13, 21, 23, 31, 32, 34, 35, 37, or 39 of such title 38.

(11) **Certain public assistance payments.–**Any amount payable to an individual as a recipient of public assistance under-

(A) title IV or title XVI (relating to supplemental security income for the aged, blind, and disabled) of the Social Security Act, or

(B) State or local government public assistance or public welfare programs for which eligibility is determined by a needs or income test.

(12) **Assistance Under Job Training Partnership Act.–**Any amount payable to a participant under the Job Training Partnership Act (29 U.S.C. 1501 *et seq.*) from funds appropriated pursuant to such Act.

(d) **Exempt Amount of Wages, Salary, or Other Income.–**

(1) **Individuals on weekly basis.–**In the case of an individual who is paid or receives all of his wages, salary, and other income on a weekly basis, the amount of the wages, salary, and other income payable to or received by him during any week which is exempt from levy under subsection (a) (9) shall be the exempt amount.

(2) **Exempt Amount.–**For purposes of paragraph (1), the term "exempt amount" means an amount equal to–

(A) the sum of–

(I) the standard deduction, and

(II) the aggregate amount of the deductions for personal exemptions allowed the taxpayer under section 151 in the taxable year in which such levy occurs, divided by

(B) 52.

Unless the taxpayer submits to the Secretary a written and properly verified statement specifying the facts necessary to determine the proper amount under subparagraph (A), subparagraph (A) shall be applied as if the taxpayer were a married individual filing a separate return with only 1 personal exemption.

(3) **Individuals on basis other than weekly.**–In the case of any individual not described in paragraph (1), the amount of wages, salary, and other income payable to or received by him during any applicable pay period or other fiscal period (as determined under regulations prescribed by the Secretary) which is exempt from levy under subsection (a) (9) shall be an amount (determined under such regulations) which as nearly as possible will result in the same total exemption from levy for such individual over a period of time as he would have under paragraph (1) if (during such period of time) he were paid or received such wages, salary and other income on a regular weekly basis.

Sec. 6343. AUTHORITY TO RELEASE LEVY AND RETURN PROPERTY.

(a) Release of Levy and Notice of Release.–

(1) **In General.**–Under regulations prescribed by the Secretary, the Secretary shall release the levy upon all, or part of, the property or rights to property levied upon and shall promptly notify the person upon whom such levy was made *(if any)* that such levy has been released if–

(A) the liability for which such levy was made is satisfied or becomes unenforceable by reason of lapse of time,

(B) release of such levy will facilitate the collection of such liability,

(C) the taxpayer has entered into an agreement under section 6159 to satisfy such liability by means of installment payments, unless such agreement provides otherwise.

(D) the Secretary has determined that such levy is creating an economic hardship due to the financial condition of the taxpayer, or

(E) the fair market value of the property exceeds such liability and release of the levy on a part of such property could be made without hindering the collection of such liability.

For purposes of subparagraph (C), the Secretary is not required to release such levy if such release would jeopardize the secured creditor status of the Secretary.

(2) **Expedited determination on certain business property.–**In the case of any tangible personal property essential in carrying on the trade or business of the taxpayer, the Secretary shall provide for an expedited determination under paragraph (1) if levy on such tangible personal property would prevent the taxpayer from carrying on such trade or business.

(3) **Subsequent levy.–**The release of levy on any property under paragraph (1) shall not prevent any subsequent levy on such property.

(b) **Return of Property.–**If the Secretary determines that property has been wrongfully levied upon, it shall be lawful for the Secretary to return-

(1) the specific property levied upon,

(2) an amount of money equal to the amount of money levied upon, or

(3) an amount of money equal to the amount of money received by the United States from a sale of such property.

Property may be returned at any time. An amount equal to the amount of money levied upon or received from such sale may be returned at any time before the expiration of 9 months from the date of such levy. For purposes of paragraph (3), if property is declared purchased by the United States at a sale pursuant to section 6335(e) (relating to manner and conditions of sale), the United States shall be treated as having received an amount of money equal to the minimum price determined pursuant to such section or (if larger) the amount received by the United States from the resale of such property.

(d) RETURN OF PROPERTY IN CERTAIN CASES-IF–

(1) any property has been levied upon, and

(2) the Secretary determines that–

(A) the levy on such property was premature or otherwise not in accordance with administrative procedures of the Secretary,

(B) the taxpayer has entered into an agreement under section 6159 to satisfy the tax liability for which the levy was imposed by means of installment payments, unless such agreement provides otherwise,

(C) the return of such property will facilitate the collection of the tax liability, or

(D) with the consent of the taxpayer or the National Taxpayer Advocate, the return of such property would be in the best interest of the taxpayer (as determined by the National Taxpayer Advocate) and the United States,

the provisions of subsection (b) shall apply in the same manner as if such property had been wrongly levied upon, except that no interest shall be allowed under subsection (c).

Form **668-W(c)(DO)** (Rev. 7-2002)

Form **668-W(c)(DO)** (Rev. July 2002)	Department of the Treasury – Internal Revenue Service **Notice of Levy on Wages, Salary, and Other Income**

DATE:

REPLY TO:

TELEPHONE NUMBER
OF IRS OFFICE:

NAME AND ADDRESS OF TAXPAYER:

TO:

IDENTIFYING NUMBER(S):

Kind of Tax	Tax Period Ended	Unpaid Balance of Assessment	Statutory Additions	Total

Employer or Other Addressee: Please complete the back of this page.

Total Amount Due ▶

We figured the interest and late payment penalty to _____

Statement of Exemptions and Filing Status *(To be completed by taxpayer; instructions are on the back of Part 5)*

My filing status for my income tax return is *(check one):* ☐ Single; ☐ Married Filing a Joint Return;
☐ Married Filing a Separate Return; ☐ Head of Household; or ☐ Qualifying Widow*(er)* with dependent child

ADDITIONAL STANDARD DEDUCTION: _____ *(Enter amount only if you or your spouse is at least 65 and/or blind.)*

I certify that I can claim the people named below as personal exemptions on my income tax return and that none are claimed on another Notice of Levy. No one I have listed is my minor child to whom (as required by court or administrative order) I make support payments that are already exempt from levy. I understand the information I have provided may be verified by the Internal Revenue Service. Under penalties of perjury, I declare that this statement of exemptions and filing status is true.

Name *(Last, First, Middle Initial)*	Relationship *(Husband, Wife, Son, Daughter, etc.)*	Social Security Number *(SSN)*

Taxpayer's Signature

Date

Part 3 — Return to IRS

Form **668-W(c)(DO)** (Rev. 7-2002)

A-133

PLEASE REMOVE THIS PAGE BEFORE COMPLETING IT.

TAXPAYER'S NAME*(S)* _____

IDENTIFYING NUMBER*(S)*
(as shown on the front) _____

SECTION 1.— Levy Acknowledgment

Signature of person responding _____

Printed name of person responding _____

Your telephone number ( ) _____

Date and time this levy received _____

SECTION 2.— Levy Results *(Check all applicable boxes.)*

☐ Check attached in the amount of $ _____

☐ Additional checks will be sent:

☐ _____ *(weekly, bi-weekly, monthly, etc.)*

☐ _____ approximate amount of each payment

☐ Taxpayer no longer employed here, as of _____ (date).

☐ Remarks

SECTION 3.— Additional Information *(Please complete this section if this levy does not attach any funds.)*

Taxpayer's latest address, if different from the one on this levy. _____

_____

Taxpayer's telephone number ( ) _____

Name and address of taxpayer's employer: _____
(if different from addressee)

Other information you believe may help us:

Form **668-W(c)(DO)** (Rev. 7-2002)

Form **668-W(c)(DO)** (Rev. July 2002)	Department of the Treasury – Internal Revenue Service **Notice of Levy on Wages, Salary, and Other Income**

DATE:

REPLY TO:

TELEPHONE NUMBER
OF IRS OFFICE:

NAME AND ADDRESS OF TAXPAYER:

TO:

IDENTIFYING NUMBER*(S)*:

Kind of Tax	Tax Period Ended	Unpaid Balance of Assessment	Statutory Additions	Total
			Total Amount Due ▶	

We figured the interest and late payment penalty to _____

Statement of Exemptions and Filing Status *(To be completed by taxpayer; instructions are on the back of Part 5)*

My filing status for my income tax return is *(check one):* ☐ Single; ☐ Married Filing a Joint Return; ☐ Married Filing a Separate Return; ☐ Head of Household; or ☐ Qualifying Widow*(er)* with dependent child

ADDITIONAL STANDARD DEDUCTION: _____ *(Enter amount only if you or your spouse is at least 65 and/or blind.)*

I certify that I can claim the people named below as personal exemptions on my income tax return and that none are claimed on another Notice of Levy. No one I have listed is my minor child to whom (as required by court or administrative order) I make support payments that are already exempt from levy. I understand the information I have provided may be verified by the Internal Revenue Service. Under penalties of perjury, I declare that this statement of exemptions and filing status is true.

Name *(Last, First, Middle Initial)*	Relationship *(Husband, Wife, Son, Daughter, etc.)*	Social Security Number *(SSN)*

Taxpayer's Signature | Date

Part 4 — For Employer or other Addressee to keep after Taxpayer completes | Form **668-W(c)(DO)** (Rev. 7-2002)

A-135

Excerpts from the Internal Revenue Code

Sec. 6331. LEVY AND DISTRAINT.

(b) **Seizure and Sale of Property.**–The term "levy" as used in this title includes the power of distraint and seizure by any means. Except as otherwise provided in subsection (e), a levy shall extend only to property possessed and obligations existing at the time thereof. In any case in which the Secretary may levy upon property or rights to property, he may seize and sell such property or rights to property (whether real or personal, tangible or intangible).

(c) **Successive Seizures.**–Whenever any property or right to property upon which levy has been made by virtue of subsection (a) is not sufficient to satisfy the claim of the United States for which levy is made, the Secretary may, thereafter, and as often as may be necessary, proceed to levy in like manner upon any other property liable to levy of the person against whom such claim exists, until the amount due from him, together with all expenses, is fully paid.

(e) **Continuing Levy on Salary and Wages.**–The effect of a levy on salary or wages payable to or received by a taxpayer shall be continuous from the date such levy is first made until such levy is released under Section 6343.

Sec. 6332. SURRENDER OF PROPERTY SUBJECT TO LEVY.

(a) **Requirement.**– Except as otherwise provided in this section, any person in possession of (or obligated with respect to) property or rights to property subject to levy upon which a levy has been made shall, upon demand of the Secretary, surrender such property or rights (or discharge such obligation) to the Secretary, except such part of the property or rights as is, at the time of such demand, subject to an attachment or execution under any judicial process.

(d) **Enforcement of Levy.**

(1) **Extent of personal liability**.–Any person who fails or refuses to surrender any property or rights to property, subject to levy, upon demand by the Secretary, shall be liable in his own person and estate to the United States in a sum equal to the value of the property or rights not so surrendered, but not exceeding the amount of taxes for the collection of which such levy has been made, together with costs and interest on such sum at the underpayment rate established under section 6621 from the date of such levy (or, in the case of a levy described in section 6331 (d)(3), from the date such person would otherwise have been obligated to pay over such amounts to the taxpayer). Any amount (other than costs) recovered under this paragraph shall be credited against the tax liability for the collection of which such levy was made.

(2) **Penalty for violation.**–In addition to the personal liability imposed by paragraph (1), if any person required to surrender property or rights to property fails or refuses to surrender such property or rights to property without reasonable cause, such person shall be liable for a penalty equal to 50 percent of the amount recoverable under paragraph (1). No part of such penalty shall be credited against the tax liability for the collection of which such levy was made.

(e) **Effect of honoring levy.**–Any person in possession of (or obligated with respect to) property or rights to property subject to levy upon which a levy has been made who, upon demand by the Secretary, surrenders such property or rights to property (or discharges such obligation) to the Secretary (or who pays a liability under subsection (d)(1)) shall be discharged from any obligation or liability to the delinquent taxpayer and any other person with respect to such property or rights to property arising from such surrender or payment.

Sec. 6333. PRODUCTION OF BOOKS.

If a levy has been made or is about to be made on any property, or right to property, any person having custody or control of any books or records, containing evidence or statements relating to the property or right to property subject to levy, shall, upon demand of the Secretary exhibit such books or records to the Secretary.

Sec. 6334. PROPERTY EXEMPT FROM LEVY.

(a) **Enumeration.**–There shall be exempt from levy

(4) **Unemployment benefits.**–Any amount payable to an individual with respect to his unemployment (including any portion thereof payable with respect to dependents) under an unemployment compensation law of the United States, of any State, or of the District of Columbia or of the Commonwealth of Puerto Rico.

(6) **Certain annuity and pension payments.**–Annuity or pension payments under the Railroad Retirement Act, benefits under the Railroad Unemployment Insurance Act, special pension payments received by a person whose name has been entered on the Army, Navy, Air Force, and Coast Guard Medal of Honor roll (38 U.S.C. 562), and annuities based on retired or retainer pay under chapter 73 of title 10 of the United States Code.

(7) **Workmen's compensation.**– Any amount payable to an individual as workmen's compensation (including any portion thereof payable with respect to dependents) under a workmen's compensation law of the United States, any State, the District of Columbia, or the Commonwealth of Puerto Rico.

(8) **Judgments for support of minor children.**–If the taxpayer is required by judgment of a court of competent jurisdiction, entered prior to the date of levy, to contribute to the support of his minor children, so much of his salary, wages, or other income as is necessary to comply with such judgment.

(9) **Minimum exemption for wages, salary and other income.**–Any amount payable to or received by an individual as wages or salary for personal services, or as income derived from other sources, during any period, to the extent that the total of such amounts payable to or received by him during such period does not exceed the applicable exempt amount determined under subsection (d).

(10) **Certain service-connected disability payments.**–Any amount payable to an individual as a service-connected (within the meaning of section 101(16) of title 38, United States Code) disability benefit under-

(A) subchapter II, III, IV, V, or VI of chapter 11 of such title 38, or

(B) Chapter 13, 21, 23, 31, 32, 34, 35, 37, or 39 of such title 38.

(11) **Certain public assistance payments.**–Any amount payable to an individual as a recipient of public assistance under-

(A) title IV or title XVI (relating to supplemental security income for the aged, blind, and disabled) of the Social Security Act, or

(B) State or local government public assistance or public welfare programs for which eligibility is determined by a needs or income test.

(12) **Assistance Under Job Training Partnership Act.**–Any amount payable to a participant under the Job Training Partnership Act (29 U.S.C. 1501 *et seq.*) from funds appropriated pursuant to such Act.

(d) **Exempt Amount of Wages, Salary, or Other Income.**–

(1) **Individuals on weekly basis.**–In the case of an individual who is paid or receives all of his wages, salary, and other income on a weekly basis, the amount of the wages, salary, and other income payable to or received by him during any week which is exempt from levy under subsection (a) (9) shall be the exempt amount.

(2) **Exempt Amount.**–For purposes of paragraph (1), the term "exempt amount" means an amount equal to–

(A) the sum of–

(I) the standard deduction, and

(II) the aggregate amount of the deductions for personal exemptions allowed the taxpayer under section 151 in the taxable year in which such levy occurs, divided by

(B) 52.

Unless the taxpayer submits to the Secretary a written and properly verified statement specifying the facts necessary to determine the proper amount under subparagraph (A), subparagraph (A) shall be applied as if the taxpayer were a married individual filing a separate return with only 1 personal exemption.

(3) **Individuals on basis other than weekly.**–In the case of any individual not described in paragraph (1), the amount of wages, salary, and other income payable to or received by him during any applicable pay period or other fiscal period (as determined under regulations prescribed by the Secretary) which is exempt from levy under subsection (a) (9) shall be an amount (determined under such regulations) which as nearly as possible will result in the same total exemption from levy for such individual over a period of time as he would have under paragraph (1) if (during such period of time) he were paid or received such wages, salary and other income on a regular weekly basis.

Sec. 6343. AUTHORITY TO RELEASE LEVY AND RETURN PROPERTY.

(a) Release of Levy and Notice of Release.–

(1) **In General.**–Under regulations prescribed by the Secretary, the Secretary shall release the levy upon all, or part of, the property or rights to property levied upon and shall promptly notify the person upon whom such levy was made *(if any)* that such levy has been released if–

(A) the liability for which such levy was made is satisfied or becomes unenforceable by reason of lapse of time,

(B) release of such levy will facilitate the collection of such liability,

(C) the taxpayer has entered into an agreement under section 6159 to satisfy such liability by means of installment payments, unless such agreement provides otherwise.

(D) the Secretary has determined that such levy is creating an economic hardship due to the financial condition of the taxpayer, or

(E) the fair market value of the property exceeds such liability and release of the levy on a part of such property could be made without hindering the collection of such liability.

For purposes of subparagraph (C), the Secretary is not required to release such levy if such release would jeopardize the secured creditor status of the Secretary.

(2) **Expedited determination on certain business property.**–In the case of any tangible personal property essential in carrying on the trade or business of the taxpayer, the Secretary shall provide for an expedited determination under paragraph (1) if levy on such tangible personal property would prevent the taxpayer from carrying on such trade or business.

(3) **Subsequent levy.**–The release of levy on any property under paragraph (1) shall not prevent any subsequent levy on such property.

(b) **Return of Property.**–If the Secretary determines that property has been wrongfully levied upon, it shall be lawful for the Secretary to return-

(1) the specific property levied upon,

(2) an amount of money equal to the amount of money levied upon, or

(3) an amount of money equal to the amount of money received by the United States from a sale of such property.

Property may be returned at any time. An amount equal to the amount of money levied upon or received from such sale may be returned at any time before the expiration of 9 months from the date of such levy. For purposes of paragraph (3), if property is declared purchased by the United States at a sale pursuant to section 6335(e) (relating to manner and conditions of sale), the United States shall be treated as having received an amount of money equal to the minimum price determined pursuant to such section or (if larger) the amount received by the United States from the resale of such property.

(d) RETURN OF PROPERTY IN CERTAIN CASES-IF–

(1) any property has been levied upon, and

(2) the Secretary determines that–

(A) the levy on such property was premature or otherwise not in accordance with administrative procedures of the Secretary,

(B) the taxpayer has entered into an agreement under section 6159 to satisfy the tax liability for which the levy was imposed by means of installment payments, unless such agreement provides otherwise,

(C) the return of such property will facilitate the collection of the tax liability, or

(D) with the consent of the taxpayer or the National Taxpayer Advocate, the return of such property would be in the best interest of the taxpayer (as determined by the National Taxpayer Advocate) and the United States,

the provisions of subsection (b) shall apply in the same manner as if such property had been wrongly levied upon, except that no interest shall be allowed under subsection (c).

Form **668-W(c)(DO)** (Rev. 7-2002)

Form **668-W(c)(DO)** (Rev. July 2002)	Department of the Treasury – Internal Revenue Service **Notice of Levy on Wages, Salary, and Other Income**

DATE:

REPLY TO:

TELEPHONE NUMBER
OF IRS OFFICE:

NAME AND ADDRESS OF TAXPAYER:

TO:

IDENTIFYING NUMBER(S):

Kind of Tax	Tax Period Ended	Unpaid Balance of Assessment	Statutory Additions	Total
			Total Amount Due ▶	

We figured the interest and late payment penalty to _____

Statement of Exemptions and Filing Status *(To be completed by taxpayer; instructions are on the back of Part 5)*

My filing status for my income tax return is *(check one):* ☐ Single; ☐ Married Filing a Joint Return;
☐ Married Filing a Separate Return; ☐ Head of Household; or ☐ Qualifying Widow*(er)* with dependent child

ADDITIONAL STANDARD DEDUCTION: _____ *(Enter amount only if you or your spouse is at least 65 and/or blind.)*

I certify that I can claim the people named below as personal exemptions on my income tax return and that none are claimed on another Notice of Levy. No one I have listed is my minor child to whom (as required by court or administrative order) I make support payments that are already exempt from levy. I understand the information I have provided may be verified by the Internal Revenue Service. Under penalties of perjury, I declare that this statement of exemptions and filing status is true.

Name *(Last, First, Middle Initial)*	Relationship *(Husband, Wife, Son, Daughter, etc.)*	Social Security Number *(SSN)*

Taxpayer's Signature | Date

Part 5 — For Taxpayer to keep   Form **668-W(c)(DO)** (Rev. 7-2002)

Instructions to the Taxpayer

A levy was served on the person named on the front of this form. The information you provide on this form will be used by that person to figure the amount of your income that is exempt from levy.

Please complete Parts 3, 4, and 5. First, indicate your filing status by checking one of the five blocks on the Statement of Exemptions and Filing Status. Then, list each person that you can claim as an exemption on your income tax return not claimed on another Notice of Levy on Wages, Salary, and Other Income. Include each person's relationship to you and Social Security Number. If the person is less than six months old and does not have a number yet, write "Less than six months old" in the Social Security Number column. If you are claimed as a dependent by someone else, write "I can't claim an exemption for myself" next to your signature on the statement. Be sure to complete, sign and date all copies of the statement.

The amount of your income that is exempt from this levy each week can be figured by adding the standard deduction you can claim on your income tax return and the amount you claim on it for exemptions. Then, this total is divided by 52.

If you or your spouse is at least 65 years old and/or blind, you can claim the additional standard deduction which increases the amount exempt from this levy. Count one for each of the following: (a) you are 65 or older, (b) you are blind, (c) your spouse is 65 or older, and (d) your spouse is blind. Enter this total (up to 4) to the right of "ADDITIONAL STANDARD DEDUCTION" on Parts 3, 4, and 5.

Also, if you are required by a court or administrative order *(made before the date of this levy)* to support your minor children, then the amount needed to pay the support established by a court or administrative order is also exempt from the levy, and these minor children can't be listed as exemptions.

Keep Parts 2 and 5 for your records. Give Parts 3 and 4 to your employer within 3 work days after you receive them. If you do not give the completed statement to your employer, then your exempt amount will be figured as if your filing status is married filing separate with only one exemption, plus the amount for paying child support established by a court or administrative order. If you subsequently submit a Statement of Exemptions and Filing Status to your employer, your exempt amount will be adjusted to correspond to your statement.

If the number of your exemptions or your filing status change while this levy is in effect, please file another Statement of Exemptions and Filing Status with the person on whom this levy was served. You can get more forms from an Internal Revenue Service office.

In addition, if this levy is still in effect next year and if the standard deduction and amount deductible for personal exemptions change in the new year for all taxpayers, you may submit a new Statement of Exemptions and Filing Status, even though there may be no change from the prior statement. Submitting a new Statement of Exemptions and Filing Status will allow your employer to use the new year's exemption table (Publication 1494).

The information you provide is submitted under penalties of perjury and may be verified by the Internal Revenue Service.

Form **668-W(c)(DO)** (Rev. 7-2002)

Form **668-W(c)(DO)** (Rev. July 2002)	Department of the Treasury – Internal Revenue Service **Notice of Levy on Wages, Salary, and Other Income**

DATE:

REPLY TO:

TELEPHONE NUMBER
OF IRS OFFICE:

NAME AND ADDRESS OF TAXPAYER:

TO:

IDENTIFYING NUMBER*(S)*:

Kind of Tax	Tax Period Ended	Unpaid Balance of Assessment	Statutory Additions	Total
			Total Amount Due ▶	

We figured the interest and late payment penalty to _____

THIS ISN'T A BILL FOR TAXES YOU OWE. THIS IS A NOTICE OF LEVY TO COLLECT MONEY OWED BY THE TAXPAYER NAMED ABOVE.

The Internal Revenue Code provides that there is a lien for the amount shown above. Although we have given the notice and demand required by the Code, the amount owed hasn't been paid. This levy requires you to turn over to us: (1) this taxpayer's wages and salary that have been earned but not paid, as well as wages and salary earned in the future until this levy is released, and (2) this taxpayer's other income that you have now or for which you are obligated.

We levy this money to the extent it isn't exempt, as shown in the instructions. Don't offset money this person owes you without contacting us at the telephone number shown above for instructions.

If you don't owe money to this taxpayer, please call us at the telephone number at the top of this form. Instead of calling us you may complete the back of Part 3, attach it as a cover to the rest of this form, and return all parts to IRS in the enclosed envelope.

If you do owe money to this taxpayer, please see the back of this page for instructions on how to act on this notice.

Signature of Service Representative	Title

Part 6 — IRS File Copy   Catalog No. 15703I   www.irs.gov   Form **668-W(c)(DO)** (Rev. 7-2002)

Form **673**
(Rev. December 2007)
Department of the Treasury
Internal Revenue Service

Statement for Claiming Exemption From Withholding on Foreign Earned Income Eligible for the Exclusion(s) Provided by Section 911

OMB No. 1545-0074

The following statement, when completed and furnished by a citizen of the United States to his or her employer, permits the employer to exclude from income tax withholding all or a part of the wages paid for services performed outside the United States.

Name *(please print or type)*

Social security number

Part I   **Qualification Information for Foreign Earned Income Exclusion**

I expect to qualify for the foreign earned income exclusion under either the bona fide residence or physical presence test for calendar year _____ or other tax year beginning _____ and ending _____ .

Please check applicable box:

☐ **Bona Fide Residence Test**

I am a citizen of the United States. I have been a bona fide resident of and my tax home has been located in _____ (foreign country or countries) for an uninterrupted period which includes an entire tax year that began on _____ , 20 _____ .
                                                       (date)

I expect to remain a bona fide resident and retain my tax home in a foreign country (or countries) until the end of the tax year for which this statement is made. Or, if not that period, from the date of this statement until _____ , 20 _____ .
         (date within tax year)

I have not submitted a statement to the authorities of any foreign country named above that I am not a resident of that country. Or, if I made such a statement, the authorities of that country thereafter made a determination to the effect that I am a resident of that country.

Based on the facts in my case, I have good reason to believe that for this period of foreign residence I will satisfy the tax home and the bona fide foreign resident requirements prescribed by section 911(d)(1)(A) of the Internal Revenue Code and qualify for the exclusion Code section 911(a) allows.

☐ **Physical Presence Test**

I am a citizen of the United States. Except for occasional absences that will not disqualify me for the benefit of section 911(a) of the Internal Revenue Code, I expect to be present in and maintain my tax home in _____ (foreign country or countries) for a 12-month period that includes the entire tax year _____ . Or, if not the entire year, for the part of the tax year beginning on _____ , 20 _____ , and ending on _____ , 20 _____ .

Based on the facts in my case, I have good reason to believe that for this period of presence in a foreign country or countries, I will satisfy the tax home and the 330 full-day requirements within a 12-month period under section 911(d)(1)(B).

Part II   **Estimated Housing Cost Amount for Foreign Housing Exclusion** (see instructions)

1 Rent	**1**	
2 Utilities (other than telephone charges)	**2**	
3 Real and personal property insurance	**3**	
4 Occupancy tax not deductible under section 164	**4**	
5 Nonrefundable fees paid for securing a leasehold	**5**	
6 Household repairs	**6**	
7 **Estimated qualified housing expenses.** Add lines 1 through 6	**7**	
8 Estimated base housing amount for qualifying period	**8**	
9 Subtract line 8 from line 7. This is your estimated housing cost amount	**9**	

Part III   **Certification**

Under penalties of perjury, I declare that I have examined the information on this form and to the best of my knowledge and belief it is true, correct, and complete. I further certify under penalties of perjury that:

● The estimated housing cost amount entered in Part II, plus the amount reported on any other statements outstanding with other employers, is not more than my total estimated housing cost amount.

● If I become disqualified for the exclusions, I will immediately notify my employer and advise what part, if any, of the period for which I am qualified.

I understand that any exemption from income tax withholding permitted by reason of furnishing this statement is not a determination by the Internal Revenue Service that any amount paid to me for any services performed during the tax year is excludable from gross income under the provisions of Code section 911(a).

Your Signature   Date

For Paperwork Reduction Act Notice, see back of form.   Cat. No. 10183Y   Form **673** (Rev. 12-2007)

Instructions

Information for Employee

File Form 673 with your U.S. employer to claim an exemption from U.S. income tax withholding on wages earned abroad to the extent of the foreign earned income exclusion and foreign housing exclusion. Your employer will then withhold the correct amount of federal income tax from your pay.

Even though you may qualify for the foreign earned income exclusion, you must file Form 2555, Foreign Earned Income, or Form 2555-EZ, Foreign Earned Income Exclusion, with your Form 1040, U.S. Individual Income Tax Return, to claim your exclusion. You must file Form 2555 to claim the foreign housing exclusion.

Estimated housing cost amount. The amount of qualified housing expenses eligible for the housing exclusion is limited depending on the location of your foreign tax home. See Pub. 54, Tax Guide for U.S. Citizens and Resident Aliens Abroad, and the Instructions for Form 2555 for more details.

Information for Employer

Once you have received Form 673 completed by the employee, you may discontinue withholding of U.S. income tax on those wages that qualify for the exclusion(s). If for any reason you believe the employee will not qualify for the exclusion(s), you should disregard Form 673.

Note. If you have questions about the exclusion(s), see Pub. 54.

Paperwork Reduction Act Notice

We ask for the information on this form to carry out the Internal Revenue laws of the United States. If you want to claim an exemption from withholding, you are required to give this form (or similar statement) to your employer.

You are not required to provide the information requested on a form that is subject to the Paperwork Reduction Act unless the form displays a valid OMB control number. Books or records relating to a form or its instructions must be retained as long as their contents may become material in the administration of any Internal Revenue law. Generally, tax returns and return information are confidential, as required by Code section 6103.

The average time and expenses required to complete and file this form will vary depending on individual circumstances. For the estimated averages, see the instructions for your income tax return.

If you have suggestions for making this form simpler, we would be happy to hear from you. See the instructions for your income tax return.

Form **843**
(Rev. August 2011)
Department of the Treasury
Internal Revenue Service

Claim for Refund and Request for Abatement

▶ **See separate instructions.**

OMB No. 1545-0024

Use Form 843 if your claim or request involves:

  (a)   a refund of one of the taxes (other than income taxes or an employer's claim for FICA tax, RRTA tax, or income tax withholding) or a fee, shown on line 3,

  (b)   an abatement of FUTA tax or certain excise taxes, or

  (c)   a refund or abatement of interest, penalties, or additions to tax for one of the reasons shown on line 5a.

Do not use Form 843 if your claim or request involves:

  (a)   an overpayment of income taxes or an employer's claim for FICA tax, RRTA tax, or income tax withholding (use the appropriate amended tax return),

  (b)   a refund of excise taxes based on the nontaxable use or sale of fuels, or

  (c)   an overpayment of excise taxes reported on Form(s) 11-C, 720, 730, or 2290.

Name(s)	Your social security number
Address (number, street, and room or suite no.)	Spouse's social security number
City or town, state, and ZIP code	Employer identification number (EIN)
Name and address shown on return if different from above	Daytime telephone number

1   **Period.** Prepare a separate Form 843 for each tax period or fee year.
    From _____ to _____

2   **Amount** to be refunded or abated:
    $ _____

3   **Type of tax or fee.** Indicate the type of tax or fee to be refunded or abated or to which the interest, penalty, or addition to tax is related.

    ☐ Employment   ☐ Estate   ☐ Gift   ☐ Excise   ☐ Income   ☐ Fee

4   **Type of penalty.** If the claim or request involves a penalty, enter the Internal Revenue Code section on which the penalty is based (see instructions). IRC section:

5a   **Interest, penalties, and additions to tax.** Check the box that indicates your reason for the request for refund or abatement. (If none apply, go to line 6.)

    ☐ Interest was assessed as a result of IRS errors or delays.

    ☐ A penalty or addition to tax was the result of erroneous written advice from the IRS.

    ☐ Reasonable cause or other reason allowed under the law (other than erroneous written advice) can be shown for not assessing a penalty or addition to tax.

  b   Date(s) of payment(s) ▶ _____

6   **Original return.** Indicate the type of fee or return, if any, filed to which the tax, interest, penalty, or addition to tax relates.

    ☐ 706   ☐ 709   ☐ 940   ☐ 941   ☐ 943   ☐ 945
    ☐ 990-PF   ☐ 1040   ☐ 1120   ☐ 4720   ☐ Other (specify) ▶

7   **Explanation.** Explain why you believe this claim or request should be allowed and show the computation of the amount shown on line 2. If you need more space, attach additional sheets.

Signature. If you are filing Form 843 to request a refund or abatement relating to a joint return, both you and your spouse must sign the claim. Claims filed by corporations must be signed by a corporate officer authorized to sign, and the officer's title must be shown.

Under penalties of perjury, I declare that I have examined this claim, including accompanying schedules and statements, and, to the best of my knowledge and belief, it is true, correct, and complete. Declaration of preparer (other than taxpayer) is based on all information of which preparer has any knowledge.

Signature (Title, if applicable. Claims by corporations must be signed by an officer.)   Date

Signature (spouse, if joint return)   Date

Paid Preparer Use Only	Print/Type preparer's name	Preparer's signature	Date	Check ☐ if self-employed	PTIN
	Firm's name ▶			Firm's EIN ▶	
	Firm's address ▶			Phone no.	

For Privacy Act and Paperwork Reduction Act Notice, see separate instructions.   Cat. No. 10180R   Form **843** (Rev. 8-2011)

Instructions for Form 843

(Rev. December 2012)

(Use the August 2011 revision of Form 843.)

Claim for Refund and Request for Abatement

Department of the Treasury
Internal Revenue Service

Section references are to the Internal Revenue Code unless otherwise noted.

General Instructions

Future developments

For the latest information about developments related to Form 843 and its instructions, such as legislation enacted after they were published, go to *www.irs.gov/form843*.

Purpose of Form

Use Form 843 to claim a refund or request an abatement of certain taxes, interest, penalties, fees, and additions to tax.

Note. If you are filing Form 843 to claim a refund of the branded prescription drug fee, please write "Branded Prescription Drug Fee" across the top of Form 843.

Do not use Form 843 to request a refund of income tax. Employers cannot use Form 843 to request a refund of Federal Insurance Contributions Act (FICA) tax, Railroad Retirement Tax Act (RRTA) tax, or income tax withholding. Also do not use Form 843 to amend a previously filed income or employment tax return. Do not use Form 843 to claim a refund of agreement fees, offer-in-compromise fees, or lien fees.

Note. You cannot use Form 843 to request an abatement of income, estate, or gift taxes. Employers cannot use Form 843 to request abatement of FICA tax, RRTA tax, or income tax withholding.

Use Form 843 to claim or request the following.

• A refund of tax, other than a tax for which a different form must be used. (See *Do not use Form 843 when you must use a different tax form,* next.)
• An abatement of tax, other than income, estate, or gift tax. Employers cannot use Form 843 to request an abatement of FICA tax, RRTA tax, or income tax withholding.
• A refund to an employee of excess social security or RRTA tax withheld by any one employer, but only if your employer will not adjust the overcollection. See the instructions for line 7.
• A refund to an employee of social security or Medicare taxes that were withheld in error, but only if your employer will not adjust the overcollection. See the instructions for Line 7. If you are a nonresident alien, see Pub. 519 for specific instructions.
• A refund of excess tier 2 RRTA tax when you had more than one railroad employer for the year and your total tier 2 RRTA tax withheld or paid for the year was more than the tier 2 limit. See the instructions for line 3.
• A refund or abatement of interest, penalties, or additions to tax, caused by certain IRS errors or delays, or certain erroneous written advice from the IRS.
• A refund or abatement of a penalty or addition to tax due to reasonable cause or other reason (other than erroneous written advice provided by the IRS) allowed under the law.
• A refund of the penalty imposed under section 6715 for misuse of dyed fuel.
• A refund or abatement of tier 1 RRTA tax for an employee representative.
• A refund of a branded prescription drug fee.

If you received an IRS notice notifying you of a change to an item on your tax return, or that you owe interest, a penalty, or addition to tax, follow the instructions on the notice. You may not have to file Form 843.

Do not use Form 843 when you must use a different tax form.

• Use Form 1040X, Amended U.S. Individual Income Tax Return, to change any amounts reported on Form 1040, 1040A, 1040EZ, 1040NR, or 1040NR-EZ, to change amounts previously adjusted by the IRS, or to make certain elections after the prescribed deadline (see Regulations sections 301.9100-1 through -3).
• Use Form 8379, Injured Spouse Allocation, to claim your portion of a joint refund used to offset your spouse's past due obligations.
• Individuals, estates, and trusts filing within 1 year after the end of the year in which a claim of right adjustment under section 1341(b)(1), a net operating loss (NOL), a general business credit, or net section 1256 contracts loss arose, can use Form 1045, Application for Tentative Refund, to apply for a "quick refund" resulting from any overpayment of tax due to the claim of right adjustment or the carryback of the loss or unused credit. Individuals also can get a refund by filing Form 1040X instead of Form 1045. An estate or trust can file an amended Form 1041, U.S. Income Tax Return for Estates and Trusts.
• Use Form 940, Employer's Annual Federal Unemployment (FUTA) Tax Return, to amend a previously filed Form 940. See the Instructions for Form 940.
• Employers must use the tax form that corresponds to the tax return previously filed to make an adjustment or claim a refund or abatement of FICA tax, RRTA tax, or income tax withholding.

IF you filed...	CORRECT using...
Form 941 or Form 941-SS	Form 941-X
Form 943	Form 943-X
Form 944 or Form 944-SS	Form 944-X
Form 945	Form 945-X
Form CT-1	Form CT-1 X
Formulario 941-PR	Formulario 941-X (PR)
Formulario 943-PR	Formulario 943-X (PR)
Formulario 944-PR	Formulario 944-X (PR)
Formulario 944 (SP)	Formulario 944-X (SP)

If you filed Schedule H (Form 1040) or Anexo H-PR (Formulario 1040-PR), see Pub. 926, Household Employer's Tax Guide, for how to correct that form.

For more information, see Treasury Decision 9405 at *www.irs.gov/irb/2008-32_IRB/ar13.html.*
• Use Form 1120X, Amended U.S. Corporation Income Tax Return, to correct Form 1120 or 1120-A as originally filed, or as later adjusted by an amended return, a claim for refund, or an examination, or to make certain elections after the prescribed deadline (see Regulations sections 301.9100-1 through -3).
• Use Form 720X, Amended Quarterly Federal Excise Tax Return, to make adjustments to liability reported on Forms 720 you have filed for previous quarters. Do not use Form 720X to

make changes to claims made on Schedule C (Form 720), except for the section 4051(d) tire credit and section 6426 fuel credits.
• Use Form 730, Monthly Tax Return for Wagers, to claim a credit or refund of wagering tax.
• Use Form 4136, Credit for Federal Tax Paid on Fuels, to claim a credit against your income tax for certain nontaxable uses (or sales) of fuel during the income tax year. Also, use Form 4136 if you are a producer claiming a credit for alcohol fuel mixtures or biodiesel mixtures. However, you can use Form 8849, Claim for Refund of Excise Taxes, to claim a periodic refund instead of waiting to claim an annual credit on Form 4136.
• Use Form 8849, Claim for Refund of Excise Taxes, to claim a refund of excise taxes other than those resulting from adjustments to your reported liabilities. See IRS Pub. 510, Excise Taxes, for the appropriate forms to use to claim excise tax refunds.
• Corporations (other than S corporations) can use Form 1139, Corporation Application for Tentative Refund, to apply for a "quick refund" of taxes from an overpayment of tax due to a claim of right adjustment under section 1341(b)(1), or the carryback of an NOL, a net capital loss, or an unused general business credit.

Separate Form Required

Generally, you must file a separate Form 843 for each tax period or fee year or type of tax or fee. There are exceptions for certain claims. See the instructions for line 5.

Who Can File

You can file Form 843 or your authorized representative can file it for you. If your authorized representative files Form 843, the original or copy of Form 2848, Power of Attorney and Declaration of Representative, must be attached. You must sign Form 2848 and authorize the representative to act on your behalf for the purposes of the request. See the Instructions for Form 2848 for more information.

If you are filing as a legal representative for a decedent whose return you filed, attach to Form 843 a statement that you filed the return and you are still acting as the decedent's representative. If you did not file the decedent's return, attach certified copies of letters testamentary, letters of administration, or similar evidence to show your authority. File Form 1310, Statement of Person Claiming Refund Due a Deceased Taxpayer, with Form 843 if you are the legal representative of a decedent.

Where To File

IF you are filing Form 843...	THEN mail the form to...
In response to an IRS notice regarding a tax or fee related to certain taxes such as income, employment, gift, estate, excise, etc.	The address shown in the notice.
For penalties, or for any other reason other than an IRS notice (see above) or Letter 4658 (see below)	The service center where you would be required to a file a current year tax return for the tax to which your claim or request relates. See the instructions for the return you are filing.
In response to Letter 4658 (notice of branded prescription drug fee) **Note.** To ensure proper processing, write "Branded Prescription Drug Fee" across the top of Form 843.	Internal Revenue Service Mail Stop 4916 1973 N. Rulon White Blvd. Ogden, UT 84404 **Caution.** *Use this address only if you are claiming a refund of the branded prescription drug fee.*

Penalty for Erroneous Claim for Refund

If you claim an excessive amount of tax refund or credit relating to income tax (other than a claim relating to the earned income credit), you may be liable for a penalty of 20% of the amount determined to be excessive. An excessive amount is the amount of the claim for refund or credit that is more than the amount of claim allowable for the tax year. The penalty may be waived if you can show that you had a reasonable basis for making the claim.

Paid Tax Return Preparer

A paid tax return preparer who files Form 843 for you must sign the form and fill in the identifying information at the bottom of the form. The tax preparer must give you a copy of the completed Form 843 for your records.

Specific Instructions

Social security number. Enter your social security number (SSN). If you are filing Form 843 relating to a joint return, enter the SSNs for both you and your spouse.

Line 1

Enter the tax period for which you are making the claim for refund or request for abatement. If you are requesting a refund of a branded prescription drug fee, enter the fee year on the "From" line.

Line 3

Check the appropriate box to show the type of tax or fee for which you are claiming a refund or requesting an abatement. If the claim relates to interest, a penalty, or addition to tax, check the box to indicate the type of tax to which the claim or request relates.

 Do not use Form 843 when another tax form must be used. See Purpose of Form.

Excess tier 2 RRTA tax. Complete lines 1 and 2. On line 3, check the box for "Employment" tax. Skip lines 4, 5, and 6. On line 7, identify the claim as "Excess tier 2 RRTA" and show your computation of the refund. You must also attach copies of your Forms W-2 for the year to Form 843. See the worksheet in Pub. 505, Tax Withholding and Estimated Tax, to help you figure the excess amount.

Branded prescription drug fee. On line 1, enter the fee year on the "From" line. Complete line 2. On line 3, check the box for "Fee." Skip lines 4 and 5. On line 6, check the "Other" box and enter "BPD Fee" in the space provided. On line 7, identify the claim as "branded prescription drug fee" and explain why you are claiming a refund.

Attach a copy of the Form 8947 that provided the basis for the fee as calculated by the IRS, as well as any additional information on the amount to be refunded. You must tell us whether you or anyone else has filed a previous claim for any amount covered by this claim. Fee claims should not be combined with any other claims.

Note. Interest related to the branded prescription drug fee cannot be abated.

Line 4

If you are requesting a refund or abatement of an assessed penalty, enter the applicable Internal Revenue Code (IRC) section. Generally, you can find the IRC section on the Notice of Assessment you received from the IRS.

Line 5

Requesting Abatement or Refund of Interest Due to IRS Error or Delay

The IRS can abate interest if the interest is caused by IRS errors or delays.

The IRS will abate the interest only if there was an unreasonable error or delay in performing a managerial or ministerial act (defined next). The taxpayer cannot have caused any significant aspect of the error or delay. In addition, the interest can be abated only if it relates to taxes for which a notice of deficiency is required. This includes income taxes, generation-skipping transfer taxes, estate and gift taxes, and certain excise taxes. Interest related to employment taxes or other excise taxes cannot be abated. See Pub. 556, Examination of Returns, Appeal Rights, and Claims for Refund, for more information.

Managerial act. The term "managerial act" means an administrative act that occurs during the processing of your case involving the temporary or permanent loss of records or the exercise of judgment or discretion relating to management of personnel. A decision regarding the proper application of federal tax law (or other federal or state law) is not a managerial act. See Regulations section 301.6404-2 for more information.

Ministerial act. The term "ministerial act" means a procedural or mechanical act that does not involve the exercise of judgment or discretion and that occurs during the processing of your case after all prerequisites of the act, such as conferences and review by supervisors, have taken place. A decision regarding the proper application of federal tax law (or other federal or state law) is not a ministerial act. See Regulations section 301.6404-2 for more information.

How To Request an Abatement of Interest

Abatement of interest on a tax. Request an abatement of interest on a tax by writing "Request for Abatement of Interest Under Section 6404(e)" at the top of Form 843.

Complete lines 1 through 3. Check the first box on line 5a. On line 5b, show the dates of any payment of interest or tax liability for the tax period involved.

On line 7 state:
- The type of tax involved,
- When you were first notified by the IRS in writing about the deficiency or payment,
- The specific period for which you are requesting abatement of interest,
- The circumstances of your case, and
- The reasons why you believe that failure to abate the interest would result in grossly unfair treatment.

Multiple tax years or types of tax. File only one Form 843 if the interest assessment resulted from the IRS's error or delay in performing a single managerial or ministerial act affecting a tax assessment for multiple tax years or types of tax (for example, where 2 or more tax years were under examination). Check the applicable box(es) on line 3 and provide a detailed explanation on line 7.

Requesting Abatement or Refund of a Penalty or Addition to Tax as a Result of Written Advice

The IRS can abate or refund any portion of a penalty or addition to tax caused by erroneous advice furnished to you in writing by

an officer or employee of the IRS acting in his or her official capacity.

The IRS will abate the penalty or addition to tax only if:

1. You reasonably relied on the written advice,

2. The written advice was in response to a specific written request for advice made by you (or your representative who is allowed to practice before the IRS), and

3. The penalty or addition to tax did not result from your failure to provide the IRS with adequate or accurate information.

How To Request an Abatement or Refund of a Penalty or an Addition to Tax as a Result of Written Advice

Request an abatement or refund of a penalty or addition to tax because of erroneous written advice by writing "Request for Abatement of Penalty or Addition to Tax Under Section 6404(f)" at the top of Form 843.

Complete lines 1 through 4. Check the second box on line 5a. On line 5b, enter the date of payment if the penalty or addition to tax has been paid.

You must attach copies of the following information to Form 843.

1. Your written request for advice.

2. The erroneous written advice you relied on that was furnished to you by the IRS.

3. The report, if any, of tax adjustments identifying the penalty or addition to tax, and the item(s) relating to the erroneous advice.

When to file. An abatement of any penalty or addition to tax as a result of written advice will be allowed only if:
- You submit the request for abatement within the period allowed for collection of the penalty or addition to tax, or
- You paid the penalty or addition to tax, within the period allowed for claiming a credit or refund of such penalty or addition to tax.

Line 6

Check the appropriate box to show the type of fee or return, if any, to which your claim or request relates. Check the box labeled "1040" to indicate other individual income tax returns (such as Form 1040A or Form 1040EZ).

 You can use Form 843 to request a refund or an abatement of interest, penalties, and additions to tax that relate to your income tax return. However, you cannot use Form 843 to request a refund or an abatement of income tax. If you are an employer, you cannot use it to request abatement of FICA tax, RRTA tax, or income tax withholding.

Check the box labeled "Other" if your claim relates to:
- Form 944, Employer's Annual Federal Tax Return. Enter "944" (or "944-SS") in the space provided.
- Form CT-2, Employee Representative's Quarterly Railroad Tax Return. Enter "CT-2" in the space provided.
- The branded prescription drug fee. Enter "BPD Fee" in the space provided.

Line 7

Explain in detail your reasons for filing this claim and show your computation for the credit, refund, or abatement. If you attach an additional sheet(s), include your name and SSN or employer identification number (EIN) on it. Also attach appropriate supporting evidence.

Instructions for Form 843 (Rev. December 2012) -3-

Refund of excess social security taxes. If you are claiming a refund of excess social security or RRTA tax withheld by one employer, you must, if possible, attach a statement from the employer. The statement should indicate the following.

• The amount, if any, the employer has repaid or reimbursed you for excess taxes withheld.

• The amount, if any, of credit or refund claimed by the employer or authorized by you to be claimed by the employer. The employer should include in the statement the fact that it is made in support of your claim for refund of employee tax paid by the employer to the IRS.

If you cannot obtain a statement from the employer, you should attach a statement with the same information to the best of your knowledge and belief and include in the statement an explanation of why you could not obtain a statement from the employer. Attach a copy of your Form W-2 to prove the amount of social security or RRTA taxes withheld.

Refund of social security and Medicare tax withheld in error. The same supporting evidence described above must be provided. If you are a nonresident alien, see Pub. 519 for additional information.

Requesting Net Interest Rate of Zero on Overlapping Tax Underpayments and Overpayments

If you have paid or are liable for interest on a tax underpayment and have received or are due interest on a tax overpayment for the same period of time, you can request the IRS compute the interest using the net interest rate of zero.

How To Request a Net Interest Rate of Zero

You can request a net interest rate of zero by writing on top of Form 843 "Request for Net Interest Rate of Zero under Rev. Proc. 2000-26." You must provide documentation to substantiate that you are the taxpayer entitled to receive the interest due on the overpayment.

Leave line 1 blank. You can enter a dollar amount on line 2 or leave it blank. Complete line 3 to indicate the type of tax. More than one box can be checked.

Do not complete lines 4 and 5. Complete line 6 to indicate the type of return filed. More than one box can be checked.

On line 7, provide all of the following information.

1. The tax periods for which you overpaid and underpaid your tax liability.

2. When you paid the tax underpayment.

3. When you received your tax refund.

4. The periods that your overpayment and underpayment overlapped and the overlapping amount.

5. A computation, to the extent possible, of the amount of interest to be credited, refunded, or abated.

6. If your claim involves more than one tax identification number, please describe the relationship between each of the parties listed in the claim during the overlapping period(s).

Privacy Act and Paperwork Reduction Act Notice. We ask for the information on this form to carry out the Internal Revenue laws of the United States. Sections 6402 and 6404 state the conditions under which you may file a claim for refund and request for abatement of certain taxes, penalties, and interest. Form 843 may be used to file your claim. Section 6109 requires that you disclose your taxpayer identification number (TIN). Routine uses of this information include giving it to the Department of Justice for civil or criminal litigation and to cities, states, the District of Columbia, and U.S. commonwealths and possessions for use in administering their tax laws. We may also give this information to Federal and state agencies to enforce Federal nontax criminal laws and to combat terrorism. You are not required to claim a refund or request an abatement; however, if you choose to do so you are required to provide the information requested on this form. Failure to provide all of the requested information may delay or prevent processing your claim or request; providing false or fraudulent information may subject you to civil or criminal penalties.

You are not required to provide the information requested on a form that is subject to the Paperwork Reduction Act unless the form displays a valid OMB control number. Books or records relating to a form or its instructions must be retained as long as their contents may become material in the administration of any Internal Revenue law. Generally, tax returns and return information are confidential, as required by section 6103.

The time needed to complete and file this form will vary depending on individual circumstances. The estimated average time is:

Recordkeeping	26 min.
Learning about the law or the form	20 min.
Preparing the form	28 min.
Copying, assembling, and sending the form to the IRS	20 min.

If you have comments concerning the accuracy of these time estimates or suggestions for making this form simpler, we would be happy to hear from you. You can write to the Internal Revenue Service, Tax Products Coordinating Committee, SE:W:CAR:MP:T:T:SP, 1111 Constitution Ave. NW, IR-6526, Washington, DC 20224. Do not send the form to this address. Instead, see *Where To File.*

Form **940 for 2012:** Employer's Annual Federal Unemployment (FUTA) Tax Return

850112

Department of the Treasury — Internal Revenue Service

OMB No. 1545-0028

Employer identification number (EIN) [ ] [ ] – [ ] [ ] [ ] [ ] [ ] [ ] [ ]

Name *(not your trade name)* [   ]

Trade name *(if any)* [   ]

Address [   ]

Number   Street   Suite or room number

[   ] [   ]

City   State   ZIP code

Type of Return
(Check all that apply.)

[ ] **a.** Amended

[ ] **b.** Successor employer

[ ] **c.** No payments to employees in 2012

[ ] **d.** Final: Business closed or stopped paying wages

Instructions and prior-year forms are available at *www.irs.gov/form940.*

Read the separate instructions before you complete this form. Please type or print within the boxes.

Part 1: **Tell us about your return. If any line does NOT apply, leave it blank.**

1a If you had to pay state unemployment tax in one state only, enter the state abbreviation .   **1a** [ ] [ ]

1b If you had to pay state unemployment tax in more than one state, you are a multi-state employer . . . .   **1b** [ ]   Check here. Complete Schedule A (Form 940).

2 If you paid wages in a state that is subject to **CREDIT REDUCTION** . . . .   **2** [ ]   Check here. Complete Schedule A (Form 940).

Part 2: **Determine your FUTA tax before adjustments for 2012. If any line does NOT apply, leave it blank.**

3 Total payments to all employees . . . .   **3** [.]

4 Payments exempt from FUTA tax . . . .   **4** [.]

Check all that apply: **4a** [ ] Fringe benefits   **4c** [ ] Retirement/Pension   **4e** [ ] Other
             4b [ ] Group-term life insurance   **4d** [ ] Dependent care

5 Total of payments made to each employee in excess of $7,000   **5** [.]

6 Subtotal (line 4 + line 5 = line 6) . . . .   **6** [.]

7 Total taxable FUTA wages (line 3 – line 6 = line 7) (see instructions) . . . .   **7** [.]

8 FUTA tax before adjustments (line 7 x .006 = line 8) . . . .   **8** [.]

Part 3: **Determine your adjustments. If any line does NOT apply, leave it blank.**

9 If ALL of the taxable FUTA wages you paid were excluded from state unemployment tax, multiply line 7 by .054 (line 7 × .054 = line 9). Go to line 12 . . . .   **9** [.]

10 If SOME of the taxable FUTA wages you paid were excluded from state unemployment tax, **OR** you paid ANY state unemployment tax late (after the due date for filing Form 940), complete the worksheet in the instructions. Enter the amount from line 7 of the worksheet . .   **10** [.]

11 If credit reduction applies, enter the total from Schedule A (Form 940) . . . .   **11** [.]

Part 4: **Determine your FUTA tax and balance due or overpayment for 2012. If any line does NOT apply, leave it blank.**

12 Total FUTA tax after adjustments (lines 8 + 9 + 10 + 11 = line 12) . . . .   **12** [.]

13 FUTA tax deposited for the year, including any overpayment applied from a prior year   **13** [.]

14 Balance due (If line 12 is more than line 13, enter the excess on line 14.)
   • If line 14 is more than $500, you must deposit your tax.
   • If line 14 is $500 or less, you may pay with this return. (see instructions) . . . . . .   **14** [.]

15 Overpayment (If line 13 is more than line 12, enter the excess on line 15 and check a box below.) . . . .   **15** [.]

▶ You **MUST** complete both pages of this form and **SIGN** it.

Check one: [ ] Apply to next return.   [ ] Send a refund.

Next ▶

For Privacy Act and Paperwork Reduction Act Notice, see the back of Form 940-V, Payment Voucher.   Cat. No. 11234O   Form **940** (2012)

850212

Name *(not your trade name)*	Employer identification number (EIN)

Part 5: Report your FUTA tax liability by quarter only if line 12 is more than $500. If not, go to Part 6.

16 Report the amount of your FUTA tax liability for each quarter; do NOT enter the amount you deposited. If you had no liability for a quarter, leave the line blank.

   16a **1st quarter** (January 1 – March 31) . . . .   16a [.   ]

   16b **2nd quarter** (April 1 – June 30) . . . .   16b [.   ]

   16c **3rd quarter** (July 1 – September 30) . . . .   16c [.   ]

   16d **4th quarter** (October 1 – December 31) . . . . . .   16d [.   ]

17 Total tax liability for the year (lines 16a + 16b + 16c + 16d = line 17) 17 [.   ] Total must equal line 12.

Part 6: May we speak with your third-party designee?

Do you want to allow an employee, a paid tax preparer, or another person to discuss this return with the IRS? See the instructions for details.

☐ **Yes.** Designee's name and phone number [   ] [   ]

Select a 5-digit Personal Identification Number (PIN) to use when talking to IRS [ ] [ ] [ ] [ ] [ ]

☐ **No.**

Part 7: Sign here. You MUST complete both pages of this form and SIGN it.

Under penalties of perjury, I declare that I have examined this return, including accompanying schedules and statements, and to the best of my knowledge and belief, it is true, correct, and complete, and that no part of any payment made to a state unemployment fund claimed as a credit was, or is to be, deducted from the payments made to employees. Declaration of preparer (other than taxpayer) is based on all information of which preparer has any knowledge.

✗ **Sign your name here** [   ]

Print your name here [   ]

Print your title here [   ]

Date [/   /   ]

Best daytime phone [   ]

Paid Preparer Use Only   Check if you are self-employed . . . ☐

Preparer's name	[ ]	PTIN	[ ]
Preparer's signature	[ ]	Date	[/ /]
Firm's name (or yours if self-employed)	[ ]	EIN	[ ]
Address	[ ]	Phone	[ ]
City	[ ] State [ ]	ZIP code	[ ]

Form 940-V, Payment Voucher

Purpose of Form

Complete Form 940-V, Payment Voucher, if you are making a payment with Form 940, Employer's Annual Federal Unemployment (FUTA) Tax Return. We will use the completed voucher to credit your payment more promptly and accurately, and to improve our service to you.

Making Payments With Form 940

To avoid a penalty, make your payment with your 2012 Form 940 **only if** your FUTA tax for the fourth quarter (plus any undeposited amounts from earlier quarters) is $500 or less. If your total FUTA tax after adjustments (Form 940, line 12) is more than $500, you must make deposits by electronic funds transfer. See *When Must You Deposit Your FUTA Tax?* in the Instructions for Form 940. Also see sections 11 and 14 of Pub. 15 (Circular E), Employer's Tax Guide, for more information about deposits.

Caution. *Use Form 940-V when making any payment with Form 940. However, if you pay an amount with Form 940 that should have been deposited, you may be subject to a penalty. See* Deposit Penalties *in section 11 of Pub. 15 (Circular E).*

Specific Instructions

Box 1—Employer Identification Number (EIN). If you do not have an EIN, you may apply for one online. Go to IRS.gov and click on the *Apply for an EIN Online* link under *Tools.* You may also apply for an EIN by calling 1-800-829-4933, or you can fax or mail Form SS-4, Application for Employer Identification Number. If you have not received your EIN by the due date of Form 940, write "Applied For" and the date you applied in this entry space.

Box 2—Amount paid. Enter the amount paid with Form 940.

Box 3—Name and address. Enter your name and address as shown on Form 940.

• Enclose your check or money order made payable to the "United States Treasury." Be sure to enter your EIN, "Form 940," and "2012" on your check or money order. Do not send cash. Do not staple Form 940-V or your payment to Form 940 (or to each other).

• Detach Form 940-V and send it with your payment and Form 940 to the address provided in the Instructions for Form 940.

Note. You must also complete the entity information above Part 1 on Form 940.

▼ **Detach Here and Mail With Your Payment and Form 940.** ▼

Form **940-V** Department of the Treasury Internal Revenue Service	**Payment Voucher** ▶ **Do not staple or attach this voucher to your payment.**	OMB No. 1545-0028 2012

1 Enter your employer identification number (EIN).	2 **Enter the amount of your payment.** ▶ Make your check or money order payable to **"United States Treasury"**	Dollars	Cents
	3 Enter your business name (individual name if sole proprietor).		
	Enter your address.		
	Enter your city, state, and ZIP code.		

Form 940 (2012)

Privacy Act and Paperwork Reduction Act Notice. We ask for the information on this form to carry out the Internal Revenue laws of the United States. We need it to figure and collect the right amount of tax. Chapter 23, Federal Unemployment Tax Act, of Subtitle C, Employment Taxes, of the Internal Revenue Code imposes a tax on employers with respect to employees. This form is used to determine the amount of the tax that you owe. Section 6011 requires you to provide the requested information if you are liable for FUTA tax under section 3301. Section 6109 requires you to provide your identification number. If you fail to provide this information in a timely manner or provide a false or fraudulent form, you may be subject to penalties and interest.

You are not required to provide the information requested on a form that is subject to the Paperwork Reduction Act unless the form displays a valid OMB control number. Books and records relating to a form or instructions must be retained as long as their contents may become material in the administration of any Internal Revenue law.

Generally, tax returns and return information are confidential, as required by section 6103. However, section 6103 allows or requires the IRS to disclose or give the information shown on your tax return to others as described in the Code. For example, we may disclose your tax information to the Department of Justice for civil and criminal litigation, and to cities, states, the District of Columbia, and U.S. commonwealths and possessions to administer their tax laws. We may also disclose this information to other countries under a tax treaty, to federal and state agencies to enforce federal non-tax criminal laws, or to federal law enforcement and intelligence agencies to combat terrorism.

The time needed to complete and file this form will vary depending on individual circumstances. The estimated average time is:

Recordkeeping . . . . 9 hr., 19 min.

Learning about the law or the form . . 1 hr., 23 min.

Preparing, copying, assembling, and sending the form to the IRS . . . . . 1 hr., 36 min.

If you have comments concerning the accuracy of these time estimates or suggestions for making Form 940 simpler, we would be happy to hear from you. You can email us at *taxforms@irs.gov*. Enter "Form 940" on the subject line. Or write to: Internal Revenue Service, Tax Products Coordinating Committee, SE:W:CAR:MP:T:M:S, 1111 Constitution Avenue, NW, IR-6526, Washington, DC 20224. **Do not** send Form 940 to this address. Instead, see *Where Do You File?* in the Instructions for Form 940.

20**12**

Instructions for Form 940

Employer's Annual Federal Unemployment (FUTA) Tax Return

Department of the Treasury
Internal Revenue Service

Section references are to the Internal Revenue Code unless otherwise noted.

Future Developments

For the latest information about developments related to Form 940 and its instructions, such as legislation enacted after they were published, go to *www.irs.gov/form940*.

What's New

FUTA tax rate. The FUTA tax rate remains 6.0%.

Credit reduction state. A state that has not repaid money it borrowed from the federal government to pay unemployment benefits is a "credit reduction state." The Department of Labor determines these states. If an employer pays wages that are subject to the unemployment tax laws of a credit reduction state, that employer must pay additional federal unemployment tax when filing its Form 940.

For 2012, there are credit reduction states. If you paid any wages that are subject to the unemployment compensation laws of any of those states, the regular .054 credit is reduced. Use Schedule A (Form 940), Multi-State Employer and Credit Reduction Information, to figure the tax. For more information, see the Schedule A (Form 940) instructions or visit IRS.gov.

Change of address. Use Form 8822-B, Change of Address—Business, to notify the IRS of an address change.

Reminders

Federal tax deposits must be made by electronic funds transfer. You must use electronic funds transfer to make all federal tax deposits. Generally, electronic funds transfers are made using the Electronic Federal Tax Payment System (EFTPS). If you do not want to use EFTPS, you can arrange for your tax professional, financial institution, payroll service, or other trusted third party to make deposits on your behalf. Also, you may arrange for your financial institution to initiate a same-day wire payment on your behalf. EFTPS is a free service provided by the Department of Treasury. Services provided by your tax professional, financial institution, payroll service, or other third party may have a fee. For more information on making federal tax deposits, see section 11 of Pub. 15 (Circular E), Employer's Tax Guide. To get more information about EFTPS or to enroll in EFTPS, visit *www.eftps.gov* or call 1-800-555-4477. Additional information about EFTPS is also available in Pub. 966, Electronic Federal Tax Payment System: A Guide to Getting Started.

Aggregate Form 940 filers. Agents must complete Schedule R (Form 940), Allocation Schedule for Aggregate Form 940 Filers, when filing an aggregate Form 940. Aggregate Forms 940 are filed by agents of home care service recipients approved by the IRS under section 3504 of the Internal Revenue Code. To request approval to act as an agent for an employer, the agent must file Form 2678, Employer/Payer Appointment of Agent, with the IRS unless you are a state or local government agency acting as agent under the special procedures provided in

Notice 2003-70, 2003-43 I.R.B. 916, available at *www.irs.gov/irb/2003-43_IRB/ar09.html*.

Disregarded entities and qualified subchapter S subsidiaries (QSubs). Business entities that are disregarded as separate from their owner, including qualified subchapter S subsidiaries, are required to withhold and pay employment taxes and file employment tax returns using the name and employer identification number (EIN) of the disregarded entity. For more information, see *Disregarded entities*, later.

State unemployment information. When you registered as an employer with your state, the state assigned you a state reporting number. If you do not have a state unemployment account and state experience tax rate, or if you have questions about your state account, you must contact your state unemployment agency. For a list of state unemployment agencies, visit the U.S. Department of Labor's website at *www.workforcesecurity.doleta.gov/unemploy/agencies.asp*.

You can file and pay electronically. Using electronic options available from the IRS can make filing a return and paying your federal tax easier. You can use IRS *e-file* to file a return and EFTPS to make deposits or pay in full whether you rely on a tax professional or prepare your own taxes.
- For IRS *e-file*, visit IRS.gov for additional information.
- For EFTPS, visit *www.eftps.gov*, or call EFTPS Customer Service at 1-800-555-4477, 1-800-733-4829 (TDD), or 1-800-244-4829 (Spanish).

Electronic funds withdrawal (EFW). If you file Form 940 electronically, you can *e-file* and e-pay (electronic funds withdrawal) the balance due in a single step using tax preparation software or through a tax professional. However, **do not** use EFW to make federal tax deposits. For more information on paying your taxes using EFW, visit the IRS website at *www.irs.gov/e-pay*. A fee may be charged to file electronically.

You can pay your balance due by credit or debit card. You may pay your FUTA tax shown on line 14 using a major credit card or debit card. However, **do not** use a credit or debit card to pay taxes that are required to be deposited (see *When Must You Deposit Your FUTA Tax*, later). For more information on paying your taxes with a credit or debit card, visit the IRS website at *www.irs.gov/e-pay*.

Photographs of missing children. The IRS is a proud partner with the National Center for Missing and Exploited Children. Photographs of missing children selected by the Center may appear in instructions on pages that would otherwise be blank. You can help bring these children home by looking at the photographs and calling 1-800-THE-LOST (1-800-843-5678) if you recognize a child.

How Can You Get More Help?

If you want more information about this form, see Pub. 15 (Circular E), visit our website at IRS.gov, or call 1-800-829-4933 (TDD/TTY for persons who are deaf, hard of hearing, or have a speech disability at 1-800-829-4059) Monday through Friday 7 a.m. to 7 p.m. local time (Alaska and Hawaii follow Pacific time).

For a list of related employment tax topics, visit the IRS website at *www.irs.gov/businesses* and click on the *Employment Taxes* link under *Businesses Topics*. You can order forms,

Nov 20, 2012   Cat. No. 13660I instructions, and publications at *www.irs.gov/formspubs* or by calling 1-800-TAX-FORM (1-800-829-3676).

_____

General Instructions: Understanding Form 940

What's the Purpose of Form 940?

Use Form 940 to report your annual Federal Unemployment Tax Act (FUTA) tax. Together with state unemployment tax systems, the FUTA tax provides funds for paying unemployment compensation to workers who have lost their jobs. Most employers pay both a federal and a state unemployment tax. Only employers pay FUTA tax. Do not collect or deduct FUTA tax from your employees' wages.

The FUTA tax applies to the first $7,000 you pay to each employee during a calendar year after subtracting any payments exempt from FUTA tax.

These instructions give you some background information about Form 940. They tell you who must file the form, how to fill it out line by line, and when and where to file it.

Who Must File Form 940?

Except as noted below, if you answer "Yes" to either one of these questions, you must file Form 940.
* Did you pay wages of $1,500 or more to employees in any calendar quarter during 2011 or 2012?
* Did you have one or more employees for at least some part of a day in any 20 or more different weeks in 2011 or 20 or more different weeks in 2012? Count all full-time, part-time, and temporary employees. However, if your business is a partnership, do not count its partners.

If your business was sold or transferred during the year, each employer who answered "Yes" to at least one question above must file Form 940. However, do not include any wages paid by the predecessor employer on your Form 940 unless you are a successor employer. For details, see *Successor employer* under *Type of Return.*

If you are not liable for FUTA tax for 2012 because you made no payments to employees in 2012, check box *c* in the top right corner of the form. Then go to Part 7, sign the form, and file it with the IRS.

If you will not be liable for filing Form 940 in the future because your business has closed or because you stopped paying wages, check box *d* in the top right corner of the form. See *Final: Business closed or stopped paying wages* under *Type of Return* for more information.

For Employers of Household Employees . . .

If you are a household employer, you must pay FUTA tax on wages that you paid to your household employees only if you paid cash wages of $1,000 or more in any calendar quarter in 2011 or 2012.

A household employee performs household work in a:
* Private home,
* Local college club, or
* Local chapter of a college fraternity or sorority.

Generally, employers of household employees must file Schedule H (Form 1040), Household Employment Taxes, instead of Form 940.

However, if you have other employees in addition to household employees, you can choose to include the FUTA taxes for your household employees on Form 940 instead of filing Schedule H (Form 1040). If you choose to include household employees on your Form 940, you must also file Form 941, Employer's QUARTERLY Federal Tax Return; Form 943, Employer's Annual Federal Tax Return for Agricultural Employees; or Form 944, Employer's ANNUAL Federal Tax Return; to report social security, Medicare, and any withheld federal income taxes for your household employees.

See Pub. 926, Household Employer's Tax Guide, for more information.

For Agricultural Employers . . .

File Form 940 if you answer "Yes" to either of these questions.
* Did you pay cash wages of $20,000 or more to farmworkers during any calendar quarter in 2011 or 2012?
* Did you employ 10 or more farmworkers during some part of the day (whether or not at the same time) during any 20 or more different weeks in 2011 or 20 or more different weeks in 2012?

Count wages you paid to aliens who were admitted to the United States on a temporary basis to perform farmwork (workers with H-2A visas). However, wages paid to "H-2A visa workers" are not subject to FUTA tax.

See Pub. 51 (Circular A), Agricultural Employer's Tax Guide, for more information.

For Indian Tribal Governments . . .

Services rendered by employees of a federally recognized Indian tribal government employer (including any subdivision, subsidiary, or business enterprise wholly owned by the tribe) are exempt from FUTA tax and no Form 940 is required. However, the tribe must have participated in the state unemployment system for the full year and be in compliance with applicable state unemployment law. For more information, see section 3309(d).

For Tax-Exempt Organizations . . .

Religious, educational, scientific, charitable, and other organizations described in section 501(c)(3) and exempt from tax under section 501(a) are not subject to FUTA tax and do not have to file Form 940.

For Employers of State or Local Governments. . .

Services rendered by employees of a state of a political subdivision or instrumentality of the state are exempt from FUTA tax and no Form 940 is required.

When Must You File Form 940?

The due date for filing Form 940 for 2012 is January 31, 2013. However, if you deposited all your FUTA tax when it was due, you may file Form 940 by February 11, 2013.

If we receive your return after the due date, we will treat your return as filed on time if the envelope containing your return is properly addressed, contains sufficient postage, and is postmarked by the U.S. Postal Service on or before the due date or sent by an IRS-designated private delivery service on or before the due date. However, if you do not follow these guidelines, we will consider your return filed when it is actually received. For a list of IRS-designated private delivery services, see Pub. 15 (Circular E).

Where Do You File?

Where you file depends on whether you include a payment (check or money order) with your return. However, mail your amended return to the *Without a payment* address even if a payment is included.

-2-

If you are in . . .		Without a payment . . .	With a payment . . .
EXCEPTION for tax-exempt organizations, Federal, State and Local Governments, and Indian Tribal Governments, regardless of your location		Department of the Treasury Internal Revenue Service Ogden, UT 84201-0046	Internal Revenue Service P.O. Box 37940 Hartford, CT 06176-7940
Connecticut Delaware District of Columbia Florida Georgia Illinois Indiana Kentucky Maine Maryland Massachusetts Michigan New Hampshire	New Jersey New York North Carolina Ohio Pennsylvania Rhode Island South Carolina Tennessee Vermont Virginia West Virginia Wisconsin	Department of the Treasury Internal Revenue Service Cincinnati, OH 45999-0046	Internal Revenue Service P.O. Box 804521 Cincinnati, OH 45280-4521
Alabama Alaska Arizona Arkansas California Colorado Hawaii Idaho Iowa Kansas Louisiana Minnesota Mississippi	Missouri Montana Nebraska Nevada New Mexico North Dakota Oklahoma Oregon South Dakota Texas Utah Washington Wyoming	Department of the Treasury Internal Revenue Service Ogden, UT 84201-0046	Internal Revenue Service P.O. Box 37940 Hartford, CT 06176-7940
Puerto Rico U.S. Virgin Islands		Internal Revenue Service P.O. Box 409101 Ogden, UT 84409	Internal Revenue Service P.O. Box 37940 Hartford, CT 06176-7940
If the location of your legal residence, principal place of business, office, or agency is not listed . . .		Internal Revenue Service P.O. Box 409101 Ogden, UT 84409	Internal Revenue Service P.O. Box 37940 Hartford, CT 06176-7940

 Private delivery services cannot deliver to P.O. boxes. You must use the U.S. Postal Service to mail an item to a P.O. box address.

Credit for State Unemployment Tax Paid to a State Unemployment Fund

You get a credit for amounts you pay to a state (including the District of Columbia, Puerto Rico, and the U.S. Virgin Islands) unemployment fund by January 31, 2013 (or February 11, 2013, if that is your Form 940 due date). Your FUTA tax will be higher if you do not pay the state unemployment tax timely. If you did not pay all state unemployment tax by the due date of Form 940, see the line 10 instructions.

State unemployment taxes are sometimes called "contributions." These contributions are payments that a state requires an employer to make to its unemployment fund for the payment of unemployment benefits. They **do not include:**
* Any payments deducted or deductible from your employees' pay;
* Penalties, interest, or special administrative taxes; and
* Voluntary amounts you paid to get a lower assigned state experience rate.

Additional credit. You may receive an additional credit if you have a state experience rate lower than 5.4% (.054). This applies even if your rate varies during the year. This additional credit is the difference between your actual state unemployment tax payments and the amount you would have been required to pay at 5.4%.

Special credit for successor employers. You may be eligible for a credit based on the state unemployment taxes paid by a predecessor. You may claim this credit if you are a successor employer who acquired a business in 2012 from a predecessor who was not an employer for FUTA purposes and, therefore, was not required to file Form 940 for 2012. See section 3302(e). You can include amounts paid by the predecessor on the *Worksheet* as if you paid them. For details on successor employers, see *Successor employer* under *Type of Return*. If the predecessor was required to file Form 940, see the line 5 instructions.

When Must You Deposit Your FUTA Tax?

Although Form 940 covers a calendar year, you may have to deposit your FUTA tax before you file your return. If your FUTA tax is more than $500 for the calendar year, you must deposit at least one quarterly payment.

You must determine when to deposit your tax based on the amount of your quarterly tax liability. If your FUTA tax is $500 or less in a quarter, carry it over to the next quarter. Continue carrying your tax liability over until your cumulative tax is more than $500. At that point, you must deposit your tax for the quarter. Deposit your FUTA tax by the last day of the month after the end of the quarter. If your tax for the next quarter is $500 or less, you are not required to deposit your tax again until the cumulative amount is more than $500.

Fourth quarter liabilities. If your FUTA tax for the fourth quarter (plus any undeposited amounts from earlier quarters) is more than $500, deposit the entire amount by January 31, 2013. If it is $500 or less, you can either deposit the amount or pay it with your Form 940 by January 31, 2013.

In years when there are credit reduction states, you must include liabilities owed for credit reduction with your fourth quarter deposit.

When To Deposit Your FUTA Tax

If your undeposited FUTA tax is more than $500 on . . .*	Deposit your tax by . . .
March 31	April 30
June 30	July 31
September 30	October 31
December 31	January 31

*Also, see the instructions for line 16.

 If any deposit due date falls on a Saturday, Sunday, or legal holiday, you may deposit on the next business day.

How Do You Figure Your FUTA Tax Liability for Each Quarter?

You owe FUTA tax on the first $7,000 of wages that you paid to each employee during the calendar year. The FUTA tax is 6.0% (.060) for 2012. Most employers receive a maximum credit of up to 5.4% (.054) against this FUTA tax. Every quarter, you must figure how much of the first $7,000 of each employee's annual wages you paid during that quarter.

-3-

Figure Your Tax Liability

Before you can figure the amount to deposit, figure your FUTA tax liability for the quarter. To figure your tax liability, add the first $7,000 of each employee's annual wages you paid during the quarter for FUTA wages paid and multiply that amount by .006.

The tax rates are based on your receiving the maximum credit against FUTA taxes. You are entitled to the maximum credit if you paid all state unemployment tax by the due date of your Form 940 or if you were not required to pay state unemployment tax during the calendar year due to your state experience rate.

Example. During first quarter, you had three employees: Employees A, B, and C. You paid $11,000 to Employee A, $2,000 to Employee B, and $4,000 to Employee C.

To figure your liability for the first quarter, add the first $7,000 of each employee's wages:

$7,000	Employee A's wages subject to FUTA tax
2,000	Employee B's wages subject to FUTA tax
+ 4,000	Employee C's wages subject to FUTA tax
$13,000	Total wages subject to FUTA tax for the first quarter
$13,000	Total wages subject to FUTA tax for the first quarter
x .006	Tax rate (based on maximum credit of 5.4%)
$78	Your liability for the first quarter

In this example, you do not have to make a deposit because your liability is $500 or less for the first quarter. However, you must carry this liability over to the second quarter.

If any wages subject to FUTA tax are not subject to state unemployment tax, you may be liable for FUTA tax at a higher rate (up to 6.0%). For instance, in certain states, wages paid to corporate officers, certain payments of sick pay by unions, and certain fringe benefits are excluded from state unemployment tax.

Example. Employee A and Employee B are corporate officers whose wages are excluded from state unemployment tax in your state. Employee C's wages are not excluded from state unemployment tax. During the first quarter, you paid $11,000 to Employee A, $2,000 to Employee B, and $4,000 to Employee C.

$ 9,000	Total FUTA wages for Employees A and B in first quarter
x .060	Tax rate
$540	Your liability for the first quarter for Employees A and B
$4,000	Total FUTA wages subject to state unemployment tax
x .006	Tax rate (based on maximum credit of 5.4%)
$24	Your liability for the first quarter for Employee C
$540	Your liability for the first quarter for Employees A and B
+ 24	Your liability for first quarter for Employee C
$564	Your liability for the first quarter for Employees A, B, and C

In this example, you must deposit $564 by April 30 because your liability for the first quarter is more than $500.

How Must You Deposit Your FUTA Tax?

You Must Deposit Your FUTA Tax Using EFT

You must deposit all depository taxes using electronic funds transfers (EFT). Generally, electronic funds transfers are made using the Electronic Federal Tax Payment System (EFTPS). To get more information or to enroll in EFTPS, visit the EFTPS website at *www.eftps.gov*, or call 1-800-555-4477. Additional information about EFTPS is also available in Pub. 966.

If your business is new, IRS will automatically pre-enroll you in EFTPS when you apply for an employer identification number (EIN). Follow the instructions on your EIN package to activate your enrollment.

 To make your EFTPS deposits on time, you must initiate the transaction by 8 p.m. Eastern time the day before the date the deposit is due.

Same-day payment option. If you fail to initiate a deposit transaction on EFTPS by 8 p.m. Eastern time the day before the date a deposit is due, you can still make your deposit on time by using the Federal Tax Application (FTA). To use the same-day wire payment method, you will need to make arrangements with your financial institution ahead of time. Please check with your financial institution regarding availability, deadlines, and costs. Your financial institution may charge you a fee for payments made this way. To learn more about the information you will need to provide your financial institution to make a same-day wire payment, visit *www.eftps.gov* to download the *Same-Day Payment Worksheet*.

Timeliness of federal tax deposits. If a deposit is required to be made on a day that is not a business day, the deposit is considered timely if it is made by the close of the next business day. A business day is any day other than a Saturday, Sunday, or legal holiday. The term "legal holiday" for deposit purposes includes only those legal holidays in the District of Columbia. Legal holidays in the District of Columbia are provided in Pub. 15 (Circular E).

How Can You Avoid Penalties and Interest?

Penalties and interest are assessed at a rate set by law on taxes paid late, returns filed late or incorrectly, insufficient payments made, and failure to make deposits using EFT.

You can avoid paying penalties and interest if you:
- Deposit or pay your tax when it is due,
- File your completed Form 940 accurately and on time, and
- Ensure your checks for tax payments are valid.

If you receive a notice about a penalty after you file this return, reply to the notice with an explanation and we will determine if you meet reasonable-cause criteria. Do not attach an explanation when you file your Form 940.

Can You Amend a Return?

You use the 2012 Form 940 to amend a return that you previously filed for 2012. If you are amending a return for a previous year, use the previous year's Form 940.

Follow the steps below to amend your return.
- Use a paper return to amend a Form 940 filed under an electronic filing program.
- Check the amended return box in the top right corner of Form 940, page 1, box a.
- Fill in all the amounts that should have been on the original form.
- Sign the form.
- Attach an explanation of why you are amending your return. For example, tell us if you are filing to claim credit for tax paid to your state unemployment fund after the due date of Form 940.
- File the amended return using the *Without a payment* address (even if a payment is included) under *Where Do You File*.
- If you file an amended return for an aggregate Form 940, be sure to attach Schedule R (Form 940). Complete Schedule R (Form 940) only for employers who have adjustments on the amended Form 940.

-4-

Completing Your Form 940

Follow These Guidelines to Correctly Fill Out the Form

To help us accurately scan and process your form, please follow these guidelines.
* Make sure your business name and EIN are on every page of the form and any attachments.
* If you type or use a computer to fill out your form, use a 12-point Courier font, if possible.
* Make sure you enter dollars to the left of the preprinted decimal point and cents to the right.
* Do not enter dollar signs or decimal points. Commas are optional.
* You may choose to round your amounts to the nearest dollar, instead of reporting cents on this form. If you choose to round, you must round all entries. To round, drop the amounts under 50 cents and increase the amounts from 50 to 99 cents to the next dollar. For example, $1.49 becomes $1.00 and $2.50 becomes $3.00. If you use two or more amounts to figure an entry on the form, use cents to figure the answer and round the answer only.
* If you have a line with the value of zero, leave it blank.

Employer Identification Number (EIN), Name, Trade Name, and Address

Enter Your Business Information at the Top of the Form

Enter your EIN, name, and address in the spaces provided. You must enter your name and EIN here and on page 2. Enter the business (legal) name that you used when you applied for your EIN on Form SS-4, Application for Employer Identification Number. For example, if you are a sole proprietor, enter "Ronald Smith" on the *Name* line and "Ron's Cycles" on the *Trade Name* line. Leave the *Trade Name* line blank if it is the same as your *Name*.

If you pay a tax preparer to fill out Form 940, make sure the preparer shows your business name exactly as it appeared when you applied for your EIN.

Employer identification number (EIN). The IRS monitors tax filings and payments by using a numerical system to identify taxpayers and to make sure that businesses comply with federal tax laws. A unique nine-digit EIN is assigned to all corporations, partnerships, and some sole proprietors. Businesses that need an EIN must apply for a number and use it throughout the life of the business on all tax returns, payments, and reports.

Your business should have only one EIN. If you have more than one and are unsure which one to use, call 1-800-829-4933 to verify your correct EIN.

If you do not have an EIN, apply for one by:
* Visiting the IRS website at IRS.gov and clicking on *Apply for an EIN Online* under *Tools*.
* Calling 1-800-829-4933 and applying by telephone, or
* Filling out Form SS-4 and mailing it to the address in the Instructions for Form SS-4 or faxing it to the number in the Instructions for Form SS-4.

If you have not received your EIN by the time a return is due, write *"Applied For"* and the date you applied in the space shown for the EIN on pages 1 and 2 of your return.

 If you are filing your tax return electronically, a valid EIN is required at the time the return is filed. If a valid EIN is not provided, the return will not be accepted. This may result in penalties.

 Always be sure the EIN on the form you file exactly matches the EIN that the IRS assigned to your business. Do not use a social security number or individual taxpayer identification number (ITIN) on forms that ask for an EIN. Filing a Form 940 with an incorrect EIN or using the EIN of another's business may result in penalties and delays in processing your return.

Tell Us if You Change Your Name or Address

Notify the IRS immediately if you change your business name or address.
* If your business name changes, write to the IRS using the *Without a payment* address under *Where Do You File?* Also see Pub. 1635, Employer Identification Number: Understanding Your EIN, for general information on EINs.
* If your address changes, complete and mail Form 8822-B, Change of Address—Business. Do not attach Form 8822-B to your Form 940. Mail Form 8822-B separately to the address indicated on Form 8822-B.

Type of Return

Review the box at the top of the form. If any line applies to you, check the appropriate box to tell us which type of return you are filing. You may check more than one box.

Amended. If this is an amended return that you are filing to correct a return that you previously filed, check box *a*.

Successor employer. Check box *b* if you are a successor employer and:
* You are reporting wages paid before you acquired the business by a predecessor who was required to file a Form 940 because the predecessor was an employer for FUTA tax purposes, or
* You are claiming a special credit for state unemployment tax paid before you acquired the business by a predecessor who was not required to file a Form 940 because the predecessor was not an employer for FUTA tax purposes.
   A successor employer is an employer who:
* Acquires substantially all the property used in a trade or business of another person (predecessor) or used in a separate unit of a trade or business of a predecessor, and
* Immediately after the acquisition, employs one or more people who were employed by the predecessor.

No payments to employees in 2012. If you are not liable for FUTA tax for 2012 because you made no payments to employees in 2012, check box *c*. Then go to Part 7, sign the form, and file it with the IRS.

Final: Business closed or stopped paying wages. If this is a final return because you went out of business or stopped paying wages and you will not be liable for filing Form 940 in the future, check box *d*. Complete all applicable lines on the form, sign it in Part 7, and file it with the IRS. Include a statement showing the address at which your records will be kept and the name of the person keeping the records.

Disregarded entities. A disregarded entity is required to file Form 940 using its name and EIN, not the name and EIN of its owner. An entity that has a single owner and is disregarded as separate from its owner for federal income tax purposes is treated as a separate entity for purposes of payment and reporting federal employment taxes. If the entity does not currently have an EIN, it must apply for one using one of the methods explained earlier. Disregarded entities include single-owner limited liability companies (LLCs) that have not elected to be taxed as a corporation for federal income tax purposes, qualified subchapter S subsidiaries, and certain foreign entities treated as disregarded entities for U.S. income tax purposes. Although a disregarded entity is treated as a separate entity for employment tax purposes, it is not subject to FUTA tax if it is owned by a tax-exempt organization under section 501(c)(3) and is not required to file Form 940. For more information, see *Disregarded entities and qualified subchapter S subsidiaries* in the *Introduction* section of Pub. 15 (Circular E).

Specific Instructions

Part 1: Tell Us About Your Return

1. If You Were Required to Pay Your State Unemployment Tax In . . .

Identify the state(s) where you were required to pay state unemployment taxes.

1a. One state only. Enter the two-letter U.S. Postal Service abbreviation for the state where you were required to pay your tax on line 1a. For a list of state abbreviations, see the Instructions for Schedule A (Form 940) or visit the website for the U.S. Postal Service at *www.usps.com*.

1b. More than one state (you are a multi-state employer). Check the box on line 1b. Then fill out Schedule A (Form 940), and attach it to your Form 940.

2. If You Paid Wages in a State That is Subject to Credit Reduction

If you paid wages that are subject to the unemployment tax laws of a credit reduction state, you may have to pay more FUTA tax when filing your Form 940.

A state that has not repaid money it borrowed from the federal government to pay unemployment benefits is called a *credit reduction state*. The U.S. Department of Labor determines which states are credit reduction states.

For tax year 2012, there are credit reduction states. If you paid wages subject to the unemployment tax laws of these states, check the box on line 2 and fill out Schedule A (Form 940). See the instructions for line 9 before completing the Schedule A (Form 940).

Part 2: Determine Your FUTA Tax Before Adjustments for 2012

If any line in Part 2 does not apply, leave it blank.

3. Total Payments to All Employees

Report the total payments you made during the calendar year on line 3. Include payments for the services of all employees, even if the payments are not taxable for FUTA. Your method of payment does not determine whether payments are wages. You may have paid wages hourly, daily, weekly, monthly, or yearly. You may have paid wages for piecework or as a percentage of profits. Include:

- **Compensation,** such as:
  —Salaries, wages, commissions, fees, bonuses, vacation allowances, and amounts you paid to full-time, part-time, or temporary employees.

- **Fringe benefits,** such as:
  —Sick pay (including third-party sick pay if liability is transferred to the employer). For details on sick pay, see Pub. 15-A, Employer's Supplemental Tax Guide.
  —The value of goods, lodging, food, clothing, and non-cash fringe benefits.
  —Section 125 (cafeteria) plan benefits.

- **Retirement/Pension,** such as:
  —Employer contributions to a 401(k) plan, payments to an Archer MSA, payments under adoption assistance programs, and contributions to SIMPLE retirement accounts (including elective salary reduction contributions).
  —Amounts deferred under a non-qualified deferred compensation plan.

- **Other payments,** such as:
  —Tips of $20 or more in a month that your employees reported to you.
  —Payments made by a predecessor employer to the employees of a business you acquired.
  —Payments to nonemployees who are treated as your employees by the state unemployment tax agency.

 Wages may be subject to FUTA tax even if they are excluded from your state's unemployment tax.

For details on wages and other compensation, see section 5 of Pub. 15-A.

Example:

You had 3 employees. You paid $44,000 to Employee A, $8,000 to Employee B, and $16,000 to Employee C.

$44,000	Amount paid to Employee A
8,000	Amount paid to Employee B
+ 16,000	Amount paid to Employee C
$68,000	Total payments to employees. You would enter this amount on line 3.

---

4. Payments Exempt from FUTA Tax

If you enter an amount on line 4, check the appropriate box or boxes on lines 4a through 4e to show the types of payments exempt from FUTA tax. **You only report a payment as exempt from FUTA tax on line 4 if you included the payment on line 3.**

Some payments are exempt from FUTA tax because the payments are not included in the definition of wages or the services are not included in the definition of employment. Payments exempt from FUTA tax may include:

- **Fringe benefits,** such as:
  —The value of certain meals and lodging.
  —Contributions to accident or health plans for employees, including certain employer payments to a Health Savings Account or an Archer MSA.
  —Employer reimbursements (including payments to a third party) for qualified moving expenses, to the extent that these expenses would otherwise be deductible by the employee.
  —Payments for benefits excluded under section 125 (cafeteria) plans.

- **Group term life insurance.**

For information about group term life insurance and other payments for fringe benefits that may be exempt from FUTA tax, see Pub. 15-B, Employer's Tax Guide to Fringe Benefits.

-6-

- **Retirement/Pension**, such as employer contributions to a qualified plan, including a SIMPLE retirement account (other than elective salary reduction contributions) and a 401(k) plan.
- **Dependent care**, such as payments (up to $5,000 per employee, $2,500 if married filing separately) for a qualifying person's care that allows your employees to work and that would be excludable by the employee under section 129.
- **Other payments**, such as:

 —All non-cash payments and certain cash payments for agricultural labor, and all payments to "H-2A" visa workers. See *For agricultural employers*, earlier, or see Pub. 51 (Circular A).
 —Payments made under a workers' compensation law because of a work-related injury or sickness. See section 6 of Pub. 15-A.
 —Payments for domestic services if you did not pay cash wages of $1,000 or more (for all domestic employees) in any calendar quarter in 2011 or 2012. See Pub. 926.
 —Payments for services provided to you by your parent, spouse, or child under the age of 21. See section 3 of Pub. 15 (Circular E).
 —Payments for certain fishing activities. See Pub. 334, Tax Guide for Small Business.
 —Payments to certain statutory employees. See section 1 of Pub. 15-A.
 —Payments to nonemployees who are treated as your employees by the state unemployment tax agency.

See section 3306 and its related regulations for more information about FUTA taxation of retirement plan contributions, dependent care payments, and other payments.

For more information on payments exempt from FUTA tax, see section 14 in Pub. 15 (Circular E) or section 10 in Pub. 51 (Circular A).

Example:

You had 3 employees. You paid $44,000 to Employee A including $2,000 in health insurance benefits. You paid $8,000 to Employee B, including $500 in retirement benefits. You paid $16,000 to Employee C, including $2,000 in health and retirement benefits.

$ 2,000	Health insurance benefits for Employee A
500	Retirement benefits for Employee B
+ 2,000	Health and retirement benefits for Employee C
$4,500	Total payments exempt from FUTA tax. You would enter this amount on line 4 and check boxes 4a and 4c.

5. Total of Payments Made to Each Employee in Excess of $7,000

Only the first $7,000 you paid to each employee in a calendar year is subject to FUTA tax. This $7,000 is called the *FUTA wage base*.

Enter on line 5 the total of the payments over $7,000 you paid to each employee during 2012 **after subtracting any payments exempt from FUTA tax shown on line 4.**

Following our example:

You had three employees. You paid $44,000 to Employee A, $8,000 to Employee B, and $16,000 to Employee C, including a total of $4,500 in payments exempt from FUTA tax for all three employees. To determine the total payments made to each employee in excess of the FUTA wage base, the payments exempt from FUTA tax and the FUTA wage base must be subtracted from total payments. These amounts are shown in parentheses.

Employees	A	B	C
Total payments to employees	$44,000	$8,000	$16,000
Payments exempt from FUTA tax	(2,000)	(500)	(2,000)
FUTA wage base	(7,000)	(7,000)	(7,000)
	$35,000	$ 500	$ 7,000

Total of payments made to each employee in excess of $7,000. You would enter this amount on line 5.	$42,500

If you are a successor employer . . . When you figure the payments made to each employee in excess of $7,000, you may include the payments that the predecessor made to the employees who continue to work for you **only** if the predecessor was an employer for FUTA tax purposes resulting in the predecessor being required to file Form 940.

Example for successor employers:

During the calendar year, the predecessor employer paid $5,000 to Employee A. You acquired the predecessor's business. After the acquisition, you employed Employee A and paid Employee A an additional $3,000 in wages. None of the amounts paid to Employee A were payments exempt from FUTA tax.

$5,000	Wages paid by predecessor employer
+ 3,000	Wages paid by you
$8,000	Total payments to Employee A. You would include this amount on line 3.
$8,000	Total payments to Employee A
− 7,000	FUTA wage base
$1,000	Payments made to Employee A in excess of $7,000.
$1,000	Payments made to Employee A in excess of $7,000.
+ 5,000	Taxable FUTA wages paid by predecessor employer
$6,000	You would include this amount on line 5.

6. Subtotal

To figure your subtotal, add the amounts on lines 4 and 5 and enter the result on line 6.

line 4
+ line 5
line 6

7. Total Taxable FUTA Wages

To figure your total taxable FUTA wages, subtract line 6 from line 3 and enter the result on line 7.

line 3
− line 6
line 7

8. FUTA Tax Before Adjustments

To figure your total FUTA tax before adjustments, multiply line 7 by .006 and then enter the result on line 8.

line 7 x .006
line 8

Part 3: Determine Your Adjustments

If any line in Part 3 does not apply, leave it blank.

9. If ALL of the Taxable FUTA Wages You Paid Were Excluded from State Unemployment Tax. . .

If all of the taxable FUTA wages you paid were excluded from state unemployment tax, multiply line 7 by .054 and enter the result on line 9.

line 7
x .054
line 9

If you were not required to pay state unemployment tax because all of the wages you paid were excluded from state unemployment tax, you must pay FUTA tax at the 6.0% (.060) rate. For example, if your state unemployment tax law excludes wages paid to corporate officers or employees in specific occupations, and the only wages you paid were to corporate officers or employees in those specific occupations, you must pay FUTA tax on those wages at the full FUTA rate of 6.0% (.060). When you figured the FUTA tax before adjustments on line 8, it was based on the maximum allowable credit (5.4%) for state unemployment tax payments. Because you did not pay state unemployment tax, you do not have a credit and must figure this adjustment.

If line 9 applies to you, lines 10 and 11 do not apply to you. Therefore, leave lines 10 and 11 blank. Do not fill out the worksheet in these instructions or Schedule A (Form 940).

10. If SOME of the Taxable FUTA Wages You Paid Were Excluded From State Unemployment Tax, or You Paid any State Unemployment Tax Late...

You must fill out the worksheet on the next page if:

- Some of the taxable FUTA wages you paid were excluded from state unemployment, or
- Any of your payments of state unemployment tax were late. The worksheet takes you step by step through the process of figuring your credit. You'll find an example of how to use it. Do not complete the worksheet if line 9 applied to you (see instructions above).

Before you can properly fill out the worksheet, you will need to gather the following information.
- Taxable FUTA wages (Form 940, line 7).
- Taxable state unemployment wages (state and federal wage bases may differ).
- The experience rates assigned to you by the states where you paid wages.
- The amount of state unemployment taxes you paid on time (*On time* means that you paid the state unemployment taxes by the due date for filing Form 940).
- The amount of state unemployment taxes you paid late. (*Late* means after the due date for filing Form 940.)

 Do not include any penalties, interest, or unemployment taxes deducted from your employees' pay in the amount of state unemployment taxes. Also, do not include as state unemployment taxes any special administrative taxes or voluntary contributions you paid to get a lower assigned experience rate or any surcharges, excise taxes, or employment and training taxes. (These items are generally listed as separate items on the state's quarterly wage report.)

For line 3 of the worksheet:
- If any of the experience rates assigned to you were less than 5.4% for any part of the calendar year, you must list each assigned experience rate separately on the worksheet.
- If you were assigned six or more experience rates that were less than 5.4% for any part of the calendar year, you must use another sheet to figure the additional credits and then include those additional credits in your line 3 total.

After you complete the worksheet, enter the amount from line 7 of the worksheet on Form 940, line 10. **Do not attach the worksheet to your Form 940.** Keep it with your records.

-8-

Worksheet—Line 10

Before you begin: Read the *Example* before completing this worksheet.

Use this worksheet to figure your credit if:

✓ Some of the wages you paid were excluded from state unemployment tax, OR
✓ You paid any state unemployment tax late.

For this worksheet, **do not round your figures**.

Before you can properly fill out this worksheet, you must gather this information:

- Taxable FUTA wages (Form 940, line 7)

- Taxable state unemployment wages

- The experience rates assigned to you by the states where you paid wages

- The amount of state unemployment taxes you paid on time. (*On time* means that you paid the state unemployment taxes by the due date for filing Form 940.) Include any state unemployment taxes you paid on nonemployees who were treated as employees by your state unemployment agency.

- The amount of state unemployment taxes you paid late. (*Late* means after the due date for filing Form 940.)

1. **Maximum allowable credit** — Enter Form 940, line 7 _____ . ___ x .054 on line 1   1. _____ . ___
(Form 940, line 7 x .054 = line 1).

2. **Credit for timely state unemployment tax payments** — How much did you pay on time?   2. _____ . ___

- If line 2 is **equal to** or **more than** line 1, **STOP here.** (STOP) You have completed the worksheet. Leave Form 940, line 10 blank.

- If line 2 is **less than** line 1, continue this worksheet.

3. **Additional credit** — Were ALL of your assigned experience rates 5.4% or more?

- **If yes,** enter zero on line 3. Then go to line 4 of this worksheet.

- **If no,** fill out the computations below. List ONLY THOSE STATES for which your assigned experience rate for any part of the calendar year was less than 5.4%.

State	Computation rate The difference between 5.4% (.054) and your assigned experience rate (.054 − .XXX (assigned experience rate) = computation rate)		Taxable state unemployment wages at assigned experience rate		Additional Credit
1. _____	_____ . ___	x	_____ . ___	=	_____ . ___
2. _____	_____ . ___	x	_____ . ___	=	_____ . ___
3. _____	_____ . ___	x	_____ . ___	=	_____ . ___
4. _____	_____ . ___	x	_____ . ___	=	_____ . ___
5. _____	_____ . ___	x	_____ . ___	=	_____ . ___

If you need more lines, use another sheet and include those additional credits in the total.

Total _____ . ___

Enter the total on line 3.

3. _____ . ___

4. **Subtotal** (line 2 + line 3 = line 4)   4. _____ . ___

- If line 4 is equal to or more than line 1, **STOP here.** (STOP) You have completed the worksheet. Leave Form 940, line 10 blank.

- If line 4 is less than line 1, continue this worksheet.

5. **Credit for paying state unemployment taxes late:**

   5a. What is your remaining allowable credit? (line 1 − line 4 = line 5a)   5a. _____ . ___

   5b. How much state unemployment tax did you pay late?   5b. _____ . ___

   5c. Which is smaller, line 5a or line 5b? Enter the smaller number here.   5c. _____ . ___

   5d. Your allowable credit for paying state unemployment taxes late (line 5c x .90 = line 5d)   5d. _____ . ___

6. **Your FUTA credit** (line 4 + line 5d = line 6)   6. _____ . ___

- If line 6 is equal to or more than line 1, **STOP here.** (STOP) You have completed the worksheet. Leave Form 940, line 10 blank.

- If line 6 is less than line 1, continue this worksheet.

7. **Your adjustment** (line 1 − line 6 = line 7)   Enter line 7 from this worksheet on Form 940, line 10.   7. _____ . ___

Do not attach this worksheet to your Form 940. Keep it for your records.

Example for using the worksheet:

Employee A and Employee B are corporate officers whose wages are excluded from state unemployment tax in your state. Employee C's wages are not excluded from state unemployment tax. During 2012, you paid $44,000 to Employee A, $22,000 to Employee B, and $16,000 to Employee C. Your state's wage base is $8,000. You paid some state unemployment tax on time, some late, and some remains unpaid.

Here are the records:

Total taxable FUTA wages (Form 940, line 7)	$21,000.00
Taxable state unemployment wages	$ 8,000.00
Experience rate for 2012	.041(4.1%)
State unemployment tax paid on time	$100.00
State unemployment tax paid late	$78.00
State unemployment tax not paid	$150.00

1. Maximum allowable credit

$21,000.00	(Form 940, line 7)		
x .054	(maximum credit rate)		
$1,134.00		**1.**	$1,134.00

2. Credit for timely state unemployment tax payments   **2.** $100.00

3. Additional credit   **3.** $104.00

.054	(maximum credit rate)	$8,000
− .041	(your experience rate)	x .013
.013	(your computation rate)	$104.00

4. Subtotal (line 2 + line 3)   **4.** $204.00

$100
+ 104
$204

5. Credit for paying state unemployment taxes late

5a.	**Remaining allowable credit: (line 1 - line 4)**	**5a.**	$930.00

$1,134.00
− 204.00
$930.00

5b.	**State unemployment tax paid late:**	**5b.**	$78.00
5c.	**Which is smaller? Line 5a or line 5b?**	**5c.**	$78.00
5d.	**Allowable credit (for paying late)**	**5d.**	$70.20

$78.00
x .90
$70.20

6. Your FUTA credit (line 4 + line 5d)   **6.** $274.20

$204.00
+ 70.20
$274.20

7. Your adjustment (line 1 - line 6)   **7.** $859.80

$1,134.00	
− 274.20	
$859.80	**You would enter this amount on Form 940, line 10.**

11. If Credit Reduction Applies . . .

If you paid FUTA taxable wages that were also subject to state unemployment taxes in any states that are subject to credit reduction, enter the total amount from Schedule A (Form 940) on Form 940, line 11. However, if you entered an amount on line 9 because all the FUTA taxable wages you paid were excluded from state unemployment tax, skip line 11 and go to line 12.

Part 4: Determine Your FUTA Tax for 2012

If any line in Part 4 does not apply, leave it blank.

12. Total FUTA Tax After Adjustments

Add the amounts shown on lines 8, 9, 10, and 11, and enter the result on line 12.

line 8
line 9
line 10
+ line 11
line 12

 If line 9 is greater than zero, lines 10 and 11 must be zero because they would not apply.

13. FUTA Tax Deposited for the Year

Enter the amount of total FUTA tax that you deposited for the year, including any overpayment that you applied from a prior year.

14. Balance Due

If line 13 is less than line 12, enter the difference on line 14.

line 12
− line 13
line 14

If line 14 is:
- More than $500, you must deposit your tax. See *When Must You Deposit Your FUTA Tax.*
- $500 or less, you can deposit your tax, pay your tax with a major credit card, debit card, or pay your tax by check or money order with your return.
- Less than $1, you do not have to pay it.

 If you do not deposit as required and pay any balance due with Form 940, you may be subject to a penalty.

How to deposit or pay the balance due. You may pay the amount shown on line 14 using EFTPS, a credit or debit card, or electronic funds withdrawal (EFW). **Do not** use a credit or debit card or EFW to pay taxes that were required to be deposited. For more information on paying your taxes with a credit or debit card or EFW, go to *www.irs.gov/e-pay*.

If you pay by EFTPS, credit or debit card, or EFW, file your return using the *Without a payment* address under *Where Do You File?* and **do not** file Form 940-V, Payment Voucher.

15. Overpayment

If line 13 is more than line 12, enter the difference on line 15.

line 13
− line 12
line 15

If you deposited more than the FUTA tax due for the year, you may choose to have us either:

-10-

- Apply the refund to your next return, or
- Send you a refund.

Check the appropriate box in line 15 to tell us which option you select. If you do not check either box, we will automatically refund your overpayment. Also, we may apply your overpayment to any past due tax account you have.

If line 15 is less than $1, we will send you a refund or apply it to your next return only if you ask for it in writing.

Part 5: Report Your FUTA Tax Liability by Quarter Only if Line 12 is More Than $500

Fill out Part 5 **only** if line 12 is more than $500. If line 12 is $500 or less, leave Part 5 blank and go to Part 6.

16. Report the Amount of Your FUTA Tax Liability for Each Quarter

Enter the amount of your FUTA tax liability for each quarter on lines 16a–d. **Do not** enter the amount you deposited. If you had no liability for a quarter, leave the line blank.

16a. 1st quarter (January 1 to March 31).
16b. 2nd quarter (April 1 to June 30).
16c. 3rd quarter (July 1 to September 30).
16d. 4th quarter (October 1 to December 31).

To figure your FUTA tax liability for the fourth quarter, complete Form 940 through line 12. Then copy the amount from line 12 onto line 17. Lastly, subtract the sum of lines 16a through 16c from line 17 and enter the result on line 16d.

Example:

You paid wages on March 28 and your FUTA tax on those wages was $200. You were not required to make a deposit for the 1st quarter because your accumulated FUTA tax was $500 or less. You paid additional wages on June 28 and your FUTA tax on those wages was $400. Because your accumulated FUTA tax for the 1st and 2nd quarters exceeded $500, you were required to make a deposit of $600 by July 31.

You would enter $200 in line 16a because your liability for the 1st quarter is $200. You would also enter $400 in line 16b to show your 2nd quarter liability.

 In years when there are credit reduction states, you must include liabilities owed for credit reduction with your fourth quarter deposit. You may deposit the anticipated extra liability throughout the year, but it is not due until the due date for the deposit for the fourth quarter, and the associated liability should be recorded as being incurred in the fourth quarter.

17. Total Tax Liability for the Year

Your total tax liability for the year **must equal** line 12. Copy the amount from line 12 onto line 17.

Part 6: May We Speak With Your Third-Party Designee?

If you want to allow an employee, your paid tax preparer, or another person to discuss your Form 940 with the IRS, check the "Yes" box. Then enter the name and phone number of the person you choose as your designee. Be sure to give us the specific name of a person — not the name of the firm that prepared your tax return.

Have your designee select a five-digit Personal Identification Number (PIN) that he or she must use as identification when talking to the IRS about your form.

By checking "Yes," you authorize us to talk to your designee about any questions that we may have while we process your return. Your authorization applies only to this form, for this year; it does not apply to other forms or other tax years.

You are authorizing your designee to:
- Give us any information that is missing from your return,
- Ask us for information about processing your return, and
- Respond to certain IRS notices that you have shared with your designee about math errors and in preparing your return. We will **not** send notices to your designee.

You are **not** authorizing your designee to:
- Receive any refund check,
- Bind you to anything (including additional tax liability), or
- Otherwise represent you before the IRS.

The authorization will automatically expire 1 year after the due date for filing your Form 940 (regardless of extensions). If you or your designee want to end the authorization before it expires, write to the IRS office for your location using the *Without a payment* address under *Where Do You File?*

If you want to expand your designee's authorization or if you want us to send your designee copies of your notices, see Pub. 947, Practice Before the IRS and Power of Attorney.

Part 7: Sign Here

You MUST Fill Out Both Pages of This Form and SIGN It

Failure to sign will delay the processing of your return.

On page 2 in Part 7, sign and print your name and title. Then enter the date and the best daytime telephone number, including area code, where we can reach you if we have any questions.

Who Must Sign Form 940?

Form 940 must be signed as follows.
- **Sole proprietorship**—The individual who owns the business.
- **Partnership (including a limited liability company (LLC) treated as a partnership) or unincorporated organization**— A responsible and duly authorized partner, member, or officer having knowledge of its affairs.
- **Corporation (including an LLC treated as a corporation)** —The president, vice president, or other principal officer duly authorized to sign.
- **Single member LLC treated as a disregarded entity for federal income tax purposes**—The owner of the LLC or a principal officer duly authorized to sign.
- **Trust or estate**—The fiduciary.

Form 940 may also be signed by a duly authorized agent of the taxpayer if a valid power of attorney or reporting agent authorization (Form 8655, Reporting Agent Authorization) has been filed.

Alternative signature method. Corporate officers or duly authorized agents may sign Form 940 by rubber stamp, mechanical device, or computer software program. For details and required documentation, see Rev. Proc. 2005-39, 2005-28 I.R.B. 82, available at *www.irs.gov/irb/2005-28_IRB/ar16.html*.

Paid preparers. A paid preparer must sign Form 940 and provide the information in the *Paid Preparer Use Only* section of Part 7 if the preparer was paid to prepare Form 940 and is not an employee of the filing entity. Paid preparers must sign paper returns with a manual signature. The preparer must give you a copy of the return in addition to the copy to be filed with IRS.

If you are a paid preparer, enter your Preparer Tax Identification Number (PTIN) in the space provided. Include your complete address. If you work for a firm, write the firm's name and the EIN of the firm. You can apply for a PTIN online or by filing Form W-12, IRS Paid Preparer Tax Identification Number (PTIN) Application and Renewal. For more information about applying for a PTIN online, visit the IRS website at *www.irs.gov/ ptin*. You cannot use your PTIN in place of the EIN of the tax preparation firm.

Generally, do not complete the Paid Preparer Use Only section if you are filing the return as a reporting agent and have a valid Form 8655 on file with the IRS. However, a reporting agent must complete this section if the reporting agent offered legal advice, for example, by advising the client on determining whether its workers are employees or independent contractors for Federal tax purposes.

Privacy Act and Paperwork Reduction Act Notice

We ask for the information on Form 940 to carry out the Internal Revenue laws of the United States. We need it to figure and collect the right amount of tax. Subtitle C, Employment Taxes, of the Internal Revenue Code imposes unemployment tax under the Federal Unemployment Tax Act. Form 940 is used to determine the amount of the taxes that you owe. Section 6011 requires you to provide the requested information if the tax is applicable to you. Section 6109 requires you to provide your identification number. If you fail to provide this information in a timely manner, or provide false or fraudulent information, you may be subject to penalties and interest.

You are not required to provide the information requested on a form that is subject to the Paperwork Reduction Act unless the form displays a valid OMB control number. Books or records relating to a form or instructions must be retained as long as their contents may become material in the administration of any Internal Revenue law.

Generally, tax returns and return information are confidential, as required by section 6103. However, section 6103 allows or requires the IRS to disclose or give the information shown on your tax return to others as described in the Code. For example, we may disclose your tax information to the Department of Justice for civil and criminal litigation, and to cities, states, the District of Columbia, and U.S. commonwealths and possessions to administer their tax laws. We may also disclose this information to other countries under a tax treaty, to federal and state agencies to enforce federal nontax criminal laws, or to federal law enforcement and intelligence agencies to combat terrorism.

If you have comments concerning the accuracy of these time estimates or suggestions for making these forms simpler, we would be happy to hear from you. You can email us at *taxforms@irs.gov*. Enter "Form 940" on the subject line. Or write to: Internal Revenue Service, Tax Products Coordinating Committee, SE:W:CAR:MP:T:M:S, 1111 Constitution Avenue, NW, IR-6526, Washington, DC 20224. Do not send Form 940 to this address. Instead, see *Where Do You File*, earlier.

Estimated average times

The time needed to complete and file this form will vary depending on individual circumstances. The estimated average time is:

Form	Recordkeeping	Learning about the law or the form	Preparing the form	Copying, assembling, and sending the form to the IRS
Schedule A (Form 940)	16 hrs., 01 min.		15 min.	
Worksheet (Form 940)	1 hr., 41 min.		21 min.	
Voucher (Form 940-V)	21 min.		4 min.	

Schedule A (Form 940) for 2012:

Multi-State Employer and Credit Reduction Information
Department of the Treasury — Internal Revenue Service

860312

OMB No. 1545-0028

See the instructions on page 2. File this schedule with Form 940.

Employer identification number (EIN) ☐☐ – ☐☐☐☐☐☐☐

Name *(not your trade name)*

Place an "X" in the box of EVERY state in which you were required to pay state unemployment tax this year. For states with a credit reduction rate greater than zero, enter the FUTA taxable wages, multiply by the reduction rate, and then enter the credit reduction amount for that state. If any states do not apply to you, leave them blank.

Postal Abbreviation	FUTA Taxable Wages	Reduction Rate	Credit Reduction	Postal Abbreviation	FUTA Taxable Wages	Reduction Rate	Credit Reduction
☐ AK	.		.	☐ NC	.		.
☐ AL	.		.	☐ ND	.		.
☐ AR	.		.	☐ NE	.		.
☐ AZ	.		.	☐ NH	.		.
☐ CA	.		.	☐ NJ	.		.
☐ CO	.		.	☐ NM	.		.
☐ CT	.		.	☐ NV	.		.
☐ DC	.		.	☐ NY	.		.
☐ DE	.		.	☐ OH	.		.
☐ FL	.		.	☐ OK	.		.
☐ GA	.		.	☐ OR	.		.
☐ HI	.		.	☐ PA	.		.
☐ IA	.		.	☐ RI	.		.
☐ ID	.		.	☐ SC	.		.
☐ IL	.		.	☐ SD	.		.
☐ IN	.		.	☐ TN	.		.
☐ KS	.		.	☐ TX	.		.
☐ KY	.		.	☐ UT	.		.
☐ LA	.		.	☐ VA	.		.
☐ MA	.		.	☐ VT	.		.
☐ MD	.		.	☐ WA	.		.
☐ ME	.		.	☐ WI	.		.
☐ MI	.		.	☐ WV	.		.
☐ MN	.		.	☐ WY	.		.
☐ MO	.		.	☐ PR	.		.
☐ MS	.		.	☐ VI	.		.
☐ MT	.		.				

Total Credit Reduction. Add all amounts shown in the *Credit Reduction* boxes. Enter the total here and on Form 940, line 11 . . . . ☐ .

For Privacy Act and Paperwork Reduction Act Notice, see the last page of Form 940.   Cat. No. 16997C   Schedule A (Form 940) 2012

Instructions for Schedule A (Form 940) for 2012:

860412

Multi-State Employer and Credit Reduction Information

For more information on completing Schedule A, see the Frequently Asked Questions, available at *www.irs.gov/form940*.

Specific Instructions: Completing Schedule A

Step 1. Check the box for every state (including the District of Columbia, Puerto Rico, and the U.S. Virgin Islands) in which you were required to pay state unemployment taxes this year even if the state's credit reduction rate is zero.

Note. Make sure that you have applied for a state unemployment number for your business. If you do not have an unemployment account number from a state in which you paid wages, contact the state office to receive one. For a list of state unemployment agencies, visit the U.S. Department of Labor's website at *www.workforcesecurity.doleta.gov/unemploy/agencies.asp*.

The table below provides the two-letter postal abbreviations used on Schedule A.

State	Postal Abbreviation	State	Postal Abbreviation
Alabama	AL	Montana	MT
Alaska	AK	Nebraska	NE
Arizona	AZ	Nevada	NV
Arkansas	AR	New Hampshire	NH
California	CA	New Jersey	NJ
Colorado	CO	New Mexico	NM
Connecticut	CT	New York	NY
Delaware	DE	North Carolina	NC
District of Columbia	DC	North Dakota	ND
Florida	FL	Ohio	OH
Georgia	GA	Oklahoma	OK
Hawaii	HI	Oregon	OR
Idaho	ID	Pennsylvania	PA
Illinois	IL	Rhode Island	RI
Indiana	IN	South Carolina	SC
Iowa	IA	South Dakota	SD
Kansas	KS	Tennessee	TN
Kentucky	KY	Texas	TX
Louisiana	LA	Utah	UT
Maine	ME	Vermont	VT
Maryland	MD	Virginia	VA
Massachusetts	MA	Washington	WA
Michigan	MI	West Virginia	WV
Minnesota	MN	Wisconsin	WI
Mississippi	MS	Wyoming	WY
Missouri	MO	Puerto Rico	PR
		U.S. Virgin Islands	VI

Step 2. You are subject to credit reduction if you paid FUTA taxable wages that were also subject to state unemployment taxes in any state listed that has a credit reduction rate greater than zero.

If you paid FUTA taxable wages that were also subject to state unemployment taxes in any states that are subject to credit reduction, find the lines for each state.

In the *FUTA Taxable Wages* box, enter the total FUTA taxable wages that you paid in that state. (The FUTA wage base for all states is $7,000.) However, do not include in the *FUTA Taxable Wages* box wages that were excluded from state unemployment tax.

Note. Do not enter your state unemployment wages in the *FUTA Taxable Wages* box.

Then multiply the total taxable FUTA wages by the reduction rate.

Enter your total in the *Credit Reduction* box at the end of the line.

Step 3. Total credit reduction

To calculate the total credit reduction, add up all of the *Credit Reduction* boxes and enter the amount in the *Total Credit Reduction* box.

Then enter the total credit reduction on Form 940, line 11.

Example 1

You paid $20,000 in wages to each of three employees in State A. State A is subject to credit reduction at a rate of .003 (.3%). Because you paid wages in a state that is subject to credit reduction, you must complete Schedule A and file it with Form 940.

Total payments to all employees in State A $60,000

Payments exempt from FUTA tax
(see the Instructions for Form 940) $0

Total payments made to each employee in
excess of $7,000 (3 x ($20,000 - $7,000)) $39,000

Total taxable FUTA wages you paid in State A entered in the *FUTA Taxable Wages* box ($60,000 - $0 - $39,000) $21,000

Credit reduction rate for State A 003

Total credit reduction for State A ($21,000 x .003) $63

Caution. *Do not include in the FUTA Taxable Wages box wages in excess of the $7,000 wage base for each employee subject to unemployment insurance in the credit reduction state. The credit reduction applies only to taxable FUTA wages.*

In this case, you would write $63.00 in the *Total Credit Reduction* box and then enter that amount on Form 940, line 11.

Example 2

You paid $48,000 ($4,000 a month) in wages to Employee A and no payments were exempt from FUTA tax. Employee A worked in State B (not subject to credit reduction) in January and then transferred to State C (subject to credit reduction) on February 1. Because you paid wages in more than one state, you must complete Schedule A and file it with Form 940.

The total payments in State B that are not exempt from FUTA tax are $4,000. Since this payment to Employee A does not exceed the $7,000 FUTA wage base, the total taxable FUTA wages paid in State B are $4,000.

The total payments in State C that are not exempt from FUTA tax are $44,000. However, $4,000 of FUTA taxable wages was paid in State B with respect to Employee A. Therefore, the total taxable FUTA wages with respect to Employee A in State C is $3,000 ($7,000 (FUTA wage base) - $4,000 (total FUTA taxable wages paid in State B)). Enter $3,000 in the *FUTA Taxable Wages* box, multiply it by the *Reduction Rate*, and then enter the result in the *Credit Reduction* box.

Attach Schedule A to Form 940 when you file your return.

860512

Schedule R (Form 940): Allocation Schedule for Aggregate Form 940 Filers

OMB No. 1545-0028

(Rev. December 2012)

Department of the Treasury — Internal Revenue Service

Employer identification number (EIN)

☐ ☐ – ☐ ☐ ☐ ☐ ☐ ☐

Name *as shown on Form 940*

Report for calendar year:

(Same as Form 940):

Read the separate instructions before you complete Schedule R (Form 940). Type or print within the boxes. Complete a separate line for the amounts allocated to each of your clients.

	(a) Client Employer Identification Number (EIN)	(b) State abbreviation from Form 940, line 1a, or Schedule A (Form 940)	(c) Total taxable FUTA wages allocated to the listed client EIN from Form 940, line 7	(d) Total adjustments to FUTA tax allocated to the listed client EIN from Form 940, line 9 or line 10	(e) Credit reduction amount allocated to the listed client EIN from Form 940, line 11	(f) Total FUTA tax after adjustments allocated to the listed client EIN from Form 940, line 12	(g) Total FUTA tax deposits from Form 940, line 13, plus any payment made with the return allocated to the listed client EIN
1			.	.	.	.	.
2			.	.	.	.	.
3			.	.	.	.	.
4			.	.	.	.	.
5			.	.	.	.	.
6			.	.	.	.	.
7			.	.	.	.	.
8			.	.	.	.	.
9			.	.	.	.	.
10			.	.	.	.	.
11			.	.	.	.	.
12			.	.	.	.	.
13			.	.	.	.	.
14			.	.	.	.	.
15			.	.	.	.	.
16 Subtotals for clients. Add all amounts on lines 1 through 15.			.	.	.	.	.
17 Enter the combined subtotal from line 26 of all Continuation Sheets for Schedule R (Form 940).			.	.	.	.	.
18 Enter Form 940 amounts for employees of the agent.			.	.	.	.	.
19 Totals. Add lines 16, 17, and 18. The column totals must match the related lines on the aggregate Form 940.			.	.	.	.	.

For Paperwork Reduction Act Notice, see the instructions.   Cat. No. 53082A   Schedule R (Form 940) (Rev. 12-2012)

Page ____ of ____

860612

Continuation Sheet for Schedule R (Form 940)

(Rev. December 2012)

| Employer identification number (EIN) | □ □ – □ □ □ □ □ □ □ |
| Name *as shown on Form 940* | |

Report for calendar year:

(Same as Form 940):

Read the separate instructions before you complete Schedule R (Form 940). Type or print within the boxes. Complete a separate line for the amounts allocated to each of your clients.

	(a) Client Employer Identification Number (EIN)	(b) State abbreviation from Form 940, line 1a, or Schedule A (Form 940)	(c) Total taxable FUTA wages allocated to the listed client EIN from Form 940, line 7	(d) Total adjustments to FUTA tax allocated to the listed client EIN from Form 940, line 9 or line 10	(e) Credit reduction amount allocated to the listed client EIN from Form 940, line 11	(f) Total FUTA tax after adjustments allocated to the listed client EIN from Form 940, line 12	(g) Total FUTA tax deposits from Form 940, line 13, plus any payment made with the return allocated to the listed client EIN
1			.	.	.	.	.
2			.	.	.	.	.
3			.	.	.	.	.
4			.	.	.	.	.
5			.	.	.	.	.
6			.	.	.	.	.
7			.	.	.	.	.
8			.	.	.	.	.
9			.	.	.	.	.
10			.	.	.	.	.
11			.	.	.	.	.
12			.	.	.	.	.
13			.	.	.	.	.
14			.	.	.	.	.
15			.	.	.	.	.
16			.	.	.	.	.
17			.	.	.	.	.
18			.	.	.	.	.
19			.	.	.	.	.
20			.	.	.	.	.
21			.	.	.	.	.
22			.	.	.	.	.
23			.	.	.	.	.
24			.	.	.	.	.
25			.	.	.	.	.
26	**Subtotals for clients.** Add lines 1 through 25. Include the subtotals from line 26 on Schedule R (Form 940), line 17.		.	.	.	.	.

Schedule R (Form 940) (Rev. 12-2012)

860712

Section references are to the Internal Revenue Code unless otherwise noted.

General Instructions

Purpose of Schedule R

Use Schedule R to allocate the aggregate information reported on Form 940, Employer's Annual Federal Unemployment (FUTA) Tax Return, to each home care service recipient client. An aggregate Form 940 may only be filed by section 3504 Agents acting on behalf of home care service recipients. If you are an agent for home care service recipients and have more than 15 clients, complete continuation sheets as necessary. Attach Schedule R, including any continuation sheets, to your aggregate Form 940 and file it with your Form 940.

Who Must File?

You must complete Schedule R if you file an aggregate Form 940. Aggregate Forms 940 are filed by agents of home care service recipients approved by the IRS under section 3504. To request approval to act as an agent for a home care service recipient, you must file Form 2678, Employer/Payer Appointment of Agent, with the IRS, unless you are a state or local government agency acting as agent under the special procedures provided in Notice 2003-70. On Schedule R, we call those home care service recipients your clients.

When Must You File?

If you are an aggregate Form 940 filer, file Schedule R with your aggregate Form 940 every year when your Form 940 is due. Schedule R may be filed electronically or by paper submission. However, agents filing for 1,000 or more clients must file a paper return.

Specific Instructions

Completing Schedule R

Enter Your Business Information

Carefully enter your employer identification number (EIN) and the name of your business at the top of the schedule. Make sure they exactly match the EIN and name shown on the attached Form 940.

Calendar Year

Enter the calendar year for which you are filing your Form 940. Make sure that the year entered on the top of Schedule R matches the year on the attached Form 940.

Client and Employee Information

On Schedule R, including any continuation sheets, you must report the following for each client.

- Your client's employer identification number (EIN).
- The state abbreviation of the client's location.

- Total taxable FUTA wages (Form 940, line 7) allocated to the client.
- Total adjustments to FUTA tax (Form 940, line 9 or line 10) allocated to the client.
- Credit reduction amount (Form 940, line 11) allocated to the client.
- Total FUTA tax after adjustments (Form 940, line 12) allocated to the client.
- Total FUTA tax deposits for the tax year plus any other payments (Form 940, line 13) allocated to the client.

You must also report the same information for your employees from line 18 of Schedule R.

Compare the total of each column on line 19 (including your information from line 18) to the amounts reported on the aggregate Form 940. For each column total, the relevant line from Form 940 is noted in the column heading.

If the totals on line 19 of the Schedule R do not match the totals on Form 940, there is an error that must be corrected before submitting Form 940 and Schedule R.

Paperwork Reduction Act Notice. We ask for the information on Schedule R to carry out the Internal Revenue laws of the United States. You are required to give us this information. We need it to ensure that you are complying with these laws and to allow us to figure and collect the right amount of tax.

You are not required to provide the information requested on a form that is subject to the Paperwork Reduction Act unless the form displays a valid OMB control number. Books or records relating to a form or its instructions must be retained as long as their contents may become material in the administration of any Internal Revenue law. Generally, tax returns and return information are confidential, as required by section 6103.

The time needed to complete and file Schedule R will vary depending on individual circumstances. The estimated average time is:

Recordkeeping . . . . 10 hrs., 45 min.

Learning about the law or the form . . . . 12 min.

Preparing, copying, and assembling the form . . . 22 min.

If you have comments concerning the accuracy of these time estimates or suggestions for making Schedule R simpler, we would be happy to hear from you. You can email us at *taxforms@irs.gov.* Enter "Schedule R (Form 940)" on the subject line. Or write to: Internal Revenue Service, Tax Products Coordinating Committee, SE:W:CAR:MP:T:M:S, 1111 Constitution Ave., NW, IR-6526, Washington, DC 20224. **Do not** send Schedule R to this address. Instead, see *Where Do You File?* in the Instructions for Form 940.

Form **941 for 2013:** Employer's QUARTERLY Federal Tax Return
(Rev. January 2013)   Department of the Treasury — Internal Revenue Service

950113

OMB No. 1545-0029

Employer identification number (EIN) [ ][ ] – [ ][ ][ ][ ][ ][ ][ ]

Name *(not your trade name)* [_____]

Trade name *(if any)* [_____]

Address [_____]
Number   Street   Suite or room number
[_____]
City   State   ZIP code

Report for this Quarter of 2013
(Check one.)

☐ **1:** January, February, March

☐ **2:** April, May, June

☐ **3:** July, August, September

☐ **4:** October, November, December

Instructions and prior year forms are available at *www.irs.gov/form941.*

Read the separate instructions before you complete Form 941. Type or print within the boxes.

Part 1:   Answer these questions for this quarter.

1. Number of employees who received wages, tips, or other compensation for the pay period including: *Mar. 12* (Quarter 1), *June 12* (Quarter 2), *Sept. 12* (Quarter 3), or *Dec. 12* (Quarter 4)   **1** [_____]

2. Wages, tips, and other compensation . . . . **2** [_____.__]

3. Income tax withheld from wages, tips, and other compensation . . . . **3** [_____.__]

4. If no wages, tips, and other compensation are subject to social security or Medicare tax   ☐ Check and go to line 6.

		Column 1			Column 2	
5a	Taxable social security wages . .	[_____.__]	× .124 =		[_____.__]	
5b	Taxable social security tips . . .	[_____.__]	× .124 =		[_____.__]	
5c	Taxable Medicare wages & tips. .	[_____.__]	× .029 =		[_____.__]	
5d	Taxable wages & tips subject to Additional Medicare Tax withholding	[_____.__]	× .009 =		[_____.__]	

5e. Add Column 2 from lines 5a, 5b, 5c, and 5d . . . . **5e** [_____.__]

5f. Section 3121(q) Notice and Demand—Tax due on unreported tips (see instructions) . . **5f** [_____.__]

6. Total taxes before adjustments (add lines 3, 5e, and 5f) . . . . . . **6** [_____.__]

7. Current quarter's adjustment for fractions of cents . . . . **7** [_____.__]

8. Current quarter's adjustment for sick pay . . . . **8** [_____.__]

9. Current quarter's adjustments for tips and group-term life insurance . . . . **9** [_____.__]

10. Total taxes after adjustments. Combine lines 6 through 9 . . . . **10** [_____.__]

11. Total deposits for this quarter, including overpayment applied from a prior quarter and overpayment applied from Form 941-X or Form 944-X filed in the current quarter . . . **11** [_____.__]

12a. COBRA premium assistance payments (see instructions) . . . . . **12a** [_____.__]

12b. Number of individuals provided COBRA premium assistance . . [_____]

13. Add lines 11 and 12a . . . . **13** [_____.__]

14. Balance due. If line 10 is more than line 13, enter the difference and see instructions . . . **14** [_____.__]

15. Overpayment. If line 13 is more than line 10, enter the difference [_____.__] Check one: ☐ Apply to next return. ☐ Send a refund.

▶ You MUST complete both pages of Form 941 and SIGN it.   Next ▶

For Privacy Act and Paperwork Reduction Act Notice, see the back of the Payment Voucher.   Cat. No. 17001Z   Form **941** (Rev. 1-2013)

950213

Name *(not your trade name)*	Employer identification number (EIN)

Part 2: Tell us about your deposit schedule and tax liability for this quarter.

If you are unsure about whether you are a monthly schedule depositor or a semiweekly schedule depositor, see Pub. 15 (Circular E), section 11.

16   Check one: ☐ Line 10 on this return is less than $2,500 or line 10 on the return for the prior quarter was less than $2,500, and you did not incur a $100,000 next-day deposit obligation during the current quarter. If line 10 for the prior quarter was less than $2,500 but line 10 on this return is $100,000 or more, you must provide a record of your federal tax liability. If you are a monthly schedule depositor, complete the deposit schedule below; if you are a semiweekly schedule depositor, attach Schedule B (Form 941). Go to Part 3.

☐ **You were a monthly schedule depositor for the entire quarter.** Enter your tax liability for each month and total liability for the quarter, then go to Part 3.

Tax liability:	Month 1		.
	Month 2		.
	Month 3		.

Total liability for quarter | | . | **Total must equal line 10.**

☐ **You were a semiweekly schedule depositor for any part of this quarter.** Complete Schedule B (Form 941), Report of Tax Liability for Semiweekly Schedule Depositors, and attach it to Form 941.

Part 3: Tell us about your business. If a question does NOT apply to your business, leave it blank.

17   If your business has closed or you stopped paying wages . . . . ☐ Check here, and

enter the final date you paid wages   /   /   .

18   If you are a seasonal employer and you do not have to file a return for every quarter of the year . . ☐ Check here.

Part 4: May we speak with your third-party designee?

Do you want to allow an employee, a paid tax preparer, or another person to discuss this return with the IRS? See the instructions for details.

☐ Yes. Designee's name and phone number | | |

Select a 5-digit Personal Identification Number (PIN) to use when talking to the IRS. ☐ ☐ ☐ ☐ ☐

☐ No.

Part 5: Sign here. You MUST complete both pages of Form 941 and SIGN it.

Under penalties of perjury, I declare that I have examined this return, including accompanying schedules and statements, and to the best of my knowledge and belief, it is true, correct, and complete. Declaration of preparer (other than taxpayer) is based on all information of which preparer has any knowledge.

X   **Sign your name here** | | Print your name here | |

Print your title here | |

Date   /   /   Best daytime phone | |

Paid Preparer Use Only   Check if you are self-employed . . . ☐

Preparer's name		PTIN	
Preparer's signature		Date	/ /
Firm's name (or yours if self-employed)		EIN	
Address		Phone	
City	State	ZIP code	

Page **2**   Form **941** (Rev. 1-2013)

Form 941-V, Payment Voucher

Purpose of Form

Complete Form 941-V, Payment Voucher, if you are making a payment with Form 941, Employer's QUARTERLY Federal Tax Return. We will use the completed voucher to credit your payment more promptly and accurately, and to improve our service to you.

Making Payments With Form 941

To avoid a penalty, make your payment with Form 941 **only if:**

• Your total taxes after adjustments for either the current quarter or the preceding quarter (Form 941, line 10) are less than $2,500, you did not incur a $100,000 next-day deposit obligation during the current quarter, and you are paying in full with a timely filed return, or

• You are a monthly schedule depositor making a payment in accordance with the Accuracy of Deposits Rule. See section 11 of Pub. 15 (Circular E), Employer's Tax Guide, for details. In this case, the amount of your payment may be $2,500 or more.

Otherwise, you must make deposits by electronic funds transfer. See section 11 of Pub. 15 (Circular E) for deposit instructions. Do not use Form 941-V to make federal tax deposits.

Caution. *Use Form 941-V when making any payment with Form 941. However, if you pay an amount with Form 941 that should have been deposited, you may be subject to a penalty. See* Deposit Penalties *in section 11 of Pub. 15 (Circular E).*

Specific Instructions

Box 1—Employer identification number (EIN). If you do not have an EIN, you may apply for one online. Go to IRS.gov and click on the *Apply for an EIN Online* link under "Tools." You may also apply for an EIN by calling 1-800-829-4933, or you can fax or mail Form SS-4, Application for Employer Identification Number. If you have not received your EIN by the due date of Form 941, write "Applied For" and the date you applied in this entry space.

Box 2—Amount paid. Enter the amount paid with Form 941.

Box 3—Tax period. Darken the circle identifying the quarter for which the payment is made. Darken only one circle.

Box 4—Name and address. Enter your name and address as shown on Form 941.

• Enclose your check or money order made payable to the "United States Treasury." Be sure to enter your EIN, "Form 941," and the tax period on your check or money order. Do not send cash. Do not staple Form 941-V or your payment to Form 941 (or to each other).

• Detach Form 941-V and send it with your payment and Form 941 to the address in the Instructions for Form 941.

Note. You must also complete the entity information above Part 1 on Form 941.

✂ ▼ **Detach Here and Mail With Your Payment and Form 941.** ▼ ✂

Form **941-V**	**Payment Voucher**	OMB No. 1545-0029
Department of the Treasury Internal Revenue Service	▶ **Do not staple this voucher or your payment to Form 941.**	2013

1 Enter your employer identification number (EIN).	2 **Enter the amount of your payment.** ▶ Make your check or money order payable to "**United States Treasury**"	Dollars	Cents

3 Tax Period		4 Enter your business name (individual name if sole proprietor).
○ 1st Quarter	○ 3rd Quarter	Enter your address.
○ 2nd Quarter	○ 4th Quarter	Enter your city, state, and ZIP code.

Form 941 (Rev. 1-2013)

Privacy Act and Paperwork Reduction Act Notice.
We ask for the information on Form 941 to carry out the Internal Revenue laws of the United States. We need it to figure and collect the right amount of tax. Subtitle C, Employment Taxes, of the Internal Revenue Code imposes employment taxes on wages, including income tax withholding. Form 941 is used to determine the amount of taxes that you owe. Section 6011 requires you to provide the requested information if the tax is applicable to you. Section 6109 requires you to provide your identification number. If you fail to provide this information in a timely manner, or provide false or fraudulent information, you may be subject to penalties and interest.

You are not required to provide the information requested on a form that is subject to the Paperwork Reduction Act unless the form displays a valid OMB control number. Books and records relating to a form or its instructions must be retained as long as their contents may become material in the administration of any Internal Revenue law.

Generally, tax returns and return information are confidential, as required by section 6103. However, section 6103 allows or requires the IRS to disclose or give the information shown on your tax return to others as described in the Code. For example, we may disclose your tax information to the Department of Justice for civil and criminal litigation, and to cities, states, the District of Columbia, and U.S. commonwealths and possessions for use in administering their tax laws. We may also disclose this information to other countries under a tax treaty, to federal and state agencies to enforce federal nontax criminal laws, or to federal law enforcement and intelligence agencies to combat terrorism.

The time needed to complete and file Form 941 will vary depending on individual circumstances. The estimated average time is:

Recordkeeping . . . . 11 hr.

Learning about the law or the form . . . . 47 min.

Preparing, copying, assembling, and sending the form to the IRS . . . . 1 hr.

If you have comments concerning the accuracy of these time estimates or suggestions for making Form 941 simpler, we would be happy to hear from you. You can email us at *taxforms@irs.gov*. Enter "Form 941" on the subject line. Or write to: Internal Revenue Service, Tax Products Coordinating Committee, SE:W:CAR:MP:T:M:S, 1111 Constitution Ave. NW, IR-6526, Washington, DC 20224. **Do not** send Form 941 to this address. Instead, see *Where Should You File?* in the Instructions for Form 941.

Instructions for Form 941

Department of the Treasury
Internal Revenue Service

(Rev. January 2012)
Employer's QUARTERLY Federal Tax Return

Section references are to the Internal Revenue Code unless otherwise noted.

What's New

Future developments. The IRS has created a page on IRS.gov for information about Form 941, at *www.irs.gov/form941*. Information about any future developments affecting Form 941 (such as legislation enacted after we release it) will be posted on that page.

Social security and Medicare tax for 2012. The employee tax rate for social security is 4.2% and the employer tax rate for social security is 6.2%, unchanged from 2011. The social security wage base limit is $110,100. The Medicare tax rate is 1.45% each for the employee and employer, unchanged from 2011. There is no wage base limit for Medicare tax.

Social security and Medicare taxes apply to the wages of household workers you pay $1,800 or more in cash or an equivalent form of compensation in 2012. Social security and Medicare taxes apply to election workers who are paid $1,500 or more in cash or an equivalent form of compensation in 2012.

VOW to Hire Heroes Act of 2011. On November 21, 2011, the President signed into law the VOW to Hire Heroes Act of 2011. This new law provides an expanded work opportunity tax credit to businesses that hire eligible unemployed veterans and, for the first time, also makes part of the credit available to certain tax-exempt organizations. Businesses claim the credit as part of the general business credit and tax-exempt organizations claim it against their payroll tax liability using Form 5884-C, Work Opportunity Credit for Qualified Tax-Exempt Organizations Hiring Qualified Veterans. The liability reported on Form 941 is not reduced by the amount of the credit. The credit is available for eligible unemployed veterans who begin work on or after November 22, 2011, and before January 1, 2013. For more information about the credit, visit *www.irs.gov/form5884c*.

Change of address. Beginning in 2012, employers must use new Form 8822-B, Change of Address—Business, for any address change.

Reminders

Section 3121(q) Notice and Demand—Tax due on unreported tips. An employer enters the amount of social security and Medicare taxes on unreported tips shown on the Section 3121(q) Notice and Demand on line 5e of the employer's Form 941 for the calendar quarter corresponding to the "Date of Notice and Demand."

Employers can choose to file Forms 941 instead of Form 944. Employers that would otherwise be required to file Form 944, Employer's ANNUAL Federal Tax Return, can notify the IRS if they want to file quarterly Forms 941 instead of annual Form 944. See Rev. Proc. 2009-51 2009-45 I.R.B. 625, available at *www.irs.gov/irb/2009-45_IRB/ar12.html*.

Correcting a previously filed Form 941. If you discover an error on a previously filed Form 941, make the correction using Form 941-X, Adjusted Employer's QUARTERLY Federal Tax Return or Claim for Refund. Form 941-X is filed separately from Form 941. For more information, see section 13 of Pub. 15 (Circular E), Employer's Tax Guide, or visit IRS.gov and enter the keywords *Correcting Employment Taxes*.

Paid preparers must sign Form 941. Paid preparers must complete and sign the paid preparer's section of Form 941.

Aggregate Form 941 filers. Agents must complete Schedule R (Form 941), Allocation Schedule for Aggregate Form 941 Filers, when filing an aggregate Form 941. Aggregate Forms 941 are filed by agents approved by the IRS under section 3504. To request approval to act as an agent for an employer, the agent files Form 2678, Employer/Payer Appointment of Agent, with the IRS.

COBRA premium assistance credit. The credit for COBRA premium assistance payments applies to premiums paid for employees involuntarily terminated between September 1, 2008, and May 31, 2010, and to premiums paid for up to 15 months. See *COBRA Premium Assistance Payments*, later.

Federal tax deposits must be made by electronic funds transfer. You must use electronic funds transfer to make all federal tax deposits. Generally, electronic funds transfers are made using the Electronic Federal Tax Payment System (EFTPS). If you do not want to use EFTPS, you can arrange for your tax professional, financial institution, payroll service, or other trusted third party to make deposits on your behalf. Also, you may arrange for your financial institution to initiate a same-day wire payment on your behalf. EFTPS is a free service provided by the Department of Treasury. Services provided by your tax professional, financial institution, payroll service, or other third party may have a fee.

For more information on making federal tax deposits, see section 11 of Pub. 15 (Circular E). To get more information about EFTPS or to enroll in EFTPS, visit *www.eftps.gov* or call 1-800-555-4477. Additional information about EFTPS is also available in Pub. 966, The Secure Way to Pay Your Federal Taxes.

 For an EFTPS deposit to be on time, you must initiate the deposit by 8 p.m. Eastern time the day before the date the deposit is due.

Same-day wire payment option. If you fail to initiate a deposit transaction on EFTPS by 8 p.m. Eastern time the day before the date a deposit is due, you can still make your deposit on time by using the Federal Tax Application (FTA). If you ever need the same-day wire payment method, you will need to make arrangements with your financial institution ahead of time. Please check with your financial institution regarding availability, deadlines, and costs. Your financial institution may charge you a fee for payments made this way. To learn more about the information you will need to provide your financial institution to make a same-day wire payment, visit *www.eftps.gov* to download the *Same-Day Payment Worksheet*.

Timeliness of federal tax deposits. If a deposit is required to be made on a day that is not a business day, the deposit is considered timely if it is made by the close of the next business day. A business day is any day other than a Saturday, Sunday, or legal holiday. The term "legal holiday"

Feb 24, 2012   Cat. No. 14625L

for deposit purposes includes only those legal holidays in the District of Columbia. Legal holidays in the District of Columbia are provided in Pub. 15 (Circular E). Previously, legal holidays for deposits included statewide legal holidays.

Electronic filing and payment. Now, more than ever before, businesses can enjoy the benefits of filing tax returns and paying their federal taxes electronically. Whether you rely on a tax professional or handle your own taxes, the IRS offers you convenient programs to make filing and paying easier. Spend less time and worry on taxes and more time running your business. Use e-file and the Electronic Federal Tax Payment System (EFTPS) to your benefit.

• For e-file, visit the IRS website at *www.irs.gov/efile* for additional information.

• For EFTPS, visit *www.eftps.gov* or call EFTPS Customer Service at 1-800-555-4477, 1-800-733-4829 (TDD), or 1-800-244-4829 (Spanish).

 If you are filing your tax return or paying your federal taxes electronically, a valid EIN is required at the time the return is filed. If a valid EIN is not provided, the return or payment will not be processed. This may result in penalties and delays in processing your return or payment.

Electronic funds withdrawal (EFW). If you file Form 941 electronically, you can e-file and e-pay (electronic funds withdrawal) the balance due in a single step using tax preparation software or through a tax professional. However, **do not** use EFW to make federal tax deposits. For more information on paying your taxes using EFW, visit the IRS website at *www.irs.gov/e-pay*. A fee may be charged to file electronically.

Credit or debit card payments. Employers can pay the balance due shown on Form 941 by credit or debit card. **Do not** use a credit or debit card to make federal tax deposits. For more information on paying your taxes with a credit or debit card, visit the IRS website at *www.irs.gov/e-pay*.

Employer's liability. Employers are responsible to ensure that tax returns are filed and deposits and payments are made, even if the employer contracts with a third party. The employer remains liable if the third party fails to perform a required action.

Where can you get telephone help? You can call the IRS Business and Specialty Tax Line toll-free at 1-800-829-4933 (TTY/TDD for the hearing impaired at 1-800-829-4059), Monday through Friday from 7 a.m. to 7 p.m. local time (Alaska and Hawaii follow Pacific time) for answers to your questions about completing Form 941, tax deposit rules, or obtaining an employer identification number (EIN).

Photographs of missing children. The Internal Revenue Service is a proud partner with the National Center for Missing and Exploited Children. Photographs of missing children selected by the Center may appear in instructions on pages that would otherwise be blank. You can help bring these children home by looking at the photographs and calling 1-800-THE-LOST (1-800-843-5678) if you recognize a child.

General Instructions:

Purpose of Form 941

These instructions give you some background information about Form 941. They tell you who must file Form 941, how to complete it line by line, and when and where to file it.

If you want more in-depth information about payroll tax topics relating to Form 941, see Pub. 15 (Circular E) or visit

the IRS website at *www.irs.gov/businesses* and click on the *Employment Taxes* link.

Federal law requires you, as an employer, to withhold taxes from your employees' paychecks. Each time you pay wages, you must withhold – or take out of your employees' paychecks – certain amounts for federal income tax, social security tax, and Medicare tax. Under the withholding system, taxes withheld from your employees are credited to your employees in payment of their tax liabilities.

Federal law also requires you to pay any liability for the employer's portion of social security and Medicare taxes. This portion of social security and Medicare taxes is not withheld from employees.

Who Must File Form 941?

Use Form 941 to report the following amounts.
• Wages you have paid.
• Tips your employees have received.
• Federal income tax you withheld.
• Both the employer's and the employee's share of social security and Medicare taxes.
• Current quarter's adjustments to social security and Medicare taxes for fractions of cents, sick pay, tips, and group-term life insurance.
• Credit for COBRA premium assistance payments.

Do not use the Form 941 to report backup withholding or income tax withholding on **nonpayroll** payments such as pensions, annuities, and gambling winnings. Report these types of withholding on Form 945, Annual Return of Withheld Federal Income Tax.

After you file your first Form 941, you must file a return for each quarter, even if you have no taxes to report, unless you filed a **final return** or one of the exceptions listed below applies.

Exceptions

Special rules apply to some employers.
• **Seasonal employers** do not have to file a Form 941 for quarters in which they have no tax liability because they have paid no wages. To tell the IRS that you will not file a return for one or more quarters during the year, check the box on line 18 **every quarter** you file Form 941. See section 12 of Pub. 15 (Circular E) for more information.
• Employers of **household employees** do not usually file Form 941. See Pub. 926, Household Employer's Tax Guide, and Schedule H (Form 1040), Household Employment Taxes, for more information.
• Employers of **farm employees** do not usually file Form 941. See Form 943, Employer's Annual Federal Tax Return for Agricultural Employees, and Pub. 51 (Circular A), Agricultural Employer's Tax Guide.

 *If none of the above exceptions applies and you have not filed a final return, you **must** file Form 941 each quarter even if you did not pay wages during the quarter. Use IRS e-file, if possible.*

What if You Reorganize or Close Your Business?

If You Sell or Transfer Your Business . . .

If you sell or transfer your business, you and the new owner must each file a Form 941 for the quarter in which the transfer occurred. Report only the wages you paid.

When two businesses merge, the continuing firm must file a return for the quarter in which the change took place and the other firm should file a **final return**.

Changing from one form of business to another—such as from a sole proprietorship to a partnership or corporation—is considered a transfer. If a transfer occurs, you may need a new EIN. See section 1 of Pub. 15 (Circular E). Attach a statement to your return with:
• The new owner's name (or the new name of the business);
• Whether the business is now a sole proprietorship, partnership, or corporation;
• The kind of change that occurred (a sale or transfer);
• The date of the change; and
• The name of the person keeping the payroll records and the address where those records will be kept.

If Your Business Has Closed . . .

If you go out of business or stop paying wages to your employees, you must file a **final return.** To tell the IRS that Form 941 for a particular quarter is your final return, check the box on line 17 and enter the date you last paid wages. Also attach a statement to your return showing the name of the person keeping the payroll records and the address where those records will be kept.

See the General Instructions for Forms W-2 and W-3 for information about earlier dates for the expedited furnishing and filing of Forms W-2, Wage and Tax Statement, when a final Form 941 is filed.

If you participated in a statutory merger or consolidation, or qualify for predecessor-successor status due to an acquisition, you should generally file Schedule D (Form 941), Report of Discrepancies Caused by Acquisitions, Statutory Mergers, or Consolidations. See the Instructions for Schedule D (Form 941) to determine whether you should file Schedule D (Form 941) and when you should file it.

When Must You File?

File your initial Form 941 for the quarter in which you first paid wages that are subject to social security and Medicare taxes or subject to federal income tax withholding. See the table below titled, *When To File Form 941.*

Then you must file for every quarter after that—every 3 months—even if you have no taxes to report, unless you are a seasonal employer or are filing your final return. See *Seasonal employers* and *If Your Business Has Closed*, earlier.

File Form 941 only once for each quarter. If you filed electronically, do not file a paper Form 941. For more information about filing Form 941 electronically, see *Electronic filing and payment*, earlier.

When To File Form 941

Your Form 941 is due by the last day of the month that follows the end of the quarter.		
The Quarter Includes . . .	**Quarter Ends**	**Form 941 Is Due**
1. January, February, March	March 31	April 30
2. April, May, June	June 30	July 31
3. July, August, September	September 30	October 31
4. October, November, December	December 31	January 31

For example, you generally must report wages you pay during the first quarter—which is January through March—by April 30. If you made timely deposits in full payment of your taxes for a quarter, you have 10 more days after the due dates shown above to file your Form 941.

If we receive Form 941 after the due date, we will treat Form 941 as filed on time if the envelope containing Form 941 is properly addressed, contains sufficient postage, and is postmarked by the U.S. Postal Service on or before the due date, or sent by an IRS-designated private delivery service on or before the due date. If you do not follow these guidelines, we will consider Form 941 filed when it is actually received. See Pub. 15 (Circular E) for more information on IRS-designated private delivery services.

If any due date for filing shown above falls on a Saturday, Sunday, or legal holiday, you may file your return on the next business day.

How Should You Complete Form 941?

Type or print your EIN, name, and address in the spaces provided. Also enter your name and EIN on the top of page 2. **Do not** use your social security number (SSN) or individual taxpayer identification number (ITIN). Generally, enter the business (legal) name you used when you applied for your EIN on Form SS-4, Application for Employer Identification Number. For example, if you are a sole proprietor, enter "Haleigh Smith" on the "Name" line and "Haleigh's Cycles" on the "Trade name" line. Leave the "Trade name" line blank if it is the same as your "Name."

Employer identification number (EIN). To make sure businesses comply with federal tax laws, the IRS monitors tax filings and payments by using a numerical system to identify taxpayers. A unique nine-digit employer identification number (EIN) is assigned to all corporations, partnerships, and some sole proprietors. Businesses needing an EIN must apply for a number and use it throughout the life of the business on all tax returns, payments, and reports.

Your business should have only one EIN. If you have more than one and are not sure which one to use, write to the IRS office where you file your returns (using the *Without a payment* address under *Where Should You File*, later) or call the IRS at 1-800-829-4933.

If you do not have an EIN, you may apply for one online. Go to IRS.gov and click on the *Apply for an EIN Online* link. You may also apply for an EIN by calling 1-800-829-4933, or you can fax or mail Form SS-4 to the IRS. If you have not received your EIN by the due date of Form 941, write "Applied For" and the date you applied in this entry space.

 If you are filing your tax return electronically, a valid EIN is required at the time the return is filed. If a valid EIN is not provided, the return will not be accepted. This may result in penalties and delays in processing your return.

 Always be sure the EIN on the form you file exactly matches the EIN the IRS assigned to your business. Do not use your social security number on forms that ask for an EIN. Filing a Form 941 with an incorrect EIN or using another business's EIN may result in penalties and delays in processing your return.

If you change your name or address... Notify the IRS immediately if you change your business name or address.
• Write to the IRS office where you file your returns (using the *Without a payment* address under *Where Should You File*, later) to notify the IRS of any name change. See Pub. 1635, Understanding Your Employer Identification Number (EIN), to see if you need to apply for a new EIN.
• Complete and mail Form 8822-B, Change of Address—Business, for any address change.

Check the Box for the Quarter

Under "Report for this Quarter of 2012" at the top of Form 941, check the appropriate box of the quarter for which you are filing. Make sure the quarter checked is the same as shown on any attached Schedule B (Form 941), Report of Tax Liability for Semiweekly Schedule Depositors.

Completing and Filing Form 941

Make entries on Form 941 as follows to enable accurate scanning and processing.
- Use 10-point Courier font (if possible) for all entries if you are typing or using a computer to complete your form.
- Omit dollar signs and decimal points. Commas are optional. Enter dollars to the left of the preprinted decimal point and cents to the right of it.
- Leave blank any data field (except lines 1, 2, and 10) with a value of zero.
- Enter negative amounts using a minus sign (if possible). Otherwise, use parentheses.
- Enter your name and EIN on all pages and attachments.
- Staple multiple sheets in the upper left corner when filing.

Other Forms You Must Use

To notify employees about the earned income credit (EIC), you must give the employees one of the following items.
- The IRS Form W-2, which has the required information about the EIC on the back of Copy B.
- A substitute Form W-2 with the same EIC information on the back of the employee's copy that is on Copy B of the IRS Form W-2.
- Notice 797, Possible Federal Tax Refund Due to the Earned Income Credit (EIC).
- Your written statement with the same wording as Notice 797.

For more information, see section 10 of Pub. 15 (Circular E) and Pub. 596, Earned Income Credit (EIC).

Reconciling Forms 941 and Form W-3

The IRS matches amounts reported on your four quarterly Forms 941 with Form W-2 amounts totaled on your yearly Form W-3, Transmittal of Wage and Tax Statements. If the amounts do not agree, you may be contacted by the IRS or the Social Security Administration (SSA). The following amounts are reconciled.
- Federal income tax withholding.
- Social security wages.
- Social security tips.
- Medicare wages and tips.

For more information, see section 12 of Pub. 15 (Circular E) and the Instructions for Schedule D (Form 941).

Where Should You File?

Where you file depends on whether you include a payment with Form 941.

If you are in . . .		Without a payment . . .	With a payment . . .
Special filing addresses for exempt organizations; federal, state, and local governmental entities; and Indian tribal governmental entities; regardless of location		Department of the Treasury Internal Revenue Service Ogden, UT 84201-0005	Internal Revenue Service P.O. Box 105083 Atlanta, GA 30348-5083
Connecticut Delaware District of Columbia Georgia Illinois Indiana Kentucky Maine Maryland Massachusetts Michigan New Hampshire	New Jersey New York North Carolina Ohio Pennsylvania Rhode Island South Carolina Tennessee Vermont Virginia West Virginia Wisconsin	Department of the Treasury Internal Revenue Service Cincinnati, OH 45999-0005	Internal Revenue Service P.O. Box 804522 Cincinnati, OH 45280-4522

If you are in . . .		Without a payment . . .	With a payment . . .
Alabama Alaska Arizona Arkansas California Colorado Florida Hawaii Idaho Iowa Kansas Louisiana Minnesota Mississippi	Missouri Montana Nebraska Nevada New Mexico North Dakota Oklahoma Oregon South Dakota Texas Utah Washington Wyoming	Department of the Treasury Internal Revenue Service Ogden, UT 84201-0005	Internal Revenue Service P.O. Box 105083 Atlanta, GA 30348-5083
No legal residence or principal place of business in any state		Internal Revenue Service P.O. Box 409101 Ogden, UT 84409	Internal Revenue Service P.O. Box 105273 Atlanta, GA 30348-5273

Depositing Your Taxes: When Must You Deposit Your Taxes?

Determine if You Are a Monthly or Semiweekly Schedule Depositor for the Quarter

The IRS uses two different sets of deposit rules to determine when businesses must deposit their social security, Medicare, and withheld federal income taxes. These schedules tell you when a deposit is due after you have a payday.

Your deposit schedule is not determined by how often you pay your employees. Your deposit schedule depends on the total tax liability you reported on Form 941 during the previous four-quarter **lookback period** (July 1 of the second preceding calendar year through June 30 of last year). See section 11 of Pub. 15 (Circular E) for details. If you filed Form 944 in either 2010 or 2011, your lookback period is the 2010 calendar year.

Before the beginning of each calendar year, determine which type of deposit schedule you must use.
- If you reported $50,000 or less in taxes during the lookback period, you are a **monthly schedule depositor**.
- If you reported more than $50,000 of taxes during the lookback period, you are a **semiweekly schedule depositor**.

 See section 11 of Pub. 15 (Circular E) for the Next Day Deposit Rule on taxes of $100,000 or more accumulated on any day during the deposit period.

How Must You Deposit Your Taxes?

You may have to deposit the federal income taxes you withheld and both the employer and employee social security taxes and Medicare taxes.
- **If your total taxes (line 10) are less than $2,500 for the current quarter or the preceding quarter, and you did not incur a $100,000 next-day deposit obligation during the current quarter.** You do not have to make a deposit. To avoid a penalty, you must pay the amount in full with a timely filed return or you must deposit the amount timely. If you are not sure your total tax liability for the current quarter will be less than $2,500 (and your liability for the preceding quarter was not less than $2,500), make deposits using the semi-weekly or monthly rules so you won't be subject to failure to deposit penalties.

- **If your total taxes (line 10) are $2,500 or more for the current quarter and the preceding quarter.**You must make deposits according to your deposit schedule. See section 11 of Pub. 15 (Circular E) for information and rules about federal tax deposits.

 The IRS has issued regulations under section 6302 which provide that you must deposit all depository taxes electronically by electronic funds transfers. For more information about electronic funds transfers, visit the IRS website at www.irs.gov/e-pay.

You may reduce your deposits during the quarter by the amount of COBRA premium assistance payments on line 12a.

What About Penalties and Interest?

Avoiding Penalties and Interest

You can avoid paying penalties and interest if you do all of the following.
- Deposit or pay your taxes when they are due.
- File your fully completed Form 941 on time.
- Report your tax liability accurately.
- Submit valid checks for tax payments.
- Furnish accurate Forms W-2 to employees.
- File Form W-3 and Copies A of Form W-2 with the Social Security Administration (SSA) on time and accurately.

Penalties and interest are charged on taxes paid late and returns filed late at a rate set by law. See sections 11 and 12 of Pub. 15 (Circular E) for details.

Use Form 843, Claim for Refund and Request for Abatement, to request abatement of assessed penalties or interest. **Do not** request abatement of assessed penalties or interest on Form 941 or Form 941-X.

 A trust fund recovery penalty may apply if federal income, social security, and Medicare taxes that must be withheld are not withheld or paid. The penalty is the full amount of the unpaid trust fund tax. This penalty may apply when these unpaid taxes cannot be collected from the employer. The trust fund recovery penalty may be imposed on all people the IRS determines to be responsible for collecting, accounting for, and paying these taxes, and who acted willfully in not doing so. For details, see section 11 of Pub. 15 (Circular E).

Specific Instructions:

Part 1: Answer These Questions for This Quarter

1. Number of Employees Who Received Wages, Tips, or Other Compensation This Quarter

Enter the number of employees on your payroll for the pay period including March 12, June 12, September 12, or December 12, **for the quarter indicated** at the top of Form 941. Do not include:
- Household employees,
- Employees in nonpay status for the pay period,
- Farm employees,
- Pensioners, or
- Active members of the Armed Forces.

 If you enter "250" or more on line 1, you must file Forms W-2 electronically. For details, call the SSA at 1-800-772-6270 or visit SSA's Employer W-2 Filing Instructions & Information website at www.socialsecurity.gov/employer.

2. Wages, Tips, and Other Compensation

Enter amounts on line 2 that would also be included in box 1 of your employees' Forms W-2. Include sick pay paid by a third party if you were given timely notice of the payments and transferred liability for the employees' taxes. See the General Instructions for Forms W-2 and W-3 for details.

If you are a third-party payer of sick pay, do not include sick pay that you paid to policyholders' employees here if you gave the policyholders timely notice of the payments.

3. Income Tax Withheld From Wages, Tips, and Other Compensation

Enter the federal income tax you withheld (or were required to withhold) from your employees on this quarter's wages, tips, taxable fringe benefits, and supplemental unemployment compensation benefits. Do not include any income tax withheld by a third-party payer of sick pay even if you reported it on Form W-2. You will reconcile this difference on Form W-3. Also include here any excise taxes you were required to withhold on golden parachute payments (section 4999).

If you are a third-party payer of sick pay, enter the federal income tax you withheld (or were required to withhold) on third-party sick pay here.

4. If No Wages, Tips, and Other Compensation are Subject to Social Security or Medicare Tax . . .

If no wages, tips, and other compensation on line 2 are subject to social security or Medicare tax, check the box on line 4. If this question does not apply to you, leave the box blank. For more information about exempt wages, see section 15 of Pub. 15 (Circular E) and section 4 of Pub. 15-A, Employer's Supplemental Tax Guide.

 If you are a government employer, wages you pay are not automatically exempt from social security and Medicare taxes. Your employees may be covered by law or by a voluntary Section 218 Agreement with the SSA. For more information, see Pub. 963, Federal-State Reference Guide.

5a–5d. Taxable Social Security and Medicare Wages and Tips

5a. Taxable social security wages. Enter the total wages, sick pay, and fringe benefits subject to social security taxes you paid to your employees during the quarter. For this purpose, sick pay includes payments made by an insurance company to your employees for which you received timely notice from the insurance company. See Section 6 in Pub. 15-A for more information about sick pay reporting.

Enter the amount before deductions. **Do not** include tips on this line. For information on types of wages subject to social security taxes, see section 5 of Pub. 15 (Circular E).

For 2012, the rate of social security tax on taxable wages is 6.2% (.062) for the employer and 4.2% (.042) for the employee or 10.4% (.104) for both. Stop paying social security tax on and entering an employee's wages on line 5a when the employee's taxable wages (including tips) reach $110,100 for the year. However, continue to withhold income and Medicare taxes for the whole year on wages and tips even when the social security wage base of $110,100 has been reached.

$$\frac{\text{line 5a (column 1)}}{\text{x} \quad .104}$$
$$\overline{\text{line 5a (column 2)}}$$

5b. Taxable social security tips. Enter all tips your employees reported to you during the quarter until the total of the tips and wages for an employee reach $110,100 for the year. Include all tips your employee reported to you even if you were unable to withhold the employee tax of 4.2%.

An employee must report cash tips to you, including tips you paid the employee for charge customers, totaling $20 or more in a month by the 10th of the next month. Employees may use Form 4070, Employee's Report of Tips to Employer (available only in Pub. 1244, Employee's Daily Record of Tips and Report to Employer), or submit a written statement or electronic tip record.

Do not include allocated tips on this line. Instead, report them on Form 8027, Employer's Annual Information Return of Tip Income and Allocated Tips. Allocated tips are not reportable on Form 941 and are not subject to withholding of federal income, social security, or Medicare taxes.

$$\frac{\text{line 5b (column 1)}}{\text{x} \quad .104}$$
$$\overline{\text{line 5b (column 2)}}$$

5c. Taxable Medicare wages & tips. Enter all wages, tips, sick pay, and taxable fringe benefits that are subject to Medicare tax. Unlike social security wages, there is no limit on the amount of wages subject to Medicare tax.

Include all tips your employees reported during the quarter, even if you were unable to withhold the employee tax of 1.45%.

$$\frac{\text{line 5c (column 1)}}{\text{x} \quad .029}$$
$$\overline{\text{line 5c (column 2)}}$$

For more information on tips, see section 6 of Pub. 15 (Circular E).

5d. Total social security and Medicare taxes. Add the social security wages tax (line 5a), social security tips tax (line 5b), and Medicare wages and tips tax (line 5c) and enter the result on line 5d.

5e. Section 3121(q) Notice and Demand—Tax on Unreported Tips

Enter the tax due from your Section 3121(q) Notice and Demand on line 5e. The IRS issues a Section 3121(q) Notice and Demand to advise an employer of the amount of tips received by employees who failed to report or underreported tips to the employer. An employer is not liable for the employer share of the social security and Medicare taxes on unreported tips until notice and demand for the taxes is made to the employer by the IRS in a Section 3121(q) Notice and Demand. The tax due may have been determined from tips reported to the IRS on employees' Forms 4137, Social Security and Medicare Tax on Unreported Tip Income, or other tips that were not reported to their employer as determined by the IRS during an examination.

Deposit the tax within the time period required under your deposit schedule to avoid any possible deposit penalty. The tax is treated as accumulated by the employer on the "Date of Notice and Demand" as printed on the Section 3121(q) Notice and Demand. The employer must include this amount on the appropriate line of the record of federal tax liability (Part 2 of Form 941 for a monthly schedule depositor

or Schedule B (Form 941) for a semiweekly schedule depositor).

6. Total Taxes Before Adjustments

Add the total federal income tax withheld from wages, tips, and other compensation (line 3), the total social security and Medicare taxes before adjustments (line 5d), and any tax due under section 3121(q) as entered on line 5e. Enter the result on line 6.

7–9. Tax Adjustments

Enter **tax amounts** on lines 7–9 that result from current quarter adjustments. Use a minus sign (if possible) to show an adjustment that decreases the total taxes shown on line 6 instead of parentheses. Doing so enhances the accuracy of our scanning software. For example, enter "-10.59" instead of "(10.59)." However, if your software only allows for parentheses in entering negative amounts, you may use them.

Current quarter's adjustments. In certain cases, you must adjust the amounts you entered as social security and Medicare taxes in column 2 of lines 5a, 5b, and 5c to figure your correct tax liability for this quarter's Form 941. See section 13 of Pub. 15 (Circular E).

7. Current quarter's adjustment for fractions of cents. Enter adjustments for fractions of cents (due to rounding) relating to the employee share of social security and Medicare taxes withheld. The employee share of amounts shown in column 2 of lines 5a, 5b, and 5c may differ slightly from amounts actually withheld from employees' paychecks due to the rounding of social security and Medicare taxes based on statutory rates.

8. Current quarter's adjustment for sick pay. Enter the adjustment for the employee share of social security and Medicare taxes that were withheld and deposited by your third-party sick pay payer with regard to sick pay paid by the third-party. These wages should be included on lines 5a and 5c. If you are the third-party sick pay payer, enter the adjustment for any employer share of these taxes required to be paid by the employer.

9. Current quarter's adjustments for tips and group-term life insurance. Enter adjustments for:
- Any uncollected employee share of social security and Medicare taxes on tips, and
- The uncollected employee share of social security and Medicare taxes on group-term life insurance premiums paid for former employees.

Prior quarter's adjustments. If you need to correct any adjustment reported on a previously filed Form 941, complete and file Form 941-X. Form 941-X is filed separately from Form 941. See section 13 of Pub. 15 (Circular E).

10. Total Taxes After Adjustments

Combine lines 6–9 and enter the result on line 10.

- **If line 10 is less than $2,500 or line 10 on the preceding quarterly return was less than $2,500, and you did not incur a $100,000 next-day deposit obligation during the current quarter.** You may pay the amount with Form 941 or you may deposit the amount. To avoid a penalty, you must pay the amount in full with a timely filed return or you must deposit the amount timely.
- **If line 10 is $2,500 or more and line 10 on the preceding quarterly return was $2,500 or more, or if you incurred a $100,000 next-day deposit obligation during the current quarter.** You must make deposits according to your deposit schedule. See section 11 of Pub. 15 (Circular E) for information and rules about federal tax deposits. The amount shown on line 10 **must** equal the "Total liability for

the quarter" shown on line 16 or the "Total liability for the quarter" shown on Schedule B (Form 941).

For more information on federal tax deposits, see *Depositing Your Taxes*, earlier, and section 11 of Pub. 15 (Circular E).

 If you are a semiweekly depositor, you must complete Schedule B (Form 941). If you fail to complete and submit Schedule B (Form 941), the IRS will assert deposit penalties based on available information.

11. Total Deposits for This Quarter

Enter your deposits for this quarter, including any overpayment from a prior quarter. Also include in the amount shown any overpayment from filing Form 941-X or Form 944-X, Adjusted Employer's ANNUAL Federal Tax Return or Claim for Refund, in the current quarter.

12a. COBRA Premium Assistance Payments

Enter 65% of the COBRA premiums for assistance eligible individuals. Take the COBRA premium assistance credit on this line only after the assistance eligible individual's 35% share of the premium has been paid. For COBRA coverage provided under a self-insured plan, COBRA premium assistance is treated as having been made for each assistance eligible individual who pays 35% of the COBRA premium. Do not include the assistance eligible individual's 35% of the premium in the amount entered on this line. For more information on the COBRA premium assistance credit, visit IRS.gov and enter the keyword *COBRA*.

 The amount entered on line 12a is treated as a deposit of taxes on the first day of your return period and must not be used to adjust line 16 or Schedule B (Form 941).

If you provided premium assistance in a prior quarter of the current year and did not report the amount of that premium assistance on Form 941 for that quarter, you may include the amount of that premium assistance in the amount entered on this line, or file form 941-X to report the amount for the prior quarter of the current year.

12b. Number of Individuals Provided COBRA Premium Assistance on Line 12a

Enter the total number of assistance eligible individuals provided COBRA premium assistance for the amount entered on line 12a. Count each assistance eligible individual who paid a reduced COBRA premium in the quarter as one individual, whether or not the reduced premium was for insurance that covered more than one assistance eligible individual. For example, if the reduced COBRA premium was for coverage for a former employee, spouse, and two children, you would include one individual in the number entered on line 12b for the premium assistance. Further, each individual is entered only once per quarter. For example, an assistance eligible individual who made monthly premium payments during the quarter would only be entered as one individual.

13. Total Deposits and Credits

Add lines 11 and 12a.

14. Balance Due

If line 10 is more than line 13, enter the difference on line 14. Otherwise, see *Overpayment* below. **You do not have to pay if line 14 is under $1.** Generally, you should have a balance due only if your total taxes (line 10) for the current quarter or preceding quarter are less than $2,500, and you did not incur a $100,000 next-day deposit obligation during the current quarter. However, see section 11 of Pub. 15

(Circular E) for information about payments made under the accuracy of deposit rule.

You may pay the amount shown on line 14 using EFTPS, a credit or debit card, a check or money order, or electronic funds withdrawal (EFW). **Do not** use a credit or debit card or EFW to pay taxes that were required to be deposited. For more information on electronic payment options, visit the IRS website at *www.irs.gov/e-pay*.

If you pay by EFTPS, credit or debit card, or EFW, file your return using the *Without a payment* address under *Where Should You File*, earlier, and **do not** file Form 941-V, Payment Voucher.

If you pay by check or money order, make it payable to the "United States Treasury." Enter your EIN, Form 941, and the tax period on your check or money order. Complete Form 941-V and enclose with Form 941.

If line 10 is $2,500 or more and you have deposited all taxes when due, the balance due on line 14 should be zero.

 If you do not deposit as required and, instead, pay the taxes with Form 941, you may be subject to a penalty.

15. Overpayment

If line 13 is more than line 10, enter the difference on line 15. **Never make an entry on both lines 14 and 15.**

If you deposited more than the correct amount for the quarter, you can choose to have the IRS either refund the overpayment or apply it to your next return. Check only one box on line 15. If you do not check either box or if you check both boxes, generally we will apply the overpayment to your account. We may apply your overpayment to any past due tax account that is shown in our records under your EIN.

If line 15 is under $1, we will send a refund or apply it to your next return only if you ask us in writing to do so.

Complete Both Pages

You must complete both pages of Form 941 and sign on page 2. An incomplete return may delay processing.

Part 2: Tell Us About Your Deposit Schedule and Tax Liability for This Quarter

16. Tax Liability for the Quarter

• If line 10 is less than $2,500 or line 10 on the preceding quarterly return was less than $2,500, and you did not incur a $100,000 next-day deposit obligation during the current quarter, check the appropriate box on line 16 and go to Part 3.

• If you reported $50,000 or less in taxes during the lookback period, you are a **monthly schedule depositor** unless the *$100,000 Next-Day Deposit Rule* discussed in section 11 of Pub. 15 (Circular E) applies. Check the appropriate box on line 16 and enter your tax liability for each month in the quarter. Add the amounts for each month. Enter the result in the *Total liability for quarter* box.

Note that your total tax liability for the quarter must equal your total taxes shown on line 10. If it does not, your tax deposits and payments may not be counted as timely. **Do not** change your tax liability on line 16 by adjustments reported on any Forms 941-X.

You are a **monthly schedule depositor** for the calendar year if the amount of your Form 941 taxes reported for the lookback period is $50,000 or less. The **lookback period** is the four consecutive quarters ending on June 30 of the prior year. For 2012, the lookback period begins July 1, 2010,

Instructions for Form 941 (Rev. 1-2012) -7-

and ends June 30, 2011. For details on the deposit rules, see section 11 of Pub. 15 (Circular E). If you filed Form 944 in either 2010 or 2011, your lookback period is the 2010 calendar year.

 *The amounts entered on line 16 are a summary of your monthly **tax liability**, not a summary of deposits you made. If you do not properly report your liabilities when required or if you are a semiweekly schedule depositor and enter your liabilities on line 16 instead of on Schedule B (Form 941), you may be assessed an "averaged" failure-to-deposit (FTD) penalty. See* Deposit Penalties *in section 11 of Pub. 15 (Circular E) for more information.*

• If you reported more than $50,000 of taxes for the lookback period, you are a **semiweekly schedule depositor.** Check the appropriate box on line 16.

You **must** complete Schedule B (Form 941) and submit it with your Form 941. **Do not** use Schedule B (Form 941) if you are a monthly schedule depositor.

Do not change your tax liability on Schedule B (Form 941) by adjustments reported on any Forms 941-X.

Part 3: Tell Us About Your Business

In Part 3, answer only those questions that apply to your business. If the questions do not apply, leave them blank and go to Part 4.

17. If Your Business Has Closed . . .

If you go out of business or stop paying wages, you must file a **final return.** To tell the IRS that a particular Form 941 is your final return, check the box on line 17 and enter the date you last paid wages in the space provided. For additional filing requirements, see *If Your Business Has Closed,* earlier.

18. If You are a Seasonal Employer . . .

If you hire employees seasonally—such as for summer or winter only—check the box on line 18. Checking the box tells the IRS not to expect four Forms 941 from you throughout the year because you have not paid wages regularly.

Generally, we will not ask about unfiled returns if you file at least one return showing tax due each year. However, you must check the box **every time** you file a Form 941.

Also, when you complete Form 941, be sure to check the box on the top of the form that corresponds to the quarter reported.

Part 4: May We Speak With Your Third-party Designee?

If you want to allow an employee, a paid tax preparer, or another person to discuss your Form 941 with the IRS, check the "Yes" box in Part 4. Then tell us the name, phone number, and the five-digit personal identification number (PIN) of the specific person to speak with—not the name of the firm who prepared your tax return. The designee may choose any five numbers as his or her PIN.

By checking "Yes," you authorize the IRS to talk to the person you named (your designee) about any questions we may have while we process your return. You also authorize your designee to:
• Give us any information that is missing from your return,
• Call us for information about processing your return, and

• Respond to certain IRS notices that you have shared with your designee about math errors and return preparation. The IRS will not send notices to your designee.

You are not authorizing your designee to bind you to anything (including additional tax liability) or to otherwise represent you before the IRS. If you want to expand your designee's authorization, see Pub. 947, Practice Before the IRS and Power of Attorney.

The authorization will automatically expire 1 year from the due date (without regard to extensions) for filing your Form 941. If you or your designee want to terminate the authorization, write to the IRS office for your location using the *Without a payment* address under *Where Should You File,* earlier.

Part 5: Sign Here

Complete all information in Part 5 and sign Form 941 as follows.

• **Sole proprietorship—** The individual who owns the business.

• **Corporation (including a limited liability company (LLC) treated as a corporation)—** The president, vice president, or other principal officer duly authorized to sign.

• **Partnership (including an LLC treated as a partnership) or unincorporated organization—** A responsible and duly authorized member, partner, or officer having knowledge of its affairs.

• **Single member LLC treated as a disregarded entity for federal income tax purposes—** The owner of the LLC or a principal officer duly authorized to sign.

• **Trust or estate—** The fiduciary.

Form 941 may also be signed by a duly authorized agent of the taxpayer if a valid power of attorney has been filed.

Alternative signature method. Corporate officers or duly authorized agents may sign Form 941 by rubber stamp, mechanical device, or computer software program. For details and required documentation, see Rev. Proc. 2005-39, 2005-28 I.R.B. 82, at *www.irs.gov/irb/2005-28_IRB/ar16.html.*

Paid Preparer Use Only

A paid preparer must sign Form 941 and provide the information in the *Paid Preparer Use Only* section of Part 5 if the preparer was paid to prepare Form 941 and is not an employee of the filing entity. Paid preparers must sign paper returns with a manual signature. The preparer must give you a copy of the return in addition to the copy to be filed with the IRS.

If you are a paid preparer, enter your Preparer Tax Identification Number (PTIN) in the space provided. Include your complete address. If you work for a firm, enter the firm's name and the EIN of the firm. You can apply for a PTIN online or by filing Form W-12, IRS Paid Preparer Tax Identification Number (PTIN) Application and Renewal. For more information about applying for a PTIN online, visit the IRS website at *www.irs.gov/ptin.* You cannot use your PTIN in place of the EIN of the tax preparation firm.

Generally, do not complete this section if you are filing the return as a reporting agent and have a valid Form 8655, Reporting Agent Authorization, on file with the IRS. However, a reporting agent must complete this section if the reporting agent offered legal advice, for example, advising the client on determining whether its workers are employees or independent contractors for federal tax purposes.

How to Order Forms and Publications from the IRS

 Call 1-800-829-3676.

 Visit *www.irs.gov/formspubs*.

Other IRS Products You May Need

- Form SS-4, Application for Employer Identification Number

- Form W-2, Wage and Tax Statement

- Form W-2c, Corrected Wage and Tax Statement

- Form W-3, Transmittal of Wage and Tax Statements

- Form W-3c, Transmittal of Corrected Wage and Tax Statements

- Form W-4, Employee's Withholding Allowance Certificate

- Form 940, Employer's Annual Federal Unemployment (FUTA) Tax Return

- Form 941-X, Adjusted Employer's QUARTERLY Federal Tax Return or Claim for Refund

- Form 943, Employer's Annual Federal Tax Return for Agricultural Employees

- Form 944, Employer's ANNUAL Federal Tax Return

- Form 944-X, Adjusted Employer's ANNUAL Federal Tax Return or Claim for Refund

- Form 4070, Employee's Report of Tips to Employer

- Form 8027, Employer's Annual Information Return of Tip Income and Allocated Tips

- Form 8655, Reporting Agent Authorization

- Notice 797, Possible Federal Tax Refund Due to the Earned Income Credit (EIC)

- Pub. 15 (Circular E), Employer's Tax Guide

- Pub. 15-A, Employer's Supplemental Tax Guide

- Pub. 15-B, Employer's Tax Guide to Fringe Benefits

- Pub. 596, Earned Income Credit

- Pub. 926, Household Employer's Tax Guide

- Schedule B (Form 941), Report of Tax Liability for Semiweekly Schedule Depositors

- Schedule D (Form 941), Report of Discrepancies Caused by Acquisitions, Statutory Mergers, or Consolidations

- Schedule H (Form 1040), Household Employment Taxes

- Schedule R (Form 941), Allocation Schedule for Aggregate Form 941 Filers

Schedule B (Form 941):

Report of Tax Liability for Semiweekly Schedule Depositors

960311

(Rev. June 2011)   Department of the Treasury — Internal Revenue Service

OMB No. 1545-0029

(EIN)
Employer identification number   ☐☐ – ☐☐☐☐☐☐☐

Name *(not your trade name)*

Calendar year   ☐☐☐☐   (Also check quarter)

Report for this Quarter...
(Check one.)

☐ **1:** January, February, March

☐ **2:** April, May, June

☐ **3:** July, August, September

☐ **4:** October, November, December

Use this schedule to show your TAX LIABILITY for the quarter; DO NOT use it to show your deposits. When you file this form with Form 941 or Form 941-SS, DO NOT change your tax liability by adjustments reported on any Forms 941-X. You must fill out this form and attach it to Form 941 or Form 941-SS if you are a semiweekly schedule depositor or became one because your accumulated tax liability on any day was $100,000 or more. Write your daily tax liability on the numbered space that corresponds to the date wages were paid. See Section 11 in Pub. 15 (Circular E), Employer's Tax Guide, for details.

Month 1

1		9		17		25		Tax liability for Month 1
2		10		18		26		
3		11		19		27		
4		12		20		28		
5		13		21		29		
6		14		22		30		
7		15		23		31		
8		16		24				

Month 2

1		9		17		25		Tax liability for Month 2
2		10		18		26		
3		11		19		27		
4		12		20		28		
5		13		21		29		
6		14		22		30		
7		15		23		31		
8		16		24				

Month 3

1		9		17		25		Tax liability for Month 3
2		10		18		26		
3		11		19		27		
4		12		20		28		
5		13		21		29		
6		14		22		30		
7		15		23		31		
8		16		24				

Fill in your total liability for the quarter (Month 1 + Month 2 + Month 3) ▶

Total must equal line 10 on Form 941 or Form 941-SS.

Total liability for the quarter

For Paperwork Reduction Act Notice, see separate instructions.   Cat. No. 11967Q   Schedule B (Form 941) (Rev. 6-2011)

Instructions for Schedule B (Form 941)

Department of the Treasury
Internal Revenue Service

(Rev. June 2011)

Report of Tax Liability for Semiweekly Schedule Depositors

Section references are to the Internal Revenue Code unless otherwise noted.

Reminders

Reporting prior period adjustments. Prior period adjustments are reported on Form 941-X, Amended Employer's QUARTERLY Federal Tax Return or Claim for Refund, and are not taken into account when figuring the tax liability for the current quarter.

When you file Schedule B (Form 941) with your Form 941 (or Form 941-SS), do not change your tax liability by adjustments reported on any Form 941-X.

Amended Schedule B. If you have been assessed a failure-to-deposit (FTD) penalty, you may be able to file an amended Schedule B (Form 941). See *Amending a Previously Filed Schedule B (Form 941)* on page 2.

General Instructions

Purpose of Schedule B (Form 941)

These instructions tell you about Schedule B (Form 941), Report of Tax Liability for Semiweekly Schedule Depositors. To determine if you are a semiweekly depositor, visit IRS.gov and type "semiweekly depositor" in the search box. Also see Pub. 15 (Circular E), Employer's Tax Guide, or Pub. 80 (Circular SS), Federal Tax Guide for Employers in the U.S. Virgin Islands, Guam, American Samoa, and the Commonwealth of the Northern Mariana Islands.

Federal law requires you, as an employer, to withhold taxes from your employees' paychecks. Each time you pay wages, you must withhold – or take out of your employees' paychecks – certain amounts for federal income tax, social security tax, and Medicare tax (payroll taxes). Under the withholding system, taxes withheld from your employees are credited to your employees in payment of their tax liabilities.

Federal law also requires employers to pay any liability for the employer's portion of social security and Medicare taxes. This portion of social security and Medicare taxes is not withheld from employees.

On Schedule B (Form 941), list your **tax liability** for each day. Your liability includes:
• The federal income tax you withheld from your employees' paychecks, and
• Both employee and employer social security and Medicare taxes.

Do not use the Schedule B (Form 941) to show federal tax deposits. The IRS gets deposit data from electronic funds transfers.

 The IRS uses Schedule B (Form 941) to determine if you have deposited your federal employment tax liabilities on time. If you do not properly complete and file your Schedule B (Form 941) with Form 941 or Form 941-SS, the IRS may propose an "averaged" failure-to-deposit penalty. See Deposit Penalties *in section 11 of Pub. 15 (Circular E) for more information.*

Who Must File?

File Schedule B (Form 941) if you are a semiweekly schedule depositor. You are a semiweekly depositor if you reported more than $50,000 of employment taxes in the lookback period or accumulated a tax liability of $100,000 or more on any given day in the current or prior calendar year. See section 11 of Pub. 15 (Circular E) for more information.

 Do not complete Schedule B (Form 941) if you have a tax liability that is less than $2,500 during the quarter.

When Must You File?

Schedule B (Form 941) is filed with Form 941, Employer's QUARTERLY Federal Tax Return, or Form 941-SS, Employer's QUARTERLY Federal Tax Return (American Samoa, Guam, the Commonwealth of the Northern Mariana Islands, and the U.S. Virgin Islands). File Schedule B (Form 941) with your Form 941 or Form 941-SS every quarter when Form 941 or Form 941-SS is due.

Do not file Schedule B (Form 941) as an attachment to Form 944, Employer's ANNUAL Federal Tax Return, or Form 944-SS, Employer's ANNUAL Federal Tax Return (American Samoa, Guam, the Commonwealth of the Northern Mariana Islands, and the U.S. Virgin Islands). Instead, if required to file a report of tax liability with either of these forms, use Form 945-A, Annual Record of Federal Tax Liability.

Specific Instructions

Completing Schedule B (Form 941)

Enter Your Business Information
Carefully enter your employer identification number (EIN) and name at the top of the schedule. Make sure that they exactly match the name of your business and the EIN that the IRS assigned to your business and also agree with the name and EIN shown on the attached Form 941 or Form 941-SS.

Calendar Year
Enter the calendar year that applies to the quarter checked.

Check the Box for the Quarter
Under *Report for this Quarter* at the top of Schedule B (Form 941), check the appropriate box of the quarter for which you are filing this schedule. Make sure the quarter checked on the top of the Schedule B (Form 941) matches the quarter checked on your Form 941 or Form 941-SS.

Enter Your Tax Liability by Month
Schedule B (Form 941) is divided into the 3 months that make up a quarter of a year. Each month has 31 numbered spaces that correspond to the dates of a typical month. Enter your tax liabilities in the spaces that correspond to the dates you **paid** wages to your employees, not the date payroll deposits were made.

For example, if your payroll period ended on December 31, 2010, and you **paid** the wages for that period on January 6, 2011, you would:
• Go to Month 1 (because January is the first month of the quarter), and

Jul 08, 2011   Cat. No. 38683X

- Enter your tax liability on line 6 (because line 6 represents the sixth day of the month).

 Make sure you have checked the appropriate box in Part 2 of Form 941 or Form 941-SS to show that you are a semiweekly schedule depositor.

Total Liability for the Quarter

To find your total liability for the quarter, add your monthly tax liabilities.

```
      Tax Liability for Month 1
     +Tax Liability for Month 2
     +Tax Liability for Month 3
      Total Liability for the Quarter
```

Your total liability for the quarter must equal line 10 on Form 941 or Form 941-SS.

Example 1. Employer A is a **semiweekly** schedule depositor who pays wages for each month on the last day of the month. On December 22, 2010, Employer A also paid its employees year-end bonuses (subject to employment taxes). Employer A must report employment tax liabilities on Schedule B (Form 941) for the 4th quarter (October, November, December), as follows.

Month	Lines for dates wages were paid
1 (October)	line 31 (pay day, last day of the month)
2 (November)	line 30 (pay day, last day of the month)
3 (December)	line 22 (bonus paid December 22, 2010)
3 (December)	line 31 (pay day, last day of the month)

Example 2. Employer B is a **semiweekly** schedule depositor who pays employees every other Friday. Employer B accumulated a $20,000 employment tax liability on each of these pay dates: 1/14/11, 1/28/11, 2/11/11, 2/25/11, 3/11/11, and 3/25/11. Employer B must report employment tax liabilities on Schedule B (Form 941) as follows.

Month	Lines for dates wages were paid
1 (January)	lines 14 and 28
2 (February)	lines 11 and 25
3 (March)	lines 11 and 25

Example 3. Employer C is a new business and **monthly** schedule depositor for 2011. Employer C pays wages every Friday and has accumulated a $2,000 employment tax liability on 1/14/11 and a $110,000 employment tax liability on 1/21/11 and on every subsequent Friday during 2011. Under the deposit rules, employers **become semiweekly schedule depositors** on the day after any day they accumulate $100,000 or more of employment tax liability in a deposit period. Employer C became a semiweekly schedule depositor on 1/22/11, because Employer C had a total accumulated employment tax liability of $112,000 on 1/21/11. For more information, see section 11 of Pub. 15 (Circular E) or section 8 of Pub. 80 (Circular SS).

Employer C must complete Schedule B (Form 941) as shown below and file it with Form 941 or 941-SS.

Month	Lines for dates wages were paid	Amount to report
1 (January)	line 14	$2,000
1 (January)	lines 21, 28	$110,000
2 (February)	lines 4, 11, 18, 25	$110,000
3 (March)	lines 4, 11, 18, 25	$110,000

Amending a Previously Filed Schedule B (Form 941)

Semiweekly schedule depositors. If you have been assessed a failure-to-deposit (FTD) penalty for a quarter and you made an error on Schedule B (Form 941) and the correction will not change the total liability for the quarter you reported on Schedule B (Form 941), you may be able to reduce your penalty by filing a corrected Schedule B (Form 941).

Example. You reported a liability of $3,000 on day 1 of month 1. However, the liability was actually for month 3. Prepare an amended Schedule B (Form 941) showing the $3,000 liability on day 1 of month 3. Also, you must enter the liabilities previously reported for the quarter that did not change. Write "Amended" at the top of Schedule B (Form 941). The IRS will refigure the penalty and notify you of any change in the penalty.

Monthly schedule depositors. You can also file an amended Schedule B (Form 941) if you have been assessed an FTD penalty for a quarter and you made an error on the monthly tax liability section of Form 941. When completing Schedule B (Form 941), only enter the monthly totals. The daily entries are not required.

Where to file. File your amended Schedule B at the address provided in the penalty notice you received. You do not have to submit your original Schedule B (Form 941).

Form 941-X

Tax decrease. If you are filing Form 941-X for a quarter, you can file an amended Schedule B (Form 941) with Form 941-X if both of the following apply.

1. You have a tax decrease.
2. You were assessed an FTD penalty.

File your amended Schedule B (Form 941) with Form 941-X. The total liability for the quarter reported on your corrected Schedule B (Form 941) must equal the corrected amount of tax reported on Form 941-X. If your penalty is decreased, the IRS will include the penalty decrease with your tax decrease.

Tax increase — Form 941-X filed timely. If you are filing a timely Form 941-X, do not file an amended Schedule B (Form 941), unless you were assessed an FTD penalty caused by an incorrect, incomplete, or missing Schedule B (Form 941). If you are filing an amended Schedule B (Form 941), do not include the tax increase reported on Form 941-X.

Tax increase — Form 941-X filed late. If you owe tax and are filing a late Form 941-X, that is, after the due date of the return for the filing period of the Form 941 in which you discovered the error, you must file an amended Schedule B (Form 941) with Form 941-X. Otherwise, the IRS may assess an "averaged" FTD penalty.

The total tax reported on the "Total liability for the quarter" line of the amended Schedule B (Form 941) must match the corrected tax (line 10 of Form 941 combined with any correction reported on line 21 of Form 941-X for the quarter), less any previous abatements and interest-free adjustments.

Paperwork Reduction Act Notice. We ask for the information on Schedule B (Form 941) to carry out the Internal Revenue laws of the United States. You are required to give us the information. We need it to ensure that you are complying with these laws and to allow us to figure and collect the right amount of tax.

You are not required to provide the information requested on a form that is subject to the Paperwork Reduction Act unless the form displays a valid OMB control number. Books or records relating to a form or its instructions must be retained as long as their contents may become material in the administration of any Internal Revenue law. Generally, tax returns and return information are confidential, as required by Code section 6103.

The time needed to complete and file Schedule B (Form 941) will vary depending on individual circumstances. The estimated average time is 2 hours, 53 minutes.

If you have comments concerning the accuracy of this time estimate or suggestions for making Schedule B (Form 941) simpler, we would be happy to hear from you. You can email us at: *taxforms@irs.gov*. Enter "Schedule B (Form 941)" on the subject line. Or write to: Internal Revenue Service, Tax Products Coordinating Committee, SE:W:CAR:MP:T:T:SP, 1111 Constitution Ave. NW, IR-6526, Washington, DC 20224. **Do not** send Schedule B (Form 941) to this address. Instead, see *Where Should You File?* in the Form 941 or Form 941-SS instructions.

Schedule D (Form 941):
Report of Discrepancies Caused by Acquisitions, Statutory Mergers, or Consolidations

(Rev. June 2011)   Department of the Treasury—Internal Revenue Service

OMB No. 1545-0029

Employer Identification Number (EIN)   ☐☐ – ☐☐☐☐☐☐☐

Name *(not your trade name)*

Trade name *(if any)*

Address
Number   Street   Suite or room number

City   State   ZIP code

Phone number

Tax Year of Discrepancies (Fill in)

☐☐☐☐ Format: YYYY

Type of Submission (Check one)

☐ Original

☐ Corrected

About this schedule

Each year the Internal Revenue Service (IRS) and the Social Security Administration (SSA) compare the totals on your Forms 941, *Employer's QUARTERLY Federal Tax Return,* with the totals on Forms W-2, *Wage and Tax Statement,* to verify that:

- The wages you reported on Forms 941 match those you reported on Forms W-2 (Copy A) so that your employees' social security earnings records are complete for benefit purposes; and
- You have paid the appropriate taxes.

Generally, the totals on your Forms W-2 (Copy A) should equal the totals you reported on Forms 941. Use this schedule if discrepancies exist between the totals you reported on those forms ONLY as a result of an acquisition, statutory merger, or consolidation. **In many cases, the information on this schedule should help the IRS resolve discrepancies without contacting you.** If you are an eligible employer who elects to use the alternate procedure set forth in Rev. Proc. 2004-53, explained in the instructions, you should file this schedule.

Read the separate instructions before you fill out this schedule.

Part 1: Answer these background questions.

1. Are you filing this schedule —

☐ After a statutory merger or consolidation? (See Rev. Rul. 62-60, 1962-1 C.B. 186 and Rev. Proc. 2004-53, 2004-2 C.B. 320.)

You are either: ☐ An acquired corporation or

☐ A surviving corporation.

OR

☐ After an acquisition and you are using the alternate procedure under Rev. Proc. 2004-53, 2004-2 C.B. 320?

You are either: ☐ A predecessor or

☐ A successor.

2. The effective date of the statutory merger/consolidation or acquisition is . . . .

MM / DD / YYYY

3. The OTHER PARTY in this transaction is . . .

Other party's EIN   ☐☐ – ☐☐☐☐☐☐☐

Other party's name

Trade name *(if any)*

Address
Number   Street   Suite or room number

City   State   ZIP code

Phone number

Next ▶

For Paperwork Reduction Act Notice, see separate instructions.   Cat. No. 38791Y   **Schedule D (Form 941)** (Rev. 6-2011)

Your EIN ☐☐ – ☐☐☐☐☐☐☐

Name *(not your trade name)* _____

Other party's EIN ☐☐ – ☐☐☐☐☐☐☐

Tax Year of Discrepancies (Fill in)

☐☐☐☐ Format: YYYY

Part 2: Tell us about the discrepancies with your returns.

	Column A	Column B	Column C
	Amount you reported to IRS for the tax year	– **Amount you reported to SSA for the tax year**	= **The difference**
	Totals from Forms 941 as corrected by any Forms 941-X	Totals from Forms W-2 (Copy A) as corrected by any Forms W-2c (Copy A)	
4. Social security wages	_____	– _____	= _____
5. Medicare wages and tips	_____	– _____	= _____
6. Social security tips	_____	– _____	= _____
7. Federal income tax withheld	_____	– _____	= _____
8. Advance earned income credit (EIC) payments (for tax years ending before January 1, 2011)	_____	– _____	= _____

If you are filing for one transaction only, STOP here. If you are filing for more than one transaction, go to Part 3.

Part 3: Fill this part out ONLY if you are filing more than one Schedule D (Form 941) for any calendar year.

9. File one Schedule D (Form 941) for each separate transaction. This is schedule ☐ of ☐ . (Example: *This is schedule 1 of 3.*)

	Column A	Column B	Column C
	Amount you reported to IRS for the tax year for the employees affected by the transaction reported on this Schedule D (Form 941)	– **Amount you reported to SSA for the tax year for the employees affected by the transaction reported on this Schedule D (Form 941)**	= **The difference**
	Totals from Forms 941 as corrected by any Forms 941-X	Totals from Forms W-2 (Copy A) as corrected by any Forms W-2c (Copy A)	
10. Social security wages	_____	– _____	= _____
11. Medicare wages and tips	_____	– _____	= _____
12. Social security tips	_____	– _____	= _____
13. Federal income tax withheld	_____	– _____	= _____
14. Advance earned income credit (EIC) payments (for tax years ending before January 1, 2011)	_____	– _____	= _____

Schedule D (Form 941) (Rev. 6-2011)

Instructions for Schedule D (Form 941)

Department of the Treasury
Internal Revenue Service

(Rev. June 2011)

Report of Discrepancies Caused by Acquisitions, Statutory Mergers, or Consolidations

Section references are to the Internal Revenue Code unless otherwise noted.

General Instructions

Understanding Schedule D (Form 941)

These instructions tell you about Schedule D (Form 941), Report of Discrepancies Caused by Acquisitions, Statutory Mergers, or Consolidations. Employers can use Schedule D (Form 941), to explain certain discrepancies (caused by acquisitions, statutory mergers, and consolidations) between Forms W-2, Wage and Tax Statement (Copy A), and Forms 941, Employer's QUARTERLY Federal Tax Return, for the totals of social security wages, Medicare wages and tips, social security tips, federal income tax withheld, and advance earned income credit (EIC) payments (for tax years ending before January 1, 2011).

What Is Schedule D (Form 941)?

Each year the Internal Revenue Service (IRS) and the Social Security Administration (SSA) compare the totals on your Forms 941 with the totals from your Forms W-2 (Copy A), to verify the following.
• The wages you reported on Forms 941 match those you reported on Forms W-2 (Copy A) so that your employees' social security earnings records are complete for benefit purposes.
• You have paid the appropriate taxes.

Generally, the totals of all your Forms W-2 (Copy A) should equal the aggregate quarterly totals you reported on Forms 941. Use Schedule D (Form 941) if discrepancies exist between the totals you reported on those forms **only** as a result of an acquisition, statutory merger, or consolidation.

 IRS uses Schedule D (Form 941) to determine if you have reported your wages and tax liabilities correctly. In many cases, the information on Schedule D (Form 941) helps the IRS resolve discrepancies without contacting you.

Who Should File Schedule D (Form 941)?

You do not need to file a Schedule D (Form 941) for every merger, acquisition, or other reorganization that occurs. File Schedule D (Form 941) **only** for those acquisitions, statutory mergers or consolidations that create discrepancies between Forms W-2 (Copy A) and Forms 941 in the totals of:
• Social security wages,
• Medicare wages and tips,
• Social security tips,
• Federal income tax withheld, and
• Advance EIC payments (for tax years ending before January 1, 2011).

 ***Each** party to an applicable transaction (see below) files its own Schedule D (Form 941).*

File Schedule D (Form 941) for:
• A statutory merger,
• A consolidation, or
• An acquisition for which you are using the alternate procedure under Rev. Proc. 2004-53. See Rev. Proc. 2004-53, 2004-34 I.R.B. 320, available at *www.irs.gov/irb/2004-34_IRB/ar13.html*.

Do NOT file a Schedule D for:
• An acquisition for which you are using the standard procedure under Rev. Proc. 2004-53, or
• An acquisition that is not a statutory merger or consolidation and that does not qualify under the predecessor-successor rules. See *Acquisitions that Qualify Under Predecessor-Successor Rules,* on page 2, for a complete discussion of the predecessor-successor rules.

Types of Mergers and Acquisitions

Mergers, acquisitions, and other reorganizations generally fall into one of three categories for purposes of reporting employment taxes.
• Statutory mergers and consolidations.
• Acquisitions that qualify under the predecessor-successor rules (see *Acquisitions that Qualify Under Predecessor-Successor Rules* on page 2).
• Other acquisitions that are not statutory mergers or consolidations and that **do not** qualify under the predecessor-successor rules (see *Acquisitions that Qualify Under the Predecessor-Successor Rules* on page 2).

Statutory Mergers and Consolidations

If you are the **surviving** corporation after a statutory merger or consolidation, you should file Schedule D (Form 941) to provide:
• The date of the statutory merger or consolidation;
• The name, trade name (doing business as or d/b/a), address, and employer identification number (EIN) of the acquired corporation; and
• An explanation of any discrepancies between Forms W-2 (Copy A) and Forms 941 in the totals of social security wages, Medicare wages and tips, social security tips, federal income tax withheld, and advance EIC payments (only for tax years ending before January 1, 2011).

If you are the **acquired** corporation after a statutory merger or consolidation and you are filing a final Form 941, you should file Schedule D (Form 941) to provide:
• The date of the statutory merger or consolidation;

Jun 27, 2011   Cat. No. 38789M

- The name, trade name (doing business as or d/b/a), address, and EIN of the surviving corporation; and
- An explanation of any discrepancies between Forms W-2 (Copy A) and Forms 941 in the totals of social security wages, Medicare wages and tips, social security tips, federal income tax withheld, and advance EIC payments (only for tax years ending before January 1, 2011).

Rev. Rul. 62-60, 1962-1 C.B. 186, provides that, for employment tax purposes, the "resultant" corporation (now called a "surviving" corporation) resulting from a statutory merger or consolidation is the same employer and taxpayer as the "absorbed" corporation (now called an "acquired" corporation). The predecessor-successor rules described in Rev. Proc. 2004-53 do not apply to these transactions.

However, Rev. Proc. 2004-53 provides guidance for using Schedule D (Form 941) by a surviving corporation or an acquired corporation to report information after a statutory merger or consolidation **only** where there is a discrepancy. If the surviving corporation completes and files Schedule D (Form 941) to explain discrepancies between the totals on Forms W-2 (Copy A) and the totals on Forms 941, filing Schedule D (Form 941) will also provide notice of a statutory merger or consolidation under Rev. Rul. 62-60.

Acquisitions that Qualify Under the Predecessor-Successor Rules

Acquisitions that qualify under the predecessor-successor rules are acquisitions in which a **successor** employer:
- Acquires substantially all the property used in a trade or business of another employer (predecessor) or in a separate unit of a trade or business of a predecessor, and
- In connection with and directly after the acquisition (but during the same calendar year) employs individuals who immediately before the acquisition were employed in the trade or business of the predecessor.

These acquisitions satisfy the conditions for predecessor-successor status set forth in section 3121(a)(1) and Regulations section 31.3121(a)(1)-1(b).

Rev. Proc. 2004-53 contains the rules that apply to employment tax reporting in a predecessor-successor situation. Two procedures can be used in an acquisition that qualifies as a predecessor-successor situation.
- **Standard procedure**—Do not file Schedule D (Form 941). No discrepancies should exist between the totals of the Forms W-2 (Copy A) and the totals of the Forms 941 as a result of the acquisition.
- **Alternate procedure**—Each party in the transaction should file Schedule D (Form 941). Forms W-2 (Copy A) filed by the successor may include amounts reported on Forms 941 filed by the predecessor.

Other Acquisitions

If you completed other acquisitions that are not statutory mergers or consolidations and that do not qualify under the predecessor-successor rules, no discrepancies should exist as a result of the acquisition. Rev. Rul. 62-60 and Rev. Proc. 2004-53 do not apply to such transactions. **Do not** file Schedule D (Form 941) for such transactions.

When Should You File?

If your business is continuing to operate, you should file Schedule D (Form 941) with your Form 941 no later than the due date of your Form 941 for the first quarter of the year after the calendar year of the transaction.

If your business is **not** continuing to operate, you should file Schedule D (Form 941) with your final Form 941.

For example, if the transaction occurred in the third quarter of 2010 and your business is continuing to operate, you would file Schedule D (Form 941) with your Form 941 no later than the due date for the first quarter of 2011. However, if your business is not continuing to operate during 2010, you would file Schedule D (Form 941) with your final Form 941 no later than the due date for the third quarter of 2010.

How Should You File?

Schedule D (Form 941) was designed to be filed electronically with your electronic submission of Form 941. Electronic filing of Schedule D (Form 941) enables IRS to process information on the form more efficiently and accurately.

However, you may file Schedule D (Form 941) on paper if necessary. When filing on paper, **do not** attach Schedule D (Form 941) to your Form 941. Instead, file Schedule D (Form 941) **separately** using the following address.

IRS Philadelphia Campus
Mail Stop 4-G08 151
2970 Market Street
Philadelphia, PA 19104
Do not use this address to file Form 941. See *Where Should You File?* in the Instructions for Form 941 for the filing address of Form 941.

Specific Instructions

Completing Schedule D (Form 941)

Your Business Information
Carefully fill in your employer identification number (EIN), name, trade name (doing business as or d/b/a), and complete address at the top of the schedule.

 Always be sure the EIN on the Schedule D (Form 941) you file exactly matches the EIN the IRS assigned to your business.

Tax Year of Discrepancies
In the box at the top of the schedule, write the tax year (not the quarter) in which the discrepancies occurred. Write the tax year using four digits. For example, if the transaction occurred on March 22, 2011, write "2011" in the box.

Make sure you fill in the correct tax year so you can reconcile the information appropriately. The tax year must be the same as the calendar year you write in Part 1, line 2.

 Be sure to fill in your EIN, business name, other party's EIN, and the tax year of the discrepancies on the top of page 2 as well.

Type of Submission

Check the appropriate box to show whether this form is the "Original" Schedule D (Form 941) for a specific transaction or corrects (mark "Corrected") a Schedule D (Form 941) you previously submitted.

Part 1: Answer these background questions

1. Check the appropriate box to explain the type of transaction for which you are submitting Schedule D (Form 941). See *Types of Mergers and Acquisitions* on page 1 for details.

File Schedule D (Form 941) after either:

a. A statutory merger or consolidation (Check whether you are an acquired corporation or a surviving corporation.), or

b. An acquisition for which you are using the alternate procedure under Rev. Proc. 2004-53. (Check whether you are a predecessor or a successor.)

2. Fill in the effective date of the transaction in the box. Make sure you write the month, day, and year in this format: MM/DD/YYYY. The year must be the same as the calendar year you write in the box at the top of the schedule.

3. Fill in the contact information about the OTHER PARTY in the transaction by including the other party's EIN, name, trade name (doing business as or d/b/a), complete address, and phone number. Verify the other party's EIN to make sure it is correct.

Part 2: Tell us about the discrepancies with your returns

Lines 4–8. Gather your information about the social security wages, Medicare wages and tips, social security tips, federal income tax withheld, and advance earned income credit (EIC) payments (for tax years ending before January 1, 2011) you reported. When entering money amounts from your Forms 941 and W-2 (Copy A) on lines 4–14, you may round to the nearest dollar. Do not show dollar signs but do use commas as appropriate. Show an amount (even if it is zero) for each column of a line.

In Column A, fill in the amount you reported to the IRS for the tax year for each of the items. Add the totals from all Forms 941, as corrected by any Forms 941-X, Adjusted Employer's QUARTERLY Federal Tax Return or Claim for Refund, and write your answers on the appropriate lines.

In Column B, fill in the amount you reported to SSA for each of the items. Add the totals from all Forms W-2 (Copy A), as corrected by any Forms W-2c, Corrected Wage and Tax Statement (Copy A), and write your answers on the appropriate lines.

Calculate the differences between the entries in the columns:

$$
\begin{array}{r}
\text{Column A} \\
-\ \underline{\text{Column B}} \\
\text{Column C}
\end{array}
$$

Enter any negative result in parentheses, if possible. For example, if line 6, Column A is "-0-" and line 6, Column B is "6,000," write "(6,000)" on line 6, Column C.

 If no Forms W-2 (Copy A) were filed by you, write "-0-" in Column B, "Amount you reported to SSA for the tax year."

If you are filing for one transaction only, stop here. If you are filing for more than one transaction, go to Part 3.

Part 3: Fill this part out ONLY if you are filing more than one Schedule D (Form 941) for any calendar year

If you are filing only one Schedule D (Form 941) for the calendar year, leave this part blank.

When more than one statutory merger, consolidation, or acquisition occurs during a calendar year, file a **separate** Schedule D (Form 941) for each transaction. Complete Part 3 for each transaction. For instance, if you have 11 different transactions in a calendar year, you need to file 11 different Schedules D (Form 941). Part 2 would be the same for each schedule. Part 3 would show one of the 11 transactions. For example, the amount entered in Part 2 on line 4 for Column C should equal the total of all 11 entries in Part 3 on line 10 for Column C.

Line 9. Show the number of schedules you are filing for the year and identify which schedule this is. For example, if you had three different transactions in a calendar year and you are filing a Schedule D (Form 941) to describe the second transaction, fill in "2" and "3" so the sentence reads: "This is schedule 2 of 3. "

Lines 10–14. For purposes of Part 3, Columns A and B, the term "employees affected by the transaction reported on this Schedule D" means those employees who received wages that were reported on Forms 941 filed by one employer but whose wages were reported on Form W-2 (Copy A) filed by another employer as a result of this particular transaction. Report the totals for social security wages, Medicare wages and tips, social security tips, federal income tax withheld, and advance earned income credit (EIC) payments (for tax years ending before January 1, 2011).

In Column A, fill in the amount you reported to the IRS for the tax year for employees affected by the transaction reported on this Schedule D (Form 941) for each of the items. Add the totals from all your Forms 941, as corrected by any Forms 941-X, and write your answers on the appropriate lines.

In Column B, fill in the amount you reported to SSA for the tax year for employees affected by the transaction reported on Form 941) for each of the items. Add the totals from all Forms W-2 (Copy A), as corrected by any Forms W-2c (Copy A), and write your answers on the appropriate lines.

Calculate the differences between the entries in the columns:

$$
\begin{array}{r}
\text{Column A} \\
-\ \underline{\text{Column B}} \\
\text{Column C}
\end{array}
$$

Enter any negative result in parentheses, if possible. For example, if line 12, Column A is "-0-" and line 12, Column B is "6,000," write "(6,000)" on line 12, Column C.

 If no Forms W-2 (Copy A) were filed by you, write "-0-" in Column B, "Amount you reported to SSA for the tax year."

Paperwork Reduction Act Notice. We ask for the information on Schedule D (Form 941) to carry out the Internal Revenue laws of the United States. You are required to give us the information. We need it to ensure you are complying with these laws and to allow us to figure and collect the right amount of tax.

You are not required to provide the information requested on a form that is subject to the Paperwork Reduction Act unless the form displays a valid OMB control number. Books or records relating to a form or its instructions must be retained as long as their contents may become material in the administration of any Internal Revenue law. Generally, tax returns and return information are confidential, as required by section 6103.

The time needed to complete and file Schedule D (Form 941) will vary depending on individual circumstances. The estimated average time is: **Recordkeeping,** 11 hr., 43 min.; **Learning about the law or the form,** 18 min.; **Preparing, copying, assembling, and sending the form to the IRS,** 30 min. If you have comments concerning the accuracy of this time estimate or suggestions for making Schedule D (Form 941) simpler, we would be happy to hear from you. You can email us at: *taxforms@irs.gov*. Enter "Schedule D (Form 941)" on the subject line. Or write to: Internal Revenue Service, Tax Products Coordinating Committee, SE:W:CAR:MP:T:T:SP, 1111 Constitution Ave. NW, IR-6526, Washington, DC 20224. **Do not** send Schedule D (Form 941) to this address. Instead, see *How Should You File?*, earlier.

Schedule R (Form 941):   **Allocation Schedule for Aggregate Form 941 Filers**

950412

OMB No. 1545-0029

(Rev. January 2012)

Department of the Treasury — Internal Revenue Service

Employer identification number (EIN) ☐☐ – ☐☐☐☐☐☐☐

Name *as shown on* Form 941 _____

Report for calendar year:

[_____]

Check the quarter (same as Form 941):

☐ **1:** January, February, March

☐ **2:** April, May, June

☐ **3:** July, August, September

☐ **4:** October, November, December

Read the instructions before you complete Schedule R (Form 941). Type or print within the boxes.
Complete a separate line for the amounts allocated to each of your clients.

(a) Client's Employer Identification Number (EIN)	(b) Wages, tips, and other compensation allocated to the listed client EIN from line 2 of Form 941	(c) Total income tax withheld from wages, tips, and other compensation allocated to the listed client EIN from line 3 of Form 941	(d) Total social security and Medicare taxes allocated to the listed client EIN from line 5d of Form 941	(e) Section 3121(q) Notice and Demand- Tax due on unreported tips allocated to the listed client EIN from line 5e of Form 941	(f) Total taxes after adjustments allocated to the listed client EIN from line 10 of Form 941	(g) Total deposits and COBRA payments from line 13 of Form 941 plus any payments made with the return allocated to the listed client EIN
1	.	.	.	.	.	.
2	.	.	.	.	.	.
3	.	.	.	.	.	.
4	.	.	.	.	.	.
5	.	.	.	.	.	.
6	.	.	.	.	.	.
7	.	.	.	.	.	.
8	.	.	.	.	.	.
9	.	.	.	.	.	.
10	.	.	.	.	.	.
11	.	.	.	.	.	.
12	.	.	.	.	.	.
13	.	.	.	.	.	.
14	.	.	.	.	.	.
15	.	.	.	.	.	.
16 Subtotals for clients. Add all amounts on lines 1 through 15	.	.	.	.	.	.
17 Enter the combined subtotal from line 26 of all Continuation Sheets for Schedule R (Form 941)	.	.	.	.	.	.
18 Enter Form 941 amounts for your employees	.	.	.	.	.	.
19 Totals. Add lines 16, 17, and 18. The column totals must match the related lines on the aggregate Form 941	.	.	.	.	.	.

For Paperwork Reduction Act Notice, see the instructions.   Cat. No. 49301K   **Schedule R (Form 941) (Rev. 1-2012)**

Page _____ of _____

Continuation Sheet for Schedule R (Form 941)

(Rev. January 2012)

950512

OMB No.

Employer identification number (EIN)	☐ ☐ – ☐ ☐ ☐ ☐ ☐ ☐ ☐
Name *as shown on Form 941*	

Report for calendar year:

[   ]

Check the quarter (same as Form 941):

☐ **1:** January, February, March

☐ **2:** April, May, June

☐ **3:** July, August, September

☐ **4:** October, November, December

	(a) Client's Employer Identification Number (EIN)	(b) Wages, tips, and other compensation allocated to the listed client EIN from line 2 of Form 941	(c) Total income tax withheld from wages, tips, and other compensation allocated to the listed client EIN from line 3 of Form 941	(d) Total social security and Medicare taxes allocated to the listed client EIN from line 5d of Form 941	(e) Section 3121(q) Notice and Demand-Tax due on unreported tips allocated to the listed client EIN from line 5e of Form 941	(f) Total taxes after adjustments allocated to the listed client EIN from line 10 of Form 941	(g) Total deposits and COBRA payments from line 13 of Form 941 plus any payments made with the return allocated to the listed client EIN
1		.	.	.	.	.	.
2		.	.	.	.	.	.
3		.	.	.	.	.	.
4		.	.	.	.	.	.
5		.	.	.	.	.	.
6		.	.	.	.	.	.
7		.	.	.	.	.	.
8		.	.	.	.	.	.
9		.	.	.	.	.	.
10		.	.	.	.	.	.
11		.	.	.	.	.	.
12		.	.	.	.	.	.
13		.	.	.	.	.	.
14		.	.	.	.	.	.
15		.	.	.	.	.	.
16		.	.	.	.	.	.
17		.	.	.	.	.	.
18		.	.	.	.	.	.
19		.	.	.	.	.	.
20		.	.	.	.	.	.
21		.	.	.	.	.	.
22		.	.	.	.	.	.
23		.	.	.	.	.	.
24		.	.	.	.	.	.
25		.	.	.	.	.	.
26	Subtotals for clients. Add lines 1 through 25. Include the subtotals from line 26 on line 17 of Schedule R (Form 941)	.	.	.	.	.	.

Schedule R (Form 941) (Rev. 1-2012)

A-191

950612

Schedule R (Form 941) (Rev. 1-2012)

Section references are to the Internal Revenue Code unless otherwise noted.

General Instructions

Purpose of Schedule R (Form 941)

Use Schedule R (Form 941) to allocate the aggregate information reported on Form 941 to each client. If you have more than 15 clients, complete as many Continuation Sheets for Schedule R (Form 941) as necessary. Attach Schedule R (Form 941), including any Continuation Sheets, to your aggregate Form 941.

Who Must File?

You must complete Schedule R (Form 941) each time you file an aggregate Form 941, Employer's QUARTERLY Federal Tax Return. Aggregate Forms 941 are filed by agents approved by the IRS under section 3504. To request approval to act as an agent for an employer, you must file Form 2678, Employer/Payer Appointment of Agent, with the IRS. On Schedule R (Form 941), we call those employers your clients.

When Must You File?

If you are an aggregate Form 941 filer, file Schedule R (Form 941) with your aggregate Form 941 every quarter when Form 941 is due. The Schedule R (Form 941) may be filed electronically or by paper submission. However, agents filing for 1,000 or more clients must file a paper return.

Note. If you are filing Schedule R (Form 941) for a quarter ending before January 1, 2011, that includes advance earned income credit (EIC) payments, you must file the January 2011 revision of Schedule R (Form 941). The January 2011 revision of Schedule R (Form 941) can be attached to a late filed Form 941 or Form 941-X, Adjusted Employer's QUARTERLY Federal Tax Return or Claim for Refund. The January 2011 revision of Schedule R (Form 941) is available on IRS.gov.

Specific Instructions

Completing Schedule R (Form 941)

Enter Your Business Information

Carefully enter your employer identification number (EIN) and the name of your business at the top of the schedule. Make sure they exactly match the EIN and name shown on the attached Form 941.

Calendar Year

Enter the calendar year that applies to the quarter checked.

Check the Box for the Quarter

Check the appropriate box of the quarter for which you are filing Schedule R (Form 941). Make sure the quarter checked on the top of the Schedule R (Form 941) matches the quarter checked on your Form 941.

Client and Employee Information

On Schedule R (Form 941), including any Continuation Sheets for Schedule R (Form 941), you must report the following for each client.

Note. When entering amounts over 999.99 on Schedule R (Form 941), do not enter commas.

- Your client's employer identification number (EIN).

- Wages, tips, and other compensation allocated to the listed client EIN from line 2 of Form 941.

- Total income tax withheld from wages, tips, and other compensation allocated to the listed client EIN from line 3 of Form 941.

- Total social security and Medicare taxes allocated to the listed client EIN from line 5d of Form 941.

- Section 3121(q) Notice and Demand—Tax due on unreported tips allocated to the listed client EIN from line 5e of Form 941.

- Total taxes after adjustments allocated to the listed client EIN from line 10 of Form 941.

- Total deposits and COBRA premium assistance payments from line 13 of Form 941 plus any payments made with the return allocated to the listed client EIN.

You must also report the same information for your employees on line 18 of Schedule R (Form 941).

Compare the total of each column on line 19 (including your information on line 18) of Schedule R (Form 941) to the amounts reported on the aggregate Form 941. For each column total of Schedule R (Form 941), the relevant line from Form 941 is noted in the column heading.

If the totals on line 19 of the Schedule R (Form 941) do not match the totals on Form 941, there is an error that must be corrected before submitting Form 941 and Schedule R (Form 941).

Paperwork Reduction Act Notice. We ask for the information on Schedule R (Form 941) to carry out the Internal Revenue laws of the United States. You are required to give us this information. We need it to ensure that you are complying with these laws and to allow us to figure and collect the right amount of tax.

You are not required to provide the information requested on a form that is subject to the Paperwork Reduction Act unless the form displays a valid OMB control number. Books or records relating to a form or its instructions must be retained as long as their contents may become material in the administration of any Internal Revenue law. Generally, tax returns and return information are confidential, as required by section 6103.

The time needed to complete and file Schedule R (Form 941) will vary depending on individual circumstances. The estimated average time is:

Recordkeeping	12 hrs., 26 min.
Learning about the law or the form	12 min.
Preparing, copying, and assembling the form	24 min.

If you have comments concerning the accuracy of these time estimates or suggestions for making Schedule R (Form 941) simpler, we would be happy to hear from you. You can email us at taxforms@irs.gov. Enter "Schedule R (Form 941)" on the subject line. Or write to: Internal Revenue Service, Tax Products Coordinating Committee, SE:W:CAR:MP:T:M:S, 1111 Constitution Ave. NW, IR-6526, Washington, DC 20224. **Do not** send Schedule R (Form 941) to this address. Instead, see *Where Should You File?* in the Instructions for Form 941.

Form **941-X:** **Adjusted Employer's QUARTERLY Federal Tax Return or Claim for Refund**
(Rev. April 2012)   Department of the Treasury — Internal Revenue Service

OMB No. 1545-0029

Employer identification number (EIN) ☐☐ – ☐☐☐☐☐☐☐

Name *(not your trade name)*

Trade name *(if any)*

Address

| Number | Street | Suite or room number |

| City | State | ZIP code |

Return You Are Correcting ...

Check the type of return you are correcting:

☐ 941

☐ 941-SS

Check the ONE quarter you are correcting:

☐ **1:** January, February, March

☐ **2:** April, May, June

☐ **3:** July, August, September

☐ **4:** October, November, December

Enter the calendar year of the quarter you are correcting:

☐☐☐☐ (YYYY)

Enter the date you discovered errors:

__ / __ / ____

(MM / DD / YYYY)

Read the instructions before completing this form. Use this form to correct errors you made on Form 941 or Form 941-SS. Use a separate Form 941-X for each quarter that needs correction. Type or print within the boxes. You MUST complete all three pages. Do not attach this form to Form 941 or Form 941-SS.

Part 1: **Select ONLY one process.**

☐ **1.** **Adjusted employment tax return.** Check this box if you underreported amounts. Also check this box if you overreported amounts and you would like to use the adjustment process to correct the errors. You must check this box if you are correcting both underreported and overreported amounts on this form. The amount shown on line 21, if less than zero, may only be applied as a credit to your Form 941, Form 941-SS, or Form 944 for the tax period in which you are filing this form.

☐ **2.** **Claim.** Check this box if you overreported amounts only and you would like to use the claim process to ask for a refund or abatement of the amount shown on line 21. Do not check this box if you are correcting ANY underreported amounts on this form.

Part 2: **Complete the certifications.**

☐ **3.** **I certify that I have filed or will file Forms W-2, Wage and Tax Statement, or Forms W-2c, Corrected Wage and Tax Statement, as required.**

Note. If you are correcting underreported amounts only, go to Part 3 on page 2 and skip lines 4 and 5.

4. **If you checked line 1 because you are adjusting overreported amounts, check all that apply.** You must check at least one box. I certify that:

☐ **a.** I repaid or reimbursed each affected employee for the overcollected federal income tax for the current year and the overcollected social security and Medicare taxes for current and prior years. For adjustments of employee social security and Medicare taxes overcollected in prior years, I have a written statement from each employee stating that he or she has not claimed (or the claim was rejected) and will not claim a refund or credit for the overcollection.

☐ **b.** The adjustments of social security tax and Medicare tax are for the employer's share only. I could not find the affected employees or each employee did not give me a written statement that he or she has not claimed (or the claim was rejected) and will not claim a refund or credit for the overcollection.

☐ **c.** The adjustment is for federal income tax, social security tax, and Medicare tax that I did not withhold from employee wages.

5. **If you checked line 2 because you are claiming a refund or abatement of overreported employment taxes, check all that apply.** You must check at least one box. I certify that:

☐ **a.** I repaid or reimbursed each affected employee for the overcollected social security and Medicare tax. For claims of employee social security and Medicare tax overcollected in prior years, I have a written statement from each employee stating that he or she has not claimed (or the claim was rejected) and will not claim a refund or credit for the overcollection.

☐ **b.** I have a written consent from each affected employee stating that I may file this claim for the employee's share of social security and Medicare tax. For refunds of employee social security and Medicare tax overcollected in prior years, I also have a written statement from each employee stating that he or she has not claimed (or the claim was rejected) and will not claim a refund or credit for the overcollection.

☐ **c.** The claim for social security tax and Medicare taxes is for the employer's share only. I could not find the affected employees; or each employee did not give me a written consent to file a claim for the employee's share of social security and Medicare taxes; or each employee did not give me a written statement that he or she has not claimed (or the claim was rejected) and will not claim a refund or credit for the overcollection.

☐ **d.** The claim is for federal income tax, social security tax, and Medicare tax that I did not withhold from employee wages.

Next ▶

For Paperwork Reduction Act Notice, see the separate instructions.   IRS.gov/form941x   Cat. No. 17025J   Form **941-X** (Rev. 4-2012)

Name *(not your trade name)*	Employer identification number *(EIN)*	Correcting quarter (1, 2, 3, 4)
		Correcting calendar year *(YYYY)*

Part 3: Enter the corrections for this quarter. If any line does not apply, leave it blank.

		Column 1	Column 2	Column 3	Column 4
		Total corrected amount (for ALL employees)	*Amount originally reported or as previously corrected (for ALL employees)*	*Difference (If this amount is a negative number, use a minus sign.)*	*Tax correction*

6. **Wages, tips, and other compensation** (Form 941, line 2)

[____ .] − [____ .] = [____ .]   Use the amount in Column 1 when you prepare your Forms W-2 or Forms W-2c.

7. **Income tax withheld from wages, tips, and other compensation** (Form 941, line 3)

[____ .] − [____ .] = [____ .]   Copy Column 3 here ▶ [____ .]

8. **Taxable social security wages** (Form 941 or Form 941-SS, line 5a, Column 1)

[____ .] − [____ .] = [____ .]   × .124* = [____ .]

*If you are correcting a 2011 or 2012 return, use .104. If you are correcting your employer share only, use .062. See instructions.

9. **Taxable social security tips** (Form 941 or Form 941-SS, line 5b, Column 1)

[____ .] − [____ .] = [____ .]   × .124* = [____ .]

*If you are correcting a 2011 or 2012 return, use .104. If you are correcting your employer share only, use .062. See instructions.

10. **Taxable Medicare wages and tips** (Form 941 or Form 941-SS, line 5c, Column 1)

[____ .] − [____ .] = [____ .]   × .029* = [____ .]

*If you are correcting your employer share only, use .0145. See instructions.

11. **Section 3121(q) Notice and Demand—Tax due on unreported tips** (Form 941 or Form 941-SS, line 5e)

[____ .] − [____ .] = [____ .]   Copy Column 3 here ▶ [____ .]

12a. **Number of qualified employees *first* paid exempt wages/tips this quarter** (Form 941 or Form 941-SS, line 6a)*

[____] − [____] = [____]

12b. **Number of qualified employees paid exempt wages/tips this quarter** (Form 941 or Form 941-SS, line 6b)*

[____] − [____] = [____]   *Complete lines 12a, 12b, and 12c only for corrections to quarters ending after March 31, 2010, and before January 1, 2011.

12c. **Exempt wages/tips paid to qualified employees this quarter** (Form 941 or Form 941-SS, line 6c)*

[____ .] − [____ .] = [____ .]   × .062 = [____ .]

13. **Tax adjustments** (Form 941 or Form 941-SS, lines 7–9 (lines 7a–7c for quarters ending before January 1, 2011))

[____ .] − [____ .] = [____ .]   Copy Column 3 here ▶ [____ .]

14. **Special addition to wages for federal income tax**

[____ .] − [____ .] = [____ .]   See instructions [____ .]

15. **Special addition to wages for social security taxes**

[____ .] − [____ .] = [____ .]   See instructions [____ .]

16. **Special addition to wages for Medicare taxes**

[____ .] − [____ .] = [____ .]   See instructions [____ .]

17. Combine the amounts on lines 7–16 of Column 4 . . . . [____ .]

18. **Advance earned income credit (EIC) payments made to employees** (Form 941, line 9; only for quarters ending before January 1, 2011)

[____ .] − [____ .] = [____ .]   See instructions [____ .]

19a. **COBRA premium assistance payments** (Form 941 or Form 941-SS, line 12a)

[____ .] − [____ .] = [____ .]   See instructions [____ .]

19b. **Number of individuals provided COBRA premium assistance** (Form 941 or Form 941-SS, line 12b)

[____] − [____] = [____]

19c. **Number of qualified employees paid exempt wages/tips March 19–31, 2010** (Form 941 or Form 941-SS, line 12c)*

[____] − [____] = [____]   *Complete lines 19c and 19d only for corrections to the second quarter of 2010.

19d. **Exempt wages/tips paid to qualified employees March 19–31, 2010** (Form 941 or Form 941-SS, line 12d)*

[____ .] − [____ .] = [____ .]   × .062 = [____ .]

20. **Total.** Combine the amounts on lines 17–19d of Column 4. Continue on next page [____ .]

Next ▶

Name *(not your trade name)*	Employer identification number *(EIN)*	Correcting quarter (1, 2, 3, 4)
		Correcting calendar year (YYYY)

Part 3: Continued

21. Amount from line 20 on page 2 . . . .

     If line 21 is less than zero:

     • If you checked line 1, this is the amount you want applied as a credit to your Form 941 or Form 941-SS for the tax period in which you are filing this form. If you are currently filing Form 944, Employer's ANNUAL Federal Tax Return, see the instructions.

     • If you checked line 2, this is the amount you want refunded or abated.

     If line 21 is more than zero, this is the amount you owe. Pay this amount by the time you file this return. For information on how to pay, see *Amount you owe* in the instructions.

Part 4: Explain your corrections for this quarter.

□ 22. **Check here if any corrections you entered on a line include both underreported and overreported amounts.** Explain both your underreported and overreported amounts on line 24.

□ 23. **Check here if any corrections involve reclassified workers.** Explain on line 24.

24. **You must give us a detailed explanation of how you determined your corrections.** See the instructions.

Part 5: Sign here. You must complete all three pages of this form and sign it.

Under penalties of perjury, I declare that I have filed an original Form 941 or Form 941-SS and that I have examined this adjusted return or claim, including accompanying schedules and statements, and to the best of my knowledge and belief, they are true, correct, and complete. Declaration of preparer (other than taxpayer) is based on all information of which preparer has any knowledge.

X   **Sign your name here**

Print your name here

Print your title here

Date   /   /

Best daytime phone

Paid Preparer Use Only

Check if you are self-employed . . . □

Preparer's name		PTIN	
Preparer's signature		Date / /
Firm's name (or yours if self-employed)		EIN	
Address		Phone	
City	State	ZIP code	

Form 941-X: Which process should you use?

Type of errors you are correcting			
Underreported amounts ONLY	**Use the adjustment process** to correct underreported amounts. • Check the box on line 1. • Pay the amount you owe from line 21 by the time you file Form 941-X.		
Overreported amounts ONLY	The process you use depends on **when** you file Form 941-X.	**If you are filing Form 941-X MORE THAN 90 days before the period of limitations on credit or refund for Form 941 or Form 941-SS expires ...**	Choose either process to correct the overreported amounts. **Choose the adjustment process** if you want the amount shown on line 21 credited to your Form 941, Form 941-SS, or Form 944 for the period in which you file Form 941-X. Check the box on line 1. OR **Choose the claim process** if you want the amount shown on line 21 refunded to you or abated. Check the box on line 2.
		If you are filing Form 941-X WITHIN 90 days of the expiration of the period of limitations on credit or refund for Form 941 or Form 941-SS ...	You must use the **claim process** to correct the overreported amounts. Check the box on line 2.
BOTH underreported and overreported amounts	The process you use depends on **when** you file Form 941-X.	**If you are filing Form 941-X MORE THAN 90 days before the period of limitations on credit or refund for Form 941 or Form 941-SS expires ...**	Choose either the adjustment process or both the adjustment process and the claim process when you correct both underreported and overreported amounts. **Choose the adjustment process** if combining your underreported amounts and overreported amounts results in a balance due or creates a credit that you want applied to Form 941, Form 941-SS, or Form 944. • File one Form 941-X, and • Check the box on line 1 and follow the instructions on line 21. OR **Choose both the adjustment process and the claim process** if you want the overreported amount refunded to you or abated. File two separate forms. **1. For the adjustment process,** file one Form 941-X to correct the underreported amounts. Check the box on line 1. Pay the amount you owe from line 21 by the time you file Form 941-X. **2. For the claim process,** file a second Form 941-X to correct the overreported amounts. Check the box on line 2.
		If you are filing Form 941-X WITHIN 90 days of the expiration of the period of limitations on credit or refund for Form 941 or Form 941-SS ...	You must use both the adjustment process and claim process. File two separate forms. **1. For the adjustment process,** file one Form 941-X to correct the underreported amounts. Check the box on line 1. Pay the amount you owe from line 21 by the time you file Form 941-X. **2. For the claim process,** file a second Form 941-X to correct the overreported amounts. Check the box on line 2.

Form **941-X** (Rev. 4-2012)

Instructions for Form 941-X

Department of the Treasury
Internal Revenue Service

(April 2012)

Adjusted Employer's QUARTERLY Federal Tax Return or Claim for Refund

Section references are to the Internal Revenue Code unless otherwise noted.

Future Developments

For the latest information about developments related to Form 941-X and its instructions, such as legislation enacted after they were published, go to *www.irs.gov/form941x*.

What's New

Social security tax rate for 2012. The employee social security tax rate is 4.2% and the employer social security tax rate is 6.2% (10.4% total). Be sure to use the correct rate when correcting amounts reported on lines 8 and 9.

Reminders

Section 3121(q) Notice and Demand—Tax due on unreported tips. An employer enters the amount of social security and Medicare taxes on unreported tips shown on the Section 3121(q) Notice and Demand on line 5e of the employer's Form 941 for the calendar quarter corresponding to the "Date of Notice and Demand." Any errors discovered on previously filed Forms 941 for these taxes are corrected on Form 941-X, line 11. In addition, any errors relating to Section 3121(q) Notice and Demand amounts reported on Form 941, line 7c (for quarters ending before January 1, 2011) should be corrected on Form 941-X, line 11.

Qualified employer's social security tax exemption expired. The qualified employer's exemption for their share (6.2%) of social security tax on wages/tips paid to qualified employees expired on December 31, 2010. Any errors discovered on previously filed Forms 941 (for quarters ending after March 31, 2010, and before January 1, 2011) for this exemption are corrected on Form 941-X, lines 12a–12c.

Advance payment of earned income credit (EIC). The option of receiving advance payroll payments of EIC expired on December 31, 2010. Any errors discovered on a previously filed Form 941 for this credit are corrected on Form 941-X, line 18.

Adjusting COBRA premium assistance payments. Employers who make COBRA premium assistance payments for assistance eligible individuals are allowed a credit for the payments on Form 941. Any errors discovered on previously filed Forms 941 for this credit are corrected on Form 941-X. See *COBRA Premium Assistance Payments*, later.

Adjusting an aggregate Form 941. Agents must complete Schedule R (Form 941), Allocation Schedule for Aggregate Form 941 Filers, when adjusting an aggregate Form 941. Schedule R (Form 941) is completed only for those clients who have adjustments reported on Form 941-X. Schedule R (Form 941) is filed as an attachment to Form 941-X. Aggregate Forms 941 are filed by agents approved by the IRS under section 3504. To request approval to act as an agent for an employer, the agent files Form 2678, Employer/Payer Appointment of Agent, with the IRS.

General Instructions: Understanding Form 941-X

What Is the Purpose of Form 941-X?

Use Form 941-X to correct errors on a Form 941 that you previously filed. Use Form 941-X to correct:
- Wages, tips, and other compensation;
- Income tax withheld from wages, tips, and other compensation;
- Taxable social security wages;
- Taxable social security tips;
- Taxable Medicare wages and tips;
- Advance earned income credit (EIC) payments made to employees (for quarters ending before January 1, 2011);
- Credits for COBRA premium assistance payments;
- Credits for qualified employer's share of social security tax on wages/tips paid to qualified employees March 19–31, 2010 (second quarter 2010 only); and
- Exemptions for qualified employer's share of social security tax on wages/tips paid to qualified employees (for quarters ending after March 31, 2010, and before January 1, 2011).

Use Form 843, Claim for Refund and Request for Abatement, to request a refund or abatement of assessed interest or penalties. **Do not** request abatement of assessed interest or penalties on Form 941 or Form 941-X.

References to Form 941 on Form 941-X and in these instructions also apply to Form 941-SS, Employer's QUARTERLY Federal Tax Return, unless otherwise noted. We use the terms "correct" and "corrections" on Form 941-X and in these instructions to include interest-free adjustments under sections 6205 and 6413 and claims for refund and abatement under sections 6402, 6414, and 6404. See Rev. Rul. 2009-39 for examples of how the interest-free adjustment and claim for refund rules apply in 10 different situations. You can find Rev. Rul. 2009-39, 2009-52, I.R.B. 951 at www.irs.gov/irb/2009-52_IRB/ar14.html.

When you discover an error on a previously filed Form 941, you must:
- Correct that error using Form 941-X,
- File a separate Form 941-X for each Form 941 that you are correcting, and
- File Form 941-X separately. Do not file Form 941-X with Form 941.

If you did not file a Form 941 for one or more quarters, **do not** use Form 941-X. Instead, file Form 941 for each of those quarters. See also *When Should You File Form 941-X*, later. However, if you did not file Forms 941 because you improperly treated workers as independent contractors or nonemployees and are now reclassifying them as employees, see the instructions for line 23, later.

Report the correction of underreported and overreported amounts for the same tax period on a single Form 941-X, unless you are requesting a refund or abatement. If you are requesting a refund or abatement and are correcting both underreported and overreported amounts, file one Form 941-X correcting the underreported amounts only and a second Form 941-X correcting the overreported amounts.

You will use the adjustment process if you underreported employment taxes and are making a payment, or if you overreported employment taxes and will be applying the credit to Form 941 for the period during which you file Form 941-X. However, see the *Caution* under *Is There a Deadline for Filing Form 941-X,* later, if you are correcting overreported amounts during the last 90 days of a period of limitations. You will use the claim process if you overreported employment taxes and are requesting a refund or abatement of the overreported amount. Follow the chart on the back of Form 941-X for help in choosing whether to use the adjustment process or the claim process. Be sure to give us a detailed explanation on line 24 for each correction that you show on Form 941-X.

Continue to report current quarter fractions of cents, third-party sick pay, tips, and group-term life insurance on Form 941, lines 7–9.

You have additional requirements to complete when filing Form 941-X, such as certifying that you filed (or will file) all applicable Forms W-2, Wage and Tax Statements, and Forms W-2c, Corrected Wage and Tax Statements, with the Social Security Administration (SSA). For corrections of overreported federal income tax, social security tax, or Medicare tax, you must make any certifications that apply to your situation.

 Do not use Form 941-X to correct Form CT-1, 943, 944, 944-SS, or 945. Instead, use the "X" form that corresponds to those forms (Form CT-1 X, 943-X, 944-X, or 945-X).

Where Can You Get Help?

For help filing Form 941-X or for questions about federal employment taxes and tax corrections, you can:
• Call the IRS Business and Specialty Tax Line toll-free at 1-800-829-4933 (TTY/TDD for hearing and speech-impaired individuals at 1-800-829-4059), Monday through Friday from 7 a.m. to 7 p.m. local time (Alaska and Hawaii follow Pacific time),
• Visit the IRS website at *www.irs.gov/businesses* and click on "Employment Taxes," or
• See Pub. 15 (Circular E), Employer's Tax Guide, for correcting Form 941, or Pub. 80 (Circular SS), Federal Tax Guide for Employers in the U.S. Virgin Islands, Guam, American Samoa, and the Commonwealth of the Northern Mariana Islands, for correcting Form 941-SS.

See also *How Can You Order Forms and Publications from the IRS,* later.

When Should You File Form 941-X?

File Form 941-X when you discover an error on a previously filed Form 941.

However, if your only errors on Form 941 relate to the number of employees who received wages or to federal tax liabilities reported on Form 941, Part 2, or on Schedule B (Form 941), do not file Form 941-X. For more information about correcting federal tax liabilities reported on Form 941, Part 2, or on Schedule B (Form 941), Report of Tax Liability for Semiweekly Schedule Depositors, see the Instructions for Schedule B (Form 941).

Due dates. The due date for filing Form 941-X depends on when you discover an error and if you underreported or overreported tax. If you underreported tax, see *Underreported tax* below. For overreported amounts, you may choose to either make an interest-free adjustment or file a claim for refund or abatement. If you are correcting overreported amounts, see *Overreported tax—credit* or *Overreported tax—claim* below.

If any due date falls on a Saturday, Sunday, or legal holiday, you may file Form 941-X on the next business day. If we receive Form 941-X after the due date, we will treat Form 941-X as filed on time if the envelope containing Form 941-X is properly addressed, contains sufficient postage, and is postmarked by the U.S. Postal Service on or before the due date, or sent by an IRS-designated private delivery service on or before the due date. If you do not follow these guidelines, we will consider Form 941-X filed when it is actually received. See

Pub. 15 (Circular E) or Pub. 80 (Circular SS) for more information on IRS-designated private delivery services.

Underreported tax. If you are correcting underreported tax, you must file Form 941-X by the due date of the return for the return period in which you discovered the error and **pay** the amount you owe by the time you file. Doing so will generally ensure that your correction is interest free and not subject to failure-to-pay or failure-to-deposit penalties. See *What About Penalties and Interest,* later. For details on how to make a payment, see the instructions for lines 20–21, later.

If Form 941-X is filed late (after the due date of the return for the return period in which you discovered the error), you must attach an amended Schedule B (Form 941) to Form 941-X. Otherwise, the IRS may assess an "averaged" failure-to-deposit penalty. The total tax reported on the "Total liability for the quarter" line of Schedule B (Form 941) must match the corrected tax (Form 941, line 10, combined with any correction entered on Form 941-X, line 17, minus any advance EIC reported on Form 941-X, line 18) for the quarter, less any previous abatements and interest-free tax assessments.

If you discover an error in	Form 941-X is due . . .
1. January, February, March	April 30
2. April, May, June	July 31
3. July, August, September	October 31
4. October, November, December	January 31
The dates shown in the table above apply only to corrections of underreported amounts. If any due date falls on a Saturday, Sunday, or legal holiday, you may file Form 941-X on the next business day.	

Example—You owe tax. On February 10, 2012, you discover that you underreported $10,000 of social security and Medicare wages on your 2011 fourth quarter Form 941. File Form 941-X and pay the amount you owe by April 30, 2012, because you discovered the error in the first quarter of 2012, and April 30, 2012, is the due date for that quarter. If you file Form 941-X before April 30, pay the amount you owe when you file.

Overreported tax—credit. If you overreported tax on Form 941 and choose to apply the credit to Form 941 or Form 944, file Form 941-X soon after you discovered the error but more than 90 days before the period of limitations on the credit or refund for Form 941 expires. See *Is There a Deadline for Filing Form 941-X?* below.

Overreported tax—claim. If you overreported tax on Form 941, you may choose to file a claim for refund or abatement on Form 941-X any time before the period of limitations on credit or refund expires on Form 941. If you need to correct **any** underreported amounts, you must file another Form 941-X reporting only corrections to the underreported amounts. See *Is There a Deadline for Filing Form 941-X?* next.

Is There a Deadline for Filing Form 941-X?

Generally, you may correct overreported taxes on a previously filed Form 941 if you file Form 941-X within 3 years of the date Form 941 was filed or 2 years from the date you paid the tax reported on Form 941, whichever is later. You may correct underreported taxes on a previously filed Form 941 if you file Form 941-X within 3 years of the date the Form 941 was filed. We call each of these time frames a "period of limitations." For purposes of the period of limitations, Forms 941 for a calendar year are considered filed on April 15 of the succeeding year if filed before that date.

Example. You filed your 2009 fourth quarter Form 941 on January 27, 2010, and payments were timely made. The IRS treats the return as if it were filed on April 15, 2010. On January

20, 2013, you discover that you overreported social security and Medicare wages on that form by $350. To correct the error you must file Form 941-X by April 15, 2013, which is the end of the period of limitations for Form 941, and use the claim process.

 If you file Form 941-X to correct overreported amounts in the last 90 days of a period of limitations (after January 15, 2013, in the example above), you must use the claim process. You cannot use the adjustment process. If you are also correcting underreported amounts, you must file another Form 941-X to correct the underreported amounts using the adjustment process and pay any tax due.

Where Should You File Form 941-X?

Send your completed Form 941-X to the Internal Revenue Service Center shown below.

IF you are in	THEN use this address . . .
Special filing addresses for exempt organizations; federal, state, and local governmental entities; and Indian tribal governmental entities; regardless of location	Department of the Treasury Internal Revenue Service Ogden, UT 84201-0005
Connecticut, Delaware, District of Columbia, Georgia, Illinois, Indiana, Kentucky, Maine, Maryland, Massachusetts, Michigan, New Hampshire, New Jersey, New York, North Carolina, Ohio, Pennsylvania, Rhode Island, South Carolina, Tennessee, Vermont, Virginia, West Virginia, Wisconsin	Department of the Treasury Internal Revenue Service Cincinnati, OH 45999-0005
Alabama, Alaska, Arizona, Arkansas, California, Colorado, Florida, Hawaii, Idaho, Iowa, Kansas, Louisiana, Minnesota, Mississippi, Missouri, Montana, Nebraska, Nevada, New Mexico, North Dakota, Oklahoma, Oregon, South Dakota, Texas, Utah, Washington, Wyoming	Department of the Treasury Internal Revenue Service Ogden, UT 84201-0005
No legal residence or principal place of business in any state	Internal Revenue Service P.O. Box 409101 Ogden, UT 84409

How Should You Complete Form 941-X?

Use a Separate Form 941-X for Each Quarter You Are Correcting

Use a separate Form 941-X for each Form 941 that you are correcting. For example, if you found errors on your Forms 941 for the third and fourth quarters of 2010, file one Form 941-X to correct the 2010 third quarter Form 941. File a second Form 941-X to correct the 2010 fourth quarter Form 941.

EIN, Name, and Address

Enter your EIN, name, and address in the spaces provided. Also enter your name and EIN on the top of pages 2 and 3, and on any attachments. If your address has changed since you filed your Form 941, enter the corrected information and the IRS will update your address of record.

Return You Are Correcting

In the box at the top of page 1, check the type of return (Form 941 or Form 941-SS) you are correcting. Check the appropriate box for the **one** quarter you are correcting. Enter the calendar year of the Form 941 you are correcting. Enter the quarter and calendar year on pages 2 and 3. Be sure to write your name,

EIN, Form 941-X, the quarter, and calendar year on the top of any attachments.

Enter the Date You Discovered Errors

You **must** enter the date you discovered errors. If you are reporting several errors that you discovered at different times, enter the earliest date you discovered them here. You discover an error when you have enough information to be able to correct it. Report any subsequent dates and related errors on line 24.

Must You Make an Entry on Each Line?

You must provide all of the information requested at the top of page 1. You must check one box (but not both) in Part 1. You must check the box on line 3 and any applicable boxes on lines 4 and 5. In Part 3, if any line does not apply, leave it blank. Complete Parts 4 and 5 as instructed.

How Should You Report Negative Amounts?

Form 941-X uses negative numbers to show reductions in tax (credits) and positive numbers to show additional tax (amounts you owe).

When reporting a negative amount in columns 3 and 4, use a minus sign instead of parentheses. For example, enter "-10.59" instead of "(10.59)." However, if you are completing the return on your computer and your software only allows you to use parentheses to report negative amounts, you may use them.

How Should You Make Entries on Form 941-X?

You can help the IRS process Form 941-X timely and accurately if you follow these guidelines.
- Type or print your entries.
- Use Courier font (if possible) for all typed or computer-generated entries.
- Omit dollar signs. You may use commas and decimal points, if desired. Enter dollar amounts to the left of any preprinted decimal point and cents to the right of it.
- Always show an amount for cents. Do not round entries to whole dollars.
- Complete all three pages and sign Form 941-X on page 3.
- Staple multiple sheets in the upper-left corner.

What About Penalties and Interest?

Generally, your correction of an underreported amount will not be subject to a failure-to-pay penalty, failure-to-deposit penalty, or interest if you:
- File on time (by the due date of the quarter in which you discover the error),
- Pay the amount shown on line 21 **by the time you file** Form 941-X,
- Enter the date you discovered the error, and
- Explain in detail the grounds and facts relied on to support the correction.

No correction will be eligible for interest-free treatment if any of the following apply.
- The amounts underreported relate to an issue that was raised in an examination of a prior period.
- You knowingly underreported your employment tax liability.
- You received a notice and demand for payment.
- You received a Notice of Determination of Worker Classification.

Overview of the Process

The process to correct a previously filed Form 941 or file a claim is outlined below.

If you underreported the tax. If you underreported the tax on a previously filed Form 941, check the box on line 1 and **pay** any additional amount you owe by the time you file Form 941-X. For details on how to make a payment, see the instructions for lines 20–21, later.

Example—You underreported employment taxes. On June 20, 2012, you discover an error that results in additional tax on your 2011 fourth quarter Form 941. File Form 941-X by

July 31, 2012, and pay the amount you owe by the time you file. See *When Should You File Form 941-X*, earlier. **Do not** attach Form 941-X to your 2012 second quarter Form 941.

If you overreported the tax. If you overreported the tax on a previously filed Form 941, you may **choose** one of the following options.
- *Use the adjustment process.* Check the box on line 1 to apply any credit (negative amount) from line 21 to Form 941 for the quarter during which you file Form 941-X.
- *Use the claim process.* Check the box on line 2 to file a claim on Form 941-X requesting a refund or abatement of the amount shown on line 21.

TIP *To ensure that the IRS has enough time to process a credit for an **overreporting adjustment** in the quarter during which you file Form 941-X, you are encouraged to file Form 941-X correcting the overreported amount in the first two months of a quarter. For example, if you discover an overreported amount in March, June, September, or December, you may want to file Form 941-X in the first two months of the next quarter. However, there must be 90 days remaining on the period of limitations when you file Form 941-X. See the Caution under* Is There a Deadline for Filing Form 941-X*, earlier. This should ensure that the IRS will have enough time to process Form 941-X so the credit will be posted before you file Form 941, thus avoiding an erroneous balance due notice from the IRS. See the example below.*

If you currently file Form 944 instead of Form 941 and will claim a credit on Form 944, file Form 941-X before December in any year before the expiration of the period of limitations on Form 941. In the year of the expiration of the period of limitations on Form 941, file Form 941-X at least 90 days before the expiration date.

Example—You want your overreported tax applied as a credit to Form 941. On June 22, 2012, you discover you overreported your tax on your 2011 fourth quarter Form 941 and want to choose the adjustment process. To allow the IRS enough time to process the credit, you file Form 941-X on July 1, 2012, and take the credit on your third quarter 2012 Form 941.

Specific Instructions:

Part 1: Select ONLY one process

Because Form 941-X may be used to file either an adjusted employment tax return or a claim for refund or abatement, you **must** check one box on either line 1 or line 2. Do not check both boxes.

1. Adjusted Employment Tax Return

Check the box on line 1 if you are correcting underreported amounts or overreported amounts and you would like to use the adjustment process to correct the errors.

If you are correcting both underreported amounts and overreported amounts on this form, you **must** check this box. If you check this box, any negative amount shown on line 21 will be applied as a credit (tax deposit) to your Form 941 or Form 944 for the period in which you are filing this form. See *Example—You want your overreported tax applied as a credit to Form 941* above.

If you owe tax. Pay the amount shown on line 21 by the time you file Form 941-X. Generally, you will not be charged interest if you file on time, pay on time, enter the date you discovered the error, and explain the correction on line 24.

If you have a credit. You overreported employment taxes (you have a negative amount on line 21) and want the IRS to apply the credit to Form 941 or Form 944 for the period during which you filed Form 941-X. The IRS will apply your credit on the first day of the Form 941 or Form 944 period during which you filed Form 941-X. However, the credit you show on line 21 of Form 941-X may not be fully available on your Form 941 or

Form 944 if the IRS corrects it during processing or you owe other taxes, penalties, or interest. The IRS will notify you if your claimed credit changes or if the amount available as a credit on Form 941 or Form 944 was reduced because of unpaid taxes, penalties, or interest.

 Do not check the box on line 1 if you are correcting overreported amounts and the period of limitations on credit or refund for Form 941 will expire within 90 days of the date you file Form 941-X. Instead, check the box on line 2. See Is There a Deadline for Filing Form 941-X*, earlier.*

2. Claim

Check the box on line 2 to use the claim process if you are correcting **overreported amounts only** and you are claiming a refund or abatement for the negative amount (credit) shown on line 21. Do not check this box if you are correcting any underreported amounts on this form.

You must check the box on line 2 if you have a credit and the period of limitations on credit or refund for Form 941 will expire within 90 days of the date you file Form 941-X. See *Is There a Deadline for Filing Form 941-X*, earlier.

The IRS usually processes claims shortly after they are filed. The IRS will notify you if your claim is denied, accepted as filed, or selected to be examined. See Pub. 556, Examination of Returns, Appeal Rights, and Claims for Refund, for more information.

Unless the IRS corrects Form 941-X during processing or you owe other taxes, penalties, or interest, the IRS will refund the amount shown on line 21, plus any interest that applies.

Part 2: Complete the Certifications

You must complete all certifications that apply by checking the appropriate boxes. If all of your corrections relate to underreported amounts, complete line 3 only; skip lines 4 and 5 and go to Part 3. If your corrections relate to overreported amounts, you have a duty to ensure that your employees' rights to recover overpaid employee social security and Medicare taxes that you withheld are protected. The certifications on lines 4 and 5 address the requirement to:
- Repay or reimburse your employees for the overcollection of employee social security and Medicare taxes, or
- Obtain consents from your employees to file a claim on their behalf.

3. Filing Forms W-2 or Forms W-2c

Check the box on line 3 to certify that you filed or will file Forms W-2 or Forms W-2c with the SSA, as required, showing your employees' correct wage and tax amounts. See the Instructions for Forms W-2 and W-3 and the Instructions for Forms W-2c and W-3c for detailed information about filing requirements. References to Form W-2 on Form 941-X and in these instructions also apply to Forms W-2AS, W-2CM, W-2GU, and W-2VI unless otherwise noted.

You must check the box on line 3 to certify that you filed Forms W-2 or Forms W-2c even if your corrections on Form 941-X do not change amounts shown on those forms. For example, if your only correction to Form 941 involves misstated tax adjustments (see the instructions for line 13, later), check the box on line 3 to certify that you already filed all required Forms W-2 and W-2c with the SSA.

4. Certifying Overreporting Adjustments

If you overreported federal income tax, social security tax, or Medicare tax and checked the box on line 1, check the appropriate box on line 4. You may need to check more than one box. If you obtained written statements from some employees but you could not locate or secure the cooperation of the remaining employees, check all applicable boxes. Provide a summary on line 24 of the amount of the corrections both for the employees who provided written statements and for those who did not.

4a. Check the box on line 4a if your overreported amount includes each affected employee's share of overcollected taxes.

You are certifying that you repaid or reimbursed the employee's share of current and prior year taxes and you received written statements from the employees stating that they did not and will not receive a refund or credit for the prior year taxes. You are certifying that you adjusted federal income tax withheld from employees for the current calendar year only.

Example. The following is an example of the written statement that is required from employees.

> *Employee name* _____
> *Employer name* _____
> *I have received a repayment of $_____ as overcollected social security and Medicare taxes for 20___. I have not claimed a refund of or credit for the overcollected taxes from the IRS, or if I did, that claim has been rejected; and I will not claim a refund or a credit of the amount.*
> *Employee signature* _____
> *Date* _____

Do not send these statements to the IRS. Keep them for your records. Generally, all employment tax records must be kept for at least 4 years.

4b. Check the box on line 4b to certify that your overreported amount is only for the employer share of taxes on those employees who you were unable to find or those who would not (or could not) give you a statement described on line 4a.

4c. Check the box on line 4c to certify that your overreported amount is only for federal income tax, social security tax, and Medicare tax that you did not withhold from your employees.

5. Certifying Claims

If you are filing a claim for refund or abatement of overreported federal income tax, social security tax, or Medicare tax and checked the box on line 2, check the appropriate box on line 5. You may need to check more than one box. If you obtained written statements or consents from some employees but you could not locate or secure the cooperation of the remaining employees, check all applicable boxes. Provide a summary on line 24 of the amount of the corrections for both the employees who provided statements or consents and for those who did not. You may not file a refund claim to correct federal income tax actually withheld from employees.

5a. Check the box on line 5a if your overreported tax includes each affected employee's share of social security and Medicare taxes. You are certifying that you repaid or reimbursed to the employees their share of social security and Medicare taxes. For refunds of employee social security and Medicare taxes overcollected in prior years, you are certifying that you received written statements from those employees stating that they did not and will not receive a refund or credit for the prior year taxes.

5b. Check the box on line 5b if your overreported tax includes each affected employee's share of social security and Medicare taxes and you have not yet repaid or reimbursed the employee share of taxes. You are certifying that you received consent from each affected employee to file a claim on the employee share of those taxes and you received written statements from those employees stating that they did not and will not receive a refund or credit for the prior year taxes.

Example. The following is an example of the consent and written statement that is required from employees when you are filing a claim for refund and have not yet paid or reimbursed the employee share of taxes.

> *Employee name* _____
> *Employer name* _____
> *I give my consent to have my employer (named above) file a claim on my behalf with the IRS requesting $_____ in overcollected social security and Medicare taxes for 20___. I have not claimed a refund of or credit for the overcollected taxes from the IRS, or if I did, that claim has been rejected; and I will not claim a refund or a credit of the amount.*
> *Employee signature* _____

Date _____

Do not send these statements to the IRS. Keep them for your records. Generally, all employment tax records must be kept for at least 4 years.

In certain situations, you may not have repaid or reimbursed your employees or obtained their consents prior to filing a claim, such as in cases where the period of limitations on credit or refund is about to expire. In those situations, file Form 941-X, but do not check a box on line 5. Tell us on line 24 that you have not repaid or reimbursed employees or obtained consents. However, you must certify that you have repaid or reimbursed your employees or obtained consents before the IRS can grant the claim.

5c. Check the box on line 5c to certify that your overreported tax is only for the employer share of social security and Medicare taxes. Affected employees did not give you consent to file a claim for refund for the employee share of social security and Medicare taxes, they could not be found, or would not (or could not) give you a statement described on line 5b.

5d. Check the box on line 5d to certify that your overreported amount is only for federal income tax, social security tax, and Medicare tax that you did not withhold from your employees.

Part 3: Enter the Corrections for This Quarter

What Amounts Should You Report in Part 3?

On lines 6–10, columns 1 and 2, show amounts for **all** of your employees, not just for those employees whose amounts you are correcting.

If a correction that you report in column 4 includes both underreported and overreported amounts (see the instructions for lines 20–21, later), give us details for each error on line 24.

Because special circumstances apply for lines 11–16 and 18–19d, read the instructions for each line carefully before entering amounts in the columns.

 If you previously adjusted or amended Form 941 by using Form 941c, Form 941-X, Form 843, an "amended" Form 941, a "supplemental" Form 941, or because of an IRS examination change, show amounts in column 2 that include those previously reported corrections.

6. Wages, Tips, and Other Compensation

If you are correcting the wages, tips, and other compensation you reported on Form 941, line 2, enter the total corrected amount for ALL employees in column 1. In column 2, enter the amount you originally reported. In column 3, enter the difference between columns 1 and 2. This line does not apply to Form 941-SS.

If you or the IRS previously corrected the amount reported on Form 941, line 2, enter in column 2 the amount after any previous corrections.

line 6 (column 1)	
- line 6 (column 2)	
line 6 (column 3)	If the amount in column 2 is larger than the amount in column 1, use a minus sign in column 3.

Example — Wages, tips, and other compensation increased. You reported $9,000 as total wages, tips, and other compensation on line 2 of your 2009 third quarter Form 941. In July of 2010, you discovered that you had overlooked $1,000 in tips for one of your part-time employees. To correct the error, figure the difference on Form 941-X as shown.

Column 1 (corrected amount)	10,000.00
Column 2 (Form 941, line 2)	- 9,000.00
Column 3 (difference)	-1,000.00

Example — Wages, tips, and other compensation decreased. You reported $9,000 as wages, tips, and other compensation on line 2 of your 2009 fourth quarter Form 941. In December of 2010, you discovered that you included $2,000 in wages for one of your employees twice. To correct the error, figure the difference on Form 941-X as shown.

Column 1 (corrected amount)	7,000.00
Column 2 (Form 941, line 2)	- 9,000.00
Column 3 (difference)	-2,000.00

Example—Auto allowance; wages, tips, and other compensation increased. You paid one of your employees a $500 monthly auto allowance from October through December 2010, and did not treat the payments as taxable wages. In February 2011, you realized that the payments were wages because they were not reimbursements of deductible business expenses that were substantiated and paid under an accountable plan. You correct the error by treating the auto allowance as wages subject to income, social security, and Medicare taxes. Report the additional $1,500 of wages on lines 6, 8, and 10.

Use the amount on line 6, column 1, when you prepare your Forms W-2 or Forms W-2c.

7. Income Tax Withheld from Wages, Tips, and Other Compensation

If you are correcting the federal income tax withheld from wages, tips, and other compensation you reported on Form 941, line 3, enter the total corrected amount in column 1. In column 2, enter the amount you originally reported or as previously corrected. In column 3, enter the difference between columns 1 and 2. This line does not apply to Form 941-SS.

line 7 (column 1)	
- line 7 (column 2)	
line 7 (column 3)	If the amount in column 2 is larger than the amount in column 1, use a minus sign in column 3.

Copy the amount in column 3 to column 4. Include any minus sign shown in column 3.

*Generally, you may correct federal income tax withholding errors **only** if you discovered the errors in the same calendar year you paid the wages. However, you may correct federal income tax withholding errors for prior years if the amounts shown on Form 941 do not agree with the amounts you actually withheld, that is, an administrative error or if section 3509 rates apply. See section 13 of Pub. 15 (Circular E) for more information about corrections during the calendar year and about administrative errors. See section 2 of Pub. 15 (Circular E) for more information about section 3509.*

Example—Failure to withhold income tax when required. You were required to withhold $400 of federal income tax from an employee's bonus that was paid in December of 2011 but you withheld nothing. You discovered the error on March 15, 2012. You cannot file Form 941-X to correct your 2011 fourth quarter Form 941 because the error involves a previous year and the amount previously reported for the employee represents the actual amount withheld from the employee during 2011.

Example—Administrative error reporting income tax. You had three employees. In the fourth quarter of 2011, you withheld $1,000 of federal income tax from employee A, $2,000 from employee B, and $6,000 from employee C. The total amount of federal income tax you withheld was $9,000. You mistakenly reported $6,000 on line 3 of your 2011 fourth quarter

Form 941. You discovered the error on March 16, 2012. This is an example of an administrative error that may be corrected in a later calendar year because the amount actually withheld from employees' wages differs from the amount reported on Form 941. Use Form 941-X to correct the error. Enter $9,000 in column 1 and $6,000 in column 2. Subtract the amount in column 2 from the amount in column 1.

Column 1 (corrected amount)	9,000.00
Column 2 (Form 941, line 3)	- 6,000.00
Column 3 (difference)	3,000.00

Report the 3,000.00 as a tax correction in column 4.

Be sure to explain the reasons for this correction on line 24.

8. Taxable Social Security Wages

The 2011 and 2012 employee tax rate for social security is 4.2%. The employer tax rate for social security is 6.2%.

If you are correcting the taxable social security wages you reported on Form 941, line 5a, column 1, enter the total corrected amount in column 1. In column 2, enter the amount you originally reported or as previously corrected. In column 3, enter the difference between columns 1 and 2.

line 8 (column 1)	
- line 8 (column 2)	
line 8 (column 3)	If the amount in column 2 is larger than the amount in column 1, use a minus sign in column 3.

Multiply the amount in column 3 by .124 (.104 for corrections to a 2011 or 2012 return) and enter that result in column 4.

line 8 (column 3)	
x .124	(Use .104 for corrections to a 2011 or 2012 return.)
line 8 (column 4)	If the amount in column 3 used a minus sign, also use a minus sign in column 4.

Note. If you are correcting only the employer share of tax on a decrease to social security wages, use .062 (6.2%) when multiplying the amount shown in column 3. If you are correcting both shares of tax for some employees and only the employer share for other employees, enter the properly calculated amount in column 4. Be sure to show your calculations on line 24.

Example—Social security wages decreased. Following *Example—Wages, tips and other compensation decreased* in the instructions for line 6, the wages that you counted twice were also taxable social security wages. To correct the error, figure the difference on Form 941-X as shown.

Column 1 (corrected amount)	7,000.00
Column 2 (Form 941, line 5a, column 1)	- 9,000.00
Column 3 (difference)	-2,000.00

Use the difference in column 3 to determine your tax correction.

Column 3 (difference)	-2,000.00
Tax rate (12.4%)	x .124
Column 4 (tax correction)	-248.00

Be sure to explain the reasons for this correction on line 24.

Note. If the example above was for a correction to a 2011 or 2012 return, the amount in column 3 would be multiplied by .104.

9. Taxable Social Security Tips

 The 2011 and 2012 employee tax rate for social security is 4.2%. The employer tax rate for social security is 6.2%.

If you are correcting the taxable social security tips you reported on Form 941, line 5b, column 1, enter the total corrected amount in column 1. In column 2, enter the amount you originally reported or as previously corrected. In column 3, enter the difference between columns 1 and 2.

line 9 (column 1)
- line 9 (column 2)
line 9 (column 3)   If the amount in column 2 is larger than the amount in column 1, use a minus sign in column 3.

Multiply the amount in column 3 by .124 (.104 for corrections to a 2011 or 2012 return) and report that result in column 4.

line 9 (column 3)
           x .124   (Use .104 for corrections to a 2011 or 2012 return.)
line 9 (column 4)   If the amount in column 3 used a minus sign, also use a minus sign in column 4.

Note. If you are correcting only the employer share of tax on a decrease to social security tips, use .062 (6.2%) when multiplying the amount shown in column 3. If you are correcting both shares of tax for some employees and only the employer share for other employees, report the properly calculated amount in column 4. Be sure to show your calculations on line 24.

Following the *Example—Wages, tips, and other compensation increased* in the instructions for line 6, the tips that you overlooked were also taxable social security tips. To correct the error, figure the difference on Form 941-X as shown.

Column 1 (corrected amount)   10,000.00
Column 2 (Form 941, line 5b, column 1)   - 9,000.00
Column 3 (difference)   1,000.00

Use the difference in column 3 to determine your tax correction.

Column 3 (difference)   1,000.00
Tax rate (12.4%)   x .124
Column 4 (tax correction) 124.00

Be sure to explain the reasons for this correction on line 24.

Note. If the example above was for a correction to a 2011 or 2012 return, the amount in column 3 would be multiplied by .104.

10. Taxable Medicare Wages and Tips

If you are correcting the taxable Medicare wages and tips you reported on Form 941, line 5c, column 1, enter the total corrected amount in column 1. In column 2, enter the amount you originally reported or as previously corrected. In column 3, enter the difference between columns 1 and 2.

line 10 (column 1)
- line 10 (column 2)
line 10 (column 3)   If the amount in column 2 is larger than the amount in column 1, use a minus sign in column 3.

Multiply the amount in column 3 by .029 (2.9% tax rate) and enter that result in column 4.

line 10 (column 3)
            x .029
line 10 (column 4)   If the amount in column 3 used a minus sign, also use a minus sign in column 4.

Note. If you are correcting only the employer share of tax on a decrease to Medicare wages and tips, use .0145 (1.45%) when multiplying the amount in column 3. If you are correcting both shares of tax for some employees and only the employer share for other employees, enter the properly calculated amount in column 4. Be sure to explain your calculations on line 24.

Example—Medicare wages and tips decreased.
Following *Example—Wages, tips and other compensation decreased* in the instructions for line 6, the wages that you counted twice were also taxable Medicare wages and tips. To correct the error, figure the difference on Form 941-X as shown.

Column 1 (corrected amount)   7,000.00
Column 2 (Form 941, line 5c, column 1)   - 9,000.00
Column 3 (difference)   -2,000.00

Use the difference in column 3 to determine your tax correction.

Column 3 (difference)   -2,000.00
Tax rate (2.9%)   x .029
Column 4 (tax correction) -58.00

Be sure to explain the reasons for this correction on line 24.

11. Section 3121(q) Notice and Demand—Tax on Unreported Tips

Enter any corrections, including amounts reported on line 7c (for quarters ending before 2011) and amounts reported on line 5e (for quarters ending after 2010), to the tax due from a Section 3121(q) Notice and Demand on line 11. The IRS issues a Section 3121(q) Notice and Demand to advise an employer of the amount of tips received by employees who failed to report or underreported tips to the employer. An employer is not liable for the employer share of the social security and Medicare taxes on unreported tips until a Section 3121(q) Notice and Demand for the taxes is made to the employer by the IRS.

 Lines 12a–12c apply only for corrections to quarters ending after March 31, 2010, and before January 1, 2011.

12. Employer's Social Security Tax Exemption

Complete lines 12a–12c to correct the payroll tax exemption for the employer's share (6.2%) of social security tax on exempt wages/tips paid to one or more qualified employees from April 1–December 31, 2010.

An employer must be a qualified employer to qualify for the employer's social security tax exemption. A **qualified employer** is any employer other than Federal, State, and any related government entities. All public institutions of higher education and Indian tribal governments are also qualified employers.

For more information regarding the employer's social security tax exemption visit IRS.gov and enter the keywords *HIRE Act* in the search box.

12a. Number of qualified employees first paid exempt wages/tips this quarter. Enter on line 12a (column 2) the number of qualified employees originally reported on Form 941, line 6a. If you are not correcting Form 941, line 6a, and are making a correction on line 12b, enter the amount from Form 941, line 6a, on line 12a.

A **qualified employee** is an employee who:
● Began employment with you after February 3, 2010, and before January 1, 2011;
● Certifies by signed affidavit (Form W-11, Hiring Incentives to Restore Employment (HIRE) Act Employee Affidavit, or similar statement) under penalties of perjury that he or she has not been employed for more than 40 hours during the 60-day period (including 2009) ending on the date the employee begins employment with you;
● Is not employed by you to replace another employee unless the other employee separated from employment voluntarily or for cause (including downsizing); and
● Is not related to you. An employee is related to you if he or she is your child or a descendant of your child, your sibling or stepsibling, your parent or ancestor of your parent, your stepparent, your niece or nephew, your aunt or uncle, or your

in-law. An employee is also related to you if he or she is related to anyone who owns more than 50% of your outstanding stock or capital and profits interest or is your dependent or a dependent of anyone who owns more than 50% of your outstanding stock or capital and profits interest. If you are an estate or trust, see section 51(i)(1) and section 152(d)(2) for more details.

Exempt wages/tips are the wages/tips paid to qualified employees for which the employer is exempt from paying the employer's 6.2% share of social security tax.

 If you make a correction on line 12a, then you must complete line 12b.

12b. Number of qualified employees paid exempt wages/tips this quarter. Enter on line 12b (column 1) the total corrected number of qualified employees paid exempt wages/tips to which you applied the social security tax exemption in the quarter you are correcting. Enter on line 12b (column 2) the total number of qualified employees originally reported on Form 941, line 6b. If you are not correcting Form 941, line 6b, and are making a correction on line 12a, enter on line 12b the amount from Form 941, line 6b. See the instructions for line 12a for definitions of qualified employee and exempt wages/tips.

 If you make a correction on line 12b, then you must complete line 12a.

12c. Exempt wages/tips paid to qualified employees this quarter. Enter the amount of exempt wages/tips paid in the quarter you are correcting to all qualified employees. Enter the corrected amount from Form 941, line 6c. Enter the corrected amount in column 1. In column 2, enter the amount you originally reported or as previously corrected. In column 3, enter the difference between columns 1 and 2. If the amount in column 2 is larger than the amount in column 1, use a minus sign in column 3. Multiply the amount in column 3 by .062 and enter the result in column 4. However, to properly show the correction as a credit or balance due item, enter a positive number in column 3 as a negative number in column 4 or a negative number in column 3 as a positive number in column 4. See the instructions for line 12a for definitions of qualified and exempt wages/tips.

13. Tax Adjustments

Use line 13 to correct any adjustments reported on Form 941, lines 7–9 (lines 7a–7c for quarters ending before 2011). Enter in column 1 the total **corrected** amount for Form 941, lines 7–9 (lines 7a–7c for quarters ending before 2011).

Enter in column 2 the total originally reported or previously corrected amounts from Form 941, lines 7–9 (lines 7a–7c for quarters ending before 2011). In column 3, enter the difference between columns 1 and 2.

line 13 (column 1)
-line 13 (column 2)
line 13 (column 3)

 You may need to report negative numbers in any column. Make sure that the difference you enter in column 3 accurately represents the change to adjustments originally reported or previously corrected on Form 941, lines 7–9 (lines 7a–7c for quarters ending before 2011).

Copy the amount in column 3 to column 4. Include any minus sign shown in column 3.

On line 24, describe what you misreported on Form 941. Tell us if your adjustment is for fractions of cents, third-party sick pay, tips, or group-term life insurance.

Example—Current quarter's third-party sick pay underreported. You reported $6,900 (shown as "-6,900.00") as a third-party sick pay adjustment (reduction to tax) on line 7b of your 2010 second quarter Form 941. You did not report any amounts on lines 7a and 7c. Your third-party sick pay adjustment should have been $9,600 (shown as "-9,600.00")

because your third-party sick pay payer withheld that amount of social security and Medicare taxes from your employees. You discovered the error in April of 2011. To correct the error, figure the difference on Form 941-X as shown.

Column 1 (corrected amount)   -9,600.00
Column 2 (Form 941, line 7b)   - (6,900.00)
Column 3 (difference)   -2,700.00

Here is how you would enter the numbers on Form 941-X.

Column 1 (corrected amount)	Column 2 (Form 941, line 7b)	Column 3 (difference)
-9,600.00	-6,900.00	-2,700.00

Report "-2,700.00" as your correction in column 4.

In this example, you are claiming a credit for $2,700 in overreported tax for your 2010 second quarter Form 941. Always enter the same amount in column 4 (including any minus sign) that you enter in column 3.

Be sure to explain the reasons for this correction on line 24.

Note. If the example above was for a correction to a 2011 or 2012 return, the references to line 7b change to line 8.

 Do not use line 13 to report corrections to amounts reported on lines 7d–7g of pre-2009 Forms 941.

14–16. Special Additions to Wages for Federal Income Tax, Social Security Tax, and Medicare Tax

Section 3509 provides special rates for the employee share of social security and Medicare taxes and income tax withholding when workers are reclassified as employees in certain circumstances. The applicable rate depends on whether you filed required information returns. An employer cannot recover any tax paid under this provision from the employees. The full employer share of social security and Medicare taxes is due for all reclassifications.

Note. Section 3509 rates are not available if you intentionally disregarded the requirements to withhold taxes from the employee, or if you withheld income tax but did not withhold social security and Medicare taxes. Section 3509 rates are also not available for certain statutory employees.

On lines 14–16 enter **only** corrections to wages resulting from reclassifying certain workers as employees when section 3509 rates are used to calculate the taxes.

If the employer issued the required information returns, use the section 3509 rates as follows.
• For social security taxes, use the employer rate of 6.2% plus 20% of the employee rate of 6.2% (4.2% for 2011 and 2012), for a total rate of 7.44% (7.04% for 2011 and 2012) of wages.
• For Medicare taxes, use the employer rate of 1.45% plus 20% of the employee rate of 1.45%, for a total rate of 1.74% of wages.
• For income tax withholding, the rate is 1.5% of wages.

If the employer did not issue the required information returns, use the section 3509 rates as follows.
• For social security taxes, use the employer rate of 6.2% plus 40% of the employee rate of 6.2% (4.2% for 2011 and 2012), for a total rate of 8.68% (7.88% for 2011 and 2012) of wages.
• For Medicare taxes, use the employer rate of 1.45% plus 40% of the employee rate of 1.45%, for a total rate of 2.03% of wages.
• For income tax withholding, the rate is 3.0% of wages.

Unlike other lines on Form 941-X, enter in column 1 only the corrected wages for workers being reclassified, **not** the amount paid to ALL employees. Enter previously reported wages to reclassified employees (if any) in column 2. To get the amount for column 4, use the applicable section 3509 rates. The tax correction in column 4 will be a positive number if you increased the amount of wages you previously reported. See the instructions for line 23 for more information.

If you misreported the taxes from worker reclassification on line 7f or line 7g on a pre-2009 Form 941, you may correct the amount using lines 14–16 of Form 941-X. Be sure to complete all of the columns and provide a detailed explanation on line 24.

17. Subtotal

Combine the amounts from column 4 on lines 7–16.

Example. You entered "1,400.00" in column 4 on line 7, "-500.00" in column 4 on line 8, and "-100.00" in column 4 on line 10. Combine these amounts and enter "800.00" in column 4 on line 17.

Line 7	1,400.00
Line 8	-500.00
Line 10	-100.00
Line 17	800.00

18. Advance EIC Payments Made to Employees

 The option of receiving advance payroll payments of EIC expired on December 31, 2010. Corrections to advance EIC can be made only for quarters ending before January 1, 2011.

If you are correcting the advance EIC payments made to your employees that you reported on Form 941, line 9 (only for quarters ending before January 1, 2011), enter the total corrected amount for ALL employees in column 1. In column 2, enter the amount you originally reported or as previously corrected. In column 3, enter the difference between columns 1 and 2. This line does not apply to Form 941-SS.

line 18 (column 1)	
- line 18 (column 2)	
line 18 (column 3)	If the amount in column 2 is larger than the amount in column 1, use a minus sign in column 3.

 Copy the amount in column 3 to column 4. However, to properly show the correction as a credit or balance due item, enter a positive number in column 3 as a negative number in column 4 or a negative number in column 3 as a positive number in column 4. Remember, negative amounts in column 4 represent credits and positive amounts in column 4 represent additional tax.

Examples. If line 18, column 3 shows "560.00," enter "-560.00" in column 4.

If line 18, column 3 shows "-990.00," enter "990.00" in column 4.

Example—Advance EIC payments increased. You filed your 2010 fourth quarter Form 941 reporting zero (line left blank) on line 9. On February 17, 2011, you discovered that you forgot to report the $1,000 in advance EIC payments you made on behalf of John Smith, one of your employees. You made no other EIC payments for your other employees. This is an example of an administrative error. To correct the error, file Form 941-X showing the following.

Column 1 (corrected amount)	1,000.00
Column 2 (Form 941, line 9)	- 0.00
Column 3 (difference)	1,000.00

Reverse the mathematical sign of the amount in column 3 and enter your correction in column 4.

Column 4 (tax correction)	-1,000.00

Be sure to explain the reasons for this correction on line 24.

 See section 13 of Pub. 15 (Circular E) for more information about administrative errors and corrections during the calendar year. The same rules that apply to withheld federal income taxes also apply to advance EIC payments made to employees.

19a. COBRA Premium Assistance Payments

If you are correcting the total COBRA premium assistance payments reported on Form 941, line 12a, report on this line 65% of the COBRA premiums for assistance eligible individuals. Report the premium assistance credit on this line only after the assistance eligible individual's 35% share of the premium has been paid. For COBRA coverage provided under a self-insured plan, COBRA premium assistance is treated as having been made for each assistance eligible individual who pays 35% of the COBRA premium.

Do not include the assistance eligible individual's 35% of the premium in the amount entered on this line. For more information on the COBRA premium subsidy, visit IRS.gov and enter the keyword *COBRA*.

Copy the amount in column 3 to column 4. However, to properly show the correction as a credit or balance due item, enter a positive number in column 3 as a negative number in column 4 or a negative number in column 3 as a positive number in column 4. This is the same procedure as the advance EIC on line 18.

19b. Number of Individuals Provided COBRA Premium Assistance on line 19a

Complete this line only if you are correcting Form 941, line 12b. Enter in column 1 on line 19b the corrected number of assistance eligible individuals provided COBRA premium assistance. Count each assistance eligible individual who paid a reduced COBRA premium in the quarter as one individual, whether or not the reduced premium was for insurance that covered more than one assistance eligible individual. For example, if the reduced COBRA premium was for coverage for a former employee, spouse, and two children, you would include one individual in the number entered on line 19b for the premium assistance entered on line 19a. Further, each individual is reported only once per quarter. For example, an assistance eligible individual who made monthly premium payments during the quarter would only be reported as one individual on line 19b for that quarter.

Enter in column 2 on line 19b the number of assistance eligible individuals provided COBRA premium assistance originally reported on Form 941, line 12b.

 Lines 19c and 19d apply only to the second quarter of 2010. These lines are used to report the number of qualified employees, amount of exempt wages/tips, and amount of employer social security tax exemption as if the exemption were allowed for the first quarter of 2010.

19c. Number of Qualified Employees Paid Exempt Wages/Tips March 19–31

Complete this line when correcting Form 941 for the second quarter of 2010 only. Enter on line 19c (column 1) the corrected number of qualified employees paid exempt wages/tips from March 19, 2010, through March 31, 2010. Include only qualified employees for whom you are claiming the exemption. Enter on line 19c (column 2) the number of qualified employees originally reported on line 12c of the second quarter 2010 Form 941. If you are not correcting line 12c of the second quarter 2010 Form 941 but you are making a correction on line 19d, enter the amount from line 12c of the second quarter 2010 Form 941 on line 19c. For the definition of qualified employee, see the instructions for line 12a.

19d. Exempt Wages/Tips Paid to Qualified Employees March 19-31

Complete this line when correcting Form 941 for the second quarter of 2010 only. Enter on line 19d the amount of exempt wages/tips paid to qualified employees from March 19, 2010, through March 31, 2010. For the definition of exempt wages/tips, see the instructions for line 12a. Enter the corrected amount in column 1. In column 2, enter the amount you originally reported or as previously corrected. In column 3, enter the difference between columns 1 and 2. If the amount in column 2 is larger than the amount in column 1, use a minus sign in column 3. Multiply the amount in column 3 by .062 and enter the result in column 4. However, to properly show the correction as a credit or balance due item, enter a positive number in column 3 as a negative number in column 4 or a negative number in column 3 as a positive number in column 4.

20–21. Total
Combine lines 17–19d of column 4 and enter the result on line 20. Copy the amount from line 20 on page 2 to line 21 on page 3.

Your credit. If the amount entered on line 21 is less than zero, for example, "-115.00," you have a credit because you overreported your federal employment taxes.
• If you checked the box on line 1, include this amount on Form 941, line 11 ("Total deposits" line), for the quarter during which you filed Form 941-X or Form 944, line 8 ("Total deposits" line), for the year during which you filed Form 941-X. Do not make any changes to your record of federal tax liability reported on Form 941, line 17, or Schedule B (Form 941), if your Form 941-X is filed timely. The amounts reported on the record should reflect your actual tax liability for the period.
• If you checked the box on line 2, you are filing a claim for refund or abatement of the amount shown.

If your credit is less than $1, we will send a refund or apply it only if you ask us in writing to do so.

Amount you owe. If the amount on line 21 is a positive number, you must pay the amount you owe by the time you file Form 941-X. You may not use any credit that you show on another Form 941-X to pay the amount you owe, even if you filed for the amount you owe and the credit at the same time.

If you owe tax and are filing a timely Form 941-X, do not file an amended Schedule B (Form 941) unless you were assessed an FTD penalty caused by an incorrect, incomplete, or missing Schedule B (Form 941). Do not include the tax increase reported on Form 941-X on any amended Schedule B (Form 941) you file.

If you owe tax and are filing a late Form 941-X, that is, after the due date for Form 941 for the quarter in which you discovered the error, you must file an amended Schedule B (Form 941) with the Form 941-X. Otherwise, the IRS may assess an "averaged" FTD penalty. The total tax reported on the "Total liability for the quarter" line of Schedule B (Form 941), must match the corrected tax (Form 941, line 10, combined with any correction reported on Form 941-X, line 17, minus any advance EIC reported on Form 941-X, line 18), less any previous abatements and interest-free tax assessments.

Payment methods. You may pay the amount you owe on line 21 electronically using the Electronic Federal Tax Payment System (EFTPS), by credit or debit card, or by a check or money order.
• The preferred method of payment is EFTPS. For more information, visit www.eftps.gov, call EFTPS Customer Service at 1-800-555-4477 toll free, or see Pub. 966, Electronic Federal Tax Payment System: A Guide to Getting Started.
• To pay by credit or debit card, visit the IRS website at www.irs.gov/e-pay.
• If you pay by check or money order, make it payable to "United States Treasury." On your check or money order, be sure to write your EIN, "Form 941-X," and the quarter and year corrected.

You do not have to pay if the amount you owe is less than $1.

Previously assessed FTD penalty. If line 21 reflects overreported tax and the IRS previously assessed a failure-to-deposit (FTD) penalty, you may be able to reduce the penalty. For more information, see the Instructions for Schedule B (Form 941).

Part 4: Explain Your Corrections for This Quarter

22. Correction of Both Underreported and Overreported Amounts
Check the box on line 22 if any corrections you entered on lines 6–19d, column 3, reflect both underreported and overreported amounts.

Example. If you had an increase to social security wages of $15,000 for employee A and a decrease to social security wages of $5,000 for employee B, you would enter $10,000 on line 8, column 3. That $10,000 represents the net change from corrections.

On line 24, you must explain the reason for both the $15,000 increase and the $5,000 decrease.

23. Did You Reclassify Any Workers?
Check the box on line 23 if you reclassified any workers to be independent contractors or nonemployees. Also check this box if the IRS (or you) determined that workers you treated as independent contractors or nonemployees should be classified as employees. On line 24, give us a detailed reason why any worker was reclassified and, if you used section 3509 rates on lines 14–16, for any worker reclassified as an employee, explain why section 3509 rates apply and what rates you used.

Return not filed because you did not treat any workers as employees. If you did not previously file Form 941 because you mistakenly treated all workers as independent contractors or as nonemployees, file a Form 941 for each delinquent quarter.

On each Form 941 for which you are entitled to use section 3509 rates, complete the following steps.
• Write "Misclassified Employees" in dark, bold letters across the top margin of page 1.
• Enter a zero on line 10 ("Total taxes after adjustments").
• Complete the signature area.
• Attach a completed Form 941-X (see instructions below).

On each Form 941-X complete the following steps.
• Complete the top of Form 941-X, including the date you discovered the error.
• Enter the wage amounts on lines 14–16, column 1.
• Enter zeros on lines 14–16, column 2.
• Complete columns 3 and 4 as instructed in Part 3.
• Provide a detailed statement on line 24.
• Complete the signature area.

⚠ **CAUTION** *If you cannot use section 3509 rates (for example, because the workers you treated as nonemployees were certain statutory employees), file a Form 941 for each delinquent quarter. Write "Misclassified Employees" in dark, bold letters across the top margin of page 1 of each Form 941. Complete Form 941 using the Instructions for Form 941. Attach a Form 941-X to each Form 941. Complete the top of Form 941-X, including the date you discovered the error, and provide a detailed explanation on line 24.*

24. Explain Your Corrections
Treasury regulations require you to explain in detail the grounds and facts relied upon to support each correction. On line 24, describe in detail each correction you entered on lines 6–19d, column 3. If you need more space, attach additional sheets, but be sure to write your name, EIN, Form 941-X, quarter, and calendar year on the top of each sheet.

You must describe the events that caused the underreported or overreported amounts. Explanations such as "social security and Medicare wages were overstated" or "administrative/payroll errors were discovered" are insufficient and may delay processing your Form 941-X because the IRS may need to ask for a more complete explanation.

Provide the following information in your explanation for each correction.
- Form 941-X line number(s) affected.
- Date you discovered the error.
- Difference (amount of the error).
- Cause of the error.

You may report the information in paragraph form. The following paragraph is an example.

"The $1,000 difference shown in column 3 on lines 6, 8, and 10 was discovered on May 16, 2011, during an internal payroll audit. We discovered that we included $1,000 of wages for one of our employees twice. This correction removes the reported wages that were never paid."

For corrections shown on lines 14–16, column 3, explain why the correction was necessary and attach any notice you received from the IRS.

Part 5. Sign Here

You must complete all three pages of Form 941-X and sign it on page 3. If you do not sign, processing of Form 941-X will be delayed.

Who must sign the Form 941-X? Form 941-X must be signed by one of the following.
- **Sole proprietorship**—The individual who owns the business.
- **Corporation (including a limited liability company (LLC) treated as a corporation)**—The president, vice president, or other principal officer duly authorized to sign.
- **Partnership (including an LLC treated as a partnership) or unincorporated organization**—A responsible and duly authorized member, partner, or officer having knowledge of its affairs.
- **Single member LLC treated as a disregarded entity for federal income tax purposes**—The owner of the LLC or a principal officer duly authorized to sign.
- **Trust or estate**—The fiduciary.

Form 941-X may also be signed by a duly authorized agent of the taxpayer if a valid power of attorney has been filed.

Alternative signature method. Corporate officers or duly authorized agents may sign Form 941-X by rubber stamp, mechanical device, or computer software program. For details and required documentation, see Rev. Proc. 2005-39. You can find Rev. Proc. 2005-39, 2005-28 I.R.B. 82, at *www.irs.gov/irb/2005-28_IRB/ar16.html*.

Paid Preparer Use Only

A paid preparer must sign Form 941-X and provide the information in the *Paid Preparer Use Only* section of Part 5 if the preparer was paid to prepare Form 941-X and is not an employee of the filing entity. Paid preparers must sign paper returns with a manual signature. The preparer must give you a copy of the return in addition to the copy to be filed with the IRS.

If you are a paid preparer, enter your Preparer Tax Identification Number (PTIN) in the space provided. Include your complete address. If you work for a firm, enter the firm's name and the EIN of the firm. You can apply for a PTIN online or by filing Form W-12, IRS Paid Preparer Tax Identification Number (PTIN) Application and Renewal. For more information about applying for a PTIN online, visit the IRS website at *www.irs.gov/ptin*. You cannot use your PTIN in place of the EIN of the tax preparation firm.

Generally, you are not required to complete this section if you are filing the return as a reporting agent and have a valid Form 8655, Reporting Agent Authorization, on file with the IRS. However, a reporting agent must complete this section if the reporting agent offered legal advice, for example, advising the client on determining whether its workers are employees or independent contractors for federal tax purposes.

How Can You Order Forms and Publications from the IRS?

 Call 1-800-829-3676.

 Visit the IRS website at *www.irs.gov/formspubs*.

Additional Information

You may find the following products helpful when using Form 941-X.
- Form W-2, Wage and Tax Statement
- Form W-3, Transmittal of Wage and Tax Statements
- Instructions for Forms W-2 and W-3
- Form W-2AS, American Samoa Wage and Tax Statement
- Form W-2CM, Wage and Tax Statement (Northern Mariana Islands)
- Form W-2GU, Guam Wage and Tax Statement
- Form W-2VI, U.S. Virgin Islands Wage and Tax Statement
- Form W-3SS, Transmittal of Wage and Tax Statements
- Instructions for Forms W-2AS, W-2GU, W-2VI, and W-3SS
- Form W-2c, Corrected Wage and Tax Statement
- Form W-3c, Transmittal of Corrected Wage and Tax Statements
- Instructions for Forms W-2c and W-3c
- Form W-11, Hiring Incentives to Restore Employment (HIRE) Act Employee Affidavit
- Instructions for Form 843
- Instructions for Form 941
- Instructions for Schedule B (Form 941)
- Instructions for Form 941-SS
- Pub. 15 (Circular E), Employer's Tax Guide
- Pub. 80 (Circular SS), Federal Tax Guide for Employers in the U.S. Virgin Islands, Guam, American Samoa, and the Commonwealth of the Northern Mariana Islands
- Pub. 966, Electronic Federal Tax Payment System: A Guide to Getting Started

Paperwork Reduction Act Notice We ask for the information on Form 941-X to carry out the Internal Revenue laws of the United States. We need it to figure and collect the right amount of tax. Subtitle C, Employment Taxes, of the Internal Revenue Code imposes employment taxes on wages, including income tax withholding. This form is used to determine the amount of taxes that you owe. Section 6011 requires you to provide the requested information if the tax is applicable to you.

You are not required to provide the information requested on a form that is subject to the Paperwork Reduction Act unless the form displays a valid OMB control number. Books and records relating to a form or instructions must be retained as long as their contents may become material in the administration of any Internal Revenue law.

The time needed to complete and file Form 941-X will vary depending on individual circumstances. The estimated average time is:

Recordkeeping	16 hr., 15 min.
Learning about the law or the form	30 min.
Preparing and sending the form to the IRS	47 min.

If you have comments concerning the accuracy of these time estimates or suggestions for making Form 941-X simpler, we would be happy to hear from you. You can email us at: *taxforms@irs.gov*. Enter "Form 941-X" on the subject line. Or write to: Internal Revenue Service, Tax Products Coordinating Committee, SE:W:CAR:MP:T:MS, 1111 Constitution Ave. NW, IR-6526, Washington, DC 20224. **Do not** send Form 941-X to this address. Instead, see *Where Should You File Form 941-X*, earlier.

Form **943**

Department of the Treasury
Internal Revenue Service

Employer's Annual Federal Tax Return for Agricultural Employees

▶ Information about Form 943 and its separate instructions is at *www.irs.gov/form943*.

OMB No. 1545-0035

2012

**Type
or
Print**

Name (as distinguished from trade name)	Calendar year
Trade name, if any	Employer identification number (EIN)
Address (number and street)	City, state, and ZIP code

If address is different from prior return, check here. ▶ ☐

If you do not have to file returns in the future, check here . . . . ▶ ☐

1	Number of agricultural employees employed in the pay period that includes March 12, 2012 ▶	**1**	

For 2012, the employee social security tax rate is 4.2% and the Medicare tax rate is 1.45%. The employer social security tax rate is 6.2% and the Medicare tax rate is 1.45%.

2	Total wages subject to social security tax (see separate instructions)	**2**	
3	Social security tax (multiply line 2 by 10.4% (.104))	**3**	
4	Total wages subject to Medicare tax (see separate instructions) . . .	**4**	
5	Medicare tax (multiply line 4 by 2.9% (.029))	**5**	
6	Federal income tax withheld (see separate instructions)	**6**	
7	Total taxes before adjustments. Add lines 3, 5, and 6	**7**	
8	Current year's adjustments (see separate instructions)	**8**	
9	Total taxes after adjustments (line 7 as adjusted by line 8)	**9**	
10	Total deposits for 2012, including overpayment applied from a prior year and Form 943-X . . .	**10**	
11a	COBRA premium assistance payments (see separate instructions)	**11a**	
11b	Number of individuals provided COBRA premium assistance **11b**		
12	Add lines 10 and 11a	**12**	
13	**Balance due.** If line 9 is more than 12, enter the difference and see the instructions . . . ▶	**13**	
14	**Overpayment.** If line 12 is more than line 9, enter the difference ▶ $ _____ Check one: ☐ Appy to next return. ☐ Send a refund.		

- **All filers:** If line 9 is less than $2,500, **do not** complete line 15 or Form 943-A.
- **Semiweekly schedule depositors:** Complete Form 943-A and check here ▶ ☐ • **Monthly schedule depositors:** Complete line 15 and check here ▶ ☐

15	**Monthly Summary of Federal Tax Liability. (Do not** complete if you were a semiweekly schedule depositor.)				
	Tax liability for month		**Tax liability for month**		**Tax liability for month**
A January . . .		**F** June		**K** November . . .	
B February . . .		**G** July		**L** December . . .	
C March		**H** August . . .		**M** Total liability for year (add lines **A** through **L**) . .	
D April		**I** September . .			
E May		**J** October . . .			

Third-Party Designee

Do you want to allow another person to discuss this return with the IRS (see separate instructions)? ☐ Yes. Complete the following. ☐ No.

Designee's name ▶	Phone no. ▶	Personal identification number (PIN) ▶ ☐☐☐☐☐

Sign Here

Under penalties of perjury, I declare that I have examined this return, including accompanying schedules and statements, and to the best of my knowledge and belief, it is true, correct, and complete. Declaration of preparer (other than taxpayer) is based on all information of which preparer has any knowledge.

Signature ▶	Print Your Name and Title ▶	Date ▶

Paid Preparer Use Only

Print/Type preparer's name	Preparer's signature	Date	Check ☐ if self-employed	PTIN
Firm's name ▶			Firm's EIN ▶	
Firm's address ▶			Phone no.	

For Privacy Act and Paperwork Reduction Act Notice, see the separate instructions.　　　Cat. No. 11252K　　　Form **943** (2012)

Form 943-V,
Payment Voucher

Purpose of Form

Complete Form 943-V, Payment Voucher, if you are making a payment with Form 943, Employer's Annual Federal Tax Return for Agricultural Employees. We will use the completed voucher to credit your payment more promptly and accurately, and to improve our service to you.

Making Payment With Form 943

To avoid a penalty, make your payment with your 2012 Form 943 **only if:**

• Your total taxes after adjustments for the year (Form 943, line 9) are less than $2,500 and you are paying in full with a timely filed return, or

• You are a monthly schedule depositor making a payment in accordance with the Accuracy of Deposits Rule. See section 7 of Pub. 51 (Circular A), Agricultural Employer's Tax Guide, for details. In this case, the amount of your payment may be $2,500 or more.

Otherwise, you must make deposits by electronic funds transfer. See section 7 of Pub. 51 (Circular A) for deposit instructions. Do not use Form 943-V to make federal tax deposits.

Caution. *Use Form 943-V when making any payment with Form 943. However, if you pay an amount with Form 943 that should have been deposited, you may be subject to a penalty. See* Deposit Penalties *in section 7 of Pub. 51 (Circular A).*

Specific Instructions

Box 1—Employer identification number (EIN). If you do not have an EIN, you may apply for one online. Go to IRS.gov and click on the *Apply for an EIN Online* link under "Tools." You may also apply for an EIN by calling 1-800-829-4933, or you can fax or mail Form SS-4, Application for Employer Identification Number. If you have not received your EIN by the due date of Form 943, write "Applied For" and the date you applied in this entry space.

Box 2—Amount paid. Enter the amount paid with Form 943.

Box 3—Name and address. Enter your name and address as shown on Form 943.

• Enclose your check or money order made payable to the "United States Treasury." Be sure to enter your EIN, "Form 943," and "2012" on your check or money order. Do not send cash. Do not attach Form 943-V or your payment to Form 943 (or to each other).

• Detach Form 943-V and send it with your payment and Form 943 to the address provided in the Instructions for Form 943.

Note. You must also complete the entity information above line 1 on Form 943.

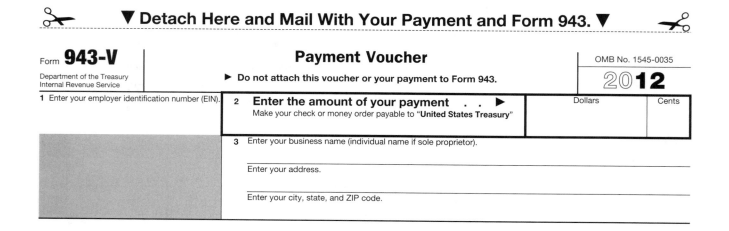

20**12**

Instructions for Form 943

Department of the Treasury
Internal Revenue Service

Employer's Annual Federal Tax Return for Agricultural Employees

Section references are to the Internal Revenue Code unless otherwise noted.

Future Developments

For the latest information about developments related to Form 943 and its instructions, such as legislation enacted after they were published, go to *www.irs.gov/form943*.

What's New

Social security and Medicare tax for 2012. The employee tax rate for social security is 4.2% and the employer tax rate for social security is 6.2%, unchanged from 2011. The social security wage base limit is $110,100. The Medicare tax rate is 1.45% each for the employee and employer, unchanged from 2011. There is no limit on the amount of wages subject to Medicare tax.

VOW to Hire Heroes Act of 2011. On November 21, 2011, the President signed into law the VOW to Hire Heroes Act of 2011. This new law provides an expanded work opportunity tax credit to businesses that hire eligible unemployed veterans and, for the first time, also makes part of the credit available to tax-exempt organizations. Businesses claim the credit as part of the general business credit and tax-exempt organizations claim it against their payroll tax liability using Form 5884-C, Work Opportunity Credit for Qualified Tax-Exempt Organizations Hiring Qualified Veterans. The liability reported on Form 943 is not reduced by the amount of the credit. The credit is available for eligible unemployed veterans who begin work on or after November 22, 2011, and before January 1, 2013. For more information about the credit, visit *www.irs.gov/form5884c*.

Social security wage base for 2013. The maximum amount of wages subject to the social security tax for 2013 will be discussed in the December 2012 revision of Publication 51 (Circular A), Agricultural Employer's Tax Guide.

Change of address. Beginning in 2012, employers must use new Form 8822-B, Change of Address—Business, for any address change.

Reminders

Correcting a previously filed Form 943. If you discover an error on a previously filed Form 943, make the correction using Form 943-X, Adjusted Employer's Annual Federal Tax Return for Agricultural Employees or Claim for Refund. Form 943-X is filed separately from Form 943. For more information, see section 9 of Pub. 51 (Circular A), or visit IRS.gov and enter the keywords *Correcting Employment Taxes*.

COBRA premium assistance credit. The credit for COBRA premium assistance payments applies to premiums paid for employees involuntarily terminated

between September 1, 2008, and May 31, 2010, and to premiums paid for up to 15 months. See *COBRA Premium Assistance Payments,* later.

Compensation paid to H-2A visa holders. Report compensation of $600 or more paid to foreign agricultural workers who entered the country on H-2A visas in box 1 of Form W-2, Wage and Tax Statement. Compensation paid to H-2A workers for agricultural labor performed in connection with this visa is not subject to social security and Medicare taxes, and therefore should not be reported as wages subject to social security tax (line 2) or Medicare tax (line 4) on Form 943, and should not be reported as social security wages (box 3) or Medicare wages (box 5) on Form W-2.

An employer is not required to withhold federal income tax from compensation it pays to an H-2A worker for agricultural labor performed in connection with this visa unless the worker asks for withholding and the employer agrees. In this case, the worker must give the employer a completed Form W-4, Employee's Withholding Allowance Certificate. Federal income tax withheld should be reported on Form 943, line 6, and in box 2 of Form W-2. These reporting rules apply when the H-2A worker provides his or her taxpayer identification number (TIN) to the employer. For the rules relating to backup withholding and reporting when the H-2A worker does not provide a TIN, see the Instructions for Form 1099-MISC and the Instructions for Form 945.

Federal tax deposits must be made by electronic funds transfer. You must use electronic funds transfer to make all federal tax deposits. Generally, electronic funds transfers are made using the Electronic Federal Tax Payment System (EFTPS). If you do not want to use EFTPS, you can arrange for your tax professional, financial institution, payroll service, or other trusted third party to make deposits on your behalf. Also, you may arrange for your financial institution to initiate a same-day wire payment on your behalf. EFTPS is a free service provided by the Department of Treasury. Services provided by your tax professional, financial institution, payroll service, or other third party may have a fee.

For more information on making tax deposits, see section 7 of Pub. 51 (Circular A). To get more information about EFTPS or to enroll in EFTPS, visit the EFTPS website at *www.eftps.gov*, or call 1-800-555-4477. Additional information about EFTPS is also available in Pub. 966, Electronic Federal Tax Payment System: A Guide to Getting Started.

Paid preparers must sign Form 943. Paid preparers must complete and sign the paid preparer's section of Form 943.

Employer's liability. Employers are responsible to ensure that tax returns are filed and deposits and payments are made, even if the employer contracts with a third party. The employer remains liable if the third party fails to perform a required action.

Credit or debit card payments. Employers can pay the balance due shown on Form 943 by credit or debit card. **Do not** use a credit or debit card to make federal tax deposits. For more information on paying your taxes with a credit or debit card, visit the IRS website at *www.irs.gov/e-pay*.

Disregarded entities and qualified subchapter S subsidiaries (QSubs). The IRS has published final regulations section 301.7701(c)(2)(iv) under which QSubs and eligible single-owner disregarded entities are treated as separate entities for employment tax purposes. For more information, see *Disregarded entities and qualified subchapter S subsidiaries* in Pub. 15 (Circular E), Employer's Tax Guide.

How to get forms and publications. You can get most IRS forms and publications by visiting IRS.gov or by calling the IRS at 1-800-TAX-FORM (1-800-829-3676).

Telephone help. You can call the IRS Business and Specialty Tax Line toll free at 1-800-829-4933 or 1-800-829-4059 (for persons who are deaf, hard of hearing, or have a speech disability) Monday–Friday 7 a.m.–7 p.m. local time (Alaska and Hawaii follow Pacific time) for answers to your questions about completing Form 943, tax deposit rules, or obtaining an employer identification number (EIN).

Photographs of Missing Children

The Internal Revenue Service is a proud partner with the National Center for Missing and Exploited Children. Photographs of missing children selected by the Center may appear in instructions on pages that would otherwise be blank. You can help bring these children home by looking at the photographs and calling 1-800-THE-LOST (1-800-843-5678) if you recognize a child.

General Instructions

Purpose of Form 943

Use Form 943 to report federal income tax withheld and employer and employee social security and Medicare taxes on wages paid to farmworkers.

If you have household employees working in your private home on your farm operated for a profit, they are not considered to be farm employees. To report social security, Medicare, and federal income tax withholding on the wages of household employees, you may either:

* File Schedule H (Form 1040), Household Employment Taxes, with your Form 1040, or
* Include the wages with your farm employees' wages on Form 943.

If you paid wages to a household employee in a home that is not on a for-profit farm, you must report the taxes on Schedule H (Form 1040). If you paid wages to other nonfarm workers, do not report these on Form 943. Taxes on wages paid to nonfarm workers are reported on Form 941/941-SS, Employer's QUARTERLY Federal Tax

Return, or Form 944, Employer's ANNUAL Federal Tax Return. See Pub. 926, Household Employer's Tax Guide, for more information about household employees.

Who Must File

File Form 943 if you paid wages to one or more farmworkers and the wages were subject to social security and Medicare taxes or federal income tax withholding under the tests discussed below. For more information on farmworkers and wages, see Pub. 51 (Circular A).

The $150 Test or the $2,500 Test

All cash wages that you pay to farmworkers are subject to social security and Medicare taxes and federal income tax withholding for any calendar year that you meet either of the tests listed below.

* You pay an employee cash wages of $150 or more in a year for farmwork.
* The total (cash and noncash) wages that you pay to all farmworkers is $2,500 or more.

If the $2,500-or-more test for the group is not met, the $150-or-more test for an individual still applies.

Exceptions. Special rules apply to certain hand-harvest laborers who receive less than $150 in annual cash wages. For more information, see section 4 of Pub. 51 (Circular A).

When To File

For 2012, file Form 943 by January 31, 2013. However, if you made deposits on time in full payment of the taxes due for the year, you may file the return as late as February 11, 2013.

Final Return

If you stop paying wages during the year and do not expect to pay wages again, file a final return for 2012. Be sure to mark the box above line 1 on the form indicating that you do not have to file returns in the future. If you later become liable for any of the taxes, notify the IRS.

Employer Identification Number (EIN)

If you do not have an EIN, you may apply for one online. Go to IRS.gov and click on the *Apply for an EIN Online* link under "Tools." You may also apply for an EIN by calling 1-800-829-4933, or you can fax or mail Form SS-4, Application for Employer Identification Number, to the IRS. If you have not received your EIN by the due date of Form 943, write "Applied For" and the date you applied in this entry space.

Forms W-2 and W-3

By January 31, 2013, give Form W-2 to each employee who was working for you at the end of 2012. If an employee stops working for you before the end of the year, give him or her Form W-2 any time after employment ends but no later than January 31 of the following year. If the employee asks you for Form W-2, give him or her the completed form within 30 days of the request or the last wage payment, whichever is later.

Compensation paid to H-2A visa holders. Report compensation of $600 or more paid to foreign agricultural workers who entered the country on H-2A visas in box 1 of Form W-2. Compensation paid to H-2A workers for agricultural labor performed in connection with H-2A visas is not subject to social security and Medicare taxes, and therefore should not be reported as wages subject to social security tax (line 2) or Medicare tax (line 4) on Form 943, and should not be reported as social security wages (box 3) or Medicare wages (box 5) on Form W-2.

An employer is not required to withhold federal income tax from compensation it pays to an H-2A worker for agricultural labor performed in connection with this visa unless the worker asks for withholding and the employer agrees. In this case, the worker must give the employer a completed Form W-4. Federal income tax withheld is reported on Form 943, line 6, and in box 2 of Form W-2. These reporting rules apply when the H-2A worker provides his or her taxpayer identification number (TIN) to the employer. For the rules relating to backup withholding and reporting when the H-2A worker does not provide a TIN, see the Instructions for Form 1099-MISC and the Instructions for Form 945.

Filing on paper forms. By February 28, 2013, send Copy A of all Forms W-2 with Form W-3, Transmittal of Wage and Tax Statements, to the Social Security Administration (SSA) if you are filing less than 250 paper Forms W-2. The mailing address can be found on Form W-3 under *Where To File Paper Forms*. If you are required to file 250 or more Forms W-2, you must file them electronically unless the IRS granted you a waiver. Even if you are required to file less than 250 Forms W-2, we encourage you to take advantage of electronic filing.

Filing electronically. Visit the SSA's Employer W-2 Filing Instructions and Information website at *www.socialsecurity.gov/employer* for information about filing Forms W-2 electronically. If you file electronically, the due date is April 1, 2013. The SSA no longer accepts any form of magnetic media for wage reporting.

Where To File

Find the state of your legal residence, principal place of business, office, or agency in the table that follows. Send your return to the address listed for your location.

Note. Where you file depends on whether or not you are including a payment. Be sure to use the correct address.

If you are in . . .		Without a payment . . .	With a payment . . .
Connecticut	New Jersey	Department of the	Internal Revenue
Delaware	New York	Treasury	Service
District of	North Carolina	Internal Revenue	P.O. Box 804523
Columbia	Ohio	Service	Cincinnati, OH
Florida	Pennsylvania	Cincinnati, OH	45280-4523
Georgia	Rhode Island	45999-0008	
Illinois	South Carolina		
Indiana	Tennessee		
Kentucky	Vermont		
Maine	Virginia		
Maryland	West Virginia		
Massachusetts	Wisconsin		
Michigan			
New Hampshire			

If you are in . . .		Without a payment . . .	With a payment . . .
Alabama	Missouri	Department of the	Internal Revenue
Alaska	Montana	Treasury	Service
Arizona	Nebraska	Internal Revenue	P. O Box 37943
Arkansas	Nevada	Service	Hartford, CT
California	New Mexico	Ogden, UT	06176-7943
Colorado	North Dakota	84201-0008	
Hawaii	Oklahoma		
Idaho	Oregon		
Iowa	South Dakota		
Kansas	Texas		
Louisiana	Utah		
Minnesota	Washington		
Mississippi	Wyoming		

If you are in . . .	Without a payment . . .	With a payment . . .
No legal residence or principal place of business in any state:	Internal Revenue Service P.O. Box 409101 Ogden, UT 84409	Internal Revenue Service P. O Box 37943 Hartford, CT 06176-7943
If you are filing Form 943 for an exempt organization or government entity (federal, state, local, or Indian tribal government), use the following addresses regardless of your location:	Department of the Treasury Internal Revenue Service Ogden, UT 84201-0008	Internal Revenue Service P. O Box 37943 Hartford, CT 06176-7943

Reconciliation of Form 943 to Forms W-2 and W-3

Certain amounts reported on Form 943 for 2012 should agree with the Form W-2 totals reported on the 2012 Form W-3. The amounts from Form 943 that should agree with the related boxes on Form W-3 are: federal income tax withheld (line 6 versus box 2), social security wages (line 2 versus box 3), and Medicare wages (line 4 versus box 5). If the totals do not agree, the IRS or SSA may require you to explain any differences and correct any errors. Keep all records that show why the totals do not match. For more information, see section 11 of Pub. 51 (Circular A).

Depositing Taxes

If your total taxes after adjustments (line 9) are less than $2,500 for the year, you can pay the tax due with your return if you file on time. If your total taxes after adjustments are $2,500 or more for the year, you must make deposits by electronic funds transfer throughout the year in accordance with your deposit schedule. There are two deposit schedules—monthly or semiweekly—for determining when you must deposit. Before the beginning of each calendar year, you must determine which of the two deposit schedules you must use. See section 7 of Pub. 51 (Circular A) for information and rules concerning federal tax deposits and to determine your status as a monthly or semiweekly schedule depositor.

Penalties and Interest

You can avoid paying penalties and interest if you do all of the following.
- Deposit or pay your taxes when they are due.
- File your fully completed Form 943 on time.
- Report your tax liability accurately.
- Submit valid checks for tax payments.
- Furnish accurate Forms W-2 to employees.

- File Form W-3 and Copies A of Form W-2 with the Social Security Administration (SSA) on time and accurately.

Penalties and interest are charged on taxes paid late and returns filed late at a rate set by law. See section 8 of Pub. 51 (Circular A) for details.

If you receive a notice about a penalty after you file this return, reply to the notice with an explanation and we will determine if you meet reasonable-cause criteria. Do **not** attach an explanation when you file your return.

Use Form 843, Claim for Refund and Request for Abatement, to request abatement of assessed penalties or interest. Do not request abatement of assessed penalties or interest on Form 943 or Form 943-X.

 If federal income, social security, and Medicare taxes that must be withheld (that is, trust fund taxes) are not withheld or are not paid to the United States Treasury, the trust fund recovery penalty may apply. The penalty is 100% of the unpaid trust fund tax. This penalty may apply to you if these unpaid taxes cannot be immediately collected from the employer or business. The trust fund recovery penalty may be imposed on all persons who are determined by the IRS to be responsible for collecting, accounting for, and paying over these taxes, and who acted willfully in not doing so. See section 7 of Pub. 51 (Circular A) for more information.

Specific Instructions

Line 1. Number of Agricultural Employees

Enter the number of agricultural employees on your payroll during the pay period that included March 12, 2012. Do not include household employees, persons who received no pay during the pay period, pensioners, or members of the Armed Forces.

An entry of 250 or more on line 1 indicates that you must file Forms W-2 electronically. Call the SSA at 1-800-772-6270 or visit the SSA's Employer W-2 Filing Instructions and Information website at *www.socialsecurity.gov/employer* for more information about filing electronically.

Line 2. Total Wages Subject to Social Security Tax

Enter the total cash wages subject to social security tax that you paid to your employees for farmwork during the calendar year. Enter the amount before deductions. Cash wages include checks, money orders, etc. Do not include the value of noncash items, such as food or lodging, or pay for services other than farmwork. See *Purpose of Form 943,* earlier, for household employee information. See section 3 of Pub. 51 (Circular A) for information on taxable wages.

For 2012, the rate of social security tax on taxable wages is 6.2% (.062) for the employer and 4.2% (.042) for the employee or 10.4% (.104) for both. Do not report an employee's social security wages over $110,100 for 2012.

If you, as a qualifying employer, receive an approved Form 4029, Application for Exemption From Social Security and Medicare Taxes and Waiver of Benefits, from one or more of your employees, write "Form 4029" to the right of the entry space.

Line 4. Total Wages Subject to Medicare Tax

Enter the total cash wages subject to Medicare tax that you paid to your employees for farmwork during the calendar year. Enter the amount before deductions. Do not include the value of noncash items, such as food or lodging, or pay for services other than farmwork. There is no limit on the amount of wages subject to Medicare tax. If you, as a qualifying employer, receive an approved Form 4029 from one or more of your employees, write "Form 4029" to the right of the entry space.

Line 6. Federal Income Tax Withheld

Enter federal income tax withheld on wages paid to your employees. Generally, you must withhold federal income tax from employees from whom you withhold social security and Medicare taxes. See sections 5 and 13 of Pub. 51 (Circular A) for more information on withholding rules.

Line 7. Total Taxes Before Adjustments

Add the total social security tax (line 3), Medicare tax (line 5), and federal income tax withheld (line 6). Enter the result on line 7.

Line 8. Adjustments to Taxes

Use line 8 to:
- Adjust for rounding of fractions of cents, or
- Adjust for the uncollected employee share of social security and Medicare taxes on third-party sick pay or group-term life insurance premiums paid for former employees. See section 9 in Pub. 51 (Circular A).

Use a minus sign (if possible) to show a decrease to the amounts reported on lines 3 or 5. Otherwise, use parentheses.

Adjustment for fractions of cents. If there is a small difference between total taxes after adjustments (line 9) and total deposits (line 10), it may be caused by rounding to the nearest cent each time you computed payroll. This rounding occurs when you figure the amount of social security and Medicare tax to be withheld from each employee's wages. If the fractions of cents adjustment is the only entry on line 8, write "Fractions Only" on the dotted line to the left of the entry space for line 8.

Adjustment for sick pay. Enter the adjustment for the employee share of social security and Medicare taxes that were withheld and deposited by your third-party sick pay payer with regard to sick pay paid by the third-party. These wages should be included on lines 2 and 4.

Increases and decreases in tax liability. Because any amount shown on line 8 increases or decreases your tax liability, the adjustment must also be included on your Monthly Summary of Federal Tax Liability on Form 943 (line 15) or Form 943-A, Agricultural Employer's Record of

Federal Tax Liability. For details on how to report adjustments on the Monthly Summary of Federal Tax Liability, see the instructions for line 15. For details on how to report adjustments on Form 943-A (for use by semiweekly depositors only), see the Form 943-A instructions.

Line 9. Total Taxes After Adjustments

Combine lines 7 and 8; enter the result on line 9.

Line 10. Total Deposits

Enter your total Form 943 deposits for the year, including any overpayment that you applied from filing Form 943-X and any overpayment that you applied from your 2011 return.

Line 11a. COBRA Premium Assistance Payments

Enter 65% of the COBRA premiums for assistance eligible individuals. Take the COBRA premium assistance credit on this line only after the assistance eligible individual's 35% share of the premium has been paid. For COBRA coverage provided under a self-insured plan, COBRA premium assistance is treated as having been made for each assistance eligible individual who pays 35% of the COBRA premium. Do not include the assistance eligible individual's 35% of the premium in the amount entered on this line. For more information on the COBRA premium assistance credit, visit IRS.gov and enter the keyword *COBRA*.

 The amount reported on line 11a is treated as a deposit of taxes on the first day of your return period and must not be used to adjust line 15 or Form 943-A.

Line 11b. Number of Individuals Provided COBRA Premium Assistance on Line 11a

Enter the total number of individuals provided COBRA premium assistance payments reported on line 11a. Count each assistance eligible individual who paid a reduced COBRA premium during the year as one individual, whether or not the reduced premium was for insurance that covered more than one assistance eligible individual. For example, if the reduced COBRA premium was for coverage for a former employee, spouse, and two children, you would include one individual in the number entered on line 11b for the premium assistance. Further, each individual is reported only once per year. For example, an assistance eligible individual who made monthly premium payments would only be reported as one individual.

Line 13. Balance Due

If line 9 is more than line 12, enter the difference on line 13. Otherwise, see *Overpayment* below. You do not have to pay if line 13 is under $1. Generally, you should show a balance due on line 13 only if your total taxes after adjustments for the year (line 9) is less than $2,500. However, see section 7 of Pub. 51 (Circular A) regarding payments made under the accuracy of deposits rule.

You may pay the amount shown on line 13 using EFTPS, a credit or debit card, or a check or money order. **Do not** use a credit or debit card to pay taxes that were required to be deposited. For more information on electronic payment options, visit the IRS website at *www.irs.gov/e-pay*.

If you pay by EFTPS or credit or debit card, file your return using the *Without a payment* address under *Where To File*, earlier. **Do not** file Form 943-V, Payment Voucher.

If you pay by check or money order, make it payable to the "United States Treasury." Enter your EIN, Form 943, and the tax period on your check or money order. Complete Form 943-V and enclose with Form 943.

 If you did not make deposits as required and instead pay the taxes with Form 943, you may be subject to a penalty.

Line 14. Overpayment

If line 12 is more than line 9, enter the difference on line 14. **Never make an entry on both lines 13 and 14.**

If you deposited more than the correct amount for the year, you can have the overpayment refunded or applied to your next return by checking the appropriate box on line 14. Check only one box on line 14. If you do not check either box or if you check both boxes, generally we will apply the overpayment to your account. We may apply your overpayment to any past due tax account that is shown in our records under your EIN.

If line 14 is under $1, we will send you a refund or apply it to your next return only if you ask us in writing to do so.

Line 15. Monthly Summary of Federal Tax Liability

This is a summary of your yearly tax liability, not a summary of deposits made. If line 9 is less than $2,500, **do not** complete line 15 or Form 943-A.

Complete line 15 only if you were a **monthly schedule depositor** for the entire year and line 9 is $2,500 or more. The amount entered on line 15M must equal the amount reported on line 9. See section 7 of Pub. 51 (Circular A) for details on the deposit rules. You are a monthly schedule depositor for the calendar year if the amount of your Form 943 taxes (line 9) reported for the lookback period is not more than $50,000. The lookback period is the second calendar year preceding the current calendar year. For example, the lookback period for 2013 is 2011.

 If you were a semiweekly schedule depositor during any part of the year, do not complete line 15. Instead, complete Form 943-A.

Reporting adjustments on line 15. If your net adjustment during a month is negative and it exceeds your total liability for the month, do not enter a negative amount for the month. Instead, enter "-0-" for the month and carry over the unused portion of the adjustment to the next month.

Additional Information

Pub. 51 (Circular A) has information that you may need about social security, Medicare, federal unemployment (FUTA), and withheld federal income taxes. It includes tables showing the federal income tax to withhold from an employee's wages.

Third-Party Designee

If you want to allow an employee, a paid tax preparer, or another person to discuss your Form 943 with the IRS, check the "Yes" box in the "Third-Party Designee" section. Then tell us the name, phone number, and the five-digit personal identification number (PIN) of the specific person to speak with—not the name of the firm who prepared your tax return. The designee may choose any five numbers as his or her PIN.

By checking "Yes," you authorize the IRS to talk to the person you named (your designee) about any questions we may have while we process your return. You also authorize your designee to:

• Give us any information that is missing from your return,
• Call us for information about processing your return, and
• Respond to certain IRS notices that you have shared with your designee about math errors and return preparation. The IRS will not send notices to your designee.

You are not authorizing your designee to bind you to anything (including additional tax liability) or to otherwise represent you before the IRS. If you want to expand your designee's authorization, see Pub. 947, Practice Before the IRS and Power of Attorney.

The authorization will automatically expire 1 year from the due date (without regard to extensions) for filing your Form 943. If you or your designee wants to terminate the authorization, write to the IRS office for your locality using the *Without a payment* address under *Where To File,* earlier.

Who Must Sign

Form 943 must be signed as follows:
• **Sole proprietorship** — The individual who owns the business.
• **Corporation (including a limited liability company (LLC) treated as a corporation)** — The president, vice president, or other principal officer duly authorized to sign.
• **Partnership (including an LLC treated as a partnership) or unincorporated organization** — A responsible and duly authorized partner, member, or officer having knowledge of its affairs.
• **Single member LLC treated as a disregarded entity for federal income tax purposes** — The owner of the LLC or a principal officer duly authorized to sign.
• **Trust or estate** — The fiduciary.

Form 943 may also be signed by a duly authorized agent of the taxpayer if a valid power of attorney has been filed.

Alternative signature method. Corporate officers or duly authorized agents may sign Form 943 by rubber stamp, mechanical device, or computer software

program. For details and required documentation, see Rev. Proc. 2005-39. You can find Rev. Proc. 2005-39 on page 82 of Internal Revenue Bulletin 2005-28 at *www.irs.gov/irb/2005-28_IRB/ar16.html*.

Paid Preparer Use Only

A paid preparer must sign Form 943 and enter the information requested in the *Paid Preparer Use Only* section if the preparer was paid to prepare Form 943 and is not an employee of the filing entity. Paid preparers must sign paper returns with a manual signature. The preparer must give you a copy of the return in addition to the copy to be filed with the IRS.

If you are a paid preparer, enter your Preparer Tax Identification Number (PTIN) in the space provided. Include your complete address. If you work for a firm, enter the firm's name and the EIN of the firm. You can apply for a PTIN online or by filing Form W-12, IRS Paid Preparer Tax Identification Number (PTIN) Application and Renewal. For more information about applying for a PTIN online, visit the IRS website at *www.irs.gov/ptin*. You cannot use your PTIN in place of the EIN of the tax preparation firm.

Generally, do not complete this section if you are filing Form 943 as a reporting agent and have a valid Form 8655, Reporting Agent Authorization, on file with the IRS. However, a reporting agent must complete this section if the reporting agent offered legal advice, for example, advising the client on determining whether its workers are employees or independent contractors for federal tax purposes.

Privacy Act and Paperwork Reduction Act Notice. We ask for the information on Forms 943, 943-A, and 943-V to carry out the Internal Revenue laws of the United States. We need it to figure and collect the right amount of tax. Subtitle C, Employment Taxes, of the Internal Revenue Code imposes employment taxes on wages, including income tax withholding. These forms are used to report the amount of taxes that you owe. Section 6011 requires you to provide the requested information if the tax applies to you. Section 6109 requires you to provide your identification number. If you fail to provide this information in a timely manner, or provide false or fraudulent information, you may be subject to penalties and interest.

You are not required to provide the information requested on a form that is subject to the Paperwork Reduction Act unless the form displays a valid OMB control number. Books or records relating to a form or its instructions must be retained as long as their contents may become material in the administration of any Internal Revenue law.

Generally, tax returns and return information are confidential, as required by section 6103. However, section 6103 allows or requires us to disclose this information to others as described in the Code. We may disclose your tax information to the Department of Justice for civil and criminal litigation, and to cities, states, the District of Columbia, and U.S. commonwealths and possessions to administer their tax laws. We may also disclose this information to other countries under a tax treaty, to federal and state agencies to enforce federal nontax criminal laws, or to federal law enforcement and intelligence agencies to combat terrorism.

The time needed to complete and file these forms will vary depending on individual circumstances. The estimated average time for **Form 943** is: Recordkeeping, 10 hr., 45 min.; Learning about the law or the form, 30 min.; Preparing and sending the form to the IRS, 42 min. The estimated average time for **Form 943-A** is: Recordkeeping, 6 hr., 42 min.; Preparing and sending the form to the IRS, 6 min. The estimated average time for

Form 943-V is 14 min. If you have comments concerning the accuracy of these time estimates or suggestions for making these forms simpler, we would be happy to hear from you. You can email us at *taxforms@irs.gov*. Enter "Form 943" on the subject line. Or write to the Internal Revenue Service, Tax Products Coordinating Committee, SE:W:CAR:MP:T:M:S, 1111 Constitution Ave. NW, IR-6526, Washington, DC 20224. **Do not** send Form 943 to this address. Instead, see *Where To File,* earlier.

Form **943-A**
(Rev. October 2012)
Department of the Treasury
Internal Revenue Service

**Agricultural Employer's Record of
Federal Tax Liability**

▶ Information about Form 943-A and its instructions is at *www.irs.gov/form943a.*
▶ File with Form 943 or Form 943-X.

OMB No. 1545-0035

__ __ __ __
Calendar Year

Name (as shown on Form 943)

Employer identification number (EIN)

You must complete this form if you are required to deposit on a semiweekly schedule or if your tax liability during any month was $100,000 or more. Show tax liability here, not deposits. (The IRS gets deposit data from electronic funds transfers.) **DO NOT change your tax liability by adjustments reported on any Forms 943-X.**

January Tax Liability				February Tax Liability				March Tax Liability			
1		16		1		16		1		16	
2		17		2		17		2		17	
3		18		3		18		3		18	
4		19		4		19		4		19	
5		20		5		20		5		20	
6		21		6		21		6		21	
7		22		7		22		7		22	
8		23		8		23		8		23	
9		24		9		24		9		24	
10		25		10		25		10		25	
11		26		11		26		11		26	
12		27		12		27		12		27	
13		28		13		28		13		28	
14		29		14		29		14		29	
15		30		15				15		30	
		31								31	

A Total liability for month ▶   **B** Total liability for month ▶   **C** Total liability for month ▶

April Tax Liability				May Tax Liability				June Tax Liability			
1		16		1		16		1		16	
2		17		2		17		2		17	
3		18		3		18		3		18	
4		19		4		19		4		19	
5		20		5		20		5		20	
6		21		6		21		6		21	
7		22		7		22		7		22	
8		23		8		23		8		23	
9		24		9		24		9		24	
10		25		10		25		10		25	
11		26		11		26		11		26	
12		27		12		27		12		27	
13		28		13		28		13		28	
14		29		14		29		14		29	
15		30		15		30		15		30	
						31					

D Total liability for month ▶   **E** Total liability for month ▶   **F** Total liability for month ▶

For Privacy Act and Paperwork Reduction Act Notice, see the separate Instructions for Form 943.   Cat. No. 17030C   Form **943-A** (Rev. 10-2012)

Form 943-A (Rev. 10-2012)   Page **2**

July Tax Liability				August Tax Liability				September Tax Liability			
1		16		1		16		1		16	
2		17		2		17		2		17	
3		18		3		18		3		18	
4		19		4		19		4		19	
5		20		5		20		5		20	
6		21		6		21		6		21	
7		22		7		22		7		22	
8		23		8		23		8		23	
9		24		9		24		9		24	
10		25		10		25		10		25	
11		26		11		26		11		26	
12		27		12		27		12		27	
13		28		13		28		13		28	
14		29		14		29		14		29	
15		30		15		30		15		30	
		31				31					

G Total liability for month ▶   **H** Total liability for month ▶   **I** Total liability for month ▶

October Tax Liability				November Tax Liability				December Tax Liability			
1		16		1		16		1		16	
2		17		2		17		2		17	
3		18		3		18		3		18	
4		19		4		19		4		19	
5		20		5		20		5		20	
6		21		6		21		6		21	
7		22		7		22		7		22	
8		23		8		23		8		23	
9		24		9		24		9		24	
10		25		10		25		10		25	
11		26		11		26		11		26	
12		27		12		27		12		27	
13		28		13		28		13		28	
14		29		14		29		14		29	
15		30		15		30		15		30	
		31								31	

J Total liability for month ▶   **K** Total liability for month ▶   **L** Total liability for month ▶

M Total tax liability for year (add lines A through L)   . . . . ▶

Form **943-A** (Rev. 10-2012)

Future Developments

For the latest information about developments related to Form 943-A and its instructions, such as legislation enacted after they were published, go to *www.irs.gov/form943a.*

Reminders

Reporting prior period adjustments. Prior period adjustments are reported on Form 943-X, Adjusted Employer's Annual Federal Tax Return for Agricultural Employees or Claim for Refund, and are not taken into account when figuring the tax liability for the current year.

When you file Form 943-A with your Form 943, **do not** change your tax liability by adjustments reported on any Forms 943-X.

Amended Form 943-A. If you have been assessed a failure-to-deposit (FTD) penalty, you may be able to file an amended Form 943-A. See *Amending a Previously Filed Form 943-A,* later.

General Instructions

Purpose of form. Use this form to report your tax liability (federal income tax withheld plus both employee and employer social security and Medicare taxes). Do not show federal tax deposits here.

Do not report taxes on wages paid to nonfarm workers on this form. Taxes on wages paid to nonfarm workers are reported on Form 941/941-SS, Employer's QUARTERLY Federal Tax Return, or Form 944, Employer's ANNUAL Federal Tax Return. Do not attach Form 943-A to your Form 941/941-SS or Form 944. Instead, use Schedule B (Form 941) or Form 945-A, Annual Return of Federal Tax Liability (with Form 944).

Caution. IRS uses Form 943-A to determine if you have timely deposited your Form 943 tax liabilities. If you are a semiweekly schedule depositor and you do not properly complete and file Form 943-A with Form 943, the IRS may propose an "averaged" failure-to-deposit penalty. See *Deposit Penalties* in section 7 of Pub. 51 (Circular A), Agricultural Employer's Tax Guide, for more information.

Who must file. Semiweekly schedule depositors are required to complete and file Form 943-A with Form 943. Monthly schedule depositors who accumulate $100,000 or more during any month become semiweekly schedule depositors on the next day and must also complete and file Form 943-A. Do not file this form if you were a monthly schedule depositor for the entire year or if your total taxes after adjustments for the year (Form 943, line 9) are less than $2,500.

Note. If you use this form, do not complete Form 943, line 15.

When to file. File Form 943-A with your Form 943 every year when Form 943 is due. See the Instructions for Form 943 for due dates.

Specific Instructions

Enter your business information. Carefully enter your employer identification number (EIN) and name at the top of the form. Make sure that they exactly match the name of your business and the EIN that the IRS assigned to your business and also agree with the name and EIN shown on the attached Form 943.

Calendar year. Enter the calendar year of the Form 943 or Form 943-X to which Form 943-A is attached.

Enter your tax liability by month. Enter your tax liabilities in the spaces that correspond to the dates you **paid** wages to your employees, not the date payroll deposits were made. The total tax liability for the year (line M) must equal total taxes after adjustments on Form 943 (line 9). Report your tax liabilities on this form corresponding to the dates of each wage payment, not to when payroll liabilities are accrued. Enter the monthly totals on lines A, B, C, D, E, F, G, H, I, J, K, and L. Enter the total for the year on line M.

For example, if your payroll period ended on December 31, 2011, and you **paid** the wages for that period on January 6, 2012, you would:

• Go to January, and

• Enter your tax liability on line 6 (because line 6 represents the sixth day of the month).

 Make sure you have checked the appropriate box below line 14 of Form 943 to show that you are a semiweekly schedule depositor.

Here are some additional examples:

• Employer A is a **semiweekly** schedule depositor. Employer A accumulated a federal tax liability of $3,000 on its January 11 and January 25 paydays. In the January column, Employer A must enter $3,000 on lines 11 and 25.

• Employer B is a **semiweekly** schedule depositor who paid wages in October, November, and December on the last day of the month. On December 22, 2012, Employer B also paid its employees year-end bonuses (subject to employment taxes). Because Employer B is a semiweekly schedule depositor, Employer B must record employment tax liabilities on Form 943-A.

Month	Lines for dates wages were paid
October	line 31 (pay day, last day of the month)
November	line 30 (pay day, last day of the month)
December	lines 22 (bonus paid) + 31 (pay day, last day of the month)

• Employer C is a new business and **monthly** schedule depositor for 2012. Employer C pays wages every Thursday. Employer C incurred a $2,000 employment tax liability on 10/11/12. Employer C incurred a $110,000 liability on 10/18/12 and on every subsequent Thursday during 2012. Under the deposit rules, employers **become semiweekly schedule depositors** on the day after any day they accumulate $100,000 or more of tax liability in a deposit period.

Because Employer C accumulated $112,000 on 10/18/12, Employer C became a semiweekly schedule depositor on the next day and must complete Form 943-A and file it with Form 943.

Month	Lines for dates wages were paid	Amount to record
October	line 11	$2,000
October	lines 18, 25	$110,000
November	lines 1, 8, 15, 22, 29	$110,000
December	lines 6, 13, 20, 27	$110,000

See *Depositing Taxes* in Pub. 51 (Circular A) for more information.

Amending a Previously Filed Form 943-A

Semiweekly schedule depositors. If you have been assessed a failure-to-deposit (FTD) penalty and you made an error on Form 943-A and the correction will not change the total liability you reported on Form 943-A, you may be able to reduce your penalty by filing an amended Form 943-A.

Example. You reported a liability of $3,000 on January 1. However, the liability was actually for March. Prepare an amended Form 943-A showing the $3,000 liability on March 1. Also, you must enter the liabilities previously reported for the year that did not change. Write "Amended" at the top of Form 943-A. The IRS will refigure the penalty and notify you of any change in the penalty.

Monthly schedule depositors. You can also file an amended Form 943-A if you have been assessed an FTD penalty and you made an error on the monthly tax liability section of Form 943. When completing Form 943-A for this situation, only enter the monthly totals. The daily entries are not required.

Where to file. File your amended Form 943-A at the address provided in the penalty notice you received. You do not have to submit your original Form 943-A.

Form 943-X

Tax decrease. If you are filing Form 943-X, you can file an amended Form 943-A with Form 943-X if both of the following apply.

1. You have a tax decrease.

2. You were assessed an FTD penalty.

File your amended Form 943-A with Form 943-X. The total liability reported on your amended Form 943-A must equal the corrected amount of tax reported on Form 943-X. If your penalty is decreased, the IRS will include the penalty decrease with your tax decrease.

Tax increase—Form 943-X filed timely. If you are filing a timely Form 943-X showing a tax increase, do not file an amended Form 943-A, unless you were assessed an FTD penalty caused by an incorrect, incomplete, or missing Form 943-A. Do not include the tax increase reported on Form 943-X on an amended Form 943-A you file.

Tax increase—Form 943-X filed late. If you owe tax and are filing Form 943-X late, that is, after the due date for Form 943 for the year in which you discovered the error, you must file an amended Form 943-A with the Form 943-X. Otherwise, IRS may assess an "averaged" FTD penalty.

The total tax reported on line M of Form 943-A must match the corrected tax (Form 943, line 9 (line 11 for years before 2011) combined with any correction reported on Form 943-X, line 14, minus any advanced EIC reported on Form 943-X, line 15) for the year, less any previous abatements and interest-free tax assessments.

Form **944 for 2012:**   **Employer's ANNUAL Federal Tax Return**

Department of the Treasury — Internal Revenue Service

OMB No. 1545-2007

Employer identification number (EIN) [ ] [ ] – [ ] [ ] [ ] [ ] [ ] [ ] [ ]

Name *(not your trade name)* [   ]

Trade name *(if any)* [   ]

Address [   ]
Number   Street   Suite or room number

[   ]
City   State   ZIP code

Who Must File Form 944

You must file annual Form 944 instead of filing quarterly Forms 941 **only if the IRS notified you in writing.** You also must file Form 944 (or Form 944 (SP)) for 2012 if you filed Form 944-SS or Form 944-PR in 2011 and you did not request to file Forms 941-SS or Forms 941-PR for 2012. Instructions and prior-year forms are available at *www.irs.gov/form944.*

Read the separate instructions before you complete Form 944. Type or print within the boxes.

Part 1:   Answer these questions for this year. Employers in American Samoa, Guam, the Commonwealth of the Northern Mariana Islands, the U.S. Virgin Islands, and Puerto Rico can skip lines 1 and 2.

1   Wages, tips, and other compensation . . . .   **1** [.   ]

2   FEDERAL income tax withheld from wages, tips, and other compensation . . . . .   **2** [.   ]

3   If no wages, tips, and other compensation are subject to social security or Medicare tax   **3** [ ] Check and go to line 5.

4   Taxable social security and Medicare wages and tips:

	Column 1		Column 2	
4a Taxable social security wages	[.]	× .104 =	[.]	For 2012, the employee social security tax rate is 4.2% and the Medicare tax rate is 1.45%. The employer social security tax rate is 6.2% and the Medicare tax rate is 1.45%.
4b Taxable social security tips	[.]	× .104 =	[.]	
4c Taxable Medicare wages & tips	[.]	× .029 =	[.]	

4d   Add *Column 2* line 4a, *Column 2* line 4b, and *Column 2* line 4c . . . .   **4d** [.   ]

5   Total taxes before adjustments (add lines 2 and 4d) . . . .   **5** [.   ]

6   Current year's adjustments (see instructions) . . . .   **6** [.   ]

7   Total taxes after adjustments. Combine lines 5 and 6 . . . .   **7** [.   ]

8   Total deposits for this year, including overpayment applied from a prior year and overpayment applied from Form 944-X, 944-X (PR), 944-X (SP), 941-X, or 941-X (PR) . .   **8** [.   ]

9a   COBRA premium assistance payments (see instructions) . . . .   **9a** [.   ]

9b   Number of individuals provided COBRA premium assistance   [   ]

10   Add lines 8 and 9a . . . .   **10** [.   ]

11   Balance due. If line 7 is more than line 10, enter the difference and see instructions . . . .   **11** [.   ]

12   Overpayment. If line 10 is more than line 7, enter the difference   [.   ]   Check one: [ ] Apply to next return.   [ ] Send a refund.

▶ **You MUST complete both pages of Form 944 and SIGN it.**   Next ▶

For Privacy Act and Paperwork Reduction Act Notice, see the back of the Payment Voucher.   Cat. No. 39316N   Form **944** (2012)

Name *(not your trade name)*

Employer identification number (EIN)

Part 2: Tell us about your deposit schedule and tax liability for this year.

13 Check one: ☐ Line 7 is less than $2,500. Go to Part 3.

☐ Line 7 is $2,500 or more. Enter your tax liability for each month. If you are a semiweekly depositor or you accumulate $100,000 or more of liability on any day during a deposit period, you must complete Form 945-A instead of the boxes below.

	Jan.		Apr.		Jul.		Oct.
13a	·	**13d**	·	**13g**	·	**13j**	·
	Feb.		May		Aug.		Nov.
13b	·	**13e**	·	**13h**	·	**13k**	·
	Mar.		Jun.		Sep.		Dec.
13c	·	**13f**	·	**13i**	·	**13l**	·

Total liability for year. Add lines 13a through 13l. Total must equal line 7.   **13m** ☐ ·

Part 3: Tell us about your business. If question 14 does NOT apply to your business, leave it blank.

14 If your business has closed or you stopped paying wages...

☐ Check here and enter the final date you paid wages. ☐

Part 4: May we speak with your third-party designee?

Do you want to allow an employee, a paid tax preparer, or another person to discuss this return with the IRS? See the instructions for details.

☐ Yes. Designee's name and phone number ☐ ☐

Select a 5-digit Personal Identification Number (PIN) to use when talking to IRS. ☐ ☐ ☐ ☐ ☐

☐ No.

Part 5: Sign Here. You MUST complete both pages of Form 944 and SIGN it.

Under penalties of perjury, I declare that I have examined this return, including accompanying schedules and statements, and to the best of my knowledge and belief, it is true, correct, and complete. Declaration of preparer (other than taxpayer) is based on all information of which preparer has any knowledge.

✗ **Sign your name here**

Print your name here

Print your title here

Date

Best daytime phone

Paid Preparer Use Only   Check if you are self-employed ☐

Preparer's name	PTIN
Preparer's signature	Date
Firm's name (or yours if self-employed)	EIN
Address	Phone
City	State	ZIP code

Page **2**   Form **944** (2012)

Form 944-V,
Payment Voucher

Purpose of Form

Complete Form 944-V, Payment Voucher, if you are making a payment with Form 944, Employer's ANNUAL Federal Tax Return. We will use the completed voucher to credit your payment more promptly and accurately, and to improve our service to you.

Making Payments With Form 944

To avoid a penalty, make your payment with your 2012 Form 944 **only if** one of the following applies.

• Your net taxes for the year (Form 944, line 7) are less than $2,500 and you are paying in full with a timely filed return.

• You already deposited the taxes you owed for the first, second, and third quarters of 2012, and the tax you owe for the fourth quarter of 2012 is less than $2,500, and you are paying, in full, the tax you owe for the fourth quarter of 2012 with a timely filed return.

• Your net taxes for the third quarter are $2,500 or more, net taxes for the fourth quarter are less than $2,500, and you did not incur a $100,000 next-day deposit obligation during the fourth quarter.

• You are a monthly schedule depositor making a payment in accordance with the Accuracy of Deposits Rule. See section 11 of Pub. 15 (Circular E), Employer's Tax Guide, for details. In this case, the amount of your payment may be $2,500 or more.

Otherwise, you must make deposits by electronic funds transfer. See section 11 of Pub. 15 (Circular E) for deposit instructions. Do not use Form 944-V to make federal tax deposits.

Caution. *Use Form 944-V when making any payment with Form 944. However, if you pay an amount with Form 944 that should have been deposited, you may be subject to a penalty. See* Deposit Penalties *in section 11 of Pub. 15 (Circular E).*

Specific Instructions

Box 1—Employer identification number (EIN). If you do not have an EIN, you may apply for one online. Go to IRS.gov and click on the *Apply for an EIN Online* link under *Tools.* You may also apply for an EIN by calling 1-800-829-4933, or you can fax or mail Form SS-4, Application for Employer Identification Number. If you have not received your EIN by the due date of Form 944, write "Applied For" and the date you applied in this entry space.

Box 2—Amount paid. Enter the amount paid with Form 944.

Box 3—Name and address. Enter your name and address as shown on Form 944.

• Enclose your check or money order made payable to the "United States Treasury" and write your EIN, "Form 944," and "2012" on your check or money order. Do not send cash. Do not staple Form 944-V or your payment to Form 944 (or to each other).

• Detach Form 944-V and send it with your payment and Form 944 to the address provided in the Instructions for Form 944. Do not send a photocopy of Form 944-V because your payment may be misapplied or delayed.

Note. You must also complete the entity information above Part 1 on Form 944.

Detach Here and Mail With Your Payment and Form 944.

✂ - - - - - ▼ - ▼ - - - - - - - - - ✂

Form **944-V**	**Payment Voucher**	OMB No. 1545-2007
Department of the Treasury Internal Revenue Service	▶ **Do not staple this voucher or your payment to Form 944.**	20**12**

1 Enter your employer identification number (EIN).	2 **Enter the amount of your payment.** ▶ Make your check or money order payable to "**United States Treasury**"	Dollars	Cents
	3 Enter your business name (individual name if sole proprietor).		
	Enter your address.		
	Enter your city, state, and ZIP code.		

Privacy Act and Paperwork Reduction Act Notice. We ask for the information on this form to carry out the Internal Revenue laws of the United States. We need it to figure and collect the right amount of tax. Subtitle C, Employment Taxes, of the Internal Revenue Code imposes employment taxes on wages, including income tax withholding. This form is used to determine the amount of the taxes that you owe. Section 6011 requires you to provide the requested information if the tax is applicable to you. Section 6109 requires you to provide your identification number. If you fail to provide this information in a timely manner, or provide false or fraudulent information, you may be subject to penalties and interest.

You are not required to provide the information requested on a form that is subject to the Paperwork Reduction Act unless the form displays a valid OMB control number. Books and records relating to a form or instructions must be retained as long as their contents may become material in the administration of any Internal Revenue law.

Generally, tax returns and return information are confidential, as required by section 6103. However, section 6103 allows or requires the IRS to disclose or give the information shown on your tax return to others as described in the Code. For example, we may disclose your tax information to the Department of Justice for civil and criminal litigation, and to cities, states, the District of Columbia, and U.S. commonwealths and possessions for use in administering their tax laws. We may also disclose this information to other countries under a tax treaty, to federal and state agencies to enforce federal nontax criminal laws, or to federal law enforcement and intelligence agencies to combat terrorism.

The time needed to complete and file Form 944 will vary depending on individual circumstances. The estimated average time is:

Recordkeeping . . . . 10 hrs., 45 min.

Learning about the law or the form . . . . 24 min.

Preparing, copying, assembling, and sending the form to the IRS . . . . 35 min.

If you have comments concerning the accuracy of these time estimates or suggestions for making Form 944 simpler, we would be happy to hear from you. You can email us at *taxforms@irs.gov.* Enter "Form 944" on the subject line. Or write to: Internal Revenue Service, Tax Products Coordinating Committee, SE:W:CAR:MP:T:M:S, 1111 Constitution Ave. NW, IR-6526, Washington, DC 20224. **Do not** send Form 944 to this address. Instead, see *Where Should You File?* in the Instructions for Form 944.

20**12**

Department of the Treasury
Internal Revenue Service

Instructions for Form 944

Employer's ANNUAL Federal Tax Return

Section references are to the Internal Revenue Code unless otherwise noted.

Future Developments

For the latest information about developments related to Form 944 and its instructions, such as legislation enacted after they were published, go to *www.irs.gov/form944*.

What's New

Forms 944-SS and 944-PR discontinued. Form 944-SS, Employer's ANNUAL Federal Tax Return—American Samoa, Guam, the Commonwealth of the Northern Mariana Islands, and the U.S. Virgin Islands, and Form 944-PR, Planilla para la Declaración Federal ANUAL del Patrono, will no longer be issued by the IRS after 2011.

Beginning with tax year 2012, employers who previously filed Form 944-SS or 944-PR will continue to file annually using Form 944 (or Form 944 (SP), Declaración Federal ANUAL de Impuestos del Patrono o Empleador, the Spanish language equivalent of Form 944). Alternatively, employers in American Samoa, Guam, the Commonwealth of the Northern Mariana Islands, and the U.S. Virgin Islands may request to file Forms 941-SS, Employer's QUARTERLY Federal Tax Return—American Samoa, Guam, the Commonwealth of the Northern Mariana Islands, and the U.S. Virgin Islands, instead of Form 944 or Form 944 (SP). Employers in Puerto Rico may request to file Forms 941-PR, Planilla para la Declaración Federal TRIMESTRAL del Patrono, instead of Form 944 or Form 944 (SP).

Social security and Medicare taxes for 2012. The employee tax rate for social security is 4.2%. The employer tax rate for social security remains unchanged at 6.2%. The Medicare tax rate is 1.45% each for the employee and employer, unchanged from 2011. The social security wage base limit is $110,100. There is no wage base limit for Medicare tax.

Social security and Medicare taxes apply to the wages of household workers you pay $1,800 or more in cash or an equivalent form of compensation. Social security and Medicare taxes apply to election workers who are paid $1,500 or more in cash or an equivalent form of compensation.

VOW to Hire Heroes Act of 2011. On November 21, 2011, the President signed into law the VOW to Hire Heroes Act of 2011. This new law provides an expanded work opportunity tax credit to businesses that hire eligible unemployed veterans and, for the first time, also makes part of the credit available to certain tax-exempt organizations. Businesses claim the credit as part of the general business credit and tax-exempt organizations claim it against their payroll tax liability using Form 5884-C, Work Opportunity Credit for Qualified Tax-Exempt Organizations Hiring Qualified Veterans. The liability reported on Form 944 is not reduced by the amount of the credit. The credit is available for eligible unemployed veterans who begin work on or after November 22, 2011, and before January 1, 2013. For more information about the credit, visit *www.irs.gov/form5884c*.

Change of address. Use Form 8822-B, Change of Address—Business, to notify the IRS of an address change.

Reminders

Employers can choose to file Forms 941, 941-SS, or 941-PR instead of Form 944. Employers required to file Form 944, who want to file Forms 941, 941-SS, or 941-PR instead, must notify the IRS they are electing to file quarterly Forms 941, 941-SS, or 941-PR and opting out of filing Form 944. See *What if you want to file Forms 941, 941-SS, or 941-PR instead of Form 944*, later.

Correcting a previously filed Form 944 or 944-SS. If you discover an error on a previously filed Form 944 or 944-SS, make the correction using Form 944-X, Adjusted Employer's ANNUAL Federal Tax Return or Claim for Refund. Form 944-X is filed separately from Form 944. For more information, see section 13 of Pub. 15 (Circular E), Employer's Tax Guide, or section 9 of Pub. 80 (Circular SS), Federal Tax Guide for Employers in the U.S. Virgin Islands, Guam, American Samoa, and the Commonwealth of the Northern Mariana Islands. You may also visit IRS.gov and enter the keywords *Correcting Employment Taxes*.

Correcting a previously filed Form 944-PR. If you discover an error on a previously filed Form 944-PR, make the correction using Form 944-X (PR), Ajuste a la Declaración Federal ANNUAL del Patrono o Reclamación de Reembolso. Form 944-X (PR) is filed separately from Form 944. For more information, see section 12 of Pub. 179 (Circular PR), Guía Contributiva Federal para Paronos Puertorriqueños. You may also visit IRS.gov and enter the keywords *Correcting Employment Taxes*.

Paid preparers must sign Form 944. Paid preparers must complete and sign the paid preparer's section of Form 944.

COBRA premium assistance credit. The credit for COBRA premium assistance payments applies to premiums paid for employees involuntarily terminated between September 1, 2008, and May 31, 2010, and to premiums paid for up to 15 months. See the instructions for line 9a, later.

Federal tax deposits must be made by electronic funds transfer. You must use electronic funds transfer to make all federal tax deposits. Generally, electronic funds transfers are made using the Electronic Federal Tax Payment System (EFTPS). If you do not want to use EFTPS, you can arrange for your tax professional, financial institution, payroll service, or other trusted third party to make deposits on your behalf. Also, you may arrange for your financial institution to initiate a same-day wire payment on your behalf. EFTPS is a free service provided by the Department of Treasury. Services provided by your tax professional, financial institution, payroll service, or other third party may have a fee.

For more information on making federal tax deposits, see section 11 of Pub. 15 (Circular E), section 8 of Pub. 80

Oct 22, 2012   Cat. No. 39820A

(Circular SS), or section 11 of Pub. 179 (Circular PR). To get more information about EFTPS or to enroll in EFTPS, visit *www.eftps.gov* or call one of the following numbers.
- 1-800-555-4477
- 1-800-733-4829 (TDD)
- 1-800-244-4829 (Spanish)
- 303-967-5916 (toll call)

Additional information about EFTPS is also available in Pub. 966, Electronic Federal Tax Payment System: A Guide to Getting Started, or Pub. 966 (SP), Sistema de Pago Electrónico del Impuesto Federal: La Manera Segura de Pagar los Impuestos Federales.

 For an EFTPS deposit to be on time, you must initiate the deposit by 8 p.m. Eastern time the day before the date the deposit is due.

Same-day wire payment option. If you fail to initiate a deposit transaction on EFTPS by 8 p.m. Eastern time the day before the date a deposit is due, you can still make your deposit on time by using the Federal Tax Application (FTA). To use the same-day wire payment method, you will need to make arrangements with your financial institution ahead of time. Please check with your financial institution regarding availability, deadlines, and costs. Your financial institution may charge you a fee for payments made this way. To learn more about the information you will need to provide to your financial institution to make a same-day wire payment, visit *www.eftps.gov* to download the *Same-Day Payment Worksheet*.

Timeliness of federal tax deposits. If a deposit is required to be made on a day that is not a business day, the deposit is considered timely if it is made by the close of the next business day. A business day is any day other than a Saturday, Sunday, or legal holiday. The term *legal holiday* for deposit purposes includes only those legal holidays in the District of Columbia. Legal holidays in the District of Columbia are provided in Pub. 15 (Circular E).

Electronic filing and payment. Now, more than ever before, businesses can enjoy the benefits of filing tax returns and paying their federal taxes electronically. Whether you rely on a tax professional or handle your own taxes, the IRS offers you convenient programs to make filing and paying easier. Spend less time and worry on taxes and more time running your business. Use e-file and Electronic Federal Tax Payment System (EFTPS) to your benefit.
- For e-file, visit *www.irs.gov/efile*.
- For EFTPS, visit *www.eftps.gov* or call EFTPS at one of the numbers provided under *Federal tax deposits must be made by electronic funds transfer*, earlier.

 If you are filing your tax return or paying your federal taxes electronically, a valid EIN is required at the time the return is filed. If a valid EIN is not provided, the return or payment will not be processed. This may result in penalties.

 If you were a semiweekly schedule depositor at any time during 2012, you must file a paper Form 944 and Form 945-A, Annual Record of Federal Tax Liability.

Electronic funds withdrawal (EFW). If you file Form 944 electronically, you can e-file and e-pay (electronic funds withdrawal) the balance due in a single step using tax preparation software or through a tax professional. However, **do not** use EFW to make federal tax deposits. For more information on paying your taxes using EFW, visit the IRS website at *www.irs.gov/e-pay*. A fee may be charged to file electronically.

Credit or debit card payments. Employers can pay the balance due shown on Form 944 by credit or debit card. **Do not** use a credit or debit card to make federal tax deposits. For more information on paying your taxes with a credit or debit card, visit the IRS website at *www.irs.gov/e-pay*. A convenience fee will be charged for this service.

Employer's liability. Employers are responsible to ensure that tax returns are filed and deposits and payments are made, even if the employer contracts with a third party. The employer remains liable if the third party fails to perform a required action.

Where can you get telephone help? For answers to your questions about completing Form 944, tax deposit rules, or obtaining an employer identification number (EIN) call the IRS at one of the numbers listed below.
- 1-800-829-4933 (Business and Specialty Tax Line) or 1-800-829-4059 (TDD/TTY for persons who are deaf, hard of hearing, or have a speech disability); Monday–Friday 7:00 a.m.–7:00 p.m. local time (Alaska and Hawaii follow Pacific time; employers in Puerto Rico receive service from 8:00 a.m.–8:00 p.m. local time).
- 267-941-1000 (toll call); Monday–Friday 6:00 a.m.–11:00 p.m. Eastern time.

Photographs of missing children. The IRS is a proud partner with the National Center for Missing and Exploited Children. Photographs of missing children selected by the Center may appear in instructions on pages that would otherwise be blank. You can help bring these children home by looking at the photographs and calling 1-800-THE-LOST (1-800-843-5678) if you recognize a child.

General Instructions

Federal law requires employers to withhold taxes from employees' paychecks. Each time wages are paid, employers must withhold — or take out of employees' paychecks — certain amounts for federal income tax, social security tax, and Medicare tax. Under the withholding system, taxes withheld from employees are credited to employees in payment of their tax liabilities.

 References to federal income tax withholding do not apply to employers in American Samoa, Guam, the Commonwealth of the Northern Mariana Islands, the U.S. Virgin Islands, and Puerto Rico.

Federal law also requires employers to pay any liability for the employer's portion of social security and Medicare taxes. This portion of social security and Medicare taxes is not withheld from employees.

What Is the Purpose of Form 944?

Form 944 is designed so the smallest employers (those whose annual liability for social security, Medicare, and withheld federal income taxes is $1,000 or less) will file and pay these taxes only once a year instead of every quarter. These instructions give you some background information about Form 944, who must file Form 944, how to complete it line by line, and when and where to file it.

For more information about annual employment tax filing and tax deposit rules, see Treasury Decision 9566, 2012-8 I.R.B. 389, at *www.irs.gov/irb/2012-08_IRB/ar09.html*.

If you want more in-depth information about payroll tax topics, see Pub. 15 (Circular E), Pub. 80 (Circular SS), Pub. 179 (Circular PR), or visit the IRS website at *www.irs.gov/businesses* and click on the *Employment Taxes* link under *Businesses Topics*.

Who Must File Form 944?

In general, if the IRS has notified you to file Form 944, you must file Form 944 instead of Forms 941, 941-SS, or 941-PR to report the following amounts.

- Wages you have paid.
- Tips your employees have received.
- Federal income tax you withheld.
- Both the employer's and the employee's share of social security and Medicare taxes.
- Current year's adjustments to social security and Medicare taxes for fractions of cents, sick pay, tips, and group-term life insurance.
- Credit for COBRA premium assistance payments.

If you received notification to file Form 944, you must file Form 944 to report your social security, Medicare, and withheld federal income taxes for the 2012 calendar year unless you contacted the IRS by April 2, 2012, to request to file Forms 941, 941-SS, or 941-PR quarterly instead and received written confirmation that your filing requirement was changed. You must file Form 944 even if you have no taxes to report (or you have taxes in excess of $1,000 to report) unless you filed a final return. See *If your business has closed...*, later. Also see *What if you want to file Forms 941, 941-SS, or 941-PR instead of Form 944*, later.

 If you have not received notification to file Form 944 but estimate your employment tax liability for calendar year 2013 will be $1,000 or less and would like to file Form 944 instead of Forms 941, 941-SS, or 941-PR, you can contact the IRS to request to file Form 944. To file Form 944 for calendar year 2013, you must call the IRS at 1-800-829-4933 or 267-941-1000 (toll call) by April 1, 2013, or send a written request postmarked by March 15, 2013. The mailing addresses for written requests are provided below under What if you want to file Forms 941, 941-SS, or 941-PR instead of Form 944. *The IRS will send you a written notice that your filing requirement has been changed to Form 944. If you do not receive this notice, you must file Forms 941, 941-SS, or 941-PR for calendar year 2013.*

New employers are also eligible to file Form 944 if they will meet the eligibility requirements. New employers filing Form SS-4, Application for Employer Identification Number, or Form SS-4PR, Solicitud de Número de Identificación Patronal (*EIN*), must complete line 13 of Form SS-4 or SS-4PR indicating the highest number of employees expected in the next 12 months and must check the box on line 14 to indicate whether they expect to have $1,000 or less in employment tax liability for the calendar year and would like to file Form 944. Generally, if you pay $4,000 or less in wages subject to social security and Medicare taxes and federal income tax withholding, you are likely to pay $1,000 or less in employment taxes. Generally, if you are an employer in Puerto Rico, American Samoa, Guam, the Commonwealth of the Northern Mariana Islands, or the U.S.

Virgin Islands and you pay $6,536 or less in wages subject to social security and Medicare taxes, you are likely to pay $1,000 or less in employment taxes. New employers are advised of their employment tax filing requirement when they are issued their EIN.

 If the IRS notified you to file Form 944 for 2012, file Form 944 (and not Forms 941, 941-SS, or 941-PR) even if your tax liability for 2012 exceeds $1,000.

What if you want to file Forms 941, 941-SS, or 941-PR instead of Form 944?

You must file Form 944 if the IRS has notified you to do so, unless you contact the IRS to request to file quarterly Forms 941, 941-SS, or 941-PR instead. To request to file quarterly Forms 941, 941-SS, or 941-PR to report your social security, Medicare, and withheld federal income taxes for the 2013 calendar year, call the IRS at 1-800-829-4933 or 267-941-1000 (toll call) by April 1, 2013, or send a written request postmarked by March 15, 2013. Written requests should be sent to:

Department of Treasury		Department of Treasury
Internal Revenue Service	or	Internal Revenue Service
Ogden, UT 84201-0038		Cincinnati, OH 45999-0038

Select one of the addresses above based on the state filing alignment for returns filed *Without a payment* under *Where Should You File*, later. After you contact the IRS, the IRS will send you a written notice that your filing requirement has been changed. If you do not receive this notice, you must file Form 944 for calendar year 2013. See Rev. Proc. 2009-51, 2009-45 I.R.B. 625, available at *www.irs.gov/irb/2009-45_IRB/ar12.html*.

Who cannot file Form 944?

The following employers **cannot** file Form 944.

- **Employers who are not notified.** If the IRS does not notify you to file Form 944, do not file Form 944. If you would like to file Form 944 instead of Forms 941, 941-SS, or 941-PR, see the *TIP* under *Who Must File Form 944*, earlier.
- **Household employers.** If you employ only household employees, do not file Form 944. For more information, see Pub. 926, Household Employer's Tax Guide, and Schedule H (Form 1040), Household Employment Taxes, or Pub. 179 (Circular PR) and Schedule H-PR (Form 1040-PR), Contribuciones sobre el Empleo de Empleados Domésticos.
- **Agricultural employers.** If you employ only agricultural employees, do not file Form 944. For more information, see Pub. 51 (Circular A), Agricultural Employer's Tax Guide, and Form 943, Employer's Annual Federal Tax Return for Agricultural Employees, or Pub. 179 (Circular PR) and Form 943-PR, Planilla para la Declaración Anual de la Contribución Federal del Patrono de Empleados Agrícolas.

What if you reorganize or close your business?

If you sell or transfer your business...

If you sell or transfer your business, you and the new owner must each file a Form 944, 941, 941-SS, or 941-PR, whichever is required, for the year in which the transfer occurred. Report only the wages you paid.

When two businesses merge, the continuing firm must file a return for the year in which the change took place and the other firm should file a **final return**.

Instructions for Form 944 (2012)   -3-

Changing from one form of business to another—such as from a sole proprietorship to a partnership or corporation—is considered a transfer. If a transfer occurs, you may need a new EIN. See section 1 of Pub. 15 (Circular E). Attach a statement to your return with all the following information.

- The new owner's name (or the new name of the business).
- Whether the business is now a sole proprietorship, partnership, or corporation.
- The kind of change that occurred (a sale or transfer).
- The date of the change.
- The name of the person keeping the payroll records and the address where those records will be kept.

If your business has closed...

If you go out of business or stop paying wages to your employees, you must file a **final return.** To tell the IRS that Form 944 for a particular year is your final return, check the box in Part 3 on page 2 of Form 944 and enter the final date you paid wages. Also attach a statement to your return showing the name of the person keeping the payroll records and the address where those records will be kept.

If you participated in a statutory merger or consolidation, or qualify for predecessor-successor status due to an acquisition, you should generally file Schedule D (Form 941), Report of Discrepancies Caused by Acquisitions, Statutory Mergers, or Consolidations. See the Instructions for Schedule D (Form 941) to determine whether you should file Schedule D (Form 941) and when you should file it.

When Must You File?

File Form 944 by January 31, after the end of the calendar year. If you made timely deposits in full payment of your taxes by January 31, you have 10 more calendar days after that date to file your Form 944.

File Form 944 only once for each calendar year. If you filed Form 944 electronically, do not file a paper Form 944. For more information about filing Form 944 electronically, see *Electronic filing and payment*, earlier.

If we receive Form 944 after the due date, we will treat Form 944 as filed on time if the envelope containing Form 944 is properly addressed, contains sufficient postage, and is postmarked by the U.S. Postal Service on or before the due date, or sent by an IRS-designated private delivery service on or before the due date. If you do not follow these guidelines, we will consider Form 944 filed when it is actually received. See Pub. 15 (Circular E), Pub. 80 (Circular SS), or Pub. 179 (Circular PR) for more information on IRS-designated private delivery services.

If any due date for filing falls on a Saturday, Sunday, or legal holiday, you may file your return on the next business day.

How Should You Complete Form 944?

Enter your EIN, name, and address in the spaces provided. Also enter your name and EIN at the top of page 2. Do not use your social security number (SSN) or individual taxpayer identification number (ITIN). Generally, enter the business (legal) name that you used when you applied for your EIN. For example, if you are a sole proprietor, enter "Tyler Smith" on the *Name* line and "Tyler's Cycles" on the *Trade name* line. Leave the *Trade name* line blank if it is the same as your *Name* line.

If you use a tax preparer to complete Form 944, make sure the preparer uses your correct business name and EIN.

Employer identification number (EIN). To make sure that businesses comply with federal tax laws, the IRS monitors tax filings and payments by using a numerical system to identify taxpayers. A unique nine-digit EIN is assigned to all corporations, partnerships, and some sole proprietors. Businesses needing an EIN must apply for a number and use it throughout the life of the business on all tax returns, payments, and reports.

Your business should have only one EIN. If you have more than one and are not sure which one to use, write to the IRS office where you file your returns (using the *Without a payment* address under *Where Should You File*, later) or call the IRS at 1-800-829-4933 or 267-941-1000 (toll call).

If you do not have an EIN, you may apply for one online. Visit IRS.gov and click on the *Apply for an EIN Online* link under *Tools*. You may also apply for an EIN by calling 1-800-829-4933 or 267-941-1000 (toll call), or you can fax or mail Form SS-4 or SS-4PR to the IRS. If you have applied for an EIN but do not have your EIN by the time a return is due, write "Applied For" and the date you applied in the space shown for the number.

 Always be sure the EIN on the form you file exactly matches the EIN the IRS assigned to your business. Do not use your SSN or ITIN on forms that ask for an EIN. Filing a Form 944 with an incorrect EIN or using another business's EIN may result in penalties and delays in processing your return.

If you change your name or address... Notify the IRS immediately if you change your business name or address.

- **Name change.** Write to the IRS office where you filed your return (using the *Without a payment* address under *Where Should You File*, later) to notify the IRS of any name change. See Pub. 1635, Employer Identification Number: Understanding Your EIN, to see if you need to also apply for a new EIN.
- **Address change.** Complete and mail Form 8822-B, Change of Address—Business, to notify the IRS of an address change.

Completing and Filing Form 944

Make entries on Form 944 as follows to enable accurate processing.

- Use 12-point Courier font (if possible) for all entries if you are using a typewriter or computer to complete Form 944.
- Do not enter dollar signs and decimal points. Commas are optional. Report dollars to the left of the preprinted decimal point and cents to the right of it.
- Leave blank any data field with a value of zero (except line 7).
- Enter negative amounts using a minus sign (if possible). Otherwise, use parentheses.
- Enter your name and EIN on **all** pages and attachments.

Other Forms You Must Use

To notify employees about the earned income credit (EIC), employers in the United States must give the employees one of the following:
- The IRS Form W-2, Wage and Tax Statement, which has the required information about the EIC on the back of Copy B.

- A substitute Form W-2 with the same EIC information on the back of the employee's copy that is on the back of Copy B of the IRS Form W-2.
- Notice 797, Possible Federal Tax Refund Due to the Earned Income Credit (EIC).
- Your written statement with the same wording as Notice 797.

For more information, see section 10 of Pub. 15 (Circular E) and Pub. 596, Earned Income Credit (EIC).

Reconciling Form 944 and Form W-3, W-3SS, or W-3PR

The IRS matches amounts reported on your Form 944 with Form W-2, W-2AS, W-2GU, W-2CM, W-2VI, or Form 499R-2/W-2PR amounts totaled on your Form W-3 or W-3SS, Transmittal of Wage and Tax Statements, or Form W-3PR. Informe de Comprobantes de Retención. If the amounts do not agree, the IRS may contact you. The following amounts are reconciled.

- Federal income tax withholding, if applicable.
- Social security wages.
- Social security tips.
- Medicare wages and tips.

For more information, see section 12 of Pub. 15 (Circular E).

Must You Deposit Your Taxes?

If your liability for social security, Medicare, and withheld federal income taxes is less than $2,500 for the year, you can pay the taxes with your return. To avoid a penalty, you should pay in full and file on time. You do not have to deposit the taxes. However, you may choose to make deposits of these taxes even if your liability is less than $2,500. If your liability for these taxes is $2,500 or more, you are generally required to deposit the taxes instead of paying them when you file Form 944. See the *Federal Tax Deposit Requirements for Form 944 Filers* chart below. If you do not deposit the taxes when required, you may be subject to penalties and interest.

The $2,500 threshold at which federal tax deposits must be made is different from the amount of annual tax liability ($1,000 or less) that makes an employer eligible to file Form 944. Form 944 filers whose businesses grow during the year may be required to make federal tax deposits (see chart below), but they will still file Form 944 for the year.

Federal Tax Deposit Requirements for Form 944 Filers	
If Your Tax Liability is:	**Your Deposit Requirement is:**
Less than $2,500 for the year	No deposit required. You may pay the tax with your return. If you are unsure that your tax liability for the year will be less than $2,500, deposit under the rules below.
$2,500 or more for the year, but less than $2,500 for the quarter	You can deposit by the last day of the month after the end of a quarter. However, if your fourth quarter tax liability is less than $2,500, you may pay the fourth quarter's tax liability with Form 944.
$2,500 or more for the quarter	You must deposit monthly or semiweekly depending on your deposit schedule. But, if you accumulate $100,000 or more of taxes on any day, you must deposit the tax by the next business day. See section 11 of Pub. 15 (Circular E), section 8 of Pub. 80 (Circular SS), or section 11 of Pub. 179 (Circular PR).

Note. When you make deposits depends on your deposit schedule, which is either monthly or semiweekly, depending on the amount of your tax liability during the lookback period. The lookback period for Form 944 filers is different than the lookback period for Form 941, 941-SS, and 941-PR filers, so your deposit schedule may have changed. For more information, see section 11 of Pub. 15 (Circular E), section 8 of Pub. 80 (Circular SS), or section 11 of Pub. 179 (Circular PR).

What About Penalties and Interest?

Avoiding penalties and interest

You can avoid paying penalties and interest if you do all of the following.

- Deposit or pay your taxes when they are due.
- File your fully completed Form 944 on time.
- Report your tax liability accurately in Part 2 of Form 944.
- Submit valid checks for tax payments.
- Give accurate Forms W-2, W-2AS, W-2GU, W-2CM, W-2VI, or Form 499R-2/W-2PR to employees.
- File Form W-3, W-3SS, or W-3PR and Copies A of Forms W-2, W-2AS, W-2GU, W-2CM, W-2VI, or Form 499R-2/W-2PR with the Social Security Administration (SSA) on time and accurately.

Penalties and interest are charged on taxes paid late and returns filed late at a rate set by law. See sections 11 and 12 of Pub. 15 (Circular E), section 8 of Pub. 80 (Circular SS), or section 11 of Pub. 179 (Circular PR) for details. Use Form 843, Claim for Refund and Request for Abatement, to request abatement of assessed penalties or interest. Do not request abatement of assessed penalties or interest on Form 944, Form 944-X, 944-X (PR), 944-X (SP), 941-X, or 941-X (PR).

If you receive a notice about a penalty after you file your return, reply to the notice with an explanation and we will determine if you meet reasonable-cause criteria. **Do not** include an explanation when you file your return.

A trust fund recovery penalty may apply if federal income, social security, or Medicare taxes that must be withheld are not withheld or paid. The penalty is the full amount of the unpaid trust fund tax. This penalty may apply when these unpaid taxes cannot be collected from the employer. The trust fund recovery penalty may be imposed on all people the IRS determines to be responsible for collecting, accounting for, and paying over these taxes, and who acted willfully in not doing so. For details, see section 11 of Pub. 15 (Circular E), section 8 of Pub. 80 (Circular SS), or section 11 of Pub. 179 (Circular PR).

Where Should You File?

Where you file depends on whether you include a payment with your form.

If you are in . . .		Without a payment . . .	With a payment . . .
Special filing address for exempt organizations; federal, state and local governmental entities; and Indian tribal governmental entities; regardless of location		Department of the Treasury Internal Revenue Service Ogden, UT 84201-0044	Internal Revenue Service P.O. Box 37944 Hartford, CT 06176-7944
Connecticut Delaware District of Columbia Florida Georgia Illinois Indiana Kentucky Maine Maryland Massachusetts Michigan New Hampshire	New Jersey New York North Carolina Ohio Pennsylvania Rhode Island South Carolina Tennessee Vermont Virginia West Virginia Wisconsin	Department of the Treasury Internal Revenue Service Cincinnati, OH 45999-0044	Internal Revenue Service P.O. Box 804522 Cincinnati, OH 45280-4522
Alabama Alaska Arizona Arkansas California Colorado Hawaii Idaho Iowa Kansas Louisiana Minnesota Mississippi	Missouri Montana Nebraska Nevada New Mexico North Dakota Oklahoma Oregon South Dakota Texas Utah Washington Wyoming	Department of the Treasury Internal Revenue Service Ogden, UT 84201-0044	Internal Revenue Service P. O Box 37944 Hartford, CT 06176-7944
No legal residence or principal place of business in any state		Internal Revenue Service P.O. Box 409101 Ogden, UT 84409	Internal Revenue Service P. O Box 37944 Hartford, CT 06176-7944

 Your filing address may have changed from that used to file your employment tax return in prior years. Do not send Form 944 or any payments to the Social Security Administration (SSA). Private delivery services cannot deliver to P.O. boxes.

Specific Instructions

Part 1: Answer These Questions for This Year

 Employers in American Samoa, Guam, the Commonwealth of the Northern Mariana Islands, the U.S. Virgin Islands, and Puerto Rico may skip lines 1 and 2.

1. Wages, Tips, and Other Compensation

Enter amounts on line 1 that would also be included in box 1 of your employees' Forms W-2. See the General Instructions for Forms W-2 and W-3 for details.

2. Federal Income Tax Withheld From Wages, Tips, and Other Compensation

Enter the federal income tax that you withheld (or were required to withhold) from your employees on this year's wages, tips, taxable fringe benefits, and supplemental unemployment compensation benefits.

 References to federal income tax withholding do not apply to employers in American Samoa, Guam, the Commonwealth of the Northern Mariana Islands, the U.S. Virgin Islands, and Puerto Rico.

3. If No Wages, Tips, and Other Compensation are Subject to Social Security or Medicare Tax

If no wages, tips, and other compensation are subject to social security or Medicare taxes, check the box on line 3 and go to line 5. If this question does not apply to you, leave the box blank. For more information about exempt wages, see section 15 of Pub. 15 (Circular E), section 12 of Pub. 80 (Circular SS), or section 15 of Pub. 179 (Circular PR). For religious exemptions, see section 4 of Pub. 15-A, Employer's Supplemental Tax Guide.

4. Taxable Social Security and Medicare Wages and Tips

4a. Taxable social security wages. Report the total wages, sick pay, and fringe benefits subject to social security taxes that you paid to your employees during the year.

Enter the amount before deductions. **Do not** include tips on this line. For information on types of wages subject to social security taxes, see section 5 of Pub. 15 (Circular E), section 4 of Pub. 80 (Circular SS), or section 5 of Pub. 179 (Circular PR).

For 2012, the rate of social security tax on taxable wages is 6.2% (.062) for the employer and 4.2% (.042) for the employee, or 10.4% (.104) for both. Stop paying social security tax on and reporting an employee's wages on line 4a when the employee's taxable wages (including tips) reach $110,100 for the year. However, continue to withhold income and Medicare taxes for the whole year on wages and tips even when the social security wage base of $110,100 has been reached.

$$
\begin{array}{r}
\text{line 4a (column 1)} \\
\times \quad .104 \\
\hline
\text{line 4a (column 2)}
\end{array}
$$

4b. Taxable social security tips. Enter all tips your employees reported to you during the year until the total of the tips and wages for an employee reach $110,100 for the year. Include all tips your employees reported to you even if you were unable to withhold the 4.2% employee's share of social security tax.

Your employee must report cash tips to you by the 10th day of the month after the month the tips are received. The report should include charged tips you paid over to the employee for charge customers, tips the employee received directly from customers, and tips received from other employees under any tip-sharing arrangement. Both directly and indirectly tipped employees must report tips to you. No report is required for months when tips are less than $20. Employees may use Form 4070, Employee's Report of Tips to Employer (available only in Pub. 1244, Employee's Daily Record of Tips and Report of Tips to Employer), or Form 4070-PR, Informe al Patrono de Propinas Recibidas por el(la) Empleado(a) (available only in Pub. 1244-PR, Registro Diario de Propinas Recibidas por el(la) Empleado(a) e Informe al Patrono), or submit a written statement or electronic tip record.

	line 4b (column 1)
x	.104
	line 4b (column 2)

4c. Taxable Medicare wages and tips. Report all wages, tips, sick pay, and taxable fringe benefits that are subject to Medicare tax. Unlike social security wages, there is no limit on the amount of wages subject to Medicare tax.

The rate of Medicare tax is 1.45% (.0145) each for the employer and employee, or 2.9% (.029) for both. Include all tips your employees reported during the year, even if you were unable to withhold the employee tax of 1.45%.

	line 4c (column 1)
x	.029
	line 4c (column 2)

For more information on tips, see section 6 of Pub. 15 (Circular E), section 5 of Pub. 80 (Circular SS), or section 6 of Pub. 179 (Circular PR).

4d. Total social security and Medicare taxes. Add the social security tax, social security tips tax, and Medicare tax.

	line 4a	(column 2)
	line 4b	(column 2)
+	line 4c	(column 2)
	line 4d	

5. Total Taxes Before Adjustments

Add the income tax withheld from wages, tips, and other compensation from line 2 and the total social security and Medicare taxes before adjustments from line 4d. Enter the result on line 5.

6. Current Year's Adjustments

Enter **tax amounts** that result from current period adjustments. Use a minus sign (if possible) to show an adjustment that decreases the total taxes shown on line 5. Otherwise, use parentheses.

In certain cases, you must adjust the amounts you reported as social security and Medicare taxes in column 2 of lines 4a, 4b, and 4c to figure your correct tax liability for this

year's Form 944. See section 13 of Pub. 15 (Circular E), section 9 of Pub. 80 (Circular SS), or section 12 of Pub. 179 (Circular PR).

If you need to adjust any amount reported on line 6 or 6a from a previously filed Form 944 or 944-SS, complete and file Form 944-X. Form 944-X is an adjusted returns and is filed separately from Form 944. See section 13 of Pub. 15 (Circular E) or section 9 of Pub. 80 (Circular SS).

If you need to adjust any amount reported on line 6 or 6a from a previously filed Form 944-PR, complete and file Form 944-X (PR). Form 944-X (PR) is an adjusted return and is filed separately from Form 944. See section 12 of Pub. 179 (Circular PR).

Fractions of cents. Enter adjustments for fractions of cents (due to rounding) relating to the employee share of social security and Medicare taxes withheld. The employee share of amounts shown in column 2 of lines 4a, 4b, and 4c may differ slightly from amounts actually withheld from employees' paychecks due to rounding social security and Medicare taxes based on statutory rates.

Sick pay. Enter the adjustment for the employee share of social security and Medicare taxes that were withheld and deposited by your third-party sick pay payer with regard to sick pay paid by the third party. These wages should be included on lines 4a and 4c. If you are the third-party sick pay payer, enter the adjustment for any employer share of these taxes required to be paid by the employer.

Adjustments for tips and group-term life insurance. Enter adjustments for both of the following items.

- Any uncollected employee share of social security and Medicare taxes on tips.
- The uncollected employee share of social security and Medicare taxes on group-term life insurance premiums paid for former employees.

7. Total Taxes After Adjustments

Combine the amounts shown on lines 5 and 6 and enter the result on line 7.

- **If line 7 is less than $2,500,** you may pay the amount with Form 944 or you may deposit the amount. See section 11 of Pub. 15 (Circular E), section 8 of Pub. 80 (Circular SS), or section 11 of Pub. 179 (Circular PR) for information about federal tax deposits.
- **If line 7 is $2,500 or more,** you generally must deposit your tax liabilities by electronic funds transfer. However, if you deposited all taxes accumulated in the first three quarters of the year and your fourth quarter liability is less than $2,500, you may pay taxes accumulated during the fourth quarter with Form 944. The amount shown on line 7 **must** equal the amount shown on line 13m.

8. Total Deposits for This Year

Enter your deposits for this year, including any overpayment that you applied from filing Form 944-X, 944-X (PR), 944-X (SP), 941-X, or 941-X (PR) in the current year. Also include in the amount shown any overpayment from a previous period that you applied to this return.

9a. COBRA Premium Assistance Payments

Report 65% of the COBRA premiums for assistance eligible individuals. Take the COBRA premium assistance credit on this line only after the assistance eligible individual's 35% share of the premium has been paid. For COBRA coverage provided under a self-insured plan, COBRA premium assistance is treated as having been made for each assistance eligible individual who pays 35% of the COBRA premium. Do not include the assistance eligible individual's 35% of the premium in the amount entered on this line. For more information on the COBRA premium assistance credit, visit IRS.gov and enter the keyword *COBRA*.

 The amount reported on line 9a is treated as a deposit of taxes on the first day of the return period and must not be used to adjust line 13 or Form 945-A.

9b. Number of Individuals Provided COBRA Premium Assistance on Line 9a

Enter the total number of assistance eligible individuals provided COBRA premium assistance reported on line 9a. Count each assistance eligible individual who paid a reduced COBRA premium in the year as one individual, whether or not the reduced premium was for insurance that covered more than one assistance eligible individual. For example, if the reduced COBRA premium was for coverage for a former employee, spouse, and two children, you would include one individual in the number entered on line 9b for the premium assistance. Further, each individual is reported only once per year. For example, an assistance eligible individual who made monthly premium payments during the year would only be reported as one individual.

10. Total Deposits and Credits

Add lines 8 and 9a.

11. Balance Due

If line 7 is more than line 10, enter the difference on line 11. Otherwise, see *Overpayment*, later.

You do not have to pay if line 11 is less than $1. Generally, you should have a balance due only if your total taxes after adjustments (line 7) are less than $2,500. See *If line 7 is $2,500 or more*, earlier, for an exception.

If line 11 is:

- Less than $1, you do not have to pay it.
- $1 or more, but less than $2,500, you can pay the amount owed with your return. Make your check or money order payable to the "United States Treasury" and write your EIN, "Form 944," and "2012" on the check or money order. Complete Form 944-V, Payment Voucher, and enclose it with your return.
- $2,500 or more, you must deposit your tax. See *Must You Deposit Your Taxes*, earlier.

You may pay the amount shown on line 11 using EFTPS, a credit or debit card, or electronic funds withdrawal (EFW). **Do not** use a credit or debit card or EFW to pay taxes that were required to be deposited. For more information on electronic payment options, visit the IRS website at *www.irs.gov/e-pay*.

If you pay by EFTPS or credit or debit card, file your return using the *Without a payment* address under *Where Should You File*, earlier. **Do not** file Form 944-V.

 If you are required to make deposits and, instead, pay the taxes with Form 944, you may be subject to a penalty.

12. Overpayment

If line 10 is more than line 7, enter the amount on line 12. **Never** make an entry on both lines 11 and 12.

If you deposited more than the correct amount for the year, you can choose to have the IRS either refund the overpayment or apply it to your next return. Check only one box on line 12. If you do not check either box or if you check both boxes, generally we will apply the overpayment to your account. We may apply your overpayment to any past due tax account that is shown in our records under your EIN.

If line 12 is less than $1, we will send a refund or apply it to your next return only if you ask us in writing to do so.

Complete both pages.

You must complete both pages of Form 944 and sign it on page 2. Failure to do so may delay processing of your return.

Part 2: Tell Us About Your Deposit Schedule and Tax Liability for This Year

13. Check One

If line 7 is less than $2,500, check the first box on line 13 and go to line 14.

If line 7 is $2,500 or more, check the second box on line 13. If you are a monthly schedule depositor, enter your tax liability for each month and figure the total liability for the year. If you do not enter your tax liability for each month, the IRS will not know when you should have made deposits and may assess an "averaged" failure-to-deposit penalty. See section 11 of Pub. 15 (Circular E), section 8 of Pub. 80 (Circular SS), or section 11 of Pub. 179 (Circular PR). If your tax liability for any month is negative (for example, if you are adjusting an overreported liability in a prior month), do not enter a negative amount for the month. Instead, enter zero for the month and subtract that negative amount from your tax liability for the next month.

Note. The amount shown on line 13m must equal the amount shown on line 7.

If you are a semiweekly schedule depositor or if you accumulate $100,000 or more in tax liability on any day in a deposit period, you must complete Form 945-A and file it with Form 944. See the *$100,000 Next Day Deposit Rule* in section 11 of Pub. 15 (Circular E), section 8 of Pub. 80 (Circular SS), or section 11 of Pub. 179 (Circular PR). Do not complete lines 13a–13m if you file Form 945-A.

Part 3: Tell Us About Your Business

In Part 3, answer question 14 only if it applies to your business. If it does not apply, leave it blank and go to Part 4.

14. If Your Business Has Closed...

If you go out of business or stop paying wages, you must file a **final return**. To notify the IRS that a particular Form 944 is your final return, check the box on line 14 and enter the date you last paid wages in the space provided.

Part 4: May We Speak With Your Third-party Designee?

If you want to allow an employee, a paid tax preparer, or another person to discuss your Form 944 with the IRS, check the "Yes" box in Part 4. Enter the name, phone number, and the 5-digit personal identification number (PIN) of the specific person to contact—not the name of the firm that prepared your tax return. The designee may choose any numbers as his or her PIN.

By checking "Yes," you authorize the IRS to talk to the person you named (your designee) about any questions we may have while we process your return. You also authorize your designee to do all of the following.

• Give us any information that is missing from your return.
• Call us for information about processing your return.
• Respond to certain IRS notices that you have shared with your designee about math errors and return preparation. The IRS will not send notices to your designee.

You are not authorizing your designee to bind you to anything (including additional tax liability) or to otherwise represent you before the IRS. If you want to expand your designee's authorization, see Pub. 947, Practice Before the IRS and Power of Attorney.

The authorization will automatically expire 1 year after the due date (without regard to extensions) for filing Form 944. If you or your designee want to terminate the authorization, write to the IRS office for your locality using the *Without a payment* address under *Where Should You File*, earlier.

Part 5: Sign Here

Complete all information in Part 5 and sign Form 944 as follows.

• **Sole proprietorship—** The individual who owns the business.

• **Corporation (including a limited liability company (LLC) treated as a corporation)—** The president, vice president, or other principal officer duly authorized to sign.

• **Partnership (including an LLC treated as a partner-ship) or unincorporated organization—** A responsible and duly authorized member, partner, or officer having knowledge of its affairs.

• **Single member LLC treated as a disregarded entity for federal income tax purposes—** The owner of the LLC or a principal officer duly authorized to sign.

• **Trust or estate—** The fiduciary.

If you have filed a valid power of attorney, your duly authorized agent may also sign Form 944.

Alternative signature method. Corporate officers or duly authorized agents may sign Form 944 by rubber stamp, mechanical device, or computer software program. For details and required documentation, see Rev. Proc. 2005-39, 2005-28 I.R.B. 82, available at *www.irs.gov/irb/2005-28_IRB/ar16.html*.

Paid Preparer Use Only

A paid preparer must sign Form 944 and provide the information in the *Paid Preparer Use Only* section of Part 5 if the preparer was paid to prepare Form 944 and is not an employee of the filing entity. Paid preparers must sign paper returns with a manual signature. The preparer must give you a copy of the return in addition to the copy to be filed with the IRS.

If you are a paid preparer, enter your Preparer Tax Identification Number (PTIN) in the space provided. Include your complete address. If you work for a firm, enter the firm's name and the EIN of the firm. You can apply for a PTIN online or by filing Form W-12, IRS Paid Preparer Tax Identification Number (PTIN) Application and Renewal. For more information about applying for a PTIN online, visit the IRS website at *www.irs.gov/ptin*. You cannot use your PTIN in place of the EIN of the tax preparation firm.

Generally, do not complete this section if you are filing the return as a reporting agent and have a valid Form 8655, Reporting Agent Authorization, on file with the IRS. However, a reporting agent must complete this section if the reporting agent offered legal advice, for example, advising the client on determining whether its workers are employees or independent contractors for federal tax purposes.

How to Order Forms, Instructions, and Publications From the IRS

 Call 1-800-TAX-FORM (1-800-829-3676).

 Visit *www.irs.gov/formspubs*.

Form **945**

Department of the Treasury
Internal Revenue Service

Annual Return of Withheld Federal Income Tax

▶ For withholding reported on Forms 1099 and W-2G.
▶ See separate instructions. For more information on income tax withholding, see Pub. 15 (Circ. E) and Pub. 15-A.
Information about Form 945 and its separate instructions is at *www.irs.gov/form945*.

OMB No. 1545-1430

20**12**

Type or Print	Name (as distinguished from trade name)	Calendar year	If address is different from prior return, check here. ▶
	Trade name, if any	Employer identification number (EIN)	
	Address (number and street)	City, state, and ZIP code	

A If you **do not have to file** returns in the future, check here ▶ ☐ and enter date final payments made. ▶ - - - - - - - - - - - - - - - - -

1	Federal income tax withheld from pensions, annuities, IRAs, gambling winnings, etc.	**1**	
2	Backup withholding	**2**	
3	**Total taxes.** If $2,500 or more, this must equal line 7M below or line M of Form 945-A	**3**	
4	Total deposits for 2012, including overpayment applied from a prior year and overpayment applied from Form 945-X	**4**	
5	**Balance due.** If line 3 is more than line 4, enter the difference and see the separate instructions .	**5**	

6 **Overpayment.** If line 4 is more than line 3, enter the difference ▶ $ _____

Check one: ☐ Apply to next return.   ☐ Send a refund.

- **All filers:** If line 3 is less than $2,500, **do not** complete line 7 **or** Form 945-A.
- **Semiweekly schedule depositors:** Complete **Form 945-A** and check here . . . . ▶ ☐
- **Monthly schedule depositors:** Complete **line 7, entries A through M,** and check here . . . . ▶ ☐

7 **Monthly Summary of Federal Tax Liability. (Do not** complete if you were a semiweekly schedule depositor.)			
	Tax liability for month	Tax liability for month	Tax liability for month
A January . . .		**F** June	**K** November . . .
B February . .		**G** July	**L** December . . .
C March . . .		**H** August	**M** Total liability for year (add lines **A** through **L**) . . .
D April		**I** September . . .	
E May		**J** October	

Third-Party Designee	Do you want to allow another person to discuss this return with the IRS (see the instructions)?	☐ Yes. Complete the following.	☐ No.
	Designee's name ▶	Phone no. ▶	Personal identification number (PIN) ▶ ☐☐☐☐☐

Sign Here

Under penalties of perjury, I declare that I have examined this return, including accompanying schedules and statements, and to the best of my knowledge and belief, it is true, correct, and complete. Declaration of preparer (other than taxpayer) is based on all information of which preparer has any knowledge.

Signature ▶   Print Your Name and Title ▶   Date ▶

Paid Preparer Use Only	Print/Type preparer's name	Preparer's signature	Date	Check ☐ if self-employed	PTIN
	Firm's name ▶			Firm's EIN ▶	
	Firm's address ▶			Phone no.	

For Privacy Act and Paperwork Reduction Act Notice, see the separate instructions.   Cat. No. 14584B   Form **945** (2012)

Form 945-V,
Payment Voucher

Purpose of Form

Complete Form 945-V, Payment Voucher, if you are making a payment with Form 945, Annual Return of Withheld Federal Income Tax. We will use the completed voucher to credit your payment more promptly and accurately, and to improve our service to you.

Making Payments With Form 945

To avoid a penalty, make your payment with your 2012 Form 945 **only if:**

• Your total taxes for the year (Form 945, line 3) are less than $2,500 and you are paying in full with a timely filed return, or

• You are a monthly schedule depositor making a payment in accordance with the Accuracy of Deposits Rule. See section 11 of Pub. 15 (Circular E), Employer's Tax Guide, for details. In this case, the amount of your payment may be $2,500 or more.

Otherwise, you must make deposits by electronic funds transfer. See section 11 of Pub. 15 (Circular E) for deposit instructions. Do not use Form 945-V to make federal tax deposits.

Caution. *Use Form 945-V when making any payment with Form 945. However, if you pay an amount with Form 945 that should have been deposited, you may be subject to a penalty. See Deposit Penalties in section 11 of Pub. 15 (Circular E).*

Specific Instructions

Box 1—Employer identification number (EIN). If you do not have an EIN, you may apply for one online. Go to IRS.gov and click on the *Apply for an EIN Online* link under "Tools." You may also apply for an EIN by calling 1-800-829-4933, or you can fax or mail Form SS-4, Application for Employer Identification Number. If you have not received your EIN by the due date of Form 945, write "Applied For" and the date you applied in this entry space.

Box 2—Amount paid. Enter the amount paid with Form 945.

Box 3—Name and address. Enter your name and address as shown on Form 945.

• Enclose your check or money order made payable to the "United States Treasury." Be sure to enter your EIN, "Form 945," and "2012" on your check or money order. Do not send cash. Do not staple Form 945-V or your payment to the return (or to each other).

• Detach Form 945-V and send it with your payment and Form 945 to the address provided in the Instructions for Form 945.

Note. You must also complete the entity information above line A on Form 945.

✂ - - - - ▼ **Detach Here and Mail With Your Payment and Form 945.** ▼ - - - - ✂

Form **945-V**	**Payment Voucher**	OMB No. 1545-1430
Department of the Treasury Internal Revenue Service	▶ **Do not attach this voucher or your payment to Form 945.**	20**12**

1 Enter your employer identification number (EIN).	2		Dollars	Cents
	Enter the amount of your payment . . ▶ Make your check or money order payable to "**United States Treasury**"			
	3 Enter your business name (individual name if sole proprietor).			
	Enter your address.			
	Enter your city, state, and ZIP code.			

20**12**
Instructions for Form 945

**Department of the Treasury
Internal Revenue Service**

Annual Return of Withheld Federal Income Tax

Section references are to the Internal Revenue Code unless otherwise noted.

Future Developments

For the latest information about developments related to Form 945 and its instructions, such as legislation enacted after they were published, go to *www.irs.gov/form945*.

What's New

Voluntary income tax withholding rates for 2013. The voluntary income tax withholding rates will be available in January 2013 at *www.irs.gov/form945.*

Reminders

Correcting a previously filed Form 945. If you discover an error on a previously filed Form 945, make the correction using Form 945-X, Adjusted Annual Return of Withheld Federal Income Tax or Claim for Refund. Form 945-X is a stand-alone form, meaning taxpayers can file Form 945-X when an error is discovered. For more information, get the Instructions for Form 945-X or visit IRS.gov and type *Correcting Employment Taxes* in the search box.

Federal tax deposits must be made by electronic funds transfer. You must use electronic funds transfer to make all federal tax deposits. Generally, electronic funds transfers are made using the Electronic Federal Tax Payment System (EFTPS). If you do not want to use EFTPS, you can arrange for your tax professional, financial institution, payroll service, or other trusted third party to make deposits on your behalf. Also, you may arrange for your financial institution to initiate a same-day wire payment on your behalf. EFTPS is a free service provided by the Department of Treasury. Services provided by your tax professional, financial institution, payroll service, or other third party may have a fee.

For more information on making federal tax deposits, see section 11 of Pub. 15 (Circular E), Employer's Tax Guide. To get more information about EFTPS or to enroll in EFTPS, visit the EFTPS website at *www.eftps.gov*, or call 1-800-555-4477. Additional information about EFTPS is also available in Pub. 966, Electronic Federal Tax Payment System: A Guide to Getting Started.

Paid preparers must sign Form 945. Paid preparers must complete and sign the paid preparer's section of Form 945.

Credit or debit card payments. Payors can pay the balance due shown on Form 945 by credit or debit card. Do not use a credit or debit card to make federal tax deposits. For more information on paying your taxes with a credit or debit card, visit the IRS website at *www.irs.gov/e-pay*.

How to get forms and publications. You can get most IRS forms and publications by accessing the IRS website at IRS.gov or by calling the IRS at 1-800-TAX-FORM (1-800-829-3676).

Telephone help. You can call the IRS Business and Specialty Tax Line toll free at 1-800-829-4933 or 1-800-829-4059 (TTY/TDD for persons who are deaf, hard of hearing, or have a speech disability) Monday–Friday 7 a.m.–7 p.m. local time (Alaska and Hawaii follow Pacific time) for answers to your questions about completing Form 945, tax deposit rules, or obtaining an employer identification number (EIN).

Additional information. Pub. 15 (Circular E) explains the rules for withholding, depositing, and reporting federal income tax. Pub. 15-A, Employer's Supplemental Tax Guide, includes information on federal income tax withholding from pensions, annuities, and Indian gaming profits. For information on withholding from gambling winnings, see the Instructions for Forms W-2G and 5754.

For a list of employment tax products, visit the IRS website at *www.irs.gov/businesses* and select click on the *Employment Taxes* link under "Businesses Topics."

Photographs of Missing Children

The Internal Revenue Service is a proud partner with the National Center for Missing and Exploited Children. Photographs of missing children selected by the Center may appear in instructions on pages that would otherwise be blank. You can help bring these children home by looking at the photographs and calling 1-800-THE-LOST (1-800-843-5678) if you recognize a child.

General Instructions

Purpose of Form 945

Use Form 945 to report withheld federal income tax from nonpayroll payments. Nonpayroll payments include:

- Pensions (including distributions from tax-favored retirement plans, for example, section 401(k), section 403(b), and governmental section 457(b) plans) and annuities;
- Military retirement;
- Gambling winnings;
- Indian gaming profits;
- Voluntary withholding on certain government payments; and
- Backup withholding.

Report all federal income tax withholding from nonpayroll payments or distributions annually on one Form 945. **Do not** file more than one Form 945 for any calendar year.

All federal income tax withholding reported on

Sep 06, 2012

Cat. No. 20534D

Forms 1099 (for example, Form 1099-R or 1099-MISC) or Form W-2G must be reported on Form 945. **Do not** report federal income tax withholding from wages on Form 945.

All employment taxes and federal income tax withholding reported on Form W-2, Wage and Tax Statement, must be reported on Form 941 or Form 944, Form 943 for agricultural employees, Schedule H (Form 1040) for household employees, or Form CT-1 for railroad employees.

Do not report on Form 945 federal income tax withheld on distributions to participants from nonqualified pension plans (including **nongovernmental** section 457(b) plans) and some other deferred compensation arrangements that are treated as wages and are reported on Form W-2. Report such withholding on Form 941 or Form 944. See Pub. 15 (Circular E) for more information.

Compensation paid to H-2A visa holders. Generally, report compensation of $600 or more paid to foreign agricultural workers who entered the country on H-2A visas on Form W-2 and Form 943, Employer's Annual Tax Return for Agricultural Employees. However, if an H-2A visa worker did not provide the employer with a taxpayer identification number, the employee is subject to backup withholding. The employer must report the wages and backup withholding on Form 1099-MISC, Miscellaneous Income. The employer must also report the backup withholding on Form 945, line 2.

Who Must File

If you withhold federal income tax (including backup withholding) from nonpayroll payments, you must file Form 945. See *Purpose of Form 945,* earlier. You do not have to file Form 945 for those years in which you do not have a nonpayroll tax liability. **Do not** report on Form 945 withholding that is required to be reported on Form 1042, Annual Withholding Tax Return for U.S. Source Income of Foreign Persons.

When To File

For 2012, file Form 945 by January 31, 2013. However, if you made deposits on time in full payment of the taxes for the year, you may file the return by February 11, 2013. Your return will be considered timely filed if it is properly addressed and mailed First-Class or sent by an IRS-designated private delivery service on or before the due date. See Pub. 15 (Circular E) for more information on IRS-designated private delivery services.

Where To File

In the list below, find the location of your legal residence, principal place of business, office, or agency. Send Form 945 to the address listed for your location.

 Where you file depends on whether or not you are including a payment with the return.

If you are in . . .		Without a payment . . .	With a payment . . .
Connecticut	New Jersey	Department of the Treasury	Internal Revenue Service
Delaware	New York		
District of	North Carolina	Internal Revenue	P. O. Box 804524
Columbia	Ohio	Service	Cincinnati, OH
Florida	Pennsylvania	Cincinnati, OH	45280-4524
Georgia	Rhode Island	45999-0042	
Illinois	South Carolina		
Indiana	Tennessee		
Kentucky	Vermont		
Maine	Virginia		
Maryland	West Virginia		
Massachusetts	Wisconsin		
Michigan			
New Hampshire			
Alabama	Missouri	Department of the Treasury	Internal Revenue Service
Alaska	Montana		
Arizona	Nebraska	Internal Revenue	P. O. Box 37945
Arkansas	Nevada	Service	Hartford, CT
California	New Mexico	Ogden, UT	06176-7945
Colorado	North Dakota	84201-0042	
Hawaii	Oklahoma		
Idaho	Oregon		
Iowa	South Dakota		
Kansas	Texas		
Louisiana	Utah		
Minnesota	Washington		
Mississippi	Wyoming		
No legal residence or principal place of business in any state:		Internal Revenue Service P.O. Box 409101 Ogden, UT 84409	Internal Revenue Service P. O. Box 37945 Hartford, CT 06176-7945
If you are filing Form 945 for an exempt organization or government entity (federal, state, local, or Indian tribal government), use the following addresses, regardless of your location:		Department of the Treasury Internal Revenue Service Ogden, UT 84201-0042	Internal Revenue Service P. O. Box 37945 Hartford, CT 06176-7945

Employer Identification Number (EIN)

If you do not have an EIN, you may apply for one online. Go to IRS.gov and click on the *Apply for an EIN Online* link under "Tools." You may also apply for an EIN by calling 1-800-829-4933, or you can fax or mail Form SS-4, Application for Employer Identification Number, to the IRS. If you have not received your EIN by the due date of Form 945, write "Applied For" and the date you applied in this entry space.

Penalties and Interest

There are penalties for filing Form 945 late and for paying or depositing taxes late, unless there is reasonable cause. See section 11 of Pub. 15 (Circular E) for more information on deposit penalties. There are also penalties for failure to furnish information returns (for example, Forms 1099-MISC, 1099-R, or W-2G) to payees and failure to file copies with the IRS. Interest is charged on taxes paid late at a rate set by law.

If you receive a notice about a penalty after you file this return, reply to the notice with an explanation and we will determine if you meet reasonable-cause criteria. Do **not** attach an explanation when you file your return.

Use Form 843, Claim for Refund and Request for Abatement, to request abatement of assessed penalties or interest. Do not request abatement of assessed penalties or interest on Form 945 or Form 945-X.

*If amounts that must be withheld are not withheld or are not deposited or paid to the United States Treasury, the **trust fund recovery penalty** may apply. The penalty is the full amount of any unpaid trust fund tax. This penalty may apply when these unpaid taxes cannot be immediately collected from the employer or business. The trust fund recovery penalty may be imposed on all persons who are determined by the IRS to have been responsible for collecting, accounting for, and paying over these taxes, and who acted willfully in not doing so. "Willfully" in this case means voluntarily, consciously, and intentionally. A responsible person acts willfully if the person knows that the required actions are not taking place.*

Voluntary Income Tax Withholding

States must allow unemployment compensation recipients to elect to have federal income tax withheld. Recipients paid under the Railroad Unemployment Insurance Act may also elect withholding.

Recipients of any of the following federal payments may request federal income tax withholding.
* Social security and Tier 1 railroad retirement benefits.
* Certain crop disaster payments.
* Commodity Credit Corporation loans.

The voluntary income tax withholding rates will be available in January 2013 at *www.irs.gov/form945.*

The payee may request withholding on Form W-4V, Voluntary Withholding Request, or you may develop your own substitute form. Any voluntary withholding on these payments must be reported on Form 945 (and on the required information return—Form 1099-G, Form SSA-1099, or Form RRB-1099) and is subject to the deposit rules.

Depositing Withheld Taxes

Deposit all nonpayroll (Form 945) withheld federal income tax, including backup withholding, by electronic funds transfer. Combine all Form 945 taxes for deposit purposes. **Do not** combine deposits for Forms 941, 943, 944, or Form CT-1 with deposits for Form 945.

Generally, the deposit rules that apply to Form 941 also apply to Form 945. However, because Form 945 is an annual return, the rules for determining your deposit schedule (discussed below) are different from those for Form 941. See section 11 of Pub. 15 (Circular E) for a detailed discussion of the deposit rules.

Determining Your Deposit Schedule

There are two deposit schedules—**monthly** or **semiweekly**— for determining when you must deposit withheld federal income tax. These schedules tell you when a deposit is due after a tax liability arises (that is, you make a payment subject to federal income tax withholding, including backup withholding). Before the beginning of each calendar year, you must determine which of the two deposit schedules you must use.

For 2013, you are a monthly schedule depositor for Form 945 if the total tax reported on your 2011 Form 945 (line 3) was $50,000 or less. If the total tax reported for 2011 exceeded $50,000, you are a semiweekly schedule depositor.

 If you are a monthly schedule depositor and accumulate a $100,000 liability or more on any day during a calendar month, your deposit schedule changes on the next day to semiweekly for the remainder of the year and for the following year. For more information, see the $100,000 Next-Day Deposit Rule in section 11 of Pub. 15 (Circular E).

Specific Instructions

Line A. Final Return

If you go out of business or end operations and you will not have to file Form 945 in the future, file a final return. Be sure to check the box on line A and enter the date that final nonpayroll payments were made.

Line 1. Federal Income Tax Withheld

Enter the federal income tax that you withheld (or were required to withhold) from pensions (including distributions from tax-favored retirement plans, for example, section 401(k), section 403(b), and governmental section 457(b) plans), annuities, IRA distributions, military retirement, Indian gaming profits, and gambling winnings (regular gambling withholding only). Also enter any voluntary amount that you withheld on certain government payments. If you are required to report federal income tax withholding on Forms 1099 (for example, Form 1099-R or 1099-MISC) or Form W-2G, you must report the federal income tax withheld on Form 945.

 *Federal income tax withholding reported on Form W-2 **must** be reported on Form 941, Form 943, Form 944, or Schedule H (Form 1040), as appropriate.*

Line 2. Backup Withholding

Enter any backup withholding, including backup withholding on gambling winnings.

Regulated investment companies (RICs) and real estate investment trusts (REITs) must report any backup withholding on Form 945 in the year that the dividends are actually paid. This includes January payments of dividends declared during October, November, and December of the prior year. See the Instructions for Form 1099-DIV for special reporting requirements.

Line 3. Total Taxes

Add lines 1 and 2. If total taxes are $2,500 or more, the amount reported on line 3 must equal the total liability for the year reported on line 7M of the Monthly Summary of Federal Tax Liability, or line M of Form 945-A, Annual Return of Federal Tax Liability.

Line 4. Total Deposits

Enter your total Form 945 deposits for the year, including any overpayment that you applied from filing Form 945-X and any overpayment that you applied from your 2011 return.

Line 5. Balance Due

If line 3 is more than line 4, enter the difference on line 5. Otherwise, see *Overpayment* below. You do not have to pay if line 5 is under $1. Generally, you should have a balance due only if your total taxes for the year (line 3) are less than $2,500. If you made payments under the accuracy of deposits rule, see section 11 of Pub. 15 (Circular E).

You may pay the amount shown on line 5 using EFTPS, a credit or debit card, or a check or money order. Do not use a credit or debit card to pay taxes that were required to be deposited. For more information on electronic payment options, visit the IRS website at *www.irs.gov/e-pay*.

If you pay by EFTPS or credit or debit card, file your return using the *Without a payment* address under *Where To File*, earlier. Do not file Form 945-V, Payment Voucher. If you pay by check or money order, make it payable to the "United States Treasury." Enter your EIN, Form 945, and the tax period on your check or money order. Complete Form 945-V and enclose with Form 945.

If line 3 is $2,500 or more and you deposited all taxes when due, the amount on line 5 should be zero.

 If you did not make deposits as required and instead pay the taxes with Form 945, you may be subject to a penalty.

Line 6. Overpayment

If line 4 is more than line 3, enter the difference on line 6. **Never make an entry on both lines 5 and 6.**

If you deposited more than the correct amount for the year, you can have the overpayment refunded or applied to your next return by checking the appropriate box. Check only one box below line 6. If you do not check either box or if you check both boxes, generally we will apply the overpayment to your account. We may apply your overpayment to any past due tax account that is shown in our records under your EIN. If line 6 is under $1, we will send a refund or apply it to your next return only on written request.

Line 7. Monthly Summary of Federal Tax Liability

 This is a summary of your monthly tax liability, not a summary of deposits made. If line 3 is less than $2,500, do not complete line 7 or Form 945-A.

Complete line 7 only if you were a **monthly schedule depositor** for the entire year and line 3 is $2,500 or more. See *Determining Your Deposit Schedule*, earlier.

 The amount entered on line 7M must equal the amount reported on line 3.

Report your liabilities on Form 945-A instead of on line 7 if either of the following apply.
• You were a **semiweekly schedule depositor** during 2012. **Do not** complete entries A through M of line 7. Instead, complete and file Form 945-A with Form 945.

• You were a **monthly schedule depositor** for 2012 and during any month you accumulated nonpayroll taxes of $100,000 or more. Because this converted you to a semiweekly schedule depositor for the remainder of 2012 (and for 2013), you must report your liabilities on Form 945-A for the entire year. **Do not** complete entries A through M of line 7. For more information, see the *$100,000 Next-Day Deposit Rule* in section 11 of Pub. 15 (Circular E).

Third-Party Designee

If you want to allow any individual, corporation, firm, organization, or partnership to discuss your 2012 Form 945 with the IRS, check the "Yes" box in the "Third-Party Designee" section of Form 945. Also, enter the name, phone number, and any five-digit personal identification number (PIN) for the specific person to speak with — not the name of the firm who prepared your return.

By checking the "Yes" box, you are authorizing the IRS to speak with the designee to answer any questions relating to the information reported on your tax return. You are also authorizing the designee to:
• Give the IRS any information that is missing from your return,
• Call the IRS for information about the processing of your return or the status of your refund or payments,
• Receive copies of notices or transcripts related to your return upon request, and
• Respond to certain IRS notices about math errors, offsets, and return preparation.

You are not authorizing the designee to receive any refund check, bind you to anything (including additional tax liability), or otherwise represent you before the IRS. If you want to expand the designee's authorization, see Pub. 947, Practice Before the IRS and Power of Attorney.

The authorization will automatically expire 1 year from the due date (without regard to extensions) for filing your 2012 Form 945. If you or your designee wants to terminate the authorization, write to the IRS office for your locality using *Without a payment* address under *Where To File*, earlier.

Who Must Sign

Form 945 must be signed as follows:
• **Sole proprietorship** — The individual who owns the business.
• **Corporation (including a limited liability company (LLC) treated as a corporation)** — The president, vice president, or other principal officer duly authorized to sign.
• **Partnership (including an LLC treated as a partnership) or unincorporated organization** — A responsible and duly authorized partner, member, or officer having knowledge of its affairs.
• **Single member LLC treated as a disregarded entity** — The owner of the limited liability company (LLC).
• **Trust or estate** — The fiduciary.

Form 945 may also be signed by a duly authorized agent of the taxpayer if a valid power of attorney has been filed.

Alternative signature method. Corporate officers or duly authorized agents may sign Form 945 by rubber stamp, mechanical device, or computer software program. For details and required documentation, see Rev. Proc. 2005-39, 2005-28 I.R.B. 82, available at *www.irs.gov/irb/2005-28_IRB/ar16.html.*

Paid Preparer Use Only

A paid preparer must sign Form 945 and provide the information in the *Paid Preparer Use Only* section if the preparer was paid to prepare Form 945 and is not an employee of the filing entity. Paid preparers must sign paper returns with a manual signature. The preparer must give you a copy of the return in addition to the copy to be filed with the IRS.

If you are a paid preparer, enter your Preparer Tax Identification Number (PTIN) in the space provided. Include your complete address. If you work for a firm, enter the firm's name and the EIN of the firm. You can apply for a PTIN online or by filing Form W-12, IRS Paid Preparer Tax Identification Number (PTIN) Application and Renewal. For more information about applying for a PTIN online, visit the IRS website at *www.irs.gov/ptin*. You cannot use your PTIN in place of the EIN of the tax preparation firm.

Generally, do not complete this section if you are filing the return as a reporting agent and have a valid Form 8655, Reporting Agent Authorization, on file with the IRS. However, a reporting agent must complete this section if the reporting agent offered legal advice, for example, advising the client on determining whether federal income tax withholding is required on certain payments.

Privacy Act and Paperwork Reduction Act Notice.
We ask for the information on Form 945 to carry out the Internal Revenue laws of the United States. We need it to figure and collect the right amount of tax. Sections 3402, 3405, and 3406 of the Internal Revenue Code require taxpayers to pay over to the IRS federal income tax withheld from certain nonpayroll payments and distributions, including backup withholding. Form 945 is used to report these withholdings. Section 6011 requires you to provide the requested information if the tax applies to you. Section 6109 requires you to provide your identification number. If you fail to provide this information in a timely manner, or provide false or fraudulent information, you may be subject to penalties and interest.

You do not have to provide the information requested on a form that is subject to the Paperwork Reduction Act unless the form displays a valid OMB control number. Books or records relating to a form or its instructions must be retained as long as their contents may become material in the administration of any Internal Revenue law.

Generally, tax returns and return information are confidential, as required by section 6103. However, section 6103 allows or requires the Internal Revenue Service to disclose or give the information shown on your tax return to others described in the Code. For example, we may disclose your tax information to the Department of Justice for civil and criminal litigation, and to cities, states, the District of Columbia, and U.S. commonwealths and possessions to administer their tax laws. We may also disclose this information to other countries under a tax treaty, to federal and state agencies to enforce federal nontax criminal laws, or to federal law enforcement and intelligence agencies to combat terrorism.

The time needed to complete and file Form 945 will vary depending on individual circumstances. The estimated average time is: **Recordkeeping,** 7 hr., 9 min.; **Learning about the law or the form,** 47 min.; and **Preparing and sending the form to the IRS,** 56 min. If you have comments concerning the accuracy of these time estimates or suggestions for making Form 945 simpler, we would be happy to hear from you. You can email us at *taxforms@irs.gov*. Enter "Form 945" on the subject line. Or write to the Internal Revenue Service, Tax Products Coordinating Committee, SE:W:CAR:MP:T:M:S, 1111 Constitution Ave. NW, IR-6526, Washington, DC 20224. **Do not** send Form 945 to this address. Instead, see *Where To File,* earlier.

Form **945-A**

(Rev. October 2012)

Department of the Treasury
Internal Revenue Service

Annual Record of Federal Tax Liability

▶ Information about Form 945-A and its instructions is at *www.irs.gov/form945*.
▶ File with Form 945, 945-X, CT-1, CT-1 X, 944, or 944-X.

OMB No. 1545-1430

___ ___ ___ ___
Calendar Year

Name (as shown on Form 945, 945-X, CT-1, CT-1 X, 944, or 944-X) | Employer identification number (EIN)

You must complete this form if you are required to deposit on a semiweekly schedule or if your tax liability during any month was $100,000 or more. Show tax liability here, not deposits. (The IRS gets deposit data from electronic funds transfers.) **DO NOT change your tax liability by adjustments reported on any Form 945-X, 944-X, or CT-1 X.**

January Tax Liability		February Tax Liability		March Tax Liability	
1 — 17		1 — 17		1 — 17	
2 — 18		2 — 18		2 — 18	
3 — 19		3 — 19		3 — 19	
4 — 20		4 — 20		4 — 20	
5 — 21		5 — 21		5 — 21	
6 — 22		6 — 22		6 — 22	
7 — 23		7 — 23		7 — 23	
8 — 24		8 — 24		8 — 24	
9 — 25		9 — 25		9 — 25	
10 — 26		10 — 26		10 — 26	
11 — 27		11 — 27		11 — 27	
12 — 28		12 — 28		12 — 28	
13 — 29		13 — 29		13 — 29	
14 — 30		14		14 — 30	
15 — 31		15		15 — 31	
16		16		16	

A Total for month ▶   **B** Total for month ▶   **C** Total for month ▶

April Tax Liability		May Tax Liability		June Tax Liability	
1 — 17		1 — 17		1 — 17	
2 — 18		2 — 18		2 — 18	
3 — 19		3 — 19		3 — 19	
4 — 20		4 — 20		4 — 20	
5 — 21		5 — 21		5 — 21	
6 — 22		6 — 22		6 — 22	
7 — 23		7 — 23		7 — 23	
8 — 24		8 — 24		8 — 24	
9 — 25		9 — 25		9 — 25	
10 — 26		10 — 26		10 — 26	
11 — 27		11 — 27		11 — 27	
12 — 28		12 — 28		12 — 28	
13 — 29		13 — 29		13 — 29	
14 — 30		14 — 30		14 — 30	
15		15 — 31		15	
16		16		16	

D Total for month ▶   **E** Total for month ▶   **F** Total for month ▶

For Paperwork Reduction Act Notice, see page 4.   Cat. No. 14733M   Form **945-A** (Rev. 10-2012)

Form 945-A (Rev. 10-2012)   Page **2**

	July Tax Liability					August Tax Liability					September Tax Liability		
1		17			1		17			1		17	
2		18			2		18			2		18	
3		19			3		19			3		19	
4		20			4		20			4		20	
5		21			5		21			5		21	
6		22			6		22			6		22	
7		23			7		23			7		23	
8		24			8		24			8		24	
9		25			9		25			9		25	
10		26			10		26			10		26	
11		27			11		27			11		27	
12		28			12		28			12		28	
13		29			13		29			13		29	
14		30			14		30			14		30	
15		31			15		31			15			
16					16					16			

G Total for month ▶   **H** Total for month ▶   **I** Total for month ▶

	October Tax Liability					November Tax Liability					December Tax Liability		
1		17			1		17			1		17	
2		18			2		18			2		18	
3		19			3		19			3		19	
4		20			4		20			4		20	
5		21			5		21			5		21	
6		22			6		22			6		22	
7		23			7		23			7		23	
8		24			8		24			8		24	
9		25			9		25			9		25	
10		26			10		26			10		26	
11		27			11		27			11		27	
12		28			12		28			12		28	
13		29			13		29			13		29	
14		30			14		30			14		30	
15		31			15					15		31	
16					16					16			

J Total for month ▶   **K** Total for month ▶   **L** Total for month ▶

M Total tax liability for the year (add lines **A** through **L**). This should equal line 3 on Form 945 (line 13 on Form CT-1, line 7 on Form 944.)   . . . . ▶

Form **945-A** (Rev. 10-2012)

Future Developments

For the latest information about developments related to Form 945-A and its instructions, such as legislation enacted after they were published, go to *www.irs.gov/form945*.

Reminders

Reporting prior period adjustments. Prior period adjustments are reported on Form 945-X, Adjusted Annual Return of Federal Income Tax or Claim for Refund; Form CT-1 X, Adjusted Employer's Annual Railroad Retirement Tax Return or Claim for Refund; and Form 944-X, Adjusted Employer's ANNUAL Federal Tax Return or Claim for Refund; respectively, and are not taken into account when figuring the tax liability for the current year.

When you file Form 945-A with your Form 945, CT-1, or 944, **do not** change your tax liability by adjustments reported on any Form 945-X, CT-1 X, or 944-X.

Amended Form 945-A. If you have been assessed a failure-to-deposit (FTD) penalty, you may be able to file an amended Form 945-A. For more information, see *Amending a Previously Filed Form 945-A,* later.

General Instructions

Purpose of form. Use Form 945-A to report your federal tax liability (based on the dates payments were made or wages were paid) for the following tax returns.

• Forms 945 and 945-X for federal income tax withholding on nonpayroll payments. Nonpayroll withholding includes backup withholding and federal income tax withholding on pensions, annuities, IRAs, Indian gaming profits, gambling winnings, and military retirement.

• Forms CT-1 and CT-1 X for both employee and employer Tier I taxes and employer Tier II taxes.

• Forms 944 and 944-X for federal income tax withheld plus both employee and employer social security and Medicare taxes.

Forms 944(SP), 944-X (SP), and 944-X (PR). If you are a semiweekly schedule depositor who files Formulario 944(SP), Declaración Federal ANUAL de Impuestos del Patrono o Empleador, you should use Formulario 943A-PR, Registro de la Obligación Contributiva Federal del Patrono Agrícola, to report your tax liability. You should also file Form 943A-PR if you file Form 944-X(SP) or Form 944-X(PR) and you need to amend a previously filed Form 943A-PR.

Who must file. Semiweekly schedule depositors must complete and file Form 945-A with their tax return. **Do not** file Form 945-A if your tax liability for the return period is less than $2,500. **Do not** file this form if you are a monthly schedule depositor unless you accumulated a tax liability of $100,000 during any month of the year. Monthly schedule depositors who accumulate $100,000 become semiweekly schedule depositors for the remainder of the year (and the next year) and must complete Form 945-A for the entire year.

The deposit rules, including the $100,000 Next-Day Deposit Rule, are explained in section 11 of Pub. 15 (Circular E), Employer's Tax Guide, and in the instructions for your tax return.

Caution. IRS uses Form 945-A to match the tax liability you reported on the returns indicated above with your deposits. The IRS also uses Form 945-A to determine if you have deposited your tax liabilities on time. Unless Form 945-A is properly completed and filed (if applicable) with your tax return, the IRS may propose an "averaged" failure-to-deposit penalty. See *Deposit Penalties* in section 11 of Pub. 15 (Circular E) for more information.

Specific Instructions

If you must report your tax liabilities on Form 945-A as discussed above, file it with your tax return. Each numbered space on Form 945-A corresponds to a date during the year. Report your tax liabilities in the spaces that correspond to the dates you made payments, not the date tax deposits were made. For example, if you became liable for a pension distribution on December 31, 2011, but did not make the distribution until January 3, 2012, the federal income tax withholding liability for the distribution must be reported on Form 945-A for 2012, on line 3 under January Tax Liability.

Enter your business information. Carefully enter your employer identification number (EIN) and name at the top of the form. Make sure that they exactly match the name of your business and the EIN that the IRS assigned to your business and also agree with the name and EIN shown on the attached Form 945, 945-X, CT-1, CT-1 X, 944, or 944-X.

Calendar year. Enter the calendar year of the Form 945, 945-X, CT-1, CT-1 X, 944, or 944-X to which Form 945-A is attached.

Form 945 filers. Do not complete entries A through M of the Monthly Summary of Federal Tax Liability (Form 945, line 7). Be sure to mark the semiweekly schedule depositor checkbox above line 7 on Form 945.

Form CT-1 filers. Do not complete the Monthly Summary of Railroad Retirement Tax Liability (Form CT-1).

Form 944 filers. On Form 944, check the box for "Line 7 is $2,500 or more" at line 13, and leave blank lines 13a–13m.

Enter your tax liability by month. Enter your tax liabilities in the spaces that correspond to the dates you **paid** wages to your employees or made nonpayroll payments, not the date deposits were made. The total tax liability for the year (line M) must equal net taxes on Form 945 (line 3), Form 944 (line 7) or Form CT-1 (line 13). Report your tax liabilities on this form corresponding to the dates of each wage payment or nonpayroll payment, **not** to when the liabilities are accrued. Enter the monthly totals on lines A, B, C, D, E, F, G, H, I, J, K, and L. Enter the total for the year on line M.

For example, if you are a Form 945 filer, your payroll period ended on December 31, 2011, and you **paid** the nonpayroll payments for that period on January 6, 2012, you would:

• Go to January (on Form 945-A filed with your 2012 return), and

• Enter your tax liability on line 6 (because line 6 represents the sixth day of the month).

 Make sure you have checked the appropriate box below line 6 of Form 945 to show that you are a semiweekly schedule depositor.

Example 1. Cedar Co., which has a semiweekly deposit schedule, makes periodic payments on gambling winnings on the 15th day of each month. On December 24, 2012, in addition to its periodic payments, it withheld from a payment on gambling winnings under the backup withholding rules. Since Cedar Co. is a semiweekly schedule depositor, it **must** record these nonpayroll withholding liabilities on Form 945-A. It must report tax liabilities on line 15 for each month and line 24 for December.

Cedar Co. enters the monthly totals on lines **A** through **L**. It adds these monthly subtotals and enters the total tax liability for the year on line **M**. The amount on line **M** should equal Form 945, line 3.

Example 2. Fir Co. is a semiweekly schedule depositor. During January, it withheld federal income tax on pension distributions as follows: $52,000 on January 10; $35,000 on January 24. Since Fir Co. is a semiweekly schedule depositor, it **must** record its federal income tax withholding liabilities on Form 945-A. It must record $52,000 on line 10 and $35,000 on line 24 for January.

Example 3. Because Elm Co. is a new business, it is a monthly schedule depositor at the beginning of 2012. During January, it withheld federal income tax on nonpayroll payments as follows: $2,000 on January 10; $99,000 on January 24. The deposit rules require that a monthly schedule depositor begin depositing on a semiweekly deposit schedule when a $100,000 or more tax liability is accumulated on any day within a month (see section 11 of Pub. 15 (Circular E) for details). Since Elm Co. accumulated $101,000 ($2,000 + $99,000) on January 24, 2012, it became a semiweekly schedule depositor on January 25, 2012. Elm Co. must complete Form 945-A and file it with Form 945. It must record $2,000 on line 10 and $99,000 on line 24 for January. **No entries** should be made on Form 945, line 7, although Elm Co. was a monthly schedule depositor until January 25.

Amending a Previously Filed Form 945-A

Semiweekly schedule depositors. If you have been assessed a failure-to-deposit (FTD) penalty and you made an error on Form 945-A and the correction will not change the total liability you reported on Form 945-A, you may be able to reduce your penalty by filing an amended Form 945-A.

Example. You reported a liability of $3,000 on January 1. However, the liability was actually for March. Prepare an amended Form 945-A showing the $3,000 liability on March 1. Also, you must enter the liabilities previously reported for the year that did not change. Write "Amended" at the top of Form 945-A. The IRS will refigure the penalty and notify you of any change in the penalty.

Monthly schedule depositors. You can also file an amended Form 945-A if you have been assessed an FTD penalty and you made an error on the monthly tax liability section of Form 945. When completing Form 945-A, only enter the monthly totals. The daily entries are not required.

Where to file. File your amended Form 945-A at the address provided in the penalty notice you received. You do not have to submit your original Form 945-A.

Forms 945-X, CT-1 X, and 944-X

Tax decrease. If you are filing Form 945-X, CT-1 X, or 944-X, you can file an amended Form 945-A with the form if **both** of the following apply.

1. You have a tax decrease.

2. You were assessed an FTD penalty.

File your amended Form 945-A with Form 945-X, CT-1 X, or 944-X. The total liability reported on your amended Form 945-A must equal the corrected amount of tax reported on Form 945-X, CT-1 X, or 944-X. If your penalty is decreased, the IRS will include the penalty decrease with your tax decrease.

Tax increase—Form 945-X, CT-1 X, or 944-X filed timely. If you are filing a timely Form 945-X, CT-1 X, or 944-X showing a tax increase, do not file an amended Form 945-A, unless you were assessed an FTD penalty caused by an incorrect, incomplete, or missing Form 945-A. Do not include the tax increase reported on Form 945-X, CT-1 X, or 944-X on an amended Form 945-A you file.

Tax increase—Form 945-X, CT-1 X, or 944-X filed late. If you owe tax and are filing late, that is, after the due date of the return for the filing period in which you discovered the error, you must file the form with an amended Form 945-A. Otherwise, IRS may assess an "averaged" FTD penalty.

The total tax reported on line M of Form 945-A must match the corrected tax (Form 945, line 3; Form 944, line 7 (line 9 for years before 2011); Form CT-1, line 13) combined with any correction reported on Form 945-X, line 5 (Form 944-X, line 16 minus any advance EIC reported on Form 944-X, line 17; Form CT-1X, line 18) for the year, less any previous abatements and interest-free tax assessments.

Paperwork Reduction Act Notice. We ask for the information on this form to carry out the Internal Revenue laws of the United States. You are required to give us the information. We need it to ensure that you are complying with these laws and to allow us to figure and collect the right amount of tax.

You are not required to provide the information requested on a form that is subject to the Paperwork Reduction Act unless the form displays a valid OMB control number. Books or records relating to a form or its instructions must be retained as long as their contents may become material in the administration of any Internal Revenue law. Generally, tax returns and return information are confidential, as required by Code section 6103.

The time needed to complete and file this form will vary depending on individual circumstances. The estimated average time is:

Recordkeeping	6 hr., 27 min.
Learning	6 min.
Preparing and sending the form to the IRS	12 min.

If you have comments concerning the accuracy of these time estimates or suggestions for making this form simpler, we would be happy to hear from you. You can write to the IRS at the address listed in the Privacy Act Notice for your tax return.

Department of The Treasury
Internal Revenue Service
[ADDRESS LINE 1]
[ADDRESS LINE 2]

IF YOU WRITE OR CALL US, refer to this information:

Notice Number: 972CG
Date of This Notice:
Taxpayer Identification Number: Form:
Tax Period: Penalty Reference Code:

||||||||||||||||||||||||||

[taxpayer name]
[address line one]
[address line two]
[city/state/zip]

For General Information,
please call: 1-800-829-1040 TOLL FREE

We're Proposing a Penalty For Your Tax Year 19XX Information Returns

ACTION REQUIRED

Our records show that you didn't file certain information returns as the law requires for the tax period shown above. The law allows us to charge you a penalty for not filing information returns correctly. We're proposing a penalty in the amount of $_____. We won't charge interest on this penalty until after we send you a bill.

Please read this entire notice carefully. It explains why we proposed the penalty and what you should do if you agree or disagree with our proposal. Our explanation of the proposed penalty begins on page 2.

HOW YOU SHOULD RESPOND TO THIS NOTICE

Please review your records related to filing the returns listed on page 2.

--If you AGREE to the full amount of the proposed penalty, do all of the following:

1. Check box (A) on the last page of this notice.
2. Sign and date the consent to the penalty assessment.
3. Enclose your payment in full, if possible. Make your check or money order payable to the *Internal Revenue Service.*
4. Check the box to show if you have or have not enclosed a payment.
5. Return the last page of this notice with your payment in the enclosed envelope.

--If YOU DON'T AGREE with our findings or believe you have a reason why we shouldn't charge all or part of this penalty, do all of the following:

1. Check box (B) or (C) on the last page of this notice.
2. Enclose a signed statement explaining why you disagree.
3. Include any supporting documents you wish us to consider.
4. If you agree to part of penalty, enclose your payment, if possible. Make your check payable to the Internal Revenue Service.
5. Check the box to show if you have or have not enclosed a payment.
6. Return the last page of this notice with your statement and documents in the enclosed envelope. Please include a telephone number, including the area code, and the best time to call you.

It's important that we receive your completed response within 45 days from the date of this notice. You have 60 days to respond if you live outside of the United States. If we don't hear from you within this period, we'll conclude that the proposed penalty is correct. Then we'll send you a bill called "Notice of Penalty Charge" for the amount of the proposed penalty. We'll charge interest from the date of the Notice of Penalty Charge to the date we receive the amount you owe in full. You may contest the Notice of Penalty Charge by sending us proof that the penalty is incorrect.

If you have any questions about this notice, you may write to us at the return address on this notice. If you prefer, you may call the telephone number shown above for general information about this notice. However, the office at the address shown on this notice is most familiar with your case.

IRS information: service center name, TIN, penalty reference code(s), tax period, date of this notice, notice #)

These information returns were not filed correctly according to our records.

1st name line of payor	Form (1099-INT,MISC,DIV,ETC)	Transmitter Control Code:
2nd name line of payor	Number received:	( )
1st address line of payor	Number amended:	
2nd address line of payor	Date received:	Proposed Penalty Type:
	How received: (paper or tape)	(late filing, magnetic Media, missing or incorrect TINs)
1st name line of payor	Form (1099-INT,MISC,DIV,ETC)	Transmitter Control Code:
2nd name line of payor	Number received:	( )
1st address line of payor	Number amended:	
2nd address line of payor	Date received:	Proposed Penalty Type:
	How received: (paper or tape)	(late filing, magnetic Media, missing or incorrect TINs)

Explanation of Penalty

We propose a penalty for each Form 1098, 1099, W-2G, or W-2 that you didn't file correctly by the due date (including extensions). This penalty may also apply if we sent timely filed returns back to you for changes and you didn't return them to us in the time we requested.

The penalty is:

- $15 for each return filed within 30 days after the due date, up to a maximum of $75,000 per year ($25,000 for small businesses as defined below),

- $30 for each return filed more that 30 days after the due date but by August 1, up to a maximum of $150,000 per year ($50,000 for small businesses), or

- $50 for each return filed after August 1.

The maximum penalty we can charge is $50 per information return, up to $250,000 per year ($100,000 for small businesses).

Lower Penalty for Small Businesses

The lower maximum penalties stated above for small businesses apply if a business had average gross receipts of $5 million or less for the three most recent tax years (or time in business, if shorter) ending before the calendar year the information returns were due. For example, if we charged you a penalty for 1992 information returns due in 1993, the three most recent tax years are 1992, 1991, and 1990. If the penalty on the notice you received is more than the maximum penalty for small businesses, we'll reduce the penalty based on evidence you give us that you're a small business as we define it here.

IRS information: service center name, TIN, penalty reference code(s), tax period, date of this notice, notice #)

These information returns were not filed correctly according to our records.

1st name line of payor	Form (1099-INT,MISC,DIV,ETC)	Transmitter Control Code:
2nd name line of payor	Number received:	( )
1st address line of payor	Number amended:	
2nd address line of payor	Date received:	Proposed Penalty Type:
	How received: (paper or tape)	(late filing, magnetic Media, missing or incorrect TINs)
1st name line of payor	Form (1099-INT,MISC,DIV,ETC)	Transmitter Control Code:
2nd name line of payor	Number received:	( )
1st address line of payor	Number amended:	
2nd address line of payor	Date received:	Proposed Penalty Type:
	How received: (paper or tape)	(late filing, magnetic Media, missing or incorrect TINs)

Explanation of Penalty

We propose a penalty for each Form 1098, 1099, W-2G, or W-2 that you didn't send to us on magnetic media as the law requires. The law requires you to file on magnetic media if you file more than 250 returns. The penalty for not filing on magnetic media is $50 for each return over 250 that you filed on paper. For example, if you filed 300 paper returns that should have been filed on magnetic media, we would apply the penalty to 50 of them. The maximum penalty we can charge is $50 per information return, up to $250,000 per year ($100,000 for small businesses as defined below).

According to our records, you didn't receive an undue hardship waiver to exempt you from filing returns on magnetic media for 19XX. If you feel that we shouldn't charge this penalty because to file on magnetic media would have caused you an undue hardship, you must send us:

1. An estimate, including the cost of preparation, of what it would have cost you to file paper returns, and

2. An estimate, including the cost of preparation, of what it would have cost you to file on magnetic media, and

3. Cost estimates from two computer service bureaus showing the cost of return preparation.

If you cannot show that an undue hardship existed, you must be able to show reasonable cause to have the penalty waived.

Lower Penalty for Small Businesses

The lower maximum penalty stated above for small businesses applies if a business had average gross receipts of $5 million or less for the three most recent tax years ending before the calendar year in which the information returns were due (or time in business, if shorter). For example, if we charged you a penalty for 1992 information returns due in 1993, the three most recent tax years are 1992, 1991, and 1990. If the penalty on the notice you received is more than the maximum penalty for small businesses, we'll reduce the penalty based on evidence you give us that you are a small business as we define it here.

Page 2   Notice 972

Magnetic Media Penalty

(IRS information: service center name, TIN, penalty reference code(s), tax period, date of this notice, notice #)

Summary of Proposed Penalty

The summary below shows the information returns on which we proposed the penalty and the amount of penalty for each penalty type. The number of returns shown in the summary may be less than the number you filed because of allowances made in computing the penalty.

PROPOSED PENALTY AMOUNT: $XXX,XXX

TYPE OF RETURNS	PENALTY TYPE AND AMOUNT						
	Late Filing	Number of Returns	Magnetic Media	Number of Returns	Payee Tax ID Number	Number of of Returns	Total Penalty Amount
1099-DIV 1099-B	$XXX,XXX $XXX,XXX	nn,nnn nn,nnn	$XXX,XXX $XXX,XXX	nn,nnn nn,nnn	$XXX,XXX $XXX,XXX	nn,nnn nn,nnn	$XXX,XXX XXX,XXX
Totals	$XXX,XXX	nn,nnn	$XXX,XXX	nn,nnn	$XXX,XXX	nn,nnn	$XXX,XXX

Proposed Penalty-- This amount may be less than the total of the individual penalty amounts shown above if more than one type of penalty applies to any of the returns you filed. For example, if you filed a return late and with a missing taxpayer identification number, we'll show the returns in both penalty columns. However, the maximum we will charge is $50 for that return. The proposed penalty may also be reduced because the total applicable penalty exceeded the $250,000 per year maximum allowed by law.

Late filing Penalty -- This penalty applies to returns filed after the due date. It may also apply to returns filed by the due date but not filed correctly.

Magnetic Media penalty -- This penalty applies to the number of paper returns over 250 that you filed.

Payee Tax Identification Number penalty -- This penalty applies to returns filed with a missing or incorrect taxpayer identification number.

If you believe you have an acceptable reason why we should not charge any part of the Total Penalty Amount shown above, please send us an explanation. If you give us an acceptable explanation for only part of the Total Penalty Amount shown, we'll send you a bill for any unexplained penalty amounts.

IRS information: service center name, TIN, penalty reference code(s), tax period, date of this notice, notice #)

These information returns were not filed correctly according to our records.

1st name line of payor	Form (1099-INT,MISC,DIV,ETC)	Transmitter Control Code:
2nd name line of payor	Number received:	( )
1st address line of payor	Number amended:	
2nd address line of payor	Date received:	Proposed Penalty Type:
	How received: (paper or tape)	(late filing, magnetic Media, missing or incorrect TINs)

1st name line of payor	Form (1099-INT,MISC,DIV,ETC)	Transmitter Control Code:
2nd name line of payor	Number received:	( )
1st address line of payor	Number amended:	
2nd address line of payor	Date received:	Proposed Penalty Type:
	How received: (paper or tape)	(late filing, magnetic Media, missing or incorrect TINs)

Explanation of Penalty

We propose a penalty for each information return you filed that had a missing or incorrect taxpayer identification number. The penalty is $50 for each Form 1098, 1099, W-2G or W-2 you sent to us with a missing or incorrect TIN.

The maximum penalty we can charge is $50 per form, up to $250,00 per year ($100,000 for small businesses as defined below).

We've enclosed a list of the information returns you filed that had missing or incorrect TINs. You should check this list against your records to see if you have an acceptable reason why we shouldn't charge the penalty.

The enclosed Publication 1586, Reasonable Cause Regulations and Requirements as they Apply to Missing and Incorrect TINs, explains what actions you must have taken in order to show reasonable cause for missing or incorrect TINs. You should also check the list and follow the guidelines in Publication 1586 to make any required solicitations (requests for TINs) to payee. This may help you establish reasonable cause to avoid penalties in future years.

Publication 1586 also contains:

-Information and guidance needed to comply with the reporting requirements for the Omnibus Budget Reconciliation Act of 1989 and gives special attention to the requirement for requesting TINs from payees.

-Regulations that apply to information returns reporting and the penalties for not filing as the law requires, and

-Regulations which explain how to have the penalties waived based on reasonable cause.

Lower Penalty for Small Businesses

The lower maximum penalty stated above for small businesses applies if a business had average gross receipts of $5 million or less for the three most recent tax years ending before the calendar year in which the information returns were due (or time in business, if shorter). For example, if we charged you a penalty for 1992 information returns due in 1993, the three most recent tax years are 1992, 1991, and 1990. If the penalty on the notice you received is more than the maximum penalty for small businesses, we'll reduce the penalty based on evidence you give us that you are a small business as we define it here.

Page 2   Notice 972

Missing and Incorrect TIN Penalty

(IRS information: service center name, TIN, penalty reference code(s), tax period, date of this notice, notice#)

Response to Proposed Penalty for Your Tax Year 19XX Information Returns

Please check the box below that applies to you. Return this page in the enclosed envelope and make sure the Internal Revenue Service address appears through the window. We've enclosed an extra copy of this page of the notice so that you will have a complete copy for your records.

Please check only one box:

[ ] (A) TOTAL AGREEMENT WITH THE PROPOSED PENALTY -- I consent to the immediate assessment and collection of the penalty amount shown in this notice, plus interest.
I Have [ ]   Have not [ ] enclosed a payment.

_____   _____
Signature   Date

[ ] (B) PARTIAL AGREEMENT WITH THE PROPOSED PENALTY -- I agree with PART of the proposed penalty shown in this notice. I have attached a signed statement and supporting documents explaining which items I disagree with and why I disagree, or why I feel you shouldn't charge part of the proposed penalty.
I Have [ ]   Have not [ ] enclosed a payment.

[ ] (C) TOTAL DISAGREEMENT WITH THE PROPOSED PENALTY -- I disagree with all of the proposed penalty shown in this notice. I've attached a signed statement and supporting documents explaining why the proposed penalty is incorrect, or an acceptable reason why you shouldn't charge this proposed penalty.

Telephone number: (   ) _____   Best hours to call: _____
(include area code)

_____
                           Please Do Not Detach

TIN   Ck digit   NC   MFT(13 or 55)   TINVal.   Chk   9212   640   0000995000

|!|!|!|!|!|!|!|!|!|!|!|!|!|!|!|!|!|!|!|

Internal Revenue Service   TIN   Date of notice
Service Center Name   Taxpayer Name
1st Address line   1st Address line
2nd Address line   2nd Address line

                        Page 4   Notice 972 (JAN. 1994)

Form **1042**

Department of the Treasury
Internal Revenue Service

Annual Withholding Tax Return for
U.S. Source Income of Foreign Persons

▶ Information about Form 1042 and its separate instructions is at *www.irs.gov/form1042*.

OMB No. 1545-0096

20**12**

If this is an amended return, check here . . . . ▶ ☐

Name of withholding agent	Employer identification number	For IRS Use Only	
		CC	FD
Number, street, and room or suite no. (if a P.O. box, see instructions)		RD	FF
		CAF	FP
City or town, province or state, and country (including postal code)		CR	I
		EDC	SIC

If you will not be liable for returns in the future, check here ▶ ☐   Enter date final income paid ▶ _____

Check if you are a: QI/Withholding foreign partnership or trust ☐   NQI/Flow-through entity ☐   (See instructions.)

Record of Federal Tax Liability (Do not show federal tax deposits here.)

Line No.	Period ending		Tax liability for period (including any taxes assumed on Form(s) 1000)	Line No.	Period ending		Tax liability for period (including any taxes assumed on Form(s) 1000)	Line No.	Period ending		Tax liability for period (including any taxes assumed on Form(s) 1000)
1	Jan.	7		21	May	7		41	Sept.	7	
2		15		22		15		42		15	
3		22		23		22		43		22	
4		31		24		31		44		30	
5	Jan. total			25	May total			45	Sept. total		
6	Feb.	7		26	June	7		46	Oct.	7	
7		15		27		15		47		15	
8		22		28		22		48		22	
9		29		29		30		49		31	
10	Feb. total			30	June total			50	Oct. total		
11	Mar.	7		31	July	7		51	Nov.	7	
12		15		32		15		52		15	
13		22		33		22		53		22	
14		31		34		31		54		30	
15	Mar. total			35	July total			55	Nov. total		
16	Apr.	7		36	Aug.	7		56	Dec.	7	
17		15		37		15		57		15	
18		22		38		22		58		22	
19		30		39		31		59		31	
20	Apr. total			40	Aug. total			60	Dec. total		

61   **No. of Forms 1042-S filed: a** On paper _____   **b** Electronically _____

62   **For all Form(s) 1042-S and 1000: a** Gross income paid   **b** Taxes withheld or assumed

63a	Total tax liability (add monthly total lines from above) . . .	**63a**	
b	Adjustments (see instructions)	**63b**	
c	Total **net tax** liability (combine lines 63a and 63b) . . . . ▶	**63c**	
64	Total paid by electronic funds transfer (or with a request for an extension of time to file) for 2012	**64**	
65	Enter overpayment applied as a credit from 2011 Form 1042 .	**65**	
66	Credit for amounts withheld by other withholding agents (see instructions)	**66**	
67	**Total payments.** Add lines 64 through 66 . . . . ▶	**67**	
68	If line 63c is larger than line 67, enter **balance due** here	**68**	
69	If line 67 is larger than line 63c, enter **overpayment** here	**69**	
70	Apply overpayment on line 69 to (check one): ☐ **Credit on 2013 Form 1042** or ☐ **Refund**		
71	Excise tax on specified federal procurement payments included on line 63a. (Total payments made _____ x 2% = _____)	**71**	

Third Party Designee   Do you want to allow another person to discuss this return with the IRS (see instructions)? ☐ **Yes. Complete the following.** ☐ **No**
Designee's name ▶ _____   Phone no. ▶ _____   Personal identification number (PIN) ▶ ☐☐☐☐☐☐☐☐

Sign Here   Under penalties of perjury, I declare that I have examined this return, including accompanying schedules and statements, and to the best of my knowledge and belief, it is true, correct, and complete. Declaration of preparer (other than withholding agent) is based on all information of which preparer has any knowledge.

Your signature ▶ _____   Date _____   Capacity in which acting ▶ _____

Daytime phone number ▶ _____

Paid Preparer Use Only

Print/Type preparer's name	Preparer's signature	Date	Check ☐ if self-employed	PTIN
Firm's name ▶			Firm's EIN ▶	
Firm's address ▶			Phone no.	

For Privacy Act and Paperwork Reduction Act Notice, see instructions.   Cat. No. 11384V   Form **1042** (2012)

20**12**
Instructions for Form 1042

Department of the Treasury
Internal Revenue Service

Annual Withholding Tax Return for U.S. Source Income of Foreign Persons

Section references are to the Internal Revenue Code unless otherwise noted.

Future Developments

For the latest information about developments related to Form 1042 and its instructions, such as legislation enacted after they were published, go to *www.irs.gov/form1042*.

General Instructions

Purpose of Form

Use Form 1042 to report the following.
- The tax withheld on certain income of foreign persons, including nonresident aliens, foreign partnerships, foreign corporations, foreign estates, and foreign trusts.
- The section 5000C 2% excise tax due on specified Federal procurement payments.

Publicly traded partnerships (section 1446 withholding tax). For purposes of reporting on Form 1042, a publicly traded partnership (PTP) must withhold section 1446 tax on distributions of effectively connected income (ECI) to its foreign partners. A nominee that receives a distribution of ECI from a PTP and is treated as the withholding agent must use Form 1042 to report the tax withheld. For this purpose, a nominee is a domestic person holding an interest in the PTP on behalf of one or more foreign partners. For more information, see Regulations section 1.1446-4 and Pub. 515, Withholding of Tax on Nonresident Aliens and Foreign Entities.

Who Must File

Every withholding agent or intermediary (see definitions next) who receives, controls, has custody of, disposes of, or pays any fixed or determinable annual or periodical income must file an annual return for the preceding calendar year on Form 1042. Also, any PTP or nominee making a distribution of ECI under section 1446 must file Form 1042 for the preceding calendar year.

You must file Form 1042 if any of the following applies.
- You are required to file Form(s) 1042-S (whether or not any tax was withheld or was required to be withheld). File Form 1042 even if you file Forms 1042-S electronically.

- You pay gross investment income to foreign private foundations that are subject to tax under section 4948(a).
- You pay any foreign person specified Federal procurement payments.

Withholding Agent

Any person required to withhold tax is a withholding agent. A withholding agent may be an individual, trust, estate, partnership, corporation, nominee (under section 1446), government agency, association, or tax-exempt foundation, whether domestic or foreign.

Liability for tax. As a withholding agent, you are personally liable for any tax required to be withheld. If you fail to withhold and the foreign payee fails to satisfy its U.S. tax liability, then both you and the foreign person are liable for tax, as well as interest and any applicable penalties.

The applicable tax will be collected only once. If the foreign person satisfies its U.S. tax liability, you are not liable for the tax but remain liable for any interest and penalties for failure to withhold.

Intermediary

An intermediary is a person who acts as a custodian, broker, nominee, or otherwise as an agent for another person, regardless of whether that other person is the beneficial owner of the amount paid, a flow-through entity, or another intermediary.

Qualified intermediary (QI). A QI is an intermediary that is a party to a withholding agreement with the IRS. An entity must indicate its status as a QI on a Form W-8IMY submitted to a withholding agent.

For information on a QI withholding agreement, see:
- Rev. Proc. 2000-12, which is on page 387 of Internal Revenue Bulletin 2000-4 at *www.irs.gov/pub/irs-irbs/irb00-04.pdf*;
- Notice 2001-4, which is on page 267 of Internal Revenue Bulletin 2001-2 at *www.irs.gov/pub/irs-irbs/irb01-02.pdf*;
- Rev. Proc. 2003-64, Appendix 3, 2003-32 I.R.B. 306, available at *www.irs.gov/irb/2003-32_IRB/ar19.html*;
- Rev. Proc. 2004-21, 2004-14 I.R.B. 702, available at *www.irs.gov/irb/2004-14_IRB/ar10.html*; and

- Rev. Proc. 2005-77, 2005-51 I.R.B. 1176, available at *www.irs.gov/irb/2005-51_IRB/ar13.html*.

Withholding foreign partnership (WP) or withholding foreign trust (WT). A WP or WT is a foreign partnership or trust that has entered into a withholding agreement with the IRS in which it agrees to assume primary withholding responsibility for all payments that are made to it for its partners, beneficiaries, or owners. For information on these withholding agreements, see Rev. Proc. 2003-64, Appendix 1 and Appendix 2. Also see Rev. Proc. 2004-21 and Rev. Proc. 2005-77.

Nonqualified intermediary (NQI). An NQI is any intermediary that is not a U.S. person and that is not a QI.

Qualified securities lender (QSL). A QSL is a foreign financial institution that is a bank, custodian, broker-dealer, or clearing organization subject to regulatory supervision in its home jurisdiction and that is:

1. Regularly engaged in the business of borrowing securities of U.S. corporations and lending such securities to unrelated customers; and

2. Subject to audit by the IRS under section 7602 or, in the case of a QI, an external auditor.

For further information about QSL status and the withholding requirements for substitute dividend payments, see Notice 2010-46, 2010-24 I.R.B. 757, available at *www.irs.gov/irb/2010-24_IRB/ar09.html*.

Where and When To File

Mail Form 1042 by March 15, 2013, to:

Ogden Service Center
P.O. Box 409101
Ogden, UT 84409

Use Form 1042-T to transmit paper Forms 1042-S.

Extension of time to file. If you need more time to file Form 1042, you may submit Form 7004, Application for Automatic Extension of Time To File Certain Business Income Tax, Information, and Other Returns.

Form 7004 does not extend the time for payment of tax.

Sep 21, 2012

Cat. No. 54843T

Additional Information

For details on the withholding of tax, see Pub. 515. You can get Pub. 515 by calling 1-800-TAX-FORM (1-800-829-3676) or by downloading it from IRS.gov. Click on "Forms and Pubs" and then on "Publication Number."

Need Assistance?

If you need help completing Form 1042, call 267-941-1000 (not a toll-free number) from 6:00 a.m. to 11:00 p.m. Eastern time or write to:

> Internal Revenue Service
> International Section
> Philadelphia, PA 19255-0725

Income Tax Withholding on Wages, Pensions, Annuities, and Certain Other Deferred Income

Use Form 941, Employer's QUARTERLY Federal Tax Return, to report income tax withheld and social security and Medicare taxes on wages paid to a nonresident alien employee.

Use Form 945, Annual Return of Withheld Federal Income Tax, to report income tax withheld under section 3405 from pensions, annuities, and certain other deferred income paid to a nonresident alien individual. However, if the recipient has elected under section 3405(a)(2) or (b)(2) not to have withholding under section 3405, these payments are subject to withholding under section 1441 and the tax withheld must be reported using Forms 1042 and 1042-S.

Use Schedule H (Form 1040), Household Employment Taxes, to report income tax withheld and social security and Medicare taxes on wages paid to a nonresident alien household employee.

Deposit Requirements

You are required to use the Electronic Federal Tax Payment System (EFTPS), discussed later, to deposit the tax withheld and required to be shown on Form 1042.

 To avoid a penalty, do not mail your deposits directly to the IRS.

The amount of tax you are required to withhold determines the frequency of your deposits. The following rules explain how often deposits must be made.

Note. If you are requesting an extension of time to file using Form 7004, follow these rules to see if you must make a deposit of any balance due or if you can pay it with Form 7004. See Form 7004 and its instructions for more information.

If at the end of any quarter-monthly period the total amount of undeposited taxes is $2,000 or more, you must deposit the taxes within 3 business days after the end of the quarter-monthly period. (A quarter-monthly period ends on the 7th, 15th, 22nd, and last day of the month.) A business day is any day other than a Saturday, Sunday, or legal holiday in the District of Columbia.

2. If at the end of any month the total amount of undeposited taxes is at least $200 but less than $2,000, you must deposit the taxes within 15 days after the end of the month. If you make a deposit of $2,000 or more during any month except December under rule 1, earlier, carry over any end-of-the-month balance of less than $2,000 to the next month. If you make a deposit of $2,000 or more during December, any end-of-December balance of less than $2,000 should be remitted with your Form 1042 by March 15, 2013.

3. If at the end of a calendar year the total amount of undeposited taxes is less than $200, you may either pay the taxes with your Form 1042 or deposit the entire amount by March 15, 2013.

Electronic deposit requirement. You must make electronic deposits of all depository tax liabilities using EFTPS. If you fail to use EFTPS, you may be subject to a 10% penalty. To enroll in or get more information about EFTPS, call 1-800-555-4477 or visit *www.eftps.gov/eftps*. Information is also available at *www.irs.gov/e-pay* .

Depositing on time. For deposits made by EFTPS to be on time, you must initiate the deposit by 8 p.m. Eastern time the day before the date the deposit is due. If you use a third party to make deposits on your behalf, they may have different cutoff times.

Same-day wire payment option. If you fail to initiate a deposit transaction on EFTPS by 8 p.m. Eastern time the day before the date a deposit is due, you still can make your deposit on time by using the Federal Tax Application. If you ever need the same-day wire payment method, you will need to make arrangements with your financial institution ahead of time. Check with your financial institution regarding availability, deadlines, and costs. Your financial institution may charge you a fee for payments made this way. To learn more about the information you will need to provide to your financial institution to make a same-day wire payment, visit *www.eftps.gov* to download the *Same-Day Payment Worksheet*.

Note. All payments should be made in U.S. dollars.

Interest and Penalties

If you file Form 1042 late, or fail to pay or deposit the tax when due, you may be liable for penalties and interest unless you can show that the failure to file or pay was due to reasonable cause and not willful neglect.

 You do not have to figure the amount of any interest or penalties you may owe. Because figuring these amounts can be complicated, we will do it for you if you want. We will send you a bill for any amount due.

If you include interest or penalties with your payment, identify and enter the amount in the bottom margin of Form 1042. Do not include interest or penalties in the balance due on line 68.

Interest. Interest is charged on taxes not paid by the due date, even if an extension of time to file is granted. Interest is also charged on penalties imposed for failure to file, negligence, fraud, and substantial understatements of tax from the due date (including extensions) to the date of payment. Interest is figured at a rate determined under section 6621.

Late filing of Form 1042. The penalty for not filing Form 1042 when due (including extensions) is 5% of the unpaid tax for each month or part of a month the return is late, up to a maximum of 25% of the unpaid tax.

Late payment of tax. The penalty for not paying tax when due is usually $1/2$ of 1% of the unpaid tax for each month or part of a month the tax is unpaid. The penalty cannot exceed 25% of the unpaid tax.

Other penalties. Penalties may be imposed for negligence, substantial understatement of tax, and fraud. See sections 6662 and 6663.

Specific Instructions

 File only one Form 1042 consolidating all Form 1042-S recipient information, regardless of the number of different clients, branches, divisions, or types of income for which you are the withholding agent. However, if you are acting in more than one capacity (for example, you are acting as a QI for certain designated accounts and as an NQI for other accounts), file a separate Form 1042 for each capacity in which you are acting.

Rounding off to whole dollars. You can round off cents to whole dollars. If you do round to whole dollars, you must round all amounts. To round, drop amounts under 50 cents and increase amounts from 50 to 99 cents to the next dollar. For example, $1.39 becomes $1 and $2.50 becomes $3. If you have to add two or more amounts to figure the amount to enter on a line, include cents when adding and only round off the total.

Employer identification number (EIN). You are generally required to enter your EIN. However, if you are filing Form 1042 as a QI, withholding foreign partnership, or withholding foreign trust, enter your QI-EIN, WP-EIN, or WT-EIN. Also, be sure to check the "QI/Withholding foreign partnership or trust" box. See *QI and NQI checkboxes*, later.

If you do not have an EIN, you can apply for one online at *www.irs.gov/businesses*. Click on "Employer ID Numbers" and then on "Apply for an EIN Online." You can apply for an EIN by telephone at 1-800-829-4933. You also can file Form SS-4, Application for Employer Identification Number, by fax or mail. File amended Forms 1042-S when you receive your EIN.

To get a QI-EIN, WP-EIN, or WT-EIN, submit Form SS-4 with your application for that status. Do not send an application for a QI-EIN, WP-EIN, or WT-EIN to the addresses listed in the Instructions for Form SS-4. Send the application along with Form SS-4 to:

> Internal Revenue Service
> LB & I: International: QI Group 1031
> 290 Broadway, 12th floor
> New York, NY 10007-1867 USA

If you are a QSL that is also a QI, enter your QI-EIN. Otherwise enter the EIN you have been assigned.

Address. Include the suite, room, or other unit number after the street address. If your post office does not deliver mail to the street address and you have a P.O. box, show the box number instead of the street address.

QI and NQI checkboxes. See page 1 for definitions of intermediary, qualified intermediary (QI), withholding foreign partnership (WP), withholding foreign trust (WT), and nonqualified intermediary (NQI). See the Form 1042-S instructions for definitions of U.S. branch treated as a U.S. person and flow-through entity.

Check the "QI/Withholding foreign partnership or trust" box if you are a QI, WP, WT, or a U.S. branch treated as a U.S. person. Check the "NQI/Flow-through entity" box if you are an NQI or a flow-through entity.

Lines 1 through 60. Except as otherwise provided in these instructions, include tax liability for the period in which the income was distributed. Do not enter any negative amounts on these lines.

Foreign partners of U.S. partnerships. To the extent that a domestic partnership has not distributed a foreign partner's

distributive share of income subject to withholding under section 1441, it should not include any tax liability on lines 1 through 60 for tax relating to the partner's distributive share in the year the partnership earns the income. For distributive shares not actually distributed, the partnership must include any tax liability on lines 1 through 60 of the Form 1042 for the following year. Include the tax liability on the line that represents the earlier of the following dates.

• The date on which the Schedule K-1 (Form 1065) is sent or otherwise furnished to the foreign partner.
• The due date for furnishing Schedule K-1 (Form 1065) to the partner.

Include such tax liability for the period that includes the date the tax was required to be withheld.

Example. In 2011, USP, a U.S. partnership, has foreign partners. The withholding tax relating to the distributive shares of the foreign partners was $120. USP made no distributions in 2011. On the 2011 Form 1042, USP did not enter any amount as tax liability on lines 1 through 60 because it did not distribute any amounts.

USP made a distribution on February 10, 2012, that related to the 2011 distributive shares of the foreign partners. USP withheld $100 at the time of the distribution. USP sent the 2011 Schedules K-1 (Form 1065) to its partners on April 2, 2012.

On the 2012 Form 1042, USP entered $100 on line 7. This is the tax liability for the period (February 8 through 15) during which it made a distribution. USP entered $20 on line 16. This is the tax liability for the period (April 1 through 7) during which it furnished the Schedules K-1 (Form 1065) to the partners.

 Use Form 8804 to report withholding tax liability on the partnership's income effectively connected with a U.S. trade or business.

Corporate distributions. Do not include on lines 1 through 60 any tax liability caused by adjustments of underwithheld tax on corporate distributions made in calendar year 2012 if the following apply.
• The distributing corporation made a reasonable estimate of accumulated and current earnings and profits under Regulations section 1.1441-3(c)(2)(ii)(A); and
• The distributing corporation or intermediary paid over the underwithheld tax by March 15, 2013.

Instead, include these payments of underwithheld tax on line 63b.

Excise tax on specified Federal procurement payments. Include on lines 1 through 60 any liability for the 2% excise

tax imposed by section 5000C on foreign persons who receive one or more specified Federal procurement payments. Report the amount on the line that corresponds with the date the payment was made.

Specified Federal procurement payment. A specified Federal procurement payment means any payment made pursuant to a contract with the United States Government entered into after January 1, 2011, for the provision of goods, if such goods are manufactured or produced in any country which is not a party to an international procurement agreement with the United States, or the provision of services, if such services are provided in any country which is not a party to an international procurement agreement with the United States.

Qualified intermediaries with no primary withholding responsibility. If you are a QI that did not assume primary withholding responsibility, enter the total amount withheld by the U.S. withholding agent(s) on line 59. Report all other amounts (that is, amounts you actually withheld) on the line that corresponds with the date the liability was incurred.

Overwithholding. If you repaid the recipient for an amount overwithheld by reducing the amount withheld on a later payment, report the reduced amount on these lines. If you used the reimbursement procedure for overwithheld amounts, see *Adjustment for Overwithholding*, later.

Line 61. Enter the number of Forms 1042-S filed on paper and electronically.

 If you file 250 or more Forms 1042-S, you must submit them electronically.

Lines 62a and 62b. Enter the amounts requested for all Forms 1042-S (regardless of whether the form was filed electronically or on paper) and for all Forms 1000, Ownership Certificate.

 Be sure to reconcile amounts on Form 1042 with amounts on Forms 1042-S (including Forms 1042-S filed electronically), to avoid unnecessary correspondence with the IRS.

Line 62a. The amount on line 62a should equal the sum of all amounts shown on Forms 1042-S, box 2, and all amounts shown as gross interest paid on Forms 1000.

Line 62b. The amount on line 62b should equal:
• The sum of all Forms 1042-S, box 9 (box 7 plus box 8), less
• The sum of all Forms 1042-S, box 10, plus

- The tax assumed from Forms 1000.

If it does not, attach a statement to Form 1042 explaining the difference.

Line 63a. The amount on line 63a must equal the sum of the monthly totals as listed on the Record of Federal Tax Liability. Do not make any adjustments on this line. Except for adjustments described in the instructions for line 63b, you may only make adjustments on the appropriate entry line of the Record of Federal Tax Liability.

Line 63b. Include on line 63b any tax liability resulting from adjustments of underwithheld tax on corporate distributions made in calendar year 2012 if:
- The distributing corporation made a reasonable estimate of accumulated and current earnings and profits under Regulations section 1.1441-3(c)(2)(ii)(A), and
- The distributing corporation or intermediary paid over the underwithheld tax by March 15, 2013.

If you are a regulated investment company (RIC), real estate investment trust (REIT), or personal holding company (PHC) that paid a dividend subject to section 852(b)(7), section 857(b)(9), or section 563(b) (relating to certain dividends declared in the preceding October, November, or December), enter your additional tax liability on those dividends declared in 2012 but paid no later than March 15, 2013, less any additional tax liability on those dividends declared in 2011 but paid no later than March 15, 2012. Show any negative amount in brackets. Attach a statement showing your calculation.

Line 64. Enter the total tax deposits you made (including amounts paid with an extension of time to file).

Line 66. You are permitted to take a credit for amounts withheld by other withholding agents that relate to the total net tax liability reported on line 63c. For example, you are a QI and the amount you entered on line 63c includes amounts withheld by a U.S. withholding agent. You may take a credit on line 66 for the amounts that were withheld by the U.S. withholding agent. The amount on line 66 should equal the sum of all Forms 1042-S, box 8, that you file for the year.

Note. All withholding agents (QIs and NQIs) must verify entries on Line 66 by attaching supporting Form(s) 1042-S, issued to you, to verify the credit amounts claimed.

 If you are a QI requesting a refund, you must attach the corresponding Form(s) 1042-S received to support the amount claimed

on line 66. Failure to do so will result in the denial of the refund or credit being claimed. If you are a PTP or a nominee withholding under section 1446, the tax paid for a payee may only be claimed as a credit by the payee.

QSL claiming a credit forward. If you are a QSL or other withholding agent claiming a credit forward of prior withholding on substitute dividends as determined under Notice 2010-46, you should attach Form(s) 1042-S issued to you to support such credits. If a credit is claimed with respect to any U.S. source substitute dividends paid to you from a withholding agent that has not issued a Form 1042-S to you for such payments, attach a supporting statement to Form 1042 indicating the following:

- The withholding agent's name, address, and EIN (if known);
- The amount of U.S. source substitute dividends received from the withholding agent; and
- The amount of credit forward you included on line 66 in connection with these substitute dividends.

Line 69. You may claim an overpayment shown on line 69 as a refund or a credit. Check the applicable box on line 70 to show which you are claiming. If you claim a credit, it can reduce your required deposits of withheld tax for 2012.

Line 71. Enter on line 71 the total amount of specified federal procurement payments multiplied by 2% (.02).

Adjustment For Overwithholding

What to do if you overwithheld tax depends on when you discover the overwithholding.

Overwithholding discovered by March 15 of the following calendar year. If you discover that you overwithheld tax by March 15 of the following calendar year, you may use any undeposited amount of tax to make any necessary adjustments between you and the recipient of the income. Repay the recipient and reduce the amount of your total deposit. Report the reduced tax liability on lines 1 through 60 for the period(s) for which you repaid the overwithheld tax.

If the undeposited amount is not enough to make any adjustments, or if you discover the overwithholding after the entire amount of tax has been deposited, you can use either the reimbursement or the set-off procedure to adjust the overwithholding.

 If March 15 is a Saturday, Sunday, or legal holiday, the next business day is the final date for these actions.

Reimbursement procedure. Under the reimbursement procedure, you repay the beneficial owner or payee the amount overwithheld. You use your own funds for this repayment. You must make the repayment by March 15 of the year after the calendar year in which the amount was overwithheld. For example, if you overwithhold tax in 2012, you must repay the beneficial owner by March 15, 2013. You must keep a receipt showing the date and amount of the repayment and provide a copy of the receipt to the beneficial owner.

You may reimburse yourself by reducing any subsequent deposits you make before the end of the year after the calendar year in which the amount was overwithheld. The reduction cannot be more than the amount you actually repaid.

Report the reduced tax liability on lines 1 through 60 for the period for which you reimbursed the overwithheld tax. Report the total tax withheld as your total deposits. Indicate on line 70 whether you want a refund or a credit.

Set-off procedure. Under the set-off procedure, you repay the beneficial owner or payee the amount overwithheld by reducing the amount you would have been required to withhold on later payments you make to that person. These later payments must be made before the earlier of:
- The date you actually file Form 1042-S for the calendar year in which the amount was overwithheld, or
- March 15 of the year after the calendar year in which the amount was overwithheld.

Report the reduced tax liability on lines 1 through 60.

Overwithholding discovered at a later date. If you discover after March 15 of the following calendar year that you overwithheld tax for the prior year, do not adjust the amount of tax liability reported on Form 1042 or on any deposit or payment for that prior year. Do not repay the beneficial owner or payee the amount overwithheld.

In this situation, the recipient will have to file a U.S. income tax return (Form 1040NR, Form 1040NR-EZ, or Form 1120-F) or, if a tax return has already been filed, a claim for refund (Form 1040X or amended Form 1120-F) to recover the amount overwithheld.

Third Party Designee

If you want to allow any individual, corporation, firm, organization, or partnership to discuss your 2012 Form 1042 with the IRS, check the "Yes" box in the Third Party Designee section of the return. Also, enter the designee's name, phone number, and any five digits the designee chooses as his or her personal identification number (PIN). The authorization applies only to the tax form upon which it appears.

If you check the "Yes" box, you are authorizing the IRS to call the designee to answer any questions relating to the information reported on your tax return. You also are authorizing the designee to:
• Exchange information concerning your tax return with the IRS, and
• Request and receive written tax return information relating to your tax return, including copies of specific notices, correspondence, and account transcripts.

You are not authorizing the designee to receive any refund check, bind you to anything (including additional tax liability), or otherwise represent you before the IRS. If you want to expand the designee's authorization, see Pub. 947, Practice Before the IRS and Power of Attorney.

The authorization automatically expires one year from the due date (without any extensions) for filing your 2012 Form 1042. If you or your designee desires to terminate the authorization, a written statement conveying your wish to revoke the authorization should be submitted to the IRS service center where the return was processed.

Amended Return

If you have to make changes to your Form 1042 after you submit it, file an amended Form 1042. Use a Form 1042 for the year you are amending. Check the "Amended Return" box at the top of the form. You must complete the entire form, including all filing information for the calendar year, and sign the return. Attach a statement explaining why you are filing an amended return (for example, you are filing because the tax liability for May was incorrectly reported due to a mathematical error).

If you also are amending Form(s) 1042-S, see *Amended Returns* in the Form 1042-S instructions.

Do not amend Form 1042 to recover taxes overwithheld in the prior year. For more information, see *Adjustment for Overwithholding*, earlier.

Privacy Act and Paperwork Reduction Act Notice. We ask for the information on this form to carry out the Internal Revenue laws of the United States. Sections 1441, 1442, and 1446 (for PTPs) require withholding agents to report and pay over to the IRS taxes withheld from certain U.S. source income of foreign persons. Form 1042 is used to report the amount of withholding that must be paid over. Form 1042-S is used to report the amount of income and withholding to the payee. Section 6109 requires you to provide your identifying number on the return. Routine uses of this information include giving it to the Department of Justice for civil and criminal litigation, and to cities, states, the District of Columbia, and U.S. commonwealths and possessions for use in administering their tax laws. We may also disclose this information to other countries under a tax treaty, to federal and state agencies to enforce federal nontax criminal laws, or to federal law enforcement and intelligence agencies to combat terrorism. If you fail to provide this information in a timely manner, you may be liable for penalties and interest.

You are not required to provide the information requested on a form that is subject to the Paperwork Reduction Act unless the form displays a valid OMB control number. Books or records relating to a form or its instructions must be retained as long as their contents may become material in the administration of any Internal Revenue law. Generally, tax returns and return information are confidential, as required by section 6103.

The time needed to complete and file these forms will vary depending on individual circumstances. The estimated average time is: **Recordkeeping,** 10 hr., 31 min.; **Learning about the law or the form,** 2 hr., 25 min.; **Preparing the form,** 4 hr., 34 min.; and **Copying, assembling, and sending the form to the IRS,** 32 min.

If you have comments concerning the accuracy of these time estimates or suggestions for making this form simpler, we would be happy to hear from you. You can write to the Internal Revenue Service, Tax Products Coordinating Committee, SE:W:CAR:MP:T:M:S, 1111 Constitution Ave. NW, IR-6526, Washington, DC 20224. Do not send the form to this address. Instead, see *Where and When To File*, earlier.

Form **1042-S** | **Foreign Person's U.S. Source Income Subject to Withholding** 20**13** | OMB No. 1545-0096

► Information about Form 1042-S and its separate instructions is at www.irs.gov/form1042.

Department of the Treasury
Internal Revenue Service

☐ **AMENDED**   ☐ **PRO-RATA BASIS REPORTING**

Copy A for
Internal Revenue Service

1 Income code	2 Gross income	3 Withholding allowances	4 Net income	5 Tax rate	7 Federal tax withheld
				6 Exemption code	8 Withholding by other agents
					9 Total withholding credit

10 Amount repaid to recipient

14 Recipient's U.S. TIN, if any ►
☐ SSN or ITIN   ☐ EIN   ☐ QI-EIN

11 Withholding agent's EIN ►
☐ EIN   ☐ QI-EIN

15 Recipient's foreign tax identifying number, if any | **16** Country code

12a WITHHOLDING AGENT'S name

17 NQI's/FLOW-THROUGH ENTITY'S name | **18** Country code

12b Address (number and street)

19a NQI's/Entity's address (number and street)

12c Additional address line (room or suite no.)

19b Additional address line (room or suite no.)

12d City or town, province or state, country, ZIP or foreign postal code

19c City or town, province or state, country, ZIP or foreign postal code

13a RECIPIENT'S name | **13b** Recipient code

20 NQI's/Entity's U.S. TIN, if any ►

13c Address (number and street)

21 PAYER'S name and TIN (if different from withholding agent's)

13d Additional address line (room or suite no.)

22 Recipient account number (optional)

13e City or town, province or state, country, ZIP or foreign postal code

23 State income tax withheld | **24** Payer's state tax no. | **25** Name of state

For Privacy Act and Paperwork Reduction Act Notice, see instructions.   Cat. No. 11386R   Form **1042-S** (2013)

U.S. Income Tax Filing Requirements

Generally, every nonresident alien individual, nonresident alien fiduciary, and foreign corporation with United States income, including income that is effectively connected with the conduct of a trade or business in the United States, must file a United States income tax return. However, no return is required to be filed by a nonresident alien individual, nonresident alien fiduciary, or foreign corporation if such person was not engaged in a trade or business in the United States at any time during the tax year and if the tax liability of such person was fully satisfied by the withholding of United States tax at the source. Corporations file Form 1120-F; all others file Form 1040NR (or Form 1040NR-EZ if eligible). You may get the return forms and instructions at any United States Embassy or consulate or by writing to: Internal Revenue Service, 1201 N. Mitsubishi Motorway, Bloomington, IL 61705-6613

En règle générale, tout étranger non-résident, tout organisme fidéicommissaire étranger non-résident et toute société étrangère percevant un revenu aux Etats-Unis, y compris tout revenu dérivé, en fait, du fonctionnement d'un commerce ou d'une affaire aux Etats-Unis, doit produire une déclaration d'impôt sur le revenu auprès des services fiscaux des Etats-Unis. Cependant aucune déclaration d'impôt sur le revenu n'est exigée d'un étranger non-résident, d'un organisme fidéicommissaire étranger non-résident, ou d'une société étrangère s'ils n'ont pris part à aucun commerce ou affaire aux Etats-Unis à aucun moment pendant l'année fiscale et si les impôts dont ils sont redevables, ont été entièrement acquittés par une retenue à la source sur leur salaire. Les sociétés doivent faire leur déclaration d'impôt en remplissant le formulaire 1120-F; tous les autres redevables doivent remplir le formulaire 1040NR (ou 1040NR-EZ s'ils en remplissent les conditions). On peut se procurer les formulaires de déclarations d'impôts et les instructions y afférentes dans toutes les Ambassades et tous les Consulats des Etats-Unis. L'on peut également s'adresser pour tout renseignement à: Internal Revenue Service, 1201 N. Mitsubishi Motorway, Bloomington, IL 61705-6613

Por regla general, todo extranjero no residente, todo organismo fideicomisario extranjero no residente y toda sociedad anónima extranjera que reciba ingresos en los Estados Unidos, incluyendo ingresos relacionados con la conducción de un negocio o comercio dentro de los Estados Unidos, deberá presentar una declaración estadounidense de impuestos sobre ingreso. Sin embargo, no se requiere declaración alguna a un individuo extranjero, una sociedad anónima extranjera u organismo fideicomisario extranjero no residente, si tal persona no ha efectuado comercio o negocio en los Estados Unidos durante el año fiscal y si la responsabilidad con los impuestos de tal persona ha sido satisfecha plenamente mediante retención del impuesto de los Estados Unidos en la fuente. Las sociedades anónimas envían el Formulario 1120-F; todos los demás contribuyentes envían el Formulario 1040NR (o el Formulario 1040NR-EZ si le corresponde). Se podrá obtener formularios e instrucciones en cualquier Embajada o Consulado de los Estados Unidos o escribiendo directamente a: Internal Revenue Service, 1201 N. Mitsubishi Motorway, Bloomington, IL 61705-6613

Im allgemeinen muss jede ausländische Einzelperson, jeder ausländische Bevollmächtigte und jede ausländische Gesellschaft mit Einkommen in den Vereinigten Staaten, einschliesslich des Einkommens, welches direkt mit der Ausübung von Handel oder Gewerbe innerhalb der Staaten verbunden ist, eine Einkommensteuererklärung der Vereinigten Staaten abgeben. Eine Erklärung, muss jedoch nicht von Ausländern, ausländischen Bevollmächtigten oder ausländischen Gesellschaften in den Vereinigten Staaten eingereicht werden, falls eine solche Person während des Steuerjahres kein Gewerbe oder Handel in den Vereinigten Staaten ausgeübt hat und die Steuerschuld durch Einbehaltung der Steuern der Vereinigten Staaten durch die Einkommensquelle abgegolten ist. Gesellschaften reichen den Vordruck 1120-F ein; alle anderen reichen das Formblatt 1040NR (oder wenn passend das Formblatt 1040NR-EZ) ein. Einkommensteuererklärungen und Instruktionen können bei den Botschaften und Konsulaten der Vereiningten Staaten eingeholt werden. Um weitere Informationen wende man sich bitte an: Internal Revenue Service, 1201 N. Mitsubishi Motorway, Bloomington, IL 61705-6613

20**13**
Instructions for Form 1042-S

Foreign Person's U.S. Source Income Subject to Withholding

 Department of the Treasury
Internal Revenue Service

Section references are to the Internal Revenue Code unless otherwise noted.

Future Developments

For the latest information about developments related to Form 1042-S, and its instructions, such as legislation enacted after they were published, go to *www.irs.gov/form1042*.

General Instructions

 Use the 2013 Form 1042-S only for income paid during 2013. Do not use the 2013 Form 1042-S for income paid during 2012.

What's New

Backup withholding rate. There are a few instances throughout these instructions where we make reference to the need to apply backup withholding on payments to payees who are presumed to be U.S. nonexempt recipients or unknown U.S. persons under the presumption rules. At the time these instructions were printed, there was uncertainty as to the specific backup withholding rate that will be in effect for 2013. To find out this specific rate, see the 2013 General Instructions for Certain Information Returns (Forms 1097, 1098, 1099, 3921, 3922, 5498, and W-2G), available at *www.irs.gov/formspubs*.

Interest on deposits. Beginning January 1, 2013, deposit interest described in section 871(i)(2)(A) aggregating $10 or more paid to certain nonresident alien individuals with respect to a deposit maintained at an office within the United States must be reported on Form 1042-S. For more information, see *Interest on deposits,* later.

Reminders

FIRE System. For files submitted on the FIRE System, it is the responsibility of the filer to check the status within 5 business days to verify the results of the transmission. The IRS will not mail error reports for files that are bad.

Substitute forms. Any substitute forms must comply with the rules set out in Pub. 1179, General Rules and Specifications for Substitute Forms 1096, 1098, 1099, 5498, W-2G, and 1042-S. A substitute of Form 1042-S, Copy A, must be an exact copy of Form 1042-S, Copy A. If it is not,

the form may be rejected as incorrect and the IRS may impose penalties. For more information, see *Substitute Forms,* later.

Purpose of Form

Use Form 1042-S to report income described under *Amounts Subject to Reporting on Form 1042-S* , later, and to report amounts withheld under Chapter 3 of the Internal Revenue Code.

Also use Form 1042-S to report distributions of effectively connected income by a publicly traded partnership or nominee. See *Publicly Traded Partnerships (Section 1446 Withholding Tax)* , later.

 Every person required to deduct and withhold any tax under Chapter 3 of the Code is liable for such tax. Every person required to deduct and withhold any tax on payments made to expatriates is liable for such tax.

Do not use Form 1042-S to report an item required to be reported on any of the following forms.
• Form W-2 (wages and other compensation made to employees (other than compensation for dependent personal services for which the beneficial owner is claiming treaty benefits), including wages in the form of group-term life insurance.
• Form 1099.
• Form 8288-A, Statement of Withholding on Dispositions by Foreign Persons of U.S. Real Property Interests, or Form 8805, Foreign Partner's Information Statement of Section 1446 Withholding Tax. Withholding agents otherwise required to report a distribution partly on a Form 8288-A or Form 8805 and partly on a Form 1042-S may instead report the entire amount on Form 8288-A or Form 8805.

Who Must File

Every withholding agent (defined in *Definitions,* later) must file an information return on Form 1042-S to report amounts paid during the preceding calendar year that are described under *Amounts Subject to Reporting on Form 1042-S,* later. However, withholding agents who are individuals are not required to report a payment on Form 1042-S if they are not making the payment as part of their trade or business and no withholding is required to be made on the payment. For example, an individual making a payment of interest

that qualifies for the portfolio interest exception from withholding is not required to report the payment if the portfolio interest is paid on a loan that is not connected to the individual's trade or business. However, an individual paying an amount that actually has been subject to withholding is required to report the payment. Also, an individual paying an amount on which withholding is required must report the payment, whether or not the individual actually withholds. See *Multiple Withholding Agent Rule,* later, for exceptions to reporting when another person has reported the same payment to the recipient. Also see *Publicly Traded Partnerships (Section 1446 Withholding Tax),* later.

You must file a Form 1042-S even if you did not withhold tax because the income was exempt from tax under a U.S. tax treaty or the Code, including the exemption for income that is effectively connected with the conduct of a trade or business in the United States, or you released the tax withheld to the recipient. For exceptions, see *Amounts That Are Not Subject to Reporting on Form 1042-S,* later.

Amounts paid to bona fide residents of U.S. possessions and territories are not subject to reporting on Form 1042-S if the beneficial owner of the income is a U.S. citizen, national, or resident alien.

 If you are required to file Form 1042-S, you also must file Form 1042, Annual Withholding Tax Return for U.S. Source Income of Foreign Persons. See Form 1042 for more information.

Where, When, and How To File

Forms 1042-S, whether filed on paper or electronically, must be filed with the Internal Revenue Service by March 15, 2014. You also are required to furnish Form 1042-S to the recipient of the income by March 15, 2014.

Copy A is filed with the Internal Revenue Service. Send all paper Forms 1042-S with Form 1042-T, Annual Summary and Transmittal of Forms 1042-S, to the address in the Form 1042-T instructions. You must use Form 1042-T to transmit paper Forms 1042-S. Use a separate Form 1042-T to transmit each type of Form 1042-S. See *Payments by*

Oct 22, 2012

Cat. No. 64278A

U.S. Withholding Agents , later, and the Form 1042-T instructions for more information. If you have 250 or more Forms 1042-S to file, follow the instructions under *Electronic Reporting*, later.

 Attach only Copy A to Form 1042-T. Copies B, C, and D should be provided to the recipient of the income. Copy E should be retained by the withholding agent.

Extension of time to file. To request an extension of time to file Forms 1042-S, file Form 8809, Application for Extension of Time To File Information Returns. See the Form 8809 instructions for where to file that form. You should request an extension as soon as you are aware that an extension is necessary, but no later than the due date for filing Form 1042-S. By filing Form 8809, you will get an automatic 30-day extension to file Form 1042-S. If you need more time, a second Form 8809 may be submitted before the end of the initial extended due date. See Form 8809 for more information.

 If you are requesting extensions of time to file for 2 or more withholding agents or payers, you must submit the extension requests electronically. See Pub. 1187, Specifications for Filing Form 1042-S, Foreign Person's U.S. Source Income Subject to Withholding, Electronically, for more information.

Recipient copies. You may request an extension of time to provide the statements to recipients by sending a letter to:

> Internal Revenue Service
> Information Returns Branch
> **Attn: Extension of Time Coordinator**
> 240 Murall Drive Mail Stop 4360
> Kearneysville, WV 25430

See *Extension to provide statements to recipients* in Pub. 515, Withholding of Tax on Nonresident Aliens and Foreign Entities.

 If you are requesting an extension of time to file for recipients of more than 10 withholding agents, you must submit the extension requests electronically. See Pub. 1187, Part D, Section 4, for more information.

Electronic Reporting

If you file 250 or more Forms 1042-S, you are required to submit them electronically.

Electronic submissions are filed using the Filing Information Returns Electronically (FIRE) System. The FIRE System operates 24 hours a day, 7 days a week, at *http://fire.irs.gov*. For more information, see Pub. 1187.

The electronic filing requirement applies separately to original and amended returns. Any person, including a corporation, partnership, individual, estate, or trust, that is required to file 250 or more Forms 1042-S must file such returns electronically. The filing requirement applies individually to each reporting entity as defined by its separate taxpayer identification number (TIN). This requirement applies separately to original and amended returns. For example, if you have 300 original Forms 1042-S, they must be filed electronically. However, if 200 of those forms contained erroneous information, the amended returns may be filed on paper forms because the number of amended Forms 1042-S is less than the 250-or-more filing requirement.

 If you file electronically, do not file the same returns on paper. Duplicate filing may cause penalty notices to be generated.

Note. Even though as many as 249 Forms 1042-S may be submitted on paper to the IRS, the IRS encourages filers to transmit forms electronically.

Hardship waiver. To receive a hardship waiver from the required filing of Forms 1042-S electronically, submit Form 8508, Request for Waiver From Filing Information Returns Electronically. Waiver requests should be filed at least 45 days before the due date of the returns. See Form 8508 for more information.

Need assistance? For additional information and instructions on filing Forms 1042-S electronically, extensions of time to file (Form 8809), and hardship waivers (Form 8508), see Pub. 1187. You also can call the Information Reporting Program at 866-455-7438 (toll free) or 304-263-8700 (not a toll-free number). Do not call the Information Reporting Program to answer tax law questions. See *Caution* below for additional information. The Information Reporting Program also can be reached by fax at 877-477-0572 (toll free) and international fax at 304-579-4105 (not a toll-free number).

 This call site does not answer tax law questions concerning the requirements for withholding of tax on payments of U.S. source income to foreign persons under Chapter 3 of the Code. If you need such assistance, you can call 267-941-1000 (not a toll-free number) from 6:00 a.m. to 11:00 p.m. Eastern time or write to:

> *Internal Revenue Service
> International Section
> Philadelphia, PA 19255-0725*

Additional Information

For more information on the withholding of tax, see Pub. 515. To order this publication and other publications and forms, call 1-800-TAX-FORM (1-800-829-3676). You also can download forms and publications from IRS.gov.

Record Retention

Withholding agents should retain a copy of the information returns filed with the IRS, or have the ability to reconstruct the data, for at least 3 years after the reporting due date.

Substitute Forms

The official Form 1042-S is the standard for substitute forms. Because a substitute form is a variation from the official form, you should know the requirements of the official form for the year of use before you modify it to meet your needs. The IRS provides several means of obtaining the most frequently used tax forms. These include the Internet and DVD. For details on the requirements of substitute forms, see Pub. 1179.

 You are permitted to use substitute payee copies of Form 1042-S (that is, copies B, C, and D) that contain more than one type of income. This will reduce the number of Forms 1042-S you send to the recipient. Under no circumstances, however, may the copy of the form filed with the IRS (copy A) contain more than one type of income.

Penalty for filing incorrect substitute form. Privately printed substitute Forms 1042-S must be exact copies of both the format and content of the official Form 1042-S. If you file a substitute for Form 1042-S, Copy A, with the IRS that is not an exact copy of the official Form 1042-S, Copy A, you may be subject to a penalty for failure to file a correct return. See *Penalties*, later.

Deposit Requirements

For information and rules concerning federal tax deposits, see *Depositing Withheld Taxes* in Pub. 515 or *Deposit Requirements* in the Instructions for Form 1042.

Definitions

Withholding agent. A withholding agent is any person, U.S. or foreign, that has control, receipt, or custody of an amount subject to withholding or who can disburse or make payments of an amount subject to withholding. The withholding agent may be an individual, corporation, partnership, trust, association, or any other entity. The term withholding agent also includes, but is not limited to, a qualified intermediary (QI), a nonqualified intermediary (NQI), a withholding foreign partnership (WP), a withholding foreign trust (WT), a flow-through entity, a U.S. branch of a foreign insurance company or foreign bank that is treated as a U.S. person, a nominee under section 1446, and an authorized foreign agent. A person may be a withholding agent even if there is no requirement to withhold from a payment or even if another person has already withheld the required amount from a payment.

In most cases, the U.S. person who pays (or causes to be paid) the item of U.S. source income to a foreign person (or to its agent) must withhold. However, other persons may be required to withhold. For example, if a payment is made by a QI (whether or not it assumes primary withholding responsibility) that knows that withholding was not done by the person from which it received the payment, then that QI is required to do the appropriate withholding. In addition, withholding must be done by any QI that assumes primary withholding responsibility under Chapter 3 of the Code, a WP, a WT, a U.S. branch of a foreign insurance company or foreign bank that agrees to be treated as a U.S. person, or an authorized foreign agent. Finally, if a payment is made by an NQI or a flow-through entity that knows, or has reason to know, that withholding was not done, that NQI or flow-through entity is required to withhold since it also falls within the definition of a withholding agent.

Authorized foreign agent. An agent is an authorized foreign agent only if all four of the following apply.

1. There is a written agreement between the withholding agent and the foreign person acting as agent.

2. The IRS International Section has been notified of the appointment of the agent before the first payment for which the authorized agent acts on behalf of the withholding agent. This notification must be sent to the following address:

> Internal Revenue Service
> International Section
> Philadelphia, PA 19255-0725

3. The books and records and relevant personnel of the foreign agent are available to the IRS so that the IRS can evaluate the withholding agent's compliance with its withholding and reporting obligations.

4. The U.S. withholding agent remains fully liable for the acts of its agent and does not assert any of the defenses that otherwise may be available.

For further details, see Regulations section 1.1441-7(c).

Beneficial owner. For payments other than those for which a reduced rate of withholding is claimed under an income tax treaty, the beneficial owner of income in most cases is the person who is required under U.S. tax principles to include the income in gross income on a tax return. A person is not a beneficial owner of income, however, to the extent that person is receiving the income as a nominee, agent, or custodian, or to the extent the person is a conduit whose participation in a transaction is disregarded. In the case of amounts paid that do not constitute income, beneficial ownership is determined as if the payment were income.

Foreign partnerships, foreign simple trusts, and foreign grantor trusts are not the beneficial owners of income paid to the partnership or trust. The beneficial owners of income paid to a foreign partnership in most cases are the partners in the partnership, provided that the partner is not itself a partnership, foreign simple or grantor trust, nominee, or other agent. The beneficial owner of income paid to a foreign simple trust (a foreign trust that is described in section 651(a)) in most cases is the beneficiary of the trust, if the beneficiary is not a foreign partnership, foreign simple or grantor trust, nominee, or other agent. The beneficial owner of a foreign grantor trust (a foreign trust to the extent that all or a part of the income of the trust is treated as owned by the grantor or another person under sections 671 through 679) is the person treated as the owner of the trust. The beneficial owner of income paid to a foreign complex trust (a foreign trust that is not a foreign simple trust or foreign grantor trust) is the trust itself.

The beneficial owner of income paid to a foreign estate is the estate itself.

A payment to a U.S. partnership, U.S. trust, or U.S. estate is not subject to 30% foreign-person withholding. A U.S. partnership, trust, or estate should provide the withholding agent with a Form W-9, Request for Taxpayer Identification Number and Certification. In most cases, these beneficial owner rules apply for purposes of section 1446; however, there are exceptions.

Disregarded entity. A business entity that has a single owner and is not a corporation under Regulations section 301.7701-2(b) is disregarded as an entity separate from its owner.

Dividend equivalent. Under section 871(m), a dividend equivalent is a payment that, directly or indirectly, is contingent on, or determined by reference to, the payment of a dividend from U.S. sources. Dividend equivalent payments include the following payments.

1. A substitute dividend made under a securities lending or sale-repurchase transaction involving a U.S. stock,

2. A payment made under a specified notional principal contract, and

3. Any payment determined by the IRS to be substantially similar to a payment in (1) or (2).

Exempt recipient. In most cases, an exempt recipient is any payee that is not required to provide Form W-9 and is exempt from the Form 1099 reporting requirements. See the Instructions for the Requester of Form W-9 for a list of exempt recipients.

Expatriate. A person is considered an expatriate if he or she relinquishes U.S. citizenship or, in the case of a long-term resident of the United States, ceases to be a lawful permanent resident as defined in section 7701(b)(6).

Fiscally transparent entity. An entity is treated as fiscally transparent with respect to an item of income for which treaty benefits are claimed to the extent that the interest holders in the entity must, on a current basis, take into account separately their shares of an item of income paid to the entity, whether or not distributed, and must determine the character of the items of income as if they were realized directly from the sources from which realized by the entity. For example, partnerships, common trust funds, and simple trusts or grantor trusts in most cases are considered to be fiscally transparent with respect to items of income received by them.

Flow-through entity. A flow-through entity is a foreign partnership (other than a withholding foreign partnership), a foreign simple or grantor trust (other than a withholding foreign trust), or, for any payments for which a reduced rate of withholding under an income tax treaty is claimed, any entity to the extent the entity is considered to be fiscally transparent under section 894 with respect to the payment by an interest holder's jurisdiction.

Foreign person. A foreign person includes a nonresident alien individual, a foreign corporation, a foreign partnership, a foreign trust, a foreign estate, and any other person that is not a U.S. person. The term also includes a foreign branch or office of a U.S. financial institution or U.S. clearing organization if the foreign branch is a QI. In most cases, a payment to a U.S. branch of a foreign person is a payment to a foreign person.

Intermediary. An intermediary is a person that acts as a custodian, broker, nominee, or otherwise as an agent for another person, regardless of whether that other person is the beneficial owner of the

Instructions for Form 1042-S (2013)

-3-

amount paid, a flow-through entity, or another intermediary.

Qualified intermediary (QI). A QI is an intermediary that is a party to a withholding agreement with the IRS. An entity must indicate its status as a QI on a Form W-8IMY submitted to a withholding agent. For information on a QI withholding agreement, see Rev. Proc. 2000-12, which is on page 387 of Internal Revenue Bulletin (IRB) 2000-4 at *www.irs.gov/pub/irs-irbs/irb00-04.pdf*. Also see the following documents.
● Notice 2001-4, which is on page 267 of Internal Revenue Bulletin 2001-2 at *www.irs.gov/pub/irs-irbs/irb01-02.pdf*.
● Rev. Proc. 2003-64, Appendix 3, 2003-32 I.R.B. 306, available at *www.irs.gov/irb/2003-32_IRB/ar19.html*.
● Rev. Proc. 2004-21, 2004-14 I.R.B. 702, available at *www.irs.gov/irb/2004-14_IRB/ar10.html*.
● Rev. Proc. 2005-77, 2005-51 I.R.B. 1176, available at *www.irs.gov/irb/2005-51_IRB/ar13.html*.

A branch of a financial institution may not act as a QI in a country that does not have approved know-your-customer (KYC) rules. Countries having approved KYC rules are listed on IRS.gov. Branches that operate in non-KYC approved jurisdictions are required to act as nonqualified intermediaries.

Nonqualified intermediary (NQI). An NQI is any intermediary that is not a U.S. person and that is not a QI.

Private arrangement intermediary (PAI). A QI may enter into a private arrangement with another intermediary under which the other intermediary generally agrees to perform all of the obligations of the QI. See Section 4 of the sample withholding agreement in Rev. Proc. 2000-12 for details.

Non-exempt recipient. A non-exempt recipient is any person who is not an exempt recipient.

Nonresident alien individual. Any individual who is not a citizen or resident of the United States is a nonresident alien individual. An alien individual meeting either the green card test or the substantial presence test for the calendar year is a resident alien. Any person not meeting either test is a nonresident alien individual. Additionally, an alien individual who is a resident of a foreign country under the residence article of an income tax treaty, or an alien individual who is a bona fide resident of Puerto Rico, Guam, the Commonwealth of the Northern Mariana Islands, the U.S. Virgin Islands, or American Samoa, is a nonresident alien individual. See Pub. 519, U.S. Tax Guide for Aliens, for more information on resident and nonresident alien status.

 Even though a nonresident alien individual married to a U.S. citizen or resident alien may choose to be treated as a resident alien for certain purposes (for example, filing a joint income tax return), such individual is still treated as a nonresident alien for withholding tax purposes.

Payer. A payer is the person for whom the withholding agent acts as a paying agent pursuant to an agreement whereby the withholding agent agrees to withhold and report a payment.

Presumption rules. The presumption rules are those rules prescribed under Chapter 3 and Chapter 61 of the Code that a withholding agent must follow to determine the status of a beneficial owner (for example, as a U.S. person or a foreign person) when it cannot reliably associate a payment with valid documentation. See, for example, Regulations sections 1.1441-1(b)(3), 1.1441-4(a), 1.1441-5(d) and (e), 1.1441-9(b)(3), 1.1446-1(c)(3), and 1.6049-5(d). Also see Pub. 515.

Publicly traded partnership (PTP). A PTP is any partnership in which interests are regularly traded on an established securities market (regardless of the number of its partners). However, it does not include a PTP treated as a corporation under section 7704.

Qualified securities lender (QSL). A QSL is a foreign financial institution that satisfies **all** of the following.
● It is a bank, custodian, broker-dealer, or clearing organization that is regulated by the government in its home jurisdiction and that regularly borrows and lends the securities of U.S. corporations to unrelated customers.
● It is subject to audit by the IRS under section 7602 or by an external auditor if it is a QI.
● It provides to the withholding agent an annual certification of its QSL status.
● It meets the requirements to qualify as a QSL provided in Notice 2010-46 for the transition period and until additional published guidance is issued. See Notice 2010-46, 2010-24 I.R.B. 757, available at *www.irs.gov/irb/2010-24_IRB/ar09.html*.

Recipient. A recipient is any of the following.
● A beneficial owner of income.
● A QI.
● A WP or WT.
● An authorized foreign agent.
● A U.S. branch of certain foreign banks or insurance companies that is treated as a U.S. person.
● A foreign partnership or a foreign trust (other than a WP or WT), but only to the extent the income is effectively connected with its conduct of a trade or business in the United States.

● A payee who is not known to be the beneficial owner, but who is presumed to be a foreign person under the presumption rules.
● A PAI.
● A partner receiving a distribution of effectively connected income from a PTP or nominee.
● A QSL.

A recipient does not include any of the following.
● An NQI.
● A nonwithholding foreign partnership, if the income is not effectively connected with its conduct of a trade or business in the United States.
● A disregarded entity.
● A foreign trust that is described in section 651(a) (a foreign simple trust) if the income is not effectively connected with the conduct of a trade or business in the United States.
● A foreign trust to the extent that all or a part of the trust is treated as owned by the grantor or other person under sections 671 through 679 (a foreign grantor trust).
● A U.S. branch that is not treated as a U.S. person unless the income is, or is treated as, effectively connected with the conduct of a trade or business in the United States.

Specified notional principal contract (SNPC). An SNPC is any notional principal contract that satisfies **one** or more of the following.
● In connection with entering into the contract, any long party to the contract transfers the underlying security to any short party to the contract.
● In connection with the termination of the contract, any short party to the contract transfers the underlying security to any long party to the contract.
● The underlying security is not readily tradable on an established securities market.
● In connection with entering into the contract, the underlying security is posted as collateral by any short party to the contract with any long party to the contract.
● The IRS identifies the contract as an SNPC.

U.S. branch treated as a U.S. person. The following types of U.S. branches (of foreign entities) may reach an agreement with the withholding agent to treat the branch as a U.S. person: (a) a U.S. branch of a foreign bank subject to regulatory supervision by the Federal Reserve Board or (b) a U.S. branch of a foreign insurance company required to file an annual statement on a form approved by the National Association of Insurance Commissioners with the Insurance Department of a State, Territory, or the District of Columbia.

The U.S. branch must provide a Form W-8IMY evidencing the agreement with the withholding agent.

 A U.S. branch that is treated as a U.S. person is treated as such solely for purposes of determining whether a payment is subject to withholding. The branch is, for purposes of information reporting, a foreign person, and payments to such a branch must be reported on Form 1042-S.

Withholding certificate. The term "withholding certificate" refers to Form W-8 or Form W-9 in most cases.

Note. Throughout these instructions, a reference to or mention of "Form W-8" is a reference to Forms W-8BEN, W-8ECI, W-8EXP, and/or W-8IMY.

Withholding foreign partnership (WP) or withholding foreign trust (WT). A WP or WT is a foreign partnership or trust that has entered into a withholding agreement with the IRS in which it agrees to assume primary withholding responsibility for all payments that are made to it for its partners, beneficiaries, or owners. For information on these withholding agreements, see Rev. Proc. 2003-64. Also see Rev. Proc. 2004-21 and Rev. Proc. 2005-77.

Amounts Subject to Reporting on Form 1042-S

Amounts subject to reporting on Form 1042-S are amounts paid to foreign persons (including persons presumed to be foreign) that are subject to withholding, even if no amount is deducted and withheld from the payment because of a treaty or Code exception to taxation or if any amount withheld was repaid to the payee. Amounts subject to withholding are amounts from sources within the United States that constitute (a) fixed or determinable annual or periodical (FDAP) income; (b) certain gains from the disposal of timber, coal, or domestic iron ore with a retained economic interest; and (c) gains relating to contingent payments received from the sale or exchange of patents, copyrights, and similar intangible property. Amounts subject to withholding also include distributions of effectively connected income by a publicly traded partnership. Amounts subject to reporting include, but are not limited to, the following U.S. source items.
• **Interest on deposits.** Interest described in section 871(i)(2)(A) aggregating $10 or more paid with respect to a deposit maintained at an office within the United States if such interest is paid to a nonresident alien individual who is a resident of a country identified, in Revenue Procedure 2012-24 (or a superseding Revenue Procedure) as of

December 31, prior to the calendar year in which the interest is paid, as a country with which the United States has in effect an income tax or other convention or bilateral agreement relating to exchange information within the meaning of section 6103(k)(4). A payor may elect to report interest described above paid to any nonresident alien individual by reporting all such interest. See Revenue Procedure 2012-24 (or superseding Revenue Procedure) for the current list of countries with which the United States has in effect an income tax or other convention or bilateral agreement relating to exchange information within the meaning of section 6103(k)(4).

When completing Form 1042-S, use income code 29 in box 1 and exemption code 02 in box 6.

On the statements furnished to the recipient, you must include a statement that the information on the form is being furnished to the United States Internal Revenue Service.
• **Corporate distributions.** The entire amount of a corporate distribution (whether actual or deemed) must be reported, regardless of any estimate of the part of the distribution that represents a taxable dividend. Any distribution, however, that is treated as gain from the redemption of stock is not an amount subject to withholding. For information on dividends paid by a qualified investment entity (QIE), see Pub. 515.
• **Interest.** This includes the part of a notional principal contract payment that is characterized as interest.
• **Rents.**
• **Royalties.**
• **Compensation for independent personal services performed in the United States.**
• **Compensation for dependent personal services performed in the United States (but only if the beneficial owner is claiming treaty benefits).**
• **Annuities.**
• **Pension distributions and other deferred income.**
• **Most gambling winnings.** However, proceeds from a wager placed in blackjack, baccarat, craps, roulette, or big-6 wheel are not amounts subject to reporting.
• **Cancellation of indebtedness.** Income from the cancellation of indebtedness must be reported unless the withholding agent is unrelated to the debtor and does not have knowledge of the facts that give rise to the payment.
• **Effectively connected income (ECI).** ECI includes amounts that are (or are presumed to be) effectively connected with the conduct of a trade or business in the United States even if no withholding certificate is required, as, for example,

with income on notional principal contracts. Note that bank deposit interest, which is not subject to Form 1042-S reporting in most cases, is subject to Form 1042-S reporting if it is effectively connected income. ECI of a PTP distributed to a foreign partner must be reported on Form 1042-S.
• **Notional principal contract income.** Income from notional principal contracts that the payer knows, or must presume, is effectively connected with the conduct of a U.S. trade or business is subject to reporting using income code 32. The amount to be reported is the amount of cash paid on the contract during the calendar year. Any amount of interest determined under the provisions of Regulations section 1.446-3(g)(4) (dealing with interest in the case of a significant non-periodic payment) is reportable as interest and not as notional principal contract income. See, however, the separate reporting for other U.S.-source dividend equivalent payments.
• **REMIC excess inclusions.** Excess inclusions from REMICs (income code 02) and withheld tax must be reported on Form 1042-S. A domestic partnership must separately state a partner's allocable share of REMIC taxable income or net loss and the excess inclusion amount on Schedule K-1 (Form 1065). If the partnership allocates all or some part of its allocable share of REMIC taxable income to a foreign partner, the partner must include the partner's allocated amount in income as if that amount was received on the earliest to occur of (1) the date of distribution by the partnership; (2) the date the foreign partner disposes of its indirect interest in the REMIC residual interest; or (3) the last day of the partnership's tax year.

The partnership must withhold tax on the part of the REMIC amount that is an excess inclusion.

An excess inclusion allocated to the following foreign persons must be included in that person's income at the same time as other income from the entity is included in income.
• Shareholder of a real estate investment trust.
• Shareholder of a regulated investment company.
• Participant in a common trust fund.
• Patron of a subchapter T cooperative organization.
• **Students, teachers, and researchers.** Amounts paid to foreign students, trainees, teachers, or researchers as scholarship or fellowship income, and compensation for personal services (whether or not exempt from tax under an income tax treaty), must be reported. However, amounts that are exempt from tax under section 117 are not subject to reporting.

Instructions for Form 1042-S (2013)

-5-

• **Amounts paid to foreign governments, foreign controlled banks of issue, and international organizations.** These amounts are subject to reporting even if they are exempt under section 892 or 895.

• **Foreign targeted registered obligations.** Interest paid on registered obligations targeted to foreign markets paid to a foreign person other than a financial institution or a member of a clearing organization is an amount subject to reporting.

• **Original issue discount (OID) from the redemption of an OID obligation.** The amount subject to reporting is the amount of OID actually includible in the gross income of the foreign beneficial owner of the income, if known. Otherwise, the withholding agent should report the entire amount of OID as if the recipient held the instrument from the date of original issuance. See Pub. 1212, Guide to Original Issue Discount (OID) Instruments.

• **Certain dispositions of U.S. real property interests.** See *Withholding on Dispositions of U.S. Real Property Interests by Publicly Traded Trusts and Qualified Investment Entities (QIEs)*, later.

• **Other U.S.-source dividend equivalent payments.** Other U.S.-source dividend equivalent payments are payments other than substitute dividends that qualify as U.S.-source dividends under section 871(m). Report these amounts using income code 40.

• **Guarantee of indebtedness.** This includes amounts paid, directly or indirectly, for the provision of a guarantee of indebtedness issued after September 27, 2010. They must be paid by a non-corporate resident or U.S. corporation or by any foreign person if the amounts are effectively connected with the conduct of a U.S. trade or business. Report these amounts using income code 41.

Amounts That Are Not Subject to Reporting on Form 1042-S

Interest and OID from short-term obligations. Interest and OID from any obligation payable 183 days or less from the date of original issue should not be reported on Form 1042-S. See, however, the reporting requirements for deposit interest described above.

Registered obligations targeted to foreign markets. Interest on a registered obligation that is targeted to foreign markets and qualifies as portfolio interest is not subject to reporting if it is paid to a registered owner that is a financial institution or member of a clearing organization and you have received the required certifications.

 Withholding is required on interest paid on any registered obligation targeted to foreign markets if the registered obligation is issued after March 18, 2012. You must file Form 1042-S to report this interest.

Bearer obligations targeted to foreign markets. Do not file Form 1042-S to report interest not subject to withholding on bearer obligations if a Form W-8 is not required.

 Withholding is required on interest paid on any bearer obligations targeted to foreign markets if the obligation is issued after March 18, 2012. You must file Form 1042-S to report this interest.

Notional principal contract payments that are not ECI. Amounts paid on a notional principal contract other than a specified notional principal contract (SNPC) that are not effectively connected with the conduct of a trade or business in the United States should not be reported on Form 1042-S. All amounts paid on an SNPC that are treated as dividend equivalent payments should be reported on Form 1042-S.

Accrued interest and OID. Interest paid on obligations sold between interest payment dates and the part of the purchase price of an OID obligation that is sold or exchanged in a transaction other than a redemption is not subject to reporting unless the sale or exchange is part of a plan, the principal purpose of which is to avoid tax, and the withholding agent has actual knowledge or reason to know of such plan.

Exception for amounts previously withheld upon. A withholding agent should report on Form 1042-S any amounts, whether or not subject to withholding, that are paid to a foreign payee and that have been withheld upon, including backup withholding, by another withholding agent under the presumption rules.

Example. A withholding agent (WA) makes a payment of bank deposit interest to a foreign intermediary that is a nonqualified intermediary (NQI-B). NQI-B failed to provide any information regarding the beneficial owners to whom the payment was attributable. Under the presumption rules, WA must presume that the amounts are paid to a U.S. non-exempt recipient. WA withholds on the payment under the backup withholding provisions of the Code and files a Form 1099-INT reporting the interest as paid to an unknown recipient. A copy of Form 1099-INT is sent to NQI-B. The beneficial owners of the bank deposit interest are two customers of NQI-B, X and Y. Both X and Y have provided NQI-B with

documentary evidence establishing that they are foreign persons and therefore not subject to backup withholding. NQI-B must file a Form 1042-S reporting the amount of bank deposit interest paid to each of X and Y and the proportionate amount of withholding that occurred.

Withholding on Dispositions of U.S. Real Property Interests by Publicly Traded Trusts and Qualified Investment Entities (QIEs)

In general, when a publicly traded trust makes a distribution to a foreign person attributable to the disposition of a U.S. real property interest, it must withhold tax under section 1445. However, this withholding liability is shifted to the person who pays the distribution to a foreign person (or to the account of the foreign person) if the special notice requirement of Regulations section 1.1445-8(f) and other requirements of Regulations section 1.1445-8(b)(1) are satisfied.

The amount subject to withholding for a distribution by a publicly traded trust is determined under the large trust rules of Regulations section 1.1445-5(c)(3).

The rate of withholding is as follows:

1. Distribution by a publicly traded trust that makes recurring sales of growing crops and timber—10%.

2. Distribution by a publicly traded trust not described in (1) above—35%.

Special rules apply to qualified investment entities (QIEs). A QIE is one of the following.
• A real estate investment trust (REIT).
• A regulated investment company (RIC) that is a U.S. real property holding corporation. The special rule for a RIC applies only for distributions by the RIC that are directly or indirectly attributable to distributions the RIC received from a REIT.

In most cases, any distribution from a QIE attributable to gain from the sale or exchange of a U.S. real property interest is treated as such gain by the nonresident alien, foreign corporation, or other QIE receiving the distribution.

A distribution by a QIE to a nonresident alien or foreign corporation that is treated as gain from the sale or exchange of a U.S. real property interest by the shareholder is subject to withholding at 35%.

Any distribution by a QIE on stock regularly traded on a securities market in the United States is not treated as gain from the sale or exchange of a U.S. real property interest if the shareholder did not

Instructions for Form 1042-S (2013)

own more than 5% of that stock at any time during the 1-year period ending on the date of the distribution. These distributions are included in the shareholder's gross income as a dividend (income code 06) from the QIE, not as long-term capital gain.

Use Forms 1042-S and 1042 to report and pay over the withheld amounts. All other withholding required under section 1445 is reported and paid over using Form 8288, U.S. Withholding Tax Return for Dispositions by Foreign Persons of U.S. Real Property Interests, and Form 8288-A, Statement of Withholding on Dispositions by Foreign Persons of U.S. Real Property Interests.

For more information on reporting income from real property interests, see *U.S. Real Property Interest* in Pub. 515.

Publicly Traded Partnerships (Section 1446 Withholding Tax)

A publicly traded partnership (PTP) (defined earlier in *Definitions*) that has effectively connected income, gain, or loss must pay a withholding tax on distributions of that income made to its foreign partners and file Form 1042-S using income code 27. A nominee that receives a distribution of effectively connected income from a PTP is treated as the withholding agent to the extent of the amount specified in the qualified notice received by the nominee. For this purpose, a nominee is a domestic person that holds an interest in a PTP on behalf of a foreign person. See Regulations section 1.1446-4 and Pub. 515 for details.

 If you are a nominee that is the withholding agent under section 1446, enter the PTP's name and other required information in boxes 17 through 20 on Form 1042-S.

Other partnerships that have effectively connected gross income allocable to foreign partners must pay a withholding tax under section 1446. These amounts are reported on Form 8804, Annual Return for Partnership Withholding Tax (Section 1446), and Form 8805, Foreign Partner's Information Statement of Section 1446 Withholding Tax.

Payments by U.S. Withholding Agents

In general. U.S. withholding agents making payments described under *Amounts Subject to Reporting on Form 1042-S* , earlier, must file a separate Form 1042-S for each recipient who receives the income. Furthermore, withholding agents filing paper Forms 1042-S are not permitted to report multiple types of

income on copy A filed with the IRS. These filers must use a separate Form 1042-S for information reportable on a single type of income.

 These filers cannot use a single Form 1042-S to report income if that income is reportable under different income, recipient, or exemption codes, or is subject to different rates of withholding.

A withholding agent may be permitted to use substitute payee copies of Form 1042-S (copies B, C, and D) that contain more than one type of income. See *Substitute Forms*, earlier, for details.

See *Payments Made to Persons Who Are Not Recipients* , later, if the payment is made to a foreign person that is not a recipient.

Payments to Recipients

Payments directly to beneficial owners. A U.S. withholding agent making a payment directly to a beneficial owner must complete Form 1042-S and treat the beneficial owner as the recipient. Boxes 17 through 20 should be left blank. A U.S. withholding agent should complete box 21 only if it is completing Form 1042-S as a paying agent acting pursuant to an agreement.

Under a grace period rule, a U.S. withholding agent may, under certain circumstances, treat a payee as a foreign person while the withholding agent waits for a valid withholding certificate. A U.S. withholding agent who relies on the grace period rule to treat a payee as a foreign person must file Form 1042-S to report all payments during the period that person was presumed to be foreign even if that person is later determined to be a U.S. person based on appropriate documentation or is presumed to be a U.S. person after the grace period ends.

In the case of foreign joint owners, you may provide a single Form 1042-S made out to the owner whose status you relied upon to determine the applicable rate of withholding (the owner subject to the highest rate of withholding). If, however, any one of the owners requests its own Form 1042-S, you must furnish a Form 1042-S to the person who requests it. If more than one Form 1042-S is issued for a single payment, the aggregate amount paid and tax withheld that is reported on all Forms 1042-S cannot exceed the total amounts paid to joint owners and the tax withheld on those payments.

Payments to a qualified intermediary, withholding foreign partnership, or withholding foreign trust. A U.S. withholding agent that makes payments to a QI (whether or not the QI assumes primary withholding responsibility), a withholding foreign partnership (WP), or a

withholding foreign trust (WT) should complete Forms 1042-S in most cases, treating the QI, WP, or WT as the recipient. However, see *Payments allocated, or presumed made, to U.S. non-exempt recipients* , later, for exceptions. The U.S. withholding agent must complete a separate Form 1042-S for each withholding rate pool of the QI, WP, or WT. For this purpose, a withholding rate pool is a payment of a single type of income, determined in accordance with the income codes used to file Form 1042-S, that is subject to a single rate of withholding. A QI that does not assume primary withholding responsibility provides information regarding the proportions of income subject to a particular withholding rate to the withholding agent on a withholding statement associated with Form W-8IMY. A U.S. withholding agent making a payment to a QI, WP, or WT must use recipient code 12 (qualified intermediary) or 04 (withholding foreign partnership or withholding foreign trust). A U.S. withholding agent must not use recipient code 13 (private arrangement intermediary withholding rate pool—general), 14 (private arrangement intermediary withholding rate pool—exempt organizations), 15 (qualified intermediary withholding rate pool—general), or 16 (qualified intermediary withholding rate pool—exempt organizations). Use of an inappropriate recipient code may cause a notice to be generated.

 A QI, WP, or WT is required to act in such capacity only for designated accounts. Therefore, such an entity also may provide a Form W-8IMY in which it certifies that it is acting as an NQI or flow-through entity for other accounts. A U.S. withholding agent that receives a Form W-8IMY on which the foreign person providing the form indicates that it is not acting as a QI, WP, or WT may not treat the foreign person as a recipient. A withholding agent must not use the EIN that a QI, WP, or WT provides in its capacity as such to report payments that are treated as made to an entity in its capacity as an NQI or flow-through entity. In that case, use the EIN, if any, that is provided by the entity on its Form W-8IMY in which it claims that it is acting as an NQI or flow-through entity.

Payments allocated, or presumed made, to U.S. non-exempt recipients. You may be given Forms W-9 or other information regarding U.S. non-exempt recipients from a QI together with information allocating all or a part of the payment to U.S. non-exempt recipients. You must report income allocable to a U.S. non-exempt recipient on the appropriate Form 1099 and not on Form

1042-S, even though you are paying that income to a QI.

You also may be required under the presumption rules to treat a payment made to a QI as made to a payee that is a U.S. non-exempt recipient from which you must withhold on the payment under the backup withholding provisions of the Code. In this case, you must report the payment on the appropriate Form 1099. See the General Instructions for Certain Information Returns.

Example 1. WA, a U.S. withholding agent, makes a payment of U.S. source dividends to QI, a qualified intermediary. QI provides WA with a valid Form W-8IMY with which it associates a withholding statement that allocates 95% of the payment to a 15% withholding rate pool and 5% of the payment to C, a U.S. individual. QI provides WA with C's Form W-9. WA must complete a Form 1042-S, showing QI as the recipient in box 13a and recipient code 12 (qualified intermediary) in box 13b, for the dividends allocated to the 15% withholding rate pool. WA also must complete a Form 1099-DIV reporting the part of the dividend allocated to C.

Example 2. WA, a withholding agent, makes a payment of U.S. source dividends to QI, a qualified intermediary. QI provides WA with a valid Form W-8IMY with which it associates a withholding statement that allocates 40% of the payment to a 15% withholding rate pool and 40% to a 30% withholding rate pool. QI does not provide any withholding rate pool information regarding the remaining 20% of the payment. WA must apply the presumption rules to the part of the payment (20%) that has not been allocated. Under the presumption rules, that part of the payment is treated as paid to an unknown foreign payee. WA must complete three Forms 1042-S: one for dividends subject to 15% withholding, showing QI as the recipient in box 13a and recipient code 12 (qualified intermediary) in box 13b; one for dividends subject to 30% withholding, showing QI as the recipient in box 13a and recipient code 12 (qualified intermediary) in box 13b; and one for dividends subject to 30% withholding, showing QI as the recipient in box 13a and recipient code 20 (unknown recipient) in box 13b.

Amounts paid to qualified securities lenders. A withholding agent that makes payments of substitute dividends to a qualified securities lender (QSL) should complete Form 1042-S treating the QSL as the recipient. Use income code 34. Use recipient code 21 or 22.

The withholding agent is not required to withhold on a substitute dividend payment that is part of a series of dividend equivalent payments if it receives, at least annually, a certificate from the QSL that

includes a statement with the following information.
- The recipient of the substitute dividend is a QSL, and
- With respect to the substitute dividend it receives from the withholding agent, the QSL states that it will withhold and remit or pay the proper amount of U.S. gross-basis tax. Use exemption code 10.

If the QSL is also a QI with primary withholding responsibility, use exemption code 10 and not exemption code 06.

Amounts paid to certain U.S. branches. A U.S. withholding agent making a payment to a "U.S. branch treated as a U.S. person" (defined in *Definitions*, earlier) completes Form 1042-S as follows:
- If a withholding agent makes a payment to a U.S. branch that has provided the withholding agent with a Form W-8IMY that evidences its agreement with the withholding agent to be treated as a U.S. person, the U.S. withholding agent treats the U.S. branch as the recipient.
- If a withholding agent makes a payment to a U.S. branch that has provided a Form W-8IMY to transmit information regarding recipients, the U.S. withholding agent must complete a separate Form 1042-S for each recipient whose documentation is associated with the U.S. branch's Form W-8IMY. If a payment cannot be reliably associated with recipient documentation, the U.S. withholding agent must complete Form 1042-S in accordance with the presumption rules.
- If a withholding agent cannot reliably associate a payment with a Form W-8IMY from a U.S. branch, the payment must be reported on a single Form 1042-S treating the U.S. branch as the recipient and reporting the income as effectively connected income.

 The rules above apply only to U.S. branches treated as U.S. persons (defined in Definitions, *earlier). In all other cases, payments to a U.S. branch of a foreign person are treated as payments to the foreign person.*

Amounts paid to authorized foreign agents. If a U.S. withholding agent makes a payment to an authorized foreign agent (defined in *Definitions*, earlier), the withholding agent files Forms 1042-S for each type of income (determined by reference to the income codes used to complete Form 1042-S) treating the authorized foreign agent as the recipient, provided that the authorized foreign agent reports the payments on Forms 1042-S to each recipient to which it makes payments. If the authorized foreign agent fails to report the amounts paid on Forms 1042-S for each recipient, the U.S. withholding agent remains responsible for such reporting.

In box 13b, use recipient code 17 (authorized foreign agent).

Amounts paid to a complex trust or an estate. If a U.S. withholding agent makes a payment to a foreign complex trust or a foreign estate, a Form 1042-S must be completed showing the complex trust or estate as the recipient. Use recipient code 05 (trust) or 10 (estate). See *Payments Made to Persons Who Are Not Recipients*, later, for the treatment of payments made to foreign simple trusts and foreign grantor trusts.

Dual claims. A U.S. withholding agent may make a payment to a foreign entity (for example, a hybrid entity) that is simultaneously claiming a reduced rate of tax on its own behalf for a part of the payment and a reduced rate on behalf of persons in their capacity as interest holders in that entity on the remaining part. If the claims are consistent and the withholding agent has accepted the multiple claims, a separate Form 1042-S must be filed for the entity for those payments for which the entity is treated as claiming a reduced rate of withholding and separate Forms 1042-S must be filed for each of the interest holders for those payments for which the interest holders are claiming a reduced rate of withholding. If the claims are consistent but the withholding agent has not chosen to accept the multiple claims, or if the claims are inconsistent, a separate Form 1042-S must be filed for the person(s) being treated as the recipient(s).

Special instructions for U.S. trusts and estates. Report the entire amount of income subject to reporting, regardless of estimates of distributable net income.

Payments Made to Persons Who Are Not Recipients

Disregarded entities. If a U.S. withholding agent makes a payment to a disregarded entity but receives a valid Form W-8BEN or W-8ECI from a foreign person that is the single owner of the disregarded entity, the withholding agent must file a Form 1042-S in the name of the foreign single owner. The taxpayer identifying number (TIN) on the Form 1042-S, if required, must be the foreign single owner's TIN.

Example. A withholding agent (WA) makes a payment of interest to LLC, a foreign limited liability company. LLC is wholly-owned by FC, a foreign corporation. LLC is treated as a disregarded entity. WA has a Form W-8BEN from FC on which it states that it is the beneficial owner of the income paid to LLC. WA reports the interest payment on Form 1042-S showing FC as the recipient. The result would be the same if LLC was a domestic entity.

A disregarded entity can claim to be the beneficial owner of a payment if it is a hybrid entity claiming treaty benefits. See Form W-8BEN and its instructions for more information. If a disregarded entity claims on a valid Form W-8BEN to be the beneficial owner, the U.S. withholding agent must complete a Form 1042-S treating the disregarded entity as a recipient and use recipient code 02 (corporation).

Amounts paid to a nonqualified intermediary or flow-through entity. If a U.S. withholding agent makes a payment to an NQI or a flow-through entity, it must complete a separate Form 1042-S for each recipient on whose behalf the NQI or flow-through entity acts as indicated by its withholding statement and the documentation associated with its Form W-8IMY. If a payment is made through tiers of NQIs or flow-through entities, the withholding agent must nevertheless complete Form 1042-S for the recipients to which the payments are remitted. A withholding agent completing Form 1042-S for a recipient that receives a payment through an NQI or a flow-through entity must include in boxes 17 through 20 of Form 1042-S the name, country code, address, and TIN, if any, of the NQI or flow-through entity from whom the recipient directly receives the payment. A copy of the Form 1042-S need not be provided to the NQI or flow-through entity unless the withholding agent must report the payment to an unknown recipient. See *Example 4* , later.

If a U.S. withholding agent makes payments to an NQI or flow-through entity and cannot reliably associate the payment, or any part of the payment, with a valid withholding certificate (Forms W-8 or W-9) or other valid appropriate documentation from a recipient (either because a recipient withholding certificate has not been provided or because the NQI or flow-through entity has failed to provide the information required on a withholding statement), the withholding agent must follow the appropriate presumption rules for that payment. If, under the presumption rules, an unknown recipient of the income is presumed to be foreign, the withholding agent must withhold 30% of the payment and report the payment on Form 1042-S. For this purpose, if the allocation information provided to the withholding agent indicates an allocation of more than 100% of the payment, then no part of the payment should be considered to be associated with a Form W-8, Form W-9, or other appropriate documentation. The Form 1042-S should be completed by entering "Unknown Recipient" in box 13a and recipient code 20 in box 13b.

Pro-rata reporting. If the withholding agent has agreed that an NQI may provide information allocating a payment to its account holders under the alternative procedure of Regulations section 1.1441-1(e)(3)(iv)(D) (no later than February 14, 2013) and the NQI fails to allocate more than 10% of the payment in a withholding rate pool to the specific recipients in the pool, the withholding agent must file Forms 1042-S for each recipient in the pool on a pro-rata basis. If, however, the NQI fails to timely allocate 10% or less of the payment in a withholding rate pool to the specific recipients in the pool, the withholding agent must file Forms 1042-S for each recipient for which it has allocation information and report the unallocated part of the payment on a Form 1042-S issued to "Unknown Recipient." In either case, the withholding agent must include the NQI information in boxes 17 through 20 on that form. See *Example 6* and *Example 7* , later.

The following examples illustrate Form 1042-S reporting for payments made to NQIs and flow-through entities.

Example 1. NQI, a nonqualified intermediary, has three account holders, A, B, and QI. All three account holders invest in U.S. securities that produce interest and dividends. A and B are foreign individuals and have provided NQI with Forms W-8BEN. QI is a qualified intermediary and has provided NQI with a Form W-8IMY and the withholding statement required from a qualified intermediary. QI's withholding statement states that QI has two withholding rate pools: one for interest described by income code 01 (interest paid by U.S. obligors—general) and one for dividends described by income code 06 (dividends paid by U.S. corporations—general). NQI provides WA, a U.S. withholding agent, with its own Form W-8IMY, with which it associates the Forms W-8BEN of A and B and the Form W-8IMY of QI. In addition, NQI provides WA with a complete withholding statement that allocates the payments of interest and dividends WA makes to NQI among A, B, and QI. All of the interest and dividends paid by WA to NQI are described by income code 01 (interest paid by U.S. obligors—general) and income code 06 (dividends paid by U.S. corporations—general). WA must file a total of six Forms 1042-S: two Forms 1042-S (one for interest and one for dividends) showing A as the recipient, two Forms 1042-S (one for interest and one for dividends) showing B as the recipient, and two Forms 1042-S (one for interest and one for dividends) showing QI as the recipient. WA must show information relating to NQI in boxes 17 through 20 on all six Forms 1042-S.

Example 2. The facts are the same as in Example 1, except that A and B are account holders of NQI2, which is an account holder of NQI. NQI2 provides NQI with a Form W-8IMY with which it associates the Forms W-8BEN of A and B and a complete withholding statement that allocates the interest and dividend payments it receives from NQI to A and B. NQI provides WA with its Form W-8IMY and the Forms W-8IMY of NQI2 and QI and the Forms W-8BEN of A and B. In addition, NQI associates a complete withholding statement with its Form W-8IMY that allocates the payments of interest and dividends to A, B, and QI. WA must file six Forms 1042-S: two Forms 1042-S (one for interest and one for dividends) showing A as the recipient, two Forms 1042-S (one for interest and one for dividends) showing B as the recipient, and two Forms 1042-S (one for interest and one for dividends) showing QI as the recipient. The Forms 1042-S issued to A and B must show information relating to NQI2 in boxes 17 through 20 because A and B receive their payments directly from NQI2, not NQI. The Forms 1042-S issued to QI must show information relating to NQI in boxes 17 through 20.

Example 3. FP is a nonwithholding foreign partnership and therefore a flow-through entity. FP establishes an account with WA, a U.S. withholding agent, from which FP receives interest described by income code 01 (interest paid by U.S. obligors—general). FP has three partners, A, B, and C, all of whom are individuals. FP provides WA with a Form W-8IMY with which it associates the Forms W-8BEN from each of A, B, and C. In addition, FP provides a complete withholding statement with its Form W-8IMY that allocates the interest payments among A, B, and C. WA must file three Forms 1042-S, one each for A, B, and C. The Forms 1042-S must show information relating to FP in boxes 17 through 20.

Example 4. NQI is a nonqualified intermediary. It has four customers: A, B, C, and D. NQI receives Forms W-8BEN from each of A, B, C, and D. NQI establishes an account with WA, a U.S. withholding agent, in which it holds securities on behalf of A, B, C, and D. The securities pay interest that is described by income code 01 (interest paid by U.S. obligors—general) and that may qualify for the portfolio interest exemption from withholding if all of the requirements for that exception are met. NQI provides WA with a Form W-8IMY with which it associates the Forms W-8BEN of A, B, C, and D. However, NQI does not provide WA with a complete withholding statement in association with its Form W-8IMY. Because NQI has not provided WA with a complete withholding statement, WA cannot reliably associate the payments of interest with the documentation of A, B, C, and D, and must apply the presumption rules. Under the presumption rules, WA must treat the interest as paid to an unknown recipient that is a foreign person. The payments of interest are subject to 30% withholding. WA must complete one Form 1042-S, entering "Unknown Recipient" in box 13a and recipient code 20 in box 13b. WA must include information relating to NQI in boxes 17 through 20 and must provide the recipient copies of the form to NQI. Because NQI has failed to provide all the information necessary for WA to accurately report the payments of interest to A, B, C, and D, NQI must report the payments on Form 1042-S. See *Amounts Paid by Nonqualified Intermediaries and Flow-Through Entities* , later. The results would be the same if WA's account holder was a flow-through entity instead of a nonqualified intermediary.

Example 5. The facts are the same as in Example 4, except that NQI provides the Forms W-8BEN of A and B, but not the Forms W-8BEN of C and D. NQI also provides a withholding statement that allocates a part of the interest payment to A and B but does not allocate the remaining part of the payment. WA must file three Forms 1042-S: one showing A as the recipient in box 13a, one showing B as the recipient in box 13a, and one showing "Unknown Recipient" in box 13a (and recipient code 20 in box 13b) for the unallocated part of the payment that cannot be associated with valid documentation from a recipient. In addition, WA must send the Form 1042-S for the unknown recipient to NQI. All Forms 1042-S must contain information relating to NQI in boxes 17 through 20. The results would be the same if WA's account holder was a flow-through entity instead of a nonqualified intermediary.

Example 6. NQI is a nonqualified intermediary. It has four customers: A, B, C, and D. NQI receives Forms W-8BEN from each of A, B, C, and D. NQI establishes an account with WA, a U.S. withholding agent, in which it holds securities on behalf of A, B, C, and D. The securities pay interest that is described by income code 01 (interest paid by U.S. obligors—general) and that may qualify for the portfolio interest exemption from withholding if all of the requirements for that exception are met. NQI provides WA with a Form W-8IMY with which it associates the Forms W-8BEN of A, B, C, and D. WA and NQI agree that they will apply the alternative procedures of Regulations section 1.1441-1(e)(3)(iv)(D). Accordingly, NQI provides a complete withholding statement that indicates that it has one 0% withholding rate pool. WA pays $100 of interest to NQI. NQI fails to provide WA with the allocation information by February 14, 2013. Therefore, WA must report 25% of the payment to each of

A, B, C, and D using pro-rata basis reporting. Accordingly, for each of the Forms 1042-S, WA must enter $25 in box 2 (gross income),"30.00" in box 5 (tax rate), $0 in box 7 (federal tax withheld), and $0 in box 9 (total withholding credit). In addition, WA must check the PRO-RATA BASIS REPORTING box at the top of the form and include NQI's name, address, country code, and TIN, if any, in boxes 17 through 20. WA must enter "30.00" in box 5 (tax rate) because without allocation information, WA cannot reliably associate the payment of interest with documentation from a foreign beneficial owner and therefore may not apply the portfolio interest exception. See the instructions for box 6 (exemption code) , later, for information on completing that box.

Example 7. The facts are the same as in Example 6, except that NQI timely provides WA with information allocating 70% of the payment to A, 10% of the payment to B, and 10% of the payment to C. NQI fails to allocate any of the payment to D. Because NQI has allocated 90% of the payment made to the 0% withholding rate pool, WA is not required to report to NQI's account holders on a pro-rata basis. Instead, WA must file Forms 1042-S for A, B, and C, entering $70, $10, and $10, respectively, in box 2 (gross income), "00.00" in box 5 (tax rate), exemption code 05 (portfolio interest) in box 6, $0 in box 7 (federal tax withheld), and $0 in box 9 (total withholding credit). WA must apply the presumption rules to the $10 that NQI has not allocated and file a Form 1042-S showing "Unknown Recipient" in box 13a and recipient code 20 in box 13b. On that Form 1042-S, WA also must enter "30.00" in box 5 (tax rate) because the portfolio interest exemption is unavailable and $0 in box 7 (federal tax withheld) and in box 9 (total withholding credit) because no amounts actually were withheld from the interest. In addition, WA must send the Form 1042-S for the unknown recipient to NQI. All Forms 1042-S must contain information relating to NQI in boxes 17 through 20.

Payments allocated, or presumed made, to U.S. non-exempt recipients. You may be given Forms W-9 or other information regarding U.S. non-exempt recipients from an NQI or flow-through entity together with information allocating all or a part of the payment to U.S. non-exempt recipients. You must report income allocable to a U.S. non-exempt recipient on the appropriate Form 1099 and not on Form 1042-S, even though you are paying that income to an NQI or a flow-through entity.

You also may be required under the presumption rules to treat a payment made to an NQI or flow-through entity as

made to a payee that is a U.S. non-exempt recipient from which you must withhold on the payment under the backup withholding provisions of the Code. In this case, you must report the payment on the appropriate Form 1099. See the General Instructions for Certain Information Returns.

Example 1. FP is a nonwithholding foreign partnership and therefore a flow-through entity. FP establishes an account with WA, a U.S. withholding agent, from which FP receives interest described by income code 01 (interest paid by U.S. obligors—general). FP has three partners, A, B, and C, all of whom are individuals. FP provides WA with a Form W-8IMY with which it associates Forms W-8BEN from A and B and a Form W-9 from C, a U.S. person. In addition, FP provides a complete withholding statement in association with its Form W-8IMY that allocates the interest payments among A, B, and C. WA must file two Forms 1042-S, one each for A and B, and a Form 1099-INT for C.

Example 2. The facts are the same as in Example 1, except that FP does not provide any documentation from its partners. Because WA cannot reliably associate the interest with documentation from a payee, it must apply the presumption rules. Under the presumption rules, the interest is deemed paid to an unknown U.S. non-exempt recipient. WA must, therefore, apply backup withholding to the payment of interest and report the payment on Form 1099-INT. WA must file a Form 1099-INT and send a copy to FP.

Amounts Paid by Qualified Intermediaries

In general. A QI reports payments on Form 1042-S in the same manner as a U.S. withholding agent. However, payments that are made by the QI directly to foreign beneficial owners (or that are treated as paid directly to beneficial owners) may be reported on the basis of reporting pools in most cases. A reporting pool consists of income that falls within a particular withholding rate and within a particular income code, exemption code, or recipient code as determined on Form 1042-S. A QI may not report on the basis of reporting pools in the circumstances described in *Recipient-by-Recipient Reporting* , later. A QI may use a single recipient code 15 (qualified intermediary withholding rate pool—general) for all reporting pools, except for amounts paid to foreign tax-exempt recipients for which recipient code 16 should be used. Note, however, that a QI should use recipient code 16 only for pooled account holders that have claimed an exemption based on their tax-exempt status and not some other exemption (tax treaty or other Code exception). See *Amounts Paid to Private Arrangement Intermediaries* , later, if a QI is reporting payments to a PAI.

Example 1. QI, a qualified intermediary, has four direct account holders, A and B, foreign individuals, and X and Y, foreign corporations. A and X are residents of a country with which the United States has an income tax treaty and have provided documentation that establishes that they are entitled to a lower treaty rate of 15% on withholding of dividends from U.S. sources. B and Y are not residents of a treaty country and are subject to 30% withholding on dividends. QI receives U.S. source dividends on behalf of its four customers. QI must file one Form 1042-S for the 15% withholding rate pool. This Form 1042-S must show income code 06 (dividends paid by U.S. corporations—general) in box 1, "15.00" in box 5 (tax rate), "Withholding rate pool" in box 13a (recipient's name), and recipient code 15 (qualified intermediary withholding rate pool—general) in box 13b. QI also must file one Form 1042-S for the 30% withholding rate pool that contains the same information as the Form 1042-S filed for the 15% withholding rate pool, except that it will show "30.00" in box 5 (tax rate).

Example 2. The facts are the same as in Example 1, except that Y is an organization that has tax-exempt status in the United States and in the country in which it is located. QI must file three Forms 1042-S. Two of the Forms 1042-S will contain the same information as in Example 1. The third Form 1042-S will contain information for the withholding rate pool consisting of the amounts paid to Y. This Form 1042-S will show income code 06 (dividends paid by U.S. corporations—general) in box 1, "00.00" in box 5 (tax rate), exemption code 02 (exempt under an Internal Revenue Code section (income other than portfolio interest)) in box 6, "Zero rate withholding pool—exempt organizations," or similar designation, in box 13a (recipient's name), and recipient code 16 (qualified intermediary withholding rate pool—exempt organizations) in box 13b.

 Under the terms of its withholding agreement with the IRS, the QI may be required to report the amounts paid to U.S. non-exempt recipients on Form 1099 using the name, address, and TIN of the payee to the extent those items of information are known. These amounts must not be reported on Form 1042-S. In addition, amounts paid to U.S. exempt recipients are not subject to reporting on Form 1042-S or Form 1099.

Amounts Paid to Private Arrangement Intermediaries

In most cases, a QI must report payments made to each private arrangement intermediary (PAI) (defined earlier in *Definitions*) as if the PAI's direct account holders were its own. Therefore, if the payment is made directly by the PAI to the recipient, the QI may report the payment on a pooled basis. A separate Form 1042-S is required for each withholding rate pool of each PAI. However, the QI must include the name and address of the PAI and use recipient code 13 or 14 in boxes 13a through 13e. If the PAI is providing recipient information from an NQI or flow-through entity, the QI may not report the payments on a pooled basis. Instead, it must follow the same procedures as a U.S. withholding agent making a payment to an NQI or flow-through entity.

Example. QI, a qualified intermediary, pays U.S. source dividends to direct account holders that are foreign persons and beneficial owners. It also pays a part of the U.S. source dividends to two private arrangement intermediaries, PAI1 and PAI2. The private arrangement intermediaries pay the dividends they receive from QI to foreign persons that are beneficial owners and direct account holders in PAI1 and PAI2. All of the dividends paid are subject to a 15% rate of withholding. QI must file a Form 1042-S for the dividends paid to its own direct account holders that are beneficial owners. QI also must file two Forms 1042-S, one for the dividends paid to the direct account holders of each of PAI1 and PAI2. Each of the Forms 1042-S that QI files for payments made to PAI1 and PAI2 must contain the name and address of PAI1 or PAI2 and recipient code 13 (private arrangement intermediary withholding rate pool—general) in boxes 13a through 13e.

Amounts Paid to Certain Related Partnerships and Trusts

A QI that is applying the rules of Section 4A.02 of the QI agreement in Rev. Proc. 2003-64 to a partnership or trust must file separate Forms 1042-S reflecting reporting pools for each partnership or trust that has provided reporting pool information in its withholding statement. However, the QI must file separate Forms 1042-S for partners, beneficiaries, or owners of such partnership or trust that are indirect partners, beneficiaries, or owners, and for direct partners, beneficiaries, or owners of such partnership or trust that are intermediaries or flow-through entities.

Recipient-by-Recipient Reporting

If a QI is not permitted to report on the basis of reporting pools, it must follow the same rules that apply to a U.S. withholding agent. A QI may not report the following payments on a reporting pool basis, but rather must complete Form 1042-S for each appropriate recipient.

Payments made to another QI, QSL, WP, or WT. The QI must complete a Form 1042-S treating the other QI, QSL, WP, or WT as the recipient.

Payments made to an NQI (including an NQI that is an account holder of a PAI). The QI must complete a Form 1042-S for each recipient who receives the payment from the NQI. A QI that is completing Form 1042-S for a recipient that receives a payment through an NQI must include in boxes 17 through 20 the name, country code, address, and TIN, if any, of the NQI from whom the recipient directly receives the payment.

Example. QI, a qualified intermediary, has NQI, a nonqualified intermediary, as an account holder. NQI has two account holders, A and B, both foreign persons who receive U.S. source dividends from QI. NQI provides QI with a valid Form W-8IMY, with which it associates Forms W-8BEN from A and B and a complete withholding statement that allocates the dividends paid to NQI between A and B. QI must complete two Forms 1042-S, one for A and one for B, and include information relating to NQI in boxes 17 through 20.

Payments made to a flow-through entity. The QI must complete a Form 1042-S for each recipient who receives the payment from the flow-through entity. A QI that is completing a Form 1042-S for a recipient that receives a payment through a flow-through entity must include in boxes 17 through 20 the name, country code, address, and TIN, if any, of the flow-through entity from which the recipient directly receives the payment.

Example. QI, a qualified intermediary, has FP, a nonwithholding foreign partnership, as an account holder. QI pays interest described by income code 01 (interest paid by U.S. obligors—general) to FP. FP has three partners, A, B, and C, all of whom are individuals. FP provides QI with a Form W-8IMY with which it associates the Forms W-8BEN from each of A, B, and C. In addition, FP provides a complete withholding statement in association with its Form W-8IMY that allocates the interest payments among A, B, and C. QI must file three Forms 1042-S, one each for A, B, and C. The Forms 1042-S must show information relating to FP in boxes 17 through 20.

Amounts Paid by Withholding Foreign Partnerships and Trusts

In general. In most cases, a withholding foreign partnership (WP) or withholding foreign trust (WT) must file a separate Form 1042-S for each direct partner, beneficiary, or owner to whom the WP or WT distributes, or in whose distributive share is included, an amount subject to withholding under Chapter 3 of the Code, in the same manner as a U.S. withholding agent. However, if the WP or WT has made a pooled reporting election in its WP or WT agreement, the WP or WT may instead report payments to such direct partners, beneficiaries, or owners on the basis of reporting pools and file a separate Form 1042-S for each reporting pool. A reporting pool consists of income that falls within a particular withholding rate and within a particular income code, exemption code, and recipient code, as determined on Form 1042-S. A WP or WT may use a single recipient code 15 (qualified intermediary withholding rate pool—general) for all reporting pools, except for amounts paid to foreign tax-exempt recipients for which a separate recipient code 16 must be used. For this purpose, a foreign tax-exempt recipient includes any organization that is not subject to withholding and is not liable to tax in its country of residence because it is a charitable organization, pension fund, or foreign government.

Amounts paid to certain related partnerships and trusts. A WP or WT that is applying the rules of Section 10.02 of the WP or WT agreement in Rev. Proc. 2003-64 to a partnership or trust must file separate Forms 1042-S reflecting reporting pools for each partnership or trust that has provided reporting pool information in its withholding statement. However, the WP or WT must apply the provisions of Regulations sections 1.1441-1 and 1.1441-5 to partners, beneficiaries, or owners of such partnership or trust that are indirect partners, beneficiaries, or owners, and to direct partners, beneficiaries, or owners of such partnership or trust that are intermediaries or flow-through entities.

Amounts Paid by Nonqualified Intermediaries and Flow-Through Entities

An NQI and a flow-through entity are withholding agents and must file Forms 1042-S for amounts paid to recipients. However, an NQI or flow-through entity is not required to file Form 1042-S if it is not required to file Form 1042-S under the *Multiple Withholding Agent Rule* , later. An NQI or flow-through entity must report payments made to recipients to the extent it has failed to provide to another withholding agent the appropriate documentation and complete withholding statement, including information allocating the payment to each recipient.

If another withholding agent withheld tax but did not report the payment on Form 1042-S to the recipient, even if the recipient should have been exempt from taxation, the NQI or flow-through entity must file Form 1042-S. Failure to file Forms 1042-S may not only result in penalties for the NQI or flow-through entity, but may result in the denial of any refund claim made by a recipient.

If another withholding agent has withheld tax on an amount that should have been exempt (for example, where the withholding agent applied the presumption rules because it did not receive proper documentation or other required information from the NQI or flow-through entity), the NQI or flow-through entity should report the correct tax rate and the combined amount of U.S. federal tax withheld by the NQI or flow-through entity and any other withholding agent and should enter the applicable exemption code using the instructions for box 6 , later.

If another withholding agent underwithholds, even though it received proper documentation from the NQI or flow-through entity, the NQI or flow-through entity must withhold additional amounts to bring the total withholding to the correct amount. Furthermore, the NQI or flow-through entity must complete Form 1042-S and must include the correct tax rate and the combined amount of U.S. federal tax withheld by the NQI or flow-through entity.

Example 1. A foreign bank acts as a nonqualified intermediary (NQI) for four different foreign persons (A, B, C, and D) who own securities from which they receive interest. The interest is paid by a U.S. withholding agent (WA) as custodian of the securities for NQI. A, B, C, and D each own a 25% interest in the securities. NQI has furnished WA a Form W-8IMY to which it has attached Forms W-8BEN from A and B. NQI's Form W-8IMY contains an attachment stating that 25% of the securities are allocable to each of A and B, and 50% to undocumented owners. WA pays $100 of interest during the calendar year. WA treats the $25 of interest allocable to A and the $25 of interest allocable to B as portfolio interest and completes a Form 1042-S for A and for B as the recipients. WA includes information relating to NQI in boxes 17 through 20 on the Forms 1042-S for A and B. WA subjects the remaining $50 of interest to 30% withholding under the presumption rules and reports the interest on a Form 1042-S by entering "Unknown Recipient" in box 13a (and recipient code 20 in box 13b), "30.00" in box 5 (tax rate), and $15 as the amount withheld in box 7 and box 9. WA also includes information relating to NQI in boxes 17 through 20 of the Form 1042-S and sends a copy of the form to NQI. Because NQI has not provided WA with beneficial owner information for C and D, NQI must report the interest paid to C and D on Forms 1042-S. (Note that under the multiple withholding agent rule, NQI is not required to file a Form 1042-S for A or B.) The Forms 1042-S for C and D should show $25 in box 2 (gross income) and $7.50 in boxes 7 and 9. The rate of tax NQI includes on the Form 1042-S for C and D depends on the rate of withholding to which they should be subject. Thus, if C and D provided NQI with documentation prior to the payment of interest that would qualify the interest as portfolio interest, the rate entered in box 5 should be "00.00." If they do not qualify for a reduced rate of withholding, NQI should enter "30.00" in box 5. In any event, NQI also must enter "99" in box 6 (exemption code) of the Forms 1042-S it prepares for C and D. See the instructions for box 6 , later.

Example 2. A U.S. withholding agent (WA) makes a $100 dividend payment to a foreign bank (NQI) that acts as a nonqualified intermediary. NQI receives the payment on behalf of A, a resident of a treaty country who is entitled to a 15% rate of withholding, and B, a resident of a country that does not have a tax treaty with the United States and who is subject to 30% withholding. NQI provides WA with its Form W-8IMY to which it associates the Forms W-8BEN from both A and B and a complete withholding statement that allocates 50% of the dividend to A and 50% to B. A's Form W-8BEN claims a 15% treaty rate of withholding. B's Form W-8BEN does not claim a reduced rate of withholding. WA, however, mistakenly withholds only 15%, $15, from the entire $100 payment. WA completes a Form 1042-S for each A and B as the recipients, showing on each form $50 of dividends in box 2, a withholding rate of "15.00" in box 5 (tax rate), and $7.50 as the amount withheld in boxes 7 and 9. Under the multiple withholding agent rule, NQI is not required to file a Form 1042-S for A. However, because NQI knows (or should know) that B is subject to a 30% rate of withholding, and assuming it knows that WA only withheld 15%, the multiple withholding agent rule does not apply to the dividend paid to B, and NQI must withhold an additional 15% from the payment to B. NQI then must file a Form 1042-S for B showing $50 of dividends in box 2, "30.00" in box 5 (the correct tax rate), and $7.50 withheld by NQI in box 7,

Instructions for Form 1042-S (2013)

$7.50 withheld by WA in box 8, and $15 in box 9 (the combined amount withheld). NQI also must enter "00" in box 6 (exemption code). See the instructions for box 6, later.

Example 3. A withholding agent (WA) receives a Form W-8IMY from a nonqualified intermediary (NQI). NQI's Form W-8IMY relates to payments of bank deposit interest. NQI collects the bank deposit interest on behalf of A, B, C, and D, but does not associate Forms W-8, W-9, or other documentary evidence with the Form W-8IMY that NQI provides WA. A, B, and C are foreign persons for whom NQI has valid documentation establishing their foreign status. D is a U.S. person and has provided NQI with a Form W-9. Under the presumption rules, WA must treat the bank deposit interest as being paid to an unknown U.S. person and apply backup withholding. WA must complete one Form 1099 for an unknown payee showing backup withholding. A copy of the form must be sent to NQI. Because NQI failed to provide the requisite documentation to WA and because the amounts have been subject to withholding, NQI must report the amounts paid to A, B, C, and D. Accordingly, NQI must file a Form 1042-S for each A, B, and C showing deposit interest (income code 29) as the type of payment in box 1; "00.00" in box 5 (the correct tax rate); "0" in box 7 (the amount withheld by NQI); the actual amount withheld by WA that is allocable to A, B, and C in box 8; the total withheld (box 7 plus box 8) in box 9; and exemption code 99 in box 6. (See the instructions for box 6 , later.) NQI also must file a Form 1099 for D to report the actual amounts paid and withheld.

Multiple Withholding Agent Rule

A withholding agent is not required to file Form 1042-S if a return is filed by another withholding agent reporting the same amount to the same recipient (the multiple withholding agent rule). If an NQI or flow-through entity has provided another withholding agent with the appropriate documentation and complete withholding statement, including information allocating the payment to each recipient, the NQI or flow-through entity may presume that the other withholding agent filed the required Forms 1042-S unless the NQI or flow-through entity knows, or has reason to know, that the required Form 1042-S reporting has not been done.

The multiple withholding agent rule does not relieve withholding agents from Form 1042-S reporting responsibility in the following circumstances.

• Any withholding agent making a payment to a QI, QSL, WP, or WT must

report that payment as made to the QI, QSL, WP, or WT.
• Any U.S. withholding agent making a payment to an authorized foreign agent must report that payment to the authorized foreign agent.
• Any withholding agent making a payment to a U.S. branch treated as a U.S. person must report the payment as made to that branch.
• Any withholding agent making a payment to a flow-through entity must report the payment as made to a beneficial owner, QI, WP, or WT that has a direct or indirect interest in that entity.
• Any withholding agent that withholds an amount from a payment under Chapter 3 of the Code must report that amount to the recipient from whom it was withheld, unless the payment is reportable on another IRS form.

Furthermore, the multiple withholding agent rule does not relieve the following from Form 1042-S reporting responsibility.
• Any QI, WP, or WT required to report an amount to a withholding rate pool.
• An NQI or flow-through entity that has not transmitted a valid Form W-8 or other valid documentation to another withholding agent together with the required withholding statement.

Penalties

The following penalties apply to the person required to file Form 1042-S. The penalties apply to both paper filers and electronic filers.

Late filing of correct Form 1042-S. A penalty may be imposed for failure to file each correct and complete Form 1042-S when due (including extensions), unless you can show that the failure was due to reasonable cause and not willful neglect. The penalty, based on when you file a correct Form 1042-S, is:
• $30 per Form 1042-S if you correctly file within 30 days after the required filing date; the maximum penalty is $250,000 per year ($75,000 for a small business). A small business, for this purpose, is defined as having average annual gross receipts of $5 million or less for the 3 most recent tax years (or for the period of its existence, if shorter) ending before the calendar year in which the Forms 1042-S are due.
• $60 per Form 1042-S if you correctly file more than 30 days after the due date but by August 1; the maximum penalty is $500,000 per year ($200,000 for a small business).
• $100 per Form 1042-S if you file after August 1 or you do not file correct Forms 1042-S; the maximum penalty is $1,500,000 per year ($500,000 for a small business).

If you intentionally disregard the requirement to report correct information, the penalty per Form 1042-S is increased

to the greater of $250 or 10% of the total amount of items required to be reported, with no maximum penalty.

Failure to furnish correct Form 1042-S to recipient. If you fail to provide statements to recipients and cannot show reasonable cause, a penalty of up to $100 may be imposed for each failure to furnish Form 1042-S to the recipient when due. The penalty also may be imposed for failure to include all required information or for furnishing incorrect information on Form 1042-S. The maximum penalty is $1,500,000 for all failures to furnish correct recipient statements during a calendar year. If you provide the correct statement on or before August 1, reduced penalties similar to those for failing to file a correct Form 1042-S with the IRS may be imposed. See *Late filing of correct Form 1042-S*, earlier. If you intentionally disregard the requirement to report correct information, each $100 penalty is increased to the greater of $250 or 10% of the total amount of items required to be reported, with no maximum penalty.

Failure to file electronically. If you are required to file electronically but fail to do so, and you do not have an approved waiver on record, you may be subject to a $50 penalty per return unless you establish reasonable cause. The penalty applies separately to original returns and amended returns. The maximum penalty is $100,000.

Avoid Common Errors

To ensure that your Forms 1042-S can be correctly processed, be sure that you:
• Carefully read the information provided in Pub. 515 and these instructions.
• Comply with the requirements in Pub. 1187 if you are an electronic filer.
• Complete all required fields. At a minimum, you must enter information in boxes 1, 2, 5, 6, 7, 9, 11, 12a through 12d, 13a, 13b, and 16. Other boxes must be completed if the nature of the payment requires it.

Note. You may leave box 5 blank if you are reporting a payment to an artist or athlete and there is a central withholding agreement. See *Exception for central withholding agreements* in the instructions for box 5. You may leave box 6 blank if you are applying backup withholding to the payment being reported.
• Use only income, recipient, exemption, and country codes specifically listed in these instructions.
• Use only tax rates that are allowed by statute, regulation, or treaty. Do not attempt to "blend" rates. Instead, if necessary, submit multiple Forms 1042-S to show changes in tax rate. See the Valid Tax Rate Table , later.

Income Codes, Exemption Codes, and Recipient Codes

Box 1. Enter the appropriate income code.

Code	Interest Income
01	Interest paid by U.S. obligors—general
02	Interest paid on real property mortgages
03	Interest paid to controlling foreign corporations
04	Interest paid by foreign corporations
05	Interest on tax-free covenant bonds
29	Deposit interest
30	Original issue discount (OID)
31	Short-term OID
33	Substitute payment—interest

Code	Dividend Income
06	Dividends paid by U.S. corporations—general
07	Dividends qualifying for direct dividend rate
08	Dividends paid by foreign corporations
34	Substitute payment—dividends
40	Other U.S.-source dividend equivalents under IRC section 871(m)

Code	Other Income
09	Capital gains
10	Industrial royalties
11	Motion picture or television copyright royalties
12	Other royalties (for example, copyright, recording, publishing)
13	Real property income and natural resources royalties
14	Pensions, annuities, alimony, and/or insurance premiums
15	Scholarship or fellowship grants
16	Compensation for independent personal services[1]
17	Compensation for dependent personal services[1]
18	Compensation for teaching[1]
19	Compensation during studying and training[1]
24	Real estate investment trust (REIT) distributions of capital gains
25	Trust distributions subject to IRC section 1445
26	Unsevered growing crops and timber distributions by a trust subject to IRC section 1445
27	Publicly traded partnership distributions subject to IRC section 1446
28	Gambling winnings[2]
32	Notional principal contract income[3]
35	Substitute payment—other
36	Capital gains distributions
37	Return of capital
38	Eligible deferred compensation items subject to IRC section 877A(d)(1)
39	Distributions from a nongrantor trust subject to IRC section 877A(f)(1)
41	Guarantee of indebtedness
42	Earnings as an artist or athlete—no central withholding agreement[4]
43	Earnings as an artist or athlete—central withholding agreement[4]
50	Other income

Box 6. If the tax rate entered in box 5 is 00.00, in most cases you must enter the appropriate exemption code from the list below (but see the **Caution** below).

Code	Authority for Exemption
01	Income effectively connected with a U.S. trade or business
02	Exempt under an Internal Revenue Code section (income other than portfolio interest)
03	Income is not from U.S. sources[5]
04	Exempt under tax treaty
05	Portfolio interest exempt under an Internal Revenue Code section
06	Qualified intermediary that assumes primary withholding responsibility
07	Withholding foreign partnership or withholding foreign trust
08	U.S. branch treated as a U.S. person
09	Qualified intermediary represents income is exempt
10	Qualified securities lender that assumes primary withholding responsibility for substitute dividends

Caution: *See the instructions for box 6, later, for information on additional codes ("00" and "99") that may be required.*

Box 13b. Enter the appropriate recipient code.

Code	Type of Recipient
01	Individual[4]
02	Corporation[4]
03	Partnership other than a withholding foreign partnership[4]
04	Withholding foreign partnership or withholding foreign trust
05	Trust
06	Government or international organization
07	Tax-exempt organization (IRC section 501(a))
08	Private foundation
09	Artist or athlete[4]
10	Estate
11	U.S. branch treated as U.S. person
12	Qualified intermediary
13	Private arrangement intermediary withholding rate pool—general[6]
14	Private arrangement intermediary withholding rate pool—exempt organizations[6]
15	Qualified intermediary withholding rate pool—general[6]
16	Qualified intermediary withholding rate pool—exempt organizations[6]
17	Authorized foreign agent
18	Public pension fund
20	Unknown recipient
21	Qualified securities lender—qualified intermediary
22	Qualified securities lender—other

[1] If compensation that otherwise would be covered under Income Codes 16 through 19 is directly attributable to the recipient's occupation as an artist or athlete, use Income Code 42 or 43 instead.

[2] Subject to 30% withholding rate unless the recipient is from one of the treaty countries listed under *Gambling winnings (Income Code 28)* in Pub. 515.

[3] Use appropriate Interest Income Code for embedded interest in a notional principal contract.

[4] If Income Code 42 or 43 is used, Recipient Code 09 (artist or athlete) should be used instead of Recipient Code 01 (individual), 02 (corporation), or 03 (partnership other than withholding foreign partnership).

[5] Non-U.S. source income paid to a nonresident alien is not subject to U.S. tax. Use Exemption Code 03 when entering an amount for information reporting purposes only.

[6] May be used only by a qualified intermediary.

All information you enter when reporting the payment must correctly reflect the intent of the statute and regulations. In most cases, you should rely on the withholding documentation you have collected (Form W-8 series, Form 8233, etc.) to complete your Form 1042-S submissions.

Also note the following:
• The gross income you report in box 2 cannot be zero.
• The income code you report in box 1 must correctly reflect the type of income you pay to the recipient.
• The withholding agent's name, address, and EIN, QI-EIN, WP-EIN, or WT-EIN must be reported in boxes 11, 12a, 12b, 12c, and 12d in all cases.
• The recipient's name, recipient code, address, and U.S. TIN, if any, must be reported in boxes 13 and 14. In most cases, you must report a foreign address. See the instructions for box 13, later. If you want, you can put the recipient's account number in box 22.
• The recipient code you report in box 13b must correctly identify the recipient's status. Use recipient code 20 only if you do not know who the recipient is.

Note. If you cannot identify the recipient, the tax withheld must be 30%.
• The recipient's country code that you report in box 16 must be present and correctly coded and cannot be "US." Additionally, do not use "OC" or "UC" except as specifically allowed in these instructions.
• The exemption code you report in box 6 must correctly identify the proper tax status for the type of income you pay to the recipient.

Note. If you use exemption code 04 (exempt under tax treaty), the country code that you report in box 16 must be a valid treaty country. Countries with which the United States has a tax treaty are shown in bold italics in the country code list, later.

 You, the withholding agent, are liable for the tax if you know, or should have known, that underwithholding on a payment has occurred.

Specific Instructions for Withholding Agents

 All amounts must be reported in U.S. dollars.

Rounding Off to Whole Dollars

You may round off cents to whole dollars. If you do round to whole dollars, you must round all amounts. To round off amounts to the nearest whole dollar, drop amounts under 50 cents and increase amounts from 50 to 99 cents to the next dollar. For example, $1.39 becomes $1 and $2.50 becomes $3. If you have to add two or more amounts to figure the amount to enter on a line, include cents when adding and only round off the total.

AMENDED Checkbox

See *Amended Returns*, later.

PRO-RATA BASIS REPORTING Checkbox

Withholding agents must check this box to notify the IRS that an NQI that used the alternative procedures of Regulations section 1.1441-1(e)(3)(iv)(D) failed to properly comply with those procedures. See *Pro-rata reporting*, earlier, for additional information and examples.

Box 1, Income Code

All filers must enter the appropriate 2-digit income code from the list, earlier. Use the income code that is the most specific. See Pub. 515 for further explanation of the income codes. Below are examples on how to use some of the income codes.

1. Use code 09 for the following types of capital gain:

a. Gains on disposal of timber, coal, or domestic iron ore with a retained economic interest, unless an election is made to treat those gains as income effectively connected with a U.S. trade or business;

b. Gains on contingent payments received from the sale or exchange after October 4, 1966, of patents, copyrights, secret processes and formulas, goodwill, trademarks, trade brands, franchises, and other like property;

c. Gains on certain transfers of all substantial rights to, or an undivided interest in, patents if the transfers were made before October 5, 1966; and

d. Certain gains from the sale or exchange of original issue discount obligations issued after March 31, 1972.

2. Use code 16 for payments for personal services performed by an independent contractor as contrasted with those performed by an employee. This includes payments that are subject to the business profits article of a treaty.

3. Use code 29 if you are paying bank deposit interest, not code 01 (interest paid by U.S. obligors—general).

4. Use code 24 for distributions of capital gains from a real estate investment trust (REIT). Use code 36 for capital gain distributions (dividends) paid or credited by mutual funds (or other regulated investment companies). Include short-term capital gain dividends (use exemption code 02 in box 6).

Note. Exempt-interest dividends should be reported under income code 01 (use exemption code 02 in box 6).

5. Use code 28 for gambling winnings. These are proceeds from a game other than blackjack, baccarat, craps, roulette, or big-6 wheel. For more information, see Pub. 515.

6. Use code 33, 34, or 35 for all substitute payment transactions. For more information, see Regulations sections 1.861-2(a)(7) and 1.861-3(a)(6) and Notice 2010-46.

7. Use code 37 for a nondividend distribution (return of capital). This is a distribution that is not paid out of the earnings and profits of a corporation. It represents a distribution in part or full payment in exchange for stock.

8. Use code 40 for other U.S.-source dividend equivalents. These are dividend equivalent payments under section 871(m) that are not substitute dividend payments identified with income code 34.

9. Use code 41 for certain guarantee of indebtedness payments. These are amounts paid for the provision of a guarantee of indebtedness that was issued after September 27, 2010.

10. Use either code 42 (earnings as an artist or athlete—no central withholding agreement) or 43 (earnings as an artist or athlete—central withholding agreement) for payments to an artist or athlete. A central withholding agreement is Form 13930, Application for Central Withholding Agreement, plus additional information specified in the instructions, that is entered into by the artist or athlete, a designated withholding agent, and the IRS. For more details, see Pub. 515.

If you paid more than one type of income to or on behalf of the same recipient, you must complete a separate Form 1042-S, Copy A, for each income type.

Note. Although income codes are provided for deposit interest, short-term OID, and notional principal contract income, those items are not always subject to reporting on Form 1042-S. For example, bank deposit interest is reportable if it is effectively connected with the conduct of a U.S. trade or business or is paid to a resident of Canada. Short-term OID or bank deposit interest may need to be reported by an NQI or flow-through entity if those amounts are paid to foreign persons and another withholding agent backup withheld on those amounts under the presumption rules. (See *Example 3* in *Amounts Paid by Nonqualified Intermediaries and Flow-Through Entities*, earlier.) Notional principal contract income is reportable if it is effectively connected with the conduct of a trade or business in the United States or results in the payment of interest under Regulations section 1.446-3(g)(4) or a dividend equivalent under section 871(m). For more information, see the regulations under Chapter 3 of the Code and Pub. 515.

Box 2, Gross Income

For each income type, enter the gross amount you paid to or on behalf of the recipient during calendar year 2012, including withheld tax. The following special procedures apply to the reporting of gross income.

• You must report the entire amount of a corporate distribution made with respect to stock even if you elect to reduce the amount of withholding on the distribution because all or a part of the distribution is nontaxable or represents a capital gain dividend.

• You must report the entire amount of a payment if you do not know at the time of payment the amount that is subject to withholding because the determination of the source of the income or the calculation of the amount of income subject to tax depends upon facts that are not known at the time of payment.

• You must report the entire amount of gains relating to the disposal of timber, coal, or domestic iron ore with a retained economic interest and gains relating to contingent payments received from the sale or exchange of patents, copyrights, and similar intangible property.

• You must report only the amount of cash paid on notional principal contracts.

Box 3, Withholding Allowances

This box should be completed only if the income code reported in box 1 is 15 (scholarship or fellowship grants), 16 (compensation for independent personal services), 17 (compensation for dependent personal services), 18 (compensation for teaching), 19 (compensation during studying and training), or 42 (earnings as an artist or athlete—no central withholding agreement). See Pub. 515 for more information.

Box 4, Net Income

Complete this box only if you entered an amount in box 3. Otherwise, leave it blank.

Box 5, Tax Rate

Enter the correct rate of withholding that applies to the income in box 2 (gross income) or box 4 (net income), as appropriate. (See Valid Tax Rate Table, later.) The correct tax rate should be included even if you withheld at a different rate. For example, if an NQI is reporting dividends paid to a beneficial owner who is a resident of a country with which the United States does not have a tax treaty and a U.S. withholding agent paid the dividend and withheld only 15% (rather than the required 30%) and the NQI withholds an additional 15%, the NQI should report "30.00" in box 5. See *Example 2* in *Amounts Paid by Nonqualified Intermediaries and Flow-Through Entities*, earlier.

The tax rate on dividends paid to a corporation created or organized in, or under the law of, the Commonwealth of Puerto Rico may be 10%, rather than 30%. See Pub. 515 for more information.

Enter the tax rate using the following format: two digits, a decimal, and two digits (for example, "30.00" for 30%). However, if the income is exempt from tax under a U.S. tax treaty or the Code, enter "00.00." If the tax rate is less than 10%, enter a zero before the tax rate (for example, "04.00" for 4%).

 If you withheld at more than one tax rate for a specific type of income that you paid to the same recipient, you must file a separate Form 1042-S, Copy A, for each amount to which a separate rate was applied.

Valid Tax Rate Table

00.00	07.00	14.00	27.50
04.00	08.00	15.00	28.00
04.90	10.00	17.50	30.00
04.95	12.00	20.00	35.00
05.00	12.50	25.00	

Exception for central withholding agreements. If you are the designated withholding agent who has entered into a central withholding agreement and you report an amount in box 2 using income code 43, you do not have to enter a tax rate in box 5.

Box 6, Exemption Code

Note. If you are filing a Form 1042-S to correct certain information already provided to you by another withholding agent on a Form 1099 or Form 1042-S (for example, as required under *Amounts Paid by Nonqualified Intermediaries and Flow-Through Entities*, earlier), see item 5 under this heading.

In most cases, if the tax rate you entered in box 5 is 00.00, you should enter the appropriate exemption code (01 through 10) from *Income Codes, Exemption Codes, and Recipient Codes*, earlier.

If an amount was withheld under Chapter 3 of the Code (the tax rate you entered in box 5 is greater than zero and is not due to backup withholding), enter "00" in box 6. If the tax rate you entered in box 5 is due to backup withholding, leave box 6 blank.

1. If exemption code 01 (income effectively connected with a U.S. trade or business) may apply, you must enter the recipient's U.S. TIN in box 14. If the recipient's U.S. TIN is unknown or unavailable, you must withhold tax at the foreign-person rate of 30% (30.00) and enter "00" in box 6.

2. A withholding agent should use exemption code 06 (qualified intermediary that assumes primary withholding responsibility) only if it is making a payment to a QI that has represented on its Form W-8IMY that it is assuming primary withholding responsibility under Chapter 3 of the Code.

3. A withholding agent should use exemption code 07 (withholding foreign partnership or withholding foreign trust) only if it is making a payment to a foreign partnership or trust that has represented that it is a withholding foreign partnership or trust.

4. A withholding agent should use exemption code 09 (qualified intermediary represents income is exempt) only if it makes a payment to a QI that has not assumed primary withholding responsibility under Chapter 3 of the Code or primary backup withholding responsibility, but has represented on a withholding statement associated with its Form W-8IMY that the income is exempt from withholding.

5. A withholding agent should use exemption code 10 (qualified securities lender that assumes primary withholding responsibility for substitute dividends) only if the withholding agent makes a substitute dividend payment to a financial institution that is a QSL.

6. If you have failed to provide another withholding agent with appropriate information regarding the status of the person to whom you are making a payment, the other withholding agent may be required to withhold on the payment based on the presumption rules. If the income is in fact exempt from withholding, you must submit a Form 1042-S providing the correct information. In this situation, you must:

Instructions for Form 1042-S (2013)

a. Indicate the correct rate at which the income should have been subject to withholding in box 5 (usually 00.00),

b. Enter "99" in box 6, and

c. Enter the actual amount of U.S. federal tax withheld by the other withholding agent in box 8.

You also must provide the correct recipient code and the name and address of the actual recipient in boxes 13a through e.

Boxes 7 Through 9, Federal Tax Withheld

Box 7. Enter the total amount of U.S. federal tax you actually withheld in box 7. If you did not withhold any tax, enter "-0-."

Box 8. If you are a withholding agent filing a Form 1042-S to report income that has already been subject to withholding by another withholding agent, enter the amount actually withheld by the other agent(s) in box 8. Further, report in box 8 any credit forward of prior withholding as determined under Notice 2010-46 with respect to substitute dividend payments.

Box 9. Enter the total amount of tax withheld by you and any other withholding agent in box 9.

 Boxes 7 and 9 must be completed in all cases, even if no tax has actually been withheld.

Box 10, Amount Repaid to Recipient

This box should be completed only if:
• You repaid a recipient an amount that was overwithheld; and
• You are going to reimburse yourself by reducing, by the amount of tax actually repaid, the amount of any deposit made for a payment period in the calendar year following the calendar year of withholding.

In most cases, a QI should not enter an amount in box 10 unless it is a QI that has represented on its Form W-8IMY that it is assuming primary withholding responsibility under Chapter 3 of the Code.

You also must state on a timely filed Form 1042 for the calendar year of overwithholding that the filing of the Form 1042 constitutes a claim for refund.

 The adjustment for amounts overwithheld does not apply to partnerships or nominees required to withhold under section 1446.

Box 11, Withholding Agent's Employer Identification Number (EIN)

In most cases, you are required to enter your EIN. However, if you are filing Form 1042-S as a QI, withholding foreign partnership, or withholding foreign trust, enter your QI-EIN, WP-EIN, or WT-EIN and check the QI-EIN box.

If you do not have an EIN, you can apply for one online at *www.irs.gov/businesses/small* or by telephone at 1-800-829-4933. Also, you can apply for an EIN by filing Form SS-4, Application for Employer Identification Number. File amended Forms 1042-S when you receive your EIN.

To get a QI-EIN, WP-EIN, or WT-EIN, submit Form SS-4 with your application for that status. (See the definitions for *Qualified intermediary (QI)* and *Withholding foreign partnership (WP) or withholding foreign trust (WT)* in *Definitions*, earlier, for more information.)

Box 12, Withholding Agent's Name and Address

Enter your name and address in the appropriate boxes. If your post office does not deliver mail to the street address and you have a P.O. box, show the box number instead of the street address.

If you are a nominee that is the withholding agent under section 1446, enter the PTP's name and other information in boxes 17 through 20.

Note. On statements furnished to Canadian recipients of U.S. source deposit interest, in addition to your name and address, you must include the telephone number of a person to contact. This number must provide direct access to an individual who can answer questions about the statement. The telephone number is not required on Copy A of paper forms or on electronically filed forms. You also must include a statement that the information on the form is being furnished to the United States Internal Revenue Service and may be furnished to Canada.

Box 13, Recipient's Name, Recipient Code, and Address

Name. Enter the complete name of the recipient in box 13a.
• If you do not know the name of the recipient, enter "Unknown Recipient."
• If Form 1042-S is being completed by a QI, WP, or WT for a withholding rate pool, enter "Withholding rate pool" in box 13a. No address is necessary.

• A QI reporting payments made to a PAI on a withholding rate pool basis must include the name and address of the PAI in boxes 13a through 13e.

Recipient code. Enter the recipient code from *Income Codes, Exemption Codes, and Recipient Codes*, earlier, in box 13b. The following special instructions apply.
• If applicable, use recipient code 09 (artist or athlete) instead of recipient code 01 (individual), 02 (corporation), or 03 (partnership other than a withholding foreign partnership).
• Use recipient code 12 if you are making a payment to a QI and 04 if you are making a payment to a WP or a WT.
• If you are making a payment to an NQI or flow-through entity, in most cases you must use the recipient code that applies to the type of recipient who receives the income from the NQI or flow-through entity.
• Use recipient code 03 (partnership other than withholding foreign partnership) only if you are reporting a payment of income that is effectively connected with the conduct of a trade or business of a nonwithholding foreign partnership in the United States. Otherwise, follow the rules that apply to payments to flow-through entities.
• Use recipient code 20 (unknown recipient) only if you have not received a withholding certificate or other documentation for a recipient or you cannot determine how much of a payment is reliably associated with a specific recipient. Do not use this code because you cannot determine the recipient's status as an individual, corporation, etc. The regulations under Chapter 3 of the Code provide rules on how to determine a recipient's status when a withholding agent does not have the necessary information.
• Use recipient code 21 (qualified securities lender—qualified intermediary) or 22 (qualified securities lender—other) if you make a payment to a QSL.
• Only QIs may use recipient codes 13 (private arrangement intermediary withholding rate pool—general), 14 (private arrangement intermediary withholding rate pool—exempt organizations), 15 (qualified intermediary withholding rate pool—general), and 16 (qualified intermediary withholding rate pool—exempt organizations). A QI should use recipient code 14 or 16 only for pooled account holders that have claimed an exemption based on their tax-exempt status and not some other exemption (for example, treaty or other Code exception). A U.S. withholding agent making a payment to a QI should use recipient code 12.

Address. In most cases, you must enter a foreign address in boxes 13c through

13e. However, there are limited exceptions. For example, you may enter a U.S. address when reporting payments of scholarship or fellowship grants (income code 15).

For addresses outside the United States or its commonwealths and possessions, follow the foreign country's practice for entering the postal code.

For addresses within the United States, use the U.S. Postal Service 2-letter abbreviation for the state name. Do not enter "United States" or "U.S."

If you want to enter the recipient's account number, use box 22.

Box 14, Recipient's U.S. Taxpayer Identification Number (TIN)

You must obtain and enter a U.S. taxpayer identification number (TIN) for any of the following recipients.
• Any recipient whose income is effectively connected with the conduct of a trade or business in the United States.

Note. For these recipients, enter exemption code 01 in box 6.
• Any foreign person claiming a reduced rate of, or exemption from, tax under a tax treaty between a foreign country and the United States, unless the income is an unexpected payment (as described in Regulations section 1.1441-6(g)) or consists of dividends and interest from stocks and debt obligations that are actively traded; dividends from any redeemable security issued by an investment company registered under the Investment Company Act of 1940 (mutual fund); dividends, interest, or royalties from units of beneficial interest in a unit investment trust that are (or were, upon issuance) publicly offered and are registered with the Securities and Exchange Commission under the Securities Act of 1933; and amounts paid with respect to loans of any of the above securities.
• Any nonresident alien individual claiming exemption from tax under section 871(f) for certain annuities received under qualified plans.
• A foreign organization claiming an exemption from tax solely because of its status as a tax-exempt organization under section 501(c) or as a private foundation.
• Any QI.
• Any WP or WT.
• Any nonresident alien individual claiming exemption from withholding on compensation for independent personal services.
• Any U.S. branch of a foreign bank or foreign insurance company that is treated as a U.S. person.

• Any QSL that was paid a substitute dividend.

In all other cases, if you know the recipient's TIN or if a foreign person provides a TIN on a Form W-8, but is not required to do so, you must include the TIN on Form 1042-S.

Box 15, Recipient's Foreign Tax Identifying Number

Enter the recipient's identifying number used in the country of residence for tax purposes (optional).

Box 16, Recipient's Country Code

You must enter the code (from *Country Codes*, later) for the country of which the recipient claims residency under that country's tax laws. Enter "OC" (other country) only when the country of residence does not appear on the list or the payment is made to an international organization (for example, the United Nations). Enter "UC" (unknown country) only if the payment is to an unknown recipient. If you are making a payment to a QI, QSL, WP, or WT, or if you are a QI, QSL, WP, or WT and are making a payment to a QI, WP, or WT withholding rate pool, enter the country code of the QI, WP, or WT.

 If exemption code 04 (exempt under tax treaty) appears in box 6 or if a reduced rate of withholding based on a tax treaty is entered in box 5, the country code entered in box 16 must be a country with which the United States has entered into an income tax treaty.

Boxes 17 Through 20, NQI's/Flow-Through Entity's Name, Country Code, Address, and TIN

If you are reporting amounts paid to a recipient whose withholding certificates or other documentation has been submitted to you with a Form W-8IMY provided by an NQI or flow-through entity, you must include the name, address, and TIN, if any, of the NQI or flow-through entity with whose Form W-8IMY the recipient's Form W-8 or other documentation is associated.

You also must provide this information about the NQI or flow-through entity when the NQI or flow-through entity provided a Form W-8IMY but you cannot associate part or all of the payment with valid documentation for a specific recipient or you cannot determine how much of the payment should be associated with a specific recipient.

Note. An NQI or flow-through entity will leave these boxes blank unless it is making the payment to an NQI or flow-through entity.

For box 18, you must enter the country code from *Country Codes*, later, for the country where the NQI or flow-through entity is located.

If you are a nominee that is the withholding agent under section 1446, enter the PTP's name and other information in these boxes.

Box 21, Payer's Name and Taxpayer Identification Number (TIN)

See the definition of a payer in *Definitions*, earlier. Include the payer's name and TIN if different from that in boxes 11 and 12.

Box 22, Recipient's Account Number

You may use this box to enter the account number assigned by you to the recipient.

Boxes 23 Through 25, State Income Tax Withheld and Related Information

Include in these boxes information relating to any state income tax withheld.

Amended Returns

If you filed a Form 1042-S with the IRS and later discover you made an error on it, you must correct it as soon as possible. To correct a previously filed Form 1042-S, you will need to file an amended Form 1042-S.

 You may be required to submit amended Forms 1042-S electronically. See Electronic Reporting, earlier, and Pub. 1187.

If any information you correct on Form(s) 1042-S changes the information you previously reported on Form 1042, you also must correct the Form 1042 by filing an amended return. To do this, see the Form 1042 instructions.

If you are filing electronically, see *Amended Returns* in Pub. 1187.

If you are not filing electronically, follow these steps to amend a previously filed Form 1042-S.

Step 1. Prepare a paper Form 1042-S.
• Enter all the correct information on the form, including the recipient name and address, money amounts, and codes.
• Enter an "X" in the AMENDED box at the top of the form.

AMENDED checkbox. Enter an "X" in the AMENDED checkbox of Copy A only if you are amending a Form 1042-S you

Instructions for Form 1042-S (2013)

previously filed with the IRS. Enter an "X" in the AMENDED checkbox on the copy you give to the recipient only if you are correcting a Form 1042-S previously furnished to the recipient. You must provide statements to recipients showing the corrections as soon as possible.

Step 2. File the amended paper Form 1042-S with a Form 1042-T. See the Form 1042-T instructions for information on filing these forms.

 If you fail to correct Form(s) 1042-S, you may be subject to a penalty. See Penalties, *earlier.*

Privacy Act and Paperwork Reduction Act Notice. We ask for the information on this form to carry out the Internal Revenue laws of the United States. Sections 1441, 1442, and 1446 (for PTPs) require withholding agents to report and pay over to the IRS taxes withheld from certain U.S. source income of foreign persons. Form

1042-S is used to report the amount of income and withholding to the payee. Form 1042 is used to report the amount of withholding that must be paid over to the IRS. Section 6109 requires you to provide your identification number. Routine uses of this information include giving it to the Department of Justice for civil and criminal litigation, and cities, states, the District of Columbia, and U.S. Commonwealths and possessions for use in administering their tax laws. We may also disclose this information to other countries under a tax treaty, to federal and state agencies to enforce federal nontax criminal laws, or to federal law enforcement and intelligence agencies to combat terrorism. If you fail to provide this information in a timely manner, you may be liable for penalties and interest.

You are not required to provide the information requested on a form that is subject to the Paperwork Reduction Act unless the form displays a valid OMB

control number. Books or records relating to a form or its instructions must be retained as long as their contents may become material in the administration of any Internal Revenue law. Generally, tax returns and return information are confidential, as required by section 6103.

The time needed to complete and file this form will vary depending on individual circumstances. The estimated average time is 34 minutes.

If you have comments concerning the accuracy of these time estimates or suggestions for making this form simpler, we would be happy to hear from you. You can write to the Internal Revenue Service, Tax Products Coordinating Committee, SE:W:CAR:MP:T:M:S, 1111 Constitution Ave. NW, IR-6526, Washington, DC 20224. Do not send the form to this address. Instead, see *Where, When, and How To File*, earlier.

Country Codes

Select the appropriate code from the following list and enter it in box 16 (country code of recipient). Also use the following codes to complete box 18 (country code of NQI), if applicable. See the instructions for box 16 (and box 18 if applicable), earlier, before selecting a country code. **Note.** Countries bolded and italicized are those with which the United States had entered into an income tax treaty at the time these instructions were printed.

Country	Code
Afghanistan	AF
Akrotiri	AX
Albania	AL
Algeria	AG
American Samoa	AQ
Andorra	AN
Angola	AO
Anguilla	AV
Antarctica	AY
Antigua and Barbuda	AC
Argentina	AR
Armenia[1]	AM
Aruba	AA
Ashmore and Cartier Islands[2]	AT
Australia	AS
Austria	AU
Azerbaijan[1]	AJ
Bahamas, The	BF
Bahrain	BA
Baker Island	FQ
Bangladesh	BG
Barbados	BB
Belarus[1]	BO
Belgium	BE
Belize	BH
Benin	BN
Bermuda	BD
Bhutan	BT
Bolivia	BL
Bosnia-Herzegovina	BK
Botswana	BC
Bouvet Island	BV
Brazil	BR
British Indian Ocean Territory	IO
Brunei	BX
Bulgaria	BU
Burkina Faso	UV
Burma	BM
Burundi	BY
Cambodia	CB
Cameroon	CM
Canada	CA
Cape Verde	CV
Cayman Islands	CJ
Central African Republic	CT
Chad	CD
Chile	CI
China	CH
Christmas Island[2]	KT
Clipperton Island	IP
Cocos (Keeling) Islands[2]	CK
Colombia	CO
Comoros	CN
Congo (Brazzaville)	CF
Congo, Democratic Republic of (Kinshasa)	CG
Cook Islands	CW
Coral Sea Islands Territory[2]	CR

Country	Code
Costa Rica	CS
Cote D'Ivoire (Ivory Coast)	IV
Croatia	HR
Cuba	CU
Cyprus	CY
Czech Republic	EZ
Denmark	DA
Dhekelia	DX
Djibouti	DJ
Dominica	DO
Dominican Republic	DR
Ecuador	EC
Egypt	EG
El Salvador	ES
Equatorial Guinea	EK
Eritrea	ER
Estonia	EN
Ethiopia	ET
Falkland Islands (Islas Malvinas)	FK
Faroe Islands	FO
Fiji	FJ
Finland	FI
France	FR
French Guiana[3]	FG
French Polynesia	FP
French Southern and Antarctic Lands	FS
Gabon	GB
Gambia, The	GA
Georgia[1]	GG
Germany	GM
Ghana	GH
Gibraltar	GI
Great Britain (United Kingdom)	UK
Greece	GR
Greenland	GL
Grenada	GJ
Guadeloupe[3]	GP
Guam	GQ
Guatemala	GT
Guernsey	GK
Guinea	GV
Guinea-Bissau	PU
Guyana	GY
Haiti	HA
Heard Island and McDonald Islands	HM
Holy See	VT
Honduras	HO
Hong Kong[5]	HK
Howland Island	HQ
Hungary	HU
Iceland	IC
India	IN
Indonesia	ID
Iran	IR
Iraq	IZ
Ireland	EI
Isle of Man	IM
Israel	IS
Italy	IT
Jamaica	JM
Jan Mayen	JN
Japan	JA
Jarvis Island	DQ
Jersey	JE
Johnston Atoll	JQ
Jordan	JO
Kazakhstan	KZ
Kenya	KE
Kingman Reef	KQ
Kiribati	KR
Korea, North	KN

Country	Code
Korea, South	KS
Kosovo	KV
Kuwait	KU
Kyrgyzstan[1]	KG
Laos	LA
Latvia	LG
Lebanon	LE
Lesotho	LT
Liberia	LI
Libya	LY
Liechtenstein	LS
Lithuania	LH
Luxembourg	LU
Macau	MC
Macedonia	MK
Madagascar (Malagasy Republic)	MA
Malawi	MI
Malaysia	MY
Maldives	MV
Mali	ML
Malta	MT
Marshall Islands	RM
Martinique[3]	MB
Mauritania	MR
Mauritius	MP
Mayotte	MF
Mexico	MX
Micronesia, Federated States of	FM
Midway Islands	MQ
Moldova[1]	MD
Monaco	MN
Mongolia	MG
Montenegro	MJ
Montserrat	MH
Morocco	MO
Mozambique	MZ
Namibia	WA
Nauru	NR
Navassa Island	BQ
Nepal	NP
Netherlands	NL
Netherlands Antilles	NT
New Caledonia	NC
New Zealand	NZ
Nicaragua	NU
Niger	NG
Nigeria	NI
Niue	NE
Norfolk Island[2]	NF
Northern Ireland[4]	UK
Northern Mariana Islands	CQ
Norway	NO
Oman	MU
Pakistan	PK
Palau	PS
Palmyra Atoll	LQ
Panama	PM
Papua New Guinea	PP
Paracel Islands	PF
Paraguay	PA
Peru	PE
Philippines	RP
Pitcairn Island	PC
Poland	PL
Portugal	PO
Puerto Rico	RQ
Qatar	QA
Reunion[3]	RE
Romania	RO

Instructions for Form 1042-S (2013)

Russia	RS	*Turkey*	TU
Rwanda	RW	*Turkmenistan*[1]	TX
St. Barthelemy	TB	Turks and Caicos Islands	TK
St. Helena	SH	Tuvalu	TV
St. Kitts (St. Christopher		Uganda	UG
and Nevis)	SC	*Ukraine*	UP
St. Lucia	ST	United Arab Emirates	AE
St. Martin	RN	*United Kingdom (England,*	
St. Pierre and Miquelon	SB	*Wales, Scotland, No.*	
St. Vincent and the		*Ireland)*	UK
Grenadines	VC	Uruguay	UY
Samoa	WS	*Uzbekistan*[1]	UZ
San Marino	SM	Vanuatu	NH
Sao Tome and Principe	TP	*Venezuela*	VE
Saudi Arabia	SA	Vietnam	VM
Senegal	SG	Virgin Islands (British)	VI
Serbia	RB	Virgin Islands (U.S.)	VQ
Seychelles	SE	Wake Island	WQ
Sierra Leone	SL	Wallis and Futuna	WF
Singapore	SN	Western Sahara	WI
Slovak Republic		Yemen	YM
(Slovakia)	LO	Zambia	ZA
Slovenia	SI	Zimbabwe	ZI
Solomon Islands	BP	Other Country	OC
Somalia	SO	Unknown Country	UC
South Africa	SF		
South Georgia and the South			
Sandwich Islands	SX		
Spain	SP		
Spratly Islands	PG		
Sri Lanka	CE		
Sudan	SU		
Suriname	NS		
Svalbard	SV		
Swaziland	WZ		
Sweden	SW		
Switzerland	SZ		
Syria	SY		
Taiwan	TW		
Tajikistan[1]	TI		
Tanzania	TZ		
Thailand	TH		
Timor-Leste	TT		
Togo	TO		
Tokelau	TL		
Tonga	TN		
Trinidad and Tobago	TD		
Tunisia	TS		

[1] These countries are former Soviet republics that are now covered by the United States treaty with the Commonwealth of Independent States, formerly known as the Union of Soviet Socialist Republics.

[2] These countries are covered under the United States treaty with Australia.

[3] These countries are covered under the United States treaty with France.

[4] Northern Ireland is covered under the United States treaty with the United Kingdom.

[5] Hong Kong is not covered under the United States treaty with China.

DO NOT STAPLE

Form **1042-T** Department of the Treasury Internal Revenue Service	**Annual Summary and Transmittal of Forms 1042-S**	OMB No. 1545-0096 20**12**

Name of withholding agent	Employer identification number

Number, street, and room or suite no.

City or town, province or state, and country (including postal code)

If you are an intermediary (see Form 1042 instructions), check if you are a: ☐ QI/Withholding foreign partnership or trust
☐ NQI/Flow-through entity

1a Type of paper Forms 1042-S attached (check only **one** box): ☐ Original ☐ Amended
Also check here if pro-rata (see instructions) ▶ ☐
b Number of paper Forms 1042-S attached ▶ _____

2a Total gross income on all paper Forms 1042-S (box 2) attached . . . . $ _____
b Total federal tax withheld on all paper Forms 1042-S (box 9) attached . . . . $ _____

Caution: _If you have already filed a Form 1042 and an attached Form 1042-S causes the gross income or tax withheld information shown on your previously filed Form 1042 to change, you must file an amended Form 1042. See the instructions below._

If this is your FINAL return, enter an "X" here (see instructions) ▶ ☐

Please return this entire page to the Internal Revenue Service.

Sign Here
Under penalties of perjury, I declare that I have examined this return and accompanying documents and, to the best of my knowledge and belief, they are true, correct, and complete.

▶ Your signature	Title	Date	Daytime phone number

Instructions

Purpose of form. Use this form to transmit paper Forms 1042-S, Foreign Person's U.S. Source Income Subject to Withholding, to the Internal Revenue Service. Use a separate Form 1042-T to transmit each type of Form 1042-S (see the instructions for line 1a).

 If you file 250 or more Forms 1042-S, you are required to submit them electronically. You also can use this method to submit less than 250 Forms 1042-S. If you submit Forms 1042-S electronically, do not use Form 1042-T. See Pub. 1187, Specifications for Filing Form 1042-S, Foreign Person's U.S. Source Income Subject to Withholding, Electronically, for information on filing electronically.

Use of this form to transmit paper Forms 1042-S does not affect your obligation to file Form 1042, Annual Withholding Tax Return for U.S. Source Income of Foreign Persons.

If you have not yet filed a Form 1042 for 2012, you may send in more than one Form 1042-T to submit paper Forms 1042-S prior to filing your Form 1042. You may submit amended Forms 1042-S even though changes reflect differences in gross income and tax withheld information of Forms 1042-S previously submitted with a Form 1042-T.

If you have already filed a Form 1042 for 2012 and an attached Form 1042-S caused the gross income or tax withheld information previously reported on line 62a or 62b of your Form 1042 to change, you must file an amended Form 1042.

Where and when to file. File Form 1042-T (and Copy A of the paper Forms 1042-S being transmitted) with the Ogden Service Center; P.O. Box 409101; Ogden, UT 84409; by March 15, 2013. Send the forms in a flat mailing (not folded).

Identifying information at top of form. The name, address, and EIN of the withholding agent or intermediary on this form must be the same as those you enter on Forms 1042 and 1042-S. See the instructions for Form 1042 for definitions of withholding agent and intermediary.

Line 1a. You must file a separate Form 1042-T for each type of paper Form 1042-S you are transmitting. Check only the Original or Amended box. If you are filing pro-rata Forms 1042-S (see Form 1042-S instructions), also check the pro-rata box. As a result, there are four possible types of Form 1042-S that may be transmitted:

- Original
- Original pro-rata
- Amended
- Amended pro-rata

Each type would be transmitted with a separate Form 1042-T. For example, you would transmit only original Forms 1042-S with one Form 1042-T and only amended Forms 1042-S with another Form 1042-T.

Line 2a. Enter the total of the gross income amounts shown on the Forms 1042-S (box 2) being transmitted with this Form 1042-T.

Line 2b. Enter the total of the federal tax withheld amounts shown on the Forms 1042-S (box 9) being transmitted with this Form 1042-T.

Final return. If you will not be required to file Forms 1042-S in the future (on paper or electronically), enter an "X" in the "FINAL return" box.

Paperwork Reduction Act Notice. The time needed to complete and file this form will vary depending on individual circumstances. The estimated average time is 12 minutes.

For more information and the Privacy Act and Paperwork Reduction Act Notice, see Form 1042-S.   Cat. No. 28848W   Form **1042-T** (2012)

Do Not Staple 6969

Form 1096

Department of the Treasury
Internal Revenue Service

Annual Summary and Transmittal of U.S. Information Returns

OMB No. 1545-0108

2012

FILER'S name	For Official Use Only
Street address (including room or suite number)	
City, state, and ZIP code	

Name of person to contact	Telephone number
Email address	Fax number

1 Employer identification number	2 Social security number	3 Total number of forms	4 Federal income tax withheld $	5 Total amount reported with this Form 1096 $

6 Enter an "X" in only one box below to indicate the type of form being filed.

7 If this is your **final return**, enter an "X" here . . . . . ▶ ☐

W-2G 32	1097-BTC 50	1098 81	1098-C 78	1098-E 84	1098-T 83	1099-A 80	1099-B 79	1099-C 85	1099-CAP 73	1099-DIV 91	1099-G 86	1099-H 71	1099-INT 92
☐	☐	☐	☐	☐	☐	☐	☐	☐	☐	☐	☐	☐	☐
1099-K 10	1099-LTC 93	1099-MISC 95	1099-OID 96	1099-PATR 97	1099-Q 31	1099-R 98	1099-S 75	1099-SA 94	3921 25	3922 26	5498 28	5498-ESA 72	5498-SA 27
☐	☐	☐	☐	☐	☐	☐	☐	☐	☐	☐	☐	☐	☐

Return this entire page to the Internal Revenue Service. Photocopies are not acceptable.

Under penalties of perjury, I declare that I have examined this return and accompanying documents, and, to the best of my knowledge and belief, they are true, correct, and complete.

Signature ▶ _____   Title ▶ _____   Date ▶ _____

Instructions

Reminder. The only acceptable method of filing information returns with Internal Revenue Service/Information Returns Branch is electronically through the FIRE system. See Pub. 1220, Specifications for Filing Forms 1097, 1098, 1099, 3921, 3922, 5498, 8935, and W-2G Electronically.

Purpose of form. Use this form to transmit paper Forms 1097, 1098, 1099, 3921, 3922, 5498, and W-2G to the Internal Revenue Service. Do not use Form 1096 to transmit electronically. For electronic submissions, see Pub. 1220.

Caution. If you are required to file 250 or more information returns of any one type, you must file electronically. If you are required to file electronically but fail to do so, and you do not have an approved waiver, you may be subject to a penalty. For more information, see part F in the 2012 General Instructions for Certain Information Returns.

Who must file. The name, address, and TIN of the filer on this form must be the same as those you enter in the upper left area of Forms 1097, 1098, 1099, 3921, 3922, 5498, or W-2G. A filer is any person or entity who files any of the forms shown in line 6 above.

Enter the filer's name, address (including room, suite, or other unit number), and TIN in the spaces provided on the form.

When to file. File Form 1096 as follows.

• With Forms 1097, 1098, 1099, 3921, 3922, or W-2G, file by February 28, 2013.

• With Form 5498, file by May 31, 2013.

Where To File

Send all information returns filed on paper with Form 1096 to the following:

If your principal business, office or agency, or legal residence in the case of an individual, is located in	Use the following three-line address
Alabama, Arizona, Arkansas, Connecticut, Delaware, Florida, Georgia, Kentucky, Louisiana, Maine, Massachusetts, Mississippi, New Hampshire, New Jersey, New Mexico, New York, North Carolina, Ohio, Pennsylvania, Rhode Island, Texas, Vermont, Virginia, West Virginia	Department of the Treasury Internal Revenue Service Center Austin, TX 73301

For more information and the Privacy Act and Paperwork Reduction Act Notice, see the 2012 General Instructions for Certain Information Returns.

Cat. No. 14400O   Form **1096** (2012)

Alaska, California, Colorado, District of Columbia, Hawaii, Idaho, Illinois, Indiana, Iowa, Kansas, Maryland, Michigan, Minnesota, Missouri, Montana, Nebraska, Nevada, North Dakota, Oklahoma, Oregon, South Carolina, South Dakota, Tennessee, Utah, Washington, Wisconsin, Wyoming

Department of the Treasury
Internal Revenue Service Center
Kansas City, MO 64999

If your legal residence or principal place of business is outside the United States, file with the Department of the Treasury, Internal Revenue Service Center, Austin, TX 73301.

Transmitting to the IRS. Group the forms by form number and transmit each group with a separate Form 1096. For example, if you must file both Forms 1098 and 1099-A, complete one Form 1096 to transmit your Forms 1098 and another Form 1096 to transmit your Forms 1099-A. You need not submit original and corrected returns separately. Do not send a form (1099, 5498, etc.) containing summary (subtotal) information with Form 1096. Summary information for the group of forms being sent is entered only in boxes 3, 4, and 5 of Form 1096.

Box 1 or 2. Complete only if you are not using a preaddressed Form 1096. Make an entry in either box 1 or 2; not both. Individuals not in a trade or business must enter their social security number (SSN) in box 2; sole proprietors and all others must enter their employer identification number (EIN) in box 1. However, sole proprietors who do not have an EIN must enter their SSN in box 2. Use the same EIN or SSN on Form 1096 that you use on Forms 1097, 1098, 1099, 3921, 3922, 5498, or W-2G.

Box 3. Enter the number of forms you are transmitting with this Form 1096. Do not include blank or voided forms or the Form 1096 in your total. Enter the number of correctly completed forms, not the number of pages, being transmitted. For example, if you send one page of three-to-a-page Forms 1098 with a Form 1096 and you have correctly completed two Forms 1098 on that page, enter "2" in box 3 of Form 1096.

Box 4. Enter the total federal income tax withheld shown on the forms being transmitted with this Form 1096.

Box 5. No entry is required if you are filing Form 1098-T, 1099-A, or 1099-G. For all other forms, enter the total of the amounts from the specific boxes of the forms listed below.

Form	Box
Form W-2G	Box 1
Form 1097-BTC	Box 1
Form 1098	Boxes 1 and 2
Form 1098-C	Box 4c
Form 1098-E	Box 1
Form 1099-B	Boxes 2a and 7
Form 1099-C	Box 2
Form 1099-CAP	Box 2
Form 1099-DIV	Boxes 1a, 2a, 3, 8, 9, and 10
Form 1099-H	Box 1
Form 1099-INT	Boxes 1, 3, and 8
Form 1099-K	Box 1
Form 1099-LTC	Boxes 1 and 2
Form 1099-MISC	Boxes 1, 2, 3, 5, 6, 7, 8, 10, 13, and 14
Form 1099-OID	Boxes 1, 2, and 6
Form 1099-PATR	Boxes 1, 2, 3, and 5
Form 1099-Q	Box 1
Form 1099-R	Box 1
Form 1099-S	Box 2
Form 1099-SA	Box 1
Form 3921	Boxes 3 and 4
Form 3922	Boxes 3, 4, and 5
Form 5498	Boxes 1, 2, 3, 4, 5, 8, 9, 10, 12b, 13a, and 14a
Form 5498-ESA	Boxes 1 and 2
Form 5498-SA	Box 1

Final return. If you will not be required to file Forms 1097, 1098, 1099, 3921, 3922, 5498, or W-2G in the future, either on paper or electronically, enter an "X" in the "final return" box.

Corrected returns. For information about filing corrections, see the 2012 General Instructions for Certain Information Returns. Originals and corrections of the same type of return can be submitted using one Form 1096.

9393   ☐ VOID   ☐ CORRECTED

PAYER'S name, street address, city or town, province or state, country, ZIP or foreign postal code, and telephone no.	**1** Gross long-term care benefits paid $	OMB No. 1545-1519 20**13** Form **1099-LTC**	**Long-Term Care and Accelerated Death Benefits**
	2 Accelerated death benefits paid $		

PAYER'S federal identification number	POLICYHOLDER'S identification number	**3** Check one: ☐ Per diem ☐ Reimbursed amount	INSURED'S social security no.	**Copy A** **For** **Internal Revenue Service Center** **File with Form 1096.**
POLICYHOLDER'S name		INSURED'S name		For Privacy Act and Paperwork Reduction Act Notice, see the **2013 General Instructions for Certain Information Returns.**
Street address (including apt. no.)		Street address (including apt. no.)		
City or town, province or state, country, and ZIP or foreign postal code		City or town, province or state, country, and ZIP or foreign postal code		
Account number (see instructions)	**4** Qualified contract ☐ (optional)	**5** Check, if applicable: (optional)	☐ Chronically ill Date certified ☐ Terminally ill	

Form **1099-LTC**   Cat. No. 23021Z   www.irs.gov/form1099ltc   Department of the Treasury - Internal Revenue Service

Do Not Cut or Separate Forms on This Page — Do Not Cut or Separate Forms on This Page

Instructions for Policyholder

A payer, such as an insurance company or a viatical settlement provider, must give this form to you for payments made under a long-term care insurance contract or for accelerated death benefits. Payments include those made directly to you (or to the insured) and those made to third parties.

A long-term care insurance contract provides coverage of expenses for long-term care services for an individual who has been certified by a licensed health care practitioner as chronically ill. A life insurance company or viatical settlement provider may pay accelerated death benefits if the insured has been certified by either a physician as terminally ill or by a licensed health care practitioner as chronically ill.

Long-term care insurance contract. Generally, amounts received under a qualified long-term care insurance contract are excluded from your income. However, if payments are made on a per diem basis, the amount you may exclude is limited. The per diem exclusion limit must be allocated among all policyholders who own qualified long-term care insurance contracts for the same insured. See Pub. 525 and Form 8853, and its instructions for more information.

Per diem basis. This means the payments were made on any periodic basis without regard to the actual expenses incurred during the period to which the payments relate.

Accelerated death benefits. Amounts paid as accelerated death benefits are fully excludable from your income if the insured has been certified by a physician as terminally ill. Accelerated death benefits paid on behalf of individuals who are certified as chronically ill are excludable from income to the same extent they would be if paid under a qualified long-term care insurance contract.

Account number. May show an account or other unique number the payer assigned to distinguish your account.

Box 1. Shows the gross benefits paid under a long-term care insurance contract during the year.

Box 2. Shows the gross accelerated death benefits paid during the year.

Box 3. Shows if the amount in box 1 or 2 was paid on a per diem basis or was reimbursement of actual long-term care expenses. If the insured was terminally ill, this box may not be checked.

Box 4. May show if the benefits were from a qualified long-term care insurance contract.

Box 5. May show if the insured was certified chronically ill or terminally ill, and the latest date certified.

Future developments. For the latest developments related to Form 1099-LTC and its instructions, such as legislation enacted after they were published, go to *www.irs.gov/form1099ltc*.

Instructions for Insured

A payer, such as an insurance company or a viatical settlement provider, must give this form to you and to the policyholder for payments made under a long-term care insurance contract or for accelerated death benefits. Payments include both benefits you received directly and expenses paid on your behalf to third parties.

If you are the insured but are not the policyholder, Copy C is provided to you for information only because these payments are not taxable to you. If you are also the policyholder, you should receive Copy B.

Account number. May show an account or other unique number the payer assigned to distinguish your account.

Box 1. Shows the gross benefits paid under a long-term care insurance contract during the year.

Box 2. Shows the gross accelerated death benefits paid during the year.

Box 3. Shows if the amount in box 1 or 2 was paid on a per diem basis or was reimbursement of actual long-term care expenses. If you are terminally ill, this box may not be checked.

Box 4. May show if the benefits were from a qualified long-term care insurance contract.

Box 5. May show if you were certified chronically ill or terminally ill, and the latest date certified.

Future developments. For the latest developments related to Form 1099-LTC and its instructions, such as legislation enacted after they were published, go to *www.irs.gov/form1099ltc*.

Instructions for Payer

General and specific form instructions are provided separately. You should use the 2013 General Instructions for Certain Information Returns and the 2013 Instructions for Form 1099-LTC to complete Form 1099-LTC. A chart in the general instructions gives a quick guide to which form must be filed to report a particular payment. To order these instructions and additional forms, go to *www.irs.gov/form1099ltc* or call 1-800-TAX-FORM (1-800-829-3676).

Caution: *Because paper forms are scanned during processing, you cannot file Forms 1096, 1097, 1098, 1099, 3921, 3922, or 5498 that you print from the IRS website.*

Due dates. Furnish Copy B of this form to the policyholder by January 31, 2014.

Furnish Copy C of this form to the insured by January 31, 2014.

File Copy A of this form with the IRS by February 28, 2014. If you file electronically, the due date is March 31, 2014. To file electronically, you must have software that generates a file according to the specifications in Pub. 1220, Specifications for Filing Forms 1097, 1098, 1099, 3921, 3922, 5498, 8935, and W-2G Electronically. The IRS does not provide a fill-in form option.

Need help? If you have questions about reporting on Form 1099-LTC, call the information reporting customer service site toll free at 1-866-455-7438 or 304-263-8700 (not toll free). Persons with a hearing or speech disability with access to TTY/TDD equipment can call 304-579-4827 (not toll free). The hours of operation are Monday through Friday from 8:30 a.m. to 4:30 p.m., Eastern time.

20**13**
Instructions for Form 1099-LTC

Department of the Treasury
Internal Revenue Service

Long-Term Care and Accelerated Death Benefits

Future Developments

For the latest information about developments related to Form 1099-LTC and its instructions, such as legislation enacted after they were published, go to *www.irs.gov/form1099ltc*.

What's New

Pilot program for truncating a policyholder's and insured's identifying number of paper payee statement has ended. Filers of Form 1099-LTC must show the policyholder's and insured's complete identifying number on all copies of the form.

Reminder

In addition to these specific instructions, you should also use the 2013 General Instructions for Certain Information Returns. Those general instructions include information about the following topics.
- Backup withholding.
- Electronic reporting requirements.
- Penalties.
- Who must file (nominee/middleman).
- When and where to file.
- Taxpayer identification numbers.
- Statements to recipients.
- Corrected and void returns.
- Other general topics.

You can get the general instructions from *www.irs.gov/form1099ltc* or by calling 1-800-TAX-FORM (1-800-829-3676).

Specific Instructions

File Form 1099-LTC, Long-Term Care and Accelerated Death Benefits, if you pay any long-term care benefits.

Long-Term Care Benefits

Long-term care benefits means:

1. Any payments made under a product that is advertised, marketed, or offered as long-term care insurance (whether qualified or not) and

2. Accelerated death benefits (excludable in whole or in part from gross income under section 101(g)) paid under a life insurance contract or paid by a viatical settlement provider.

Who Must File

File Form 1099-LTC if you paid any long-term care benefits, including accelerated death benefits. Payers include insurance companies, governmental units, and viatical settlement providers.

Viatical Settlement Providers

A viatical settlement provider is any person who:

1. Is regularly engaged in the trade or business of purchasing or taking assignments of life insurance contracts on the lives of terminally or chronically ill individuals and

2. Is licensed in the state where the insured lives. If licensing is not required in the state, the provider must meet other requirements (including those below) depending on whether the insured is terminally or chronically ill.

a. If the insured is terminally ill, the provider must meet the requirements of sections 8 and 9 of the Viatical Settlements Model Act of the National Association of Insurance Commissioners (NAIC), relating to disclosure and general rules. The provider must also meet the requirements of the Model Regulations of the NAIC for evaluating the reasonableness of amounts paid in viatical settlement transactions with terminally ill individuals.

b. If the insured is chronically ill, the provider must meet requirements similar to those of sections 8 and 9 of the Viatical Settlements Model Act of the NAIC and must also meet any standards of the NAIC for evaluating the reasonableness of amounts paid in viatical settlement transactions with chronically ill individuals.

 However, if a state enacts a licensing requirement but does not permit viatical settlement providers to engage in business until the licenses are granted, the provider will not be considered as licensed under section 101(g)(2)(B)(i) (I). See Rev. Rul. 2002-82, which is on page 978 of Internal Revenue Bulletin 2002-51 at www.irs.gov/pub/irs-irbs/irb02-51.pdf.

Qualified Long-Term Care Insurance Contract

A contract issued after 1996 is a qualified long-term care insurance contract if it meets the requirements of section 7702B, including the requirement that the insured must be a chronically ill individual (see *Chronically ill Individual* below). A contract issued before 1997 generally is treated as a qualified long-term care insurance contract if it met state law requirements for long-term care insurance contracts and it has not been materially changed.

Accelerated Death Benefits

An accelerated death benefit is any amount paid under a life insurance contract for an insured individual who is terminally or chronically ill. It also includes any amount paid by a viatical settlement provider for the sale or assignment of a death benefit under a life insurance contract for a chronically or terminally ill individual.

Chronically ill Individual

A chronically ill individual is someone who has been certified (at least annually) by a licensed health care practitioner as:

1. Being unable to perform, without substantial assistance from another individual, at least two daily living activities (eating, toileting, transferring, bathing, dressing, and continence) for at least 90 days due to a loss of functional capacity or

2. Requiring substantial supervision to protect the individual from threats to health and safety due to severe cognitive impairment.

Sep 26, 2012   Cat. No. 27981Y

Terminally ill Individual

A terminally ill individual is someone who has been certified by a physician as having an illness or physical condition that can reasonably be expected to result in death in 24 months or less after the date of certification.

Reporting

Report payments only if the policyholder is an individual. Reportable payments are those made to the policyholder, to the insured, or to a third party.

You may report benefits paid from each contract on a separate Form 1099-LTC. At your option, you may aggregate benefits paid under multiple contracts on one Form 1099-LTC if the same information is reportable on the form for each contract (other than the amount of benefits paid).

Policyholder

The policyholder is the individual who owns the contract, including the owner of a contract sold or assigned to a viatical settlement provider. In the case of a group contract, the term policyholder includes the certificate holder (or similar participant). You must report long-term care benefits to the policyholder even if the payments were made to the insured or to a third party (for example, a nursing home, caretaker, or physician). The policyholder also may be the insured.

Enter the name, address, and taxpayer identification number (TIN) of the policyholder on Form 1099-LTC. If the policyholder is not an individual, no reporting is required.

Insured

The insured is the chronically or terminally ill individual on whose behalf long-term care benefits are paid.

Enter the name, address, and TIN of the insured on Form 1099-LTC.

Statement to Policyholder and Insured

If you are required to file Form 1099-LTC, you must furnish a statement or acceptable substitute to both the policyholder and to the insured as shown.

IF the statement is for the ...	THEN use...
Policyholder	Copy B
Insured	Copy C
Policyholder and the policyholder is the insured	Copy B (Copy C is optional)

For more information about the requirement to furnish a statement to the policyholder and to the insured, see part M in the 2013 General Instructions for Certain Information Returns.

Account Number

The account number is required if you have multiple accounts for a recipient for whom you are filing more than one Form 1099-LTC. Additionally, the IRS encourages you to designate an account number for all Forms 1099-LTC that you file. See part L in the 2013 General Instructions for Certain Information Returns.

Box 1. Gross Long-Term Care Benefits Paid

Enter the gross long-term care benefits paid this year (other than accelerated death benefits). These benefits are all amounts paid out on a *per diem* or other periodic basis or on a reimbursed basis. It includes amounts paid to the insured, to the policyholder, and to third parties. You are not required to determine whether any benefits are taxable or nontaxable.

Box 2. Accelerated Death Benefits Paid

Enter the gross accelerated death benefits paid under a life insurance contract this year to or on behalf of an insured who has been certified as terminally or chronically ill. Include the amount paid by a viatical settlement provider for the sale or assignment of the insured's death benefit under a life insurance contract.

Box 3. Check if *Per Diem* or Reimbursed Amount

Check a box to indicate whether the payments were made on a *per diem* or other periodic basis or on a reimbursed basis. For accelerated death benefits, do not check a box if you made payments on behalf of a terminally ill person. *Per diem* basis means payments made on any periodic basis without regard to actual expenses. Reimbursed basis means payments made for actual expenses incurred.

Box 4. Qualified Contract (Optional)

Check the box to indicate whether long-term care insurance benefits are paid from a qualified long-term care insurance contract. See *Qualified Long-Term Care Insurance Contract* earlier.

Box 5. Check if Chronically ill or Terminally ill (Optional)

Check the box to indicate whether the insured was chronically or terminally ill. Also, enter the latest date certified. If the insured was neither chronically nor terminally ill, leave this box blank. See *Chronically ill Individual* and *Terminally ill Individual* earlier.

9595   ☐ VOID   ☐ CORRECTED

PAYER'S name, street address, city or town, province or state, country, ZIP or foreign postal code, and telephone no.		1 Rents $	OMB No. 1545-0115	Miscellaneous Income
		2 Royalties $	2013 Form **1099-MISC**	
		3 Other income $	4 Federal income tax withheld $	**Copy A**
PAYER'S country code	Check if branch reporting elected ☐	5 Fishing boat proceeds	6 Medical and health care payments	**For Internal Revenue Service Center**
PAYER'S federal identification number	RECIPIENT'S identification number	$	$	**File with Form 1096.**
RECIPIENT'S name		7 Nonemployee compensation	8 Substitute payments in lieu of dividends or interest	For Privacy Act and Paperwork Reduction Act Notice, see the
Street address (including apt. no.)		$	$	**2013 General Instructions for Certain Information Returns.**
		9 Payer made direct sales of $5,000 or more of consumer products to a buyer (recipient) for resale ▶ ☐	10 Crop insurance proceeds $	
City or town, province or state, country, and ZIP or foreign postal code		11 Foreign tax paid $	12 Foreign country or U.S. possession	
Account number (see instructions)	2nd TIN not. ☐	13 Excess golden parachute payments $	14 Gross proceeds paid to an attorney $	
15a Section 409A deferrals $	15b Section 409A income $	16 State tax withheld $ $	17 State/Payer's state no.	18 State income $ $

Form **1099-MISC**   Cat. No. 14425J   www.irs.gov/form1099misc   Department of the Treasury - Internal Revenue Service

Do Not Cut or Separate Forms on This Page — Do Not Cut or Separate Forms on This Page

Instructions for Recipient

Account number. May show an account or other unique number the payer assigned to distinguish your account.

Amounts shown may be subject to self-employment (SE) tax. If your net income from self-employment is $400 or more, you must file a return and compute your SE tax on Schedule SE (Form 1040). See Pub. 334 for more information. If no income or social security and Medicare taxes were withheld and you are still receiving these payments, see Form 1040-ES (or Form 1040-ES(NR)). Individuals must report these amounts as explained in the box 7 instructions on this page. Corporations, fiduciaries, or partnerships must report the amounts on the proper line of their tax returns.

Form 1099-MISC incorrect? If this form is incorrect or has been issued in error, contact the payer. If you cannot get this form corrected, attach an explanation to your tax return and report your income correctly.

Box 1. Report rents from real estate on Schedule E (Form 1040). However, report rents on Schedule C (Form 1040) if you provided significant services to the tenant, sold real estate as a business, or rented personal property as a business.

Box 2. Report royalties from oil, gas, or mineral properties, copyrights, and patents on Schedule E (Form 1040). However, report payments for a working interest as explained in the box 7 instructions. For royalties on timber, coal, and iron ore, see Pub. 544.

Box 3. Generally, report this amount on the "Other income" line of Form 1040 (or Form 1040NR) and identify the payment. The amount shown may be payments received as the beneficiary of a deceased employee, prizes, awards, taxable damages, Indian gaming profits, or other taxable income. See Pub. 525. If it is trade or business income, report this amount on Schedule C or F (Form 1040).

Box 4. Shows backup withholding or withholding on Indian gaming profits. Generally, a payer must backup withhold if you did not furnish your taxpayer identification number. See Form W-9 and Pub. 505 for more information. Report this amount on your income tax return as tax withheld.

Box 5. An amount in this box means the fishing boat operator considers you self-employed. Report this amount on Schedule C (Form 1040). See Pub. 334.

Box 6. For individuals, report on Schedule C (Form 1040).

Box 7. Shows nonemployee compensation. If you are in the trade or business of catching fish, box 7 may show cash you received for the sale of fish. If the amount in this box is SE income, report it on Schedule C or F (Form 1040), and complete Schedule SE (Form 1040). You received this form instead of Form W-2 because the payer did not consider you an employee and did not withhold income tax or social security and Medicare tax. If you believe you are an employee and cannot get the payer to correct this form, report the amount from box 7 on Form 1040, line 7 (or Form 1040NR, line 8). You must also complete Form 8919 and attach it to your return. If you are not an employee but the amount in this box is not SE income (for example, it is income from a sporadic activity or a hobby), report it on Form 1040, line 21 (or Form 1040NR, line 21).

Box 8. Shows substitute payments in lieu of dividends or tax-exempt interest received by your broker on your behalf as a result of a loan of your securities. Report on the "Other income" line of Form 1040 (or Form 1040NR).

Box 9. If checked, $5,000 or more of sales of consumer products was paid to you on a buy-sell, deposit-commission, or other basis. A dollar amount does not have to be shown. Generally, report any income from your sale of these products on Schedule C (Form 1040).

Box 10. Report this amount on Schedule F (Form 1040).

Box 11. Shows the foreign tax that you may be able to claim as a deduction or a credit on Form 1040. See the Form 1040 instructions.

Box 12. Shows the country or U.S. possession to which the foreign tax was paid.

Box 13. Shows your total compensation of excess golden parachute payments subject to a 20% excise tax. See the Form 1040 (or Form 1040NR) instructions for where to report.

Box 14. Shows gross proceeds paid to an attorney in connection with legal services. Report only the taxable part as income on your return.

Box 15a. May show current year deferrals as a nonemployee under a nonqualified deferred compensation (NQDC) plan that is subject to the requirements of section 409A, plus any earnings on current and prior year deferrals.

Box 15b. Shows income as a nonemployee under an NQDC plan that does not meet the requirements of section 409A. This amount is also included in box 7 as nonemployee compensation. Any amount included in box 15a that is currently taxable is also included in this box. This income is also subject to a substantial additional tax to be reported on Form 1040 (or Form 1040NR). See "Total Tax" in the Form 1040 (or Form 1040NR) instructions.

Boxes 16–18. Shows state or local income tax withheld from the payments.

Future developments. For the latest information about developments related to Form 1099-MISC and its instructions, such as legislation enacted after they were published, go to *www.irs.gov/form1099misc*.

Instructions for Payer

General and specific form instructions are provided separately. You should use the 2013 General Instructions for Certain Information Returns and the 2013 Instructions for Form 1099-MISC to complete Form 1099-MISC. A chart in the general instructions gives a quick guide to which form must be filed to report a particular payment. To order these instructions and additional forms, go to *www.irs.gov/form1099misc* or call 1-800-TAX-FORM (1-800-829-3676).

Caution: *Because paper forms are scanned during processing, you cannot file with the IRS Forms 1096, 1097, 1098, 1099, 3921, 3922, or 5498 that you print from the IRS website.*

Due dates. Furnish Copy B of this form to the recipient by January 31, 2014. The due date is extended to February 18, 2014, if you are reporting payments in boxes 8 or 14.

File Copy A of this form with the IRS by February 28, 2014. If you file electronically, the due date is March 31, 2014. To file electronically, you must have software that generates a file according to the specifications in Pub. 1220, Specifications for Filing Forms 1097, 1098, 1099, 3921, 3922, 5498, 8935, and W-2G Electronically. The IRS does not provide a fill-in form option.

Need help? If you have questions about reporting on Form 1099-MISC, call the information reporting customer service site toll free at 1-866-455-7438 or 304-263-8700 (not toll free). Persons with a hearing or speech disability with access to TTY/TDD equipment can call 304-579-4827 (not toll free). The hours of operation are Monday through Friday from 8:30 a.m. to 4:30 p.m., Eastern time.

20**13**
Instructions for
Form 1099-MISC

Miscellaneous Income

Department of the Treasury
Internal Revenue Service

Section references are to the Internal Revenue Code unless otherwise noted.

Future Developments

For the latest information about developments related to Form 1099-MISC and its instructions, such as legislation enacted after they were published, go to *www.irs.gov/ form1099misc*.

What's New

Truncating recipient's identification number on paper payee statements. Pursuant to proposed regulations §§ 1.6042-4(b) and 301.6109-4 (REG-148873-09), all filers of this form may truncate a recipient's identification number (social security number (SSN), individual taxpayer identification number (ITIN), or adoption taxpayer identification number (ATIN)) on payee statements. See part M in the 2013 General Instructions for Certain Information Returns.

Reminder

In addition to these specific instructions, you should also use the 2013 General Instructions for Certain Information Returns. Those general instructions include information about the following topics.
* Backup withholding.
* Electronic reporting requirements.
* Penalties.
* Who must file (nominee/middleman).
* When and where to file.
* Taxpayer identification numbers.
* Statements to recipients.
* Corrected and void returns.
* Other general topics.

You can get the general instructions from *www.irs.gov/ form1099misc* or by calling 1-800-TAX-FORM (1-800-829-3676).

Specific Instructions

File Form 1099-MISC, Miscellaneous Income, for each person to whom you have paid during the year:
* At least $10 in royalties (see the instructions for box 2) or broker payments in lieu of dividends or tax-exempt interest (see the instructions for box 8);
* At least $600 in rents, services (including parts and materials), prizes and awards, other income payments, medical and health care payments, crop insurance proceeds, cash payments for fish (or other aquatic life) you purchase from anyone engaged in the trade or business of catching fish, or, generally, the cash paid from a notional principal contract to an individual, partnership, or estate;

* Any fishing boat proceeds; or
* Gross proceeds of $600 or more paid to an attorney. See *Payments to attorneys*, later.

In addition, use Form 1099-MISC to report that you made direct sales of at least $5,000 of consumer products to a buyer for resale anywhere other than a permanent retail establishment. You must also file Form 1099-MISC for each person from whom you have withheld any federal income tax under the backup withholding rules regardless of the amount of the payment.

 Be sure to report each payment in the proper box because the IRS uses this information to determine whether the recipient has properly reported the payment.

Trade or business reporting only. Report on Form 1099-MISC only when payments are made in the course of your trade or business. Personal payments are not reportable. You are engaged in a trade or business if you operate for gain or profit. However, nonprofit organizations are considered to be engaged in a trade or business and are subject to these reporting requirements. Other organizations subject to these reporting requirements include trusts of qualified pension or profit-sharing plans of employers, certain organizations exempt from tax under section 501(c) or (d), farmers' cooperatives that are exempt from tax under section 521, and widely held fixed investment trusts. Payments by federal, state, or local government agencies are also reportable.

Exceptions. Some payments do not have to be reported on Form 1099-MISC, although they may be taxable to the recipient. Payments for which a Form 1099-MISC is not required include all of the following.
* Generally, payments to a corporation. But see *Reportable payments to corporations*, later.
* Payments for merchandise, telegrams, telephone, freight, storage, and similar items.
* Payments of rent to real estate agents. But the real estate agent must use Form 1099-MISC to report the rent paid over to the property owner. See Regulations section 1.6041-1(e)(5), Example 5, and the instructions for box 1.
* Wages paid to employees (report on Form W-2, Wage and Tax Statement).
* Military differential wage payments made to employees while they are on active duty in the Armed Forces or other uniformed services (report on Form W-2).
* Business travel allowances paid to employees (may be reportable on Form W-2).
* Cost of current life insurance protection (report on Form W-2 or Form 1099-R, Distributions From Pensions,

Jan 23, 2013   Cat. No. 27982J

Annuities, Retirement or Profit-Sharing Plans, IRAs, Insurance Contracts, etc.).
- Payments to a tax-exempt organization including tax-exempt trusts (IRAs, HSAs, Archer MSAs, and Coverdell ESAs), the United States, a state, the District of Columbia, a U.S. possession, or a foreign government.
- Payments made to or for homeowners from the HFA Hardest Hit Fund or the Emergency Homeowners' Loan Program or similar state program (report on Form 1098-MA).

Form 1099-K. Payments made with a credit card or payment card and certain other types of payments, including third party network transactions, must be reported on Form 1099-K by the payment settlement entity under section 6050W and are not subject to reporting on Form 1099-MISC. See the separate Instructions for Form 1099-K.

Fees paid to informers. A payment to an informer as an award, fee, or reward for information about criminal activity does not have to be reported if the payment is made by a federal, state, or local government agency, or by a nonprofit organization exempt from tax under section 501(c)(3) that makes the payment to further the charitable purpose of lessening the burdens of government. For more information, see Regulations section 1.6041-3(l).

Scholarships. Do not use Form 1099-MISC to report scholarship or fellowship grants. Scholarship or fellowship grants that are taxable to the recipient because they are paid for teaching, research, or other services as a condition for receiving the grant are considered wages and must be reported on Form W-2. Other taxable scholarship or fellowship payments (to a degree or nondegree candidate) do not have to be reported by you to the IRS on any form. See section 117(b)-(d) and Regulations section 1.6041-3(n) for more information.

Difficulty-of-care payments. Do not use Form 1099-MISC to report difficulty-of-care payments that are excludable from the recipient's gross income. Difficulty-of-care payments to foster care providers are not reportable if paid for fewer than 11 children under age 19 and fewer than six individuals age 19 or older. Amounts paid for more than 10 children or more than five other individuals are reportable on Form 1099-MISC.

Canceled debt. A canceled debt is not reportable on Form 1099-MISC. Canceled debts must be reported on Form 1099-C, Cancellation of Debt, by financial institutions, credit unions, Federal Government agencies, certain agencies connected with the Federal Government, and an organization where the lending of money (such as finance and credit card companies) is a significant trade or business. See the Instructions for Forms 1099-A and 1099-C.

Reportable payments to corporations. The following payments made to corporations generally must be reported on Form 1099-MISC.
- Medical and health care payments reported in box 6.
- Fish purchases for cash reported in box 7.
- Attorneys' fees reported in box 7.
- Gross proceeds paid to an attorney reported in box 14.
- Substitute payments in lieu of dividends or tax-exempt interest reported in box 8.

- Payments by a federal executive agency for services (vendors) reported in box 7.

 Federal executive agencies may also have to file Form 8596, Information Return for Federal Contracts, and Form 8596-A, Quarterly Transmittal of Information Returns for Federal Contracts, if a contracted amount for personal services is more than $25,000. See Rev. Rul. 2003-66, which is on page 1115 of Internal Revenue Bulletin 2003-26 at www.irs.gov/pub/irs-irbs/irb03-26.pdf for details.

Payments to attorneys. The term attorney includes a law firm or other provider of legal services. Attorneys' fees of $600 or more paid in the course of your trade or business are reportable in box 7 of Form 1099-MISC.

Gross proceeds paid to attorneys. Under section 6045(f), report in box 14 payments that:
- Are made to an attorney in the course of your trade or business in connection with legal services, for example, as in a settlement agreement,
- Total $600 or more, and
- Are not reportable by you in box 7.

Generally, you are not required to report the claimant's attorney's fees. For example, an insurance company pays a claimant's attorney $100,000 to settle a claim. The insurance company reports the payment as gross proceeds of $100,000 in box 14. The insurance company does not have a reporting requirement for the claimant's attorney's fees subsequently paid from these funds.

These rules apply whether or not the legal services are provided to the payer and whether or not the attorney is exclusive payee (for example, the attorney's and claimant's names are on one check) or other information returns are required for some or all of a payment under section 6041A(a)(1). For example, a person who, in the course of a trade or business, pays $600 of taxable damages to a claimant by paying that amount to a claimant's attorney is required to furnish Form 1099-MISC to the claimant under section 6041 and furnish Form 1099-MISC to the claimant's attorney under section 6045(f). For more examples and exceptions relating to payments to attorneys, see Regulations section 1.6045-5.

However, these rules do not apply to wages paid to attorneys that are reportable on Form W-2 or to profits distributed by a partnership to its partners that are reportable on:
- Schedule K-1 (Form 1065), Partner's Share of Income, Deductions, Credits, etc., or
- Schedule K-1 (Form 1065-B), Partner's Share of Income (Loss) From an Electing Large Partnership.

Payments to corporations for legal services. The exemption from reporting payments made to corporations does not apply to payments for legal services. Therefore, you must report attorneys' fees (in box 7) or gross proceeds (in box 14) as described earlier to corporations that provide legal services.

Taxpayer identification numbers (TINs). To report payments to an attorney on Form 1099-MISC, you must obtain the attorney's TIN. You may use Form W-9, Request for Taxpayer Identification Number and Certification, to obtain the attorney's TIN. An attorney is required to promptly supply its TIN whether it is a corporation or other entity, but the attorney is not required to certify its TIN. If the attorney fails to provide its TIN, the attorney may be subject to a penalty under section 6723 and its regulations, and you must backup withhold on the reportable payments.

Fish purchases. If you are in the trade or business of purchasing fish for resale, you must report total cash payments of $600 or more paid during the year to any person who is engaged in the trade or business of catching fish. Report these payments in box 7. You are required to keep records showing the date and amount of each cash payment made during the year, but you must report only the total amount paid for the year on Form 1099-MISC.

"Fish" means all fish and other forms of aquatic life. "Cash" means U.S. and foreign coin and currency and a cashier's check, bank draft, traveler's check, or money order. Cash does not include a check drawn on your personal or business account.

Deceased employee's wages. If an employee dies during the year, you must report the accrued wages, vacation pay, and other compensation paid after the date of death. If you made the payment in the same year the employee died, you must withhold social security and Medicare taxes on the payment and report them only as social security and Medicare wages on the employee's Form W-2 to ensure that proper social security and Medicare credit is received. On the Form W-2, show the payment as social security wages (box 3) and Medicare wages and tips (box 5) and the social security and Medicare taxes withheld in boxes 4 and 6; do not show the payment in box 1 of Form W-2.

If you made the payment after the year of death, do not report it on Form W-2, and do not withhold social security and Medicare taxes.

Whether the payment is made in the year of death or after the year of death, you also must report the payment to the estate or beneficiary on Form 1099-MISC. Report the payment in box 3 (rather than in box 7 as specified in Rev. Rul. 86-109, 1986-2 C.B. 196). See the *Example* that follows. Enter the name and TIN of the payment recipient on Form 1099-MISC. For example, if the recipient is an individual beneficiary, enter the name and social security number of the individual; if the recipient is the estate, enter the name and employer identification number of the estate. The general backup withholding rules apply to this payment.

Death benefits from nonqualified deferred compensation plans or section 457 plans paid to the estate or beneficiary of a deceased employee are reportable on Form 1099-MISC. Do not report these death benefits on Form 1099-R. However, if the benefits are from a qualified plan, report them on Form 1099-R. See the Instructions for Forms 1099-R and 5498.

Example. Before Employee A's death on June 15, 2013, A was employed by Employer X and received $10,000 in wages on which federal income tax of $1,500 was withheld. When A died, X owed A $2,000 in wages and $1,000 in accrued vacation pay. The total of $3,000 (less the social security and Medicare taxes withheld) was paid to A's estate on July 20, 2013. Because X made the

payment during the year of death, X must withhold social security and Medicare taxes on the $3,000 payment and must complete Form W-2 as follows.

- Box 1—10000.00 (does not include the $3,000 accrued wages and vacation pay)
- Box 2—1500.00
- Box 3—13000.00 (includes the $3,000 accrued wages and vacation pay)
- Box 4—Social security tax withheld on the amount in box 3
- Box 5—13000.00 (includes the $3,000 accrued wages and vacation pay)
- Box 6—Medicare tax withheld on the amount in box 5

Employer X also must complete Form 1099-MISC as follows.

- Boxes for recipient's name, address, and TIN—the estate's name, address, and TIN.
- Box 3—3000.00 (Even though amounts were withheld for social security and Medicare taxes, the gross amount is reported here.)

If Employer X made the payment after the year of death, the $3,000 would not be subject to social security and Medicare taxes and would not be shown on Form W-2. However, the employer would still file Form 1099-MISC.

Employee business expense reimbursements. Do not use Form 1099-MISC to report employee business expense reimbursements. Report payments made to employees under a nonaccountable plan as wages on Form W-2. Generally, payments made to employees under an accountable plan are not reportable on Form W-2, except in certain cases when you pay a *per diem* or mileage allowance. For more information, see the Instructions for Forms W-2 and W-3; Pub. 463, Travel, Entertainment, Gift, and Car Expenses; and Pub. 1542, Per Diem Rates. For information on reporting employee moving expense reimbursements on Form W-2, see the Instructions for Forms W-2 and W-3.

Independent contractor or employee. Generally, you must report payments to independent contractors on Form 1099-MISC in box 7. See the instructions for box 7.

 Section 530 of the Revenue Act of 1978 as extended by section 269(c) of P.L. 97-248 deals with the employment tax status of independent contractors and employees. To qualify for relief under section 530, employers must file Form 1099-MISC. Additional requirements for relief are discussed in Rev. Proc. 85-18, 1985-1 C.B. 518. Also see Pub. 15-A, Employer's Supplemental Tax Guide, for special rules that may apply to technical service specialists and test proctors and room supervisors.

Transit passes and parking for independent contractors. Although you cannot provide qualified transportation fringes to independent contractors, the working condition and *de minimis* fringe rules for transit passes and parking apply to independent contractors. Tokens or farecards that enable an independent contractor to commute on a public transit system (not including privately operated van pools) are excludable from the independent contractor's gross income and are not reportable on Form 1099-MISC if their value in any month is $21 or less. However, if the value of a pass provided in a month is greater than $21, the full value is includible in gross income and is reportable on Form 1099-MISC. The value of parking may be excludable from an independent contractor's gross income, and, therefore, not reportable on Form 1099-MISC if certain requirements are met. See Regulations section 1.132-9(b), Q/A-24.

Directors' fees. You must report directors' fees and other remuneration, including payments made after retirement, on Form 1099-MISC in the year paid. Report them in box 7.

Commissions paid to lottery ticket sales agents. A state that has control over and responsibility for online and instant lottery games must file Form 1099-MISC to report commissions paid, whether directly or indirectly, to licensed sales agents. For example, State X retains control over and liability for online and instant lottery games. For online ticket sales, State X pays commissions by allowing an agent to retain 5% of the ticket proceeds the agent remits to State X. For instant ticket sales, State X pays commissions by providing tickets to the agent for 5% less than the proceeds to be obtained by the agent from the sale of those tickets. If the commissions for the year total $600 or more, they must be reported in box 7 on Form 1099-MISC. See Rev. Rul. 92-96, 1992-2 C.B. 281.

Escrow agent; construction project. When an escrow agent maintains owner-provided funds in an escrow account for a construction project, performs management and oversight functions relating to the construction project, and makes payments for the owner and the general contractor, the escrow agent must file Form 1099-MISC for reportable payments of $600 or more. This requirement applies whether or not the escrow agent is a bank. If the contractor is the borrower of the funds, do not report on Form 1099-MISC any loan payments made to the contractor/borrower.

Indian gaming profits, payments to tribal members. If you make payments to members of Indian tribes from the net revenues of class II or class III gaming activities conducted or licensed by the tribes, you must withhold federal income tax on such payments. File Form 1099-MISC to report the payments and withholding to tribal members. Report the payments in box 3 and the federal income tax withheld in box 4. Pub. 15-A contains the necessary "Tables for Withholding on Distributions of Indian Gaming Profits to Tribal Members."

State or local sales taxes. If state or local sales taxes are imposed on the service provider and you (as the buyer) pay them to the service provider, report them on Form 1099-MISC as part of the reportable payment. However, if sales taxes are imposed on you (as the buyer) and collected from you by the service provider, do not report the sales taxes on Form 1099-MISC.

Widely held fixed investment trusts (WHFITs). Trustees and middlemen of WHFITs must report items of gross income attributable to a trust income holder (TIH) on the appropriate Form 1099. A tax information statement that includes the information provided to the IRS on Forms 1099, as well as additional information identified in Regulations section 1.671-5(e), must be furnished to TIHs. For details, see the 2013 General Instructions for Certain Information Returns.

Statements to recipients. If you are required to file Form 1099-MISC, you must provide a statement to the recipient. For more information about the requirement to furnish a statement to each recipient, see part M in the 2013 General Instructions for Certain Information Returns.

2nd TIN not. You may enter an "X" in this box if you were notified by the IRS twice within 3 calendar years that the payee provided an incorrect TIN. If you mark this box, the IRS will not send you any further notices about this account. However, if you received both IRS notices in the same year, or if you received them in different years but they both related to information returns filed for the same year, do not check the box at this time. For purposes of the two-notices-in-3-years rule, you are considered to have received one notice. You are not required to send a second "B" notice upon receipt of the second notice. See part N in the 2013 General Instructions for Certain Information Returns for more information.

 For information on the TIN Matching System offered by the IRS, see the 2013 General Instructions for Certain Information Returns.

Recipient's Identification Number

Enter the recipient's identification number using hyphens in the proper format. SSNs, ITINs, and ATINs should be in the XXX-XX-XXXX format. EINs should be in the XX-XXXXXXX format. You should make every effort to insure that you have the correct type of number reported in the correct format.

Account Number

The account number is required if you have multiple accounts for a recipient for whom you are filing more than one Form 1099-MISC. Additionally, the IRS encourages you to designate an account number for all Forms 1099-MISC that you file. See part L in the 2013 General Instructions for Certain Information Returns.

Box 1. Rents

Enter amounts of $600 or more for all types of rents, such as any of the following.
• Real estate rentals paid for office space. However, you do not have to report these payments on Form 1099-MISC if you paid them to a real estate agent. But the real estate agent must use Form 1099-MISC to report the rent paid over to the property owner. See Regulations section 1.6041-1(e)(5), Example 5.
• Machine rentals (for example, renting a bulldozer to level your parking lot). If the machine rental is part of a contract that includes both the use of the machine and the operator, prorate the rental between the rent of the machine (report that in box 1) and the operator's charge (report that as nonemployee compensation in box 7).
• Pasture rentals (for example, farmers paying for the use of grazing land).

Public housing agencies must report in box 1 rental assistance payments made to owners of housing projects. See Rev. Rul. 88-53, 1988-1 C.B. 384.

Coin-operated amusements. If an arrangement between an owner of coin-operated amusements and an owner of a business establishment where the amusements are placed is a lease of the amusements or the amusement space, the owner of the amusements or the owner of the space, whoever makes the payments, must report the lease payments in box 1 of Form 1099-MISC if the payments total at least $600. However, if the arrangement is a joint venture, the joint venture must file a Form 1065, U.S. Return of Partnership Income, and provide each partner with the information necessary to report the partner's share of the taxable income. Coin-operated amusements include video games, pinball machines, jukeboxes, pool tables, slot machines, and other machines and gaming devices operated by coins or tokens inserted into the machines by individual users. For more information, see Rev. Rul. 92-49, 1992-1 C.B. 433.

Box 2. Royalties

Enter gross royalty payments (or similar amounts) of $10 or more. Report royalties from oil, gas, or other mineral properties before reduction for severance and other taxes that may have been withheld and paid. Do not include surface royalties. They should be reported in box 1. Do not report oil or gas payments for a working interest in box 2; report payments for working interests in box 7. Do not report timber royalties made under a pay-as-cut contract; report these timber royalties on Form 1099-S, Proceeds From Real Estate Transactions.

Use box 2 to report royalty payments from intangible property such as patents, copyrights, trade names, and trademarks. Report the gross royalties (before reduction for fees, commissions, or expenses) paid by a publisher directly to an author or literary agent, unless the agent is a corporation. The literary agent (whether or not a corporation) that receives the royalty payment on behalf of the author must report the gross amount of royalty payments to the author on Form 1099-MISC whether or not the publisher reported the payment to the agent on its Form 1099-MISC.

Box 3. Other Income

Enter other income of $600 or more required to be reported on Form 1099-MISC that is not reportable in one of the other boxes on the form.

Also enter in box 3 prizes and awards that are not for services performed. Include the fair market value (FMV) of merchandise won on game shows. Also include amounts paid to a winner of a sweepstakes not involving a wager. If a wager is made, report the winnings on Form W-2G, Certain Gambling Winnings.

Illustrated example.

The completed Form 1099-MISC illustrates the following example. Z Builders is a contractor that subcontracts drywall work to Ronald Green, a sole proprietor who does business as Y Drywall. During the year, Z Builders pays Mr. Green $5,500. Z Builders must file Form 1099-MISC because they paid Mr. Green $600 or more in the course of their trade or business, and Mr. Green is not a corporation.

9595	☐ VOID	☐ CORRECTED	

PAYER'S name, street address, city or town, province or state, country, ZIP or foreign postal code, and telephone no. Z Builders 123 Maple Avenue Oaktown, AL 00000 555-555-1212	**1** Rents $	OMB No. 1545-0115 **20**13 Form **1099-MISC**	**Miscellaneous Income**
	2 Royalties $		
	3 Other income $	**4** Federal income tax withheld $	Copy A **For Internal Revenue Service Center**

PAYER'S federal identification number	RECIPIENT'S identification number	**5** Fishing boat proceeds $	**6** Medical and health care payments $	File with Form 1096.
10-9999999	123-00-6789			

RECIPIENT'S name Ronald Green dba/ Y Drywall	**7** Nonemployee compensation $ 5500.00	**8** Substitute payments in lieu of dividends or interest $	For Privacy Act and Paperwork Reduction Act Notice, see the **2013 General Instructions for Certain Information Returns.**
Street address (including apt. no.) 456 Flower Lane	**9** Payer made direct sales of $5,000 or more of consumer products to a buyer (recipient) for resale ▶ ☐	**10** Crop insurance proceeds $	
City or town, province or state, country, and ZIP or foreign postal code Oaktown, AL 00000	**11** Foreign tax paid $	**12** Foreign country or U.S. possession	
Account number (see instructions)	2nd TIN not. ☐	**13** Excess golden parachute payments $	**14** Gross proceeds paid to an attorney $	

15a Section 409A deferrals $	**15b** Section 409A income $	**16** State tax withheld $	**17** State/Payer's state no.	**18** State income $ $

Form **1099-MISC**   Cat. No. 14425J   www.irs.gov/form1099misc   Department of the Treasury - Internal Revenue Service

Do Not Cut or Separate Forms on This Page — Do Not Cut or Separate Forms on This Page

If, not later than 60 days after the winner becomes entitled to the prize, the winner can choose the option of a lump sum or an annuity payable over at least 10 years, the payment of winnings is considered made when actually paid. If the winner chooses an annuity, file Form 1099-MISC each year to report the annuity paid during that year.

Do not include prizes and awards paid to your employees. Report these on Form W-2. Do not include in box 3 prizes and awards for services performed by nonemployees, such as an award for the top commission salesperson. Report them in box 7.

Prizes and awards received in recognition of past accomplishments in religious, charitable, scientific, artistic, educational, literary, or civic fields are not reportable if:
• The winners are chosen without action on their part,
• The winners are not expected to perform future services, and
• The payer transfers the prize or award to a charitable organization or governmental unit under a designation made by the recipient. See Rev. Proc. 87-54, 1987-2 C.B. 669.

Other items required to be reported in box 3 include the following.

1. Payments as explained earlier under *Deceased employee's wages*.

2. Payments as explained earlier under *Indian gaming profits, payments to tribal members*.

3. A payment or series of payments made to individuals for participating in a medical research study or studies.

4. Termination payments to former self-employed insurance salespeople. These payments are not subject to self-employment tax and are reportable in box 3 (rather than box 7) if all the following apply.

a. The payments are received from an insurance company because of services performed as an insurance salesperson for the company.

b. The payments are received after termination of the salesperson's agreement to perform services for the company.

c. The salesperson did not perform any services for the company after termination and before the end of the year.

d. The salesperson enters into a covenant not to compete against the company for at least 1 year after the date of termination.

e. The amount of the payments depends primarily on policies sold by the salesperson or credited to the salesperson's account during the last year of the service agreement or to the extent those policies remain in force for some period after termination, or both.

f. The amount of the payments does not depend at all on length of service or overall earnings from the company (regardless of whether eligibility for payment depends on length of service).

If the termination payments do not meet all these requirements, report them in box 7.

5. Generally, all punitive damages, any damages for nonphysical injuries or sickness, and any other taxable damages. Report punitive damages even if they relate to physical injury or physical sickness. Generally, report all compensatory damages for nonphysical injuries or sickness, such as employment discrimination or defamation. However, do not report damages (other than punitive damages):

a. Received on account of personal physical injuries or physical sickness;

b. That do not exceed the amount paid for medical care for emotional distress;

c. Received on account of nonphysical injuries (for example, emotional distress) under a written binding agreement, court decree, or mediation award in effect on or issued by September 13, 1995; or

d. That are for a replacement of capital, such as damages paid to a buyer by a contractor who failed to complete construction of a building.

Damages received on account of emotional distress, including physical symptoms such as insomnia, headaches, and stomach disorders, are not considered received for a physical injury or physical sickness and are reportable unless described in b or c above. However, damages received on account of emotional distress due to physical injuries or physical sickness are not reportable.

Also report liquidated damages received under the Age Discrimination in Employment Act of 1967.

 *Taxable back pay damages may be wages and reportable on Form W-2. See Pub. 957, Reporting Back Pay and Special Wage Payments to the Social Security Administration.*

Foreign agricultural workers. Report in box 3 compensation of $600 or more paid in a calendar year to an H-2A visa agricultural worker who did not give you a valid taxpayer identification number. You must also withhold federal income tax under the backup withholding rules. For more information, go to IRS.gov and enter "foreign agricultural workers" in the search box.

Box 4. Federal Income Tax Withheld

Enter backup withholding. For example, persons who have not furnished their TIN to you are subject to withholding on payments required to be reported in boxes 1, 2 (net of severance taxes), 3, 5 (to the extent paid in cash), 6, 7 (except fish purchases for cash), 8, 10, and 14. For more information on backup withholding, including the rate, see part N in the 2013 General Instructions for Certain Information Returns.

Also enter any income tax withheld from payments to members of Indian tribes from the net revenues of class II or class III gaming activities conducted or licensed by the tribes.

Box 5. Fishing Boat Proceeds

Enter the individual's share of all proceeds from the sale of a catch or the FMV of a distribution in kind to each crew member of fishing boats with normally fewer than 10 crew members. A fishing boat has normally fewer than 10 crew members if the average size of the operating crew was fewer than 10 on trips during the preceding 4 calendar quarters.

In addition, report cash payments of up to $100 per trip that are contingent on a minimum catch and are paid solely for additional duties (such as mate, engineer, or cook) for which additional cash payments are traditional in the industry. However, do not report on Form 1099-MISC any wages reportable on Form W-2.

Box 6. Medical and Health Care Payments

Enter payments of $600 or more made in the course of your trade or business to each physician or other supplier or provider of medical or health care services. Include payments made by medical and health care insurers under health, accident, and sickness insurance programs. If payment is made to a corporation, list the corporation as the recipient rather than the individual providing the services. Payments to persons providing health care services often include charges for injections, drugs, dentures, and similar items. In these cases the entire payment is subject to information reporting. You are not required to report payments to pharmacies for prescription drugs.

The exemption from issuing Form 1099-MISC to a corporation does not apply to payments for medical or health care services provided by corporations, including professional corporations. However, you are not required to report payments made to a tax-exempt hospital or extended care facility or to a hospital or extended care facility owned and operated by the United States (or its possessions), a state, the District of Columbia, or any of their political subdivisions, agencies, or instrumentalities.

 Generally, payments made under a flexible spending arrangement (as defined in section 106(c)(2)) or a health reimbursement arrangement which is treated as employer-provided coverage under an accident or health plan for purposes of section 106 are exempt from the reporting requirements of section 6041.

Box 7. Nonemployee Compensation

Enter nonemployee compensation of $600 or more. Include fees, commissions, prizes and awards for services performed as a nonemployee, other forms of compensation for services performed for your trade or business by an individual who is not your employee, and fish purchases for cash. Include oil and gas payments for a working interest, whether or not services are performed. Also include expenses incurred for the use of an entertainment facility that you treat as compensation to a nonemployee. Federal executive agencies that make payments to vendors for services, including payments to corporations, must report the payments in this box. See Rev. Rul. 2003-66, which is on page 1115 of Internal Revenue Bulletin 2003-26 at *www.irs.gov/pub/irs-irbs/ irb03-26.pdf*.

What is nonemployee compensation? If the following four conditions are met, you must generally report a payment as nonemployee compensation.
- You made the payment to someone who is not your employee;
- You made the payment for services in the course of your trade or business (including government agencies and nonprofit organizations);
- You made the payment to an individual, partnership, estate, or, in some cases, a corporation; and
- You made payments to the payee of at least $600 during the year.

Self-employment tax. Generally, amounts reportable in box 7 are subject to self-employment tax. If payments to individuals are not subject to this tax and are not reportable elsewhere on Form 1099-MISC, report the payments in box 3. However, report section 530 (of the Revenue Act of 1978) worker payments in box 7.

Examples. The following are some examples of payments to be reported in box 7.
- Professional service fees, such as fees to attorneys (including corporations), accountants, architects, contractors, engineers, etc.
- Fees paid by one professional to another, such as fee-splitting or referral fees.
- Payments by attorneys to witnesses or experts in legal adjudication.
- Payment for services, including payment for parts or materials used to perform the services if supplying the parts or materials was incidental to providing the service. For example, report the total insurance company payments to an auto repair shop under a repair contract showing an amount for labor and another amount for parts, if furnishing parts was incidental to repairing the auto.
- Commissions paid to nonemployee salespersons that are subject to repayment but not repaid during the calendar year.
- A fee paid to a nonemployee, including an independent contractor, or travel reimbursement for which the nonemployee did not account to the payer, if the fee and reimbursement total at least $600. To help you determine whether someone is an independent contractor or an employee, see Pub. 15-A.
- Payments to nonemployee entertainers for services. Use Form 1042-S, Foreign Person's U.S. Source Income Subject to Withholding, for payments to nonresident aliens.
- Exchanges of services between individuals in the course of their trades or businesses. For example, an attorney represents a painter for nonpayment of business debts in exchange for the painting of the attorney's law offices. The amount reportable by each on Form 1099-MISC is the FMV of his or her own services performed. However, if the attorney represents the painter in a divorce proceeding, this is an activity that is unrelated to the painter's trade or business. The attorney must report on Form 1099-MISC the value of his or her services. But the painter need not report on Form 1099-MISC the value of painting the law offices because the work is in exchange for legal services that are separate from the painter's business.

Instructions for Form 1099-MISC (2013)   -7-

- Taxable fringe benefits for nonemployees. For information on the valuation of fringe benefits, see Pub. 15-B, Employer's Tax Guide to Fringe Benefits.
- Gross oil and gas payments for a working interest.
- Payments to an insurance salesperson who is not your common law or statutory employee. See Pub. 15-A for the definition of employee. However, for termination payments to former insurance salespeople, see the instructions for box 3.
- Directors' fees as explained under *Directors' fees*, earlier.
- Commissions paid to licensed lottery ticket sales agents as explained under *Commissions paid to lottery ticket sales agents*, earlier.
- Payments to section 530 (of the Revenue Act of 1978) workers. See the *TIP* under *Independent contractor or employee*, earlier.
- Fish purchases for cash. See *Fish purchases*, earlier.

Nonqualified deferred compensation (Section 409A) income. Include in box 7 the amount of all deferrals (plus earnings) reported in box 15b that are includible in gross income because the nonqualified deferred compensation (NQDC) plan fails to satisfy the requirements of section 409A. See Regulations sections 1.409A-1 through 1.409A-6.

Golden parachute payments. A parachute payment is any payment that meets all of the following conditions.

1. The payment is in the nature of compensation.

2. The payment is to, or for the benefit of, a disqualified individual.

3. The payment is contingent on a change in the ownership of a corporation, the effective control of a corporation, or the ownership of a substantial portion of the assets of a corporation (a change in ownership or control).

4. The payment has (together with other payments described in 1, 2, and 3, above, made to the same individual) an aggregate present value of at least three times the individual's base amount.

A disqualified individual is one who at any time during the 12-month period prior to and ending on the date of the change in ownership or control of the corporation (the disqualified individual determination period) was an employee or independent contractor and was, in regard to that corporation, a shareholder, an officer, or a highly compensated individual.

For more details, see Regulations section 1.280G-1. Also, see Rev. Proc. 2003-68, which is on page 398 of Internal Revenue Bulletin 2003-34 at *www.irs.gov/pub/irs-irbs/irb03-34.pdf*, concerning the valuation of stock options for purposes of golden parachute payment rules. For the treatment of unvested shares of restricted stock, see Rev. Rul. 2005-39, available at *www.irs.gov/irb/2005-27_IRB/ar08.html*.

Independent contractor. Enter in box 7 the total compensation, including any golden parachute payment. For excess golden parachute payments, see the box 13 reporting instructions.

For employee reporting of these payments, see Pub. 15-A.

Payments not reported in box 7. Do not report in box 7, nor elsewhere on Form 1099-MISC, the cost of current life insurance protection (report on Form W-2 or Form 1099-R); an employee's wages, travel or auto allowance, or bonuses (report on Form W-2); or the cost of group-term life insurance paid on behalf of a former employee (report on Form W-2).

Box 8. Substitute Payments in Lieu of Dividends or Interest

Enter aggregate payments of at least $10 received by a broker for a customer in lieu of dividends or tax-exempt interest as a result of a loan of a customer's securities. For this purpose, a customer includes an individual, trust, estate, partnership, association, company, or corporation. See Notice 2003-67, which is on page 752 of Internal Revenue Bulletin 2003-40 at *www.irs.gov/pub/irs-irbs/irb03-40.pdf*. It does not include a tax-exempt organization, the United States, any state, the District of Columbia, a U.S. possession, or a foreign government. File Form 1099-MISC with the IRS and furnish a copy to the customer for whom you received the payment. Also, file Form 1099-MISC for and furnish a copy to an individual for whom you received a payment in lieu of tax-exempt interest.

Substitute payment means a payment in lieu of (a) a dividend or (b) tax-exempt interest to the extent that interest (including OID) has accrued while the securities were on loan.

Box 9. Payer Made Direct Sales of $5,000 or More

Enter an "X" in the checkbox for sales by you of $5,000 or more of consumer products to a person on a buy-sell, deposit-commission, or other commission basis for resale (by the buyer or any other person) anywhere other than in a permanent retail establishment. Do not enter a dollar amount in this box.

If you are reporting an amount in box 7, you may also check box 9 on the same Form 1099-MISC.

The report you must give to the recipient for these direct sales need not be made on the official form. It may be in the form of a letter showing this information along with commissions, prizes, awards, etc.

Box 10. Crop Insurance Proceeds

Enter crop insurance proceeds of $600 or more paid to farmers by insurance companies unless the farmer has informed the insurance company that expenses have been capitalized under section 278, 263A, or 447.

Box 11. Foreign Tax Paid

Enter the name of the foreign country or U.S. Possession to which the withheld tax applies.

Box 12. Foreign Country or U.S. Possession

Enter the name of the foreign country or U.S. possession to which the withheld tax applies.

Box 13. Excess Golden Parachute Payments

Enter any excess golden parachute payments. An excess parachute payment is the amount of the excess of any parachute payment over the base amount (the average annual compensation for services includible in the individual's gross income over the most recent 5 tax years). See Q/A-38 through Q/A-44 of Regulations section 1.280G-1 for how to compute the excess amount.

See *Golden parachute payments*, earlier, for more information.

Box 14. Gross Proceeds Paid to an Attorney

Enter gross proceeds of $600 or more paid to an attorney in connection with legal services (regardless of whether the services are performed for the payer). See *Payments to attorneys*, earlier.

Box 15a. Section 409A Deferrals

You do not have to complete this box. For details, see Notice 2008-115, available at *www.irs.gov/irb/ 2008-52_IRB/ar10.html*.

If you complete this box, enter the total amount deferred during the year of at least $600 for the nonemployee under all nonqualified plans. The deferrals during the year include earnings on the current year and prior year deferrals. For additional information, see Regulations sections 1.409A-1 through 1.409A-6.

For deferrals and earnings under NQDC plans for employees, see the Instructions for Forms W-2 and W-3.

Box 15b. Section 409A Income

Enter all amounts deferred (including earnings on amounts deferred) that are includible in income under section 409A because the NQDC plan fails to satisfy the requirements of section 409A. Do not include amounts properly reported on a Form 1099-MISC, corrected Form 1099-MISC, Form W-2, or Form W-2c for a prior year. Also, do not include amounts that are considered to be subject to a substantial risk of forfeiture for purposes of section 409A. For additional information, see Regulations sections 1.409A-1 through 1.409A-6; Notice 2008-113, available at *www.irs.gov/irb/2008-51_IRB/ar12.html*; Notice 2008-115; Notice 2010-6, which is available at *www.irs.gov/irb/2010-03_IRB/ar08.html*; and Notice 2010-80, available at *www.irs.gov/irb/2010-51_IRB/ ar08.html*.

The amount included in box 15b is also includible in box 7.

Boxes 16–18. State Information

These boxes, and Copies 1 and 2, are provided for your convenience only and need not be completed for the IRS. Use the state information boxes to report payments for up to two states. Keep the information for each state separated by the dash line. If you withheld state income tax on this payment, you may enter it in box 16. In box 17, enter the abbreviated name of the state and the payer's state identification number. The state number is the payer's identification number assigned by the individual state. In box 18, you may enter the amount of the state payment. Use Copy 1 to provide information to the state tax department. Give Copy 2 to the recipient for use in filing the recipient's state income tax return.

To help us develop a more useful index, please let us know if you have ideas for index entries.
See "Comments and Suggestions" in the "Introduction" for the ways you can reach us.

Index

9898 ☐ VOID ☐ CORRECTED

PAYER'S name, street address, city or town, province or state, country, and ZIP or foreign postal code	1 Gross distribution $	OMB No. 1545-0119 **2013** Form **1099-R**	Distributions From Pensions, Annuities, Retirement or Profit-Sharing Plans, IRAs, Insurance Contracts, etc.
	2a Taxable amount $		

	2b Taxable amount not determined ☐	Total distribution ☐	Copy A For Internal Revenue Service Center
PAYER'S federal identification number RECIPIENT'S identification number	3 Capital gain (included in box 2a) $	4 Federal income tax withheld $	File with Form 1096.
RECIPIENT'S name	5 Employee contributions /Designated Roth contributions or insurance premiums $	6 Net unrealized appreciation in employer's securities $	For Privacy Act and Paperwork Reduction Act Notice, see the **2013 General Instructions for Certain Information Returns.**
Street address (including apt. no.)	7 Distribution code(s) IRA/ SEP/ SIMPLE ☐	8 Other $ %	
City or town, province or state, country, and ZIP or foreign postal code	9a Your percentage of total distribution %	9b Total employee contributions $	
10 Amount allocable to IRR within 5 years $ 11 1st year of desig. Roth contrib.	12 State tax withheld $ ---- $	13 State/Payer's state no.	14 State distribution $ ---- $
Account number (see instructions)	15 Local tax withheld $ ---- $	16 Name of locality	17 Local distribution $ ---- $

Form **1099-R**   Cat. No. 14436Q   www.irs.gov/form1099r   Department of the Treasury - Internal Revenue Service

Do Not Cut or Separate Forms on This Page — Do Not Cut or Separate Forms on This Page

Instructions for Recipient

Generally, distributions from pensions, annuities, profit-sharing and retirement plans (including section 457 state and local government plans), IRAs, insurance contracts, etc., are reported to recipients on Form 1099-R.

Qualified plans. If your annuity starting date is after 1997, you must use the simplified method to figure your taxable amount if your payer did not show the taxable amount in box 2a. See the instructions for Form 1040 or 1040A.

IRAs. For distributions from a traditional individual retirement arrangement (IRA), simplified employee pension (SEP), or savings incentive match plan for employees (SIMPLE), generally the payer is not required to compute the taxable amount. See the Form 1040 or 1040A instructions to determine the taxable amount. If you are at least age 70½, you must take minimum distributions from your IRA (other than a Roth IRA). If you do not, you may be subject to a 50% excise tax on the amount that should have been distributed. See Pub. 590 for more information on IRAs.

Roth IRAs. For distributions from a Roth IRA, generally the payer is not required to compute the taxable amount. You must compute any taxable amount on Form 8606. An amount shown in box 2a may be taxable earnings on an excess contribution.

Loans treated as distributions. If you borrow money from a qualified plan, section 403(b) plan, or governmental section 457(b) plan, you may have to treat the loan as a distribution and include all or part of the amount borrowed in your income. There are exceptions to this rule. If your loan is taxable, Code L will be shown in box 7. See Pub. 575.

Recipient's identification number. For your protection, this form may show only the last four digits of your social security number (SSN), individual taxpayer identification number (ITIN), or adoption taxpayer identification number (ATIN). However, the issuer has reported your complete identification number to the IRS and, where applicable, to state and/or local governments.

Account number. May show an account or other unique number the payer assigned to distinguish your account.

Box 1. Shows the total amount you received this year. The amount may have been a direct rollover, a transfer or conversion to a Roth IRA, a recharacterized IRA contribution; or you may have received it as periodic payments, as nonperiodic payments, or as a total distribution. Report the amount on Form 1040 or 1040A on the line for "IRA distributions" or "Pensions and annuities" (or the line for "Taxable amount"), and on Form 8606, as applicable. However, if this is a lump-sum distribution, see Form 4972. If you have not reached minimum retirement age, report your disability payments on the line for "Wages, salaries, tips, etc." on your tax return. Also report on that line permissible withdrawals from eligible automatic contribution arrangements and corrective distributions of excess deferrals, excess contributions, or excess aggregate contributions except if you are self-employed.

If a life insurance, annuity, qualified long-term care, or endowment contract was transferred tax free to another trustee or contract issuer, an amount will be shown in this box and Code 6 will be shown in box 7. If a charge or payment was made against the cash value of an annuity contract or the cash surrender value of a life insurance contract for the purchase of qualified long-term care insurance, an amount will be shown in this box and Code W will be shown in box 7. You need not report these amounts on your tax return.

Box 2a. This part of the distribution is generally taxable. If there is no entry in this box, the payer may not have all the facts needed to figure the taxable amount. In that case, the first box in box 2b should be checked. You may want to get one of the free publications from the IRS to help you figure the taxable amount. See *Additional information* on the back of Copy 2. For an IRA distribution, see *IRAs* and *Roth IRAs* on this page. For a direct rollover, other than from a qualified plan to a Roth IRA, zero should be shown, and you must enter zero (-0-) on the "Taxable amount" line of your tax return.

(Continued on the back of Copy C.)

Instructions for Recipient *(Continued)*

If this is a total distribution from a qualified plan and you were born before January 2, 1936 (or you are the beneficiary of someone born before January 2, 1936), you may be eligible for the 10-year tax option. See the Form 4972 instructions for more information.

If you are an eligible retired public safety officer who elected to exclude from income distributions from your eligible plan used to pay certain insurance premiums, the amount shown in box 2a has not been reduced by the exclusion amount. See the instructions for Form 1040 or 1040A for more information.

Box 2b. If the first box is checked, the payer was unable to determine the taxable amount, and box 2a should be blank, except for an IRA. It is your responsibility to determine the taxable amount. If the second box is checked, the distribution was a total distribution that closed out your account.

Box 3. If you received a lump-sum distribution from a qualified plan and were born before January 2, 1936 (or you are the beneficiary of someone born before January 2, 1936), you may be able to elect to treat this amount as a capital gain on Form 4972 (not on Schedule D (Form 1040)). See the Form 4972 instructions. For a charitable gift annuity, report as a long-term capital gain as explained in the instructions for Form 8949.

Box 4. Shows federal income tax withheld. Include this amount on your income tax return as tax withheld, and if box 4 shows an amount (other than zero), attach Copy B to your return. Generally, if you will receive payments next year that are not eligible rollover distributions, you can change your withholding or elect not to have income tax withheld by giving the payer Form W-4P.

Box 5. Generally, this shows the employee's investment in the contract (after-tax contributions), if any, recovered tax free this year; the portion that is your basis in a designated Roth account; the part of premiums paid on commercial annuities or insurance contracts recovered tax free; or the nontaxable part of a charitable gift annuity. This box does not show any IRA contributions. If the amount shown is your basis in a designated Roth account, the year you first made contributions to that account may be entered in box 11.

Box 6. If you received a lump-sum distribution from a qualified plan that includes securities of the employer's company, the net unrealized appreciation (NUA) (any increase in value of such securities while in the trust) is taxed only when you sell the securities unless you choose to include it in your gross income this year. See Pub. 575 and the Form 4972 instructions. If you did not receive a lump-sum distribution, the amount shown is the NUA attributable to employee contributions, which is not taxed until you sell the securities.

Box 7. The following codes identify the distribution you received. For more information on these distributions, see the instructions for your tax return. Also, certain distributions may be subject to an additional 10% tax. See the instructions for Form 5329.

1—Early distribution, no known exception (in most cases, under age 59½).

2—Early distribution, exception applies (under age 59½).

3—Disability.

4—Death.

5—Prohibited transaction.

6—Section 1035 exchange (a tax-free exchange of life insurance, annuity, qualified long-term care insurance, or endowment contracts).

7—Normal distribution.

8—Excess contributions plus earnings/excess deferrals (and/or earnings) taxable in 2013.

9—Cost of current life insurance protection.

A—May be eligible for 10-year tax option (see Form 4972).

B—Designated Roth account distribution.

Note. If Code B is in box 7 and an amount is reported in box 10, see the instructions for Form 5329.

D—Annuity payments from nonqualified annuities that may be subject to tax under section 1411.

(Continued on the back of Copy 2.)

Instructions for Recipient *(Continued)*

E—Distributions under Employee Plans Compliance Resolution System (EPCRS).

F—Charitable gift annuity.

G—Direct rollover of a distribution (other than a designated Roth account distribution) to a qualified plan, a section 403(b) plan, a governmental section 457(b) plan, or an IRA.

H—Direct rollover of a designated Roth account distribution to a Roth IRA.

J—Early distribution from a Roth IRA, no known exception (in most cases, under age 59½).

L—Loans treated as distributions.

N—Recharacterized IRA contribution made for 2013 and recharacterized in 2013.

P—Excess contributions plus earnings/excess deferrals (and/or earnings) taxable in 2012.

Q—Qualified distribution from a Roth IRA.

R—Recharacterized IRA contribution made for 2012 and recharacterized in 2013.

S—Early distribution from a SIMPLE IRA in first 2 years, no known exception (under age 59½).

T—Roth IRA distribution, exception applies.

U—Dividend distribution from ESOP under sec. 404(k).

   Note. This distribution is not eligible for rollover.

W—Charges or payments for purchasing qualified long-term care insurance contracts under combined arrangements.

   If the IRA/SEP/SIMPLE box is checked, you have received a traditional IRA, SEP, or SIMPLE distribution.

Box 8. If you received an annuity contract as part of a distribution, the value of the contract is shown. It is not taxable when you receive it and should not be included in boxes 1 and 2a. When you receive periodic payments from the annuity contract, they are taxable at that time. If the distribution is made to more than one person, the percentage of the annuity contract distributed to you is also shown.

You will need this information if you use the 10-year tax option (Form 4972). If charges were made for qualified long-term care insurance contracts under combined arrangements, the amount of the reduction in the investment (but not below zero) in the annuity or life insurance contract is reported here.

Box 9a. If a total distribution was made to more than one person, the percentage you received is shown.

Box 9b. For a life annuity from a qualified plan or from a section 403 (b) plan (with after-tax contributions), an amount may be shown for the employee's total investment in the contract. It is used to compute the taxable part of the distribution. See Pub. 575.

Box 10. If an amount is reported in this box, see the instructions for Form 5329 and Pub. 575.

Box 11. The 1st year you made a contribution to the designated Roth account reported on this form is shown in this box.

Boxes 12—17. If state or local income tax was withheld from the distribution, boxes 14 and 17 may show the part of the distribution subject to state and/or local tax.

Future developments. For the latest information about developments related to Form 1099-R and its instructions, such as legislation enacted after they were published, go to *www.irs.gov/form1099r.*

Additional information. You may want to see:

Form W-4P, Withholding Certificate for Pension or Annuity Payments,

Form 4972, Tax on Lump-Sum Distributions,

Form 5329, Additional Taxes on Qualified Plans (Including IRAs) and Other Tax-Favored Accounts,

Form 8606, Nondeductible IRAs,

Pub. 560, Retirement Plans for Small Business (SEP, SIMPLE, and Qualified Plans),

Pub. 571, Tax-Sheltered Annuity Plans (403(b) Plans),

Pub. 575, Pension and Annuity Income,

Pub. 590, Individual Retirement Arrangements (IRAs),

Pub. 721, Tax Guide to U.S. Civil Service Retirement Benefits,

Pub. 939, General Rule for Pensions and Annuities,

Pub. 969, Health Savings Accounts and Other Tax-Favored Health Plans.

Instructions for Payer

We provide general and specific form instructions separately. You should use the 2013 General Instructions for Certain Information Returns and the 2013 Instructions for Forms 1099-R and 5498 to complete Form 1099-R. A chart in the general instructions gives a quick guide to which form must be filed to report a particular payment. To order these instructions and additional forms, go to *www.irs.gov/form1099r* or call 1-800-TAX-FORM (1-800-829-3676).

Caution: *Because paper forms are scanned during processing, you cannot file with the IRS Forms 1096, 1097, 1098, 1099, 3921, 3922, or 5498 that you print from the IRS website.*

Due dates. Furnish Copies B, C, and 2 of this form to the recipient by January 31, 2014.

File Copy A of this form with the IRS by February 28, 2014. If you file electronically, the due date is March 31, 2014. To file

electronically, you must have software that generates a file according to the specifications in Pub. 1220, Specifications for Filing Forms 1097, 1098, 1099, 3921, 3922, 5498, 8935, and W-2G Electronically. The IRS does not provide a fill-in form option.

Need help? If you have questions about reporting on Form 1099-R, call the information reporting customer service site toll free at 1-866-455-7438 or 304-263-8700 (not toll free). Persons with a hearing or speech disability with access to TTY/TDD equipment can call 304-579-4827 (not toll free). The hours of operation are Monday through Friday from 8:30 a.m. to 4:30 p.m., Eastern time.

20**13**

Department of the Treasury
Internal Revenue Service

Instructions for Forms 1099-R and 5498

Distributions From Pensions, Annuities, Retirement or Profit-Sharing Plans, IRAs, Insurance Contracts, etc., and IRA Contribution Information

Section references are to the Internal Revenue Code unless otherwise noted.

Future Developments

For the latest information about developments related to Form 1099-R and 5498 and their instructions, such as legislation enacted after they were published, go to *www.irs,gov/form1099r* or *www.irs.gov/form5498*.

What's New

Truncating recipient's identification number on paper payee statements. Pursuant to proposed regulations §§ 1.6042-4(b) and 301.6109-4 (REG-148873-09), all filers of Forms 1099-R and 5498 may truncate a recipient's identification number (social security number (SSN), individual taxpayer identification number (ITIN), or adoption taxpayer identification number (ATIN)) on payee statements. See part M in the 2013 General Instructions for Certain Information Returns.

New distribution code. Use Distribution Code D to identify nonqualified annuity payments that may be subject to tax under section 1411. See Guide to Distribution Codes on page 16.

Airline payment amount. Certain airline payment amounts may be contributed or rolled over to traditional and Roth IRAs, subject to limitations. See *Airline payment amount* on page 19.

Reminder

In addition, see the 2013 General Instructions for Certain Information Returns for information on the following topics.
- Backup withholding.
- Electronic reporting requirements.
- Penalties.
- Who must file (nominee/middleman).
- When and where to file.
- Taxpayer identification numbers.
- Statements to recipients.
- Corrected and void returns.
- Other general topics.

You can get the general instructions at *www.irs.gov/form1099r* or *www.irs.gov/form5498* or call 1-800-TAX-FORM (1-800-829-3676).

Specific Instructions for Form 1099-R

File Form 1099-R, Distributions From Pensions, Annuities, Retirement or Profit-Sharing Plans, IRAs, Insurance Contracts, etc., for each person to whom you have made a designated distribution or are treated as having made a

distribution of $10 or more from profit-sharing or retirement plans, any individual retirement arrangements (IRAs), annuities, pensions, insurance contracts, survivor income benefit plans, permanent and total disability payments under life insurance contracts, charitable gift annuities, etc.

Also, report on Form 1099-R death benefit payments made by employers that are not made as part of a pension, profit-sharing, or retirement plan. See *Box 1* on page 9. See nonqualified plans below for distributions from nongovernmental section 457(b) plans to beneficiaries of deceased participants.

Reportable disability payments made from a retirement plan must be reported on Form 1099-R.

Generally, do not report payments subject to withholding of social security and Medicare taxes on this form. Report such payments on Form W-2, Wage and Tax Statement.

Generally, do not report amounts totally exempt from tax, such as workers' compensation and Department of Veterans Affairs (VA) payments. However, if part of the distribution is taxable and part is nontaxable, report the entire distribution.

 There is no special reporting for qualified charitable distributions under section 408(d)(8), qualified health savings account (HSA) funding distributions described in section 408(d)(9) or for the payment of qualified health and long-term care insurance premiums for retired public safety officers described in section 402(l).

Military retirement annuities. Report payments to military retirees or payments of survivor benefit annuities on Form 1099-R. Report military retirement pay awarded as a property settlement to a former spouse under the name and taxpayer identification number (TIN) of the recipient, not that of the military retiree.

Governmental section 457(b) plans. Report on Form 1099-R, not Form W-2, income tax withholding and distributions from a governmental section 457(b) plan maintained by a state or local government employer. Distributions from a governmental section 457(b) plan to a participant or beneficiary include all amounts that are paid from the plan. For more information, see Notice 2003-20 which is on page 894 of Internal Revenue Bulletin 2003-19, at *www.irs.gov/pub/irs-irbs/irb03-19.pdf*. Also see *Section 457(b) plan distributions* on page 14 for information on distribution codes.

Nonqualified plans. Report any reportable distributions from commercial annuities. Report distributions to

Feb 08, 2013   Cat. No. 27987M

employee plan participants from section 409A nonqualified deferred compensation plans including nongovernmental section 457(b) plans on Form W-2, not on Form 1099-R; for nonemployees, these payments are generally reportable on Form 1099-MISC. Also, generally report distributions to beneficiaries of deceased plan participants on Form 1099-MISC. However, distributions to beneficiaries of deceased participants from nongovernmental section 457(b) plans are reported on Form 1099-R.

Section 404(k) dividends. Distributions of section 404(k) dividends from an employee stock ownership plan (ESOP), including a tax credit ESOP, are reported on Form 1099-R. Distributions other than section 404(k) dividends from the plan must be reported on a separate Form 1099-R.

Section 404(k) dividends paid directly from the corporation to participants or their beneficiaries are reported on Form 1099-DIV. See Announcement 2008-56, 2008-26 I.R.B. 1192, available at *www.irs.gov/ irb/2008-26_IRB/ar11.html*.

Charitable gift annuities. If cash or capital gain property is donated in exchange for a charitable gift annuity, report distributions from the annuity on Form 1099-R. See *Charitable gift annuities* on page 11.

Life insurance, annuity, and endowment contracts. Report payments of matured or redeemed annuity, endowment, and life insurance contracts. However, you do not need to file Form 1099-R to report the surrender of a life insurance contract if it is reasonable to believe that none of the payment is includible in the income of the recipient. If you are reporting the surrender of a life insurance contract, see *Code 7* on page 16.

Report premiums paid by a trustee or custodian for the cost of current life or other insurance protection. Costs of current life insurance protection are not subject to the 10% additional tax under section 72(t). See *Cost of current life insurance protection* on page 10.

Report charges or payments for a qualified long-term care insurance contract against the cash value of an annuity contract or the cash surrender value of a life insurance contract, which is excludible from gross income under section 72(e)(11). See *Code W* on page 17.

Section 1035 exchange. A tax-free section 1035 exchange is the exchange of (a) a life insurance contract for another life insurance contract, or for an endowment or annuity contract, or for a qualified long-term care insurance contract; or (b) a contract of endowment insurance for another contract of endowment insurance that provides for regular payments to begin no later than they would have begun under the old contract, or for an annuity contract, or for a qualified long-term care insurance contract; or (c) an annuity contract for an annuity contract or for a qualified long-term care insurance contract; or (d) a qualified long-term care insurance contract for a qualified long-term care insurance contract. A contract shall not fail to be treated as an annuity contract or as a life insurance contract solely because a qualified long-term care insurance contract is a part of or a rider on such contract. However, the distribution of other property or the cancellation of a contract loan at the time

of the exchange may be taxable and reportable on a separate Form 1099-R.

These exchanges of contracts are generally reportable on Form 1099-R. However, reporting on Form 1099-R is not required if (a) the exchange occurs within the same company, (b) the exchange is solely a contract for contract exchange, as defined above, that does not result in a designated distribution, and (c) the company maintains adequate records of the policyholder's basis in the contracts. For example, a life insurance contract issued by Company X received in exchange solely for another life insurance contract previously issued by Company X does not have to be reported on Form 1099-R as long as the company maintains the required records. See Rev. Proc. 92-26, 1992-1 C.B. 744, for certain exchanges for which reporting is not required under section 6047(d). Also see Rev. Rul. 2007-24, 2007-21 I.R.B. 1282, available at *www.irs.gov/irb/2007-21_IRB/ ar15.html* for certain transactions that do not qualify as tax-free exchanges. For more information on partial exchanges of annuity contracts, see Rev. Proc. 2011-38, 2011-30 I.R.B. 66, available at *www.irs.gov/irb/ 2011-30_IRB/ar09.html*.

For more information on reporting taxable exchanges, see *Box 1* on page 9.

Prohibited transactions. If an IRA owner engages in a prohibited transaction with respect to an IRA, the assets of the IRA are treated as distributed on the first day of the tax year in which the prohibited transaction occurs. IRAs that include, or consist of, non-marketable securities and/or closely held investments, in which the IRA owner effectively controls the underlying assets of such securities or investments, have a greater potential for resulting in a prohibited transaction. Report the distribution as you normally would for the type of IRA that has engaged in the prohibited transaction. Enter Code 5 in box 7.

Designated Roth Account Distributions

An employer offering a section 401(k), 403(b), or governmental section 457(b) plan may allow participants to contribute all or a portion of the elective deferrals they are otherwise eligible to make to a separate designated Roth account established under the plan. Contributions made under a section 401(k) plan must meet the requirements of Regulations section 1.401(k)-1(f) (Regulations section 1.403(b)-3(c) for a section 403(b) plan). Under the terms of the section 401(k) plan, section 403(b) plan, or governmental section 457(b) plan, the designated Roth account must meet the requirements of section 402A.

Distributions allocable to an in-plan Roth rollover (IRR). The distribution of an amount allocable to the taxable amount of an in-plan Roth rollover (IRR), made within the 5-year period beginning with the first day of the participant's tax year in which the rollover was made, is treated as includible in gross income for purposes of applying section 72(t) to the distribution. The total amount allocable to such an IRR is reported in box 10. See the instructions for *Box 10* on page 14.

Instructions for Forms 1099-R and 5498 (2013)

A separate Form 1099-R must be used to report the total annual distribution from a designated Roth account.

IRA Distributions

 For deemed IRAs under section 408(q), use the rules that apply to traditional IRAs or Roth IRAs as applicable. Simplified employee pension (SEP) IRAs and savings incentive match plan for employees (SIMPLE) IRAs, however, may not be used as deemed IRAs.

Deemed IRAs. A qualified employer plan may allow employees to make voluntary employee contributions to a separate account or annuity established under the plan. Under the terms of the qualified employer plan, the account or annuity must meet the applicable requirements of section 408 or 408A for a traditional IRA or Roth IRA. Under section 408(q), the "deemed IRA" portion of the qualified employer plan is subject to the rules applicable to traditional and Roth IRAs, and not to those of the applicable plan under section 401(a), 403(a), 403(b), or 457.

Accordingly, the reporting and withholding rules on plan and IRA distributions apply separately depending on whether the distributions are made from the deemed IRA or the qualified employer plan. For example, the reporting rules for required minimum distributions (RMDs) apply separately for the two portions of the plan. A total distribution of amounts held in the qualified employer plan portion and the deemed IRA portion is reported on two separate Forms 1099-R — one for the distribution from the deemed IRA portion and one for the rest of the distribution. Also, the 20% withholding rules of section 3405(c) do not apply to a distribution from the deemed IRA portion but would apply to a distribution from the qualified employer plan portion, and section 72(t) applies separately to the two portions.

IRAs other than Roth IRAs. Unless otherwise instructed, distributions from any IRA, except a Roth IRA, must be reported in boxes 1 and 2a. Check the "Taxable amount not determined" box in box 2b. But see:
- *Traditional, SEP, or SIMPLE IRA* on page 11 for how to report the withdrawal of IRA contributions under section 408(d)(4),
- *Transfers* on page 6 for information on trustee-to-trustee transfers, including recharacterizations,
- Reporting a corrective distribution from an IRA under section 408(d)(5) on page 11,
- Reporting IRA revocations or account closures due to Customer Identification Program failures on this page, and
- Reporting a transfer from a SIMPLE IRA to a non-SIMPLE IRA within the first 2 years of plan participation on page 6.

The direct rollover provisions beginning later do not apply to distributions from any IRA. However, taxable distributions from traditional IRAs and SEP IRAs may be rolled over into an eligible retirement plan. See section 408(d)(3). SIMPLE IRAs may also be rolled over into an eligible retirement plan, but only after the 2-year period described in section 72(t)(6).

An IRA includes all investments under one IRA plan or account. File only one Form 1099-R for distributions from all investments under one plan that are paid in 1 year to one recipient, unless you must enter different codes in box 7. You do not have to file a separate Form 1099-R for each distribution under the plan.

Roth IRAs. For distributions from a Roth IRA, report the gross distribution in box 1 but generally leave box 2a blank. Check the "Taxable amount not determined" box in box 2b. Enter Code J, Q, or T as appropriate in box 7. Do not use any other codes with Code Q or Code T. You may enter Code 8 or P with Code J. For the withdrawal of excess contributions, see *Roth IRA* on page 11. It is not necessary to mark the IRA/SEP/SIMPLE checkbox.

Roth IRA conversions. You must report a traditional, SEP, or SIMPLE IRA distribution that you know is converted or reconverted this year to a Roth IRA in boxes 1 and 2a (checking box 2b "Taxable amount not determined" unless otherwise directed elsewhere in these instructions), even if the conversion is a trustee-to-trustee transfer or is with the same trustee. Enter Code 2 or 7 in box 7 depending on the participant's age.

IRA Revocation or Account Closure

If a traditional or Roth IRA is revoked during its first 7 days (under Regulations section 1.408-6(d)(4)(ii)) or is closed at any time by the IRA trustee or custodian due to a failure of the taxpayer to satisfy the Customer Identification Program requirements described in section 326 of the USA PATRIOT Act, the distribution from the IRA must be reported. In addition, Form 5498, IRA Contribution Information, must be filed to report any regular, rollover, Roth IRA conversion, SEP IRA, or SIMPLE IRA contribution to an IRA that is subsequently revoked or closed by the trustee or custodian.

If a regular contribution is made to a traditional or Roth IRA that later is revoked or closed, and a distribution is made to the taxpayer, enter the gross distribution in box 1. If no earnings are distributed, enter 0 (zero) in box 2a and Code 8 in box 7 for a traditional IRA and Code J for a Roth IRA. If earnings are distributed, enter the amount of earnings in box 2a. For a traditional IRA, enter Codes 1 and 8, if applicable, in box 7; for a Roth IRA, enter Codes J and 8, if applicable. These earnings could be subject to the 10% early distribution tax under section 72(t). If a rollover contribution is made to a traditional or Roth IRA that later is revoked or closed, and distribution is made to the taxpayer, enter in boxes 1 and 2a of Form 1099-R the gross distribution and the appropriate code in box 7 (Code J for a Roth IRA). Follow this same procedure for a transfer from a traditional or Roth IRA to another IRA of the same type that later is revoked or closed. The distribution could be subject to the 10% early distribution tax under section 72(t).

If an IRA conversion contribution or a rollover from a qualified plan is made to a Roth IRA that later is revoked or closed, and a distribution is made to the taxpayer, enter the gross distribution in box 1 of Form 1099-R. If no earnings are distributed, enter 0 (zero) in box 2a and Code J in box 7. If earnings are distributed, enter the amount of the earnings in box 2a and Code J in box 7.

These earnings could be subject to the 10% early distribution tax under section 72(t).

If an employer SEP IRA or SIMPLE IRA plan contribution is made and the SEP IRA or SIMPLE IRA is revoked by the employee or is closed by the trustee or custodian, report the distribution as fully taxable.

For more information on IRAs that have been revoked, see Rev. Proc. 91-70, 1991-2 C.B. 899.

Deductible Voluntary Employee Contributions (DVECs)

If you are reporting a total distribution from a plan that includes a distribution of DVECs, you may file a separate Form 1099-R to report the distribution of DVECs. If you do, report the distribution of DVECs in boxes 1 and 2a on the separate Form 1099-R. For the direct rollover (explained later) of funds that include DVECs, a separate Form 1099-R is not required to report the direct rollover of the DVECs.

Direct Rollovers

You must report a direct rollover of an eligible rollover distribution. A direct rollover is the direct payment of the distribution from a qualified plan, section 403(b) plan, or a governmental section 457(b) plan to a traditional IRA, Roth IRA, or other eligible retirement plan. For additional rules regarding the treatment of direct rollovers from designated Roth accounts, see *Designated Roth accounts* on page 5. A direct rollover may be made for the employee, for the employee's surviving spouse, for the spouse or former spouse who is an alternate payee under a qualified domestic relations order (QDRO) or for a nonspouse designated beneficiary, in which case the direct rollover can only be made to an inherited IRA. If the distribution is paid to the surviving spouse, the distribution is treated in the same manner as if the spouse were the employee. See Part V of Notice 2007-7, 2007-5 I.R.B. 395, available at *www.irs.gov/irb/2007-05_IRB/ar11.html*, which has been modified by Notice 2009-82, 2009-41 I.R.B. 491, available at *www.irs.gov/irb/2009-41_IRB/ar12.html* for guidance on direct rollovers by nonspouse designated beneficiaries. See also Notice 2008-30, Part II, 2008-12 I.R.B. 638, available at *www.irs.gov/irb/2008-12_IRB/ar11.html*, which has been amplified and clarified by Notice 2009-75, 2009-39 I.R.B. 436, available at *www.irs.gov/irb/2009-39_IRB/ar15.html*, for questions and answers covering rollover contributions to Roth IRAs.

 Notice 2007-7 and Notice 2008-30 do not reflect changes made to section 402 by the Worker, Retiree, and Employer Recovery Act of 2008.

An eligible rollover distribution is any distribution of all or any portion of the balance to the credit of the employee (including net unrealized appreciation (NUA)) from a qualified plan, a section 403(b) plan or a governmental section 457(b) plan except:

1. One of a series of substantially equal periodic payments made at least annually over:

a. The life of the employee or the joint lives of the employee and the employee's designated beneficiary,

b. The life expectancy of the employee or the joint life and last survivor expectancy of the employee and the employee's designated beneficiary, or

c. A specified period of 10 years or more.

2. An RMD (under section 401(a)(9)). A plan administrator is permitted to assume there is no designated beneficiary for purposes of determining the minimum distribution.

3. Elective deferrals (under section 402(g)(3)), employee contributions, and earnings on each returned because of the section 415 limits.

4. Corrective distributions of excess deferrals (under section 402(g)) and earnings.

5. Corrective distributions of excess contributions under a qualified cash or deferred arrangement (under section 401(k)) and excess aggregate contributions (under section 401(m)) and earnings.

6. Loans treated as deemed distributions (under section 72(p)). But plan loan offset amounts can be eligible rollover distributions. See Regulations section 1.402(c)-2, Q/A-9.

7. Section 404(k) dividends.

8. Cost of current life insurance protection.

9. Distributions to a payee other than the employee, the employee's surviving spouse, a spouse or former spouse who is an alternate payee under a QDRO, or a nonspouse designated beneficiary.

10. Any hardship distribution.

11. A permissible withdrawal under section 414(w).

12. Prohibited allocations of securities in an S corporation that are treated as deemed distributions.

13. Distributions of premiums for accident or health insurance under Regulations section 1.402(a)-1(e).

Amounts paid under an annuity contract purchased for and distributed to a participant under a qualified plan can qualify as eligible rollover distributions. See Regulations section 1.402(c)-2, Q/A-10.

Automatic rollovers. Eligible rollover distributions may also include involuntary distributions that are more than $1,000 but $5,000 or less and are made from a qualified plan to an IRA on behalf of a plan participant. Involuntary distributions are generally subject to the automatic rollover provisions of section 401(a)(31)(B) and must be paid in a direct rollover to an IRA, unless the plan participant elects to receive the distribution directly.

For information on the notification requirements, see *Explanation to Recipients Before Eligible Rollover Distributions (Section 402(f) Notice)*, later. For additional information, also see Notice 2005-5, 2005-3 I.R.B. 337, available at *www.irs.gov/irb/2005-03_IRB/ar10.html*, modified by Notice 2005-95, 2005-51 I.R.B. 1172, available at *www.irs.gov/irb/2005-51_IRB/ar12.html*.

Reporting a direct rollover. Report a direct rollover in box 1 and a 0 (zero) in box 2a, unless the rollover is a direct rollover of a qualified rollover contribution other than from a designated Roth account. See *Qualified rollover contributions as defined in section 408A(e)*, later. You do not have to report capital gain in box 3 or NUA in box 6.

Enter Code G in box 7 unless the rollover is a direct rollover from a designated Roth account to a Roth IRA. See *Designated Roth accounts* below. If the direct rollover is made by a nonspouse designated beneficiary, also enter Code 4 in box 7.

Prepare the form using the name and social security number (SSN) of the person for whose benefit the funds were rolled over (generally the participant), not those of the trustee of the traditional IRA or other plan to which the funds were rolled.

If you receive a direct rollover to an IRA, you must prepare Form 5498. If you receive a direct rollover to a qualified plan, section 403(b) plan or a governmental section 457(b) plan, no report is required.

If part of the distribution is a direct rollover and part is distributed to the recipient, prepare two Forms 1099-R.

For more information on eligible rollover distributions, including substantially equal periodic payments, RMDs, and plan loan offset amounts, see Regulations sections 1.402(c)-2 and 1.403(b)-7(b). Also, see Rev. Rul. 2002-62 which is on page 710 of Internal Revenue Bulletin 2002-42 at *www.irs.gov/pub/irs-irbs/irb02-42.pdf* for guidance on substantially equal periodic payments that began after December 31, 2002.

 For information on distributions of amounts attributable to rollover contributions separately accounted for by an eligible retirement plan and if permissible timing restrictions apply, see Rev. Rul. 2004-12, 2004-7 I.R.B. 478, available at www.irs.gov/irb/2004-07_IRB/ar08.html.

Designated Roth accounts. A direct rollover from a designated Roth account may only be made to another designated Roth account or to a Roth IRA. A distribution from a Roth IRA, however, cannot be rolled over into a designated Roth account. In addition, a plan is permitted to treat the balance of the participant's designated Roth account and the participant's other accounts under the plan as accounts held under two separate plans for purposes of applying the automatic rollover rules of section 401(a)(31)(B) and Q/A-9 through Q/A-11 of Regulations section 1.401(a)(31)-1. Thus, if a participant's balance in the designated Roth account is less than $200, the plan is not required to offer a direct rollover election or to apply the automatic rollover provisions to such balance.

A distribution from a designated Roth account that is a qualified distribution is tax-free. A qualified distribution is a payment that is made both after age 59¹⁄₂ (or after death or disabililty) and after the 5-taxable-year period that begins with the first day of the first taxable year in which the employee makes a designated Roth contribution. Certain amounts, including corrective distributions, cannot be qualified distributions. See Regulations section 1.402A-1.

If any portion of a distribution from a designated Roth account that is not includible in gross income is to be rolled over into a designated Roth account under another plan, the rollover must be accomplished by a direct rollover. Any portion not includible in gross income that is distributed to the employee, however, cannot be rolled over to another designated Roth account, though it can be rolled over into a Roth IRA within the 60-day period

described in section 402(c)(3). In the case of a direct rollover, the distributing plan is required to report to the recipient plan the amount of the investment (basis) in the contract and the first year of the 5-taxable-year period, or that the distribution is a qualified distribution.

For a direct rollover of a distribution from a designated Roth account to a Roth IRA, enter the amount rolled over in box 1 and 0 (zero) in box 2a. Use Code H in box 7. For all other distributions from a designated Roth account, use Code B in box 7, unless Code E applies. If the direct rollover is from one designated Roth account to another designated Roth account, also enter Code G in box 7.

For a direct rollover of a distribution from a section 401(k) plan, a section 403(b) plan, or a governmental section 457(b) plan to a designated Roth account in the same plan, enter the amount rolled over in box 1, the taxable amount in box 2a, and any basis recovery amount in box 5. Use Code G in box 7.

Qualified rollover contributions as defined in section 408A(e). A qualified rollover contribution as defined in section 408A(e) is:

• A rollover contribution to a Roth IRA from another IRA that meets the requirements of section 408(d)(3) or

• A rollover contribution to a Roth IRA from an eligible retirement plan (other than an IRA) that meets the requirements of section 408A(e)(2)(B).

For reporting a rollover from an IRA other than a Roth IRA to a Roth IRA, see *Roth IRA conversions* on pages 3 and 11.

For a direct rollover of an eligible rollover distribution to a Roth IRA (other than from a designated Roth account), report the total amount rolled over in box 1, the taxable amount in box 2a, and any basis recovery amount in box 5. (See the instructions for *Box 5* on page 13.) Use Code G in box 7. If the direct rollover is made on behalf of a nonspouse designated beneficiary, also enter Code 4 in box 7.

For reporting instructions for a direct rollover from a designated Roth account, see *Designated Roth accounts*, earlier.

Explanation to Recipients Before Eligible Rollover Distributions (Section 402(f) Notice)

For qualified plans, section 403(b) plans, and governmental section 457(b) plans, the plan administrator must provide to each recipient of an eligible rollover distribution an explanation using either a written paper document or an electronic medium (section 402(f) notice). The explanation must be provided no more than 180 days and no fewer than 30 days before making an eligible rollover distribution or before the annuity starting date. However, if the recipient who has received the section 402(f) notice affirmatively elects a distribution, you will not fail to satisfy the timing requirements merely because you make the distribution fewer than 30 days after you provided the notice as long as you meet the requirements of Regulations section 1.402(f)-1, Q/A-2. The electronic section 402(f) notice must meet the consumer consent requirements as provided in Regulations section 1.401(a)-21(b).

The notice must explain the rollover rules, the special tax treatment for lump-sum distributions, the direct rollover option (and any default procedures), the mandatory 20% withholding rules, and an explanation of how distributions from the plan to which the rollover is made may have different restrictions and tax consequences than the plan from which the rollover is made. The notice and summary are permitted to be sent either as a written paper document or through an electronic medium reasonably accessible to the recipient; see Regulations section 1.402(f)-1, Q/A-5.

For periodic payments that are eligible rollover distributions, you must provide the notice before the first payment and at least once a year as long as the payments continue. For section 403(b) plans, the payer must provide an explanation of the direct rollover option within the time period described earlier or some other reasonable period of time.

Notice 2009-68, 2009-39 I.R.B. 423, available at *www.irs.gov/irb/2009-39_IRB/ar14.html*, contains two safe harbor explanations that may be provided to recipients of eligible rollover distributions from an employer plan in order to satisfy section 402(f). See also Notice 2009-75, and, if the plan offers IRRs, Notice 2010-84, Q/A-5, 2010-51 I.R.B. 872, which is available at *www.irs.gov/irb/2010-51_IRB/ar11.html*.

Involuntary distributions. For involuntary distributions paid to an IRA in a direct rollover (automatic rollover) you may satisfy the notification requirements of section 401(a)(31)(B)(i) either separately or as a part of the section 402(f) notice. The notification must be in writing and may be sent using electronic media in accordance with Q/A-5 of Regulations section 1.402(f)-1. Also see Notice 2005-5, Q/A-15.

Transfers

Generally, do not report a transfer between trustees or issuers that involves no payment or distribution of funds to the participant, including a trustee-to-trustee transfer from one IRA to another IRA, valid transfers from one section 403(b) plan in accordance with paragraphs 1 through 3 of Regulations section 1.403(b)-10(b), or for the purchase of permissive service credit under section 403(b)(13) or section 457(e)(17) in accordance with paragraph 4 of Regulations section 1.403(b)-10(b) and Regulations section 1.457-10(b)(8). However, you must report:
- Recharacterized IRA contributions;
- Roth IRA conversions; and
- Direct rollovers from qualified plans, section 403(b) plans or governmental section 457(b) plans, including any direct rollovers from such plans that are qualified rollover contributions described in section 408A(e).

IRA recharacterizations. You must report each recharacterization of an IRA contribution. If a participant makes a contribution to an IRA (first IRA) for a year, the participant may choose to recharacterize the contribution by transferring, in a trustee-to-trustee transfer, any part of the contribution (plus earnings) to another IRA (second IRA). The contribution is treated as made to the second IRA (recharacterization). A recharacterization may be made with the same trustee or with another trustee. The trustee of the first IRA must report the recharacterization

as a distribution on Form 1099-R and the contribution to the first IRA and its character on Form 5498.

Enter the fair market value (FMV) of the amount recharacterized in box 1, 0 (zero) in box 2a, and Code R in box 7 if reporting a recharacterization of a prior-year (2012) contribution or Code N if reporting a recharacterization of a contribution in the same year (2013). It is not necessary to check the IRA/SEP/SIMPLE checkbox. For more information on how to report, see Notice 2000-30 on page 1266 of Internal Revenue Bulletin 2000-25 at *www.irs.gov/pub/irs-irbs/irb00-25.pdf*.

Section 1035 exchange. You may have to report exchanges of insurance contracts, including an exchange under section 1035, under which any designated distribution may be made. For a section 1035 exchange that is in part taxable, file a separate Form 1099-R to report the taxable amount. See *Section 1035 exchange* on page 2.

SIMPLE IRAs. Do not report a trustee-to-trustee transfer from one SIMPLE IRA to another SIMPLE IRA. However, you must report as a taxable distribution in boxes 1 and 2a a trustee-to-trustee transfer from a SIMPLE IRA to an IRA that is not a SIMPLE IRA during the 2-year period beginning on the day contributions are first deposited in the individual's SIMPLE IRA by the employer. Use Code S in box 7 if appropriate.

Transfer of an IRA to spouse. If you transfer or re-designate an interest from one spouse's IRA to an IRA for the other spouse under a divorce or separation instrument, the transfer or re-designation as provided under section 408(d)(6) is tax free. Do not report such a transfer on Form 1099-R.

Corrective Distributions

You must report on Form 1099-R corrective distributions of excess deferrals, excess contributions and excess aggregate contributions under section 401(a) plans, section 401(k) cash or deferred arrangements, section 403(a) annuity plans, section 403(b) salary reduction agreements, and salary reduction simplified employee pensions (SARSEPs) under section 408(k)(6). Excess contributions that are recharacterized under a section 401(k) plan are treated as distributed. Corrective distributions must include earnings through the end of the year in which the excess arose. These distributions are reportable on Form 1099-R and are generally taxable in the year of the distribution (except for excess deferrals under section 402(g)). Enter Code 8 or P in box 7 (with Code B if applicable) to designate the distribution and the year it is taxable.

Use a separate Form 1099-R to report a corrective distribution from a designated Roth account.

 The total amount of the elective deferral is reported in box 12 of Form W-2. See the Instructions for Forms W-2 and W-3 for more information.

For more information about reporting corrective distributions see: the *Guide to Distribution Codes* on pages 15, 16, and 17; Notice 89-32, 1989-1 C.B. 671; Notice 88-33, 1988-1 C.B. 513; Notice 87-77, 1987-2 C.B.

Instructions for Forms 1099-R and 5498 (2013)

385; and the Regulations under sections 401(k), 401(m), 402(g), and 457.

Excess deferrals. Excess deferrals under section 402(g) can occur in section 401(k) plans, section 403(b) plans or SARSEPs. If distributed by April 15 of the year following the year of deferral, the excess is taxable to the participant in the year of deferral (other than designated Roth contributions), but the earnings are taxable in the year distributed. Except for a SARSEP, if the distribution occurs after April 15, the excess is taxable in the year of deferral and the year distributed. The earnings are taxable in the year distributed. For a SARSEP, excess deferrals not withdrawn by April 15 are considered regular IRA contributions subject to the IRA contribution limits. Corrective distributions of excess deferrals are not subject to federal income tax withholding or social security and Medicare taxes. For losses on excess deferrals, see *Losses*, below. See the regulations under section 457 for special rules for excess deferrals under governmental section 457(b) plans.

Excess contributions. Excess contributions can occur in a section 401(k) plan or a SARSEP. All distributions of the excess contributions plus earnings (other than designated Roth contributions), including recharacterized excess contributions, are taxable to the participant in the year of distribution. Report the gross distribution in box 1 of Form 1099-R. In box 2a, enter the excess contribution and earnings distributed less any designated Roth contributions. For a SARSEP, the employer must notify the participant by March 15 of the year after the year the excess contribution was made that the participant must withdraw the excess and earnings. All distributions from a SARSEP are taxable in the year of distribution. An excess contribution not withdrawn by April 15 of the year after the year of notification is considered a regular IRA contribution subject to the IRA contribution limits.

 Regulations have not been updated for SARSEPs.

Excess aggregate contributions. Excess aggregate contributions under section 401(m) can occur in section 401(a), section 401(k), section 403(a), and section 403(b) plans. A corrective distribution of excess aggregate contributions plus earnings is taxable to the participant in the year the distribution was made. Report the gross distribution in box 1 of Form 1099-R. In box 2a, enter the excess and earnings distributed less any after-tax contributions.

Losses. If a corrective distribution of an excess deferral is made in a year after the year of deferral and a net loss has been allocated to the excess deferral, report the corrective distribution amount in boxes 1 and 2a of Form 1099-R for the year of the distribution with the appropriate distribution code in box 7. If the excess deferrals consist of designated Roth contributions, report the corrective distribution amount in box 1, 0 (zero) in box 2a, and the appropriate distribution code in box 7. However, taxpayers must include the total amount of the excess deferral (unadjusted for loss) in income in the year of deferral, and they may report a loss on the tax return for the year the corrective distribution is made.

Distributions under Employee Plans Compliance Resolution System (EPCRS)

The procedure for correcting excess annual additions under section 415 is explained in the latest EPCRS revenue procedure, Rev. Proc. 2008-50, 2008-35 I.R.B. 464, available at *www.irs.gov/irb/2008-35_IRB/ar10.html*.

Distributions to correct a section 415 failure are not eligible rollover distributions although they are subject to federal income tax withholding under section 3405. They are not subject to social security, Medicare, or Federal Unemployment Tax Act (FUTA) taxes. In addition, such distributions are not subject to the 10% early distribution tax under section 72(t).

You may report the distribution of elective deferrals (other than designated Roth contributions) and employee contributions (and earnings attributable to such elective deferrals and employee contributions) on the same Form 1099-R. However, if you made other distributions during the year, report them on a separate Form 1099-R. Because the distribution of elective deferrals (other than designated Roth contributions) is fully taxable in the year distributed (no part of the distribution is a return of the investment in the contract), report the total amount of the distribution in boxes 1 and 2a. Leave box 5 blank, and enter Code E in box 7. For a return of employee contributions (or designated Roth contributions) plus earnings, enter the gross distribution in box 1, the earnings attributable to the employee contributions (or designated Roth contributions) being returned in box 2a, and the employee contributions (or designated Roth contributions) being returned in box 5. Enter Code E in box 7. For more information, see Rev. Proc. 92-93, 1992-2 C.B. 505.

Similar rules apply to other corrective distributions under EPCRS. Also, special Form 1099-R reporting is available for certain plan loan failures. See Rev. Proc. 2008-50 for details.

If excess employer contributions (other than elective deferrals), and the earnings on them, under SEP, SARSEP, or SIMPLE IRA plans are returned to an employer (with the participant's consent), enter the gross distribution (excess and earnings) in box 1 and 0 (zero) in box 2a. Enter Code E in box 7.

Failing the ADP or ACP Test After a Total Distribution

If you make a total distribution in 2013 and file a Form 1099-R with the IRS and then discover in 2014 that the plan failed either the section 401(k)(3) actual deferral percentage (ADP) test for 2013 and you compute excess contributions or the section 401(m)(2) actual contribution percentage (ACP) test and you compute excess aggregate contributions, you must recharacterize part of the total distribution as excess contributions or excess aggregate contributions. First, file a CORRECTED Form 1099-R for 2013 for the correct amount of the total distribution (not including the amount recharacterized as excess contributions or excess aggregate contributions). Second, file a new Form 1099-R for 2013 for the excess contributions or excess aggregate contributions and allocable earnings.

To avoid a late filing penalty if the new Form 1099-R is filed after the due date, enter in the bottom margin of Form 1096, Annual Summary and Transmittal of U.S. Information Returns, the words "Filed To Correct Excess Contributions."

You must also issue copies of the Forms 1099-R to the plan participant with an explanation of why these new forms are being issued. ADP and ACP test corrections are exempt from the 10% early distribution tax under section 72(t).

Loans Treated as Distributions

A loan from a qualified plan under sections 401(a) and 403(a) and (b), and a plan maintained by the United States, a state or political subdivision, or any of its subsidiary agencies made to a participant or beneficiary is not treated as a distribution from the plan if the loan satisfies the following requirements.

1. The loan is evidenced by an enforceable agreement,

2. The agreement specifies that the loan must be repaid within 5 years, except for a principal residence,

3. The loan must be repaid in substantially level installments (at least quarterly), and

4. The loan amount does not exceed the limits in section 72(p)(2)(A) (maximum limit is equal to the lesser of 50% of the vested account balance or $50,000).

Certain exceptions, cure periods, and suspension of the repayment schedule may apply.

The loan agreement must specify the amount of the loan, the term of the loan, and the repayment schedule. The agreement may include more than one document.

If a loan fails to satisfy 1, 2, or 3, the balance of the loan is a deemed distribution. The distribution may occur at the time the loan is made or later if the loan is not repaid in accordance with the repayment schedule.

If a loan fails to satisfy 4 at the time the loan is made, the amount that exceeds the amount permitted to be loaned is a deemed distribution.

Deemed distribution. If a loan is treated as a deemed distribution, it is reportable on Form 1099-R using the normal taxation rules of section 72, including tax basis rules. The distribution also may be subject to the 10% early distribution tax under section 72(t). It is not eligible to be rolled over to an eligible retirement plan nor is it eligible for the 10-year tax option. On Form 1099-R, complete the appropriate boxes, including boxes 1 and 2a, and enter Code L in box 7. Also, enter Code 1 or Code B, if applicable.

Interest that accrues after the deemed distribution of a loan is not an additional loan, and, therefore, is not reportable on Form 1099-R.

Loans that are treated as deemed distributions or that are actual distributions are subject to federal income tax withholding. If a distribution occurs after the loan is made, you must withhold only if you distributed cash or property (other than employer securities) at the time of the deemed or actual distribution. See section 72(p), section 72(e)(4)(A), and Regulations section 1.72(p)-1.

Subsequent repayments. If a participant makes any cash repayments on a loan that was reported on Form 1099-R as a deemed distribution, the repayments increase the participant's tax basis in the plan as if the repayments were after-tax contributions. However, such repayments are not treated as after-tax contributions for purposes of section 401(m) or 415(c)(2)(B).

For a deemed distribution that was reported on Form 1099-R but was not repaid, the deemed distribution does not increase the participant's basis.

If a participant's accrued benefit is reduced (offset) to repay a loan, the amount of the account balance that is offset against the loan is an actual distribution. Report it as you would any other actual distribution. Do not enter Code L in box 7.

Permissible Withdrawals Under Section 414(w)

For permissible withdrawals from an eligible automatic contribution arrangement (EACA) under section 414(w):
• The distribution (except to the extent the distribution consists of designated Roth contributions) is included in the employee's gross income in the year distributed;
• Report principal and earnings in boxes 1 and 2a except, in the case of a distribution from a designated Roth account, report only earnings in box 2a;
• The distribution is not subject to the 10% additional tax, indicated by reporting Code 2 in box 7; and
• The distribution must be elected by the employee no later than 90 days after the first default elective contribution under the EACA, as specified in Regulations section 1.414(w)-1(c)(2).

If the distribution is from a designated Roth account, enter Code B as well as Code 2 in box 7.

Corrected Form 1099-R

If you filed a Form 1099-R with the IRS and later discover that there is an error on it, you must correct it as soon as possible. For example, if you transmit a direct rollover and file a Form 1099-R with the IRS reporting that none of the direct rollover is taxable by entering 0 (zero) in box 2a, and you then discover that part of the direct rollover consists of RMDs under section 401(a)(9), you must file a corrected Form 1099-R reporting the eligible rollover distribution as the direct rollover and file a new Form 1099-R reporting the RMD as if it had been distributed to the participant. See part H in the 2013 General Instructions for Certain Information Returns or Pub. 1220, if filing electronically.

Filer

The payer, trustee, or plan administrator must file Form 1099-R using the same name and employer identification number (EIN) used to deposit any tax withheld and to file Form 945, Annual Return of Withheld Federal Income Tax.

Beneficiaries

If you make a distribution to a beneficiary, trust, or estate, prepare Form 1099-R using the name and TIN of the beneficiary, trust, or estate, not that of the decedent. If there are multiple beneficiaries, report on each Form 1099-R only the amount paid to the beneficiary whose name appears on the Form 1099-R, and enter the percentage in box 9a, if applicable.

Disclaimers. A beneficiary may make a qualified disclaimer of all or some of an IRA account balance if the disclaimed amount and income are paid to a new beneficiary or segregated in a separate account. A qualified disclaimer may be made after the beneficiary has previously received the RMD for the year of the decedent's death. For more information, see Rev. Rul. 2005-36, 2005-26 I.R.B. 1368, available at *www.irs.gov/ irb/2005-26_IRB/ar11.html*.

Alternate Payee under a Qualified Domestic Relations Order (QDRO)

Distributions to an alternate payee who is a spouse or former spouse of the employee under a QDRO are reportable on Form 1099-R using the name and TIN of the alternate payee. If the alternate payee under a QDRO is a nonspouse, enter the name and TIN of the employee. However, this rule does not apply to IRAs; see *Transfer of an IRA to spouse* on page 6.

Nonresident Aliens

If income tax is withheld under section 3405 on any distribution to a nonresident alien, report the distribution and withholding on Form 1099-R. Also file Form 945 to report the withholding. See the Presumption Rules in part S of the 2013 General Instructions for Certain Information Returns.

However, any payments to a nonresident alien from any trust under section 401(a), any annuity plan under section 403(a), any annuity, custodial account, or retirement income account under section 403(b), or any IRA account under section 408(a) or (b) are subject to withholding under section 1441, unless there is an exception under a tax treaty. Report the distribution and withholding on Form 1042, Annual Withholding Tax Return for U.S. Source Income of Foreign Persons, and Form 1042-S, Foreign Person's U.S. Source Income Subject to Withholding.

For guidance regarding covered expatriates, see Notice 2009-85, 2009-45 I.R.B. 598, available at *www.irs.gov/irb/2009-45_IRB/ar10.html*.

Statements to Recipients

If you are required to file Form 1099-R, you must furnish a statement to the recipient. For more information about the requirement to furnish a statement to each recipient, see part M in the 2013 General Instructions for Certain Information Returns.

 Do not enter a negative amount in any box on Form 1099-R.

Account Number

The account number is required if you have multiple accounts for a recipient for whom you are filing more than one Form 1099-R. Additionally, the IRS encourages you to designate an account number for all Forms 1099-R that you file. See part L in the 2013 General Instructions for Certain Information Returns.

Box 1. Gross distribution

Enter the total amount of the distribution before income tax or other deductions were withheld. Include direct rollovers, IRA rollovers to accepting employer plans, premiums paid by a trustee or custodian for the cost of current life or other insurance protection, including a recharacterization and a Roth IRA conversion. Also include in this box distributions to plan participants from governmental section 457(b) plans. However, in the case of a distribution by a trust representing certificates of deposit (CDs) redeemed early, report the net amount distributed. Also, see *Box 6* on page 13.

Include in this box the value of U.S. Savings Bonds distributed from a plan. Enter the appropriate taxable amount in box 2a. Furnish a statement to the plan participant showing the value of each bond at the time of distribution. This will provide him or her with the information necessary to figure the interest income on each bond when it is redeemed.

Include in box 1 amounts distributed from a qualified retirement plan for which the recipient elects to pay health insurance premiums under a cafeteria plan or that are paid directly to reimburse medical care expenses incurred by the recipient (see Rev. Rul. 2003-62 on page 1034 of Internal Revenue Bulletin 2003-25 at *www.irs.gov/pub/irs-irbs/irb03-25.pdf*). Also include this amount in box 2a.

Include in box 1 charges or payments for qualified long-term care insurance contracts under combined arrangements. Enter Code W in box 7.

In addition to reporting distributions to beneficiaries of deceased employees, report here any death benefit payments made by employers that are not made as part of a pension, profit-sharing, or retirement plan. Also enter these amounts in box 2a; enter Code 4 in box 7.

 Do not report accelerated death benefits on Form 1099-R. Report them on Form 1099-LTC, Long-Term Care and Accelerated Death Benefits.

For section 1035 exchanges that are reportable on Form 1099-R, enter the total value of the contract in box 1, 0 (zero) in box 2a, the total premiums paid in box 5, and Code 6 in box 7.

Designated Roth account distributions. If you are making a distribution from a designated Roth account, enter the gross distribution in box 1, the taxable portion of the distribution in box 2a, the basis included in the distributed amount in box 5, any amount allocable to an IRR made within the previous 5 years (unless an exception to section 72(t) applies) in box 10, and the first year of the 5-taxable-year period for determining qualified distributions in box 11. Also, enter the applicable code(s) in box 7.

Employer securities and other property. If you distribute employer securities or other property, include in box 1 the FMV of the securities or other property on the date of distribution. If there is a loss, see *Losses* on page 10.

If you are distributing worthless property only, you are not required to file Form 1099-R. However, you may file and enter 0 (zero) in boxes 1 and 2a and any after-tax employee contributions or designated Roth contributions in box 5.

Charitable gift annuities. If cash or capital gain property is donated in exchange for a charitable gift annuity, report the total amount distributed during the year in box 1. See *Charitable gift annuities* under *Box 3* on page 11.

Box 2a. Taxable amount

 When determining the taxable amount to be entered in box 2a, do not reduce the taxable amount by any portion of the $3,000 exclusion for which the participant may be eligible as a payment of qualified health and long-term care insurance premiums for retired public safety officers under section 402(l).

Generally, you must enter the taxable amount in box 2a. However, if you are unable to reasonably obtain the data needed to compute the taxable amount, leave this box blank. Do not enter excludable or tax-deferred amounts reportable in boxes 5, 6, and 8. Enter 0 (zero) in box 2a for:

• A direct rollover (other than a qualified rollover contribution under section 408A(e) or an IRR) from a qualified plan, section 403(b) plan, a governmental section 457(b) plan, or a rollover from a designated Roth account into a Roth IRA,
• A traditional, SEP, or SIMPLE IRA directly transferred to an accepting employer plan,
• An IRA recharacterization,
• A nontaxable section 1035 exchange of life insurance, annuity, endowment or long-term care insurance contracts, or
• A nontaxable charge or payment, for the purchase of a qualified long-term care insurance contract, against the cash value of an annuity contract or the cash surrender value of a life insurance contract.

For more information on qualified rollover contributions under section 408A(e), see *Qualified rollover contributions as defined in section 408A(e)* on page 5.

Annuity starting date in 1998 or later. If you made annuity payments from a qualified plan under section 401(a), 403(a), or 403(b) and the annuity starting date is in 1998 or later, you must use the simplified method under section 72(d)(1) to figure the taxable amount. Under this method, the expected number of payments you use to figure the taxable amount depends on whether the payments are based on the life of one or more than one person. See Notice 98-2, 1998-1 C.B. 266, and Pub. 575, Pension and Annuity Income, to help you figure the taxable amount to enter in box 2a.

Annuity starting date after November 18, 1996, and before 1998. Under the simplified method for figuring the taxable amount, the expected number of payments is based only on the primary annuitant's age on the annuity starting date. See Notice 98-2.

Annuity starting date before November 19, 1996. If you properly used the rules in effect before November 19, 1996, for annuities that started before that date, continue to report using those rules. No changes are necessary.

Corrective distributions. Enter in box 2a the amount of excess deferrals, excess contributions, or excess aggregate contributions (other than employee contributions or designated Roth contributions). See *Corrective Distributions* on page 6.

Cost of current life insurance protection. Include current life insurance protection costs (net premium costs) that were reported in box 1. However, do not report these costs and a distribution on the same Form 1099-R. Use a separate Form 1099-R for each. For the cost of current life insurance protection, enter Code 9 in box 7.

DVECs. Include DVEC distributions in this box. Also see *Deductible Voluntary Employee Contributions (DVECs)* on page 4.

Designated Roth account. Generally, a distribution from a designated Roth account that is not a qualified distribution is taxable to the recipient under section 402 in the case of a plan qualified under section 401(a), under section 403(b)(1) in the case of a section 403(b) plan and under section 457(a)(1)(B) in the case of a governmental section 457(b) plan. For purposes of section 72, designated Roth contributions are treated as employer contributions as described in section 72(f)(1) (that is, as includible in the participant's gross income).

Examples. Participant A received a nonqualified distribution of $5,000 from the participant's designated Roth account. Immediately before the distribution, the participant's account balance was $10,000, consisting of $9,400 of designated Roth contributions and $600 of earnings. The taxable amount of the $5,000 distribution is $300 ($600/$10,000 x $5,000). The nontaxable portion of the distribution is $4,700 ($9,400/$10,000 x $5,000). The issuer would report on Form 1099-R:
• Box 1, $5,000 as the gross distribution;
• Box 2a, $300 as the taxable amount;
• Box 4, $60 ($300 x 20%) as the withholding on the earnings portion of the distribution;
• Box 5, $4,700 as the designated Roth contribution basis (nontaxable amount);
• Box 7, Code B; and
• The first year of the 5-taxable-year period in box 11.

Using the same facts as in the example above, except that the distribution was a direct rollover to a Roth IRA, the issuer would report on Form 1099-R:
• Box 1, $5,000 as the gross distribution;
• Box 2a, 0 (zero) as the taxable amount;
• Box 4, no entry;
• Box 5, $4,700 as the designated Roth contribution basis (nontaxable amount);
• Box 7, Code H; and
• The first year of the 5-taxable-year period in box 11.

Losses. If a distribution is a loss, do not enter a negative amount in this box. For example, if an employee's 401(k) account balance, consisting solely of stock, is distributed but the value is less than the employee's remaining after-tax contributions or designated Roth contributions, enter the value of the stock in box 1, leave box 2a blank, and enter the employee's contributions or designated Roth contributions in box 5.

For a plan with no after-tax contributions or designated Roth contributions, even though the value of the account may have decreased, there is no loss for reporting purposes. Therefore, if there are no employer securities distributed, show the actual cash and/or FMV of property distributed in boxes 1 and 2a, and make no entry in box 5. If only employer securities are distributed, show the FMV of the securities in boxes 1 and 2a and make no entry in box 5 or 6. If both employer securities and cash or other property are distributed, show the actual cash and/or FMV of the property (including employer securities) distributed in box 1, the gross less any NUA on employer securities in box 2a, no entry in box 5, and any NUA in box 6.

Qualified rollover contributions. See *Direct Rollovers* on page 4 for information on qualified rollover contributions.

Roth IRA. For a distribution from a Roth IRA, report the total distribution in box 1 and leave box 2a blank except in the case of an IRA revocation or account closure (see page 3) and a recharacterization (see page 6). Use Code J, Q, or T as appropriate in box 7. Use Code 8 or P, if applicable, in box 7 with Code J. Do not combine Code Q or T with any other codes.

However, for the distribution of excess Roth IRA contributions, report the gross distribution in box 1 and only the earnings in box 2a. Enter Code J and Code 8 or P in box 7.

Roth IRA conversions. Report the total amount converted or reconverted from a traditional IRA, SEP IRA, or SIMPLE IRA to a Roth IRA in box 2a. Check the "Taxable amount not determined" box in box 2b. A conversion or reconversion is considered a distribution and must be reported even if it is with the same trustee and even if the conversion is done by a trustee-to-trustee transfer. When an individual retirement annuity described in section 408(b) is converted to a Roth IRA, the amount that is treated as distributed is the FMV of the annuity contract on the date the annuity contract is converted. This rule also applies when a traditional IRA holds an annuity contract as an account asset and the traditional IRA is converted to a Roth IRA. Determining the FMV of an individual retirement annuity issued by a company regularly engaged in the selling of contracts depends on the timing of the conversion as outlined in Q/A-14 of Regulations section 1.408A-4.

For a Roth IRA conversion, use Code 2 in box 7 if the participant is under age 59½ or Code 7 if the participant is at least age 59½. Also check the IRA/SEP/SIMPLE box in box 7.

Traditional, SEP, or SIMPLE IRA. Generally, you are not required to compute the taxable amount of a traditional, SEP, or SIMPLE IRA nor designate whether any part of a distribution is a return of basis attributable to nondeductible contributions. Therefore, except as provided below or elsewhere in these instructions, report the total amount distributed from a traditional, SEP, or SIMPLE IRA in box 2a. This will be the same amount reported in box 1. Check the "Taxable amount not determined" box in box 2b.

However, for a distribution by a trust representing CDs redeemed early, report the net amount distributed. Do not include any amount paid for IRA insurance protection in this box.

For a distribution of contributions plus earnings from an IRA before the due date of the return under section 408(d)(4), report the gross distribution in box 1, only the earnings in box 2a, and enter Code 8 or P, whichever is applicable, in box 7. Enter Code 1 or 4 also, if applicable.

For a distribution of excess contributions without earnings after the due date of the individual's return under section 408(d)(5), leave box 2a blank, and check the "Taxable amount not determined" box in box 2b. Use Code 1 or 7 in box 7 depending on the age of the participant.

For a traditional IRA or a SEP IRA directly rolled over to an accepting employer plan, or a SIMPLE IRA directly rolled over to an accepting employer plan after the 2-year period (see section 72(t)(6)), enter the gross amount in box 1, 0 (zero) in box 2a, and Code G in box 7.

Box 2b. Taxable amount not determined
Enter an "X" in this box only if you are unable to reasonably obtain the data needed to compute the taxable amount. If you check this box, leave box 2a blank; but see *Traditional, SEP, or SIMPLE IRA,* on this page. Except for IRAs, make every effort to compute the taxable amount.

Box 2b. Total distribution
Enter an "X" in this box only if the payment shown in box 1 is a total distribution. A total distribution is one or more distributions within 1 tax year in which the entire balance of the account is distributed. If periodic or installment payments are made, mark this box in the year the final payment is made.

Box 3. Capital gain (included in box 2a)
If any amount is taxable as a capital gain, report it in box 3.

Charitable gift annuities. Report in box 3 any amount from a charitable gift annuity that is taxable as a capital gain. Report in box 1 the total amount distributed during the year. Report in box 2a the taxable amount. Advise the annuity recipient of any amount in box 3 subject to the 28% rate gain for collectibles and any unrecaptured section 1250 gain. Report in box 5 any nontaxable amount. Enter Code F in box 7. See Regulations section 1.1011-2(c), Example 8.

Special rule for participants born before January 2, 1936 (or their beneficiaries). For lump-sum distributions from qualified plans only, enter the amount in box 2a eligible for the capital gain election under section 1122(h)(3) of the Tax Reform Act of 1986 and section 641(f)(3) of the Economic Growth and Tax Relief Reconciliation Act of 2001. Enter the full amount eligible for the capital gain election. You should not complete this box for a direct rollover.

To compute the months of an employee's active participation before 1974, count as 12 months any part of a calendar year in which an employee actively participated under the plan; for active participation after 1973, count as 1 month any part of a month in which the employee actively participated under the plan. See the *Example*, on the this page.

Active participation begins with the first month in which an employee became a participant under the plan and ends with the earliest of:
- The month in which the employee received a lump-sum distribution under the plan;
- For an employee, other than a self-employed person or owner-employee, the month in which the employee separates from service;
- The month in which the employee dies; or
- For a self-employed person or owner-employee, the first month in which the employee becomes disabled within the meaning of section 72(m)(7).

Example for Computing Amount Eligible for Capital Gain Election (See **Box 3.**)

Step 1. Total Taxable Amount

A. Total distribution		XXXXX
B. Less:		
1. Current actuarial value of any annuity	XXXX	
2. Employee contributions or designated Roth contributions (minus any amounts previously distributed that were not includible in the employee's gross income)	XXXX	
3. Net unrealized appreciation in the value of any employer securities that was a part of the lump-sum distribution.	XXXX	
C. Total of lines 1 through 3		XXXXX
D. Total taxable amount. Subtract line C from line A.		XXXXX

Step 2. Capital Gain

$$\text{Line D} \times \frac{\text{Months of active participation before 1974}}{\text{Total months of active participation}} = \text{Capital gain}$$

(Total taxable amount = Line D)

Box 4. Federal income tax withheld

Enter any federal income tax withheld. This withholding under section 3405 is subject to deposit rules and the withholding tax return is Form 945. Backup withholding does not apply. See Pub. 15-A, Employer's Supplemental Tax Guide, and the Instructions for Form 945 for more withholding information.

Even though you may be using Code 1 in box 7 to designate an early distribution subject to the 10% additional tax specified in section 72(q), (t), or (v), you are not required to withhold that tax.

 The amount withheld cannot be more than the sum of the cash and the FMV of property (excluding employer securities) received in the distribution. If a distribution consists solely of employer securities and cash ($200 or less) in lieu of fractional shares, no withholding is required.

To determine your withholding requirements for any designated distribution under section 3405, you must first determine whether the distribution is an eligible rollover distribution. See *Direct Rollovers* on page 4 for a discussion of eligible rollover distributions. If the distribution is not an eligible rollover distribution, the rules for periodic payments or nonperiodic distributions apply. For purposes of withholding, distributions from any IRA are not eligible rollover distributions.

Eligible rollover distribution; 20% withholding. If an eligible rollover distribution is paid directly to an eligible retirement plan in a direct rollover, do not withhold federal income tax. If any part of an eligible rollover distribution is not a direct rollover, you must withhold 20% of the part that is paid to the recipient and includible in gross income. This includes the earnings portion of any nonqualified designated Roth account distribution that is not directly rolled over. The recipient cannot claim exemption from the 20% withholding but may ask to have additional amounts withheld on Form W-4P, Withholding Certificate for Pension or Annuity Payments. If the recipient is not asking that additional amounts be withheld, Form W-4P is not required for an eligible rollover distribution because 20% withholding is mandatory.

Employer securities and plan loan offset amounts that are part of an eligible rollover distribution must be included in the amount multiplied by 20%. However, the actual amount to be withheld cannot be more than the sum of the cash and the FMV of property (excluding employer securities and plan loan offset amounts). For example, if the only part of an eligible rollover distribution that is not a direct rollover is employer securities or a plan loan offset amount, no withholding is required. However, any cash that is paid in the distribution must be used to satisfy the withholding on the employer securities or plan loan offset amount.

Depending on the type of plan or arrangement, the payer or, in some cases, the plan administrator is required to withhold 20% of eligible rollover distributions from a qualified plan's distributed annuity and on eligible rollover distributions from a governmental section 457(b) plan. For additional information, see section 3405(d) and Regulations sections 35.3405-1T, A-13; and 31.3405(c)-1, Q/A 4 and 5. For governmental section 457(b) plans only, see Notice 2003-20.

Any NUA excludable from gross income under section 402(e)(4) is not included in the amount of any eligible rollover distribution that is subject to 20% withholding.

You are not required to withhold 20% of an eligible rollover distribution that, when aggregated with other eligible rollover distributions made to one person during the year, is less than $200.

IRAs. The 20% withholding does not apply to distributions from any IRA, but withholding does apply to IRAs under the rules for periodic payments and nonperiodic distributions. For withholding, assume that the entire amount of an IRA distribution is taxable (except for the distribution of contributions under section 408(d)(4), in which only the earnings are taxable, and section 408(d)(5), as applicable). Generally, Roth IRA distributions are not subject to withholding except on the earnings portion of excess contributions distributed under section 408(d)(4).

An IRA recharacterization is not subject to income tax withholding.

Periodic payments. For periodic payments that are not eligible rollover distributions, withhold on the taxable part as though the periodic payments were wages, based on the recipient's Form W-4P. The recipient may request additional withholding on Form W-4P or claim exemption from withholding. If a recipient does not submit a Form W-4P, withhold by treating the recipient as married with three withholding allowances. See Circular E, Employer's Tax Guide (Pub. 15), for wage withholding tables.

 Rather than Form W-4P, military retirees should give you Form W-4, Employee's Withholding Allowance Certificate.

Nonperiodic distributions. Withhold 10% of the taxable part of a nonperiodic distribution that is not an eligible rollover distribution. In most cases, designated distributions from any IRA are treated as nonperiodic distributions subject to withholding at the 10% rate even if the distributions are paid over a periodic basis. See Regulations section 35.3405-1T, Q/A F-15. The recipient may request additional withholding on Form W-4P or claim exemption from withholding.

Failure to provide TIN. For periodic payments and nonperiodic distributions, if a payee fails to furnish his or her correct TIN to you in the manner required, or if the IRS notifies you before any distribution that the TIN furnished is incorrect, a payee cannot claim exemption from withholding. For periodic payments, withhold as if the payee was single claiming no withholding allowances. For nonperiodic payments, withhold 10%. Backup withholding does not apply.

Box 5. Employee contributions/designated Roth contributions or insurance premiums

Enter the employee's contributions, designated Roth contributions, or insurance premiums that the employee may recover tax free this year (even if they exceed the box 1 amount). The entry in box 5 may include any of the following: (a) designated Roth contributions or contributions actually made on behalf of the employee over the years under the plan that were required to be included in the income of the employee when contributed (after-tax contributions), (b) contributions made by the employer but considered to have been contributed by the employee under section 72(f), (c) the accumulated cost of premiums paid for life insurance protection taxable to the employee in previous years and in the current year under Regulations section 1.72-16 (cost of current life insurance protection) (only if the life insurance contract itself is distributed), and (d) premiums paid on commercial annuities. Do not include any DVECs, elective deferrals, or any contribution to a retirement plan that was not an after-tax contribution.

Generally, for qualified plans, section 403(b) plans, and nonqualified commercial annuities, enter in box 5 the employee contributions or insurance premiums recovered tax free during the year based on the method you used to determine the taxable amount to be entered in box 2a. On a separate Form 1099-R, include the portion of the employee's basis that has been distributed from a designated Roth account. See the _Examples_ in the instructions for box 2a on page 10.

If periodic payments began before 1993, you are not required to, but you are encouraged to, report in box 5.

 If you made periodic payments from a qualified plan and the annuity starting date is after November 18, 1996, you must use the simplified method to figure the tax-free amount each year. See Annuity starting date in 1998 or later on page 10.

If a total distribution is made, the total employee contributions or insurance premiums available to be recovered tax free must be shown only in box 5. If any previous distributions were made, any amount recovered tax free in prior years must not appear in box 5.

If you are unable to reasonably obtain the data necessary to compute the taxable amount, leave boxes 2a and 5 blank, and check the first box in box 2b.

For more information, see Rev. Proc. 92-86, 1992-2 C.B. 495 and section 72(d).

For reporting charitable gift annuities, see _Charitable gift annuities_ on page 11.

Box 6. Net unrealized appreciation (NUA) in employer's securities

Use this box if a distribution from a qualified plan (except a qualified distribution from a designated Roth account) includes securities of the employer corporation (or a subsidiary or parent corporation) and you can compute the NUA in the employer's securities. Enter all the NUA in employer securities if this is a lump-sum distribution. If this is not a lump-sum distribution, enter only the NUA in employer securities attributable to employee contributions. See Regulations section 1.402(a)-1(b) for the determination of the NUA. Also see Notice 89-25, Q/A-1, 1989-1 C.B. 662. Include the NUA in box 1 but not in box 2a except in the case of a direct rollover to a Roth IRA (see Notice 2009-75, Q/A 1). You do not have to complete this box for a direct rollover.

Box 7. Distribution code(s)

Enter an "X" in the IRA/SEP/SIMPLE checkbox if the distribution is from a traditional IRA, SEP IRA, or SIMPLE IRA. Do not check the box for a distribution from a Roth IRA or for an IRA recharacterization.

Enter the appropriate code(s) in box 7. Use the _Guide to Distribution Codes_ on pages 15, 16, and 17 to determine the appropriate code(s) to enter in box 7 for any amounts reported on Form 1099-R. Read the codes carefully and enter them accurately because the IRS uses the codes to help determine whether the recipient has properly reported the distribution. If the codes you enter are incorrect, the IRS may improperly propose changes to the recipient's taxes.

When applicable, enter a numeric and an alpha code. For example, when using Code P for a traditional IRA distribution under section 408(d)(4), you must also enter

Code 1, if it applies. For a normal distribution from a qualified plan that qualifies for the 10-year tax option, enter Codes 7 and A. For a direct rollover to an IRA or a qualified plan for the surviving spouse of a deceased participant, or on behalf of a nonspouse designated beneficiary, enter Codes 4 and G (Codes 4 and H if from a designated Roth account to a Roth IRA). If two or more distribution codes are not valid combinations, you must file more than one Form 1099-R.

 Enter a maximum of two alpha/numeric codes in box 7. See the Guide to Distribution Codes *on pages 15, 16, and 17 for allowable combinations. Only three numeric combinations are permitted on one Form 1099-R: Codes 8 and 1, 8 and 2, or 8 and 4. If two or more other numeric codes are applicable, you must file more than one Form 1099-R. For example, if part of a distribution is premature (Code 1) and part is not (Code 7), file one Form 1099-R for the part to which Code 1 applies and another Form 1099-R for the part to which Code 7 applies. In addition, for the distribution of excess deferrals, parts of the distribution may be taxable in 2 different years. File separate Forms 1099-R using Code 8 or P to indicate the year the amount is taxable.*

Even if the employee/taxpayer is age 59¹⁄₂ or over, use Code 1 if a series of substantially equal periodic payments was modified within 5 years of the date of the first payment (within the meaning of section 72(q)(3) or (t)(4)), if you have been reporting distributions in previous years using Code 2.

For example, Mr. B began receiving payments that qualified for the exception for part of a series of substantially equal periodic payments under section 72(t)(2)(A)(iv) when he was 57. When he was 61, Mr. B substantially modified the payments. Because the payments were modified within 5 years, use Code 1 in the year the payments were modified, even though Mr. B is over 59¹⁄₂.

If you do not know that the taxpayer meets the requirements for substantially equal periodic payments under section 72(t)(2)(A)(iv), use Code 1 to report the payments.

 For further guidance on what makes a series of substantially equal periodic payments, see Notice 89-25, Q/A-12, as modified by Rev. Rul. 2002-62, 2002-42 I.R.B. 710. Notice 2004-15, 2004-9 I.R.B. 526, available at www.irs.gov/irb/2004-09_IRB/ar09.html, allows taxpayers to use one of three methods in Notice 89-25, as modified by Rev. Rul. 2002-62, to determine whether a distribution from a nonqualified annuity is part of a series of substantially equal periodic payments under section 72(q)(2)(D).

If part of an eligible rollover distribution is paid in a direct rollover and part is not, you must file a separate Form 1099-R for each part showing the appropriate code on each form. If part of a distribution is an eligible rollover distribution and part is not (for example, a minimum distribution required by section 401(a)(9)) and the part that is an eligible rollover distribution is directly rolled over, you must file a separate Form 1099-R to report each part.

Section 457(b) plan distributions. Generally, a distribution from a governmental section 457(b) plan is not subject to the 10% additional tax under section 72(t). However, an early distribution from a governmental section 457(b) plan of an amount that is attributable to a rollover from another type of eligible retirement plan or IRA is subject to the additional tax as if the distribution were from a plan described in section 401(a). See section 72(t)(9). If the distribution consists solely of amounts that are not attributable to such a rollover, enter Code 2 in box 7. If the distribution consists solely of amounts attributable to such a rollover, then enter the appropriate code in box 7 as if the distribution were from a plan described in section 401(a). If the distribution is made up of amounts from both sources, you must file separate Forms 1099-R for each part of the distribution unless Code 2 would be entered on each form.

Box 8. Other

Enter the current actuarial value of an annuity contract that is part of a lump-sum distribution. Do not include this item in boxes 1 and 2a.

To determine the value of an annuity contract, show the value as an amount equal to the current actuarial value of the annuity contract, reduced by an amount equal to the excess of the employee's contributions over the cash and other property (not including the annuity contract) distributed.

If an annuity contract is part of a multiple recipient lump-sum distribution, enter in box 8, along with the current actuarial value, the percentage of the total annuity contract each Form 1099-R represents.

Also, enter in box 8 the amount of the reduction in the investment (but not below 0 (zero)) against the cash value of an annuity contract or the cash surrender value of a life insurance contract due to charges or payments for qualified long-term care insurance contracts.

Box 9a. Your percentage of total distribution

If this is a total distribution and it is made to more than one person, enter the percentage received by the person whose name appears on Form 1099-R. You need not complete this box for any IRA distributions or for a direct rollover.

Box 9b. Total employee contributions

You are not required to enter the total employee contributions or designated Roth contributions in box 9b. However, because this information may be helpful to the recipient, you may choose to report them.

If you choose to report the total employee contributions or designated Roth contributions, do not include any amounts recovered tax free in prior years. For a total distribution, report the total employee contributions or designated Roth contributions in box 5 rather than in box 9b.

Box 10. Amount allocable to IRR within 5 years

Enter the amount of the distribution allocable to an IRR made within the 5-year period beginning with the first day of the year in which the rollover was made. Do not complete this box if an exception under section 72(t) applies.

For further guidance on determining amounts allocable to an IRR, see Notice 2010-84, Q/A-13.

Box 11. 1st year of desig. Roth contrib.

Enter the first year of the 5-taxable-year period. This is the year in which the designated Roth account was first established by the recipient.

Boxes 12–17. State and local information

These boxes and Copies 1 and 2 are provided for your convenience only and need not be completed for the IRS. Use the state and local information boxes to report distributions and taxes for up to two states or localities. Keep the information for each state or locality separated by the broken line. If state or local income tax has been withheld on this distribution, you may enter it in boxes 12 and 15, as appropriate. In box 13, enter the abbreviated name of the state and the payer's state identification number. The state number is the payer's identification number assigned by the individual state. In box 16, enter the name of the locality. In boxes 14 and 17, you may enter the amount of the state or local distribution. Copy 1 may be used to provide information to the state or local tax department. Copy 2 may be used as the recipient's copy in filing a state or local income tax return.

Guide to Distribution Codes		
Distribution Codes	**Explanations**	***Used with code ...(if applicable)**
1—Early distribution, no known exception.	Use Code 1 only if the employee/taxpayer has not reached age $59\frac{1}{2}$, and you do not know if any of the exceptions under Code 2, 3, or 4 apply. Use Code 1 even if the distribution is made for medical expenses, health insurance premiums, qualified higher education expenses, a first-time home purchase, or a qualified reservist distribution under section 72(t)(2)(B), (D), (E), (F), or (G). Code 1 must also be used even if a taxpayer is $59\frac{1}{2}$ or older and he or she modifies a series of substantially equal periodic payments under section 72(q), (t), or (v) prior to the end of the 5-year period which began with the first payment.	8, B, L, or P
2—Early distribution, exception applies.	Use Code 2 **only if** the employee/taxpayer has not reached age $59\frac{1}{2}$ **and you know** the distribution is: • A Roth IRA conversion (an IRA converted to a Roth IRA). • A distribution made from a qualified retirement plan or IRA because of an IRS levy under section 6331. • A section 457(b) plan distribution that is not subject to the additional 10% tax. But see *Section 457(b) plan distributions* on page 14 for information on distributions that may be subject to the 10% additional tax. • A distribution from a qualified retirement plan after separation from service in or after the year the taxpayer has reached age 55. • A distribution from a governmental defined benefit plan to a public safety employee after separation from service in or after the year the employee has reached age 50. • A distribution that is part of a series of substantially equal periodic payments as described in section 72(q), (t), (u), or (v). • A distribution that is a permissible withdrawal under an eligible automatic contribution arrangement (EACA). • Any other distribution subject to an exception under section 72(q), (t), (u), or (v) that is not required to be reported using Code 1, 3, or 4.	8, B, or P
3—Disability.	For these purposes, see section 72(m)(7).	None
4—Death.	Use Code 4 regardless of the age of the employee/taxpayer to indicate payment to a decedent's beneficiary, including an estate or trust. Also use it for death benefit payments made by an employer but not made as part of a pension, profit-sharing, or retirement plan.	8, A, B, G, H, L, or P
5—Prohibited transaction.	Use Code 5 if there was a prohibited transaction involving the account. Code 5 means the account is no longer an IRA.	None
6—Section 1035 exchange.	Use Code 6 to indicate the tax-free exchange of life insurance, annuity, long-term care insurance, or endowment contracts under section 1035.	W

Guide to Distribution Codes		
Distribution Codes	**Explanations**	***Used with code ...(if applicable)**
7—Normal distribution.	Use Code 7: (a) for a normal distribution from a plan, including a traditional IRA, section 401(k), or section 403(b) plan, if the employee/taxpayer is at least age 59 $^1/_2$, (b) for a Roth IRA conversion if the participant is at least age 59$^1/_2$, and (c) to report a distribution from a life insurance, annuity, or endowment contract and for reporting income from a failed life insurance contract under sections 7702(g) and (h). See Rev. Proc. 2008-42, 2008-29 I.R.B. 160, available at *www.irs.gov/irb/ 2008-29_IRB/ar19.html*. Generally, use Code 7 if no other code applies. Do not use Code 7 for a Roth IRA. **Note:** *Code 1 must be used even if a taxpayer is 59$^1/2$ or older and he or she modifies a series of substantially equal periodic payments under section 72(q), (t), or (v) prior to the end of the 5-year period which began with the first payment.*	A or B
8—Excess contributions plus earnings/excess deferrals (and/or earnings) taxable in 2013.	Use Code 8 for an IRA distribution under section 408(d)(4), unless Code P applies. Also use this code for corrective distributions of excess deferrals, excess contributions, and excess aggregate contributions, unless Code P applies. See *Corrective Distributions* on page 6 and *IRA Revocation or Account Closure* on page 3 for more information.	1, 2, 4, B, or J
9—Cost of current life insurance protection.	Use Code 9 to report premiums paid by a trustee or custodian for current life or other insurance protection. See the instructions for box 2a on page 10 for more information.	None
A—May be eligible for 10-year tax option.	Use Code A only for participants born before January 2, 1936, or their beneficiaries to indicate the distribution may be eligible for the 10-year tax option method of computing the tax on lump-sum distributions (on Form 4972, Tax on Lump-Sum Distributions). To determine whether the distribution may be eligible for the tax option, you need not consider whether the recipient used this method (or capital gain treatment) in the past.	4 or 7
B—Designated Roth account distribution.	Use Code B for a distribution from a designated Roth account. But use Code E for a section 415 distribution under EPCRS (see Code E) or Code H for a direct rollover to a Roth IRA.	1, 2, 4, 7, 8, G, L, P, or U
D—Annuity payments from nonqualified annuities that may be subject to tax under section 1411.	Use Code D for a distribution from any plan or arrangement not described in sections 401(a), 403(a), 403(b), 408, 408A, or 457(b).	None
E—Distributions under Employee Plans Compliance Resolution System (EPCRS).	See *Distributions under Employee Plans Compliance Resolutions System (EPCRS)* on page 7.	None
F—Charitable gift annuity.	See *Charitable gift annuities* on page 11.	None
G—Direct rollover and rollover contribution.	Use Code G for a direct rollover from a qualified plan, section 403(b) plan or a governmental section 457(b) plan to an eligible retirement plan (another qualified plan, a section 403(b) plan, a governmental section 457(b) plan, or an IRA). See *Direct Rollovers* on page 4. Also use Code G for IRA rollover contributions to an accepting employer plan and for IRRs. **Note:** *Do not use Code G for a direct rollover from a designated Roth account to a Roth IRA. Use Code H.*	4 or B
H—Direct rollover of a designated Roth account distribution to a Roth IRA.	Use Code H for a direct rollover of a distribution from a designated Roth account to a Roth IRA.	4
J—Early distribution from a Roth IRA.	Use Code J for a distribution from a Roth IRA when Code Q or Code T does not apply. But use Code 2 for an IRS levy and Code 5 for a prohibited transaction.	8 or P

Guide to Distribution Codes		
Distribution Codes	**Explanations**	***Used with code ...(if applicable)**
L—Loans treated as deemed distributions under section 72(p).	Do not use Code L to report a loan offset. See *Loans Treated as Distributions* on page 8.	1, 4, or B
N—Recharacterized IRA contribution made for 2013.	Use Code N for a recharacterization of an IRA contribution made for 2013 and recharacterized in 2013 to another type of IRA by a trustee-to-trustee transfer or with the same trustee.	None
P—Excess contributions plus earnings/excess deferrals taxable in 2012.	See the explanation for Code 8. The IRS suggests that anyone using Code P for the refund of an IRA contribution under section 408(d)(4), including excess Roth IRA contributions, advise payees, at the time the distribution is made, that the earnings are taxable in the year in which the contributions were made.	1, 2, 4, B, or J
Q—Qualified distribution from a Roth IRA.	Use Code Q for a distribution from a Roth IRA if you know that the participant meets the 5-year holding period and: • The participant has reached age $59^1/2$, • The participant died, or • The participant is disabled. **Note:** *If any other code, such as 8 or P, applies, use Code J.*	None
R—Recharacterized IRA contribution made for 2012.	Use Code R for a recharacterization of an IRA contribution made for 2012 and recharacterized in 2013 to another type of IRA by a trustee-to-trustee transfer or with the same trustee.	None
S—Early distribution from a SIMPLE IRA in the first 2 years, no known exception.	Use Code S only if the distribution is from a SIMPLE IRA in the first 2 years, the employee/taxpayer has not reached age $59^1/2$, and none of the exceptions under section 72(t) are known to apply when the distribution is made. The 2-year period begins on the day contributions are first deposited in the individual's SIMPLE IRA. Do not use Code S if Code 3 or 4 applies.	None
T—Roth IRA distribution, exception applies.	Use Code T for a distribution from a Roth IRA if you do not know if the 5-year holding period has been met but: • The participant has reached age $59^1/2$, • The participant died, or • The participant is disabled. **Note:** *If any other code, such as 8 or P, applies, use Code J.*	None
U—Dividends distributed from an ESOP under section 404(k).	Use Code U for a distribution of dividends from an employee stock ownership plan (ESOP) under section 404(k). These are not eligible rollover distributions. **Note:** Do **not** report dividends paid by the corporation directly to plan participants or their beneficiaries. Continue to report those dividends on Form 1099-DIV.	B
W—Charges or payments for purchasing qualified long-term care insurance contracts under combined arrangements.	Use Code W for charges or payments for purchasing qualified long-term care insurance contracts under combined arrangements which are excludible under section 72(e)(11) against the cash value of an annuity contract or the cash surrender value of a life insurance contract.	6

*See the first **Caution** for box 7 instructions on page 14.

Specific Instructions for Form 5498

File Form 5498, IRA Contribution Information, with the IRS by June 2, 2014, for each person for whom in 2013 you maintained any individual retirement arrangement (IRA), including a deemed IRA under section 408(q).

An IRA includes all investments under one IRA plan. It is not necessary to file a Form 5498 for each investment under one plan. For example, if a participant has three certificates of deposit (CDs) under one IRA plan, only one Form 5498 is required for all contributions and the fair market values (FMVs) of the CDs under the plan. However, if a participant has established more than one IRA plan with the same trustee, a separate Form 5498 must be filed for each plan.

Contributions. You must report contributions to any IRA on Form 5498. See the instructions under boxes 1, 2, 3, 4, 8, 9, 10, 13a, and 14a on pages 21 and 22. If no reportable contributions were made for 2013, complete only boxes 5 and 7, and boxes 11, 12a, and 12b, if applicable.

 You are required to file Form 5498 even if required minimum distributions (RMDs) or other annuity or periodic payments have started.

Report contributions to a spousal IRA under section 219(c) on a separate Form 5498 using the name and taxpayer identification number (TIN) of the spouse.

For contributions made between January 1 and April 15, 2014, trustees and issuers should obtain the participant's designation of the year for which the contributions are made.

Direct rollovers, transfers, and recharacterizations. You must report the receipt of a direct rollover from a qualified plan, section 403(b) plan or governmental section 457(b) plan to an IRA. Report a direct rollover in box 2. For information on direct rollovers of eligible rollover distributions, see *Direct Rollovers* on page 4.

If a rollover or trustee-to-trustee transfer is made from a savings incentive match plan for employees (SIMPLE) IRA to an IRA that is not a SIMPLE IRA and the trustee has adequately substantiated information that the participant has not satisfied the 2-year period specified in section 72(t)(6), report the amount as a regular

Index

To help us develop a more useful index, please let us know if you have ideas for index entries. See "Comments and Suggestions" in the "Introduction" for the ways you can reach us.

9494 ☐ VOID ☐ CORRECTED

TRUSTEE'S/PAYER'S name, street address, city or town, province or state, country, ZIP or foreign postal code, and telephone number			OMB No. 1545-1517	**Distributions From an HSA, Archer MSA, or Medicare Advantage MSA**
			20**13** Form **1099-SA**	
PAYER'S federal identification number	RECIPIENT'S identification number	**1** Gross distribution $	**2** Earnings on excess cont. $	**Copy A** For **Internal Revenue Service Center** **File with Form 1096.**
RECIPIENT'S name		**3** Distribution code	**4** FMV on date of death $	For Privacy Act and Paperwork Reduction Act Notice, see the
Street address (including apt. no.)		**5** HSA ☐ Archer MSA ☐		**2013 General Instructions for Certain Information Returns.**
City or town, province or state, country, and ZIP or foreign postal code		MA MSA ☐		
Account number (see instructions)				

Form **1099-SA** Cat. No. 38471D www.irs.gov/form1099sa Department of the Treasury - Internal Revenue Service

Do Not Cut or Separate Forms on This Page — Do Not Cut or Separate Forms on This Page

Instructions for Recipient

Distributions from a health savings account (HSA), Archer MSA, or Medicare Advantage (MA) MSA are reported to you on Form 1099-SA. File Form 8853 or Form 8889 with your Form 1040 to report a distribution from these accounts even if the distribution is not taxable. The payer is not required to compute the taxable amount of any distribution.

An HSA or Archer MSA distribution is not taxable if you used it to pay qualified medical expenses of the account holder and family or you rolled it over. An HSA may be rolled over to another HSA; an Archer MSA may be rolled over to another Archer MSA or an HSA. An MA MSA is not taxable if you used it to pay qualified medical expenses of the account holder only. If you did not use the distribution from an HSA, Archer MSA, or MA MSA to pay for qualified medical expenses, or in the case of an HSA or Archer MSA, you did not roll it over, you must include the distribution in your income (see Form 8853 or Form 8889). Also, you may owe a penalty.

For more information, see the separate instructions for Form 8853 and Form 8889. Also see Pub. 969.

Spouse beneficiary. If you inherited an Archer MSA or MA MSA because of the death of your spouse, special rules apply. See the Instructions for Form 8853. If you inherited an HSA because of the death of your spouse, see the Instructions for Form 8889.

Estate beneficiary. If the HSA, Archer MSA, or MA MSA account holder dies and the estate is the beneficiary, the fair market value (FMV) of the account on the date of death is includible in the account holder's gross income. Report the amount on the account holder's final income tax return.

Nonspouse beneficiary. If you inherited the HSA, Archer MSA, or MA MSA from someone who was not your spouse, you must report as income on your tax return the FMV of the account as of the date of death. Report the FMV on your tax return for the year the account owner died even if you received the distribution from the account in a later year. See the instructions for Form 8853

or Form 8889. Any earnings on the account after the date of death (box 1 minus box 4 of Form 1099-SA) are taxable. Include the earnings on the "Other income" line of your tax return.

Account number. May show an account or other unique number the payer assigned to distinguish your account.

Box 1. Shows the amount received this year. The amount may have been a direct payment to the medical service provider or distributed to you.

Box 2. Shows the earnings on any excess contributions you withdrew from an HSA or Archer MSA by the due date of your income tax return. If you withdrew the excess, plus any earnings, by the due date of your income tax return, you must include the earnings in your income in the year you received the distribution even if you used it to pay qualified medical expenses. This amount is included in box 1. Include the earnings on the "Other income" line of your tax return. An excise tax of 6% for each tax year is imposed on you for excess individual and employer contributions that remain in the account. See Form 5329, Additional Taxes on Qualified Plans (Including IRAs) and Other Tax-Favored Accounts.

Box 3. These codes identify the distribution you received: 1—Normal distribution; 2—Excess contributions; 3—Disability; 4—Death distribution other than code 6; 5—Prohibited transaction; 6—Death distribution after year of death to a nonspouse beneficiary.

Box 4. If the account holder died, shows the FMV of the account on the date of death.

Box 5. Shows the type of account that is reported on this Form 1099-SA.

Future developments. For the latest information about developments related to Form 1099-SA, such as legislation enacted after this form and instruction were published, go to *www.irs.gov/form1099sa*.

Instructions for Trustee/Payer

General and specific form instructions are provided separately. You should use the 2013 General Instructions for Certain Information Returns and the 2013 Instructions for Forms 1099-SA and 5498-SA to complete Form 1099-SA. A chart in the general instructions gives a quick guide to which form must be filed to report a particular payment. To order these instructions and additional forms, go to *www.irs.gov/form1099sa* or call 1-800-TAX-FORM (1-800-829-3676).

Caution: *Because paper forms are scanned during processing, you cannot file Forms 1096, 1097, 1098, 1099, 3921, 3922, or 5498 that you print from the IRS website.*

Due dates. Furnish Copy B of this form to the recipient by January 31, 2014.

File Copy A of this form with the IRS by February 28, 2014. If you file electronically, the due date is March 31, 2014. To file electronically, you must have software that generates a file according to the specifications in Pub. 1220, Specifications for Filing Forms 1097, 1098, 1099, 3921, 3922, 5498, 8935, and W-2G Electronically. The IRS does not provide a fill-in form option.

Need help? If you have questions about reporting on Form 1099-SA, call the information reporting customer service site toll free at 1-866-455-7438 or 304-263-8700 (not toll free). Persons with a hearing or speech disability with access to TTY/TDD equipment can call 304-579-4827 (not toll free). The hours of operation are Monday through Friday from 8:30 a.m. to 4:30 p.m., Eastern time.

20**13**

Instructions for Forms 1099-SA and 5498-SA

Department of the Treasury
Internal Revenue Service

Distributions From an HSA, Archer MSA, or Medicare Advantage MSA, and HSA, Archer MSA, or Medicare Advantage MSA Information

Section references are to the Internal Revenue Code unless otherwise noted.

Future Developments

For the latest information about developments related to Forms 1099–SA and 5498–SA and their instructions, such as legislation enacted after they were published, go to *www.irs.gov/form1099sa* and *www.irs.gov/form5498sa*.

What's New

Pilot program for truncating an individual's identifying number on paper payee statements has ended. Filers of Form 1099-H must show the recipient's complete identifying number on all copies of the form.

Reminder

General instructions. In addition to these specific instructions, you should also use the 2013 General Instructions for Certain Information Returns. Those general instructions include information about the following topics.
* Backup withholding.
* Electronic reporting requirements.
* Penalties.
* Who must file (nominee/middleman).
* When and where to file.
* Taxpayer identification numbers.
* Statements to recipients.
* Corrected and void returns.
* Other general topics.

   You can get the general instructions from *www.irs.gov/form1099sa*, *www.irs.gov/form5498sa*, or by calling 1-800-TAX-FORM (1-800-829-3676).

Specific Instructions for Form 1099-SA

File Form 1099-SA, Distributions From an HSA, Archer MSA, or Medicare Advantage MSA, to report distributions made from an HSA, Archer MSA, or Medicare Advantage MSA (MA MSA). The distribution may have been paid directly to a medical service provider or to the account holder. A separate return must be filed for each plan type.

Transfers. Do not report a trustee-to-trustee transfer from one Archer MSA or MA MSA to another Archer MSA or MA MSA, one Archer MSA to an HSA, or from one HSA to another HSA. For reporting purposes, contributions and rollovers do not include transfers.

HSA mistaken distributions. If amounts were distributed during the year from an HSA because of a mistake of fact due to reasonable cause, the account beneficiary may repay the mistaken distribution no later than April 15 following the first year the account beneficiary knew or should have known the distribution was a mistake. For example, the account beneficiary reasonably, but mistakenly, believed that an expense was a qualified medical expense and was reimbursed for that expense from the HSA. The account beneficiary then repays the mistaken distribution to the HSA.

   Under these circumstances, the distribution is not included in gross income, is not subject to the additional 20% tax, and the payment is not subject to the excise tax on excess contributions. Do not treat the repayment as a contribution on Form 5498-SA.

TIP *As the trustee or custodian, you do not have to allow beneficiaries to return a mistaken distribution to the HSA. However, if you do allow the return of the mistaken distribution, you may rely on the account beneficiary's statement that the distribution was in fact a mistake. See Notice 2004-50, 2004-33 I.R.B. 196, Q/A-76, available at www.irs.gov/irb/2004-33_IRB/ar08.html. Do not report the mistaken distribution on Form 1099-SA. Correct any filed Form 1099-SA with the IRS and the account beneficiary as soon as you become aware of the error. See Corrected Returns on Paper Forms in the 2013 General Instructions for Certain Information Returns for more information.*

Death of Account Holder

Archer MSAs and MA MSAs. When the account holder dies and the designated beneficiary is the spouse:
* The spouse becomes the account holder of the Archer MSA,
* An MA MSA is treated as an Archer MSA of the spouse for distribution purposes, and
* Distributions from these accounts are subject to the rules that apply to Archer MSAs.

   If the designated beneficiary is not the spouse or there is no named beneficiary, the account ceases to be an MSA as of the date of death and the fair market value (FMV) on that date is reported.

   If there is more than one recipient, the FMV should be allocated among them, as appropriate.

   If the beneficiary is the estate, enter the estate's name and taxpayer identification number (TIN) in place of the recipient's on the form.

   Distribution in year of death. If you learn of the account holder's death and make a distribution to the beneficiary in the year of death, issue a Form 1099-SA and enter in:
* Box 1, the gross distribution;
* Box 3, code 4 (see page 2); and
* Box 4, the FMV of the account on the date of death.

   Distribution after year of death. If you learn of the death of the account holder and make a distribution after the year of death, issue a Form 1099-SA in the year you learned of the death of the account holder. Enter in:
* Box 1, the gross distribution;
* Box 3, one of the following codes (see page 2):
   1—if the beneficiary is the spouse,
   4—if the beneficiary is the estate, or
   6—if the beneficiary is not the spouse or estate;
* Box 4, the FMV of the account on the date of death.

HSAs. When the account holder dies and:
* The designated beneficiary is the surviving spouse, the spouse becomes the account holder of the HSA.
* The spouse is not the designated beneficiary, the account ceases to be an HSA on the date of the account holder's death. The FMV of the account as of the date of death is required to be reported in

box 4. Follow the rules and coding above under *Distribution in year of death* and *Distribution after year of death*.

Statements to Recipients

If you are required to file Form 1099-SA, you must provide a statement to the recipient. For more information about the requirement to furnish a Form 1099-SA or acceptable substitute statement to recipients, see part M in the 2013 General Instructions for Certain Information Returns.

Account Number

The account number is required if you have multiple accounts for a recipient for whom you are filing more than one Form 1099-SA. Additionally, the IRS encourages you to designate an account number for all Forms 1099-SA that you file. See part L in the 2013 General Instructions for Certain Information Returns.

Box 1. Gross Distribution

Enter the total amount of the distribution. Include any earnings separately reported in box 2. You are not required to determine the taxable amount of a distribution. Do not report a negative amount in box 1. Do not report the withdrawal of excess employer contributions (and the earnings on them) returned to an employer as a distribution from an employee's HSA. Do not report excess MA MSA contributions returned to the Secretary of Health and Human Services or his or her representative.

Box 2. Earnings on Excess Contributions

Enter the total earnings distributed with any excess HSA or Archer MSA contributions returned by the due date of the account holder's tax return. Include this amount in box 1. Report earnings on other distributions only in box 1.

 For HSAs and Archer MSAs, if you are reporting earnings on a distribution of excess contributions, use the method under Regulations section 1.408-11 for calculating the net income attributable to IRA contributions that are distributed as a returned contribution. If the amount in box 2 includes earnings on excess contributions, enter distribution code 2 in box 3.

Box 3. Distribution Code

Enter the appropriate distribution code from the list below that shows the type of distribution.

1—Normal distributions	Use this code for normal distributions to the account holder and any direct payments to a medical service provider. Use this code if no other code applies. Also, see *Distribution after year of death* on page 1.
2—Excess contributions	Use this code for distributions of excess HSA or Archer MSA contributions to the account holder.
3—Disability	Use this code if you made distributions after the account holder was disabled (see section 72(m)(7)).
4—Death distribution other than code 6	Use this code for payments to a decedent's estate in the year of death. Also use this code for payments to an estate after the year of death. Do not use with code 6. See *Death of Account Holder* on page 1.

5—Prohibited transaction	See sections 220(e)(2) and 223(e)(2).
6—Death distribution after year of death to a nonspouse beneficiary	Use this code for payments to a decedent's nonspouse beneficiary, other than an estate, after the year of death. Do not use with code 4.

Box 4. FMV on Date of Death

Enter the FMV of the account on the date of death. See *Death of Account Holder* on page 1.

Box 5. Checkbox

Check the box to indicate if this distribution was from an HSA, Archer MSA, or MA MSA.

Specific Instructions for Form 5498-SA

File Form 5498-SA, HSA, Archer MSA, or Medicare Advantage MSA Information, with the IRS on or before June 2, 2014, for each person for whom you maintained an HSA, Archer MSA, or Medicare Advantage MSA (MA MSA) during 2013. You are required to file if you are the trustee or custodian of an HSA, Archer MSA, or MA MSA. A separate form is required for each type of plan.

For HSA or Archer MSA contributions made between January 1, 2014, and April 15, 2014, you should obtain the participant's designation of the year for which the contributions are made.

For repayment of a mistaken distribution amount, see *HSA mistaken distributions* on page 1.

Rollovers

You must report the receipt of a rollover from one Archer MSA to another Archer MSA, and receipt of a rollover from an Archer MSA or an HSA to an HSA in box 4.

Transfers

Do not report a trustee-to-trustee transfer from one Archer MSA or MA MSA to another Archer MSA or MA MSA, from an Archer MSA to an HSA, or from one HSA to another HSA. For reporting purposes, contributions and rollovers do not include these transfers. However, see box 2 on this page for the reporting of a trustee-to-trustee transfer from an IRA to an HSA.

Total Distribution, No Contributions

Generally, if a total distribution was made from an HSA or Archer MSA during the year and no contributions were made for that year, you need not file Form 5498-SA nor furnish a statement to the participant to reflect that the FMV on December 31 was zero.

Death of Account Holder

In the year an HSA, Archer MSA, or MA MSA owner dies, generally you must file a Form 5498-SA and furnish a statement for the decedent. If the designated beneficiary is the spouse:
- The spouse becomes the account holder of the HSA or Archer MSA.
- An MA MSA is treated as an Archer MSA of the spouse for distribution purposes, but no new contributions may be made to the account.

If the designated beneficiary is not the spouse or there is no designated beneficiary, the account ceases to be an HSA, Archer MSA, or MA MSA.

Statements to Participants

If you are required to file Form 5498-SA, you must provide a statement to the participant (generally Copy B) by June 2, 2014. You may, but you are not required to, provide participants with a statement of the December 31, 2013, FMV of the participant's account by January 31, 2014. For more information about statements to participants, see part M in the 2013 General Instructions for Certain Information Returns.

If you furnished a statement of the FMV of the account to the participant by January 31, 2014, and no reportable contributions, including rollovers, were made for 2013, you need not furnish another statement (or Form 5498-SA) to the participant to report zero contributions. However, you must file Form 5498-SA with the IRS by June 2, 2014, to report the December 31, 2013, FMV of the account.

 If you do not furnish another statement to the participant because no reportable contributions were made for the year, the statement of the FMV of the account must contain a legend designating which information is being furnished to the Internal Revenue Service.

Account Number

The account number is required if you have multiple accounts for a recipient for whom you are filing more than one Form 5498-SA. Additionally, the IRS encourages you to designate an account number for all Forms 5498-SA that you file. See part L in the 2013 General Instructions for Certain Information Returns.

Box 1. Employee or Self-Employed Person's Archer MSA Contributions Made in 2013 and 2014 for 2013

Enter the employee's or self-employed person's regular contributions to the Archer MSA made in 2013 and through April 15, 2014, for 2013. Report gross contributions, including any excess contributions, even if the excess contributions were withdrawn. No HSA information is to be reported in box 1.

Box 2. Total Contributions Made in 2013

Enter the total HSA or Archer MSA contributions made in 2013. Include any contribution made in 2013 for 2012. Also include qualified HSA funding distributions (trustee-to-trustee transfers from an IRA to an HSA under section 408(d)(9)) received by you during 2013. Any excess employer contributions (and the earnings on them) withdrawn by the employer pursuant to Notice 2008-59, Q/A 24, available at *www.irs.gov/irb/2008-29_IRB/ar11.html*, should not be reported as a contribution. You may, but you are not required to, report the total MA MSA contributions the Secretary of Health and Human Services or his or her representative made in 2013. Do not include amounts reported in box 4.

Box 3. Total HSA or Archer MSA Contributions Made in 2014 for 2013

Enter the total HSA or Archer MSA contributions made in 2014 for 2013.

Box 4. Rollover Contributions

Enter rollover contributions to the HSA or Archer MSA received by you during 2013. These amounts are not to be included in box 2.

Box 5. Fair Market Value of HSA, Archer MSA, or MA MSA

Enter the FMV of the account on December 31, 2013.

Box 6. Checkbox

Check the box to indicate if this account is an HSA, Archer MSA, or MA MSA.

Form **2032**

(Rev. November 2010)

Department of the Treasury
Internal Revenue Service

Contract Coverage Under Title II
of the Social Security Act

For use by an American employer to extend social security coverage to
U.S. citizens and resident aliens employed by its foreign affiliates.

OMB No. 1545-0137

**File three copies
of this form**

Name of American employer	Employer identification number

Address number and street (P.O. Box if no mail delivery to street address)	Apt. or suite no.

City, state, and ZIP code

This Form 2032 is filed as (check applicable box(es)):

1 ☐ An original (new) agreement.

This agreement is effective for services performed on and after (for original agreements only, check one):

a ☐ The first day of the calendar quarter in which the submission processing field director signs this agreement.

b ☐ The first day of the calendar quarter following the calendar quarter in which the submission processing field director signs this agreement.

2 ☐ An amendment to an agreement previously entered into.

3 ☐ An election to apply the rules in effect after April 20, 1983, to agreements in effect on that date. By making this election, U.S. resident aliens as well as U.S. citizens will be covered by social security.

If this is an amended election or agreement, provide the following information:

on

(Location where previous Form 2032 was filed)   (Date submission processing field director signed original agreement on Form 2032)

4 This agreement extends the federal insurance system under Title II of the Social Security Act to certain services performed outside the United States by U.S. citizens and resident aliens employed by any of the foreign affiliates listed below. If you checked the box on line 2 and did not check the box on line 3 above, this amendment extends Title II social security coverage to certain services performed outside the United States by U.S. citizens employed by any of the foreign affiliates listed below.

Note. Enter foreign affiliate addresses below in the following order: city, province or state, and country. Do not abbreviate the country name, and follow the country's practice for entering the postal code. If this agreement includes more than four foreign affiliates, attach a separate sheet of paper identified as part of this agreement with the name and address of each additional foreign affiliate.

a Name and address of foreign affiliate	**c** Name and address of foreign affiliate
b Name and address of foreign affiliate	**d** Name and address of foreign affiliate

5 Estimated number of employees to be initially covered by this agreement, amendment, or election:
Nonagricultural employees ▶   Agricultural employees ▶

This agreement applies to all services performed outside the United States by each U.S. citizen or resident alien employed by any of the foreign affiliates named above. However, the agreement applies only to the extent that payments to each employee for the services would be considered wages if paid by the employer for services performed in the United States. This agreement does not apply to any service that is considered employment for purposes of the employee tax and the employer tax under the Federal Insurance Contributions Act.

For an original agreement, an amendment to an agreement that was entered into after April 20, 1983, or an election to apply the rules in effect after April 20, 1983, to agreements in effect on that date, the American employer declares that it owns at least a 10% interest (directly or through one or more entities) in the voting stock or profits of each foreign entity named above. It also declares that section 3121(l) does not prevent this agreement.

For an amendment to an agreement in effect on April 20, 1983, without making the election to apply the new rules in effect after that date, the domestic corporation declares that **(a)** it owns at least 20% of the voting stock of each foreign corporation named above, or **(b)** it owns at least 20% of the voting stock of a foreign corporation that owns more than 50% of the voting stock of each foreign corporation named above. It also declares that section 3121(l) does not prevent this agreement.

The American employer agrees:

1. To pay amounts equal to the taxes that would be imposed by sections 3101 and 3111 if the payment for the services was considered wages;

2. To pay, on written notification and demand, amounts equal to the interest, additions to taxes, and penalties that would apply if the payment for the services were considered wages; and

3. To comply with the applicable regulations under section 3121(l).

This agreement (or amended agreement or election) is entered into under the provisions of section 3121(l) of the Internal Revenue Code and the applicable regulations.

Signature of individual authorized to enter into this agreement for the American employer	Title	Date

Field Director, Submission Processing	Location	Date

For Privacy Act and Paperwork Reduction Act Notice, see back of form.   Cat. No. 49954D   Form **2032** (Rev. 11-2010)

General Instructions

Section references are to the Internal Revenue Code.

Before April 21, 1983, only domestic corporations could enter into this agreement to cover only U.S. citizens employed by foreign subsidiaries. For this agreement, a foreign subsidiary was defined as a foreign corporation in which:

• at least 20% of the voting stock was owned by the domestic corporation, or

• more than 50% of the voting stock was owned by another foreign corporation in which the domestic corporation owned at least 20% of the voting stock.

After April 20, 1983, any American employer (no longer limited to a domestic corporation) can enter into this agreement to cover U.S. resident aliens as well as U.S. citizens employed by a foreign affiliate. For this agreement, a foreign affiliate is any foreign entity (no longer limited to a foreign corporation) in which the American employer owns at least a 10% interest in the voting stock or profits. This interest must be owned directly or through one or more entities.

A domestic corporation having an agreement in effect that was entered into before April 21, 1983, can elect to apply the post-April 20,1983 rules to such agreements. If a domestic corporation makes this election, social security coverage will be extended to U.S. resident alien employees of any foreign subsidiary for which U.S. citizens are currently covered by an existing agreement. In addition, the election allows a domestic corporation to extend social security and Medicare coverage to U.S. citizens and resident aliens employed by a foreign entity that did not qualify for coverage under the old 20% ownership rules, but that now qualifies under the 10% ownership rules.

Note. The United States has social security (totalization) agreements with specific countries. These agreements ensure that social security taxes are paid to only one country. However, these agreements may affect the withholding requirements resulting from filing Form 2032. For more information, see Social Security and Medicare Taxes in Pub. 54, Tax Guide for U.S. Citizens and Resident Aliens Abroad.

Purpose of form. An American employer uses this form to:

• Enter into the agreement specified in 3121(l) to extend coverage under Title II of the Social Security Act to U.S. citizens and resident aliens abroad by foreign affiliates,

• Amend a previous agreement, or

• Elect to apply the rules in effect after April 20, 1983, to agreements in effect on that date.

For this agreement, an American employer is an employer that is:

• The United States or any instrumentality thereof,

• An individual who is a resident of the United States,

• A partnership if two-thirds or more of the partners are residents of the United States,

• A trust if all the trustees are residents of the United States, or

• A corporation organized under the laws of the United States or of any state.

Where To File

Send three copies of this form to:
   Internal Revenue Service
   Ogden, UT 84201-0023

An American employer already filing Form 941, Employer's Quarterly Federal Tax Return, should file Form 2032 with the Internal Revenue Service where the employer files Form 941 (generally their principal place of business). For electronic Form 941 filers, send Form 2032 to Internal Revenue Service, Cincinnati, OH 45999-0038. Enter on Form 2032 the employer identification number (EIN) as shown on Form 941. This will help the IRS process your form faster.

Completing Form 2032

Complete Form 2032 in triplicate. Each copy of the form must be signed and dated by the individual authorized to enter into the agreement, amendment, or election. Attach to each form evidence showing the authority for such individual to sign the form. For example, corporations must include a certified copy of the minutes of the board of directors' meeting.

After the director signs and dates the form, it constitutes the agreement, amendment, or election authorized by section 3121(l). The IRS will return one copy of Form 2032 to the American employer, send one copy to the Social Security Administration, and keep one copy with all related papers.

Original agreements. Check the box on line 1. Also check the applicable box on line 1a or b to designate when the agreement will take effect.

Amending agreements. You may amend an agreement at any time to extend coverage to any foreign affiliate not covered by an existing agreement. File Form 2032 in triplicate, and check the box on line 2. If you amend an agreement entered into on or before April 20, 1983, without making the election to apply the rules in effect after that date, the agreement and amendments will continue to be governed by the rules in effect before April 21, 1983.

Effective date. If you file an amendment to an agreement on Form 2032 to include foreign affiliates not previously covered, and if the field director signs the amendment during the quarter for which the original agreement is first effective or during the first month following that quarter, the amendment will be effective as of the effective date of the original agreement. But if the amendment is signed by the field director after the end of the 4th month for which the original agreement is in effect, the amendment will not be effective until the first day of the quarter following the one in which the field director signed the amendment.

Election to apply post-April 20, 1983 rules. A domestic corporation having an agreement in effect that was entered into before April 21, 1983 (old agreement), may elect to have the rules in effect after April 20, 1983, apply to the old agreement. File Form 2032 in triplicate, and check the box on line 3.

If you make this election, it will be effective for all foreign entities covered by the agreement. By making the election, U.S. resident alien employees as well as U.S. citizen employees will be covered by the agreement.

To extend coverage to any foreign affiliate not covered by an agreement, indicate the name and address of the foreign affiliate on line 4 and check the box on line 2 for the amended agreement, and the box on line 3 for the election.

Effective date. Generally, the election will be effective on the day following the quarter in which the election is signed by the field director.

No Termination of Agreement

Once you enter into an agreement, you cannot terminate it, either in its entirety or with respect to any foreign affiliate. However, the agreement will terminate for a foreign entity at the end of any quarter in which the foreign entity, at any time in that quarter, ceased to be your foreign affiliate.

Privacy Act and Paperwork Reduction Act Notice. We ask for the information on this form to carry out the Internal Revenue laws of the United States. We need it to figure and collect the right amount of tax. Section 6109 requires you to provide your taxpayer identification number (SSN or EIN). Section 3121 of the Internal Revenue Code allows employees of foreign affiliates to be covered under social security. Routine uses of this information include giving it to the Social Security Administration for use in calculating social security benefits, the Department of Justice for civil and criminal litigation, and cities, states, and the District of Columbia for use in administering their tax laws. We may also disclose this information to federal and state agencies to enforce federal nontax criminal laws and to combat terrorism. We may also give the information to foreign countries under tax treaties. If you want this coverage, you are required to give us this information. If you fail to provide this information in a timely manner, or you provide incorrect or fraudulent information, you may be denied this coverage and you may be liable for penalties and interest.

You are not required to provide the information requested on a form that is subject to the Paperwork Reduction Act unless the form displays a valid OMB control number. Books or records relating to a form or its instructions must be retained as long as their contents may become material in the administration of any Internal Revenue law. Generally, tax returns and return information are confidential, as required by section 6103.

The time needed to complete and file this form will vary depending on individual circumstances. The estimated average time is: **Recordkeeping,** 4 hr., 46 min.; **Learning about the law or the form,** 35 min.; **Preparing and sending the form to the IRS,** 42 min. If you have comments concerning the accuracy of these time estimates or suggestions for making this form simpler, we would be happy to hear from you. You can write to: Internal Revenue Service, Tax Products Coordinating Committee, SE:W:CAR:MP:T:T:SP, 1111 Constitution Ave. NW, IR-6526, Washington, DC 20224. Do not send Form 2032 to this address. Instead, see *Where To File* above.

Form **2159**
(Rev. January 2007)

Department of the Treasury — **Internal Revenue Service**
Payroll Deduction Agreement
(See Instructions on the back of this page.)

TO: *(Employer name and address)*

Regarding: *(Taxpayer name and address)*

Contact Person's Name   Telephone *(Include area code)*

Social security or employer identification number
(Taxpayer)   *(Spouse)*

EMPLOYER—*See the instructions on the back of Part 2.* The taxpayer identified above on the right named you as an employer. Please read and sign the following statement to agree to withhold amount*(s)* from the taxpayer's *(employee's)* wages or salary to apply to taxes owed.

I agree to participate in this payroll deduction agreement and will withhold the amount shown below from each wage or salary payment due this employee. I will send the money to the Internal Revenue Service every: *(Check one box.)*

☐ WEEK ☐ TWO WEEKS ☐ MONTH ☐ OTHER *(Specify.)* _____

Signed: _____

Title: _____ Date: _____

Your telephone number *(Include area code)*
(Home)   *(Work or business)*

For assistance, call: **1-800-829-0115** *(Business)* or
1-800-829-8374 *(Individual – Self-Employed/Business Owners)*, or
1-800-829-0922 *(Individuals – Wage Earners)*

Or write: _____ **Campus**
            (City, State, and ZIP Code)

Financial Institution*(s)* *(Name and address)*

Kinds of taxes *(Form numbers)*	Tax Periods	Amount owed as of _____
		$ _____ , plus all penalties and interest provided by law.

I am paid every: *(Check one):* ☐ WEEK ☐ TWO WEEKS ☐ MONTH ☐ OTHER *(Specify.)* _____

I agree to have $_____ deducted from my wage or salary payment beginning _____ until the total liability is paid in full. I also agree and authorize this deduction to be increased or decreased as follows:

Date of increase *(or decrease)*	Amount of Increase *(or decrease)*	New installment payment amount

Terms of this agreement—By completing and submitting this agreement, you *(the taxpayer)* agree to the following terms:

- You will make each payment so that we *(IRS)* receive it by the monthly due date stated on the front of this form. **If you cannot make a scheduled payment, contact us immediately.**
- This agreement is based on your current financial condition. We may modify or terminate the agreement if our information shows that your ability to pay has significantly changed. You must provide updated financial information when requested.
- While this agreement is in effect, you must file all federal tax returns and pay any *(federal)* taxes you owe on time.
- We will apply your federal tax refunds or overpayments *(if any)* to the amount you owe until it is fully paid.
- You must pay a $105 user fee, which we have authority to deduct from your first payment*(s)*.
- If you default on your installment agreement, you must pay a $45 reinstatement fee if we reinstate the agreement. We have the

- authority to deduct this fee from your first payment*(s)* after the agreement is reinstated.
- We will apply all payments on this agreement in the best interests of the United States.
- **We can terminate your installment agreement if:**
  - You do not make monthly installment payments as agreed.
  - You do not pay any other federal tax debt when due.
  - You do not provide financial information when requested.
- If we terminate your agreement, we may collect the entire amount you owe by levy on your income, bank accounts or other assets, or by seizing your property.
- We may terminate this agreement at any time if we find that collection of the tax is in jeopardy.
- This agreement may require managerial approval. We'll notify you when we approve or don't approve the agreement.

Additional Terms *(To be completed by IRS)*

Note: Internal Revenue Service employees may contact third parties in order to process and maintain this agreement.

Your signature	Title *(If Corporate Officer or Partner)*	Date
Spouse's signature *(If a joint liability)*		Date
Agreement examined or approved by *(Signature, title, function)*		Date

FOR IRS USE ONLY

FOR IRS USE ONLY:

AGREEMENT LOCATOR NUMBER: ___ ___ ___ ___
Check the appropriate boxes:
☐ RSI "1" no further review
☐ RSI "5" PPIA IMF 2 year review
☐ RSI "6" PPIA BMF 2 year review
Agreement Review Cycle: __ __ __ __ __ __
Earliest CSED: _____
☐ Check box if pre-assessed modules included

☐ AI "0" Not a PPIA
☐ AI "1" Field Asset PPIA
☐ AI "2" All other PPIAs

Originator's ID #: _____ Originator Code: _____
Name: _____ Title: _____

A NOTICE OF FEDERAL TAX LIEN *(Check one box.)*
☐ **HAS ALREADY BEEN FILED**
☐ **WILL BE FILED IMMEDIATELY**
☐ **WILL BE FILED WHEN TAX IS ASSESSED**
☐ **MAY BE FILED IF THIS AGREEMENT DEFAULTS**

Part 1— Acknowledgement Copy *(Return to IRS)*   Catalog No. 21475H   www.irs.gov   Form **2159** (Rev. 1-2007)

Reset Form Fields

Agreement Locator Number Designations

XX Position *(the first two numbers)* **denotes either the Initiator or Type of Agreement. The XX values are:**

00	Form 433-D initiated by AO on an ACS case
01	Service Center and Toll-free initiated agreements
02	AO Field Territory *(revenue officer)* initiated agreements
03	Direct Debit agreements initiated by any function
06	Exam initiated agreements
07	Submission Processing initiated agreements
08	Agreements initiated by other functions
11	Form 2159 agreement initiated by AO or ACS
12	AO or ACS agreement with multiple conditions
20	Status 22/24 accounts – Call Site/SCCB
90	SCCB initiated agreements – other than status 22 or 26
91	Form 2159 agreement initiated by SCCB
92	SCCB agreement with multiple conditions
99	Up to 120 days extensions

YY Position (the second two numbers) denotes Conditions Affecting the Agreement. The YY values are:

08	Continuous Wage Levy *(from ACS and RO)*
09	All other conditions
12	One year rule *(use for specific BAL DUE module agreements)*
15	In Business Trust Fund *(IBTF)* monitoring required
27	Restricted Interest/Penalty condition present
32	Unassessed modules to be included in agreement
36	Streamlined agreements, less than 60 months, up to $25,000
41	BMF in Business Deferral Level *(SCCB USE ONLY)*
53	*Report Currently Not Collectible (CNC)* if agreement defaults
63	Cross-reference TIN *(Status 63)*
66	File lien in event of default
70	Secondary TP responsible for Joint Liability
80	Review and revise payment amount
99	Up to 120 days extensions

When an agreement has more than one condition, use either 12 or 92 in the "XX" position and assign the primary condition *(YY)* based on the following priorities:

#1-53, #2-08, #3-27, or #4-15

The remaining multiple conditions will be input as a history item on IDRS by SCCB. For example, to construct a history item to record an unassessed module, use the following format:

UM309312 *(Unassessed module, MFT 30, 9312 Tax Period);* or
UMFILE LIEN *(Unassessed module, file Lien, if appropriate)*

Installment Agreement Originator Codes

20	Collection field function regular agreement
21	Collection field function streamlined agreement
30	Reserved
31	Reserved
50	Field assistance regular agreement
51	Field assistance streamlined agreement
58	Field Assistance ICS – regular agreement
59	Field Assistance ICS – streamlined agreement
60	Examination regular agreement
61	Examination streamlined agreement
70	Toll-free regular agreement
71	Toll-free streamlined agreement
72	Paper regular agreement
73	Paper streamlined agreement
74	Voice Response Unit (system generated)
75	Automated Collection Branch regular
76	Automated Collection Branch streamlined
77	Automated Collection Branch Voice Response Unit regular *(system generated)*
78	Automated Collection Branch Voice Response Unit streamlined *(system generated)*
80	Other function regular agreement
81	Other function-streamlined agreement
90-91	Reserved for vendors – all streamlined agreements

Form **2159**
(Rev. January 2007)

Department of the Treasury — **Internal Revenue Service**

Payroll Deduction Agreement

(See Instructions on the back of this page.)

TO: *(Employer name and address)*

Regarding: *(Taxpayer name and address)*

Contact Person's Name | Telephone *(Include area code)*

Social security or employer identification number
(Taxpayer)   *(Spouse)*

EMPLOYER—*See the instructions on the back of Part 2.* The taxpayer identified above on the right named you as an employer. Please read and sign the following statement to agree to withhold amount*(s)* from the taxpayer's *(employee's)* wages or salary to apply to taxes owed.

I agree to participate in this payroll deduction agreement and will withhold the amount shown below from each wage or salary payment due this employee. I will send the money to the Internal Revenue Service every: *(Check one box.)*

☐ WEEK ☐ TWO WEEKS ☐ MONTH ☐ OTHER *(Specify.)* _____

Signed: _____

Title: _____ Date: _____

Your telephone number *(Include area code)*
(Home)   *(Work or business)*

For assistance, call: **1-800-829-0115** *(Business)* or
1-800-829-8374 *(Individual – Self-Employed/Business Owners),* or
1-800-829-0922 *(Individuals – Wage Earners)*

Or write: _____ **Campus**
            (City, State, and ZIP Code)

Financial Institution*(s)* *(Name and address)*

Kinds of taxes *(Form numbers)*	Tax Periods	Amount owed as of _____

$ _____ , plus all penalties and interest provided by law.

I am paid every: *(Check one)*: ☐ WEEK ☐ TWO WEEKS ☐ MONTH ☐ OTHER *(Specify.)* _____

I agree to have $_____ deducted from my wage or salary payment beginning _____ until the total liability is paid in full. I also agree and authorize this deduction to be increased or decreased as follows: _____

Date of increase *(or decrease)*	Amount of Increase *(or decrease)*	New installment payment amount

Terms of this agreement—By completing and submitting this agreement, you *(the taxpayer)* agree to the following terms:

- You will make each payment so that we *(IRS)* receive it by the monthly due date stated on the front of this form. *If you cannot make a scheduled payment, contact us immediately.*
- This agreement is based on your current financial condition. We may modify or terminate the agreement if our information shows that your ability to pay has significantly changed. You must provide updated financial information when requested.
- While this agreement is in effect, you must file all federal tax returns and pay any *(federal)* taxes you owe on time.
- We will apply your federal tax refunds or overpayments *(if any)* to the amount you owe until it is fully paid.
- You must pay a $105 user fee, which we have authority to deduct from your first payment*(s)*.
- If you default on your installment agreement, you must pay a $45 reinstatement fee if we reinstate the agreement. We have the

authority to deduct this fee from your first payment(s) after the agreement is reinstated.
- We will apply all payments on this agreement in the best interests of the United States.
- **We can terminate your installment agreement if:**
  - You do not make monthly installment payments as agreed.
  - You do not pay any other federal tax debt when due.
  - You do not provide financial information when requested.
- If we terminate your agreement, we may collect the entire amount you owe by levy on your income, bank accounts or other assets, or by seizing your property.
- We may terminate this agreement at any time if we find that collection of the tax is in jeopardy.
- This agreement may require managerial approval. We'll notify you when we approve or don't approve the agreement.

Additional Terms *(To be completed by IRS)*

Note: Internal Revenue Service employees may contact third parties in order to process and maintain this agreement.

Your signature	Title *(If Corporate Officer or Partner)*	Date
Spouse's signature *(If a joint liability)*		Date
Agreement examined or approved by *(Signature, title, function)*		Date

FOR IRS USE ONLY:

FOR IRS USE ONLY

AGREEMENT LOCATOR NUMBER: ___ ___ ___ ___
Check the appropriate boxes:
☐ RSI "1" no further review
☐ RSI "5" PPIA IMF 2 year review
☐ RSI "6" PPIA BMF 2 year review
☐ AI "0" Not a PPIA
☐ AI "1" Field Asset PPIA
☐ AI "2" All other PPIAs
Agreement Review Cycle: ___ ___ ___ ___ ___
Earliest CSED: _____
☐ Check box if pre-assessed modules included

Originator's ID #:_____ Originator Code:_____
Name: _____ Title: _____

A NOTICE OF FEDERAL TAX LIEN *(Check one box.)*
☐ **HAS ALREADY BEEN FILED**
☐ **WILL BE FILED IMMEDIATELY**
☐ **WILL BE FILED WHEN TAX IS ASSESSED**
☐ **MAY BE FILED IF THIS AGREEMENT DEFAULTS**

Part 2 — Employer's Copy   Catalog No. 21475H   www.irs.gov   Form **2159** (Rev. 1-2007)

INSTRUCTIONS TO EMPLOYER

This payroll deduction agreement requires your approval. If you agree to participate, please complete the spaces provided under the employer section on the front of this form.

WHAT YOU SHOULD DO

- Enter the name and telephone number of a contact person. *(This will allow us to contact you if your employee's liability is satisfied ahead of time.)*

- Indicate when you will forward payments to IRS.

- Sign and date the form.

- After you and your employee have completed and signed the form, please return it *(all parts)* to IRS. Use the IRS address on the letter the employee received with the form or the address shown on the front of the form.

HOW TO MAKE PAYMENTS

- ☐ Please deduct the amount your employee agreed with the IRS to have deducted from each wage or salary payment due the employee.

- ☐ Make your check payable to the "United States Treasury." To insure proper credit, please write your employee's name and social security number on each payment.

- ☐ Send the money to the IRS mailing address printed on the letter that came with the agreement. Your employee should give you a copy of this letter. If there is no letter, use the IRS address shown on the front of the form.

Note: The amount of the liability shown on the form may not include all penalties and interest provided by law. Please continue to make payments unless IRS notifies you that the liability has been satisfied. When the amount owed, as shown on the form, is paid in full and IRS hasn't notified you that the liability has been satisfied, please call the appropriate telephone number below to request the final balance due.

If you need assistance, please call the telephone number on the letter that came with the agreement or write to the address shown on the letter. If there's no letter, please call the appropriate telephone number below or write IRS at the address shown on the front of the form.

For assistance, call: **1-800-829-0115** *(Business),* or
1-800-829-8374 *(Individual – Self-Employed/Business Owners),* or
1-800-829-0922 *(Individuals – Wage Earners)*

THANK YOU FOR YOUR COOPERATION

Catalog No. 21475H   Form **2159** (Rev. 1-2007)

Form **2159** (Rev. January 2007)	Department of the Treasury — **Internal Revenue Service** **Payroll Deduction Agreement** *(See Instructions on the back of this page.)*

TO: *(Employer name and address)*

Regarding: *(Taxpayer name and address)*

Contact Person's Name   Telephone *(Include area code)*

Social security or employer identification number
(Taxpayer)   *(Spouse)*

EMPLOYER—*See the instructions on the back of Part 2.* The taxpayer identified above on the right named you as an employer. Please read and sign the following statement to agree to withhold amount*(s)* from the taxpayer's *(employee's)* wages or salary to apply to taxes owed.

I agree to participate in this payroll deduction agreement and will withhold the amount shown below from each wage or salary payment due this employee. I will send the money to the Internal Revenue Service every: *(Check one box.)*

☐ WEEK ☐ TWO WEEKS ☐ MONTH ☐ OTHER *(Specify.)* _____

Signed: _____

Title: _____ Date: _____

Your telephone number *(Include area code)*
(Home)   *(Work or business)*

For assistance, call: **1-800-829-0115** *(Business)* or
1-800-829-8374 *(Individual – Self-Employed/Business Owners)*, or
1-800-829-0922 *(Individuals – Wage Earners)*

Or write: _____ **Campus**
(City, State, and ZIP Code)

Financial Institution*(s)* *(Name and address)*

Kinds of taxes *(Form numbers)*	Tax Periods	Amount owed as of _____ $ _____ , plus all penalties and interest provided by law.

I am paid every: *(Check one)*: ☐ WEEK ☐ TWO WEEKS ☐ MONTH ☐ OTHER *(Specify.)* _____

I agree to have $_____ deducted from my wage or salary payment beginning _____ until the total liability is paid in full. I also agree and authorize this deduction to be increased or decreased as follows: _____

Date of increase *(or decrease)*	Amount of Increase *(or decrease)*	New installment payment amount

Terms of this agreement—By completing and submitting this agreement, you *(the taxpayer)* agree to the following terms:

- You will make each payment so that we *(IRS)* receive it by the monthly due date stated on the front of this form. **If you cannot make a scheduled payment, contact us immediately.**
- This agreement is based on your current financial condition. We may modify or terminate the agreement if our information shows that your ability to pay has significantly changed. You must provide updated financial information when requested.
- While this agreement is in effect, you must file all federal tax returns and pay any *(federal)* taxes you owe on time.
- We will apply your federal tax refunds or overpayments *(if any)* to the amount you owe until it is fully paid.
- You must pay a $105 user fee, which we have authority to deduct from your first payment*(s)*.
- If you default on your installment agreement, you must pay a $45 reinstatement fee if we reinstate the agreement. We have the

authority to deduct this fee from your first payment(s) after the agreement is reinstated.
- We will apply all payments on this agreement in the best interests of the United States.
- **We can terminate your installment agreement if:**
  - You do not make monthly installment payments as agreed.
  - You do not pay any other federal tax debt when due.
  - You do not provide financial information when requested.
- If we terminate your agreement, we may collect the entire amount you owe by levy on your income, bank accounts or other assets, or by seizing your property.
- We may terminate this agreement at any time if we find that collection of the tax is in jeopardy.
- This agreement may require managerial approval. We'll notify you when we approve or don't approve the agreement.

Additional Terms *(To be completed by IRS)*

Note: Internal Revenue Service employees may contact third parties in order to process and maintain this agreement.

Your signature	Title *(If Corporate Officer or Partner)*	Date

Spouse's signature *(If a joint liability)*		Date

Agreement examined or approved by *(Signature, title, function)*		Date

FOR IRS USE ONLY

AGREEMENT LOCATOR NUMBER: ___ ___ ___ ___

Check the appropriate boxes:

☐ RSI "1" no further review   ☐ AI "0" Not a PPIA
☐ RSI "5" PPIA IMF 2 year review   ☐ AI "1" Field Asset PPIA
☐ RSI "6" PPIA BMF 2 year review   ☐ AI "2" All other PPIAs
Agreement Review Cycle: __ __ __ __ __
Earliest CSED: _____
☐ Check box if pre-assessed modules included

FOR IRS USE ONLY:

Originator's ID #:_____ Originator Code:_____
Name: _____ Title: _____

A NOTICE OF FEDERAL TAX LIEN *(Check one box.)*
☐ HAS ALREADY BEEN FILED
☐ WILL BE FILED IMMEDIATELY
☐ WILL BE FILED WHEN TAX IS ASSESSED
☐ MAY BE FILED IF THIS AGREEMENT DEFAULTS

Part 3 — Taxpayer's Copy   Catalog No. 21475H   www.irs.gov   Form **2159** (Rev. 1-2007)

INSTRUCTIONS TO TAXPAYER

If not already completed by an IRS employee, please fill in the information in the spaces provided on the front of this form for the following items:

- Your employer's name and address

- Your name(s) *(plus spouse's name if the amount owed is for a joint return)* and current address.

- Your social security number or employer identification number. *(Use the number that appears on the notice(s) you received.)* Also, enter your spouse's social security number if this is a joint liability.

- Your home and work telephone number*(s)*

- The complete name and address of your financial institution*(s)*

- The kind of taxes you owe *(form numbers)* and the tax periods

- The amount you owe as of the date you spoke to IRS

- When you are paid

- The amount you agreed to have deducted from your pay when you spoke to IRS

- The date the deduction is to begin

- The amount of any increase or decrease in the deduction amount, if you agreed to this with IRS; otherwise, leave BLANK

After you complete, sign *(along with your spouse if this is a joint liability)*, and date this agreement form, give it to your participating employer. If you received the form by mail, please give the employer a copy of the letter that came with it.

Your employer should mark the payment frequency on the form and sign it. Then the employer should return all parts of the form to the IRS address on your letter or the address shown in the "For assistance" box on the front of the form.

If you need assistance, please call the appropriate telephone number below or write IRS at the address shown on the form. However, if you received this agreement by mail, please call the telephone number on the letter that came with it or write IRS at the address shown on the letter.

For assistance, call: **1-800-829-0115** *(Business),* or
1-800-829-8374 *(Individual – Self-Employed/Business Owners),* or
1-800-829-0922 *(Individuals – Wage Earners)*

Note: This agreement **will not** affect your liability *(if any)* for backup withholding under Public Law 98-67, the Interest and Dividend Compliance Act of 1983.

Catalog No. 21475H

Form **2159** (Rev. 1-2007)

Form **2555**

Department of the Treasury
Internal Revenue Service

Foreign Earned Income

▶ **Attach to Form 1040.**
▶ **Information about Form 2555 and its separate instructions is at** *www.irs.gov/form2555.*

OMB No. 1545-0074

20**12**

Attachment
Sequence No. **34**

For Use by U.S. Citizens and Resident Aliens Only

Name shown on Form 1040

Your social security number

Part I   **General Information**

1   Your foreign address (including country)

2 Your occupation

3   Employer's name ▶

4a Employer's U.S. address ▶

 b Employer's foreign address ▶

5   Employer is (check ▶   **a** ☐ A foreign entity   **b** ☐ A U.S. company   **c** ☐ Self
     any that apply):   **d** ☐ A foreign affiliate of a U.S. company   **e** ☐ Other (specify) ▶

6a If you previously filed Form 2555 or Form 2555-EZ, enter the last year you filed the form. ▶

 b If you did not previously file Form 2555 or 2555-EZ to claim either of the exclusions, check here ▶ ☐ and go to line 7.

 c Have you ever revoked either of the exclusions? . . . . ☐ **Yes** ☐ **No**

 d If you answered "Yes," enter the type of exclusion and the tax year for which the revocation was effective. ▶

7   Of what country are you a citizen/national? ▶

8a Did you maintain a separate foreign residence for your family because of adverse living conditions at your
     tax home? See **Second foreign household** in the instructions . . . . ☐ **Yes** ☐ **No**

 b If "Yes," enter city and country of the separate foreign residence. Also, enter the number of days during your tax year that you
     maintained a second household at that address. ▶

9   List your tax home(s) during your tax year and date(s) established. ▶

Next, complete either Part II or Part III. If an item does not apply, enter "NA." If you do not give the information asked for, any exclusion or deduction you claim may be disallowed.

Part II   **Taxpayers Qualifying Under Bona Fide Residence Test** (see instructions)

10   Date bona fide residence began ▶   , and ended ▶

11   Kind of living quarters in foreign country ▶   **a** ☐ Purchased house   **b** ☐ Rented house or apartment   **c** ☐ Rented room
                                     d ☐ Quarters furnished by employer

12a Did any of your family live with you abroad during any part of the tax year? . . . . ☐ **Yes** ☐ **No**
  b If "Yes," who and for what period? ▶

13a Have you submitted a statement to the authorities of the foreign country where you claim bona fide
      residence that you are not a resident of that country? See instructions . . . . ☐ **Yes** ☐ **No**

  b Are you required to pay income tax to the country where you claim bona fide residence? See instructions . ☐ **Yes** ☐ **No**

     If you answered "Yes" to 13a and "No" to 13b, you do not qualify as a bona fide resident. Do not complete the rest of this part.

14   If you were present in the United States or its possessions during the tax year, complete columns **(a)–(d)** below. **Do not**
     include the income from column **(d)** in Part IV, but report it on Form 1040.

(a) Date arrived in U.S.	**(b)** Date left U.S.	**(c)** Number of days in U.S. on business	**(d)** Income earned in U.S. on business (attach computation)	**(a)** Date arrived in U.S.	**(b)** Date left U.S.	**(c)** Number of days in U.S. on business	**(d)** Income earned in U.S. on business (attach computation)

15a List any contractual terms or other conditions relating to the length of your employment abroad. ▶

  b Enter the type of visa under which you entered the foreign country. ▶

  c Did your visa limit the length of your stay or employment in a foreign country? If "Yes," attach explanation . ☐ **Yes** ☐ **No**

  d Did you maintain a home in the United States while living abroad? . . . . ☐ **Yes** ☐ **No**

  e If "Yes," enter address of your home, whether it was rented, the names of the occupants, and their relationship
     to you. ▶

For Paperwork Reduction Act Notice, see the Form 1040 instructions.   Cat. No. 11900P   Form **2555** (2012)

Form 2555 (2012)   Page **2**

Part III Taxpayers Qualifying Under Physical Presence Test (see instructions)

16 The physical presence test is based on the 12-month period from ▶ _____ through ▶ _____

17 Enter your principal country of employment during your tax year. ▶ _____

18 If you traveled abroad during the 12-month period entered on line 16, complete columns **(a)–(f)** below. Exclude travel between foreign countries that did not involve travel on or over international waters, or in or over the United States, for 24 hours or more. If you have no travel to report during the period, enter "Physically present in a foreign country or countries for the entire 12-month period." **Do not** include the income from column **(f)** below in Part IV, but report it on Form 1040.

(a) Name of country (including U.S.)	**(b)** Date arrived	**(c)** Date left	**(d)** Full days present in country	**(e)** Number of days in U.S. on business	**(f)** Income earned in U.S. on business (attach computation)

Part IV All Taxpayers

Note: *Enter on lines 19 through 23 all income, including noncash income, you earned and actually or constructively received during your 2012 tax year for services you performed in a foreign country. If any of the foreign earned income received this tax year was earned in a prior tax year, or will be earned in a later tax year (such as a bonus), see the instructions. **Do not** include income from line 14, column (d), or line 18, column (f). Report amounts in U.S. dollars, using the exchange rates in effect when you actually or constructively received the income.*

> **If you are a cash basis taxpayer, report on Form 1040 all income you received in 2012, no matter when you performed the service.**

2012 Foreign Earned Income		Amount (in U.S. dollars)	
19	Total wages, salaries, bonuses, commissions, etc.	**19**	
20	Allowable share of income for personal services performed (see instructions):		
a	In a business (including farming) or profession	**20a**	
b	In a partnership. List partnership's name and address and type of income. ▶ _____		
		20b	
21	Noncash income (market value of property or facilities furnished by employer—attach statement showing how it was determined):		
a	Home (lodging)	**21a**	
b	Meals	**21b**	
c	Car	**21c**	
d	Other property or facilities. List type and amount. ▶ _____		
		21d	
22	Allowances, reimbursements, or expenses paid on your behalf for services you performed:		
a	Cost of living and overseas differential	**22a**	
b	Family	**22b**	
c	Education	**22c**	
d	Home leave	**22d**	
e	Quarters	**22e**	
f	For any other purpose. List type and amount. ▶ _____		
		22f	
g	Add lines 22a through 22f	**22g**	
23	Other foreign earned income. List type and amount. ▶ _____		
		23	
24	Add lines 19 through 21d, line 22g, and line 23	**24**	
25	Total amount of meals and lodging included on line 24 that is excludable (see instructions) . .	**25**	
26	Subtract line 25 from line 24. Enter the result here and on line 27 on page 3. This is your **2012 foreign earned income** . . . . ▶	**26**	

Form **2555** (2012)

Part V   **All Taxpayers**

27	Enter the amount from line 26	**27**	

Are you claiming the housing exclusion or housing deduction?

☐ **Yes.** Complete Part VI.
☐ **No.** Go to Part VII.

Part VI   **Taxpayers Claiming the Housing Exclusion and/or Deduction**

28	Qualified housing expenses for the tax year (see instructions)	**28**	
29a	Enter location where housing expenses incurred (see instructions) ▶ ---------------------		
b	Enter limit on housing expenses (see instructions)	**29b**	
30	Enter the **smaller** of line 28 or line 29b	**30**	
31	Number of days in your qualifying period that fall within your 2012 tax year (see instructions) . . . . **31** **days**		
32	Multiply $41.57 by the number of days on line 31. If 366 is entered on line 31, enter $15,216.00 here	**32**	
33	Subtract line 32 from line 30. If the result is zero or less, do not complete the rest of this part or any of Part IX	**33**	
34	Enter employer-provided amounts (see instructions) **34**		
35	Divide line 34 by line 27. Enter the result as a decimal (rounded to at least three places), but do not enter more than "1.000"	**35**	× .
36	**Housing exclusion.** Multiply line 33 by line 35. Enter the result but do not enter more than the amount on line 34. Also, complete Part VIII . . . . ▶	**36**	

Note: *The housing deduction is figured in Part IX. If you choose to claim the foreign earned income exclusion, complete Parts VII and VIII before Part IX.*

Part VII   **Taxpayers Claiming the Foreign Earned Income Exclusion**

37	Maximum foreign earned income exclusion	**37**	$95,100 00
38	• If you completed Part VI, enter the number from line 31. • All others, enter the number of days in your qualifying period that fall within your 2012 tax year (see the instructions for line 31). } **38** **days**		
39	• If line 38 and the number of days in your 2012 tax year (usually 366) are the same, enter "1.000." • Otherwise, divide line 38 by the number of days in your 2012 tax year and enter the result as a decimal (rounded to at least three places). }	**39**	× .
40	Multiply line 37 by line 39	**40**	
41	Subtract line 36 from line 27	**41**	
42	**Foreign earned income exclusion.** Enter the **smaller** of line 40 or line 41. Also, complete Part VIII ▶	**42**	

Part VIII   **Taxpayers Claiming the Housing Exclusion, Foreign Earned Income Exclusion, or Both**

43	Add lines 36 and 42	**43**	
44	Deductions allowed in figuring your adjusted gross income (Form 1040, line 37) that are allocable to the excluded income. See instructions and attach computation	**44**	
45	Subtract line 44 from line 43. Enter the result here and in parentheses on **Form 1040, line 21.** Next to the amount enter "Form 2555." On Form 1040, subtract this amount from your income to arrive at total income on Form 1040, line 22	**45**	

Part IX   **Taxpayers Claiming the Housing Deduction**—Complete this part only if **(a)** line 33 is more than line 36 and **(b)** line 27 is more than line 43.

46	Subtract line 36 from line 33	**46**	
47	Subtract line 43 from line 27	**47**	
48	Enter the **smaller** of line 46 or line 47	**48**	

Note: *If line 47 is **more than** line 48 and you could not deduct all of your 2011 housing deduction because of the 2011 limit, use the housing deduction carryover worksheet in the instructions to figure the amount to enter on line 49. Otherwise, go to line 50.*

49	Housing deduction carryover from 2011 (from housing deduction carryover worksheet in the instructions)	**49**	
50	**Housing deduction.** Add lines 48 and 49. Enter the total here and on Form 1040 to the left of line 36. Next to the amount on Form 1040, enter "Form 2555." Add it to the total adjustments reported on that line . . . . ▶	**50**	

Form **2555** (2012)

20**12**
Instructions for Form 2555

Foreign Earned Income

Department of the Treasury
Internal Revenue Service

Section references are to the Internal Revenue Code unless otherwise noted.

Future Developments

For the latest information about developments related to Form 2555 and its instructions, such as legislation enacted after they were published, go to *www.irs.gov/form2555*.

What's New

Exclusion amount. For 2012, the maximum exclusion has increased to $95,100.

General Instructions

 Do not include on Form 1040, line 62 (federal income tax withheld), any taxes a foreign employer withheld from your pay and paid to the foreign country's tax authority instead of to the U.S. Treasury.

Purpose of Form

If you qualify, you can use Form 2555 to figure your foreign earned income exclusion and your housing exclusion or deduction. You cannot exclude or deduct more than your foreign earned income for the year.

You may be able to use Form 2555-EZ, Foreign Earned Income Exclusion, if you did not have any self-employment income for the year, your total foreign earned income did not exceed $95,100, you do not have any business or moving expenses, and you do not claim the housing exclusion or deduction. For more details, see Form 2555-EZ and its separate instructions.

General Information

If you are a U.S. citizen or a U.S. resident alien living in a foreign country, you are subject to the same U.S. income tax laws that apply to citizens and resident aliens living in the United States.

Note. Specific rules apply to determine if you are a resident or nonresident alien of the United States. See Pub. 519, U.S. Tax Guide for Aliens, for details.

Foreign country. A foreign country is any territory under the sovereignty of a government other than that of the United States.

The term "foreign country" includes the country's territorial waters and airspace, but not international waters and the airspace above them. It also includes the seabed and subsoil of those submarine areas adjacent to the country's territorial waters over which it has exclusive rights under international law to explore and exploit the natural resources.

The term "foreign country " does not include U.S. possessions or territories. It does not include the Antarctic region.

Who Qualifies

You qualify for the tax benefits available to taxpayers who have foreign earned income if both of the following apply.
*   You meet the tax home test (discussed later on this page).
*   You meet either the bona fide residence test or the physical presence test, discussed later.

Note. Income from working abroad as an employee of the U.S. Government does not qualify for either of the exclusions or the housing deduction. Do not file Form 2555.

Tax home test. To meet this test, your tax home must be in a foreign country, or countries (see *Foreign country*, earlier), throughout your period of bona fide residence or physical presence, whichever applies. For this purpose, your period of physical presence is the 330 full days during which you were present in a foreign country, not the 12 consecutive months during which those days occurred.

Your tax home is your regular or principal place of business, employment, or post of duty, regardless of where you maintain your family residence. If you do not have a regular or principal place of business because of the nature of your trade or business, your tax home is your regular place of abode (the place where you regularly live).

You are not considered to have a tax home in a foreign country for any period during which your abode is in the United States. However, if you are temporarily present in the United States, or you maintain a dwelling in the United States (whether or not that dwelling is used by your spouse and dependents), it does not necessarily mean that your abode is in the United States during that time.

Example. You are employed on an offshore oil rig in the territorial waters of a foreign country and work a 28-day on/ 28-day off schedule. You return to your family residence in the United States during your off periods. You are considered to have an abode in the United States and do not meet the tax home test. You cannot claim either of the exclusions or the housing deduction.

Travel to Cuba

Generally, if you were in Cuba in violation of U.S. travel restrictions, the following rules apply.
*   Any time spent in Cuba cannot be counted in determining if you qualify under the bona fide residence or physical presence test.
*   Any income earned in Cuba is not considered foreign earned income.
*   Any housing expenses in Cuba (or housing expenses for your spouse or dependents in another country while you were in Cuba) are not considered qualified housing expenses.

Note. If you performed services at the U.S. Naval Base at Guantanamo Bay, you were not in violation of U.S. travel restrictions.

Additional Information

Pub. 54, Tax Guide for U.S. Citizens and Resident Aliens Abroad, has more information about the bona fide residence test, the physical presence test, the foreign earned income exclusion, and the housing exclusion and deduction. You can get this publication from most U.S. Embassies and consulates or by writing to: National Distribution Center, 1201 N. Mitsubishi Motorway, Bloomington, IL 61705-6613. You can also download this publication (as well as other forms and publications) at IRS.gov.

Waiver of Time Requirements

If your tax home was in a foreign country and you were a bona fide resident of, or physically present in, a foreign country and had to leave because of war, civil unrest, or similar adverse conditions, the minimum time requirements specified under the bona fide residence and physical presence tests may be waived. You must be able to show that you reasonably could have expected to meet the minimum time requirements if you had not been required to leave. Each year the IRS will publish in the Internal Revenue Bulletin a list of the only countries that qualify for the waiver for the previous year

Nov 06, 2012

Cat. No. 11901A

and the dates they qualify. If you left one of the countries during the period indicated, you can claim the tax benefits on Form 2555, but only for the number of days you were a bona fide resident of, or physically present in, the foreign country.

If you can claim either of the exclusions or the housing deduction because of the waiver of time requirements, attach a statement to your return explaining that you expected to meet the applicable time requirement, but the conditions in the foreign country prevented you from the normal conduct of business. Also, enter "Claiming Waiver" in the top margin on page 1 of Form 2555.

When To File

A 2012 calendar year Form 1040 is generally due April 15, 2013.

However, you are automatically granted a 2-month extension of time to file (to June 17, 2013, for a 2012 calendar year return) if, on the due date of your return, you live outside the United States and Puerto Rico and your tax home (defined earlier) is outside the United States and Puerto Rico. If you take this extension, you must attach a statement to your return explaining that you meet these two conditions.

The automatic 2-month extension also applies to paying the tax. However, you will owe interest on any tax not paid by the regular due date of your return.

When to claim the exclusion(s). The first year you plan to take the foreign earned income exclusion and/or the housing exclusion or deduction, you may not yet have met either the physical presence test or the bona fide residence test by the due date of your return (including the automatic 2-month extension, discussed earlier). If this occurs, you can either:

1. Apply for a special extension to a date after you expect to qualify, or

2. File your return timely without claiming the exclusion and then file an amended return after you qualify.

Special extension of time. To apply for this extension, complete and file Form 2350, Application for Extension of Time To File U.S. Income Tax Return, with the Department of the Treasury, Internal Revenue Service Center, Austin, TX 73301-0045, before the due date of your return. Interest is charged on the tax not paid by the regular due date as explained earlier.

Amended return. File Form 1040X, Amended U.S. Individual Income Tax Return, to change a return you already filed. Generally, Form 1040X must be filed within 3 years after the date the original return was filed or within 2 years after the date the tax was paid, whichever is later.

Choosing the Exclusion(s)

To choose either of the exclusions, complete the appropriate parts of Form 2555 and file it with your Form 1040 or Form 1040X, Amended U.S. Individual Income Tax Return. Your initial choice to claim the exclusion must usually be made on a timely filed return (including extensions) or on a return amending a timely filed return. However, there are exceptions. See Pub. 54 for details.

Once you choose to claim an exclusion, that choice remains in effect for that year and all future years unless it is revoked. To revoke your choice, you must attach a statement to your return for the first year you do not wish to claim the exclusion(s). If you revoke your choice, you cannot claim the exclusion(s) for your next 5 tax years without the approval of the Internal Revenue Service. See Pub. 54 for more information.

Figuring tax on income not excluded. If you claim either of the exclusions or the housing deduction, you must figure the tax on your nonexcluded income using the tax rates that would have applied had you not claimed the exclusions. See the Instructions for Form 1040 and complete the Foreign Earned Income Tax Worksheet to figure the amount of tax to enter on Form 1040, line 44. When figuring your alternative minimum tax on Form 6251, you must use the Foreign Earned Income Tax Worksheet in the instructions for Form 6251.

Earned income credit. You cannot take the earned income credit if you claim either of the exclusions or the housing deduction.

Foreign tax credit or deduction. You cannot take a credit or deduction for foreign income taxes paid or accrued on income that is excluded under either of the exclusions. If all of your foreign earned income is excluded, you cannot claim a credit or deduction for the foreign taxes paid or accrued on that income. If only part of your income is excluded, you cannot claim a credit or deduction for the foreign taxes allocable to the excluded income. See Pub. 514, Foreign Tax Credit for Individuals, for details on how to figure the amount allocable to the excluded income.

IRA deduction. If you claim either of the exclusions, special rules apply in figuring the amount of your IRA deduction. For details, see Pub. 590, Individual Retirement Arrangements (IRAs).

Specific Instructions

Part I

Line 1. Enter entire address including city, province or state, country, and postal code. If using a military or diplomatic address, include the country in which you are living or stationed.

Part II

Bona Fide Residence Test

To meet this test, you must be one of the following:
* A U.S. citizen who is a bona fide resident of a foreign country, or countries, for an uninterrupted period that includes an entire tax year (January 1–December 31, if you file a calendar year return), or
* A U.S. resident alien who is a citizen or national of a country with which the United States has an income tax treaty in effect and who is a bona fide resident of a foreign country, or countries, for an uninterrupted period that includes an entire tax year (January 1–December 31, if you file a calendar year return). See Pub. 901, U.S. Tax Treaties, for a list of countries with which the United States has an income tax treaty in effect.

Whether you are a bona fide resident of a foreign country depends on your intention about the length and nature of your stay. Evidence of your intention may be your words and acts. If these conflict, your acts carry more weight than your words. Generally, if you go to a foreign country for a definite, temporary purpose and return to the United States after you accomplish it, you are not a bona fide resident of the foreign country. If accomplishing the purpose requires an extended, indefinite stay, and you make your home in the foreign country, you may be a bona fide resident. See Pub. 54 for more information and examples.

Line 10. Enter the dates your bona fide residence began and ended. If you are still a bona fide resident, enter "Continues" in the space for the date your bona fide residence ended.

Lines 13a and 13b. If you submitted a statement of nonresidence to the authorities of a foreign country in which you earned income and the authorities hold that you are not subject to their income tax laws by reason of nonresidency in the foreign country, you are not considered a bona fide resident of that country.

If you submitted such a statement and the authorities have not made an adverse determination of your nonresident status, you are not considered a bona fide resident of that country.

Part III

Physical Presence Test

To meet this test, you must be a U.S. citizen or resident alien who is physically present in a foreign country, or countries, for at least 330 full days during any period of 12 months in a row. A full day means the 24-hour period that starts at midnight.

To figure 330 full days, add all separate periods you were present in a foreign country during the 12-month period shown on line 16. The 330 full days can be interrupted by periods when you are traveling over international waters or are otherwise not in a foreign country. See Pub. 54 for more information and examples.

Note. A nonresident alien who, with a U.S. citizen or U.S. resident alien spouse, chooses to be taxed as a resident of the United States can qualify under this test if the time requirements are met. See Pub. 54 for details on how to make this choice.

Line 16. The 12-month period on which the physical presence test is based must include 365 or 366 days, part of which must be in 2012. The dates may begin or end in a calendar year other than 2012.

 You must enter dates in both spaces provided on line 16. Do not enter "Continues" in the space for the ending date.

Part IV

Foreign Earned Income

Enter in this part the total foreign earned income you earned and received (including income constructively received) during the tax year. If you are a cash basis taxpayer, include in income on Form 1040, the foreign earned income you received during the tax year regardless of when you earned it. (For example, include wages on Form 1040, line 7.)

Income is earned in the tax year you perform the services for which you receive the pay. But if you are a cash basis taxpayer and, because of your employer's payroll periods, you received your last salary payment for 2011 in 2012, that income may be treated as earned in 2012. If you cannot treat that salary payment as income earned in 2012, the rules explained under *Income earned in prior year*, discussed later, apply. See Pub. 54 for more details.

Foreign earned income for this purpose means wages, salaries, professional fees, and other compensation received for personal services you performed in a foreign country during the period for which you meet the tax home test and either the bona fide residence test or the physical presence test. It also includes noncash

income (such as a home or car) and allowances or reimbursements.

Foreign earned income does not include amounts that are actually a distribution of corporate earnings or profits rather than a reasonable allowance as compensation for your personal services. It also does not include the following types of income.
• Pension and annuity income (including social security benefits and railroad retirement benefits treated as social security).
• Interest, ordinary dividends, capital gains, alimony, etc.
• Portion of 2011 moving expense deduction allocable to 2012 that is included in your 2012 gross income. For details, see *Moving Expense Attributable to Foreign Earnings in 2 Years* under *Moving Expenses* in Pub. 54.
• Amounts paid to you by the U.S. Government or any of its agencies if you were an employee of the U.S. Government or any of its agencies.
• Amounts received after the end of the tax year following the tax year in which you performed the services.
• Amounts you must include in gross income because of your employer's contributions to a nonexempt employees' trust or to a nonqualified annuity contract.

Income received in prior year. Foreign earned income received in 2011 for services you performed in 2012 can be excluded from your 2011 gross income if, and to the extent, the income would have been excludable if you had received it in 2012. To claim the additional exclusion, you must amend your 2011 tax return. To do this, file Form 1040X.

Income earned in prior year. Foreign earned income received in 2012 for services you performed in 2011 can be excluded from your 2012 gross income if, and to the extent, the income would have been excludable if you had received it in 2011.

If you are excluding income under this rule, do not include this income in Part IV. Instead, attach a statement to Form 2555 showing how you figured the exclusion. Enter the amount that would have been excludable in 2011 on Form 2555 to the left of line 45. Next to the amount enter "Exclusion of Income Earned in 2011." Include it in the total reported on line 45.

Note. If you claimed any deduction, credit, or exclusion on your 2011 return that is definitely related to the 2011 foreign earned income you are excluding under this rule, you may have to amend your 2011 income tax return to adjust the amount you claimed. To do this, file Form 1040X.

Line 20. If you engaged in an unincorporated trade or business in which

both personal services and capital were material income-producing factors, a reasonable amount of compensation for your personal services will be considered earned income. The amount treated as earned income, however, cannot be more than 30% of your share of the net profits from the trade or business after subtracting the deduction for the employer-equivalent portion of self-employment tax.

If capital is not an income-producing factor and personal services produced the business income, the 30% rule does not apply. Your entire gross income is earned income.

Line 23. List other foreign earned income not included on lines 19-22. You can write "Various" on the dotted lines to the left of the entry space if you have other foreign earned income from multiple sources.

Line 25. Enter the value of meals and/or lodging provided by, or on behalf of, your employer that is excludable from your income under section 119. To be excludable, the meals and lodging must have been provided for your employer's convenience and on your employer's business premises. In addition, you must have been required to accept the lodging as a condition of your employment. If you lived in a camp provided by, or on behalf of, your employer, the camp may be considered part of your employer's business premises. See *Exclusion of Meals and Lodging* in Pub. 54 for details.

Part VI

Line 28. Enter the total reasonable expenses paid or incurred during the tax year by you, or on your behalf, for your foreign housing and the housing of your spouse and dependents if they lived with you. You can also include the reasonable expenses of a second foreign household (defined later). Housing expenses are considered reasonable to the extent they are not lavish or extravagant under the circumstances.

Housing expenses include rent, utilities (other than telephone charges), real and personal property insurance, nonrefundable fees paid to obtain a lease, rental of furniture and accessories, residential parking, and household repairs. You can also include the fair rental value of housing provided by, or on behalf of, your employer if you have not excluded it on line 25.

Do not include deductible interest and taxes, any amount deductible by a tenant-stockholder in connection with cooperative housing, the cost of buying or improving a house, principal payments on a mortgage, or depreciation on the house. Also, do not include the cost of domestic labor, pay television, or the cost of buying furniture or accessories.

Include expenses for housing only during periods for which:
• The value of your housing is not excluded from gross income under section 119 (unless you maintained a second foreign household as defined later), and
• You meet the tax home test and either the bona fide residence or physical presence test.

Second foreign household. If you maintained a separate foreign household for your spouse and dependents at a place other than your tax home because the living conditions at your tax home were dangerous, unhealthful, or otherwise adverse, you can include the expenses of the second household on line 28.

Married couples. The following rules apply if both you and your spouse qualify for the tax benefits of Form 2555.

Same foreign household. If you and your spouse lived in the same foreign household and file a joint return, you must figure your housing amounts (line 33) jointly. If you file separate returns, only one spouse can claim the housing exclusion or deduction.

In figuring your housing amount jointly, either spouse (but not both) can claim the housing exclusion or housing deduction. However, if you and your spouse have different periods of residence or presence,

and the one with the shorter period of residence or presence claims the exclusion or deduction, you can claim as housing expenses only the expenses for that shorter period. The spouse claiming the exclusion or deduction can aggregate the housing expenses of both spouses, subject to the limit on housing expenses (line 29b), and subtract his or her base housing amount.

Separate foreign households. If you and your spouse lived in separate foreign households, you each can claim qualified expenses for your own household only if:
• Your tax homes were not within a reasonable commuting distance of each other, and
• Each spouse's household was not within a reasonable commuting distance of the other spouse's tax home.

Otherwise, only one spouse can claim his or her housing exclusion or deduction. This is true even if you and your spouse file separate returns.

See Pub. 54 for additional information.

Line 29a. Enter the city or other location (if applicable) and the country where you incurred foreign housing expenses during the tax year only if your location is listed in the table at the end of the instructions; otherwise, leave this line blank.

Line 29b. Your housing expenses may not exceed a certain limit. The limit on housing expenses varies depending upon

the location in which you incur housing expenses. In 2012, for most locations, this limit is $28,530 (30 percent of $95,100) if your qualifying period includes all of 2012 (or $77.95 per day if the number of days in your qualifying period that fall within your 2012 tax year is less than 366).

The table at the end of the instructions lists the housing expense limits based on geographic differences in foreign housing costs relative to housing costs in the United States. If the location in which you incurred housing expenses is listed in the table, or the number of days in your qualifying period that fall within the 2012 tax year is less than 366, use the *Limit on Housing Expenses Worksheet* to figure the amount to enter on line 29b. If the location in which you incurred housing expenses is not listed in the table, and the number of days in your qualifying period is 366, enter $28,530 on line 29b.

Example. For 2012, because your location is not listed in the table at the end of the instructions, your limit on housing expenses is $77.95 per day ($28,530 divided by 366). If you file a calendar year return and your qualifying period is January 1, 2012, to October 1, 2012 (275 days), you would enter $21,436 on line 29b ($77.95 multiplied by 275 days).

More than one foreign location. If you moved during the 2012 tax year and incurred housing expenses in more than one foreign location as a result, complete the *Limit on Housing Expenses Worksheet* for each location in which you incurred housing expenses, entering the number of qualifying days during which you lived in the applicable location on line 1. Add the results shown on line 4 of each worksheet, and enter the total on line 29b.

 If you moved during the 2012 tax year and are completing more than one Limit on Housing Expenses Worksheet, *the total number of days entered on line 1 of your worksheets may not exceed the total number of days in your qualifying period that fall within the 2012 tax year (that is, the number of days entered on Form 2555, line 31).*

Line 31. Enter the number of days in your qualifying period that fall within your 2012 tax year. Your qualifying period is the period during which you meet the tax home test and either the bona fide residence or the physical presence test.

Example. You establish a tax home and bona fide residence in a foreign country on August 14, 2012. You maintain the tax home and residence until January 31, 2014. You are a calendar year taxpayer. The number of days in your qualifying period that fall within your 2012 tax year is 140 (August 14 through December 31, 2012).

Limit on Housing Expenses Worksheet—Line 29b

Keep for Your Records

Note. If the location in which you incurred housing expenses is not listed in the table at the end of the instructions, and the number of days in your qualifying period that fall within the 2012 tax year is 366, DO NOT complete this worksheet. Instead, enter $28,530 on line 29b.

1. Enter the number of days in your qualifying period that fall within the 2012 tax year (see the instructions for line 31) . . . . **1.** _____

2. Did you enter 366 on line 1?

  ☐ **No.** If the amount on line 1 is less than 366, skip line 2 and go to line 3.

  ☐ **Yes.** Locate the amount under the column *Limit on Housing Expenses (full year)* from the table at the end of the instructions for the location in which you incurred housing expenses. This is your **limit on housing expenses**. Enter the amount here and on line 29b.

  (STOP) Do not complete the rest of this worksheet . . . . **2.** _____

3. Enter the amount under the column *Limit on Housing Expenses (daily)* from the table at the end of the instructions for the location in which you incurred housing expenses. If the location is not listed in the table, enter $77.95 . . . . **3.** _____

4. Multiply line 1 by line 3. This is your **limit on housing expenses**. Enter the result here and on line 29b . . . . **4.** _____

Instructions for Form 2555 (2012)

Nontaxable U.S. Government allowances. If you or your spouse received a nontaxable housing allowance as a military or civilian employee of the U.S. Government, see Pub. 54 for information on how that allowance may affect your housing exclusion or deduction.

Line 34. Enter any amount your employer paid or incurred on your behalf that is foreign earned income included in your gross income for the tax year (without regard to section 911).

Examples of employer-provided amounts are:
• Wages and salaries received from your employer.
• The fair market value of compensation provided in kind (such as the fair rental value of lodging provided by your employer as long as it is not excluded on line 25).
• Rent paid by your employer directly to your landlord.
• Amounts paid by your employer to reimburse you for housing expenses, educational expenses of your dependents, or as part of a tax equalization plan.

Self-employed individuals. If all of your foreign earned income (Part IV) is self-employment income, skip lines 34 and 35 and enter -0- on line 36. If you qualify for the housing deduction, be sure to complete Part IX.

Part VII

Married couples. If both you and your spouse qualify for, and choose to claim, the foreign earned income exclusion, figure the amount of the exclusion separately for each of you. You each must complete Part VII of your separate Forms 2555.

Community income. The amount of the exclusion is not affected by the income-splitting provisions of community property laws. The sum of the amounts figured separately for each of you is the total amount excluded on a joint return.

Part VIII

If you claim either of the exclusions, you cannot claim any deduction (including moving expenses), credit, or exclusion that is definitely related to the excluded income. If only part of your foreign earned income is excluded, you must prorate such items based on the ratio that your excludable earned income bears to your total foreign earned income. See Pub. 54 for details on how to figure the amount allocable to the excluded income.

The exclusion under section 119 and the housing deduction are not considered definitely related to the excluded income.

Line 44. Report in full on Form 1040 and related forms and schedules all deductions allowed in figuring your adjusted gross income (Form 1040, line 37). Enter on line 44 the total amount of those deductions (such as the deduction for moving expenses, the deductible part of self-employment tax, and the expenses claimed on Schedule C or C-EZ (Form 1040)) that are not allowed because they are allocable to the excluded income. This applies only to deductions definitely related to the excluded earned income. See Pub. 54 for details on how to report your itemized deductions (such as unreimbursed employee business expenses) that are allocable to the excluded income.

Part IX

If line 33 is more than line 36 and line 27 is more than line 43, complete this part to figure your housing deduction.

Line 49. Use the housing deduction carryover worksheet on this page to figure your carryover from 2011.

One-year carryover. If the amount on line 46 is more than the amount on line 47, you can carry the difference over to your 2013 tax year. If you cannot deduct the excess in 2013 because of the 2013 limit, you cannot carry it over to any future tax year.

Housing Deduction Carryover Worksheet—Line 49 *Keep for Your Records*

1. Enter the amount from your 2011 Form 2555, line 46 .... **1.** _____

2. Enter the amount from your 2011 Form 2555, line 48 .... **2.** _____

3. Subtract line 2 from line 1. If the result is zero, **stop;** enter -0- on line 49 of your 2012 Form 2555. You do not have any housing deduction carryover from 2011 .... **3.** _____

4. Enter the amount from your 2012 Form 2555, line 47 .... **4.** _____

5. Enter the amount from your 2012 Form 2555, line 48 .... **5.** _____

6. Subtract line 5 from line 4 .... **6.** _____

7. Enter the **smaller** of line 3 or line 6 here and on line 49 of your 2012 Form 2555. If line 3 is **more than** line 6, you **cannot** carry the difference over to any future tax year .... ▶ **7.** _____

2012 LIMITS ON HOUSING EXPENSES			
Country	City or Other Location	Limit on Housing Expenses (daily)	Limit on Housing Expenses (full year)
Angola	Luanda	229.51	84,000
Argentina	Buenos Aires	154.37	56,500
Australia	Adelaide	89.62	32,800
	Brisbane	88.52	32,400
	Darwin, Northern Country	83.61	30,600
	Gold Coast	88.52	32,400
	Melbourne	113.39	41,500
	Oakey	88.52	32,400
	Perth	121.31	44,400
	Sydney	89.57	32,782
	Toowoomba	88.52	32,400
Austria	Vienna	96.72	35,400
Bahamas, The	Nassau	135.79	49,700
Bahrain		120.22	44,000
Barbados		103.01	37,700
Belgium	Antwerp	98.63	36,100
	Brussels	130.33	47,700
	Gosselies	118.31	43,300
	Hoogbuul	98.63	36,100
	Mons	118.31	43,300
	SHAPE/Chievres	118.31	43,300
Bermuda		245.90	90,000
Bosnia-Herzegovina	Sarajevo	83.61	30,600
Brazil	Brasilia	144.26	52,800
	Rio de Janeiro	95.90	35,100
	Sao Paulo	154.64	56,600
Canada	Calgary	109.02	39,900
	Dartmouth	93.44	34,200
	Edmonton	96.99	35,500
	Halifax	93.44	34,200
	London, Ontario	82.79	30,300
	Montreal	154.37	56,500
	Ottawa	136.07	49,800
	Toronto	134.70	49,300
	Vancouver	128.42	47,000
	Victoria	91.53	33,500
	Winnipeg	90.16	33,000
Cayman Islands	Grand Cayman	131.15	48,000
Chile	Santiago	140.16	51,300
China	Beijing	194.54	71,200
	Hong Kong	312.30	114,300
	Shanghai	155.74	57,001
Colombia	Bogota	147.81	54,100
	All cities other than Bogota	134.97	49,400
Costa Rica	San Jose	87.43	32,000
Denmark	Copenhagen	119.41	43,704
Dominican Republic	Santo Domingo	124.32	45,500
Ecuador	Guayaquil	84.15	30,800
	Quito	88.52	32,400
Estonia	Tallinn	127.32	46,600
France	Garches	231.69	84,800
	Le Havre	96.17	35,200
	Lyon	133.88	49,000
	Marseille	124.86	45,700
	Montpellier	107.92	39,500
	Paris	231.69	84,800
	Sevres	231.69	84,800
	Suresnes	231.69	84,800
	Versailles	231.69	84,800

Instructions for Form 2555 (2012)

	2012 LIMITS ON HOUSING EXPENSES		
Country	**City or Other Location**	**Limit on Housing Expenses (daily)**	**Limit on Housing Expenses (full year)**
Germany	Babenhausen	113.66	41,600
	Bad Aibling	96.99	35,500
	Bad Nauheim	90.98	33,300
	Baumholder	108.47	39,700
	Berlin	138.80	50,800
	Birkenfeld	108.47	39,700
	Boeblingen	137.70	50,400
	Bonn	114.75	42,000
	Butzbach	88.80	32,500
	Cologne	153.55	56,200
	Darmstadt	113.66	41,600
	Frankfurt am Main	118.58	43,400
	Friedberg	90.98	33,300
	Garmisch-Partenkirchen	103.55	37,900
	Gelnhausen	143.17	52,400
	Germersheim	85.79	31,400
	Giebelstadt	98.09	35,900
	Giessen	98.36	36,000
	Grafenwoehr	111.75	40,900
	Hanau	143.17	52,400
	Hannover	84.70	31,000
	Heidelberg	107.65	39,400
	Idar-Oberstein	108.47	39,700
	Ingolstadt	160.11	58,600
	Kaiserslautern, Landkreis	139.07	50,900
	Kitzingen	98.00	35,900
	Leimen	107.65	39,400
	Ludwigsburg	137.70	50,400
	Mainz	153.55	56,200
	Mannheim	107.65	39,400
	Munich	160.11	58,600
	Nellingen	137.70	50,400
	Neubruecke	108.47	39,700
	Ober Ramstadt	113.66	41,600
	Oberammergau	103.55	37,900
	Pirmasens	139.07	50,900
	Rheinau	107.65	39,400
	Schwetzingen	107.65	39,400

A-343

2012 LIMITS ON HOUSING EXPENSES			
Country	City or Other Location	Limit on Housing Expenses (daily)	Limit on Housing Expenses (full year)
Germany (*Continued*)	Seckenheim	107.65	39,400
	Sembach	139.07	50,900
	Stuttgart	137.70	50,400
	Vilseck	111.75	40,900
	Wahn	114.75	42,000
	Wertheim	98.09	35,900
	Wiesbaden	153.55	56,200
	Wuerzburg	98.09	35,900
	Zweibruecken	139.07	50,900
	All cities other than Augsburg, Babenhausen, Bad Aibling, Bad Kreuznach, Bad Nauheim, Baumholder, Berchtesgaden, Berlin, Birkenfeld, Boeblingen, Bonn, Bremen, Bremerhaven, Butzbach, Cologne, Darmstadt, Delmenhorst, Duesseldorf, Erlangen, Flensburg, Frankfurt am Main, Friedberg, Fuerth, Garlstedt, Garmisch-Partenkirchen, Geilenkirchen, Gelnhausen, Germersheim, Giebelstadt, Giessen, Grafenwoehr, Grefrath, Greven, Gruenstadt, Hamburg, Hanau, Handorf, Hannover, Heidelberg, Heilbronn, Herongen, Idar-Oberstein, Ingolstadt, Kaiserslautern, Landkreis, Kalkar, Karlsruhe, Kerpen, Kitzingen, Koblenz, Leimen, Leipzig, Ludwigsburg, Mainz, Mannheim, Mayen, Moenchen-Gladbach, Muenster, Munich, Nellingen, Neubruecke, Noervenich, Nuernberg, Ober Ramstadt, Oberammergau, Osterholz-Scharmbeck, Pirmasens, Rheinau, Rheinberg, Schwabach, Schwetzingen, Seckenheim, Sembach, Stuttgart, Twisteden, Vilseck, Wahn, Wertheim, Wiesbaden, Worms, Wuerzburg, Zirndorf, and Zweibruecken	110.11	40,300
Ghana	Accra	98.36	36,000
Greece	Argyroupolis	88.52	32,400
	Athens	113.66	41,600
	Elefsis	113.66	41,600
	Ellinikon	113.66	41,600
	Mt. Hortiatis	88.52	32,400
	Mt. Parnis	113.66	41,600
	Mt. Pateras	113.66	41,600
	Nea Makri	113.66	41,600
	Perivolaki	88.52	32,400
	Piraeus	113.66	41,600
	Tanagra	113.66	41,600
	Thessaloniki	88.52	32,400
Guatemala	Guatemala City	115.03	42,100
Guyana	Georgetown	95.63	35,000
Holy See, The		154.37	56,500
Hungary	Budapest	88.80	32,500
	Papa	121.58	44,500
India	Mumbai	185.57	67,920

Instructions for Form 2555 (2012)

	2012 LIMITS ON HOUSING EXPENSES		
Country	**City or Other Location**	**Limit on Housing Expenses (daily)**	**Limit on Housing Expenses (full year)**
India (*Continued*)	New Delhi	82.66	30,252
Indonesia	Jakarta	103.21	37,776
Ireland	Dublin	134.15	49,100
	Shannon Area	106.01	38,800
Israel	Tel Aviv	138.80	50,800
Italy	Catania	90.16	33,000
	Genoa	114.21	41,800
	Gioia Tauro	85.25	31,200
	La Spezia	110.38	40,400
	Leghorn	96.72	35,400
	Milan	230.60	84,400
	Naples	146.45	53,600
	Parma	117.21	42,900
	Pisa	96.72	35,400
	Pordenone-Aviano	117.21	42,900
	Rome	154.37	56,500
	Sardinia	79.23	29,000
	Sigonella	90.16	33,000
	Turin	115.30	42,200
	Vicenza	118.31	43,300
	All cities other than Avellino, Brindisi, Catania, Florence, Gaeta, Genoa, Gioia Tauro, La Spezia, Leghorn, Milan, Mount Vergine, Naples, Nettuno, Parma, Pisa, Pordenone-Aviano, Rome, Sardinia, Sigonella, Turin, Verona, and Vicenza	92.62	33,900
Jamaica	Kingston	112.57	41,200
Japan	Akashi	116.67	42,700
	Akizuki	102.73	37,600
	Atsugi	150.55	55,100
	Camp Zama	150.55	55,100
	Chiba-Ken	150.55	55,100
	Fussa	150.55	55,100
	Gifu	203.01	74,300
	Gotemba	111.48	40,800
	Haneda	150.55	55,100
	Iwakuni	117.76	43,100
	Kanagawa-Ken	150.55	55,100
	Komaki	203.01	74,300
	Machida-Shi	150.55	55,100
	Misawa	126.50	46,300
	Nagoya	203.01	74,300
	Okinawa Prefecture	202.73	74,200
	Osaka-Kobe	247.72	90,664
	Sagamihara	150.55	55,100
	Saitama-Ken	150.55	55,100
	Sasebo	126.23	46,200
	Tachikawa	150.55	55,100
	Tokyo	349.73	128,000
	Tokyo-to	150.55	55,100
	Yokohama	189.34	69,300
	Yokosuka	175.68	64,300
	Yokota	150.55	55,100
Kazakhstan	Almaty	131.15	48,000

A-345

2012 LIMITS ON HOUSING EXPENSES			
Country	City or Other Location	Limit on Housing Expenses (daily)	Limit on Housing Expenses (full year)
Korea	Camp Carroll	83.06	30,400
	Camp Colbern	143.44	52,500
	Camp Market	143.44	52,500
	Camp Mercer	143.44	52,500
	K-16	143.44	52,500
	Kimhae	78.14	28,600
	Kimpo Airfield	143.44	52,500
	Munsan	87.98	32,200
	Osan AB	90.71	33,200
	Pusan	78.14	28,600
	Pyongtaek	89.07	32,600
	Seoul	143.44	52,500
	Suwon	143.44	52,500
	Taegu	86.07	31,500
	Tongduchon	78.96	28,900
	Uijongbu	84.97	31,100
	Waegwan	83.06	30,400
	All cities other than Ammo Depot #9, Camp Carroll, Camp Colbern, Camp Market, Camp Mercer, Changwon, Chinhae, Chunchon, K-16, Kimhae, Kimpo Airfield, Kunsun, Kwangju, Munsan, Osan AB, Pusan, Pyongtaek, Seoul, Suwon, Taegu, Tongduchon, Uijongbu, and Waegwan	82.79	30,300
Kuwait	Kuwait City	175.96	64,400
	All cities other than Kuwait City	157.65	57,700
Luxembourg	Luxembourg	126.50	46,300
Macedonia	Skopje	96.72	35,400
Malaysia	Kuala Lumpur	126.23	46,200
	All cities other than Kuala Lumpur	92.08	33,700
Malta		137.98	50,500
Mexico	Mazatlan	84.70	31,000
	Merida	103.55	37,900
	Mexico City	118.58	43,400
	Monterrey	90.71	33,200
	All cities other than Ciudad Juarez, Cuernavaca, Guadalajara, Hermosillo, Matamoros, Mazatlan, Merida, Metapa, Mexico City, Monterrey, Nogales, Nuevo Laredo, Reynosa, Tapachula, Tijuana, Tuxtla Gutierrez, and Veracruz	107.65	39,400
Mozambique	Maputo	107.92	39,500
Namibia	Windhoek	87.70	32,100
Netherlands	Amsterdam	144.54	52,900
	Aruba	98.36	36,000
	Brunssum	108.74	39,800
	Eygelshoven	108.74	39,800
	Hague, The	183.88	67,300
	Heerlen	108.74	39,800
	Hoensbroek	108.74	39,800
	Hulsberg	108.74	39,800
	Kerkrade	108.74	39,800
	Landgraaf	108.74	39,800
	Maastricht	108.74	39,800
	Papendrecht	110.93	40,600
	Rotterdam	110.93	40,600
	Schaesburg	108.74	39,800
	Schinnen	108.74	39,800
	Schiphol	144.54	52,900
	Ypenburg	183.88	67,300
	All cities other than Amsterdam, Aruba, Brunssum, Coevorden, Eygelshoven, The Hague, Heerlen, Hoensbroek, Hulsberg, Kerkrade, Landgraaf, Maastricht, Margraten, Papendrecht, Rotterdam, Schaesburg, Schinnen, Schiphol, and Ypenburg	110.93	40,600

	2012 LIMITS ON HOUSING EXPENSES		
Country	**City or Other Location**	**Limit on Housing Expenses (daily)**	**Limit on Housing Expenses (full year)**
Netherlands Antilles	Curacao	125.14	45,800
New Zealand	Auckland	97.54	35,700
	Wellington	92.35	33,800
Nicaragua	Managua	86.89	31,800
Nigeria	Abuja	98.36	36,000
Norway	Oslo	141.26	51,700
	Stavanger	119.95	43,900
	All cities other than Oslo and Stavanger	103.01	37,700
Panama	Panama City	96.99	35,500
Philippines	Cavite	106.56	39,000
	Manila	106.56	39,000
Poland		80.33	29,400
Portugal	Alverca	141.26	51,700
	Lisbon	141.26	51,700
Qatar	Doha	99.08	36,264
	All cities other than Doha	88.52	32,400
Russia	Moscow	295.08	108,000
	Saint Petersburg	163.93	60,000
	Sakhalin Island	211.75	77,500
	Vladivostok	211.75	77,500
	Yekaterinburg	129.51	47,400
Rwanda	Kigali	86.07	31,500
Saudi Arabia	Jeddah	83.79	30,667
	Riyadh	109.29	40,000
Singapore		184.43	67,500
South Africa	Pretoria	107.38	39,300
Spain	Barcelona	110.93	40,600
	Madrid	188.25	68,900
	Rota	113.39	41,500
	Valencia	108.20	39,600
	All cities other than Barcelona, Madrid, Rota, Seville, Seville Province, and Valencia	81.69	29,900
Suriname	Paramaribo	90.16	33,000
Switzerland	Bern	181.69	66,500
	Geneva	257.10	94,100
	Zurich	107.16	39,219
	All cities other than Bern, Geneva, and Zurich	89.89	32,900
Taiwan	Taipei	126.20	46,188
Tanzania	Dar Es Salaam	120.22	44,000
Thailand	Bangkok	161.20	59,000
Trinidad and Tobago	Port of Spain	148.91	54,500
Turkey	Izmir-Cigli	86.34	31,600
	Yamanlar	86.34	31,600
Ukraine	Kiev	196.72	72,000
United Arab Emirates	Abu Dhabi	135.76	49,687
	Dubai	156.21	57,174

2012 LIMITS ON HOUSING EXPENSES			
Country	City or Other Location	Limit on Housing Expenses (daily)	Limit on Housing Expenses (full year)
United Kingdom	Basingstoke	112.29	41,099
	Bath	112.02	41,000
	Bracknell	169.67	62,100
	Bristol	105.74	38,700
	Brookwood	116.12	42,500
	Cambridge	117.49	43,000
	Caversham	201.64	73,800
	Cheltenham	140.98	51,600
	Croughton	117.21	42,900
	Fairford	116.94	42,800
	Farnborough	149.45	54,700
	Felixstowe	111.75	40,900
	Gibraltar	121.90	44,616
	Harrogate	123.50	45,200
	High Wycombe	169.67	62,100
	Kemble	116.94	42,800
	Lakenheath	145.90	53,400
	Liverpool	106.01	38,800
	London	228.42	83,600
	Loudwater	173.50	63,500
	Menwith Hill	123.50	45,200
	Mildenhall	145.90	53,400
	Oxfordshire	115.85	42,400
	Plymouth	115.85	42,400
	Portsmouth	115.85	42,400
	Reading	169.67	62,100
	Rochester	120.22	44,000
	Southampton	120.77	44,200
	Surrey	132.25	48,402
	Waterbeach	119.67	43,800
	Wiltshire	113.66	41,600
	All cities other than Basingstoke, Bath, Belfast, Birmingham, Bracknell, Bristol, Brookwood, Brough, Cambridge, Caversham, Chelmsford, Cheltenham, Chicksands, Croughton, Dunstable, Edinburgh, Edzell, Fairford, Farnborough, Felixstowe, Ft. Halstead, Gibraltar, Glenrothes, Greenham Common, Harrogate, High Wycombe, Hythe, Kemble, Lakenheath, Liverpool, London, Loudwater, Menwith Hill, Mildenhall, Nottingham, Oxfordshire, Plymouth, Portsmouth, Reading, Rochester, Southampton, Surrey, Waterbeach, Welford, West Byfleet, and Wiltshire	116.12	42,500
Venezuela	Caracas	155.74	57,000
Vietnam	Hanoi	127.87	46,800
	Ho Chi Minh City	114.75	42,000

A-348

Form **2555-EZ**

Department of the Treasury
Internal Revenue Service (99)

Foreign Earned Income Exclusion

► **Attach to Form 1040.**
► **Information about Form 2555-EZ and its separate instructions is at *www.irs.gov/form2555*.**

OMB No. 1545-0074

20**12**

Attachment
Sequence No. **34A**

Name shown on Form 1040 | Your social security number

You May Use This Form If You:
- Are a U.S. citizen or a resident alien.
- Earned wages/salaries in a foreign country.
- Had total foreign earned income of $95,100 or less.
- Are filing a calendar year return that covers a 12-month period.

And You:
- Do not have self-employment income.
- Do not have business/moving expenses.
- Do not claim the foreign housing exclusion or deduction.

Part I — Tests To See If You Can Take the Foreign Earned Income Exclusion

1   Bona Fide Residence Test

a   Were you a bona fide resident of a foreign country or countries for a period that includes an entire tax year (see page 2 of the instructions)? . . . . ☐ **Yes** ☐ **No**
- If you answered "Yes," you meet this test. Fill in line 1b and then go to line 3.
- If you answered "No," you **do not** meet this test. Go to line 2 to see if you meet the Physical Presence Test.

b   Enter the date your bona fide residence began ► _____ , and ended (see instructions) ► _____ .

2   Physical Presence Test

a   Were you physically present in a foreign country or countries for at least 330 full days during—
{ 2012 **or**
{ any other period of 12 months in a row starting or ending in 2012? } . . . . ☐ **Yes** ☐ **No**
- If you answered "Yes," you meet this test. Fill in line 2b and then go to line 3.
- If you answered "No," you **do not** meet this test. You **cannot** take the exclusion unless you meet the Bona Fide Residence Test above.

b   The physical presence test is based on the 12-month period from ► _____ through ► _____ .

3   Tax Home Test. Was your tax home in a foreign country or countries throughout your period of bona fide residence or physical presence, whichever applies? . . . . ☐ **Yes** ☐ **No**
- If you answered "Yes," you can take the exclusion. Complete Part II below and then go to page 2.
- If you answered "No," you **cannot** take the exclusion. **Do not** file this form.

Part II — General Information

4 Your foreign address (including country) | **5** Your occupation

6 Employer's name | **7** Employer's U.S. address (including ZIP code) | **8** Employer's foreign address

9   Employer is (check any that apply):
a   A U.S. business . . . . ☐
b   A foreign business . . . . ☐
c   Other (specify) ► _____ ☐
10a   If you previously filed Form 2555 or 2555-EZ, enter the last year you filed the form. ► _____
b   If you did not previously file Form 2555 or 2555-EZ, check here ► ☐ and go to line 11a now.
c   Have you ever revoked the foreign earned income exclusion? . . . . ☐ **Yes** ☐ **No**
d   If you answered "Yes," enter the tax year for which the revocation was effective. ► _____
11a   List your tax home(s) during 2012 and date(s) established. ► _____

b   Of what country are you a citizen/national? ► _____

For Paperwork Reduction Act Notice, see the Form 1040 instructions.   Cat. No. 13272W   Form **2555-EZ** (2012)

Part III   **Days Present in the United States—** Complete this part if you were in the
United States or its possessions during 2012.

12 (a) Date arrived in U.S.	(b) Date left U.S.	(c) Number of days in U.S. on business	(d) Income earned in U.S. on business (attach computation)

Part IV   **Figure Your Foreign Earned Income Exclusion**

13	Maximum foreign earned income exclusion	**13**	$95,100 00
14	Enter the number of days in your qualifying period that fall within 2012 . |**14**| **days**		
15	Did you enter 366 on line 14?		
	☐ **Yes.** Enter "1.000."		
	☐ **No.** Divide line 14 by 366 and enter the result as }	**15**	× .
	a decimal (rounded to at least three places). }		
16	Multiply line 13 by line 15	**16**	
17	Enter, in U.S. dollars, the total foreign earned income you earned and received in 2012 (see instructions). Be sure to include this amount on Form 1040, line 7	**17**	
18	**Foreign earned income exclusion.** Enter the **smaller** of line 16 or line 17 here and in parentheses on **Form 1040, line 21.** Next to the amount enter "2555-EZ." On Form 1040, subtract this amount from your income to arrive at total income on Form 1040, line 22 . . . . ▶	**18**	

Form **2555-EZ** (2012)

20**12**
Instructions for Form 2555-EZ

Foreign Earned Income Exclusion

Department of the Treasury
Internal Revenue Service

Section references are to the Internal Revenue Code unless otherwise noted.

Future Developments

For the latest information about developments related to Form 2555-EZ and its instructions, such as legislation enacted after they were published, go to *www.irs.gov/form2555*.

What's New

Exclusion amount. For 2012, the maximum exclusion has increased to $95,100.

General Instructions

 Do not include on Form 1040, line 62 (federal income tax withheld), any taxes a foreign employer withheld from your pay and paid to the foreign country's tax authority instead of to the U.S. Treasury.

Purpose of Form

If you qualify, you can use Form 2555-EZ instead of Form 2555, Foreign Earned Income, to figure your foreign earned income exclusion. You cannot exclude more than your foreign earned income for the year.

General Information

If you are a U.S. citizen or a U.S. resident alien living in a foreign country, you are subject to the same U.S. income tax laws that apply to citizens and resident aliens living in the United States.

Note. Specific rules apply to determine if you are a resident or nonresident alien of the United States. See Pub. 519, U.S. Tax Guide for Aliens, for details.

Foreign country. A foreign country is any territory under the sovereignty of a government other than that of the United States.

The term "foreign country" includes the country's territorial waters and airspace, but not international waters and the airspace above them. It also includes the seabed and subsoil of those submarine areas adjacent to the country's territorial waters over which it has exclusive rights under international law to explore and exploit the natural resources.

The term "foreign country" does not include U.S. possessions or territories. It does not include the Antarctic region.

Who Qualifies

You can use Form 2555-EZ to claim the foreign earned income exclusion if all of the following apply.

- You meet the seven conditions listed at the top of Form 2555-EZ.
- Your total foreign earned income received in 2012 is reported on Form 1040, line 7.
- You do not have a housing deduction carryover from 2011.
- You meet either the bona fide residence test (see the instructions for lines 1a and 1b, later) or the physical presence test (see the instructions for lines 2a and 2b, later).
- You meet the tax home test (see the instructions for line 3, later).

Note. Income from working abroad as an employee of the U.S. Government does not qualify for the foreign earned income exclusion. Do not file Form 2555-EZ.

Married Couples

If both you and your spouse qualify for, and choose to claim, the foreign earned income exclusion, figure the amount of the exclusion separately for each of you. You must each complete separate Forms 2555-EZ.

Community income. The amount of the exclusion is not affected by the income-splitting provisions of community property laws. The sum of the amounts figured separately for each of you is the total amount excluded on a joint return.

Travel to Cuba

Generally, if you were in Cuba in violation of U.S. travel restrictions, the following rules apply.

- Any time spent in Cuba cannot be counted in determining if you qualify under the bona fide residence or physical presence test.
- Any income earned in Cuba is not considered foreign earned income.

Note. If you performed services at the U.S. Naval Base at Guantanamo Bay, you were not in violation of U.S. travel restrictions.

Additional Information

Pub. 54, Tax Guide for U.S. Citizens and Resident Aliens Abroad, has more information about the bona fide residence test, the physical presence test, and the foreign earned income exclusion. You can get this publication from most U.S. Embassies and consulates or by writing to: National Distribution Center, 1201 N. Mitsubishi Motorway, Bloomington, IL 61705-6613. You can also download this publication (as well as other forms and publications) at IRS.gov.

Waiver of Time Requirements

If your tax home was in a foreign country and you were a bona fide resident of, or physically present in, a foreign country and had to leave because of war, civil unrest, or similar adverse conditions, the minimum time requirements specified under the bona fide residence and physical presence tests may be waived. You must be able to show that you reasonably could have expected to meet the minimum time requirements if you had not been required to leave. Each year the IRS will publish in the Internal Revenue Bulletin a list of the only countries that qualify for the waiver for the previous year and the dates they qualify. If you left one of the countries during the period indicated, you can claim the foreign earned income exclusion on Form 2555-EZ, but only for the number of days you were a bona fide resident of, or physically present in, the foreign country.

If you can claim the foreign earned income exclusion because of the waiver of time requirements, attach a statement to your return explaining that you expected to meet the applicable time requirement, but the conditions in the foreign country prevented you from the normal conduct of business. Also, enter "Claiming Waiver" in the top margin on page 1 of your Form 2555-EZ.

When To File

Form 1040 is generally due April 15, 2013.

However, you are automatically granted a 2-month extension of time to file (to June 17, 2013) if, on the due date of your return, you live outside the United States and Puerto Rico and your tax home (defined later) is outside the United States and Puerto Rico. If you take this extension, you must attach a statement to your return explaining that you meet these two conditions.

The automatic 2-month extension also applies to paying the tax. However, interest is charged on the unpaid tax from the regular due date until it is paid.

When to claim the exclusion(s). The first year you plan to take the foreign earned income exclusion, you may not yet have met either the physical presence test or the bona fide residence test by the due date of your return (including the automatic 2-month extension, discussed earlier). If this occurs, you can either:

1. Apply for a special extension to a date after you expect to qualify, or

2. File your return timely without claiming the exclusion and then file an amended return after you qualify.

Special extension of time. To apply for this extension, complete and file Form 2350, Application for Extension of Time To File U.S. Income Tax Return, with the Department of the Treasury, Internal Revenue Service Center, Austin, TX 73301-0045, before the due date of your return. Interest is charged on the tax not paid by the regular due date as explained earlier.

Amended return. File Form 1040X, Amended U.S. Individual Income Tax Return, to change a return you already filed. Generally, Form 1040X must be filed within 3 years after the date the original return was filed or within 2 years after the date the tax was paid, whichever is later.

Choosing the Exclusion

To choose the foreign earned income exclusion, complete the appropriate parts of Form 2555-EZ and file it with your Form 1040 or Form 1040X. Your initial choice to claim the exclusion must usually be made on a timely filed return (including extensions) or on a return amending a timely filed return. However, there are exceptions. See Pub. 54 for more information.

Once you choose to claim the exclusion, that choice remains in effect for that year and all future years unless it is revoked. To revoke your choice, you must attach a statement to your return for the first year you do not wish to claim the exclusion. If you revoke your choice, you cannot claim the exclusion for your next 5 tax years without the approval of the Internal Revenue Service. See Pub. 54 for details.

Figuring tax on income not excluded. If you claim the foreign earned income exclusion, you must figure the tax on your nonexcluded income using the tax rates that would have applied had you not

claimed the exclusion. See the Instructions for Form 1040 and complete the Foreign Earned Income Tax Worksheet to figure the amount of tax to enter on Form 1040, line 44. When figuring your alternative minimum tax on Form 6251, you must use the Foreign Earned Income Tax Worksheet in the instructions for Form 6251.

Earned income credit. You cannot take the earned income credit if you claim the exclusion.

Foreign tax credit or deduction. You cannot claim a credit or deduction for foreign income taxes paid on income you exclude. If all of your foreign earned income is excluded, you cannot claim a credit or deduction for the foreign taxes paid on that income. If only part of your income is excluded, you cannot claim a credit or deduction for the foreign taxes allocable to the excluded income. For details on how to figure the amount allocable to the excluded income, see Pub. 514, Foreign Tax Credit for Individuals.

IRA deduction. If you claim the exclusion, special rules apply in figuring the amount of your IRA deduction. For details, see Pub. 590, Individual Retirement Arrangements (IRAs).

Specific Instructions

Lines 1a and 1b

Bona Fide Residence Test

To meet this test, you must be one of the following:
• A U.S. citizen who is a bona fide resident of a foreign country, or countries, for an uninterrupted period that includes an entire tax year (January 1–December 31), or
• A U.S. resident alien who is a citizen or national of a country with which the United States has an income tax treaty in effect and who is a bona fide resident of a foreign country, or countries, for an uninterrupted period that includes an entire tax year (January 1–December 31). See Pub. 901, U.S. Tax Treaties, for a list of countries with which the United States has an income tax treaty in effect.

Whether you are a bona fide resident of a foreign country depends on your intention about the length and nature of your stay. Evidence of your intention may be your words and acts. If these conflict, your acts carry more weight than your words. Generally, if you go to a foreign country for a definite, temporary purpose and return to the United States after you accomplish it, you are not a bona fide resident of the foreign country. If accomplishing the purpose requires an

extended, indefinite stay, and you make your home in the foreign country, you may be a bona fide resident. See Pub. 54 for more information and examples.

If you submitted a statement of nonresidence to the authorities of a foreign country in which you earned income and the authorities hold that you are not subject to their income tax laws by reason of nonresidency in the foreign country, you are not considered a bona fide resident of that country.

If you submitted such a statement and the authorities have not made an adverse determination of your nonresident status, you are not considered a bona fide resident of that country.

Line 1b. If you answered "Yes" on line 1a, enter the dates your bona fide residence began and ended. If you are still a bona fide resident, enter "Continues" in the space for the date your bona fide residence ended.

Lines 2a and 2b

Physical Presence Test

To meet this test, you must be a U.S. citizen or resident alien who is physically present in a foreign country, or countries, for at least 330 full days during any period of 12 months in a row. A full day means the 24-hour period that starts at midnight.

Line 2a. To figure 330 full days of presence, add all separate periods you were present in a foreign country during the 12-month period in which those days occurred. The 330 full days can be interrupted by periods when you are traveling over international waters or are otherwise not in a foreign country. See Pub. 54 for more information and examples.

Line 2b. The 12-month period on which the physical presence test is based must include 365 or 366 days, part of which must be in 2012. The dates may begin or end in a calendar year other than 2012.

 You must enter dates in both spaces provided on line 2b. Do not enter "Continues" in the space for the ending date.

Note. A nonresident alien who, with a U.S. citizen or U.S. resident alien spouse, chooses to be taxed as a resident of the United States can qualify under this test if the time requirements are met. See Pub. 54 for details on how to make this choice.

Line 3

Tax Home Test

To meet this test, your tax home must be in a foreign country, or countries (see *Foreign country*, earlier), throughout your period of bona fide residence or physical presence, whichever applies. For this purpose, your period of physical presence is the 330 full days during which you were present in a foreign country, not the 12 consecutive months during which those days occurred.

Your tax home is your regular or principal place of business, employment, or post of duty, regardless of where you maintain your family residence. If you do not have a regular or principal place of business because of the nature of your trade or business, your tax home is your regular place of abode (the place where you regularly live).

You are not considered to have a tax home in a foreign country for any period during which your abode is in the United States. However, if you are temporarily present in the United States, or you maintain a dwelling in the United States (whether or not that dwelling is used by your spouse and dependents), it does not necessarily mean that your abode is in the United States during that time.

Example. You are employed on an offshore oil rig in the territorial waters of a foreign country and work a 28-day on/28-day off schedule. You return to your family residence in the United States during your off periods. You are considered to have an abode in the United States and do not meet the tax home test. You cannot claim the foreign earned income exclusion.

Line 4

Enter your entire address including city, province or state, country, and postal code. If using a military or diplomatic address, include the country in which you are living or stationed.

Line 12

Complete columns (a) through (d) if you were present in the United States or any of its possessions in 2012. Do not include time spent in the United States or its possessions before your period of bona fide residence or physical presence, whichever applies, began or after it ended.

Column (d). Enter, in U.S. dollars, the amount of income earned in the United

States on business (such as meetings or conventions). Attach a statement showing how you determined the amount. Do not include this income on line 17. Even if you live and work in a foreign country, any income earned during the time spent in the United States on business is considered U.S. source income and cannot be excluded.

Line 14

Enter the number of days in your qualifying period that fall within 2012. Your qualifying period is the period during which you meet the tax home test and either the bona fide residence test or the physical presence test.

Example. You establish a tax home and bona fide residence in a foreign country on August 14, 2012. You maintain the tax home and residence until January 31, 2014. The number of days in your qualifying period that fall within 2012 is 140 (August 14 through December 31, 2012).

Line 17

Enter the total foreign earned income you earned and received in 2012. Report the amount in U.S. dollars using the exchange rates in effect when you actually received the income. If you are a cash-basis taxpayer, include in income on Form 1040 the foreign earned income you received in 2012 regardless of when you earned it. (For example, include wages on Form 1040, line 7.)

Income is earned in the year you performed the services for which you received the pay. But if you received your last wage or salary payment for 2011 in 2012 because of your employer's payroll period, that income can be treated as earned in 2012. If you cannot treat that wage or salary payment as earned in 2012, the rules explained later under *Income earned in prior year* apply. See Pub. 54 for more details.

Foreign earned income. For purposes of this form, foreign earned income means only the following types of income received for personal services you performed in a foreign country during the period for which you meet the tax home

test and either the bona fide residence test or the physical presence test.
- Wages, salaries, tips, and bonuses.
- Noncash income (such as a home or car) if reported as income on Form 1040, line 7.
- Allowances or reimbursements if reported as income on Form 1040, line 7.

Foreign earned income does not include:
- Income earned in the United States on business (Form 2555-EZ, line 12, column (d)),
- Amounts paid to you by the U.S. Government or any of its agencies if you were an employee of the U.S. Government or any of its agencies,
- Amounts that are actually a distribution of corporate earnings or profits rather than a reasonable allowance as compensation for your personal services,
- Amounts received after the end of the tax year following the tax year in which you performed the services, or
- Amounts you must include in gross income because of your employer's contributions to a nonexempt employees' trust or to a nonqualified annuity contract.

Income earned in prior year. Foreign earned income received in 2012 for services you performed in 2011 can be excluded from your 2012 gross income if, and to the extent, the income would have been excludable if you had received it in 2011.

If you are excluding income under this rule, do not include this income on line 17. Instead, attach a statement to Form 2555-EZ showing how you figured the exclusion. Enter the amount that would have been excludable in 2011 on Form 2555-EZ to the left of line 18. Next to the amount enter "Exclusion of Income Earned in 2011." Include it in the total reported on line 18.

Note. If you claimed any deduction, credit, or exclusion on your 2011 return that is definitely related to the 2011 foreign earned income you are excluding under this rule, you may have to amend your 2011 income tax return to adjust the amount claimed. To do this, file Form 1040X.

Form **2678**
(Rev. October 2012)

Employer/Payer Appointment of Agent

Department of the Treasury — Internal Revenue Service

OMB No. 1545-0748

Use this form if you want to request approval to have an agent file returns and make deposits or payments of employment or other withholding taxes or if you want to revoke an existing appointment.

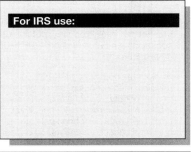

For IRS use:

- If you are an employer or payer who wants to request approval, complete Parts 1 and 2 and sign Part 2. Then give it to the agent. Have the agent complete Part 3 and sign it.

  Note. This appointment is not effective until we approve your request. See the instructions for filing Form 2678 on page 3.

- If you are an employer, payer, or agent who wants to revoke an existing appointment, complete all three parts. In this case, only one signature is required.

Part 1: Why you are filing this form...

(Check one)

☐ You want to **appoint** an agent for tax reporting, depositing, and paying.

☐ You want to **revoke** an existing appointment.

Part 2: Employer or Payer Information: Complete this part if you want to appoint an agent or revoke an appointment.

1 Employer identification number (EIN)

☐☐ – ☐☐☐☐☐☐☐

2 Employer's or payer's name
(not your trade name)

3 Trade name (if any)

4 Address

Number	Street		Suite or room number

City		State	ZIP code

5 Forms for which you want to appoint an agent or revoke the agent's appointment to file.
(*Check all that apply.*)

	For ALL employees/ payees	For SOME employees/ payees
Form 940, 940-PR (Employer's Annual Federal Unemployment (FUTA) Tax Return)*	☐	☐
Form 941, 941-PR, 941-SS (Employer's QUARTERLY Federal Tax Return)	☐	☐
Form 943, 943-PR (Employer's Annual Federal Tax Return for Agricultural Employees)	☐	☐
Form 944, 944(SP) (Employer's ANNUAL Federal Tax Return)	☐	☐
Form 945 (Annual Return of Withheld Federal Income Tax)	☐	☐
Form CT-1 (Employer's Annual Railroad Retirement Tax Return)	☐	☐
Form CT-2 (Employee Representative's Quarterly Railroad Tax Return)	☐	☐

*Generally you cannot appoint an agent to report, deposit, and pay taxes reported on Form 940, Employer's Annual Federal Unemployment (FUTA) Tax Return, unless you are a home care service recipient.

☐ Check here if you are a home care service recipient, and you want to appoint the agent to report, deposit, and pay FUTA taxes for you. See the instructions.

I am authorizing the IRS to disclose otherwise confidential tax information to the agent relating to the authority granted under this appointment, including disclosures required to process Form 2678. The agent may contract with a third party, such as a reporting agent or certified public accountant, to prepare or file the returns covered by this appointment, or to make any required deposits and payments. Such contract may authorize the IRS to disclose confidential tax information of the employer/payer and agent to such third party. If a third party fails to file the returns or make the deposits and payments, the agent and employer/payer remain liable.

X Sign your name here

Date _____ / _____ / _____

Print your name here _____

Print your title here _____

Best daytime phone _____

Now give this form to the agent to complete. ▶

For Paperwork Reduction Act Notice, see the instructions.   IRS.gov/form2678   Cat. No. 18770D   Form **2678** (Rev. 10-2012)

Part 3:   Agent Information: If you will be an agent for an employer or payer, or want to revoke an appointment, complete this part.

6   **Agent's employer identification number (EIN)**   ☐ ☐ – ☐ ☐ ☐ ☐ ☐ ☐ ☐

7   **Agent's name** (not trade name)

8   **Trade name** (if any)

9   **Address**

Number   Street   Suite or room number

City   State   ZIP code

☐   Check here if the employer is a home care service recipient receiving home care services through a program administered by a federal, state, or local government agency.

Under penalties of perjury, I declare that I have examined this form and any attachments, and to the best of my knowledge and belief, it is true, correct, and complete.

✗ Sign your name here

Print your name here

Print your title here

Date   /   /

Best daytime phone

Instructions for Form 2678

Section references are to the Internal Revenue Code.

Future Developments

For the latest information about developments related to Form 2678 and its instructions, such as legislation enacted after they were published, go to *www.irs.gov/form2678*.

Purpose of Form

Use this form if you want to request approval to have an agent file returns and make deposits or payments of employment or other withholding taxes or if you want to revoke an existing appointment. You cannot use a prior version of this form. All prior versions are obsolete and will not be accepted.

• If you want to appoint an agent, check the box in Part 1 that says, "You want to **appoint** an agent for tax reporting, depositing, and paying," and complete Part 2.

Note. Generally, employers cannot appoint an agent to report, deposit, and pay FUTA taxes. If you are a home care service recipient, you may request approval to have an agent act on your behalf for FUTA tax purposes by checking the box in the footnote on line 5.

• If you are an agent and you want to accept an appointment, complete Part 3. If you are a corporate officer, partner, or tax matters partner, you must have the authority to execute this appointment of agent.

Note. If the employer/payer will be making payments not covered by the appointment, the employer/payer must file all related returns and deposit and pay taxes for those payments. When completing line 5, check the box(es) "For SOME employees/payees."

• If you are an employer, payer, or agent and you want to revoke an existing appointment of an agent, check the box in Part 1 that says, "You want to **revoke** an existing appointment," and complete Parts 2 and 3. However, only one signature is required. If an existing appointment is revoked, the IRS cannot disclose confidential tax information to anyone other than the employer/payer for periods after the appointment is revoked.

Filing Form 2678

Send Form 2678 to the address for your location in the *Where To File Chart*, later. We will send a letter to the agent after we have approved the request. Until we approve the request, the agent is not liable for filing any tax returns or making any deposits or payments.

Filing Schedule R (Form 940) and Schedule R (Form 941)

An agent for a home care service recipient that files an aggregate Form 940 must complete Schedule R (Form 940), Allocation Schedule for Aggregate Form 940 Filers, and file it with the aggregate Form 940.

An agent that files an aggregate Form 941 must complete Schedule R (Form 941), Allocation Schedule for Aggregate Form 941 Filers, and file it with the aggregate Form 941.

What are the reporting, deposit, and payment requirements after the IRS approves the appointment?

Agents must follow the procedures in Revenue Procedure 70-6 for employment taxes (unless you are a subagent for a state agent under Notice 2003-70) and Revenue Procedure 84-33 for

backup withholding. Agents for employers who are home care service recipients receiving home care services through a program administered by a federal, state, or local government agency may also use this form. These agents are often referred to as "fiscal/employer agents" and "household employer agents." All agents, employers, and payers remain liable for filing all returns and making all tax deposits and payments while this appointment is in effect. If an agent contracts with a third party, such as a reporting agent or certified public accountant, to prepare or file the returns covered by this appointment or to make any required tax deposits or payments and the third party fails to do so, the agent, employer, and payer remain liable.

Privacy Act and Paperwork Reduction Act Notice. We ask for the information on Form 2678 to carry out the Internal Revenue laws of the United States. The principal purpose of this information is to permit you to appoint an agent to act on your behalf. You do not have to appoint an agent; however, if you choose to appoint an agent, you must provide the information requested on Form 2678. Our authority to collect this information is section 3504. Section 6109 requires you and the agent to provide your identification numbers. Failure to provide this information could delay or prevent processing your appointment of agent. Intentionally providing false information could subject you and the agent to penalties.

You are not required to provide the information requested on a form that is subject to the Paperwork Reduction Act unless the form displays a valid OMB control number. Books or records relating to a form or its instructions must be retained as long as their contents may become material in the administration of any Internal Revenue law.

Generally, tax returns and return information are confidential, as required by section 6103. However, section 6103 allows or requires the IRS to disclose or give the information shown on this form to others as described in the Code. For example, we may disclose your tax information to the Department of Justice for civil and criminal litigation, and to cities, states, the District of Columbia, and U.S. commonwealths and possessions for use in administering their tax laws. We may also disclose this information to other countries under a tax treaty, to federal and state agencies to enforce federal nontax criminal laws, or to federal law enforcement and intelligence agencies to combat terrorism.

The time needed to complete and file Form 2678 will vary depending on individual circumstances. The estimated average time is:

Recordkeeping . . . . 1 hr., 5 min.

Learning about the law or the form . . . . 54 min.

**Preparing, copying, assembling, and
sending the form to the IRS** . . . . 13 min.

If you have any comments concerning the accuracy of these time estimates or suggestions for making Form 2678 simpler, we would be happy to hear from you. You can email us at *taxforms@irs.gov.* Enter "Form 2678" on the subject line. Or write to: Internal Revenue Service, Tax Products Coordinating Committee, SE:W:CAR:MP:T:M:S, 1111 Constitution Ave. NW, IR-6526, Washington, DC 20224. **Do not** send Form 2678 to this address. Instead, see the *Where To File Chart* next.

Form 2678 (Rev. 10-2012)   Page **4**

Where To File Chart

If you are in ...

						Then use this address ...
Connecticut Delaware District of Columbia	Illinois Indiana Kentucky Maine	Maryland Massachusetts Michigan New Hampshire	New Jersey New York North Carolina Ohio	Pennsylvania Rhode Island South Carolina Vermont	Virginia West Virginia Wisconsin	Department of the Treasury, Internal Revenue Service, Cincinnati, OH 45999
Alabama Alaska Arizona Arkansas California	Colorado Florida Georgia Hawaii Idaho	Iowa Kansas Louisiana Minnesota Mississippi	Missouri Montana Nebraska Nevada New Mexico	North Dakota Oklahoma Oregon South Dakota Tennessee	Texas Utah Washington Wyoming	Department of the Treasury, Internal Revenue Service, Ogden, UT 84201
No legal residence or place of business in any state						Department of the Treasury, Internal Revenue Service, Ogden, UT 84201
Exempt organization or government entity						Department of the Treasury, Internal Revenue Service, Ogden, UT 84201-0046

Form **2848**	**Power of Attorney**	OMB No. 1545-0150
(Rev. March 2012) Department of the Treasury Internal Revenue Service	**and Declaration of Representative** ▶ **Type or print.** ▶ **See the separate instructions.**	**For IRS Use Only** Received by: Name _____ Telephone _____ Function _____ Date / /

Part I **Power of Attorney**

Caution: *A separate Form 2848 should be completed for each taxpayer. Form 2848 will not be honored for any purpose other than representation before the IRS.*

1 Taxpayer information. Taxpayer must sign and date this form on page 2, line 7.

Taxpayer name and address	Taxpayer identification number(s)	
	Daytime telephone number	Plan number (if applicable)

hereby appoints the following representative(s) as attorney(s)-in-fact:

2 Representative(s) must sign and date this form on page 2, Part II.

Name and address

CAF No. _____
PTIN _____
Telephone No. _____
Fax No. _____

Check if to be sent notices and communications ☐   Check if new: Address ☐   Telephone No. ☐   Fax No. ☐

Name and address

CAF No. _____
PTIN _____
Telephone No. _____
Fax No. _____

Check if to be sent notices and communications ☐   Check if new: Address ☐   Telephone No. ☐   Fax No. ☐

Name and address

CAF No. _____
PTIN _____
Telephone No. _____
Fax No. _____

Check if new: Address ☐   Telephone No. ☐   Fax No. ☐

to represent the taxpayer before the Internal Revenue Service for the following matters:

3 Matters

Description of Matter (Income, Employment, Payroll, Excise, Estate, Gift, Whistleblower, Practitioner Discipline, PLR, FOIA, Civil Penalty, etc.) (see instructions for line 3)	Tax Form Number (1040, 941, 720, etc.) (if applicable)	Year(s) or Period(s) (if applicable) (see instructions for line 3)

4 Specific use not recorded on Centralized Authorization File (CAF). If the power of attorney is for a specific use not recorded on CAF, check this box. See the instructions for Line 4. **Specific Uses Not Recorded on CAF** . . . . ▶ ☐

5 Acts authorized. Unless otherwise provided below, the representatives generally are authorized to receive and inspect confidential tax information and to perform any and all acts that I can perform with respect to the tax matters described on line 3, for example, the authority to sign any agreements, consents, or other documents. The representative(s), however, is (are) not authorized to receive or negotiate any amounts paid to the client in connection with this representation (including refunds by either electronic means or paper checks). Additionally, unless the appropriate box(es) below are checked, the representative(s) is (are) not authorized to execute a request for disclosure of tax returns or return information to a third party, substitute another representative or add additional representatives, or sign certain tax returns.

☐ Disclosure to third parties;   ☐ Substitute or add representative(s);   ☐ Signing a return; _____

☐ Other acts authorized: _____
(see instructions for more information)

Exceptions. An unenrolled return preparer cannot sign any document for a taxpayer and may only represent taxpayers in limited situations. An enrolled actuary may only represent taxpayers to the extent provided in section 10.3(d) of Treasury Department Circular No. 230 (Circular 230). An enrolled retirement plan agent may only represent taxpayers to the extent provided in section 10.3(e) of Circular 230. A registered tax return preparer may only represent taxpayers to the extent provided in section 10.3(f) of Circular 230. See the line 5 instructions for restrictions on tax matters partners. In most cases, the student practitioner's (level k) authority is limited (for example, they may only practice under the supervision of another practitioner).

List any specific deletions to the acts otherwise authorized in this power of attorney: _____
_____
_____
_____

For Privacy Act and Paperwork Reduction Act Notice, see the instructions.   Cat. No. 11980J   Form **2848** (Rev. 3-2012)

6   **Retention/revocation of prior power(s) of attorney.** The filing of this power of attorney automatically revokes all earlier power(s) of attorney on file with the Internal Revenue Service for the same matters and years or periods covered by this document. If you **do not** want to revoke a prior power of attorney, check here . . . . ▶ ☐
YOU MUST ATTACH A COPY OF ANY POWER OF ATTORNEY YOU WANT TO REMAIN IN EFFECT.

7   **Signature of taxpayer.** If a tax matter concerns a year in which a joint return was filed, the husband and wife must each file a separate power of attorney even if the same representative(s) is (are) being appointed. If signed by a corporate officer, partner, guardian, tax matters partner, executor, receiver, administrator, or trustee on behalf of the taxpayer, I certify that I have the authority to execute this form on behalf of the taxpayer.

▶ **IF NOT SIGNED AND DATED, THIS POWER OF ATTORNEY WILL BE RETURNED TO THE TAXPAYER.**

Signature	Date	Title (if applicable)
Print Name	PIN Number	Print name of taxpayer from line 1 if other than individual

Part II   Declaration of Representative

Under penalties of perjury, I declare that:

• I am not currently under suspension or disbarment from practice before the Internal Revenue Service;

• I am aware of regulations contained in Circular 230 (31 CFR, Part 10), as amended, concerning practice before the Internal Revenue Service;

• I am authorized to represent the taxpayer identified in Part I for the matter(s) specified there; and

• I am one of the following:

  a Attorney—a member in good standing of the bar of the highest court of the jurisdiction shown below.

  b Certified Public Accountant—duly qualified to practice as a certified public accountant in the jurisdiction shown below.

  c Enrolled Agent—enrolled as an agent under the requirements of Circular 230.

  d Officer—a bona fide officer of the taxpayer's organization.

  e Full-Time Employee—a full-time employee of the taxpayer.

  f Family Member—a member of the taxpayer's immediate family (for example, spouse, parent, child, grandparent, grandchild, step-parent, step-child, brother, or sister).

  g Enrolled Actuary—enrolled as an actuary by the Joint Board for the Enrollment of Actuaries under 29 U.S.C. 1242 (the authority to practice before the Internal Revenue Service is limited by section 10.3(d) of Circular 230).

  h Unenrolled Return Preparer—Your authority to practice before the Internal Revenue Service is limited. You must have been eligible to sign the return under examination and have signed the return. **See Notice 2011-6 and Special rules for registered tax return preparers and unenrolled return preparers in the instructions.**

  i Registered Tax Return Preparer—registered as a tax return preparer under the requirements of section 10.4 of Circular 230. Your authority to practice before the Internal Revenue Service is limited. You must have been eligible to sign the return under examination and have signed the return. **See Notice 2011-6 and Special rules for registered tax return preparers and unenrolled return preparers in the instructions.**

  k Student Attorney or CPA—receives permission to practice before the IRS by virtue of his/her status as a law, business, or accounting student working in LITC or STCP under section 10.7(d) of Circular 230. See instructions for Part II for additional information and requirements.

  r Enrolled Retirement Plan Agent—enrolled as a retirement plan agent under the requirements of Circular 230 (the authority to practice before the Internal Revenue Service is limited by section 10.3(e)).

  ▶ **IF THIS DECLARATION OF REPRESENTATIVE IS NOT SIGNED AND DATED, THE POWER OF ATTORNEY WILL BE RETURNED. REPRESENTATIVES MUST SIGN IN THE ORDER LISTED IN LINE 2 ABOVE.** See the instructions for Part II.

Note: For designations d-f, enter your title, position, or relationship to the taxpayer in the "Licensing jurisdiction" column. See the instructions for Part II for more information.

Designation— Insert above letter (a–r)	Licensing jurisdiction (state) or other licensing authority (if applicable)	Bar, license, certification, registration, or enrollment number (if applicable). See instructions for Part II for more information.	Signature	Date

Instructions for Form 2848

Department of the Treasury
Internal Revenue Service

(Rev. March 2012)

Power of Attorney and Declaration of Representative

Section references are to the Internal Revenue Code unless otherwise noted.

General Instructions

What's New

Joint returns. Joint filers must now complete and submit separate Forms 2848 to have the power of attorney recorded on the IRS's Centralized Authorization File (CAF).

Copies of notices and communications. You must check the box next to your representative's name and address if you want to authorize the IRS to send copies of all notices and communications to your representative.

Acts authorized. Check boxes have been added to assist you in identifying certain specific acts that your representative may perform. The CAF no longer records authorizations allowing your representative to receive but not endorse your refund check; the check box authorizing this act has been eliminated.

Representative designations. A new designation (i) has been added for registered tax return preparers. Also, the designations for student attorneys and student certified public accountants (CPA) have been combined into one designation (k). See the instructions for Part II.

Future developments. The IRS has created a page on IRS.gov for Form 2848 and its instructions, at *www.irs.gov/form2848*. Information about any future developments affecting Form 2848 (such as legislation enacted after we release it) will be posted on that page.

Purpose of Form

Use Form 2848 to authorize an individual to represent you before the IRS. See "Substitute Form 2848" for information about using a power of attorney other than a Form 2848 to authorize an individual to represent you before the IRS. The individual you authorize must

be an individual eligible to practice before the IRS. Eligible individuals are listed in Part II, Declaration of Representative, items a-r. You may authorize a student who works in a qualified Low Income Taxpayer Clinic (LITC) or Student Tax Clinic Program (STCP) to represent you under a special order issued by the Office of Professional Responsibility, see the instructions for Part II, later. Your authorization of an eligible representative will also allow that individual to receive and inspect your confidential tax information. See the instructions for line 7.

Use Form 8821, Tax Information Authorization, if you want to authorize an individual or organization to receive or inspect your confidential tax return information, but do not want to authorize an individual to represent you before the IRS. Use Form 4506T, Request for Transcript of Tax Return, if you want to authorize an individual or organization to receive or inspect transcripts of your confidential return information, but do not want to authorize an individual to represent you before the IRS. This form is often used by third parties to verify your tax compliance.

Use Form 56, Notice Concerning Fiduciary Relationship, to notify the IRS of the existence of a fiduciary relationship. A fiduciary (trustee, executor, administrator, receiver, or guardian) stands in the position of a taxpayer and acts as the taxpayer, not as a representative. If a fiduciary wishes to authorize an individual to represent or perform certain acts on behalf of the entity, the fiduciary must file a power of attorney that names the eligible individual(s) as representative(s) for the entity. Because the fiduciary stands in the position of the entity, the fiduciary signs the power of attorney on behalf of the entity.

Note. Authorizing someone to represent you does not relieve you of your tax obligations.

Where To File

Except as provided in this paragraph, completed Forms 2848 should be mailed or faxed directly to the IRS office identified in the *Where To File Chart* below. The exceptions are listed as follows:

Where To File Chart

IF you live in...	THEN use this address...	Fax number*
Alabama, Arkansas, Connecticut, Delaware, District of Columbia, Florida, Georgia, Illinois, Indiana, Kentucky, Louisiana, Maine, Maryland, Massachusetts, Michigan, Mississippi, New Hampshire, New Jersey, New York, North Carolina, Ohio, Pennsylvania, Rhode Island, South Carolina, Tennessee, Vermont, Virginia, or West Virginia	Internal Revenue Service P.O. Box 268, Stop 8423 Memphis, TN 38101-0268	901-546-4115
Alaska, Arizona, California, Colorado, Hawaii, Idaho, Iowa, Kansas, Minnesota, Missouri, Montana, Nebraska, Nevada, New Mexico, North Dakota, Oklahoma, Oregon, South Dakota, Texas, Utah, Washington, Wisconsin, or Wyoming	Internal Revenue Service 1973 N. Rulon White Blvd. MS 6737 Ogden, UT 84404	801-620-4249
All APO and FPO addresses, American Samoa, nonpermanent residents of Guam or the U.S. Virgin Islands**, Puerto Rico (or if excluding income under Internal Revenue Code section 933), a foreign country: U.S. citizens and those filing Form 2555, 2555-EZ, or 4563.	Internal Revenue Service International CAF Team 2970 Market Street MS:3-E08.123. Philadelphia, PA 19104	267-941-1017

* These numbers may change without notice.

**Permanent residents of Guam should use Department of Taxation, Government of Guam, P.O. Box 23607, GMF, GU 96921; permanent residents of the U.S. Virgin Islands should use: V.I. Bureau of Internal Revenue, 6115 Estate Smith Bay, Suite 225, St. Thomas, V.I. 00802.

Mar 21, 2012

Cat. No. 11981U

- If Form 2848 is for a specific use, mail or fax it to the office handling the specific matter. For more information on specific use, see the instructions for line 4.
- Your representative may be able to file Form 2848 electronically via the IRS website. For more information, go to *IRS.gov* and under the *Tax Professionals* tab, click on *e-services — for Tax Pros*. If you complete Form 2848 for electronic signature authorization, do not file Form 2848 with the IRS. Instead, give it to your representative, who will retain the document. When a power of attorney is mailed or faxed to the IRS using the *Where To File Chart*, the power of attorney will be recorded on the CAF. Unless when the power of attorney is revoked or withdrawn earlier, a power of attorney recorded on the CAF generally will be deleted from the CAF seven years after it is first recorded. However, you may re-establish the record of the authorization for representation by resubmitting the power of attorney to the IRS using the *Where To File Chart*. In the case of a power of attorney held by a student of an LITC or an STCP, the CAF record will be deleted 130 days after it is received and you generally must submit a new power of attorney to the IRS if you want to authorize the same student or another student of an LITC or an STCP to represent you.

Authority Granted

Except as specified below or in other IRS guidance, this power of attorney authorizes the listed representative(s) to receive and inspect confidential tax information and to perform all acts (that is, sign agreements, consents, waivers or other documents) that you can perform with respect to matters described in the power of attorney. However, this authorization, does not include the power to receive a check issued in connection with any liability for tax or any act specifically excluded on line 5 of the power of the attorney. Additionally, unless specifically provided in the power of attorney, this authorization does not include the power to substitute another representative or add another representative, the power to sign certain returns or the power to execute a request for disclosure of tax returns or return information to a third party. See instructions to line 5 for more information regarding specific authorities.

Note. The power to sign tax returns only may be granted in limited situations. See instructions to line 5 for more information.

Special rules for registered tax return preparers and unenrolled return preparers

Registered tax return preparers and unenrolled return preparers may only represent taxpayers before revenue agents, customer service representatives, or similar officers and employees of the Internal Revenue Service (including the Taxpayer Advocate Service) during an examination of the taxable period covered by the tax return they prepared and signed. Registered tax return preparers and unenrolled return preparers cannot represent taxpayers, regardless of the circumstances requiring representation, before appeals officers, revenue officers, counsel or similar officers or employees of the Internal Revenue Service or the Department of Treasury. Registered tax return preparers and unenrolled return preparers cannot execute closing agreements, extend the statutory period for tax assessments or collection of tax, execute waivers, execute claims for refund, or sign any document on behalf of a taxpayer.

A registered tax return preparer is an individual who has passed an IRS competency test. A registered tax return preparer may prepare and sign Form 1040 series tax returns as a paid return preparer. An unenrolled return preparer is an individual other than an attorney, CPA, enrolled agent, enrolled retirement plan agent, enrolled actuary, or registered tax return preparer who prepares and signs a taxpayer's return as the preparer, or who prepares a return but is not required (by the instructions to the return or regulations) to sign the return.

If a registered tax return preparer or an unenrolled return preparer does not meet the requirements for limited representation, you may authorize the unenrolled return preparer to inspect and/or receive your taxpayer information, by filing Form 8821. Completing the Form 8821 will not authorize the unenrolled return preparer to represent you. See Form 8821.

Revocation of Power of Attorney/ Withdrawal of Representative

If you want to revoke an existing power of attorney and do not want to name a new representative, or if a representative wants to withdraw from representation, mail or fax a copy of the previously executed power of attorney to the IRS, using the *Where To File Chart*, or if the power of attorney is for a specific matter, to the IRS office handling the matter. If the taxpayer is revoking the power of attorney, the taxpayer must write "REVOKE " across the top of the first page with a current signature and date below this annotation. If the representative is withdrawing from the representation, the representative must write "WITHDRAW " across the top of the first page with a current signature and date below this annotation. If you do not have a copy of the power of attorney you want to revoke or withdraw, send a statement to the IRS. The statement of revocation or withdrawal must indicate that the authority of the power of attorney is revoked, list the matters and periods, and must be signed and dated by the taxpayer or representative as applicable. If the taxpayer is revoking, list the name and address of each recognized representative whose authority is revoked. When the taxpayer is completely revoking authority, the form should state "remove all years/periods" instead of listing the specific tax matter, years, or periods. If the representative is withdrawing, list the name, TIN, and address (if known) of the taxpayer.

Substitute Form 2848

The IRS will accept a power of attorney other than Form 2848 provided the document satisfies the requirements for a power of attorney. See Pub. 216, Conference and Practice Requirements, section 601.503(a). These alternative powers of attorney cannot, however, be recorded on the CAF unless a completed Form 2848 is attached. See Instruction to Line 4 for more information. You are not required to sign the Form 2848 when it is attached to an alternative power of attorney that has been signed by you, but your representative must sign the Declaration of Representative on the Form 2848. See Pub. 216, Conference and Practice Requirements, section 601.503(b)(2).

Representative Address Change

If the representative's address has changed, a new Form 2848 is not required. The representative can send a written notification that includes the new information and the representative's signature to the location where the Form 2848 was filed.

Additional Information

Additional information concerning practice before the IRS may be found in:
- Treasury Department Circular No. 230, Regulations Governing the Practice before the Internal Revenue Service (Circular 230), and
- Pub. 216, Conference and Practice Requirements.

For general information about taxpayer rights, see Pub. 1, Your Rights as a Taxpayer.

Specific Instructions

Part I. Power of Attorney

Line 1. Taxpayer Information

Enter the information requested about you. Do not enter information about any other person, including your spouse, except as stated in the specific instructions below.

Individuals. Enter your name, social security number (SSN), individual taxpayer identification number (ITIN), and/or employer identification number (EIN), if applicable, and your street address or post office box. Do not use your representative's address or post office box for your own. If you file a tax return that includes a sole proprietorship business (Schedule C) and the matters that you are authorizing the listed representative(s) to represent you include your individual and business tax matters, including employment tax liabilities, enter both your SSN (or ITIN) and your business EIN as your taxpayer identification numbers. If you, your spouse, or former spouse are submitting powers of attorney to the CAF in connection with a joint return that you filed, you must submit separate Forms 2848 even if you are authorizing the same representative(s) to represent you.

Corporations, partnerships, or associations. Enter the name, EIN, and business address. If this form is being prepared for corporations filing a consolidated tax return (Form 1120) and the representation concerns matters related to the consolidated return, do not attach a list of subsidiaries to this form. Only the parent corporation information is required on line 1. Also, for line 3 only list Form 1120 in the Tax Form Number column. A subsidiary must file its own Form 2848 for returns that must be filed separately from the consolidated return, such as Form 720, Quarterly Federal Excise Tax Return, Form 940, Employer's Annual Federal Unemployment (FUTA) Tax Return, and Form 941, Employer's QUARTERLY Federal Tax Return.

Exempt organization. Enter the name, address, and EIN of the exempt organization.

Trust. Enter the name, title, and address of the trustee, and the name and EIN of the trust.

Deceased Individual. For Form 1040: Enter the name and SSN (or ITIN) of the decedent as well as the name, title, and address of the decedent's executor or personal representative.

Estate. Enter the name of the decedent as well as the name, title, and address of the decedent's executor or personal representative. For Forms 706: Enter the decedent's SSN (or ITIN) for the taxpayer identification number. For all other IRS forms: Enter the estate's EIN for the taxpayer identification number, or, if the estate does not have an EIN, enter the decedent's SSN (or ITIN).

Gifts. Enter the name, address, and SSN (or ITIN) of the donor.

Employee plan. Enter the name, address, and EIN or SSN of the plan sponsor. Also, enter the three-digit plan number. If the plan's trust is under examination, see the instructions relating to trust above. If both the plan and trust are being represented by the same representative, separate Forms 2848 are required.

Line 2. Representative(s)

Enter your representative's full name. Only individuals who are eligible to practice before the IRS may be named as representatives. Use the identical full name on all submissions and correspondence. If you want to name more than three representatives, indicate so on this line and attach an additional Form(s) 2848.

Enter the nine-digit CAF number for each representative. If a CAF number has not been assigned, enter "None," and the IRS will issue one directly to your representative. The CAF number is a unique nine-digit identification number (not the SSN, EIN, PTIN, or enrollment card number) that the IRS assigns to representatives. The CAF number is not an indication of authority to practice. The representative should use the assigned CAF number on all future powers of attorney. CAF numbers will not be assigned for employee plans and exempt organizations application requests.

Enter the PTIN, if applicable, for each representative. If a PTIN has not been assigned, but one has been applied for, then write "applied for" on the line.

Check the appropriate box to indicate if either the address, telephone number, or fax number is new since a CAF number was assigned.

Check the box on the line for up to two representatives to indicate that you want original and other written correspondence to be sent to you and a copy to the indicated representative(s). You must check the box next to a representative's name and address if you want to authorize this representative to receive copies of all notices and communications sent to you by the IRS. If you do not want any notices sent to your representative(s) then do not check the box. By checking this box you are not changing your last known address with the IRS. To change your last known address, use Form 8822 for your home address and use Form 8822-B to change your business address. Both forms are available at *IRS.gov*. Also, by checking this box, you are replacing any prior designation of a different representative to receive copies of written correspondence related to the matters designated on line 3.

Note. Representatives will not receive forms, publications, and other related materials with the notices.

If the representative is a former employee of the federal government, he or she must be aware of the postemployment restrictions contained in 18 U.S.C. 207 and in Circular 230, section 10.25. Criminal penalties are provided for violation of the statutory restrictions, and the Office of Professional Responsibility is authorized to take disciplinary action against the practitioner.

Students in LITCs and the STCP. The lead attorney or CPA must be listed as a representative. List the lead attorney or CPA first on line 2, then the student on the next line. Also see *Declaration of Representative* later, to complete *Part II*.

Line 3. Description of Matters

Enter the description of the matter, and where applicable, the tax form number, and the year(s) or period(s) in order for the power of attorney to be valid. For example, you may list "Income, 1040" for calendar year "2010" and "Excise, 720" for "2010" (this covers all quarters in 2010). For multiple years or a series of inclusive periods, including quarterly periods, you may list 2008 through (thru or a hyphen) 2010. For example, "2008 thru 2010" or "2nd 2009 - 3rd 2010." For fiscal years, enter the ending year and month, using the YYYYMM format. Do not use a general reference such as "All years," "All periods," or "All taxes." Any power of attorney with a general reference will be returned. Representation only applies for the years or periods listed on line 3. Only tax forms directly related to the taxpayer may be listed on line 3.

You may list the current year/period and any tax years or periods that have already ended as of the date you sign the power of attorney. However, you may include on a power of attorney only future tax periods that end no later than 3 years after the date the power of attorney is received by the IRS. The 3 future periods are determined starting after December 31 of the year the power of attorney is received by the IRS. You must enter the description of the matter, the tax form number, and the future year(s) or period(s). If the matter relates to estate tax, enter the date of the decedent's death instead of the year or period. If the matter relates to an employee plan, include the plan number in the description of the matter.

If the matter is not a tax matter, or if the tax form number, or years or periods does not apply to the matter (for example, representation for a penalty or filing a ruling request or a determination letter, or Application for Award for Original Information under section 7623, Closing Agreement on Final Determination Covering Specific Classification Settlement Program (CSP), Form 8952, Application for Voluntary Classification Settlement Program (VSCP), or FOIA) specifically describe the matter to which the power of attorney pertains (including, if applicable, the name of the employee benefit plan) and enter "Not Applicable" in the appropriate column(s).

Civil penalty representation (including the trust fund recovery penalty). Unless you specifically provide otherwise on line 5, representation for return-related penalties and interest is presumed to be included when representation is authorized for the related tax return on line 3. However, if the penalty is not related to a return, you must reference "civil penalties" or the specific penalties for which representation is authorized on line 3. For example, Joann prepares Form 2848 authorizing Margaret to represent her before the IRS in connection with the examination of her 2009 and 2010 Forms 1040. Margaret is authorized to represent Joann with respect to the accuracy-related penalty that the revenue agent is proposing for the 2009 tax year. Similarly, if Diana authorizes John to represent her in connection with his Forms 941 and W-2 for 2010, John is authorized to represent in connection with the failure to file Forms W-2 penalty that the revenue agent is considering imposing for 2010. However, if Diana only authorizes John to represent her in connection with her Form 1040 for 2010, he is not authorized to represent her when the revenue agent proposes to impose a trust fund recovery penalty against her in connection with the employment taxes owed by the Schedule C business she owns.

How to complete line 3. If you are authorizing this representative to represent you *only with respect to penalties and interest* due on the penalties, enter "civil penalties" on line 3. The description of matter column and the year(s) to which the penalty applies in the year(s) or period(s) column. Enter "Not Applicable" in

Instructions for Form 2848 (Rev. 3-2012)   -3-

the tax form number column. You do not have to enter the specific penalty.

Note. If the taxpayer is subject to penalties related to an individual retirement account (IRA) (for example, a penalty for excess contributions), enter "IRA civil penalty" on line 3.

Line 4. Specific Uses Not Recorded on CAF

Generally, the IRS records powers of attorney on the CAF system. The CAF system is a computer file system containing information regarding the authority of individuals appointed under powers of attorney. The system gives IRS personnel quicker access to authorization information without requesting the original document from the taxpayer or representative. However, a specific-use power of attorney is a one-time or specific-issue grant of authority to a representative or is a power of attorney that does not relate to a specific tax period (except for civil penalties) that is not recorded in the CAF. Examples of specific issues include but are not limited to the following:
- Requests for a private letter ruling or technical advice,
- Applications for an EIN,
- Claims filed on Form 843, Claim for Refund and Request for Abatement,
- Corporate dissolutions,
- Circular 230 Disciplinary Investigations and Proceedings,
- Requests to change accounting methods or periods,
- Applications for recognition of exemption under sections 501(c)(3), 501(a), or 521 (Forms 1023, 1024, or 1028),
- Request for a determination of the qualified status of an employee benefit plan (Forms 5300, 5307, 5316, or 5310),
- Application for Award for Original Information under section 7623,
- Voluntary submissions under the Employee Plans Compliance Resolution System (EPCRS), and
- Freedom of Information Act requests.

Check the box on line 4 if the power of attorney is for a use that will not be listed on the CAF. If the box on line 4 is checked, the representative should mail or fax the power of attorney to the IRS office handling the matter. Otherwise, the representative should bring a copy of the power of attorney to each meeting with the IRS.

A specific-use power of attorney will not revoke any prior powers of attorney recorded on the CAF or provided to the IRS in connection with an unrelated specific matter.

Line 5. Acts Authorized

Use line 5 to modify the acts that your named representative(s) can perform. Check the box for the acts authorized that you intend to authorize or specifically not authorize your representative to perform on your behalf. In the space provided, describe any specific additions or deletions.

Substituting or adding a representative . Your representative cannot substitute or add another representative without your written permission unless this authority is specifically delegated to your representative on line 5. If you authorize your representative to substitute another representative, the new representative can send in a new Form 2848 with a copy of the Form 2848 you are now signing attached and you do not need to sign the new Form 2848.

Disclosure of returns to a third party. A representative cannot execute consents that will allow the IRS to disclose your tax return or return information to a third party unless this authority is specifically delegated to the representative on line 5.

Authority to sign your return. Treasury regulations section 1.6012-1(a)(5) permits another person to sign a return for you only in the following circumstances:
(a) Disease or injury,
(b) Continuous absence from the United States (including Puerto Rico), for a period of at least 60 days prior to the date required by law for filing the return, or
(c) Specific permission is requested of and granted by the IRS for other good cause.
Authority to sign your income tax return may be granted to (1) your representative or (2) an agent (a person other than your representative).

Authorizing your representative. Check the box on line 5 authorizing your representative to sign your income tax return and include the following statement on the line provided: "This power of attorney is being filed pursuant to Treasury regulations section 1.6012-1(a)(5), which requires a power of attorney to be attached to a return if a return is signed by an agent by reason of [enter the specific reason listed under (a), (b), or (c) under Authority to sign your return, *earlier*]. No other acts on behalf of the taxpayer are authorized."

Authorizing an agent. To authorize an agent you must do all four of the following:
1. Complete lines 1-3.
2. Check the box on line 4.
3. Write the following statement on line 5:
"This power of attorney is being filed pursuant to Treasury regulations section 1.6012-1(a)(5), which requires a power of attorney to be attached to a return if a return is signed by an agent by reason of [enter the specific reason listed under (a), (b), or (c) under Authority to sign your return, *earlier*]. No other acts on behalf of the taxpayer are authorized."
4. Sign and date the form. If your return is electronically filed, your representative should attach Form 2848 to Form 8453, U.S. Individual Income Tax Transmittal for an IRS *e-file* Return, and send to the address listed in the instructions for Form 8453. If you file a paper return, Form 2848 should be attached to your return. See the instructions for line 7 for more information on signatures. The agent does not complete Part II of Form 2848.

Other. List any other acts you want your representative to be able to perform on your behalf.

Tax matters partner. The tax matters partner (TMP) (as defined in section 6231(a)(7)) is authorized to perform various acts on behalf of the partnership. The following are examples of acts performed by the TMP that cannot be delegated to the representative:
- Binding nonnotice partners to a settlement agreement under section 6224 and, under certain circumstances, binding all partners to a settlement agreement under Tax Court Rule 248 and
- Filing a request for administrative adjustment on behalf of the partnership under section 6227.

Check the box for deletions and list the act or acts you do not want your representative to perform on your behalf.

Line 6. Retention/Revocation of Prior Power(s) of Attorney

If this power of attorney is filed on the CAF system, it generally will revoke any earlier power of attorney previously recorded on the system for the same matter. If this power of attorney is for a specific use or is not filed on the CAF, this power of attorney only will revoke an earlier power of attorney that is on file with the same office and for the same matters. For example, you previously provided the IRS's Office of Chief Counsel with a power of attorney authorizing Attorney A to represent you in a PLR matter. Now, several months later you decide you want to have Attorney B handle this matter for you. By providing the IRS' Office of Chief Counsel with a power of attorney designating Attorney B to handle the same PLR matter, you are revoking the earlier power of attorney given to Attorney A. If you do not want to revoke any existing power(s) of attorney check the box on this line and attach a copy of the power(s) of attorney. The filing of a Form 2848 will not revoke any Form 8821 that is in effect.

Line 7. Signature of Taxpayer(s)

Individuals. You must sign and date the power of attorney. If a joint return has been filed, your spouse must execute his or her own power of attorney on a separate Form 2848 to designate a representative.

Corporations or associations. An officer having authority to bind the taxpayer must sign.

Partnerships. All partners must sign unless one partner is authorized to act in the name of the partnership. A partner is authorized to act in the name of the partnership if, under state law, the partner has authority to bind the partnership. A copy of such authorization must be attached. For purposes of executing Form 2848, the TMP is authorized to act in the name of the partnership. However, see *Tax matters partner,* earlier. For dissolved partnerships, see 26 CFR 601.503(c)(6).

Estate. If there is more than one executor, only one co-executor having the authority to bind the estate is required to sign. See 26 CFR 601.503(d).

Employee plan. If the plan is listed as the taxpayer on line 1, a duly authorized individual having authority to bind the taxpayer must sign and that individual's exact title must be entered. If the trust is the taxpayer listed on line 1, a trustee having the authority to bind the trust must sign with the title of trustee entered. A Form 56, Notice Concerning Fiduciary Relationship, must also be completed to identify the current trustee.

All others. If the taxpayer is a dissolved corporation, decedent, insolvent, or a person for whom or by whom a fiduciary (a trustee, guarantor, receiver, executor, or administrator) has been appointed, see 26 CFR 601.503(d).

Note. Generally the taxpayer signs first, granting the authority and then the representative signs, accepting the authority granted. The date between when the taxpayer signs and when the representative subsequently signs must be within 45 days for domestic authorizations and within 60 days for authorization from taxpayers residing abroad. If the taxpayer signs after the representative signs, there is no time requirement.

PIN number. If you are submitting this form electronically through the IRS's e-services portal, enter the PIN number you used to sign the form you submitted electronically on the copy of the form you retain. You should not provide your PIN number to your representative(s) or include it on the copy of the form your representative(s) will retain.

Part II. Declaration of Representative

The representative(s) you name must sign and date this declaration and enter the designation (for example, items a-r) under which he or she is authorized to practice before the IRS. Representatives must sign in the order listed in line 2 earlier. In addition, the representative(s) must list the following in the "Licensing jurisdiction (state) or other licensing authority" and "Bar, license, certification, registration, or enrollment number" columns:

a Attorney—Enter the two-letter abbreviation for the state (for example, "NY" for New York) in which admitted to practice and associated bar or license number, if any.

b Certified Public Accountant—Enter the two-letter abbreviation for the state (for example, "CA" for California) in which licensed to practice and associated certification or license number, if any.

c Enrolled Agent—Enter the enrollment card number issued by the Office of Professional Responsibility.

d Officer—Enter the title of the officer (for example, President, Vice President, or Secretary).

e Full-Time Employee—Enter title or position (for example, Comptroller or Accountant).

f Family Member—Enter the relationship to taxpayer (generally, must be a spouse, parent, child, brother, sister, grandparent, grandchild, step-parent, step-child, step-brother, or step-sister).

g Enrolled Actuary—Enter the enrollment card number issued by the Joint Board for the Enrollment of Actuaries.

h Unenrolled Return Preparer—Enter your PTIN.

i Registered Tax Return Preparer —Enter your PTIN.

k Student—Enter LITC or STCP.

r Enrolled Retirement Plan Agent—Enter the enrollment card number issued by the Office of Professional Responsibility.

Students in LITCs and the STCP. You must receive permission to practice before the IRS by virtue of your status as a law, business, or accounting student working in a Low Income Taxpayer Clinic or the Student Tax Clinic Program under section 10.7(d) of Circular 230. Be sure to attach a copy of the letter from the Office of Professional Responsibility authorizing practice before the IRS.

Note. In many cases, the student practitioner's authority is limited (for example, they may only practice under the supervision of another practitioner). At the end of 130 days after input to the CAF, they are automatically purged from the CAF.

 Any individual may represent an individual or entity before personnel of the IRS when such representation occurs outside the United States. Individuals acting as representatives must sign and date the declaration; leave the Licensing jurisdiction (state) or other licensing authority column blank. See section 10.7(c)(1)(vii) of Circular 230.

Privacy Act and Paperwork Reduction Act Notice. We ask for the information on this form to carry out the Internal Revenue laws. Form 2848 is provided by the IRS for your convenience and its use is voluntary. If you choose to designate a representative to act on your behalf, you must provide the requested information. Section 6109 requires you to provide your identifying number; section 7803 authorizes us to collect the other information. We use this information to properly identify you and your designated representative and determine the extent of the representative's authority. Failure to provide the information requested may delay or prevent honoring your Power of Attorney designation.

The IRS may provide this information to the Department of Justice for civil and criminal litigation, and to cities, states, the District of Columbia, and U.S. possessions to carry out their tax laws. We may also disclose this information to other countries under a tax treaty, to federal and state agencies to enforce federal nontax criminal laws, or to federal law enforcement and intelligence agencies to combat terrorism.

You are not required to provide the information requested on a form that is subject to the Paperwork Reduction Act unless the form displays a valid OMB control number. Books or records relating to a form or its instructions must be retained as long as their contents may become material in the administration of any Internal Revenue law.

The time needed to complete and file Form 2848 will vary depending on individual circumstances. The estimated average time is: **Recordkeeping,** 11 min.; **Learning about the law or the form,** 53 min.; **Preparing the form,** 77 min.; **Copying and sending the form to the IRS,** 58 min.

If you have comments concerning the accuracy of these time estimates or suggestions for making Form 2848 simpler, we would be happy to hear from you. You can write to the Internal Revenue Service, Individual and Specialty Forms and Publications Branch, SE:W:CAR:MP:T:I, 1111 Constitution Ave. NW, IR-6526, Washington, DC 20224. Do not send Form 2848 to this address. Instead, see the *Where To File Chart.*

Form **3903**	**Moving Expenses**	OMB No. 1545-0074
Department of the Treasury Internal Revenue Service (99)	▶ Information about Form 3903 and its instructions is available at *www.irs.gov/form3903*. ▶ **Attach to Form 1040 or Form 1040NR.**	**20**12 Attachment Sequence No. **170**

Name(s) shown on return	Your social security number

Before you begin:
  ✓ See the **Distance Test** and **Time Test** in the instructions to find out if you can deduct your moving expenses.
  ✓ See **Members of the Armed Forces** in the instructions, if applicable.

1	Transportation and storage of household goods and personal effects (see instructions) . . .	**1**	
2	Travel (including lodging) from your old home to your new home (see instructions). **Do not** include the cost of meals	**2**	
3	Add lines 1 and 2	**3**	
4	Enter the total amount your employer paid you for the expenses listed on lines 1 and 2 that is **not** included in box 1 of your Form W-2 (wages). This amount should be shown in box 12 of your Form W-2 with code **P**	**4**	
5	Is line 3 **more than** line 4?		
	☐ **No.** You **cannot** deduct your moving expenses. If line 3 is less than line 4, subtract line 3 from line 4 and include the result on Form 1040, line 7, or Form 1040NR, line 8.		
	☐ **Yes.** Subtract line 4 from line 3. Enter the result here and on Form 1040, line 26, or Form 1040NR, line 26. This is your **moving expense deduction**	**5**	

For Paperwork Reduction Act Notice, see your tax return instructions.   Cat. No. 12490K   Form **3903** (2012)

General Instructions

Future Developments

For the latest information about developments related to Form 3903 and its instructions, such as legislation enacted after they were published, go to *www.irs.gov/form3903*.

What's New

For 2012, the standard mileage rate for using your vehicle to move to a new home is 23 cents a mile.

Purpose of Form

Use Form 3903 to figure your moving expense deduction for a move related to the start of work at a new principal place of work (workplace). If the new workplace is outside the United States or its possessions, you must be a U.S. citizen or resident alien to deduct your expenses.

If you qualify to deduct expenses for more than one move, use a separate Form 3903 for each move.

For more details, see Pub. 521, Moving Expenses.

Moving Expenses You Can Deduct

You can deduct the reasonable expenses of moving your household goods and personal effects and of traveling from your old home to your new home. Reasonable expenses can include the cost of lodging (but not meals) while traveling to your new home. You cannot deduct the cost of sightseeing trips.

Who Can Deduct Moving Expenses

If you move to a new home because of a new principal workplace, you may be able to deduct your moving expenses whether you are self-employed or an employee. But you must meet both the distance and time tests that follow. Also, your move must be closely related both in time and place to the start of work at your new job location. For more details, see Pub. 521.

 Members of the Armed Forces may not have to meet the distance and time tests. See Members of the Armed Forces *later in the instructions.*

Distance Test

Your new principal workplace must be at least 50 miles farther from your old home than your old workplace was. For example, if your old workplace was 3 miles from your old home, your new workplace must be at least 53 miles from that home. If you did not have an old workplace, your new workplace must be at least 50 miles from your old home. The distance between the two points is the shortest of the more commonly traveled routes between them.

 To see if you meet the distance test, you can use the worksheet below.

Distance Test Worksheet

Keep a Copy for Your Records

1. Number of miles from your **old home** to your **new workplace** . . . . **1.** _____ miles	
2. Number of miles from your **old home** to your **old workplace** . . . . **2.** _____ miles	
3. Subtract line 2 from line 1. If zero or less, enter -0- . . . . **3.** _____ miles	
Is line 3 at least 50 miles?	
☐ **Yes.** You meet this test.	
☐ **No.** You do not meet this test. You **cannot** deduct your moving expenses. **Do not** complete Form 3903.	

Time Test

If you are an employee, you must work full time in the general area of your new workplace for at least 39 weeks during the 12 months right after you move. If you are self-employed, you must work full time in the general area of your new workplace for at least 39 weeks during the first 12 months and a total of at least 78 weeks during the 24 months right after you move.

What if you do not meet the time test before your return is due? If you expect to meet the time test, you can deduct your moving expenses in the year you move. Later, if you do not meet the time test, you must either:

• Amend your tax return for the year you claimed the deduction by filing Form 1040X, Amended U.S. Individual Income Tax Return, or

• For the year you cannot meet the time test, report as income the amount of your moving expense deduction that reduced your income tax for the year you moved.

If you did not deduct your moving expenses in the year you moved and you later meet the time test, you can take the deduction by filing an amended return for the year you moved. To do this, use Form 1040X.

Exceptions to the time test. You do not have to meet the time test if any of the following apply.

• Your job ends because of disability.

• You are transferred for your employer's benefit.

• You are laid off or discharged for a reason other than willful misconduct.

• You are in the Armed Forces and the move is due to a permanent change of station (see below).

• You meet the requirements (explained later) for retirees or survivors living outside the United States.

• You are filing this form for a decedent.

Members of the Armed Forces

If you are in the Armed Forces, you do not have to meet the distance and time tests if the move is due to a permanent change of station. A permanent change of station includes a move in connection with and within 1 year of retirement or other termination of active duty.

How To Complete This Form If You Are In the Armed Forces

Do not include on lines 1 and 2 any expenses for moving or storage services that were provided by the government. If you and your spouse and dependents are moved to or from different locations, treat the moves as a single move.

On line 4, enter the total reimbursements and allowances you received from the government in connection with the expenses you claimed on lines 1 and 2. Do not include the value of moving or storage services provided by the government. Complete line 5 if applicable.

Retirees or Survivors Living Outside the United States

If you are a retiree or survivor who moved to a home in the United States or its possessions and you meet the following requirements, you are treated as if you moved to a new principal workplace located in the United States. You are subject only to the distance test.

Retirees

You can deduct moving expenses for a move to a new home in the United States when you permanently retire if both your old principal workplace and your old home were outside the United States.

Survivors

You can deduct moving expenses for a move to a home in the United States if you are the spouse or dependent of a person whose principal workplace at the time of his or her death was outside the United States. The expenses must be for a move (a) that begins within 6 months after the decedent's death, and (b) from a former home outside the United States that you lived in with the decedent at the time of his or her death.

Reimbursements

You can choose to deduct moving expenses in the year you are reimbursed by your employer, even though you paid the expenses in a different year. However, special rules apply. See *When To Deduct Expenses* in Pub. 521.

Filers of Form 2555

If you file Form 2555, Foreign Earned Income, to exclude any of your income or housing costs, report the full amount of your deductible moving expenses on Form 3903 and on Form 1040. Report the part of your moving expenses that is not allowed because it is allocable to the excluded income on the appropriate line of Form 2555. For details on how to figure the part allocable to the excluded income, see Pub. 54, Tax Guide for U.S. Citizens and Resident Aliens Abroad.

Specific Instructions

You can deduct the following expenses you paid to move your family and dependent household members. Do not deduct expenses for employees such as a maid, nanny, or nurse.

Line 1

Moves within or to the United States or its possessions. Enter the amount you paid to pack, crate, and move your household goods and personal effects. You can also include the amount you paid to store and insure household goods and personal effects within any period of 30 days in a row after the items were moved from your old home and before they were delivered to your new home.

Moves outside the United States or its possessions. Enter the amount you paid to pack, crate, move, store, and insure your household goods and personal effects. Also, include the amount you paid to move your personal effects to and from storage and to store them for all or part of the time the new workplace continues to be your principal workplace.

Storage fees. Do not file Form 3903 if all of the following apply:

• You moved in an earlier year,

• You are claiming only storage fees during your absence from the United States, and

• Any amount your employer paid for the storage fees is included in box 1 of your Form W-2 (wages).

   Instead, enter the storage fees on Form 1040, line 26, or Form 1040NR, line 26, and write "Storage" on the dotted line next to line 26.

Line 2

Enter the amount you paid to travel from your old home to your new home. This includes transportation and lodging on the way. Include costs for the day you arrive. The members of your household do not have to travel together or at the same time. But you can only include expenses for one trip per person. Do not include any househunting expenses.

   If you use your own vehicle(s), you can figure the expenses by using either:

• Actual out-of-pocket expenses for gas and oil, or

• Mileage at the rate of 23 cents a mile.

   You can add parking fees and tolls to the amount claimed under either method.

2525 ☐ VOID ☐ CORRECTED

TRANSFEROR'S name, street address, city, state, and ZIP code	**1** Date option granted	OMB No. 1545-2129	**Exercise of an Incentive Stock Option Under Section 422(b)**
		Form 3921	
	2 Date option exercised	(Rev. October 2010)	

TRANSFEROR'S federal identification number	EMPLOYEE'S identification number	**3** Exercise price per share	**4** Fair market value per share on exercise date	**Copy A**
EMPLOYEE'S name		$	$	**For Internal Revenue Service Center**
		5 No. of shares transferred		**File with Form 1096.**
Street address (including apt. no.)		**6** If other than TRANSFEROR, name, address, and EIN of corporation whose stock is being transferred		For Privacy Act and Paperwork Reduction Act Notice, see the **most current version of the General Instructions for Certain Information Returns.**
City, state, and ZIP code				
Account number (see instructions)				

Form **3921** (Rev. October 2010) Cat. No. 41179O Department of the Treasury - Internal Revenue Service

Do Not Cut or Separate Forms on This Page — Do Not Cut or Separate Forms on This Page

Instructions for Employee

You have received this form because your employer (or transfer agent) transferred your employer's stock to you pursuant to your exercise of an incentive stock option (ISO). You must recognize (report) gain or loss on your tax return for the year in which you sell or otherwise dispose of the stock. Keep this form and use it to figure the gain or loss. For more information, see Pub. 525, Taxable and Nontaxable Income.

When you exercise an ISO, you may have to include in alternative minimum taxable income a portion of the fair market value of the stock acquired through the exercise of the option. For more information, see Form 6251, Alternative Minimum Tax—Individuals, and its instructions.

Account number. May show an account or other unique number your employer or transfer agent assigned to distinguish your account.

Box 1. Shows the date the option to purchase the stock was granted to you.

Box 2. Shows the date you exercised the option to purchase the stock.

Box 3. Shows the exercise price per share of stock.

Box 4. Shows the fair market value (FMV) of a share of stock on the date the option was exercised.

Box 5. Shows the number of shares of stock transferred to you pursuant to the exercise of the option.

Box 6. Shows the name, address, and employer identification number (EIN) of the corporation whose stock is being transferred (if other than the corporation shown in TRANSFEROR boxes in the upper left corner of the form).

Instructions for Transferor

General and specific form instructions are provided as separate products. The products you should use to complete Form 3921 are the most current General Instructions for Certain Information Returns and the most current Instructions for Forms 3921 and 3922. A chart in the general instructions gives a quick guide to which form must be filed to report a particular payment. To order these instructions and additional forms, visit IRS.gov or call 1-800-TAX-FORM (1-800-829-3676).

Caution: *Because paper forms are scanned during processing, you cannot file with the IRS Forms 1096, 1097, 1098, 1099, 3921, 3922, or 5498 that you print from the IRS website.*

Due dates. Furnish Copy B of this form to the employee by January 31 of the year following the year of exercise of the ISO.

Furnish Copy C of this form to the corporation whose stock is being transferred by January 31 of the year following the year of exercise of the ISO.

File Copy A of this form with the IRS by February 28 of the year following the year of exercise of the ISO. If you file electroncially, the due date is March 31 of the year following the year of exercise of the ISO. To file electronically, you must have software that generates a file according to the specifications in Pub. 1220, Specifications for Filing Forms 1097, 1098, 1099, 3921, 3922, 5498, 8935, and W-2G Electronically. IRS does not provide a fill-in form option.

Need help? If you have questions about reporting on Form 3921, call the information reporting customer service site toll free at 1-866-455-7438 or 304-263-8700 (not toll free). For TTY/TDD equipment, call 304-579-4827 (not toll free). The hours of operation are Monday through Friday from 8:30 a.m. to 4:30 p.m., Eastern time.

2626 ☐ VOID ☐ CORRECTED

CORPORATION'S name, street address, city, state, and ZIP code	**1** Date option granted	OMB No. 1545-2129	**Transfer of Stock Acquired Through an Employee Stock Purchase Plan Under Section 423(c)**
	2 Date option exercised	**Form 3922** (Rev. October 2010)	

CORPORATION'S federal identification number	EMPLOYEE'S identification number	**3** Fair market value per share on grant date $	**4** Fair market value per share on exercise date $	**Copy A** **For Internal Revenue Service Center** File with Form 1096.
EMPLOYEE'S name		**5** Exercise price paid per share $	**6** No. of shares transferred	For Privacy Act and Paperwork Reduction Act Notice, see the **most current version of the General Instructions for Certain Information Returns.**
Street address (including apt. no.)		**7** Date legal title transferred		
City, state, and ZIP code		**8** Exercise price per share determined as if the option was exercised on the date shown in box 1. $		
Account number (see instructions)				

Form **3922** (Rev. October 2010)   Cat. No. 41180P   Department of the Treasury - Internal Revenue Service

Do Not Cut or Separate Forms on This Page   —   Do Not Cut or Separate Forms on This Page

Instructions for Employee

You have received this form because (1) your employer (or its transfer agent) has recorded a first transfer of legal title of stock you acquired pursuant to your exercise of an option granted under an employee stock purchase plan and (2) the exercise price was less than 100 percent of the value of the stock on the date shown in box 1 or was not fixed or determinable on that date.

No income is recognized when you exercise an option under an employee stock purchase plan. **However**, you must recognize (report) gain or loss on your tax return for the year in which you sell or otherwise dispose of the stock. Keep this form and use it to figure the gain or loss. For more information, see Pub. 525, Taxable and Nontaxable Income.

Account number. May show an account or other unique number your employer or transfer agent assigned to distinguish your account.

Box 1. Shows the date the option to purchase the stock was granted to you.

Box 2. Shows the date you exercised the option to purchase the stock.

Box 3. Shows the fair market value (FMV) per share on the date the option to purchase the stock was granted to you.

Box 4. Shows the FMV per share on the date you exercised the option to purchase the stock.

Box 5. Shows the price paid per share on the date you exercised the option to purchase the stock.

Box 6. Shows the number of shares to which legal title was transferred by you.

Box 7. Shows the date legal title of the shares was first transferred by you.

Box 8. If the exercise price per share was not fixed or determinable on the date entered in box 1, box 8 shows the exercise price per share determined as if the option was exercised on the date in box 1. If the exercise price per share was fixed or determinable on the date shown in box 1, then box 8 will be blank.

Instructions for Corporation

General and specific form instructions are provided as separate products. The products you should use to complete Form 3922 are the most current General Instructions for Certain Information Returns and the most current Instructions for Forms 3921 and 3922. A chart in the general instructions gives a quick guide to which form must be filed to report a particular payment. To order these instructions and additional forms, visit IRS.gov or call 1-800-TAX-FORM (1-800-829-3676).

Caution: *Because paper forms are scanned during processing, you cannot file with the IRS Forms 1096, 1097, 1098, 1099, 3921, 3922, or 5498 that you print from the IRS website.*

Due dates. Furnish Copy B of this form to the employee by January 31 of the year following the year of first transfer of the stock acquired through the employee stock purchase plan.

File Copy A of this form with the IRS by February 28 of the year following the year of first transfer of the stock acquired through the employee stock purchase plan. If you file electronically, the due date is March 31 of the year following the year of first transfer of the stock acquired through the employee stock purchase plan. To file electronically, you must have software that generates a file according to the specifications in Pub. 1220, Specifications for Filing Forms 1097, 1098, 1099, 3921, 3922, 5498, 8935, and W-2G Electronically. IRS does not provide a fill-in form option.

Need help? If you have questions about reporting on Form 3922, call the information reporting customer service site toll free at 1-866-455-7438 or 304-263-8700 (not toll free). For TTY/TDD equipment, call 304-579-4827 (not toll free). The hours of operation are Monday through Friday from 8:30 a.m. to 4:30 p.m., Eastern time.

Instructions for Forms 3921 and 3922

(Rev. December 2011)

Department of the Treasury
Internal Revenue Service

Section references are to the Internal Revenue Code unless otherwise noted.

Reminders

General instructions. In addition to these specific instructions, you should also use the current version of the General Instructions for Certain Information Returns. Those general instructions include information about the following topics.

- Backup withholding.
- Electronic reporting requirements.
- Penalties.
- Who must file (nominee/middleman).
- When and where to file.
- Taxpayer identification numbers.
- Statements to recipients.
- Corrected and void returns.
- Other general topics.

You can get the general instructions from IRS.gov or by calling 1-800-TAX-FORM (1-800-829-3676).

How to get the latest information. If there are changes to the tax law that affects these forms, you can find them at *www.irs.gov/form3921* and *www.irs.gov/form3922*.

Specific Instructions for Form 3921

Who Must File

Every corporation which in any calendar year transfers to any person a share of stock pursuant to that person's exercise of an incentive stock option described in section 422(b) must, for that calendar year, file Form 3921 for each transfer made during that year.

Exception. A Form 3921 is not required for the exercise of an incentive stock option by an employee who is a nonresident alien (as defined in section 7701(b)) and to whom the corporation is not required to provide a Form W-2, Wage and Tax Statement, for any calendar year within the time period beginning with the first day of the calendar year in which the option was granted to the employee and ending on the last day of the calendar year in which the employee exercised the option. For this purpose, the term "corporation" is defined in section 7701(a) and includes, but is not limited to:

- The corporation issuing the stock,
- A related corporation of the corporation,
- Any agent of the corporation,
- Any party distributing shares of stock or other payments in connection with the plan (for example, a brokerage firm), and
- Any party in control of the payment of remuneration for employment to the employee.

Statements to Transferees

If you are required to file Form 3921, you must provide a statement to the person whose name is set forth on Form 3921. For more information, see part M in the current

version of the General Instructions for Certain Information Returns.

Employee's Name, Address, and Identification Number

Enter the name, address, and identifying number of the person to whom the share or shares were transferred pursuant to the exercise of the option.

Account Number

The account number is required if you have multiple accounts for a person for whom you are filing more than one Form 3921. Additionally, the IRS encourages you to designate an account number for all Forms 3921 that you file. See part L in the current version of the General Instructions for Certain Information Returns.

Box 1. Date option granted

Enter the date the option was granted.

Box 2. Date option exercised

Enter the date the option was exercised.

Box 3. Exercise price per share

Enter the exercise price per share of stock.

Box 4. Fair market value per share on exercise date

Enter the fair market value (FMV) per share of stock on the date the option was exercised.

Box 5. Number of shares transferred

Enter the number of shares of stock transferred pursuant to the exercise of the option.

Box 6. If other than TRANSFEROR, name, address, and EIN of corporation whose stock is being transferred

Enter the name, address, and employer identification number (EIN) of the corporation whose stock is being transferred pursuant to the exercise of the option. Enter this information only if the corporation is not the entity shown in the TRANSFEROR boxes in the upper left corner of Form 3921.

Specific Instructions for Form 3922

Who Must File

Every corporation, which in any calendar year records, or has by its agent recorded, a transfer of the legal title of a share of stock acquired by the transferor (person who acquires the shares pursuant to the exercise of the option) pursuant to the transferor's exercise of an option granted under an employee stock purchase plan and described in section 423(c) (where the exercise price is less than 100% of the value of the stock on the date of grant, or is not fixed or determinable on the date of

Dec 22, 2011

Cat. No. 23069T

grant), must, for that calendar year, file Form 3922 for each transfer made during that year.

A return is required by reason of a transfer described in section 6039(a)(2) only for the first transfer of legal title of the shares by the transferor, including the first transfer of legal title to a recognized broker or financial institution. If a contractual agreement exists or is entered into with a recognized broker or financial institution pursuant to which shares acquired upon exercise of the option will be immediately deposited into a brokerage account established on behalf of the transferor, then the deposit of shares by the transferor into the brokerage account following the exercise of the option is the first transfer of legal title of the shares acquired by the transferor, and the corporation is only required to file a return relating to that transfer of legal title.

Shares of stock transferred as a result of the exercise of an option described above must be identified in a manner sufficient to enable the accurate reporting of the transfer of legal title to such shares. This identification can be made by assigning to the share certificates of stock issued pursuant to such options a special serial number or color.

The corporation whose stock is being transferred must file Form 3922.

Exception. A Form 3922 is not required for the first transfer of legal title of a share of stock by an employee who is a nonresident alien (as defined in section 7701(b)) and to whom the corporation is not required to provide a Form W-2, Wage and Tax Statement, for any calendar year within the time period beginning with the first day of the calendar year in which the option was granted to the employee and ending on the last day of the calendar year in which the employee first transferred legal title to shares acquired under the option. For this purpose, the term "corporation" is defined in section 7701(a) and includes, but is not limited to:
- The corporation issuing the stock,
- A related corporation of the corporation,
- Any agent of the corporation,
- Any party distributing shares of stock or other payments in connection with the plan (for example, a brokerage firm), and
- Any party in control of the payment of remuneration for employment to the employee.

Statements to Transferors

If you are required to file Form 3922, you must provide a statement to the transferor. For more information, see part M in the current version of the General Instructions for Certain Information Returns.

Employee's Name, Address, and Identification Number

Enter the name, address, and identifying number of the transferor.

Account Number

The account number is required if you have multiple accounts for a transferor for whom you are filing more than one Form 3922. Additionally, the IRS encourages you to designate an account number for all Forms 3922 that you file. See part L in the current version of the General Instructions for Certain Information Returns.

Box 1. Date option granted

Enter the date the option was granted.

Box 2. Date option exercised

Enter the date the option was exercised.

Box 3. Fair market value per share on grant date

Enter the fair market value (FMV) per share of stock on the date the option was granted.

Box 4. Fair market value per share on exercise date

Enter the FMV per share of stock on the date the option to purchase the stock was exercised.

Box 5. Exercise price paid per share

Enter the price paid per share on the date the option was exercised.

Box 6. Number of shares transferred

Enter the number of shares to which legal title was transferred.

Box 7. Date legal title transferred

Enter the date legal title of the shares was first transferred.

Box 8. Exercise price per share determined as if the option was exercised on the date shown in box 1

If the exercise price per share was not fixed or determinable on the date of grant entered in box 1, enter the exercise price per share determined as if the option was exercised on the date of grant entered in box 1. If the exercise price per share is fixed or determinable on the date of grant entered in box 1, then leave box 8 blank.

Form **4070**
(Rev. August 2005)
Department of the Treasury
Internal Revenue Service

Employee's Report of Tips to Employer

OMB No. 1545-0074

Employee's name and address	Social security number
Employer's name and address (include establishment name, if different)	**1** Cash tips received
	2 Credit and debit card tips received
	3 Tips paid out
Month or shorter period in which tips were received from , , to ,	**4** Net tips (lines **1** + **2** - **3**)
Signature	Date

For Paperwork Reduction Act Notice, see the instructions on the back of this form.

Cat. No. 41320P

Form **4070** (Rev. 8-2005)

Purpose. Use this form to report tips you receive to your employer. This includes cash tips, tips you receive from other employees, and debit and credit card tips. You must report tips every month regardless of your total wages and tips for the year. However, you do not have to report tips to your employer for any month you received less than $20 in tips while working for that employer.

Report tips by the 10th day of the month following the month that you receive them. If the 10th day is a Saturday, Sunday, or legal holiday, report tips by the next day that is not a Saturday, Sunday, or legal holiday.

See Pub. 531, Reporting Tip Income, for more details.

You can get additional copies of Pub. 1244, Employee's Daily Record of Tips and Report to Employer, which contains both Forms 4070A and 4070, by calling 1-800-TAX-FORM (1-800-829-3676) or by downloading the pub from the IRS website at *www.irs.gov.*

Paperwork Reduction Act Notice. We ask for the information on these forms to carry out the Internal Revenue laws of the United States. You are required to give us the information. We need it to ensure that you are complying with these laws and to allow us to figure and collect the right amount of tax.

You are not required to provide the information requested on a form that is subject to the Paperwork Reduction Act unless the form displays a valid OMB control number. Books or records relating to a form or its instructions must be retained as long as their contents may become material in the administration of any Internal Revenue law. Generally, tax returns and return information are confidential, as required by Code section 6103.

The average time and expenses required to complete and file this form will vary depending on individual circumstances. For the estimated averages, see the instructions for your income tax return.

If you have suggestions for making this form simpler, we would be happy to hear from you. See the instructions for your income tax return.

Instructions

You must keep sufficient proof to show the amount of your tip income for the year. A daily record of your tip income is considered sufficient proof. Keep a daily record for each workday showing the amount of cash and credit card tips received directly from customers or other employees. Also keep a record of the amount of tips, if any, you paid to other employees through tip sharing, tip pooling or other arrangements, and the names of employees to whom you paid tips. Show the date that each entry is made. This date should be on or near the date you received the tip income. You may use Form 4070A, Employee's Daily Record of Tips, or any other daily record to record your tips.

Reporting tips to your employer. If you receive tips that total $20 or more for any month while working for one employer, you must report the tips to your employer. Tips include cash left by customers, tips customers add to debit or credit card charges, and tips you receive from other employees. You must report your tips for any one month by the 10th of the month after the month you receive the tips. If the 10th day falls on a Saturday, Sunday, or legal holiday, you may give the report to your employer on the next business day that is not a Saturday, Sunday, or legal holiday.

You must report tips that total $20 or more every month regardless of your total wages and tips for the year. You may use Form 4070, Employee's Report of Tips to Employer, to report your tips to your employer. See the instructions on the back of Form 4070.

You must include all tips, including tips not reported to your employer, as wages on your income tax return. You may use the last page of this publication to total your tips for the year.

Your employer must withhold income, social security, and Medicare (or railroad retirement) taxes on tips you report. Your employer usually deducts the withholding due on tips from your regular wages.

(continued on inside of back cover)

Instructions *(continued)*

Unreported Tips. If you received tips of $20 or more for any month while working for one employer but did not report them to your employer, you must figure and pay social security and Medicare taxes on the unreported tips when you file your tax return. If you have unreported tips, you must use Form 1040 and Form 4137, Social Security and Medicare Tax on Unreported Tip Income, to report them. You may not use Form 1040A or 1040EZ. Employees subject to the Railroad Retirement Tax Act cannot use Form 4137 to pay railroad retirement tax on unreported tips. To get railroad retirement credit, you must report tips to your employer.

If you do not report tips to your employer as required, you may be charged a penalty of 50% of the social security and Medicare taxes (or railroad retirement tax) due on the unreported tips unless there was reasonable cause for not reporting them.

Additional Information. Get Pub. 531, Reporting Tip Income, and Form 4137 for more information on tips. If you are an employee of certain large food or beverage establishments, see Pub. 531 for tip allocation rules.

Recordkeeping. If you do not keep a daily record of tips, you must keep other reliable proof of the tip income you received. This proof includes copies of restaurant bills and credit card charges that show amounts customers added as tips.

Keep your tip income records for as long as the information on them may be needed in the administration of any Internal Revenue law.

(See Instructions on back)

Form **4419** (Rev. June 2012)	Department of the Treasury – Internal Revenue Service **Application for Filing Information Returns Electronically (FIRE)** ▶ IRS/IRB encourages transmitters who file for multiple payers to submit one application and use the assigned TCC for all payers.	**IRS Use Only**	OMB No. **1545-0387**

1. Transmitter and/or Payer Information

Legal Name (associated with EIN in Box 3)

Mailing Address

City	State	ZIP

2. Person to contact about this request

Name	Title

Email Address	Telephone Number

3. Employer Identification Number **(EIN)** Social Security Number Not Permitted	**4.** Is the request for a Foreign Transmitter without a TIN? ☐ Yes	**5.** What **Tax Year** will electronic filing begin?

6. Will TCC be used for **Electronic Extension of Time Files only?** ☐ Yes

7. Type of return to be reported **(Check the box(es) next to the returns you will file electronically.)**

Important: Form W-2 information is sent to the Social Security Administration (SSA) only. Do not use Form 4419 to request authorization to file this information electronically. Contact SSA for W-2 electronic filing information at 1-800-772-6270.

Note: For the forms referenced below, electronic filing does not refer to online fill-in forms.

☐ Forms 1097, 1098, 1099, 3921, 3922, 5498 and W-2G	☐ Form 1042-S, Foreign Person's U.S. Source Income Subject to Withholding	☐ Form 8027, Employer's Annual Information Return of Tip Income and Allocated Tips	☐ Form 8955-SSA, Annual Registration Statement Identifying Separated Participants with Deferred Vested Benefits
See Publication 1220	See Publication 1187	See Publication 1239	See Publication 4810

8. Check the appropriate box:

☐ I have or will have software. (Name of software if known) _____

☐ I have a service provider who will file my data for me.

Under penalties of perjury, I declare that I have examined this document, including any accompanying statements, and, to the best of my knowledge and belief, it is true, correct, and complete.

9. Person responsible for preparation of tax reports	Name	Title
	Signature (A computer generated signature is not acceptable.)	Date

General Instructions

Paperwork Reduction Act Notice. We ask for the information on these forms to carry out the Internal Revenue Laws of the United States. You are not required to provide the information requested on a form that is subject to the Paperwork Reduction Act unless the form displays a valid OMB control number. Books or records relating to a form must be retained as long as their contents may become material in the administration of any Internal Revenue law. Generally, tax returns and return information are confidential, as required by Code section 6103.

The time needed to provide this information would vary depending on individual circumstances. The estimated average time is:

Preparing Form 4419 . . . . **20 min.**

If you have comments concerning the accuracy of this time estimate or suggestions for making this form simpler, we would be happy to hear from you. You can write to the Internal Revenue Service, Tax Forms Committee, Western Area Distribution Center, Rancho Cordova, CA 95743-0001. DO NOT SEND THE FORM TO THIS OFFICE. Instead, see the instructions below on where to file. **When completing this form, please type or print clearly.**

Purpose of Form. File Form 4419 to request authorization to file any of the forms shown in Block 7 electronically. Please be sure to complete all appropriate blocks. Transmitters who file for multiple payers may submit **one** application and use the assigned TCC for all payers. If your application is approved, a five-character alphanumeric Transmitter Control Code (TCC) will be assigned to your organization. If any information on the form should change, please write to IRS/Information Returns Branch so we can update our database. It is not necessary to submit a new Form 4419.

Forms W-2: Do **not** use Form 4419 to request authorization to file Forms W-2 electronically, since Form W-2 information is only sent to the Social Security Administration (SSA). **Contact SSA if you have any questions concerning the filing of Forms W-2 electronically at 1-800-772-6270.**

Specific Instructions

Due Date: In order to ensure timely filing, submit Form 4419 at least 45 days before the due date of the return.

Block 1
Enter the legal name (associated with the EIN in box 3) and the complete address of the organization that will submit the electronic files (transmitter and/or payer).

Block 2
Enter the name, title, email address (if available) and telephone number (with area code) of the person to contact about this application. This should be a person who is knowledge able about electronic filing of information returns.

Block 3
Enter the Employer Identification Number (EIN) of the organization transmitting the electronic files. Social Security Numbers are not permitted.

Block 4
If you are a foreign transmitter who does not have a nine-digit Taxpayer Identification Number, check this box.

Block 5
Enter the tax year that you wish to begin filing electronically.

Block 6
Indicate if you are requesting this transmitter control code solely for filing electronic files for an extension of time to file information returns.

Block 7
Only check the box next to the returns you need to file with IRS electronically. A separate TCC will be assigned for each box checked in Block 7. Please be sure to submit your electronic files using the correct TCC. For further information concerning the electronic filing of information returns, access IRS.gov for the current tax year publications. These are:

Publication 1220, *Specifications for Filing Form 1097, 1098, 1099, 3921, 3922, 5498, 8935, and W2-G Electronically*

Publication 1187, *Specifications for Filing Form 1042-S, Foreign Person's U.S. Source Income Subject to Withholding, Electronically*

Publication 1239, *Specifications for Filing Form 8027, Employers Annual Information Return of Tip Income and Allocated Tips, Electronically*

Publication 4810, *Specifications for Filing Form 8955-SSA, Annual Registration Statement Identifying Separated Participants and Deferred Vested Benefits, Electronically*

Block 8
Indicate if your company will be filing your data with a software package (and provide the name of the software) or if you have contracted to have a service provider file your data for you.

Note: The FIRE System does not provide an on-line fill-in option for the forms listed in Box 7. You must transmit your data in a specific format required by IRS.

Block 9
The form must be signed and dated by an official of the company or organization requesting authorization to report electronically.

Mailing Address:

Send your Form 4419 to the address below:

> Internal Revenue Service
> Information Reporting Program
> 230 Murall Drive Mail Stop 4360
> Kearneysville, WV 25430

If you prefer, Form 4419 can be faxed to the IRS, Information Returns Branch at (877) 477-0572 from within the U.S. or (304) 579-4105 from outside the U.S.

You may contact the IRS, Information Returns Branch at (866) 455-7438 from within the U.S. or (304) 263-8700 from outside the U.S., Monday through Friday, between the hours of 8:30 a.m. and 4:30 p.m. Eastern Time (ET).

We will not issue a TCC over the phone or by email. If you do not receive a reply from IRS within 45 days, contact us at the telephone number shown above. Do not submit any files until you receive your TCC.

2727   ☐ VOID   ☐ CORRECTED

TRUSTEE'S name, street address, city, state, and ZIP code		**1** Employee or self-employed person's Archer MSA contributions made in 2012 and 2013 for 2012 $	OMB No. 1545-1518 20**12** Form **5498-SA**	**HSA, Archer MSA, or Medicare Advantage MSA Information**
		2 Total contributions made in 2012 $		
TRUSTEE'S federal identification number	PARTICIPANT'S social security number	**3** Total HSA or Archer MSA contributions made in 2013 for 2012 $		**Copy A** **For**
PARTICIPANT'S name		**4** Rollover contributions $	**5** Fair market value of HSA, Archer MSA, or MA MSA $	**Internal Revenue Service Center** **File with Form 1096.**
Street address (including apt. no.)		**6** HSA ☐ Archer MSA ☐		For Privacy Act and Paperwork Reduction Act
City, state, and ZIP code		MA MSA ☐		Notice, see the **2012 General**
Account number (see instructions)				**Instructions for Certain Information Returns.**

Form **5498-SA**   Cat. No. 38467V   Department of the Treasury - Internal Revenue Service

Do Not Cut or Separate Forms on This Page — Do Not Cut or Separate Forms on This Page

Instructions for Participant

This information is submitted to the Internal Revenue Service by the trustee of your health savings account (HSA), Archer MSA, or Medicare Advantage MSA (MA MSA).

Generally, contributions you make to your Archer MSA are deductible. Employer contributions are excluded from your income and are not deductible by you. If your employer makes a contribution to one of your Archer MSAs, you cannot contribute to any Archer MSA for that year. If you made a contribution to your Archer MSA when your employer has contributed, you cannot deduct your contribution, and you will have an excess contribution. If your spouse's employer makes a contribution to your spouse's Archer MSA, you cannot make a contribution to your Archer MSA if your spouse is covered under a high deductible health plan that also covers you.

Contributions that the Social Security Administration makes to your MA MSA are not includible in your gross income nor are they deductible. Neither you nor your employer can make contributions to your MA MSA.

Generally, contributions you or someone other than your employer make to your HSA are deductible on your tax return. Employer contributions to your HSA may be excluded from your income and are not deductible by you. You and your employer can make contributions to your HSA in the same year.

See Form 8853 and its instructions or Form 8889 and its instructions. Any employer contributions made to an Archer MSA are shown on your Form W-2 in box 12 (code R); employer contributions made to an HSA are shown in box 12 (code W). For more information, see Pub. 969.

Participant's identification number. For your protection, this form may show only the last four digits of your social security number (SSN), individual taxpayer identification number (ITIN), or adoption taxpayer identification number (ATIN).

However, the issuer has reported your complete identification number to the IRS, and, where applicable, to state and/or local governments.

Account number. May show an account or other unique number the trustee assigned to distinguish your account.

Box 1. Shows contributions you made to your Archer MSA in 2012 and through April 15, 2013, for 2012. You may be able to deduct this amount on your 2012 Form 1040. See the Form 1040 instructions.

Note. The information in boxes 2 and 3 is provided for IRS use only.

Box 2. Shows the total contributions made in 2012 to your HSA or Archer MSA. See Pub. 969 for who can make contributions. This includes qualified HSA funding distributions (trustee-to-trustee transfers) from your IRA to fund your HSA. The trustee of your MA MSA is not required to, but may, show contributions to your MA MSA.

Box 3. Shows the total HSA or Archer MSA contributions made in 2013 for 2012.

Box 4. Shows any rollover contribution from an Archer MSA to this Archer MSA in 2012 or any rollover from an HSA or Archer MSA to this HSA. See Form 8853 or Form 8889 and their instructions for information about how to report distributions. This amount is not included in box 1, 2, or 3.

Box 5. Shows the fair market value of your HSA, Archer MSA, or MA MSA at the end of 2012.

Box 6. Shows the type of account that is reported on this Form 5498-SA.

Other information. The trustee of your HSA, Archer MSA, or MA MSA may provide other information about your account on this form.

Note. Do not attach Form 5498-SA to your income tax return. Instead, keep it for your records.

Instructions for Trustee

General and specific form instructions are provided as separate products. The products you should use to complete Form 5498-SA are the 2012 General Instructions for Certain Information Returns and the 2012 Instructions for Forms 1099-SA and 5498-SA. A chart in the general instructions gives a quick guide to which form must be filed to report a particular payment. To order these instructions and additional forms, visit IRS.gov or call 1-800-TAX-FORM (1-800-829-3676).

Caution: *Because paper forms are scanned during processing, you cannot file Forms 1096, 1097, 1098, 1099, 3921, 3922, or 5498 that you print from the IRS website.*

Due dates. Furnish Copy B of this form to the participant by May 31, 2013.

File Copy A of this form with the IRS by May 31, 2013. To file electronically, you must have software that generates a file according to the specifications in Pub. 1220, Specifications for Filing Forms 1097, 1098, 1099, 3921, 3922, 5498, 8935, and W-2G Electronically. IRS does not provide a fill-in form option.

Need help? If you have questions about reporting on Form 5498-SA, call the information reporting customer service site toll free at 1-866-455-7438 or 304-263-8700 (not toll free). For TTY/TDD equipment, call 304-579-4827 (not toll free). The hours of operation are Monday through Friday from 8:30 a.m. to 4:30 p.m., Eastern time.

Form **7004**
(Rev. December 2012)
Department of the Treasury
Internal Revenue Service

Application for Automatic Extension of Time To File Certain Business Income Tax, Information, and Other Returns

▶ File a separate application for each return.

▶ Information about Form 7004 and its separate instructions is at *www.irs.gov/form7004.*

OMB No. 1545-0233

Print or Type	Name		Identifying number
	Number, street, and room or suite no. (If P.O. box, see instructions.)		
	City, town, state, and ZIP code (If a foreign address, enter city, province or state, and country (follow the country's practice for entering postal code)).		

Note. *File request for extension by the due date of the return for which the extension is granted. See instructions before completing this form.*

Part I   Automatic 5-Month Extension

1a Enter the form code for the return that this application is for (see below) . . . . □□

Application Is For:	Form Code	Application Is For:	Form Code
Form 1065	09	Form 1041 (estate other than a bankruptcy estate)	04
Form 8804	31	Form 1041 (trust)	05

Part II   Automatic 6-Month Extension

b Enter the form code for the return that this application is for (see below) . . . . □□

Application Is For:	Form Code	Application Is For:	Form Code
Form 706-GS(D)	01	Form 1120-ND (section 4951 taxes)	20
Form 706-GS(T)	02	Form 1120-PC	21
Form 1041 (bankruptcy estate only)	03	Form 1120-POL	22
Form 1041-N	06	Form 1120-REIT	23
Form 1041-QFT	07	Form 1120-RIC	24
Form 1042	08	Form 1120S	25
Form 1065-B	10	Form 1120-SF	26
Form 1066	11	Form 3520-A	27
Form 1120	12	Form 8612	28
Form 1120-C	34	Form 8613	29
Form 1120-F	15	Form 8725	30
Form 1120-FSC	16	Form 8831	32
Form 1120-H	17	Form 8876	33
Form 1120-L	18	Form 8924	35
Form 1120-ND	19	Form 8928	36

2 If the organization is a foreign corporation that does not have an office or place of business in the United States, check here . . . . ▶ □

3 If the organization is a corporation and is the common parent of a group that intends to file a consolidated return, check here . . . . ▶ □

If checked, attach a statement, listing the name, address, and Employer Identification Number (EIN) for each member covered by this application.

Part III   All Filers Must Complete This Part

4 If the organization is a corporation or partnership that qualifies under Regulations section 1.6081-5, check here . ▶ □

5a The application is for calendar year 20___, or tax year beginning _____, 20___, and ending _____, 20___

b **Short tax year.** If this tax year is less than 12 months, check the reason: □ Initial return □ Final return □ Change in accounting period □ Consolidated return to be filed □ Other (see instructions-attach explanation)

6	Tentative total tax	**6**	
7	**Total** payments and credits (see instructions)	**7**	
8	**Balance due.** Subtract line 7 from line 6 (see instructions)	**8**	

For Privacy Act and Paperwork Reduction Act Notice, see separate Instructions.   Cat. No. 13804A   Form **7004** (Rev. 12-2012)

Instructions for Form 7004
(Rev. December 2012)

Department of the Treasury
Internal Revenue Service

Application for Automatic Extension of Time To File Certain Business Income Tax, Information, and Other Returns

Section references are to the Internal Revenue Code unless otherwise noted.

Future Developments

For the latest information about developments related to Form 7004 and its instructions, such as legislation enacted after they were published, go to *www.irs.gov/form7004*.

What's New

Short tax year. On line 5b, if none of the reasons listed apply, the applicable entity can check the "Other" box and attach an explanation.

Where to file. Beginning January 1, 2013, for certain filers with a principal business, office, or agency located in Florida, the address to mail Form 7004 has changed. See the *Where To File* chart later.

General Instructions

Purpose of Form

Use Form 7004 to request an automatic extension of time to file certain business income tax, information, and other returns. The extension will be granted if you complete Form 7004 properly, make a proper estimate of the tax (if applicable), file the form by the due date of the return to which the Form 7004 applies, and pay any tax that is due.

Automatic 5-month extension. All the returns shown in Part I, line 1a of Form 7004 are eligible for an automatic 5-month extension of time to file from the due date of the return.

Automatic 6-month extension. All the returns shown in Part II, line 1b of Form 7004 are eligible for an automatic 6-month extension of time to file from the due date of the return. However, see the instructions for lines 2 and 4 for exceptions.

When to File

Generally, Form 7004 must be filed on or before the due date of the applicable tax return. The due dates of the returns can be found in the instructions for the applicable return.

Exceptions. See the instructions for line 2 for foreign corporations with no office or place of business in the United States. See the instructions for line 4 for foreign and certain domestic corporations and for certain partnerships.

Termination of Extension

The IRS may terminate the automatic extension at any time by mailing a notice of termination to the entity or person that requested the extension. The notice will be mailed at least 10 days before the termination date given in the notice.

How and Where To File

Form 7004 can be filed electronically for most returns. However, Form 7004 cannot be filed electronically for Forms 8612, 8613, 8725, 8831, 8876, or 706-GS(D). For details on electronic filing, visit *www.irs.gov/Filing*.

If you do not file electronically, file Form 7004 with the Internal Revenue Service Center at the applicable address for your return as shown in the table, *Where To File*, later in the instructions.

Signature. No signature is required on this form.

No Blanket Requests

File a separate Form 7004 for each return for which you are requesting an extension of time to file. This extension will apply only to the specific return identified on line 1a or line 1b. For consolidated group returns, see the instructions for line 3.

 Do not complete both Part I, line 1a and Part II, line 1b, of this form. See the instructions for lines 1a and 1b.

Extension Period

The IRS will no longer be sending notifications that your extension has been approved. We will notify you only if your request for an extension is disallowed. Properly filing this form will automatically give you the maximum extension allowed from the due date of your return to file the return (except as noted below in the instructions for lines 2 and 4 with regard to foreign corporations, certain domestic corporations, and certain partnerships with their books and records outside of the United States and Puerto Rico). See the instructions for the applicable return for its due date.

Rounding Off to Whole Dollars

The entity can round off cents to whole dollars on its return and schedules. If the entity does round to whole dollars, it must round all amounts. To round, drop amounts under 50 cents and increase amounts from 50 to 99 cents to the next dollar (for example, $1.39 becomes $1 and $2.50 becomes $3).

If two or more amounts must be added to figure the amount to enter on a line, include cents when adding the amounts and round off only the total.

Payment of Tax

Form 7004 does not extend the time for payment of tax. Generally, payment of any balance due on line 8 of Form 7004 is required by the due date of the return for which this extension is filed. See the instructions for line 8.

Penalty for late filing of return. Generally, a penalty is charged if a return is filed after the due date (including extensions) unless you can show reasonable cause for not filing on time.

Penalty for late payment of tax. Generally, a penalty of $1/2$ of 1% of any tax not paid by the due date is charged for each month or part of a month that the tax remains unpaid. The penalty cannot exceed 25% of the amount due. The penalty will not be charged if you can show reasonable cause for not paying on time.

If a corporation is granted an extension of time to file a corporation income tax return, it will not be charged a late payment penalty if the tax shown on line 6 (or the amount of tax paid by the regular due date of the return) is at least 90% of the tax shown on the total tax line of your return, and the balance due shown on the return is paid by the extended due date.

Nov 21, 2012   Cat. No. 51607V

Interest. Interest is charged on any tax not paid by the regular due date of the return from the due date until the tax is paid. It will be charged even if you have been granted an extension or have shown reasonable cause for not paying on time.

Forms 1065, 1065-B, and 1066. A penalty may be assessed against the partnership or REMIC if it is required to file a return, but fails to file it on time, including extensions, or files a return that fails to show all the information required, unless the entity can show reasonable cause for not filing on time. See the Instructions for Forms 1065, 1065-B, or 1066 for more information.

Reasonable cause. If you receive a notice about a penalty after you file your return, send the IRS an explanation and we will determine if you meet reasonable-cause criteria. Do not attach an explanation when you file your return.

Specific Instructions

Name and identifying number. If your name has changed since you filed your tax return for the previous year, enter on Form 7004 your name as you entered it on the previous year's income tax return. If the name entered on Form 7004 does not match the IRS database and/or the identifying number is incorrect, you will not have a valid extension. Enter the applicable employer identification number (EIN) or social security number.

Address. Include the suite, room, or other unit number after the street address. If the post office does not deliver mail to the street address and the entity has a P.O. box, show the box number instead of the street address.

If the entity's address is outside the United States or its possessions or territories, enter in the space for "city or town, state, and ZIP code," the information in the following order: city, province or state, and country. Follow the country's practice for entering the postal code. Do not abbreviate the country name.

If your mailing address has changed since you filed your last return, use Form 8822, Change of Address, or Form 8822-B, Change of Address—Business, to notify the IRS of the change. A new address shown on Form 7004 will not update your record.

Part I Automatic 5-Month Extension

Line 1a

If you are applying for an automatic 5-month extension, enter the appropriate Form Code in the boxes on line 1a to indicate the type of return for which you are requesting an extension. Enter only one Form Code. If you make a Form Code entry on line 1a, do not make a Form Code entry on line 1b.

Part II Automatic 6-Month Extension

Line 1b

If you are applying for an automatic 6-month extension, enter the appropriate Form Code in the boxes on line 1b to indicate the type of return for which you are requesting an extension. Enter only one Form Code. If you make a Form Code entry on line 1b, do not make a Form Code entry on line 1a.

Note. If an association is electing to file Form 1120-H, U.S. Income Tax Return for Homeowners Associations, it should file for the extension on Form 7004 using the original form type assigned to the entity. See the Instructions for Form 1120-H.

Line 2

Check the box on line 2 if you are requesting an extension of time to file for a foreign corporation that does not have an office or place of business in the United States. The entity should file Form 7004 by the due date of the return (the 15th day of the 6th month following the close of the tax year) to request the automatic 6-month extension.

Line 3

Note. This is applicable to corporations only.
Only the common parent of a consolidated group can request an extension of time to file the group's consolidated return.

Attach a list of all members of the consolidated group showing the name, address, and EIN for each member of the group. If you file a paper return, you must provide this information using the following format: 8.5 x 11, 20 lb. white paper, 12 point font in Courier, Arial, or Times New Roman; black ink; one sided printing, and at least $^1/_2$ inch margin. Information is to be presented in a two column format, with the left column containing affiliates' names and addresses, and the right column containing the TIN with $^1/_2$ inch between the columns. There should be two blank lines between listed affiliates.

Generally, all members of a consolidated group must use the same taxable year as the common parent corporation. If, however, a particular member of a consolidated group is required to file a separate income tax return for a short period and seeks an extension of time to file the return, that member must file a separate Form 7004 for that period. See Regulations section 1.1502-76 for details.

 Any member of either a controlled group of corporations or an affiliated group of corporations not joining in a consolidated return must file a separate Form 7004.

Note. Failure to list members of the affiliated group on an attachment may result in the group's inability to elect to file a consolidated return. However, see Regulations sections 301.9100-1 through 301.9100-3 for information about extensions of time for making elections.

Part III All Filers Must Complete This Part

Line 4. Corporations or Certain Partnerships That Qualify Under Regulations Section 1.6081-5

Exceptions for foreign and certain domestic corporations. Certain foreign and domestic corporations (as described below) are entitled to a 3-month extension of time to file and pay under Regulations section 1.6081-5. These entities do not need to file Form 7004 to take this 3-month extension and must file (or request an additional extension of time to file) and pay any balance due by the 15th day of the 6th month following the close of the tax year.

This includes:
- A foreign corporation that maintains an office or place of business in the United States,
- A domestic corporation that transacts its business and keeps its books and records of account outside the United States and Puerto Rico, or
- A domestic corporation whose principal income is from sources within the possessions of the United States.

Attach a statement to the corporation's tax return stating the corporation qualifies for the extension to file and pay. If the corporation is unable to file its return within the 3-month extension, check box 4 on Form 7004 to request an additional 3-month extension.

Exceptions for certain partnerships. Partnerships that keep their books and records outside the United States and Puerto Rico are entitled to a 2-month extension of time to file and pay, if applicable.

You do not need to file Form 7004 if the partnership is taking the 2-month extension of time to file and pay. Attach a statement to the partnership's tax return stating that the partnership qualifies for the extension of time to file and pay. If the partnership is unable to file its return within the 2-month period, check box 4 on Form 7004 to request an additional extension (3 months for partnerships filing Form 1065, and 4 months for partnerships filing Form 1065-B).

Line 5a

If you do not use a calendar year, complete the lines showing the tax year beginning and ending dates.

Line 5b

Check the applicable box for the reason for the short tax year.

If the box for "Change in accounting period" is checked, the entity must have applied for approval to change its tax year unless certain conditions have been met. For more information, see Form 1128, Application To Adopt, Change, or Retain a Tax Year, and Pub. 538, Accounting Periods and Methods.

If you have a short tax year and none of the reasons listed apply, check the box for "Other" and attach a statement explaining the reason for the short tax year. Clearly explain the circumstances that caused the short tax year.

Line 6

Enter the total tax, including any nonrefundable credits, the entity expects to owe for the tax year. See the specific instructions for the applicable return to estimate the amount of the tentative tax. If you expect this amount to be zero, enter -0-.

Line 7

Enter the total payments and refundable credits. For more information about "write-in" payments and credits, see the instructions for the applicable return.

Line 8

Form 7004 does not extend the time to pay tax. If the entity is a corporation or affiliated group of corporations filing a consolidated return, the corporation must remit the amount of the unpaid tax liability shown on line 8 on or before the due date of the return.

Most entities must use electronic funds transfer to make all federal tax deposits, including deposits for corporate income taxes. Forms 8109 and 8109-B, Federal Tax Deposit Coupon, can no longer be used. Generally, electronic funds transfers are made using the Electronic Federal Tax Payment System (EFTPS). To get more information about EFTPS or to enroll in EFTPS, visit *www.eftps.gov* or call 1-800-555-4477.

If the entity does not want to use EFTPS, it can arrange for its tax professional, financial institution, payroll service, or other trusted third party to make deposits on its behalf.

If you file Form 7004 electronically, you can pay by Electronic Funds Withdrawal (EFW). See Form 8878-A, IRS *e-file* Electronic Funds Withdrawal Authorization for Form 7004. If the corporation expects to have a net operating loss carryback, the corporation can reduce the amount to be deposited to the extent of the overpayment resulting from the carryback, provided all other prior year tax liabilities have been fully paid and Form 1138, Extension of Time for Payment of Taxes by a Corporation Expecting a Net Operating Loss Carryback, is filed with Form 7004.

Foreign corporations that maintain an office or place of business in the United States should pay their tax as described above.

Foreign corporations that do not maintain an office or place of business in the United States, see the instructions for the corporation's applicable tax return (Form 1120-F or Form 1120-FSC) for information on depositing any tax due.

A trust (Form 1041), electing large partnership (Form 1065-B), or REMIC (Form 1066) will be granted an extension even if it cannot pay the full amount shown on line 8. But it should pay as much as it can to limit the amount of penalties and interest it will owe.

If you are requesting an extension of time to file Form 1042, see the deposit rules in the instructions for the form to determine how payment must be made.

Privacy Act and Paperwork Reduction Act Notice. We ask for the information on this form to carry out the Internal Revenue laws of the United States. We need it to ensure that you are complying with these laws and to allow us to figure and collect the right amount of tax. This information is needed to process your application for the requested extension of time to file. You are not required to request an extension of time to file. However, if you do so, Internal Revenue Code sections 6001, 6011(a), 6081, and 6109 require you to provide the information requested on this form, including identification numbers. Failure to provide the information may delay or prevent processing your application; providing any false information may subject you to penalties.

You are not required to provide the information requested on a form that is subject to the Paperwork Reduction Act unless the form displays a valid OMB control number. Books or records relating to a form or its instructions must be retained as long as their contents may become material in the administration of any Internal Revenue law. Generally, tax returns and return information are confidential, as required by section 6103.

However, section 6103 allows or requires the Internal Revenue Service to disclose or give such information to the Department of Justice for civil or criminal litigation, and to cities, states, the District of Columbia, and United States possessions and commonwealths for use in administering their tax laws. We may also disclose this information to other countries under a tax treaty, to Federal and state agencies to enforce Federal nontax criminal laws, or to Federal law enforcement and intelligence agencies to combat terrorism.

The time needed to complete and file this form will vary depending on individual circumstances. The estimated average time is:

Recordkeeping	3 hr., 21 min.
Learning about the law or the form	1 hr., 3 min.
Preparing the form	2 hr., 6 min.
Copying, assembling, and sending the form to the IRS	16 min.

If you have comments concerning the accuracy of these time estimates or suggestions for making this form simpler, we would be happy to hear from you. You can write to the Internal Revenue Service, Tax Products Coordinating Committee, 1111 Constitution Ave. NW, IR-6526, Washington, DC 20224. Do not send the tax form to this address. Instead, see *Where To File*, below.

Where To File

IF the form is . . .	AND the settler is (or was at death) . . .	THEN file Form 7004 at:
706-GS(D) & 706-GS(T)	A resident U.S. citizen, resident alien, nonresident U.S. citizen, or alien	Department of the Treasury, Internal Revenue Service Center, Cincinnati, OH 45999-0045, or for private delivery service: 201 W. Rivercenter Blvd., Covington, KY 41011-1424

IF the form is . . .	AND your principal business, office, or agency is located in . . .	THEN file Form 7004 at:	
1041, 1120-H	Connecticut, Delaware, District of Columbia, Florida, Georgia, Illinois, Indiana, Kentucky, Maine, Maryland, Massachusetts, Michigan, New Hampshire, New Jersey, New York, North Carolina, Ohio, Pennsylvania, Rhode Island, South Carolina, Tennessee, Vermont, Virginia, West Virginia, Wisconsin	Department of the Treasury Internal Revenue Service Center Cincinnati, OH 45999-0045	
	Alabama, Alaska, Arizona, Arkansas, California, Colorado, Hawaii, Idaho, Iowa, Kansas, Louisiana, Minnesota, Mississippi, Missouri, Montana, Nebraska, Nevada, New Mexico, North Dakota, Oklahoma, Oregon, South Dakota, Texas, Utah, Washington, Wyoming	Department of the Treasury Internal Revenue Service Center Ogden, UT 84201-0045	
	A foreign country or U.S. possession	Internal Revenue Service Center P.O. Box 409101, Ogden, UT 84409	
1041-QFT, 8725, 8831, 8876, 8924, 8928	Any location	Department of the Treasury Internal Revenue Service Center Cincinnati, OH 45999-0045	
1042, 1120-F, 1120-FSC, 3520-A, 8804	Any location	Internal Revenue Service Center P.O. Box 409101, Ogden, UT 84409	
1066, 1120-C, 1120-PC	The United States	Department of the Treasury Internal Revenue Service Center Ogden, UT 84201-0045	
	A foreign country or U.S. possession	Internal Revenue Service Center P.O. Box 409101, Ogden, UT 84409	
1041-N, 1065-B, 1120-POL	Any location	Department of the Treasury Internal Revenue Service Center Ogden, UT 84409-0045	
1065, 1120, 1120-L, 1120-ND, 1120-REIT, 1120-RIC, 1120S, 1120-SF, 8612, 8613	Connecticut, Delaware, District of Columbia, Florida, Georgia, Illinois, Indiana, Kentucky, Maine, Maryland, Massachusetts, Michigan, New Hampshire, New Jersey, New York, North Carolina, Ohio, Pennsylvania, Rhode Island, South Carolina, Tennessee, Vermont, Virginia, West Virginia, Wisconsin	**And the total assets at the end of the tax year are:** Less than $10 million	Department of the Treasury Internal Revenue Service Center Cincinnati, OH 45999-0045
		$10 million or more	Department of the Treasury Internal Revenue Service Center Ogden, UT 84201-0045
	Alabama, Alaska, Arizona, Arkansas, California, Colorado, Hawaii, Idaho, Iowa, Kansas, Louisiana, Minnesota, Mississippi, Missouri, Montana, Nebraska, Nevada, New Mexico, North Dakota, Oklahoma, Oregon, South Dakota, Texas, Utah, Washington, Wyoming	Department of the Treasury Internal Revenue Service Center Ogden, UT 84201-0045	
	A foreign country or U.S. possession	Internal Revenue Service Center P.O. Box 409101, Ogden, UT 84409	

-4-

Form **8027**

Department of the Treasury
Internal Revenue Service

Employer's Annual Information Return of Tip Income and Allocated Tips
► See the separate instructions.
► Information about Form 8027 and its separate instructions is available at *www.irs.gov/form8027.*

OMB No. 1545-0714

20**12**

Check **if:**
Amended Return ☐
Final Return ☐

Name of establishment

Number and street (see instructions)

City or town, state, and ZIP code

Employer identification number

Type of establishment **(check only one box)**

☐ **1** Evening meals only

☐ **2** Evening and other meals

☐ **3** Meals other than evening meals

☐ **4** Alcoholic beverages

Employer's name (name as shown on Form 941)

Establishment number (see instructions)

Number and street (P.O. box, if applicable)

Apt. or suite no.

City, state, and ZIP code (if a foreign address, see instructions)

Does this establishment accept credit cards, debit cards, or other charges? ☐ Yes (lines 1 and 2 **must** be completed) ☐ No

1	Total charged tips for calendar year 2012	**1**	
2	Total charge receipts showing charged tips (see instructions)	**2**	
3	Total amount of service charges of less than 10% paid as wages to employees	**3**	
4a	Total tips reported by indirectly tipped employees	**4a**	
b	Total tips reported by directly tipped employees	**4b**	
	Note. Complete the **Employer's Optional Worksheet for Tipped Employees** in the instructions to determine potential unreported tips of your employees.		
c	Total tips reported (add lines 4a and 4b)	**4c**	
5	Gross receipts from food or beverage operations (not less than line 2—see instructions) . .	**5**	
6	Multiply line 5 by 8% (.08) or the lower rate shown here ► _____ granted by the IRS. Attach a copy of the IRS determination letter to this return	**6**	

Note. If you have allocated tips using other than the calendar year (semimonthly, biweekly, quarterly, etc.), mark an "**X**" on line 6 and enter the amount of allocated tips from your records on line 7.

7	Allocation of tips. If line 6 is more than line 4c, enter the excess here	**7**	

► This amount must be allocated as tips to tipped employees working in this establishment. Check the box below that shows the method used for the allocation. Show the portion, if any, allocated to each employee in box 8 of the employee's Form W-2.

a Allocation based on hours-worked method (see instructions for restriction) . . . . . ☐
Note. If you marked the checkbox on line 7a, enter the average number of employee hours worked per business day during the payroll period. (see instructions) _____

b Allocation based on gross receipts method . . . . ☐

c Allocation based on good-faith agreement. Attach a copy of the agreement . . . . . ☐

8 Enter the total number of directly tipped employees at this establishment during 2012 ►

Under penalties of perjury, I declare that I have examined this return, including accompanying schedules and statements, and to the best of my knowledge and belief, it is true, correct, and complete.

Signature ►   Title ►   Date ►

For Privacy Act and Paperwork Reduction Act Notice, see the separate instructions.   Cat. No. 49989U   Form **8027** (2012)

20**12**
Instructions for Form 8027

**Employer's Annual Information Return of
Tip Income and Allocated Tips**

Department of the Treasury
Internal Revenue Service

Section references are to the Internal Revenue Code unless otherwise noted.

Future Developments

For the latest information about developments related to Form 8027 and its instructions, such as legislation enacted after they were published, go to *www.irs.gov/form8027*.

Reminders

• You must check one of the "Yes" or "No" boxes under employer's name and address to indicate whether or not the establishment accepts credit cards, debit cards, or other charges. If the "Yes" box is checked, lines 1 and 2 of Form 8027 must be completed. Also see the instructions for lines 1 and 2.

• Complete the *Worksheet for Determining Whether To File Form 8027* (below) to determine if you must file Form 8027.

• You may want to use the *Employer's Optional Worksheet for Tipped Employees*, later, as a means of determining if your employees are reporting all of their tip income to you.

Electronic filing. If you file 250 or more Forms 8027, you **must** file the returns electronically. See Pub. 1239, Specifications for Filing Form 8027, Employer's Annual Information Return of Tip Income and Allocated Tips, Electronically, for more information.

Expiration of the Attributed Tip Income Program (ATIP). The Attributed Tip Income Program (ATIP) expired on December 31, 2011.

General Instructions

Purpose of Form

Form 8027 is used by large food or beverage establishments when the employer is required to make annual reports to the IRS on receipts from food or beverage operations and tips reported by employees.

All employees receiving $20 or more a month in tips must report 100% of their tips to their employer.

Who Must File

You must file Form 8027 if you are an employer who operates a large food or beverage establishment. If you own more than one establishment, you must file Form 8027 for each one. There may be more than one establishment (business activity providing food or beverages) operating within a single building, and, if gross receipts are recorded separately, each activity is required to file a Form 8027.

A return is required only for establishments in the 50 states and the District of Columbia.

If you are required to report for more than one establishment, you must complete and file Form 8027-T, Transmittal of Employer's Annual Information Return of Tip Income and Allocated Tips, with Forms 8027.

A large food or beverage establishment is one to which all of the following apply.

• Food or beverage is provided for consumption on the premises.
• Tipping is a customary practice.
• More than 10 employees who work more than 80 hours were normally employed on a typical business day during the preceding calendar year.

Worksheet for Determining Whether To File Form 8027

Complete the worksheet below to determine if you had more than 10 employees on a typical business day during 2011 and, therefore, must file Form 8027 for 2012. It is the **average number of employee hours worked on a typical business day** that determines whether or not you employed more than 10 employees.

1. Enter **one-half** of the **total** employee hours worked during the month in 2011 with the **greatest** aggregate gross receipts from food and beverages . . . . _____

2. Enter the number of **days opened for business** during the month shown in line 1 . . . . _____

3. Enter **one-half** of the **total** employee hours worked during the month in 2011 with the **least** aggregate gross receipts from food and beverages . . . . . _____

4. Enter the number of **days opened for business** during the month shown in line 3. . . . . _____

5. Divide line 1 by line 2. . . . . _____

6. Divide line 3 by line 4. . . . . _____

7. Add lines 5 and 6. If line 7 is greater than 80 (hours), you must file Form 8027 for 2012. . . . . _____

Note. The filing requirement (more than 10 employees) is based on the total of all employees who provided services in connection with the provision of food and beverages at the establishment, not just the number of directly tipped employees. Include employees such as waitstaff, bussers, bartenders, seat persons, wine stewards, cooks, and kitchen help. See Regulations section 31.6053-3(j)(10) for more information.

A person who owns 50% or more in value of the stock of a corporation that runs the establishment is not considered an employee when determining whether the establishment normally employs more than 10 individuals.

New large food or beverage establishment. File Form 8027 for a new large food or beverage establishment if, during any 2 consecutive calendar months, the average number of hours worked each business day by all employees is more than 80 hours. To figure the average number of employee hours worked each business day during a month, divide the total hours all employees worked during the month by the number of days the establishment was open for business. After the test is met for 2 consecutive months, you must file a return covering the rest of the year, beginning with the next payroll period.

Exceptions To Filing

A return is not required for:
• Establishments operated for less than 1 month in calendar year 2012.
• Fast food restaurants and operations where tipping is not customary such as cafeterias or operations where 95% of the total sales are carryout sales or sales with a service charge of 10% or more.

When To File

File Form 8027 (and Form 8027-T when filing more than one Form 8027) by February 28, 2013. However, if you file electronically, the due date is April 1, 2013.

Extension of time to file. Filers of Form 8027 submitted on paper or electronically may request an extension of time to file on Form 8809, Application for Extension of Time To File Information Returns. File Form 8809 as soon as you know an extension of time to file is necessary, but not later than February 28, 2013 (April 1, 2013 if you file electronically).

Note. When filing a paper Form 8027 attach a copy of your extension approval. If an approval has not been received by the time you file, attach a copy of your timely filed Form 8809.

Where To File

Mail Form 8027 to:

Department of the Treasury
Internal Revenue Service
Cincinnati, OH 45999

Note. When filing a paper Form 8027, attach a copy of your extension approval (or a copy of your timely filed Form 8809 if an extension is not received by the time you file), a copy of your approved waiver from filing Form 8027 electronically, a copy of your "lower rate" determination letter from the IRS, and/or a copy of your good-faith agreement. Do not attach any unrelated correspondence. See line 6 of Form 8027.

Reporting and filing electronically. If you are the employer and you file 250 or more Forms 8027, you must file the returns electronically. See Pub. 1239 for information on filing Form 8027 electronically.

Penalties

The law provides for a penalty if you do not file Form 8027 (and Form 8027-T) on time unless you can show reasonable cause for the delay. You may be charged penalties for each failure to:
• Timely file a correct information return including failure to file electronically if required, and
• Timely provide a correct Form W-2, Wage and Tax Statement, to the employee.

For more information on penalties for untimely or incorrect Forms W-2 or 8027, see Pub. 1239 and the General Instructions for Forms W-2 and W-3.

Gross Receipts

Gross receipts include all receipts (other than nonallocable receipts, see definition below) from cash sales, charge receipts, charges to a hotel room (excluding tips charged to the hotel room if your accounting procedures allow these tips to be separated), and the retail value of complimentary food or beverages served to customers as explained below.

Also include charged tips in gross receipts, but only to the extent that you reduced your cash sales by the amount of any cash you paid to tipped employees for any charged tips due them. However, if you did not reduce cash sales for charged tips paid out to employees, do not include those charged tips in gross receipts. Do not include state or local taxes in gross receipts.

 Remind all directly and indirectly tipped employees to include all charged tips and all cash tips received in the tip amount that they must report to you.

Nonallocable receipts. These are receipts for carryout sales and receipts with a service charge added of 10% or more. Nonallocable receipts generally include all sales on which tipping is not customary.

Complimentary items. Food or beverages served to customers without charge must be included in gross receipts if (a) tipping for providing them is customary at the establishment, and (b) they are provided in connection with an activity that is engaged in for profit and whose receipts would not be included in the amount on line 5 of Form 8027.

For example, you would have to include in gross receipts the retail value of the complimentary drinks served to customers in a gambling casino because tipping is customary, the gambling casino is an activity engaged in for profit, and the gambling receipts of the casino are not included in the amount on line 5.

However, you would not have to include the retail value of complimentary hors d'oeuvres at your bar or a complimentary dessert served to a regular patron of your restaurant in gross receipts because the receipts of the bar or restaurant would be included in the amount on line 5. You would not have to include the value of a fruit basket placed in a hotel room in gross receipts since, generally, tipping for it is not customary.

Allocation of Tips

You must allocate tips among employees who receive them if the total tips reported to you during any payroll period are less than 8% (or the approved lower rate) of this establishment's gross receipts for that period.

Generally, the amount allocated is the difference between the total tips reported by employees and 8% (or the lower rate) of the gross receipts, other than nonallocable receipts.

Lower rate. You (or a majority of the employees) may request a lower rate (but not lower than 2%) by submitting a petition to:

Internal Revenue Service
National Tip Reporting Compliance
3251 North Evergreen Dr. NE
Grand Rapids, MI 49525

Do not mail Form 8027 to this address. See *Where To File,* earlier.

The burden of supplying sufficient information to allow the IRS to estimate with reasonable accuracy the actual tip rate

of the establishment rests with the petitioner. Your petition for a lower rate must clearly demonstrate that a rate less than 8% should apply. It must include the following information.
* Employer's name, address, and EIN.
* Establishment's name, address, and establishment number.
* Detailed description of the establishment that would help to determine the tip rate. The description should include the type of restaurant, days and hours of operation, type of service including any self-service, the person (waiter or waitress, cashier, etc.) to whom the customer pays the check, whether the check is paid before or after the meal, and whether alcohol is available.
* Past year's information shown on lines 1 through 6 of Form 8027 as well as total carryout sales; total charge sales; percentage of sales for breakfast, lunch, and dinner; average dollar amount of a guest check; service charge, if any, added to the check; and the percentage of sales with a service charge.
* Type of clientele.
* Copy of a representative menu for each meal.

The petition must contain the following statement and be signed by a responsible person who is authorized to make and sign a return, statement, or other document.

"Under penalties of perjury, I declare that I have examined this petition, including accompanying documents, and to the best of my knowledge and belief, the facts presented in support of this petition are true, correct, and complete."

You must attach to the petition copies of Form 8027 (if any) filed for the 3 years before your petition. If you are petitioning for more than one establishment or you want to know your appeal rights, see Rev. Proc. 86-21, 1986 1 C.B. 560 for additional information. Also include with your petition a check or money order made payable to the "United States Treasury" for the amount of the user fee required for determination letters.

For the current user fee amount, consult the first revenue procedure of the year (for example, Rev. Proc. 2012-1, 2012-1 I.R.B. 1, available at *www.irs.gov/irb/2012-01_IRB/ar06.html*). This revenue procedure is updated annually as the first revenue procedure of the year, but it may be modified or amplified during the year. The user fees are posted in Appendix A of the revenue procedure. Since the taxpayer is requesting a letter ruling determination, the payment for the user fee must be submitted along with the petition for the rate reduction.

A majority of all the directly tipped employees must consent to any petition written by an employee. A "majority of employees" means more than half of all directly tipped employees employed by the establishment at the time the petition is filed. Employee groups must follow the procedures in Regulations section 31.6053-3(h); Pub. 531, Reporting Tip Income; and Rev. Proc. 86-21.

The IRS will notify you when and for how long the reduced rate is effective.

Note. You must attach a copy of your "lower rate" determination letter from the IRS when filing a paper Form 8027. See Pub. 1239 for instructions on submitting a copy of your "lower rate" determination letter from the IRS when filing electronically.

Reporting Allocated Tips To Employees

Give each employee who has been allocated tips a Form W-2 that shows the allocated amount in box 8. The form must be furnished to the employee by January 31 of the following year. If employment ends before the end of the year and the employee asks for the Form W-2, a tip allocation is not required on the early Form W-2. However, you may include on the early Form W-2 the employee's actual tip allocation or a good-faith estimate of the allocation. Signify a good-faith estimate by writing "estimate" next to the allocated amount in box 8 of the Form W-2.

If no allocation was shown on the early Form W-2 or if the estimated allocation on the early form differs from the actual amount by more than 5%, give the employee a new Form W-2 marked "CORRECTED" with the correct information during January of the next year.

If you allocate tips among employees by the methods described in the instructions for lines 7a through 7c, you are not liable to any employee if any amount is improperly allocated. However, if the allocation shown on the employee's Form W-2 differs from the correct allocation by more than 5%, you must adjust that employee's allocation and must review the allocable amount of all other employees in the same establishment to assure that the error did not distort any other employee's share by more than 5%.

Use the current version of Form W-2c, Corrected Wage and Tax Statement, to report the corrected allocation on a previously filed Form W-2. However, if you discover the allocation error on Form W-2 after you issue it to your employee but before you send it to the Social Security Administration (SSA), prepare a new Form W-2 with the correct information, and send Copy A to the SSA. Write "CORRECTED" on the employee's new copies (B, C, and 2), and furnish them to the employee. Do not write "CORRECTED" on Copy A of Form W-2.

You do not need to send to the IRS separate copies of Forms W-2 showing allocated tips. The IRS will use the information shown on the Forms W-2 that you file with the SSA.

Tip allocations have no effect on withholding income tax, social security tax, or Medicare tax from employees' wages. Allocated tips are not subject to withholding and are not to be included in boxes 1, 3, 5, and 7 of Form W-2.

Specific Instructions

File a separate Form 8027 for each large food or beverage establishment. Use Form 8027-T when filing more than one Form 8027.

Name and Address of Establishment and Employer Identification Number

Type or print the name and address of the establishment. They may be different from your mailing address, as in the case of employers who have more than one establishment. If mail is not delivered to the street address of the establishment, enter the P.O. box number. The employer identification number (EIN) should be the same as the number on the Forms W-2 that you give to the employees and the Form 941, Employer's QUARTERLY Federal Tax

Return, that you file to report wages and taxes for employees working for the establishment.

Type of Establishment

Check the box (check only one box) on the form that best describes the food or beverage operation at this establishment.

- An establishment that serves evening meals only (with or without alcoholic beverages).
- An establishment that serves evening and other meals (with or without alcoholic beverages).
- An establishment that serves only meals other than evening meals (with or without alcoholic beverages).
- An establishment that serves food, if at all, only as an incidental part of the business of serving alcoholic beverages.

Employer's Name and Address

Enter the name and address of the entity or individual whose EIN was provided earlier. Enter foreign addresses as follows: city, province or state, and country. Do not abbreviate the name of the country.

Establishment Number

Enter a five-digit number to identify the individual establishments that you are reporting under the same EIN. Give each establishment a separate number. For example, each establishment could be numbered consecutively, starting with 00001.

Lines 1 Through 8

Credit Card Sales

If the credit or debit charge receipts reflect tips, then you **must** enter on lines 1 and 2 the appropriate amounts shown on the credit card or debit card charge statements. See instructions for line 1 below.

Rounding Off to Whole Dollars

You may round off cents to whole dollars on your Form 8027. If you do round to whole dollars, you must round all amounts. To round, drop amounts under 50 cents and increase amounts from 50 to 99 cents to the next dollar. For example, $1.39 becomes $1 and $2.50 becomes $3.

If you have to add two or more amounts to figure the amount to enter on a line, include cents when adding the amounts and round off only the total.

Line 1. Charged Tips for Calendar Year 2012

Enter the total amount of tips that are shown on charge receipts for the year.

Line 2. Charge Receipts Showing Charged Tips

Enter the total sales (other than nonallocable receipts as defined earlier) from charge receipts that had a charged tip shown. Include credit card charges and other credit arrangements and charges to a hotel room unless your normal accounting practice consistently excludes charges to a hotel room. Do not include any state or local taxes in the amounts reported.

Line 3. Total Amount of Service Charges of Less Than 10% Paid as Wages to Employees

Enter the total amount of service charges of less than 10% that have been added to customers' bills and have been

distributed to your employees for the year. In general, service charges added to the bill are not tips since the customer does not have a choice. These service charges are treated as wages and are includible on Form W-2.

Line 4a. Tips Reported by Indirectly Tipped Employees

Enter the total amount of tips reported for the year by indirectly tipped employees, such as cooks, bussers, and service bartenders. Indirectly tipped employees generally receive their tips from other tipped employees and not directly from the customer.

Line 4b. Tips Reported by Directly Tipped Employees

Enter the total amount of tips reported for the year by directly tipped employees, such as bartenders and waitstaff. Directly tipped employees receive tips directly from customers.

Line 4c. Total Tips Reported

Add the amounts on lines 4a and 4b and enter the result on line 4c. This amount cannot be a negative amount.

```
   Line 4a
 + Line 4b
   Line 4c
```

 In figuring the tips you should report for 2012, do not include tips received by employees in December 2011, but not reported until January 2012. However, include tips received by employees in December 2012, but not reported until January 2013.

Line 5. Gross Receipts from Food or Beverage Operations

Enter the total gross receipts from the provision of food or beverages for this establishment for the year.

If you do not charge separately for providing food or beverages along with other goods or services (such as a package deal for food and lodging), make a good-faith estimate of the gross receipts from the food or beverages. This estimate must reflect the cost to the employer for providing the food or beverage plus a reasonable profit factor.

Line 6

Enter the result of multiplying line 5 by 8% (.08) or a lower rate (if the establishment was granted a lower rate by the IRS).

If a lower percentage rate was granted, write the rate in the space provided and attach a copy of the IRS determination letter. If you file Form 8027 electronically, see Pub. 1239 for instructions on submitting a copy of the IRS determination letter.

 The 8% rate (or lower rate) is used for tip allocation purposes only. Using this rate does not mean that directly tipped employees must report only 8%. They should report the amount of actual tips received.

If you have allocated tips using other than the calendar year, put an "X" on line 6 and enter the amount of allocated tips (if any) from your records on line 7. This may occur if you allocated tips based on the time period for which wages were paid or allocated on a quarterly basis.

Line 7. Allocation of Tips

If the amount shown on line 6 is more than the amount of tips reported by your employees on line 4c, you must allocate the excess to those employees. Enter the excess on line 7. There are three methods by which you may allocate tips. Check the box on line 7a, b, or c to show the method used.

Line 7a. Hours-Worked Method

Establishments that employ fewer than the equivalent of 25 full-time employees (both tipped and nontipped employees) during a payroll period may use the hours-worked method to allocate tips. You will be considered to have employed fewer than the equivalent of 25 full-time employees during a payroll period if the average number of employee hours worked (both tipped and nontipped employees) per business day during a payroll period is less than 200 hours.

To allocate tips by the hours-worked method, follow the steps explained in *Line 7b. Gross Receipts Method* below. However, for the fraction in step 3 of the gross receipts method, substitute in the numerator (top number) the number of hours worked by each employee who is tipped directly, and in the denominator (bottom number) the total number of hours worked by all employees who are directly tipped for the payroll period. See Regulations section 31.6053-3(f)(1)(iv) for details.

If you use the hours-worked method, be sure to enter on line 7a the average number of employee (both tipped and nontipped) hours worked per business day during the payroll period. If the establishment has more than one payroll period, you must use the payroll period in which the greatest number of workers (both tipped and nontipped) were employed.

Line 7b. Gross Receipts Method

If no good-faith agreement (as explained below) applies to the payroll period, you must allocate the difference between total tips reported and 8% of gross receipts using the gross receipts method (or hours-worked method (line 7a)) as follows (see *Example for Line 7b. Gross Receipts Method,* later).

1. Multiply the establishment's gross receipts (other than nonallocable receipts) for the payroll period by 8% (.08) or the lower rate.

2. Subtract from the amount figured in step 1 the total amount of tips reported by employees who were tipped indirectly for the payroll period. This difference is the directly tipped employees' total share of 8% (or the lower rate) of the gross receipts of the establishment. Indirectly tipped employees do not receive tips directly from customers. Examples are bussers, service bartenders, and cooks. Directly tipped employees, such as waitstaff and bartenders, receive tips directly from customers. Employees, such as maitre d's, who receive tips directly from customers and indirectly through tip splitting or pooling, are treated as directly tipped employees.

3. For each employee who is tipped directly, multiply the result in step 2 by the following fraction: the numerator (top number) is the amount of the establishment's gross receipts attributable to the employee, and the denominator (bottom number) is the gross receipts attributable to all directly tipped employees. The result is each directly tipped employee's share of 8% (or the lower rate) of the gross receipts for the payroll period.

4. From each directly tipped employee's share of 8% or the lower rate of the gross receipts figured in step 3, subtract the tips the employee reported for the payroll period. The result is each directly tipped employee's shortfall (if any) for the period.

5. From the amount figured in step 1, subtract the total tips reported by both directly and indirectly tipped employees. The result is the amount that has to be allocated among the directly tipped employees who had a shortfall for the payroll period as figured in step 4.

6. For each directly tipped employee who had a shortfall for the period as figured in step 4, multiply the amount in step 5 by the following fraction: the numerator is the employee's shortfall (figured in step 4), and the denominator is the total shortfall of all directly tipped employees. The result is the amount of allocated tips for each directly tipped employee.

Line 7c. Good-Faith Agreement

An allocation can be made under a good-faith agreement. This is a written agreement between you and at least two-thirds of the employees of each occupational category of employees who receive tips (for example, waitstaff, bussers, and maitre d's) working in the establishment when the agreement is adopted. The agreement must:

1. Provide for an allocation of the difference between total tips reported and 8% (or the lower rate) of gross receipts among employees who receive tips that approximates the actual distribution of tip income among the employees;

2. Be effective the first day of a payroll period that begins after the date the agreement is adopted, but no later than January 1 of the next year;

3. Be adopted when there are employees in each occupational category who would be affected by the agreement; and

4. Allow for revocation by a written agreement adopted by at least two-thirds of the employees in occupational categories affected by the agreement when it is revoked. The revocation is effective only at the beginning of a payroll period.

Note. You must attach a copy of your good-faith agreement when filing a paper Form 8027. Pub. 1239 provides instructions on submitting a copy of your good-faith agreement when filing electronically.

Line 8. Total Number of Directly Tipped Employees

Enter the total number of directly tipped employees who worked at the establishment during 2012. This is the cumulative total of all directly tipped employees who worked at the establishment at any time during the year. If you have a large turnover of directly tipped employees, this number may be large. Do not use this number to determine if you must file Form 8027. Instead, see the *Worksheet for Determining Whether To File Form 8027,* earlier.

-5-

Signature

Sign your name and include your title. Then enter the date signed and the best daytime telephone number where the IRS can reach you, including area code.

Who Must Sign?

Form 8027 must be signed as follows.

• **Sole proprietorship.** The individual who owns the business.

• **Corporation (including a limited liability company (LLC) treated as a corporation).** The president, vice president, or other principal officer duly authorized to sign.

• **Partnership (including an LLC treated as a partnership) or unincorporated organization.** A responsible and duly authorized member, partner, or officer having knowledge of its affairs.

• **Single member limited liability company (LLC) treated as a disregarded entity for federal income tax purposes.** The owner of the LLC or principal officer duly authorized to sign.

• **Trust or estate.** The fiduciary.

Form 8027 may also be signed by a duly authorized agent of the taxpayer if a valid power of attorney has been filed.

Alternative signature method. Corporate officers or duly authorized agents may sign Form 8027 by rubber stamp, mechanical device, or computer software program. For details and required documentation, see Rev. Proc. 2005-39, 2005-28 I.R.B. 82, available at *www.irs.gov/irb/2005-28_IRB/ar16.html*.

Example for Line 7b. Gross Receipts Method

A large food or beverage establishment has gross receipts for a payroll period of $100,000 and has tips reported for the payroll period of $6,200. Directly tipped employees reported $5,700, while indirectly tipped employees reported $500.

Directly tipped employees	Gross receipts for payroll period	Tips reported
A	$18,000	$1,080
B	16,000	880
C	23,000	1,810
D	17,000	800
E	12,000	450
F	14,000	680
Totals	$100,000	$5,700

1. $100,000 (gross receipts) x .08 = $8,000
2. $8,000 - $500 (tips reported by indirectly tipped employees) = $7,500
3.

Directly tipped employees	Directly tipped employee's share of 8% of the gross	(Times) Gross receipts ratio	Employee's share of 8% of gross
A	$7,500	18,000/100,000 =	$1,350
B	$7,500	16,000/100,000 =	1,200
C	$7,500	23,000/100,000 =	1,725
D	$7,500	17,000/100,000 =	1,275
E	$7,500	12,000/100,000 =	900
F	$7,500	14,000/100,000 =	1,050
	Total		$7,500

4.

Directly tipped employees	Employee's share of 8% of the gross	(Minus) Tips reported	Employee shortfall
A	$1,350	$1,080 =	$270
B	$1,200	880 =	320
C	$1,725	1,810 =	–
D	$1,275	800 =	475
E	$900	450 =	450
F	$1,050	680 =	370
	Total shortfall		$1,885

5. $8,000 less $6,200 (total tips reported) = $1,800 (amount allocable among employees who had a shortfall)

6.

Shortfall employees	Allocable amount	(Times) Shortfall ratio	Amount of allocation
A	$1,800	$270/1,885 =	$258
B	$1,800	320/1,885 =	306
D	$1,800	475/1,885 =	454
E	$1,800	450/1,885 =	430
F	$1,800	370/1,885 =	353

Since employee C has no shortfall, there is no allocation to C.

 In this example, the total amount of allocation is $1,801 resulting from the rounding off to whole numbers.

Employer's Optional Worksheet for Tipped Employees

Unreported tip income can lead to additional employer liability for FICA taxes. As a means of determining if your employees are reporting all of their tips to you, please take a few minutes to voluntarily complete the following worksheet. Completing this worksheet is only for the employer's information (it is not sent to the IRS).

1. Enter amount from Form 8027, line 1 ...... 1. _____
2. Enter amount from Form 8027, line 2 ...... 2. _____
3. Divide line 1 by line 2, enter as a decimal (at least 4 decimal places) .... 3. _____
4. Enter amount from Form 8027, line 4c ...... 4. _____
5. Enter amount from Form 8027, line 5 ...... 5. _____
6. Divide line 4 by line 5, enter as a decimal (at least 4 decimal places) .... 6. _____
7. Subtract line 6 from line 3; if zero or less, stop here .... 7. _____
8. Potential unreported tips. Multiply line 7 by line 5 .... 8. _____

Once you have completed the worksheet:

• If the entry on line 7 is zero or less, your employees are probably accurately reporting their tips; however,

- If the entry on line 8 is greater than zero, depending on the type of operation you have and whether or not you have allocated tips, it is possible that your employees are not reporting all of their tip income to you.

 Another quick method to determine if your employees are properly reporting all of their tips to you is to compare the rate of tips reported on credit sales to the rate of tips reported on cash sales. For example, if line 3 in the worksheet above greatly exceeds the rate determined from dividing reported cash tips by reportable cash receipts (that is, total cash receipts less nonallocable cash receipts), some of your employees may not be reporting all of their tips to you and you generally should be showing an amount on line 7 ("Allocation of tips") of Form 8027.

Need Help?

If it appears that not all tips are being reported to you, the IRS offers a service called the Tip Rate Determination & Education Program. This program can assist you, the employer, in implementing more effective methods of tip income reporting. The program also offers assistance in educating tipped employees concerning their obligations relating to the reporting of any tip income they receive. To find out more about this program or to participate in a voluntary tip compliance agreement, visit IRS.gov and type "restaurant" in the search box. You may also call 1-800-829-4933 or send an email to *TIP.Program@irs.gov* and request information on this program.

Privacy Act and Paperwork Reduction Act Notice. We ask for the information on this form to carry out the Internal Revenue laws of the United States. You are required to give us the information. We need it to ensure that you are complying with these laws and to allow us to figure and collect the right amount of tax.

Chapter 61, Information and Returns, of Subtitle F, Procedure and Administration, requires certain employers to report gross receipts, tips reported to them, and any allocated tips; and to furnish the amount of any allocated tips to affected employees. Section 6053 and its related regulations provide the definitions and methodology to be used in completing these forms. If you fail to provide this information in a timely manner, you may be liable for penalties as provided by section 6721.

You are not required to provide the information requested on a form that is subject to the Paperwork Reduction Act unless the form displays a valid OMB control number. Books or records relating to a form or its instructions must be retained as long as their contents may become material in the administration of any Internal Revenue law.

Generally, tax returns and return information are confidential, as required by section 6103. However, section 6103 allows or requires the Internal Revenue Service to disclose or give the information shown on your tax return to others as described in the Code. For example, we may disclose your tax information to the Department of Justice for civil and criminal litigation, and to cities, states, the District of Columbia, and U.S commonwealths and possessions to administer their tax laws. We may also disclose this information to other countries under a tax treaty, to federal and state agencies to enforce federal nontax criminal laws, or to federal law enforcement and intelligence agencies to combat terrorism.

The time needed to complete and file these forms will vary depending on individual circumstances. The estimated average times are:

Forms	8027	8027-T
Recordkeeping	9 hr., 33 min.	43 min.
Learning about the law or the form	53 min.	
Preparing and sending the form to the IRS	1 hr., 5 min.	

If you have comments concerning the accuracy of these time estimates or suggestions for making these forms simpler, we would be happy to hear from you. You can email us at *taxforms@irs.gov*. Enter "Form 8027" on the subject line. Or write to the Internal Revenue Service, Tax Products Coordinating Committee, SE:W:CAR:MP:T:M:S, 1111 Constitution Ave. NW, IR-6526, Washington, DC 20224. **Do not** send the tax forms to this address. Instead, see *Where To File*, earlier.

-7-

Form **8027-T**

Department of the Treasury
Internal Revenue Service

**Transmittal of Employer's Annual
Information Return of Tip Income and Allocated Tips**

▶ For Privacy Act and Paperwork Reduction Act Notice, see
the Instructions for Form 8027.

OMB No. 1545-0714

20**12**

Type or print employer's name, address, and employer identification number as shown on Form 941.	Employer's name		Employer identification number
	Number and street (or P.O. box number, if mail is not delivered to street address.)	Apt. or suite no.	Number of accompanying Forms 8027
	City or town, state, and ZIP code		

Use Form 8027-T to send Forms 8027 to the Internal Revenue Service if you have more than one establishment for which you have to file Form 8027.

File Form 8027-T along with accompanying Forms 8027 with the Department of the Treasury, Internal Revenue Service, Cincinnati, OH 45999 by February 28, 2013.

Cat. No. 61006A

Form **8027-T** (2012)

Form **8233**	**Exemption From Withholding on Compensation**	
(Rev. March 2009)	**for Independent (and Certain Dependent) Personal**	
Department of the Treasury Internal Revenue Service	**Services of a Nonresident Alien Individual** ▶ **See separate instructions.**	OMB No. 1545-0795

Who Should Use This Form?	**IF** you are a nonresident alien individual who is receiving . . .	**THEN,** if you are the beneficial owner of that income, use this form to claim . . .
Note: *For definitions of terms used in this section and detailed instructions on required withholding forms for each type of income, see* **Definitions** *on pages 1 and 2 of the instructions.*	Compensation for independent personal services performed in the United States	A tax treaty withholding exemption (Independent personal services, Business profits) for part or all of that compensation and/or to claim the daily personal exemption amount.
	Compensation for dependent personal services performed in the United States	A tax treaty withholding exemption for part or all of that compensation. **Note:** *Do not* use Form 8233 to claim the daily personal exemption amount.
	Noncompensatory scholarship or fellowship income **and** personal services income **from the same withholding agent**	A tax treaty withholding exemption for part or all of **both** types of income.
DO NOT Use This Form. . .	**IF** you are a beneficial owner who is . . .	**INSTEAD,** use . . .
	Receiving compensation for dependent personal services performed in the United States **and** you are **not** claiming a tax treaty withholding exemption for that compensation	Form W-4 (See page 2 of the Instructions for Form 8233 for how to complete Form W-4.)
	Receiving noncompensatory scholarship or fellowship income **and** you are **not** receiving any personal services income **from the same withholding agent**	Form W-8BEN or, if elected by the withholding agent, Form W-4 for the noncompensatory scholarship or fellowship income
	Claiming only foreign status or treaty benefits with respect to income that is **not** compensation for personal services	Form W-8BEN

This exemption is applicable for compensation for calendar year _____ , or other tax year beginning _____ and ending _____ .

Part I	**Identification of Beneficial Owner** (See instructions.)	
1 Name of individual who is the beneficial owner	**2** U.S. taxpayer identifying number	**3** Foreign tax identifying number, if any (optional)

4 Permanent residence address (street, apt. or suite no., or rural route). **Do not use a P.O. box.**

City or town, state or province. Include postal code where appropriate.	Country (do not abbreviate)

5 Address in the United States (street, apt. or suite no., or rural route). **Do not use a P.O. box.**

City or town, state, and ZIP code

Note: *Citizens of Canada or Mexico are not required to complete lines 7a and 7b.*

6 U.S. visa type	**7a** Country issuing passport	**7b** Passport number
8 Date of entry into the United States	**9a** Current nonimmigrant status	**9b** Date your current nonimmigrant status expires

10 If you are a foreign student, trainee, professor/teacher, or researcher, check this box . . . . ▶ ☐
    Caution: *See the* **line 10 instructions** *for the required additional statement you must attach.*

For Privacy Act and Paperwork Reduction Act Notice, see separate instructions.   Cat. No. 62292K   Form **8233** (Rev. 3-2009)

Part II   Claim for Tax Treaty Withholding Exemption and/or Personal Exemption Amount

11   Compensation for independent (and certain dependent) personal services:

  a   Description of personal services you are providing _____

_____

  b   Total compensation you expect to be paid for these services in this calendar or tax year $ _____

12   If compensation is exempt from withholding based on a tax treaty benefit, provide:

  a   Tax treaty **and treaty article** on which you are basing exemption from withholding _____

_____

  b   Total compensation listed on line 11b above that is exempt from tax under this treaty $ _____

  c   Country of permanent residence

    Note: *Do not complete lines 13a through 13c unless you also received compensation for personal services **from the same withholding agent.***

13   Noncompensatory scholarship or fellowship income:

  a   Amount $ _____

  b   Tax treaty **and treaty article** on which you are basing exemption from withholding _____

_____

  c   Total income listed on line 13a above that is exempt from tax under this treaty $ _____

14   Sufficient facts to justify the exemption from withholding claimed on line 12 and/or line 13 (see instructions) _____

_____

_____

_____

_____

_____

_____

_____

_____

_____

    Note: *Lines 15 through 18 are to be completed only for certain independent personal services (see instructions).*

15   Number of personal exemptions claimed ▶ | **16**   How many days will you perform services in the United States during this tax year? ▶

17   Daily personal exemption amount claimed (see instructions) ▶

18   Total personal exemption amount claimed. Multiply line 16 by line 17 ▶

Part III   Certification

Under penalties of perjury, I declare that I have examined the information on this form and to the best of my knowledge and belief it is true, correct, and complete. I further certify under penalties of perjury that:

- I am the beneficial owner (or am authorized to sign for the beneficial owner) of all the income to which this form relates.
- The beneficial owner is not a U.S. person.
- The beneficial owner is a resident of the treaty country listed on line 12a and/or 13b above within the meaning of the income tax treaty between the United States and that country.

Furthermore, I authorize this form to be provided to any withholding agent that has control, receipt, or custody of the income of which I am the beneficial owner or any withholding agent that can disburse or make payments of the income of which I am the beneficial owner.

Sign Here ▶ _____   _____
      Signature of beneficial owner (or individual authorized to sign for beneficial owner)   Date

Part IV   Withholding Agent Acceptance and Certification

Name | **Employer identification number**

Address (number and street) (Include apt. or suite no. or P.O. box, if applicable.)

City, state, and ZIP code | Telephone number

Under penalties of perjury, I certify that I have examined this form and any accompanying statements, that I am satisfied that an exemption from withholding is warranted, and that I do not know or have reason to know that the nonresident alien individual is not entitled to the exemption or that the nonresident alien's eligibility for the exemption cannot be readily determined.

Signature of withholding agent ▶   Date ▶

Form **8233** (Rev. 3-2009)

Instructions for Form 8233

 Department of the Treasury
Internal Revenue Service

(Rev. June 2011)

(Use with the March 2009 revision of Form 8233.)

Exemption From Withholding on Compensation for Independent (and Certain Dependent) Personal Services of a Nonresident Alien Individual

General Instructions

Section references are to the Internal Revenue Code unless otherwise noted.

 If you are a "resident of a treaty country," you must know the terms of the tax treaty between the United States and the treaty country to properly complete Form 8233.

Purpose of Form

In general, section 1441 requires 30% income tax withholding on compensation for independent personal services (defined later). Sections 1441, 3401, and 3402 require withholding, sometimes at 30% and sometimes at graduated rates, on compensation for dependent personal services (defined later). However, some payments may be exempt from withholding because of a tax treaty or because the payments are not more than your personal exemption amount (defined later). Complete and give Form 8233 to your withholding agent if some or all of your compensation is exempt from withholding.

You can use Form 8233 to claim a tax treaty withholding exemption for noncompensatory scholarship or fellowship income only if you also are claiming a tax treaty withholding exemption for compensation for personal services (including compensatory scholarship or fellowship income) received from the same withholding agent.

 Do not use Form 8233 if you have an office in the United States regularly available to you for performing personal services.

Additional information. You can download the complete text of most U.S. tax treaties at IRS.gov. Enter "tax treaties" in the search box. Technical explanations for many of those treaties are also available on that site. Also, see Pub. 901, U.S. Tax Treaties, for a quick reference guide to the provisions of U.S. tax treaties. You can get any of the forms or publications referred to in these instructions by calling 1-800-TAX-FORM (1-800-829-3676) or by downloading them from *www.irs.gov/formspubs.*

Jun 07, 2011

Giving Form 8233 to the Withholding Agent

You must complete Form 8233:
• For each tax year (be sure to specify the tax year in the space provided above Part I of the form),
• For each withholding agent, and
• For each type of income. However, you can use one Form 8233 to claim a tax treaty withholding exemption for both compensation for personal services (including compensatory scholarship or fellowship income) and noncompensatory scholarship or fellowship income received from the same withholding agent.

Give the form to the withholding agent. The withholding agent's responsibilities are discussed in the Part IV instructions.

Example. A nonresident alien is primarily present in the United States as a professor, but also is occasionally invited to lecture at another educational institution. These lectures are not connected with his teaching obligations but are in the nature of self-employment. For each tax year, the professor must complete two Forms 8233 and give one to each withholding agent to claim tax treaty benefits on the separate items of income.

Definitions

Nonresident Alien

If you are an alien individual (that is, an individual who is not a U.S. citizen), specific rules apply to determine if you are a resident alien or a nonresident alien for tax purposes. Generally, you are a resident alien if you meet either the "green card test" or the "substantial presence test" for the calendar year. Any person not meeting either test is generally a nonresident alien. Additionally, an alien individual who qualifies as a "resident of a treaty country" (defined later) or a bona fide resident of Puerto Rico, Guam, the Commonwealth of the Northern Mariana Islands, the U.S. Virgin

Cat. No. 22663B

Islands, or American Samoa is a nonresident alien individual.

For more information on the tests used to determine resident alien or nonresident alien status, see Pub. 519, U.S. Tax Guide for Aliens.

 Even though a nonresident alien individual married to a U.S. citizen or resident alien may choose to be treated as a resident alien for certain purposes (for example, filing a joint income tax return), such individual is still treated as a nonresident alien for withholding tax purposes on all income except wages.

U.S. Person

For purposes of this form, a U.S. person is a U.S. citizen or resident alien.

Tax Treaty Withholding Exemption

This term refers to an exemption from withholding permitted by IRS regulations under section 1441 that is based on a tax treaty benefit. See *Resident of a Treaty Country* next for requirements for claiming a tax treaty benefit on this form.

See the instructions for line 4 for additional information for determining residence for purposes of claiming a tax treaty withholding exemption on this form.

Resident of a Treaty Country

An alien individual may claim to be a resident of a treaty country if he or she qualifies as a resident of that country under the terms of the residency article of the tax treaty between the United States and that country. See *Nonresident Alien,* earlier.

A nonresident alien may claim a tax treaty benefit on this form only if that individual is the beneficial owner of the income and meets the residency requirement and all other requirements for benefits under the terms of the tax treaty.

Compensation for Independent Personal Services

Independent personal services are services performed as an independent contractor in the United States by a nonresident alien who is self-employed rather than an employee. Compensation for such services includes payments for contract labor; payments for professional services, such as fees to an attorney, physician, or accountant, if the payments are made directly to the person performing the services; consulting fees; honoraria paid to visiting professors, teachers, researchers, scientists, and prominent speakers; and generally, payments for performances by public entertainers.

Business profits. Certain treaties do not have an independent personal services article. Payments for independent personal services may be covered under the business profits article of an applicable income tax treaty. If you are eligible to claim exemption from withholding on this type of income, complete and give Form 8233 to the withholding agent.

Public entertainers. Special restrictions on exemption from or reduction of withholding apply to nonresident alien public entertainers (such as actors, musicians, artists, and athletes). Generally, Form 8233 cannot be accepted because the exemption may be based on factors that cannot be determined until after the end of the year. These individuals are subject to 30% withholding from gross income paid for personal services performed unless a reduced rate of withholding is applied for using Form 13930, Application for Central Withholding Agreement. In addition, many tax treaties contain separate articles that apply to public entertainers. If present, these articles take precedence over the "independent personal services" and "dependent personal services" articles of the treaties.

Required Withholding Form

For compensation you receive for independent personal services, complete Form 8233 to claim a tax treaty withholding exemption for part or all of that income and/or to claim the daily personal exemption amount.

Compensation for Dependent Personal Services

Dependent personal services are services performed as an employee in the United States by a nonresident alien. Dependent personal services include compensatory scholarship or fellowship income (defined later).

Compensation for such services includes wages, salaries, fees, bonuses, commissions, and similar designations for amounts paid to an employee.

Required Withholding Form(s)

Complete Form 8233 for compensation you receive for dependent personal services only if you are claiming a tax treaty withholding exemption for part or all of that income. Do not use Form 8233 to claim the daily personal exemption amount. For compensation for which you are not claiming a tax treaty withholding exemption, use Form W-4, Employee's Withholding Allowance Certificate.

Completing Form W-4. You should complete Form W-4 as follows:

Line 2. You are required to enter a social security number (SSN) on line 2 of Form W-4. If you do not have an SSN but are eligible to get one, you should apply for it. Get Form SS-5, Application for a Social Security Card, online at *www.socialsecurity.gov*, from your local Social Security Administration (SSA) office, or by calling the SSA at 1-800-772-1213.

 You cannot enter an individual taxpayer identification number (ITIN) on line 2 of Form W-4.

Line 3. Check the single box regardless of your actual marital status.

Line 5. In most cases, you should claim one withholding allowance. However, if you are a resident of Canada, Mexico, or South Korea; a student from India; or a U.S. national; you may be able to claim additional withholding allowances for your spouse and children. See Pub. 519 for more information.

If you are completing Form W-4 for more than one withholding agent (for example, you have more than one employer), figure the total number of allowances you are entitled to claim (see the previous paragraph) and claim no more than that amount on all Forms W-4 combined. Your withholding usually will be most accurate when all allowances are claimed on the Form W-4 for the highest-paying job and zero allowances are claimed on the others.

Line 6. Write "nonresident alien" or "NRA" above the dotted line on line 6. If you would like to have an additional amount withheld, enter the amount on line 6.

Line 7. Do not claim that you are exempt from withholding on line 7 of Form W-4 (even if you meet both of the conditions listed on that line).

Compensatory Scholarship or Fellowship Income

In general, scholarship or fellowship income is compensatory to the extent it represents payment for past, present, or future services (for example, teaching or research) performed by a nonresident alien as an employee and the performance of those services is a condition for receiving the scholarship or fellowship (or tuition reduction).

Example. XYZ University awards a scholarship to N, a nonresident alien student. The only condition of the scholarship is that N attends classes and maintains a minimum level of academic performance. The scholarship income is not compensatory because N is not required to perform services as an employee as a condition for receiving the scholarship.

Required Withholding Form(s)

Compensatory scholarship or fellowship income is considered to be dependent personal services income. Therefore, complete Form 8233 for this income only if you are claiming a tax treaty withholding exemption for part or all of that income. Do not complete Form 8233 to claim the daily personal exemption amount.

For any part of this compensatory income for which you are not claiming a tax treaty withholding exemption, use Form W-4. See *Completing Form W-4,* earlier.

Noncompensatory Scholarship or Fellowship Income

Noncompensatory scholarship or fellowship income is scholarship or fellowship income that is not compensatory scholarship or fellowship income (defined earlier).

In most cases, the taxable portion of noncompensatory scholarship or fellowship income (defined later) paid to a nonresident alien is subject to withholding at a rate of 30% (in most cases, the rate is 14% for a nonresident alien temporarily present in the United States under an "F," "J," "M," or "Q" visa).

Taxable portion of noncompensatory scholarship or fellowship income. If you were a degree candidate, the amount of this type of income that you used for expenses other than tuition and course-related expenses (fees, books, supplies, and equipment) is taxable in most cases. For example, in most cases amounts used for room, board, and travel are taxable. If you were not a degree candidate, the full amount of the scholarship or fellowship income is taxable in most cases.

Required Withholding Form

In most cases, you should complete Form W-8BEN, Certificate of Foreign Status of Beneficial Owner for United States Tax Withholding, to claim a tax treaty withholding exemption for this type of income. No Form W-8BEN is required unless a treaty benefit is being claimed.

Exception. If you are receiving both compensation for personal services (including compensatory scholarship or fellowship income) and noncompensatory scholarship or fellowship income from the same withholding agent, you may use one Form 8233 for both types of income. However, this exception applies only if you are claiming a tax treaty withholding exemption for both types of income.

Alternate withholding election. A withholding agent may elect to withhold on the taxable portion of noncompensatory scholarship or fellowship income of a nonresident alien temporarily present in the United States under an "F," "J," "M," or "Q" visa as if it were compensatory scholarship or fellowship income (provided the nonresident alien is not claiming treaty benefits with respect to that income). The withholding agent makes this election by requesting that the nonresident alien complete Form W-4 using the instructions in Rev. Proc. 88-24, 1988-1 C.B. 800. Indian students also should see Rev. Proc. 93-20, 1993-1 C.B. 528.

Withholding Agent

Any person, U.S. or foreign, that has control, receipt, or custody of an amount subject to withholding or that can disburse or make payments of an amount subject to withholding is a withholding agent. The withholding agent may be an individual, corporation, partnership, trust, association, or any other entity, including (but not limited to) any foreign intermediary, foreign partnership, and U.S. branch of certain foreign banks and insurance companies. In most cases, the person who pays (or causes to be paid) the amount subject to withholding to the nonresident alien individual (or to his or her agent) must withhold.

Beneficial Owner

For payments other than those for which a reduced rate of withholding is claimed under an income tax treaty, the beneficial owner of income is in most cases the person who is required under U.S. tax principles to include the income in gross income on a tax return. A person is not a beneficial owner of income, however, to the extent that

person is receiving the income as a nominee, agent, or custodian, or to the extent the person is a conduit whose participation in a transaction is disregarded. In the case of amounts paid that do not constitute income, beneficial ownership is determined as if the payment were income.

Avoid Common Errors

To ensure that your Form 8233 is promptly accepted, be sure that you:
• Answer all applicable questions completely.
• Specify the tax year for which this form will be effective in the space provided above Part I of the form.
• Enter your complete name, addresses, and identifying number(s) in Part I.
• Have attached the required statement described in the line 10 instructions if you are a foreign student, trainee, professor/teacher, or researcher.
• Are not trying to claim tax treaty benefits for a country with which the United States does not have a ratified tax treaty.
• Are not trying to claim tax treaty benefits that do not exist in your treaty.
• Complete lines 11 through 14 in sufficient detail to allow the IRS to determine the tax treaty benefit you are claiming.
• Claim the proper number of personal exemptions on line 15.
• Complete the required certification in Part III.

Specific Instructions

Part I

Line 2

You are required to furnish a U.S. taxpayer identifying number on this form. In most cases, you are required to enter your social security number (SSN) on line 2. See *Line 2* in *Completing Form W-4* for instructions on how to get an SSN.

If you do not have an SSN and are not eligible to get one, you must get an individual taxpayer identification number (ITIN). To apply for an ITIN, file Form W-7, Application for IRS Individual Taxpayer Identification Number, with the IRS. In most cases, you apply for an ITIN when you file your tax return for which the ITIN is needed. However, if the reason for your ITIN request is because you need to provide Form 8233 to the withholding agent, you must file Form W-7 and provide proof that you are not eligible for an SSN (your Form SS-5 was rejected by the SSA) and include a Form 8233. It

usually takes about 6 to 10 weeks to get an ITIN.

For details on how to apply for an ITIN, see Form W-7 and its instructions. Get Form W-7 online at IRS.gov. Click on *Individuals*, then *Individual Taxpayer Identification Numbers*.

If you have applied for an SSN or ITIN but have not yet received it, you may attach a copy of a completed Form W-7 or SS-5 showing that a number has been applied for.

 An ITIN is for tax use only. It does not entitle you to social security benefits or change your employment or immigration status under U.S. law.

Line 3

If your country of residence for tax purposes has issued you a tax identifying number, enter it here. For example, if you are a resident of Canada, enter your Social Insurance Number.

Line 4

Your permanent residence address is the address in the country where you claim to be a resident for purposes of that country's income tax. If you are completing Form 8233 to claim a tax treaty withholding exemption, you must determine your residency in the manner required by the treaty. Do not show the address of a financial institution, a post office box, or an address used solely for mailing purposes. If you are an individual who does not have a tax residence in any country, your permanent residence is where you normally reside.

Most tax treaties that provide for a tax treaty withholding exemption require that the recipient be a resident of the treaty country at the time of, or immediately prior to, entry into the United States. Thus, in most cases, a student or researcher can claim the withholding exemption even if he or she no longer has a permanent address in the treaty country after entry into the United States. If this is the case, you may provide a U.S. address on line 4 and still be eligible for the withholding exemption if all other conditions required by the tax treaty are met. You also must identify on line 12a and/or line 13b the tax treaty country of which you were a resident at the time of, or immediately prior to, your entry into the United States.

Line 6

Enter your U.S. visa type. For example, foreign students are usually granted an "F-1" visa. Foreign professors, teachers, or researchers are usually granted a "J-1" visa. Business/vocational trainees are usually granted an "M-1" visa; however, some persons granted a "J-1" visa also may be considered business/vocational trainees (for example, a person admitted to complete a postgraduate residency in medicine).

If you do not have, or do not require, a visa, write "None."

 Spouses and dependents admitted on secondary visas (for example, "F-2," "J-2," "H-4," and "O-3" visas) usually are not eligible to claim the same treaty benefits as the primary visa holder.

Line 8

In most cases, you are required to enter your date of entry into the United States that pertains to your current nonimmigrant status. For example, enter the date of arrival shown on your current Immigration Form I-94, Arrival-Departure Record.

Exception. If you are claiming a tax treaty benefit that is determined by reference to more than one date of arrival, enter the earlier date of arrival. For example, you are currently claiming treaty benefits (as a teacher or a researcher) under article 15 of the tax treaty between the United States and Norway. You previously claimed treaty benefits (as a student) under article 16(1) of that treaty. Under article 16(4) of that treaty, the combination of exemptions under articles 15 and 16(1) may not extend beyond 5 tax years from the date you entered the United States. If article 16(4) of that treaty applies, enter on line 8 the date you entered the United States as a student.

Line 9a

Enter your current nonimmigrant status. For example, enter your current nonimmigrant status shown on your current Immigration Form I-94.

Line 9b

Enter the date your current nonimmigrant status expires. For example, you may enter the date of expiration shown on your current Immigration Form I-94. Enter "DS" on line 9b if the date of expiration is based on "duration of status."

Line 10

Nonresident alien students, trainees, professors/teachers, and researchers using Form 8233 to claim a tax treaty withholding exemption for compensation for personal services must attach to Form 8233 a statement. The format and contents of the required statements are shown in Appendix A and Appendix B in Pub. 519.

Part II

Line 11a

For compensation for independent personal services, examples of acceptable descriptions to enter on this line include: "Consulting contract to design software" or "give three lectures at XYZ University."

For compensation for dependent personal services, examples of acceptable descriptions to enter on this line include:
- A nonresident alien student may enter "part-time library assistant," "part-time restaurant worker," or "teaching one chemistry course per semester to undergraduate students."
- A nonresident alien professor or teacher may enter "teaching at ABC University."
- A nonresident alien researcher may enter "research at ABC University's school for liquid crystal research."
- A nonresident alien business/ vocational trainee may enter "neurosurgical residency at ABC Hospital" or "one-year internship in hydraulic engineering at XYZ Corporation."

Line 11b

Enter the total amount of compensation for personal services you will receive from this withholding agent during the tax year. Enter an estimated amount if you do not know the exact amount.

Line 12a

Enter the specific treaty and article on which you are basing your claim for exemption from withholding (for example, "U.S./Germany tax treaty, Article 20(4)" or "U.S./Belgium tax treaty, Article 7 (business profits)").

Line 12b

If all income received for the services performed to which this Form 8233 applies is exempt, write "All." If only part is exempt, enter the exact dollar amount that is exempt from withholding.

Line 12c

Generally, you may claim a withholding exemption based on a U.S. tax treaty with the country in which you claim permanent (or indefinite) residence. This is the foreign country in which you live most of the time. It is not necessarily the country of your citizenship. For example, you are a citizen of Pakistan but maintain your home in England. You cannot claim a withholding exemption based on the U.S./Pakistan tax treaty. Any withholding exemption you claim must be based on the U.S./United Kingdom tax treaty.

Line 13b

Enter the specific treaty and article on which you are basing your claim for exemption from withholding (for example, "U.S./Germany tax treaty, Article 20(3)").

Line 14

Provide sufficient facts to justify the exemption from withholding claimed on line 12 and/or line 13. Be sure you provide enough details to allow the IRS to determine the tax treaty benefit you are claiming.

Lines 15 through 18 (for certain independent personal services)

Do not complete lines 15 through 18 if you are claiming an exemption from withholding based on the "business profit" article of a treaty or claiming on line 12b that all of the compensation you are receiving for independent personal services is exempt from withholding.

Line 15

For compensation for independent personal services for which an exemption from withholding is not available, 30% must be withheld from that compensation after subtracting the value of one personal exemption. In most cases, you will enter "1" on line 15; however, if the exception described next applies to you, enter the total number of personal exemptions you are entitled to on line 15.

Exception. If you are a resident of Canada, Mexico, or South Korea; a student from India; or a U.S. national; you may be able to claim additional personal exemptions for your spouse and children. See Pub. 519 for more information.

Lines 16 and 17

Each allowable personal exemption must be prorated for the number of days during the tax year you will perform the personal services in the United States. Enter the number of days on line 16 that pertain to the independent personal services described in line 11a. To figure the daily personal exemption amount to enter on line 17, divide the personal exemption amount for the tax year ($3,700 for 2011) by 365 (366 for leap year) and multiply the result by the amount you entered on line 15. For example, if you are entitled to one personal exemption for 2011, enter $10.14 (that is, $3,700 / 365 days = $10.14 x 1 personal exemption = $10.14) on line 17.

-4-

Part IV

Withholding Agent's Responsibilities

When the nonresident alien individual gives you Form 8233, review it to see if you are satisfied that the exemption from withholding is warranted. If you are satisfied, based on the facts presented, complete and sign the certification in Part IV.

You will need three copies of the completed Form 8233. Each copy of Form 8233 must include any attachments submitted by the nonresident alien individual. Give one copy of the completed Form 8233 to the nonresident alien individual. Keep a copy for your records. Within 5 days of your acceptance, forward one copy to:

 Department of the Treasury
Internal Revenue Service
Philadelphia, PA 19255-0725

 You also can fax Form 8233 to: (267) 941-1365. You are limited to 25 pages at one time.

The exemption from withholding is effective for payments made retroactive to the date of the first payment covered by Form 8233, even though you must wait at least 10 days after you have properly mailed Form 8233 to the IRS to see whether the IRS has any objections to the Form 8233.

You must not accept Form 8233, and you must withhold, if either of the following applies:
• You know, or have reason to know, that any of the facts or statements on Form 8233 may be false, or
• You know, or have reason to know, that the nonresident alien's eligibility for the exemption from withholding cannot be readily determined (for example, you know the nonresident alien has a fixed base or permanent establishment in the United States).

If you accept Form 8233 and later find that either of the situations described above applies, you must promptly notify the IRS (by writing to the address provided earlier) and you must begin withholding on any amounts

not yet paid. Also, if you are notified by the IRS that the nonresident alien's eligibility for the exemption from withholding is in doubt or that the nonresident alien is not eligible for exemption from withholding, you must begin withholding immediately. See Regulations section 1.1441-4(b)(2)(iii) for examples illustrating these rules.

If you submit an incorrect Form 8233, you will be notified by the IRS that the form submitted is not acceptable and that you must begin withholding immediately. Examples of incorrect Forms 8233 include:
• Any Form 8233 that claims a tax treaty benefit that does not exist or is obviously false.
• Any Form 8233 that has not been completed in sufficient detail to allow determination of the correctness of the tax treaty benefit or exemption claimed.

Signature

You or your authorized agent must sign and date Form 8233. See Regulations section 1.1441-7(c) for information about authorized agents.

Privacy Act and Paperwork Reduction Act Notice. We ask for the information on this form to carry out the Internal Revenue laws of the United States. You are not required to request a tax treaty withholding exemption. However, if you want to receive exemption from withholding on compensation for independent (and certain dependent) personal services, you are required to give us this information so that we can verify eligibility under the relevant tax treaty and confirm proper tax treatment. Our legal right to ask for this information is Internal Revenue Code sections 1441, 3401, and 3402. We need this information to ensure that you are complying with these laws and to allow us to figure and collect the right amount of tax. Code section 6109 requires taxpayers and withholding agents to provide their identification number. Routine uses of this information include giving it to the Department of Justice for civil and criminal litigation, and cities, states, the District of Columbia, and

U.S. commonwealths and possessions for use in administering their tax laws. We may also disclose this information to other countries under a tax treaty, to federal and state agencies to enforce federal nontax criminal laws, or to federal law enforcement and intelligence agencies to combat terrorism. If a nonresident alien fails to provide a properly completed form, the withholding agent cannot accept it and is required to withhold. If a withholding agent accepts a Form 8233 as completed and later finds that any of the facts or statements made on the form are false, or that a nonresident alien's eligibility for the exemption is in doubt, the withholding agent is required to notify the IRS and begin withholding; failure to do so may result in penalties.

You are not required to provide the information requested on a form that is subject to the Paperwork Reduction Act unless the form displays a valid OMB control number. Books or records relating to a form or its instructions must be retained as long as their contents may become material in the administration of any Internal Revenue law. Generally, tax returns and return information are confidential, as required by section 6103.

The time needed to complete and file this form will vary depending on individual circumstances. The estimated average time is: **Recordkeeping,** 1 hr. 5 min.; **Learning about the law or the form,** 31 min.; **Preparing and sending the form to IRS,** 57 min.

If you have comments concerning the accuracy of these time estimates or suggestions for making this form simpler, we would be happy to hear from you. You can write to the Internal Revenue Service, Tax Products Coordinating Committee, SE:W:CAR:MP:T:T:SP, 1111 Constitution Ave. NW, IR-6526, Washington, DC 20224. Do not send the tax form to this address. Instead, give it to your withholding agent.

-5-

Form 8508
(Rev. 1-2012)
Internal Revenue Service
Department of the Treasury

Request for Waiver From Filing
Information Returns Electronically

(Forms W-2, W-2G, 1042-S, 1097-BTC, 1098 Series, 1099 Series, 3921, 3922, 5498 Series, and 8027)
*(Please type or print in **black ink** when completing this form - see instructions on back.)*

OMB Number
1545-0957

Note: Only the person required to file electronically can file Form 8508. A transmitter cannot file Form 8508 for the payer, unless he or she has a power of attorney. If you have a power of attorney, attach a letter to the Form 8508 stating this fact.

1. Type of submission   ☐ Original   ☐ Reconsideration

2. Payer name, **complete** address, and contact person. (A **separate** Form 8508 must be filed for **each payer** requesting a waiver.)

Name _____

Address _____

City _____ State _____ ZIP _____

Contact Name _____

3. Taxpayer Identification Number
(9-digit EIN/SSN)

4. Telephone number

(_____) _____

Email Address _____

5. Waiver Requested for	Enter the Number of Returns That:		Waiver Requested for	Enter the Number of Returns That:	
	(a) You wish to file on paper	(b) You expect to file next tax year		(a) You wish to file on paper	(b) You expect to file next tax year
☐ 1042-S			☐ 1099-PATR		
☐ 1097-BTC			☐ 1099-Q		
☐ 1098			☐ 1099-R		
☐ 1098-C			☐ 1099-S		
☐ 1098-E			☐ 1099-SA		
☐ 1098-T			☐ 3921		
☐ 1099-A			☐ 3922		
☐ 1099-B			☐ 5498		
☐ 1099-C			☐ 5498-ESA		
☐ 1099-CAP			☐ 5498-SA		
☐ 1099-DIV			☐ 8027		
☐ 1099-G			☐ W-2		
☐ 1099-H			☐ W-2AS		
☐ 1099-INT			☐ W-2G		
☐ 1099-K			☐ W-2GU		
☐ 1099-LTC			☐ W-2PR		
☐ 1099-MISC			☐ W-2VI		
☐ 1099-OID					

6. Is this waiver requested for corrections ONLY?   ☐ Yes   ☐ No

7. Is this the first time you requested a waiver from the electronic filing requirements for any of the forms listed in Block 5?
☐ Yes *(Skip to signature line)*   ☐ No *(Complete Block 9 if your request is due to undue hardship)*

8. Enter **two current cost estimates** given to you by third parties for software, software upgrades or programming for your current system, or costs for preparing your files for you.

$ _____

Cost estimates for any reason other than the preparation of electronic files will not be acceptable.

*Attach these **two written cost estimates** to the Form 8508. Failure to provide **current** cost estimates and/or signature will result in denial of your waiver request.*

$ _____

Under penalties of perjury, I declare that I have examined this document, including any accompanying statements, and, to the best of my knowledge and belief, it is true, correct, and complete.

9. Signature	Title	Date

For Paperwork Reduction Act Notice, see back of this form.   Catalog Number 63499V   Form **8508** (Rev. 1-2012)

General Instructions

Paperwork Reduction Act Notice. We ask for the information on these forms to carry out the Internal Revenue Laws of the United States. You are not required to provide the information requested on a form that is subject to the Paperwork Reduction Act unless the form displays a valid OMB control number. Books or records relating to a form must be retained as long as their contents may become material in the administration of any Internal Revenue law. Generally, tax returns and return information are confidential, as required by Code section 6103.

The time needed to provide this information would vary depending on individual circumstances. The estimated average time is:

Preparing Form 8508 . . . . **15 min.**

If you have comments concerning the accuracy of these time estimates or suggestions for making this form simpler, we would be happy to hear from you. You can write to the Internal Revenue Service, Tax Products Coordinating Committee, SE:W:CAR:MP:T:T:SP, 1111 Constitution Ave. NW, IR-6406, Washington, DC 20224.
DO NOT SEND THE FORMS TO THIS OFFICE. Instead, see the instructions below on where to file. **When completing this form, please type or print clearly in** <u>**BLACK**</u> **ink.**

Purpose of Form. Use this form to request a waiver from filing Forms W-2, W-2AS, W-2G, W-2GU, W-2PR, W-2VI, 1042-S, 1097-BTC, 1098 Series, 1099 Series, 3921, 3922, 5498 Series, or 8027 electronically for the current tax year. Complete a Form 8508 for each Taxpayer Identification Number *(TIN)*. You may use one Form 8508 for multiple types of forms. After evaluating your request, IRS will notify you as to whether your request is approved or denied.

Specific Instructions

Block 1. –Indicate the type of submission by checking the appropriate box. An original submission is your first request for a waiver for the current year. A reconsideration indicates that you are submitting additional information to IRS that you feel may reverse a denial of an originally submitted request.

Block 2. –Enter the name and complete address of the payer and person to contact if additional information is needed by IRS.

Block 3. –Enter the Taxpayer Identification Number *(TIN)* [Employer Identification Number *(EIN)* or the Social Security Number *(SSN)*] of the payer. The number must contain 9-digits.

Block 4. –Enter the telephone number and Email address of the contact person.

Block 5. –Check the box*(es)* beside the form*(s)* for which the waiver is being requested.

Block 5a. –For each type of information return checked, enter the total number of forms you plan to file.

Block 5b. –Provide an estimate of the total number of information returns you plan to file for the following tax year.

Block 6. –Indicate whether or not this waiver is requested for corrections only. If you request a waiver for original documents and it is approved, you will automatically receive a waiver for corrections. However, if you can submit your original returns electronically, but not your corrections, a waiver must be requested for corrections only.

Block 7. –If this is the first time you have requested a waiver for any of the forms listed in Block 5, for any tax year, check "YES" and skip to Block 9. However, if you have requested a waiver in the past and check "NO," complete Block 8 to establish undue hardship. Waivers, after the first year, are granted only in case of undue hardship or catastrophic event.
Note: Under Regulations Section 301.6011-2(c)(2), "The principal factor in determining hardship will be the amount, if any, by which the cost of filing the information returns in accordance with this section exceeds the cost of filing the returns on other media."

Block 8. –Enter the cost estimates from two service bureaus or other third parties. These cost estimates must reflect the total amount that each service bureau will charge for software, software upgrades or programming for your current system, or costs to produce your electronic file only. If you do not provide two written cost estimates from service bureaus or other third parties, we will automatically deny your request. Cost estimates from prior years will not be accepted.
Note: If your request is not due to undue hardship, as defined above, attach a detailed explanation of why you need a waiver.

Block 9. –The waiver request must be signed by the payer or a person duly authorized to sign a return or other document on his behalf.

Filing Instructions

When to File. – You should file Form 8508 at least 45 days before the due date of the returns for which you are requesting a waiver. See Publication 1220, Part A for the due dates. Waiver requests will be processed beginning January 1st of the calendar year the returns are due.

Where to File –
By Mail: Internal Revenue Service
Information Returns Branch
Attn: Extension of Time Coordinator
240 Murall Drive Mail Stop 4360
Kearneysville, WV 25430

By Fax: **1-877-477-0572**

Please either fax or mail, do not do both.

For further information concerning the filing of information returns to IRS electronically, contact the IRS Enterprise Computing Center at the address above or by telephone at **866-455-7438** between 8:30 a.m. and 4:30 p.m. Eastern Standard Time.

Penalty. – If you are required to file electronically but fail to do so and you do not have an approved waiver on record, you may be subject to a penalty of $100 per return unless you establish reasonable cause.

Catalog Number 63499V   Form **8508** (Rev. 1-2012)

Form **8655**
(Rev. December 2012)
Department of the Treasury
Internal Revenue Service

Reporting Agent Authorization

▶ **Information about Form 8655 is at** *www.irs.gov/form8655.*

OMB No. 1545-1058

Taxpayer

1a Name of taxpayer (as distinguished from trade name)

2 Employer identification number (EIN)

1b Trade name, if any

4 If you are a seasonal employer, check here . . . . ☐

3 Address (number, street, and room or suite no.)

5 Other identification number

City or town, state, and ZIP code

6 Contact person

7 Daytime telephone number

8 Fax number

Reporting Agent

9 Name (enter company name or name of business)

10 Employer identification number (EIN)

11 Address (number, street, and room or suite no.)

City or town, state, and ZIP code

12 Contact person

13 Daytime telephone number

14 Fax number

Authorization of Reporting Agent To Sign and File Returns

15 Use the entry lines below to indicate the tax return(s) to be filed by the reporting agent. Enter the beginning year of annual tax returns or beginning quarter of quarterly tax returns. See the instructions for how to enter the quarter and year. Once this authority is granted, it is effective until revoked by the taxpayer or reporting agent.

| 940 _____ | 941 _____ | 940-PR _____ | 941-PR _____ | 941-SS _____ | 943 _____ |
| 943-PR _____ | 944 _____ | 945 _____ | 1042 _____ | CT-1 _____ | |

Authorization of Reporting Agent To Make Deposits and Payments

16 Use the entry lines below to enter the starting date (the first month and year) of any tax return(s) for which the reporting agent is authorized to make deposits or payments. See the instructions for how to enter the month and year. Once this authority is granted, it is effective until revoked by the taxpayer or reporting agent.

| 940 _____ | 941 _____ | 943 _____ | 944 _____ | 945 _____ | 720 _____ |
| 1041 _____ | 1042 _____ | 1120 _____ | CT-1 _____ | 990-PF _____ | 990-T _____ |

Disclosure of Information to Reporting Agents

17a Check here to authorize the reporting agent to receive or request copies of tax information and other communications from the IRS related to the authorization granted on lines 15, 16, and/or line 18 . . . . ☐

b Check here if the reporting agent also wants to receive copies of notices from the IRS . . . . ☐

Disclosure Authorization

18a The reporting agent is authorized to receive otherwise confidential taxpayer information from the IRS to assist in responding to certain IRS notices relating to the Form W-2 series information returns. This authority is effective for calendar year forms beginning _____ .

b The reporting agent is authorized to receive otherwise confidential taxpayer information from the IRS to assist in responding to certain IRS notices relating to the Form 1099 series information returns. This authority is effective for calendar year forms beginning _____ .

c The reporting agent is authorized to receive otherwise confidential taxpayer information from the IRS to assist in responding to certain IRS notices relating to the Forms 3921 and 3922. This authority is effective for calendar year forms beginning _____ .

State or Local Authorization

19 Check here to authorize the reporting agent to sign and file state or local returns related to the authorization granted on line 15 and/or line 16 ☐

Authorization Agreement

I understand that this agreement does not relieve me, as the taxpayer, of the responsibility to ensure that all tax returns are filed and that all deposits and payments are made. If line 15 is completed, the reporting agent named above is authorized to sign and file the return indicated, beginning with the quarter or year indicated. If any starting dates on line 16 are completed, the reporting agent named above is authorized to make deposits and payments beginning with the period indicated. Any authorization granted remains in effect until it is revoked by the taxpayer or reporting agent. I am authorizing the IRS to disclose confidential tax information to the reporting agent relating to the authority granted on line 15 and/or line 16, including disclosures required to process Form 8655. Disclosure authority is effective upon signature of taxpayer and IRS receipt of Form 8655. The authority granted on Form 8655 will not revoke any Power of Attorney (Form 2848) or Tax Information Authorization (Form 8821) in effect.

Sign Here

I certify I have the authority to execute this form and authorize disclosure of otherwise confidential information on behalf of the taxpayer.

▶ _____ ▶ _____ ▶ _____
Signature of taxpayer   Title   Date

For Privacy Act and Paperwork Reduction Act Notice, see page 2.   Cat. No. 10241T   Form **8655** (Rev. 12-2012)

General Instructions

What's New

Beginning in 2012, Form 944-PR and Form 944-SS have been deleted from line 15. Taxpayers who would otherwise file Form 944-PR or Form 944-SS will file Form 944 or Form 944(SP) unless they request to file quarterly Forms 941-PR or 941-SS.

Purpose of Form

Use Form 8655 to authorize a reporting agent to:

• Sign and file certain returns. Reporting agents must file returns electronically except as provided under Rev. Proc. 2012-32. You can find Rev. Proc. 2012-32 on page 267 of Internal Revenue Bulletin 2012-34 at *www.irs.gov/pub/irs-irbs/irb12-34.pdf*;

• Make deposits and payments for certain returns;

• Receive duplicate copies of tax information, notices, and other written and/ or electronic communication regarding any authority granted; and

• Provide IRS with information to aid in penalty relief determinations related to the authority granted on Form 8655.

Authority Granted

Once Form 8655 is signed, any authority granted is effective beginning with the period indicated on lines 15 or 16 and continues indefinitely unless revoked by the taxpayer or reporting agent. A new authorization must be submitted to the Service for any increase or decrease in the authority of a reporting agent to act for its client. The preceding authorization remains in effect except as modified by the new one. No authorization or authority is granted for periods prior to the period(s) indicated on Form 8655.

Where authority is granted for any form, it is also effective for related forms such as the corresponding non-English language form, amended return, (Form 941-X, 941-X(PR), 943-X, 944-X(PR), 945-X, or CT-1X), or payment voucher. In addition to the returns shown on lines 15 and 16, Form 8655 can be used to provide authorization for Form 944-SP using the entry spaces for Form 944. The form also can be used to authorize a reporting agent to make deposits and payments for other returns in the Form 1120 series, such as Form 1120-C, using the entry space for Form 1120 on line 16.

Disclosure authority granted on line 17a is effective on the date Form 8655 is signed by the taxpayer. Any authority granted on Form 8655 does not revoke and has no effect on any authority granted on Forms 2848 or 8821, or any third-party designee checkbox authority.

Where To File

Send Form 8655 to:

> Internal Revenue Service
> Accounts Management Service Center
> MS 6748 RAF Team
> 1973 North Rulon White Blvd.
> Ogden, UT 84404

You can fax Form 8655 to the IRS. The number is 801-620-4142.

Additional Information

Additional information concerning reporting agent authorizations may be found in:

• **Pub. 1474,** Technical Specifications Guide for Reporting Agent Authorizations and Federal Tax Depositors.

• Rev. Proc. 2012-32.

Substitute Form 8655

If you want to prepare and use a substitute Form 8655, see Pub. 1167, General Rules and Specifications for Substitute Forms and Schedules. If your substitute Form 8655 is approved, the form approval number must be printed in the lower left margin of each substitute Form 8655 you file with the IRS.

Revoking an Authorization

If you have a valid Form 8655 on file with the IRS, the filing of a new Form 8655 revokes the authority of the prior reporting agent beginning with the period indicated on the new Form 8655. However, the prior reporting agent is still an authorized reporting agent and retains any previously granted disclosure authority for the periods prior to the beginning period of the new reporting agent's authorization unless specifically revoked.

If the taxpayer wants to revoke an existing authorization, send a copy of the previously executed Form 8655 to the IRS at the address under *Where To File*, above. Re-sign the copy of the Form 8655 under the original signature. Write "REVOKE" across the top of the form. If you do not have a copy of the authorization you want to revoke, send a statement to the IRS. The statement of revocation must indicate that the authority of the reporting agent is revoked and must be signed by the taxpayer. Also, list the name and address of each reporting agent whose authority is revoked.

Withdrawing from reporting authority. A reporting agent can withdraw from authority by filing a statement with the IRS, either on paper or using a delete process. The statement must be signed by the reporting agent (if filed on paper) and identify the name and address of the taxpayer and authorization(s) from which the reporting agent is withdrawing. For information on the delete process, see Pub. 1474.

Specific Instructions

Line 15

Use the "YYYY" format for annual tax returns. Use the "MM/YYYY" format for quarterly tax returns, where "MM" is the ending month of the quarter the named reporting agent is authorized to sign and file tax returns for the taxpayer. For example, enter "09/2012" on the line for "941" to indicate you are authorizing the named reporting agent to sign and file Form 941 for the July–September quarter of 2012 and subsequent quarters.

Line 16

Use the "MM/YYYY" format to enter the starting date, where "MM" is the first month the named reporting agent is authorized to make deposits or payments for the taxpayer. For example, enter "08/2012" on the line for "720" to indicate you are authorizing the named reporting agent to make deposits or payments for Form 720 starting in August 2012 and all subsequent months.

Who Must Sign

Sole proprietorship. The individual owning the business.

Corporation (including a limited liability company (LLC) treated as a corporation). Generally, Form 8655 can be signed by: (a) an officer having legal authority to bind the corporation, (b) any person designated by the board of directors or other governing body, (c) any officer or employee on written request by any principal officer, and (d) any other person authorized to access information under section 6103(e).

Partnership (including an LLC treated as a partnership) or an unincorporated organization. Generally, Form 8655 can be signed by any person who was a member of the partnership during any part of the tax period covered by Form 8655.

Single member LLC treated as a disregarded entity. The owner of the LLC.

Trust or estate. The fiduciary.

Privacy Act and Paperwork Reduction Act Notice. We ask for the information on this form to carry out the Internal Revenue laws of the United States. Our authority to request this information is Internal Revenue Code sections 6011, 6061, 6109, and 6302 and the regulations thereunder. We use this information to identify you and record your reporting agent authorization. You are not required to authorize a reporting agent to act on your behalf. However, if you choose to authorize a reporting agent, you are required to provide the information requested, including your identification number. Failure to provide all the information requested may prevent or delay processing of your authorization; providing false or fraudulent information may subject you to penalties.

Routine uses of this information include giving it to the Department of Justice for civil and criminal litigation, and to cities, states, the District of Columbia, and U.S. commonwealths and possessions for use in administering their tax laws. We may also disclose this information to other countries under a tax treaty, to federal and state agencies to enforce federal nontax criminal laws, or to federal law enforcement agencies and intelligence agencies to combat terrorism.

You are not required to provide the information requested on a form that is subject to the Paperwork Reduction Act unless the form displays a valid OMB control number. Books or records relating to a form or instructions must be retained as long as their contents may become material in the administration of any Internal Revenue law.

The time needed to complete and file Form 8655 will vary depending on individual circumstances. The estimated average time is 1 hour, 7 minutes.

If you have comments concerning the accuracy of this time estimate or suggestions for making Form 8655 simpler, we would be happy to hear from you. Email us at *taxforms@irs.gov* and enter "Form 8655" on the subject line or write to: Internal Revenue Service, Tax Products Coordinating Committee, SE:W:CAR:MP:T:T:SP, 1111 Constitution Ave. NW, IR-6526, Washington, DC 20224. **Do not** send Form 8655 to this address. Instead, see *Where To File* above.

Form 8802

(Rev. April 2012)

Department of the Treasury
Internal Revenue Service

Application for United States Residency Certification

▶ **See separate instructions.**

OMB No. 1545-1817

Important. For applications filed after March 31, 2012, the user fee is $85 per application.

☐ **Additional request** (see instructions)

☐ **Foreign claim form attached**

Electronic payment confirmation no. ▶

For IRS use only:

Pmt Amt $ _____

Deposit Date: ___ /___ /___

Date Pmt Vrfd: ___ /___ /___

Applicant's name	Applicant's U.S. taxpayer identification number
If a joint return was filed, spouse's name (see instructions)	If a joint return was filed, spouse's U.S. taxpayer identification number

If a separate certification is needed for spouse, check here ▶ ☐

1 Applicant's name and taxpayer identification number as it should appear on the certification if different from above

2 Applicant's address during the calendar year for which certification is requested, including country and ZIP or postal code. If a P.O. box, see instructions.

3a Mail Form 6166 to the following address:

b Appointee Information (see instructions):

Appointee Name ▶ _____   CAF No. ▶ _____

Phone No. ▶ (_____)   Fax No. ▶ (_____)

4 Applicant is (check appropriate box(es)):

a ☐ Individual. Check all applicable boxes.

  ☐ U.S. citizen ☐ U.S. lawful permanent resident (green card holder) ☐ Sole proprietor

  ☐ Other U.S. resident alien. Type of entry visa ▶ _____

  Current nonimmigrant status ▶ _____ and date of change (see instructions) ▶ _____

  ☐ Dual-status U.S. resident (see instructions). From ▶ _____ to ▶ _____

  ☐ Partial-year Form 2555 filer (see instructions). U.S. resident from ▶ _____ to ▶ _____

b ☐ Partnership. Check all applicable boxes. ☐ U.S. ☐ Foreign ☐ LLC

c ☐ Trust. Check if: ☐ Grantor (U.S.) ☐ Simple ☐ Rev. Rul. 81-100 Trust ☐ IRA (for Individual)

  ☐ Grantor (foreign) ☐ Complex ☐ Section 584 ☐ IRA (for Financial Institution)

d ☐ Estate

e ☐ Corporation. If incorporated in the United States only, go to line 5. Otherwise, continue.

  Check if: ☐ Section 269B ☐ Section 943(e)(1) ☐ Section 953(d) ☐ Section 1504(d)

  Country or countries of incorporation ▶ _____

  If a dual-resident corporation, specify other country of residence ▶ _____

  If included on a consolidated return, attach page 1 of Form 1120 and Form 851.

f ☐ S corporation

g ☐ Employee benefit plan/trust. Plan number, if applicable ▶ _____

  Check if: ☐ Section 401(a) ☐ Section 403(b) ☐ Section 457(b)

h ☐ Exempt organization. If organized in the United States, check all applicable boxes.

  ☐ Section 501(c) ☐ Section 501(c)(3) ☐ Governmental entity

  ☐ Indian tribe ☐ Other (specify) ▶ _____

i ☐ Disregarded entity. Check if: ☐ LLC ☐ LP ☐ LLP ☐ Other (specify) ▶ _____

j ☐ Nominee applicant (must specify the type of entity/individual for whom the nominee is acting) ▶

For Privacy Act and Paperwork Reduction Act Notice, see separate instructions.   Cat. No. 10003D   Form **8802** (Rev. 4-2012)

Applicant name:

5   Was the applicant required to file a U.S. tax form for the tax period(s) on which certification will be based?

    Yes.   Check the appropriate box for the form filed and **go to line 7.**

☐ 990   ☐ 990-T   ☐ 1040   ☐ 1041   ☐ 1065   ☐ 1120   ☐ 1120S   ☐ 3520-A   ☐ 5227   ☐ 5500

☐ Other (specify) ▶ --

    No.   Attach explanation (see instructions). Check applicable box and go to line 6.

☐ Minor child   ☐ QSub   ☐ U.S. DRE   ☐ Foreign DRE   ☐ Section 761(a) election

☐ FASIT   ☐ Foreign partnership   ☐ Other ▶ ---

6   Was the applicant's parent, parent organization or owner required to file a U.S. tax form? **(Complete this line only if you checked "No" on line 5.)**

    Yes.   Check the appropriate box for the form filed by the parent.

☐ 990   ☐ 990-T   ☐ 1040   ☐ 1041   ☐ 1065   ☐ 1120   ☐ 1120S   ☐ 5500

☐ Other (specify) ▶ --

Parent's/owner's name and address ▶ --

----

and U.S. taxpayer identification number ▶ --

    No.   Attach explanation (see instructions).

7   Calendar year(s) for which certification is requested.

Note. If certification is for the current calendar year or a year for which a tax return is not yet required to be filed, a penalties of perjury statement from Table 2 of the instructions must be entered on line 10 or attached to Form 8802 (see instructions).

8   Tax period(s) on which certification will be based (see instructions).

9   Purpose of certification. Must check applicable box (see instructions).

☐ Income tax   ☐ VAT (specify NAICS codes) ▶ --

☐ Other (must specify) ▶ --

10   Enter penalties of perjury statements and any additional required information here (see instructions).

Sign here

Keep a copy for your records. ▶

Under penalties of perjury, I declare that I have examined this application and accompanying attachments, and to the best of my knowledge and belief, they are true, correct, and complete. If I have designated a third party to receive the residency certification(s), I declare that the certification(s) will be used only for obtaining information or assistance from that person relating to matters designated on line 9.

Applicant's signature (or individual authorized to sign for the applicant)   Applicant's daytime phone no.:

--   -------------------------------   ---

          Signature   Date

     Name and title (print or type)

    Spouse's signature. If a joint application, **both** must sign.

         Name (print or type)

Form 8802 (Rev. 4-2012)   **Worksheet for U.S. Residency Certification Application**   Page **3**

Applicant Name	Applicant TIN

Appointee Name (If Applicable)

Calendar year(s) for which certification is requested (must be the same year(s) indicated on line 7)

11   Enter the number of certifications needed in the column to the right of each country for which certification is requested.

Note. If you are requesting certifications for more than one calendar year per country, enter the total number of certifications for all years for each country (see instructions).

Country	CC	#	Country	CC	#	Country	CC	#	Country	CC	#
Column A			**Column B**			**Column C**			**Column D**		
Armenia	AM		Finland	FI		Latvia	LG		South Africa	SF	
Australia	AS		France	FR		Lithuania	LH		Spain	SP	
Austria	AU		Georgia	GG		Luxembourg	LU		Sri Lanka	CE	
Azerbaijan	AJ		Germany	GM		Mexico	MX		Sweden	SW	
Bangladesh	BG		Greece	GR		Moldova	MD		Switzerland	SZ	
Barbados	BB		Hungary	HU		Morocco	MO		Tajikistan	TI	
Belarus	BO		Iceland	IC		Netherlands	NL		Thailand	TH	
Belgium	BE		India	IN		New Zealand	NZ		Trinidad and Tobago	TD	
Bermuda	BD		Indonesia	ID		Norway	NO		Tunisia	TS	
Bulgaria	BU		Ireland	EI		Pakistan	PK		Turkey	TU	
Canada	CA		Israel	IS		Philippines	RP		Turkmenistan	TX	
China	CH		Italy	IT		Poland	PL		Ukraine	UP	
Cyprus	CY		Jamaica	JM		Portugal	PO		United Kingdom	UK	
Czech Republic	EZ		Japan	JA		Romania	RO		Uzbekistan	UZ	
Denmark	DA		Kazakhstan	KZ		Russia	RS		Venezuela	VE	
Egypt	EG		Korea, South	KS		Slovak Republic	LO				
Estonia	EN		Kyrgyzstan	KG		Slovenia	SI				
Column A - Total			**Column B - Total**			**Column C - Total**			**Column D - Total**		

12   Enter the total number of certifications requested (add columns A, B, C, and D of line 11) . . . . ▶

Instructions for Form 8802
(Rev. October 2012)

(Use with the April 2012 revision of Form 8802)
Application for United States Residency Certification

Department of the Treasury
Internal Revenue Service

Section references are to the Internal Revenue Code unless otherwise noted.

Future Developments

For the latest information about developments related to Form 8802 and its instructions, such as legislation enacted after they were published, go to *www.irs.gov/form8802*.

What's New

User fee. For applications filed after March 31, 2012, the user fee is $85 per application. See *User Fee*, later.

Teaching or research activities. If you receive payments for teaching or research activities, see *Individuals With Residency Outside the United States*, later.

U.S. Residency Certification

Income Tax Treaty

Many foreign countries withhold tax on certain types of income paid from sources within those countries to residents of other countries. The rate of withholding is set by that country's internal law. An income tax treaty between the United States and a foreign country often reduces the withholding rates (sometimes to zero) for certain types of income paid to residents of the United States. This reduced rate is referred to as the treaty-reduced rate. For more information on reduced rates, see *Tax Treaty Tables* in Pub. 515, Withholding of Tax on Nonresident Aliens and Foreign Entities.

Many U.S. treaty partners require the IRS to certify that the person claiming treaty benefits is a resident of the United States for federal tax purposes. The IRS provides this residency certification on Form 6166, a letter of U.S. residency certification. Form 6166 is a computer-generated letter printed on stationary bearing the U.S. Department of Treasury letterhead, and the facsimile signature of the Field Director, Philadelphia Accounts Management Center.

Form 6166 will only certify that, for the certification year (the period for which certification is requested), you were a resident of the United States for purposes of U.S. taxation, or in the case of a fiscally transparent entity, that the entity, when required, filed an information return and its partners/members/owners/beneficiaries filed income tax returns as residents of the United States.

Upon receiving Form 6166 from the IRS, unless otherwise directed, you should send Form 6166 to the foreign withholding agent or other appropriate person in the foreign country to claim treaty benefits. Some foreign countries will withhold at the treaty-reduced rate at the time of payment, and other foreign countries will initially withhold tax at their statutory rate and will refund the amount that is more than the treaty-reduced rate on receiving proof of U.S. residency.

Other conditions for claiming treaty benefits. In order to claim a benefit under a tax treaty, there are other requirements in addition to residence. These include the requirement that the person claiming a treaty-reduced rate of

Oct 11, 2012   Cat. No. 10827V

withholding be the beneficial owner of the item of income and meet the limitation on benefits article of the treaty, if applicable.

The IRS cannot certify whether you are the beneficial owner of an item of income or that you meet the limitation on benefits article, if any, in the treaty. You may, however, be required by a foreign withholding agent to establish directly with the agent that these requirements have been met.

 You should examine the specific income tax treaty to determine if any tax credit, tax exemption, reduced rate of tax, or other treaty benefit or safeguards apply.

Value Added Tax (VAT)

Form 6166 may also be used as proof of U.S. tax residency status for purposes of obtaining an exemption from a VAT imposed by a foreign country. In connection with a VAT request, the United States can certify only to certain matters in relation to your U.S. federal income tax status, and not that you meet any other requirements for a VAT exemption in a foreign country.

General Instructions

Purpose of Form

Form 8802 is used to request Form 6166, a letter of U.S. residency certification for purposes of claiming benefits under an income tax treaty or VAT exemption. You cannot use Form 6166 to substantiate that U.S. taxes were paid for purposes of claiming a foreign tax credit.

You cannot claim a foreign tax credit to reduce your U.S. tax liability with respect to foreign taxes that have been reduced or eliminated by reason of a treaty. If you receive a refund of foreign taxes paid with the benefit of Form 6166, you may need to file an amended return with the IRS adjusting any foreign tax credits previously claimed for those taxes.

When To Apply

You should mail your application, including full payment of the user fee, at least 45 days before the date you need Form 6166. We will contact you after 30 days if there will be a delay in processing your application. You can call (267) 941-1000 (not a toll free number) and select the U.S. residency option if you have questions regarding your application.

Early submission for a current year certification. The IRS cannot accept an early submission for a current year Form 6166 that has a postmark date before December 1. Requests received with a postmark date earlier than December 1 will be returned to the sender. For example, a Form 6166 request for 2012:
- Received with a postmark date before December 1, 2011, cannot be processed.
- Received with a postmark date on or after December 1, 2011, can be processed with the appropriate documentation.

User Fee

Form 8802 application(s) will not be processed until the non-refundable user fee is paid. The user fee is $85 for a Form 8802 filed after March 31, 2012.

Additional request. Additional requests for Form 6166 submitted on a separate Form 8802, following the procedures established under *Additional Requests*, later, will require the payment of an $85 user fee.

 Applicants are advised to request all Forms 6166 on a single Form 8802 to avoid paying the $85 user fee charged for processing a second Form 8802.

Method of Payment

Payment of the user fee can be by check, money order, or electronic payment.

Check or Money Order

Form 8802 must be accompanied by a check or money order in U.S. dollars, payable to the United States Treasury, in the appropriate amount. Do not send cash.

Multiple Forms 8802. If you are submitting multiple Forms 8802, you may submit a single check or money order payment to cover the aggregate amount of the user fee for all Forms 8802. No more than 200 Forms 8802 can be associated with one check or money order.

Note. If you pay by check, it will be converted into an electronic funds transfer (EFT). This means we will copy your check and use the account information on it to electronically debit your account for the amount of the check. The debit from your account will usually occur within 24 hours, and will be shown on your regular account

statement. You will not receive your original check back. We will destroy your original check, but we will keep a copy of it. If the EFT cannot be processed for technical reasons, you authorize us to process the copy in place of your original check.

Electronic Payment (e-payment)

Visit the IRS website at IRS.gov and enter "e-pay" in the search box. Click on the search result, Electronic Payment Options Home Page. Choose "User Fees" at the bottom of the page, and then click on U.S. Residency User Fee. Complete the form and submit online the information requested on the website.

Once your electronic payment has been processed, you will receive an electronic payment confirmation number for the transaction. Enter the electronic payment confirmation number on page 1 of Form 8802 before you submit the application. You can use either the Agency Tracking ID or the Pay.gov ID as the electronic payment confirmation number. Either one is acceptable. If you make an electronic payment covering multiple Forms 8802, the same electronic payment confirmation number must be written on each form. Form 8802 will not be processed if the electronic payment confirmation number has not been entered on the application.

The user fee website requires the entry of the following information.
- Applicant's name.
- Applicant's TIN or EIN.
- Submitter's name (name of person or entity submitting the payment).
- Contact email address.
- Number of Form(s) 6166 requested.
- Payment amount.
- Selection of Automatic Clearing House (ACH) debit or credit card will open a window for account information.

Supplemental User Fee Payment

If you have been contacted by the U.S. Residency Certification Unit to make a supplemental payment, you can use the e-payment system on IRS.gov by checking the supplemental user fee checkbox.

Where To Apply

The method by which you can submit Form 8802 to the IRS depends upon how you choose to pay the user fee.

Payment by Check or Money Order

If you are paying the user fee by check or money order, send the payment, Form 8802, and all required attachments to:

> Internal Revenue Service
> P.O. Box 71052
> Philadelphia, PA 19176-6052

Or, by private delivery service to:

> Internal Revenue Service
> 2970 Market Street
> BLN# 3-G23.100
> Philadelphia, PA 19104-5002

Electronic Payment

After the electronic confirmation number has been entered on page 1 of Form 8802, you can submit Form 8802 and all required attachments by mail, private delivery service, or fax (see below for limitations on the use of faxed transmissions).

If you are paying the user fee by e-payment, send Form 8802 and all required attachments to:

> Department of the Treasury
> Internal Revenue Service
> Philadelphia, PA 19255-0625

Or, by private delivery service to:

> Internal Revenue Service
> 2970 Market Street
> BLN# 3-G23.100
> Philadelphia, PA 19104-5002

Fax. You can fax up to 10 Forms 8802 (including all required attachments) for a maximum of 50 pages to the fax numbers below. A fax cover sheet stating the number of pages included in the transmission must be used.

The following fax numbers are not toll-free:
- (267) 941-1035
- (267) 941-1366

Who Is Eligible for Form 6166

In general, under an income tax treaty, an individual or entity is a resident of the United States if the individual or entity is subject to U.S. tax by reason of residence, citizenship, place of incorporation, or other similar criteria. U.S. residents are subject to tax in the United States on their worldwide income. An entity may be considered subject to tax on its worldwide income even if it is statutorily exempt from tax, such as a pension fund or charity. Similarly, individuals are considered subject to tax even if their income is less than the amount that would require that they file an income tax return.

In general, Form 6166 is issued only when the IRS can verify that for the year for which certification is requested one of the following applies:
- You filed an appropriate income tax return (for example, Form 1120 for a domestic corporation),
- In the case of a certification year for which a return is not yet due, you filed a return for the most recent year for which a return was due, or
- You are not required to file an income tax return for the tax period on which certification will be based and other documentation is provided.

Who Is Not Eligible for Form 6166

In general, you are not eligible for Form 6166 if, for the tax period for which your Form 6166 is based, any of the following applies:
- You did not file a required U.S. return.
- You filed a return as a nonresident (including Form 1040NR, U.S. Nonresident Alien Income Tax Return; Form 1040NR-EZ, U.S. Income Tax Return for Certain Nonresident Aliens With No Dependents; Form 1120-F, U.S. Income Tax Return of a Foreign Corporation; Form 1120-FSC, U.S. Income Tax Return of a Foreign Sales Corporation; or any of the U.S. possession tax forms).
- You are a dual resident individual who has made (or intends to make), pursuant to the tie breaker provision within an applicable treaty, a determination that you are not a resident of the United States and are a resident of the other treaty country. For more information and examples, see Reg. section 301.7701(b)-7.
- You are a fiscally transparent entity organized in the United States (that is, a domestic partnership, domestic grantor trust, or domestic LLC disregarded as an entity separate from its owner) and you do not have any U.S. partners, beneficiaries, or owners.
- The entity requesting certification is an exempt organization that is not organized in the United States.

Special Rules

Form 8802 Filed Before Return Posted by the IRS

If your return has not been posted by the IRS by the time you file Form 8802, you will receive a request to provide a signed copy of your most recent return. If you recently filed your return, it may take less time to process your application if you include a copy of the income tax return with your Form 8802. Write "COPY — do not process" on the tax return.

Individuals With Residency Outside the United States

If you are in any of the following categories for the current or prior tax year for which certification is requested, you must submit a statement and documentation, as described below, with Form 8802.

1. You are a resident under the internal law of both the United States and the treaty country for which you are requesting certification (you are a dual resident).

2. You are a green card holder or U.S. citizen who filed Form 2555, Foreign Earned Income.

3. You are a bona fide resident of a U.S. possession.

If you are a dual resident described in category 1, above, your request may be denied unless you submit evidence to establish that you are a resident of the United States under the tie breaker provision in the residence article of the treaty with the country for which you are requesting certification.

If you are described in category 2 or 3, attach a statement and documentation to establish why you believe you should be entitled to certification as a resident of the U.S. for purposes of the relevant treaty. Under many U.S. treaties, U.S. citizens or green card holders who do not have a substantial presence, permanent home, or habitual abode in the United States during the tax year are not entitled to treaty benefits. U.S. citizens or green card holders who reside outside the United States must examine the specific treaty to determine if they are eligible for treaty benefits and U.S. residency certification. See *Exceptions*, below.

If you are described in category 2 and are claiming treaty benefits under a provision applicable to payments received in consideration of teaching or research activities, see Table 2 for the penalties of perjury statement you must either enter on line 10 of Form 8802 or attach to the form.

Exceptions

You do not need to attach the additional statement or documentation requested if you:
• Are a U.S. citizen or green card holder; and
• Are requesting certification only for Bangladesh, Bulgaria, Cyprus, Hungary, Iceland, India, Kazakhstan, Malta, New Zealand, Russia, South Africa, Sri Lanka, Ukraine; and
• The country for which you are requesting certification and your country of residence are not the same.

Form 1116, Foreign Tax Credit

If you have filed or intend to file a Form 1116, Foreign Tax Credit, claiming either a foreign tax credit amount in excess of $5,000 U.S. or a foreign tax credit for any amount of foreign earned income for the tax period for which certification is requested, you must submit evidence that you were (or will be if the request relates to a current year) a resident of the United States and that the foreign taxes paid were not imposed because you were a resident of the foreign country.

In addition, individuals who have already filed their federal income tax return must submit a copy of it, including any information return(s) relating to income, such as Form W-2 or Form 1099, along with the Form 1116. Your request for U.S. residency certification may be denied if you do not submit the additional materials.

United Kingdom

If you are applying for relief at source from United Kingdom (U.K.) income tax or filing a claim for repayment of U.K. income tax, you may need to complete a U.K. certification form (US/Individual 2002 or US/Company 2002) in addition to Form 8802. For copies of these forms, contact HM Revenue and Customs:
• On the Internet at *www.hmrc.gov.uk/cnr/usdownload.htm*, or
• Telephone at: 44-115-974-0897 if calling from outside the U.K., or 0115-974-0897 if calling from the U.K.

Send the completed U.K. form to the IRS with your completed Form 8802.

Specific Instructions

Check Boxes at Top of Page 1

Additional Requests

Check this box if Form 8802 is being submitted to request additional Form(s) 6166 for a tax period for which the IRS has previously issued a Form 6166 to you. Additional requests on a separate Form 8802 will require a non-refundable user fee of $85. See *User Fee*, earlier.

An applicant can only use this additional request procedure if there are no changes to the applicant's tax information provided on the original Form 8802. An applicant may use this procedure to obtain a Form 6166 for any country or countries, whether or not the country was identified on a previously filed Form 8802. An additional request for Form 6166 using this procedure must be made within 12 months of the most recently issued Form 6166 relating to the same tax period.

Additional documentation. If you are requesting certification for a previously identified country and if additional documentation was necessary for the original application, it does not need to be resubmitted with the request for an additional Form 6166. In the signature line of the additional request form, write "See attached copy of the original Form 8802." Attach a copy of the original Form 8802.

If you are requesting Form 6166 for a country not identified on a previously filed Form 8802 that requires documentation not previously submitted, you must include that documentation with the additional request. Sign and date the additional request form. Attach a copy of the original Form 8802.

Additional request made by third party appointees. Third party appointees cannot use this special procedure to request additional Form(s) 6166 for countries that were not originally authorized by the taxpayer in their previously signed and dated Form 8802. If you anticipate using the additional request procedure to authorize a third party appointee to request additional Forms 6166 for a country not identified in your current Form 8802, you must include in line 10, a written statement authorizing the third party appointee to request Form 6166 covering the same tax period for any country.

Foreign Claim Form

Check the box if you have included with Form 8802 a foreign claim form sent to you by a foreign country. The submission or omission of a foreign claim form will not affect your residency certification. If the IRS does not have an agreement with the foreign country to date stamp, or otherwise process the form, we will not process it and such foreign claim form will be mailed back to you.

Note. For more information about foreign countries with which the IRS has an agreement to process a foreign claim form, call the U.S. residency certification unit at (267) 941-1000 (not a toll-free number).

Applicant's Name and U.S. Taxpayer Identification Number

As part of certifying U.S. residency, the IRS must be able to match the name(s) and taxpayer identification number(s) (TIN(s)) on this application to those previously verified on either the U.S. return filed for the tax period for which certification is to be based or on other documentation you provide.

Enter the applicant's name and TIN **exactly** as they appear on the U.S. return filed for the tax period(s) for which certification will be based. If the applicant was not required to file a U.S. return, enter the applicant's name and TIN as they appear on documentation previously provided to the IRS (for example, Form 8832, Entity Classification Election) or on documentation provided by the IRS (for example, a determination letter).

Joint return. If a joint income tax return was filed for a tax period for which certification will be based, enter the spouse's name and TIN **exactly** as they appear on the return filed.

Change in taxpayer's name. If the taxpayer's name has changed since the most recent Form 8802 was filed with the IRS, the Form 8802 and tax disclosure authorization for each individual or entity must be submitted under the taxpayer's new name. In addition, documentation of the name change must be submitted with Form 8802 (for example, trust agreement, corporate charter).

Certification will not be issued if the name change has not been updated in the IRS database. For information on how to update the IRS on your new name, contact customer service. For businesses, the number is 1-800-829-4933. For individuals, the number is 1-800-829-1040.

Line 2. Applicant's Address

 Do not enter a P.O. box number or C/O address. Certification may be denied if the applicant enters a P.O. box or C/O address.

Enter your address for the calendar year for which you are requesting certification. If you are an individual who lived outside the United States during the year for which certification is requested, the special rules under *Individuals With Residency Outside the United States*, earlier, may apply to you.

Line 3a. Mailing Address

Form 6166 and any related correspondence may be mailed to you or to a third party appointee. If you provide an address on line 3a, it will be used for all mail correspondence relating to your Form 6166 request. If you do not indicate a mailing address on line 3a, Form 6166 will be mailed to the address on line 2.

Line 3b. Third Party Appointee's Information

If the mailing address entered on line 3a is for a third party appointee, you must provide written authorization for the IRS to release the certification to the third party. By filling out the appointee's information in lines 3a and 3b (name and address), written authorization will be deemed to have been provided when you sign and date the Form 8802. You are not required to enter a phone number or a fax number of your third party appointee. However, by providing a phone number or fax number, you are authorizing the IRS to call or fax your third party appointee.

The Centralized Authorization File (CAF) contains information on third parties authorized to represent taxpayers before the IRS and/or receive and inspect confidential tax information. If your appointee has a CAF number, enter it on line 3b.

In general, you do not need to fill out line 3b if you have attached Form 2848 or Form 8821. In line 3b, write "See attached authorization." Attach a Form 2848 or Form 8821 for each additional third party that you wish to authorize to receive your tax information.

Form 8821, Taxpayer Information Authorization, and Form 2848, Power of Attorney and Declaration of Representative. Form 8821 is used to authorize disclosure of tax information to a third party designee of the taxpayer. Form 8821 cannot be used to authorize a third party to sign Form 8802 on your behalf, and it does not authorize a third party to represent you before the IRS. Pursuant to section 6103(c) and the regulations thereunder, authorization on Form 8821 will not be accepted if it covers matters other than federal tax matters.

Form 2848 authorizes a third party to represent you before the IRS. Only individuals who are recognized to practice before the IRS can be authorized to represent you. The only individuals who can be recognized representatives are the following:
- Attorneys
- Certified Public Accountants
- Enrolled Agents
- Enrolled Actuaries (the authority to practice before the IRS is limited)
- Registered Tax Return Preparer under section 10.4 of Circular 230 (the authority to practice before the IRS is limited)
- Student attorney or CPA (must receive permission to practice before the IRS)
- Enrolled Retirement Plan Agents (the authority to practice before the IRS is limited)
- Certain individuals who have a special relationship or status with the taxpayer

For more information, see Pub. 947, Practice Before the IRS and Power of Attorney.

Line 4a. Individual

Green card holder. If you are a resident alien with lawful permanent resident status who recently arrived in the United States and you have not yet filed a U.S. income tax return, you should provide a copy of your current Form I-551, Alien Registration Receipt Card (green card). Instead of a copy of your green card, you can attach a statement from U.S. Citizenship and Immigration Services (USCIS) that gives your alien registration number, the date and port of entry, date of birth, and classification. For more information in determining your U.S. resident status for tax purposes, see *Nonresident Alien or Resident Alien*, in Pub. 519, U.S. Tax Guide for Aliens.

Sole proprietor. Include on line 6 the type of tax return, name, TIN, and any other information that would be required if certification were being requested for the individual owner that filed the Schedule C (Form 1040), Profit or Loss From Business.

U.S. resident alien. An individual who is not a lawful permanent resident of the United States but who meets the "substantial presence test" under section 7701(b) is a resident alien for purposes of U.S. taxation. If you are a resident alien under the substantial presence test and you have not yet filed a U.S. income tax return for the year for which certification is requested, you must attach a copy of your current Form I-94, Arrival-Departure Record. Enter the date (YYYYMMDD) your status changed on the line provided. For information on determining your period of residency, see *Substantial Presence Test* in Pub. 519.

Students, teachers, and trainees. If you filed Form 1040, U.S. Individual Income Tax Return, and you are in the United States under an "F1,""J1,""M1," or "Q1" visa, include the following with Form 8802.

1. A statement explaining why Form 1040 was filed.

2. A statement and documentation showing that you reported your worldwide income.

First-year election. If you are an individual who made or intends to make the first-year election under section 7701(b)(4) applicable to the year for which certification is requested, enter the date (YYYYMMDD) your status as a U.S. resident for tax purposes will begin. For more information regarding the first-year election and determining your period of residency, see *First-Year Choice* in Pub. 519.

- If you have made a first-year residence election under section 7701(b)(4) applicable to the year for which you are requesting certification, attach to Form 8802 the election statement you filed with your income tax return for the taxable year of election.
- If, for the calendar year for which certification is requested, you have not yet filed a first-year residence election statement, attach to Form 8802 a statement that you intend to file such statement and that you are eligible to make the election.

Dual-status alien. An individual is a dual-status alien for U.S. tax purposes if the individual is a part-year resident alien and a part-year nonresident alien during the calendar year(s) for which certification is requested. Dual-status generally occurs in the year an individual acquires status as a U.S. resident or terminates such status. For example, you are a dual-status alien if you are a U.S. citizen or green card holder and you lost citizenship or green card holder status during the same calendar year. You may also be a dual-status alien if you are a non-resident alien but due to meeting the substantial presence test become a resident alien during the same calendar year.

The dual-status alien classification does not occur merely due to a temporary absence from the United States, nor will multiple periods of temporary absence and re-entry into the United States create multiple periods of U.S. resident and non-resident status. For information and examples of a dual-status alien, and to determine your period of residency, see Pub. 519.

If you checked the dual-status box, enter the dates (YYYYMMDD) that correspond to the period that you were a resident of the United States during the year(s) for which certification is requested.

Partial-year Form 2555 filer. Check this box if you filed a Form 2555 that covered only part of a year for which certification is requested. For each year that this applies, enter the eight-digit dates (YYYYMMDD) that correspond to the beginning and ending of the period you were a resident of the United States.

Line 4b. Partnership

Partnerships are not considered U.S. residents within the meaning of the residence article of U.S. income tax treaties. Treaty benefits are only available to a partner who is a U.S. resident.

Note. The Form 6166 issued to partnerships will include an attached list of partners that are U.S. residents. The IRS does not certify the percentage of ownership interest of the listed partners. It is the responsibility of the partnership to provide such information to the withholding agent.

Include the following with Form 8802:

1. The name and TIN of each partner for which certification is requested and any additional information that would be required if certification were being requested for each of those partners.

2. Authorization (for example, Form 8821) from each partner, including all partners listed within tiered partnerships. Each authorization must explicitly allow the third party requester to receive the partner's tax information and must not address matters other than federal tax matters.

3. Unless the requester is a partner in the partnership during the tax year for which certification is requested, authorization from the partnership must explicitly allow the third party requester to receive the partnership's tax information. The authorization must not address matters other than federal tax matters.

An LLC that is classified as a partnership follows the above procedures. Members of the LLC are treated as partners.

Nominee partnership. Do not check the partnership box on line 4b. Instead, check line 4j and attach the information required by the instructions.

Line 4c. Trust

Domestic and foreign grantor trusts and simple trusts can be certified for U.S. residency, to the extent the owner of the grantor trust or beneficiaries of simple trusts are U.S. residents. Domestic complex trusts may be certified without regard to the residence of the settler or beneficiaries.

A trust is domestic if a court within the U.S. is able to exercise primary supervision over the administration of the trust and one or more U.S. persons has authority to control all substantial decisions of the trust.

Grantor trust. Include the following with Form 8802:

1. The name and TIN of each owner and any information that would be required if certification were being requested for each owner.

2. Authorization (for example, Form 8821) from each owner. Each authorization must explicitly allow the third party requester to receive the owner's tax information and must not address matters other than federal tax matters.

3. Unless the requester is a trustee of the trust, authorization from the trust must explicitly allow the third party requester to receive the trust's tax information. The authorization must not address matters other than federal tax matters.

4. If the grantor trust is a foreign trust, also include a copy of Form

3520-A, Annual Information Return of Foreign Trust With a U.S. Owner, including a copy of the foreign grantor trust owner statement.

Domestic complex trust. Unless the requester is a trustee of the trust during the tax year for which certification is requested, authorization from the trust must explicitly allow the third party requester to receive the trust's tax information. The authorization must not address matters other than federal tax matters.

Simple trust. Include the following with Form 8802:

1. The name and TIN of each beneficiary and any information that would be required if certification were being requested for each beneficiary.

2. Authorization (for example, Form 8821) from each beneficiary. Each authorization must explicitly allow the third party requester to receive the beneficiary's tax information and must not address matters other than federal tax matters.

3. Unless the requester is a trustee of the trust, authorization from the trust must explicitly allow the third party requester to receive the trust's tax information. The authorization must not address matters other than federal tax matters.

Group trust arrangement, described in Rev. Rul. 81-100. A group trust arrangement that has received a determination letter recognizing its exempt status under section 501(a) must attach a copy of that letter to Form 8802.

A group trust arrangement that is seeking benefits from Switzerland with respect to dividends paid by a Swiss corporation must also attach to Form 8802 the name of each participant and a statement that each participant listed is a trust forming part of a plan described in section 401(a), 403(b), or 457(b).

IRA. Domestic individual retirement arrangements (individual retirement accounts within the meaning of section 408(a) and Roth IRAs within the meaning of section 408A) (collectively referred to as IRAs) may be certified as residents (without regard to the residence of the IRA holder). Either the IRA holder or the trustee of the IRA may request certification on behalf of the IRA.

An IRA holder requesting certification on behalf of an IRA must provide the IRA account name (that is, the IRA holder's name) and number, the IRA holder's TIN, and a copy of Form 8606, Nondeductible IRAs, or Form 5498, IRA Contribution Information. Complete the remainder of Form 8802 as if certification were being requested by the IRA.

A bank or financial institution acting as the trustee for IRAs may request certification for multiple IRAs grouped by year and by country for which certification is requested. The bank or financial institution must include the following with Form 8802:

1. A list of IRA account names and account numbers for which certification is requested.

2. A statement that each IRA account name and number listed is an IRA within the meaning of section 408(a) or 408A.

3. A statement that the bank or financial institution is a trustee of the IRA.

Common trust fund as defined in section 584. Include the following with Form 8802:

1. The name and TIN of each participant and any information that would be required if certification were being requested for each participant.

2. Authorization (for example, Form 8821) from each participant. Each authorization must explicitly allow the third party requester to receive the participant's tax information and must not address any matters other than federal tax matters. If a pass-through entity is a participant, you must list the partners/shareholders/owners/ participants/members/beneficiaries in the pass-through entity and obtain authorization from each such participant.

3. Unless the requester is a trustee of the trust, authorization from the trust must explicitly allow the third party requester to receive the trust's tax information. The authorization must not address matters other than federal tax matters.

A common trust fund that is seeking benefits from Switzerland with respect to dividends paid by a Swiss corporation must also attach to Form 8802 the name of each participant and a statement that each participant listed is a trust forming part of a plan that is described in section 401(a), 403(b), or 457(b), or is a trust forming part of a plan described in section 401(a), 403(b), or 457(b) that is within a group trust arrangement described in Rev. Rul. 81-100, 1981-13

I.R.B. 33, as clarified and modified by Rev. Rul. 2004-67, 2004-28 I.R.B. 28 and modified by Rev. Rul. 2011-1, 2011-2 I.R.B. 251. Also, see Notice 2012-6.

Line 4d. Estate

If you are filing a Form 8802 on behalf of the estate of a decedent, you must include proof that you are the executor or administrator of the decedent's estate. Form 8802 can be submitted on behalf of an estate for the year of the taxpayer's death or any prior year. Proof can include a court certificate naming you executor or administrator of the estate. U.S. residency certification will be based on the tax information and residency of the decedent.

Line 4e. Corporation

Generally, a corporation that is not incorporated in the United States is not entitled to U.S. residency certification. However, there are exceptions for certain corporations that are treated as U.S. corporations under sections 269B, 943(e)(1), 953(d), or 1504(d). Only Canadian and Mexican corporations are eligible to be treated as domestic corporations under section 1504(d).

Corporations requesting U.S. residency certification on behalf of their subsidiaries must attach a list of the subsidiaries and the Form 851, Affiliations Schedule, filed with the corporation's consolidated return.

Dual-resident corporation. If you are requesting certification for treaty benefits in the other country of residence named on line 4e, certification depends on the terms of the residence article of the relevant treaty. If the treaty provides that benefits are available only if the competent authorities reach a mutual agreement to that effect, request competent authority assistance in accordance with Rev. Proc. 2006-54, 2006-49 I.R.B. 1035, or its successor, prior to seeking certification.

 Effective January 1, 2005, the special rules for financial asset securitization investment trusts (FASITs) were repealed. However, the special rules still apply to any FASIT in existence on October 22, 2004, to the extent that regular interests issued by the FASIT before that date continue to remain outstanding in accordance with the original terms of issuance.

Line 4f. S Corporation

S corporations are not considered U.S. residents within the meaning of the residence article of U.S. income tax treaties. Treaty benefits are only available to a shareholder who is a U.S. resident for purposes of the applicable treaty.

Include the following with Form 8802:

1. The name and TIN of each shareholder for which certification is requested and any additional information that would be required if certification were being requested for each of those shareholders.

2. Authorization (for example, Form 8821) from each shareholder. Each authorization must explicitly allow the third party requester to receive the shareholder's tax information and must not address any matters other than federal tax matters.

3. Unless the requester is a shareholder in the S corporation during the tax year for which certification is requested, authorization from an officer with legal authority to bind the corporation must explicitly allow the third party requester to receive the corporation's tax information. The authorization must not address matters other than federal tax matters.

Line 4g. Employee Benefit Plan/Trust

Trusts that are part of an employee benefit plan that is required to file Form 5500, Annual Return/Report of Employee Benefit Plan, must include a copy of the signed Form 5500 with Form 8802.

An employee plan that is not subject to the Employee Retirement Income Security Act (ERISA) or is not otherwise required to file Form 5500 must include with Form 8802 a copy of the employee benefit plan determination letter.

An employee plan that is not required to file Form 5500 and does not have a determination letter must provide evidence that it is entitled to certification. It must also provide a statement under penalties of perjury explaining why it is not required to file Form 5500 and why it does not have a determination letter.

Line 4h. Exempt Organization

Generally, an organization that is exempt from U.S. income tax must attach to Form 8802 a copy of either the organization's determination letter from the IRS or the determination letter for the parent organization.

An exempt organization that is not required to file a U.S. income tax return and that has not received a determination letter will not be issued a Form 6166, unless such organization has other means of proving U.S. residency for tax treaty purposes. For such an entity, include with Form 8802 the entity's bylaws, corporate charter, trust agreement, partnership agreement, etc.

Governmental entity. Federal, state, or local government agencies requesting U.S. residency certification that have not obtained a determination letter, private letter ruling, revenue ruling, etc., can submit in writing, on official government letterhead, a letter under penalties of perjury from a legally authorized government official stating that the organization is a government agency.

Line 4i. Disregarded Entity

Disregarded entities (DRE) are not considered U.S. residents within the meaning of the residence article of U.S. income tax treaties. Treaty benefits will only be available to a DRE owner who is a U.S. resident. The DRE type must be specified on line 4i.

Note. See line 5 for more information regarding the DRE's owner information that may be required to be included with your Form 8802.

Line 4j. Nominee Applicant

If you act as a nominee for another person or entity, you must provide all certification information required for each individual or entity for which you are acting as a nominee. For example, if you are acting as a nominee for a resident alien, you must attach the information required of applicants that are resident aliens. Similarly, if one of the entities for which you are acting as a nominee is a partnership, then you must submit the certification information for each of the partners requesting certification. In addition, you must include the following with Form 8802.

1. Authorization (for example, Form 8821) from each individual or entity. Each authorization must explicitly allow the nominee applicant to receive the individual's or entity's tax information and must not address any matters other than federal tax matters.

2. A statement under penalties of perjury signed by an individual with legal authority to bind the nominee applicant, explicitly stating the nominee applicant is acting as an agent on behalf of the above-named individual(s) or entity(ies) for whom the Form 6166 is being requested.

Note. If you are a nominee partnership, please do not provide information concerning your partners. The residence of your partners will not be verified.

Line 5. Statement Required If Applicant Did Not File a U.S. Income Tax Return

If the applicant was not required to file a U.S. income tax return for the tax period(s) for which certification will be based, check the applicable box next to "No." If the applicant does not fit in any of the categories listed, check "Other" and on the dotted line that follows, enter the code section that exempts the applicant from the requirement to file a U.S. income tax return. See Table 1 for the statement required if the applicant did not file a U.S. income tax return.

Table 1. Statement Required If Applicant Did Not File a U.S. Income Tax Return

IF the applicant was not required to file a U.S. income tax return and the applicant is...	THEN ...
an individual	attach proof of income (for example, an income statement, Form W-2, Form 1099, etc.) and a written statement that explains why the individual is not required to file an income tax return for the tax period(s) for which certification is based. If the individual is a U.S. citizen, the written statement must be made under penalties of perjury.
a child under age 19, or under age 24 if a full-time student, whose parent(s) elected to report the child's income on their return	attach a signed copy of the Form 8814, Parents' Election To Report Child's Interest and Dividends.
a qualified subchapter S subsidiary (QSub) (include the parent S corporation information on line 6 of Form 8802)	attach proof of the election made on Form 8869, Qualified Subchapter S Subsidiary Election, and all other requirements listed in the instructions for line 4f that apply to the parent S corporation.
a trust or estate	attach an explanation of why the trust or estate is not required to file Form 1041.
a common trust fund	attach a copy of the determination letter or proof that a participant is not required to file.
a group trust arrangement	attach a copy of the determination letter or private letter ruling.
a partnership described in section 761(a)	attach a copy of the section 761(a) election submitted with Form 1065, U.S. Return of Partnership Income, or a statement from a general partner that is signed and dated under penalties of perjury. See Table 2, Current Year Penalties of Perjury Statements.
a financial asset securitization investment trust (FASIT) (include the parent C corporation information on line 6 of Form 8802)[1]	attach a copy of the statement of election made by the parent C corporation requesting that the entity be treated as a FASIT under section 860L(a)(3). See Table 2.
a government entity	submit in writing, on official government letterhead, an explanation of why the government entity is exempt from a filing requirement. The letter must be signed and dated under penalty of perjury by a government official with the authority to bind the organization or agency.
a foreign partnership	include all information indicated in the instructions for line 4b for each partner requesting certification.
a domestic disregarded entity (domestic DRE)	include the entity's single owner information on line 6 of Form 8802. Include with Form 8802: the owner's name and entity type (e.g., corporation, partnership), TIN, and all other certification information required for the owner's type of entity. If the DRE is either newly formed, was established before 2001, or was established by default (no Form 8832 was filed), also include a statement from the owner, signed under penalties of perjury (see Table 2).
a foreign disregarded entity (foreign DRE)	For tax years beginning on or after January 1, 2004, if the disregarded entity is organized outside the United States and the owner is a U.S. person, attach a copy of the Form 8858, Information Return of U.S. Persons With Respect To Foreign Disregarded Entities, filed with the U.S. owner's income tax return for the calendar year(s) for which certification is requested. If the owner has not identified the foreign DRE on the Form 8858, the foreign DRE cannot be certified. Include the foreign DRE's owner information on line 6. Include with Form 8802, the owner's name and entity type, TIN, and all other certification information required for the owner's type of entity. If certification is being requested for tax years prior to January 1, 2004, the U.S. owner is not required to attach a copy of the Form 8858, but must attach proof that the foreign DRE is owned by a U.S. resident. For example, if the foreign DRE is owned by a U.S. corporation, attach a copy of Schedule N (Form 1120), Foreign Operations of U.S. Corporations, filed with the owner's income tax return for the calendar year for which certification is requested. If the owner has not identified the DRE on an attachment to its Schedule N, the foreign DRE cannot be certified.
1 See *Caution* under *Line 4e. Corporation*, earlier.	

Line 6. Parent, Parent Organization, or Owner

If you answered "Yes" to line 5, do **not** complete line 6.

If you answered "No" to line 5, you must complete line 6.

If you answered "Yes" to line 6, check the appropriate box and enter the parent's, parent organization's, or owner's information. If the applicant is a minor child, enter the name, address, and TIN of the parent who reported the child's income.

If you answered "No" to line 6, attach proof of the parent's, parent organization's, or owner's income and an explanation of why the parent is not required to file a tax return for the tax period(s) for which certification is based.

Line 7. Calendar Year of Request

The certification period is generally 1 year. You can request certification for both the current year and any number of prior years.

If you entered the most recent prior year on this line, see *Form 8802 Filed Before Return Posted by the IRS*, earlier.

Enter the four-digit (YYYY) calendar year(s) for which you are requesting certification. However, see the *Exception* below.

Exception. If you were a dual-status alien during any year for which you are requesting certification, enter instead the eight-digit dates (YYYYMMDD) that correspond to the beginning and ending of the period you were a resident of the United States. You must show the specific period of residence for each year for which you are requesting certification. For information on determining your period of residency, see Pub. 519.

Current year certification. If certification is requested for purposes of claiming benefits under an income tax treaty or VAT exemption for any period during the current calendar year or a year for which a tax return is not yet required to be filed with the IRS, penalties of perjury statement(s) will be required from all applicants stating that such applicant is a U.S. resident and will continue to be so throughout the current tax year. See Table 2 for the current year penalties of perjury statement you must enter on line 10 of Form 8802 or attach to the form.

Note. For VAT certification, a statement that the business activity has not changed is also required. For more information, see the instructions for line 10 below.

Line 8. Tax Period(s)

If you are requesting certification for a tax period for which a tax return is not yet due, enter the four-digit year and two-digit month (YYYYMM) that corresponds to the end of the most recent tax period for which you filed a tax return. For a prior year certification, the four-digit year and two-digit month should correspond to the end of the prior year tax period for which certification is requested.

Example 1. A Form 1040 filer who is completing Form 8802 for certification year 2012 on January 1, 2012, would enter 201012 on line 8. This is because on January 1, 2012, the 2010 Form 1040 is the latest return required to have been filed by an individual requesting certification for 2012.

Example 2. On May 1, 2012, the same Form 1040 filer would enter 201112 as the tax period for a certification year of 2011 (the 2011 Form 1040 was required to have been filed before May 1, 2012).

Example 3. On January 1, 2012, a Form 1040 filer completing Form 8802 for a certification year of 2009 would enter 200912.

If you were not required to file a U.S. tax return for the tax period for which certification is requested, enter the tax period that would have been applicable, if you were required to file a U.S. tax return. After the tax period, add "(not required to file)."

Line 9. Purpose of Certification

You must indicate the purpose of the certification.

 Your application will be returned to you for completion if you do not include a purpose on the application.

Income tax treaty. If you are requesting certification to obtain benefits under an income tax treaty but you have requested certification for a non-treaty country, your application will be returned to you for correction.

VAT. The North American Industry Classification System (NAICS) codes can be found in the instructions for your tax return (for example, Form 1120 or Schedule C (Form 1040)). If you do not provide a NAICS code on Form 8802 and one was not provided on the return you filed, one will not be entered automatically. Form 6166 will only certify that you filed a return with a particular NAICS code if it matches the NAICS code on your application. If you provide a code that does not match, Form 6166 will state that you represent that your NAICS code is as stated on Form 8802.

Line 10. Penalties of Perjury Statements and Attachments

Penalties of perjury statements from Table 2 may be entered in the space provided under line 10 or as an attachment to Form 8802. Penalties of perjury statements submitted independently of Form 8802 must have a valid signature and date. See Table 3.

VAT. For VAT certifications, the penalties of perjury statement must also include a statement that the business activity (NAICS code) has not changed since your last filed return.

Attachments. If any attachment is submitted independently of Form 8802 and is prepared by someone other than the person signing Form 8802, the attachment must be signed and dated under penalties of perjury by an individual who has authority to sign Form 8802. See Table 3.

Additional information. If additional information is required to be submitted with Form 8802, use the space provided under line 10 or attach the information to the form.

Table 2. Current Year Penalties of Perjury Statements

IF the applicant is...	THEN the Form 8802 penalties of perjury statement must include...	STATING: "This certification is given under penalties of perjury and to the best of my knowledge and belief, the statements are true, correct, and complete."
an individual	a statement from the individual	*[Insert name of individual and TIN]* is a U.S. resident and will continue to be throughout the current tax year.
an individual claiming treaty benefits for teaching or research activities	a statement from the individual	**Countries other than Japan:** *[Insert name of individual and TIN]* was a U.S. resident within the meaning of Article *[#]* of the U.S.-*[country]* treaty (including, in some cases, physical presence in the United States) immediately before entering *[country]*. The assignment began on *[date]* and ends on *[date]*. Article *[#]* of the U.S.-*[country]* treaty provides a *[2 or 3]* year exemption from income tax. **Japan:** *[Insert name of individual and TIN]* is (and will continue to be) a U.S. resident within the meaning of Article 4(1) of the U.S.-Japan treaty. The assignment began on *[date]* and ends on *[date]*. Article 20 of the U.S.-Japan treaty provides a 2 year exemption from income tax.
a partnership	a statement from each individual partner for which certification is requested	*[Insert name of partner and TIN]* is a U.S. resident and will continue to be throughout the current tax year, **and**
	a statement from a general partner	*[Insert name of partnership and EIN]* has filed its required return and the entity classification has not changed since the return was filed.
an S corporation	a statement from each individual shareholder for which certification is requested	*[Insert name of shareholder and TIN]* is a U.S. resident and will continue to be throughout the current tax year, **and**
	a statement from an officer of the corporation with the authority to legally bind the corporation	*[Insert name of S corporation and EIN]* has filed its required return and the entity classification has not changed since the return was filed.
a common trust fund, grantor trust, or simple trust	a statement from each individual participant/ beneficiary/ owner	*[Insert name and TIN]* is a U.S. resident and will continue to be throughout the current tax year, **and**
	a statement from the trustee with authority to legally bind the trust	*[Insert name of trust and EIN]* has filed its required return and the entity classification has not changed since the return was filed. **Note:** When the participant, beneficiary, or owner, is other than an individual, use the statement that corresponds to the type of entity.
a trust	a statement from the trustee with authority to legally bind the trust	*[Insert name of trust and EIN]* is a U.S. resident and will continue to be throughout the current tax year.
a corporation	a statement from an officer of the corporation with the authority to legally bind the corporation	*[Insert name of corporation and EIN]* is a U.S. resident and will continue to be throughout the current tax year.
an exempt organization	a statement from an officer of the organization with authority to legally bind the organization	*[Insert name of organization and EIN]* is a U.S. resident and will continue to be throughout the current tax year.

-11-

IF the applicant is...	THEN the Form 8802 penalties of perjury statement must include...	STATING: "This certification is given under penalties of perjury and to the best of my knowledge and belief, the statements are true, correct, and complete."
an estate of a decedent	a statement from the personal representative	*[Insert name of estate and EIN]* is a U.S. resident and will continue to be throughout the current tax year.
an employee benefit plan/trust	a statement from an officer of the plan/trust with authority to legally bind the plan/trust	*[Insert name of plan/trust and EIN]* is a U.S. resident and will continue to be throughout the current tax year.
a partnership under IRC section 761(a) election	a statement from each partner for which certification is requested	*[Insert name of partner and TIN]* is a U.S. resident and will continue to be throughout the current tax year, **and**
	a statement from a general partner	a. *[Insert name of partnership and EIN]* has made an election pursuant to IRC section 761(a). As a result, it is not required to file Form 1065 on an annual basis and all of its partners report their respective shares of income, gain, loss, deductions, and credits on their tax returns as required. b. The *[insert name of partnership]* 's entity classification has not changed since the filing of the partners' returns.
a foreign partnership under Regulations section 1.6031(a)-1(b)	an additional statement from a general partner	*[Insert name of partnership and EIN]* is not required to file Form 1065 under Regulations section 1.6031(a)-1(b) and the entity classification has not changed since the filing of the partners' returns.
a financial asset securitization investment trust (FASIT) [1]	a statement from an officer of the corporation with the authority to legally bind the corporation	a. *[Insert name of corporation and EIN]* is the corporate owner of *[insert name of FASIT and EIN]* which is treated as a FASIT under IRC section 860H, and as such, *[insert name of corporation]* reports all of *[insert name of FASIT]* 's income, gain, loss, deductions, and credits on *[insert name of corporate owner]* 's Form 1120, U.S. Corporation Income Tax Return. b. The corporation is a U.S. resident and will continue to be throughout the current tax year.
a FASIT not required to file a U.S. tax return[1]	a statement from an officer of the corporation with the authority to legally bind the corporation	*[Insert name of corporation and EIN]* is the corporate owner of *[insert name of FASIT and EIN]* which is treated as a FASIT under IRC section 860H, and as such, *[insert corporate owner]* reports all of *[insert name of FASIT]* 's income, gain, loss, deductions, and credits on *[insert name of corporate owner]* 's Form 1120, U.S. Corporation Income Tax Return.
a disregarded entity (DRE)	a statement from the owner of the DRE	This certifies that *[insert name and TIN of the owner of the DRE corporation, partnership, or individual]* trading as *[insert name of limited liability company]* is a single-owner limited liability company that is treated as a disregarded entity for U.S. income tax purposes, that *[insert name of corporation, partnership, or individual]* is the single owner of *[insert name of limited liability company]*, and, as such, *[insert name of corporation, partnership, or individual]* is required to take into account all the income, gain, loss, deductions, and credits of *[insert name of limited liability company]* on its/his/her U.S. federal income tax or information return.
a nominee	a statement from each individual or entity for whom the nominee is acting	*[Insert name and TIN of individual(s)/entity(ies) on whose behalf the nominee is acting]* is a U.S. resident and will continue to be throughout the current year.

1 See *Caution* under *Line 4e. Corporation*, earlier.

Signature and Date

Form 8802 will not be considered complete and valid if the application is not signed and dated by an individual who has the authority to sign Form 8802. A third party representative with authorization to sign Form 8802 must attach documentation (for example, Form 2848) of the authorization. See Table 3 to determine who has authority to sign Form 8802.

To avoid processing delays and possible rejection of Form 8802, if Form 8802 is signed by an individual who is not identified in the instructions, enter a statement in line 10 and attach any appropriate documentation to indicate such individual's authority to sign Form 8802. If you are granting authority to a third party, you must sign and date the documentation.

Table 3. Who Has Authority To Sign Form 8802

IF the applicant is...	THEN the individual with authority to sign Form 8802 is...
an individual	the individual.
a married couple	both the husband and the wife.
a minor child who cannot sign	either parent by signing the child's name and adding "By (your signature), parent for minor child."
a child under age 19, or under age 24 if a full-time student, whose parent(s) reported the child's income on Form 8814	the parent who filed Form 8814 with his/her income tax return.
a partnership	any partner or partners duly authorized to act for the partnership (general partner or tax matters partner). Each partner must certify that he or she has such authority.
an S corporation	any corporate officer, for example, president, vice president, treasurer, chief accounting officer, etc., duly authorized by the corporation to bind the corporation in accordance with applicable state law.
a trust, common trust fund, grantor trust or simple trust	the fiduciary (trustee, executor, administrator, receiver, or guardian).
an estate of a decedent	the personal representative (executor or administrator).
a corporation	any corporate officer, for example, president, vice president, treasurer, chief accounting officer, etc., duly authorized by the corporation to bind the corporation in accordance with applicable state law.
an employee benefit plan or trust	any organization officer, for example, president, vice president, treasurer, chief accounting officer, etc., duly authorized by the plan or trust to bind the plan or trust in accordance with applicable state law.
an exempt organization	any organization officer, for example, president, vice president, treasurer, chief accounting officer, etc., duly authorized by the organization to bind the organization in accordance with applicable state law.
a partnership under an IRC 761(a) election	any partner or partners duly authorized to act for the partnership. Each partner must certify that he or she has such authority.
a financial asset securitization investment trust (FASIT)[1]	any corporate officer, for example, president, vice president, treasurer, chief accounting officer, etc., duly authorized by the owner corporation to bind the owner corporation in accordance with applicable state law.
a governmental organization	an officer of the governmental organization with authority in the course of his or her official duties to bind the organization.

1 See *Caution* under *Line 4e. Corporation*, earlier.

Daytime Phone Number

Providing your daytime phone number can help speed the processing of Form 8802. We may have questions about items on your application, such as the NAICS code, type of applicant, etc. By answering our questions over the phone, we may be able to continue processing your Form 8802 without mailing you a letter. If you are filing a joint application, you can enter either your or your spouse's daytime phone number.

Line 11. Number of Certifications (Forms 6166) Requested for Each Country

Enter the number of certifications (Forms 6166) requested for each country listed in columns A, B, C, and D. For any country not listed, enter the country in the blank spaces at the bottom of Column D. If you are requesting certifications for more than one calendar year for a country, enter the number of certifications requested for all years to get the total number of certifications requested for that country.

Example. You are requesting certifications for Germany. You need 3 certifications for 2009, 2 certifications for 2010, and 4 certifications for 2011. Enter 9 as the total number of certifications requested for Germany.

Line 12. Total Number of Certifications (Forms 6166) Requested

Add the total number of certifications requested in columns A, B, C, and D of line 11, and enter the total on line 12.

When To Seek U.S. Competent Authority Assistance

If your request for Form 6166 is denied and you believe you are entitled to treaty benefits under a specific treaty article, you can request U.S. competent authority assistance following the procedures established in Rev. Proc. 2006-54, 2006-49 I.R.B. 1035, or its successor. A request for U.S. competent authority assistance regarding a residency issue will be

-13-

accepted for consideration only if it is established that the issue requires consultation with the foreign competent authority to ensure consistent treatment by the United States and the applicable treaty partner. The U.S. competent authority does not make unilateral determinations with respect to residency. Residency determinations are made by mutual agreement between the two competent authorities.

 The U.S. competent authority cannot consider requests involving countries with which the United States does not have an income tax treaty.

Your request for U.S. competent authority assistance should be mailed to the address indicated in Rev. Proc. 2006-54, or its successor. Rev. Proc. 2006-54 is available at *www.irs.gov/irb/2006-49_IRB/ar13.html*.

Comments and Suggestions

Do **not** send Form 8802 to this address. This address is only for comments or suggestions about Form 8802 and its separate instructions.

Internal Revenue Service
Office of Tax Treaty
SE:LB:IN:TAIT
1111 Constitution Avenue NW, MA
Washington, DC 20224
U.S.A.

Privacy Act and Paperwork Reduction Act Notice. We ask for the information on this form under sections 6103 and 6109 of the Internal Revenue Code. You are required to provide the information requested on this form only if you wish to have your U.S. residency for tax purposes certified in order to claim VAT exemption or to claim certain benefits under a tax treaty between the United States and the foreign country (countries) indicated on Form 8802. We need this information to determine if the applicant can be certified as a U.S. resident for tax purposes for the period specified. Failure to provide the requested information may prevent certification. Providing false or fraudulent information may subject you to penalties. If you designate an appointee to receive Form 6166, but do not provide all of the information requested, we may be unable to honor the designation.

Generally, tax returns and return information are confidential, as required by section 6103. However, section 6103 authorizes or requires us to disclose this information in certain circumstances. We may disclose the information to the tax authorities of other countries pursuant to a tax treaty. We may disclose this information to the Department of Justice for civil and criminal litigation. We may also disclose this information to cities, states, the District of Columbia, and U.S. commonwealths and possessions for use in administering their tax laws, to federal and state agencies to enforce federal nontax criminal laws, or to federal law enforcement and intelligence agencies to combat terrorism.

You are not required to provide the information requested on a form that is subject to the Paperwork Reduction Act unless the form displays a valid OMB control number. Books or records relating to a form or its instructions must be retained as long as their contents may become material in the administration of any Internal Revenue law.

The time needed to complete and file this form will vary depending on individual circumstances. The estimated average time is:

Recordkeeping	33 min.
Learning about the law or the form	1hr., 13 min.
Preparing the form . . .	1 hr., 3 min.
Copying, assembling, and sending the form to the IRS	48 min.

If you have comments concerning the accuracy of these time estimates or suggestions for making this form simpler, we would be happy to hear from you. You can write to the Internal Revenue Service, Tax Products Coordinating Committee, SE:W:CAR:MP:T:M:S, 1111 Constitution Ave. NW, IR-6526, Washington, DC 20224. Do **not** send the form to this address. Instead, see *Where To Apply*, earlier.

Form **8809**

(Rev. May 2011)

Department of the Treasury
Internal Revenue Service

Application for Extension of Time
To File Information Returns

(For Forms W-2, W-2G, 1042-S, 1097, 1098, 1099, 3921, 3922, 5498, and 8027)
▶ **Requests for more than one filer must be filed through the Filing Information Returns
Electronically (FIRE) System.** See *How to file* below.

OMB No. 1545-1081

Caution: *Do not use this form to request an extension of time to (1) provide statements to recipients (see Extensions under Section M of the General Instructions for Certain Information Returns or see Part D, Section 4, of Publication 1220), (2) file Form 1042 (use Form 7004), or (3) file Form 1040 (use Form 4868).*

1 Filer information. **Type or print clearly in black ink.**

Filer name

Address

City   State   ZIP Code

Contact name   Telephone number

Email address

2 Taxpayer identification number
(Enter your nine-digit number. Do not enter hyphens.)

3   Check this box only if you already received the automatic extension and you now need an additional extension. See instructions. ▶ ☐

4   Check the box(es) that apply. **Do not** enter the number of returns.

Form(s)	✓ here	Form(s)	✓ here	Form	✓ here
W-2		5498		8027	
1097, 1098, 1099, 3921, 3922, W-2G		5498-ESA			
1042-S		5498-SA			

5   If you checked the box on line 3, state in detail why you need an additional extension of time. You must give a reason or your request will be denied. If you need more space, attach additional sheets. Include your name and taxpayer identification number on each additional page.

Under penalties of perjury, I declare that I have examined this form, including any accompanying statements, and, to the best of my knowledge and belief, it is true, correct, and complete.

Signature ▶   Title ▶   Date ▶

General Instructions

Purpose of form. Use Form 8809 to request an extension of time to file any forms shown in line 4 for the current tax year.

How to file. Extensions may be requested:

• Online by completing a fill-in Form 8809 through the FIRE system at *http://fire.irs.gov* for an automatic 30-day extension. Approvals are automatically displayed online if the request is made by the due date of the return.

• Electronically through the FIRE system in a file formatted according to the specifications in Publication 1220, Part D.

• On paper Form 8809, if the request is for one filer. Mail the form to the address shown in *Where to file,* later, or fax it to 1-877-477-0572 (toll free). Requesters will receive an approval or denial letter. You are encouraged to submit your request via the online fill-in form.

Where to file. Send Form 8809 to Internal Revenue Service, Information Returns Branch, Attn: Extension of Time Coordinator, 240 Murall Dr., Mail Stop 4360, Kearneysville, WV 25430.

If you are requesting an extension for more than one filer, you must submit the request electronically or online as a fill-in form.

Information Reporting Customer Service Site. If you have questions about Form 8809, you may call a toll-free number, 1-866-455-7438. You may still use the original telephone number, 304-263-8700 (not toll free). For TTY/TDD equipment, call 304-579-4827 (not toll free). The hours of operation are Monday through Friday from 8:30 a.m. to 4:30 p.m., Eastern time.

Also, see Pub. 1220, Specifications for Filing Forms 1097, 1098, 1099, 3921, 3922, 5498, 8935, and W-2G Electronically; and Pub. 1187, Specifications for Filing Form 1042-S, Foreign Person's U.S. Source Income Subject to Withholding, Electronically. For additional information, see Topic 803, Waivers and Extensions, at *www.irs.gov/taxtopics.*

Note. Specifications for filing Forms W-2, Wage and Tax Statement, electronically are only available from the Social Security Administration (SSA). Call 1-800-772-6270 for more information or visit the SSA's Employer W-2 Filing Instructions & Information page at *www.socialsecurity.gov/employer.*

For Privacy Act and Paperwork Reduction Act Notice, see page 2.   Cat. No. 10322N   Form **8809** (Rev. 5-2011)

When to file. File Form 8809 as soon as you know an extension of time to file is necessary. However, Form 8809 must be filed by the due date of the returns. See the chart below that shows the due dates for filing this form on paper or electronically. Filers and transmitters of Form W-2 whose business has terminated should see *Terminating a business* in the *Special Reporting Situations for Form W-2* section of the General Instructions for Forms W-2 and W-3 to request an extension.

If you are requesting an extension of time to file several types of forms, you may use one Form 8809, but you must file Form 8809 by the earliest due date. For example, if you are requesting an extension of time to file both Forms 1099 and 5498, you must file Form 8809 by February 28 (March 31 if you file electronically). You may complete more than one Form 8809 to avoid this problem. An extension cannot be granted if a request is filed after the due date of the original returns.

The due dates for filing Form 8809 are shown below.

IF you file Form(s) . . .	ON PAPER, then the due date is . . .	ELECTRONICALLY, then the due date is . . .
W-2	Last day of February	March 31
W-2G	February 28	March 31
1042-S	March 15	March 15
1097	February 28	March 31
1098	February 28	March 31
1099	February 28	March 31
3921	February 28	March 31
3922	February 28	March 31
5498	May 31	May 31
8027	Last day of February	March 31

If any due date falls on a Saturday, Sunday, or legal holiday, file by the next business day.

Caution: *You do not have to wait for a response before filing your returns. File your returns as soon as they are ready. For all forms shown in line 4, if you have received a response, do not send a copy of the letter or Form 8809 with your returns. If you have not received a response by the end of the extension period, file your returns. When filing Form 8027 on paper only, attach a copy of your approval letter. If an approval letter has not been received, attach a copy of your timely filed Form 8809.*

Extension period. The automatic extension is 30 days from the original due date. You may request one additional extension of not more than 30 days by submitting a second Form 8809 before the end of the first extension period (see *Line 3*, later). Requests for an additional extension of time to file information returns are not automatically granted. Generally, requests for additional time are granted only in cases of extreme hardship or catastrophic event. The IRS will send you a letter of explanation approving or denying your request for an additional extension.

Note. The automatic and any approved additional request will only extend the due date for filing the returns. It will not extend the due date for furnishing statements to recipients.

Penalty. If you file required information returns late and you have not applied for and received an approved extension of time to file, you may be subject to a late filing penalty. The amount of the penalty is based on when you file the correct information return. For more information on penalties, see part O in the General Instructions for Certain Information Returns, and *Penalties* in the Instructions for Form 1042-S, the Instructions for Form 8027, and the General Instructions for Forms W-2 and W-3.

Specific Instructions

Line 1. Enter the name and complete mailing address, including room or suite number of the filer requesting the extension of time. Use the name and address where you want the response sent. For example, if you are a preparer and want to receive the response, enter your client's complete name, care of (c/o) your firm, and your complete mailing address.

The name and taxpayer identification number (TIN) must be consistent with the name and TIN used on your other returns. Do not use abbreviations.

Enter the name of someone who is familiar with this request whom the IRS can contact if additional information is required. Please provide your telephone number and email address.

Note. Approval or denial notification will be sent only to the person who requested the extension.

Line 2. Enter your nine-digit employer identification number (EIN) or qualified intermediary employer identification number (QI-EIN). If you are not required to have an EIN or QI-EIN, enter your social security number. Do not enter hyphens.

Line 3. Check this box if you have already received the automatic 30-day extension, but you need an additional extension for the same year and for the same forms. Do not check this box unless you received an original extension.

If you check this box, be sure to complete line 5. Then sign and date the request.

Signature. No signature is required for the automatic 30-day extension. For an additional extension, Form 8809 must be signed by you or a person who is duly authorized to sign a return, statement, or other document.

Privacy Act and Paperwork Reduction Act Notice. We ask for the information on this form to carry out the Internal Revenue laws of the United States. Form 8809 is provided by the IRS to request an extension of time to file information returns. Section 6081 and its regulations require you to provide the requested information if you desire an extension of time for filing an information return. If you do not provide the requested information, an extension of time for filing an information return may not be granted. Section 6109 requires you to provide your taxpayer identification number (TIN). Routine uses of this information include giving it to the Department of Justice for civil and criminal litigation, and to cities, states, the District of Columbia, and U.S. commonwealths and possessions for use in administering their tax laws. We may also disclose this information to other countries under a tax treaty, or to federal and state agencies to enforce federal nontax criminal laws, or to federal law enforcement and intelligence agencies to combat terrorism.

You are not required to provide the information requested on a form that is subject to the Paperwork Reduction Act unless the form displays a valid OMB control number. Books or records relating to a form or its instructions must be retained as long as their contents may become material in the administration of any Internal Revenue law. Generally, tax returns and return information are confidential, as required by Code section 6103.

The time needed to complete and file this form will vary depending on individual circumstances. The estimated average time is: Recordkeeping, 4 hrs., 4 min.; Learning about the law or the form, 18 min.; Preparing and sending the form to the IRS, 22 min.

If you have comments concerning the accuracy of these time estimates or suggestions for making this form simpler, we would be happy to hear from you. You can write to the Tax Products Coordinating Committee, SE:W:CAR:MP:T:T:SP, 1111 Constitution Ave. NW, IR-6526, Washington, DC 20224. Do not send the form to this address. Instead, see *Where to file* on page 1.

Form **8846**	Credit for Employer Social Security and Medicare Taxes Paid on Certain Employee Tips	OMB No. 1545-1414

Department of the Treasury
Internal Revenue Service

► **Attach to your tax return.**
► **Information about Form 8846 and its instructions is at** *www.irs.gov/form8846*

2012
Attachment
Sequence No. **98**

Name(s) shown on return	Identifying number

Note. Claim this credit **only** for social security and Medicare taxes paid by a food or beverage establishment where tipping is customary for providing food or beverages. See the instructions for line 1.

1	Tips received by employees for services on which you paid or incurred employer social security and Medicare taxes during the tax year (see instructions)	**1**	
2	Tips not subject to the credit provisions (see instructions)	**2**	
3	Creditable tips. Subtract line 2 from line 1	**3**	
4	Multiply line 3 by 7.65% (.0765). If you had any tipped employees whose wages (including tips) exceeded $110,100, see instructions and check here . . . . . ► ☐	**4**	
5	Credit for employer social security and Medicare taxes paid on certain employee tips from partnerships and S corporations	**5**	
6	Add lines 4 and 5. Partnerships and S corporations, report this amount on Schedule K. All others, report this amount on Form 3800, line 4f	**6**	

For Paperwork Reduction Act Notice, see instructions.   Cat. No. 16148Z   Form **8846** (2012)

General Instructions

Section references are to the Internal Revenue Code.

Future Developments

For the latest information about developments related to Form 8846 and its instructions, such as legislation enacted after they were published, go to *www.irs.gov/form8846*.

Purpose of Form

Certain food and beverage establishments (see *Who Should File,* below) use Form 8846 to claim a credit for social security and Medicare taxes paid or incurred by the employer on certain employees' tips. The credit is part of the general business credit.

You can claim or elect not to claim the credit any time within 3 years from the due date of your return on either your original return or on an amended return.

Taxpayers, other than partnerships or S corporations, whose only source of this credit is from those pass-through entities, are not required to complete or file this form. Instead, report this credit directly on the applicable line of Form 3800, General Business Credit.

Who Should File

File Form 8846 if you meet both of the following conditions.

1. You had employees who received tips from customers for providing, delivering, or serving food or beverages for consumption if tipping of employees for delivering or serving food or beverages is customary.

2. During the tax year, you paid or incurred employer social security and Medicare taxes on those tips.

How the Credit Is Figured

Generally, the credit equals the amount of employer social security and Medicare taxes paid or incurred by the employer on tips received by the employee. However, the amount of tips for any month that are used to figure the credit must be reduced by the amount by which the wages that would have been payable during that month at $5.15 an hour exceed the wages (excluding tips) paid by the employer during that month.

For example, an employee worked 100 hours and received $450 in tips for October 2012. The worker received $375 in wages (excluding tips) at the rate of $3.75 an hour. If the employee had been paid $5.15 an hour, the employee would have received wages, excluding tips, of $515. For credit purposes, the $450 in tips is reduced by $140 (the difference between $515 and $375), and only $310 of the employee's tips for October 2012 is taken into account.

Specific Instructions

Figure the current year credit from your trade or business on lines 1 through 4.

Line 1

Enter the tips received by employees for services on which you paid or incurred employer social security and Medicare taxes during the tax year.

Include tips received from customers for providing, delivering, or serving food or beverages for consumption if tipping of employees for delivering or serving food or beverages is customary.

Line 2

If you pay each tipped employee wages (excluding tips) equal to or more than $5.15 an hour, enter zero on line 2.

Figure the amount of tips included on line 1 that are not creditable for each employee on a monthly basis. This is the total amount that would be payable to the employee at $5.15 an hour reduced by the wages (excluding tips) actually paid to the employee during the month. Enter on line 2 the total amounts figured for all employees.

Line 4

If any tipped employee's wages and tips exceeded the 2012 social security tax wage base of $110,100 subject to the 6.2% rate, check the box on line 4 and attach a separate computation showing the amount of tips subject to only the Medicare tax rate of 1.45%. Subtract these tips from the line 3 tips, and multiply the difference by .0765. Then, multiply the tips subject only to the Medicare tax by .0145. Enter the sum of these amounts on line 4.

Reduce the income tax deduction for employer social security and Medicare taxes by the amount on line 4.

Form **8919**

Department of the Treasury
Internal Revenue Service

Uncollected Social Security and Medicare Tax on Wages

▶ Information about Form 8919 and its instructions is at *www.irs.gov/form8919.*

▶ Attach to your tax return.

OMB No. 1545-0074

2012

Attachment
Sequence No. **72**

Name of person who must file this form. If married, complete a separate Form 8919 for each spouse who must file this form. | Social security number

Who must file. You must file Form 8919 if **all** of the following apply.
- You performed services for a firm.
- You believe your pay from the firm was not for services as an independent contractor.
- The firm did not withhold your share of social security and Medicare taxes from your pay.
- One of the reasons listed below under *Reason codes* applies to you.

Reason codes: For each firm listed below, enter in column (c) the applicable reason code for filing this form. If none of the reason codes apply to you, but you believe you should have been treated as an employee, enter reason code G, and **file Form SS-8 on or before the date you file your tax return.**

A I filed Form SS-8 and received a determination letter stating that I am an employee of this firm.

C I received other correspondence from the IRS that states I am an employee.

G I filed Form SS-8 with the IRS and have not received a reply.

H I received a Form W-2 and a Form 1099-MISC from this firm for 2012. The amount on Form 1099-MISC should have been included as wages on Form W-2. **(Do not file Form SS-8 if you select reason code H.)**

	(a) Name of firm	(b) Firm's federal identification number (see instructions)	(c) Enter reason code from above	(d) Date of IRS determination or correspondence (MM/DD/YYYY) (see instructions)	(e) Check if Form 1099-MISC was received	(f) Total wages received with no social security or Medicare tax withholding and not reported on Form W-2
1					☐	
2					☐	
3					☐	
4					☐	
5					☐	

6	**Total wages.** Combine lines 1 through 5 in column (f). Enter here and include on Form 1040, line 7; Form 1040NR, line 8; or 1040NR-EZ, line 3	**6**	
7	Maximum amount of wages subject to social security tax . . .	**7**	110,100 00
8	Total social security wages and tips (total of boxes 3 and 7 on Form(s) W-2) or railroad retirement (tier 1) compensation, and unreported tips subject to social security tax from Form 4137, line 10	**8**	
9	Subtract line 8 from line 7. If line 8 is more than line 7, enter -0- here and on line 10	**9**	
10	Wages subject to social security tax. Enter the smaller of line 6 or line 9	**10**	
11	Multiply line 10 by .042 (social security tax rate for 2012)	**11**	
12	Multiply line 6 by .0145 (Medicare tax rate)	**12**	
13	Add lines 11 and 12. Enter here and on Form 1040, line 57; Form 1040NR, line 55; or Form 1040NR-EZ, line 16. (Form 1040-SS and Form 1040-PR filers, see instructions) . . . ▶	**13**	

For Paperwork Reduction Act Notice, see your tax return instructions. | Cat. No. 37730B | Form **8919** (2012)

Future Developments

For the latest information about developments related to Form 8919 and its instructions, such as legislation enacted after they were published, go to *www.irs.gov/form8919*.

What's New

Changes to reason codes. Former reason codes B, D, E, and F have been eliminated. Enter only one reason code on each line of column (c). Previously, more than one reason code could be entered.

Increase in wage amount subject to social security tax. On line 7, the maximum amount of wages subject to social security tax has increased from $106,800 to $110,100 for 2012.

Continuation of 4.2% social security tax rate. On line 11, the social security tax rate remains at 4.2% for 2012.

General Instructions

Purpose of form. Use Form 8919 to figure and report your share of the uncollected social security and Medicare taxes due on your compensation if you were an employee but were treated as an independent contractor by your employer. By filing this form, your social security and Medicare taxes will be credited to your social security record. For an explanation of the difference between an independent contractor and an employee, see Pub. 1779, Independent Contractor or Employee, available at IRS.gov.

 Do not use this form:

• *For services you performed as an independent contractor. Instead, use Schedule C (Form 1040), Profit or Loss From Business, or Schedule C-EZ (Form 1040), Net Profit From Business, to report the income. And use Schedule SE (Form 1040), Self-Employment Tax, to figure the tax on net earnings from self-employment.*

• *To figure the social security and Medicare tax owed on tips you did not report to your employer, including any allocated tips shown on your Form(s) W-2 that you must report as income. Instead, use Form 4137, Social Security and Medicare Tax on Unreported Tip Income.*

Firm. For purposes of this form, the term "firm" means any individual, business enterprise, company, nonprofit organization, state, or other entity for which you performed services. This firm may or may not have paid you directly for these services.

Form SS-8, Determination of Worker Status for Purposes of Federal Employment Taxes and Income Tax Withholding. File Form SS-8 if you want the IRS to determine whether you are an independent contractor or an employee. See the form instructions for information on completing the form. **If you select reason code G, you must file Form SS-8 on or before the date you file Form 8919. Do not attach Form SS-8 to your tax return. Form SS-8 must be filed separately.**

Specific Instructions

Lines 1 through 5. Complete a separate line for each firm. If you worked as an employee for more than five firms in 2012, attach additional Form(s) 8919 with lines 1 through 5 completed. Complete lines 6 through 13 on only one Form 8919. The line 6 amount on that Form 8919 should be the combined totals of all lines 1 through 5 of all your Forms 8919.

Column (a). Enter the name of the firm for which you worked. If you received a Form 1099-MISC from the firm, enter the firm's name exactly as it is entered on Form 1099-MISC.

Column (b). The federal identification number for a firm can be an employer identification number (EIN) or a social security number (SSN) (if the firm is an individual). An EIN is a nine-digit number assigned by the IRS to a business. Enter an EIN like this: XX-XXXXXXX. Enter an SSN like this: XXX-XX-XXXX. If you received a Form 1099-MISC from the firm, enter the firm's federal identification number that is entered on Form 1099-MISC. If you do not know the firm's federal identification number, you can use Form W-9, Request for Taxpayer Identification Number and Certification, to request it from the firm. If you are unable to obtain the number, enter "unknown."

Column (c). Enter the reason code for why you are filing this form. If none of the reason codes apply to you, but you believe you should have been treated as an employee, enter reason code G, and **file Form SS-8 on or before the date you file your tax return. Do not attach Form SS-8 to your tax return. Form SS-8 must be filed separately.**

Enter reason code C if you were designated as a "section 530 employee" by the IRS. You are a section 530 employee, for these purposes, if you were determined to be an employee by the IRS prior to January 1, 1997, but your employer was granted relief from payment of employment taxes under Section 530 of the Revenue Act of 1978.

Enter reason code H if you received both a Form W-2 and a Form 1099-MISC from the firm and the amount on the Form 1099-MISC should have been included as wages on Form W-2 as an amount you received for services you provided as an employee. If reason code H applies to your situation, **do not file Form SS-8.** Examples of amounts that are sometimes erroneously included on Form 1099-MISC that should be reported as wages on Form W-2 include employee bonuses, awards, travel expense reimbursements not paid under an accountable plan, scholarships, and signing bonuses. Generally, amounts paid by an employer to an employee are not reported on Form 1099-MISC. Form 1099-MISC is used for reporting nonemployee compensation, rents, royalties, and certain other payments.

 If you enter reason code G, you or the firm that paid you may be contacted for additional information. Use of this reason code is not a guarantee that the IRS will agree with your worker status determination. *If the IRS does not agree that you are an employee, you may be billed for the additional tax, penalties, and interest resulting from the change to your worker status.*

Column (d). Complete only if reason code A or C is entered in column (c).

Line 13. Form 1040-SS and Form 1040-PR filers, the amount on line 13 should be included in the line 5 amount on your Form 1040-SS or Form 1040-PR, whichever you file. See the instructions for those forms for directions on how to report the tax due on line 5 of those forms.

Form **8952**

(Rev. December 2012)

Department of the Treasury
Internal Revenue Service

Application for Voluntary
Classification Settlement Program (VCSP)

▶ **Do not** send payment with Form 8952.

▶ **Information about Form 8952 and its separate instructions is at** *www.irs.gov/form8952.*

OMB No. 1545-2215

Caution. *Taxpayer must make certain representations in order to be eligible to participate in the VCSP. These representations can be found in Part V on page 2.*

Part I   Taxpayer Information

1 Taxpayer's name

2 Employer identification number (EIN)

3 Number and street (or P.O. box number if mail is not delivered to a street address)

Room/Suite

4 City, town or post office, state, and ZIP code

5 Telephone number

6 Website address (optional)

7 Fax number (optional)

8 Email address (optional)

9 Type of entity.   Check the applicable box:
- ☐ Sole proprietorship
- ☐ Joint venture
- ☐ Partnership
- ☐ C corporation
- ☐ S corporation
- ☐ Cooperative organization described in section 1381 of the Internal Revenue Code
- ☐ Tax-exempt organization
- ☐ State or local government (for worker class or position not covered under a section 218 agreement)
- ☐ Other (specify here) _____

10 Are you a member of an affiliated group?
☐ Yes   ☐ No
If "Yes," complete the common parent information on lines 11-14.
If "No," skip to Part II.

11 Name of common parent of the affiliated group

12 EIN of common parent

13 Number and street (or P.O. box number if mail is not delivered to a street address) of common parent

14 City, town or post office, state, and ZIP code of common parent

Part II   Contact Person

Attach a properly completed Form 2848, Power of Attorney and Declaration of Representative, if applicable.
- Name and title of contact person _____
- Contact person's number and street (or P.O. box number if mail is not delivered to a street address) _____
- Contact person's city, town or post office, state, and ZIP code _____
- Contact person's telephone number _____
- Contact person's fax number (optional) _____
- Contact person's email address (optional) _____

Part III   General Information About Workers To Be Reclassified

15 Enter the total number of workers from all classes to be reclassified. A class of workers includes all workers who perform the same or similar services.

16 Enter a description of the class or classes of workers to be reclassified. If more space is needed, attach separate sheets (see instructions).

17 Enter the beginning date of the employment tax period (calendar year or quarter) for which you want to begin treating the class or classes of workers as employees. This date should be at least 60 days after the date you file Form 8952 (see instructions).

      /   /

For Privacy Act and Paperwork Reduction Act Notice, see separate instructions.   Cat. No. 37772H   Form **8952** (Rev. 12-2012)

Taxpayer's name	Employer identification number (EIN)

Part IV Payment Calculation Using Section 3509(a) Rates (see instructions)

18	Enter total compensation paid in the most recently completed calendar year to all workers to be reclassified (see instructions)	18		
19	Multiply line 18 by 3.24% (.0324)		19	
20	Enter any compensation included on line 18 that exceeded the social security wage base for any worker or workers for the most recently completed calendar year (see instructions)	20		
21	Subtract line 20 from line 18	21		
22	Multiply line 21 by 7.04% (.0704)		22	
23	Add lines 19 and 22		23	
24	Multiply line 23 by 10% (.10). This is the VCSP payment you will pay when you submit your signed closing agreement (see instructions)		24	

Part V Taxpayer Representations

Caution. *Since the representations include the penalty of perjury statement, the representations under Part V must be signed by the taxpayer, not the taxpayer's representative.*

A Treatment of Workers

1. Taxpayer wants to voluntarily reclassify certain workers as employees for federal income tax withholding, Federal Insurance Contributions Act, and Federal Unemployment Tax Act taxes (collectively, federal employment taxes) for future tax periods.
2. Taxpayer is presently treating the workers as nonemployees.
3. Taxpayer has filed all required Forms 1099 for each of the workers to be reclassified for the 3 preceding calendar years ending before the date of this application.
4. Taxpayer has consistently treated the workers as nonemployees.
5. There is no current dispute between the taxpayer and the IRS as to whether the class or classes of workers are nonemployees or employees for federal employment tax purposes.

B Examination

1. Taxpayer or, if applicable, any member of the taxpayer's affiliated group, is not under employment tax examination by the IRS.
2. Taxpayer is not under examination by the Department of Labor or any state agency concerning the proper classification of the class or classes of workers.
3a. Taxpayer has not been examined previously by the IRS or the Department of Labor concerning the proper classification of the class or classes of workers; or,
   b. Taxpayer has been examined previously by the IRS or the Department of Labor concerning the proper classification of the class or classes of workers and the taxpayer has complied with the results of the prior examination.

Caution. *Do not send payment with Form 8952. You will submit payment later with your signed closing agreement. If you submit payment with Form 8952, it may cause a processing delay.*

Sign Here	Under penalties of perjury, I declare that I have examined this submission, including any accompanying documents, and to the best of my knowledge and belief, all of the facts contained herein are true, correct, and complete.		
	Taxpayer's signature ▶		Date

Paid Preparer Use Only	Print/Type preparer's name	Preparer's signature	Date	Check ☐ if self-employed	PTIN
	Firm's name ▶		Firm's EIN ▶		
	Firm's address ▶		Phone no.		

Form **8952** (Rev. 12-2012)

Instructions for Form 8952

(Rev. December 2012)

Department of the Treasury
Internal Revenue Service

Application for Voluntary Classification Settlement Program (VCSP)

Section references are to the Internal Revenue Code unless otherwise noted.

General Instructions

Future Developments

For the latest information about developments related to Form 8952 and its instructions, such as legislation enacted after they were published, go to *www.irs.gov/form8952*.

Purpose of Form

Use Form 8952 to apply for the Voluntary Classification Settlement Program.

 DO NOT *send payment with Form 8952. You will submit payment later with a signed closing agreement. If you submit payment with Form 8952, it may cause a processing delay.*

Voluntary Classification Settlement Program (VCSP)

The VCSP provides an opportunity for taxpayers to voluntarily reclassify workers as employees for federal employment tax purposes. The VCSP allows eligible taxpayers to obtain relief similar to that available through the Classification Settlement Program (CSP) for taxpayers under examination.

The VCSP is an optional program that provides taxpayers not under an employment tax examination with an opportunity to voluntarily reclassify their workers as employees for future tax periods with limited federal employment tax liability for past non-employee treatment. To participate in the program, the taxpayer must meet certain eligibility requirements, apply to participate in the VCSP, and enter into a closing agreement with the IRS.

For more information on the VCSP, see Announcement 2012-45 in Internal Revenue Bulletin 2012-51 available at *www.irs.gov/irb*.

Eligibility Requirements

To participate in the VCSP, taxpayers must meet certain eligibility requirements and certify on Form 8952 that they meet these requirements.

Specifically, to be eligible for the VCSP, a taxpayer must:

1. Want to voluntarily reclassify certain workers as employees for federal income tax withholding, Federal Insurance Contributions Act (FICA), and Federal Unemployment Tax Act (FUTA) taxes (collectively, federal employment taxes) for future tax periods;

2. Be presently treating the workers as non-employees;

3. Have filed all required Forms 1099 for each of the workers to be reclassified for the 3 preceding calendar years ending before the date Form 8952 is filed. A taxpayer will meet this requirement if it filed all required Forms 1099 for the workers being reclassified for the period of time that the workers worked for the taxpayer. For example, a taxpayer

who has only been in business for 2 years meets this requirement if the taxpayer filed all required Forms 1099 for the workers being reclassified for those 2 years;

 Taxpayers who are otherwise eligible but have not filed all required Forms 1099 may apply for a modified version of the VCSP available through June 30, 2013. For details, see Announcement 2012-46 in Internal Revenue Bulletin 2012-51 available at www.irs.gov/ irb.

4. Have consistently treated the workers as non-employees;

5. Have no current dispute with the IRS as to whether the workers are non-employees or employees for federal employment tax purposes;

6. Not be under employment tax examination by the IRS. If the taxpayer is a member of an affiliated group, this requirement is met only if no member of the affiliated group is under employment tax examination by the IRS;

7. Not be under examination by the Department of Labor or any state agency concerning the proper classification of the class or classes of workers; and

8.

a. Not have been examined previously by the IRS or the Department of Labor concerning the proper classification of the class or classes of workers; or

b. If the taxpayer has been examined previously by the IRS or the Department of Labor concerning the proper classification of the class or classes of workers, the taxpayer must have complied with the results of the prior examination.

When To File

File Form 8952 at any time. However, Form 8952 should be filed at least 60 days before the date you want to begin treating the class or classes of workers as employees.

Where To File

Mail Form 8952 to the following address.

Internal Revenue Service
Government Entities Compliance Unit
P.O. Box 12220
Ogden, UT 84412

Private delivery services. You can use certain private delivery services designated by the IRS. These private delivery services include only the following.
• DHL Express (DHL): DHL Same Day Service.
• Federal Express (FedEx): FedEx Priority Overnight, FedEx Standard Overnight, FedEx 2Day, FedEx International Priority, and FedEx International First.
• United Parcel Service (UPS): UPS Next Day Air, UPS Next Day Air Saver, UPS 2nd Day Air, UPS 2nd Day Air A.M., UPS Worldwide Express Plus, and UPS Worldwide Express.

The private delivery service can tell you how to get written proof of the mailing date.

Dec 05, 2012   Cat. No. 58045V

Private delivery services cannot deliver items to P.O. boxes. When using a private delivery service, mail Form 8952 to the following address.

Internal Revenue Service
Government Entities Compliance Unit
1973 N. Rulon White Blvd.
Mail Stop 7700
Ogden, UT 84404

Who Must Sign

Form 8952 must be signed by the taxpayer under penalties of perjury. The taxpayer's representative may not sign for the taxpayer. By signing Form 8952, including all representations in Part V, you (see below) are representing that the taxpayer is eligible for this program and that all information presented is correct to the best of your knowledge.

For a sole proprietorship, the form must be signed and dated by the individual who owns the business.

For a corporation (including a limited liability company (LLC) treated as a corporation), the form must be signed and dated by:
• The president, vice president, treasurer, assistant treasurer, chief accounting officer; or
• Any other corporate officer (such as tax officer) authorized to sign.

For a partnership, the form must be signed and dated by a general partner. For an LLC classified as a partnership, the form must be signed by a member or manager who would be authorized to sign the partnership's Form 1065. For more information on who can sign for a partnership, see the Instructions for Form 1065.

For an estate or trust, the form must be signed and dated by the fiduciary or an authorized representative. If there are joint fiduciaries or representatives, only one is required to sign the form.

If the form is filed on behalf of the taxpayer by a receiver, trustee, or assignee, the fiduciary must sign the form.

Assembling the Application

To ensure the application is both timely and correctly processed, attach all documents in the following order.

1. Form 8952.
2. Form 2848, Power of Attorney and Declaration of Representative, if applicable. See the instructions for Part II.

Complete every applicable entry space on Form 8952. Do not enter "See Attached" instead of completing the entry spaces. If more space is needed, attach separate sheets using the same size and format as the printed forms. If there are supporting statements and attachments, arrange them in the same order as the lines they support and attach them last. Show the total dollar figure on Part IV of Form 8952. Enter the taxpayer's name and EIN at the top of each supporting statement or attachment.

Specific Instructions

Line 2. Employer Identification Number (EIN)

Enter the taxpayer's EIN. If the taxpayer does not have an EIN, the taxpayer must apply for one. An EIN can be applied for in one of the following ways.

• Online–Click on the EIN link at *www.irs.gov/businesses/small*. The EIN is issued immediately once the application information is validated.
• By telephone at 1-800-829-4933.
• By faxing or mailing Form SS-4, Application for Employer Identification Number.

The taxpayer must have received an EIN by the time Form 8952 is filed for the form to be processed. For more information about EINs, see Publication 1635, Understanding Your EIN.

Line 10

Check the box that applies. If you are not a member of an affiliated group, you can skip lines 11-14.

An affiliated group is one or more chains of includible corporations (section 1504(a)) connected through stock ownership with a common parent corporation. The common parent must be an includible corporation and the following requirements must be met.
• The common parent must own directly stock that represents at least 80% of the total voting power and at least 80% of the total value of the stock of at least one of the other includible corporations.
• Stock that represents at least 80% of the total voting power and at least 80% of the total value of the stock of each of the other corporations (except for the common parent) must be owned directly by one or more of the other includible corporations.

For this purpose, the term "stock" generally does not include any stock that (a) is nonvoting, (b) is nonconvertible, (c) is limited and preferred as to dividends and does not participate significantly in corporate growth, and (d) has redemption and liquidation rights that do not exceed the issue price of the stock (except for a reasonable redemption or liquidation premium). See section 1504(a)(4).

Part II

The contact person is the person the IRS may contact if there is an issue with the application. If the contact person does not have legal authority to bind the taxpayer, the taxpayer must attach to Form 8952 a properly executed Form 2848. On Form 2848, line 3, enter "Voluntary Classification Settlement Program" as the type of tax. Leave the entry spaces for Tax Form Number and for Year(s) or Period(s) blank. Check the box on line 4 of the Form 2848.

Line 16

If more space is needed, attach separate sheets. Enter the taxpayer's name and EIN at the top of each sheet.

Line 17

Enter the beginning date of the employment tax period (calendar year or quarter) for which you want to begin treating the class or classes of workers as employees. To allow the IRS time to process your application, this date should be at least 60 days after the date you file Form 8952.

 The IRS will make every effort to process Form 8952 with sufficient time to allow for the voluntary reclassification on the requested date.

Example. If you want to begin treating a class or classes of workers as employees for the first quarter of 2013, you will enter January 1, 2013. In this case, you should file Form 8952 as soon as possible.

If you want to begin treating a class or classes of workers as employees for the fourth quarter of 2013, you will enter October 1, 2013. In this case you should file Form 8952 at least 60 days before October 1, 2013, or by August 2, 2013.

Line 18

Enter total compensation paid in the most recently completed calendar year to all workers to be reclassified.

 Nonemployee compensation of $600 or more can generally be found reported in box 7 of the Form 1099-MISC, Miscellaneous Income, filed for the worker for the most recently completed calendar year. See the instructions for box 7 of Form 1099-MISC for details.

Line 20

The social security wage base is applied on an employee by employee basis. The social security wage base for calendar year 2011 was $106,800. The social security wage base for calendar year 2012 is $110,100. The social security wage base for calendar year 2013 will be $113,700.

Example. A taxpayer filing Form 8952 in December of 2012 with one worker would look to compensation paid to the worker in 2011 because 2011 is the most recently completed calendar year. If the worker received $125,000 in compensation in 2011, the taxpayer would subtract $106,800 from $125,000 and enter $18,200 on line 20.

Line 24

Multiply the amount on line 23 by 10% (.10). This is the amount required to be paid upon IRS acceptance of your application and execution of your VCSP closing agreement. **DO NOT** send payment with Form 8952. You will submit payment later with a signed closing agreement. If you submit payment with Form 8952, it may cause a processing delay.

Paid Preparer Use Only

A paid preparer must sign Form 8952 and provide the information in the *Paid Preparer Use Only* section at the end of the form if the preparer was paid to prepare the form and is not an employee of the filing entity. Paid preparers must sign paper forms with a manual signature. The preparer must give you a copy of the form in addition to the copy to be filed with the IRS.

If you are a paid preparer, enter your Preparer Tax Identification Number (PTIN) in the space provided. If you work for a tax preparation firm, you must also enter the firm's name, address, and EIN. However, you cannot use the PTIN of the tax preparation firm in place of your PTIN.

You can apply for a PTIN online or by filing Form W-12, IRS Paid Preparer Tax Identification Number (PTIN) Application and Renewal. For more information about applying for a PTIN online, visit the IRS website at *www.irs.gov/taxpros*.

Generally, do not complete this section if you are filing the form as a reporting agent and have a valid Form 8655, Reporting Agent Authorization, on file with the IRS. However, a reporting agent must complete this section if the reporting agent offered legal advice, for example, advising the client on determining whether its workers are employees or independent contractors for federal tax purposes.

Privacy Act and Paperwork Reduction Act Notice. We ask for the information on this form to carry out the Internal Revenue laws of the United States. We need this information to determine your eligibility to participate in this program and to calculate the appropriate payment under the VCSP. Our authority to ask for the information on this form is Subtitle C, Employment Taxes, of the Internal Revenue Code. Section 6109 requires you to provide your identifying number. You are not required to apply for the VCSP; however, if you apply you must provide the information requested. Failure to provide all the requested information may prevent the processing of your application; providing false or fraudulent information may subject you to penalties. We may disclose this information to the Department of Justice for civil or criminal litigation, and to cities, states, the District of Columbia, and U.S. commonwealths and possessions for use in administering their tax laws. We may also disclose this information to other countries under a tax treaty, to federal and state agencies to enforce federal non-tax criminal laws and to intelligence agencies to combat terrorism.

You are not required to provide the information requested on a form that is subject to the Paperwork Reduction Act unless the form displays a valid OMB control number. Books or records relating to a form or its instructions must be retained as long as their contents may become material in the administration of any Internal Revenue law. Generally, tax returns and return information are confidential, as required by section 6103.

The time needed to complete and file this form will vary depending on individual circumstances. The estimated burden for taxpayers who file this form is shown below:

Recordkeeping	6 hrs., 56 min.
Learning about the law or the form	18 min.
Preparing and sending the form to the IRS . . .	25 min.

If you have comments concerning the accuracy of these time estimates or suggestions for making this form simpler, we would be happy to hear from you. You can write to the Internal Revenue Service, Tax Products Coordinating Committee, SE:W:CAR:MP:T:M:S, 1111 Constitution Ave. NW, IR-6526, Washington, DC 20224. Do not send this form to this office. Instead, see *Where To File*, earlier.

Instructions for Form 8952 -3-

Form **14196** (November 2010)	Department of the Treasury — Internal Revenue Service **Filing Statement**

Complete the following information:

Establishment name

_____

Establishment address

_____

Employer Identification Number	Daytime telephone number (including area code) ( )

Complete and sign the following statement:

I, _____ , under penalties of perjury, do certify that I did not meet
       (Print Name and Title)
any of the Requirements, as explained in this letter, for filing Form 8027, *Employer's Annual Information Return of Tip*

Income and Allocated Tips, for the year _____ .

I did not meet the requirements because _____

_____

_____

_____

_____

NOTE: If you were not required to file because you did not employ more than 10 employees who together worked more than 80 hours on a typical business day, please send us a completed copy of the Worksheet for Determining Whether to File Form 8027 (included in the instructions for completing the Form 8027 return), when you send us the completed statement.

_____	_____
Signature and Title	**Date**

INCOME WITHHOLDING FOR SUPPORT

- ☐ **ORIGINAL INCOME WITHHOLDING ORDER/NOTICE FOR SUPPORT (IWO)**
- ☐ **AMENDED IWO**
- ☐ **ONE-TIME ORDER/NOTICE FOR LUMP SUM PAYMENT**
- ☐ **TERMINATION of IWO**   Date: _____

☐ Child Support Enforcement (CSE) Agency   ☐ Court   ☐ Attorney   ☐ Private Individual/Entity   (Check One)

NOTE: This IWO must be regular on its face. Under certain circumstances you must reject this IWO and return it to the sender (see IWO instructions http://www.acf.hhs.gov/programs/cse/newhire/employer/publication/publication.htm - forms). If you receive this document from someone other than a State or Tribal CSE agency or a Court, a copy of the underlying order must be attached.

State/Tribe/Territory _____   Remittance Identifier (include w/payment) _____
City/County/Dist./Tribe _____   Order Identifier_____
Private Individual/Entity _____   CSE Agency Case Identifier _____

RE: _____

Employer/Income Withholder's Name   Employee/Obligor's Name (Last, First, Middle)

Employer/Income Withholder's Address   Employee/Obligor's Social Security Number

                                                      Custodial Party/Obligee's Name (Last, First, Middle)

Employer/Income Withholder's FEIN _____

Child(ren)'s Name(s) (Last, First, Middle)   Child(ren)'s Birth Date(s)

ORDER INFORMATION: This document is based on the support or withholding order from _____ (State/Tribe). You are required by law to deduct these amounts from the employee/obligor's income until further notice.

$ _____ Per_____ current child support
$ _____ Per_____ past-due child support - **Arrears greater than 12 weeks?** ☐ Yes ☐No
$ _____ Per_____ current cash medical support
$ _____ Per_____ past-due cash medical support
$ _____ Per_____ current spousal support
$ _____ Per_____ past-due spousal support
$ _____ Per_____ other (must specify) _____.
for a **Total Amount to Withhold** of $ _____ per _____.

AMOUNTS TO WITHHOLD: You do not have to vary your pay cycle to be in compliance with the *Order Information*. If your pay cycle does not match the ordered payment cycle, withhold one of the following amounts:
$ _____ per weekly pay period $ _____ per semimonthly pay period (twice a month)
$ _____ per biweekly pay period (every two weeks)$_____ per monthly pay period
$ _____ **Lump Sum Payment:** Do not stop any existing IWO unless you receive a termination order.

REMITTANCE INFORMATION: If the employee/obligor's principal place of employment is_____(State/Tribe), you must begin withholding no later than the first pay period that occurs_____days after the date of_____. Send payment within_____working days of the pay date. If you cannot withhold the full amount of support for any or all orders for this employee/obligor, withhold up to_____% of disposable income for all orders. If the employee/obligor's principal place of employment is not_____(State/Tribe), obtain withholding limitations, time requirements, and any allowable employer fees at http://www.acf.hhs.gov/programs/cse/newhire/employer/contacts/contact_map.htm for the employee/obligor's principal place of employment.

Document Tracking Identifier_____   OMB 0970-0154

A-434

For electronic payment requirements and centralized payment collection and disbursement facility information (State Disbursement Unit [SDU]), see http://www.acf.hhs.gov/programs/cse/newhire/employer/contacts/contact_map.htm.

Include the **Remittance Identifier** with the payment and if necessary this FIPS code: _____ .

Remit payment to _____ (SDU/Tribal Order Payee)
at _____ (SDU/Tribal Payee Address)

☐ **Return to Sender [Completed by Employer/Income Withholder].** Payment must be directed to an SDU in accordance with 42 USC §666(b)(5) and (b)(6) or Tribal Payee (see Payments to SDU below). If payment is not directed to an SDU/Tribal Payee or this IWO is not regular on its face, you *must* check this box and return the IWO to the sender.

Signature of Judge/Issuing Official (if required by State or Tribal law): _____
Print Name of Judge/Issuing Official: _____
Title of Judge/Issuing Official: _____
Date of Signature: _____

If the employee/obligor works in a State or for a Tribe that is different from the State or Tribe that issued this order, a copy of this IWO must be provided to the employee/obligor.
☐ If checked, the employer/income withholder must provide a copy of this form to the employee/obligor.

ADDITIONAL INFORMATION FOR EMPLOYERS/INCOME WITHHOLDERS

State-specific contact and withholding information can be found on the Federal Employer Services website located at:
http://www.acf.hhs.gov/programs/cse/newhire/employer/contacts/contact_map.htm

Priority: Withholding for support has priority over any other legal process under State law against the same income (USC 42 §666(b)(7)). If a Federal tax levy is in effect, please notify the sender.

Combining Payments: When remitting payments to an SDU or Tribal CSE agency, you may combine withheld amounts from more than one employee/obligor's income in a single payment. You must, however, separately identify each employee/obligor's portion of the payment.

Payments To SDU: You must send child support payments payable by income withholding to the appropriate SDU or to a Tribal CSE agency. If this IWO instructs you to send a payment to an entity other than an SDU (e.g., payable to the custodial party, court, or attorney), you must check the box above and return this notice to the sender. Exception: If this IWO was sent by a Court, Attorney, or Private Individual/Entity and the initial order was entered before January 1, 1994 or the order was issued by a Tribal CSE agency, you must follow the "Remit payment to" instructions on this form.

Reporting the Pay Date: You must report the pay date when sending the payment. The pay date is the date on which the amount was withheld from the employee/obligor's wages. You must comply with the law of the State (or Tribal law if applicable) of the employee/obligor's principal place of employment regarding time periods within which you must implement the withholding and forward the support payments.

Multiple IWOs: If there is more than one IWO against this employee/obligor and you are unable to fully honor all IWOs due to Federal, State, or Tribal withholding limits, you must honor all IWOs to the greatest extent possible, giving priority to current support before payment of any past-due support. Follow the State or Tribal law/procedure of the employee/obligor's principal place of employment to determine the appropriate allocation method.

Lump Sum Payments: You may be required to notify a State or Tribal CSE agency of upcoming lump sum payments to this employee/obligor such as bonuses, commissions, or severance pay. Contact the sender to determine if you are required to report and/or withhold lump sum payments.

Liability: If you have any doubts about the validity of this IWO, contact the sender. If you fail to withhold income from the employee/obligor's income as the IWO directs, you are liable for both the accumulated amount you should have withheld and any penalties set by State or Tribal law/procedure. _____
_____
_____

Anti-discrimination: You are subject to a fine determined under State or Tribal law for discharging an employee/obligor from employment, refusing to employ, or taking disciplinary action against an employee/obligor because of this IWO.
_____
_____

OMB Expiration Date – 05/31/2014. The OMB Expiration Date has no bearing on the termination date of the IWO; it identifies the version of the form currently in use.

Employer's Name: _____   Employer FEIN: _____

Employee/Obligor's Name: _____

CSE Agency Case Identifier: _____   Order Identifier: _____

Withholding Limits: You may not withhold more than the lesser of: 1) the amounts allowed by the Federal Consumer Credit Protection Act (CCPA) (15 U.S.C. 1673(b)); or 2) the amounts allowed by the State or Tribe of the employee/obligor's principal place of employment (see *REMITTANCE INFORMATION*). Disposable income is the net income left after making mandatory deductions such as: State, Federal, local taxes; Social Security taxes; statutory pension contributions; and Medicare taxes. The Federal limit is 50% of the disposable income if the obligor is supporting another family and 60% of the disposable income if the obligor is not supporting another family. However, those limits increase 5% - to 55% and 65% - if the arrears are greater than 12 weeks. If permitted by the State or Tribe, you may deduct a fee for administrative costs. The combined support amount and fee may not exceed the limit indicated in this section.

For Tribal orders, you may not withhold more than the amounts allowed under the law of the issuing Tribe. For Tribal employers/income withholders who receive a State IWO, you may not withhold more than the lesser of the limit set by the law of the jurisdiction in which the employer/income withholder is located or the maximum amount permitted under section 303(d) of the CCPA (15 U.S.C. 1673 (b)).

Depending upon applicable State or Tribal law, you may need to also consider the amounts paid for health care premiums in determining disposable income and applying appropriate withholding limits.

Arrears greater than 12 weeks? If the *Order Information* does not indicate that the arrears are greater than 12 weeks, then the Employer should calculate the CCPA limit using the lower percentage.

Additional Information: _____
_____
_____

NOTIFICATION OF EMPLOYMENT TERMINATION OR INCOME STATUS: If this employee/obligor never worked for you or you are no longer withholding income for this employee/obligor, an employer must promptly notify the CSE agency and/or the sender by returning this form to the address listed in the Contact Information below:

☐   This person has never worked for this employer nor received periodic income.

☐   This person no longer works for this employer nor receives periodic income.

Please provide the following information for the employee/obligor:

Termination date: _____   Last known phone number: _____

Last known address: _____
_____

Final payment date to SDU/ Tribal Payee:_____   Final payment amount: _____

New employer's name:_____

New employer's address:_____

CONTACT INFORMATION:

To Employer/Income Withholder: If you have any questions, contact _____(Issuer name) by phone at_____, by fax at_____, by email or website at: _____ .

Send termination/income status notice and other correspondence to: _____
_____ (Issuer address).

To Employee/Obligor: If the employee/obligor has questions, contact_____(Issuer name) by phone at_____, by fax at_____, by email or website at _____ .

IMPORTANT: The person completing this form is advised that the information may be shared with the employee/obligor.

INCOME WITHHOLDING FOR SUPPORT - Instructions

The Income Withholding for Support (IWO) is the OMB-approved form used for income withholding in Tribal, intrastate, and interstate cases as well as all child support orders which are initially issued in the State on or after January 1, 1994, and all child support orders which are initially issued (or modified) in the State before January 1, 1994 if arrearages occur. This form is the standard format prescribed by the Secretary in accordance with USC 42 §666(b)(6)(A)(ii). Except as noted, the following information must be included.

Please note:
- For the purpose of this IWO form and these instructions, "State" is defined as a State or Territory.

COMPLETED BY SENDER:

1a.   **Original Income Withholding Order/Notice for Support (IWO).** Check the box if this is an original IWO.

1b.   **Amended IWO.** Check the box to indicate that this form amends a previous IWO. Any changes to an IWO must be done through an amended IWO.

1c.   One-Time Order/Notice For **Lump Sum Payment.** Check the box when this IWO is to attach a one-time collection of a lump sum payment. When this box is checked, enter the amount in field 14, Lump Sum Payment, in the *Amounts to Withhold* section. Additional IWOs must be issued to collect subsequent lump sum payments.

1d.   **Termination of IWO.** Check the box to stop income withholding on an IWO. Complete all applicable identifying information to aid the employer/income withholder in terminating the correct IWO.

1e.   **Date.** Date this form is completed and/or signed.

1f.   **Child Support Enforcement (CSE) Agency, Court, Attorney, Private Individual/Entity (Check One).** Check the appropriate box to indicate which entity is sending the IWO. If this IWO is **not** completed by a State or Tribal CSE agency, the sender should contact the CSE agency (see http://www.acf.hhs.gov/programs/cse/newhire/employer/contacts/contact_map.htm) to determine if the CSE agency needs a copy of this form to facilitate payment processing.

NOTE TO EMPLOYER/INCOME WITHHOLDER:

This IWO must be regular on its face. Under the following circumstances, the IWO must be rejected and returned to sender:
- IWO instructs the employer/income withholder to send a payment to an entity other than a State Disbursement Unit (e.g., payable to the custodial party, court, or attorney). Each State is required to operate a State Disbursement Unit (SDU), which is a centralized facility for collection and disbursement of child support payments. Exception: If this IWO is issued by a Court, Attorney, or Private Individual/Entity and the initial child support order was entered before January 1, 1994 or the order was issued by a Tribal CSE agency, the employer/income withholder must follow the payment instructions on the form.
- Form does not contain all information necessary for the employer to comply with the withholding.
- Form is altered or contains invalid information.
- Amount to withhold is not a dollar amount.
- Sender has not used the OMB-approved form for the IWO (effective May 31, 2012).
- A copy of the underlying order is required and not included.

If you receive this document from an Attorney or Private Individual/Entity, a copy of the underlying order containing a provision authorizing income withholding must be attached.

COMPLETED BY SENDER:

1g. **State/Tribe/Territory.** Name of State or Tribe sending this form. This must be a governmental entity of the State or a Tribal organization authorized by a Tribal government to operate a CSE program. If you are a Tribe submitting this form on behalf of another Tribe, complete line 1i.

1h. **Remittance Identifier (include w/payment).** Identifier that employers must include when sending payments for this IWO. The remittance identifier is entered as the case identifier on the Electronic Funds Transfer/Electronic Data Interchange (EFT/EDI) record.

NOTE TO EMPLOYER/INCOME WITHHOLDER:

The employer/income withholder must use the Remittance Identifier when remitting payments so the SDU or Tribe can identify and apply the payment correctly. The remittance identifier is entered as the case identifier on the EFT/EDI record.

COMPLETED BY SENDER:

1i. **City/County/Dist./Tribe.** Name of the city, county or district sending this form. This must be a governmental entity of the State or the name of the Tribe authorized by a Tribal government to operate a CSE program for which this form is being sent. (A Tribe should leave this field blank unless submitting this form on behalf of another Tribe.)

1j. **Order Identifier.** Unique identifier that is associated with a specific child support obligation. It could be a court case number, docket number, or other identifier designated by the sender.

1k. **Private Individual/Entity.** Name of the private individual/entity or non-IV-D Tribal CSE organization sending this form.

1l. **CSE Agency Case Identifier.** Unique identifier assigned to a State or Tribal CSE case. In a State CSE case, this is the identifier that is reported to the Federal Case Registry (FCR). For Tribes this would be either the FCR identifier or other applicable identifier.

Fields 2 and 3 refer to the employee/obligor's employer/income withholder and specific case information.

2a. **Employer/Income Withholder's Name.** Name of employer or income withholder.

2b. **Employer/Income Withholder's Address.** Employer/income withholder's mailing address including street/PO box, city, state and zip code. (This may differ from the employee/obligor's work site.) If the employer/income withholder is a federal government agency, the IWO should be sent to the address listed under Federal Agencies – Addresses for Income Withholding Purposes at http://www.acf.hhs.gov/programs/cse/newhire/contacts/iw_fedcontacts.htm.

2c. **Employer/Income Withholder's FEIN.** Employer/income withholder's nine-digit Federal Employer Identification Number (FEIN) (if available).

3a. **Employee/Obligor's Name.** Employee/obligor's last name, first name, middle name.

3b. **Employee/Obligor's Social Security Number.** Employee/obligor's Social Security number or other taxpayer identification number.

3c. **Custodial Party/Obligee's Name.** Custodial party/obligee's last name, first name, middle name.

3d. **Child(ren)'s Name(s).** Child(ren)'s last name(s), first name(s), middle name(s). (Note: If there are more than six children for this IWO, list additional children's names and birth dates in field 33 - Additional Information).

3e.   **Child(ren)'s Birth Date(s).** Date of birth for each child named.

3f.   **Blank box.** Space for court stamps, bar codes, or other information.

ORDER INFORMATION - Fields 5 through 12 identify the dollar amount to withhold for a specific kind of support (taken directly from the support order) for a specific time period.

NOTE TO EMPLOYER/INCOME WITHHOLDER:

Payments are forwarded to the SDU within each State, unless the order was issued by a Tribal CSE agency. If the order was issued by a Tribal CSE agency, the employer/income withholder must follow the remittance instructions on the form.

COMPLETED BY SENDER:

4.   **State/Tribe.** Name of the State or Tribe that issued the order.

5a-b.   **Current Child Support.** Dollar amount to be withheld **per** the time period (e.g., week, month) specified in the underlying order.

6a-b.   **Past-due Child Support.** Dollar amount to be withheld **per** the time period (e.g., week, month) specified in the underlying order.

6c.   **Arrears Greater Than 12 Weeks?** The appropriate box (Yes/No) must be checked indicating whether arrears are greater than 12 weeks so the employer/income withholder can determine the withholding limit.

7a-b.   **Current Cash Medical Support.** Dollar amount to be withheld **per** the time period (e.g., week, month) specified in the underlying order.

8a-b.   **Past-due Cash Medical Support.** Dollar amount to be withheld **per** the time period (e.g., week, month) specified in the underlying order.

9a-b.   **Current Spousal Support.** (Alimony) dollar amount to be withheld **per** the time period (e.g., week, month) specified in the underlying order.

10a-b. **Past-due Spousal Support.** (Alimony) dollar amount to be withheld **per** the time period (e.g., week, month) specified in the underlying order.

11a-c. **Other.** Miscellaneous obligations dollar amount to be withheld **per** the time period (e.g., week, month) specified in the underlying order. **Must specify.** Description of the obligation.

12a-b. **Total Amount to Withhold.** The total amount of the deductions **per** the corresponding time period. Fields 5a, 6a, 7a, 8a, 9a, 10a, and 11a should total the amount in 12a.

AMOUNTS TO WITHHOLD - Fields 13a through 13d specify the dollar amount to be withheld for this IWO if the employer/income withholder's pay cycle does not correspond with field 12b.

13a.   **Per Weekly Pay Period.** Total amount an employer/income withholder should withhold if the employee/obligor is paid weekly.

13b.   **Per Semimonthly Pay Period.** Total amount an employer/income withholder should withhold if the employee/obligor is paid twice a month.

13c.   **Per Biweekly Pay Period.** Total amount an employer/income withholder should withhold if the employee/obligor is paid every two weeks.

13d.   **Per Monthly Pay Period.** Total amount an employer/income withholder should withhold if the employee/obligor is paid once a month.

14.   **Lump Sum Payment.** Dollar amount to be withheld when the IWO is used to attach a lump sum payment. This field should be used when field 1c is checked.

REMITTANCE INFORMATION

15.   **State/Tribe.** Name of the State or Tribe sending this document.

16.   **Days.** Number of days after the effective date noted in field 17 in which withholding must begin according to the State or Tribal laws/procedures for the employee/obligor's principal place of employment.

17.   **Date.** Effective date of this IWO.

18.   **Working Days.** Number of working days within which an employer/income withholder must remit amounts withheld pursuant to the State or Tribal laws/procedures of the principal place of employment.

19.   **% of Disposable Income.** The percentage of disposable income that may be withheld from the employee/obligor's paycheck.

NOTE TO EMPLOYER/INCOME WITHHOLDER:

For State orders, the employer/income withholder may not withhold more than the lesser of: 1) the amounts allowed by the Federal Consumer Credit Protection Act (15 U.S.C. § 1673(b)); or 2) the amounts allowed by the State of the employee/obligor's principal place of employment.

For Tribal orders, the employer/income withholder may not withhold more than the amounts allowed under the law of the issuing Tribe. For Tribal employer/income withholders who receive a State order, the employer/income withholder may not withhold more than the limit set by the law of the jurisdiction in which the employer/income withholder is located or the maximum amount permitted under section 303(d) of the Federal Consumer Credit Protection Act (15 U.S.C. §1673 (b)).

A federal government agency may withhold from a variety of incomes and forms of payment, including voluntary separation incentive payments (buy-out payments), incentive pay, and cash awards. For a more complete list, see 5 Code of Federal Regulations (CFR) 581.103.

COMPLETED BY SENDER:

20.   **State/Tribe.** Name of the State or Tribe sending this document.

21.   **Document Tracking Identifier.** Optional unique identifier for this form assigned by the sender.

22.   **FIPS Code.** Federal Information Processing Standards (FIPS) code.

23.   **SDU/Tribal Order Payee.** Name of SDU (or payee specified in the underlying Tribal support order) to which payments are required to be sent. Federal law requires payments made by IWO to be sent to the SDU except for payments in which the initial child support order was entered before January 1, 1994 or payments in Tribal CSE orders.

24. **SDU/Tribal Payee Address.** Address of the SDU (or payee specified in the underlying Tribal support order) to which payments are required to be sent. Federal law requires payments made by IWO to be sent to the SDU except for payments in which the initial child support order was entered before January 1, 1994 or payments in Tribal CSE orders.

COMPLETED BY EMPLOYER/INCOME WITHHOLDER:

25. **Return to Sender Checkbox.** The employer/income withholder should check this box and return the IWO to the sender if this IWO is not payable to an SDU or Tribal Payee or this IWO is not regular on its face. Federal law requires payments made by IWO to be sent to the SDU except for payments in which the initial child support order was entered before January 1, 1994 or payments in Tribal CSE orders.

COMPLETED BY SENDER:

26. **Signature of Judge/Issuing Official.** Signature (if required by State or Tribal law) of the official authorizing this IWO.

27. **Print Name of Judge/Issuing Official.** Name of the official authorizing this IWO.

28. **Title of Judge/Issuing Official.** Title of the official authorizing this IWO.

29. **Date of Signature.** Optional date the judge/issuing official signs this IWO.

30. **Copy of IWO checkbox.** If checked, the employer/income withholder is required to provide a copy of the IWO to the employee/obligor.

ADDITIONAL INFORMATION FOR EMPLOYERS/INCOME WITHHOLDERS

The following fields refer to Federal, State, or Tribal laws that apply to issuing an IWO to an employer/income withholder. State- or Tribal-specific information may be included only in the fields below.

COMPLETED BY SENDER:

31. **Liability.** Additional information on the penalty and/or citation of the penalty for an employer/income withholder who fails to comply with the IWO. The State or Tribal law/procedures of the employee/obligor's principal place of employment govern the penalty.

32. **Anti-discrimination.** Additional information on the penalty and/or citation of the penalty for an employer/income withholder who discharges, refuses to employ, or disciplines an employee/obligor as a result of the IWO. The State or Tribal law/procedures of the employee/obligor's principal place of employment govern the penalty.

33. **Additional Information.** Any additional information, e.g., fees the employer/income withholder may charge the obligor for income withholding or children's names and DOBs if there are more than six children on this IWO. Additional information must be consistent with the requirements of the form and the instructions.

COMPLETED BY EMPLOYER/INCOME WITHHOLDER:

NOTIFICATION OF EMPLOYMENT TERMINATION OR INCOME STATUS

The employer must complete this section when the employee/obligor's employment is terminated, income withholding ceases, or if the employee/obligor has never worked for the employer.

Please Note: Employer's Name, FEIN, Employee/Obligor's Name, CSE Agency Case Identifier, and Order Identifier must appear in the header on the page with the Notification of Employment Termination or Income Status.

34a-b.   **Employment/Income Status Checkbox.** Check the employment/income status of the employee/obligor.

35.   **Termination Date.** If applicable, date employee/obligor was terminated.

36.   **Last Known Phone Number.** Last known (home/cell/other) phone number of the employee/obligor.

37.   **Last Known Address.** Last known home/mailing address of the employee/obligor.

38.   **Final Payment Date.** Date employer sent final payment to SDU/Tribal payee.

39.   **Final Payment Amount.** Amount of final payment sent to SDU/Tribal payee.

40.   **New Employer's Name.** Name of employee's/obligor's new employer (if known).

41.   **New Employer's Address.** Address of employee's/obligor's new employer (if known).

COMPLETED BY SENDER:

CONTACT INFORMATION

42.   **Issuer Name (Employer/Income Withholder Contact).** Name of the contact person that the employer/income withholder can call for information regarding this IWO.

43.   **Issuer Phone Number.** Phone number of the contact person.

44.   **Issuer Fax Number.** Fax number of the contact person.

45.   **Issuer Email/Website.** Email or website of the contact person.

46.   **Termination/Income Status and Correspondence Address.** Address to which the employer should return the Employment Termination or Income Status notice. It is also the address that the employer should use to correspond with the issuing entity.

47.   **Issuer Name (Employee/Obligor Contact).** Name of the contact person that the employee/obligor can call for information.

48.   **Issuer Phone Number.** Phone number of the contact person.

49.   **Issuer Fax Number.** Fax number of the contact person.

50.   **Issuer Email/Website.** Email or website of the contact person.

The Paperwork Reduction Act of 1995
This information collection and associated responses are conducted in accordance with 45 CFR 303.100 of the Child Support Enforcement Program. This form is designed to provide uniformity and standardization. Public reporting for this collection of information is estimated to average two to five minutes per response. An agency may not conduct or sponsor, and a person is not required to respond to, a collection of information unless it displays a currently valid OMB control number.

NATIONAL MEDICAL SUPPORT NOTICE - PART A
NOTICE TO WITHHOLD FOR HEALTH CARE COVERAGE

This Notice is issued under section 466(a)(19) of the Social Security Act, section 609(a)(5)(C) of the Employee Retirement Income Security Act of 1974 (ERISA), and for State and local government and church plans, sections 401(e) and (f) of the Child Support Performance and Incentive Act of 1998. Receipt of this Notice from the Issuing Agency constitutes receipt of a Medical Child Support Order under applicable law. The information on the Custodial Parent and Child(ren) contained on this page is confidential and should not be shared or disclosed with the employee. NOTE: For purposes of this form, the Custodial Parent may also be the employee when the State opts to enforce against the Custodial Parent.

Issuing Agency: _____
Issuing Agency Address: _____
_____
Notice Date: _____
CSE Agency Case Identifier: _____
Telephone Number: _____
FAX Number: _____

Court or Administrative Authority: _____
Order Date: _____
Order Identifier: _____
Document Tracking Identifier: _____
Employer web site: _____
See NMSN Instructions: www.acf.hhs.gov/programs/cse/forms/

RE:

_____
Employer/Withholder's Federal EIN Number

_____
Employer/Withholder's Name
_____
_____
Employer / Withholder's Address

_____
Custodial Parent's Name (Last, First, MI)

_____
Custodial Parent's Mailing Address
_____
_____

Child(ren)'s Mailing Address (if different from
Custodial Parent's)

Name and Telephone of a Representative of the
Child(ren)

Child(ren)'s Name(s   Gender   DOB   SSN
_____ _____ _____ _____
_____ _____ _____ _____
_____ _____ _____ _____

_____
Employee's Name (Last, First, MI)

_____
Employee's Social Security Number
_____
_____
Employee's Mailing Address

_____
Substituted Official/Agency Name
_____
_____
Substituted Official/Agency Address
(Required if Custodial Parent's mailing address is left blank)

_____
_____

Mailing Address of a Representative of the Child(ren)

Child(ren)'s Name(s)   Gender   DOB   SSN
_____ _____ _____ _____
_____ _____ _____ _____
_____ _____ _____ _____

The order requires the child(ren) to be enrolled in ☐ all health coverages available; or only the following coverage(s):
☐ Medical; ☐ Dental; ☐ Vision; ☐ Prescription drug; ☐ Mental health; ☐ Other specify): _____

LIMITATIONS ON WITHHOLDING

The total amount withheld for both cash and medical support cannot exceed _____% of the employee's aggregate disposable weekly earnings. The employer may not withhold more under this National Medical Support Notice than the lesser of:

1. The amounts allowed by the Federal Consumer Credit Protection Act (15 U.S.C., section 1673(b));

2. The amounts allowed by the State of the employee's principal place of employment; or

3. The amounts allowed for health insurance premiums by the child support order, as indicated here:_____.

The Federal limit applies to the aggregate disposable weekly earnings (ADWE). ADWE is the net income left after making mandatory deductions such as State, Federal, local taxes; Social Security taxes; and Medicare taxes. As required under section 2.b.2 of the Employer Responsibilities on page 4, complete item 5 of the Employer Response to notify the Issuing Agency that enrollment cannot be completed because of prioritization or limitations on withholding.

PRIORITY OF WITHHOLDING

If withholding is required for employee contributions to one or more plans under this notice and for a support obligation under a separate notice and available funds are insufficient for withholding for both cash and medical support contributions, the employer must withhold amounts for purposes of cash support and medical support contributions in accordance with the law, if any, of the State of the employee's principal place of employment requiring prioritization between cash and medical support, as described here: _____.
As required under section 2.b.2 of the Employer Responsibilities on page 4, complete item 5 of the Employer Response to notify the Issuing Agency that enrollment cannot be completed because of prioritization or limitations on withholdings.

EMPLOYER RESPONSE

If 1, 2, 3, 4 or 5 below applies, check the appropriate box and return this Part A to the Issuing Agency within 20 business days after the date of the Notice, or sooner if reasonable. NO OTHER ACTION IS NECESSARY. If 1 through 5 does not apply, complete item 7 and forward **Part B** to the appropriate Plan Administrator(s) within 20 business days after the date of the Notice, or sooner if reasonable. This includes any organization or labor union that provides group health care benefits to the employee. Check number 5 and return this **Part A** to the **Issuing Agency** if the Plan Administrator informs you that the child(ren) would be enrolled in or qualify(ies) for an option under the plan for which you have determined that the employee contribution exceeds the amount that may be withheld from the employee's income due to State or Federal withholding limitations and/or prioritization. You are required to respond to the Issuing Agency by returning this **Employer Response** regardless of whether you provide group health benefits or the employee named herein is no longer employed by your organization. Information for the Plan Administrator and the Employer Representative at the bottom of this section is required.

☐ 1. The employee named in this Notice has never been employed by this employer.

☐ 2. We, the employer, do notoffer our employees the option of purchasing dependent or family health care coverage as a benefit of their employment.

☐ 3. The employee is among a class of employees (for example, part-time or non-union) that are not eligible for family health coverage under any group health plan maintained by the employer or to which the employer contributes. Do not check this box if the employee is only temporarily ineligible for health care coverage.

☐ 4. Health care coverage is not available because employee is no longer employed by the employer:

> Date of termination: _____
>
> Last known telephone number: _____
>
> Last known address: _____
>
> New employer (if known): _____
>
> New employer telephone number: _____
>
> New employer address: _____

☐ 5 State or Federal withholding limitations and/or prioritization prevent the withholding from the employee's income of the amount required to obtain coverage under the terms of the plan.

☐ 6 The participant is subject to a waiting period that expires _____ (more than 90 days from the date of receipt of this Notice), or has not completed a waiting period, which is determined by some measure other than the passage of time, such as the completion of a certain number of hours worked (describe here: _____). At the completion of the waiting period, the Plan Administrator will process the enrollment.

☐ 7. Employer forwarded Part B to Plan Administrator on _____.
MM/DD/YY

CONTACT FOR QUESTIONS

Plan Administrator Name: _____ FAX Number: _____
Contact Person: _____ Telephone Number: _____

Employer Name: _____ Telephone Number: _____
Employer Representative Name/Title: _____ Federal EIN: _____
                                                           (if not provided on Page 1 of this Notice)
Employee Name: _____ Date: _____

INSTRUCTIONS TO EMPLOYER

This document serves as legal notice that the employee identified on this National Medical Support Notice is obligated by a court or administrative child support order to provide health care coverage for the child(ren) identified on this Notice. This National Medical Support Notice replaces any Medical Support Notice that the Issuing Agency has previously served on you with respect to the employee and the children listed on this Notice.

The document consists of **Part A - Notice to Withhold for Health Care Coverage** for the employer to withhold any employee contributions required by the group health plan(s) in which the child(ren) is/are enrolled; and **Part B - Medical Support Notice to the Plan Administrator**, which **must** be forwarded to the Administrator of each group health plan identified by the employer to enroll the eligible child(ren), or completed by the employer, if the employer serves as the health Plan Administrator.

An employer receiving this legal Notice is required to complete and return **Part A**. If group health coverage is not available to the employee named herein, or the employee was never or is no longer employed, the employer is still required to complete **Part A – Employer Response** and return it to the Issuing Agency with the appropriate response checked. If you, the employer, provide the health care benefits to the employee, forward **Part B – Plan Administrator Response** to the health Plan Administrator of your organization. If the employee's health care benefits are administered through another organization, including a labor union, forward Part B of the Notice to the labor union or other organization acting as the Plan Administrator for completion. If the employee has already enrolled the child(ren) in health care coverage, the employer must forward Part B to the Plan Administrator for completion and submittal to the Issuing Agency.

Keep a copy of **Part A** as it may be used to notify the Issuing Agency if the employee separates from service for any reason including retirement or termination.

EMPLOYER RESPONSIBILITIES

1. If the individual named in this Notice is not your employee, or if the family health care coverage is not available, please complete item 1, 2, 3, 4 or 5 of the Employer Response as appropriate, and return it to the Issuing Agency. NO OTHER ACTION IS NECESSARY.

2. If family health care coverage is available for which the child(ren) identified above may be eligible, you are required to:

    a. Transfer, not later than 20 business days after the date of this Notice, a copy of **Part B - Medical Support Notice to the Plan Administrator** to the Administrator of each appropriate group health plan for which the child(ren) may be eligible, complete item 7, and

    b. Upon notification from the Plan Administrator(s) that the child(ren) is/are enrolled, either

        1) withhold from the employee's income any employee contributions required under each group health plan, in accordance with the applicable law of the employee's principal place of employment and transfer employee contributions to the appropriate plan(s), or

        2) complete item 5 of the Employer Response to notify the Issuing Agency that enrollment cannot be completed because of prioritization or limitations on withholding.

    c. If the Plan Administrator notifies you that the employee is subject to a waiting period that expires more than 90 days from the date of its receipt of **Part B** of this Notice, or whose duration is determined by a measure other than the passage of time (for example, the completion of a certain number of hours worked), complete item 6 of the Employer Response to notify the Issuing Agency of the enrollment timeframe and notify the Plan Administrator when the employee is eligible to enroll in the plan and that this Notice requires the enrollment of the child(ren) named in the Notice in the plan.

Page 4 of 5

A-446

DURATION OF WITHHOLDING

The child(ren) shall be treated as dependents under the terms of the plan. Coverage of a child as a dependent will end when conditions for eligibility for coverage under terms of the plan no longer apply. However, the continuation coverage provisions of ERISA may entitle the child to continuation coverage under the plan. The employer must continue to withhold employee contributions and may not disenroll (or eliminate coverage for) the child(ren) unless:

1. The employer is provided satisfactory written evidence that:
   a. The court or administrative child support order referred to in this Notice is no longer in effect; or
   b. The child(ren) is or will be enrolled in comparable coverage which will take effect no later than the effective date of disenrollment from the plan; or

2. The employer eliminates family health coverage for all of its employees.

POSSIBLE SANCTIONS

An employer may be subject to sanctions or penalties imposed under State law and/or ERISA for discharging an employee from employment, refusing to employ, or taking disciplinary action against any employee because of medical child support withholding, or for failing to withhold income, or transmit such withheld amounts to the applicable plan(s) as the Notice directs. Sanctions or penalties may be imposed under State law against an employer for failure to respond and/or for non-compliance with this Notice.

NOTICE OF TERMINATION OF EMPLOYMENT

In any case in which the above employee's employment terminates, the employer must promptly notify the Issuing Agency listed above of such termination. This requirement may be satisfied by sending to the Issuing Agency a copy of Part A with response 4 checked or any notice the employer is required to provide under the continuation coverage provisions of ERISA or the Health Insurance Portability and Accountability Act.

EMPLOYEE LIABILITY FOR CONTRIBUTION TO PLAN

The employee is liable for any employee contributions that are required under the plan(s) for enrollment of the child(ren) and is subject to appropriate enforcement. The employee may contest the withholding under this Notice based on a mistake of fact (such as the identity of the obligor). Should an employee contest the withholding under this Notice, the employer must proceed to comply with the employer responsibilities in this Notice until notified by the Issuing Agency to discontinue withholding. To contest the withholding under this Notice, the employee should contact the Issuing Agency at the address and telephone number listed on the Notice. With respect to plans subject to ERISA, it is the view of the Department of Labor that Federal Courts have jurisdiction if the employee challenges a determination that the Notice constitutes a Qualified Medical Child Support Order.

CONTACT FOR QUESTIONS

If you have any questions regarding this Notice, you may contact the Issuing Agency at the address and telephone number listed on page 1 of this Notice.

NATIONAL MEDICAL SUPPORT NOTICE
PART B
MEDICAL SUPPORT NOTICE TO PLAN ADMINISTRATOR

This Notice is issued under section 466(a)(19) of the Social Security Act, section 609(a)(5)(C) of the Employee Retirement Income Security Act of 1974, and for State and local government and church plans, sections 401(e) and (f) of the Child Support Performance and Incentive Act of 1998. Receipt of this Notice from the Issuing Agency constitutes receipt of a Medical Child Support Order under applicable law. The rights of the parties and the duties of the plan administrator under this Notice are in addition to the existing rights and duties established under such law. The information on the Custodial Parent and Child(ren) contained on this page is confidential and should not be shared or disclosed with the Noncustodial Parent.

Issuing Agency: _____	Court or Administrative Authority: _____
Issuing Agency Address: _____	Date of Support Order: _____
_____	Support Order Number: _____
Date of Notice: _____	
Case Number: _____	
Telephone Number: _____	
FAX Number: _____	
Employer Web Site: _____	

_____   RE: _____
Employer/Withholder's Federal EIN Number   Employee's Name (Last, First, MI)

_____   _____
Employer/Withholder's Name   Employee's Social Security Number

_____   _____
Employer/Withholder's Address   Employee's Address

_____
Custodial Parent's Name (Last, First, MI)

_____   _____
Custodial Parent's Mailing Address   Substituted Official/Agency Name and Address
                                         (Required if Custodial Parent's mailing address is left blank)

_____
Child(ren)'s Mailing Address (if Different from Custodial Parent's)
_____
_____

_____
Name(s), Mailing Address, and Telephone
Number of a Representative of the Child(ren)

Child(ren)'s Name(s)	DOB	SSN	Child(ren)'s Name(s)	DOB	SSN
_____	_____	_____	_____	_____	_____
_____	_____	_____	_____	_____	_____
_____	_____	_____	_____	_____	_____

The order requires the child(ren) to be enrolled in [] any health coverages available; or [] only the following coverage(s): __medical; __dental; __vision; __prescription drug; __mental health; __other (specify):_____

THE PAPERWORK REDUCTION ACT OF 1995 (P.L. 104-13) public reporting burden for this collection of information is estimated to average 20 minutes per response, including the time reviewing instructions, gathering and maintaining the data needed, and reviewing the collection of information. An agency may not conduct or sponsor, and a person is not required to respond to, a collection of information unless it displays a currently valid OMB control number.

OMB control number: 1210-0113 Expiration Date: 10/31/2012.

PLAN ADMINISTRATOR RESPONSE
(To be completed and returned to the Issuing Agency within 40 business days after the date of the Notice, or sooner if reasonable)

Case #_____ (to be completed by the issuing agency)

This Notice was received by the plan administrator on _____.

1. This Notice was determined to be a "qualified medical child support order," on _____. Complete **Response 2 or 3, and 4**, if applicable.

2. The participant (employee) and alternate recipient(s) (child(ren)) are to be enrolled in the following family coverage.
      a. The child(ren) is/are currently enrolled in the plan as a dependent of the participant.
      b. There is only one type of coverage provided under the plan. The child(ren) is/are included as dependents of the participant under the plan.
      c. The participant is enrolled in an option that is providing dependent coverage and the child(ren) will be enrolled in the same option.
      d. The participant is enrolled in an option that permits dependent coverage that has not been elected; dependent coverage will be provided.

Coverage is effective as of __/__/____(includes waiting period of less than 90 days from date of receipt of this Notice).   The child(ren) has/have been enrolled in the following option (if plan is insured, identify provider, policy and group numbers): _____. Any necessary withholding should commence if the employer determines that it is permitted under State and Federal withholding and/or prioritization limitations.

3. There is more than one option available under the plan and the participant is not enrolled. The Issuing Agency must select from the available options. Each child is to be included as a dependent under one of the available options that provide family coverage. If the Issuing Agency does not reply within 20 business days of the date this Response is returned, the child(ren), and the participant if necessary, will be enrolled in the plan's default option, if any: _____.

4. The participant is subject to a waiting period that expires __/__/____ (more than 90 days from the date of receipt of this Notice), or has not completed a waiting period which is determined by some measure other than the passage of time, such as the completion of a certain number of hours worked (describe here: _____). At the completion of the waiting period, the plan administrator will process the enrollment.

5. This Notice does not constitute a "qualified medical child support order" because:
        The name of the child(ren) or participant is unavailable.
        The mailing address of the child(ren) (or a substituted official) or participant is unavailable.
        The following child(ren) is/are at or above the age at which dependents are no longer eligible for coverage under the plan _____ (insert name(s) of child(ren)).
Plan Administrator or Representative:

Name: _____   Telephone Number: _____

Title: _____   Date: _____

Address:_____

INSTRUCTIONS TO PLAN ADMINISTRATOR

This Notice has been forwarded from the employer identified above to you as the plan administrator of a group health plan maintained by the employer (or a group health plan to which the employer contributes) and in which the noncustodial parent/participant identified above is enrolled or is eligible for enrollment.

This Notice serves to inform you that the noncustodial parent/participant is obligated by an order issued by the court or agency identified above to provide health care coverage for the child(ren) under the group health plan(s) as described on **Part B**.

(A) If the participant and child(ren) and their mailing addresses (or that of a Substituted Official or Agency) are identified above, and if coverage for the child(ren) is or will become available, this Notice constitutes a "qualified medical child support order"(QMCSO) under ERISA or CSPIA, as applicable. (If any mailing address is not present, but it is reasonably accessible, this Notice will not fail to be a QMCSO on that basis.) You must, within 40 business days of the date of this Notice, or sooner if reasonable:

> (1) Complete Part B - Plan Administrator Response - and send it to the Issuing Agency:

> (a) if you checked Response 2:

>> (i) notify the noncustodial parent/participant named above, each named child, and the custodial parent that coverage of the child(ren) is or will become available (notification of the custodial parent will be deemed notification of the child(ren) if they reside at the same address);

>> (ii) furnish the custodial parent a description of the coverage available and the effective date of the coverage, including, if not already provided, a summary plan description and any forms, documents, or information necessary to effectuate such coverage, as well as information necessary to submit claims for benefits;

> (b) if you checked Response 3:

>> (i) if you have not already done so, provide to the Issuing Agency copies of applicable summary plan descriptions or other documents that describe available coverage including the additional participant contribution necessary to obtain coverage for the child(ren) under each option and whether there is a limited service area for any option;

>> (ii) if the plan has a default option, you are to enroll the child(ren) in the default option if you have not received an election from the Issuing Agency within 20 business days of the date you returned the Response. If the plan does not have a default option, you are to enroll the child(ren) in the option selected by the Issuing Agency.

(c) if the participant is subject to a waiting period that expires more than 90 days from the date of receipt of this Notice, or has not completed a waiting period whose duration is determined by a measure other than the passage of time (for example, the completion of a certain number of hours worked), complete Response 4 on the Plan Administrator Response and return to the employer and the Issuing Agency, and notify the participant and the custodial parent; and upon satisfaction of the period or requirement, complete enrollment under Response 2 or 3, and

(d) upon completion of the enrollment, transfer the applicable information on Part B - Plan Administrator Response to the employer for a determination that the necessary employee contributions are available. Inform the employer that the enrollment is pursuant to a National Medical Support Notice.

(B) If within 40 business days of the date of this Notice, or sooner if reasonable, you determine that this Notice does not constitute a QMCSO, you must complete Response 5 of Part B - Plan Administrator Response and send it to the Issuing Agency, and inform the noncustodial parent/participant, custodial parent, and child(ren) of the specific reasons for your determination.

(C) Any required notification of the custodial parent, child(ren) and/or participant may be satisfied by sending the party a copy of the Plan Administrator Response, if appropriate. You may choose to furnish these notifications electronically in accordance with the requirements of the Department of Labor's electronic disclosure regulation codified at 29 C.F.R. 2520.104b-1(c).

UNLAWFUL REFUSAL TO ENROLL

Enrollment of a child may not be denied on the ground that: (1) the child was born out of wedlock; (2) the child is not claimed as a dependent on the participant's Federal income tax return; (3) the child does not reside with the participant or in the plan's service area; or (4) because the child is receiving benefits or is eligible to receive benefits under the State Medicaid plan. If the plan requires that the participant be enrolled in order for the child(ren) to be enrolled, and the participant is not currently enrolled, you must enroll both the participant and the child(ren) regardless of whether the participant has applied for enrollment in the plan. All enrollments are to be made without regard to open season restrictions.

PAYMENT OF CLAIMS

A child covered by a QMCSO, or the child's custodial parent, legal guardian, or the provider of services to the child, or a State agency to the extent assigned the child's rights, may file claims and the plan shall make payment for covered benefits or reimbursement directly to such party.

PERIOD OF COVERAGE

The alternate recipient(s) shall be treated as dependents under the terms of the plan. Coverage of an alternate recipient as a dependent will end when similarly situated dependents are no longer eligible for coverage under the terms of the plan. However, the continuation coverage provisions of ERISA or other applicable law may entitle the alternate recipient to continue coverage under the plan. Once a child is enrolled in the plan as directed above, the alternate recipient may not be disenrolled unless:

    (1) The plan administrator is provided satisfactory written evidence that either:
        (a) the court or administrative child support order referred to above is no longer in effect, or
        (b) the alternate recipient is or will be enrolled in comparable coverage which will take effect no later than the effective date of disenrollment from the plan;

    (2) The employer eliminates family health coverage for all of its employees; or

    (3) Any available continuation coverage is not elected, or the period of such coverage expires.

CONTACT FOR QUESTIONS

If you have any questions regarding this Notice, you may contact the Issuing Agency at the address and telephone number listed above.

Paperwork Reduction Act Notice

The Issuing Agency asks for the information on this form to carry out the law as specified in the Employee Retirement Income Security Act or the Child Support Performance and Incentive Act, as applicable. You are required to give the Issuing Agency the information. You are not required to respond to this collection of information unless it displays a currently valid OMB control number. The Issuing Agency needs the information to determine whether health care coverage is provided in accordance with the underlying child support order. The average time needed to complete and file the form is estimated below. These times will vary depending on the individual circumstances.

__Learning about the law or the form__	....	__Preparing the form__
First Notice 1 hr.__	....	1 hr., 45 min.
Subsequent Notices -----	....	20 min.

Standard Response to Verification of Employment

Employers will provide requested information normally maintained on employees. If additional information not listed on this form is needed, please contact the employer.

PAYROLL SECTION - Employee Personal Information

Full Name:

_____
Last   First   M.I.

Residential Address, if known:

_____
Street Address   Apartment/Unit #

_____
City   State   ZIP Code

Mailing Address, if known:

_____
Street Address   Apartment/Unit #

_____
City   State   ZIP Code

Home Phone: _____ **Alternate Phone:** _____

Email Address, if known: _____

Social Security Number: _____ **Date of Birth:** _____

Employer and Job Information

Employment Status: ☐ Currently Employed   ☐ Terminated   ☐ Never Employed

Title: _____ **Dates of Employment:** _____

Employer Name: _____ **Employer Address:** _____

Employer Phone Number: _____ **Employer Fax Number:** _____

Federal EIN: _____

Full/Part Time or Seasonal: ☐ Full Time ☐ Part Time ☐ Seasonal

Begin Date: _____ **End Date:** _____

Return to Work Date: _____

Employee Work Site or Location: _____

Termination Reason: ☐ Voluntary   ☐ Involuntary

Wage Information

Pay Cycle/Frequency: _____ **Rate of Pay:** $ _____

Gross Pay Per Period: $ _____ **Net Disposable Pay Per Period:** $ _____

Current Year-to-Date Earnings: $ _____

1

A-454

Previous Calendar Year Earnings: $ _____

Union Name: _____   Local Number: _____

Mandatory Union Dues: $ _____   Mandatory Retirement: $ _____

Tax Filing Status: ☐ Single   ☐ Married   ☐ Head of Household

Number of Dependents: _____

Workers' Compensation: ☐ Yes   ☐ No

Name of Workers' Compensation
Company and Contact Information: _____

_____

Certification Information

Completed by:

Employer Name (Employee's Employer) _____

Name: _____

Title: _____

Signature: _____

Date: _____

Phone number: _____

If additional information is needed, please contact the person listed above.

A-455

HEALTH INSURANCE SECTION - Employee Personal Information

Full Name: _____
         Last   *First*   *M.I.*

Last 4 digits of Social Security Number: _____

Health Insurance Availability

Does the employer offer health insurance?   ☐ Yes ☐ No

If not available currently to the employee, when will it be available?   _____

Is health insurance available for dependents or spouse?   ☐ Yes ☐ No

Is this paid by: ☐ Payroll Deduction   ☐ Payment

Has the employee enrolled self and/or dependents?   ☐ Self ☐ Dependents

Medical Insurance

Insurance Provider's Name: _____

Insurance Provider's Address: _____

_____

Insurance Provider's Phone: _____ Fax: _____

Policy/Contract Number: _____ Cost for Employee Coverage: $ _____

Policy Group Name/Number: _____ Cost for Listed Children: $ _____

                                                Cost for Employee/Family: $ _____

                                                Cost Frequency: _____

Complete the following information for each dependent:

Name (Last, First, Middle)	Social Security Number	Date of Birth	Group Number	Policy Number	Start Date	End Date

Dental Insurance

Insurance Provider's Name: _____

Insurance Provider's Address: _____

_____

Insurance Provider's Phone: _____ Fax: _____

Policy/Contract Number: _____ Cost for Employee Coverage: $ _____

Policy Group Name/Number: _____ Cost for Listed Children: $ _____

                                                Cost for Employee/Family: $ _____

                                                Cost Frequency: _____

A-456

Complete the following information for each dependent:

Name (Last, First, Middle)	Social Security Number	Date of Birth	Group Number	Policy Number	Start Date	End Date

Vision Insurance

Insurance Provider's Name: _____

Insurance Provider's Address: _____

_____

Insurance Provider's Phone: _____ Fax: _____

Policy/Contract Number: _____ Cost for Employee Coverage: $ _____

Cost for Listed Children: $ _____

Policy Group Name/Number: _____ Cost for Employee/Family: $ _____

Cost Frequency: _____

Complete the following information for each dependent:

Name (Last, First, Middle)	Social Security Number	Date of Birth	Group Number	Policy Number	Start Date	End Date

Prescription Drug Insurance

Insurance Provider's Name: _____

Insurance Provider's Address: _____

_____

Insurance Provider's Phone: _____ Fax: _____

Policy/Contract Number: _____ Cost for Employee Coverage: $ _____

Cost for Listed Children: $ _____

Policy Group Name/Number: _____ Cost for Employee/Family: $ _____

Cost Frequency: _____

Complete the following information for each dependent:

Name (Last, First, Middle)	Social Security Number	Date of Birth	Group Number	Policy Number	Start Date	End Date

A-457

Mental Health Insurance

Insurance Provider's Name: _____

Insurance Provider's Address: _____

_____

Insurance Provider's Phone: _____ Fax: _____

Policy/Contract Number: _____ Cost for Employee Coverage: $ _____

Policy Group Name/Number: _____ Cost for Listed Children: $ _____

Cost for Employee/Family: $ _____

Complete the following information for each dependent: Cost Frequency: _____

Name (Last, First, Middle)	Social Security Number	Date of Birth	Group Number	Policy Number	Start Date	End Date

Other Health Insurance (specify type here):

Insurance Provider's Name: _____

Insurance Provider's Address: _____

_____

Insurance Provider's Phone: _____ Fax: _____

Policy/Contract Number: _____ Cost for Employee Coverage: $ _____

Policy Group Name/Number: _____ Cost for Listed Children: $ _____

Cost for Employee/Family: $ _____

Complete the following information for each dependent: Cost Frequency: _____

Name (Last, First, Middle)	Social Security Number	Date of Birth	Group Number	Policy Number	Start Date	End Date

Certification Information

Completed by:

Name and Title: _____

Company Name: _____

Signature: _____

Date: _____ Phone Number: _____

A-458